The El-Amarna Correspondence

Handbook of Oriental Studies
Handbuch der Orientalistik

SECTION 1, ANCIENT NEAR EAST

Editor-in-Chief

W.H. van Soldt (*Leiden*)

Editors

G. Beckman (*Ann Arbor*)
C. Leitz (*Tübingen*)
P. Michalowski (*Ann Arbor*)
P. Miglus (*Heidelberg*)
H. Gzella (*Leiden*)

VOLUME 110

The titles published in this series are listed at brill.com/ho1

The El-Amarna Correspondence

A New Edition of the Cuneiform Letters from the Site of El-Amarna based on Collations of all Extant Tablets

VOLUME 1

Collated, Transcribed and Translated by

Anson F. Rainey Z"L

Edited by

William M. Schniedewind

TUTA SUB AEGIDE PALLAS · 1683 ·

BRILL

LEIDEN · BOSTON
2015

Library of Congress Cataloging-in-Publication Data

The El-Amarna correspondence : a new edition of the cuneiform letters from the site of El-Amarna based on collations of all extant tablets / collated, transcribed and translated by Anson F. Rainey ; edited by William M. Scheidewind.

pages cm. – (Handbook of Oriental studies = Handbuch der orientalistik, section 1, ancient Near East ; 110)

Includes bibliographical references.

ISBN 978-90-04-28145-5 (hardback : alk. paper : set) – ISBN 978-90-04-28147-9 (hardback : volume one) – ISBN 978-90-04-28146-2 (hardback : volume two) – ISBN 978-90-04-28154-7 (e-book) 1. Assyro-Babylonian letters. 2. Assyro-Babylonian letters–Translations into English. 3. Akkadian language–Texts. 4. Tell el-Amarna tablets. 5. Egypt–History–Eighteenth dynasty, ca. 1570-1320 B.C.–Sources. 6. Palestine–History–To 70 A.D.–Sources. 7. Middle East–History–To 622–Sources. I. Rainey, Anson F., 1930-2011, translator. II. Schniedewind, William M., editor. III. Tell el-Amarna tablets. IV. Tell el-Amarna tablets. English.

PJ3886.E5S36 2014
492'.1–dc23

2014029901

This publication has been typeset in the multilingual "Brill" typeface. With over 5,100 characters covering Latin, IPA, Greek, and Cyrillic, this typeface is especially suitable for use in the humanities. For more information, please see www.brill.com/brill-typeface.

ISSN 0169-9423
ISBN 978-90-04-28145-5 (hardback, set)
ISBN 978-90-04-28147-9 (hardback, volume 1)
ISBN 978-90-04-28146-2 (hardback, volume 2)
ISBN 978-90-04-28154-7 (e-book)

PRINTED BY DRUKKERIJ WILCO B.V. - AMERSFOORT, THE NETHERLANDS

This edition of the el-Amarna Correspondence is dedicated to the members of my family:

Zipora, my wife, and Yoni, my son,
my parents, Anson and Bertie Mae,
and my cousin Kay Welch

CONTENTS

VOLUME 1

VOLUME 2

FOREWORD

The collection of cuneiform documents discovered at the site now known as el-Amarna ('Amârnah) preserve both cultural and historical information that shed light on the affairs of the late Eighteenth Dynasty in the fourteenth century BCE. Thus they are important to the Egyptologist. On the other hand, since they are by their nature, exemplars of the Mesopotamian writing practices, they are also of the highest significance to the Assyriologist, especially those concerned with the Fertile Crescent in the Late Bronze Age. The need for a new edition of the Amarna texts has been deeply felt for many decades. World conditions throughout the twentieth century were not particularly conducive to the task of re-collating the tablets, scattered as they are among several museums. The magisterial edition of J.A. Knudtzon served world scholarship for a century and, in spite of its shortcomings discernable today, gave the qualified Assyriologist access to the gold mine of data that has illuminated so many aspects of the regimes, the peoples and the geography of the Fertile Crescent, especially of the eastern Mediterranean littoral.

A new edition of all the Amarna correspondence needs no justification. The non-epistolary documents have been ably collated and republished by Sh. Izre'el (1997). Therefore, this present work is focused entirely on the letters. The one tablet found at Tell el-Ḥesī (EA 333) was copied in the Istanbul Arkeoloji Müzeleri in February, 1971. A few texts were examined at the British Museum in 1973. In 1980–1981 it was my privilege to collate the tablets in the Cairo Museum. But work really began in earnest during some terminal sabbatical leave at the British Museum in the fall of 1999. The discovery that corrections and new readings were possible in an appreciable number of tablets was a stimulant to continue this activity. During 1999, 2000, 2001 and 2002, the texts in New York, London, Oxford, and Chicago, as well as the remainder of the London tablets, were duly collated and edited. During ten months in 2003–2004, collations were achieved for all the texts in Berlin, Paris and Brussels. There remained the three letters in the Pushkin Museum in Moscow; those were collated during July 2007. The present edition is meant to make the results of that activity accessible to the scholarly public. It must be stressed that it is an edition for professionals; the translations are intended for those who can critique them independently by comparison with the transcriptions. There is no attempt to emulate the style of the late W.L. Moran (1992). Most translations are virtually "off the cuff," but they are an attempt to grasp the real message that the scribe (or his master) wished to convey. Although consistency in the choice of terminology was sought, there may be instances when such was not achieved. The corresponding transcription will serve to clarify the intention of the scribe.

It is a pleasant duty to acknowledge the many scholars and institutions that have made the edition possible by their generous academic and financial support.

Many fine people have contributed to the success of my efforts in producing this work. A great indebtedness must be acknowledged to the late W.L. Moran, both for his writings and for the privilege of participating in his seminar at Harvard University during the 1976–1977 academic year.

It is also a pleasure to acknowledge the kindness and encouragement of the late Erica Reiner and her staff at the Assyrian Dictionary Project in the University of Chicago's Oriental Institute. During several visits in 1976–1977, I was permitted to use the dictionary files as well as the proof copy of volumes M/1–2 and the manuscript of volumes N/1–2. Both the information and the hospitality contributed to the pleasure of this research task.

Through the generosity of G. Buccellati, a mainframe computer printout of a sign concordance for nearly all of the Amarna texts (i.e., Knudtzon's edition) was made available to me. In spite of its limitations as a pioneer work, it has proven useful in tracking down the occurrences of many particles, e.g. *lā*, and many cuneiform signs, such as LAL. Our thanks are due to Buccellati and his energetic assistants for producing such a tool.

My graduate students at Tel Aviv University, and later at Bar Ilan University, and also those in Moran's seminar mentioned above, have provided stimulation and, not infrequently, correction of various errors. The challenge of giving them a head start towards the advancement of Amarna studies has been the chief motivation for all my work in this area.

A further obligation must be recognized towards those institutions that have facilitated my lifetime of Amarna research. First and foremost, to Tel Aviv University, which granted me five sabbatical leaves, 1970–1971, 1976–1977, 1983–1984, 1988–1989, and 1995–1996 that could be devoted to EA research and writing. Through the good offices of A. Shapira, then Dean of the Faculty of Humanities at Tel Aviv University, I was awarded a grant from the Irene Young Endowment Fund for Scientific Publications. This subvention was for expenses incurred in the preparation of scholarly works for publication and it was used to support the work by L. Meiberg on the Bibliography and Index of my initial project, *Canaanite in the Amarna Tablets* (Rainey 1996). The American Council of Learned Societies provided a generous grant towards my sabbatical expenses in 1976–1977. The Research for Peace Project of Tel Aviv University furnished stipends in 1980, -81 and -82, that made possible the collation of the Amarna texts at the Egyptian Museum in Cairo. Both Harvard University (1976–1977) and the University of Pennsylvania (1983–1984, 1988–1989, 1995–1996) awarded me visiting research status that made available to me their extensive library collections.

In 1976–1977, a sabbatical from Tel Aviv University made it possible to participate in a seminar by W.L. Moran at Harvard University. It is a pleasant duty to acknowledge the hospitality of the Department of Near Eastern Languages and Civilizations at Harvard University (1976–1977) and the Department of Asian and Middle East Studies at the University of Pennsylvania (1983–1984, 1988–1989, 1995–1996) for granting the status of visiting researcher during the sabbatical leaves which I spent at their respective institutions. During those two decades I was engaged in an intensive study of the grammar of the Amarna letters that embodied the hybrid language used by the scribes in Canaan. Throughout the work on that project (Rainey 1996), the lack of up-to-date collations was sorely felt.

The Cairo texts had already been collated during the euphoria of the new Peace Treaty with Egypt. A few of the London texts were collated during a brief visit to London in 1973. But a comprehensive collation of all the extant Amarna texts seemed at that time like an impossible dream. As an emeritus professor from Tel Aviv University, I found that the dream might be realized. Starting with a two month stay in London including a few days in Berlin, the drive to personally collate all of the Amarna letters became a virtual obsession.

Collation of the London tablets was begun seriously in September 1999 (a few tablets had been collated in 1973) during some final sabbatical leave from Tel Aviv University. Further work was done in January–February of 2000 and April, 2001. This latter trip was made possible by a travel allowance from the Jeselson Fund of Bar Ilan University.

The two texts at the Metropolitan Museum were collated in November, 1999. The fragment at the University of Chicago was collated in February, 2000. Later, when the other part of this letter, EA 26 was on exhibition in Chicago, J. Brinkman was able to join the two pieces and photograph and collate them together. The remainder of the entire Berlin collection of letters was collated during the academic year 2003–2004, financed by a generous grant from the Thyssen Stiftung.

During May 2004, the tablets in the Musée d'Louvre were collated and the one tablet in the Musées Royaux d'Art et d'Histoire in Brussels was made available to me.

The three tablets in the Moscow Museum were collated recently by Sh. Izre'el who agreed to furnish his transliterations to the project. Nevertheless, those three texts were personally collated by me in July 2007, during the 53rd Rencontre Assyriologue and photographs were made.

Over the years, collation of the various tablets has been made possible by the courtesy of numerous curators: the late E. Sollberger of the British Museum (1973); M. Çiğof the Istanbul Arkeoloji Müzeleri (1971, 1976); M. Saleḥ, at that time curator of the New Kingdom section of The Egyptian Museum, Cairo (1980–1981); Ch. Walker of the British Museum, London (1999, 2000, 2002, 2003, 2004); J. Allen at the Metropolitan Museum of Art, New York (1999); J.A. Brinkman of the Oriental Institute of the University of Chicago (2000); H. Whitehouse of the Ashmolean Museum, Oxford (2002); J. Marzahn at the Vorderasiatische Museum, Berlin (1999, 2003–2004, 2005); B. Salvni of the Louvre, Paris (2004) and E. Gubel of the Musées Royeaux d'Art et d'Histoire, Brussels (2004) and finally S. Hodjash at the Pushkin Museum, Moscow (2007).

G. Wilhelm has generously agreed to permit the incorporation of his latest version of the Hurrian letter (EA 24) into this edition. I. Singer has prepared the two texts in the Hittite language (EA 31 and 32). All the texts in the various dialects of Akkadian are the result of my personal collation of every extant text (for the few texts that have been destroyed or just disappeared cf. the Introduction, *infra*).

The E.J. Brill publishing house took on the job of producing my previous contribution at Amarna research (Rainey 1996). That four volume monograph was accepted into the *Handbuch der Orientalistik*, Erste Abteilung, Der Nahe und Mittlere Osten as Band 52. Throughout my career as a student and teacher/researcher, various contributions of that series had played an important role in my research. As a student, I never dreamed that one day, my own work would join the prestigious corpus. Now I am once again in debt to Brill for accepting this present study into the *Handbuch*.

Anson F. Rainey

This project was entrusted to me by Anson a few months before he passed away. I had known Anson for many years, first studying historical geography with him at the Institute for Holy Land Studies (now, Jerusalem University College); later, while a post-doctoral fellow at the Albright Institute, I sat in on his Amarna Seminar at Tel Aviv University. I have put most of my efforts into the editing of volume 1 (which included creating a glossary), and I am especially grateful that his wife, Zipora Cochavi-Rainey, took on the task of completing volume 2, which was only in notes when Anson asked me to oversee this project to completion. Zipora also supplied corrections to the first volume based on her commentary in volume 2. I am also grateful to Jana Mynářová who worked with Rainey and provided a discussion of the discovery, research, and excavation of the tablets for the Introduction. In principle, I have tried to be as faithful as possible in representing Anson's work in volume 1. I especially appreciate the work of my graduate research assistants, Alice Mandell and Timothy Hogue, who have also helped in completing this work. I am particularly grateful to Alice Mandell who did most of the work on the glossary.

William M. Schniedewind

INTRODUCTION

A central component in the documented cultural and political life of the Ancient Near Eastern Late Bronze Age is the collection of cuneiform documents known as the Amarna Tablets. The year 2007 marked the one hundred twentieth anniversary since antiquities dealers in Egypt began to acquire cuneiform tablets and fragments from the site known today as Tell el-Amarna (*Tell el-ʿAmârnah*).

The present toponym is a late, artificial invention based on a misunderstanding of the village name et-Tîl and the tribal name *banû ʿAmram*. The name Tell el-Amarna first appears on the map by J.G. Wilkinson (1830).

The semi-legendary accounts of their discovery just over one hundred and twenty years ago are fairly well known to the scholarly world but less so today to the general public (Knudtzon 1915:1–15; cf. Sayce 1917 and Campbell 1964:32–34). Be that as it may, in the acquisitions journal of the then Bulaq Museum, objects that obviously originated from the site (including the cartouches of Akhenaton and the Aten) were listed in 1887 prior to the arrival of cuneiform tablets as recently discovered by Jana Mynářová. This strongly suggests that the original report about a peasant woman who was seeking organic soil for her garden may have been nothing but a cover up to hide clandestine antiquities theft (cf. Petrie 1898:1, who already sensed this).

Discovery and Publication

Today three hundred and eighty two texts and fragments are known although several have disappeared or been destroyed during the twentieth century. Three hundred and forty nine of them are letters in varied states of preservation, some complete, others fragmentary. This present edition includes all of the letters plus one scribal exercise text (EA 380) that was used as a sample template for a letter. As fate would have it, most of the tablets made their way to major museums of Europe. Wallis Budge brought about eighty-two texts to the British Museum. A certain Theodore Graf brought two hundred and one texts to Vienna and sold them to the new royal museum in Berlin. The Assyriologist, Hugo Winckler, made the purchase with a generous grant from James Simon, a textile magnet and friend of the Kaiser. A few other texts made their way into the hands of private collectors (see the publication record below) several of which were eventually purchased by the British Museum. The excavations by Flinders Petrie in 1891–1892 produced a handful of texts and fragments, mostly scribal exercises; these were donated to the Ashmolean Museum of Oxford University. Two tablets reached the Metropolitan Museum of New York and the fragment of one letter found its way to the Oriental Institute of the University of Chicago. Six other letters were acquired by the Louvre and one found its way to the Musées Royaux d'Art et d'Histoire in Brussels. Subsequent excavations at the site by German and later British expeditions found a small number of tablets. Those from the latter went to the British Museum. The two German finds were copied in Berlin and repatriated to Cairo in 1926. One tablet included in the "Amarna corpus" is EA 333, a chance find in the archaeological excavations by Fredrick Bliss at Tell el-Ḥesī in 1891. Because that text mentioned personalities known from the Amarna letters, Knudtzon included it in his edition. The tablet is in the Istanbul Arkeoloji Müzeleri. Various other tablets, some from the Amarna period, have been found in the southern Levant, e.g. the Taanach letters, two texts from Shechem and now numerous texts from the excavations at Hazor are not included in this edition. They have all been assembled in a convenient volume by Horowitz and Oshima (2006).

The archaeological site now called Tell el-Amarna (properly *ʿAmârnah*) is located about three hundred kilometers (ca. one hundred and eighty miles) south of Cairo in Middle Egypt. It is about half way between the southern (No-Amon = Luxor) and the northern (Moph/Memphis = Mît Rahîna) capitals of Egypt in pharaonic times. Napolean's savants called it et-Tell. Early explorers focused on the tomb caves in the cliffs to the east of the site. According to the earliest maps of the region, the site of el-Amarna has always been visible to travelers and visitors. It is the largest and most accessible of the few Egyptian cities that have been preserved. Its remains are visible on the surface. Therefore, it is in many ways the most convenient focus for the study of urbanism in the ancient historical periods of Egyptian history.

A drawing of Amarna Boundary Stela A at Tuna el-Gebel was published in 1714, by Claude Sicard, a French Jesuit missionary. The Napoleonic scientific expedition visited the region in 1799, and Edmé Jomard produced a plan of the site under the name El-Tell in the *Description de l'Égypte*, the magnificent volumes summarizing the results of the Napoleonic expedition (1817). The English scholar John Gardner Wilkinson produced plans of the entire city based on his surveys in 1824 and 1826. During the next two decades, copies of the tombs of Akhenaten's nobles were produced by Robert Hay, James Burton, and Nestor L'Hôte. Further plans of the city of el-Amarna were published by the Prussian Expedition led by Richard Lepsius based on their researches there between 1843 and 1845.

The first modern archaeological excavations at el-Amarna were conducted in 1891–1892 by W.M. Flinders Petrie. His desire to dig there was due to the sensational discovery of the cuneiform tablets a few years earlier. It proved to be basically a one period site with few stratigraphic difficulties. Unfortunately, one such problem did arise with regard to Petrie's description of his few cuneiform finds. He excavated a building (his No. 19) the bricks of which bore the inscription: "The place of the letters of the Pharaoh, *ʿ.w.ś*" (hieroglyphs in Petrie 1894: pl. XLII; also Petrie 1898: 1). Two particular rooms yielded fragments of cuneiform texts. Petrie claimed that most of the fragments that he found had come from the two rubbish pits beneath the complex of these rooms. Petrie suggested that the rubbish pits "had been filled up before the walls were built". Serious doubts have been raised about his conclusion (Kühne 1973: 70 n. 345). Pendlebury, who excavated Amarna in the 1930's, describes the poor condition of the walls and the floor of the same building (his Q.42.21). Doubts about the accuracy of Petrie's stratigraphic conclusions have justifiably remained to this day (Moran 1992: xvi n. 20). Given Petrie's notorious lack of stratigraphic comprehension, one may entertain serious doubt that the tablet collection was all thrown into a pit, or pits, that were later sealed under the walls of the building. The implications for the chronology of the tablets vis à vis the use of building 19 (Q.42.21) will be discussed below.

Several minor expeditions followed in the ensuing years, but the next really serious undertaking was the methodical survey and excavations conducted by Ludwig Borchardt (1907, 1911–1914), on behalf of the Deutsche Orient-Gesellschaft. The expedition was financed by James Simon, whose name was on the license. Some of the most famous artistic works of the Amarna style were uncovered during that period, including the famous bust of Nefertiti, which stood for some time in the saloon of James Simon until it was donated to the Kaiser's museum. The Borchardt/Simon expedition found only two cuneiform tablets, neither in house 19 (Q.42.21). One was a broken lexical text (EA 379) and the other was the now famous legend, the *Šar tamḫari*, "The King of Battle" about a presumed campaign into central Anatolia by Sargon the Great. The language and ductus of that text are totally different from the normal Amarna collection. The clay has yet to be examined petrographically, but the odds are that the text was brought to Egypt by an envoy from Anatolia, either Ḫatti or Arzawa.

Between 1901 and 1907, Egyptologists from The Egypt Exploration Fund (now the Egypt Exploration Society) copied and published the private tombs in the eastern ridges and the boundary stelae around the circumference of the Amarna plain. They resumed work in 1921, this time in proper excavations at the site. The directors, in turn, were T.E. Peet, H. Frankfort, F.L. Griffith, and finally J.D.S. Pendlebury. Their explorations ranged widely over the site, from peripheral regions such as the workers' village, the "river temple," in the south and the northern palace and finally concentrated on the central city. Pendlebury, the last excavator, had his final season in 1936 and finished his publication in 1939.

Another EES archaeologist, G.T. Martin, reinvestigated the royal tomb east of el-Amarna in the wadi behind the eastern ridges, during the early 70's. Then in 1977, the Egypt Exploration Society launched a long term project under the direction of B.J. Kemp and this work has continued at the site since. Kemp commenced excavation at the workers' village but has moved his focus to the main city area since 1987. As mentioned above, Amarna is an ideal venue for the study of the layout of an ancient Egyptian city in spite of its unusual character as the capital of the heretic king, Amenḥotep IV/Akhenaton. Prospects for finding more inscriptions have pretty well dwindled.

It would appear that the original venue of the tablet finds was truly the "House of Pharaoh's letters." At least some of the original "discoverers" came to work for Petrie in his excavation four years after the initial find. The following anecdote is a reliable witness (also cited by Izre'el 1997:6).

> The cuneiform tablets bearing the royal correspondence with Syria, were found in the block of chambers No. 19 (pls. XXXV, XLII). From the appearance of the chambers I believe the tablets were in the S.W. room. This site was shewn to Prof. Sayce in a previous year as the place where the tablets were found. Some natives, while I was at Tell el Amarna, offered to shew me a valuable site if I would employ them; I replied, as I always do to such offers, by telling them to go and get something from it, and I would pay them well and employ them. They went and dug a block of building; I watched them: they found nothing then, as it was exhausted, but it shewed me the spot which they deemed valuable. Afterwards I enquired of a man, where the tablets were found, and he led me to this place. Lastly, when we dug here I found one piece of a tablet in a chamber, and two rubbish pits, *which had been filled up before the walls were built* (italics mine), and which contained the other fragments …
>
> There cannot therefore be any doubt as to the site of this great discovery, which was so lamentably spoilt by the present conditions attaching to such discoveries in Egypt. (Petrie 1894: 23–24)

It has been convincingly argued that the texts were not only stored there but that scribes were trained there as well (Izre'el 1997:9–13). Except for a letter or two addressed to Tutankhamon (and maybe Semenkhareʿ), the epistles were all addressed to either Amenḥotep III and his widow, Teye (EA 26), or Amenḥotep IV (Akhenaton). Theories that Amenḥotep III spent time at Amarna, based on an assumed co-regency with his son, have been thoroughly dispelled by the proper collation of the hieratic date on EA 27, which shows that in the second year of Amenḥotep IV, Amenḥotep III was already dead and that his son was still in No-Amon.

All this indicates that when the royal entourage moved to the new capital city of Akhetaton (Amarna), the scribes brought with them a number of texts, both international and Levantine, that had been sent to the deceased pharaoh, Amenḥotep III. By the time the site was abandoned in the early reign of Tutankhamon, even a large group of letters to the deceased Akhenaton were obsolete and of no use to the bureaucrats and diplomats. Therefore, they were all discarded. In effect, most of the surviving letters consist of "closed cases," matters that had previously transpired but had come to their final consummation. They were no longer deemed worthy of transport to the new destination of the Egyptian Foreign Office. Most of, nearly all in fact, were probably disposed of in Petrie's rubbish pits. A few fragments were scattered on the floors or just outside the building. The clandestine diggers may even have dropped a fragment or two. Certain other texts, e.g. the "King of Battle," were found in other buildings. Demolition activities by the ancient Egyptian workman under the Nineteenth Dynasty, who stripped the site of its best building material for use elsewhere, and especially the work of the anonymous antiquities thieves in the nineteenth century CE, must have left Petrie's tablet house in a most disorderly state. The disturbed nature of his building 19 (Q42.21) possibly deceived Petrie into thinking that those same pits were stratigraphically covered by walls of the "House of Pharaoh's Letters," a view on which Pendelbury cast serious doubt. There is no hope of solving the enigma of the tablet venue, but the internal evidence of the texts themselves must carry some weight in the discussion.

Considering the circumstances of the initial discovery and the subsequent dispersal of the tablets to different museums and private collectors, the publication of the bulk of the Amarna tablets was accomplished in a fairly short time. The news of the discovery and the implications for biblical history no doubt served as a stimulus to European scholars to make their contents available to professional and lay audiences as soon as possible.

The history of their publication is an interesting commentary on the Assyriological profession during its formative stages and subsequent development. One tablet (now EA 260) was published in transcription only by Oppert (1888:253). The text was later collated personally by J.A. Knudtzon, who republished it in transcription (cf. *infra*). However, the cuneiform text never saw publication and the tablet cannot be located now (cf. Artzi, 1968:170, where an improved transcription is given). Most of the tablets that had reached the museums of Berlin and Cairo, plus the first one acquired by the Louvre (now EA 209) and the three in the possession of Vladimir Golenischeff (now EA 70, 137, 160; all in the Pushkin Museum, Moscow) were published by H. Winckler from autographs by L. Abel (Winckler 1889–1890). There are occasional mistakes; whole lines were even missed in one or two places. Those texts obtained for the British Museum in London were prepared for publication by C. Bezold and published jointly with E.A.W. Budge (Bezold and Budge 1892). Unfortunately, they were printed in the notoriously unsuccessful cuneiform type instead of hand copies. Four tablets in the hands of Rostovitz Bey (now EA 28, 82, 230, 292) and one belonging to Chauncey Murch (now recognized as a join to make EA 26) were published in autograph and transcription by V. Scheil (1892:298–309). The Rostovitz tablets were eventually acquired by the British Museum in 1903. The Murch fragment was also published by L. Abel (1892:117 ff.); but after that it seems to have disappeared until it was found by Dr. T.G. Allen in the Murch collection (mostly small objects from Egypt) at the Art Institute of Chicago. Records show that it had been acquired by the Institute in 1894. Subsequent republication by D.D. Luckenbill and T.G. Allen, (1916:1–8), made possible an improvement in understanding the text. In the year 2000, EA 26 was brought to Chicago as part of an Amarna exhibition from the British Museum. J.A. Brinkman was alerted to this fact, and he was able to join the Murch Fragment with the British tablet and in order to make photographs and a hand copy and translation (still unpublished). Photographs of the two pieces were made separately by the West Semitic Research photographic team, and the pictures have been joined digitally. A new tablet discovered by F.J. Bliss during excavations at Tell el-Ḥesī (southern Palestine) in 1891 and placed in the Istanbul Arkeoloji Müzeleri (now EA 333) was also published by V. Scheil (1893:137–138). It was included in Knudtzon's monumental edition. The same text, in a more reliable copy and with photographs, was later published by H.V. Hilprecht (1896: P1. LXIV, No. 147, and Pl. XXIV, Nos. 66–67). The text was collated by Rainey in September 1976. Recently it was collated anew and published by W. Horowitz and T. Oshima (2006:92–94, 214 [hand copy]). The tablets and fragments published up to this point were re-edited by Hugo Winckler (1896a), whose work consisted only of transcriptions though these were mostly based on a fresh examination of the texts.

An English translation of Winckler's work by J.P. Metcalf appeared that same year (Winckler 1896b). Meanwhile, Petrie's excavations at el-Amarna had produced twenty-two more texts, mostly fragments, which went to the Ashmolean Museum in Oxford and which were published in very inadequate hand copies by A.H. Sayce and W.M.F. Petrie (1894:34 ff., Pls. XXXI–XXXIII). They included one fragment that joined to make EA 14, a large tablet in the Berlin Museum; there were another six fragmentary letters, EA 43, 61, 135, 184, 190, 236, and a dozen scribal texts EA 342, 344, 345, 346, 347, 348, 350, 351, 352, 353, 354, 355; reference is made to two other unpublished fragments, later known as EA 343 and 349, and also to an un-inscribed tablet (Izre'el 1997). The director of the French school of archaeology in Cairo, M. Chassinat, obtained two more tablets (now EA 15, 153) that were published by V. Scheil (1902:113–116). The texts were subsequently acquired by the Metropolitan Museum of New York. Later they were republished with new hand copies by W.L. Moran in Ira Spar, ed. (1988:Plates 112–115).

All of the publications mentioned thus far, plus the many scholarly annotations and essays, were superseded by the magisterial work of J.A. Knudtzon (1915; Neudruck: Aalen, 1964). He had patiently collated personally all of the texts and fragments except for those acquired by C. Murch and M. Chassinat (cf. *supra*). Beside the fact that Knudtzon was the last person ever to see all those tablets, his own outstanding ability at reading texts and his thorough mastery of the contents of the Amarna archive made his work a priceless treasure that stood as the only reliable witness to most of the original tablets throughout the twentieth century. Sadly, Knudtzon explained that he was unable, for health as well as financial reasons, to publish hand copies of the cuneiform texts. Therefore, he had to content himself with transliterations. To aid the cuneiformist in identifying the signs that he had seen with his own eyes, a system of transcription was adopted whereby any one sign was usually rendered by its most well-known value at that time. The TUM-sign, for example, was always written *tum*, even though it appeared in some contexts where the mimation could not have been pronounced. In certain cases where he could not decide or where there is some special problem, Knudtzon provided a list of autographs at the end of his text edition to which he referred in his footnotes. However, his transcription method (for which he apologized) was not a reliable representation of the phonetic structure of the words. Comparison with previous text editions, especially those of Winckler-Abel, Scheil and Sayce, shows that Knudtzon's transcriptions represent a tremendous advance in precision. Signs, and sometimes whole lines, that previous copyists had missed, were properly recorded by Knudtzon. In a myriad of cases, Knudtzon's sharp eye corrected the interpretation of a particular sign. Today it is no secret that the transliterations of Knudtzon are usually more reliable than the autographs of his predecessors! Nevertheless, modern collation has shown that there were instances in which Abel or Bezold were correct contrary to Knudtzon. There are also many places where Knudtzon either failed to discern the signs or where he made a wrong interpretation of the traces preserved. Another significant contribution of Knudtzon's edition is his arrangement of all the tablets in a logical order based on geographical, chronological and functional considerations. His numerical system has stood the test of time and is the only accepted method of designating the texts today. By common agreement they are cited under the prefix EA plus Knudtzon's tablet number. The total number of texts in his edition was 358.

While Knudtzon's work was appearing, a new edition of hand copies made from the tablets in the Berlin Museum was published by O. Schroeder (1914–1915). Schroeder also added a fragment not included by Knudtzon (now EA 360) as well as two texts discovered in the Borchardt excavations at Amarna in 1913–1914 (now EA 359, 379). Schroeder's new facsimiles constitute a valuable, independent witness to the Berlin texts but comparison with Knudtzon's sample autographs suggests that Schroeder tended to present the signs in his own somewhat normalized ductus. Nevertheless, Schroeder took careful note of regional differences in the form of specific signs and presented them graphically in a rather complete sign list. However, recent collation has shown that when in doubt about a sign, Schroeder seems to have drawn the sign that Knudtzon had transcribed into Latin characters. Here and there, one must correct both Knudtzon and Schroeder (which must be used with great caution). An additional fragment was published by O. Schroeder (1917, cols. 105–106; now EA 361).

Additional letters appeared in a variety of venues. Six more epistles from the Amarna collection were acquired by the Louvre in 1918. Their definitive publication was by F. Thureau-Dangin, (1922:91–108; now EA 362–367). For good measure a fresh copy of the other Louvre text (EA 209) was added. Although Thureau-Dangin was one of the leading cuneiformists of his day, he did not specialize in Amarna studies but took on the publication of the Louvre texts as a side issue. Therefore, even his work can be critiqued by direct collation (cf. e.g. EA 362:1 where he mis-transcribed the name of the ruler of Byblos). Further excavation at Amarna by the renewed British expedition produced one more tablet that was added to the collection of the Ashmolean Museum, Oxford. It was a lexical list including Egyptian vocables in syllabic cuneiform. It was published in facsimile and in transliteration by S. Smith and C.J. Gadd (1925:230–240; now EA 368). The two tablets from

Amarna written in the Hittite language (EA 31 and 32) were republished in facsimile by A. Goetze (1930: Nos. 1 and 2) and recollated by L. Rost (1956). Jean Capart heard about an Amarna tablet in the hands of a dealer in Paris and by 1934 he had acquired it for the Musées Royeaux d'Art et d'Histoire in Brussels. This very important letter was published in cuneiform and transliteration by G. Dossin (1934:125–136; now EA 369). At this stage, S.A.B. Mercer published an edition of all the Amarna texts available (Mercer 1939). Basically, his was only a translation of Knudtzon's work into English with many errors introduced in the process. Mercer had seen the value of Knudtzon's edition but lacked the critical acumen to improve upon it. As for the tablets that had appeared subsequent to Knudtzon's work, Mercer added some of them at the end of the numerical sequence, viz. Nos. 359–361. On the other hand, he tried rather unsuccessfully to insert the epistles in their logical place among the Knudtzon texts. In the meantime, the Egypt Exploration Society had unearthed eight new fragments from el-Amarna during the excavation campaign of 1933–1934. Mercer had applied for permission to include these texts in his edition but was refused. They were finally published for the Society by C.H. Gordon (1947:1–21). Gordon also proposed to renumber all texts that appeared after Knudtzon's edition by adding them at the end of the latter's numerical sequence, a method only partially adopted by Mercer. E.F. Campbell (1964:79–80, n. 29) accepted Gordon's suggestion. Therefore, when A.R. Millard published a newly found tablet from the stores of the British Museum (1965:140–143), he readily assigned the newly discovered text its number (EA 378) in accordance with the new system. Finally, a perusal of the various editions led the late P. Artzi to the discovery that Gordon had overlooked one tablet when he revised the numbering of Mercer. This latter was Schroeder's No. 190 which Mercer had called 354a. It was duly pointed out by Artzi (1967:432), that the correct number of this neglected text should be EA 379. The tablets EA 359–379, that is, all those not in Knudtzon's edition, were published in transcription and translation by A.F. Rainey (1970; revised edition 1978).

All of the non-epistolary texts, that is, the so-called "Scholarly Tablets," have been restudied by Sh. Izre'el (1997). They consist of scribal exercises and reference lists and some important literary texts (and fragments). Two of these latter, "The King of Battle" (EA 359) and "Adapa and the South Wind" (EA 356), were first made known to the Assyriological world by the Amarna finds. Izre'el also included two letter fragments, one of which joins EA 56 (EA 361) and the other hitherto unpublished (EA 381).

As of this date a few tablets and fragments have disappeared or been destroyed. The one letter in the possession of J. Oppert (EA 260) disappeared; his original publication (1888) and the transcription and translation by J.A. Knudsen (1915) are all the personal collations we have. Another text (EA 7) was destroyed in 1945 during the bombing of Berlin. There was a leak in the ceiling of the Ashmolean Museum and water entered the display case and melted one fragmentary letter (EA 135) and a few of the scribal exercises. Fortunately, all of the latter were still extant when Izre'el made his new edition. The records in the Vorderasitische Museum in Berlin show that another fragmentary letter (EA 128) has been missing since an inventory in 1963.

Knudtzon's arrangements of the letters is followed explicitly in this edition and the texts that came to light after his work appear in sequence as proposed by C.H. Gordon (1947) and followed by all subsequent editions and translations (e.g. Rainey 1978; Moran 1992).

Language and Writing

It must have been something of a shock to western scholars when they finally realized that the Egyptians really did use Akkadian as a diplomatic language. But in the 1890's when the Amarna texts became available to them in reasonable editions, the study of the native Akkadian dialects was still in its infancy. The standard in the profession was mainly that of the Assyrian royal inscriptions and of other texts from Asshurbanipal's library or from the display inscriptions of other Assyrian monarchs. Nevertheless, Sayce was already able to discern that the Amarna texts were written in a Babylonian ductus, not Assyrian. The Code of ʿAmmurapi, composed in classical Old Babylonian, was only discovered at the beginning of the twentieth century and its syntactical and grammatical analysis was achieved a few years later (Ungnad 1903, 1904). Henceforth, the grammar of Old Babylonian from the days of the First Dynasty of Babylon was placed on a firm basis and became the standard for understanding the grammar of this classic dialect.

One letter, EA 24 was seen to be written in a strange language which we now know is Hurrian. Two other letters are in Hittite (EA 31 & 32). Knudtzon recognized early on that they were in a European language (Knudtzon 1902, 1916; Singer 2005). All the rest are in dialects of Akkadian. Only one letter, EA 16, is in Middle Assyrian (Grayson 1972:48–49; for grammar, cf. Mayer 1971); the Cassite correspondence is in Middle Babylonian (Aro 1955), and in fact it includes some of the best examples of that dialect (EA 6–13). It is Middle Babylonian that came to be borrowed throughout the Fertile Crescent in the Late Bronze Age. The local and regional dialects of Peripheral Akkadian (from Nuzi to Boghazköi and the Levant) were all based on Middle Babylonian with local variations, especially Hurro-Akkadian.

In the wake of Knudtzon's careful edition, it was recognized (Böhl 1909:21) that the letters from North Syria represented a different linguistic tradition from that of the texts from the southeastern Mediterranean littoral (i.e., Canaan). Now the dialect of those "northern letters" is frequently called Hurro-Akkadian because of the strong Hurrian influence on all levels of the language (script, phonology, syntax and occasional glosses). During the twentieth century, other tablet collections have been discovered with similar Akkadian dialectical features and grammatical studies of the respective groups have been written: the Boghazköi archives of the Hittite empire (Labat 1932), the Nuzi tablets (Gordon 1938; Wilhelm 1970), the Alalakh texts, especially from Stratum IV (Giacumakis 1970), the Carchemish letters found at Ugarit (Huehnergard 1979), the Ugaritian Akkadian documents including many from Hittite sources (Huehnergard 1989; van Soldt 1991), and recently the local texts from Emar (Ikeda 1995). The backbone of Hurro-Akkadian studies is the corpus of Mitanni letters from the Amarna collection (Adler 1976). The locally written texts from Ugarit and Emar do not necessarily contain any marked Hurrian influence, probably because the principal language of the local population was Semitic.

As for the texts from Amurru, a newly organized state standing between the Hurro-Akkadian states of the north and Canaan to the south, there are sub dialects among the various letters, ranging from Canaano-Akkadian to Hurro-Akkadian, which comprise the majority (Izre'el 1991). Letters from Amurru included not only the Amarna tablets but also thirteenth century texts found in Ugarit and Hattusas.

The Amarna letters written by Egyptian scribes represent a fair attempt to write Middle Babylonian, with only minor West Semitic or Egyptian influences (Cochavi-Rainey 1988, 1989, 1990a, 1990b, 1993, 2005). The study of Egyptian scribal practices also included later texts from the thirteenth century BCE, namely those sent by the royal family of Ramesses II to the royal family of Ḫattusili III. Influence from the Egyptian language is more pronounced in the nineteenth dynasty texts.

The Amarna tablets from Alashia include examples in Canaano-Akkadian besides Hurro-Akkadian though two of them (EA 36, 37) seem to come from a scribe trained in the true Middle Babylonian tradition. The texts of the Alashia corpus, including two texts found at Ugarit are a fruitful field of study (Cochavi-Rainey 2003), especially when the newest discoveries from Ugarit are published.

Most scholarly interest was focused, however, on the texts written by scribes from Canaan. Their verbal system, their many West Semitic glosses, and their very un-Akkadian syntax indicated that the native language of the authors was West Semitic; for lack of a better term, we have called it "Canaanite." It must be recognized that three linguistic strands are interwoven in the dialect(s) of these Canaano-Akkadian texts. First, it became clear that the scribes did not choose to base their "interlanguage" on the current Middle Babylonian (as did the scribes at Nuzi, Mitanni, Hattusas et al.). Instead, they chose a dialect of Old Babylonian that even contained some forms typical of Archaic Old Babylonian. The most surprising factor in that choice is that most of the cuneiform texts and fragments discovered thus far in Canaan (apart from the Tell el-Ḥesī, Tanaach, and Kâmed el-Lôz tablets) have come from the late Middle Bronze Age and belong by script and language to the Old Babylonian cuneiform horizon (for linguistic discussion of the texts from Hazor, Hebron, Shechem, cf. Rainey 1996a: vol. 2,28–31; now Horowitz and Oshima 2006). The second strand in the hybrid language of Canaan consists of local modifications of the Old Babylonian base language. Sometimes, these "colloquialisms" have been wrongly confused with West Semitic features.

The third strand, and naturally the most interesting from an historical (and cultural) point of view, is the use of "Canaanite" verbal inflection on Akkadian stems. The morphosyntactic system reflected in this strand was largely discovered by W.L. Moran (1950; republished 2003). The entire modal system of the prefix and suffix conjugations and the West Semitic functions of the prefix conjugation and the infinitive are now fairly well defined (Rainey 1996a: vol. 2).

The earliest attestations of Canaano-Akkadian are in the Taanach letters from the late fifteenth century BCE (Rainey 1977; 1999; Horowitz and Oshima 2006:127–151).

So somewhere between the end of the Middle Bronze Age and the beginning of the Late Bronze Age, the scribes of Canaan came to some kind of agreement as to the method to be employed whereby "Cananite" inflection would be applied to the Old Babylonian stems. How we would like to know just where and when that happened! Was it due to some dominant, creative personality in one of the scribal schools? Did this result in, or was it the result of, a spoken "interlanguage" that developed among the local administrators (according to Moran)? The answers to these and other questions must remain wrapped in obscurity. Perhaps the discovery of a real local archive will shed some light on them. The Jerusalem scribe reveals an amazing mixture of Middle Assyrian, Middle Babylonian and hybrid West

Semitized forms unlike any other author in the Amarna corpus (Moran 1975; Cochavi-Rainey and Rainey 2009).

The handful of literary works and school texts, including a short list of Egyptian words and their Sumerian equivalents (EA 368) stem from the Mesopotamian tradition but some of the compositions have strong Hurrianizing influence (e.g. EA 359; cf. Izre'el 1995).

The proper nouns, i.e. personal, divine and geographic names, have all been restudied and presented in modern format by R. Hess (1984, 1993).

The Collection and Its Contents

The Egyptian scribes certainly maintained an administrative archive, not only of the many documents written in hieratic on papyrus, but also of the cuneiform correspondence in which they had to be engaged. The composition of the staff of scribes that served in "The House of Pharaoh's Letters" remains an enigma. Some of the Amarna tablets have hieratic notations in black ink. Two of the literary pieces have a system of red dots like those sometimes employed in hieratic literary texts (cf. Izre'el 1997:11). So, of course, there were native Egyptians trained in the standard curriculum of the pharaonic administration. On the other hand, the "office copies" of cuneiform letters that were written in Egypt and sent abroad testify to the need to assume that trained cuneiformists were also present. Were there two sets of scribes, one for hieratic and one for cuneiform? Or were they basically an integrated cadre? Perhaps some graduates of the Egyptian school were selected to learn a new specialization, viz. how to read and write cuneiform. Given the varied nature of the texts received (Middle Babylonian, Hurro-Akkadian, Canaano-Akkadian), the cuneiformists would have had to be especially skilled in interpretation. The ruler of Arzawa even asked that all correspondence between the two states be conducted in Hittite (EA 32:24–25)! One of the Hittite letters is actually from pharaoh to the ruler of Arzawa. And then there is the one great Hurrian letter (EA 24) and some Hurrian glosses on texts in Hurro-Akkadian. Of special interest is the question of the hybrid language used by scribes in the Southern Levant. The letters by Egyptian scribes in the Amarna collection show a fairly good knowledge of Middle Babylonian with a ductus resembling that of the northern Levant or of the Hittite sphere. Were those same scribes, trained in Middle Babylonian, able to read the letters from Canaan without assistance? An occasional Middle Babylonian gloss to verbs in the hybrid dialect suggest that the Levantine scribe wanted to be sure that the recipient in Egypt understood the exact verbal nuance intended. So were there some Canaanites working in the same office? And how about Hurrians or Hittites? All these questions will have to remain unanswered. In spite of many conjectures, no one can estimate just how many tablets have been lost.

In any case, the surviving tablets are due to the happenstance of discovery. They were all thrown away when Akhetaten was abandoned in the early years of Tutankhamun. The various groups of letters dealing with one principal event had become "closed cases." Some of the correspondents were dead by that time, e.g. Tushrata, king of Mittani. In fact the kingdom of Mittani was no longer in existence. It had been conquered by the Hittites and split between them and the Assyrians.

One can hardly call our corpus an "archive." What we have are remnants of an archive. Their nature is suggestive of the contents and perhaps organization of that archive. There is no comparison, however, with the vast archive discovered at Ebla, where thousands of texts were found lying in a huge pile just as they had fallen when the storage room was destroyed by fire and the wooden shelves consumed. Therefore, throughout this present edition, our corpus is generally referred to as the "Amarna collection."

The Near East during the Fourteenth Century BCE

The peace with Mittani that was achieved under Thutmose IV was inherited by his son, Amenḥotep III (prenomen: *Nb-mȝʿt-Rʿ* = cuneiform *Nibmuarea/Nimmuria*). This latter pharaoh enjoyed what was in many respects the golden age of Egyptian history, certainly the peak of New Kingdom cultural, social and economic development (Fletcher 2000; O'Connor and Cline 1998). Except for one campaign to Nubia (O'Connor 1998:264–268), this pharaoh found no necessity to wage war. Canaan was in his hands (Weinstein 1998) and Mittani was at peace. He enjoyed diplomatic and commercial relations with Babylon and Mittani (Kitchen 1998), Alashia (on Cyprus), Crete and the Aegean kingdoms, especially Mycenae, and Arzawa in southern Anatolia (Cline 1998). Abundant harvests and a steady flow of gold and other resources from Nubia gave him a senior position in the world economy. During his thirty-eight year reign he expended vast sums on public buildings, including his own mortuary temple. The sun god Reʿ from Heliopolis was joined with Amon, the secluded god of Karnak, thus signifying some new symbiosis between the chief cults of north and south. Amenḥotep III liked to call himself "the dazzling Sun King" (Berman 1998).

That dazzling era came to a dramatic denouement with the accession of the next ruler, Amenḥotep IV (prenomen *Nfr-ḫprw-Rꜥ* = cuneiform *Napḫur[u]Rea*) whose seventeen year reign ended in chaos both at home and in the Levant. The new pharaoh expanded a theme in his father's poetic inscriptions, namely the reference to the Aten, the disc of the sun. A new temple was built (or begun) just east of the Amon temple at Karnak but soon the king felt it necessary to move his entire royal entourage to a new capital. He chose the site now known as Tell el-Amarna (ʿAmârnah) about midway between No-Amon and Memphis. The work was begun there by regnal year four and by regnal six or eight, the king and all his people had moved to the new site. During the ensuing years, it was decided to close the temple of Amon in No-Amon as well as other temples throughout Egypt.

Amenḥotep IV changed his name to Akhenaten "Beneficial to the Aten" and made the single focus of his capital city (named Akhetaten "Horizon of the Sun Disc") the worship of the Aten, the disc of the sun. From the banks of the Nile, a view to the eastern ridge that encircled the semicircular plain with the wadi in the center resembled the hieroglyph of the sun rising between two mountains and signifying the horizon.

His senior ministers all seem to have had military rank and one gets the feeling that the entire "Amarna Revolution" in religion was also a move by the military sector against the formal religious/financial sector (which controlled vast economic resources).

Late in his reign, Akhenaten appointed a son, Smenkhkare (prenomen *ʿnḫ-ḫprw-Rꜥ* = cuneiform *Ḫuʾurea*?), as coregent but both of them seem to have disappeared from the scene together and were succeeded by Tutankhaten who soon changed his name to Tutankhamun (prenomen *Nb-ḫprw-Rꜥ* = cuneiform *Nibḫurirea*) and abandoned the capital city of Amarna while moving to restore the traditional religious institutions. His proclamation explains that the country had been reduced to chaos. The judiciary was corrupt and the military failed to achieve any of its objectives.

The events documented for the Levantine littoral during the fourteenth century BCE are closely linked to the events in Egypt. The testimony to those events derives mainly from the collection of cuneiform letters discovered in the ruins of the Amarna site. Over a century of studying those texts has produced a reasonable synthesis of several "case histories" concerning city-states and other elements in Central Syria and in the province of Canaan (the southern Levant) as well as a limited number of international communications between the major political states of the region. Of course, the publication of texts from Ḫattusa (Boghazköi) has led to a much more detailed history of the period. Texts from Ugarit, including some sent there from the Hittite rulers, can be coordinated with the information of the Amarna tablets. These will be elucidated and illustrated in the ensuing discussion (cf. Rainey apud Rainey and Notley 2006:77–87).

International Correspondence

Babylon and Egypt

The correspondence between Kadashman-Enlil I and Amenḥotep III has to do mainly with negotiations for royal intermarriage. Things did not run so smoothly. The Cassite ruler was anxious to receive the maximum amount of precious gold in exchange for his daughter (EA 4:36–50).

Kadashman-Enlil was followed by Burnaburiash II, who also made overtures to Amenḥotep III for the continuance of diplomatic relations (EA 6:8–10).

With the accession of Amenḥotep IV, Burnaburiash approached him in order to continue the political and commercial ties (EA 7:37–39). However, the Babylonian king professed ignorance of the great distance involved in the journey from Egypt to Mesopotamia (EA 7:14–32).

The amazing list of items sent from Egypt (EA 14) is lacking its introductory lines, and the name of the sender is not certain; it is obviously a vast caravan of gifts sent to Babylon for a princess who was pledged to the Egyptian harem (Cochavi-Rainey 1999:7–38). The robbing of Babylonian caravans by local officials in Canaan will be discussed below.

Mittani and Egypt

Tushratta approached the king of Egypt, Amenḥotep III, as soon as he had gained firm control over his own government (EA 17:1–29). He also mentions that there had been an encounter with Hittite forces and he sent some of the spoil to Amenḥotep (EA 17:30–38). The economic aspect of the Egypt-Mittani relationship is underlined by Tushratta:

> And in the land of my brother gold is plentiful like dirt. (EA 19:59–61)

Two texts (EA 22, EA 25) are lists of luxury items sent from Mittani to Egypt. Like EA 14 from Egypt, the collections of objects, implements, clothes, etc., in these lists are extraordinary (Cochavi-Rainey 1999:51–162). The proposed royal marriage with a daughter of Tushratta, Tadu-Kheba, is a central theme of the correspondence, including the one letter written in the Hurrian language (EA 24). Tushratta's sister, Kelu-Kheba, was already in the Egyptian harem.

With the death of Amenḥotep III, Tushratta took steps to assure continuity in the close political and economic connections between Egypt and his country. He wrote to Teye, the wife of Amenḥotep III, to confirm the stability of these ties (EA 26). At the same time, he wrote to the new pharaoh, Amenḥotep IV, and urged him to ask his mother if he needed to be briefed on the Mittani-Egypt diplomatic relations (EA 29:6–10). In response to a letter with gifts from Amenḥotep IV, Tushratta had replied by sending gifts (EA 27). The hieratic colophon at the end of this letter reads, according to new collation and photographs:

> [Ye]ar 2, first month of winter, day [9?], when one (pharaoh) was in the southern city, in the castle of *Ḫʿ-m-ꜣḫt*; copy of the Nahrina letter that the messenger Pirissi and the messenger [Tulubri] brought.

It is thus crystal clear that by the second year of Amenḥotep IV, his father was already dead (Fritz 1991:Pl. 7; *contra* Giles 2001:31–32). Thus, there is no evidence whatsoever to support a long co-regency between Amenḥotep III and IV (*contra* Giles 1997, 2001).

As discussed above, the death of Tushratta led to the eventual conquest of Mittani and North Syria by Suppiluliuma. Those events are described in the texts from Ḫattusa.

Alashia

The handful of letters from Alashia reflect the relations with Egypt at approximately the time of transition between Amenḥotep III and IV. The name of the Alashian king is not given, nor is the name of the pharaoh. But allusions to the latter's celebrations and inauguration on the throne show that the recipient had just entered into office (cf. Helbing 1979:8–12). The letters probably represent a period of several years during the reign of Amenḥotep IV. All of the tablets were made of clay from the southern coast of Cyprus (Goren, Finkelstein and Na'aman 2004:48–73). There are three dialects represented in the letters (Cochavi-Rainey 2003). On one occasion, it looks as though pharaoh may have accused the Alashians of some act of piracy. The ruler of Alashia seems to be putting the blame on the Lukku people (classical Lycians) (EA 38:7–12).

All of the Alashia letters deal with shipments of copper for Egypt. The ruler of Alashia generally asks for silver (not gold!) and other Egyptian products, including manufactured goods. However, one very broken passage in a letter written in the Middle Babylonian dialect (Rainey 1995–1996:111), indicates that there was a three way channel of trade (EA 36:12–16). The copper went from Alashia to Egypt, perhaps in return for shipments of grain to Alashia from Canaan.

It has been suggested (Helbing 1979:14–16) that the reference to a plague ("the hand of Nergal [= Resheph])" may indicate that the letter was sent during the very end of Akhenaten's reign (EA 35:10–15, 30–39). Perhaps the Alashian who had died in Egypt was also a victim to the plague.

Levantine Correspondence

The Amurru Affairs

Nearly seventy letters in the Amarna collection are from Byblos (Gubla; known today by its Arabic name Jubail), situated on the Mediterranean seacoast about 32 km (20 miles) N of Beirut, mainly from its ruler, Rib-Haddi. From the internal evidence the texts may be divided into two groups, the first dating to the reign of Amenḥotep III and the second to the time of Amenḥotep IV. In both cases, Rib-Haddi is trying to warn the Egyptian king and his ministers of imminent danger to the Egyptian interests and territory. During the course of events reflected in his correspondence, one can trace the changes in Egyptian policy which finally, under Amenḥotep IV, resulted in the establishment of the hereditary state of Amurru and its subsequent apostasy to the king of the Hittites, Suppiluliuma.

The first enemy to Egyptian interests was a man of unnamed ancestry or origin, ʿAbdi-Ashirta, bearer of a transparently Semitic name. Both Rib-Haddi and ʿAbdi-Ashirta express concern for the safety of Ṣumur (Simyra = Tell Kazel north of the Nahr el Kebîr) the headquarters of the Egyptian commissioner in N. Lebanon. Rib-Haddi blames the danger on the *ʿapîru* men (EA 68:9–26).

On the other hand, ʿAbdi-Ashirta claims to be protecting Ṣumur from a threat by the "kings of the Hurrian army," undoubtedly the rulers of such states as Niyi and Nughasse in inland Syria (EA 60:7–32). In another, badly broken text, ʿAbdi-Ashirta wrote to Paḫamnata that he had rushed from neighboring ʿIrqatu to rescue the Egyptian base at Ṣumur from an attack by the "troops of the city of Sheḫlali" (EA 62:19–24 *et passim* also in EA 371). This Sheḫlali has been compared unconvincingly to *tȝ šȝśw Śá-ʿ-ra-r* from the Amarah temple of Ramesses II (Astour 1979:22–23). This latter appears in the company of other Shâsu territories but the suggestion does not seem likely.

But Rib-Haddi explains to Ḫaya, the vizier of Egypt, that ʿAbdi-Ashirta is supported by the lawless *ʿapîru* men (EA 71:10–31). He also explains to

Aman-appa, his own immediate "handler" in the Egyptian foreign office, how ʿAbdi-Ashirta is undermining the local rulers of Amurru (EA 73:14–33). In subsequent letters, Rib-Haddi recounted how ʿAbdi-Ashirta was advancing on Byblos by taking successive port towns along the northern coast, e.g. Ambi, Baṭrôna and Shigata. After a long period of complaints and urgings, Amenḥotep III and his advisors apparently decided to act. Aman-appa had come with a limited auxiliary force but was ineffective. Then Ḫaya was sent with an expeditionary force of regular Egyptian sea borne troops. Yet Ḫaya seemed reluctant to commit them to battle. Thus he is accused by Rib-Haddi of acting against the better interests of Egypt (EA 101:1–10, 18–37; collated 27.8.99; *contra* Liverani 1998). In later flashbacks, Rib-Haddi makes mention of the final result of that expedition (EA 117:21–28; cf. Moran 1992:194 nn. 2–3), viz. that ʿAbdi-Ashirta was taken.

However, something went wrong. The Arvadians, who were supporting Egypt's adversaries, were not detained in Egypt, and they were instrumental in obtaining ʿAbdi-Ashirta's property for his sons. Not only that, but they also assisted the sons in seizing coastal towns and in laying siege to the Egyptian governor's headquarters at Ṣumur. But most startling of all, the military equipment of the Egyptian expeditionary force, including their ships, was turned over to ʿAbdi-Ashirta's sons! This has the smell of an under-the-table arms deal! No wonder Ḫaya was not anxious to move against ʿAbdi-Ashirta. He was sympathetic to what ʿAbdi-Ashirta sought to do. One is led to wonder if Ḫaya may not have benefited personally from the transfer of the ships and armaments to the sons of ʿAbdi-Ashirta. Henceforth, the sons of ʿAbdi-Ashirta continued the program of their father, whose ultimate fate is not revealed in the texts; cf. (EA 104:6–54). Ullasa was evidently classical Orthosia (at modern day Tripoli), and the other towns mentioned are all north of Byblos, mostly along the coast. ʿIbirta (Youngblood 1961:249) was a crossing point on the Nahr el-Kebîr.

Pu-Baʿlu's brother, ʿAziru (Hess 1993:46), was the senior partner and as such, he is their spokesman. He consistently promises the king and his chief minister, Tutu, that he will supply their every request (EA 156:4–14; EA 158:5–19; cf. Izreʾel 1991: II, 22). It would seem that Tutu and some other high ranking Egyptian officials had come to the conclusion that it would serve Egypt's best interests if ʿAziru and his brothers could establish a buffer state on the northern border of Canaan. On the one hand, Suppiluliuma's forces were making their presence felt in N. Syria. On the other hand, an Amurru buffer state would control the plain bisected by the Nahr el-Kebîr and also the pass between the Lebanese mountains and the Jebel Anṣariyeh; that is, the corridor linking the Mediterranean coast with central Syria.

Control of that passageway could enable ʿAziru to acquire vast sums of tariff customs from the lucrative caravan trade. Thus, ʿAziru promised the king and Tutu (and probably other officials) a generous share in the profits.

One senior government official, Yanḫamu, was closer to the situation in the field and he held ʿAziru in great suspicion. Yanḫamu was known as a straight arrow (EA 171:3–13). Perhaps Yanḫamu's influence led to the "invitation" to ʿAziru to visit Egypt. The visit is mentioned retrospectively (EA 161:4–6; Izreʾel 1991: II, 35; Singer 1991:151). While he was in Egypt, ʿAziru received a letter from his brother, Baʿluya and his son, Bêti-ʿilu apprising him of a Hittite invasion of the land of ʿAmqi and of the reported arrival of a large army in central Syria led by Zitana, the brother of Suppiluliuma (EA 170). They also wrote to the king(?) and to Tutu (EA 169:12–34). ʿAziru's family had paid a ransom for his release, and they insist that his presence was needed in Amurru in order to protect Egypt's interests in the face of the Hittite threat. When ʿAziru was released, he immediately began to take steps towards his eventual desertion to Suppiluliuma. By now pharaoh had become suspicious and urged ʿAziru to return (EA 162), but the wily fox kept putting it off on the pretext of the Hittite threat.

Meanwhile, the hapless Rib-Haddi, whose warnings and entreaties were ignored by pharaoh, was forced to abandon his city due to his own brother's perfidy (EA 137:14–26; EA 138:39–50). He sought asylum in Beirut where a new ruler, ʿAmmunīri, received him grudgingly (EA 142:15–24). Later he even approached ʿAziru to try to make a pact (EA 162:2–4), but the last he is heard of, he was in Sidon and ʿAziru handed him over to the local rulers who presumably put him to death (EA 162:12–14).

The brother who had ousted Rib-Haddi was Ilirapiʾ who wrote to pharaoh to complain about the behavior of ʿAziru (EA 139, EA 140). Ousting Rib-Haddi left him exposed to further aggression by ʿAziru. He also complains about ʿAziru's crime after(?) his "visit" to Egypt (EA 140:20–24) when he got back to Amurru (EA 140:24–30).

So ʿAziru was working hand in hand with Aitakkama of Qidshi to gain control of the Lebanese Beqʿa. This would probably explain the two letters from Kāmed el-Lôz that were sent by Ilirapiʾ. Neither of these latter show a proper command of cuneiform orthography. Each one is full of mistakes, graphic and orthographic.

> To the senior official, my lord, speak: the message of Ilirapʾ (ᴵ*E-lì-ra-pí*), your servant; at the foot of my lord I have fallen. Behold, the men of Byblos(!) (ᵁᴿᵁGUB[!MAḪ]-*la*; Huehnergard 1996:100) the city of the king, my lord …
> (KL 74:300:1–7; Edzard 1982:131; Naʾaman 1988:192–193)

The other text has surfaced in the antiquities market (Huehnergard 1996). It accuses ʿAmmunīra and some other people (including a certain ʿAmmurapiʾ) of taking an oath with ʿAziru. These two letters were probably addressed to Puḫuru, who was the Egyptian commissioner at Kômidi.

In answer to pharaoh's demands that he present himself (again) to the king in Egypt, ʿAziru made the excuse that Suppiluliuma was too close. He ostensibly wanted to protect Egyptian controlled territory (EA 166:21–29). What he really did is spelled out in the preamble to the treaty between him and Suppiluliuma:

> ʿAziru, the king of [Amurru] abandoned the gate of Egypt and became subservient to the Sun, the ki[ng of Ḫat]ti. And the Sun, the great king, rejoiced […] that ʿAziru fell at the feet of the Sun. He (ʿAziru) came from the gate of Egypt and he fell at the feet of the Sun. I, the Sun, the great king, [received] ʿAziru and I added him to his colleagues …
>
> (Hittite version, I, 23–26; Singer 1990:146–147)

Henceforth, Amurru was a vassal state of the Hittite empire (with a few periods of defection; cf. Singer 1991). The Egyptian response, the planning of a military campaign, will be discussed below.

The Lebanese Biqʿa (*ʿAmqi*) *and the Damascene* (*Upe*)

In parallel with the subversive activities of Aziru in Amurru, Aitakkama in Qidshu was actively furthering the interests of Suppiluliuma. Originally, Aitakkama had gone forth with his father Shutatarra to confront Suppiluliuma when the latter had made a foray into Syria; they were defeated on the field of battle and finally captured after seeking refuge in a certain Abzu(ya) a central Syrian town (*CTH* 51:40–43 = Weidner 1923:114; Beckman 1996b:39–40), possibly to be located at Ḥoms or just north of it (Klengel 1970:109 n. 79). Evidently, Aitakkama was allowed to return to Qidshu as its ruler. In that capacity, he worked deceitfully to expand his own territory while claiming to be a loyal vassal of Egypt. His actions brought him into conflict with Biryawaza, who had responsibility for the Damascus area (EA 189) and who probably ruled in Damascus. While Aitakkama claims that Biryawaza had burned towns in the land of Taḫsi (the northern Biqʿa) and in Ôpe (Upe; the Damascene), Biryawaza makes the opposite claim, viz. that Aitakkama has caused the defection of Qidshi (Qissu) and that he is supported by Arsawuya from Rôǵiṣu, who (using troops from Aziru!) captured a town named Shaddu. On the other hand, a rival named Biridashwa, ruler of ʿAshtartu (Ashtaroth), had incited the town of Yanoʿam, which has to be located in the Bashan or the Hauran, possibly on one of the branches of the

Yarmuk River (Tell esh-Shiḥâb? Na'aman 1977; 1988:183), and stirred up other cities in the Bashan area, viz. Buṣruna and ʿAlunnu.

Against the background of these deeds, it must be noted that at one time, Rib-Haddi reported that ʿAziru son of ʿAbdi-Ashirta, with all his brothers, was in Damascus (EA 107:26–28). What ʿAziru was doing there is anybody's guess, but it surely was not supporting Egyptian interests.

Two lengthy epistles (EA 185 and EA 186) were found among the Amarna texts from Mayarzana, the ruler of Ḫasi (Tell Ḥizzîn? Kuschke 1958:99) in the northern Biqʿa valley. He complains bitterly about the behavior of a neighboring ruler, an Egyptian named Amanḫatpe, located at Tushultu (unidentified; Kuschke 1958:100). It seems that a band of *ʿapîru* raiders were attacking and plundering cities in the Biqʿa Valley and then taking refuge with Amanḫatpe (EA 185:16–20). Mayarzana repeats the same refrain about several other towns: Gilôni (EA 185:21–27), Magdali (EA 185:28–36; Tell Mejlûn near Baalbek, Kuschke 1958:110), and Ušte (EA 185:37–410). Finally, the *ʿapîrû* besieged Ḫasi, but Mayarzana's forces beat them off. Some of them took refuge with Amanḫatpe, and charioteers and troops from Mayarzana tried to force Amanḫatpe to hand them over but to no avail. Who these *ʿapîrû* were is not known. Were they forces sent by Aitakama? Were they forces sent by ʿAziru? They were not tribesmen of any kind.

Identical letters were sent from four local rulers in the Biqʿa, viz. Bi'eri of Ḫašabu (EA 174), Andaya of Ḫasi (EA 175; successor of Mayarzana?), ʿAbdirēša of ʿÊ‹ni›-šasi (EA 363; Rainey 1978a:24–25; cf. Rainey 1975) and another sender whose name and venue are broken off from the tablet (EA 176). They all give an identical report. This would appear to be a reference to a foray by the Hittites deep into Egyptian territory assisted by Aitakama of Qidshu.

The excavations at Kâmed el-Lôz, Kômidi of the Amarna texts, in Syria (Badre 1997; Hachmann 1986, 1989) have brought to light several cuneiform texts more or less contemporary with the Amarna collection (Edzard 1970, 1976, 1980, 1982, 1986; Wilhelm 1973, 1982); two other texts have also appeared via the antiquities market (Arnaud 1991; Huehnergard 1996). It is difficult to correlate them with the Amarna texts (cf. Na'aman 1988).

Southern Canaan

There are also groups of texts pertaining to affairs in southern Canaan. Some of these events can be more or less coordinated with the happenings up north, but there are less specific references to a particular king than, for example, in the ʿAbdi-Ashirta/ʿAziru case histories. One way to attempt a chronological linkage is through the Egyptian officials mentioned in both north and south (Campbell 1965:90–105). Yanḫamu, a very senior representative of the Egyptian authorities is the main personality in this connection. Nevertheless, some of the main "case histories" can be dated to the end of the reign of Amenḥotep III or the beginning of the reign of Amenḥotep IV.

A key player in the early stages of action in the south was Milkilu, the ruler of Gezer (Gazru). One of the texts sent by the older king is EA 369 and exemplifies the kind of requests made by pharaoh from his vassals. He asked that Milkilu "send women cupbearers (who are) very beautiful, of whom there is no guile in their hearts":

> Now, Amon has placed the Upper Land and the Lower Land, the Sunrise and the Sunset, under the two feet of the king.

The reference to the god Amon (written ^{d}*A-ma-nu*) assures that the letter was written by Amenḥotep III. A letter to Yidia of Ashkelon, sent near the end of the Amarna period, has a modified formulation without reference to Amon:

> And may [you be apprised that] the king is fine (well) l[ike the sun]in heaven. [His infantry and] his chariotry are great (or: very [well?]). From the upper land to [the lower land], from the sunrise to the sunset, it is very well.
> (EA 370:23–29)

On the other hand, Milkilu protested vociferously against Yanḫamu (EA 270). The commissioner is accused of saying to the vassal, "Give me your wife and your sons or else I will smite (you)." The occasion of this incident and pharaoh's response are unknown.

Another player in the southern intrigues was the ruler of Gath-padalla (*Gitti-padalla* = Jatt in the Sharon Plain, Rainey 2004; Rainey apud Rainey and Notley 2006:89c–99c), whose name is, in accordance with common practice of the time, written with Sumerian ideograms, ${}^{\text{I.d}}$IŠKUR.UR.SAG which means "the storm god is a hero (warrior)." This name can hardly be anything else but the Canaanite Baʿlu-meher, which means "Baal is the warrior." Baʿlu-meher complained bitterly that his supporters were being commandeered by Milkilu (EA 249:4–17). Baʿlu-meher is caught between Milkilu to his south and the latter's father-in-law, Tagi, in the Carmel area. According to an allusion in a Jerusalem letter (EA 289:18–20), there is a town called Gath-carmel which belongs to Tagi and thus places him somewhere on the plan of Acco. That reference does not necessarily mean that Gath-carmel is the seat of Tagi's rule but only that Gath-carmel is one of his towns, in fact the formulation seems to suggest that Gath-Carmel is not his main place of residence. Evidently, Tagi is also being credited with furnishing the personnel for the Egyptian garrison at Beth-shean. Gath-carmel is certainly the *Getta* mentioned by Plinius (*Nat. Hist.* V, xviii, 74; Tsafrir, de Segni and Green 1994:135). It is somewhere near Mt. Carmel (*contra* Goren, Finklestein and Na'aman 2002:249–250). It need not have been Tagi's main base but only a town that belonged to him. Possibly it could be located at Tell Abū Huwâm or Tel Nahal (Tell en-Nahl; personal communication J. Balensi 1999). Tagi himself may have ruled at some other significant town such as Tel Muʿammer (Tell ʾAmr).

Baʿlu-meher also requests a reply from pharaoh but in such a way that neither Milkilu nor another man, Lab'ayu, would hear about it. That could well explain why his letter was written on clay at Beth-shean to be sent via caravan to Acco and from there to Egypt by sea, thus avoiding the trunk route passing Gezer. Milkilu is, therefore, linked with his father-in-law in the Carmel area and with this other person, Lab'ayu. The latter is presumed to be located at Shechem on the basis of another allusion in the Jerusalem letters. The passage deals with the behavior of Milkilu and the sons of Lab'ayu, i.e. after Lab'ayu's demise.

> "Or should we do like Lab'ayu," they are giving the land of Shakmu to the *ʿapîru* men!
> (EA 289:21–24; Adamthwaite 1992:4)

The chance find of a clay cylinder from Beth-shean, which bears a cuneiform inscription that is at least a partial excerpt from a letter sent by Tagi to Lab'ayu (Horowitz 1996), provides further evidence for the connection between these two figures who appear in the letter from Baʿlu-meher. This is a valid observation even if the formula on the cylinder is merely a practice text (Rainey 1998:239–242).

Lab'ayu's own texts do not reveal his venue, but they provide some details that would best suit a location at Shechem (Tell el-Balâṭah). Furthermore, the clay of his tablets suggests the central hills of Samaria either near or not far from Shechem (Goren, Finkelstein and Na'aman 2004:262–265). One letter has to do with a local conflict about which Lab'ayu has asked counsel from the king. Hostile elements have "seized the town ‹and› my god, the plunderers of my father" (EA 252; collated 26.8.99). It has been conjectured (Reviv 1966a) that Lab'ayu's town that was taken by his enemies may have been somewhere in the hill country but not at Shechem. The town in question must have been Lab'ayu's patrimony because his house and his family deity (a statue) had been plundered; his enemies were "the plunderers of my father."

Two other letters from Lab'ayu deal with an undefined accusation against him. It would seem that he had been involved in some business frowned upon by the Egyptian authorities, probably over stepping his bounds with regard to royal territory, and that he had been severely fined (EA 254:6–29; cf. EA 253:7–24). Milkilu of Gezer may have been an accomplice but seems to have avoided the fine. Perhaps he had turned the state's evidence? One may be led to wonder if Lab'ayu's aggression against towns in the Dothan and Jezreel Valleys (discussed below) may have been the main cause of his falling into disfavor. In any case, the same letter sheds more light on the social conditions prevailing in Lab'ayu's home territory. His son was accused of complicity to act against Egyptian interests by associating with the renegade *ʿApîru* (EA 254:30–37). Lab'ayu's professed ignorance and innocence are not convincing. There were apparently bands of *ʿApîru* in the region around Lab'ayu's venue and his son was deeply involved in their activities. All this makes sense in view of other correspondence discussed below which associates Lab'ayu with the *ʿApîru*. It also makes more sense if he is really located at Shechem. The hill country (biblical: "Hill country of Ephraim") would have been a natural place for such stateless refugees or renegades to seek refuge. The suspect son was turned over to Addaya, who was an officer located at Gaza. On other occasions, he carried out similar missions.

Clear testimony to Lab'ayu's further activities is given by the ruler of Gath-padalla in a flashback after the sons of Lab'ayu were seeking to reactivate their father's program (EA 250:4–14). From the quotation of Lab'ayu's sons, Gath-padalla had been taken by their father. It would seem that at one time, Baʿl-meher had been reduced to subservience to Lab'ayu. The next move by the ruler of Shechem took a northerly direction: "… he attacked Shunem, Burquna and ʿArabu and depopulated two of them …, and seized Gitti-rimmuni (Gath-rimmon) and cultivated the ⸢fields⸣ of the king, your lord" (EA 250:40–47). Two of these towns were in the Valley of Dothan and the two others were in the Jezre'el Valley. The latter, at least, were responsible for crown lands (Na'aman 1981, 1988c), and the former may have been also. But they also controlled one branch of the trunk route from the Sharon Plain to Beth-shean and all points east.

It must have been after this move that Megiddo came under pressure from Lab'ayu. The ruler of Megiddo, Biridiya, reported to Pharaoh that Lab'ayu has "set his face to take Megiddo" (EA 244:8–43).

There had been a unit of the regular Egyptian army posted at Megiddo, probably encamped outside the city. For some reason, that unit was called home. Was it for something like a Sed festival of Amenḥotep III or perhaps was it to assist in the transition from the older king to the young Amenḥotep IV? Whatever the cause, Lab'ayu saw this as an opportunity to make a move on Megiddo. At about this time, Yashdata, a neighbor of Biridiya, was forced from his home by "the men of Taa[nach]," which led him to seek asylum at Megiddo (EA 248:9–22). This tends to suggest that the men of Taanach had joined Lab'ayu at about the time when the latter had seized those towns in the Dothan and Jezre'el Valleys. There are hints in the texts that Tagi was in collusion with Lab'ayu. The sample protocol for a letter discovered on the cylinder from Beth-shean immediately comes to mind:

> *ana Lab'aya, bēliya, qibīma umma Tagi ana šarri bēliya išteme šapārka ana iaši....*
>
> To Lab'ayu, my lord, speak: the word of Tagi to the king, my lord; I have heard your message to me ... (Horowitz 1996:210)

If the original editor is correct in assuming that in this letter Tagi is calling Lab'ayu by the title "king" (which is not certain; Rainey 1998b:239–240), then it puts a new twist on the Lab'ayu affair.

Ultimately, Pharaoh issued an order to arrest Lab'ayu and to send him alive to Egypt to answer for his actions. The rulers in the region carried out the warrant, but it was Surata, the ruler of Acco, who took a bribe and released the culprit. When Lab'ayu tried to escape back to his home base at Shechem, he was trapped by an ambush and slain. Apparently, his colleagues did not want him to reach Egypt alive (EA 245)

Since Lab'ayu had seized towns in the Jezreel Valley and depopulated them, the harvest had to be tended. Further orders must have gone out to the local rulers to provide forced labor for cultivating the crown lands in that area. Biridiya announced his compliance (EA 365:8–29).

There is no way to ascertain how much time elapsed before the sons of Lab'ayu began to actively initiate a new round of intrigues. The ruler of Gath-padalla reported to pharaoh that he was obedient (EA 257:7–22; *contra* Na'aman 1998:52). Confirmation of Milkilu's co-operation with the sons of Lab'ayu comes from 'Abdi-Kheba, ruler of Jerusalem (EA 289:21–24; Moran 1987:518; Campbell 1965:201–202; Adamthwaite 1992; Rainey 1995–1996:119–120).

The outcome of this second phase of the conflict is not documented among the surviving tablets. There are, however, some texts that shed light on intercity tensions and conflicts in the southern part of Canaan. The letters from 'Abdi-Kheba, ruler of Jerusalem, reflect the dispute over sites controlling the main routes from the coastal plain to the central watershed route in the mountains. That ruler's name, written partially with Sumerian ideograms, meaning "Servant of Kheba," must be Semitic even though the theophoric element is the Hurrian goddess corresponding to Pidray in the

Ugaritic god lists (Pardee 2002:14, line C 16). Hurrian personal names are not built on the "Servant of …" pattern. Letters from his arch-rival, Shuwardata, give the opposing view. This later person was evidently the ruler of Gath (Tell eṣ-Ṣâfī = Tel Zafit), which seems to be confirmed by the clay of his tablets (Goren, Finkelstein and Na'aman 2004:279–286). Shuwardata claimed that Keilah belonged under his hegemony (EA 280:9–15). The site in question is in the trough valley at the foot of the Judean hills; it suits the biblical data (Josh 15:44).

On the other hand, ʿAbdi-Kheba gives a different view of the conflict, claiming that Keilah was lured away from him (EA 290:5–28; Zimmern 1891:141 n.; Greenberg 1955:151, 162 n. 42; Rainey 1978c:149; *contra* Moran 1992:334 n. 2). Another town in the Jerusalem/Gath controversy was Rubbotu. It may possibly be identified with Hārabbāh (Josh. 15:60; Aharoni 1969:35, 383 nn. 95, 96) but it certainly must be the *Ra-bú-tu* that follows Gezer in the Thutmose III topographical list (No. 105). Whether it should be located in the Shephelah (near modern Latrun) or further up in the hills (near Kiriath-yearim) is an open question. It is a place that ʿAbdi-Kheba hints should belong to Jerusalem's sphere of influence. Another disputed town was Bīt-NINIB, which remains a point of intense controversy. The ideographic writing (URU É.NINIB) indicated "the town of the House of (deity name)." The question is which deity. The ideogram can stand for the Akkadian Ninurta, god of pestilence and war. It hardly seems credible that a place in Canaan would be named after a Mesopotamian deity. So which West Semitic deity was equated with NINIB = Ninurta? In spite of some comparative god lists from Ugarit, none gives the equation for NINIB. Today the best suggestion is that of Albright, elaborated by Kallai and Tadmor (1969), to see here Beth-horon. Little is known about the deity Horon (Ḥôrôn ‹Ḥawrân), but the presence of Upper and Lower Beth-horon in various biblical passages (identified certainly with Bêt ʿûr el-Fôqā and Bêt ʿûr et-Taḥta respectively) in various biblical passages, strengthens the impression that ʿAbdi-Kheba is complaining about the loss of three towns that dominated the main routes from the coastal plain to the hills around Jerusalem. This would make sense out of the entire controversy between Jerusalem and its coastal neighbors: Gezer and Gath. Some of ʿAbdi-Kheba's letters deal with the difficulties encountered when trying to send caravans to Egypt; one of his caravans was captured as it passed Ayalon, just north of Gezer (EA 287:52–57). That could explain why one of his letters was sent via Beth-shean (Goren, Finkelstein and Na'aman 2004:268). ʿAbdi-Kheba sees his enemies as conspirators who wish to seize lands belonging to the king, i.e. to form a coalition opposed to loyal city rulers like himself. The major towns on the southern coastal plain,

Gezer, Ashkelon and Lachish, are involved (EA 287:14–16). But the leaders are his direct neighbors to the west and to the north, viz. Milkilu and the sons of Lab'ayu (EA 287:29–31). As for Lachish, it must have been related to the sedition reported in the tablet discovered at Tel Ḫasi (Tell el-Ḥesī; EA 333:4–26).

There are no texts in the collection to tell how the case of Milkilu and the sons of Lab'ayu finally turned out. Another ruler of Gezer named Baʿlu-dānu (van Soldt 2002; usually read Baʿlu-shipṭi;) reports a dispute with an Egyptian official over possession of a newly refurbished fort (EA 292:26–40). He also complained that another official, named Pe'ya, had commandeered some of his men, whom Baʿlu-dānu had assigned to guard the Egyptian storehouse at Joppa (EA 294:16–24).

A third ruler of Gezer is known, probably chronologically the last, viz. Yapaʿ-Haddi. He complained about a younger brother who has entered into a town named Môḫazu (EA 298:20–29; Rainey 2003:193*-194*; *contra* Na'aman 1979:679 n. 28 and Moran 1992:340 n. 2).

A Planned Egyptian Campaign

Some seventy texts out of the 349 letters are replies to an order from pharaoh. Some of the letters mention that an envoy from Egypt had delivered the message. Two "office copies" of just such orders have survived. One is to Indaruta the ruler of Achshaph (EA 367:14–17). The concluding declaration (lines 22–25) does not mention the god Amon as did the formula in the days of Amenḥotep III; it uses the formula typical of letters from Amenḥotep IV, though the letters might have been sent out by Tutankhamun (or Semenkhare). The reply from Indaruta is apparently (EA 223). A similar letter was discovered in the British excavations. It was addressed to Yidiya, ruler of Ashkelon. The crucial paragraph stipulating the preparations for the coming of the troops is broken off from the bottom of the obverse and the top of the reverse. But there is a letter from Yidiya that gives an explicit response (EA 324:10–19).

Among the other identifiable towns that replied in the same manner were Yurza (EA 315), Lachish (EA 328) on the southern coastal plain, Megiddo (EA 247), Achshaph (EA 223), Acco (EA 233), Sidon (EA 144) and Beirut (EA 141) along the northern coastal route, Ṣiri-bashani (EA 201), Shasḫimi (EA 203), Qanû (EA 204) and Ṭôb (EA 205) in the Bashan, and Damascus/Kômidi (EA 195), Labana (EA 193) and Rôǵiṣu (EA 191) on the eastern route via Bashan and then up through the Lebanese Biqʿa Valley. If all these similar replies do relate to one planned campaign (Schulman 1964a; Reviv

1966b), the preparations have to be dated to a time when Rib-Haddi was still alive. He had sought political asylum with ʿAmmunira of Beirut who reports his preparations to pharaoh (EA 142:11–17).

Admittedly, there is no clear documentation to prove that such a campaign was actually carried out. Some have doubted that a unified campaign is reflected in this group of seventy texts; they assume that merely routine activities at various times were involved (Liverani 1971:257–263; Pintore 1972:115–117, 130). However, many chronological indications throughout these letters point to a date late in the period covered by the Amarna texts (Na'aman 1990:398–400). Furthermore, a letter from pharaoh to ʿAziru indicates that the king was contemplating a personal trip to Canaan (EA 162:40–41; Na'aman 1990:405 *contra* Moran 1992:249).

All this points strongly to a single planned campaign and not to sporadic orders concerning local situations. There may even be a witness to Hittite preparations for such an attack. The Hittites seem to have posted forces in Amurru, along the Nahr el-Kebîr, in anticipation of pharaoh's arrival with his army. That may be illustrated by a text discovered at Ugarit, "the General's Letter" (RS 20.33; *Ug.* 5, No. 20), which provides on linguistic grounds a fourteenth century dating (Izre'el and Singer 1990; Singer 1990: 162, 166).

> Since this last (month of) Sivan, I keep writing to my lord: "Send it forth! three pairs of chariots, may they each be consigned and may they be posted as a *replacement*(?); may they come straight into Ḫalba as soon as they are ready …" [It is for] these five ⌜months⌝ that I have been located in the land of Amurru and I keep watch on them day and night. And thus I am keeping watch over them, their roads and their entrances. I am keeping watch over them: half of my chariots are placed on the coast and half of my chariots are placed at the foot of Mt. Lebanon, while I, myself, am stationed here on the plain … as far as Ardat [and] my men [re]pulsed them in the middle of the night [and] conducted a fierce onslaught among them, their equipment and their personnel. From the stronghold itself they forced them out and captured one man among them. And I have been interrogating him concerning the king of Egypt. Thus he said: "The king of Egypt is going forth, but he is going forth sanctified. On the coming monthly festival his equipment will start out, and the king will come in the wake of his equipment".
>
> (RS 20.33; Ug. V, No. 20; *passim*; cf. Rainey 1971:133, 135)

This particular Ḫalba is not Aleppo but rather a town in northern Lebanon (Schaeffer 1968:678–686); the local village still has the same name. Ardat (today Ardât/Ardeh) is known from the Byblos letters (EA 104:10; et al.). The commander, therefore, was posted in Amurru (mainly the plain south of the Nahr el-Kebîr) and charged with guarding the coastal approach to the pass leading to central Syria or northwards towards Ugarit. If Izreʾel and Singer are correct, then the author of this letter, or his family, saved it in the family archive after he had served the Hittites during the late fourteenth century. The text has often been associated with the battle of Qidshu under Ramses II (e.g. Rainey 1971a; Dietrich 2003; et al.). However, the linguistic arguments of Izreʾel suggest a fourteenth century date.

It is hard to place this planned Egyptian campaign chronologically between the later years of Amenḥotep IV's reign and the death of Tutankhamun. The style of EA 367 suggests Amenḥotep IV as the sender. But the letter from Acco (EA 233) is from Satatna, the son of Surata, so obviously we are dealing with a later stage of the Amarna correspondence. A distinct possibility is that the plans for the campaign were made during the last year of Amenḥotep IV's life. But even if this campaign was postponed because of the pharaoh's demise, it seems certain that Egyptian military action was taken in response to the defection of Amurru and Qidshu. The "Deeds of Suppiluliuma" makes mention of an Egyptian attack on Qidshu (Güterboch 1956:93). The response led to the ill-advised Hittite aggression into recognized Egyptian territory and this eventually brought a plague on Suppiluliuma himself and on his people (Goetze 1955:394–396; Güterbock 1960). The discussion of the Qidshu campaign is followed in the next column by the report of the Egyptian pharaoh's death (Güterboch 1956:94). Nevertheless, the time frame is not spelled out.

Recently, new evidence has been presented to suggest that it was Nefertiti after all, who wrote to Suppiluliuma for a prince to be her consort (Miller 2007). There are still many imponderables in the equation and it still may turn out that the author of the letter was ʿAnkhesnpaAten, wife of Tutankhamun.

Tutankhamun's own "Restoration Stele" decries the previous woeful state of affairs:

> The gods were ignoring this land: if an army [was] sent to Djahy to broaden the boundaries of Egypt, no success of theirs came to pass.
>
> (Murnane 1995:213)

Details are lacking as to just how much military action had been attempted prior to the restoration and reconciliation with the Amon priesthood. Obviously there was nothing to boast about and thus no reason to erect monuments commemorating any victories. It is well to remember that the regime of Amenḥotep IV was strongly supported by the military (cf. e.g. Schulman 1964, 1978). But the Egyptian forces were now faced with a series of failures. Aziru and Qidshi were not retrieved.

Tutankhamon's untimely death was evidently caused by a kick in the chest by a horse. This has been indicated by the new CT examination of his corpse.

Perhaps, when Ay and the other generals of the Atenist regime came face to face with this military reality, they realized that they could not field an aggressive army unless they had a stable society and, most important of all, a dynamic economy behind them. The chaos within Egypt that had resulted from the Atenist "revolution" could no longer be tolerated. Was it the military failures abroad that led senior officials such as Ay to press for a reconciliation with the priesthoods of Amon and the other deities?

The final years of the fourteenth century BCE saw Egypt striving to overcome the many internal stresses caused by the abortive reign of Amenḥotep IV. Tutankhamun's aged successor, the general and senior minister, Ay, was in turn followed by a senior military officer related to the royal family only by marriage, Horemheb. He devoted most of the years of his reign to correcting the social and economic evils engendered by the Atenist experiment. Only with the establishment of Dynasty XIX would Egypt begin to reassert its claim to hegemony in the southern Levant.

Historical aspects of the various texts will receive some treatment in the Collation Notes. But this is primarily a linguistic and philological edition, and it is only hoped that it will be useful to the historians.

The Problem of the ʿApîrû

During the very first decade of Amarna studies, scholars took note of a social or ethnic element mentioned in the Jerusalem letters the name of which was spelled *ḫa-bi-ru* (EA 286:56; EA 288:38) or *ḫa-bi-ri* (EA 286:19; *et al.*). It was soon identified with the *ʿibrîm* "Hebrews" (Zimmern 1891:137–138), and H. Winckler had notified the Kaiser that at last the ancient Hebrews were documented in ancient cuneiform texts! That view still prevails among people who do not know the real details of the evidence.

Two comprehensive works, the doctoral dissertation of Greenberg (1955) and the papers from an Assyriological conference edited by Bottéro (1954), reviewed all the evidence known up to the middle of the twentieth century. In these two works, all the documentation from Nuzi beyond the Tigris, to Anatolia, Northern Syria, Canaan (the southern Levantine coast of the Eastern Mediterranean) and Egypt was cited and thoroughly discussed. From all that material, any objective observer would have seen that there is nothing in the nature of the *ʿapîrû* that would suggest a connection with the ancient *ʿib̲rîm* (*ʿib̲riyîm*). But if anyone thought that all this high level scholarly research would finally settle the matter, they were mistaken. The subsequent decades saw a number of attempts to reinterpret the material or to strengthen one of the older views. The most influential of these was the theory propounded by Mendenhall (1962, 1973) to the effect that the *ʿapîrû* were former Canaanite peasants who had fled from the oppression of their Canaanite overlords in order to find freedom in the mountains of Canaan. This thesis was expounded further by Gottwald (1979). Their "revolting peasant theory" (Rainey 1987c; 1987d; 1991:60; 1995) held sway in non-conservative biblical studies for over twenty years. It was also adopted by archaeologists who misinterpreted the material evidence of the mountain sites that sprang up in the early twelfth century BCE (Rainey 2007).

Linguistic Background

Rivers of ink have been spilt on the subject of the origin and meaning of the term *ʿapîru*. It is not our intention to review the exhausting trail of theories and counter theories (cf. Loretz 1984). Just a few pieces of evidence will be discussed here, those which are decisive in settling the issues of the root, form and semantics of *ʿapîru*. The equation discovered in texts from Ugarit established beyond all doubt that the ubiquitous Sumerian logograms LÚ.SA.GAZ(.MEŠ), LÚ.GAZ.(MEŠ), etc. really did stand for the West Semitic *ʿapîru*. Administrative texts from Ugarit in the Akkadian language had the (faulty) logogram LÚ.SAG.GAZ.MEŠ and obvious translations of the same administrative entries in the Ugaritic script had *ʿprm* (Virolleaud 1940a; 1940b). This meant that the syllabic spellings such as LÚ.MEŠ *ḫa-pí-ru* (EA 286:56), must be normalized with *ʿayin* and *pe* with the resulting **ʿapîru*; the plural at Ugarit was undoubtedly **ʿapîrûma*. This equation is also confirmed by the Egyptian references to *ʿpr* people, e.g. in the lists of prisoners brought back by Amenḥotep II. The Egyptian examples are not to be confused with the Egyptian word *ʿprw*, which means "crew" of sailors or workmen, from the root *ʿpr* "to equip"; the orthographies are entirely different. A point not stressed in the literature is that the preservation of both internal vowels should be an indication that one or the other vowel is long and/or that the middle radical is geminated. The second consonant is never written double, so that possibility is hardly likely. One never finds **ʿapru*. This can only mean that one of the vowels is long, either *ʿâpiru* or *ʿapîru*. The most likely of the two is certainly *ʿapîru* "dirty, dusty" (Borger 1958).

There is no validity to the assumption that the original was *ʿapir from the stative form with no long vowels (Mendenhall 1973:141; Weippert 1971:82). In short, the plethora of attempts to find some way to relate *ʿapîru* to the gentilic *ʿib̲rî* are all nothing but wishful thinking (e.g. Na'aman 1986). The two terms never were related (Rainey 1987), and it will be seen that the social status and the activities of the *ʿapîrû* bear no valid resemblance to the ancient Hebrews. Furthermore, scholars have rightly ignored Cazelles' attempt to relate Hebrew to the Akkadian term *ubru*, an Assyrian term (from *wabāru*) also attested at Ugarit (Cazelles 1958; 1973:20). In fact, Cazelles' summary of the problem (Cazelles 1973) is a classic example of unbridled imagination totally lacking in linguistic or semantic acumen.

Social Background

As is well known, the *ʿapîru* (West Semitic term) and its ideographic Sumerian reflex, SA.GAZ (sometimes just GAZ in the Amarna texts), are documented through 800 years of history, from Ur III down to the 20th Egyptian dynasty. They are never mentioned as pastoralists, and the preserved personal names of people bearing this designation are from no single linguistic group. There are Semites, Hurrians and others. They never belong to tribes. They may worship various deities. Geographically they are known from east of the Tigris, to Anatolia, to Egypt, in short, over the entire Ancient Near East. There is absolutely nothing to suggest an equation with the biblical Hebrews! On the other hand, they are also not to be equated with "revolting peasants" throwing off the yoke of their feudal Canaanite overlords. The *ʿapîru* men are people who have behaved disloyally towards pharaoh. In the correspondence of ʿAbdi-Kheba of Jerusalem and the letters from his opponents, *ʿapîru* serves as a pejorative designating the opposing parties, who are accused of acting against the interests of pharaoh. Neither do the documented *ʿapîru* want to escape to the mountains in order to "retribalize." It is true that they are often found seeking refuge in mountainous areas (Rowton 1965), e.g. those political refugees at Ammia who rallied around Idrimi, himself a runaway royal charioteer, the example *par excellance* of an *ʿapîru* (Rainey apud Rainey and Notley 2006:62). More *ʿapîru* men are found a century later in the same general area where ʿAbdi-Ashirta recruited them to become his militia; the Rib-Haddi correspondence makes it clear that many of the *ʿapîru* men were qualified charioteers (like Idrimi). They continued to support his son, ʿAziru and shared in the founding of the dynastic feudal state of Amurru. More *ʿapîru* show up in the hill country around

Shechem; Lab'ayu used them to carry out his aggressions against towns in the Dothan and Jezreel Valleys. As a reward, he was giving his *ʿapîru* men lands and estates (among the rich agricultural lands in the Jezreel Valley which were actually a pharaonic possession). Instead of seeking to "retribalize," quite the contrary, they sought to find a place in the good old Late Bronze feudal social structure. Usually their best option, as males with military training, was to become mercenaries and as such they appear in the personnel lists of Alalakh and Ugarit. Sometimes they signed on with a charismatic adventurer such as Lab'ayu of Shechem or ʿAbdi-Ashirta of Amurru or Idrimi of Alalakh. But they were also hired by the Egyptian authorities. They formed part of the Egyptian "foreign legion." A local ruler who had responsibilities as a district overseer for pharaoh in the Damascus region, had such troops under his command (EA 195:24–32; Rainey 1995:490). Biryawaza, the author of that letter, had hired mercenaries, who surely were outcasts from the urban city-state society, alongside a unit of nomadic warriors, the *Sutû*. Incidentally, this shows that nomadic mercenaries were never confused with urbanized *ʿapîru* men (*contra* Na'aman 1982). The Egyptian government also recruited *ʿapîru* mercenaries for service in the foreign legion at bases in Cush (Sudan). The following letter from Kâmed el-Lôz deals with just such a situation—Pharaoh to the ruler of Damascus:

> *šanītam šūbilanni awīlī ʿapīrī*(SA.GAZ.ZA) *Aburra* (= *Amurra*) *ša ašpurakku elīšunu ummā anandinšunūti ina ālāni Kāša ana ašābi ina libbišu kīmū ša aḫtabatšunūti*
>
> Furthermore, send me the *ʿapîru* men of Amurru(!) concerning which I wrote to you, saying "I will cause them to dwell in the towns of Cush instead of those whom I carried off". (KL 69:277:5–11; Cochavi-Rainey 1988:42*–43* [Hebrew]; *contrast* Edzard 1970:55–60)

Cushite mercenaries, in turn, were often stationed in Canaan (cf. EA 287:33–37).

In this light one must understand the references to *ʿapîru* in Egypt, e.g.

> *ỉmy dỉ ỉty nꜣ n rmṯ mšʿ ḥnʿ nꜣ ʿprw*
>
> Cause to be given the grain of the army personnel with the *ʿapîrû*.
> (Pap. Leiden 349:14–15; Greenberg 1955:56–57)

These *ʿapîru* men are getting rations alongside troops of the regular army. Both groups are engaged in some public construction project (but not the building of Per-Ramesses or Per-Atum!). The records indicate that army personnel were being employed and alongside them, mercenary personnel of the "foreign legion" were also serving in these tasks. There is no reason whatever to equate such *ʿapîru* with the Hebrews in Egypt, neither socially, historically nor especially linguistically!

DISCOVERY, RESEARCH, AND EXCAVATION OF THE AMARNA TABLETS—THE FORMATIVE STAGE

Jana Mynářová

As it has been already stated in the Introduction, the corpus of Amarna tablets which is, or had been in the past, available for study counts altogether three hundred and eighty two texts and fragments. Unfortunately, it is only in case of thirty one of these texts that we can, more or less reliably, reconstruct their original find-spots. These thirty one inscribed and three uninscribed tablets or fragments were excavated at the site of Tell el-Amarna during a series of archaeological works conducted by several archaeological missions starting with the excavation directed by William M. Flinders Petrie in 1891 (Petrie 1892a; 1982b; 1894). Petrie arrived to the site in November 1891 and in spite of the gloomy archaeological situation he inaugurated his excavations already shortly after his arrival. With respect to the site Petrie himself refers to, among other things, previous activities carried out by both the Museum authorities and an infamous antiquities dealer (Petrie 1892b:356). It is only at the end of January 1892 that Petrie mentions in his unpublished journal, at present kept in the Archive of the Griffith Institute in Oxford: "At last I have got touch of the cuneiform tablets" (Petrie MSS, 24–30 January 1892—XIII, 94). What follows is the famous description of old rubbish pits under the house walls in which the tablets were supposed to have been found (also Petrie 1892b:356; id. 1894:23–24). He also mentions that "a bit of one (tablet) was found in re-clearing the house in which they were said to have been found" (so-called Block No. 19; Q 42.21). Over the course of his work Petrie was able to uncover altogether twenty one texts of both an epistolary and school nature (plus an uninscribed tablet; Ash. 1893.1–41 [429]); all of them presently housed in the collection of the Ashmolean Museum in Oxford (Ash. 1893.1–41 [408–428]). An inscribed cylinder seal (Ash. 1893.1–41 [416]; EA 355) represents due to its specific shape a unique piece among these objects. As far as the Amarna corpus is concerned it is rather unfortunate that neither in his publications relating to the excavations at Amarna nor in his journal Petrie specifies which tablets have been discovered in the individual rubbish-pits and which is the tablet discovered in the so-called Block No. 21. The situation is even more blurred with regards to the two texts (EA 343 and EA 349) that were not included in Sayce's study (Sayce

1894:34–37, XXXI–XXXIII). In general his description of the discovery is not exhaustive and despite the fact that his words have been steadily repeated in both scholarly and more popular treaties of the Amarna tablets' discovery, the genuine context of the discovery might well remain partially unreconstructable.

As far as indisputable find-spot(s) of the remaining Amarna tablets are concerned both the excavations of the German Oriental Society (Deutsche Orient-Gesellschaft), under the directorship of Ludwig Borchard, and the excavations of the Egypt Exploration Society, headed first by Thomas E. Peet and subsequently by John D.S. Pendlebury, bring us more authoritative data. During Borchard's work in the area of the Main City two more inscribed tablets were uncovered, while the EES excavations enriched the collection by means of nine more inscribed and two more uninscribed tablets or their respective fragments. It was already 1913 when the D.O.G. mission discovered the two fragments (Borchardt 1914:34–36; Schroeder 1914; OLZ 1914–1918). Both of these school texts were discovered in a more remote area of the Main City and in both cases the tablets were found in a non-official context—EA 359 in O 47.2 (at present in the Egyptian Museum in Cairo; J.48396, SR 4/12223/0) and EA 379 in N 47.3 (Egyptian Museum in Cairo; J.48397; SR 4/12224/0). In the area of the Main City, or more particularly in O 49.23, another school text—EA 368 (at present in the Ashmolean Museum in Oxford; Ash. 1921.1154)—was discovered in the course of the very first excavation season carried out by the Egypt Exploration Society (then Egypt Exploration Fund) headed by the British Egyptologist Thomas Eric Peet (Peet 1921). Later on, during the 1933–1934 excavation season, eight more inscribed (plus two more uninscribed; BM 134867 and BM 13486) tablets were discovered by the EES mission, then lead by John D.S. Pendlebury. With the exception of a single tablet (EA 371; BM 13468) all the others were once again discovered in the administrative quarter located to the east of the Royal Palace in the Central City, previously excavated by W.M.F. Petrie—i.e. in the area of the royal archive and scriptorium (see Pendlebury 1951:I, 114, 150; II, Pls. LXXXIII, LXXXV). Unfortunately, leaving aside the published data of the discovery of the EES tablets, no other details could be elicited from the documents kept in the archive of the Egypt Exploration Society.

In light of this it is very unfortunate that, with respect to the total number of all Amarna tablets and respective fragments, the tablets with known find-spot represent less than ten percent of the material at our disposal.

The earliest modern history of the collection of the Amarna tablets is closely related to private excavations carried on at the site by the antiquities dealer Farag Ismaïn of Giza. Contrary to reports, referred to by J.A. Knudtzon

(1963²: 4), that the tablets were discovered either during the autumn or by the end of 1887, there are certain indications that the tablets might have actually been found already during late spring or over the summer of that year. The main evidence can be found in the documents housed in the Egyptian Museum in Cairo, more precisely in the *Journal d'entrée*, in which several registration entries for objects coming from the region of Middle Egypt, Akhmim or even the site of Amarna itself and clearly identifiable within the reign of Amenhotep IV-Akhenaten can be recognized (J.IV:330 f.; esp. J.28028–28030, J.28035–28037). Not all those entries are precisely dated but it is obvious that the earliest objects of Amarna provenience were registered in the Museum since May 1887 (Mynářová 2007: 13, fn. 10) with the name of Farag Ismaïn mentioned as the man who sold some them to the authorities. Contrary to various scenarios transmitted both in scholarly and more popular literature, the discovery of the Amarna tablets can hence no longer be interpreted as purely "accidental" since we can reliably trace its history back to the aforementioned private excavations.

The British Museum in London was to be the first official institution to host a rather extensive collection of the Amarna tablets. In this particular case it is linked to the activities of E.A. Wallis Budge who, as an Assistant Keeper of the Department of Egyptian and Assyrian Antiquities, was able to obtain a first set of the Amarna tablets already during his second mission to Egypt and Mesopotamia (1887–1888). Despite the eloquent description of his travels in the narrative autobiography *By Nile and Tigris* (Budge 1920), the probable scenario of his acquisition of the tablets can most clearly be decuded from the archival materials (especially letters addressed to Sir Edward A. Bond, Principal Librarian, and Sir Peter Le Page Renouf, Keeper of Oriental Antiquities; Mynářová 2007:16–26; Cathcart 2004:247–248) housed in the Archive of the British Museum. Immediately after his arrival to Cairo (via Marseilles and Alexandria) Budge met some of the antiquities dealers, including Marius Panayiotis Tano, a Cypriot dealer of Greek origin, whom he probably met a year before during his first mission to Egypt, as well as a newly appointed Director of the Antiquities Service and Mission archéologique in Cairo, Eugène Grébaut, only promoted in 1886 when G. Maspero returned to Paris. Among other things it was the general atmosphere of the strong Anglo-French rivalry of the 1880's and 1890's that made Grébaut's attitude towards Budge as an Englishman rather problematic, and his behaviour can be adequately described as undiplomatic.

On the evening of December 19 Budge boarded the train to Asyut, accompanied by a certain Frenchman and a Maltese and arrived at Asyut on December 20. According to the narrative of Budge, the Frenchman left the train earlier at Deir Mawas which, by that time, served as a train station for Hajj Qandil, in order "to set out to try to buy some of the tablets said to have been found at Tell 'al-'Amârnah" (Budge 1920 I:134–135). On his journey to the south Budge embarked on a steamer and after harbouring for the night at Akhmim he reached Qena. It was in Qena where he met some antiquity dealers including an unnamed Frenchman, "an owner of a flour-mill in Cairo", supposedly to be identified with Mr. Frénay, who was acting as an agent for the Louvre. It seems that on December 22 the steamer made a stop in Luxor where Budge conducted more business and it cannot be ruled out that he also met with an important collector of antiquities, the American missionary, the Rev. Chauncey Murch. Documents kept in the archives of the British Museum indicate that on several occasions Ch. Murch was involved in financial dealings conducted by the representatives of the British Museum in Egypt.

Contrary to the tradition, presented in Budge's own eloquent autobiography, the Amarna tablets were not purchased on his return from Aswan to Cairo but already during his travels upstream to Aswan. In his letter, dispatched on December 27 from Daraw in Upper Egypt, Budge mentions his business conducted in Luxor, including a clear reference to the tablets: "A certain man had 71 cuneiform tablets written in a remarkable script, and when I had spent a night examining them I decided to bring them with me to make sure of securing them. They were found at a place whose name I will give in the future. Four of them were stolen by a Copt and the Paris authorities bought them for £40 and sent out a man on purpose to buy the remainder. The Copt did not know to whom they were going and so the Frenchman was baulked" (letter kept in the Central Archives, British Museum, see also the copy of the Minutes of the Trustees of the British Museum, Department of Oriental Antiquities 1888:2195; Mynářová 2007:18). On the basis of this document we can suppose that Budge purchased at least 71 of these tablets already at the very first occasion, that means still on his way south. In respect to the ambiguity of the information presented by him on several occasions, the possibility exists that he first studied and made a reservation for the tablets and only afterwards "secured" them for the British Museum. In such case the tablets would have been safeguarded by a trustworthy individual in Luxor.

The very same set of tablets also appears in the Minutes of the Trustees of the British Museum which took place on January 14, 1888. A clear reference to Budge's communication is made, quoting that he "has secured 71 cuneiform Tablets in a remarkable script." (see above) More details can be found in the Minutes from the committee of February 11 with reference to

Budge's letter of January 8 sent from Cairo. In this particular letter Budge mentions the reactions of the authorities of the Cairo (= Boulaq) museum, including their attempts to intercept the tablets, "fortunately in Mr. Budge's own possession" (the copy of the Minutes of the Trustees of the British Museum, Department of Oriental Antiquities 1888:2204; Mynářová 2007:18). As far as the actual number of tablets held by Budge is concerned there are some discrepancies in the data. In his letter of December 27, 1887 Budge mentions 71 tablets. In his autobiography we can read that by means of two sets from two different people Budge examined 76 tablets in order "to say, whether they were genuine or forgeries" (Budge 1920 I:140) but then he was "allowed to take possession of the eighty-two tablets forthwith" (Budge 1920 I:141).

In this respect the most reliable source is formed by the documents kept in the British Museum. The Minutes of the Trustees dated October 13, 1888 contain a report of Peter Le Page Renouf recommending the purchase of a set of the tablets from "Shipping Merchants and Agents" Messrs. Bywater, Tanqueray & Co. The Minutes mentions, literally, "A very valuable collection of 81 cuneiform tablets found near Tell-el-Amarna, in Upper Egypt (*selected by Mr. Budge during recent missions to Egypt), being a series of letters and dispatches from Kings of Mesopotamia, Syria, and Phoenicia, to Amenophis III and his son Amenophis IV, BC 1530–1450. The tablets illustrate the relations in which the correspondents stood to the Egyptian monarchs, either as relatives, allies, or vassals. One of them proves the correctness of the tradition that the wife of Amenophis III was a foreign lady, the King of Mitanni, North East of Palestine, addressing him as his "son-in-law". As a further illustration of the historical importance of the collection, Mr. Renouf quotes the substance of three of the tablets. The character of the writing is unique, and several new words occur. The price of the collection is £512, payable on the passing of the Museum vote for the current year" (see copy of the Minutes of the Trustees of the British Museum, Department of Oriental Antiquities 1888:2359–2360; Mynářová 2007:21). The purchase was sanctioned and on the very same day 81 Amarna tablets were registered in the collection. To understand the difference between the number given by Budge in his letter (71) and the number actually registered by the museum authorities (81), one has to keep in mind that the existence of the tablets was probably known already before Budge's arrival to Egypt. The original find—those tablets discovered during the private excavations of F. Ismaïn—might, in fact, have already been dispersed among various antiquities dealers by that time. It seems that between his Luxor purchase and the moment he dispatched the tablets to London, Budge might have purchased yet another set consisting of ten tablets, whose origin still remains unknown. It is obvious that at the very end of 1887 and early in 1888 tablets were still up for sale, and it would not have been difficult for Budge to arrange another purchase. The same holds for the latter part of 1888, as witnessed by a letter of Ch. Murch addressed to P. Le Page Renouf and dated November 23, 1888:

> ... Reference to my correspondence with Mr. Budge concerning some of the purchases he made here last year will show that since about the 1st of August I have had to urge very energetically that payment be speedily made. Though the full expectation here was that the money would be paid June 1st, I managed to satisfy those concerned here they should be patient as long as the delay was unavoidable. According to Mr. Budge's account £650 were paid to Messrs. Bywater, Tanqueray & Co. on Sept. 15th. Though this payment was made, there have been various delays which it is unnecessary to explain at length, and to the present time only £100 have been received by us. On Oct. 8th, I wrote a most explicit letter to Messrs. Bywater, Tanqueray & Co. I insisted most urgently that the whole £650 be sent out immediately. I followed this letter by one to Mr. Budge three days later. It is a great pity that Mr. Budge did not see the Bywaters, as they have obeyed my instructions only so far as to send is a cheque for £100. Your creditor has been forced to borrow money from Greek usurers at the rate of 7 per cent per month. I have just returned after an absence of twenty days at Assouan, and I went to see him last night. I find that he is now in the state of mind which I have been fearing, and which I have more that once suggested in my correspondence about the matter, viz., he is afraid I am deceiving him about the money, and he is afraid he will never get it. As high as £20 have been offered here for the Clay Cuneiform tablets. He feels that the first lot was taken from him at too low a rate. On the whole I found him in a very bad humor last night.
>
> (Archive of the Department of Oriental Antiquities, British Museum; Mynářová 2007:22)

After he finished his tasks in Egypt and Mesopotamia Budge returned from Baghdad to London on April 24, 1888. In his autobiography he clearly states that among the objects purchased during his second mission were "eighty-two tablets from Tall al-ʿAmârnah" (Budge 1920 I:338), providing yet another number. In this particular case, it is possible to trace the origin of the single tablet. The tablet, at present BME 29829, was—as distinct from the first subset—registered only on May 9, 1891, as the publication of the material by C. Bezold and E.A.W. Budge clearly indicates (Bezold—Budge 1892:No. 46; EA 176). Once again, a report signed by P. Le Page Renouf but undisputedly written by Budge himself, on May 4, 1891 and pertaining to his fourth mission for the British Museum conducted between 1890 and 1891, contains a list of "the most interesting" objects, including "one Tell el-Amarna tablet" (copy of the report, Central Archives, British Museum, 5 May 1891, 1700–1701/22–24; Mynářová 2007:23).

At the same time that the collection of the Amarna tablets, presently housed in the British Museum, was created due to the activities of E.A.W. Budge in Egypt at the very end of 1887 and in early weeks of 1888, the tablets also captivated the attention of scholars and representatives of other institutions. The Egyptian Museum in Cairo and its director Eugène Grébaut play an crucial part in these developments. The formation of the Cairo Amarna collection is, similarly to the collection of the British Museum and the Royal Museum in Berlin (nowadays Staatliche Museen zu Berlin, see below), linked to private excavations conducted at the site of Tell el-Amarna in 1887. In a significant way, the Cairo, London and Berlin collections represent part and parcel of the majority of the whole Amarna corpus and their respective histories constitute in fact one, single story.

The authorities of the Egyptian Museum were not ignorant of the private excavations at the site of Tell el-Amarna during the year of 1887 as several objects discovered were subsequently registered in its collections. The very first mention of the Amarna tablets in Museum documents (or more precisely in the respective volume of the *Journal d'entrée*) dates to the early weeks and months of 1888 (Mynářová 2007:26–28). The earliest mention—J.28151—represents two tablets (CG 4765 = EA 148, CG 4777 = EA 320), purchased in January 1888 from an otherwise unidentified man called "Philip" (*Journal d'entrée* IV:342–343). Three more tablets arrived to the Museum shortly afterwards and, in contrast to the first purchase, the provenance is mentioned as the region of Akhmim (*Journal d'entrée* IV:343–342). The three tablets (CG 4753 = EA 113, CG 4761 = EA 195, CG 4770 = EA 240, later joined to a tablet in Berlin, see VAT 2709) were registered as J.28160. A more precise date for the registration could not be established, but it seems that it was not too long after the registration of the first set, probably during February 1888. The background of the acquisition of the third and by far the most numerous set—J.28179—is well-known (*Journal d'entrée* IV:344–345; Mynářová 2007:26–27). Documents kept in the Egyptian Museum mention that 17 complete and 14 fragments of cuneiform tablets were seized in Giza. This information is further elaborated by Knudtzon (1964[2]:7, n. 1) who links this set with the aforementioned antiquities dealer Farag Ismaïn. This was obviously the moment when the precise origin of the tablets was established. The origin of the tablets at Tell el-Amarna in Middle Egypt is mentioned with the last set—J.28185—registered in the Museum in February 1888 and consisting of 16 more cuneiform tablets (*Journal d'entrée* IV:344–345; Mynářová 2007:27–28).

It was also in early months of 1888 that the largest set of Amarna tablets, today part of the collection of the Vorderasiatisches Museum in Berlin, started to take shape. The Austrian antiquities dealer Theodor Graf played an essential role in this process (Bierbrier 2012[4]:219–220). Th. Graf was the owner of a prosperous carpet business, but during the second half of the 19th century he also came to be known as a very competent antiquities dealer. His connection to Josef von Karabacek was in light of this essential as it established a contact with Archduke Rainer of Austria and, particularly, his voluminous collection of antiquities, especially papyri from Medinet el-Fayum and Heracleopolis and mummy portraits (the so-called Faiyum portraits). According to his correspondence with J. von Karabacek (Hunger 1962) Th. Graf left Triest for Alexandria at the end of October 1887, reaching Cairo around mid-November. In his letter to Karabacek, dated November 19, 1887 and sent from El Faiyum, he mentions his plan for an early return back to Cairo (Hunger 1962:75–76, No. 52). His return is confirmed by another letter of November 21, dispatched from Cairo, in which he reports in detail on papyri from Akhmim and requests Karabacek for instructions concerning their purchase (Hunger 1962:76–77, No. 53). After two weeks in Cairo, Th. Graf returned in the fall of the year 1887 via Alexandria and Triest to Vienna. Not a single mention of cuneiform tablets appears in Graf's correspondence of 1887 and it seems that he was unaware of their existence. Unlike Budge, Graf did not travel further south to Luxor, where the tablets might have been available at that time, but spent his time only in the areas of Cairo and the Faiyum. This changed during another visit to Egypt in 1888. On November 9, 1888 Graf wrote to Karabacek in Vienna:

> Was S. Keiserl. Hoheit Bemerkug in Betreff eines Verkaufes nach Berlin anbetrifft, so haben Sie Recht gehabt zu versichern, daß es sich um Papyri nicht handeln könne! Ich werde Ihnen jedoch sehr dankbar sein, wenn Sie bei erster Gelegenheit S. Kaiserl. Hoheit mittheilen wollten, daß das Königl. Museum in Berlin, wie auch aus Zeitugsberichten ersichtlich was, von mir Thontafeln mit Keilschriften, welche in Ober-Egypten gefunden wurden, gekauft hat, aber erst, nachdem dieselben hier, wo ich sie zuerst zeigte, als falsch erklärt worden waren! Ich war in Folge dessen gezwungen, damit in's Ausland zu gehen!
> (Hunger 1962:84–85, No. 58)

Based on the list of acquisitions in the Registerbuch kept in the Vorderasiatisches Museum the tablets were acquired by different means, among these 58 VAT inventory numbers are clearly identified as purchases from Graf in Vienna in 1888. At the same time the Museum also purchased an extensive set of Amarna tablets, originally in the collection of Daninos Pasha in Alexandria, and consisting of 45 VAT inventory numbers. The by far largest set is identified as a gift of J. Simon. Among Simon's tablets occurs also VAT 1605 (EA 12), with the lower half further identified as a gift of von

Niemeyer in Cairo (Acc. 23/1890). At that time Felix von Niemeyer was acting as a diplomat ("Dragoman") at the German consulate in Cairo and it is interesting to observe that VAT 323 (EA 144) and VAT 324 (EA 76) were both acquired by Dr. Winckler using funds of the German consulate in Cairo. The data given in the Registerbuch also reveal the origin of tablet VAT 249 (EA 164). In this case the tablet was purchased directly from a certain "Todrus" in Luxor, surely to be identified with the Egyptian antiquities dealer Todrous Boulos (Bierbrier 2012[4]:542; 2695/88 Acc. Journ. 2/1889).

The common sources for both the Berlin and Cairo collections are also confirmed by the reciprocal exchange of some Amarna fragments documented by Knudtzon (1964[2]: 7–9).

The origin and modern history of other collections of the Amarna letters is known slightly better. The origin of the first of the Amarna tablets to come to the Louvre (now lost) can be traced to the antiquities dealer Elias who sold a collection of thirteen or fourteen tablets to the French mill owner and consular agent in Akhmim, M. Frénay (Capart 1936:204, 348), despite the fact that in the correspondence and journals of Charles E. Wilbour a reference to the Amarna tablets and their non-availability in relation to Frénay is mentioned: "His (= E. Grèbaut's, JM) main object was to get the cuneiform tablets said to be found at Amarna, but Consul Frénay tells me he got none." (Capart 1936:461). Nevertheless, the tablets later belonged to the collection of Urbain Bouriant and it he probably sent one (EA 260) for examination to Jules Oppert in the Louvre (Sayce 1917; Knudtzon 1964[2]:8; Mynářová 2007:25). Tablet EA 209 (AO 2036), presented to the Louvre by Gaston Maspero, represents the earliest entry among the Louvre Amarna collection (Scheil 1890). It is beyond dispute that in the early decades of the 20th century individual Amarna tablets were still available on the antiquities market. One can suppose that in most cases these objects still derived from the very early stages of the exploration of the site by means of the private excavations (Mynářová 2007:36–39). This includes the so-called Murch fragment, now in the collection of the Oriental Institute in Chicago (EA 26, A 9356) and the two tablets in the Metropolitan Museum of Art in New York, bought in Cairo in 1924 (EA 15, MMA 24.2.11; EA 153, MMA 24.2.12). Four tablets originally in the collection of Alexandros Rostovitz Bey were registered in the British Museum on May 11, 1903. These tablets probably passed through the hands of the antiquities dealer Panayotis Kyticas. Another tablet (EA 378, BME 50745) was also purchased through him or his family in 1925. A single Amarna tablet (EA 380, BM 58364) might originally have come from the excavations of W.M.F. Petrie in 1891–1892, according to the study of C.B.F. Walker (Walker 1979). In 1911 the tablets from the collection of the Russian Egyptologist

V.S. Golenischeff were ceded to the Pushkin Museum of Fine Arts in Moscow. Finally, in January 1918 the Louvre collection was enlarged to altogether seven tablets, including that of Maspero, by means of a purchase conducted by G. Bénedict. The very last museum acquisition of an Amarna tablet can be identified in the records of the Musées Royaux d'Art et d'Histoire in Brussels in 1933 (EA 369, E.6753).

This brief overview of the modern history of the Amarna tablets indicates that the early formative stages were rather "wild," and it is highly probable that one will never be able to fully reconstruct the wanderings of the individual tablets. It is however clear that in order to complete the picture of the discovery itself and its context archival data must be studied and taken into consideration.

BIBLIOGRAPHY

Adamthwaite, Murray. R. 1992. "Lab'ayu's Connection with Shechem Reassessed." *Abr-Nahrain* 30: 1–19.

Adler, Hans-Peter. 1976. *Das Akkadische des Königs Tušratta von Mittanni. Alter Orient und Altes Testament* 201. Kevelaer, Neukirchen-Vluyn.

Aharoni, Yohanan. 1969. "Rubute and Ginti-kirmil." *Vetus Testamentum* 19: 137–145.

Arnaud, Daniel. 1991. "Une lettre de Kamid-el-Loz." *Semitica* 40: 7–16.

Artzi, Pinhas. 1967. "The Exact Number of the Published Amarna Documents." *Orientalia* 36: 432

———. 1968. "Some Unrecognized Syrian Amarna Letters (EA 260, 317, 318)." *Journal of Near Eastern Studies* 27: 163–171.

Astour, Michael C. 1979. "Yahweh in Egyptian Topographic Lists." In *Festschrift Emar Edel: 12. März 1979.*, eds. M. Görg and E. Pusch, 17–34. Bamberg: M. Görg.

Badre, Leila. 1997. *Excavations of the American University of Beirut Museum 1993–1996*. BAAL 2.

Beckman, Gary M., and Harry A. Hoffner. 1996. *Hittite Diplomatic Texts*. Atlanta, Ga: Scholars Press.

Berman, Larry M. 1998. "Overview of Amenhotep III and His Reign." In *Amenhotep III perspectives on his reign*. David B. O'Connor and Eric H. Cline., 1–25. Ann Arbor: University of Michigan Press.

Bierbrier, Morris. 2012. *Who was who in Egyptology*. 4th ed. London: The Egypt Exploration Society.

Böhl, Franz M. 1909. *Die Sprache der Amarnabriefe mit besonderer Berücksichtigung der Kanaanismen*. LSS 5/2. Leipzig. Reprinted, 1968.

Borchardt, Ludwig. 1914. *Ausgrabungen in Tell el-Amarna 1913–114*. Vorliiufiger Bericht. *Mitteilingen des Instituts für Vorderasiatich-Ägyptischen Gesellschaft* 55: 3–38.

Borger, Rykle. 1958. "Das Problem der ʿapīru ('Ḫabiru')." *Zeitschrift des Deutschen Palästina Vereins* 74: 121–132.

———. 2004. *Mesopotamisches Zeichenlexikon*. Münster: Ugarit-Verlag.

Bottéro, Jean. 1954. *Le problem des Ḫabiru à la 4e Rencontre Assyriologique Internationale*, (Paris, 20 juin-1er juillet 1953). Chaiers de la societé asiatique XII. Paris.

Budge, E.A. Wallis. 1920. *By Nile and Tigris, a narrative of journeys in Egypt and Mesopotamia on behalf of the British museum between the years 1886 and 1913*. London: J. Murray.

Campbell, Edward. F. 1964. *The Chronology of the Amarna Letters*. Baltimore.

———. 1965. *Shechem in the Amarna Archive*. G.E. Wright ed., 191–213. *Shechem: The Biography of a Biblical City*. New York.

Capat, Jean. 1936. *Travels in Egypt* [December 1880 to May 1891]. Letters of Charles Edwin Wilbour, Brooklyn: Brooklyn Museum.

Cathcart, K.J. (ed.) 2004. *The Letters of Peter le Page Renouf (1822–1897)*, Vol. IV, Dublin: University College Dublin Press.

Cazelles, Henri. 1958. "Hébreu, Ubru et Ḫapiru." *Syria* 35: 198–217.

———. 1973. "De l'idéologie royale." *Journal of the Ancient Near Eastern Society* 5: 59–73.

Cochavi-Rainey, Zippora. 1988. "The Akkadian Dialect of the Egyptian Scribes in the 14th–13th Centuries BCE" PhD diss., Tel Aviv University. 2 volumes. [Hebrew with English summary].

———. 1989. "Canaanite Influence in the Akkadian Texts written by Egyptian Scribes in the 14th and 13th Centuries, BCE" *Ugarit-Forschungen* 21: 39–46.

———. 1990a. "Egyptian Influence in the Akkadian Texts written by Egyptian Scribes in the 14th and 13th Centuries, BCE" *Journal of Near Eastern Studies* 49: 57–65.

———. 1990b. "Tenses and Modes in Cuneiform Texts Written by Egyptian Scribes in the Late Bronze Age." *Ugarit-Forschungen* 22: 5–23.

———. 2003. *The Alashia Texts from the 14th and 13th Centuries BCE: a Textual and Linguistic Study*. Münster: Ugarit-Verlag.

Cochavi-Rainey, Z and C. Lilyquist. 1999. *Royal gifts in the late Bronze Age, fourteenth to thirteenth centuries BCE: selected texts recording gifts to royal personages*. Beersheba: Ben-Gurion University of the Negev Press.

Cochavi-Rainey, Z. and Rainey. A.F. 2009. "Comparative Grammatical Notes on the Treaty between Ramses II and Hattusili III." In S. Israelit-Groll, ed., 796–823. *Studies in Egyptology: presented to Miriam Lichtheim*. II. Jerusalem: Magnes Press, Hebrew University.

Dassow, Eva von. 2004. "Canaanite in Cuneiform." *Journal of the American Oriental Society* 124:641–674.

———. 2010. "Peripheral Akkadian dialects, or Akkadography of local languages?" In *Language in the Ancient Near East. Proceedings of the 53rd Rencontre Assyriologique Internationale* = (Moscow, Russia, July 23, 2007), vol. I/2, ed. L. Kogan, et al., 895–926. *Babel und Bibel* 4/2. Winona Lake, IN: Eisenbrauns.

Dietrich, Manfried. 2003. "Der Ugariter Šumiyānu an der südsyrischen Front gegen den Pharao: Zu den Nachwehen der Schlacht bei Qadeš 1275 v. Chr. ed., 45–74." In A.I. Blöbaum et al. in *Kulturwissenschaftliche Studien zu Ägypten, dem Vorderen Orient und verwandten Gebieten*. Wiesbaden.

Dossin, Georges. 1934. "Une Nouvelle Lettre d'el-Amarna." *Revues d'assyriologie et d'archéologie orientale* 31: 125–136.

Edzard, Dietz O. 1970. "Die Tontafeln von Kāmid el-Loz." D.O. Edzard, *et al.*, eds., 55–62, Pls. 10–11 *Kamid el-Loz-Kumidi*. Bonn.

———. 1976 "Ein Brief an dem "Grossen" von Kumidi aus Kāmid el-Loz." *Zeitschrift für Assyriologie* 66:62–67.

———. 1980 "Ein neues Tontafelfragment (Nr. 7) aus Kāmid el-Loz." *Zeitschrift für Assyriologie* 70:52–54.

———. 1982 "Ein Brief an dem 'Grossen' von Kumidi aus Kāmid el-Loz." R. Hachmann, R., ed., 131–135. In *Bericht über die Ergebnissse des Ausgrabungen in Kāmid el-Loz in den Jahren 1971 bis 1974. Saarbrücker Beiträge zur Altertumskunde*, 32. Bonn.

———. 1986. "Ein neues Tontafelfragment (Nr. 7) aus Kāmid el-Loz." R. Hachmann ed., 145–147 in *Bericht über die Ergebnissse des Ausgrabungen in Kāmid el-Loz in den Jahren 1977 bis 1981. Saarbrücker Beiträge zur Altertumskunde* 36. Bonn.

Fletcher, Joann. 2000. *Chronicle of a Pharaoh: the Intimate Life of Amenhotep III*. New York: Oxford University Press.

Fritz, W. 1991. "Bermerkungen zum Datierungsvermerk auf der Amarnatafel KN 27." *Studien zur altägyptischen Kultur* 18: 207–214, Pl. 7.

Giacumakis, George. 1970. *The Akkadian of Alalaḫ*. The Hague: Mouton.

Giles, Frederick J. 1997. *The Amarna Age: Western Asia. The Australian Centre for Egyptology Studies* 5. Warminster.

———. 2001. *The Amarna Age: Egypt. Australian Centre for Egyptology Studies* 6. Warminster.

Goetze, Albrecht. 1930. *Versteute Boghazköi-Texte*. Marburg.

———. 1955. *Hittite Prayers*. J.B. Pritchard ed., 393–401. in *Ancient Near Eastern Texts Relating to the Old Testament*. 2nd edition. Princeton, NJ.

Gordon, Cyrus H. 1938. "The Dialect of the Nuzi Tablets." *Orientalia* 7: 32–63, 215–232.

———. 1947. "The New Amarna Tablets." *Orientalia* 16: 1–14.

Goren, Yuval, Israel Finkelstein, and Nadav Na'aman. 2002a. "The Seat of Three Disputed Canaanite Rulers according to petrographic Investigation of the Amarna Tablets." *Tel Aviv* 29: 221–237.

———. 2002b. "Petrographic Investigation of the Amarna tablets." *Near Eastern Archaeology* 65: 196–205.

Goren, Yuval, Israel Finkelstein, Nadav Na'aman, and Michal Artzy. 2004. *Inscribed in Clay: Provenance Study of the Amarna Tablets and Other Ancient Near Eastern Texts*. Tel Aviv: Emery and Claire Yass Publications in Archaeology.

Gottwald, Norman K. 1979. *The Tribes of Yahweh: a Sociology of the Religion of Liberated Israel, 1250–1050 B.C.E.* Maryknoll, N.Y.: Orbis Books.

Grayson, Albert K. 1972. *Assyrian Royal Inscriptions. Vol* I. *From the Beginning to Ashur-rêsh-ishi* H. Goedicke ed., *Records of the Ancient Near East*. Wiesbaden.

Greenberg, Moshe. 1955. *The Ḫab/piru*. New Haven, Conn: American Oriental Society.

Güterboch, Hans Gustav. 1956a. "The Deeds of Suppiluliuma as Told by His Son, Mursili II." *Journal of Cuneiform Studies* 10: 41–68.

———. 1956b. "The Deeds of Suppiluliuma as Told by His Son, Mursili II (Continued)." *Journal of Cuneiform Studies* 10: 75–98.

———. 1960. "Mursili's Accounts of Suppiliuliuma's Dealings with Egypt." *Revue Hittite et asianique 66: 57–63*.

Hachmann, Rolf. 1986. *Bericht über die Ergebnisse der Ausgrabungen in Kāmid el-Lōz in den Jahren 1977 bis 1981*. Bonn: R. Habelt.

———.1989. *Kāmid el-Lōz, 1963–1981: German Excavations in Lebanon. Part 1 Part 1.* Beirut, Lebanon: Faculty of Arts and Sciences, the American University Beirut.

Hellbing, Lennart. 1979. *Alasia problems*. Göteborg: P. Åström.

Hess, Richard S. "Amarna Proper Names." PhD diss., The Hebrew Union College-Jewish Institute of Religion.

———. 1993. *Amarna personal names*. Winona Lake: Eisenbrauns.

Horowitz, Wayne. 1996. "An Inscribed Clay Cylinder from Amarna Age Beth Shean." Israel Exploration Journal 46: 208–218.

Horowitz, Wayne, Takayoshi Oshima, and Seth L. Sanders. 2006. *Cuneiform in Canaan: Cuneiform Sources from the Land of Israel in Ancient Times*. Jerusalem: Israel Exploration Society.

Huehnergard, John. 1979. *The Akkadian Dialects of Carchemish and Ugarit.* PhD. diss., Harvard University, Cambridge.

———. 1989. *The Akkadian of Ugarit. Harvard Semitic Studies* 34. Atlanta.

———. 1996. "A Byblos Letter, Probably from Kāmid el-Loz." *Zeitschrift für Assyriologie* 86: 97–113.

Hunger, H. 1962. *Aus der Vorgeschichte der Papyrussamlung der Österreichischen Nationalbibliothek. Briefe Theodor Grafs, Josef von Karabaceks, Erzherzog Rainers und anderer*, Wien: Georg Prachner Verlag.

Izre'el, Shlomo. 1991. *Amurru Akkadian: A Linguistic Study*. 2 vols. *Harvard Semitic Studies* 41. Atlanta Ga.

Izre'el, Shlomo. 1995. "The Amarna Letters from Canaan." Vol IV J.M. Sasson ed., 2411–2419 in *Civilizations of the Ancient Near East*. New York.

———. 1997. *The Amarna Scholarly Tablets*. Groningen: Styx.

———. "The Amarna Glosses: Who Wrote What for Whom? Some Sociolinguistic Considerations." *Israel Oriental Studies* 15 (1995): 101–122.

———. "Amarna Tablets in the Collection of the Pushkin Museum of Fine Arts." *Journal for Semitics* 7 (1995): 125–161.

Izre'el, Shlomo and Itamar Singer. 1990. *The General's Letter from Ugarit. A Linguistic and Historical Reevaluation of RS 20.33. Ugaritica V, No 20*. Tel Aviv.

Kallai, Zecharia and Tadmor, Hayim. 1969. "Bit Ninurta = Beth Horon—On the History of the Kingdom of Jerusalem in Amarna Period." *Eretz Israel* 9:138–147 (Hebrew).

Klengel, Horst. 1970. *Geschichte Syriens im 2. Jahrtausend v.u.Z. 3*. Berlin: Deutsch Akademie der Wissenschaften.

Knudtzon, Jørgen A. 1915. *Die El-Amarna Tafeln. Vorderasiatische Bibliothek* vols. 1–2. Leipzig: Hinrichs. (2nd ed. 1963).

———. 1907–1915/ 1963/4. *Die El-Amarna-Tafeln mit Einleitung und Erläuterungen*, 2 Vols., Aalen: Otto Zeller Verlagsbuchhandlung [Vorderasiatisches Bibliothek 2].

Knudtzon, Jørgen A., Sophus Bugge, and Alf Torp. 1902. *Die zwei Arzawa-Briefe: Die ältesten Urkunden in indogermanischer Sprache: Von J.A. Knudtzon*, Leipzig.

Kühne, Cord. 1973. *Die Chronologie Der Internationalen Korrespondenz Von El Amarna*. Kevelaer: Butzon & Bercker.

Kuschke, Arnulf. 1958. "Beiträge zur Siedlungsgeschi-chte der Bikāʿ." *Zeitschrift des Deutschen Palästina-Vereins* 74: 81–120.

Labat, René. 1932. *L'Akkadien de Boghaz-köi: étude sur la langue des lettres, traités et vocabulaires akkadiens trouvés à Boghaz-köi*. Bordeaux: Librairie Delmas. Labat René, and Florence Malbran-Labat. 1995. *Manuel d'épigraphie akkadienne: signes, syllabaire, idéogrammes*. Paris: Librairie orientalisle P. Geuthner.

Liverani, Mario. 1971. "Le Lettere del faraone a Rib-Adda." *Oriens Antiquus* 10: 253–268.

———. 1998. "How to kill Abdi-Ashirta. EA 101, Once Again." *Israel Oriental Studies* 18: 387–394.

Loretz, Oswald. 1984. *Habiru-Hebraeer*. Beihefte zur Zeitschrift fuer die alttestamentliche Wissenschaft 160.

Luckenbill, Daniel D. and T.G. Allen. 1916. "The Murch Fragment of an el-Amarna Letter." *American Journal of Semitic Languages* 33: 1–6.

Mayer, Walter. 1971. *Untersuchungen zur Grammatik des Mittelassyrischen*. Kevelaer: Butzon u. Bercker.
Mendenhall, George E. 1962. "The Hebrew Conquest of Palestine." *The Biblical Archaeologist* 25: 66–87.
———. 1973. *The Tenth Generation: The Origins of Biblical Tradition*. Baltimore: Johns Hopkins University Press.
Mercer, Samuel A.B. 1939. *The Tell el-Amarna tablets*. Toronto: Macmillan Co. of Canada. Millard, Alan. R. "A Letter from the Ruler of Gezer." *Palestine Exploration Quarterly* 97: 140 43, PL. XXV.
Moran, William L. 1950; republished 2003. *A Syntactical Study of the Dialect of Byblos as Reflected in the Amarna Tablets*. Ph.D Dissertation, John Hopkins University.
———. 1975. "The Syrian Scribe of the Jerusalem Amarna Letters." In *Unity and Diversity Essays in the History, Literature, and Religion of the Ancient Near East*. eds. H. Goedicke and J.J.M. Roberts, 146–166. Baltimore: Johns Hopkins Press, 1975.
———. 2002. *The Amarna Letters*. Baltimore: Johns Hopkins University.
Moran, William L., Dominique Collon, and Henri Cazelles. 1987. *Les lettres d'El Amarna: correspondance diplomatique du pharaon*. Paris: Editions du Cerf.
Moran, William L., John Huehnergard, Shlomo Izre'el, and William L. Moran. 2003. *Amarna Studies: Collected Writings*. Winona Lake, Ind: Eisenbrauns.
Murnane, William J., and Edmund S. Meltzer. 1995. *Texts from the Amarna period in Egypt*. Atlanta, Ga: Scholars Press.
Mynářová, Jana. 2009. *Language of Amarna—Language of Diplomacy. Perspectives on the Amarna Letters*, Prague: Charles University in Prague, Faculty of Arts, Czech Institute of Egyptology.
Na'aman, Nadav. 1977. "Yano'am." *Tel Aviv* 4: 166–177.
———. 1979. "The Origin and Historical Background of Several Amarna Letters." *Ugarit Forschungen* 11: 673–684.
———. 1981. "Royal Estates in the Jezreel Valley in the Late Bronze Age and under the Israelite Monarchy." *Eretz Israel* 15:140–144 (Hebrew; English summary * 81).
———. 1982. "The Town of Ibirta and the Relations of the 'Apiru and the Shosu." *Göttinget Miszellen* 57: 27–33.
———. 1986. "Ḫabiru and Hebrews: The Transfer of a Social Term to a Literacy Sphere." *Journal of Near Eastern Studies* 45: 271–288.
———. 1988. "Biryawaza of Damascus and the Date of the 1977 'Apiru Letters." *Ugarit Forschungen* 20: 179–193.
———. 1990. "Praises to the Pharaoh in Response to his Plans for a Campaign to Canaan." In *Lingering Over Words, Studies Ancient Near Eastern Literature in Honor of William L. Moran*. eds. T. Abush et. al., 253–256. Atlanta, Ga: Scholars Press.
———. 1998. "Collations of Some Amarna Tablets in the Berlin Museum." *NABU* 2: 51–53.
O'Connor, David B., and Eric H. Cline. 1998. *Amenhotep III: perspectives on his reign*. Ann Arbor: University of Michigan Press.
OLZ (1914–1918) Altertums-Berichte. Aegypten, *Orientalistische Literaturzeitung* X/8, 377.
Oppert, Jules. 1888. *Les Tablettes de Tell-Amarna. Comptes rendues de séance de l'Académie des inscriptions et belles-lettres*.

Peet, Thomas.E. 1921. "Excavations at Tell el-Amarna: a preliminary report." *Journal of Egyptian Archaeology* 7: 169–185.

Pendlebury, John D.S. 1951. *The City of Akhenaten. Part III: The Central City and the Official Quarters: The Excavations at Tell el-Amarna During the Seasons 1926–1927 and 1931–1936*, 2 Vols., London: Egypt Exploration Society [Fourty-Fourth Excavation Memoir].

Petrie, William M.F. 1892a. *Ten Years' Digging in Egypt 1881–1891*, London: The Religious Tract Society.

———. 1892b. "Excavations at Tell el-Amarna." *Academy* 41/1040, 356–357.

———. 1894 *Tell el-Amarna*. London: Methuen & Co.

———. 1898. *Syria and Egypt from the Tell el-Amarna Letters*. London: Methuen & Co.

Pintore, F. 1972. "Transiti di truppe e schemi epistolary nella Siria Egiziana dell'età di el Amarna." *Oriens Antiquus* 11: 101–131.

Rainey, Anson F. 1970; revised edition 1978. *El-Amarna tablets, 359–379: suppl. to J.A. Knudtzon, Die El-Amarna-Tafeln*. Kevelaer: Butzon und Bercker: Neukirchen Vluyn: Neukirchener Verlag.

———. 1971. "A Front Line Report from Amurru." *Ugarit-Forschungen* 3: 131–149.

———. 1975. "Toponymic Problems, 'Ain Shasu." *Tel Aviv* 2: 13–16.

———. 1977. "Verbal Usages in the Tanaach Letters." *Israel Oriental Studies* 7: 33–64.

———. 1978. "The Toponymy of Eretz Israel." *Bulletin of the American Schools of Oriental Research* 213: 1–17.

———. 1987a. "Review of Gottwald, N.K. 1979. *The tribes of Yahweh: a sociology of the religion of liberated Israel, 1250–1050 B.C.E.*"." *Journal of the American Oriental Society* 101: 541–543.

———. 1987b. "Review of Loretz, O. 1984. *Habiru-Hebraeer*. Beihefte zur Zeitschrift fuer die alttestamentliche Wissenschaft 160." *Journal of the American Oriental Society* 101: 539–541.

———. "Rainey's Challenge." *Biblical Archaeology Review* 17: 56–60, 93.

———. 1995–1996. "A New English Translation of the Amarna Letters." *Archiv für Orientforshung 42/43: 109–121.*

———. 1996 *Canaanite in the Amarna Tablets: A Lingustic Analysis of the Mixed Dialect Used by Scribes from Canaan*. in *Handbuch der Orientalistik. Der Nahe und Mittlere Osten* 25. 4 vols. Leiden: Brill.

———. 1998. "Syntax, Hemeneutics and History." *Israel Exploration Journal* 48: 239–251.

———. 1999. "Taanak Letters" *Eretz Israel 26: 153*-162.**

———. 2003. "Some Amarna Collations." *Eretz Israel* 27: 192*-202.*

———. 2004. "Publish it not as Gath." *Israel Exploration Journal* 54: 100–104.

———. 2007. "Whence Came the Israelites and Their Language?" *Israel Exploration Journal* 57: 41–64

Rainey, Anson F., and R. Steven Notley. 2006. *The Sacred Bridge: Carta's Atlas of the Biblical World*. Jerusalem: Carta.

Reviv, Hanoch. 1966. "The Government of Shechem in the El-Amama Period and in the Days of Abimelech." *Israel Exploration Journal* 16: 252–257.

———. 1966b. "The Planning of an Egyptian Campaign to Canaan in the Reign of Amenhotep IV." *Yediot* 30: 45–51 (Hebrew).

Rost, Liane. 1956. "Die ausserhalb von Boğazköy gefundenen hethitischen Briefen." *Mitteilungen des Instituts für Orientforschung* 4: 328–350.

Rowton, M.B. 1965. "The Topographical Factor in the Ḫapiru Problem." Pp. 375–388 in *Studies in honor of Benno Landsberger on his seventy-fifth birthday, April 21, 1965*. Chicago: University of Chicago Press.

Sayce, Archibald H. 1894. "The Cuneiform Tablets." Pp. 34–37 in Petrie, W.M.F., *Tell el-Amarna*. London: Methuen & Co.

———. 1917. "The Discovery of the Tel el-Amarna Tablets." *American Journal of Semitic Languages and Literatures* 33/2: 89–90.

Schaeffer, Claude. F.A. 1968. "Commentaires sur les lettres et documents trouvés dans les bibliothèques prives d'Ugarit." ed. J. Nougayrol et al., 607–768. *Ugaritica V*. Vol XVI of *Mission de Ras Shamra*. Paris.

Scheil, Jean-Vincent. 1890. "Une tablette de Tel-Amarna." *Recueil de travaux relatifs à la philologie et à l'archéologie égyptiennes et assyriennes* 13: 73–74.

Schroeder, Otto. 1914. "Die beiden neuen Tontafeln." *Mitteilungen der Deutschen Orient Gesellschaft* 55: 39–45.

———. 1914–1915. *Die Tontafeln von El-Amarna: 1.-2. Teil.*

———. 1917. "Zu Berliner Amarnatexten." *Orientalistische Literaturzeitung* 20, 105–106.

———. 1978. " 'Ankhesenamun, Nofretity, and the Amka Affair." *Journal of the American Research Center in Egypt 15: 43–48.*

Singer, Itamar. 1990, "Aziru's Apostast an the Historical Setting of the General's Letter." Izre'el S. and Singer, I. eds., 113–183. in *The General's Letter from Ugarit. A Linguistic and Historical Reevaluation of RS 20.33. Ugaritica V, No 20*. Tel Aviv.

———. 1991. "A Concise History of Amurru." Izre'el, S ed., 135–195. in *Amurru Akkadian: A Linguistic Study. Harvard Semitic Studies*. 41. Atlanta, GA.

———. 2005. "The 100th Anniversary of Knudtzon's Identification of Hittite as an Indo-European Language," in A. Süel, ed., 651–659. *Acts of the Vth International Congress of Hittitology (Corum, September 2–8, 2002)*, Ankara.

Smith, S. and C.J. Gadd. 1925. "A Cuneiform Vocabulary of Egyptian Words." *Journal of Egyptian Archaeology* 11: 230–239.

Soden, Wolfram von, and Bruno Meissner. 1965. Akkadisches Handwörterbuch; unter Benutzung des lexikalischen Nachlasses von Bruno Meissner (1868–1947). Wiesbaden: Harrassowitz.

Thureau-Dangin, François. 1922. "Nouvelles letres d'el-Amarna." *Revue d'assyriologie et d'archéologie orientale* 19: 91–108.

Tropper, Joseph and Juan-Pablo Vita. 2010. *Das Kanaano-Akkadische der Amarnazeit*. Münster: Ugarit-Verlag.

Tsafrir, Yoram, L. Di Segni, Judith Green, Israel Roll, and Tsevikah Tsuk. 1994. *Tabula Imperii Romani. Eretz Israel in the Hellenistic, Roman and Byzantine periods: maps and gazetteer*. Jerusalem: Israel Academy of Sciences and Humanities.

Ungnad, Arthur. 1903. "Zur Syntax der Gesetze Hammurabis." *Zeitschrift für Assyriologie* 17: 353–378.

———. 1904. "Zur Syntax der Gesetze Hammurabis." *Zeitschrift für Assyriologie* 18: 1–67.

Soldt, Wilfred H. van. 1991. *Studies in the Akkadian of Ugarit: dating and grammar*. Kevelaer: Butzon & Bercker.

Virolleaud, Charles. 1940a. "Les villes et les corporations du royaume d'Ugarit." *Syria*. 21 (2): 123–151.

———. 1940b. "Surs les nouveaux textes de Ras-Shamra." *Revue des études sémitiques*. 68–78.

Walker, C.B.F. 1979. "Another Fragment from El-Amarna (EA 380)." *Journal of Cuneiform Studies* 31/4: 249.

Weidner, Ernst. F. 1923. *Politische Dokumente aus Kleinasien. Boghazköi-Studien* 8 und 9. Leipzig.

Weinstein, James M. 1998. "Egypt and the Levant in the Reign of Amenhotep III." In *Amenhotep III Perspectives on His Reign*. Editors D. O'Connor and E. Cline, E, 223–238. Ann Arbor: University of Michigan Press.

Weippert, Manfred. 1971. *The settlement of the Israelite tribes in Palestine; a critical survey of recent scholarly debate*. Naperville, Ill: A.R. Allenson.

Wilhelm, Gernot. 1970. *Untersuchengen zum Ḫurro-Akkadischen von Nuzi. Alter Orient und Altes Testament* 9 Kevelaer, Neukirchen-Vluyn.

———. 1973. "Ein Brief der Amarna-Zeit aus Kāmid el-Lōz." *Zeitschrift für Assyriologie* 63: 69–75.

———. 1982. "Die Fortsetzungstafel eines Briefes aus Kāmid el-Lōz." edited by R. Hachman Hachmann, Rolf, and Rudolf Echt, 123–128. *Bericht über die Ergebnisse der Ausgrabungen in Kāmid el-Lōz in den Jahren 1971 bis 1974*. Bonn: R. Habelt.

Winckler, Hugo. (1896). *The Tell-el-Amarna Letters*. New York: Lemcke & Buechner.

Youngblood, Ronald F. 1961. *The Amarna Correspondence of Rib-Haddi, Prince of Byblos (EA 68–96)*. PhD, diss. Dropsie College, Philadelphia.

Zimmern, Heinrich. 1891. "Palästina um das Jahr 1400 v. Chr. nach neuen Quellen." *Zeitschrift des Deutschen Palästina-Vereins* 13: 133–147.

TECHNICAL APPARATUS

[ ]	restored text
[...]	missing text
.....	obscure or greatly damaged text
‹ ›	scribal omission
› ‹	sign(s) repeated by error
⌜ ⌝	signs damaged, but traces evident
( )	supplied by editor to clarify translation
\	single Glossenkeil
\\	double Glossenkeil

Sumerograms are transcribed in caps without normalizations. They follow Borger 2003. The Sumerograms KUR and URU are assumed to have been read as Akkadian words and thus are not raised above the line. The corresponding translations are “the land of ...,” and “the city of ...,” respectively even though this may make for a somewhat clumsy style. Normalizations of proper nouns in the translations usually seek to represent the true conjectured form, e.g. Yapaʿu instead of Yapaḫu. Still, some well-known GN’s such as Jerusalem, have the customary English form. In such matters, the only consistency is inconsistency.

THE EL-AMARNA CORRESPONDENCE

EA 1

TRANSCRIPTION

Obv.

01) [*a-n*]*a* ^{I}*Ka-dá-aš*!-*ma-an-En-líl šàr* KUR *Ka-ra-an-du-n*[*i*]-*še!*
02) ⸢ŠEŠ⸣-*ia qí-bí-ma um-ma* ^{I}*Ni-ib-mu-a-re-a* LUGAL GAL
03) *šàr* KUR *Mi-iṣ-ri-i* ^{KI} ŠEŠ-*ka-ma a-na maḫ-ri-ia šul-mu*
04) *a-na maḫ-ri-ka* ⸢*lu*⸣-*ú šul-mu a-na* É-*ka a-na* DAM.MEŠ-*ka*
05) *a-na* DUMU.MEŠ-*ka a-na* LÚ.MEŠ GAL.GAL.MEŠ-*ka* ANŠE.KUR.RA.MEŠ-*ka*
06) GIŠ.GIGIR.MEŠ-*ka a-na lìb-bi* KUR.KUR-*ka da-an-ni-iš lu-ú šul-mu*
07) *a-na ia-a-ši šul-mu a-na* É-*ia a-na* DAM.MEŠ-*ia a-na* DUMU.MEŠ-*ia*
08) *a-na* LÚ.MEŠ GAL.GAL.MEŠ-*ia* ANŠE.KUR.RA.MEŠ-*ia* GIŠ.GIGIR.MEŠ-*ia*
09) ÉRIN.MEŠ‹-*ia*› *ma-ad šul-mu ù* ‹*a-na*› *lìb-bi* KUR.KUR-*ia ma-gal šul-mu*
10) *a-nu-um-ma aš-te-me a-wa-ta*$_5$ *ša ta-aš-pu-ra* UGU-*še a-na ia-ši*
11) *um-ma-a-mi a-nu-um-ma tu-ba-a* DUMU.MUNUS-*ia a-na* DAM-*ut-ti-ka*
12) *ù a-ḫa-ti-ia ša id-di-na-ku a-bi-ia aš-ra-nu it-ti-ka*
13) *ù ma-am-ma ú-ul i-mu-ur-ši i-na-an-na šum-ma ba-a*[*l*]-*ṭá*-[*a*]*t*
14) *šum-ma mi-ta-at ša ta-aš-pu-ra-an-ni i-na lìb-bi* DUB-*ka*
15) *an-nu-tu*$_4$ *a-wa-tí-ka ù im-ma-ti ta-aš-pu-ra* LÚ-*ka* DUGUD
16) *ša i-de*$_4$ *a-ḫa-at-*⸢*ka*⸣ *ša i-dáb-bu-ub it-ti-še*
17) *ù ú-ma-an-de-še* ⸢*ù*⸣ *li-id-bu-ub it-ti-še*
18) LÚ.MEŠ *ša ta-ša-ap-pa-ra ri-i-qa* ⸢LÚ⸣[…]
19) *ša* ^{I}*Za-qa-ra* I-*en* LÚ.SIPA.ANŠE.ḪI.A [*š*]a ⸢KUR⸣[.....*ša-n*]*u-ú*
20) *i-ia-nu* I-*en lìb-bi-šu-n*[*u š*]*a*[*i-de*$_4$-*še š*]*a qé-ri-ib*
21) *a-na a-bi-ka ù š*[*a ú-ma-an-de-še*] *ap-pu-na-ma*
22) LÚ.MEŠ.DUMU.KIN ⸢*ša*⸣ ⸢*i*⸣[-*tu-ru i*]*t-ti-ka ù*[*iq-ta*]-*bi ši-i*
23) [*la-a*] ⸢*a*⸣-*ḫa-at-k*[*a i-ia-nu*]*lìb-bi-š*[*i-na ša i-de*$_4$]-*a-ši*
24) [*ù i-qa-ba-ak-ku a*]*p-pu*[-*na-ma šal-ma-at*]-*ma ù* TI *na-din*
25) [*mi-ma*]*a*[-*n*]*a* ŠU-⸢*ti*⸣-[*šu a*]-*na la-q*[*í-šu*] ⸢*a*⸣-*na um-mi-še*

EA 1

TRANSLATION

(1–6) Speak to Kadashman-Enlil, king of the land of Karaduniash, my brother! Thus Nibmuʿareʿa, the great king, king of the land of Egypt, your brother: With me all is well; may all be well with you. With your house, with your wives, with your sons, with your senior officials, with your horses and with your chariotry, (and) in the midst of your territories, may all be exceedingly well.

(7–9) With me all is well, with my house, my wives, with my sons, with my senior officials, my horses, my chariotry (and) ‹my› troops, it is all very well and within my territories it is very well.

(10–17) Now I have heard the message which you sent to me concerning it, saying: "You seek my daughter for your wife and my sister whom my father gave to you is there with you but no one has seen her now, whether she is alive, whether she is dead." (This) is what you sent me in your tablet; these are your words. When have you sent your dignitary who knows your sister, who can converse with her and identify her and let him converse with her?

(18–21) The men whom you send are nonentities. One was the [...] of Zaqara, the other was an ass herd of the land of [...]. There was not one among them who [knows her] who was close to your father and who [can identify her].

(21–25) Moreover, as for the envoys that re[turned t]o you and [sai]d she is [not] your sister, [there was none a]mong the t[wo that knew her, and could tell you, m]ore[over, she is well] and alive. Was there given [something] in[to his] hand in order to deli[ver it] to her mother?

26) *ù i-nu-ma ta-aš-pu-ra um-ma-*⸢*a*⸣*-mi ta-aq-ta-bi-mi*
27) *a-na* LÚ.MEŠ.DUMU.[KIN]*-ia ù* DAM.MEŠ*-ka pu-ḫu-rù iz-za-a-zu*
28) *i-na pa-ni-ka um-ma-a a-mur be-el-ti-ku-nu ša iz-za-az*
29) *i-na pa-ni-ku-nu ù* LÚ.MEŠ.DUMU.KIN*-ia ú-ul i-de*$_4$*-ši*
30) *ši-i a-ḫa-ti-ia ša ki-ka-ša a-nu-um-ma at-ta-ma*
31) *ta-aš-pu-ra um-ma-a ú-ul i-du-ši* LÚ.MEŠ. DUMU.KIN*-ia*
32) *ù ma-an-nu ú*(!)*-mé-di-ši-ma ta-qa-ab-bi am-mi-n*[*i*]
33) *la ta-šap-pa-ra* LÚ*-ka* DUGUD *ša i-qáb-ba-ku a-wa-at ki-ti*
34) *šu-ul-ma-ni ša a-ḫa-ti-ka ša an-ni-ka-a*
35) *ù ta-qa-ap ša ir-ru-ub a-na-›na‹-ma-ri*!(RA) É*-še*
36) *ù ṭe*$_4$*-em-še it-ti* LUGAL *ù i-nu-ma ta-aš-pu-ra*
37) *um-ma-a-mi mi-in*$_4$*-de* DUMU.MUNUS I*-en mu-uš-ke-nu*
38) *ù šum-ma* I*-en* KUR *Ga-‹-aš›-ga-ia šum-ma* DUMU.MUNUS KUR *Ḫa-ni-gal*$_9$*-bat-i‹a›*
39) *ù mi-in*$_4$*-de ša* KUR *Ú-ga-ri-it*⸢KI!⸣ *ša i-mu-rù*
40) LÚ.MEŠ.DUMU.MEŠ.KIN*-ia ù ma-an-nu i-qa-ap-šu-nu*
41) *ša ki-ka-ša a*[*n-ni-*]*‹tu› ú-ul ip-t*[e$_9$] *pí-še*
42) *ù mi-im-ma ú-ul i-qa-ap-šu*[*-nu ù*] *an-nu-tu* $_4$
43) *a-wa-tí-ka ù šum-ma mi-ta-a*[*t a-ḫa-at*]*-*⸢*ka*⸣
44) *ù ma-mi-nu ú-ka-ta-mu m*[*u-ta-še ù ma-mi-nu*]
45) *nu-še-zi-iz ša-ni-*[*ta…lu i-de*$_4$]
46) […]^{d}*A-ma-nu-um a-*[*ḫa-at-ka bal-ṭá-at*]

Lo.ed.

47) [*a-*]*ḫa-at* DAM*-ti ra*[*-bi-ti aš-ku-un-še*]
48) [*a-n*]*a be-el-ti* É*-t*[*i*] [............]
49) [1] *kál-la-ti ša i*[..................]

Rev.

50) UGU *ka-li* DAM.M[EŠ][*-ia*............]
51) *ša* LUGAL.MEŠ *ša* KUR *Mi-iṣ-r*[*i-i*.....]
52) *i-na* KUR *Mi*[*-iṣ-r*]*i-*⸢*i*⸣ *ù i-nu-ma* ⸢*ta*⸣*-*⸢*aš*⸣*-*⸢*pu*⸣*-*⸢*ra*⸣ *um-*⸢*ma*⸣*-a*
53) DUMU.MUNUS.MEŠ*-i*[*a š*]*a i-na* DAM*-ut-ti it-ti* LUGAL.MEŠ *ša l*[*i*]!*-m*[*e*]!*-*⸢*ti*⸣!*-*[*ia*]

(26–36) And as for your writing, saying "You spoke to my envoys while your wives were assembled, standing before you, saying 'Behold your mistress who is standing before you,' while my envoys did not recognize her; was it my sister who is like her?" And now you wrote, saying "My envoys did not recognize her," and you say, "So who has identified her?" Why don't you send your dignitary who will tell you the truth, the welfare of your sister who is here? Then you can trust the one who enters in to see(!) her house and her relationship with the king.

(36–46) And when you write saying: "Perhaps it was the daughter of some lowly person either one of the Kaskeans or a daughter of the land of Khanigalbat, or perhaps of the land of Ugarit which my envoys saw. Who can trust those that she is like her? ⸢This⸣ one did not open her mouth. One can not trust them in anything." These are your words. And if yo[ur sister is] dead then why would they conceal [her] de[ath and why] would we present anoth[er? ... Surely the great god(?)] Amon [knows your] sis[ter is alive!]

Lo.ed.
(47–49) [I have appointed her si]ster to the que[en mother a]s the mistress of a house [...one] bride of [...].

Rev.
(50–53) [...] concerning all of [my] wives [...] which the kings of the land of Egyp[t...] in the land of E[gyp]t. And as you wrote saying, "As for my daughters who are married to kings that are my neighbors,

54) *ù šum-ma [i-la-ku]* LÚ.MEŠ.DUMU.KIN-*ia aš-ra-nu ù i-dáb-bu-bu*
55) *it-ti-ši-[na ù ú-š]e-bé-lu-ni-in*$_4$*-ni šu-ul-ma-na*
56) *ša itti*(KI)-*ka[...an-n]u-tu* $_4$ *a-wa-te-ka mi-in*$_4$*-de*$_9$ LUGAL.MEŠ
57) *ša li-mi[-ti-ka š]a-ru-ti ra-bu-ti* DUMU.MUNUS.MEŠ-*ka*
58) *i-ra-aš-šu-*⸢*ú*⸣ ⸢*mi*⸣-⸢*im*⸣*-ma it-ti-šu-nu ù ú-še-bé-lu-ni-ku*
59) *ù mi-ni it-ti-še a-ḫa-at-ka ša it-ti-ia ù*
60) ⸢*ta*⸣*-ka-ša-ad mi-im-ma ù ú-še-bé-la-ak-ku*
61) SIG$_5$ *ki-i ta-na-an-*⸢*din*⸣ DUMU.MUNUS.MEŠ-*ka a-na ra-ši* TÚG-*ta*
62) *ša li-mi-ti-ka ù i-nu-ma ta-aš-pu-ra a-wa-te*^{MEŠ}
63) *ša a-bi-ia e-zi-ib la ta-qáb-bi a-wa-te-šu*
64) ⸢*ap*⸣*-pu-na-ma šu-ku-un at-ḫu-ut-ti* DUG.GA-*ti i-na bi-ri-*⸢*ni*!⸣
65) ⸢*ša*⸣ *ta-aš-pu-ra an-nu-tu* $_4$ *a-wa-tí-ka a-*⸢*nu*⸣-⸢*um*⸣*-ma at-ḫa-nu*
66) ⸢*a*⸣-⸢*na*⸣-⸢*ku*⸣ *ù at-*⸢*ta*⸣ *ki-la-li-nu ù aṣ-ṣé-el* UGU
67) ⸢LÚ⸣.⸢MEŠ⸣.DUMU.KIN-*ka ki-i i-qa-ab-bu-ú ‹i-na› pa-ni-ka um-ma-a mi-im-ma*
68) ⸢*ú*⸣*-ul i-na-an-di-*⸢*nu*⸣*-na-ši ša i-la-ku i-na* KUR *Mi-iṣ-ri-i*
69) *[š]a il*$_5$*-la-ku-ni*$_7$ *mu-ḫi-ia ù i-la-ak* I-*en lìb-bi ši-na*
70) *[ù la] il*$_5$*-te-qé* KÙ.BABBAR.ḪI.A KÙ.GI.MEŠ Ì.ḪI.A TÚG.MEŠ!(ME).ḪI.A *ka-li mi-ma* \SIG$_5$
71) [UGU *ša i-na*] ⸢KUR⸣ *ša-ni-ti ù i-qa-ab-bi la ki-ti*
72) *a-na ša [i-š]ap-pár-šu* I-*en-nu-tu* $_4$ *it-ta-at-la-ku*
73) LÚ.MEŠ.DUMU.KIN *a-na* ⸢*a*⸣*[-bi-]*⸢*ka*⸣ *ù pí-šu-nu sà-ru-ti i-dáb-bu-bu*
74) *ša-nu-ti it-tal-ku [ù] sà-ru-ti i-dáb-bu-bu-ni-ik-ku*
75) *ù aq-bi a-na-ku šum-*⸢*ma*⸣ *[a-na-an]-*⸢*di*⸣*-na-aš-šu-nu-ti mi-im-ma*
76) *šum-ma ú-ul a-na-an-din-šu-nu* ⸢*sà*⸣*[-ru-]*⸢*ti*⸣ ⸢*i*⸣*-‹dáb›-bu-bu ka-na-ma*
77) *ù aš-ku-un-šu-nu-ti ú-ul ad-*⸢*di*⸣*[-in a-na m]u[-ḫ]i-šu-nu ap-pu-na-ma*
78) *ù i-nu-ma ta-aš-pu-ra um-ma-a ta-aq[-bi-]*⸢*ma*⸣
79) *a-na* LÚ.MEŠ.DUMU.KIN-*ia um-ma-a i-ia-nu* ÉRIN.MEŠ *a-na be-l[i-ku-ni]*
80) *ù ú-ul ba-na-at ṣú-ḫa-ar-ti id-di-nu-ni*
81) *an-nu-tu* $_4$ *a-wa-tu-ka i-ia-nu la ki-ti i-dáb-bu-bu-ka*
82) LÚ.DUMU.MEŠ.KIN-*ka ka-an-na-ma šum-ma i-ba-aš-ši* ERÍN.MEŠ *ḫu-r[a-d]ì*
83) *šum-ma la i-ba-aš-ši ud-dú-ni mi-nu-ni aš-ša-a-li-*⸢*šu*⸣
84) *šum-ma* ERÍN.MEŠ *i-ba-aš-ši at-tu-ka šum-ma i-ba-aš-ši*
85) ANŠE.KUR.RA.MEŠ *at-tu-ka-ma e la te-še-me ši-na*
86) LÚ.DUMU.⸢MEŠ⸣.⸢KIN⸣-*ka ša pí-šu-ni sà-a-ru* ⸢*ša*⸣ *ta-šap-pár*
87) *an-ni-ka-a šum-ma pal-ḫu-ni-ik-ku ù i-‹dáb›-bu-bu sà-ra-ti*
88) *aš-šum a-ṣé-e i-na* ŠU-*ti-ka i-nu-ma táq-ba-a*

(54–61) if my envoys [go] there, they converse with the[m, and they se]nd to me a present. The one that is thus [....]" These are your words. Perhaps the kings who are [your ne]ighbors are rich and mighty; your daughters acquire something with them and they send it to you, but what does she have, your sister who is with me? But as soon as she acquires something, then she will send it to you. Is it fitting that you give your daughters in order to acquire a garment from your neighbors?

(62–77) And as for your citing the words of my father, leave it! Don't speak of his words! Moreover, "Establish friendly brotherhood between us." This is what you wrote; these are your words. Now, we are brothers, I and you, both of us, but I got angry concerning your envoys because they speak to you, saying, "Nothing is given to us who go to Egypt." Those who come to me, does one of the two go [without] taking silver, gold, oil, garments, every thing nice [more than from] another country, but he speaks untruth to the one who sends him? The first time the envoys went off to your f[ath]er and their mouths were speaking untruths. The second time they went forth [and] they are speaking lies to you. So I myself said, "If [I gi]ve them something or if I don't give them, they will speak lies likewise," so I made up my mind about them; I did not gi[ve to] them further.

(78–88) And as you wrote, saying, "You said to my envoys, 'Has [your] master no troops? The girl he gave to me is not beautiful!'" These are your words. Not so! Your envoys are speaking to you untruths in this manner! If there are warriors or if there are not, it is known to me. Why is it necessary to ask him if you have troops or if you have horses? No! Don't listen to your two envoys that you send here in whose mouths are lies! Perhaps they are afraid of you, so that they tell lies so as to escape your punishment?

89) *um-ma-a it-ta-din* GIŠ.GIGIR.MEŠ-*ia i-na lìb-bi* GIŠ.⸢GIGIR⸣.⸢MEŠ⸣
90) LÚ.MEŠ *ḫa-za-nu-ti ú-ul ta-mu-ur-šu-nu a-ḫi-ta*$_5$
91) *tu-ṭe*$_4$*-pí-il*$_5$*-šu-nu a-na pa-ni ma-a-ti ša ki-ka* (\)*ù?*
92) *ú-ul ta-mu‹-ur›-šu-nu a-ḫi-ta*$_5$ *lu-ú an-ni-ka*
93) GIŠ.GIGIR.MEŠ *lu-ú an-ni-ka-a* ANŠE.KUR.RA.MEŠ
94) [*m*]*a-ti-ia e-ri-šu gáb-ba* ANŠE.KUR.RA.MEŠ \-*ia*
95) GIŠ.GIGIR.MEŠ *i-nu-ma ta-aš-pu-ra a-na*

Up.ed.
96) ⸢*qa*⸣*-ti-**ia*(!) *ri-qà a-na ša-ka-an* Ì.ḪI.A⸢*a*⸣-⸢*na*⸣ [S]A[G]
97) *ṣú-ḫa-ar-ti at-ta ta-aš-pu-r*[*a-*]*ni*
98) 1 NÍG.BA Ì *ṣa-aḫ*

(88–95) As you spoke, saying, "He placed my chariots among the chariots of the city rulers, you did not review them separately! You humiliated them before the throng which is thus and(?) you did not rev[ie]w them separately." Verily the chariots are here; verily the horses of my country are here! All the chariot horses had to be supplied!

(96–98) When you sent to

Up. ed.

my hand a vessel to anoint the head of the girl, you sent to me one gift of pure oil.

EA 2

TRANSCRIPTION

Obv.

01) ⸢*a*⸣-*na* ^{I}*Ni-mu-wa-re-ia* LUGAL KUR ⸢*Mi*⸣-⸢*iṣ*⸣-*ri-i* ⸢ŠEŠ⸣-[*ia qí-bi-ma*]
02) *um-ma* ^{I}⸢*Ka*⸣-⸢*da*⸣-*aš*-⸢*ma*⸣-[*an-En*]-*lil* LUGAL KUR *Ka-ra*[*-du-ni-ia-aš*]
03) *a-na ia-ši ù ma*-⸢*ti*⸣-[*ia*] *da-an-ni-iš* [*šu-ul-mu*]
04) *a-na ka-a-ša* ⸢DAM⸣.[MEŠ-*k*]*a a-na* DUMU.MEŠ-*ka a*[*-na* LÚ.GAL.MEŠ-*ka*]
05) ⸢ANŠE⸣.KUR.RA.MEŠ-*ka* [GIŠ.GIGIR-*ka*] *ù ma-ti-ka ga-ab-bi-ša da-an-ni-iš lu šu*-[*ul-mu*]

---

06) ⸢*aš*⸣-⸢*šum*⸣ ŠEŠ-*ia a*[*-na a-ḫu-za-ti*] *iš-pu-ra*
07) ⸢*um*⸣-*ma-a* [DUMU.MUNUS-*ka a-ḫa-aš-še-e*]*ḫ am-mi-ni la ta-aḫ-ḫa-az*
08) [..........*k*]*a* ⸢DUMU.⸢MUNUS⸣.MEŠ-*ú-a i*-⸢*ba*⸣-*aš-ša-a*
09) [*mu-tu-ši-na lu-ú* LUGAL *ù l*]*u*-⸢*ú*⸣ *ze-er* ⸢LUGAL⸣ *šu-nu*
10) [*šu-nu-ma ša a-na* DUMU.MUNUS.MEŠ-*ia e-le-eq-qa-a*]*š-šu-nu-ti*
11) [LUGAL *ma-am-ma a-na la ze-er* LUGAL DUMU.MUNUS. MEŠ-*šu ul i*]*d-di-in-ši-na-t*[*i*]

---

12) [DUMU.MUNUS.MEŠ-*ka i-ba-aš-ša am-mi-ni la ta-a*]*d-di-na*
13) [......................................ME]Š

Rev.

01) [..]
02) [..]
03) [..........................ANŠE.KUR.]⸢RA⸣.MEŠ ⸢SIG$_5$⸣
04) [..]
05) 20 GIŠ[............................] KÙ.GI
06) 120 GÍN[.......................................]
07) *a-na šu-ul*-⸢*ma*⸣[*-ni-ka ul-te-bi-la-a*]*k-ku*
08) 1 ŠU GÍN NA$_4$.ZA.[GÌN.MEŠ *a-na šu-ul-ma-an a-ḫ*]*a*-⸢*ti*⸣-*ia*
09) [*aš*]-⸢*šum*⸣ DAM-*ka š*[*i-i ul-te-bil*]

EA 2

TRANSLATION

Obv.

(1–5) To Nimuwareia, king of the land of Egypt, [my] brother, [speak!] Thus (speaks) Kadashma[n-En]lil, king of the land of Kara[duniyash]: For me and for my land, all is very [well]. For you, your wive[s], for your sons, for [your senior officials,] your horses, [your chariotry] and your entire land may all be very we[ll.]

(6–11) Inasmuch as my brother has written to me a[bout marriage], saying "[I desi]re [your daughter,"] why should you not marry (her)? [...] My daughters are available, [but their husbands must be a king o]r of royal descent. [These are the only ones whom I take for my daughters. No king] gives them [to one who is not of royal descent].

(12–13) [Your daughters are available. Why have you not gi]ven me (one)? [.....]

Rev.

(1–9) [...] fine horses [...] 20 wooden [...] of gold. 120 shekels [...I send] to you as [your] greeting [gift]. 60 shekels of lapis la[zuli I send as the greeting-gift of]my ⸢sister⸣ [...be]cause sh[e] is your wife [have I sent].

EA 3

TRANSCRIPTION

Obv.

01) [*a-na* ^{I}*Ni-ib-m*]*u-ʾ-wa-re-ia šàr* KUR *Mi-iṣ-r*[*i-i* ŠEŠ-*i*]*a*
02) [*qí-*]*bí-ma*
03) [*um-ma* ^{I}*Ka-d*]*a-aš-ma-an-*^{d}*En-líl šàr* KUR *Ka-ra-an-du-n*[*i-*]*aš* ŠEŠ-*ka-ma*
04) [*a-na ia-ši lu š*]*u-ul-mu a-na ka-a-ša* É-*ka* DAM.MEŠ-*ka*
05) [*a-na* DUMU.MEŠ-*k*]*a* KUR-*ka* GIŠ.GIGIR.MEŠ-*ka* ANŠE.KUR.A.MEŠ-*ka*
06) [LÚ.GA]L.MEŠ-*ka da-an-ni-iš lu šu-ul-mu*

---

07) *aš-šum* ^{MUNUS}*ṣu-ḫa-ar-ti* DUMU.MUNUS.A.NI-*ia ša a-na a-ḫ̮u-za-ti ta-aš-pu-ra*
08) MUNUS *ir-ta-bi ša zi-ka-ri ši-i šu-up-ra-am-ma li-il-qu-ú*
09) *i-na pa-na* DUMU *ši-ip-ri a-bu-ú-a i-ša-ap-pa-ra-*[*k*]*u*[*-u*]*m-ma*
10) UD.MEŠ *ma-ʾa-du-ti ul ta-ka-al-la-šu ḫa-m*[*u-u*]*t-*[*t*]*a*
11) *tu-ka-ša-da-aš-šu ù šu-ul-ma-na ba-na-a*
12) *a-na a-bi-ia tu-še-eb-bé-la-am*

---

13) *i-na-na a-na-ku* DUMU *ši-ip-ri ki aš-pu-ra-ak-ku*
14) MU.6.KAM^{v} *ta-ak-ta-la-šu ù ša-a* MU 6-[K]AM^{v}
15) 30 *ma-na* KÙ.GI *ša ki* KÙ.BABBAR *ep-šu a-na šu-ul-ma-ni-ia tu-ul-te-bi-la*
16) KÙ.GI *ša-a-šu a-na pa-an* ^{I}*Ka-si-i* DUMU *ši-ip-ri-ka*
17) *uṣ-ṣi-id-du-ma i-ta-ma-ar*
18) *i-si-in-na ra-ba-a ki ta-aš-ku-nu* DUMU *ši-ip-ri-ka*
19) *ul ta-aš-pu-ra um-ma a-al-ka-am-m*[*a a-ku-ul*] ⸢*ù*⸣ ⸢*ši*⸣*-ti*
20) *ù šul-ma-ni ša-a i-si-in-ni u*[*l tu-še-bi-la*]
21) [*a*]*n-nu-ú* 30 *ma-na* KÙ.GI *ša tu*[*-še-bi-la*]
22) *šul-ma-ni ša-a e-em* MU.1[KAM^{v} *ú-še-bi-la-ak-ku ul ma-ṣi-*]*i*

EA 3

TRANSLATION

(1–6) [Sp]eak [to Nibm]uʿareʿa king of the land of Egyp[t m]y [brother]; [thus Kad]ashman-Enlil, king of the land of Karaduniash, your brother. [It is w]ell [with me]. With you, your house, your wives, [with yo]ur [sons,] your land, your chariotry, your horses, your [senior officia]ls, may it be very well.

(7–12) Concerning the young woman, my daughter, about whom you wrote concerning a marriage relationship, the girl is grown up, she is nubile. Send and let them take (her) away. In the past, my father used to send an envoy and you would not detain him many days. You used to set him on his way quickly and you used to send a lovely greeting gift to my father.

(13–17) Now, when I sent an envoy to you, six years have you detained him, but in the sixth year you have sent thirty minas of gold that looks like silver for my greeting gift. They melted down that gold in the presence of Kasî, your envoy and he witnessed (it).

(18–22) When you celebrated a great festival, you did not send your envoy, saying: "Come[, eat] and drink and a greeting gift of the festival [you did] no[t send]." These thirty minas of gold which yo[u sent, are not equ]al to the [gr]eeting gift that I sent to you in any sing[le] year.

23) [É *eš-š*]*a e-te-pu-uš i-na li*[*-ib-bi* É*-ia*]
24) [GIŠ.GI.IG *r*]*a-bi-ta e-te-pu-uš* [É*-ia eš-ša*]
Lo.ed. 25) [DUMU.ME]Š *ši-pi-ri-ka i-ta-am*[*-ru ù*]
26) [*i-na-an-n*]*a te-ru-ba-at* É *a-ša-ka-an*
27) [*ù at-ta*] *al-ka-am-ma it-ti-ia*
28) [*a-ku-ul*] ⸢*ù*⸣ *ši-i-ti*

Rev. 29) [*ul ep-pu-uš š*]*a at-ta te-pu-šu*
30) [25 LÚ.MEŠ *ù*] 25 MUNUS.MEŠ ŠU+NÍGIN 50 *a-m*[*i-lu-ta a-na*]
31) [*šu-ul-ma-ni-ka*] *ul-te-bi-la*[*-ak-ku*]

---

32) [...*š*]*a* 10 GIŠ.GIGIR.MEŠ GIŠ.MEŠ [*ù*]
33) [10 LÁ *ša* ANŠ]E.⸢KUR⸣.RA *a-na šu-ul-ma-ni-ka*
34) *ul-te-bi-la-ak-ku*

(23–28) I have built a [ne]w [house]. Wi[thin my house] I have built a [l]arge [door]. Your [en]voys have seen [the new house and no]w I am making the entry of the house. [So you,] come hither, [eat] with me and drink!

(29–31) [I am not doing wh]at you did. [twenty five men and] twenty five women, a total of fifty pe[ople, for your greeting gift,] have I sent [to you].

(32–34) [...o]f ten chariots, of wood, [and ten teams of ho]rses for your greeting gift have I sent.

EA 4

TRANSCRIPTION

Obv. 01) [.........]⸢*it-ʾti-ia*⸣ DUMU.⸢MEŠ⸣[*ši-ip-ri*.........]

02) [......]-⸢*i*⸣ *ki-i a*[..........]

03) [*ù* LÚ.]MEŠ GAL.MEŠ *ša i-ša-ap-pa-ru-ni* [..........]

---

04) [*ap-pu-na-m*]*a at-ta* ŠEŠ-*ia* ⸢*ki*⸣-*i la na-d*[*a-ni-im-ma*]

05) [*a-*]*na* DUMU.MUNUS-*ka a-na a-ḫa-zi ki-i áš-pu-ra*[*-ak-ku tal-ta-ap-ra*]

06) *um-ma-a ul-tu*$_4$ *pa-na* ⸢DUMU⸣.⸢MUNUS⸣ LUGAL *ša* KUR *Mi-iṣ*[*-ri-i*]

07) *a-na ma-am-ma ul in-na-ad-di-in am-mi-ni l*[*a in-na-ad-di-in*]

08) LUGAL *at-ta ki-i* ŠÀ-*ka te-ep*[*-pu-uš*]

09) *šum-ma* ⸢*ta*⸣*-at-ta-di-in ma-an-nu mi-na-a* ⸢*i*⸣[*-qa-ab-bi*]

10) *ki-i an-ni-ta a-ma-ta iq-bu-ni a-na-ku* ⸢*a*⸣[*-na* ŠEŠ-*ia*]

11) *a-ka-an-na al-ta-*⸢*ap*⸣*-ra um-ma-a* DUMU.MUNUS.MEŠ GAL.M[EŠ *ša ma-am-ma*]

12) MUNUS.MEŠ *ba-na-tu*$_4$ *i-ba-aš-ša-a* 1 MUNUS *ba-ni-ta ki-*⸢*i*⸣ [DUMU.MUNUS-*k*]*a* ⸢*ši*⸣*-i šu-bi-la*

13) *ma-an-nu i-qa-ab-bi um-ma-a ul* DUMU.MUNUS LUGAL ⸢*ši*⸣-⸢*i*⸣

14) *at-ta ki-i la šu-bu-li-im-ma ul tu-še-bi-la*

15) *at-ta ul aḫ-ḫu-ta-a ù ṭa-bu-ta tu-bé-ʾi-i-ma*

16) *ki-i a-na a-ḫa-mi-iš qé-re-bi-ni a-na a-ḫu-za-ti ta-aš-pu-ra*

17) *ù a-na-ku aš-šum an-ni-ti-im-ma a-na aḫ-ḫu-ti ù* ⸢*ṭa*⸣*-bu-ti*

18) *aš-šum a-na a-ḫa-mi-iš qé-re-bi-ni a-na a-ḫu-za-ti aš-pu-ra-ak-ku*

19) ŠEŠ-*ia* 1 MUNUS *am-mi-ni la ú-še-bi-la*

20) *mi-in-de at-ta* 1 MUNUS *ul tu-še-bi-la*

21) *a-na-ku ki-i ka-ša-ma-a* MUNUS *lu-uk-la-ak-ku-um-ma l*[*a-a ú-še-bi-il-ši*]

22) DUMU.MUNUS.MEŠ-*ú-a i-ba-aš-ša-a ul a-ka-al-la-a*[*k-ku-uš-ši*]

---

23) *mi-in-de-e-ma a-na a-ḫu-za-ti ki-i aš-*[*pu-ra-ak-ku ù*]

24) ⸢*a*⸣-[*na*] ⸢*ú*⸣*-ma-mi ki-i aš-pu-ra-ak-ku* [*at-ta ta-aq-ta-bi*]

25) [*it-ti* LÚ] GAL.MEŠ-*ka* ⸢*ki*⸣*-i ḫ*[*a-mu-ut-ta*.........]

EA 4

TRANSLATION

(1–3) [...] with me, the amba[ssadors...] when [.....the sen]ior officials whom he sends to me [.......]

(4–9) [Furthermor]e you, my brother, when [you wrote to me] about not gi[ving] (a daughter) when I wr[ote to you] for a daughter for marriage, saying: "From of old a daughter of the king of Egypt has never been given to anyone," why [has one] never [been given]? You are a king; you can [do] whatever you want. If you were to give (a daughter) who c[ould say] anything?

(10–13) When they told me this message, I wrote t[o my brother] thus, saying "There are grown daughters [of someone], beautiful women. Send one as if she were [yo]ur [daughter]. Who will say, 'She is not the king's daughter'?"

(14–19) You, because of (the policy of) not sending, have not sent. Did you not seek brotherhood and friendship? And you wrote to me about marriage so that we might become closer together. And I, because of this, for brotherhood and friendship, wrote to you about marriage, in order that we might become closer together. As for my brother, why did he not send just one woman?

(20–22) Perhaps, (since) you did not send one woman, I for that reason, may hold back a woman from you? My daughters are not available, that I should with[hold her from you]?

(23–25) Perhaps, too, when I [wrote to you] about marriage [and] when I wrote you about the animals, [you have spoken with] your [senior offic]ials that s[peedily may they.....]

Rev. 31) [..]
32) *i*[*t-ti* LÚ GA]L.MEŠ-*ka iq-bu-*⸢*ni*⸣[...............]
33) *i-na-an-na ša* DUMU.MUNUS-*ia ša ú-*⸢*še*⸣[*-bal-la-ak-ku*]
34) *at-ta ze-ra-ša ul ta-ṣa-*⸢*ab*⸣[*-ba-at ù*]
35) *ša ú-ma-mi mi-nu-um-ma e-ri-iš-ka š*[*u-bi-la*]

---

36) *ù aš-šum* KÙ.GI *ša aš-pu-ra-ak-ku* KÙ.GI.DIRI-*k*[*a*]
37) *ma-ʾa-da la-am* DUMU *ši-ip-ri-ka a-na mu-uḫ-ḫi-ia* ⸢*i*⸣[*-la-kam*]
38) *i-na-an-na ḫa-mu-ut-ta i-na* ŠÀ BURU$_{14}$ *an-ni-i*
39) *lu-ú i-na* ITI ŠU.NUMUN.NA *lu-ú i-na* ITI NE.NE.GAR
40) *šu-bi-la-am-ma du-ul-la ša ṣa-ab-ta-ku lu-*⸢*pu*⸣*-*⸢*uš*⸣
41) *šum-ma i-na* BURU$_{14}$ *an-ni-i i-na* ITI ŠU.NUMUN.NA *ù* ⸢ITI ⸣[NE.NE.]GAR
42) KÙ.GI *ša aš-pu-ra-ak-ku tu-ul-te-bi-la-a*[*m*]
43) DUMU.MUNUS-*ti a-na-di-na-ak-ku ù at-ta i-na ṭú-bi* KÙ.GI.[DIRI]-*ka šu-bi-la*
44) *ù šum-ma i-na* ITI ŠU.NUMUN.NA *ù* ITI NE.[NE.GAR]
45) KÙ.GI *la tu-ul-te-bi-la-am-ma du-ul-la ša ṣa-ab-ta-ku la e-te-pu-uš*
46) *ù i-na ṭú-bi a-na mi-ni-i tu-še-bé-la-am*
47) *ul-tu*$_{4}$ *du-ul-la ša ṣa-ab-ta-ku e-te-ep-šu*
48) KÙ.GI *a-na mi-ni-i lu-uḫ-ši-iḫ*
49) *lu-ú* 3 *lim* GUN *ša* KÙ.GI *šu-bi-la ul a-ma-aḫ-ḫa-a*[*r*]
50) *ú-ta-ar-*⸢*ra*⸣*-ak-ku ù* DUMU.MUNUS-*ti a-na a-ḫu-za-ti ul a-na-*⸢*di*⸣[*-in*]

(31–35) [...] they spoke wi[th] your [seni]or officials [...]. Now, as for my daughter which I am [sending to you], you may not acce[pt] her offspring, [but] s[end] whatever animals I have requested of you.

(36–40) And as for the gold that I wrote to you about, [yo]ur very best gold, a lot, before your envoy [comes to me], now quickly during this harvest season send to me, either in the month of Tammuz or in the month of Ab! So that the work that I have started, I may carry [out]!

(41–46) If, during this harvest, in the month of Tammuz or the month of Ab, you have sent to me the gold of which I have written to you, I will give my daughter to you. So you, as a favor, send to me your [very best] gold! But if in the month of Tammuz or the month of Ab you do not send me the gold, so that I do not finish the work I have started, then why should you send to me as a favor?

(47–50) After I have finished the work that I have started, why should I need gold? Then send me even 3000 talents of gold; I would not accept it! I would send it back to you and I would not gi[ve] my daughter in marriage!

EA 5

TRANSCRIPTION

Obv. 01) [*um-ma* ^{I}*Ni-ib-mu-a-re*]*-i*[*a* LUGAL GAL]

02) [*šàr* KUR *Mi-iṣ-ri-i a-na* ^{I}]*Ka*[*-da-aš-ma-an-En-líl*]

03) [LUGAL GAL *šàr* KUR *Ka-ra-*^{d}*du-*]*ni-ia*[*-aš* ŠEŠ*-ia*]

04) [*qí-bí-ma a-na maḫ-ri-i*]*a šul‹-mu› a*[*-na maḫ-ri-ka*]

05) [*lu-ú šul-mu a-na* É.ḪI.A*-k*]*a* DAM.M[EŠ*-ka*]

06) [DUMU.MEŠ*-ka* LÚ.MEŠ GAL.GAL*-k*]*a* ÉRIN.MEŠ*-k*[*a*]

07) [ANŠE.KUR.RA.MEŠ*-k*]*a* GI[Š.GIGIR.MEŠ-]*ka ù i-n*[*a lìb-bi*]

08) [KUR.MEŠ*-ka lu-ú šu*]*l-*⌜*mu*⌝

09) [*a-na ia-ši š*]*ul-mu* ⌜*a*⌝*-*⌜*na*⌝ É.ḪI.A*-ia* DAM.M[EŠ*-ia*]

10) [DUMU.MEŠ*-ia* LÚ.]MEŠ GAL.GAL*-ia* ERÍN.MEŠ*-ia ma-*[*a-ad*]

11) [ANŠE.KUR.RA*-i*]*a* GIŠ.GIGIR.MEŠ*-ia ù i-na lìb-b*[*i*]

12) [KUR.MEŠ*-i*]*a ma-gal ma-gal lu-ú šul-mu*

---

13) [*a-nu-um-ma*] *aš-me um-ma-a tá-te-pu-uš* É.ḪI.A GI[BIL.MEŠ?]

14) ⌜*a*⌝*-*⌜*nu*⌝*-*⌜*um*⌝*-*⌜*ma*⌝ *mi-im-*⌜*ma*⌝ ⌜*uš*⌝*-*⌜*te*⌝*-bi-la-ak-ku*

15) *te*$_{9}$*-er-sí-ti ša* É*-*⌜*ka*⌝ ⌜*ù*⌝ *a-nu-um-ma*

16) *ú-še-eš-šar mi-im-ma ma-a-ad a-na pa-ni*

17) LÚ.DUMU.KIN*-ka ša i-le-qé* DUMU.MUNUS*-ka ù šum-ma*
LÚ.DUMU.KIN*-ka is-sà-ḫur ù ú-še-bé-la-*⌜*ku*⌝

EA 5

TRANSLATION

(1–12) [Thus Nibmuʿar]ey[a, Great King, king of the land of Egypt, to Ka[dašman-Enlil, Great King, king of the land of Karadu]niya[š, my brother, speak: With me all is we‹ll›. W[ith you may all be well. With yo]ur [palace, [your] wiv[es, your sons, yo]ur [senior officials, yo[ur infantry, yo]ur [horses], your ch[ariots] and wi[thin your lands, may it be w]ell. [With me it is] well; with my palace, [my] wiv[es, my sons,] my [se]nor officials, my va[st] infantry, [m]y [horses, my chariotry, and withi[n m]y [lands], it is very, very well.

(13–17) [Now] I heard, saying: You have been building a n[ew] palace. Now I have sent you possessions, necessities for your house and now I am preparing abundant possessions in anticipation of your envoy who is bringing your daughter and when your envoy will return, I will send (them) to you.

18) *a-nu-um-ma uš-te-bi-la-ak-ku šu-ul-ma-na*
19) ⸢*ša*⸣ É ⸢GIBIL⸣ *a-na qa-ti* ^{I}*Šu-ut-ti*
20) [1] GIŠ.NÁ *ša* GIŠ.ESI ZU$_{9}$(KAxUD) *pí-ri* KÙ.GI GAR.RA
21) 3 GIŠ.⸢N⸣Á *ša* GIŠ.ESI KÙ.GI GAR.RA
22) 1 ^{GIŠ}*ú-*⸢*ru*⸣-[*u*]*š-ša ša* GIŠ.ESI KÙ.GI GAR.RA
23) 1 GIŠ.GU.ZA GA[L *š*]*a* GIŠ.ESI KÙ.GI GAR.RA
24) 5 GIŠ.GU.ZA *ša* GIŠ ESI KÙ.GI GAR.RA
25) 4 GIŠ.GU.ZA *ša* GIŠ.E[SI] KÙ.GI GAR.RA
26) *an-nu-ut-ti gáb-bu* K[Ù.G]I KI.LÁ-*šu*$_{13}$ 7 MA.NA 9 GÍN("ZU").GÍN("ZU") KÙ.GI
27) KI.LÁ.BI *ša* KÙ.BABBAR x [M]A.NA 8 ZU.ZU (sic!) ⸢KÙ⸣.[BABBAR]?
28) *ù* 1/2 ZU.ZU KÙ.BABBAR 10 GIŠ.GÌR.GUB *ša* GIŠ.ESI
29) [...] 1 MURUB$_{4}$ *ša* GIŠ.ESI KÙ.GI GAR.RA
30) [x GIŠ]GÌR.GUB *ša* GIŠ.ESI KÙ.[G]I GAR.RA

Rev. 31) [*an-nu-*]*t*[*ù š*]*a* ⸢*ṭup*⸣-*pí š*[*a*]KÙ.GI
32) [ŠU.NÍGIN x] MA.NA *ù* 10 ZU.⸢ZU⸣(sic!) *ù* 7 ZU.[ZU] (sic!) KÙ.GI

(18–33) Now I have sent to you a greeting gift for the new house in the charge of Šutti:

[1] bed of ebony, adorned with elephant ivory and gold.
3 beds of ebony, adorned with gold.
1 headrest of ebony, adorned with gold.
1 lar[ge] chair [o]f ebony, adorned with gold.
5 chairs of e[bo]ny, adorned with gold.
4 chairs of ebo[ny] adorned with gold.

These things, all the go[l]d, its weight: 7 minas, 9 shekels, of gold.
The weight of the silver: *x* [mi]nas, 8 1/2 shekels, of silver.

10 footrests of ebony, [...],
1 MURUB$_4$ of ebony, adorned with gold,
[*x*] footrests of ebony, adorned with gold.

[The]s[e are o]f the tablet o[f] the gold; [total: *x*] minas, 10 ⸢she⸣kels and 7 shekels of gold.

EA 6

TRANSCRIPTION

Obv. 01) *[a-]⸢na⸣* ^{I}*Ni-⸢mu⸣-⸢a⸣-⸢re⸣-⸢a⸣* L[UGAL KUR *Mi-iṣ-ri-i*]
02) ŠEŠ-*ia* *qí-b[í-ma]*
03) *um-ma Bur-ra-bu-ri-ia-aš šàr* ⸢KUR⸣ [*Ka-ra-du-ni-ia-aš*]
04) ŠEŠ-*ka-ma a-na ia-ši šu-ul-m[u]*
05) *a-na ka-ša* É-*ka* DAM.MEŠ-*ka* DUMU.MEŠ[-*ka*]
06) KUR-*ka* LÚ.GAL.MEŠ-*ka* ANŠE.KUR.RA.M[EŠ-*ka*]
07) GIŠ.GIGIR.MEŠ-*ka lu šu-ul[-mu]*

---

08) *ki ša pa-na at-ta ù a-bu-ú[-a]*
09) *it-ti a-ḫa-mi-iš ṭa-ba-t[u-nu]*
10) *i-na-an-na a-na-ku ù ka-ša i[t-ti a-ḫa-mi-iš lu ṭa-ba-nu]*
11) *i-na bi-ru-un-ni a-ma-tu[-um-ma]*
12) *ša-ni-tum-ma la iq[qa-ab-bi]*

---

13) *ša ḫa-aš-ḫa-ta i-na* KUR-*ia šu-u[p-ra-am-ma]*
14) *li-il-qu-ni-ik-ku*
15) *ù ša a-na-ku ḫa-aš-ḫa-ku i-na* KUR-*ka*
16) *⸢lu⸣-uš-pu-ra-am-ma li-il-qu[-ni]*

Rev. 17) ....(traces)...............
18) *⸢i⸣?-qì-ip-pá-a[k-ku-ma]*
19) *šu-up-ra-am-ma li-[il-qu-ni-ik-ku]*

---

20) *ù a-na šu-ul-ma-n[i-ka......]*
21) *ù* 1 [................................]
22) [..]....*u[l-t]e-⸢bi⸣-l[a-ak-ku]*

EA 6

TRANSLATION

(1–7) Sp[eak t]o Nimuʿarea, k[ing of Egypt], my brother: Thus Burraburiash, king of [Babylon], your brother. It is well with me. With you, with your house, your wives, [your] children, your land, your senior official, [your] hors[es], your chariotry, may it be well.

(8–12) As formerly, you and m[y] father were mutually on good terms, now [may] I and you [be mutually on good terms]. Between us may another word never be spo[ken].

(13–16) What you desire from my country, wri[te to me] that they may bring it to you. And what I desire from your country, let me write that [they] may bring (it) [to me].

(17–19) ....⌜he⌝(?) will entrust to you, write to me that [they] may [bring to you].

(20–22) And as [your] greeting gift [.....] and one [.....] I ha[ve] se[nt [to you⌝.

EA 7

TRANSCRIPTION

Obv.

01) [*a-na Na-ap-ḫu-*]*ru-re-ia* LUGAL GAL *šàr* KUR *Mi-i*[*ṣ-ri-i*]
02) [ŠEŠ-*ia qí-bí-*]*ma um-ma Bur-ra-bu-ri-ia-*[*aš*]
03) [LUGAL GAL *šà*]*r* KUR *Ka-ra-*^{d}*du-ni-ia-aš a-ḫ*[*u-ka-ma*]

---

04) [*a-na i*]*a-ši ù* É-*ia a-na* ANŠE.KUR.RA-*ia ù* G[IŠ.GIGIR.MEŠ-*ia*]
05) [*a-na r*]*a-ab-bu-ti-ia ù ma-ti-ia da-an-ni*[*-iš šu-ul-mu*]

---

06) *a-na a-ḫi-ia ù* É-*šu a-na* ANŠE.KUR.RA-*šu ù* G[IŠ.GIGIR.MEŠ-*šu*]
07) *a-na ra-ab-bu-ti-šu ù ma-ti-šu da-an-ni-iš l*[*u šu-ul-mu*]

---

08) *ul-tu u*$_4$*-mi ša* DUMU *ši-ip-ri ša a-ḫi-ia ik*[*-šu-da-an-ni*]
09) ⸢*ši*⸣-[*i*]*-ri ul ṭa-ba-an-ni-ma* DUMU *ši-ip-ri-šu ayi-i*[*-ka-am-ma*]
10) [*i-na p*]*a-ni-ia a-ka-la ul i-*⸢*ku*⸣*-ul ù ši-ka-ra* [*ul iš-ti*]
11) [*i-nu-*]*ú* DUMU *ši-ip-ri-ka ta-ša-ʾa-al-ma i-q*[*á-ab-bi-ka*]
12) [*ki-i ši*]*-i-ri la ṭa-ba-an-ni-ma a-na na-a*[*b-la-ṭi-ia*]
13) [*a-di-ni mi-i*]*m-ma-ma la uš*[*-ta-al-li-mu*]
14) [*ù*] *ki-i ši-i-ri la ṭa-ba-an-ni-ma a-ḫu-ú-a re-e*[*-ši la iš-šu*]
15) *a-na-ku* ⸢*li*⸣*-ib-ba-ti ša a-ḫi-ia am*[*-ta-la*]
16) *um-ma-a* ⸢*ki*⸣*-i ma-ar-ṣa-ku a-ḫu-ú-a ul iš* [*-me-e*]
17) *am-mi-ni re-e-ši la iš* [*-ši*]
18) DUMU *ši-ip-ri-šu am-mi-ni la iš-pu-ra-am-ma la i-mu*[*-ra-an-ni*]
19) DUMU *ši-ip-ri ša a-ḫi-ia an-ni-ta iq-ta-ba-a*
20) *u*[*m-m*]*a-a ul qá-aq-qá-ru qé-er-bu-um-ma*
21) *a-ḫu-ka i-še-em-me-ma šu-ul-ma i-ša-ap-pa-ra-ak-ku*
22) *ma-tu*$_4$ *ru-qá-at a-na a-ḫi-ka ma-an-nu i-qá-ab-ba-aš-šu-um-ma*
23) *šu-ul-ma ḫa-mu-ut-ta i-ša-ap-pa-ra-ak-ku*
24) *ki-i ma-ar-ṣa-ta-a a-ḫu-ka i-še-em-me-e-ma*
25) *ù* DUMU *ši-ip-ri-*⸢*šu*⸣ *ul i-ša-ap-pa-ra-ak-ku*
26) *a-na-ku a-ka-an-na aq-ta-ba-aš-šu um-ma-a a-na a-ḫi-ia*
27) LUGAL GAL *ma-tu*$_4$ *ru-uq-tu-ú i-ba-aš-ši ù qé-ru-ub-tu*$_4$ *i-ba-aš-ši*
28) *šu-*⸢*ú*⸣ [*a-k*]*a-an-na iq-ta-ba-a um-ma-a* DUMU *ši-ip-ri-ka* ⸢*ša*⸣*-a-al*
29) *ki-i ma-tu*$_4$ *ru-qá-tu-ma aš-šu-mi-ka a-ḫu-ka la iš-mu-ú-ma*
30) ⸢*a*⸣*-*⸢*na*⸣ [*šu-*]*ul-mi-ka la iš-pu-ra*

EA 7

TRANSLATION

(1–3) [Speak to Napḫu]rureia, the great king, the king of the land of Eg[ypt, my brother;] thus Burraburiash, [the great king, ki]ng of the land of Karaduniash, [your] bro[ther].

(4–5) It is very [well with m]e, with my horses and [my] ch[ariots, with] my [s]enior officials and my land.

(6–7) M[ay it be] exceedingly [well] with my brother and his household, with his horses and [his] c[hariotry] with his senior officials and his land

---

(8–13) From the day that my brother's envoy re[ached me], my body has been unwell and his envoy has not on any [occasion in] my presence eaten food or drunk spirits. [Whe]n you ask your envoy, he will tell you. Concerning [my] re[covery,] I am [still] not fully re[stored to health].

(14–25) [And] when my [b]ody was unwell and my brother [did not express concern] for [me], I (myself) was fi[lled] with anger, saying: "That I am sick, has my brother not he[ard]? Why has he not shown con[cern] for me? His envoy, why did he not send and did not lo[ok into my situation]?" The envoy of my brother said this to me, sa[yi]ng: "It is not a territory close by that your brother should hear and that he should send greeting to you. The land is far away. To your brother, who would tell him that he should send an urgent greeting to you? If your brother would hear you are sick, would he not send his envoy to you?"

(26–28) I thus spoke to him, saying, "Does my brother, the great king, have a distant land or is it close by?" He spoke to me thus, saying "Ask your envoy

(29–30) Because the land is far distant and your brother has not heard concerning you, (thus) he did not send concerning your [well] being."

31) *i-na-an-na ki-i* DUMU *ši-ip-ri-ka a-ša-lu-ma iq-⸢ba⸣-a*

32) *ki-i ge-er-ru ru-qá-a-tu*$_4$ *li-ib-ba-at a-ḫi-ia ul am-la as-s[a-k]u-[ut]*

33) *ù ⸢ki⸣-i iq-bu-ni i-na ma-ti ša a-ḫi-ia*

34) *ga-ab-bu i-ba-aš-ši ù a-ḫu-ú-a mi-im-ma-ma ul ḫa-ši-⸢iḫ⸣*

35) *ù i-na ma-ti-ia ga-ab-bu-um-ma i-ba-aš-ši*

36) *ù a-na-ku mi-im-ma-ma ul ḫa-aš-ḫa-[ku]*

37) *a-ma-ta ba-ni-ta ša ul-tu pa-na i-na qá-at šar-ra-ni*

38) *ma-aḫ-ra-nu-ma šu-ul-ma a-na a-ḫa-mi-iš ni-ša-ap-pa-[ra]*

39) *ši-i-ma a-ma-tu*$_4$ *i-na bi-ri-ni lu ka-a-a-na-a[t]*

40) *[šu]-⸢ul⸣-mi a-na mu-⸢uḫ⸣-⸢ḫi⸣-⸢ka⸣ [a-ša-ap-pa-ra ù]*

41) *[at-ta šu-ul-ma-ka a-na mu-uḫ-ḫi-ia ta-ša-ap-pa-ra]*

Lo.ed. 42) [..]

43) [..]

Rev. 44) [..]

45) [..]

46) [..]

47) *⸢ša⸣(?) [................] ⸢ša⸣ na-⸢ad⸣-n[u......]*

48) *šu-⸢ul⸣-m[i.............]ù šu-lum-ka i-q[á-ab-bi]*

49) *at-ta i-na-an-[na la-am t]e-re-ed-du-ú ši-it-ta* [MU.MEŠ]

50) *ma-ar ši-ip-ri-ia ta-ak-ta-[la]*

51) DUMU *ši-ip-ri-ka ṭe-e-ma al-ta-ka-an-ma al-ta-ap-[ra-ak-ku]*

52) DUMU *ši-ip-ri-ia ḫa-mu-ut-ta ṭe-e-ma šu-ku-un-ma li-i[l-li-ka]*

53) *ù ki-i iq-bu-ni-im-ma ge-er-ru da-an-n[a-at]*

54) *mu-ú ba-at-qu ù u*$_4$*-mu em[-mu]*

55) *šu-ul-ma-na ma-ʾa-da ba-na-a ul ú-še-bi-la-ak[-ku]*

56) 4 *ma-na* NA$_4$.ZA.GÌN *ba-na-a ki-i šu-ul-ma-an qá-ti*

57) *a-na a-ḫi-ia ul-te-bi-la*

58) *ù* 5 *ṣi-mi-it-ta ša si-si-i a-na a-ḫi-ia ul-te-bi-la*

59) *ki-i u*$_4$*-mu iṭ-ṭi-bu* DUMU *ši-ip-ri-ia ar-ku-ú ša il-la-ka*

60) *šu-ul-ma-na ba-na-a ma-ʾa-da a-na a-ḫi-ia ú-še-bé-la*

61) *ù mi-nu-ú ša a-ḫu-ú-a ḫa-aš-ḫu a-ḫu-ú-a li-iš-pu-ra-am-ma*

62) *ul-tu bi-ti-šu-nu li-il-qu-ni-iš-šu*

63) *du-ul-la ṣa-ab-ta-ku-ma a-na a-ḫi-ia aš-pu-ra*

64) *a-ḫu-ú-a* KÙ.GI *ba-na-a ma-ʾa-da li-še-bi-la-am-ma*

65) *a-na du-ul-li-ia lu-uš-ku-un*

66) *ù* KÙ.GI *ša a-ḫu-ú-a ú-še-eb-bé-la*

67) *a-ḫu-ú-a a-na pa-an qá-ayi-pa-ni ma-am-ma la ú-ma-ša-ar*

(31–46) Now, since I asked your envoy and he said to me that it is a long journey, I was not angry against my brother. I kept silent. And in as much as he told me, in the land of my brother there is everything and my brother doesn't want for anything and in my land everything is found and I myself lack for nothing, it is a beautiful thing that we have received from the past from the hand of the former kings; we sen[d] greetings mutually. May it be this thing that prevails between us. My [gr]eeting [I will send] to you [and you will send your greeting to me].

(42–46) *According to Knudtzon (1915:82), line 41 must have been the last line on the obverse. The lower edge could have held two or three lines and at the top of the reverse about three lines are missing.*

(47–48) which [...] that was given [...] m[y] greeting [...] he will sp[eak] your greeting.

(49–52) You, no[w, before yo]u escort (him), you have detain[ed] my envoy two [years]. As for your envoy, I have given (him) leave and I have sent (him) [to you]. Grant my envoy leave quickly and let him c[ome hither].

(53–58) And since they said, "The trip is difficu[lt,] water is scarce and the weather is ho[t]." I have not sent to [you] a nice large greeting gift. Four minas of lapiz lazuli have I sent to my brother as a small greeting gift and five teams of horses have I sent to my brother.

(59–62) When the weather has improved, my next envoy that goes forth, I will have him carry a nice large greeting gift. And whatever that my brother needs, may my brother write to me so they may be taken out of their (store) house.

(63–67) I have undertaken a project and I have written to my brother.

68) [IGI.II] ⸢*ša*⸣ *a-ḫi-ia li-mu-ra-ma a-ḫu-ú-a li-ik-nu-uk-ma li-še-bi-la*
69) ⸢KÙ.GI⸣ *ma-aḫ-ra-a ša a-ḫu-ú-a ú-še-bi-la ki-ša a-ḫu-ú-a ul i-mu-ur*
70) *qá-*[*a*]*-a-pa-nu-um-ma ša a-ḫi-ia ik-nu-uk-ma ú-še-bi-la*
71) 40 *ma-na* KÙ.GI *ša na-šu-ni a-na ú-tu-ni ki-i aš-k*[*u-nu*]
72) [x *ma-na š*]*a-ar-ru-um-ma ul i-la*[*-a*]
73) [*ù*] [I]*Ṣa-al-mu* DUMU *ši-ip-ri-ia ša aš-pu-ra-a*[*k-ku*]
74) [*ši*]*-ni-šu ge-er-ra-šu ḫa-ab-t*[*a-at*]
75) [*i*]*l-te-et* [I]*Bi-ri-ia-ma-za iḫ-ta-ba-*[*at*]
76) [*ù š*]*a-ni-ta ge-er-ra-šu* [I]*Pa-ma-ḫu*[???]
77) [*ša-ki-*]⸢*in*⸣ *ma-ti-ka ša ma-at Ki-iṣ-ri iḫ-ta-ba-*[*at*]
78) [*ma-ti*] *di-na ša-a-šu a-ḫu-ú-a* ⸢*i*⸣[*-da-an*]
79) [*ki-i*] DUMU *ši-ip-ri-ia a-na pa-an a-ḫi-ia it*[*-bu-ú*]
80) [*a-ka*]*-an-na* [I]*Ṣa-al-mu a-na pa-an a-ḫi-ia li-id-b*[*u-ub*]
81) [*ú-*]⸢*de*⸣*-e-šu li-te-er-ru-ni-i*[*š-šu*]
82) [*ù*] *ḫi-bi-il-ta-šu li-ša-al-li-mu*

May my brother send me much high quality gold that I may employ it in my project. And as for the gold that my brother sends, my brother, don't entrust it to the charge of any deputy.

(68–72) May the [eyes] of my brother see to it and may my brother seal it and may he send it. As for the previous gold that my brother sent, evidently my brother did not see to it. It was a deputy of my brother who sealed it and sent it. As for the forty minas of gold that they brought, when I ca[st] it into the kiln, [fo]r sure [only *x* minas] came fort[h].

(73–82) [And] as for Ṣalmu, my envoy whom I sent to [you], [tw]ice has his caravan has been robb[ed]. The [fi]rst, Biryawaza robbed [and] his [se]cond caravan, Pamaḫu[…], your governor of the land of Kiṣri robb[ed]. [When] will my brother ad[judicate] this case? [When] my envoy has st[ood up (in court), [th]us may Ṣalmu spe[ak] before my brother. His eq[uipment] may they return [to him and] his losses may they make good.

EA 8

TRANSCRIPTION

Obv. 01) [*a-na*] *Na-ap-ḫu-ʾ-ru-re-*[*ia*]
02) [LUG]AL KUR *Mi-iṣ-ri-i* ŠEŠ-*ia q*[*í-bí-ma*]
03) *um-ma Bur-ra-bu-ri-ia-aš* LUGAL KUR *Ka-ra*[*-du-ni-aš*]
04) ŠEŠ-*ka-ma a-na ia-a-ši šu-ul-mu*
05) *a-na ka-ša* KUR-*ka* É-*ka* DAM.MEŠ-*ka* DUMU.MEŠ[-*ka*]
06) LÚ.⸢GAL⸣.MEŠ-*ka* ANŠE.KUR.RA.MEŠ-*ka* GIŠ.GIGIR.MEŠ-*ka*
07) *da-an-ni-iš lu šu-ul-mu*

---

08) *a-na-ku ù* ŠEŠ-*ia it-ti a-ḫa-mi-iš*
09) ⸢*ṭa*⸣-*bu-ta ni-id-da-bu-ub*
10) *ù an-ni-ta ni-iq-ta-bi*
11) *um-ma-a ki-i ab-bu-ni it-ti a-ḫa-mi-iš ṭa-a-bu*
12) *ni-i-nu lu ṭa-ba-nu*
13) *i-na-an-na* DAM.GÀR.MEŠ-*ú-a*
14) *ša it-ti* ŠEŠ-*ṭa-a-bu te-bu-ú*
15) *i-na* KUR *Ki-na-aḫ-ḫi a-na ši-ma-a-ti it-*⸢*ta*⸣-*ak-lu-ú*
16) *ul-tu* ŠEŠ-*ṭa-a-bu a-na mu-uḫ-ḫi* ŠEŠ-*ia i-ti-qu*
17) *i-na* URU.KI *Ḫi-*⸢*in*⸣-⸢*na*⸣-⸢*tu*⸣-*ni ša* KUR *Ki-na-aḫ-ḫi*
18) ^{I}*Šu-um-ad-da* DUMU ^{I}*Ba-lum-me-e*
19) ^{I}*Šu-ta-at-na* DUMU ^{I}*Ša-ra-a-*tu_4 *ša* ⸢URU⸣ ⸢*Ak*⸣-⸢*ka*⸣
20) LÚ.MEŠ-*šu-*⸢*nu*⸣ *ki iš-pu-ru* LÚ.DAM.GÀR.MEŠ-*ia*
21) *id-du-ku ù* ⸢KÙ⸣.BABBAR-⸢*šu*⸣-*nu it-tab-lu*
22) [^{I}.....]-⸢*ḫu*⸣ *a-na pa-*[*ni-k*]*a ki-i* [*ka-al-le-e*]

Lo.ed. 23) [*a*]*l-ta-ap-ra-*⸢*ak*⸣-⸢*ku*⸣ *ši-ta-*[*al-šu-ma*]
24) ⸢*li*⸣-*iq-ba-ak-*[*ku*]

Rev. 25) [KUR *K*]*i-na-aḫ-ḫi* KUR-⸢*ka*⸣ ⸢*ù*⸣ LUGAL.⸢MEŠ⸣[-*ša* ÌR.MEŠ-*ka*]
26) [*i-n*]*a* KUR-*ka ḫu-um-mu-ṣa-ku su-ni-iq*[*-šu-nu-ti*]
27) KÙ.BABBAR *ša it-ba-lu šu-ul-l*[*i-im-šu*]
28) *ù* LÚ.MEŠ *ša* ÌR.MEŠ-*ia i*[*-du-ú-*]⸢*ku*⸣
29) *du-uk-šu-nu-ti-ma da-mi-*⸢*šu*⸣-⸢*nu*⸣ *te-e-er*

EA 8

TRANSLATION

(1–7) Sp[eak to] Napḫu'rure[ia], king of the land of Egypt, my brother. Thus (says) Burraburiyash, king of the land of Kara[duniash]: My brother, it is well with me. With you, your land, your household, your wives, [your] sons, your senior officials, your horses, your chariotry, may all be very well.

(8–12) I and my brother made a mutual declaration of friendship and this is what we said, saying: "Just as our fathers were mutual friends, let us be friends."

(13–24) Now, my merchants who had set out with Aḫu-ṭābu, were detained in the land of Canaan on business matters. After Aḫu-ṭābu went on to my brother, in the town of Ḫinnatōna (Hannathon) in the land of Canaan, Shum-Hadda son of Baʿlumme (and) Sutatna son of Sarātu of the town of ʿAkkā (Acco) sent their men and they attacked (slew) my merchants and they carried off their silver. In as much as I have sent po[sthaste PN] to [yo]ur pre[sence], inter[rogate him]; let him tell [you].

(25–29) [The land of C]anaan is your land and [its] kings [are your servants. I]n your land I have been despoiled. Investigate [them]; pa[y] the money that they took away and as for the men who s[lew]my servants, kill them; requite their blood.

30) *ù šum-ma* LÚ.MEŠ *an-nu-ti ul ta-ad-du-*⸢*uk*⸣
31) *i-tu-ur-ru-ma lu-ú* KASKAL *at-tu-ú-a*
32) *ù lu* LÚ.MEŠ DUMU.MEŠ *ši-ip-ri-ka i-du-ku-ú-ma*
33) *i-na bi-ri-ni* DUMU *ši-ip-ri ip-pa-ar-ra-as*
34) *ù šum-*⸢*ma*⸣ *i-na-ak-ki-ru-ka*
35) 1 LÚ *at-tu-ú-a* ^{I}*Šu-um-ad-da*
36) GÌR.MEŠ-*šu ki-i ú-na-ak-ki-su*
37) *i-tu-šu ik-ta-la-šu*
38) *ù* LÚ *ša-na-a* ^{I}⸢*Šu*⸣*-ta-at-na Ak-ka-aya-ú*
39) *i-na re-ši ki-i ul-zi-zu-šu*
40) *a-na pa-ni-šu iz-za-az* LÚ.MEŠ *ša-šu-nu*
41) ⸢*li*⸣-⸢*il*⸣-⸢*ku*⸣*-ni-ik-ku-um-ma a-mu-ur-ma*
42) *k*[*i-i mi-*]*tu ša-al-ma lu ti-i-de*
43) [*a-na šu-ul*]-⸢*ma*⸣*-ni* 1 *ma-na* NA$_4$ ZA.GÌN ⸢*uš*⸣-⸢*te*⸣-⸢*bi*⸣-⸢*la*⸣*-ak-ku*
44) [DUMU *ši-ip-*]*ri-ia ḫa-mu-ut-ta* ⸢*ku*⸣[*-ši-da-š*]*u*
45) [*ṭe-e*]*-ma ša* ŠEŠ-*ia lu i-d*[*e-ma*]
46) [DUMU *ši-*]*ip-ri-ia la ta-ka-*⸢*al*⸣[*-la-šu*]
47) [*ḫa-*]⸢*mu*⸣*-ut-ta li-*⸢*it*⸣-⸢*ta*⸣-⸢*al*⸣[*-la-ak*]

(30–33) But if you do not execute these men, they will do it again; they will attack either my caravan or your envoys. The envoy will be cut off between us.

(34–42) But if they dispute you, Shum-Hadda, having constrained one man of mine, has detained him with him and as for another man, Sutatna of ʿAkkā having forced him into service, he is still serving him. Let these men come to you; investigate and ask [if they are de]ad so that you may be apprised.

(43) [For a greet]ing gift I have sent to you one mina of lapis lazuli

(44–47) Ex[pedi]te my [ambass]ador; so that I may be apprised of my brother's [deci]sion. As for my [ambass]ador, do not hold [him back]; may he depart with [ha]ste.

EA 9

TRANSCRIPTION

Obv. 01) *a-na Ni-ib-ḫu-ur-re-re-ia šàr* KUR *M[i-iṣ-ri-i* ŠEŠ-*i]a*
02) *qí-bí-m[a]*
03) *um-ma Bur-ra-bu-ri-ia-aš šàr* KUR *Ka-ra-d[u-n]i-ia-aš*
04) ŠEŠ-*ka-ma a-na ia-a-ši šu-ul-mu*
05) *a-na ka-a-ša* É-*ka* DAM.MEŠ-*ka* DUMU.MEŠ-*ka* KUR-*ka*
06) LÚ.⸢GAL⸣.MEŠ-*ka* ANŠE.KUR.RA.MEŠ-*ka* GIŠ.GIGIR.MEŠ-*ka da-an-[ni-i]š lu šu-ul-mu*

---

07) *ul-tu ab-bu-ú-a-a ù ab-bu-ka it-ti a-ḫa-mi[-iš]*
08) *ṭa-bu-ta id-bu-bu*
09) *šu-ul-ma-na ba-na-a a-na a-ḫa-mi-iš ul-te-bi-i-lu*
10) *ù me-re-el-ta ba-ni-ta a-na a-ḫa-mi-iš ul ik-l[u-]ú*
11) *i-na-an-na a-ḫu-ú-a-a* 2 *ma-na* KÙ.GI *a-na šu-ul-ma-ni-ia ul-te-bi-i-la*
12) *i-na-an-na ‹šum›-ma* KÙ.GI *ma-a-ad ma-la ša ab-bi-ka šu-bi-la*
13) *ù šum-ma mi-i-iṣ mi-ši-il*$_5$ *ša ab-bi-ka šu-bi-i-la*
14) *am-mi-ni* 2 *ma-na* KÙ.GI *tu-še-bé-e-la*
15) *i-na-an-na du-ul-li i-na* É DINGIR *ma-a-ad ù ma-gal*
16) *ṣa-ab-ta-ku-ú-ma ep-pu-uš* KÙ.GI *ma-a-da šu-bi-la*
17) *ù at-ta mi-im-ma ša ḫa-aš-ḫa-a-ta i-na* KUR-*ia*
18) *šu-up-ra-am-ma li-il*$_5$*-qu-ni-ik-ku*

---

19) *i-na Ku-ri-gal-zu a-bi-ia Ki-na-ḫa-a-a-ú ga-ab-bi-šu-nu*
20) *a-na mu-uḫ-ḫi-šu il*$_5$*-ta-ap-ru-ni um-ma-a a-na qa-an-ni* KUR
21) *k[u-uš]-da-am-ma i ni-ba-al-ki-ta-am-ma*
Lo.ed. 22) *[it]-⸢ti⸣-ka i ni-ša-ki-in a-⸢bu⸣-ú-a-a*
23) *⸢an⸣-ni-ta il*$_5$*-ta-ap-ra-šu-nu-ti*
24) *um-ma-a*

EA 9

TRANSLATION

(1–2) To Nibḫurrereya, king of the land of E[gypt, m]y [brother,] speak:

(3–6) Thus Burraburiyaš, king of the land of Kard[un]iaš, your brother: To me all is well. To you, your house, your wives, your sons, your land, your senior officials, your horses, your chariots, may it be very well.

(7–10) From the time my fathers and your fathers mutually spoke in friendliness, they sent lovely greeting gifts to each other and they did not hold b[ack] any lovely request.

(11–14) Now, my brother has sent two minas of gold as a greeting gift. Now ‹i›f gold is plentiful, send as much as your fathers. But if it is scarce, send half of what your fathers (sent). Why do you send me only two minas of gold?

(15–18) Now, my work on the god's house is extensive and I am seriously engaged in carrying it out. Send me much gold. And as for you, whatever you desire from my country, write to me and let them bring it to you.

(19–24) In (the time of) Kurigalzu, my father, all the Canaanites wrote to him, saying: "C[om]e to the border of the land; let us revolt and let us be allied [wit]h you." My father wrote this to them, saying:

Rev. 25) *mu-uš-še-er it-ti-ia a-na na-aš-ku-ú-ni*
26) *šum-ma it-ti* LUGAL *ša Mi-iṣ-ri-i a-ḫi-ia ta-at-*⸢*ta*⸣*-ak-ra-ma*
27) *it-ti ša-ni-im-ma ta-at-ta-aš-ka-na*
28) *a-na-ku ul al-la-ka-am-ma ul a-ḫa-ba-at-ku-nu-ši-i*
29) *ki-i it-ti-ia na-aš-ku-nu a-bu-ú-a-a*
30) *aš-šum a-bi-ka ul iš-mé-šu-nu-ti*
31) *i-na-an-na Aš-šur-ra-a-a-ú da-gi-*⸢*il*⸣ *pa-ni-ia*
32) *a-na-ku ul aš-pu-ra-ak-ku ki-i ṭe-mi-šu-nu*
33) *a-na* KUR*-ka am-mi-ni il*$_5$*-li-ku-ú-ni*
34) *šum-ma ta-ra-á-ma-an-ni ši-ma-a-ti mi-im-ma*
35) *la ip-pu-ú-šu ri-qu-ti-šu-nu ku-uš-ši-da-šu-nu-ti*

Uninscribed space for about five lines

36) *a-na šu-ul-ma-ni-ka* 3 *ma-na* NA$_4$.ZA.GÌN KUR
37) *u* 5 LÁ *ša* ANŠE.KUR.RA.MEŠ *ša* 5 GIŠ.GIGIR GIŠ.MEŠ
38) *ul-te-bi-la-ak-ku*

"Leave being allied with me! If you become estranged from the king of Egypt, my brother, and become allied with another, will I not come and will I not plunder you? How can there be an alliance with me?" My father, because of your father, heeded them not.

(31–35) Now, as for the Assyrian, my vassal, it was not I who sent him to you. Why on their own initiative have they come to your country? If you love me, they will conduct no business whatsoever. Send them off to me empty handed.

(36–38) As your greeting gift I have sent 3 minas of genuine lapis lazuli and five teams of horses for five wooden chariots.

EA 10

TRANSCRIPTION

Obv.

01) [*a-na Na-ap*]-⌜*ḫur*⌝-*ra-r*[*e-i*]*a šàr* KUR *M*[*i-iṣ-ri-i qí-bí-ma*]
02) [*u*]*m-ma Bur-ra-bu-ri-ia-aš šàr* KUR *Ka-ra*-^{d}⌜*du*⌝-*n*[*i-ia-aš*]
03) *a-na ia-a-ši* *šu-ul-m*[*u*]
04) *a-na ka-a-ša a-na bi-ti-ka a-na aš-ša-ti-ka a-n*[*a* DUMU.MEŠ-*ka*]
05) *a-na ra-ab*-⌜*bu*⌝-*ti-ka a-na ṣa-bi-ka*
06) *a-na* GIŠ.GIGIR.ḪI.A-*ka a-na si-si-ka ù a-na ma-ti-ka*
07) *da-an-ni-iš* *lu šu-ul-mu*

---

08) *iš-tu Ka-ra-in-da-aš iš-tu* DUMU.MEŠ *ši-ip-ri*
09) *ša ab-bi-ka a-na mu-uḫ-ḫi ab-bi-ia it-ta-al-la-ku-ni*
10) *a-di i-na-an-na ṭa-bu-tu šu-nu*
11) *i-na-an-na a-na-ku ù ka-ša ṭa-bu-tu ni-nu*
12) DUMU.MEŠ *ši-ip-ri-ka a-di* 3-*šu it-ta-al-ku-ni*
13) *ù šu-ul-ma-na ba-na-a mi-im-ma ul tu-še-bi-lam*
14) *ù a-na-ku-ma šu-ul-ma-na ba-na-a*
15) *mi-im-ma* *ul ú-še-bi-la-ku*
16) *a-na ia-a-ši-ma mi-im-ma ul aq-ra*
17) *ù a-na ka-ša-ma mi-im-ma ul a-qar-ku*
18) DUMU *ši-ip-ri-ka ša ta-aš-pu-ra*
19) 20 MA.NA KÙ.GI *ša na-ša-a ul ma-li*
20) ⌜*ù*⌝ *a-na ú-tu-ni ki-i iš-ku-nu* 5 MA.NA KÙ.GI *ul i-la-a*
21) [KÙ.GI]⌜*ša*⌝ *i-la-a i-na ṣa-la-mi pa-an ṭi-ki-ni* ⌜*ša*⌝-⌜*ki*⌝-*in*
22) [KÙ.GI *im-ma*-]⌜*ti*⌝-*ma-a uʾ-e-du*-[*ú*]-*š*[*i*]
23) [*ù i-na-an-na ni-n*]*u*? *ṭa-bu-tu it-ti a*[*-ḫa-mi-iš*]
24) [———————]⌜*ul*⌝ *i-pu*-[*šu*?]
25) broken off
26) " "

Rev.

27) [..............................]
28) [...........] traces [...........]

EA 10

TRANSLATION

(1–7) [To Nap]ḫurar[ey]a, king of the land [Egypt, speak:] [T]hus Burrrabu-riyaš, king of the land of Karad[uniyaš]. With me all is well. With you, with your house, with your wives, wit[h your sons], with your senior officials, with your infantry, with your chariotry, with your horses and with your land, may all be very well.

(8–24) From the time of Karaindaš, since the envoys of your fathers were coming to my fathers up to now, they have been friends. Now, as for me and you, we are friends. Three times your envoys have come hither, but you have not sent me any really nice greeting gift and I also have not sent you any really nice greeting gift. As for me, there is nothing lacking, and as for you, there is nothing that you lack. As for the envoy whom you sent, the twenty minas of gold that were sent were not complete. And when they put them in the kiln, not five minas came out! [The gold] which did come out had the look of ashes when it turned dark (cooled). [As for the gold, wh]en did they ever verify it? [But now, as for u]s(?) we are friends, mu[tually‒‒‒‒‒‒] have [they] not done?

(25–28) *Broken off*

29) [.....]*e ša ri-mi a-na* ⌜KUR⌝?*M*[*i-iṣ-ri*]
30) [*ša ú-s*]*í*-⌜*i*⌝-*mu-šu-nu-ti* DUMU *ši-ip-ri*-⌜*ka* ⌝ *ki-i il-l*[*a*]-*k*[*a*]
31) *li il- qa- a*
32) *ù* NAGAR.MEŠ *le-ú-tu i-tu-ka i-ba-aš-šu-ú*
33) *ú-ma-ma lu ša ta-ba-li lu ša* ÍD
34) *a-na* ⌜*pí*⌝-*i ba-al-ṭi li-ma-aš-ši-lu-ma ma-aš-ku*
35) *ki-i* ⌜*ša*⌝ *ba-al-ṭi-ma lu e-pu-uš* DUMU *ši-ip-ri-ka li-il-qa-a*
36) *ù šum-ma la-bi-ru-tu ep-šu-tu i-ba-aš-šu-ú*
37) *ki-i* ^{I}*Ši-in-di-šu-ga-ab* DUMU *ši-ip-ri-ia ik-ta-al*-⌜*da*⌝-*ku*
38) GIŠ.GIGIR.MEŠ *ki-i ka-al-le-e ḫa-mu-ut-ta li-iš-ša-am-ma*
39) *a-na mu*-⌜*uḫ*⌝-*ḫi-ia li-ik-šu-da*
40) *ù* ⌜*eš* ⌝-⌜*šu*⌝-*ti ar-ku-ti li-pu-šu-ma*
41) *ki-i* DUMU *ši-ip-ri-ia ù* DUMU *ši-ip-ri-ka il-la-ka*
42) *it-ti a-ḫa-mi-iš li-il-qú-ni*
43) *a-na šu-ul-ma-ni-ka* 2 MA.NA ^{NA_4}ZA.GÌN *ul-te-bi-la-ku*
44) ⌜*ù*⌝ *aš*-⌜*šu*⌝ ⌜DUMU.MUNUS-*ka* ^{MUNUS}*Ma-i-ia-ti ki-i eš-mu-ù*
45) 1 NA$_4$.GÚ *ša ṭì-im-bu-e-ti ša* ^{NA_4}ZA.GÌN
46) 1 *lim* 40 *ù* 8 *mi-nu-ši-na*
47) *a-na šu-ul-ma-ni-ša ul-te-bi-la-ši*
48) *ù ki-i* DUMU *ši-ip-ri-ka it-ti* ^{I}*Ši-in-di-šu-ga-ab*
49) [*i-la-ka šu-ul*]-*ma*-⌜*na*⌝-⌜*ši*⌝ *e-pu-uš-ma ú-še*-⌜*ba*⌝-⌜*la*⌝-*aš*-⌜*ši*⌝

(27–35) [....] of a wild ox to the land of E[gypt, that they have] reddened them. When your envoy comes, may he bring (them). And there are capable carpenters there where you are; so let them fashion animals either terrestrial or aquatic, as in real life. May the hide be exactly like that of a live animal. May your envoy bring (them) hither.

(36–42) And if there are some old ones already made, when Sindišugab, my envoy, reaches you, let him appropriate chariots with all haste, and may he come to me. And let them make new ones for the future and when my envoy and your envoy come hither, may they bring them together.

(43–49) For our greeting gift I have sent 2 minas of lapis lazuli. And when I heard concerning your daughter Mayati, a necklace of lapis lazuli crickets, 1048 in number, have I sent as her greeting gift. And when your envoy [com]es with Šindišugab, I will make ⸢her⸣ [a greet]ing ⸢gift⸣(?) and he will br[ing it to her(?)]

EA 11

TRANSCRIPTION

Obv. 01) *a-na* ^{I}*Na-ap-ḫu-ru-r*[*e-a*] *šàr* KUR *Mi-iṣ-ri-i* ŠEŠ[*-ia qí-bí-ma*]
02) ⸢*um*⸣-[*ma* ^{I}*Bur*]*-na-*⸢*bu*⸣-[*ri-*]*ia-aš šàr* KUR *Ka-ra-du-ni-i*[*a-aš*]
03) *a-*[*na ia-a-ši šu-u*]*l-mu a-na ka-a-ša* DAM.MEŠ*-ka* É[*-ka* DUMU.MEŠ-*ka*]
04) ⸢*a*⸣[*-na* ANŠE.KUR.RA.MEŠ-]⸢*ka*⸣ GIŠ.GIGIR*-ka da-an-ni-iš lu* [*šu-ul-mu*]

---

05) [*ul-tu aš-ša-at a*]*-bi-ka* ⸢*qu*⸣-⸢*ub*⸣*-ba-tu*$_4$ ^{I}*Ḫu-ʾ-a* DUMU *š*[*i-ip-ri-ia*]
06) [*ù* ^{I}*Mi-ḫu-ni ta-ar-g*]*u-ma-*⸢*na*⸣ *al-ta-ap-ra*[*-ak-ku*]
07) [*a-ka-an-na al-t*]*a-ap-ra* ⸢*um*⸣*-ma-a* DUMU.MUNUS LUGAL *ša* [...]
08) [*a-na a-bi-ka il-*]*qu-ni* ⸢*ša*⸣*-ni-ta-am-ma li-*[*il-qu-ni-ku*]

---

09) [*ù at-ta* ^{I}*Ḫa-a-ma-aš-*]*ši* ⸢DUMU⸣ [*ši*]*-ip-ri-i-ka ù* ^{I}[.......]
10) [*ù* ^{I}*Mi-ḫu-ni ta-ar-gu-ma-an-na*] *ta-al-ta-a*[*p-ra*]
11) [*um-ma-a aš-ša-at a-bi-*]*ia qu-ub-ba-a-tu*$_4$ *a*[*n-na-a-tu*$_4$]
12) [............*aš-*]⸢*ša*⸣*-tu*$_4$ *an-na-a-tu*$_4$ ⸢*ša*⸣[............]
13) [...............*a*]-⸢*mi*⸣*-il-ta ša-a-ši a*[-................]
14) [................*i-n*]*a mu-ta-ni mi-ta-*[*at*.........]*iš-ši*
15) [*a-ka-an-na al-ta-ap-*]⸢*ra*⸣ ⸢*um*⸣*-ma-a a-*⸢*mi*⸣*-il-ta ša-*⸢*a*⸣[*-ši li-il-qu-ni-ku*]

---

16) [^{I}*Ḫa-a-ma-aš-ši* DUMU *ši-i*]*p-ri-i-ka ù* ^{I}*Mi-*⸢*ḫu*⸣*-ni t*[*a-ar-ga-ma-an-n*]*a*
17) [DUMU.MUNUS*-ti ki-i*] *ú-ka-li-mu-šu-*⸢*nu*⸣-⸢*ti*⸣ *a-na qa-qa-*⸢*ad*⸣ DU[MU].MU[NUS*-ti-ia*]
18) ⸢Ì⸣.[GIŠ *it-t*]*a-du-ú ù ša a-na mu-uḫ-ḫi-i-*⸢*ka*⸣
19) *le-q*[*u-ú-ši ma*]*-an-nu i-le-qa-ak-ku-uš-ši it-ti* [^{I}]*Ḫa-a-a*
20) 5 GIŠ.GIGIR *i-na* ⸢5⸣ GIŠ.GIGIR *i-le-qu-ni-ik-ku-uš-ši i-na-an-na-a-ma*
21) [*i-na* É*-i*]*a lu-še-bi-la-*⸢*ak*⸣-⸢*ku*⸣*-uš-ši* LUGAL.MEŠ *ša li-mi-ti-ia*
22) [*i-qa-ab-bu u*]*m-*⸢*ma*⸣*-a* DUMU.MUNUS ⸢LUGAL⸣ GAL *i-na* 5 GIŠ.⸢GIGIR⸣ [*a-n*]*a* ⸢KUR⸣ ⸢*Mi*⸣-⸢*iṣ*⸣-⸢*ri*⸣-⸢*i*⸣ ⸢*na*⸣-⸢*šu*⸣-⸢*ú*⸣-⸢*ši*⸣

EA 11

TRANSLATION

(1–4) [Speak] to Napḫurureʿa, king of the land of Egypt, [my] brother; the mess[age of Bur]naburiash, king of Karaduni[ash]: I[t is we]ll wi[th me.] With you, your wives, [your] household, [your sons], wi[th] your [horses,] your chariotry, may all be very [well].

(5–8) [After the wife of] your [fa]ther was mourned, I sen[t to you] Ḫuʾa, [my] en[voy,] and [Miḫuni, the tran]slator. [I wr]ote [as follows], saying "The royal princess who [...], they [brou]ght to your father. Let [them bring] another [to you]".

(9–15) [And you] sent [Ḫaamaš]ši, your envoy, [--- and Miḫuni the tran]slator, [saying] "T[his] mourned [wife of] my [father] [...]this [wi]fe who [...]that [wo]man [...] died [i]n the plague." [Thus, I wro]te, saying, "[May they bring] tha[t] woman [to you]."

(16–22) [As for Ḫaamašši] your [en]voy and Miḫuni the t[ranslat]or, [when] I showed them [my daughter], they [po]ured o[il] on the hea[d of my daughter. But as for the one ta[king her] to you, [w]ho will be taking [her] to you? With Ḫaya there are only five chariots. With five chariots will they take her to you? But now, should I send her to you [from m]y [house], the neighboring kings [will say, sa]ying "The daughter of the great king have they borne to Egypt with (only) five chariots!"

---

23) [*u*$_{4}$*-um a-bu-ú-a-a* DUMU.MUNUS-*šu il-*]*qu* ⌜*a*⌝*-na a-bi-ka ú-š*[*e-bi-*]⌜*i*⌝*-lu*
24) [LÚ.DUMU *ši-ip-ri-*]*ka* 3 *lim* ÉR[IN.MEŠ *it-t*]*i-i-šu*
25) [*it-ta-al-ka*.........] ⌜*lu*⌝*-ul-l*[*i*[......]*a-bu-ú-a-a*
26) [.......................*i-ša-ap-*]⌜*pa*⌝*-ar*
27) [.......................................]⌜*qi*⌝
28) [.................................]⌜*šu*⌝*-up-ra-am-ma*

Rev. 01) [.....................................]MEŠ-*šu-nu*
02) [.....................................]⌜*aš*⌝*-šu*
03) [...................................*li-*]*il-pu-tu*$_{4}$
04) [...........]⌜*li*⌝*-il-qu*[*-ni*.............*li-*]*il-pu-tu*$_{4}$
05) [*ša a-na*.....M]EŠ *ba-al-ṭú-t*[*i ma-aš-lu*....]⌜*li*⌝*-il-qu-ni*
06) *šum-ma la-bi-ru-tu*$_{4}$ *ga-mi-ru-tu*$_{4}$ *i*[*-ba-aš-š*]*u ḫ*[*a-mu-t*]*a šu-bi-i-la*!
07) *šum-ma la-bi-ru-tu*$_{4}$ *ia-*⌜*a*⌝*-nu eš-šu-ú-ti* ⌜*li*⌝*-il-*⌜*pu*⌝*-tu-ú-ma*
08) ᴵ*Ṣa-al-ma* DAM.GÀR *šu-bi-i-la šum-ma* ᴵ*Ṣa-al-mu* ⌜DAM⌝.⌜GÀR⌝ *it-ta-at-la-ka*
09) DUMU *ši-ip-ri-i-ka ša il-la-ka li-il-qa-a*
10) GIŠ.MEŠ ⌜*ša*⌝ *ši-in-ni li-il-pu-tu*$_{4}$ *ù li-iṣ-ru-ú-pu*
11) *ša-am-mi ša ṣe-e-ri ša a-na a-ḫa-mi-iš ma-aš-lu ša ši-in-ni*
12) *li-il-pu-tu*$_{4}$ *ù li-iṣ-ru-pu-ú-ma li-il-qu-ni*

---

13) ⌜ᴵ⌝*Ḫa-a-a ra-ba-a-ka ša ta-aš-pu-ra* GIŠ.GIGIR *ù* ÉRIN.MEŠ *ša it-ti-i-šu mi-i-ṣu*
14) [GIŠ.GI]GIR *ù* ÉRIN.MEŠ *ma-ʾa-da šu-up-ra-am-ma* ᴵ*Ḫa-a-a-ma* DUMU.MUNUS LUGA[L *li-il-q*]*a-ak-ku*
15) [*ra-b*]*a-a ša-na-am-ma la ta-ša-ap-pa-ra* DUMU.MUNUS LUGAL *ša* Ì.GIŠ [*a-na qa-q*]*a-di-ša*
16) [*na-du-*]⌜*ú*⌝ *i-tu-ú-a-a la uḫ-ḫa-ar šu-up-ra-am-ma ḫa-mu-ut-t*[*a li-il-q*]*u-*⌜*ú*⌝[*-ni-ši*]
17) [*ù šum-m*]*a i-na* ŠÀ *ša-at-ti an-ni-ti* GIŠ.GIGIR *ù* ÉRIN.MEŠ *ta-ša-ap-pa-*[*ra*]
18) [DUMU.KI]N *ki-i ka-al-le-e li-ṣa-am-ma ṭe-e-ma li-iq-b*[*a-a*]

(23–28) [When my father to]ok [his daughter] and sent to your father, your [envoy went], three thousand troops being with him [...]my father [...he will s]end [...]send to me [....]

Rev.

(1–5) [...]their [...]to him [....may] they fashion [...]may they bring [to me...may] they fashion [that resemble] live [...]may they bring to me.

(6–12) If [there i]s a full quota of old ones, have them brought to me im[mediate]ly. If there are no old ones, let them fashion new ones and send Ṣalmu, the merchant. If Ṣalmu, the merchant has already departed, let your envoy who is coming bring (them) to me. Let them fashion and color trees of ivory. Plants of the countryside that match let them fashion of ivory and may they color (them) and may they bring them to me.

(13–18) As for Ḫaya, your senior official, who you sent, the chariots and troops who are with him are too few. Send here many [chariots] and troops and [let] Ḫaya [br]ing the roy[al] princess to you. Do not send another [sen]ior official. May he not delay the royal princess of mine on whose [he]ad oil [has been pou]red. Send to me and [let] them [ta]ke her quickly. [I]f within this year you are sending chariots and troops, let an [env]oy come forth in haste that he may inform me.

---

19) [*ki-i a-*]*bu-ka a-na Ku-ri-gal-zu* KÙ.GI *ma-ʾa-da ú-še-bi-i-lu*
20) [*šu-ul-ma-na*]*ša Ku-ri-gal-zu mi-nu-ú i-ta-ti-ir-ma i-na* É.GAL [*a-bi-ia*]
21) [*mi-nu-ú i*]*n-da-ṭi aš-*⌜*šum*⌝ LUGAL.MEŠ *ša li-mi-ti še-mé-e um-ma-a* KÙ.[GI *ma-ʾa-du i-na*]
22) [*bi-ri*] LUGAL.MEŠ *aḫ-ḫu-*tu_4 *ṭa-bu-*tu_4 *sa-li-mu ù a-ma-*tu_4 [*ba-ni-*tu_4]
23) [*šu-ú-ma k*]*a-bi-it* NA_4.MEŠ *ka-bi-it* KÙ.BABBAR *ka-bi-it* [KÙ.GI]

---

24) 10 ⌜*ku*⌝*-ur-ba-né-e ša* [N]A_4.ZA.GÌN KUR *a-na šu-ul-ma-ni-ka ul*[*-te-bi-la-ak-ku*]
25) *a-na be-el-ti* É-*ka* 20 *ti-im-bu-e-ti ša* NA_4.ZA.GÌN KUR [*ul-te-bi-la-aš-ši*]
26) *ki-i* ^{MUNUS}*Ma-ia-tu-ma la i-pu-ša-an-ni ša a-na-ku šu-u*[*l-lu-ma-ku*]
27) *ù ši-i re-e-ši la iš-šu-ú ki-i du-lu-uḫ-t*[*i-iš*]
28) KÙ.GI *ma-ʾa-da at-tu-ka-a-ma li-il-qu-ni* [KÙ.GI *ma-ʾa-da*]
Up.ed. 29) ⌜*li*⌝*-il-qu-ni a-na ku-ta-al ša-at-ti* [*an-ni-ti-im-ma*]
30) *du-ul-li ḫa-mu-ut-ta lu-uk-šu-ud ù* [ŠEŠ-*ú-a-a*]
31) *la i-qa-ab-bi um-ma-a šu-ul-ma-na ma-a*[*ʾ-da ba-na-a*]
32) DUMU *ši-ip-ri-ka il-te-qe šu-ú a-ḫi*[...]
Lft.ed. 33) [.........]*ki-i lu-še-bi-la-ak-*[*ku* KÙ.GI *ma-ʾa-da šu-bi-*]*la-am-ma*
34) [*a-na-ku šu-ul-m*]*a-na ma-a-da a-na k*[*a-a-ša lu-še-bi-la-ak-ku*]

(19–23) [When] your [fa]ther sent much gold to Kurigalzu, what was more than the [greeting gift] of Kurigalzu? In the palace of [my father, what was] lacking? In order that the neighboring kings might hear, saying: "The go[ld is plentiful. Between] the kings there are brotherhood, amity and [good] relations. [It is he] who is rich in precious stones, rich in silver, rich in [gold]!"

(24–34) Ten lumps of genuine lapis lazuli have I sent as your greeting gift, and to the "mistress of the house" [I have sent] twenty "crickets" of genuine lapis lazuli. Because it was Mayatu who did nothing for me by which [I was restored to h]ealth and she did not show concern for me, with utmost has[te] let them bring to me much gold that is yours alone. May they bring [much gold]. By the end of [this very] year I want to complete my work in a hurry. And, may [my brother] not say, saying: "Your envoy has taken an extensive [and beautiful] greeting gift." He, my brother [.....]when I sent to you. [Se]nd me [much gold]. [I will send to you an] extensive [greet]ing gift.

EA 12

TRANSCRIPTION

Obv. 01) *a-na* ^{I}*bé-lí-ia*
02) *qí-bí-ma um-ma*
03) DUMU.MUNUS LUGAL-*ma*
04) *a-na ka-ša* GIŠ.GIG[IR.ME]Š-*ka*
05) [*a*]-⸢*mi*⸣-⸢*lu*⸣-*ti* ⸢*ù*⸣ [É-*ka*]
06) *lu-*⸢*ú*⸣ ⸢*šu*⸣-⸢*ul*⸣-⸢*mu*⸣
07) DINGIR.MEŠ *ša* ^{I}*Bur-ra-*⸢*bur*⸣*-ia-aš*
08) *it-ti-ka li-li-ku*
09) *šal-mi-iš a-li-ik*
10) *ù i-na ša-la-mì*
11) *ʾi-ir-ma* É-*ka a-mur*
12) *i-na pa-*[*ni* ^{I}*bé-lí-ia*]

Rev. 13) *a-ka-an-n*[*a*] ⸢*ul*⸣-[*ta-ki-in*]
14) *um-ma-a ul-*tu_4 *G*[*i*...]
15) DUMU *šip-ri-ia ṣi-ir-pa*
16) *ú-še-bi-la a-na*
17) URU.DIDLI-*ka ù* É-*ti-ka*
18) *lu-ú* ‹*šu*›*-ul-mu*
19) *it-ti li-bi-ka*
20) ⸢*la*⸣⸢*ta*⸣-⸢*da*⸣*-bu-u*[*b*]
21) *ù ia-a-ši et-ku-*⸢*la*⸣
22) *te-te-en-da-ni*

---

23) ÌR-*ka* ^{I}*Ki-din-*^{d}IŠKUR
24) *i-ša-ak-ni*

Up.ed. 25) *a-na di-na-an*
26) *be-lí-ia lu-ul-lik*

EA 12

TRANSLATION

(1–6) Speak to my lord; thus the princess: To you, your ch[ariot]s, the [m]en and [your house] may it be well.

(7–12) May the gods of Burraburiash go with you. Go safely and in peace go forward, see your house.

(12–22) In the pre[sence of my lord], thu[s,] I [prostrate myself], saying, "Since G[...] my envoy has brought colored cloth, to your cities and your house, may it be ‹w›ell. Do not murmur in your heart and impose darkness on me."

Your servant, Kidin-Adad, is located with me(?), as the substitute of my lord, I would verily go.

EA 13

TRANSCRIPTION

Obv. 01) [.........^{NA_4}*ú-*]*ḫi-nu* ⸢^{NA_4}⸣⸢GUG⸣ *zi-mìn-z*[*u*]
02) [*ù*.......] *be-ra* KÙ.[GI]
03) [..................]IGI.MEŠ ^{NA_4}BABBAR.DILI KU[R]
04) [..................]IGI.MEŠ ^{NA_4}MUŠ.G[ÍR]
05) [..................*t*]*u* ⸢*ši*⸣-⸢*ik*⸣-*ka-tu* [ZA.GÌN KU]R
06) [..................]*ù be-r*[*a*..............KÙ.GI]
07) [.......]*zi-mìn-zu* TUR(?).MEŠ ^{NA_4}ZA.GÌN ^{NA_4}M[UŠ.GÍR]
08) [.....^{NA_4}*ta-r*]*a-am-ba-nu* *ù* [KÙ.GI]
09) [.....*tu-di-it-*]*tu* GÚ.TUR ^{NA_4}ZA.GÌN *ù* ^{NA_4}MUŠ.G[ÍR]
10) [.....^{NA_4}*ta-r*]*a-am-ba-nu* *ù* K[Ù.GI]
11) [............^{N}]$^{A}{}_{4}$ZA.GÌN ^{NA_4}MUŠ. GÍR.TAB *ù* K[Ù.GI]
12) [..............]x *ka-ak-ku-su*^{NA_4}ZA.GÌN *ù* ^{NA_4}MU[Š.GÍR]
13) [.....^{NA_4}*ta-r*]*a-am-ba-nu* *ù* K[Ù.GI]
14) [......KÙ.GI]x *tù-tù-ur-ru* ^{NA_4}ZA.GÌN *ù* ^{NA_4}M[UŠ.GÍR]
15) [.....^{NA_4}*ta-r*]*a-am-ba-nu* *ù* K[Ù.GI]
16) [...KÙ.GI]x *tù-tù-ur-ru* ^{NA_4}ZA.GÌN KUR ^{NA_4}[MUŠ.GÍR]
17) [...............]*de-e-tu* ^{NA_4}ZA.GÌN *ù* ^{NA_4}M[UŠ.GÍR] KUR
18) [.....^{NA_4}*ta-ra-a*]*m-ba-nu ù* KÙ.GI *i-na lìb-bi*[*-šu*] KA KUR
19) [..................^{NA_4}Z]A.GÌN KUR *iḫ-zu ù be-ra* KÙ.GI
20) [............KÙ.[GI] *ra-bi-tu*
21) [..................] *ṣe-eḫ-ḫe-er-*⸢*tu*⸣
22) [..................] *tam-lu-ú*
23) [..................] *tam-lu-ú*
24) [..................]
25) [..................] KÙ.GI
26) [..................] *ra-bi-tu*
27) [.........*na-pa-*]*du ši-in-nu ša* 1 *na-pa-du* GIŠ.ESI
28) [..................] KÙ.GI
29) [.................*b*]*i*
30) [..................]KIB *iḫ-zu* ⸢KÙ.GI⸣
31) [..................]*ù pa-*[*ru*]*-ti*
32) [..................]*su*

EA 13

TRANSLATION

Obv. 01) [.........date]stone of carnelian, *zimìnzu* beads
02) [and] in between, gol[d]
03) [...]eye stones of genu[ine] *pappardilu* stone
04) [...]eye stones of ony[x]? stone
05) [....] a flask of [genui]ne [lapis lazuli
06) [....]and in between [of gold]
07) [...]small *ziminzu* beads of lapis lazuli and on[yx](?)
08) [....*tar*]*abbanu* colored glass and [gold]
09) [......dress p]in of lentil stones, lapis lazuli and on[yx](?)
10) [....*tar*]*abbanu* colored glass and g[old]
11) [.....] lapis lazuli, onyx(?) and go[ld]
12) [.....]*kakkusu*-stone, lapis lazuli and on[yx](?)
13) [........*tar*]*abbanu* colored glass and g[old]
14) [......gold] leaf, lapis lazuli and on[yx](?)
15) [........*tar*]*abbanu* colored glass and g[old]
16) [...gold] leaf, genuine lapis lazuli and [onyx](?)
17) [...dress] pins(?), lapis lazuli and genuine o[nyx](?)
18) [..*tar*]*abbanu* colored glass and gold in the midst of [it], genuine obsidian
19) [...] genuine lapis lazuli, mounting and in between, gold.
20) [..................gol]d large
21) [..................] small
22) [..................] inlay
23) [..................] inlay
24) [..................]
25) [..................] gold
26) [..................] large
27) [.......ivory [cl]asps of which one clasp is of ebony
28) [..................] gold
29) [..................]
30) [..................]*x* inlay of gold
31) [..................]and alabaster
32) [..................]

33) [..................*ta*]*m-l*[*u-ú*]

Rev. 01) [.......................*ka*]*m-mu*[*-ša-ak-ku*]
02) [.................^{GIŠ}*a-ma-r*]*a-a-tu* x[......]
03) [..............*kam-m*]*u-ša-ak-ku* x[....] KÙ.BABBAR
04) [....................^{G}]^{IŠ}*a-ma-ra-t*[*u a-di ṣú-up*]*-ri*
05) [.....................]ZUR.MEŠ *kam-m*[*u-ša*]*-ak-ku*
06) [.................] x *in-di ù* 10 ⌜*ṣú*⌝*-up-ri* KÙ.BABBAR
07) [.....................] KÙ.GI
08) [.................*i-n*]*a* GÚ.ZI-*ša* KÙ.GI
09) [NÍG.ŠU.LUḪ.ḪA ŠU *i-n*]*a* GÙ.ZI-*ši-na* KÙ.BABBAR
10) [NÍG.ŠU.LUḪ.ḪA G]ÌR KÙ.BABBAR
11) [.............*mu-s*]*a-li-ḫa-tu* KÙ.BABBAR
12) [.....................]*na-tu* KÙ.BABBAR
13) [.....................] KÙ.BABBAR
14) [.....................] ZABAR
15) [............*ḫu-lu-pa-a*]*q-qú* ZABAR
16) [...*al-ta-*]*pí-pu* IZI.GAR-*šu-nu* ZABAR
17) [............*n*]*a-ar-ma-ak-tu* ZABAR
18) [.........^{DUG}*t*]*a-al-lu*$_4$ ZABAR
19) [.........^{DUG}*t*]*a-al-lu*$_4$ ZABAR
20) [..........Š]EN URUDU
21) [...........*g*]*áb-bu* ZABAR
22) [.............*š*]*a-li-in-nu* ZABAR
23) [..........]*an-gu-ri-in-nu* ZABAR
24) [N]ÍG.ŠU.LUḪ.ḪA ŠU *i-na* GÙ.ZI-*ši-na* ZA[BAR]
25) [...]NÍG.ŠU.LUḪ.ḪA GÌR [...........ZABAR]
26) [.........*s*]*i* $^{\text{NA}}{}_4$ZA.GÌN *i-ki*[..............]
27) [............]$^{\text{NA}}{}_4$[ZA.GÌN *iḫ-zu* KÙ.G[I]
28) [..*mu-š*]*a-lu*$_4$ $^{\text{NA}}{}_4$DUḪ.ŠI.A *iḫ-zu* KÙ.GI
29) [..*mu-*]*ša-lu*$_4$ $^{\text{NA}}{}_4$ZA.GÌN *iḫ-zu* KÙ.GI

33) [..................in]la[y]

Rev. 01) [...].*kamm*[*uššakku*-bed]
02) [....side] boards[......]
03) [.....*kamm*]*uššakku*-bed....] silver
04) [......]side boar[ds with cla]w-feet
05) [.......]cubs(?) *kamm*[*ušš*]*akku*-bed
06) [.......] supports and ten [claw-fe]et of silver
07) [.....................] gold
08) [.................in]a its cup, gold
09) [..wash basins for hands, in]their cups, silver
10) [wash basins for fe]et silver
11) [.....li]bation vssels silver
12) [.....................] silver
13) [.....................] silver
14) [.....................] bronze
15) [.......bra]zier bronze
16) [...ch]est, their lamps bronze
17) [.............e]wer bronze
18) [.........c]ruse bronze
19) [.........c]ruse bronze
20) [...........ke]ttle, copper
21) [............a]ll bronze
22) [........*š*]*ālinnu* vessel bronze
23) [.......]*angurinnu* vessel, bronze
24) [wa]sh basin for hands, in their cups, br[onze]
25) [ ]wash basin for feet [............bronze]
26) [..........] lapis lazuli [...................]
27) [............]lapi[lazuli inlay gol]d
28) [..mir]ror of quartze inlay gold
29) [..mir]ror of lapis lazuli inlay gold

EA 14

TRANSCRIPTION

COL. I

(1) [*an-nu-tu ú-nu-tu*^{MEŠ} *ša* ^{I}*Na-ap-ḫu-ru-*]*re-ia* LUGAL GAL
(2) [LUGAL KUR *Mi-iṣ-ri-i a-na* ŠEŠ-*šu* ^{I}*Bur-na-*]*bu-ra-ri-ia-aš*
(3) [LUGAL GAL LUGAL KUR *Ka-ra-an-du-ni-ia-aš u*]*l-te-*⸢*bi*⸣*-il*
(4) [*i-nu-ma* DUMU.MUNUS-*sú id-di-na-aš-*]*šu*

---

(5) [...]*na*
(6) [...]*na*
(7) [...]*ma-na*

---

(8) [...] *šu-uk-ku-kà-at*
(9) [...]
(10) [..................*tam-lu-*]*u* KÙ.GI *ša* DUMU.MEŠ LUGAL
(11) [..$^{\text{NA}_4}$*eḫ-l*]*i-pa-ak-ki*
(12) [.................................. KÙ.GI *tam-*]*lu-u*
(13) [.............................K]Ù.GI GÚ.TUR *tam-lu-u*
(14) [.............................*ša ti-ik*]*-ki* KÙ.GI *ma-šu-ia*
(15) [.............................]NA$_4$.ḪI.A *súm-mu-ḫu ú-iz-za*
(16) [..................*ša*] *ti-ik-ki* KÙ.GI NA$_4$.ḪI.A *súm-mu-ḫu*
(17) [..................................*š*]*a* KÙ.GI
(18) [..................................*š*]*a* KÙ.GI
(19) [...................................]*du* KÙ.GI *tam-lu-u*
(20) [.......................................]*šu-nu*
(21) [.....................................]KÙ.GI *tam-lu-u*
(22–31) broken
(32) [x *ku-ku-bu ša* KÙ.GI Ì DÙ]G *ma-lu-ú* ⸢*na*⸣-⸢*am*⸣-*š*[*a*]
(33) [...........................KÙ.GI *ta*]*m-lu-u ku-*⸢*ú*⸣*-bu*
(34) [..........................KÙ.G]I *tam-lu-u* [*ḫ*]*a-t*[*ap-p*]*í*
(35) [...........................KÙ.GI] *tam-lu-u*
(36) [.........................]KÙ.GI *tam-lu-u a*!*-na-ḫu-u*
(37) [.............................] *ša* URUDU
(38) [........................]ŠU-*ti* KÙ.GI *tam-lu-u šu-zu-ta*

EA 14

TRANSLATION

COL. I

(1) [These items Napḫuru]reʿa, great king,
(2) [king of Egypt, s]ent [to his brother, Burna]burariash
(3) [great king, king of Karaduniash]
(4) [when he (Burnaburiash) gave his daughter to] him.

---

(5) [...]...
(6) [...]...
(7) [...]...

---

(8) [..] strung
(9) [with [..]
(10) [........................inla]id of gold, of sons of the king.
(11) [...r]aw glass.
(12) [.......................................gold in]laid.
(13) [..............................of g]old, "lentil" stones inlaid.
(14) [..........................ne]cklace of gold, (called) *mašuya.*
(15) [............................] assorted stones, (called) *wizza.*
(16) [..............ne]cklace, of gold inlaid with assorted stones.
(17) [..o]f gold.
(18) [..o]f gold
(19) [..]of gold, inlaid.
(20) [..their [...]
(21) [..of gold, inlaid.
(22–31) *broken*
(32) [*x kukkubu* vessels, of gold] filled with "[sw]eet [oil]" (called) *namša*
(33) [...........................], of gold, inlaid, (called) *kubu.*
(34) [.......................of gol]d, inlaid, (called) [*ḫ*]*at*[*app*]*i*
(35) [................................ of gold], inlaid.
(36) [...], of gold, inlaid, (called) *anaḫu.*
(37) [...] of copper.
(38) [...], for the hand, of gold, (called) *šuzuta.*

(39) [...KÙ.]GI *tam-lu-u i-na lìb-*⸢*bi*⸣*-šu-nu* KÙ.BABBAR *ù* KÙ.GI

(40) [..........................]KÙ.GI *ù* 1 *ku-ku*[*-bu*] *ṣé-eḫ-ru*

(41) [..........................*na-aḫ-*]*bu-ú ša* KÙ.GI

(42) [..........................*tú-dì-n*]*é-tù*

(43) [...................................]*na-da-ni* GAL *na-aš-ši*

(44) [.................................]*ša* KÙ.GI

(45) [.................................*ša* K]Ù.GI *ù* 1 *ṣé-eḫ-*⸢*ru*⸣

(46) [.................................*š*]*a* KÙ.GI *ra-aḫ-dá*

(47) [....................]⸢*ù*⸣ ⸢*ša*⸣ [KÙ.BABBAR *š*]*a ra-ma-ki*

(48) [.........*š*]*a* KÙ.GI [*ù ša* KÙ.]BABBAR KÙ.GI *súm-mu-ḫu da-*[*š*]*i*

(49) [x] [GAL.ḪI.A *ša* K]Ù.BABBAR KÙ.[GI...] *šu-nu tam-lu-u* ⸢*ḫa*⸣*-*⸢*ra-ga*⸣*-*⸢*bá*⸣*-aš*

(50) [...]*e ša* [.............................*š*]*a*

(51) [...]⸢*ka*⸣*-ar* [................................*z*]*i*

(52) [...*ša*] KÙ.BABBAR KÙ.[GI...................]*re-e*

(53) [...*š*]*a* KUR *Ki-n*[*a-aḫ-ḫi*............................]

(54) [..]

(55) ⸢2⸣ ^{d}LAMA$_2$ [..........................] *tam-lu-u ša* ⸢É⸣

(56) 15 É(!) Ì *š*[*a* KÙ.GI] *tam-lu-u*

(57) 1 *qí-iš-*⸢*šu*⸣*-*⸢*ú*⸣ [*ša* É Ì] KÙ.GI *tam-lu-u*

(58) 1 *ḫu-bu-*⸢*un*⸣*-*⸢*nu*⸣ [...] ⸢*ša*⸣ ⸢KÙ.GI⸣

(59) *la-ma-*⸢*as*⸣*-*⸢*sà*⸣ [..........]*at* KÙ.BABBAR *ša iz-za-az*

(60) 1 *ḫu-bu-u*[*n-nu š*]*a* ⸢KÙ.GI⸣

(61) 1 *mu-bal-*[*li-i*]*t-tù ṣí-iḫ-*[*ru*] *ša* KÙ.GI

(62) 1 *tù-ra-ḫ*[*u i-n*]*a q*[*á*]*-ab-la-t*[*ù-u*]*š-šu ra-bi-iṣ*

(63) 8 GAL.ḪI.A [*ra-ab-ba-*]*tù ša* KÙ.GI *ḫa-ra-ga-ba-aš*

(64) ⸢*ù*⸣ 1 *ṣ*[*é-eḫ-ru*]

(65) [x] [...*r*]*a ša* KÙ.GI *ù* 1 *ṣé-eḫ-ru*

(66) [x] *na*[*-aḫ-b*]*u-u ša* KÙ.GI *ù* 1 *ṣé-eḫ-ru*

(67) [x] [...]xx *ša* KÙ.BABBAR KÙ.GI *gáb-ga-bu na-am-ša šum-šu*

(68) [x] [...]x-*sú ša* KÙ.GI URUDU *mi-iḫ-ḫu-uṣ i-na lìb-bi-šu zi-mi-ú šum-šu*

(69) [1] *ku-ku-bu ṣé-eḫ-ḫe-r*[*u*] ⸢*ša*⸣ ⸢*ra*⸣*-*⸢*ma*⸣*-*⸢*ki*⸣ ⸢*ša*⸣ KÙ.GI

(70) [1] [*t*]*a-lu ṣé-eḫ-ru* ⸢*ša*⸣ ⸢KÙ.GI⸣

(71) [1] ⸢É⸣ *mé-qí-ti ša* ⸢KÙ.GI⸣ *tam-lu-u* ⸢*da*⸣*-*⸢*ba*⸣*-u-*⸢*ḫi*⸣ *šu*[*m-š*]*u*

(72) [x] *un-qá-tù ra-bu-ti ša* KÙ.GI

(73) [x] *un-qá-tù tá-at-bi-ku ša* KÙ.GI

(74) [x] ḪAR ŠU-*ti ša* KÙ.GI *tam-lu-u pu-a-ti šum-šu*

(75) 19 *in-ṣa-bá-ti ša* KÙ.GI *ša ú-ba-ni*

(76) 3 *mé-še-nu ša* GÌR *ša* KÙ.GI

(39) [...of g]old, inlaid; with silver and gold in their middle.
(40) [..............] of gold and one small *kukku*[*bu*] vessel.
(41) [.........................a p]ail, of gold.
(42) [........................togg]le pins.
(43) [............................]..., large, (called) *naššì.*
(44) [..........................] of gold.
(45) [........................, of gol]d, and one small one.
(46) [............................o]f gold, (called) *raḫda.*
(47) [.....................]and of [silver, fo]r bathing.
(48) [..., of] gold [and si]lver, inlaid with gold, (called) *da*[*š*]*i.*
(49) [*x*] [goblets of si]lver (and) g[old...], their [...], inlaid, (called) *ḫara-gabaš*
(50–51) broken
(52) [....of] silver, go[ld................................]
(53) [....o]f the land ofCan[aan..........................]
(54) [..]
(55) 2 female figurines [.........] inlaid of the container.
(56) 15 containers of oil, [of gold], inlaid.
(57) 1 "cucumber" [that is] an oil-container, of gold, inlaid.
(58) 1 *ḫubunnu*-container, [...], of gold.
(59) (with) a female figurine [...]..., silver, standing.
(60) 1 *ḫubun*[*nu*-container, o]f gold.
(61) 1 sma[ll] container (of aromatics) of gold (with),
(62) 1 Ibe[x] crouching in its center.
(63) 8 [lar]ge goblets of gold, (called) *ḫaragabaš.*
(64) [and] one small one (like it).
(65) [*x*] [...] of gold, and one small one (like it).
(66) [x] pails of gold and one small one (like them).
(67) [*x*] [...]...of silver and gold entirely(?); its name *namša.*
(68) [*x*] [...]...of gold, which is studded (with) copper in the center; its name *zimiu.*
(69) [1] small *kukkubu*-container, for bath[ing], of gold.
(70) [1] small *tallu*-jar, of gold.
(71) [1] [con]tainer for eye-paint, of gold inlaid; *dabaʾuḫi* is its name.
(72) [*x*] large finger rings of gold.

(73) [x] finger-rings, plating of gold.
(74) [x] hand bracelets, of gold, with inlays; *puati* is its name.
(75) 19 rings, of gold, for the finger.
(76) 3 (pairs) sandals, of gold.

(77) 10 ḪAR ŠU-*ti ra-ap-pa-šu-tù ša* NA$_4$.ḪI.A *šu-uk-ku-ku ma-aḫ-*⸢*da*⸣ *šum-šu-nu*

(78) 3 *tá-pal* ḪAR *ša* GÌR *ša* KÙ.GI NA$_4$.ḪI.A *šu-uk-ku-ku*

(79) [x] *na-ag-la-bu ša* KÙ.GI

(80) [x] [*na-*]*ag-la-bu ša* ZABAR ŠU-*ti-šu-nu* KÙ.BABBAR KÙ.GI

COL. II

(1) 13 *sà-aḫ-ḫa-ru ša* KÙ.GI *ṣí-il-la-aḫ-tá šum-*⸢*šu*⸣

(2) 9 *le-e-u$_5$ ša ti-ik-ki ša* KÙ.GI NA$_4$.AN.GUG.MI

(3) 7 *qá-nu-u ša mé-qí-tá ma-lu-ú ša* KÙ.GI

(4) *ù* 3 *qá-nu-u tá-at-bi-ku ša* KÙ.GI

(5) 1 É *ṣí-ip-pa-ra-ti* ša KÙ.GI

(6) 1 *qá-nu-u ša* É *mé-qí-ti ki-ba-ni ša* KÙ.GI *maš-ši* ⸢*ki*⸣-⸢*ti*⸣-⸢*ni*⸣

(7) 6 *qup-pu-ú ša* KÙ.GI SAG.DU-*šu-nu lu-ri-mé-tù*

(8) 1 *mu-bal-li-it-tù ṣí-iḫ-ru ša* KÙ.GI

(9) *ù na-ku-ú ša* NA$_4$.ZA.GÌN *i-na qá-ab-›uš‹-la-tù-uš-šu*

(10) 4 *na-al-pát-tù ṣú-up-ri ša* KÙ.GI

(11) 1 ALAM GAL *ša* KÙ.GI GAR.RA *ša* LUGAL

(12) *ù šu-pá-al* GÌR.MEŠ-*šu* KÙ.BABBAR GAR.RA

(13) 1 ^{d}LAMMA KÙ.GI GAR.RA *ša* DAM LUGAL

(14) 1 ^{d}LAMMA KÙ.GI GAR.RA *ša* DUMU.MUNUS-*ti* LUGAL

(15) 2 GIŠ.GIGIR.MEŠ *ša* GIŠ *šu-uš-šu-gi$_5$* KÙ.GI GAR.RA

(16) 2 GIŠ.GIGIR.MEŠ *ša* GIŠ *šu-uš-šu-gi$_5$* KÙ.GI *uḫ-ḫu-zu*

(17) 1 GIŠ.MÁ *ša* GIŠ EREN *e-re-ni* KÙ.GI *uḫ-ḫu-zu qa-du gáb ú-nu-te*^{MEŠ}-*šu*

(18) *ù* 6 GIŠ.MÁ.ḪI.A *ru-ku-bu ṣé-ḫe-ru-ti ša i-ša-ad-dá-du*

(19) 1 GIŠ.NÁ KÙ.GI GAR.RA GÌR.MEŠ-*šu* ^{d}LAMMA.ḪI.A

(20) 1 GIŠ.NÁ KÙ.GI GAR.RA 1 *ša re-e-ši* KÙ.GI GAR.RA

(21) 5 ^{GIŠ}*pa-ra-ak-ku* KÙ.GI GAR.RA

(22) 1 ^{GIŠ}*pa-ra-ak-ku* KÙ.GI *ù ša-aḫ-pu uḫ-ḫu-zu*

(23) 2 GIŠ.GU.ZA *ša* KÙ.GI *uḫ-ḫu-zu*

(24) 1 GIŠ.⸢GU⸣.⸢ZA⸣ [..........................]

(25) [...]

(26) [............KÙ.GI GAR.]RA *ša* KUR *Ki-na-aḫ-ḫi*

(27) [x] [ḪAR ŠU-*ti*] NA$_4$ ^{d}UTU *pu-a-ti šum-šu*

(28) [x] [ḪAR ŠU-*ti*]...] *šu-nu ša* KÙ.GI *pu-a-ti šum-šu*

(29) [x] [.............K]Ù.GI GAR.RA

(30) [...]

(77) 10 very wide hand-bracelets that are strung with stones; *maḫda* is their name.
(78) 3 pairs of anklets, of gold, strung with stones.
(79) [x] razors, of gold.
(80) [x] razors, of bronze; their handles, of silver (and) gold.

COL. II

(1) 13 gold bowls; *ṣillaḫta* is its name.
(2) 9 necklace-plaques, of gold andAN.GUG.MI-stone.
(3) 7 tubes, full of eye-paint of gold.
(4) and three tubes, plating of gold.
(5) 1 gold box of *ṣippar*(*r*)*ātu*-cosmetics.
(6) 1 tube for eye-paint with *kibbu*-ornaments of polished gold (called) *kitini*.
(7) 6 knives of gold, their heads are pomegranates.
(8) 1 small container (of aromatics), of gold,
(9) and a stopper of lapis lazuli in its middle.
(10) 4 spatulas (or: clips), of gold.
(11) 1 large statuette of the king that is overlaid with gold,
(12) and its feet overlaid with silver.
(13) 1 female figurine, overlaid with gold, of the king's wife.
(14) 1 female figurine, overlaid with gold, of the king's daughter.
(15) 2 chariots, of *šuššugu*-wood, overlaid with gold.
(16) 2 chariots, of *šuššugu*-wood, overlaid with gold.
(17) 1 boat, of cedar, overlaid with gold, along with all its gear.
(18) and 6 small boats that one tows.
(19) 1 bed, overlaid with gold; female figurines for its feet.
(20) 1 bed, overlaid with gold; 1 headrest, overlaid with gold.
(21) 5 thrones, overlaid with gold.

(22) 1 throne, overlaid with gold and *šaḫpu*.
(23) 2 chairs, overlaid with gold.
(24) 1 chair [.................................].
(25) [...]
(26) [....................with gold over]laid, of Canaan.
(27) [*x*] [hand-bracelets], of "sun"-stone; its name *puati*.
(28) [*x*] [hand-bracelets,] their [...] of gold; its name *puati*.
(29) [............] overlaid with gold.
(30) [...]

(31) [x] [...KÙ.GI GAR.R]A *du-ul-lu* ⸢*qá*⸣*-at-nu*

(32) [..].

(33) [*ù*]⸢*na*⸣*-ap*[*-ḫa-ru ša gáb-bi* KÙ.GI]

(34) 1 LIM 2 *me ma*[*-na*...GÍ]N([Z]U).GÍN(ZU) KÙ.GI

(35) 1 DUG *na-ma-a*[*n-du ra-b*]*u-*[*ú ša* KÙ.BABBAR]

(36) 3 *na-an-sé-tù* [*ra-bu-ú*] *ša* K[Ù.BABBAR]

(37) 1 *ma-ap-ru-u* [*ra-bu-ú š*]*a* KÙ.BABBER

(38) 1 DUG *ra-bu-ú š*[*a* KÙ.BABBAR *u*]*z-na-šu š*[*a*...]

(39) 10 GAL.ḪI.A *ša* KÙ.BA[BBAR...]*ma i*[...*š*]*u* ⸢*ša*⸣[KÙ.GI]

(40) 1 *dì-qá-ru ra-b*[*i-tù š*]*a* KÙ.BABBAR

(41) 1 *ku-ku-bu ša* 1 *l*[*i-im š*]*a* KÙ.BABBAR [*q*]*a-du na-ak-ta-mi-šu*

(42) 3 *na-ma-an-du-u ṣ*[*é-eḫ-r*]*u-ti ša* KÙ.BABBAR *bu-u-me-er šum-šu-nu*

(43) 1 *ḫa-ra-ga-ba-aš š*[*a* KÙ.BA]BBAR

(44) 1 *na-aḫ-bu-u ša* KÙ.BABBAR

(45) 1 *ma-aš-ḫa-lu*$_4$ *ša* KÙ. BAB[BAR]

(46) 1 *ta-lu ša* KÙ.BABBAR *ša* [*k*]*i-nu-ni ṣé-eḫ-ru*

(47) 1 *nu-ri-im-tù ša* KÙ.BABBAR

(48) 1 *pa-gu*$_5$*-tù ù* DUMU.MUNUS-*šu i-na*[*sú-n*]*i-ši ša* KÚ.BABBAR

(49) 1 *dì-qá-ru a-ri-ik-tù ša k*[*i-*]*nu-ni ša* KÚ.BABBAR *dì-ni-tá šum-šu*

(50) 23 *ku-ku-bu ša* KÙ.BABBAR Ì DÙG.‹GA› *ma-lu-ú na-am-ša šum-šu*

(51) 6 *ḫu-bu-un-ni-tù ša* KÚ.BABBAR ⸢*ù*⸣ 1 *ḫu-bu-un-nu* GAL *ša* KÙ.BABBAR-*ma*

(52) 1 *ḫa-nu-ú-nu ša-ḫu-ú ša* ⸢KÙ⸣.⸢BABBAR⸣ *tam-lu-u*

(53) 1 *na-al-pát-tù ša* KÙ.BABBAR *ša e-ni wa-ad-ḫa šum-šu*

(54) 12 *sà-aḫ-ḫa-ru ša* KÙ.BABBAR *ṣí*[*-l*]*a-aḫ-tá* ‹*šum-šu*›

(55) 29 *na-al-pát-tù ša* KÙ.BABBAR *qa-a*[*t-š*]*u-nu* GIŠ.TAŠKARIN *ù* GIŠ.ESI

(56) *ša še-er-tá i-ke-ez-zi-ru i-na lìb-bi-šu-nu*

(57) 1 *tup-ni-nu ša* KÙ.BABBAR *za-ki-i*

(58) 3 *mé-še-nu ša še-e-ni* ša KÚ.BABBAR

(59) [1] [*ku-k*]*u-bu ša* KÙ.BABBAR *ap-pa-šu ša* KÙ.GI

(60) [1] [É *ṣ*]*í-ip-pa-ra-tù* KÙ.BABBAR KÙ.GI *uḫ-ḫu-zu*

(61) [x] [*na-al-pát-t*]*ù ša* LÚ.ŠU.I *ša* [KÙ].BABBAR

(62) [x] [......]*a-tù ša* KÙ.BABBAR ⸢*ù*⸣ KÙ.GI

(63) 3 GIŠ.[NÁ KÙ.BABBAR *za-ku-ú*] 1 *ša re-*⸢*e*⸣*-š*]*i* KÙ.BABBAR *za-ku-ú*

(64) 1 ^{GIŠ}*p*[*a-*]*ra*[*-ak-ku* KÙ.GI *ù* KÙ.BABBAR] GAR.RA

(65) 1 *na-*[*ma*]*-a*[*r pa-ni ša* KÙ.BABBAR N]A$_4$.‹ḪI.A› ⸢*súm*⸣*-m*[*u-*]*ḫu*

(66) 1 *na-*[*m*]*a-a*[*r pa-ni ša*] KÙ.BABBAR K[Ù.G]I

(67) 18 N[A$_4$.ḪI.A] *ša* [................]KAxU-*šu-nu ša* KÙ.GI

(31) [*x*] [............] overlaid with gold, delicate work.
(32) [..]
(33) [and the]tot]al of all the gold]:
(34) 1200 mi[nas,...............*x*] shekels of gold.
(35) 1 [large] measuring-ves[sel, of silver].
(36) 3 [large] washing-bowls, of s(ilver)].
(37) 1 large *maprû* vessel [of] silver.
(38) 1 large pot, o[f silver], its [han]dles o[f...].
(39) 10 goblets, of sil[ver...]...[...].
(40) 1 lar[ge] pot, of silver.
(41) 1 *kukkubu*-container, of 1 thou[sand o]f silver [al]ong with its cover.
(42) 3 s[mal]l measuring-vessels, of silver; *bumer* is its name.
(43) 1 *ḫaragabaš*, o[f silv]er.
(44) 1 pail, of silver.
(45) 1 sieve, of silver.
(46) 1 small *tallu*-jar, of silver, for a brazier.
(47) 1 "pomegranate," of silver.
(48) 1 female monkey, with its daughter on its [la]p, of silver.
(49) 1 tall pot, for a brazier, of silver; *dinīta* is its name.
(50) 23 *kukkubu*-containers, of silver, full of "sweet oil," *namša* is its name.
(51) 6 *ḫubunnu*-containers, [and] 1 large *ḫubunnu*-container, also of silver.
(52) 1 chest(?), upright, of silver, inlaid.
(53) 1 spatula, of silver, for the eyes; *wadḫa* is its name.
(54) 12 bowls, of silver, *ṣi*[*l*]*laḫta* ‹is its name›.
(55) 29 spatulas, of silver, handles of boxwood and ebony,
(56) with which one curls the hair.
(57) 1 box of pure silver.
(58) 3 (pairs) of sandals, of silver.
(59) [1] *kukkubu*-container, of silver; its spout of gold.
(60) [1 box of *ṣ*]*ippar*(*r*)*ātu*-cosmetics, overlaid with silver (and) gold.
(61) [*x* spatu]las, for a barber, of silver.
(62) [...]..., of silver and gold.
(63) 3 b[eds, of pure silver?]; 1 headre[st], of pure silver.
(64) 1 [throne], overlaid [with silver(?) and gold(?)].
(65) 1 mi[rr]o[r of silver], set with [ston]es(?).
(66) 1 mi[rr]o[r] of silver (and) g[ol]d.
(67) 18 st[ones...], their [m]outh, of gold,

(68) ⸢ù⸣[...].
(69) 1 m[u-bal-li-it-t]ù ṣí-iḫ-ru [ša KÙ.BABBAR]
(70) ù na-[ku-ú i-]na [lì]b-bi-šu ša [KÙ.BABBAR]
(71) $^{\text{SU.NÍGIN}}$na-a[p-ḫa-a]r ⸢gáb⸣-bi KÙ.BABBAR
(72) 2 me 9⸢2⸣ [ma-na] ⸢ù⸣ 3 GÍN(ZU).GÍN(ZU)
(73) na-ap-ḫa[-ar] gáb-bi KÙ.BABBAR ù KÙ.[GI]
(74) 1 lim 5 ⸢me⸣ [+ x] ma-na [ù] 46 GÍN(ZU).GÍN(ZU) 1/2 GÍN(ZU)
(75) 20 na-m[a-ar pa]-ni ša ZABAR
(76) 12 na-m[a-a]r p[a]-ni ra-ab-bu-tù ša ZABAR
(77) na-ap-ḫa[-ru] ⸢3⸣2 na-ma-ar p[a]-ni
(78) 80 na-m[a-ar ša ZABAR]
(79) 90 n[a-ma-ar š]a ZABAR
(80) 5 ku[-ku-bu] 2 me ⸢un⸣-qa-ti [ša ZABAR] na-aš-š[a šu]m-šu-nu
(81) 5 ma[...š]a ZABAR.
(82) 3 ⸢NA$_4$⸣[...š]a ZABAR ḫu-⸢ni⸣-ma ⸢šum⸣-šu
(83) 5 q[á-x]-x-tù+ ar-ra-kà-t[ù š]a [ZABAR]
(84) 3 dì[-qá-ra-t]ù [GA]L-⸢ti⸣ ar-kà-t[ù š]a [ZABAR š]a ki-[nu]-ni
(85) 2 d[ì-qá-r]a-tù ša-qa-⸢ti⸣ [š]a ZABAR
(86) 3 š[i...] ṣé-ḫe-ru-ti ša ra-ma-ki ša ZABAR
(87) 2 [...t]i ša ki-nu-ni ša ZABAR ku-ul-du ⸢šum⸣-⸢šu⸣
(88) 20 [...] ša ZABAR ša ú-e-a

COL. III

(1) 2 m[a..............]
(2) 6 d[ì-qá-ra-tù................š]a ZABAR [..........]
(3) 12 [......................]KAxU ANŠE.KUR.RA.ḪI.A
(4) 16 n[a]-ag-l[a-bu ša Z]ABA[R qa-]at-šu-nu ša KÙ.BABBAR
(5) 5 ⸢na⸣-ag-l[a-bu] ⸢ša⸣ ZABA[R]
(6) 41 na-al-pát-[t]ù ša LÚ.ŠU.[I] ša ZABAR
(7) 5 na-a[l]-pát-tù ša ZABAR [qa-a]t-šu-nu ša GIŠ.ESI
(8) na-ap[-ḫa-]ar [ú]-nu-te^{MEŠ} ša [ZA]BAR gáb-bu
(9) 3 me [+ x] ú-n[u]-tù KI.LÁ-šu$_{13}$ ša ZABAR
(10) 8 me š[u-ši m]a-né-e 20 GÍN(ZU).[GÍ]N([Z]U)

---

(11) 1 GAD lu[-bá-ru SIG š]a 2 TÚG.⸢NÍG.LAM⸣ lu-bu-ul-tù š[a LUGAL]
(12) 20 GAD lu[-bá-ru S]IG lu-bu-ul-tù [ša] ⸢LUGAL⸣
(13) 20 GAD lu[-bá-ru SI]G lu-bu-ul-tù š[a LUGAL] ⸢ṣé⸣-eḫ-ḫ[e-er-tu]

(68) an[d...].
(69) 1 small con[tainer(?) (of aromatics), of silver],
(70) and a st[opper in the cen]ter, of s[ilver](?)
(71) The to[ta]l of all the silver:
(72) 292 [minas], and 3 shekels [of silver].
(73) The tota[l] of all the silver and g[old]:
(74) 1500 (+ x) minas and 46 1/2 shekels.
(75) 20 mi[rr]ors, of bronze.
(76) 12 large mi[rr]ors, of bronze.
(77) To[tal]: ⌜3⌝2 mirrors.
(78) 80 mi[rrors of bronze].
(79) 90 mi[rrors..., o]f bronze.
(80) 5 *ku*[*kubu* vessels], 2 hundred rings [of bronze]; its name *našša*.
(81) 5 ...[...o]f bronze.
(82) 3 ...[...], of bronze; its name *ḫunima*.
(83) 5 very long...[...]..., [o]f bronze.
(84) 3 [lar]ge, tall p[ot]s, o[f bronze, fo]r a brazier.
(85) 2 tall p[o]ts, [o]f bronze.
(86) 3 small...[...], for bathing, of bronze.
(87) 2 [...]..., for a brazier, of bronze; *kuldu* is its name.
(88) 20 [...], of bronze, fo[r...].

COL. III

(1) 2 ...[...].
(2) 6 p[ots(?)............., o]f bronze, [..........].
(3) 12 [............................] mouth, horses.
(4) 16 r[a]z[ors,...of bronz]e; their [hand]les, of silver.
(5) 5 razo[rs, o]f bron[ze].
(6) 41 spatulas, for a bar[ber], of bron[ze].
(7) 51 spatulas of bronze; their [han]dles, of ebony.
(8) T[ot]al of the [ob]jects of [bron]ze, all together:
(9) 300 [(+x) objects. the weight of the bronze:
(10) 8[60 m]inas, 20 sh[eke]ls.

---

(11) 1 piece of [fine] linen cloth for two festive garments, byssos (quality).
(12) 20 pieces of [fi]ne linen cloth; byssos (quality).
(13) 20 [s]ma[ll] pieces of [fine] linen cloth, byssos (quality).

(14) 40 GAD [................................]

(15) 35 G[Ú.È.]A SIG *lu-bu-u*[*l-tù ša* LUGAL]

(16) 3 GAD *l*[*u-bá-ru*]SIG *id-rù ša* 6 GAD *l*[*u-bá-ru* SIG]

(17) 1 GAD *lu*[*-bá-ru*]SIG *id-rù ša* 2 GAD *l*[*u-bá-ru* SIG]

(18) 15 TÚ[G!.GÚ].È.A SIG *id-rù*[..................]

(19) 1 *me* GAD *l*[*u-bá-*]*ru* GAL *ták-ti-mu*

(20) [1] *me* 50 GAD [*lu-*]*bá-ru* SIG [*a-da-ḫa*]

(21) 1 *me* GAD *lu*[*-b*]*á-ru* SIG *ṣe-eḫ-ḫe-ru-ti a-da-ḫa*

(22) 2 *me* 50 [TÚ]G.GÚ.È.A SIG ‹*a-da-ḫa*›

(23) 2 *me* 50 ⸢GADA⸣.ŠAG$_4$.DÙ.A SIG ‹*a-da-ḫa*›

(24) 1 *me* ⸢21⸣ [^{TÚ}]^{G}*tu-un-zu*

(25) ⸢5⸣ [^{TÚG}*tu*]*-un-zu* GAL *ša* GIŠ.NÁ *ša* LUGAL

(26) [1] [GAD *lu*]*-bá-ru ša pa-ni* SU GAR *ták*(!)*-mu-us-sé-e*

(27) [x] [*bur-*]*ru-ma-at ša ku-sí-ti ta-bar-ra la a-*⸢*mi*⸣

(28) [KÙ].GI *gáb-bi* NA$_4$.ḪI.A-ti *súm-mu-ḫu*

(29) [1] [G]AD *lu-bá-ru* SIG *ša pa-ni* SU GAR *ták*(!)*-mu-sé-e a-me-e ṣa-bi*

(30) ⸢6⸣ GAD *lu-‹bá›-ru* SIG *ša ta-bar-ri*

(31) 6 SA$_9$ *mi-iš-lu ul-lu-u ša* GAD ⸢*lu*⸣*-bá-ru*

(32) *a-na mu-ra-ki-šu-nu ša ta-bar-ri pa-qa*

(33) *na-ap-ḫa-ar* GAD *lu-bá-ru-u* 1 *lim* 92 *ù* 6 SA$_9$ *mi-iš-lu* ‹*ul*›*-lu-u*

(34) 1 NA$_4$ DUG *ḫu-ut-tù ša* Ì DÙG.GA *ma-li a-zi-da*

(35) 19 NA$_4$ DUG Ì DÙG.GA *ma-lu-ú ku!-ú-bu šum-šu*

(36) 20 DUG NA$_4$ *a-ku-nu ša* Ì DÙG.GA *ma-lu-ú*

(37) 9 *ku-ku-bu ša* NA$_4$ Ì DÙG.GA *ma-*⸢*lu*⸣*-ú na-am-ša šum-šu*

(38) 1 NA$_4$ *qí-iš-še-e ša* Ì DÙG.GA *ma-li*

(39) ⸢6⸣ NA$_4$ *ú-nu-tù ra-ab-bu-tù* ⸢Ì⸣ DÙG.GA *ma-lu-ú*

(40) [x] [N]A$_4$ *ku-ku-bu ša* Ì DÙG.GA *ma-lu-ú ma-*⸢*ṣí*⸣*-iq-tá šum-ši*

(41) [x] [N]A$_4$ *na-aš-pa-ku ša* Ì DÙG.GA *ma-lu-ú ku-u-bá šum-šu*

(42) [x] [NA$_4$] *ku-ku-bu* Ì DÙG.GA *ma-li ku-u-bá pu-wa-na-aḫ šum-ša*

(43) [x] [NA$_4$] *ku-ku-bu* Ì DÙG.GA *ma-lu-ú ku-i-iḫ-ku šum-šu*

(44) [x] [NA$_4$ *k*]*i-ir-re-tù* Ì DÙG.GA *ma-li aš-ša šum-šu*

(45) [^{NIGIN}*n*]*a-ap-ḫa-ar ú-nu-te*$^{\ulcorner\text{MEŠ}\urcorner}$ *ša* NA$_4$ *ša* Ì DÙG.G[A *ma-lu-ú*]

(46) [x] *lim ù* 7 *ú-nu-tu*$_4$

(14) 40 pieces of [fine] linen cloth, [byssos (quality)].
(15) 35 thin ma[ntl]es, bys[sos (quality)].
(16) 3 pieces of fine linen cloth, *idru* (quality), in size (equal to) 6 pieces of [fine] li[nen cloth].
(17) 1 piece of fine linen cloth, *idru* (quality), in size (equal to) 2 pieces of [fine] li[nen cloth].
(18) 15 thin mantles, *idru* (quality) [..................].
(19) 100 large pieces of ‹fine› linen cloth, (for) shawl(s).
(20) 150 pieces of fine l[ine]n cloth, [*adaḫa*] (quality).
(21) 100 small pieces of fine linen cloth, *adaḫa* (quality).
(22) 250 thin mantles, ‹*adaḫa*› (quality).
(23) 250 thin girdles, ‹*adaḫa*› (quality).
(24) 121 *t*]*unzu*-cloaks.
(25) 5 large [*tu*]*nzu*-cloaks, for the king's bed.
(26) [1] linen cloth, for the front of the body, decorated on the borders.
(27) [*x*] [...]...robe, *tabarru*-red, not *ami*-red.
(28) [go]ld, all set with stones.
(29) [1] piece of fine [li]nen cloth, for the front of the body, decorated with borders, colored *ami*-red.
(30) 6 pieces of fine linen cloth, *tabarru*-red.
(31) 6 ½ (half) supurb pieces of linen cloth,
(32) for their length (wise strips?), *tabarru*-red, *paqa* (quality).
(33) The total of all the linen cloth: 1092 and 6 1/2 ‹su›purb pieces.
(34) 1 stone *ḫuttu*-jar, full of "sweet oil," (called) *azida*.
(35) 19 stone jars, full of "sweet oil"; *kubu* is its name.
(36) 20 stone jars, (called) *akunu*, which are full of "sweet oil."
(37) 9 *kukkubu*-containers, of stone, full of "sweet oil"; *namša* is its name.
(38) 1 "gourd," of stone, full of "sweet oil."
(39) 6 very large stone vessels, full of "sweet oil."
(40) [*x*] *kukkubu*-containers of stone, full of "sweet oil"; *maṣiqta* is its name.
(41) [*x*] jugs, of stone, full of "sweet oil"; *kuba* is its name.
(42) [*x*] *kukkubu*-containers of stone, full of "sweet oil"; *kuba-puwanaḫ* is its name.
(43) [*x*] *kukkubu*-containers of stone, full of "sweet oil"; *kuiḫku* is its name.
(44) [*x*] [j]ars full of "sweet oil."
(45) [the t]otal of the stone vessels full of "sweet oil":
(46) [*x*] thousand and seven vessels

(47) [x] [*tu*]*p-ni-nu ša* NA$_4$ *ri-q*[*ú-tù*..........................]
(48) [1] [N]A$_4$ *ku-ku-bu na-aš-ša šum-šu* [*ù*] 1 *ṣe-eḫ-rù*! *k*[*i š*]*a-šu-ma*
(49) [x] [N]A$_4$ *pa-re-e ša* NA$_4$ ⸢*ù*⸣1 *ṣe*[*-eḫ-rù*] *ki ša-šu-ma*
(50) ⸢1⸣ [N]A$_4$ *ga-al-tù ša* ⸢NA$_4$⸣[...]*u šum-šu*
(51) [*ù* x *ṣ*]*e-eḫ-ḫe-ru-tu$_4$ k*[*i-i*] *ša-šu-nu-ma* 35 *ḫa-ra-*⸢*ga*⸣*-bá-aš ša* ⸢NA$_4$⸣
(52) [1] [...]*tu$_4$ ša* NA$_4$ GA[L-*tu$_4$*] *ḫa-ia šum-šu*
(53) [*ù* x *ṣe-e*]*ḫ-ḫe-ru-t*[*u$_4$ ša*] NA$_4$ *ú-nu-tu$_4$ pu-ú-ú-ḫa ù* 2 *i-š*[*u*]*m*
(54) [x] [..........*qa-du*] *kà-an-dú-ri-šu-nu sà-ab-na-ku-u šum-šu*
(55) [x] [..............] *ku-iḫ-ku šum-šu*
(56) [x] [................*š*]*a* NA$_4$
(57) [x] [.......................................]*an šum-šu*
(58) *ù* 1 *ṣé-eḫ-*⸢*ru*⸣ *k*[*i ša-šu-ma*]
(59) 21 ^{d}LAMMA *ša* NA$_4$ *na-an-*⸢*pa*⸣*-*⸢*ka*⸣*-aš*
(60) 1 ^{LÚ}*pé-es-sú-u ša* NA$_4$ *ki-ir-re-tù i-na* [Š]U-*ti-šu*
(61) 1 *ku-ku-bu ša* NA$_4$ *šu-i-ib-tá šum-šu*
(62) 3 *kí-ra-tù ša* NA$_4$ 2 GAL *ra-bu-ú ša* NA$_4$ *ḫi-na*
(63) 3 *na-aḫ-bu-ú ša* NA$_4$ ⸢1⸣ *ma-aš-ḫa-lu$_4$ ša* NA$_4$
(64) 1 *kà-an-dú-ru ar-ku ša* NA$_4$
(65) 2 *a-ga-nu ša* NA$_4$ 38 *iš-qí-il-la-tù ša* NA$_4$
(66) 1 É Ì *ša* NA$_4$ *wa-ad-ḫa-a šum-šu*
(67) 3 *ku-ku-bu ša* NA$_4$ *na-am-ša šum-šu*
(68) 2 *ša re-e-ši* SAG.DU *ša* NA$_4$
(69) 1 *ša re-e-ši* SAG.DU *ša* NA$_4$ *du-še-e*
(70) 1 *sà-aḫ-ḫa-ru ša* NA$_4$ BABBAR *ṣí-la-aḫ-tá šum-šu*
(71) 9 É Ì *ša* NA$_4$ BABBAR *wa-ad-ḫa šum-šu*
(72) *na-ap-ḫa-ar ú-nu-te*^{MEŠ} *ri-qú-tù ša* NA$_4$
(73) 1 *me šu-ši ù* 3
(74) 1 *me* 17 NA$_4$ *ma-še-el-tù ša* LÚ.ŠU.I
(75) 9 ^{GIŠ}*tup-ni-nu ša* GIŠ.ESI KAxUD *pí-ri du-ul-*⸢*lu*⸣ SIG
(76) 2 ^{GIŠ}*tup-ni-nu ša* GIŠ.ESI KAxUD *pí-ri du-ul-lu* SIG *za-a* (= *sà-a*)

COL. IV

(1) [x] [...]*ḫu ša* GIŠ.ESI KAxUD *pí-ri du-ul-l*[*u-t*]*i$_4$*
(2) 6 *kap-pí ú-ma-mi ša* KAxUD *pí-ri bá-aš-lu*
(3) 9 *ša-am-mu ša* KAxUD *pí-ri bá-aš-lu* ⸢*ša*⸣ *ep-ši-ma*
(4) 10 ^{Ú}*ú-ub súm-mu-ḫu ša* KAxUD *pí-ri bá-aš-lu*

(47) [*x*] em[pty] boxes, of stone, [..........................].
(48) [1] *kukkubu*-container, of stone; *naššа* is its name, [and] 1 small one just li[ke i]t.
(49) [*x*] onagers, of stone, [and] 1 sm[all one] just like it.
(50) [*x*] *galtu*, of stone, [...] is its name.
(51) [and *x* sm]all ones ju[st li]ke them; 35 *ḫaragabaš* of stone.
(52) [1 lar]ge one, of stone; its name...,
(53) [and *x* smal]l ones, of stone; *puwuḫa* vessels and 2....
(54) [*x*] [..........with] their stands; its name *sabnakû*.
(55) [x] [.............]; its name *kuiḫku*.
(56) [x] [..........o]f stone.
(57) [x] [...................................]; its name....
(58) and 1 sma[ll one]
(59) 21 female figurines, of stone,...[...].
(60) 1 cripple, of stone, with a jar in his hand.
(61) 1 *kukkubu*-container, of stone; *šuibta* is its name.
(62) 3 jars of stone; 2 large goblets, of stone, the *hin*.
(63) 3 pails, of stone; 1 sieve, of stone.
(64) 1 tall stand, of stone.
(65) 2 *agannu* jars, of stone; 38 *išqillatu*-vessels, of stone.
(66) 1 container of oil; *wadḫa* is its name.
(67) 3 *kukkubu*-containers, of stone; *namša* is its name.
(68) 2 headrests, of stone.
(69) 1 headrest, of *dušû*-stone
(70) 1 bowl, of white stone; its name *ṣilliḫta*.
(71) 9 containers of oil, of white stone; its name *wadḫa*.
(72) The total of empty stone-vessels:
(73) 160 and 3.
(74) 117 whetstones, for a barber.
(75) 9 boxes of ebony and ivory, delicate work.
(76) 2 boxes, of ebony and ivory,
(77) delicate work called *sa*

COL. IV

(1) [...]..., of ebony and ivory, delicate work.
(2) 6 (pairs of) animal paws, of stained(?) ivory.
(3) 9 plants, of stained(?) ivory for working
(4) 10 plants, various sorts, of stained(?) ivory.

(5) 29 *qí-iš-šu-u ša* É Ì ⸢*ša*⸣ ⸢KAxUD⸣ ⸢*pí*⸣*-ri bá-aš-lu*

(6) 44 É Ì *súm-mu-ḫu* ‹GIŠ›.ḪAŠḪUR *nu-ri-im-*[*tu*$_4$ *s*]*u-lu-pu*

(7) *ku-ru-ma-nu ša* KAxUD *pí-ri bá-aš-lu*

(8) 3 *me* 75 É Ì KAxUD *pí-ri bá-aš-lu* [...*s*]*à-a*

(9) 19 GIŠ.GA.RÍG *ša* KAxUD *pí-ri bá-aš-lu*

(10) 19 *tù-dì-ni-tù ša* KAxUD *pí-ri bá-aš-lu*

(11) 13 *tup-ni-na-tù ša* KAxUD *pí-ri bá-aš-lu up-ṭa*

(12) ⸢3⸣ *ša re-e-ši ša* KAxUD *pí-ri bá-aš-lu*

(13) ⸢3⸣ *ku-ku-bu ša* KAxUD *pí-ri bá-aš-lu ku-ú-bá šum-šu*

(14) 3 GU$_4$ *ša* É Ì *ša* KAxUD *pí-ri bá-aš-lu*

(15) 3 *tù-ra*!(ŠA)*-ḫu ša* É Ì *ša* KAxUD *pí-ri bá-aš-lu*

(16) 1 *m*[*u-ba*]*l-li-it-tù* TUR-*tu*$_4$ *ša* KAxUD *pí-ri bá-aš-lu*

(17) *ù* [......] *i-na lìb-bi-šu ù* 1 GU$_4$ *i-na* UGU-*ḫi-šu*

(18) [x] [.....*sà-a*]*ḫ-ḫa-ru ša* KAxUD *pí-ri bá-aš-lu*

(19) [x] [..........*š*]*a* KAxUD *pí-ri bá-aš-lu*

(20) [x] [*tup-ni-na-tù ša* GIŠ.]ESI *ma-ḫa-an*

(21) [x] [KAxUD *pí-ri du-ul-lu* SIG] *gáb-bi* NA$_4$.ḪI.A

(22) [*súm-mu-ḫu*...]*-ši i-na lìb-bi-šu-nu*

(23) [x] [............................*k*]*u-ú-b*[*u*]

(24–31) (missing)

(32) [x] [..............................*šum-š*]*u*

(33) [x] [....................................]

(34) [x] [*tup-ni-na-tù ša* GIŠ.ESI *ma-ḫa*]*-an šum-šu*

(35–57) (missing)

(58) [...]⸢*ti*⸣*-ib-nu*

(59) [...]

(60) [..........................*b*]*á-aš-la-at*

(61) [..........................] *bá-aš-la-at*

(62) [..........................] *tù-ra-ḫu*

(5) 29 "gourds," containers of oil, of stained(?) ivory.
(6) 44 containers of oil, decorated with apples, pomegranates, dates,
(7) (and) *kurumānu*, of stained(?) ivory.
(8) 375 containers of oil, of stained(?) ivory, [...] (called) [*s*]*â*.
(9) 19 combs, of stained(?) ivory.
(10) 19 toggle pins, of stained(?) ivory.
(11) 13 boxes, of stained ivory, (called) *upṭa*.
(12) 3 headrests, of stained(?) ivory.
(13) 3 *kukkubu*-containers, of stained(?) ivory; *kuba* is its name.
(14) 3 oxen, containers of oil, of stained(?) ivory.
(15) 3 ibexes(!), containers of oil, of stained(?) ivory.
(16) 1 small container (of aromatics), of stained(?) ivory,
(17) and [.....] in its center, and 1 ox on top.
(18) [x ......bo]wls of stained(?) ivory.
(19) [*x*] [...]..., of stained(?) ivory.
(20) [*x*] [boxes of] ebony (called) *maḫan*.
(21) [*x* ivory, fine, delicate work] all sorts of stones
(22) [various,........................]...in their midst.
(23) [*x*] [............................] *kûbu* [its name]
(24–31) *missing*
(32) [*x*] [................................i[ts] [name]
(33) [*x*] [..]
(34) [*x*] [boxes of ebony, its name [*maḫ*]*an*
(35–57) *scattered signs and phrases or missing entirely*
(58) [...]straw
(59) [...]
(60) [.........................col]ored
(61) [.........................] colored
(62) [.........................] wild goat

EA 15

TRANSCRIPTION

Obv. 01) *a-na* LUGAL KUR *M*[*i-iṣ-*(*ṣa*)*-ri*]
02) *qí-bi-*[*ma*]
03) *um-ma* ^{Id}*A-šur*-TI.L[A LUGAL KUR ^{d}*A*]*-šur-ma*
04) *a-na ka-ša* É*-ka a-na* [KU]R*-ka*
05) *a-na* GIŠ.GIGIR.MEŠ*-ka ù* ERÍN.MEŠ*-ka*
06) *lu-ú šul-mu*
07) DUMU *ši-ip-ri-ia al-tap-ra-ak-ku*
08) *a-na a-ma-ri-ka ù* KUR*-ka a-na a-ma-ri*
09) *a-di an-ni-ša ab-ba-ú-ia*
10) *la iš-pu-ru*
11) u_4*-ma a-na-ku al-tap-ra-ak-ku*
12) 1 GIŠ.GIRIG SIG$_5$*-ta* 2 ANŠE.KUR.RA.MEŠ
13) ⸢*ù*⸣ 1 ^{NA_4}*ú-ḫi-na ša* NA$_4$.ZA.GÌN KUR*-e*
14) [*a-n*]*a šul-ma-ni-ka*
15) [*ú*]*-še-bi-la-*⸢*ku*⸣
Lo.ed. 16) [DUMU *ši*]*-ip-ri ša aš-pu-ra-ku-ni*
17) [*a-*]*na a-ma-ri*
Rev. 18) [*l*]*a tu*$_4$*-ka-*⸢*as*⸣*-sú*
19) [*l*]*i-mu-ur ù li-it-tal-ka*
20) [*ṭ*]*é-em-ka ù ṭé-em*
21) *ma-ti-ka li-mur*
22) *ù li-it-ta-al-ka*

EA 15

TRANSLATION

(1–6) Say to the king of the land of E[gypt]: Thus Aššur-ubal[liṭ, the king of the land of (the god) A]ššur: For you, your house, for your land, for your chariotry and your troops, may all be well.

(7–15) I have sent my envoy to you to see you and to see your land. Up to now, my fathers have not written. Today, I have written to you. [I] have sent to you an excellent chariot, two horses and one date-stone of genuine lapis lazuli as your greeting gift.

(16–22) Do [n]ot delay the envoy whom I have sent to you for a visit. May he see and may he depart. May he see your behavior (nature) and the behavior (nature) of your land and may he depart.

EA 16

TRANSCRIPTION

Obv. 01) ˹*a*˺-˹*na*˺ $^{\ulcorner\text{I}\urcorner}$˹*Na*˺-˹*ap*˺-˹*ḫu*˺-˹*ri*˺-*i-ia*!(TU?) [LUGAL GAL]
02) *šàr* KUR *Mi-iṣ-ṣa-ri* ˹ŠEŠ˺-*ia* ˹*qí*˺[*-bí-ma*]
03) *um-ma* ^{Id}*A-šur*-TI.LA *šàr* KU[R] $^{\ulcorner\text{d}\urcorner}$˹*A*˺-[*šu*]r
04) LUGAL GAL ŠEŠ-*ka*

---

05) *a-na ka-a-ša a-na* É-*ka ù* KUR-*ka lu šul-mu*

---

06) [D]UMU.MEŠ *ši-i*[*p-r*]*i-ka ki-i a-mu-ru*
07) *ḫa-da-*˹*a*˺-˹*ku*˺ *da-ni-iš* DUMU.MEŠ *ši-ip-ri-ka*
08) *a-na* ˹*tek*˺*-né-e i-na maḫ-ri-ia lu aš-bu*

---

09) GIŠ.GIGIR *b*[*a*]*-ni-ta ša* LUGAL-*ti ša ṣ*[*a*]-˹*ma*˺*-di-ia*
10) *ù* 2 ANŠE.KUR.RA.MEŠ *pe-ṣú-ti š*[*a*] *ṣa-ma-di-ia-ma*
11) 1 GIŠ.GIGIR *la ṣa-mu-ut-ta ù* 1 $^{\text{NA}_4}$KISIB ZA.GÌN KUR-*e*
12) *a-na šul-ma-ni-ka ú-še-bi-la-ak-ku*

---

13) *ša* LUGAL GAL-*i šu-bu-ul-tu ka-an-na-a*
14) KÙ.GI *i-na* KUR-*ka e-pe-ru šu-ú*
15) *i-is-si-pu-uš am-mi-ni-i i-na* IGI.MEŠ-*ka*
16) *i-sa-aḫ-ḫu-ur* É.GAL-*la* GIBIL *ú-ka-al i-ip-pu-uš*
17) KÙ.GI *ma-la uḫ-ḫu-zi-ša*
18) *ù ḫi-še-eḫ-ti-ša šu-bi-la*

---

19) *un-du* ^{Id}*A-šur-na-din*-ŠEŠ.MEŠ *a-bi*
20) *a-na* KUR *Mi-iṣ-ri iš-pu-ru*
21) 20 GÚ.UN KÙ.GI *ul-te-bi-lu-šu*

---

22) [*u*]*n-du* LUGAL *Ḫa-ni-gal-ba-tu-ú*
23) [*a*]*-na* UGU *a-bi-ka a-na* KUR *Mi-i*[*ṣ-ri*]
24) [*iš*]-˹*pu*˺*-ru* 20 GÚ.UN KÙ.[GI]
25) [*u*]*l-te-bi-la-aš-š*[*u*]

EA 16

TRANSLATION

(1–4) Sp[eak] to Napḫuriya [the great king], king of the land of Egypt, my brother. Thus (speaks) Ashur-uballit, king of the land of Assyria, the great king, your brother:

---

(5) May it be well with you, with your household and your land.

(6–8) When I saw your [am]bassadors I rejoiced greatly. May your envoys dwell in my presence in great ⸢soli⸣citude.

(9–12) A beautiful chariot for royalty, accoutered for me and two white horses accoutered for me, one chariot not accoutered and one cylinder seal of real lapis lazuli have I sent to you as your greeting gift.

(13–18) Thus is the gift of a great king? Gold in your land is dirt. They gather it up. Why does it delay with your approval? I am engaged in building a new palace. Send as much gold as needed for its adornment and its needs.

(19–21) When my father Ashur-nadin-aḫḫē sent to the land of Egypt, they sent to him twenty talents of gold.

(22–25) When the Ḫanigalbatian king sent to your father, to the land of Egypt, they sent to him twenty talents of gold

---

Rev. 26) [*a-na-ku*] *a-na* LUGAL *Ḫa-*⌜*ni*⌝[*-gal*]*-*⌜*ba*⌝*-t*[*i-i*]
27) [*me-eḫ-re-*]*ku ù a-na* UGU*-ia*
28) [x *ma-na* KÙ].GI *tu-še-eb-bi-l*[*a-ni*]
29) [*ù š*]*a a-la-ki ù ta-ri-*⌜*im*⌝*-*⌜*ma*⌝
30) *a-*[*n*]*a i-di ša* DUMU.MEŠ *ši-ip-ri-ia*
31) *ul i-ma-aṣ-ṣi*

---

32) *šu*[*m*]-[*m*]*a ṭa-bu-ut-ta pa-nu-ka da-am-qí-iš*
33) K[Ù.G]I *ma-da šu-bi-la ù* É*-ka šu-ú*
34) *šu-up-ra-am-ma ša ḫa-aš-ḫa-ta li-il-qu-ú*

---

35) *ma-ta-*tu_4 *ru-qa-*tu_4 *ni-i-nu*
36) DUMU.MEŠ *ši-ip-ri-ni ka-am-ma-a li-it-tal-la-ku*

---

37) *ša* DUMU.MEŠ *ši-ip-ri-ka*
38) *ú-uḫ-ḫi-ru-ni-ik-ku* LÚ.MEŠ *Su-*tu_4*-ú*
39) *ra-du-*[*š*]*u-nu mi-*tu_4 *a-di áš-pu-ru-ma*
40) LÚ.MEŠ *Su-ti-i ra-de-e il-qu-ú-ni*
41) ⌜*ak*⌝-[*t*]*a-la-šu-nu* DUMU.MEŠ *ši-ip-ri-ia*
42) *lu la ú-uḫ-ḫa-ru-ni*

---

43) [DU]MU.MEŠ *ši-ip-ri i-na ṣe-ti*
44) *am-mi-ni-i ul-ta-na-za-zu-ma*
45) *i-na ṣe-ti i-ma-at-*tu_4
46) ⌜*šum*⌝*-ma i-na ṣe-ti i-zu-uz-zu*
47) *a-na* LUGAL *né-me-lu i-*⌜*ba*⌝*-aš-ši*
48) *ù li-zi-iz-ma i-na* ⌜*ṣe*⌝*-t*[*i-m*]*a*
49) *li-mu-ut a-na* LUGAL*-ma* ⌜*lu*⌝ *né-me-lu*
50) *ù ia-a-nu-*[*um-m*]*a-a am-mi-ni-*[*i*]
51) [*i-na ṣ*]*e-ti* [*i*]*-ma-at-*⌜*tu*⌝
52) DU[MU.M]EŠ *ši-i*[*p-r*]*i ša ni-*⌜*il*⌝*-*[*ta-na-ap-pa-ru*]
53) ⌜*ù*⌝ ⌜2⌝*-šu* ⌜DUMU⌝.MEŠ *ši-ip*[*-r*]*i*
54) *ú-*⌜*bal*⌝*-*[*l*]*a-ṭù-ú* [*i-n*]*a ṣ*[*e-ti*]
55) *uš-ma-at-*tu_4

(26–31) [I] am [equ]al to a Ḫanigalbatian king but you send [to me] [*x* minas of go]ld. It is not sufficient for the going and returning and the wages of my envoys.

(32–34) ⌜If⌝ your intention is truly genuine, send much g[ol]d and as for that house of yours, send to me so that they may bring what you need.

(35–36) We are countries far apart. May our envoys thus continue to go back and forth.

(37–42) That your envoys delayed coming to you, the Sutû who were their guides died. Until I could send (them) and they could take (new) Sutû guides, I delayed them. May my envoys not delay in coming.

(43–55) As for the [am]bassadors, why are they continually standing outside so that they will die outside? If their standing outside is profitable to the king, then let them stand outside. Outside, let them die! Profit for the king or no[t], why should they die [outs]ide? As for the envoys that we [continually] se[nd,] then doubly, they should keep the envoys alive. [Ou]ts[ide] they are killing (them).

EA 17

TRANSCRIPTION

Obv. 01) *a-na* ^{I}*Ni-ib-mu-a-re-ia* L[UGAL KUR *Mi-iṣ-ri-i*]
02) ŠEŠ-*ia qí-b*[*í-ma*]
03) *um-ma* ^{I}*Tu-iš-e-rat-ta* LUGAL KUR [*Mi-*]*it-ta-*⸢*an*⸣-[*n*]*i*
04) ŠEŠ-*ka-ma a-na ia-ši* ⸢*šul*⸣*mu*
05) *a-na ka-a-ša lu-ú šul-mu a-na* ^{MUNUS}*Kè-lu-ḫé-bá*
06) *a-ḫa-ti-ia lu-ú šul-mu a-na* É-*ka*
07) *a-na* DAM.MEŠ-*ka a-na* DUMU.MEŠ-*ka a-na* LÚ.GAL.MEŠ-*ka*
08) *a-na* ERÍN.MEŠ *ḫu-ra-dì-ka a-na* ANŠE.KUR.RA.MEŠ-*ka*
09) *a-na* GIŠ.GIGIR.MEŠ-*ka ù a-na lìb-bi* KUR-*ka*
10) *dá-an-ni-iš lu-ú šul-mu*

---

11) *iš-tu i-na* GIŠ.GU.ZA *ša a-bi-ia ú-ši-bu*
12) *ù ṣe-eḫ-re-ku ù* ^{I}*Pir-ḫi a-ma-ta*
13) *la bá-ni-ta a-na* KUR-*ti-ia i-te-pu-uš-ma*
14) *ù be-el-šu id-du-uk ù aš-šum an-ni-tì*
15) *ia-ši it-ti ša i-ra-ʾa-ma-an-ni-ni ṭa-bu-ú-ta*
16) *la ú-ma-aš-ša-ra-an-ni ù a-na-ku ap-pu-na-ma*
17) *aš-šum a-ma-a-ti an-na-tì la bá-na-a-tì*
18) *ša i-na* KUR-*ti-ia in-né-ep-šu ul em-te-ki*
19) *ù* LÚ.MEŠ *dá-i-ka*$_4$*-ni-*⸢*šu*⸣ *ša* ^{I}*Ar-ta-aš-*⸢*šu*⸣*-ma-ra*
20) ŠEŠ-*ia qa-du mi-im-*⸢*mu*⸣*-šu-nu ad-du-uk-šu-nu-ti*

---

21) *ki-i at-ta it-ti a-bi-ia ṭa-ba-a-ta*
22) *ù aš-šum an-ni-tì al-ta-pár-ma aq-ta-ba-ak-ku*
23) *ki-me-e* ŠEŠ-*ia i-še-em-me-šu-nu-ma*
24) *ù i-ḫa-ad-du a-bu-ia i-ra-ʾa-am-ka*
25) *ù at-ta ap-pu-na-ma a-bu-ia*
26) *ta-ra-ʾa-am-šu ù a-bu-ia*
27) ⸢*ki*⸣-⸢*i*⸣ *ra-a-mi a-ḫa-a-ti a-na ka-a-*⸢*ša*⸣
28) [*it*]*-ta-na-*⸢*ak*⸣*-ku* ⸢*ù*⸣ ⸢*ma*⸣-⸢*an*⸣*-nu-um-ma ša-n*[*u-ú*]
29) [*ša k*]*i-*⸢*i*⸣ *ka-a-ša it-*⸢*ti*⸣ *a-bi-ia*

EA 17

TRANSLATION

(1–10) To Nibmuʿareya, k[ing of the land of Egypt], my brother, speak: Thus (says) Tuisheratta, king of the land of [Mi]ttan[n]i, your brother. It is well with me. May it be well with you. May it be well with Kelu-Ḫeba, my sister. With your house, with your wives, with your sons, with your senior officials, with your infantry, with your horses, with your chariotry, and within your land, may it be very well.

(11–20) When I sat on the throne of my father, and I was young, then Pirḫi did some unseemly deeds in my land and slew his lord. And because of this he was not permiting me friendship with anyone who loved me. But I, moreover, because of these unseemly things that were done in my land, was not remiss and as for the people who murdered Artashumara, my brother, with all that belonged to them, I slew them.

(21–29) Inasmuch as you were friendly with my father, then because of that I have written and I have spoken to you so that my brother may hear of these things and so that he may rejoice. My father loved you and you, moreover, as for my father, you loved him and my father, because of (that) love, [g]ave to you my sister. And who else was with my father like you?

Lo.ed. 30) [*i-n*]*a* TI-*ma ap-pu-na-ma ša* ŠEŠ-⸢*ia*⸣

31) [*k*]*i*-⸢*i*⸣ *it-tù-ú*-⸢*ra*⸣?-⸢*am*⸣? KUR *Ḫa-at-ti*

Rev. 32) *gáb-bá-am-ma ki-i* LÚ.KÚR.MEŠ *a-na* KUR-*ti-i*[*a*]

33) *it-ta-al-ka* ^{d}IŠKUR *be-li a-na qa-ti-ia*

34) *id-din-šu-ma ù ad-du-uk-šu*

35) *iš-tu lìb-bi-šu*-⸢*nu*⸣ *ša i-na* KUR-*ti-šu ša i-tù-ru* ⸢*i*⸣*a-nu*

---

36) *a-nu-um-ma* 1 GIŠ.GIGIR 2 ANŠE.KUR.RA.MEŠ

37) 1 ^{LÚ}*ṣú-ḫa-ru* 1 ^{MUNUS}*ṣú-ḫa-ar-tu*$_4$

38) *ša ḫu-ub-ti ša* KUR *Ḫa-at-ti ul-te-bi-la-ak-ku*

---

39) *a-na šul-ma-ni ša* ŠEŠ-*ia* 5 GIŠ.GIGIR.MEŠ

40) 5 *ṣi-mi-it-tu*$_4$ ANŠE.KU.RA.MEŠ *ul-te-bi-la-ak-ku*

---

41) *ù a-na šul-ma-ni ša* ^{MUNUS}*Kè-lu-ḫé-bá*

42) *a-ḫa-ti-ia* 1-*nu-tu*$_4$ *dú-dì-na-tu*$_4$ KÙ.GI

43) 1-*nu-tu*$_4$ *an-ṣa-ba-tu*$_4$ KÙ.GI 1 *ma-áš-ḫu* KÙ.GI

44) *ù* 1 ^{NA}4*ta-pá-tu*$_4$ *ša* Ì.DUG.GA *ma-lu-ù*

45) *ul-te-bi-la-aš-ši*

---

46) *a-nu-um-ma* ^{I}*Kè-li-ia* LÚ SUKKAL-*li*

47) *ù* ^{I}*Tu*$_4$*-ni-ip-ib-ri al-ta-pár-šu-nu* ŠEŠ-*ia ḫa-mu-ut-ta*

48) *li-me-eš-šèr-šu-nu-ma ṭe*$_4$*-e-ma ḫa-mu-ut-ta*

49) *li-te-ru-ni-im-ma ki-me-e šul-ma-an-šu*

50) *ša* ŠEŠ-*ia e-še-em-me-ma ù a-ḫa-ad-du*

---

51) ŠEŠ-*ia ṭa-bu-ú-ta it-ti-ia li-bé-ʾi-i*

52) *ù* ŠEŠ-*ia* DUMU.MEŠ KIN-*ri-šu li-iš*-⸢*pu*⸣*-ra-am-ma*

53) *ki-me-e šul-ma-an-šu ša* ŠEŠ-*ia*

54) *i-li-ik-ku-ni-im-ma ù e-še-em-me*

(30–35) [Du]ring the life, moreover, of my brother, when it returned, when the land of Ḫatti in its entirety came as enemies against my land; Teshub, my lord, gave it into my hand and I slew it. Among them there was none that returned to their land.

(36–38) Now, one chariot, two horses, one lad and one maiden from the spoil of the land of Ḫatti have I sent to you.

(39–40) For my brother's greeting gift five chariots, (and) five teams of horses, have I sent to you.

(41–45) And for the greeting gift of Kelu-Ḫeba, my sister, one set of gold toggle pins, one set of gold earrings, one gold *mašḫu* ring, and one stone scent container that is full of sweet oil, have I sent to her.

(46–50) Now, as for Kelia, my chief minister, and Tunip-iwri, I have sent them. May my brother let them go quickly that they may bring back a report to me so that I may hear of the welfare of my brother and rejoice.

(51–54) May my brother seek friendship with me, and may my brother send his messengers to me so that the greeting of my brother may come to me and I may hear.

EA 18

TRANSCRIPTION

Obv. 01) [*a-na*......................................]*qí-bí-ma*
02) [*um-ma*................................ŠEŠ-*k*]*a-ma*
03) [*a-na ia-ši šul-mu a-na ka-a-ša*............*lu*]-*ú šul-mu*
04) [..................................GA]L.MEŠ-⸢*ka*⸣
05) [...]
06) [....................................*lu-ú šul*]-*mu*

---

07) [...]-*i*
08) ^{I}*A*[*r-ta-aš-š*]*u*[*-ma-r*]*a* [..........................].MEŠ
09) *ša* K[UR *Ḫ*]*a*-[*ni*-]⸢*gal*⸣[*ba*]*t* [.....................]x
10) ⸢*ú*⸣(?)[......*š*]*a tù*[..................................]

Rev. 01) *ù* MÚR-*šu*[...]
02) *ù* MÚR-*šu* ZÁ.DUB [................................]
03) ^{NA_4}*ḫi-li-bá tam-lu-ú*[.................................]
04) ⸢1⸣-⸢*nu*⸣-⸢tu_4⸣ *áš-ki-ru-uš-ḫ*[*u*..........................]

---

05) [*a-nu-um-m*]*a* ^{I}*Pu-u-ḫi* [.....................*a-na š*]*ul-ma-ni*
06) [*ša* ŠEŠ-*i*]*a al*-⸢*ta*⸣-*pár-š*[*u ù* ŠEŠ-*ia ḫa-mu-ut-t*]*a li-me-eš-šèr-šu*
07) [*šul-ma-*]*an-šu* [*ša* ŠEŠ-*ia lu-*]⸢*ub*⸣-*la*

EA 18

TRANSLATION

Obv. 01) [To......................................]speak!
02) [The message of......................yo]ur [brother,]
03) [It is well with me; with you............m]ay it be well
04) [..............................]your [senior] officials
05) [..]
06) [.................................... may it be] well

---

07) [..]
08) A[rtash]*u*[*mar*]a [....................................]
09) of the l[and of Ḫ]a[nigal[ba]t [.........................]
10) ⸢and⸣(?)[......whi]ch you[..........................]

Rev. 01) and in its midst[.....................................]
02) and in its midst a ––– stone[............................]
03) *ḫiliba* stone inlay [....................................]
04) A single set of *aškirušḫ*[*u*] utensils [......................]

---

05) [No]w Puḫi [.....................for the we]ll being
06) [of [m]y [brother]have I sent hi[m and] may [my brother] send him [quickly].
07) [the greeting gif]t [of my brother will]I send

EA 19

TRANSCRIPTION

Obv.

01) [*a-*]*na Nì-im-mu-re-ia* LUGAL GAL *šàr* KUR *Mi-iṣ-ri-i* ⸢ŠEŠ⸣-[*ia*]
02) [*ḫ*]*a-ta-ni-ia ša i-ra-ʾa-am-an-ni ù ša a-ra-a*[*m-mu-uš*]
03) *qí-bí-ma um-ma* ^{I}*Tu-uš-rat-ta* LUGAL GAL *e-mi-i-*[*ka*]
04) *ša i-ra-ʾa-a-mu-ú-ka šàr* KUR *Mi-i-it-ta-an-ni* ŠEŠ-*ka-ma*
05) *a-na ia-ši šul-mu a-na ka-a-ša lu-ú šul-mu a-na* ⸢É⸣-⸢*ka*⸣
06) *a-na a-ḫa-ti-ia ù a-na re-e-ḫé-ti* DAM.MEŠ-*ka a-na* DU[MU.MEŠ]-⸢*ka*⸣
07) *a-na* GIŠ.GIGIR.MEŠ-*ka a-na* ANŠE.KUR.RA.MEŠ-*ka a-na* ÉRIN.GAL-*ka*
08) *a-na* KUR-*ka ù a-na mim-mu-ka dan-níš dan-níš lu-ú šul-*⸢*mu*⸣

---

09) *a-di* AB.BA.MEŠ-*ka-ma šu-nu it-ti* AB.BA.MEŠ-*ia dan-níš*
10) *ir-ta-ta-ʾa-a-mu at-ta ap-pu-na-ma* DIRI-*ma it-ti a-bi-ia*
11) *ma-a-dì-iš da-an-ni-iš ta-ar-ta-ta-ʾa-a-am*
12) *i-na-an-na at-ta ki-i it-ti-ia a-ḫa-miš ni-ir-ta-na-ʾa-a-mu*
13) *a-na* 10-*šu el a-bi-ia tu-uš-te-em-ʾi-id*
14) DINGIR.MEŠ *li-me-eš-še-ru-šu-nu-ti-ma ša ni-ir-ta-ʾa-a-mu an-ni-k*[*a-a*]
15) ^{d}IŠKUR *be-e-li ù* ^{d}*A-ma-nu-um a-na da-ra-a-ti ki-i ša i-*⸢*na*⸣-[*an-na*]
16) *lu-ú li-né-ep-pí-*[*šu*]

---

17) *ù* ^{I}*Ma-né-e* DUMU.KIN-*ra-šu* ŠEŠ-*ia ki-i iš-pu-r*[*u*]
18) *um-ma lu-ú* ŠEŠ-*ia-ma* DUMU.MUNUS-*ka a-na* DAM-*ut-ti-ia bi-lam-mì*
19) *a-na* NIN-*et* KUR *Mi-iṣ-ri-i-im-mì ul ul-*⸢*te*⸣*-em-ri-iṣ* ŠÀ-*šu*
20) *ša* ŠEŠ-*ia ù i-na bá-na-tim-ma a-a-an-ni-ma-*⸢*a*⸣-⸢*ku*⸣*aq-ta-bi*
21) *ù ša* ŠEŠ-*ia i-ri-šu uk-te-el-li-im-ši a-na* ^{I}*Ma-né-e*
22) *ù i-ta-mar-ši ki-i i-mur*(*u*)*-ši ù ut-te-ʾi-is-*[*s*]*í dan-níš*
23) *ù i-na ša-la-a-mi i-na* KUR *ša* ŠEŠ-*ia lu-*⸢*ú*⸣ *lu-ú-*[*r*]*u-ši*
24) ^{d}INANNA *ù* ^{d}*A-ma-nu-um ki-i* ŠÀ-*šu ša* ŠEŠ-*ia li-me-eš-še-el-ši*

EA 19

TRANSLATION

(1–8) [T[o Nimmureya, the Great King, king of the land of Egypt, [my] brother, my [s]on-in-law who loves me and whom I lo[ve], speak; Message of Tuishratta, the Great King, your father-in-law who loves you, king of the land of Mittani, your brother: All is well with me; may it be well with you, with your house, with my sister and with the rest of your wives, with your sons, with your chariots, with your horses, with your great army, with your land and with whatever else belongs to you, may all be very, very well.

(9–16) Since (the time of) your fathers, they always loved my fathers very much. You, moreover, did more and always showed even more love to my father. Now, you, inasmuch as we continue to love one another in mutual affection, have increased ten fold greater than to my father. May the gods permit those very things that we have loved here (= up to now). May Teshub, my lord, and Amon, mak[e] it amenable forever just as now.

(17–23) Inasmuch as my brother sent Mane, his envoy, saying: "Please, my brother, send me your daughter for wife, to be the mistress of the land of Egypt," I caused no distress to my brother's heart but said, "with pleasure! Yes!" And as for the one whom my brother requested, I showed her to Mane and he saw her. Inasmuch as he saw her and he praised her greatly, I will convey her in safety to the land of my brother.

May Shaushga and Amon make her the image of my brother's desire.

25) ^{I}*Ké-li-ia* DUMU.KIN-*ia a-ma-te-šu ša* ŠEŠ-*ia a-na* ⸢*ia*⸣-*ši it-ta-b*[*í*]*l*
26) *ki-i eš-mu-ú ù ṭá-a-bu dan-níš ù aḫ-tá-du ki-i ma-du-ti*
27) *da-an-níš um-ma lu-ú a-na-ku-ma an-nu-ú šu-ú šu-ur-ru-um-ma*
28) *ša i-na be-ri-ni ša it-ti a-ḫa-miš ša ni-ir-ta-na-ʾa-a-mu*
29) *a-nu-um-ma i-na am-mu-ti a-ma-a-ti a-na da-ra-tim-ma lu ni-ir-ta-ʾa-am*

---

30) *a-na* ŠEŠ-*ia ki-i aš-pu-ru ù aq-ta-bi um-ma lu-ú a-na-ku-ma*
31) *ki-ma ma-a-du-ti dá-an-ni-iš*$_6$ *lu ni-ir-ta-na-ʾa-am ù i-na be-ri-ni*
32) *lu-ú ṭá-a-bá-nu ù a-na* ŠEŠ-*ia aq-ta-bi um-ma-a* ŠEŠ-*ia*
33) *el a-bi-ia* 10-*šu lu-ú ú-te-et-te-ra-an-ni*

---

34) *ù a-na* ŠEŠ-*ia* KÙ.GI.MEŠ *ma-a-at-ta e-te-ri-iš um-ma-a el* ⸢*a*⸣-*bi-ia*
35) *lu ú-še-em-ʾ*[*i-i*]*d-an-ni-ma* ŠEŠ-*ia lu-ú ú-še-bíl-an-ni*
36) *ù a-*⸢*bu*⸣-*ia* KÙ.GI.MEŠ *ma-a-at-ta tù-ul-te-bi-la-aš-šu*
37) NAM.ḪA.RA KÙ.GI.MEŠ GAL.MEŠ *ù* GIŠ.KIRI$_6$ KÙ.GI.MEŠ GAL.MEŠ *tul-te-*⸢*bíl*⸣-*aš-šu*
38) SIG$_4$ KÙ.GI.MEŠ *ki-ma ša* URUDU.MEŠ *ma-ṣú-ú tù-ul-te-b*[*íl-aš-šu*]

---

39) *un-dú* ^{I}*Ké-li-ia a-na* ŠEŠ-*ia aš-pu-ru ù* ⸢KÙ.GI⸣.[MEŠ]
40) *e-te-ri-iš um-ma lu-ú a-na-ku-ma* ŠEŠ-*ia el a-bi-ia* [10-*šu*]
41) *lu-ú ú-te-et-te-ra-an-ni ù* KÙ.GI.MEŠ *ma-a-a*[*t-ta*]
42) *ša ši-ip-ra la ep-šu li-še-e-bi-l*[*a-an-ni*]

Rev. 43) ŠEŠ-*ia el a-bi-ia ma-a-dì-iš li-še-bi-la-an-*[*ni*]
44) *ù a-ka-an-na a-na* ŠEŠ-*ia aq-ta-bi um-ma-a ka-ra-aš-k*[*a*]
45) *ša a-ba a-bi-ia e-ep-pu-uš um-ma lu-ú a-na-ku-ma ki-me-e*
46) *ki-i-ni a-an*!(AŠ)-*ni ú-nu-ú-ta e-ep-pu-uš-ma-a-ku*
47) *ù a-ka-an-na ap-pu-na aq-ta-bi* KÙ.GI.MEŠ *ša* ŠEŠ-*ia ú-*⸢*še*⸣-*bé-lu*
48) *a-na te-er-ḫa-tim-ma li-še-e-bi-il*

---

49) *i-na-an-na* ŠEŠ-*ia* KÙ.GI.MEŠ *ul-te-bíl a-qáb-bi-i um-ma-a*
50) *mi-i-iṣ-ma-a-ku ù la la mi-i-iṣ ma-a-ad ù a-na ši-ip-ri*
51) ⸢*ep*⸣-*še-et ù šum-ma ap-pu-na a-na ši-ip-ri-im-ma ep-še-et*
52) *ù aš-šum an-ni-ti aḫ-tá-du dan-níš-ma ù mi-nu-um-me-e*
53) *ša* ŠEŠ-*ia ú-še-bé-lu ù am-mi-ti dan-níš ḫa-da-a-ku*

(25–29) Kelya, my envoy, brought my brother's words to me. When I heard (them), and they were very pleasing, then I rejoiced exceedingly, and verily I said: "This is it for sure! viz. that which is between us, that which is mutual, that we love one another. Now, with such words let us love one another forevermore."

(30–33) When I wrote to my brother, then I verily said: "Let us always love one another very, very much and between us may we be in friendship. And to my brother I said: May my brother always surpass ten times what he did for my father!"

(34–38) And I requested of my brother much gold, saying: "May he exceed for me what was done for my father; may my brother send to me. And as for my father, you sent much gold to him: large golden pithoi, large golden jars, you sent to him. Bricks of gold, just like copper ones in size, you se[nt to him]."

(39–42) When I sent Keliya to my brother and I requested gold, I verily said: "May my brother exceed for me by [ten times] what was done for my father, and may he send me much gold that has not been worked."

(43–46) May my brother send to [me] much more than to my father and thus did I say to my brother, saying: "I am building the mausoleu[m] of my grandfather." Saying, verily I said: "In accordance with a truly positive response (an oracle) I am making the accoutrements."

And thus, moreover I said: "As for the gold which my brother is sending, it is for the bride price that he should send."

(49–53) Now, my brother has sent the gold. I say: "Be it little or not, not little but much, but it has been worked." But if, nevertheless, it is worked, then as for this, I rejoiced greatly and whatever my brother sends then I am very happy about that!

54) *a-⸢nu⸣-um-ma i-na-an-na a-na* ŠEŠ-*ia al-ta-pár ù* ŠEŠ-*ia*
55) *el ša a-bi-ia re-⸢e'⸣-mu-ú-ta li-še-em-'i-id-an-ni a-nu-um-ma*
56) KÙ.GI.MEŠ *a-na* ŠEŠ-*ia e-te-ri-iš ù* KÙ.GI.MEŠ *ša a-na* ŠEŠ-*ia*
57) *e-ri-šu a-na* 2-*šu a-na e-re-ši i-il-la-ak* 1-*tu*$_4$
58) *a-na ša ka-ra-aš-ki ù i-na ša-nu-ut-ti-šu a-na te-er-ḫa-ti*

---

59) *ù* ŠEŠ-*ia* KÙ.GI.MEŠ *ma-'a-dì-iš dan-níš ša a-na ši-ip-ri la ep-šu*
60) ŠEŠ-*ia li-še-bíl-an-ni ù* ŠEŠ-*ia el ša a-bi-ia* KÙ.GI *li-še-bi-la*
61) *ù i-na lìb-bi* KUR *ša* ŠEŠ-*ia* KÙ.GI.MEŠ *ki-i e-pè-ri ma-a-dá-at*
62) DINGIR.MEŠ *li-me-eš-še-ru-šu-ma ki-i-me-e ki-i ša i-na-an-na i-na* KUR
63) *ša* ŠEŠ-*ia* KÙ.GI.MEŠ *ma-'a-dá-at ù* 10-*šu el ki-i ša i-na-an-na*
64) ⸢KÙ.GI⸣.MEŠ *li-še-em-'i-id ù* KÙ.GI.MEŠ *ša e-ri-šu i-na* ŠÀ ŠEŠ-*ia*
65) *lu-ú la-a im-mar-ra-aṣ ù at-tù-ia lìb-bi* ŠEŠ-*ia lu-ú la-a*
66) *ú-ša-am-ra-aṣ ù* ⸢ŠEŠ⸣-*ia* KÙ.GI.MEŠ *ša a-na ši-ip-ri la ep-šu*
67) *ma-a-dì-iš da-an-ni-iš li-še-e-bi-la-an-ni*
68) *ù mi-nu-um-me-e ša* ŠEŠ-*ia ḫa-aš-ḫu a-na* É-*šu li-iš-pur-ma*
69) *li-il-qè ù a-na-ku* 10-TA.ÀM ša ŠEŠ-*ia i-ri-šu lu-ud-dì-in*
70) KUR *an-ni-tu*$_4$ *ša* ŠEŠ-*ia* KUR-*sú ù* É *an-ni-tu*$_4$ *ša* ŠEŠ-*ia* É-*sú*

---

71) *a-nu-um-ma* DUMU.KIN-*ia a-na* ŠEŠ-*ia al-ta-pár* ^{I}*Ké-li-ia ù* ŠEŠ-*ia*
72) *lu-ú la-a i-kál-la-a-šu* ⸢*ḫa*⸣-⸢*mut*⸣-*ta li-mèš-šèr-šu-ma li-il-li-ik*
73) *ki-me-e ša* ŠEŠ-*ia šul-*⸢*ma*⸣-⸢*an*⸣-*šu e-še-em-me ma-a-dì-iš dan-níš lu-ḫé-ed-di*$_{12}$
74) *a-na da-a-ra-tim-ma š*[*a*] ⸢ŠEŠ⸣-*ia šul-ma-an-šu lu-ul-te-em-me*
75) *ù a-ma-a-tu*$_4$ *an-na-a-tu*$_4$ *ša ni-il-ta-nap-pa-ru* ^{d}IŠKUR *be-e-li*
76) *ù* ^{d}*A-ma-nu-um li-mèš-šèr-šu-nu-ti-ma ù i-na pa-ṭì-i-šu-nu*
77) *li-ik-šu-du ù ki-i ša i-na-an-na a-di šu-nu-ma lu-ù ma-aš-lu*
78) *ki-i-me-e i-na-an-na ni-ir-ta-na-'a-*⸢*am*⸣ *ù ki-i ša i-na-an-na*
79) *a-na da-a-ra-ti-im-ma lu-ù ni-ir-ta-na-'a-am*

(54–58) Now I have written to my brother so may my brother increase affection much more than for my father. Now I have requested gold of my brother and as for the gold which I requested of my brother, it will be expended to meet two requirements; the first (part) is for the mausoleum and in the second place it is for the bride price.

(59–70) So, my brother, very much gold that is not worked, may my brother send to me; and may my brother send gold, more than to my father. And in the land of my brother gold is plentiful like dirt. May the gods grant it that just as now gold is plentiful in my brother's land, may he increase the gold ten times what it is now. And the gold that I requested, may it not be distressing to my brother's heart. And may my brother not cause distress to my heart. So may my brother send to me very much gold that has not been worked. And whatever my brother needs for his house, let him write and let him take and I will verily give ten times what my brother requested. This land is my brother's land and this house is my brother's house.

(71–79) Now my envoy, Keliya, have I sent to my brother and may my brother not detain him, may he release him swiftly so that he may go. As soon as I hear of my brother's well being, I will rejoice greatly. Forevermore may I continually hear that it is well with my brother. And as for these words that we will continually write, may Teshub, my lord, and Amon grant them and may they attain their goals, and may they be, as long as they exist, like they are now. Just as now we continually love (one another), so just as now may we love (one another) forever!

80) *a-nu-um-ma a-na šul-ma-a-ni-šu ša* ŠEŠ-*ia* 1 GAL KÙ.GI *tam-lu-ú* NA$_4$.ZA.GÌN KUR

81) *ša-kàr-ši* 1 *ma-ni-in-nu kab-bu-ut-tu*$_4$ 20 NA$_4$.ZA.GÌN KUR 19 KÙ.GI.MEŠ

82) *ša* MURUB-*šu* NA$_4$.ZA.GÌN KUR KÙ.GI GAR.RA 1 *ma-ni-in-nu kab-bu-tu*$_4$ 42 NA$_4$.NÍR KUR

83) 40 KÙ.GI *ša sú-uḫ-sí* [d]INANNA *ša* MURUB-*šu* NA$_4$.NÍR KUR KÙ.GI GAR.RA

84) 10 *ṣi-mi-it-tu*$_4$ ANŠE.KUR.RA.MEŠ 10 GIŠ.GIGIR.MEŠ GIŠ.MEŠ *qa-du mim-mu-šu-nu*

85) *ù* 30 MUNUS.NITA.MEŠ *a-na šul-ma-a-ni ša* ŠEŠ-*ia ul-te-*⸢*bíl*⸣

(80–85) Now for the greeting gift of my brother have I sent: one large gold cup, its handle inlaid with genuine lapis lazuli, one heavy *maninnu* necklace with twenty genuine lapis lazuli stones and nineteen gold ones, its center piece of genuine lapis lazuli set in gold, one heavy *maninnu* necklace with 42 geniuine *ḫulalu* stones, 40 gold pubic triangle*s* of Shaushga, of which the center piece is on genuine *ḫulalu* stones set in gold, ten teams of horses, ten wooden chariots with their accoutrements and 30 women (and) men, as the greeting gift of my brother.

EA 20

TRANSCRIPTION

Obv. 01) [*a-na* ^{I}*Ni-im-*]*mu-ú-a-re-ia šàr* KUR [*Mi-iṣ-ri-i*] ŠEŠ-*ia ḫa-ta-ni-ia*

02) [*ša a-ra*]-*'a-a-mu ša i-ra-'a-a*[*m-an-ni*] *qí-bí-ma*

03) [*um-ma* ^{I}*T*]*ù-uš-rat-ta šàr* KUR *Mi-i-t*[*a-an-ni*] *e-mu-ú-ka*

04) [*ša i-r*]*a-'a-a-mu-ú-ka* ŠEŠ-*ka*[*-ma a-n*]*a ia-ši šul-mu a-na ka-a-ša*

05) [*lu-ú š*]*ul-mu a-na* É-*ka a-na* DAM.MEŠ[-*ka*] *a-na* [DU]MU.MEŠ-*ka a-na* LÚ.MEŠ GAL-*ka*

06) [*a-na* GIŠ.]GIGIR.MEŠ-*ka a-na* ANSE.KUR.RA.MEŠ-*ka a-na* ERÍN.GAL.MEŠ-*ka*

07) [*a-n*]*a* KUR-*ka ù mi-im-mu-ka da-an-ni-iš da-an-ni-iš lu-ú šul-mu*

---

08) ^{I}*Ma-né-e* LÚ.KIN-*šu ša* ŠEŠ-*ia it-ta-*[*a*]*l-ka a-*[*n*]*a at-te-ru-ti a-na* DAM-*šu*

09) *ša* ŠEŠ-*ia a-na be-el-ti* KUR *Mi-iṣ-ri-*⸢*i*⸣ *a-na le-qè-e ú ṭup-pa*

10) *ša il-qà-a al-ta-ta-as-sí-ma* [*ú a*]*-ma-t*[*i-*]*šu el-te-me*

11) *ù* [*ṭ*]*a-a-bá da-a*[*n-n*]*i-iš-ma a-ma-a-ti*[-*š*]*u ša* ŠÉŠ-*ia ki-i ša* ŠEŠ-*ia-ma*

12) *a-mu-ru ù aḫ-ta-du i-na* u_4*-mi š*[*a-a*]*-ši ma-'a-dá da-an-ni-iš*

13) u_4*-ma ù mu-ša ša-a-ši* [*bá-*]*na-a e-te-pu*[*-uš*]

---

14) *ù ša* ŠEŠ-*ia a-ma-a-ti-šu gáb*[*-bá š*]*a* ^{I}*Ma-né-e il-qà-*⸢*a*⸣

15) *e-ep-pu-uš a-na ša-at-ti a*[*n-ni-t*]*i i-na-an-na ša* ŠEŠ-*ia* DAM-*sú*

16) *ša* KUR *Mi-iš-ri-i be-la-as-sú a-n*[*a-an-din*]*-ma ù a-na* ŠEŠ-*ia ub-bá-lu*

17) [1-*en a-mi*]-⸢*lu*⸣-⸢*ú*⸣-*t*[*u*] *i-na* u_4*-mi š*[*a-a-ši*] KUR *Ḫa-ni-gal-bat ù* KUR *Mi-i-iṣ-ri-i*

---

18) *ù aš-šum an-ni-ti* ^{I}*Ma-*[*n*]*é-e i*[*k-ka-la-a*] *ú-bá-an* ŠEŠ-*ia* ^{I}*Ké-li-ia*

19) *ù* ^{I}*Ma-né-e ḫa-mu-ut-*⸢*ta*⸣ [*ú-ma-aš-š*]*ar-šu-nu-ti ù la aq-ti-ip*!*-šu-nu*

20) ⸢*a*⸣-⸢*ka*⸣*-an-na* ŠEŠ-*ia a-na dú-u*[*l-li-i*]*m-ma a-na mu-uš-šu-r*[*i*]

21) *ù dú-ul-la ul e-pu-uš a-na* [*e-pé-eš*] 10-*šu a-na* DAM-*šu ša* ŠEŠ-*ia*

22) *ù i-na-an-na dú-ul-la e-ep*[*pu-uš*]

EA 20

TRANSLATION

(1–7) Speak [to Nim]muareʿia, king of the land of [Egypt], my son-in-law [whom I l]ove, who loves [me]. [The message of T]ushratta, king of the land of Mitt[anni], your father-in-law [who l]oves you, your brother. It is well [wi]th me. With you [may it be w]ell; with your household, with [your] wives, with your [so]ns, with your senior officials, [with] your chariotry, with your horses, with your warriors, [wit]h your land and your possessions, may it be very, very well.

(8–13) Mane, the envoy of my brother came in friendship in order to take the wife of my brother, the lady of the land of Egypt, and I read over and over the tablet which he brought [and] I heard its [w]ords and they were very sweet; the words of my brother were as if I saw my brother himself. And I rejoiced on that day very much. And I made that day and night a celebration.

(14–17) I will carry out every word of my brother that Mane brought to me. In t[his] very year, now, I will hand over my brother's wife, the mistress of Egypt, and they will bring her to my brother. On t[hat] day will Ḫanigalbat and Egypt be as [one man].

(18–22) And because of this, Mane will [be delayed] for a bit. My brother, Keliya and Mane [will I]release promptly and I will not encumber them [t]hus, my brother, with the task of finishing the work. I have not carried out the work in order [to do] ten times (more) for the wife of my brother but now I will carry out the work.

23) *i-na* ITI 6-KAMV ^{I}*Ké-li-ia* LÚ.KIN-*ia ù* ^{I}*Ma-né-e* L[Ú.KIN-*šu*]
24) [*š*]*a* ŠEŠ-*ia ú-ma-aš-ša-ar-šu-nu ša* ŠEŠ-*ia* DAM-*sú a-n*[*a-an-din*]
25) [*ù*] *a-na* ŠEŠ-*ia ú-ub-ba-lu* ^{d}‹IŠ$_{8}$›-T[ÁR] *be-el-ti be-le-*[*et* KUR.KUR *ù*]
26) [ŠEŠ-*i*]*a ù* ^{d}*A-ma-a-nu il-šu ša* ŠEŠ-*ia ki-i* [ŠÀ *ša* ŠEŠ-*ia*]
27) [*li*]-*me-eš*$_{15}$-*ši-il*[-*ši*]

---

28) [DAM-*s*]*ú a-na* ŠEŠ-*ia ú-ub-ba-lu ù* ŠEŠ-*ia ki-*⌜*i*⌝ [*ú-kál-la-mu-ši*]
29) [*ù i-im-*]*ma-ar-šu ir-ta-bi da-an-ni-iš-ma ù i-še*[-*e*ʾ-*i-ši-ma*]
30) [*ši-i*]⌜*ki*⌝-⌜*i*⌝ *lìb-bi ša* ŠEŠ-*ia ep-še-et ù* [*ap-pu-na-ma*]
31) [*šul-ma-*]*na ša a-na-an-di-nu* ŠEŠ-*ia* [*i-im-ma-ar*]
32) [*ki-i-me*]-⌜*e*⌝ *el ša pa-na-a-nu* [*ra-bi*]
33) [*a-nu-um-m*]*a* ^{I}*Ḫa-a-ra-ma-aš-š*[*i š*]*a* ŠEŠ-*ia-a-ma a-na* [*ia-ši iš-pu-ru*]
34) [*al-ta-pár-*]*šu ù ṭup-pa a-na qa-ti-šu at-ta-din ṭ*[*e-e-ma a-na* ŠEŠ-*ia*]
35) [*lil-ta-a*]*s-si-ma ù a-ma-ti-šu li-iš-me* [*ù a-nu-um-ma*]
36) [^{I}*Ḫa-a-ra-*]*ma-aš-ši a-na* ŠEŠ-*ia al-ta-pár a*[*š-šum*........]
37) [*ù* Š]EŠ-*ia* ÉRIN.MEŠ-*šu ú-ul ú-ba-an*[-*ni*.............]
38) [........] ⌜*i*⌝-*na* [.................................]
39) [............] *a-na* ŠEŠ-*ia* [.......................]
40) [............*a*]*m-ma* [............................]
41) [..]

Rev. 42) [.................*u*]*n-du* [..........].^{I}[...........]
43) [...................*b*]*i a-na* ^{I}*Ma-n*[*é-e* LÚ.KIN-*šu*]
44) [*ša* ŠEŠ-*ia*............]MEŠ *gáb-ba-ši-n*[*a*........]
45) [................*ma*]-*a-at-ta i-na pa-ni-i*[*a*]

(23–24) In six months Keliya, my envoy, and Mane, the envoy of my brother will I release. The wife of my brother will I ha[nd over] and they will bring her to my brother. [May] ‹Sha›ushka, my lady, the mister[ss of the lands and] of [m]y [brother, and Amon, the god of my brother, make [her] correspond to [my brother's desire].

28–32) They will bring [hi]s [wife] to my brother, and my brother, when [they present her] then [he will] see her; she has become very matured, and he [will desire her]. [She] is formed according to my brother's desire. And [moreover], the [greeting gi]ft that I am giving, my brother [will see], [as being greater] than can be reckoned.

33–38) [Now] Ḫaramashi, [wh]om my brother himself [sent] to [me, have I sent], and I have entrusted a tablet to him. [May he re]ad the me[ssage to my brother] and may be listen to his words. [And now Ḫara[mashi have I sent to my brother in [order to…And,] my [br]other, did I not treat we[ll] his troops [….].

39–41) […] to my brother […]

42–45) […]w]hen…]to Man[ê, the envoy of my brother…] all of them […d]ied before me [……]

46) [*ù aš-šum* KÙ.GI] *ša* ŠEŠ-*ia ú-se-bi-lu*

47) [*ú-ba-ru-t*]*u$_4$-ia gáb-bá up-te-eḫ-ḫé-er* ŠEŠ[-*ia* KÙ.GI]

48) [*ša ú-še-bi-lu*] *a-na pa-ni gáb-bi-šu-nu-ma a-ni-na is-*⸢*sal*⸣-[*ṭú*]

49) [.........*g*]*áb-bi-šu-nu-ma ka-an-ku$_8$-tu$_4$ ša-šu-nu ù* KÙ.GI *l*[*a ep-ša*]

50) [*li-ib-ba-ta im-ta*]-*lu-ú-me ù ib-te-ku$_8$-ú ma-ʾa-dá dá-an-n*[*i-iš-ma*]

51) [*um-ma-a lu*]-*ú šu-nu-ma-a-me an-nu-tum-me-e gáb-bá-šu-nu-ma-a-me* ⸢KÙ.GI⸣ *la ep-š*[*a-ma-a-me*]

52) [*ù*] *iq-ta-bu-ú i-na* KUR *Mi-iṣ-ri-im-ma-a-me* KÙ.GI *el e-pé-ri ma-a*[-*ad*]

53) [*ù*] ŠEŠ-*ia ap-pu-na i-ra-ʾa-a-am-ka da-an-ni-iš-me a-wi-lu-tu$_4$-m*[*a-a-me*]

54) [*šu-*]*ú ša i-ra-ʾa-a-mu ù a-na ša*!(ÁS)-*šu an-na-a-ti ú-ul i-na-a*[*n-din*]

55) [*ma-a*]*n-ni-ma-a-me ḫa-še-eḫ-ma-a-me el e-pé-ri i-na* KUR *Mi-iṣ-ri-i ma-a-ad*

56) [*ù*] *ma-an-nu an-na-ti a-na ma-an-ni i-na-an-din-me ša ma-la an-ni-i ma-ṣ*[*u-ú*]

57) [*ù p*]*a-na ù ba-a-ba la i-šu-ú um-ma lu-ú a-na-ku-ma ki-i-ma-a-me a-dáb-*[*bu-bu*]

58) [*a-n*]*a pa-ni-ku-nu-me ul a-dáb-bu-ub i-ra-ʾa-a-ma-an-ni ma-ʾa-dá dan-niš*[-*ma*]

59) [ŠE]Š-*ia šàr* KUR *Mi-iṣ-ri-im-*[*ma*]

---

60) *ù* ŠEŠ-*ia i-na* ŠÀ-*šu i-ṣa-ab-*⸢*ba*⸣-*ta-an-ni ki-i lìb-bi im-ra-ṣu mi-im-ma*

61) *ù la lu-ú pa-aš-ra im-ma-ti-ma* ⸢^{d}⸣⸢IŠKUR⸣ *be-li lu-ú la ú-ma-aš-ša-ra-an-ni-ma*

62) *it-ti* ŠEŠ-*ia lu-ú la ut-ta-az-za-am ka-a-am-ma a-na* ŠEŠ-*ia aq-ta-*⸢*bi*⸣

63) *ki-i-me-e* ŠEŠ-*ia i-du-ú*

---

64) ^{I}*Ma-né-e* LÚ.KIN-*šu ša* ŠEŠ-*i*[*a ù* ER]ÍN[.MEŠ-*š*]*u ša* ŠEŠ-*ia ša it-ti* ^{I}*Ma-né-e*

65) il-li-ka uk-te-eb-⸢*bi*⸣-*i*[*t a-na-k*]*u* [*g*]*á*[*b-b*]*i-šu-nu ù uk-te-eb-bi-ir-šu-nu*

66) *da-an-ni-iš a-nu-um-ma* ^{I}*Ma-né-e i-il-la-* kamV-*ma ù* ŠEŠ-*ia*

67) ⸢*il*⸣-*ta-na-ʾa-al-šu ki-i-me-e uk-*⸢*te*⸣*eb-bi-is-sú ma-ʾa-dá dá-an-ni-iš*

68) *a-na* ŠEŠ-*ia-ma i-dáb-bu-ub-ma ù* ŠEŠ-*ia il-te-nim-me-e-šu-nu-ti ki-i-me-e*

69) *e-te-pu-us-sú-nu ki-i lu-ú ḫa-šiḫ* ^{I}*Ma-né-e ul i-ma-a-*⸢*at*⸣

70) *a-di šu-ú-ma šu-ú ù la-a i-ma-ar-ra-aṣ*

46–59) [And with regard to the gold] which my brother sent, I assembled all my [foreign gue]sts. [My] brother, [the gold that he sent] in the presence of all of them, now, they were cut open, [....a]ll of them, they were sealed and the gold was u[nworked!]. [They became f]ull [of anger] and they wept grievously, [saying,] "Are all of these [tru]ly of gold? It is unworked!" [And] they said. "In the land of Egypt, gold is more plentiful than dirt." [And[, my brother, furthermore, "He loves you very much. As for mankind, [he] who loves, then to him(!) things like these he would not gi[ve]. Whoever desires, it is more plentiful than dirt in the land of Egypt, but who would give to someone things like these of which the sum is so mi[serly! But (rather)] with out reckoning (would he give)." I verily said thus, "I cannot say before you, 'My [broth]er, the king of the land of Egypt, loves me very much.'"

60–63) But, my brother will take it to heart that my heart was somewhat distressed. And only may he be mollified. Never again may Teshub permit me that I should rage thus at my brother. Thus have I spoken to my brother in order that he may know.

64–70) Mane, my brother's envoy, and the ⌜troops⌝ of my brother that accompanied him, I have honored them all and I have treated them with great distinction. Now Mane is coming and my brother can interrogate him extensively about how I honored him greatly. He will recount to my brother and my brother can listen to them in accordance with what I did to them. As if Mane lacked anything he was not going to die. He is still himself and he is not getting sick.

71) *ù* ŠEŠ-*ia* KÙ.GI *ma-ʾa-dá ša* KIN *la ep-ša li-še-e-bi-la ù aq-qa-at*

72) *a-bi-ia* ŠEŠ-*ia li-i-te-er-an-ni ki-i-me* ŠEŠ-*ia ra-ʾa-mu-ti ú-kál-lam*

73) *ki-i-me-e* ŠEŠ-*ia a-na pa-ni* KUR-*ia ki-i-me-e a-na pa-ni* LÚ.MEŠ *ú-bá-ru-ti-ia*

74) ŠEŠ-*ia ma-ʾa-dá ú-šar*!(*BAR*)-*ra-ḫa-an-ni* ^{d}IŠKUR *ù* ⸢^{d}⸣*A-m*[*a-n*]*u li-id-din-ma*

75) *a-na da-ra-tim-ma ša* ŠEŠ-*ia ša lìb-bi-šu lu-pu-uš ù* ŠEŠ-*ia*

76) *at-tù-ia ša lìb-bi-ia li-pu-uš ki-i-me-e a-mi-lu-ú-tu*$_4$

77) ^{d}UTU *i-ra-ʾa-am-šu ù ki-i* [*i-n*]*a-an-na ni-i-nu* DINGIR.MEŠ-*ú*

78) [*li-m*]*èš-še-ru-un-na-a-ši-ma a-na da-a-ra-tim-ma*

79) [*i-na lìb-b*]*i-ni i ni-ir-ta-ʾa-a-am*

---

80) [*ù a-nu-um-m*]*a a-na šul-ma-an-ni ša* ŠEŠ-*ia* 1 GIŠ.ÉŠ.SAG.KUL

81) [........] *ù i-ši-is-sú* NA$_4$ *ḫi-li-ba* KÙ.GI GAR.RA

82) [..........] *i-na qa-ti-šu i-ṣa-ab-bá-tu*$_4$

83) [........]IGI.MEŠ NA$_4$ NÌR KUR KÙ.GI GAR *ša a-na qa-ti*

84) [.........]*a-si i-il*[-*l*]*a-ku a-na* ŠEŠ-*ia ul-te-*⸢*bil*⸣

71–79) So, my brother, may he send me much gold that has not been worked; may my brother exceed the allotment of my father. May Teshub and Amon grant that my brother reveal love of me, that my brother cause me to be glorified(!) in the presence of my country and in the presence of my foreign guests.

75–79) May I fulfill my brother's heart's desire forever. And may my brother fulfill my own heart's desire. As mankind loves the sun god, so as for us now—may the gods grant us—that we may continue to love [in] our [hear]ts.

80–84) [And no]w as the greeting gift of my brother have I sent: one rope lock [the…of which is of…]and its base is of *ḫiliba* stone set in gold; […that] holds in its hand […]; […]with beads of genuine *ḫulalu* stone set in gold, that is for the hand […]…they will go.

EA 21

TRANSCRIPTION

Obv. 01) *a-na* ^{I}*Ni-im-*⸢*mu*⸣*-re-ia* LUGAL GAL
02) *šàr* KUR *Mi-iṣ-ri-i* ŠEŠ-*ia*
03) *ḫa-ta-ni-ia ša a-ra-am-mu-uš*
04) *ù ša i-ra-ʾa-a-ma-an-ni qí-bí-ma*
05) *um-ma* ^{I}*Tù-uš-rat-ta* LUGAL GAL
06) *šàr* KUR *Mi-ta-an-ni* ŠEŠ-*ka e-mu-ka*
07) *ù ša i-ra-ʾa-a-mu-ka-ma*
08) *a-na ia-ši šul-mu a-na* ŠEŠ-*ia ù a-na ḫa-ta-ni-ia*
09) *lu-ú šul-mu a-na* É.MEŠ-*ka a-na* DAM.⸢MEŠ⸣-*ka*
10) *a-na* DUMU.MEŠ-*ka a-na* LÚ.MEŠ-*ka a-na* GIŠ.GIGIR.MEŠ-*ka*
11) *a-na* ANŠE.KUR.RA.MEŠ-*ka a-na* KUR-*ka*
12) *ù a-na mim-mu-ka dan-niš lu-ú šul-mu*

---

13) *ša* ŠEŠ-*ia ša a-ra-am-mu-uš*
14) DAM-*sú* DUMU.MUNUS-*ti at-*⸢*ta*⸣*-an-na-aš-*⸢*šu*⸣
15) ^{d}UTU *ù* ^{d}INNIN *a-na* ⸢*pa*⸣-⸢*ni*⸣*-ša l*[*i-i*]*l-lik*
16) ⸢*ki*⸣*-i lìb-bi ša* ŠEŠ-*ia li-me-*⸢*eš*$_{15}$⸣?-[*ši-l*]*u-*⸢*uš*⸣
17) ⸢*ù*⸣ ŠEŠ-*ia i-na u*$_{4}$*-mi š*[*a-a-š*]*i*
18) *l*[*i-*]*iḫ-du* ^{d}UTU *ù* ^{d}I[NNIN *a-na*]
19) ŠEŠ-*ia ka-ra-ba ra-*[*ba-a*]
Lo.ed. 20) ⸢*ḫi*⸣*-du-ú-*⸢*ta*⸣ ⸢*ba*⸣*-ni-*⸢*i*⸣[*-ta*]
21) *li-id-din-ú-níš-šu li*[*k-ru-bu-šu*]
22) *ù* ŠEŠ-*ia lu-ú bal-ṭ*[*á-ta*]
Rev. 23) *a-na da-a-ra-a-tim-*[*ma*]

EA 21

TRANSLATION

(1–12) Speak to Nimmureʿa, the great king, the king of the land of Egypt, my brother, my son-in-law, whom I love and who loves me; thus (spoke) Tushratta, the great king, the king of the land of Mittanni, your brother, your father-in-law and one who loves you: It is well with me. With my brother and with my son-in-law may it be well. With your household and your wiv[es], with your sons, with your men, with your chariotry, with your horses, with your land and with your possessions may it be very well.

(13–23) My daughter as the wife of my brother whom I love, have I given to him. May Shimigi and Shaushka go before her. May they make her the image of my brother's heart. And, may my brother rejoice on t[ha]t day. May Shimigi and Shau[shka] give [to] my brother a gre[at] blessing and wonder[ful] joy. May [they bless him], and may my brother li[ve] forever.

24) [I]*Ma-né-e* LÚ.DUMU.KIN-*šu š*[*a* ŠEŠ-*ia*]
25) *ù* [I]*Ḫa-né-e tar-gu-ma-an*[*-na-šu*]
26) *ša* ŠEŠ-*ia ki-i i-li ur-te-e*[*b-bi-ma*]
27) NÍG.⌜BA⌝.MEŠ *ma-ʾa-dá at-ta-ta-ad-din-š*[*u-ni-ma*]
28) ⌜*ub*⌝-⌜*te*⌝*-en-ni-šu-nu dan-níš*
29) *ki-i ṭe*$_4$*-em-šu-nu ba-nu-ú aš-šum kal-li-šu-*⌜*nu*⌝
30) *a-mi-lu-ú-ta ša ka-an-na ep-šu*
31) *im-ma-ti-ma ú-ul a-mur* DINGER.MEŠ-*ia*
32) *ù* DINGER.MEŠ *ša* ŠEŠ-*ia li-iṣ-ṣú-ru-šu-nu*
33) *a-nu-um-ma* 1 *na-aḫ-ra ma-*⌜*aš*⌝*-ši*
34) *ša ta-am-ra‹-ta›*(?) *a-na e-pé-ši a-na* ŠEŠ-ia
35) *al-ta-pár-šu ù* 1*-en ma-ni-in-nu*
36) *ša* NA$_4$.ZA.GÌN KUR NA$_4$.ZA.GÌN ⌜KUR⌝
37) *ù ša* KÙ.GI *a-na šul-ma-ni*
38) *ša* ŠEŠ-*ia ul-te-bíl*
39) *ù a-na* 1 *me-at li-im* MU.MEŠ-*ti*
40) *a-na ti-ik-ki ša* ŠEŠ-*ia*
41) *lu-ú na-dì*

(24–32) Mane, the envoy o[f my brother], and Ḫane, the interpre[ter] of my brother have I ex[alted] like gods.have I given [to them]. I have treated the two of them really well because their report was excellent. I have never at any time seen men, both of whom are so well formed. May my gods and the gods of my brother protect them.

(33–41) Now, one polished *naḫra* for making mirror‹s› for my brother have I sent to him, and one *maninnu* necklace of pure lapis lazuli, pure lapis lazuli and of gold, have I sent and may it rest on the neck of my brother for one hundred thousand years!

EA 22

TRANSCRIPTION

COL. I

(1)	[x]	[...A]NŠE.KUR.RA.MEŠ ⸢*ba*⸣-⸢*nu*⸣-*tu*$_4$ *ša i-la-as-sú-mu-ú-n*[*i*]
(2)	1	GIŠ.GIGIR *ṭù-le-e-mi-šu mar-ši-šu ù si-iḫ-pí-šu gáb-bá*
(3)		KÙ.GI 3 *me* 20 SU KÙ.GI *ša i-na* ŠÀ-*šu na-du-ú*
(4)	1	^{GIŠ}*il-tuḫ-ḫu ša pi-ša-iš* KÙ.GI GAR *pa-ra-ti-ti-na-šu*
(5)		NA$_4$.NÍR KUR 1 NA$_4$.KIŠIB NA$_4$.NÍR KUR *i-na lìb-bi-šu šuk-ku-uk*
(6)	5	SU KÙ.GI *i-na lìb-bi-šu na-di*
(7)	2	*ša bu-ur-ḫi* KÙ.GI GAR 6 SU KÙ.GI
(8)	4	SU KÙ.BABBAR *i-na lìb-bi-šu-nu na-di*
(9)	2	*ša* ^{KUŠ}*ú-ḫa-ta-a-ti* KÙ.GI KÙ.BABBAR GAR.RA
(10)		MÚRUB-*šu-nu* ZA.GÌN *ša-ki-in* 10 SU KÙ.GI
(11)	20	SU KÙ.BABBAR *i-na lìb-bi-šu-nu na-di*
(12)	2	*ma-ni-i-in-nu ša* ANŠE.KUR.RA.MEŠ NA$_4$.⸢NÍR⸣
(13)		KÙ.GI GAR 88 *i-na* ŠID-*ti* 44 ⸢SU⸣ ⸢KÙ.GI⸣
(14)		*ša i-na* ŠÀ-*šu-nu na-du-ú*
(15)	1	ŠU KUŠ.KA.TAB ANŠE.KU[NGI *ú*]-⸢*ḫa*⸣-⸢*ti*⸣-*šu-nu gi-la-mu*
(16)		*pu-uq-dá-a-ti-šu-nu* KÙ.[GI...] *t*[*a*]-*ab-na-a-ni a-sal*
(17)		*ù ger-*[*r*]*a-a*[*s-sú-nu š*]*a* NA$_4$.GIŠ.NU$_{11}$.GAL
(18)		[*ù*] *ú-ḫa-*[*ta-as-sú-n*]*u ku*$_8$*-uš-tap-pa-a-an-ni-šu-nu*
(19)		*pa-š*[*e*......-*šu-n*]*u gi-la-a-mu*
(20)		*ù* [.......]-*šu-nu* KÙ.GI *ša da-ma šu-lu-ú*
(21)	2	*na-at-tul-la-a-tu*$_4$ *ša* KUŠ
(22)		*ša ki-i a-ra-aš-ša-a-an-ni bur-ru-mu*

EA 22

TRANSLATION

COL. I

(1) 4 beautiful horses that run (swiftly).

(2) 1 chariot, its *ṭulemu*'s, its *thongs*, its covering, all
(3) of gold. It is 320 shekels of gold that have been used on it

(4) 1 whip of *pišaiš*, overlaid with gold; its *parattitinu*,
(5) of genuine *ḫulalu*-stone; 1 seal of genuine *ḫulalu*-stone is strung on it.
(6) 5 shekels of gold have been used on it.

(7) 2 *ša burḫi*, overlaid with gold. 6 shekels of gold (and)
(8) 4 shekels of silver have been used on them.

(9) 2 (leather) *uḫatati*, overlaid with gold and silver;
(10) their center is made of lapis lazuli. 10 shekels of gold (and)
(11) 20 shekels of silver have been used on them.

(12) 2 *maninnu*-necklaces, for horses; genuine *ḫulalu*-stone
(13) mounted on gold; 88 (stones) per string. It is 44 shekels
(14) that have been used on them.

(15) 1 set of bridles for mules(?), of *gilamu*-ivory;
(16) their "thorns," of go[ld;...]...,
(17) and...[...o]f alabaster;
(18) [...]..., their *kuštappanni*;
(19) [...]..., [...] of *gilamu*-ivory;
(20) and their [...], of gold *with a reddish tinge*.

(21) 2 leather *nattullu*,
(22) that are variegated like a wild dove.

(23) 1 ŠU *gu*$_5$*-ú-ḫa-as-sú ša* ZABAR

(24) 1 [KUŠ]*ap-pa-tu*$_4$ *i-ši-is-sú ù ma-ra-as-sú*
(25) KÙ.GI GAR *ta-a-aš-li* KÙ.GI *ša dá-m[a] šu-ú-lu-ú*
(26) *mu-uḫ-ḫa-šu gáb-ba* ALAM KÙ.[GI…]*-la-aš-ši*
(27) *bá-a-ab a-ṣa-am pa-an-ša ra-*[*x*]*-a*[*n*]*-ni* [*x*]-⸢*ma*⸣
(28) *dá-ar-dá-ra-aḫ ša* KÙ.GI *mu-uḫ-*[*ḫ*]*u-*⸢*uṣ*⸣
(29) *ù* É *šum-mu-ḫi dar*$_6$*-dá-ra-aḫ-šu ša* KÙ.GI
(30) *mu-uḫ-ḫu-uṣ* 1 *šu-ši* SU *i-na* ŠÀ*-šu na-di*

(31) [x] GI.MEŠ *šar-mu* ⸢*ba*⸣*-nu-ú*

(32) [1] GÍR *ša* EME*-sú* ⸢*ḫa*⸣-⸢*bal*⸣-⸢*ki*⸣-⸢*i*⸣-⸢*in*⸣-⸢*nu*⸣
(33) [*g*]*u-mu-ú-ri-šu* KÙ.GI *u*[*ṣ-ṣu*]*-ru* [K]IN-⸢*šu*⸣
(34) [GIŠ.]ESI *ša* AMAR.MEŠ KÙ.GI GA[R SA]G-*sú* NA$_4$.AN.GUG.ME
(35) [*x*]*-ṭu-šu* KÙ.GI GAR *uṣ-ṣú-*[*ru*] 6 SU KÙ.[GI *i-na*] ŠÀ *na-di*

(36) [x] BAN *a-pí-sa-a-mu-*[*u*]*š-ḫé* [……..] K[Ù.G]I GAR
(37) 4 SU KÙ.GI *ša i-na* ŠÀ*-šu* ⸢*na*⸣-⸢*du*⸣*-ú*

(38) 1 GIŠ.TUKUL.DINGIR *ša* AN.BAR KÙ.GI GAR 15 SU GUŠ[KI]N [*i-n*]*a* ŠÀ *na-di*

(39) 1 *za-a-al-le-e-wi* ZABAR [KI]N*-šu* KÙ.GI GAR
(40) 3 SU KÙ.GI *i-na* ŠÀ*-šu na-di*

(41) 1 *ad-du ša pí-ša-iš* KÙ.GI GAR 2 SU KÙ.GI *i-na* ŠÀ *na-di*

(42) 1 *til-pa-a-nu ša za-mi-ri a-na* 4*-šu* KÙ.GI GAR
(43) 6 SU KÙ.GI *i-na* ŠÀ*-šu na-di*

(44) 2 *sa-dì-in-nu bi-ir-mu*

(45) 1 ŠU *ši-ri-in-na-a-*⸢*tu*$_4$⸣ KÙ.BABBAR 50(?) SU *i-na* KI.LÁ.BI

(23) 1 set of torques, of bronze.

---

(24) 1 (set of) reins; its base and *straps*
(25) overlaid with gold; the *tašli* of gold *with a reddish tinge*;
(26) its entire upper part is a gold figure [...]...;
(27) the *opening...its surface*...[...];
(28) It is studded with *dardaraḫ*-ornaments of gold;
(29) and the "house"...is studded with *dardaraḫ*-ornaments, also of gold.
(30) 60 shekels (of gold) were used on it.

---

(31) [x] good, sharp arrows.

---

(32) [1] dagger, the blade of which is of i[r]on;
(33) its guard, of gold, with dESIns; its haft,
(34) of ebony with calf figurines; overlaid with gold; its [pomm]el is of...-stone;
(35) its [...]..., overlaid with gold, with dESIns. 6 shekels of go[ld] have been used on it.

---

(36) [1] bow, of the *apisamuš*-type [...], overlaid with gold.
(37) It is 4 shekels of gold that have been used on it.

---

(38) 1 mace, of iron overlaid with gold. 15 shekels of gold have been used on it.

---

(39) 1 *zallewe*-knife, of bronze; its [ha]ft overlaid with gold.
(40) 3 shekels of gold have been used on it.

---

(41) 1 *addu*-throw stick, of *pišaiš*, overlaid with gold. 2 shekels of gold have been used on it.

---

(42) 1 *tilpānu*-bow, of *zamiri*; 4 times overlaid with gold.
(43) 6 shekels of gold have been used on it.

---

(44) 2 multicolored *shirts*.

---

(45) 1 set of snaffles, of silver; [5]0 shekels in weight.

---

(46) 1 ŠU *pí-ti-in-ka-ak ša* SÍG.GAN.ME.TA *ṣú-up-pu-ru*

(47) 1 ^{KUŠ}*a-ri-tu*$_4$ *ú-ru-uk-ma-a-an-nu* KÙ.BABBAR 10 SU *i-na* KI.LÁ.BI

(48) 1 ^{KUŠ}*pa-a-gu-mu* NA$_4$.GÍR.ZÚ-*šu* NA$_4$.NÍ[R] KUR
(49) *tam-lu-ú-šu* NA$_4$.ZA.GÌN KUR *ta-a-aš*-[*l*]*i tam-lu-ú* [NA$_4$.ZA.GÌN] KUR
(50) MURUB$_4$-*šu* $^{\text{NA}_4}$*ḫi-l*[*i*]*-ba* GAR *ù* MURUB$_4$-*šu š*[*a*] [$^{\text{NA}_4}$*ḫi*]-*l*[*i*]-[*b*]*a*
(51) NA$_4$.ZA.GÌN KUR GAR 2 NA$_4$.NÍR KUR *kab-bu-tu*$_4$ [KÙ.G]I GAR
(52) *ša i-na mar-ši-šu š*[*uk-ku*]-*ku* 1 NA$_4$.KIŠIB NA$_4$.ZA.GÌN KUR
(53) KÙ.GI GAR 1 NA$_4$.NÍR KUR *kab-bu-tu*$_4$ *ša i-na* EGIR-*šu šuk-ku-ku*
(54) 10 SU KÙ.GI *i-na* ŠÀ-*šu na-di*

(55) 1 *la-ḫa-nu ša* ANŠE.KUR.RA.MEŠ *ša a-mu-*⸢*ú*⸣*-ti*
(56) *ša* Á.MUŠEN.MEŠ KÙ.GI *tam-lu-ú ùtam-lu-ú-šu* NA$_4$.ZA.GÌN.KUR
3 *me* SU *i-na* KI.LAL.BI

(58) 1 *ša zu-ub-bi šu-ú-li-i* KÙ.GI *qa-du* GADA-*šu*
(59) 3 SU *i-na* KI.LÁ.BI

(60) [1] *kab-bu-ut-tu*$_4$ KÙ.GI 10 SU *i-na* KI.LÁ.BI

(61) [1] [x x]-*ḫa-lu* KÙ.GI 20 SU *i-na* KI.LÁ.B[I]

(62) [x] […*ša*] NA$_4$ SAG-*sú* NA$_4$.MUŠ.[GÌR…]
(63) [.......] KIN-*šu* KÙ.GI GAR *a-na* 2-*šu*
(64) [........-*z*]*i-in-šu* NA$_4$ ŠI.TIR [.....]
(65) [........x] KÙ.GI *i-du-uz-za-ri-ma* [......]
(66) [x SU] *i-na* ŠÀ-*šu na-*[*di*]

(46) 1 pair of gloves that are trimmed with red wool.

(47) 1 shield…of silver, 10 shekels in weight.

(48) 1 leather *halter*, its "flint-blade" of genuine *ḫulalu*-stone;,
(49) its inlay, of genuine lapis lazuli; the *tašli*, (*with*) inlay of genuine [lapis lazuli].
(50) Its centerpiece is set with *ḫiliba*-stone, and (*this*) centerpiece *o*[*f ḫili*]*b*[*a*-stone]
(51) is mounted on genuine lapis lazuli. 2 genuine *ḫulalu*-stones mounted [on gol]d,
(52) which are strung on its *straps*. 1 seal of genuine lapis lazuli, mounted
(53) on gold. 1 *ḫulalu*-stone, a *counterweight*, which is strung on its rear.
(54) 10 shekels of gold have been used on it.

(55) 1 bottle, horse-*shaped*, of *amutu*-metal,
(56) with eagles of gold as inlay; and (*also*) its inlay genuine lapis lazuli.
(57) 300 shekels in weight.

(58) 1 fly whisk, of gold, along with its linen cloth.
(59) 3 shekels in weight.

(60) [1] *counterweight*, 10 shekels in weight.

(61) [1 *si*]*eve*, of gold, 20 shekels in weight.

(62) [1 …], of stone; its top of *muš*[*šaru*]-stone;

(63) […] its haft, overlaid with gold; 2 times […];
(64) its […]…, of *pendu*-stone […];
(65) […], of gold,…[…]
(66) [x] shekels of gold have been [used] on it.

COL. II

(1) 1 ⸢ḪUR⸣.⸢ŠU⸣ *ša* AN.BAR K[Ù.GI GAR] *me-e-su-uk-ki-i-šu*

(2) *tam-lu-*[*ú*] NA$_4$.ZA.GÌN ⸢KUR⸣ 6 SU KÙ.GI *i-na* ŠÀ-*šu na-di*

---

(3) 1 ḪUR.ŠU *ša* AN.BAR KÙ.GI GAR *me-e-su-uk-ki-i-šu*

(4) NA$_4$.ZA.GÌN KUR 5 SU KÙ.GI *i-na* ŠÀ-*šu na-di*

---

(5) 1 ḪUR.GÌR KÙ.GI *tam-lu-ú* 5 SU KÙ.GI *i-na* ŠÀ-*šu na-di*

---

(6) 1 *ma-*⸢*ni*⸣*-i-in-ni šar-mu* 35 NA$_4$.ZA.GÌN KUR

(7) 35 ^{NA_4}*ḫi-li-ba* MURUB$_4$ ^{NA_4}NÍR KUR

(8) KÙ.GI *ša dá-ma šu-ú-lu-ú uḫ-ḫu-uz*

---

(9) 1 ŠU *ša* ŠU IGI.MEŠ NA$_4$.NÍR KUR 6 *i-na* ŠID-ti

(10) KÙ.GI GAR 6 SU KÙ.GI *i-na* ŠÀ-*šu-nu na-di*

---

(11) 1 ŠU *ka-rat-na-an-nu* KÙ.GI 2 SU *i-na* KI.LÁ.BI

---

(12) 1 *pa-as-ka-a-ru* KÙ.GI *ša ki-i gu*$_5$*-ḫa-az-zi*

(13) *ṣu-up-pu-ru* 14 SU *i-na* KI.LÁ.BI

---

(14) 1 ŠU *a-ra-ap-ša-a-an-na* 6 *i-du-u-uz-za-*⸢*ar*⸣*-ra*

(15) K[Ù.G]I *ša dá-ma šu-ú-lu-ú* 12 SU *i-na* KI.LÁ.BI

---

(16) 1 GÍR ša ⸢EME⸣-*sú* ⸢AN⸣.BAR KIN-*šu tam-lu-ú* [$^{N]A_4}$[......].

(17) KÙ.GI GAR SAG.DU-*sú* NA$_4$.[AN].GUG.ME *ma-lik-šu* KÙ.GI GAR

(18) *ma-aṭ-ru-ú-šu* GÙN.A *ša t*[*a-k*]*íl-ti a-na* 2-*šu*

(19) KÙ.GI GAR 14 SU KÙ.GI *i-na* ŠÀ-*šu-nu na-di*

---

(20) 1 *zal-lu-*[*la*]*m* KIŠIB.LÁ-*šu* ^{NA_4}*ḫi-li-ba ù* NA$_4$.ZAGÌN KUR GAR

(21) KIN-*šu* ⸢ALAM⸣ *a-mi-il-tu*$_4$ NA$_4$.GIŠ.NU$_{11}$.GAL *tam-lu-ú*

(22) NA$_4$.ZAGÌN KUR 6 SU KÙ.GI *i-na* ŠÀ-*šu na-*⸢*di*⸣

COL. II

(1) 1 ha[nd-brac]elet, of i[ro]n, [*overlaid with gol*]*d*; its *mesukku*-birds
(2) (have) an inlay of genuine lapis lazuli. 6 shekels of gold have been used on it.

(3) 1 hand-bracelet, of iron, overlaid with gold; its *mesukku*-birds
(4) (have) an inlay of genuine lapis lazuli. 5 shekels of gold have been used on it.

(5) 1 anklet, of gold, inlaid. 5 shekels of gold were used on it.

(6) 1 *maninnu*-necklace, cut from 35 genuine lapis lazuli stones.
(7) 35 *ḫiliba*-stones; in the center, a genuine *ḫulalu*-stone,
(8) mounted on gold *with a reddish tinge.*

(9) 1 set for the hand, beads of genuine lapis lazuli, 6 per string,
(10) mounted on gold. 6 shekels of gold have been used on it.

(11) 1 set of *karatnannu*, of gold, 2 shekels in weight.

(12) 1 head-binding, of gold,
(13) twisted like a torque, 14 shekels in weight.

(14) 1 set of *arapšanna*, 6 *iduzzarra*,
(15) of gold *with a reddish tinge*. 12 shekels in weight.

(16) 1 dagger, the blade of which is of iron; the haft has an inlay of ...-st[one],
(17) overlaid with gold; its pommel, of...-stone; its..., mounted in gold;

(18) its *maṭru*, (with) variegated trim of blue-purple wool, 2 times
(19) overlaid with gold. 14 shekels have been used on it.

(20) 1 *zallulu*, its *rettu* overlaid with *ḫiliba*-stones and genuine lapis lazuli;
(21) the handle, the figure of a woman, of alabaster; the inlay
(22) of genuine lapis lazuli. 6 shekels of gold were used on it.

(23) 1 ŠU KUŠ.E.SÍR *ša* DU$_8$.ŠI.A *ù dar$_6$-dá-ra-aḫ-m*[*a*]
(24) *ša* K[Ù.G]I *mu-uḫ-ḫu-ṣú bu-ú-tin-ni-šu-nu* ^{NA_4}*ḫi-l*[*i-ba*]
(25) *ka-r*[*at-n*]*a-an-na-al-la* NA$_4$.ZA.GÌN KUR *ti-ša-ak-k*[*u-un*]
(26) 13 SU KÙ.GI *i-na* ŠÀ-*šu-nu na-di* 1 ŠU ^{TÚG}*ka-pal-lu š*[*a i-li*]

---

(27) 1 ŠU ^{KUŠ}*bat-t*[*a-t*]*u$_4$ dar$_6$-dá-ra-aḫ ša* KÙ.GI *ma-lu-*[*ú*]
(28) 6 SU KÙ[.GI *i-n*]*a* ŠÀ-*šu-nu na-*[*di*]

---

(29) 1 ŠU ^{KUŠ}E.SÍR *ša ta-kíl-ti k*[*i-iz*]*-zi-šu-nu*
(30) *ù ta-a-*[(*diš*)]*-šu-nu* KÙ.[GI *bu*]*-ú-tin-ni-i-šu-nu*
(31) ^{NA_4}*ḫi-l*[*i*]*-ba* MURUB$_4$ *tam-lu-ú* $^{NA_4.ZA.GÌN}$ KUR
(32) 4 SU KÙ.GI *i-na* ŠÀ-*šu-nu na-di* 1 ŠU ^{TÚG}*ka-pa-lu ša i-*[*li*]

---

(33) 1 KUŠ.E.SÍR *ša* GADA GÙN.A *ša i-du-uz-za-ri-šu-nu*
(34) 1 ŠU ^{TÚG}*ka-pa-lu* *ša i-li*

---

(35) 1 ŠU KUŠ.E.SÍR *ša* GADA GÙN.A 1 ŠU ^{TÚG}⸢*ka*⸣-⸢*pal*⸣-⸢*lu*⸣ ⸢*ša*⸣ *i-li*

---

(36) 1 TÚG *ša ta-kil-ti* 1 ŠU TÚG.GÚ [*ḫur*]*-ri ša* URU

---

(37) 1 TÚG.GÚ URU *ša Tuk-ur-iš* 1 ŠU TÚG.Í[B].LÁ
(38) *ša* SÍG.GAN.ME.TA DIR

---

(39) 1 TÚG.GADA *a-aš-ši-a-an-ni* 1 ŠU TÚG.GÚ [*ḫ*]*ur-‹ri› ša* GADA
(40) 1 TÚG.GÚ URU GADA 1 TÚG.BAR.DUL *ša* GADA

---

(41) 1 ^{TÚG}*ḫa-ṣú-ra* 1 ŠU TÚG.GÚ *ḫur-ri* 1 ŠU T[ÚG].G[Ú UR]U
(42) 1 TÚG.BAR.DUL *ù* 1 TÚG.SAG *ša t*[*a-k*]*íl-t*[*i*]

---

(43) 1 *š*[*a z*]*u-ub-bi ku$_8$-uš-šu-dì* KIŠIB.LÁ-*š*[*u......*]
(44) NA$_4$.ZA.GÌN KUR *gu-ub-gu-bi* ^{NA_4}*ḫi-li-ba* KIN-[*šu* KÙ.GI GAR]

(23) 1 pair of shoes, of *dušu*-color (leather), and studded with *dardaraḫ*-ornaments
(24) of gold; their buttons of *ḫiliba*-stone;
(25) with *kar*[*atn*]*annalla*-ornaments, of genuine lapis lazuli, set here and [there].
(26) 13 shekels of gold have been used on them. 1 pair of leggings, o[f *shaggy wool*].

(27) 1 pair of *betatu*-shoes, well provided with gold *dardaraḫ*-ornaments
(28) 6 shekels of gold have been used on them.

(29) 1 pair of shoes, of blue-purple wool; their...[...].
(30) and their...[...], of gold; their buttons
(31) of *ḫiliba*-stone; the center, an inlay of genuine lapis lazuli.
(32) 4 shekels of gold have been used on them. 1 pair of *leggings*, of *shaggy* [*wool*].

(33) 1 pair of shoes, of colored linen, which have *iduzzarri*.
(34) 1 pair of *leggings*, of *shaggy wool*.

(35) 1 pair of shoes, of colored linen. 1 pair of leggings, of *shaggy wool*.

(36) 1 garment of blue-purple wool. 1 pair of shirts, Hurrian-style, [*for*] *the city*.

(37) 1 *city*-shirt, *Tukriš*-style. 1 pair of s[as]hes,
(38) of red wool, adorned.

(39) 1 linen garment, *aššianni*-type. 1 pair of shirts, Hur‹rian›-style, of linen.
(40) 1 city-shirt, of linen. 1 robe, of linen.

(41) 1 *ḫaṣuru*-garment. 1 pair of shirts, Hurrian-style, of linen. 1 pair of city-shirts.
(42) 1 robe and 1 cap, of blue-purple wool.

(43) 1 fly-whisk. Its *rettu* (has) an *in*[*lay*]
(44) of genuine lapis lazuli...*ḫiliba*-stone. [Its] haft, [overlaid with go]ld,

(45)		*a-na* 3-*šu tam-lu-ú* NA$_4$.ZA.GÌN KUR *i-ši-is-sú* [NA$_4$.ZA.GÌN KUR]
(46)		TÚG*ás-sa-ás-ta-ra-an-ni* *ku-ḫa-as-sú* [......]
(47)	25	SU KÙ.GI *i-na* ŠÀ-*šu* [*na-di*]
(48)	1	*mu-me-e*[*r*]-*ri-tu*$_4$ *ša per*$_6$-*a-zi* ⸢*ù*⸣ [*dar*$_6$-*dá-ra-aḫ*]
(49)		*ša* KÙ.GI *mu*-[*uḫ*]-*ḫu-uṣ* KIN-*šu* GIŠ.ESI [............]
(50)	6	SU KÙ.GI *i-na lìb-bi-šu* [*na-di*]
(51)	1	⸢NÍG⸣.ŠU.LUḪ.ḪA KÙ.BABBAR 1 *me* 40 SU *i-na* ⸢KI⸣.⸢LÁ⸣.⸢BI⸣
(52)	1	NA$_4$.AN.GI *gi-la-mu* 80 SU *i-na* KI.LÁ.BI
(53)	1	GI KÙ.BABBAR *gi-la-mu* 77 1/2 *i-na* KI.LÁ.BI
(54)	2	BAN.MEŠ *ša pa-at-ti* AB. ZU *ki-ṣa-al-li-šu-nu*
(55)		KÙ.[GI GAR *ù* 1-*en i-na lìb-bi-šu a-na* 2-[*šu*]
(56)		KÙ.GI *pa*-[*a*]-*az-na-a-an-ni* 10 SU KÙ.GI *i-na* ŠÀ-*šu-nu na*-[*d*]*i*
(57)	1	⸢*šu*⸣-*kùr-ru* ZABAR *a-na* 2-*šu* KÙ.GI GAR
(58)	6	SU KÙ.GI *i-na* ŠÀ-*šu na-di*
(59)	1	*ma-ak-ka-sú* ZABAR KIN-*šu a-na* 2-*šu* KÙ.GI GAR
(60)	3	SU KÙ.GI *i-na* ŠÀ-*šu na-di*
(61)	10	GA.ZUM.ME[Š] GAL.MEŠ *ša* NA$_4$.MEŠ
(62)	1	*la-ḫa-an-nu ša* NA$_4$ 1 *ḫu-li-am ša* NA$_4$.GIŠ.NU$_{11}$.GAL
(63)		*tam-lu-ú* NA$_4$.[ZA.GÌ]N KUR *ša pa-as-sú* KÙ.GI GAR
(64)	3	SU KÙ.GI *i-na* ŠÀ-*šu na-di*
(65)	1	*ḫu*-[*l*]*i-am ša* NA$_4$.IŠ.ME.KUM KÙ.GI GAR
(66)	4	[S]U KÙ.GI *i-na* ŠÀ-*šu na-di*
(67)	1	[...NA$_4$]*mar-ḫal-lu* 1 *ku-u-ni-i-nu* NA$_4$*mar-ḫal-lu*
(68)		[......NA$_4$.]NÍR KUR 1 *kab-bu-ut-tu*$_4$ *ša* NA$_4$

(45) 3 times; its inlay, of genuine lapis lazuli; its base, of [genuine l]apis lazu[li.]
(46) Its *cloth streamers* (held by) wire […].
(47) 25 shekels of gold have been used on it.

(48) 1 A *mumerritu*-scraper, of…, a[nd] it is studded [with *dardaraḫ*-ornaments]
(49) of gold. Its haft, of ebony […].
(50) 6 shekels of gold hav[e been used] on it.

(51) 1 washbasin, of silver, 140 shekels in weight.

(52) 1 stone-…, (with) *gilamu*-ivory, 70 shekels in weight.

(53) 1 silver tube, (with) *gilamu*-ivory, 77 1/2 shekels in weight.

(54) 2 *bows…*; their astragal-ornaments
(55) overlaid with gold, and on 1 of them is the o[ver]lay double.
(56) 10 shekels of gold have been used on them.

(57) 10 spears of bronze with a double overlay of gold
(58) 6 shekels of gold have been used on it.

(59) 1 *makkasu*-ax, of bronze, its handle 2 times overlaid with gold.
(60) 3 shekels of silver have been used on it.

(61) 10 large combs, of (various) stones.

(62) 1 bottle, of stone. 1 helmet-container, of alabaster,(with)
(63) an inlay of genuine lapis lazuli, its rim overlaid with gold
(64) 3 shekels of gold have been used on it.

(65) 1 helmet-container, of *malachite*, overlaid with gold.
(66) 4 [shekels] of gold have been used on it.

(67) [1] […] of *marḫallu*-stone. 1 *kuninnu*-bowl, of *marḫallu*-stone.
(68) […], of *ḫulalu*-stone. 1 *counterweight*, of stone.

(69) [x] [............GI]Š. ESI *qà-ab-la-šu gi$_5$-il-tù-*[*šu?*]
(70) [KÙ.GI GAR *iš-tu e-li-i*]*š ù iš-tu šap-*[*l*]*iš*
(71) [......................] *ù* ZÚ.SÚN KÙ.GI [GAR]

COL. III

(1) [..]*ne*(?)

---

(2) [x] [....................................] *gi$_5$-il-tù-šu-nu*
(3) KÙ.GI [GAR *iš-tu e-li-iš ù*] *iš-tu šap-li-iš*
(4) KÙ.BABBAR GAR.RA 1 *šu-ši* SU KÙ.GI 40 SU KÙ. BABBAR *i-na* ŠÀ-*šu-nu na-di*

---

(5) 1 GIŠ.DUB.DUB *ša* ALAM.MEŠ *ù ša a-bu-ú-bi*
(6) *ša* GIŠ.ESI KÙ.GI GAR 30 SU KÙ.GI *i-na* ŠÀ-*šu na-di*

---

(7) 1 GÍR *ša* EME-*sú ḫa-bal-ki-nu gu-mu-ú-ra-šu*
(8) KÙ.GI *uṣ-ṣu-ru* KIN-*šu ša* ḪÉ.TUR.MEŠ *tam-lu-ú*
(9) NA$_4$.ZA.GÌN KUR SAG-*sú* [NA$_4$]*ḫi-li-ba* 5 SU KÙ.GI *i-na* ŠÀ *na-di*

---

(10) 1 ŠU *ša* MUN *ša* AMAR.MEŠ *ù ša* UR.MA.MEŠ [NA$_4$]*ḫi-li-ba*

---

(11) 1 *pa-aš-‹šu!›-ru* KÙ.BABBAR GAR 1 *šu-ši* SU KÙ.BABBAR *i-na* ŠÀ-*šu na-di*

---

(12) 1 GIŠ.BUGIN.TUR KÙ.BABBAR GAR 40 SU KÙ.BABBAR *i-na* ŠÀ-*šu na-di*

---

(13) 1 *pur-sí-tu$_4$* KÙ.GI 10 SU [*i-na*] KI.LÁ.BI 10 ⸢*pur*⸣-⸢*sí*⸣-⸢*tu$_4$*⸣ ⸢KÙ.GI⸣
(14) 1 *pur-sí-tu$_4$* KÙ.BABBAR 10 SU *i-na* ⸢KI⸣.⸢LÁ⸣.⸢BI⸣
(15) 1 BUGIN.TUR KÙ.BABBAR ›TUR‹ 10 SU *i-na* ⸢KI⸣.LÁ.BI

---

(16) 1 MAR.NINDA KIŠIB.LÁ-*šu* NA$_4$.AN.GUG.ME KIN-*šu* KÙ.G]I] GAR
(17) SAG-*sú me-su-uk-ku$_8$* NA$_4$.AN.GUG.ME 2 SU KÙ.G]I] *i-na* ŠÀ *na-di*

---

(69) [*x*] […], of ebony; its center and [its] rungs,
(70) [*overlaid with gold; abov*]e and below […],
(71) and ivory [mounted on] go[ld…].

COL. III

(1) [………………………………………………]

(2) [*x*] [……………………………………] their rungs
(3) [overlaid with] gold, [above and] below
(4) overlaid with silver. 60 shekels of gold, 40 shekels of silver, have been used on them.

(5) 1 plaque with winged disks and Deluge monster(s),
(6) of ebony, overlaid with gold. 30 shekels of gold are used on it.

(7) 1 dagger, the blade, of iron; its hilt,
(8) of gold, with dESIns; its haft, of…; an inlay
(9) of genuine lapis lazuli; its pommel, of *ḫiliba*-stone.
5 shekels of gold have been used on it.

(10) 1 set of salt (containers, in the form) of bull-calves and lions, of *ḫiliba* stone.

(11) 1 *tr‹a›y*, overlaid with silver. 60 shekels of silver used on it.

(12) 1 small trough, overlaid with silver. 40 shekels of silver were used on it.

(13) 1 bowl, of gold, 10 shekels [in] weight. 10 bowls, of gold;
(14) 1 bowl, of silver, 10 shekels in weight.
(15) 1 small trough of silver, 10 shekels in weight.

(16) 1 bread shovel; its *rettu*, of…-stone; its hilt, overlaid with gold,
(17) its pommel, a *mesukku*-bird, of…-stone. 2 shekels of gold have been used on it.

(18) 1 MAR.NINDA KÙ.GI 5 SU *i-na* KI.LÁ.BI

1 MAR.NINDA KÙ.BABBAR [x S]U [*i-n*]*a* KI.LÁ.BI

---

(19) 1 MAR.NINDA GIŠ.ESI 1 MAR.NINDA ZÚ.SÚN 1 MAR. NINDA GIŠ.TÚG

(20) 1 *a-ú-a-ta-a-mu-lu-u-uš-ḫé ša* ZÚ.SÚN

---

(21) 1 *ša* IZI KÙ.BABBAR 1 *šu-ši* 6 SU *i-na* KI.LÁ.BI

---

22) 1 ^{GIŠ}*al-ta-pí-pu la kat-mu* ^{GIŠ}ESI ALAM KÙ.GI KÙ. BABBAR GAR

(23) 2 SU KÙ.GI 40 SU KÙ.BABBAR *ša i-na* ŠÀ-*šu na-du-ú*

---

(24) 10 TÚG.MEŠ *nam-rù* 10 ŠU TÚG.GÚ *ḫur-ri* 10 ŠU TÚG.GÚ URU

(25) 10 TÚG.BAR.DUL.MEŠ 10 ŠU KUŠ.ŠUḪUB.MEŠ

---

(26) 10 ŠU ^{TÚG}*ta-aḫ-bá-tu*$_4$ 10 ŠU [KU]Š.E.SÍR *be-ta-*[*t*]*u*$_4$

(27) 1 *ša bur-ki* GÙN.A 1 ŠU.ZU.UB *ša* GADA *ša* GÙN.A *kub-bu-ú*

---

(28) 1 TÚG.ŠU.ZU.UB *ša* GÙN.A *ku-ub-bu-ú*

---

(29) 1 $^{\text{NA}_4}$*ta-a-pa-te ša mu-ur-ri* 1 $^{\text{NA}_4}$*ta-a-pa-tu*$_4$

(30) *ša* ZI.⸢KÍL⸣ 1 $^{\text{NA}_4}$*ta-a-pa-tu*$_4$ *ša ia-ru-ut-ti*

(31) 1 $^{\text{NA}_4}$*ta-a-pa-tu*$_4$ *ša* ŠIM.AZ 1 $^{\text{NA}_4}$*ta-a-pa-tu*$_4$

(32) [*š*]*a ka-na-a-at-ki* 1 $^{\text{NA}_4}$*ta-a-pa-te ša sú-ʾ-a-ti*

(33) 1 $^{\text{NA}_4}$*ta-a-pa-tu*$_4$ *ša* ŠIM.BÚL 1 $^{\text{NA}_4}$*ta-a-pa-tu*$_4$

(34) *ša* ⸢*per*$_6$⸣*-ša-an-ti* 1 $^{\text{NA}_4}$*ta-a-pa-te w*[*u*]-⸢*ú*⸣-*ḫi-iz-zi*

(35) 1 $^{\text{NA}_4}$*ta-a-pa-tu*$_4$ *sú-um-mu-ḫu*

---

(36) 10 ^{DUG}*ki-ra-tu*$_4$ *ša* Ì DÙG.GA *ma-lu-ú*

---

(37) 1 ŠU *sà-ri-am* ZABAR 1 *gur-sí-*[*i*]*p* [ZABAR *ša*] LÚ

(38) 1 ŠU *sà-ri-am ša* ⸢KUŠ⸣ 1 *gur-sí-*[*i*]*p* [UD.K]A.BAR

(39) *ša* ^{LÚ}*sà-ar-ku*$_8$*-t*[*i*] 1-*nu-tu*$_4$ *sà-ri-am š*[*a*] KUŠ

(40) *ša* ANŠE.KUR.RA.MEŠ *qu-*[*l*]*a-a-na ša* ZABAR *mu-uḫ-ḫu-ṣú*

(18) 1 bread shovel, of gold, 5 shekels in weight. 1 bread shovel, of silver, [x sh]ekels in weight.

---

(19) 1 bread shovel, of ebony. 1 bread shovel, of ivory. 1 bread shovel, of *boxwood.*

(20) 1 *awatamulušḫe*, of ivory.

---

(21) 1 *brazier*, of silver, 66 shekels in weight.

---

(22) 1 chest, without a cover, of ebony, with a winged disk, overlaid with gold and silver.

(23) It is 2 shekels of gold, 40 shekels of silver, were used on it.

---

(24) 10 bright garments; 10 pairs of shirts Hurrian-style; 10 pairs of *city*-shirts,

(25) 10 robes, 10 pairs of boots.

---

(26) 10 pair of *leggings*; 10 pair of *betatu*-shoes.

---

(27) 1 loincloth, of colored cloth. 1 *šusuppu*-cloth, of linen, trimmed with colored cloth.

---

(28) 1 *šusuppu* cloth trimmed with colored cloth.

---

(29) 1 stone scent container, with myrrh-scented oil. 1 stone scent container

(30) with pure oil. 1 stone scent container with *iaruttu*-oil.

(31) 1 stone scent container with myrtle oil. 1 stone scent container

(32) with *kanatku*-oil. 1 stone scent container with *su'adi* oil.

(33) 1 stone scent container with styrax-oil. 1 stone scent container

(34) with *peršanti*-oil. 1 stone scent container…

(35) 1 stone scent container with a *mixture* (of various oils).

---

(36) 10 *kirru*-pots, full of "sweet oil."

---

(37) 1 cuirass set, of bronze. 1 helmet, of bronze, [f]or a man.

(38) 1 cuirass set, of leather. 1 helmet, [of br]onze,

(39) for the *sarku*-soldiers. 1 cuirass set, of leather,

(40) for horses, set with *ri*[*ng*]*s* of bronze.

(41) 2 *gur-si-ip ša* ZABAR *š*[*a* A]NŠE.KUR.RA.MEŠ

(42) 1 ^{KUŠ}*a-ri-tu*$_4$ *ú-ru-uk-ma-a-an-*[*n*]*a* KÙ.BABBAR GAR
(43) 10 SU KÙ.BABBAR *ša i-na* ŠÀ-*šu na-du-ú*

(44) 9 ^{KUŠ}*a-ri-tu*$_4$ *ša ú-*⌜*ru*⌝*-uk-ma-an-ni-šu-nu* ZABAR

(45) 1 *me-at* BAN.MEŠ *a-pí-sa-a-mu-ú-uš* KÙ.[GI GAR]
(46) *e-ra-at-ti-a-an-*[*ni*]

(47) 1 *li-im* GI.MEŠ *šar-mu* 2 *li-im* GI.M[EŠ...]

(48) 3 *li-im* GI.MEŠ [...]

(49) 10 ^{GI}*ia-ka-a-tu*$_4$ *ša ḫa-b*[*al-ki-ni*]

(50) 10 ^{GI}ia-*ka-a-tu*$_4$ *ša* [UD].KA.BAR

(51) 20 GI.MEŠ *ḫu-ut-ti* ^{GI}[*ia-ka*]*-a-tu*$_4$

(52) 20 GI.MEŠ *pu-uq*[*-da-tu*$_4$.................................]

(53) ⌜20⌝ ⌜GI⌝.⌜MEŠ⌝ ⌜*šu*⌝*-ku-ú-*[*du*]

(54) 20 GI.MEŠ *ša* IZI 20 GI.MEŠ *wa-an-tar*(?)-[*ta*(?)]

(55) 10 GIŠ.TUKUL.DINGIR .MEŠ *ša* [...........]

(56) 10 *za-a-al-le-e-we-na ša* U[D.KA.BAR]

(57) 10 ŠU ^{SI}*ka-za-tu*$_4$ *ša* GU$_4$.MEŠ *ša* UD.[KA.BAR]
(58) ⌜*ù*⌝ 1 BAN *a-na* 2-*šu* KÙ.BABBAR GAR 2 SU KÙ.BABBAR
(59) *ša i-na lìb-bi-šu-nu na-du-ú*

(60) 10 ⌜*šu*⌝-⌜*kùr*⌝-⌜*ru*⌝ [....................]
(61) [..............................]

(41) 2 helmets of bronze, f[or ho]rses.

(42) 1 shield, its *urukmannu* overlaid with silver.
(43) 10 shekels of silver have been used on it.

(44) 9 shields, their *urukmannu*, of bronze.

(45) 100 bows, of the *apisamuš*-type, of go[ld…]
(46) ……

(47) 1000 arrows, sharp. 2000 arrows […]

(48) 3000 arrows […].

(49) 10 *javelins*, with *ir*[*on*] tips.

(50) 10 *javelins*, with [bro]nze tips.

(51) 20 arrows…[…*jav*]elins…

(52) 20 arrows, with "thor[ns"…]

(53) 20 arrows, *šuku*[*du*-type]

(54) 20 arrows (to be shot) flaming. 20 arrows…[…].

(55) 10 maces of […].

(56) 10 *zallewe*-knives, of b[ronze].

(57) 10 "bull-toes," *bound together*, of br[onze],
(58) [and 1 bo]w 2 times overlaid with silver. 2 shekels of silver
(59) have been used on them.

(60) 10 spears […].
(61) [……………………………………………………]

COL. IV

(1) [.......M]EŠ *ša be/bad(?)-du-ú* [........]

(2) [.......] MEŠ *ṣe-eḫ-ḫe-ru-ú-tu*$_4$ *š*[*a* .. ....]
(3) [.............]-*lu-le-e* [.............]

(4) [........... *ša*] LÚ *e-rat-ti-i-in-ni-šu* KÙ.GI [....]
(5) [.............*lu*]-*ú-le-e-ti* 8 SU *i-na* KI.LÁ.BI

(6) 1 GIŠ.DÍLIM *ša e-lam-ma-ki* 1 *ṣu-um-bi-ru* ^{NA_4}*ia-áš-pu*

(7) 1 ŠU *te-la-a-an-nu ša* NA$_4$.GIŠ.NU$_{11}$.GAL
(8) 5 UR.GI$_7$.MEŠ KÙ.GI 5 SU *i-na* KI.LÁ.BI

(9) 5 UR.GI$_7$.MEŠ KÙ.BABBAR 5 SU *i-na* KI.LÁ.BI

(10) 6 *ša-a-ar-ra ša* NA$_4$.GIŠ.NU$_{11}$.GAL

(11) 1 AN.TA KI.TA *ṭe*$_4$*-mu-ú*

(12) 3 TÚG.SIG$_4$.ZA.MEŠ *ra-ab-bu-ú-tu*$_4$

(13) 1 TÚG GÍD.DA *ša* GIŠ.NÁ.MEŠ

(14) 1 TÚG LÚGUD!(PÚ).DA *ša sú-nu-šu* GÙN.A *ša* GIŠ.NÁ.

(15) 1 TÚG.SIG$_4$.ZA SAG 1 TÚG.SIG$_4$.ZA GÌR

(16) 1 *ḫu-li-am* ZABAR *ša* IZI 1 ŠU DAḪ(?).KÍL *ša* GIŠ

(17) 1 *na-ar-ma-ak-tu*$_4$ *qa-du na-ak-ta-mi-šu ša* ZABAR

(18) 1 *du-ú-du* ZABAR 1 *ša me-e šu-ú-li-i* ZABAR

(19) 10 DUG.MEŠ ZABAR 10 *kà-an-nu* ZABAR

(20) 1 ⸢GUNNI⸣ ZABAR 10 *wu-ut-ru* ZABAR

COL. IV

(1) […] of…[…].

(2) [x] small […] o[f…]…[…].
(3) […]

(4) […fo]r a man; its *erattinnu*, of gold […]
(5) […]…8 shekels in weight.

(6) 1 spoon, of *elammakku*-wood. 1 *sumbiru*, of jasper.

(7) 1 set of *telannu*, of alabaster.
(8) 5 dogs, of gold, 5 shekels in weight.

(9) 5 dogs, of silver, 5 shekels in weight.

(10) 6 *sarra*, of alabaster.

(11) 1 (fabric) with *cording* above and below.

(12) 3 large blankets.

(13) 1 long spread, for beds.

(14) 1 short spread, of which the trimmings are many-colored, for a bed.

(15) 1 wrap, for the head. 1 wrap, for the foot.

(16) 1 bronze helmet as a *brazier*. 1 set of…, of wood.

(17) 1 ewer, together with its cover, of bronze.

(18) 1 kettle, of bronze. 1 water-dipper, of bronze.

(19) 10 jars, of bronze, 10 stands, of bronze.

(20) 1 brazier, of bronze. 10 *wutru*, of bronze.

(21) 10 *šu-kúr-rù* ZABAR 10 *sà-ap-lu* ZABAR

(22) 10 N[ÍG.Š]U.LUḪ.ḪA ZABAR 10 *ša* IZI ZABAR

(23) 2 SAG.KUL ZABAR 30 ZA.AG.GI ZABAR

(24) 10 ⸢ŠEN⸣ ZABAR 10 ŠU *an-gu*$_5$*-ri-in-nu* ZABAR

(25) [x] [......] ZABAR 10 *ap-pa-na-a-an-nu* ZABAR

(26) [*x*] IGI/ŠI(?) UD.[KA.BAR] 5 *ša sa-la-ḫi* ZABAR

(27) ⸢1⸣ ⸢*nam*⸣*-si-tu*$_4$ ZABAR 1 *pu-ul-lu-uš-tu*$_4$ ZABAR

(28) [*x*] [......] ZABAR *qa-du ḫu-lu-up-pa-a-ak-ku*$_8$ ZABAR

(29) [x] [...]*-bi-ir-du-u-uš-ḫé* ZABAR 1 *níg-na-ag-gu* ZABAR

(30) [x] [...]*-li-na* ZABAR 1 *kà-an-nu ša* ÚTUL ZABAR

(31) [x] [...]*-u-lu-uš-ḫé* ZABAR 1 *ka-l*[*a*]*-ak-ku*$_8$ ZABAR

(32) 10 [......] UD.[KA.BAR] 6 *gu-un-gu-bu* ZABAR GAR

(33) *ša* 10 *ṣi-m*[*i*]*-it-tu*$_4$ [....] *si-iḫ-pu ša* GIŠ.GIGIR

(34) 4 GIŠ.BÚGIN.TUR *e-lam-ma-ku*$_{13}$ 1 BÚGIN.TUR GIŠ.TÚG

(35) 5 GIŠ.DÍLIM.MEŠ 5 *me gu-un-te me-me-e-tu*$_4$ GAL.M[EŠ]*-tu*$_4$

(36) 5 *li-im gu-un-te me-e-me-tu*$_4$ TUR.M[EŠ] ⸢*ša*⸣ [*i*]*-ši-tu*$_4$

(37) 10 NÍG.GÍD.DA GIGIR 10 ^{NÍG}*bu-bu-*[*t*]*u*$_4$ GIGIR

(38) [x] [*ṣ*]*i-mi-it-tu*$_4$ [*ša*]GIGIR [......] KI.KAL.GIGIR

(39) *qa-du* [......]*-šu-nu* 12 *ni-i-ru* [*ša*] GIGIR

(40) 10 *ṣi-mi-it-tu*$_4$ [.........]*-ar-ma-ak*(*?*)^{MEŠ} GIGIR

(21)	10	"spears," of bronze. 10 bowls, of bronze.
(22)	10	washbasins, of bronze. 10 braziers, of bronze.
(23)	2	bolts, of bronze. 30 *sakku*, of bronze.
(24)	10	kettles, of bronze. 10 sets of *angurinu*, of bronze.
(25)	[*x*]	[...], of bronze. 10 *appananu*, of bronze.
(26)	[*x*]	..., of bronze. 5 sprinklers, of bronze.
(27)	1	washing-bowl, of bronze. 1 *pulluštu*, of bronze.
(28)	[x]	[...]...-vessels, of bronze, along with a brazier, of bronze.
(29)	[*x*]	[...]...-vessels, of bronze. 1 censer, of bronze.
(30)	[*x*]	[...]...-vessels, of bronze. 1 stand for a pot, of bronze.
(31)		[...]...-vessels, of bronze. 1 chest, of bronze.
(32)	10	[...], of bronze. 6 *gungubu*, overlaid with bronze.
(33)		For 10 teams: [...] coverings of a chariot.
(34)	4	small troughs of *elammakku*-wood, 1 small trough of *boxwood.*
(35)	5	spoons. 500 large *gunte memetu.*
(36)	5000	small *gunte memetu* of the [st]oreroom
(37)	10	*chariot-poles.* 10 chariot-frames.
(38)	[*x*]	[y]okes [for a ch]ariot,...the chariot-platform,
(39)		along with their [...]. 12 yokes [for] a chariot.
(40)	10	teams [......] of a chariot.

(41) 10 *ṣi-mi-it-tu*$_4$ $_{[.........]}$ MEŠ *kiš-ka-nu-u*

---

(42) 4 *me-at* NÍG(?) [......]

---

(43) *an-nu-ti* NÍG.BA.MEŠ MUNUS.UŠ.MEŠ *gáb-bá-šu-nu-ma*
(44) *mi-im-ma šum-šú* ^{I}*Tù-uš-rat-ta* LUGAL *Mi-i-ta-a-an-ni*
(45) *a-na* ^{I}*Ni-im-mu-re-ia* LUGAL *Mi-iṣ-ri-i* ŠEŠ-*šu*
(46) *ḫa-ta-ni-i-šu it-ta-din un-d*[*u*$_4$] $^{\mathrm{DUMU.MU[NUS]}}$[*Ta*]*-a-du*$_4$*-Ḫ*[*é*]*-bá*
(47) DUMU.MUNUS-*sú a-na* KUR *Mi-iṣ-ri-i* [*a-n*]*a* ^{I}*N*[*i-i*]*m-mu-re-ia*
(48) *a-na* DAM-*ut-ti id-di-*⸢*nu*⸣-[*ú*]*-ši*
(49) *i-na u*$_4$*-mi-šu it-ta-din-*⸢*šu*⸣*-nu*

---

(41) 10 teams…[…] of *kiškanu*-wood.

(42) 400 [(…)]…[…].

(43–49) It is all of these wedding-gifts, of every sort, that Tushratta, the king of Mittani, gave to Nimmureya, the king of Egypt, his brother and his son-in-law. He gave them at the same time that he gave Tadu-Kheba, his daughter, to Egypt and to Nimmureya for marriage.

EA 23

TRANSCRIPTION

Obv. 01) [*a-n*]*a* ^{I}*Ni-im-mu-re-ia šàr* KUR *Mi-iṣ-ri-*⸢*i*⸣
02) ŠEŠ-*ia ḫa-ta-ni-ia ša a-ra-ʾa-a-mu*
03) *ù ša i-ra-ʾa-a-ma-an-ni qí-bí-ma*
04) *um-ma* ^{I}*Tù-uš-rat-ta šàr Mi-i-ta-an-ni*
05) *ša i-ra ʾa-a-mu-ka e-mu-ka-ma*
06) *a-na ia-ši šul-mu a-na ka-a-ša lu-ú šul-mu*
07) *a-na* É-*ka a-na* ^{MUNUS}*Ta-a-du*$_{4}$*-Ḫé-bá* DUMU.MUNUS-*ia*
08) *a-na* DAM-*ka ša ta-ra-ʾa-a-mu lu-ú šul-mu*
09) *a-na* DAM.MEŠ-*ka a-na* DUMU.MEŠ-*ka a-na* LÚ.MEŠ GAL-*ka*
10) *a-na* GIŠ.GIGIR.MEŠ-*ka a-na* ANŠE.KUR.RA.MEŠ-*ka*
11) *a-na* ÉRIN.MEŠ-*ka a-na* KUR-*ka ù a-na*
12) *mim-mu-ka dan-níš dan-níš dan-níš lu-ú šul-mu*

---

13) *um-ma* ^{d}INANNA *ša* URU *Ni-i-na-a* NIN.KUR.KUR
14) *gáb-bi-i-ši-na-ma a-na* KUR *Mi-iṣ-ri-i*
15) *i-na* KUR *ša a-ra-ʾa-a-mu lu-ul-lik-ma-mì*
16) *lu-us-sà-ḫé-er-mì a-nu-um-ma i-na-an-na*
17) *ul-te-e-bíl-ma it-tal-ka*

---

18) ⸢*a*⸣*-nu-um-ma i-na tir-ṣi a-bi-ia-ma*
19) ⸢^{d}⸣?⸢INANNA⸣? BAD-*tu*$_{4}$ *i-na* KUR *ša-a-ši it-tal-ka*
Lo.ed. 20) ⸢*ù*⸣ *ki-i-me-e i-na pa-na-a-nu-um-*⸢*ma*⸣
21) ⸢*it*⸣*-ta-šab-ma uk-te-eb-bi-du-ši*
Rev. 22) [*ù*] ⸢*i*⸣-⸢*na*⸣*-an-*⸢*na*⸣ ŠEŠ-*ia* ⸢*a*⸣-⸢*na*⸣ 10-⸢*šu*⸣
23) UGU *ša pa-na-*⸢*a*⸣*-nu* ⸢*li*⸣*-kè-eb-bi-is-si*
24) ŠEŠ-*ia li-kè-eb-bi-is-sú i-na ḫa-de-e*
25) *li-mèš-šèr-šu-ma li-tù-u-ra*

EA 23

TRANSLATION

(1–3) Speak [t]o Nimmureya, king of the land of Egypt, my brother, my son-in-law, whom I love and who loves me;

(4–12) Thus (speaks) Tušratta, king of Mitanni, who loves you, your father-in-law: For me all is well, for you may it be well. For your house, for Tadu-Ḫeba, my daughter, for your wife whom you love, may it be well. For your wives, for your sons, for your senior officials, for your chariots, for your horses, for your troops, for your country and for whatever is yours, may it be very, very well.

(13–17) Thus (spoke) Šauška of the city of Nineveh, mistress of all lands: "To the land of Egypt, to the country which I love, I verily would go and then I would verily return." Now I have sent (her), she has gone forth.

(18–25) Now, it was in the time of my father that Šauška(!) the lady went forth to that land, and just as formerly she resided there and they honored her, so now, as for my brother, may he honor her ten times more than before. As for my brother, may he honor her; in joy may he release her and may she return.

26) ^{d}INANNA NIN *ša-me-e* ŠEŠ-*ia ù ia-ši*
27) *li-iṣ-ṣur-an-na-ši* 1 *me li-im* MU.MEŠ
28) *ù ḫé-du-ta ra-bi-ta* NIN-*ni*$_5$
29) *a-na ki-la-*⸢*a*⸣*-al-li-ni li-id-din-an-*⸢*na*⸣*-*⸢*ši*⸣*-ma*
30) *ù ki-i ṭá-a-bi i ni-pu-uš*

---

31) ^{d}INANNA *a-na ia-ši-ma-a i-*⸢*li*⸣
32) *ù a-na* ⸢ŠEŠ-*ia la-a* ⸢*il*⸣*-šu*

[*ḥꜣ.*]*t-sp* 36 4 *ꜣbd* [...]1 *ỉw.tw m pꜣ* ⸢*b*⸣*ẖn rsy pr-ḥʿ*.... ....

(26–30) May Šauška, the mistress of heaven, protect us, my brother and me, for a hundred thousand years; and may our mistress grant us, to both of us, great joy and may we act as friends.

(31–32) Is Shaushka my deity and not my brother's deity?

[Regn]al year 36, 4th month, [day] 1; One (the king) was in the southern villa of the house of rejoicing....................

EA 24

TRANSCRIPTION (by G. Wilhelm)

§1

Obv.

I 1) [*a-na* ^{I}*Ni-im-*]*m*[*u*]*-u-ri-*[*ia*....................................]

2) [*ḫa-ta-ni-i*]*a* [..]

3) [..]

4) [..*a-na i*]*a-ši šul-*[*m*]*u*

5) [.................] *š*[*u*]*l-m*[*u a-na ḫa*]*-ta-n*[*i-i*]*a a-na* DAM.MEŠ[*-k*]*a*

6) [...*-k*]*a* [*a-na*] LÚ.MEŠ GAL.MEŠ-[*k*]*a* [*a-na*] ANŠE.KUR.RA.MEŠ-*ka a-na* GIŠ.GIGIR.MEŠ-*ka*

7) [*a-na* ÉRIN.MEŠ-*k*]*a a-na* KUR *-ka ù a-na* [*mim*]*-mu-ka dan-níš lu-ú šul-mu*

§2

8) [a-ti-i-ni-i]-⸢in⸣ ⸢ma-a-an-na-al⸣-[la-m]a-an at-⸢ta-a⸣-ar-ti-íw-wa-aš^{MEŠ}

9) [šu$^{?}$-u$^{?}$-we$^{?}$-na$^{?}$-m]a-⸢a-an⸣ še-⸢e-ni-íw-wu-ú-e⸣[-na-a-a]n ta-a-du-⸢ka$^{!}$⸣-a-ru-ši-il-la-a-an

10) [..(.)] šu-ú-⸢al⸣-la-ma-an ⸢ka⸣[-..]*x*-ša KUR ma-a-áš-ri-a-an-né-e-en

11) [KUR u-u-mi-i-in]-n[é-e]-en K[UR] ⸢ḫa⸣-a[d-d]u-u-ḫé-[m]a-a-an ḫur-wu-u-ḫé-⸢né⸣-e-we-na$^{!}$

12) [KUR u-u-mi-i-in-né-e-we-na] ḫé$^{?}$-ri-.-(.-)[i]n ⸢ma⸣-a-an-ni

13) [...............]-*⸢an⸣ ⸢te-a$^{?}$-a$^{?}$-al⸣*(over erasure)-la-a-an i-nu-‹ú-›me-e-ni-i-in

14) [.......KUR ḫa-ad-d]u-u-⸢ḫé⸣-ma-⸢a⸣-an KUR ḫur-ru-u-ḫé-né-e-wa

15) [ew-re-en$^{?}$-né-e-wa.....] ma-*x* du-ru-bi-i-in-ni

EA 24

TRANSLATION (by G. Wilhelm)

§ 1

Obv.

(**I**, 1–7) [Say to Nim]murey[a, the king of Egypt, my brother, my son-in-law], wh[om I love (and) who loves me: Thus (speaks) Tu]šra[tt]a, the ki[ng of the land of Mittani, your father-in-law, who loves you, your brother]. All goes well with me. [May all] go we[ll with you]. For m[y son-in-law, your wives, [your children, your] senior officials, your [hor]ses, your chariotry, yo[ur troops], your land and your [pos]ssessions, may all be very well.

§ 2

(8–15) Truly, our forefathers, [those of mine(?) an]d those of my brother, were in friendly relations. [...] all...from(?) the land of Egypt. The Hittites are the *ḫeri*(?) of the Ḫurrian [land....]...they are numerous(?). Like [...] The Ḫittite is(!?) the enemy of the Ḫurrian [king].

§3

16) [..........] a-ti-i-ni-i-i[n] ma-a-an-ni-i-im-ma-ma-an
17) [..........]-an du-ru-bi-i-in-nu-uk-ku
18) [..........] še-e-ni-íw-we an-za-a-an-nu-u-ḫ̮u-ši tiš-ša-an
19) [wa-aḫ̮-ru-uš-til-la-a-an t]a-a-⸢du⸣-ka-a-r[i]-iš KUR ḫ̮ur-⸢wu-u⸣-ḫ̮é-e-e[n]
20) [KUR u-u-mi-i-ni KUR ma-a-áš-ri-a-a-ni]-ma-a-an KUR u-u-mi-i-né-e-em-ma-m[a]-an
21) [.........]u$^{?}$-k[u$^{?}$]-la-an [bi]-id-du-ka-a-ra-a-l[a-a]n
22) [..........-l]a$^{?}$-an šu-e-né-e-[ta]n$^{?}$
23) [.............]ša-a-a[t-t]i iš-ta-ni-íw-w[a-š]a
24) [.........-a]n ^{d}Te-e-eš-šu-pa-a[š]
25) [^{d}A-ma-a-nu-(?).........u]l-lu-ú-un-za-a-til-la-⟨a-⟩a[n$^{?}$]
26) [.........] tiš-⸢ša⸣-an tiš-š[a-an]
27) [..........................]*x* *x*-at$^{?}$-[..............] Lines 28–40 are completely destroyed.

---

§4

41) [.......]-⸢a-an⸣ a[r$^{?}$-]*x*[
42) [....(.)]-ta-la-an ú-ru-u[k$^{?}$-ku$^{?}$
43) [.......]-un-na-a-an ⸢šu-ra⸣-a-[m$^{?}$-
44) [....(.)]*x* ta-a-na-aš-ta-a-ú [....(.)]- ⸢re-e⸣-ta-un-na-a-a[n]
45) x-⸢en⸣$^{?}$-⸢na⸣$^{?}$-a-an du-um-ni/né-en a-[_ _ (_)-a]n gu-ru-u-u-[ša$^{?}$]
46) *x*-⸢bi$^{?}$⸣-[i$^{?}$-r]i-en-na-a-an a-ru-u-u-ša

---

§ 3

16–20) [...] Thus it is. [...]..(It) is not as an enemy. [...] my brother has given(?)...[And we want to be good to one another] (and) to love one another.

(21–27) The Ḫurrian [land] and [the Egyptian] land [...]...Teshob and Amon(?)...and]...we/us [...] very, very [...]...[...].

§ 4

(41–46) [...]...[......]they do [not?] exist [...]...[......] I am doing, and I will [...] it. [...]...four..[...]...and he has given....

§ 5

47) [.....(.)-i]n g[u?-ru? a]t-[ta-í]w-wu-ú-e mŠu-ut-tar-na-a-we ša-a-la
48) [....(.)] -⸢a⸣-ni [...]-mu-u-ša-ma-a-an am-ma-ti-íw-wu-⸢ú⸣-e-né-tan
49) [(.)]*x*[......-m]a-a-an ši-ni še-e-ni-íw-we
50) [.........(.)-ni]-i-in šu-⸢ú⸣-ta-ma-an pa-aš-šu-ši
51) [......]-⸢a-an⸣ ša-a-la-pa-an ⸢aš⸣?-ti-íw-wu-ú-un-na a-ri
52) [.....]-⸢ta?-ma?⸣-an mAš-šu-⸢te-mi⸣-wa u-i̯a ḫi-il-lu-ši-ik-kat-ta-a-an
53) [.....]-un IMa-né-e-ta pa-[aš]-⸢ši⸣-i-it-ḫi̯-wu-ú-ta
54) [.....š]e-e-ni-íw-wu-ú-e-na-a-še-e-e[n]? ši-i-!i-e-e
55) [.....]-⸢še⸣?-e ni-i-ru-ša-e a-la-še-[e?-me?]-⸢e⸣?-ni-i-in
56) [.....]**x*-⸢ša⸣ ma*-a-na-at-ta-a-an šu-e-ni [tiš-š]a-an tiš-ša-an
57) [.......]*x*-*x*-ta šu-e-e-en an-⸢ti⸣
58) [...-]⸢ma-a-an⸣ [n]i-i-ru-ša-e ta-a-nu-ša-a-ú

§ 6

59) [..-a]n šu-ug-g[e?-..] ⸢u⸣-ul-le-en IMa-né-en pa-⸢aš-ši⸣-i-it-ḫi̯-ip
60) [ke-ba-nu]⸢šu-a-an⸣ ḫa-a-aš-[ra] pa-a-ḫi̯-i-i-wa wa-aḫ̯-⸢ru-ša⸣ né-eš-ši
61) [....]-⸢e?-ta⸣ g[e]-u-šu-a-an ḫa-a-aš-ra pa-a-ḫi̯-i-ta še-e-ni-íw-wu-ú-e
62) [aš-ti-i-in-na] K[UR]⸢Mi⸣-zi-ir-re-e-we KUR u-u-mi-i-in-né-e-we al-la-i
63) *x* [..(.)-e]n-⸢na-a-an⸣ šu-ú-an-na-ma-an
64) [...(.)-we?-]néš? né-eš-ši-iš ša-⸢ad⸣-du-u-ša

§ 5

(47–58) ...again, my father Šuttarna's daughter [......]by contrast, he did [ten times] for my grandfather. [...]...[...]two...my brother [...] When he sent to me (with the words:) "Tado-Ḫeba,] your daughter, give to me as wife." [...] I did not say "No!" to Aššutemi, and [...] to Mane, your envoy, [......] of the (pl.)...my brother..., which [...] graciously [...] whether(?) [...]...I/me everything [ve]ry, very [...] all that [...] I did graciously.

§ 6

(59–64) [...] Mane, your envoy, [...] and you have sent a gift of in the form of fine oil for her head [...] and you have anointed her head with oil; my brother's [wife] is? the Lady of the land of Egypt, and...all [...] has he taken [...].

§7

65) [....] ḫ[é$^{?}$]-⸢en-né-e-en⸣ še-⸢e⸣-ni-íw-we pa-aš-šu-ši ú-⸢a⸣-du-ra-a-an-ni-ma-a-an
66) [....](-) ⸢še-el-li⸣-íw-we-en-na-a-an šu-ú-an-⸢na⸣-ma-an
67) [..]*x*-⸢e⸣ še-e-ni-íw-wu-uš šu-u-u-ša tiš-⸢ša⸣-an tiš-ša-an
68) [...ma-a-na š]u-e-ni ⸢ KUR u-u⸣-mi-i-ni-íw-we šu-ú-⸢an-na⸣-ma-an tiš-[š]a-an tiš-ša-an
69) [....] i-ša-aš-ša-a-an ma-a-na šu-e-ni šu-e an-ti
70) [.....] ni-i-ru-ša-e tiš-ša-an tiš-ša-an (..)[ta]-a-⸢nu⸣-u-⸢ša⸣-a-ú
71) [....]-ti-íw-wu-ra ta-a-ta-uš-še-na-a-šu-ra ^{I}Ma-né-e-⸢el⸣-la-ma-an
72) ⸢pa-aš-ši-i-it-ḫi⸣-wu-uš wu-ru-u-ša-a-al-la-a-an
73) ma-⸢a⸣-na šu-e-ni ⸢ti⸣-we-e-e-na ta-⸢a-nu⸣-ša-⸢a⸣-uš-še-na

§8

74) ⸢i⸣-n[u-ú]-ut-ta-a-ni-i-in [ḫ]é-en-ni še-e-ni-íw-wu-uš ta-a-ti-a
75) [i-n]u-⸢ú⸣-me-e-ni-i-in [ḫ]é-en-ni še-e-ni-íw-we i-ša-aš ta-a-ta-ú
76) ⸢a-nam⸣-mi-til-la-a-an $^{⸢d⸣}$[T]e-e-eš-šu-pa-aš ^{d}Ša-uš-kaš ^{d}A-ma-a-nu-ú-ti-la-an
77) ^{d}[Š]i-⸢mi⸣-i-ge-né-⸢e⸣-[t]i-la-an ^{d}E-a-a-šar-ri-né-e-ti-la-an ma-a[n-š]u-u-til-la-a-an
78) DIN[GIR.ME]Š ⸢e⸣-e-⸢en-na⸣-[š]u-uš ti-ši-a-ša-an tiš-ša-an tiš-ša-an ta-⸢a⸣-ta-aš-ti-te-en
79) g[e]-⸢ra-aš⸣-še-n[a-ša-til-l]a-a-an ša-wa-al-la-ša bi-su-un-né-en tiš-ša-an tiš-ša-an
80) b[i]-su-u[š]-⸢ta-iš⸣ ú-ú-ra-ú-ša-a-aš-še-na-a-ma-a-an ti-we-e-e^{MEŠ}
81) wa-aḫ-r[u]-un-né-en iš-ta-ni-íw-wa-ša ag-gu-uš a-gu-ú-a
82) e-ti-i-⸢i⸣-ta ta-a-na-aš-ti-en ni-i-ru-ša-e tiš-ša-an

§ 7

(65–73) […] now my brother has sent. And the bride price […] and my entire […] my brother us(?) very, very […] and I did all that totally […] very, very graciously with my […] (and) with those whom I love. Mane, your envoy, has seen everything, the things that I have done.

§ 8

(74–82) As now my brother loves me, as now I love my brother, so may Teššop, Šauška, Amanu, Šimīge, Eâ-šarri and all the gods love us in their hearts very, very much so that [we] for long years
joyfully. And the things that we desire for ourselves, may we graciously do generously, one for the other, between us.

§ 9

83) ^{I}Ge-l[i]-⸢i⸣-aš-ša-a-an pa-aš-ši-i-it-ḫi-‹íw-›wu-uš ti-wi an-ti gu-lu-u-u-ša
84) ma-a-an-⸢na⸣-a-an ḫi-il-li še-e-na-wu-ša-an ^{I}Ni-im-mu-u-ri-i-aš
85) KUR Mi-zi-ir-re-e-we-né-eš éw-ri-iš ta-še ap-li ta-a-a-nu-u-ša
86) URU I-u-be(nu$^{!?}$)-né URU Ši-mi-i-ge-né-e-we-né-e-ma-a-an ú-nu-u-u-ša
87) ^{d}Ši-mi-i-ge-né-e-wa-ma-a-an e-e-ni-i-wa at-ta-⸢i-i⸣-wa a-ku-u-ša
88) at-ta-a-ar-ti-i-we-na-a-ma-a-an šu-ú-al-la-ma-an ta-⸢še⸣-e-e-na^{MEŠ}
89) tiš-ša-an tiš-⸢ša-an⸣ ge-lu-u-šu-a za-ar-ra-ma-a-an še-e-na-a-ab-be
90) KUR u-u-mi-i-ni ši-u-u-ši a-ti-i-ni-i-in ta-še-e-en id-du-u-uš-ta
91) še-e-na-pa-an e-ti-i-e-e-em-ma-ma-an ta-še-e-né-e-wa wu-ri-i-ta
92) ši-ia ir-ka-a-mu-u-ša-ma-a-an tiš-ša-an ^{I}Ge-li-i-aš ta-še-e-né-e-we
93) id-du-um-mi ma-a-na-an ḫi-il-li nu-be-e-né-na-an ḫa-a-ar-re-en
94) na-a-zu-u-ša a-ti-i-ni-‹i›-in ^{d}Ši-mi-i-ge-né-e-we-⸢né-e⸣-em-ma-ma-an
95) am-mu-u-u-ša ša-pu-ú-ḫa-a-at-⸣ta⸣-a-an tiš-ša-an ⸢a-ti⸣i-ni-i-in
96) ta-a-an-ki-⸢i⸣-[i]n ka-du-u-ša ⸢i⸣-i-al-la-a-ni-i-in
97) še-e-ni-í[w-wu]-ú-e-né-e-we KUR u-u-[m]i-i-ni-i-we e-ru-uš-ki-i-in-na
98) e-ti-i-⸢i⸣-[e]-⸢e⸣ ta-a-na-aš-še-na i-i-al-le-e-ni-i-in
99) še-e-ni-íw-[wu-u]š ta-še-e-né-e-wa e-ti-⸢i⸣-ta ti-we-e-na^{MEŠ}
100) e-ru-u-u[š]-⸢ki⸣-[n]a ta-a-nu-u-ša-a-aš-še-na ⸢an⸣-til-l[a]-⸢a⸣-⸢a-⸣an
101) ^{d}Ši-mi-i-g[e-néš] ^{d}A-ma-a-nu-ú-la-an ^{d}E-a-a-šar-ri-né-e-el-la-a-an
102) še-e-ni-íw-wu-[ú]-⸢a⸣ KUR u-u-mi-i-ni-i-wa-al-la-a-an e-ti-i-ta ḫu-tan-na
103) be-en-ti-tén$^{!}$ ⸢*x*⸣-⸢*x*(-*x*)⸣-[i]r$^{?}$-ša-a-al-la-a-an še-ḫur-na-a-al-la-a-an
104) i-i-al-la-⸢a-ni-i-in še⸣-e-ni-íw-⸢wu⸣-uš ta-še-e-né-e-wa e-ti-i-ta
105) ti-we-e-na^{M}[^{EŠ}] t[a]-a-⸢nu⸣-u-ša-a-aš-še-na ^{d}Ši-mi-i-ge-né-e-wa e-ni-i-wa
106) at-ta-i-i-⸢wa e⸣-ti-⸢i⸣-ta an-til-la-⸢a-an⸣ ^{d}Ši -mi-i-ge-néš a-re-e-ta
107) še-e-ni-íw-wu-⸢ú⸣-a še-e-ni-⸢íw⸣-[w]u-ú-u[l]-la-a-an ti-ša-a-an-na
108) ú-ú-ri-a-a-aš-še-na ti-⸢we⸣-e-na^{MEŠ} ⸢šu⸣-ú-al-la-ma-an^{MEŠ}
109) ta-a-ni-il-le-⸢e⸣-ta-a-al-la-a-an a-ti-i-ni-i-in ma-a-an-na-al-la-ma-an

§ 9

(83–107) And Keliya, my enjoy, has spoken the following word, and he had spoken as follows: "Your brother, Nimmureya, the lord of Egypt has made an *abli* gift and to Ionu(?), the city of Šimīge, he had it come. And to Šimīge, his god, his father, has he conducted (it). And he has joyfully carried out all the *gifts* of his forefathers." And the land of your brother was amazed at all the booty objects(?). So the *gift* was sent and your brother himself was delighted(?) in view of the gifts. And Keliya had observed its departure and he said as follows: "He has from/by means of ten thousand *ḫari* ... Thus has he caused it to reach the city of Šimīge, and I...very much." Thus has he written (literally spoken) his deed. As for the (things which) he is making for himself from the land of my brother as *eroški*, i.e. the *eroški* which my brother has made concerning his gifts, may Šimīge, Amon and Eâ-šarri send gloriously, in [...] and in life. The things which my brother has made as gifts for Šimīge his god, his father, which Šimīge will give to my brother, and everything that my brother from the heart desires, will he tackle. So may it be (lit.: Thus is it).

§10

110) a-nu-ú-a-⌜ma-a⌝-an ⌜ti-we-e⌝-né-⌜e⌝-wa še-e-ni-íw-we ḫi-su-ú-ḫu-⌜lu-ú-en⌝

111) ⌜i-ia$^{?}$-al-le-e⌝-[ni-i-in] ⌜še-e⌝-ni-⌜íw-wu⌝-ú-e-na pa-aš-ši-i-⌜it⌝-ḫi^{M}[^{EŠ}]

112) *x*[-(*x*-)]*x*-a-ú[..š]a-ú ⌜a⌝-ni-il-l[a-a-a]n be-kán kàr-ḫu-ša-[a$^{??}$]-⌜ú⌝$^{??}$

113) [a$^{?}$-ni]-i-la-⌜an⌝ ⌜še-e⌝-ni-íw-wu-ú-u[l]-l[a-a]-an ḫa-ši-en WA-ḫa-*x*-[..]

114) [^{I}G]e-li-i-⌜an⌝ [pa-a]š-⌜ši⌝-i-it-ḫi-íw-⌜we $^{I⌝}$M[a-né]-en-na-a-an pa-aš-ši-i-it-⌜ḫi⌝-ip

115) [na-a]k-ku-ša-a-ú ú-ú-na-a-al-la-a-an še-e-ni-íw-wu-ta

Obv. II

1) [....(..)] (traces)

2) [....(..)] (traces)

3) [...-]*x x x*[*x*] ⌜iš⌝$^{?}$ ⌜*x x x x x x x x x x x*⌝ [. (.)]

4) *x*[..]*x*-⌜u-ša-a-al-la-a-⌜an še-e-ni⌝-íw-wu-uš šu-ra-a-ma-a-al⌝-l[a-a-a]n

5) ⌜tiš-ša-an be-en-ta i-ia-at-ta-ma-an ta-a-nu-ši-ik$^{!}$-kat-ta-a-an⌝

6) še-e-ni-íw-⌜wu⌝-ú-⌜e-né⌝-e-wa aš-⌜ti-i-i-wa in-na-ma-a-ni-i⌝-[in]

7) ⌜^{I}⌝Ge-li-i-an ^{I}Ma-né-en-na-a-an ⌜ḫa-šu-u-ša-ú⌝ ⌜it-ta⌝-aš-[š]a

8) ma-az-za-ḫa-a-at-ta-a-an ⌜ḫa-a-rat-ta-ma-an še-e-ni-íw-wu-ú-e-né-e-wa⌝-[a$^{?}$-tan$^{?}$]

9) aš-ti-i-i-we ni-ḫa-a-ri-i-ta ⌜ta-a-kat$^{?}$ ú-ru⌝-u-muš-⌜te-e-wa-a-tan⌝

10) tiš-ša-an tiš-ša-an ⌜še-e-ni⌝-íw-⌜wu-ú-e-né-e-en-nu-uḫ⌝-ḫa ti-⌜ša-a-an-nu-uḫ⌝-ḫa

11) u-u-lu-u-⌜ḫé⌝-e-wa-a-ti-la-an zu-⌜kán⌝ e-⌜e-ši-íw-wa-a⌝-aš-tan a-a-wa-⌜ad-du-tan⌝

§11

12) še-e-ni-⌜íw⌝-wu-ta-a-ma-a-an ti-wi šu-uk-ku kul-le še-e-ni-íw-wu-⌜uš-ša⌝-[a-a]n

§ 10

110–114) So may my brother not distress himself about that matter. The envoys of my brother which I...and..., those have I(?) in no way(?) delayed(?), and may my brother hear them, [he may(?)...; Keliya, my envoy, and Mane, your envoy, have I allowed to depart, and they are coming to my brother.

II, 1–11) [...] and my brother has...them...and very quickly may they turn back. As for what I have not (yet) done for the wife of my brother, when I heard Keliya and Mane (by word of mouth), when they left, I was/did...and... to the dowry of my brother's wife I am ...and I will be very, very occupied(??) in a manner according to my brother's heart, and...we might...from our...soil(?).

§ 11

(12) And I want to say something else to my brother and may my brother

13) ḫa-ši-en a-ti-i-⸢ni-i-in⸣ ^{m}⸢Ma-né⸣-e-na-⸢an še⸣-e-ni-íw-⸢wu-ú⸣-[e]
14) pa-aš-ši-⸢i-it-ḫi⸣ ú-ú-na ⸢in-na⸣-ma-a-ni-i-⸢in ni-ḫa⸣-a-ri a-k[u$^{?}$]-⸢-u-u-li$^{?}$⸣
15) ú-a-du-ra-a-an-ni-ma-a-an še-e-ni-íw-wu-uš ma-⸢ka⸣-a-an-ni-íw-wu-⸢ú$^{?}$⸣-[un$^{?}$-na]$^{?}$
16) ge-pa-a-nu-u-ša-a-aš-še in-na-ma-a-ni-i-in ^{I}Ma-né-eš a-⸢ru$^{!??}$-u$^{?}$⸣-*x*-[ša$^{?}$-an$^{?}$]
17) pu-uk-lu-ša-a-un-na-a-an ^{KUR} u-u-mi-i-ni-íw-we ⸢šu-ú⸣-an-⸢na-ma-an⸣ [^{ME}]^{Š}
18) wi-i-ra-tar-ti-íw-we-la-an tup-pa-aš-še-na tub-be ḫi-⸢il-lu⸣-ši-⸢i-it⸣-[ta]-⸢a⸣-[a]n
19) ^{I}ma-né-e-ta i-i-al-le-e-ni-i-in še-e-ni-íw-wu-⸢uš du-be⸣-[e$^{?}$-na$^{?MEŠ?}$]
20) šu-ú-al-la-ma-an ge-pa-a-⸢nu⸣-u-š[a]-⸢a⸣-aš-še-na i-i-al-le-⸢e-ni⸣-[i-in]
21) tup-pa-ku-u-uš-ḫé-na^{MEŠ} šu-ú-al-la-ma-an ⸢še-e-ni⸣-[íw-wu-...(..)]
22) [g]e-pa-a-nu-u-ša-a-aš-še-na ḫu-up-⸢pu-ta⸣-aš-ša-⸢a-al-la-a-an⸣ [.....(.)]
23) [.]-šu-u-u-li-u-u-mu ⸢ḫu-up-lu-lu-uš-te-la-an šu-ú⸣-a[l-la-ma-an]
24) *x*[..](-)na-a-ku-lu-uš-te-la-an be-te-eš-te-el-la-a-an za-a-⸢ar⸣$^{??}$-[...(.)]

§12

25) [ta$^{?}$-a$^{?}$-n]u-u-ša-a-al-la-a-an tiš-ša-an ⸢ka-dup⸣$^{?}$-pu-ú-⸢uš-šu⸣-uḫ-ḫa *x*[..]
26) [...]*x* ḫi-il-lu-ši-i-it-ta-a-an KUR u-u-mi-⸢i⸣-ni-íw-w[u-uš]
27) [..(.)]*x*-e-ta-at-ta-ma-an wi-i-ra-ta-ar-ti-íw-wu-u[š$^{?}$]
28) *x*[...–e]-⸢ta-at⸣-ta-ma-an a-a-el-le-e-ni-i-in ⸢an⸣$^{?}$-[.(.)]
29) ⸢tup-pa-ku-u⸣-[u]š-⸢ḫé-na⸣^{MEŠ} du-be-na-a-ma-a-an šu-⸢ú⸣-[a]l-la-ma-an du-u-pu-š[i$^{?}$-na$^{??}$]
30) *x x* [...]*x*-e-la-an ⸢šu-ú-al-la-ma-an⸣ *x x x x*-ú-an-na-a-an [(..)]
31) [.....(.)]*x* KUR u-u-mi-i-ni-íw-⸢wu-ú-a wi-i-ra⸣-tar-ti-íw-wu-⸢ú⸣$^{?}$-[a$^{?}$]
32) [........(.)]-⸢u-ša-ú⸣ ⸢i-nu-ú⸣-u[l]$^{?}$-l[e$^{?}$-e-ni-i-in]$^{?}$
33) [........]*x x* ⸢tiš-ša⸣-a[n....(..)]

(13–24) heed it. Thus, (now) Mane, my brother's envoy is coming. When a dowry is brought (?)—the bride price which my brother [as] my gift has sent, when Mane [handed it](?) over, I will assembled my entire land. and my foreign guests, as many as there are, were there; and I said to Mane: "All the vessels(?), which my brother has sent, all of the tablet containers(?) which my brother has brought, they are undamaged(?) [The seal/sealed containers(??)] should all be broken, they should be inventoried(??), the gifts ("booty items") (??) should be spread out."

§ 12

And he di[d] very much in the manner mentioned . [......] and I have said: "My land will...me, my (foreign) honored guests were...me. If all th[ese(?)] [...]..Tablet containers(?) and all vessels(?)...have I all...for my land (and) for my (foreign) honored guest...As th[ey...ve[ry...].

§13

34) [....(.)] *x x x x* (*x x*) [*x* š]a-⌜un⌝$^{?}$ *x x* ⌜un⌝ ⌜i⌝ [.....]
35) [....(.)]*x*-⌜ka⌝-*x*[..(.)]-u$^{?}$-ša *x*[.] *x* [...] *x* [. (.)]
36) [....(.)]*x x x x x x x x x x x x* (*x x*) [....(.)]
37) [.........(..)]*x x*
38–47) (ganz zerstört)
48) [......(.)]*x x x x* ⌜a⌝$^{?}$-ri ⌜še⌝-[e]-⌜ni⌝-[íw-WA(-).....(..)]
49) [..(.)]*x*-la-a-ú a-i-⌜tan⌝ te-u-u-na-e tiš-ša-an tiš-š[a-an....(..)]
50) [...]-a še-⌜e-ni-íw-wu-ú-ut-ta⌝-a-an ka-til-le-e-t[a.....(..)]
51) [.]-⌜i⌝-aš-⌜ša⌝-a-at-ta-ma-an pa-ta-a-⌜ra⌝-a-al-[l]a-a-an i[n$^{?}$-....(.)]
52) DINGER.MEŠ e-e-en-⌜na-šu-uš⌝ na-ak-ki-du-u-we-en ḫi-su-ú-ḫu-uš-*x*[..]
53) a-i-i-in ur-⌜du-le⌝-e-wa ge-ep-še-ma-a-an KÚ.SIG$_{17}$ še-e-ni-íw-[wu-uš]
54) ma-ka-a-an-ni-íw-wu-ú-⌜un-na⌝ ge-pa-a-né-e-ta an-du-ú-a-at-ta-a-[an]
55) te-u-u-na-e tiš-ša-an ⌜tiš-ša-an⌝ bi-su-uš-te-e-wa ti-ši-íw-wa-an ma-⌜a⌝-[na]
56) šu-⌜e⌝-ni a-nam-mil-la-a-an un-du še-e-ni-íw-wu-ta gu-lu-ša-ú pa-li-i-[en$^{?}$]

§14

57) un-du-ma-a-an ^{I}Ma-né-en-na-ma-an še-e-ni-íw-wu-ú-e pa-aš-ši-i-it-[ḫi]
58) še-e-ni-íw-wu-uš-ša-ma-an a-gu-ka-ra-aš-ti-en a-i-la-an [d]u-⌜be⌝-n[a^{MEŠ}]
59) du-um-ni i-i-ši-iḫ-ḫé-na ši-in ši-ni-be-e-ru-uḫ-ḫé-⌜na⌝ *x*[....]
60) KÚ.SIG$_{17}$ šu-aš-še-na an-zu-gal-la a-ku-u-ša-a-an-ni i-nu-ú-ut-[ta-a]-⌜ni$^{?}$-i⌝$^{?}$-[in]
61) ag-gu-tan ni-ḫa-a-ar-re-e-tan ta-la-me-né-e-tan an-[š]u$^{?}$-u-a-[......]
62) bi-su-uš-ta te-u-na-⌜e⌝ tiš-ša-an i-i-e-me-e-ni-[i-i]n
63) še-e-ni-íw-wu-uš ge-pa-a-né-e-ta-a-am-ma-ma-an an-du-⌜ú-e-né⌝-[e-t]a-⌜an⌝
64) [e]-ti-i-e-e te-u-na-e tiš-ša-an [(.) .] *x*

§ 13

(34–56) [...]...I [have(?)] him/them/it(?)...[...] (lines 35–37 are extensively damaged, lines 38–47 completely destroyed). [...]...m[y] brother [...]...I. If I in exceedingly much [...].., my brother will inform me immediately(?), that (?) I/me [...] and as for the terrible things(?), may the gods not permit. [I...] offended [...]. If it should come about that my brother would send a shipment of gold as my gift, for it I would rejoice in my heart, exceedingly, totally. And thus have I now said them (these words) to my brother, (and may(?) he) know (them).

§ 14

(57–64) Now, however, may my brother expedite Mane, his envoy. If he would bring here vessels(?), four out of ebony(?), two out of ivory, [...] out of gold, in all [...], as I have rejoiced exceedingly over the one large dowry...—what my brother will send, regarding this will I [rejoice](?) exceedingly.

§15

65) ⸢ti⸣-[we]-e-na-a-an iš-ta-ni-íw-wa-ša ^{d}Te-e-eš-šu-pa-aš ^{d}A-ma-a-⸢nu⸣-[ú]-⸢ul⸣-[la-a-an]

66) [t]a-⸢a⸣-[n]u-u-ša-a-aš-še-na an-za-a-an-ni ú-nu-ú-me-e-ni-i-in za-a[l$^{??}$-p]u$^{?}$-u$^{?}$-[u]n$^{?}$-[..(.)-n]a$^{?}$

67) t[a]-a-du-ka-a-ri a-nam-mi-til-la-a-an ša-a-at-⸢ti⸣ iš-ta-ni-íw-⸢wa-ša⸣-ti[l]-⸢la-a$^{?}$-an$^{?}$⸣

68) [iš]-ta-ni-íw-wa-[š]a$^{?}$-til-la-a-an šu-uk-ku-u-ut-ti [ḫu]r-wu-u-⸢ḫé⸣-e-⸢en⸣ [K]UR u-[u-mi-i-n]i

69) [KUR] ma-a-áš-ri-a-a-ni-ma-a-an KUR u-u-mi-i-ni a-nu-ú-ta-ni-i[l-l]a-[a-an..]*x*

70) [iš]-ta-ni-a-ša šu-ka šug-gu-ú-ud-du-u-⸢u-ḫa⸣ bi-[id]-⸢du⸣-[ka-ra]-⸢a⸣-an

71) [i]š-⸢te⸣-e-⸢en⸣ [KUR] ma-a-áš-ri-a-an-né-e-we K[UR u-u]-mi-i-in-né-e-we é[w-ri-in-n]i

72) še-e-ni-íw-we-en-na-a-an ḫur-wu-u-ḫé-né-e-we [K]UR u-u-‹mi›-i-in-⸢né-e⸣-we ⸢éw-ri⸣-[in]-⸢ni⸣

73) ia-a-la-an ú-ú-rík-ki KUR u-u-mi-i-in-n[a] an-ni š[i]-⸢né-e⸣-[el$^{?}$ šu$^{?}$-e$^{?}$] -na-a-an

74) ia-ti-la-⸢a-⸣an ú-ú-rík-ki ša-a-at-ti-[la-a]n éw-⸢ra$^{?}$-ar⸣$^{?}$-⸢ti⸣$^{?}$-[ia]-aš

75) a-i-[l]a-an ti-we-e-na an-ni ta-la-me-na [..-z]u$^{?}$-u-u-un-na š[a-a]-ša

76) aš-du-ka-a-ri-íw-wa-ša DINGIR.MEŠ e-e-ni-íw-wa-šu-uš (erasure) u[š]-t[a-a]-⸢nu-u⸣-[u]š-ta

77) DINGIR e-⸢en-ni⸣-íw-wa-⸢a⸣-še-⸢e⸣-en ⸢^{d}Te⸣-e-eš-šu-u-ub-be ^{d}A-m[a]-⸢a-nu-ú-e⸣ *x*[..]-⸢i-in⸣-ni

78) be-en-⸢ti⸣-úw-wu-⸢ša⸣ a-we-en-⸢na⸣-ma-an at-ta-a-ar-ti-⸢íw⸣-w[u-ú-un-na] ⸢šu⸣-u-un-na

79) ta-a-du-ka-a-ru-ši-ik-ki i-i-e-e-en u-u-⸢li ti-wi en⸣$^{?}$-za-[..]-⸢aš⸣$^{??}$-še$^{??}$-e-na-a-an

80) ti-we-e-na^{MEŠ} šu-ú-al-la-ma-an e-ti-⸢íw-wa-ša⸣ *x x x x x x x x* -[al]-la-a-an

81) a-⸢ti⸣-i-ni-i-in ma-a-an-na-⸢al⸣-l[a]-ma-an KUR u-‹u›-mi-⸢i⸣-[......*x*]-la-a-*x*-*x*[..]-⸢it⸣-ta

82) e-ti-íw-wa-[š]al-la-a-an i-[..(.)]-e-wa ia-a-⸢la-an ta-a⸣-[.-i]n [u-u-u]l-la

83) KUR u-u-mi-i-in-na šu-ú-al-l[a-m]a-an ⸢še-e-ni-íw-wu-ú⸣-[a-al-la-a-]$^{?}$-an

84) šuk-kán-né-e-wa-an ti-wi-i-wa-an e-ti-⸢i⸣-tan ⸢še-e⸣-[ni-í]w-w[u]-⸢ú⸣$^{?}$-[ra-m]a-an

85) ta-a-du-ka-a-ar-re-e‹-wa› a-ti-i-ni-⸢i⸣-[i]n [m]a-a-an-⸢na⸣-at-ta-ma-an

§ 15

(65–83) And the things which Teshub and Amon have done between us, should…Just as…love one another, so we between us, and between us, are we one. The Hurrian land and the Egyptian land are therefore between them as one single land and support(?) one another. I am like the l[ord] of the Egyptian land and my brother is like the l[ord] of the Hurrian land. So both these entire lands, as well as we, their lords, if the great things as…in our equality of rank, our deities have brought about, we send not the…of our deities, Teshub and Amon? No one has cultivated affectionate contact in the manner of my forefathers (and) I. Another matter is: And all things, which…, for/by us…, for real!…land…For us may they….

(84–85) all…other lands, which my brother…in view of/concerning his(?) only words, will I cultivate with my brother affectionate contact. So shall it be (lit. so am I).

§16

86) ^{I}Ma -né-en-na-ma-an še-e-ni-íw-wu-uš a-⸢gu⸣-ú-⸢ka-ra⸣-aš-⸢ti-en⸣ ⸢a⸣-i-i-in

87) tup-pu-u-un-ni ki-im-ra-a-at-ta-a-an be-en-du-u[n]$^{?}$-⸢na⸣$^{?}$ ⸢a-ru-u-ši⸣ u-u-ul-la-a-an

88) KUR u-u-mi-i-in-na pa-aš-ši-i-it-ḫé-na šu-ú-al-la-ma-an ⸢tub⸣-be ⸢a⸣-⸢lu⸣$^{??}$-en-na-a-an

89) u-u-ul-la KUR u-u-mi-i-in-na šu-ú-al-la-ma-an [p]u-ú-⸢ra⸣-mar-ti-íw-we tub-be

90) a-i-tan a-ú-ú-rat-ta-ma-an a-a-al-šu-li pa-a-ḫi-⸢íw-wu⸣-ú-a-at-ta-ma-an a-i-i-⸢in⸣

91) ^{I}Ma-né-en-na-ma-an ma-a-an-nu-uk-ku a-a-lum-pu-ú-uš-še ⸢bi-i⸣-il-la-aš-ša-a-am-ma-ma-an

92) ia-a-la-an ta-a-na-ú u-u-ul-la a-⸢we⸣-e-eš-ši-⸢il⸣-la-ma-an a-⸢ti-i-ni-i-in⸣

93) ⸢še⸣-e-ni-íw-we-e-en ta-a-du-ka-a-ri-⸢iš⸣ šu-ú-ú-ra ḫi-⸢na⸣-ši [K]UR u-u-⸢mi-i-in⸣-na-⸢a⸣-an

94) ⸢šu-ú⸣-al-la-ma-an *x*$^{?}$ i-i-u-ta-a-al-la-ma-an wu-ri-⸢íw-WA⸣

---

§17

95) ^{I}Ma-né-en-na-ma-an pa-aš-ši-i-it-ḫi-ip ni-i-ri tiš-ša-an-⸢na-ma-an⸣ ú-ru-uk-⸢ku⸣-[u-u]n

96) ⸢tar⸣-šu-a-a-ni ⸢KUR⸣u-u-mi-i-in-na-ša šu-⸢ú⸣-a-ni-a-ša-a-⸢am-ma-ma-an⸣ a-nam š[i$^{?}$-ra$^{?}$-aš-š]e

97) a-⸢ti⸣-i-ni-i-in ^{KUR} u-u-mi-i-ni-íw-wa-a-an še-e-ni-íw-wu-uš ⸢pa⸣$^{??}$-aš-⸢ša⸣$^{??}$-⸢a⸣$^{??}$-⸢ri⸣$^{??}$-⸢en⸣$^{??}$

98) ⸢pa⸣-zi-i-ma-a-an i-i-im-ma-ma-an wu-ru-u-ša-⸢uš-še⸣ ⸢*x*-*x*-du-um-mi⸣

§16

(86–94) May my brother send off Mane. When he was present, I had given a reception(??) in the proper manner, and the other countries (and) all the envoys were present, and he spoke(??), (and) all the other countries (and) my vassals, were present. When I...my head..., when Mane is not there,...all other (things), which I do. So may my brother nurture a cordial association...and all countries....

§17

(95–98) Mane, my envoy, is very good: there exists no other [ma]n(!) like (him) in the entirety of the lands, so may my brother send him back once again to my land....which I have seen,

99) i-i-um-mi-⸢i-im⸣-ma-ma-an KUR u-u-mi-i-ni-íw-wa ta-a-nu-u-ša-a-aš-⸢še⸣ ⸢ú-ru-uk-ku⸣

100) še-e-ni-íw-wu-uš-ša-ma-an ^{I}Ma-né-en te-ḫu-u-⸢u⸣-ša an-⸢du⸣-ú-⸢e-ma-a-an⸣ [..]-⸢ri⸣

101) pa-zi-i-ma-a-an i-i-im-ma-ma-an ú-ru-uk-ku ⸢i-i-e⸣-ma-a-ni-i-[i]n ⸢ti-wi⸣

102) ^{I}ma -né-eš še-e-ni-íw-wu-ta ka-til-le-e-t[a]-⸢a⸣-[am]-ma-ma-an wa-aḫ-⸢ru⸣-*x x x x*

103) ur-ḫi-ma-a-an še-e-ni-íw-wu-uš-ša-a-an ki-i-pu-⸢u⸣?-[ḫa??]-⸢a⸣-la-a-⸢en⸣ šur-⸢wu-uš-ti-ik-ki-i-in⸣

104) ul-lu-⸢ḫu⸣-ug-gu-ú-un še-e-ni-íw-wu-ú-an t[i]-⸢wi-i-tan⸣ u[l]-⸢lu⸣-ḫu-⸢ug-gu⸣-[ú-u]n

105) ⸢šu⸣-u-wa-an ti-wi-íw-wa-an gu-li-a-⸢a⸣-[ma-a]-⸢an⸣ ḫa-š[a-]⸢ú⸣? ⸢ti⸣?-⸢wi⸣?

106) ur-ḫé-e-en pa-a-la ⸢gu-li⸣-a-a-ma pa-a-⸢li-ma-a-an⸣ ⸢ur-ḫa⸣ g[u]-⸢li-a-a⸣-[m]a

---

§18

107) un-du-ma-a-an še-e-ni-í[w-w]e-⸢e-en pa-aš⸣-š[u-ši ^{I}ma]-⸢né-en-na-a-an⸣ š[e-e]-⸢ni⸣-[íw-wu-u]š

108) pa-aš-šu-u-u-ša ḫu-ra-⸢a-til-la-a⸣-an še-e-[n]i-í[w-wu-uš ^{I}ma-*n]é?-e-r[a] ⸢šu?-u?-wa?⸣*

109) pa-aš-šu-u-u-ša ú-*a-⸢du⸣?-[ra-a-an-ni-ma-a-an(?) še-e-ni(?)-í]w-w[u-u]š a-[k]u??-⸢u⸣?[-u??-ša?]*

110 ú-ú-nu-u-⸢uš⸣-ta-⸢ma-a⸣-[a]n [(......) še-e]-⸢ni-íw⸣-w[u-u]š-ša-⸢a⸣?[-an? _]*x*

111) ^{I}ma-né-⸢en-na-a⸣-an še-⸢e⸣-[ni-í]w-w[u-ú-e p]a-⸢aš⸣-š[i]-⸢i⸣-[-i]t-⸢ḫi⸣ **x x x x x** [...]*x*

112) te-u-u-na-e tiš-ša-an tiš-š[a]-⸢an-na⸣?-[m]a?-a[n? (.)] **x*-⸢ḫu-uḫ⸣-ḫa-⸢a⸣*-⸢an⸣ *⸢wi-i-ra-ti??⸣-*x**

113) ta-a-nu-ši-úw-wu ⸢ú-nu-ú-ul⸣-[le-*e-ni-i-in K]UR ⸢u-u⸣-m[i]-⸢i⸣-[n]i-⸢íw⸣-[wu]-ú-⸢e-na⸣

114) ki-i-pa-aš-ši-[í]w-WA *⸢ta-a-nu-⸢ub⸣?-⸢be⸣??-e-n[a]?-ma⸣-[a-an * ....]

115) ḫi-ši-im-du-⸢ḫa⸣-ú-ú-un ⸢ḫi-iš-ma⸣-aš-ši-⸢íw⸣-[WA......–m]a?-an? [...-]⸢ma⸣-a-⸢pa⸣?

(99–106) ......, that he has done in my land, does not exist; my brother himself has done a great deal for Mane. Of the [...]......does not exist. The word that Mane will say to my brother is grac[ious and true, and my brother must him/it..., he does no evil, he changes nothing to my brother fro[m] his w[ord], he changes not a word to me. He speaks (and) I heed [h]is [wor]d(?). He does not exchange falsehood for truth and falsehood he does not repeat as truth.

§18

(107–115) Now, however, [has] m[y] brother [se]nt, and (surely) has [my br]other sent [Ma]ne, and *ḫuradi*-soldiers has m[y] brother sent to me along with [Man]e. The bride[price] ha[s m]y brother [sent](?) hither. It has happened [...] a[nd] my brother [...] to Mane, m[y] br[others en]voy...[...]... exceedingly. [...] guest...have I not done. As [...] my...my land...[...]...I...my ......[...]...

§19

116) ^{I}Ma -né-e-ra-⸢la-an⸣ ú-⸢na-aš-še-na še-e-ni-íw-wu-ú-e-na⸣ x-⸢ta-a⸣-[..]x x x
117) *ḫi-[i]š-⸢mi-i-x-x*-a⸣?-ul-la-ma-an tiš-ša-an za-a-zu-lu-u-ša[-ú] x x[...]
118) še-e-ni-[í]w-wu-ú-e-en ḫu-ra-[a?-a?]-ti šu-ú-x-ši [......(..)]
119) ⸢ni-i-ru-ša⸣-e še-e-du-⸢u-ḫu-ša-a⸣-[u]l-la-a-an bi-x-x-x-x-x-⸢a-an⸣ [..]-a-an
120) a-nam-m[i-i]l-[l]a-ma-an za-⸢a⸣-z[u]-⸢ul⸣-[lu]?-[ša]?-[u]l?-l[a]?-⸢a⸣?-a[n? a-ti-i-ni-i]?-⸢in⸣
121) ma-⸢a-an⸣-na-al-la-ma-an ⸢a⸣-ti-i-ni-⸢i⸣-[in ma-a-an-na-al-la-m]a?-an
122) an-ti-il-la-ma-an ma-a-an-nu-⸢le⸣-e-wa-⸢a-al⸣-[l]a-a-an [(.-)]⸢ú⸣?-x x x x x
123) i-nu-ú-mi-e-ni-i-i[n] še-e-ni-íw-[wu-ú-e-en]
124) ḫu-ra-a-a-⸢ti⸣ [(...)] za-a-zu-lu-u-š[a-a-ú]?
125) i-nu-ú-me-e-ni-i-in še-e-du-u-ḫu-⸢ša⸣-[a-ú]?

§19a

Rev.

III 1) še-e-ni-íw-wu-uš-ša-a-an aš-ti ša-a-ru-u-ša *KUR Mi!*-zìr-re-e-[we] a[l?-la-i]
2) un-du-ma-a-an a-ru-u-ša-ú-ú-un id-du-u-uš-ta-ma-⸢a⸣-an še-e-n[i-í]w-[wu-ta]
3) i-nu-ú-un ḫé-ri an-ti šu-e ši-ra a-we-eš-še-e-ni-i-in wu-ur-⸢ra-a-an-ni⸣
4) šu-e an-ti bi-su-u-u-ni-i-in ta-la-mi ta-duḫ-ḫu-li-ik-ki-⸢in-na-a-an⸣
5) a-ti-i-ni-i-in ma-a-an-ni-i-im-ma-ma-‹an› ia-a-an ú-ú-rík-ki ma-a-na šu-⸢e⸣-ni
6) ḫur-ru-u-ḫé KUR u-u-mi-i-ni ia-a-an ú-ú-rík-ki ma-a-na šu-e-ni
7) KUR Ma-a-áš-ri-a-a-‹an-›ni KUR u-u-mi-i-ni še-e-ni-íw-wu-ú-e-néš aš-ti-iš
8) še!-e-ni-íw-wu-ta ti-i-ḫa-nu-u-lu-ma-a-aš-še-ni šu-e-ni na-wu-⸢ug⸣-gu-ú-un
9) an-du-ú-e-e šu-e-né-e-e wu-ri-ik-ku-u-un-ni a-ti-i-ni-i-in
10) ma-a-an-ni-⸢i⸣-im-ma-ma-an ma-ra-a-du-ur-ku-na-a-an a-ti-i-ni-‹i›-in ma-a-an-ni-i-im-ma-ma-an

§ 19

(116–125) That which...my brothers, which come with Mane, have I greatly honored, have I entertained [...] The troop of my brother had [...] I have fattened them up in a good manner, thus have I entertained them. Thus is it true, thus is it true, these can..., as I have entertained my brother's troop, as I fattened (them) up.

§ 19a

(Rev. III, 1–10) And my brother has wanted a wife, a pr[incess of] Egyp[t], and I have given her, and she has gone [to my] broth[er]. As she these...all has been measured(?), everyone should see it all! These are (?) all a great joy, and...in truth! As well as (concerns) the Hurrian land in every respect, so also what (pertains) to the Egyptian land, throughout, was the wife of my brother shows(?) to my brother, in relation to all of this...it is not blind. Truthfully,..., truthfully.

§ 20

11) un-du-ma-a-an še-e$^{!}$(*Text*: en)-ni-íw-wu-ú-e-en aš-ti a-ru-u-ša-ú id-du-u-uš-ta-ma-a-an
12) še-e-ni-íw-wu-ta in-na-a-ma-a-ni-i-in (erasure) ú-ú-‹né›-e-et-ta
13) še-e-ni-íw-wu-uš-ša-a-an wu-re-e-ta ⸢a-ru-u-ma-a⸣-aš-šu-uḫ-ḫa ú-na-a-an
14) še-e-ni-íw-wu-ú-a ši-ra-a-an še-e-ni-íw-⸢wu-ú-e⸣-né-e-en-na ti-ša-a-an-na
15) ni-ḫa-a-ri-ma-a-an gu-ru še-e-ni-íw-wu-uš wu-re-e-e-ta
16) a-ru-u-ši-im-pu-ú-uš-ḫa u-u-lu-u-ḫa-a-ti-la-an zu$^{!}$(SU)-kán e-ši-íw-wa-a-aš-tan
17) ma-a-an-nu-uk-ka-ti-la-an a-a-wa-ad-duḫ-ḫa še-e-ni-íw-wu-ú-a-al-la-a-an
18) ge-pa-a-nu-ša-a-uš-še-na ge-pa-a-nu-ša-a-ul-la-ma-an wu-re-e-ta-a-al-la-a-an
19) še-e-ni-íw-wu-uš (erasure) ú-na-a-la-an
20) še-e-ni-íw-wu-ú-a ti-i-ḫa-^{ni}níš-ḫa-la-an ip-šu-ši-i-la-an

§ 20

(11–20) And now have I given a wife to my brother and she has gone to my brother. When she comes, will my brother see her, *that she is given*(??). And she comes to my brother, she corresponds to the desire of my brother, *as she is given*(??). And again will my brother see the dowry, *that it is given*(??), And we…from our…. (The things) which I have sent to my brother, have I sent, and my brother will see them, they come to my brother, and they…, and they….

§ 21

21) un-du-ma-a-an in-na-me-e-ni-i-in še-e-ni-íw-wu-ú-e aš-ti ú-né-e-et-ta
22) in-na-ma-a-ni-i-in še-e-ni-íw-wu-ta ti-i-ḫa-nu-u-ul-le-e-et-ta
23) ú-ši-íw-wu-ú-un-na-ma-a-an šu-u-we-né-e-en-na it-ti-ten ú-ši-íw-wu-un-na-a-an
24) ti-i-ḫa-ni-ten še-e-ni-íw-wu-uš-ša-a-an KUR u-‹u-›mi-i-ni šu-ú-an-na-ma-an
25) pu-uk-lu-uš-ti-en u-u-ul-la-a-an KUR u-u-mi-i-in-na šu-ú-al-la-ma-an
26) wi-i-ra-te-e-na-a-an pa-aš-ši-i-it-ḫé-na^{MEŠ} šu-ú-al-la-ma-an tup-pu-la-in
27) ti-i-ḫa-ni-i-ten-na-a-an še-e-ni-íw-wu-ta ni-ḫa-a-ri-i-in
28) še-e-ni-íw-wu-ú-e-né-e a-a-i-e-e be-te-eš-ti-ten šu-ú-an-na-ma-an
29) in-na-ma-a-ni-i-in še-e-ni-íw-wu-ú-e-né-e a-a-i-e-e be-te-eš-te-e-et-ta
30) ta-ri-i-te-na-an šuk-kán-ni e-e-še-ni ḫa-i-e-ni-la-an še-e-ni-íw-wu-uš
31) wi-i-ra-te-e-na šu-ú-al-la-ma-an pa-aš-ši-i-it-ḫé-na-a-an šu-ú-al-la-ma-an
32) u-u-ul-la-a-an KUR u-u-mi-i-in-na šu-ú-al-la-ma-an ma-ri-a-an-na-ar-ti-la-an
33) še-e-ni-íw-wu-uš ú-ú-ri-a-a-aš-še-na wa-ša-i-na-an še-e-ni-íw-we
34) be-te-eš-ti-e-na-an ni-ḫa-a-a-ri ši-RI-en-na-a-an

§ 22

35) un-du-ma-a-an at-ta-íw-wu-ú-e-en ša-a-la e-e-li-íw-we ma-a-né-e-em-ma-ma-an
36) tub-be tub-bi(over erasure)-ma-a-an ni-ḫa-a-ri-i-we ma-a-né-e-em-ma-ma-an tub-be
37) am-ma-t[i-í]w-wu-ú-e-e-en ša-a-la at-ta-íw-wu-ú-e e-⸢e⸣-la
38) ma-a-né-e-em-ma-ma-an tub-be tub-bi-ma-a-an ni-ḫa-a-ri-i-we ma-a-né-e-em-ma-ma-an
39) gu-ru tub-be a-ra-an-ni-e-ni-la-an še-e-ni-íw-wu-uš tub-bi-aš
40) ši-ni-a-še-na-a-am-ma-ma-an ḫa-ši-e-ni-il-la-a-an šu-u-we-ma-a-an tub-be
41) ni-ḫa-a-ar-re-e-we a-ru-u-ša-uš-še-né-e-we a-ra-an-ni-en-na-ma-an
42) še-e-ni-íw-wu-uš ḫa-ši-en-na-an a-la-a-še-me-e-ni-i-in ni-ḫa-a-ri te-⸢a⸣
43) a-la-a-še-me-e-ni-i-in ni-i-ri a-la-a-še-me-e-ni-i-in še-e-ni-íw-wu-ú-uz-zi

§ 21

(21–34) And now, when the wife of my brother comes, when she will be shown to my brother, may she be attired as my flesh(?) of my (flesh), and as my flesh may she be shown. And may my brother assemble the entire land and all the other countries and the honored guests (and) all envoys should be present. And may they show his dowry to my brother, and may they spread out everything in the sight on my brother. When it is spread out before my brother's sight, may they...in one place. And may my brother take all the noble guests and all the envoys and all the other lands and the chariot warriors that my brother desires, and may my brother enter and may he spread out the dowry and may they be suitable (to his wishes).

§ 22

(35–43) Now, my father's daughter. my sister, is herself there, and the tablet of her dowry is itself available; and my grandfather's daughter, the sister of my father, is herself there. May my brother have the tablets of both of them given to him and may he hear their words. And the tablet of the dowry that I gave, may he also have given to him and may my brother listen to it (and learn) that the dowry is extensive, that it is splendid, that it is befitting my brother.

§ 23

44) a-i-i-in ul-lu-i e-e-la-ar-ti-íw-wu-ú-e-na-a-še-e-em-ma-ma-an
45) ni-ḫa-a-ri-a-a-še tub-bi-aš tup-pu-uk-ku še-e-ni-íw-we-en-na-a-an
46) e-ti-i-tan-na-ma-an ši-mi$^{!}$(LUM)-i-ki pa-li-a-ma-a-aš-še-ma-a-an ú-ru-uk-ku
47) pa-li-a-al-la-a-an e-ti-i-ta-ni-il-la-ma-an še-e-ni-íw-wu-⌜uš⌝
48) tup-pu-pa-a-ta-a-al-la-ma-an i-i-in éw-re-en-na-šu-uš pal-du-pa-a-te

§ 24

49) še-e-ni-íw-wu-ta-a-ma-‹a-›an ti-wi šuk-ku kul-le še-e-ni-íw-wu-uš-⌜ša⌝-a-an ḫa-ši-en
50) še-e-ni-íw-we-e-en at-ta-ar-ti-íw-wu-tan tiš-ša-an-na-ma-an an-za-an-nu-u-ḫu-ša-ú
51) ta-a-ta-ra-aš-ka-e a-nam-ma-a-an an-za-a-an-nu-u-ḫu-ša-a-ú kul-li-ma-a-an
52) i-i-al-le-e-ni-i-in ^{I}Ar-ta-ta-a-maš am-ma-ti-íw-wu- uš at-ta-i-ip-pa
53) ⌜e-ti⌝-i-i-ta ti-we-e-na^{MEŠ} ta-a-nu-u-ša-a-aš-še-na *x x*-a-ru-ša-a-an-na-al-la-ma-an
54) i-šal-la-a-an šuk-kán-né-e-el-la-ma-an pa-aš-ši-ḫi-íw-we e-e-ma-na-a-mu-ša-a-ú
55) i-i-al-la-a-ni-i-in gu-ru at-ta-íw-wu-uš we-e-wa e-ti-i-da$^{!}$(WA)
56) ti-we-e-na^{MEŠ} ta-a-nu-u-ša-a-aš-še-na an-til-la-a-an šuk-kán-né-e-el-la-ma-an
57) pa-aš-ši-ḫi-íw-we i-ša-aš e-e-ma-na-a-mu-ša-a-ú i-i-al-la-a-ni-i-in
58) am-ma-ti-íw-wu-uš at-ta-íw-wu-uš at-ta-i-ip-pa we-e-wa ma-*ka-a* (over erasure)-an-na
59) ge-pa-a-nu-lu-u-uš-ta-a-aš-še-na a-ti-i-ni-i-in še-eḫ-ra-a-al-la-ma-an
60) pu-ud-du-ú-uk-ki-a-šu-u-un-na-a-al-la-a-an šu-u-we-na-a-šu-u-un-na ir-nu-uk-ku
61) wu-re-e-ta-a-la-an un-du še-e-ni-íw-wu-ú-ul-la-ma-an ge-pa-a-nu-ša-uš-še-na
62) še-e-ni-íw-wu-ú-a a-nam-mi-it-ta-ma-an še-e-ni-íw-wu-ú-a
63) ge-pa-a-nu-ul-›ul‹-le-e-wa-a-at-ta-a-an a-ti-i-ni-i-in ma-a-an-na-at-ta-ma-an
64) a-nam-mi-it-ta-ma-an še-e-ni-íw-wu-ra ur-ḫu-up-du-ši-le-wa a-nam-mi-it-ta-ma-an
65) ta-a-du-ka-a-ar-re-e-wa a-ti-i-ni-i-in ma-a-an-na-at-‹ta-›ma-an

§ 23

(44–48) If, on the other hand, the tablets of the dowry of my sister and my father's sister are not available,—my brother…himself not (!?), and and there is no one who does not know it, and my brother himself knows that no (tablet) exists, concerning the kings and he is not informed.

§ 24

(49–50) To my brother will I just say (one thing) and may my brother heed it. I have given(?) to my brother much more than my forefathers,

(51–65) in a loving manner…, and I have with a single (shipment) done ten times as much. Again the (things) that my grandfather (and) my father have sent to your father and to you as a gift, now they were generous(?), but they were according to their worth(?) were not equal to the (worth(?)) the (shipment) from me. And now my brother will see (the things) himself which I have dispatched. Thus will I send to my brother (gifts) for sure! So will I treat my brother faithfully. Thus will I show reciprocal love, for sure!

§25

66) iš-ši-na-a-an še-e-ni-íw-wu-uš at-ta-a-ar-ti-íw-wu-ú-un-na ḫi-i‹a›-ru-uḫ-ḫa-e

67) ir-n[u]-⸢u⸣ḫu-ši-a-a-ma še-e-er-re-e-we-‹ni-›⸢i⸣-in KÚ.SIG$_{17}$ at-ta-i-wu-uš am-ma-ti-íw-wu-ú-a

68) ú-⸢a⸣-du-ra-a-an-na ge-pa-a-nu-u-ša-a-aš-še we-e-eš-ša-a-an at-ta-íw-wu-ú-a

69) ú-⸢a⸣-[d]u-ra-a-an-na ge-pa-a-nu-u-šu-u-uš-še te-a at-ta-i-ib-be-né-e-tan

70) t[iš-š]a-an-na-ma-an šu-u-wa-ma-a-an še-e-ni-íw-wu-uš ir-nu-u-ḫu-ši-a-a-ma

§ 25

(66–70) And as for the horses(?) has my brother not plated with gold in the manner of my forefathers. The gold of the…, that your father sent to my grandfather as the bride price, the (gold), that you have sent to my father as bride price was much more than that of your father. And my brother has not done the same for me,

71) ⸢at⸣-ta-íw-wu-ú-e-né-e-en-na ge-pa-a-nu-u-ša-a-aš-še še-e-ni-íw-wu-ú-ut-ta-a-an

72) ⸢su⸣-bi-a-a-maš-ti-en éw-re-en-na-a-ša i-ri-i-in-na-ar-ti-íw-wu-ú-a

73) u-u-ul-la-a-ša KUR u-u-mi-i-in-na-a-ša wu-ri-a-ša ḫi-ia-ru-uḫ-ḫa-a-at-ta-a-an

74) t[e]-u-u-na‹-e› še-e-ni-íw-wu-uš ge-pa-a-nu-en wu-ur-te-ni-it-ta-a-an še-e-ni-íw-‹wu-›uš-ša-a-an

75) ul-⸢lu⸣-i ti-wi-íw-we šuk-ku ta-a-na-aš-ti-en ti-ši-íw-we-en-na-a-an

76) ḫi-[su-ú-ḫ]i-wa-a-en ša-a-li-íw-wu-ú-e-en še-e-ni-íw-wu-ú-e-né-e-we aš-ti-i-we

77) ⸢š[e-e-ni-íw-w]u-uš⸣ za-lam-ši ḫi-ia-ru-uḫ-ḫé na-⸢ak⸣-k[a-a]š-[š]a ku-*x*[(.)]*x*

78) [še-e-ni-íw-wu-u]š ta-a-na-aš-ti-en ma-a-nu-ú-⸢un⸣-na-a-a[l-la-a-a]n [....]

79) [........(...)-]⸢ši?-ru⸣-[.]-in-[n]a-a-an u-lu-*x x x x x*-en(-)[(...)]

80) [.......(..)]*x x*[...a?-nam?]-⸢mil? -la-ma⸣-an ut-ta-aš-ti-te-e[n]

81) [.....(..)-n]i-⸢i⸣-in še-[e-ni-í]w-⸢wu⸣-[u]š ⸢be⸣ ti-ša-a-tan ta-a-ni-⸢a⸣

82) [....(.)]-⸢un⸣-na-a-ma-a-an e-t[i]-⸢i⸣-tan-*x*-[.]*x*-an e-el-mi-i-ḫi ú-ru-uḫ-l[i]

83) [....-t]a-ma-a-an e-ti-i-ta[n-n]a-ma-an [. (.)-g]u-ú-un-na [...]-a-an

84) u-u-[ul?] -lu-⸢ḫi-duk⸣-ku-u-un i-⸢i-duk⸣-[ku]-un-na-ma-an še-e-ni-íw-wu-ú-an [......]

85) ḫi-i-*x x* ⸢ti-ši-íw-we-en-na⸣-a-an ḫi-su-ú-ḫi-wa-⸢a-en⸣ a-ri-en-na-a-an še-e-⸢ni-íw⸣-w[u-uš]

86) ša-a-ru-ši-⸢im⸣-p[u]-⸢ú⸣?-[u]š-[šu]-uḫ-ḫa ti-ši-íw-wu-ú-un-nu-uḫ-ḫa ši-ra-[aš-še]

87) an-za-a-an-nu-u-[ḫi-e-ni-tan] še-e-ni-íw-wu-uš at-ta-a-ar-ti-íw-wu-tan tiš-ša-ni-it-[ta-a]-⸢an⸣

88) ti[š]-š[a-na-an]? su-bi-a-maš-ti-e-⸢ni-tan⸣ še-e-ni-íw-wu-uš KUR u-‹u-›mi-i-ni-íw-wu-ú-a wu-ri-[i]-ta

89) t[i-ši-í]w-we-en-⸢na-a-an⸣ še-e-ni-íw-[wu]-uš ḫi-su-ú-ḫi-wa-a-en an-du-ú-a-na-an [šuk?-k]án

90) še-e-ni-íw-wu-tan za-lam-ši MUNUSša-a-⸢li⸣-íw-wu-ú-e ḫi-ia-ru-uḫ-ḫa na-⸢ak-ka-aš⸣-ša

91) ša-a-ru-ša-a-ú ia-me-e-ni-i-in⸢-in⸣ e-ti-íw-we pa-la-a-ú še-e-ni-⸢íw-wu-uš⸣

(71–91) like that which he has sent to my father as bride price. And may my brother make me glorious in the eyes of the kings, my colleagues (and) the other lands. With gold in large quantity may my brother see that I am supplied and they may behold me. And may my brother, moreover(?) see to my foreign relations for once and may he not distress my heart. And may my brother give, in the desired manner in ac[cordance with my heart, [that which] (corresponds to my wishes). And may my brother grant(?) to me much more than my forefathers, and may my brother make (me) very splendid in the eyes (lit. singular) of my lands, and may my brother not distress my heart! Incidentally, I have at one time desired a molten gold image of my daughter,

92) te-u-u-na-e tiš-ša-an tiš-⸢ša⸣-an ta-a-ti-a-⸢a-aš⸣-š[a] ⸢ti-ša⸣-a-tan še-e-[ni-í]w-⸢wu-ú-a⸣-m[a]-⸢a⸣-[an]
93) gu-ru KUR u-u-mi-i-ni-i-ta ḫi-ia-ru-uḫ-⸢ḫé⸣ pa-la-a-ú ⸢a-i-i-in⸣ [......(.)]
94) te-a še-e-⸢ni-íw⸣-wu-ú-a-ma-a-an wu-ri-i-ta i-i-uk-ku-un-na-ma-an še-⸢e-ni-íw-wu-uš⸣-[ša-a-an]
95) ul-li-wa-a-en ⸢ti⸣-ši-íw-⸢we-e-en⸣ ḫi-su-ú-ḫ[i-w]a-a-en ú-ri-im-pu-ú-⸢uš-šu-uḫ-ḫa-ma-a-an⸣
96) na-ḫu-ul-li-im-pu-ú-uš-šu-‹uḫ-›?ḫa ši-ra-aš-[še š]e-e-ni-íw-wu-uš a-ri-en ši-⸢in-nu-ma-a-an⸣
97) za-lam-ši ši-in-ni-be-e-ru-uḫ-⸢ḫé še-e-ni⸣-íw-wu-uš a-ri-en i-nu-ú-me-e-ni-i-⸢in⸣
98) URU Ni-i-nu-a-a-we ᵈŠa-uš-k[a]-⸢a⸣-wa DINGIR e-e-ni-íw-wu-ú-a a-⸢a-i-i-ta⸣
99) ka-te-e-ta-ú ḫi-ia-ru-uḫ-ḫé-ma-a-an za-lam-ši šu-u-WA še-[..(.)]-íw-WA
100) tup-pu-le-e-wa a-ti-i-ni-i-in ma-a-an-ni-i-im-ma-ma-an e-e-še-né-e-ra
101) ⸢ḫa⸣-a-wu-ru-[u]n-né-e-ra te-e-e-na ka-ti-i-⸢in⸣-na i-⸢nu-ul-le-e-ni-i⸣-[i]n
102) ḫ[i-i]l-[lu-l]e-e-wa a-ti-i-ni-i-in ma-a-an-na-al-la-ma-an ⸢an-ni-i⸣-in ⸢za-lam-ši⸣
103) ḫ[i-ia-ru-u]ḫ-ḫé na-ak-ka-‹aš-›še ᴹᵁᴺᵁˢTa-a-du-ḫé-e-pa-an ma-a-an-ni ⸢ ᴵDu-uš-rat-ta-a-we⸣
104) KUR M[i]-⸢i⸣-it-ta-a-*⸢an-né⸣*-e-we éw-ri-i-we ša-a-la ᴵIm-mu-u-⸢ri-ia-we⸣
105) KUR M[i]-zi-ir-re-e-⸢we-né⸣-e-we éw-ri-⸢i⸣-we aš-ti-i-in-na a-ru-u-ša-a-aš-še
106) ᴵI[m]-mu-u-ri-aš-ša-a-an za! -lam-ši ta-⸢a-nu-u⸣-ša ḫi-ia-ru-uḫ-ḫa na-ak-⸢ka-aš-ša⸣
107) ᴵ⸢Du⸣-uš-rat-ta-a-wa-ma-a-an ge-pa-a-nu-u-ša ta-a-ta-ra-aš-ka-e

(92–107) I know that my brother loves me exceedingly, but I also know, for my brother, gold, if it is…in his land, is plentiful; in the eyes of my brother it is not expensive, so may my brother not hold it back, may he not distress my heart, and in the quantity that is available…may my brother give in accordance (with my wishes). And for another(?), may my broher give an ivory image. As I will speak to my deity, Sha(w)oshka of Niniveh, "A golden image should for me as mine…be available!" So shall it be (lit. so it is). Before the Earth and before Heaven are the words spoken(?), as they are spoken, so may it be (lit. so it is)! "This molten image is Taduḫeba, the daughter of Tushratta, the lord of Mittani, that he has given as wife of Immoriya, the lord of Egypt. And Immoriya has made a molten image from gold and he has lovingly sent it to Tushratta."

§26

108) ⸢ša⸣-a-at-ti-la-an an-nu-tan ⸢šu-e-né-e-tan⸣ iš-ta-ni-íw-wa-ša šug-gu-ú-ud-du-u-ḫa

109) ⸢ta⸣-a-du-ka-a-ri-i-til-la-a-an ⸢te-u-u-na-e⸣ tiš-ša-an tiš-ša-an KUR u-u-mi-i-ni-íw-wa-aš-ša-a-an

110) ⸢iš⸣-ta-ni-a-ša bi-id-du-ka-a-ra in-na-a-am-ma-ma-an še-e-ni-íw-wu-ú-e

111) ⸢du⸣-ru-bi ú-ru-u-we-en a-i-ma-a-ni-i-in šuk-ku-u-um-ma-ma-an du-ru-be

112) ⸢še⸣-e-ni-⸢íw-wu⸣-ú-a KUR u-u-mi-i-ni-i-ta wa-še-e-wa pa-aš-ši-na-an še-e-ni-íw-we

113) šu-ú-ú-ta ḫur-wu-u-ḫé-ma-a-an KUR u-u-mi-i-ni^{MEŠ} kar$_4$-kar$_4$-ni^{MEŠ} nu-ú-ú-li^{MEŠ}

114) šuk-kán-ni-ma-a-an šu-e-ni še-e-ni-íw-wu-ú-e-né-e-wa du-ru-bi-i-i-wa

115) e-ti-i-ta [tub$^{?}$-b]i-in ú-ru-le-e-wa-ma-a-ni-i-in gu-ru šu-u-u-⸢we⸣

116) du-u-ru-b[i] ⸢du-ru⸣-bi-íw-⸢we⸣ in-na-a-am-ma-ma-an ú-ru-u-we-en pa-aš-še-ti-i-tan

117) še-e-ni-í[w-wu]-⸢ta⸣ [g]e-pa-a-né-e-ta-ma-a-an še-e-ni-íw-wu-uš KUR ma-a-áš-ri-a-a-an-ni

118) KUR u-u-mi-i-⸢ni⸣^{MEŠ} kar$_4$-kar$_4$-ni^{MEŠ} nu-ú-ú-li^{MEŠ} šuk-kán-ni-ma-a-an šu-e-ni du-ru-bi-íw-wu-‹ú-›a

119) e-ti-i-⸢ta⸣ ú-be-e-ti (erasure) i-i-ma-a-an gu-ru ḫa-a-ra-a-am-ma-ma-an dur-bi-íw-‹wa›-aš

120) ši-né-e-W[A..]-⸢i⸣-in ew-re-en-na ta-li-im-te-na KUR u-u-mi-i-⸢ni⸣ [^{ME}]^{Š}

121) ta-li-im-te-na du-ru-pa ti-i-ti a-ú-un-ni-ma-a-an an-ni du-ru-bi

122) e-ti-iš ta-a-ar-ra-ša ḫu-ši-a-a-aš-še du-ru-bi-íw-w[e............]

123) ú-ru-uk-ku (erasure) i-i-ri-i-in-‹ni-›íw-wa-aš-ša-⸢a⸣-[an]

124) ú-ru-uk-ku-un-na-ma-an an-nu-tan šu-e-né-e-t[an]

§ 26

(108–109) And because of all this, we are of one mind with each other and both of us love one another exceedingly. And our lands

(110–124) help(?) one another. If only an enemy of my brother did not exist! But in case sometime an enemy of my brother invades his land, (and) my brother writes to me and the Hurrian land, armor, weapons and all together everything that pertains to the enemy of my brother will be at his disposition. However, on the other hand, should there be an enemy of mine—if only he did not exist!—I will write to my brother, and my brother will send the Egyptian land, armor, weapons and and all together everything that pertains to my (!) enemy. ....our enemy...great(?) kings, great(?) lands...enemy......that enemy, which...an enemy of ours is not present, and there is none equal to us in spite of all that.

§ 27

IV 1) ti-we-e-ma-a-an šuk-ku ⸢še-e⸣-n[i-í]w-⸢wu-ta⸣ kul-le še-e-ni-íw-wu-⸢ú-a-an⸣

2) a-a-i-⸢i⸣-ta ti-wi šur-wi te-a ka-ti-ik-ku-u-un-ni ma-a-an-nu-⸢uk-kal-la⸣-a-an

3) an-ti ú! -ú-nu-uk-ka-la-an ta-la-me-né-e-wa a-a-i-⸢i⸣-ta éw-⸢re⸣-e[n-né?-e?-wa?-a]n?

4) šur-wi ti-wi ka-t[i-i]š? ḫi-il-lu-ši-i-in ḫi-il-lu-ši-ik-⸢ku-u⸣-[un-n]i

5) še-e-ni-íw-wu-ta e-ti-íw-wu-ú-e ni-i-ru-pa-a-ta-e gu-lu-u-ša-a-at-ta-a-an

§ 27

(IV, 1–5) And I want to say one thing more to my brother: In the presence of my brother evil words are numerous; one, who speaks (to him), is not (however,) at hand, those (evil words) do not come before the sight of a great one. (Now, however) an evil word was spoken(?) to the king; a babbler(?) has in a bad manner spoken to my brother ‹concerning› my person, he has denounced me,

6) ni-i-ru-pa-a-ta-e ḫa-šu-u-ša-un-na-a-an gu-ru še-e-ni-íw-wu-uš ti-wi-i-te$^{?}$-na

7) ta-a-nu-u-ša-a-aš-ša na-wa-a-an ta-la-ma še-e-ni-íw-wu-uš ni-i-nu-šu-ú-a

8) a-ú-a-a-ar-ḫé-na-a-ša-ma-a-an ge-u-u-ša a-a-ad-du-u-uš-ta-ma-a-an

9) ḫa-šu-u-ša$^{?}$-ú-ú-un bi-sa-an-du-ši-i-it-ta-a-an a-i-ma-a-ni-i-in

10) še-e-ni-íw-wu-uš a-nam ta-a-nu-ši-i-wa-al-la-a-an-ni ḫi-su-ú-ḫul-le-e-et-ta-a-an

11) tiš-ša-an ḫé-en-ni-ma-a-an gu-ru ḫi-il-lu-ši-ik-ku-u-un-ni ḫi-il-lu-ši

12) ^{I}Pár-ad-du i-i-ra-a-an-na-la$^{!}$-an ka-ti-a-ma-a-an še-e-ni-íw-we še-e-na-a-an-na-e

13) ma-a-an-ni-i-ni-i-in ti-wi an-ti ú-na-a-ni-i-in pa-ḫé an-ti a-nam

14) ḫi-il-lu-ši-iš ka-tup-pa-a-ni-i-in ti-wi an-ti za-a-lu-ša-e še-e-ni-íw-wu-ša-an

15) KUR u-u-mi-i-ni-wa a-a-i-i-ta na-wa ta-la-ma e-ti-i-ta ta-a-na-aš-du-‹wa›-en

16) pa-nu-ú-ul-le-e-ni-i-in i-i-iš-ḫé-e-wa ti-w[a]-a-al-la-a-an šur-WA še-e-ni-íw-wu-ta

17) ka-ti-ik-ki še-e-ni-íw-wu-ta-a-ma-a-an a-we-en-né-e-ni-i-in ti-wi šur-WA

18) i-ia-am-ma-ma-an ka-ti-le-e-wa šu-u-we-né-e e-ti-íw-wu-ú-e

19) KUR u-u-mi-i-ni-íw-wu-ú-e-né-e e-ti-i-e-e še-e-ni-íw-wu-ú-ul-la-a-an ti-we

20) a-né-e-na-a-am-ma-ma-an ḫa-ša-a-ši-wa-a-en a-i-la-an ^{I}Ma-né-eš ^{I}Ge-li-ia-al-la-a-an

21) gu-li-a-a-ma i-i-e-na-a-ma-a-ni-i-in ^{I}Ma-né-eš ^{I}Ge-‹li›-ia-al-la-a-an ka-til-le-ta

22) šu-u-we-né-e e-ti-íw-wu-ú-e-e KUR u-u-mi-i-ni-íw-wu-ú-e-né-e e-ti-i-e

23) ur-ḫal-la-a-an pal-ta-a-la-an ḫa-ša-a-ši-il-la-a-i-ni-il-la-a-an še-e-ni-íw-wu-uš

24) a-we-en-na-a-ni-i-in gu-ru šu-ú-ú-ta i-ia-am-ma-ma-an ḫi-il-lu-le-e-wa

25) še-e-ni-íw-wu-ú-e-né-e e-ti-i-e-e KUR u-u-mi-i-ni-i-we-né-e e-ti-i-e-e

26) ḫa-ša-a-ši-wa-al-li-i-il-la-a-an a-i-la-an ^{I}Ge-li-i-⸢aš⸣ ^{I}Ma-né-e-el-la-a-an

27) gu-li-a-a-ma i-i-e-ma-a-ni-i-in ^{I}Ge-li-i-aš ^{I}Ma-né-eš-ša-a-an gu-le-e-ta

28) še-e-ni-íw-‹wu›-ú-e-né-e e-ti-i-e-e KUR u-u-mi-i-ni-i-we-né-e e-ti-i-e-e

29) ur-ḫa-al-la-a-an pa-al-ta-a-la-an ḫa-ša-a-ši-il-li-i-il-la-a-an

(6–27) and I have, on the other hand, heard, that my brother has done a…thing and a great…has my brother…And for (or among) the peop[le] of Awari he has made provision and he has…' I heard about it, and I have rejoiced. If my brother had not behaved in this manner, I would have been very sad. And not again has a babbler(?) spoken; Parattuiranna said it(! sc. the word?): My brother is brotherly (minded). The relevant word is at hand, the relevant word is in…manner spoken, and may my brother…it in his land concerning the great…they for instance…, one has not spoken an evil word to my brother. As for an evil word which someone, for instance, spoke to my brother concerning me (or) concerning my land, that word may I not heed if Mane and Keliya do not say them. As for the (word), however, that Mane and Keliya say concerning me (or) concerning my land, that is true and correct, so may my brother heed them! As for that too that anyone might express to me concerning my brother (or) concerning his land, will I not heed. If Keliya and Mane will speak

(28–29) concerning my brother (or) concerning his land, it (sc. the word) is true and correct and I will heed it!

§ 28

30) un-du-ma-a-an i-i-al-le-e-ni-i-in ti-we-e-na^{MEŠ} šu-ú-al-la-ma-an
31) še-e-ni-íw-wu-uš ka-⸢du-u-ša⸣-a-aš-še-na ú-ú-ri-a-a-aš-še-na an-til-la-a-an
32) e-e-ma-na-a-am-ḫa ⸢ta-a-nu⸣-ša-a-ú ti-ša-a-ma-a-an še-e-ni-íw-wu-ú-e šuk-kán-né-en
33) pa-ti ti-[w]e-e-né-en ḫi-su-ú-ḫu-ši-úw-wu aš-ti-i-in še-e-ni-íw-wu-ú-e
34) a-ru-u-ša-ú še-e-ni-íw-wu-ú-e-né-e-en ti-ša-a-an-na ši-ra-aš-še
35) un-du-u-un ^{m}Ma-né-e-na-an še-e-ni-íw-wu-ú-e pa-aš-ši-i-it-ḫi un-du-u-un
36) ^{I}Ge-li-ia-na-an ^{I}Ar-te-e-eš-šu-pa-na-an ^{I}A-sa-a-li-in-na-a-an pa-aš-ši-i-it-ḫi-íw-we
37) ^{I}G e-li-ia-na-an ta-la-mi ^{I}A-sa-a-li-in-na-a-an tup-šar-ri-íw-wu-ú-un-ni
38) ki-i-pu-šu-ú-uš-ši še-e-ni-íw-wu-ta-al-la-a-an ni-i-ru-ša-e tiš-ša-an
39) pa-aš-šu-ša-a-ú še-e-ni-íw-wu-ú-ul-la-a-an wu-re-e-e-ta

§ 29

40) še-e-ni-íw-wu-ú-ul-⸢la-a⸣-an pa-aš-ši-i-it-ḫi-íw-we ku-su-uš-ti-wa-a-en kar-ḫaš-ti-wa-a-en
41) še-e-ni-íw-wu-ú-ut-ta-⸢a⸣-an ši-la-a-ḫu-šu-uš-ti-wa-a-en pa-aš-ši-i-it-ḫi-íw-WA-la-an
42) še-e-ni-íw-wu-uš šu-ra-a-maš-ti-en na-ak-ki-en ti-wa-a-at-ta-a-an gu-ru-ú-wa
43) še-e-ni-íw-wu-ú-e-ma-a-an ge-e-el-ti ni-i-ri-še ḫa-ši-i-i-le
44) bi-sa-an-ti-iš-tin-na-a-an tiš-ša-an še-e-ni-íw-wu-ú-e-né-e-wa ge-el-ti-i-wa

§ 28

(30–39) And now. all the things that my brother has named (and) wants, these have I done tenfold. And with not a single word have I distressed my brother's heart. My brother's wife have I given, who matches my brother's desire. Now have I sent off Mane, my brother's envoy most magnificently. Now too, (have I dispatched) Keliya and Ar-Teššob and Asali—Keliya is a senior official and Asali is as my tablet scribe…, to my brother and my brother will see them.

§ 29

(40–44) And may my brother not detain my envoys, may he not …(them), and may my brother not…me. And may my brother release them speedily, and a word…I. Concerning the welfare (and the) good situation of my brother may I hear, and I will rejoice greatly over the welfare of my brother.

§ 30

45) še-e-ni-íw-we-en-na-a-an ḫi-il-lu-⸢le⸣-e-wa e-ta-la-an pa-aš-ši-i-it-ḫi-íw-we ku-⸢su⸣?-u-šu
46) u-ia-ma-a-an ku-su!(Text:zu)-u-ši-úw-wu-la-an še-e-ni-íw-wu-ú-e-né-e-wa-a-tan aš-ti-i-i-we
47) ni-ḫa-a-ri-i-ta ú-ru-u-mu wu-re-e-ta-a-an še-e-ni-íw-wu-uš-ša-ma-an
48) še-e-ni-íw-wu-ú-e-né-e-we aš-ti-i-we ni-ḫa-a-ri a-ru-u-ša-uš-še
49) ip-šu-ši-i-in ti-i-ḫa-níš-ḫi-i-in ú-ú-na-a-an še-e-ni-íw-wu-‹ú›-e-né-e
50) a-a-i-i-e-e be-te-eš-ta-iš

§ 31

51) še-e-ni-íw-wu-ú-ul-la-a-an pa-aš-ši-i-it-ḫi-íw-we šu-ra-a-maš-ti-en na-ak-ki-en
52) it-ta-i-šal-la-a-an ^{I}Ma-né-en-na-a-an še-e-ni-íw-wu-uš šu-ka pa-aš-ši-en
53) it-ta-in-na-a-an pa-aš-ši-i-it-ḫi-íw-wu-ra šu-ka u-u-le-e-en še-e-ni-íw-wu-uš
54) pa-aš-ši-i-it-ḫé pa-aš-ša-ri-i-wa-a-en ^{I}Ma-né-en-na-ma-an pa-aš-ši-en a-i-ma-a-ni-i-in
55) ^{I}Ma a-né-en še-e-ni-íw-wu-uš pa-aš-ši-a-a-ma u-u-li-ma-a-an pa-aš-še-e-e-ta
56) ú-ú-ri-úw-wu-un-na-a-an še-e-ni-íw-wu-uš-ša-a-an pal-la-a-en
57) u-ia-ma-a-an še-e-ni-íw-wu-ša-an ^{I}Ma-né-en-na-ma-an pa-aš-ši-en

§ 30

(45–50) My brother may say: "You yourself have also detained my envoys!" No, I have not detained them. I was occupied(??) with the dowry of the wife of my brother and my brother himself will see the dowry of the wife of my brother, which I have given;...(It is) coming, therewith will it be spread out in the view of my brother.

§ 31

(51–57) May my brother release my envoys as soon as possible so they can leave. And only may my brother send Mane so that he may travel with my envoy. May my brother not send another envoy; may he only send Mane. If my brother does not send Mane and would send another, I don't want him, and my may brother know this! No, may my brother send only Mane!

§ 32

58) še-e-ni-íw-wu-ú-e-ma-a-an aš-ti an-ni a-ru-u-ša-uš-še ta-a-ki-⸢ma-a⸣-an an-ti

59) ma-a-an-ni še-e-ni-íw-wu-uš-ša-a-an pal-la-en ⸢a-i⸣-ma-⸢a-ni-i⸣-in ma-a-an-nu-pa-a-ta-e

60) u-u-⸢lu-u⸣-[ḫ]é-e-et-ta gu-le-e-⸢et⸣-ta ta-a-an-ki-ma-a-an an-ti ma-a-an-ni

61) me-⸢e-na-a⸣-an ma-a-an-na-a-an še-wa-a-an-⸢ši-íw-wu⸣-ú-un-na-al-la-a-an zu-tar-ḫi-íw-wa-al-la-ma-an

62) ši-né-e-el-la-ma-an ša-ta-a-al-la-a-an ^{MUNUS}né-e-ri-íw-wu-ú-la-an e-ti-i-ta

63) ap-su-u-ša i-šal-la-a-an ap-su-ša-a-ul-la-ma-an me-e-na-ma-a-an ki-ka-e

64) wa-a-aš-na-e ma-a-nu-tan ta-al-la DINGIR.MEŠ e-e-ni-íw-wa-al-la-a-an pal-la-in

65) DINGIR.MEŠ e-e-ni-il-la-a-an še-e-ni-íw-wu-ú-e-na pal-la-i-šal-la-ma-an a-i-i-in

66) me-e-na ak-ki ma-a-nu-ú-un-na ši-la-a-ḫu-uš-ḫa ir-ni a-i-i-in ni-i-ir-ša-e

67) ⸢^{MUNUS}Ta-a⸣-[d]u-⸢ḫé-e-pa⸣-a-an-na a-za-al-ta zu-kán pa-ti a-i-i-in

68) ⸢^{MUNUS}WA-du-ú-uk⸣-ki-i-ta zu-kán pa-ti ú-ú-ul-ša

§ 33

69) [..(.)-i]t-ti-a-a-⸢an-né⸣-e-we-e-en šu-uk-ku u-u-li tub-be zu-ku-u-u-un

70) [.]-uk-ku-un-⸢nam⸣-ma-a-an ⸢gu-ru⸣ ak-kíl-la-a-an *x x x*-⸢aš⸣-š[e]-n[é]-⸢e⸣-w[e]^{MEŠ}

71) [šu]-⸢ú⸣-al-la-ma-⸢an⸣ zu-ge-et-ta-al-[l]a-a-an a-*x*[....(..) g]u-ru

72) [.]-ú-ul-šu-⸢ú⸣$^{?}$-⸢a⸣$^{?}$ zu-kán pa-⸢ti⸣ aš-ti-*x*[........(..)]*x*

73) *x x x x*-aš-ti-en-na-a-an *x*[.....................................]

74) [šu]-⸢ú-al⸣-l[a-m]a-⸢an⸣ ti-W[A-.........................]

§ 32

(58–60) And as for this wife of my brother, which I have given, this (woman) is pure/unstained. And may my brother know it. If…she…were, she(?) would speak. Which is relevant…

(61–68) and she is also a twin(?), as my….., my…both of them…my mother has…them and I have…them. And the twin(?)…three from him…so that my deities know, and so that the deities of my brother know, that in in a good manner Tadoḫeba is……, that she is……to her.

§ 33

(69–74) Yet another matter of…is at hand,……again. The one, from…, all…, …again…wife……may…all…

§ 34

75) [še-e-ni-í]w-⸢wu-ú-e-né-e⸣-we/a-ma-a-an aš-t[i-i-we/a...........]
76) [...š]e-⸢e⸣-ni-íw-wu-ta-a-ma-a-an *x*[.....]
77) [še-e-ni]-íw-wu-[t]a-a-ma-a-an u-u-la-e-⸢e⸣[-em-.................]
78) [an-ti]-⸢ma⸣-a-an ⸢ma⸣-a-an-ni ta-a-an-ki ⸢a⸣-[...................]
79) [..-]ma-a-an ⸢ša-a⸣-ru-ši-⸢i⸣-in-ni [ki?]
80) [..-]⸢e⸣-el-la-⸢a-an u-u-ul⸣-la *x*[ ]
81) [...]*x x*[ ]
82–84) destroyed

§ 34

(75–84) [The] wife of my [brothe]r...[...] To my brother [...] To my brother another [...] [This] is...[...] [...] has he has demanded [...] [...] another [...] (*gap*)

85) [ᴵ]⌜Ma-né-eš⌝
86) [ ]-i-in
87) [-k]u-u-ni-i-in
88) [..........(-r)e-e]-⌜en⌝ u[r-..-n]a-⌜ma⌝- an t[a?-a?] -na-a-an
89) [......... (-a-ni-i)]-in ⌜ḫa⌝-[š]u-⌜u⌝-ša MUNUSTa-a-⌜du-ḫé-e⌝-[pa-na?-an?]
90) [........(x-a-an-nu)]-⌜u-*ḫu⌝-u*-ša-⌜a⌝-[u]š-ša i-šu-ú-ḫu-ši-i-in
91) [.........(-an)] ⌜a-a-i⌝-i-t[a] uš-ta-a-an ši-ia-ma-a-an
92) [........a-(⌜a⌝-i-i-tan) . ḫ]a-šu-u-⌜ša⌝-ú-un i-šu-ú-⌜ḫu⌝-ši-ik-ku-u-un-na
93) [.........š(i-i-it-ta)-..(.)]-⌜e⌝-ta-ma-an i-ši ša-a-la-pa-an
94) [.........-(du-ú)-..(.)]-⌜e⌝-wa-a-ni-i-in KUR u-u-⌜mi-i-in⌝-n[i-..]
95) [......(..) (e-ni)-..] ⌜a-ru⌝-la-ú KUR Ša-an-ḫar-ra-ša-⌜ni⌝-‹i-›[i]n
96) [........(...)] ⌜ta-a-du-ka-a⌝-ri-im-pu-ú-uš-še-né-e-⌜ra-a⌝-an
97) [.......(...) -n]i pa-li-u-mu-u-li-i-in KUR Ma-a-[áš-ri-a-a]n-na
98) [.......(...)]-an at-ta-⌜a-ar-ti⌝-[íw-w]u-raMEŠ
99) [....t(a)....(.) pa]-li-u-mu-u-li-i-in at-ta-[a-ar-t]i-íw-wu-uš
100) [....(a?-al)....z]u-ge-et-ta-ar-ti-aš [...]-⌜ta⌝-a-aš-še-na
101) [....(.-ša)...-]x-ta-a-aš-ša ḫé-en-né-⌜e⌝-ma-a-ni-i-in
102) [....(.)-(íw-we)...-i]l-ta ḫu-ši ḫa-šu-u-[ši?]-a?-ma-a-al-la-a-an
103) [...(. ma-a-an-na-a)-an] ḫi-il-li ú-pu-u-šu-u-⌜ti⌝-[i]-in an-til-la-a-an
104) [...(ma-⌜a⌝-an-nu-uk-ku)(-)..(.)]-i-in ki-nam-ri-na-⌜an⌝ i[t]-ti-i-wa-an tap-pu-šu-ú
105) [...-m(a-a-ni-i-in KU)R ma]-⌜a⌝-áš-ri-a-an-na-ša [z]a?-ru-u-⌜a⌝? ⌜za-ru-a⌝-ma-a-la-an
106) [..-í(w-we i-ši-i-ma-a-)an?] ḫi-i-šu-ša-a-un-na-a-an ⌜e⌝?-mi-i-wa-an e-ti-i-tan
107) [še-e-ni-(íw-wu-ú-an-na-ma)-a]n be-kán an-ti-ma-a-an [m]a-a-an-ni ti-we
108) [ša-a-ru-š(i-im-pu-ú-uš-še še)-e-n]i-íw-wu-uš-ša-a-an [pa]l-la-en i-nu-ú-ma-a-ni-i-in
109) [(x)..(⌜ú-a⌝)...(⌜ri-i⌝?)-i]t? ka-til-le-e-et-t[a-a]-⌜am⌝-ma-ma-an u-u-la-e
110) x-x-[u]k-⌜ku⌝-[u]n-⌜na-a-an še-e⌝-[ni-íw-w]u-ú-ul-la-a-an ḫa-ša-a-ši-wa-a-en

(85–110) [...] Mane...he has [...] heard. Tadoḫe[ba] has in the manner, which I have given(?) her,...[...]before his view is she opened up....[...] I have heard it.......Your daughter...perhaps. To the(?) land(s) [......] have I given. On the Babylonians [...]...[...]and to those allied in mutual desire [...]...the Egyptians [...] with my ancestors [...]...my ancestors [...] your..., which he [...] will [...] which he [...] will, now my [...] has not heard it [...] This he said:...these [...] are not.........to the Egyptians...they in minew [...] he/her, and I have him/her concerning hin...my brother in no way(?)...That is the thing, which [has been demanded], and may my brother know it. Likewise [...]...as an informant(?) speaks in some other way, may my brother not heed it (sc. the words)!

§ 35

111) [še-(⸢e⸣)-n]i-íw-wu-ra-a-ma-a-an ti-ši-íw-wa-an [t]e-u-u-na-e tiš-ša-an wa-aḫ-ru-um-me

112) [ta-a-d]u-ka-a-ru-um-me ú-ú-[r]a-ú še-e-ni-í[w-w]e-en-na-a-an ur-ḫu-up-ti-in

113) [te-u-u]-na-e tiš-ša-[a]n wa-aḫ-ru-uš-til-la-a-an ta-[a]-du-ka-a-‹ri›-iš ti-ši-íw-wa-ša-an

114) [ ]-*x*-ti-l[a$^{?}$-]-⸢zu⸣-uš KUR [u]-⸢u-mi-i-ni-íw-wu⸣-‹ú-›[d]il-la-a-an ka-šu-u-ul-la-in

115) [..-š]a-a aš-d[u- .]-ip-ri-íw-wa-š[a i-nu-ú-me]-⸢e⸣-ni-i-in še-e-er-re-e-tan

116) [DINGIR.MEŠ]e-e-en-ni-ip-tan še-ḫur-ni-í[w-w]a-aš ḫu-tan-ni-íw-wa-aš ša-a-ri-il-le-et-ta

117) [ša]-a-a[t]-til-la-a-an ši-né-e-til-la-ma-an [DINGIR].MEŠ e-e-en-na-šu-uš na-ak-ki-te-en

118) ^{d}Te-e-eš-šu-pa-aš ‹^{d}›A-ma-a-nu-ú-til-la-a-an éw-ri-íw-wa-šu-uš at-ta-íw-wa-šu-uš

119) še-eḫ-ru-uš-til-la-a-an a-ti-i-ni-i-in [m]a-a-an-na-til-la-ma-an u-ru-uḫ-ḫi-iš-til-la-a-an

120) kàr-ḫas-tiš-⸢til⸣-la-a-an a-ti-i-ma-ni-i-in k[ar]$^{?}$-ra-a-ti-la-an

121) še-e-en-nu-uḫ-ḫa ḫé-šal-lu-uḫ-ḫa-a-til-la-a-an ta-a-du-ka-a-ri-iš i-nu-ú-me-e-ni-i-in

122) ^{d}Ši-mi-ge tar-šu-an-néš wu-ri-i-ma-in ta-a-ti-a a-nam-mi-til-la-a-an iš-ta-ni-íw-wa-ša

123) ta-a-du-ka-a-ar-re-e-wa ag-gu-uš-ša-a-an a-gu-ú-e iš-⸢ta⸣-ni-íw-wa-ša-an

124) [ḫ]u-tan$^{?}$-[n]i$^{?}$ ša-a-ri-il-le-e-ta i-i-al-la-a-ni-i-in KUR u-u-mi-i-in-na^{MEŠ}

125) [šu-ú]-al-la-ma-an e-e-še-ni tup-pa-aš-še-na ^{d}Ši-mi-i-ge-néš ḫ[u$^{?}$-š]u-[u]d-du-u-la-a-aš-še-na

126) [an-ti-il-la]-a-an šu-ú-a[l]-la-ma-an e-ti-íw-wa-ša i-i-il-le-e-wa a-nam-mil-la-a-an

127) [ ]-e-wa [ú]-ú-rík-ki ^{d}Du-uš-rat-[ta-an] KUR ḫur-wu-u-ḫé e-we-er-ni

128) [-i]š ^{I}I m-mu-u-ri-i-an KUR ma-a-áš-ri-[a-a(n)]-ni e-we-er-ni a-i-la-a[n]

129) [-n]i$^{?}$ iš-ta-ni-a-ša an-za-a-an-nu-uḫ-ḫa-[ša] in-na-al-la-ma-a[n]

130) [-p]a-a-duḫ-ḫa ta-a-du-ka-a-ri t[e]-u-u-la-e tiš-ša-an

§ 35

(111–128) In my heart I wish to be on the best of terms with my brother and to love one another. And may my brother keep faith perfectly. And we wish to be friendly (to each other), (and) we would love one another and in our hearts [...]...[...], therewith my land [...] us [...]in our......As from..., (and) from your god our life (and) our glory will be desired, may the gods let both of us be—Teššob and Amanu, our lords, our fathers—(that) we may live. So be it (lit. so we are)! My we...and may we...! So...we/us, and between us may we in a brotherly and collegial manner love one another. As man loves the sun god when he sees him, so do we want, between us, to love one another, and between us may we desire the glory of one another. All the lands that exist, which the sun god unites, all of [which] may they serve(?) us, this...may they...[Bot]h Tušratta, the Hurrian king, [and al]so Immoriya, the Egyptian king, if they...

(129–130) between them ...as long as they are..., love one another exceedingly.

EA 25

TRANSCRIPTION

COL. I

(1–5) [...]

---

(6) [.......................N]A$_4$.ZA.GÌN KUR 33.[........]
(7) [.......................N]A$_4$.ZA.GÌN KUR 20(?) [......]

---

(8) [......................N]A$_4$.ZA.GÌN KUR. N[A$_4$.......]

---

(9) [..........................] - *i*-[.....................]

---

(10) [...................... *-t*]*i ù te*$_9$*-ri-*[*in-na-ti-šu-*(*nu*)]
(11) [..]

---

(12) [................................*te*$_9$*-ri-i*]*n-na-ti-šu-nu* NA$_4$.ZA.GÌN KUR
(13) [..] *tam-lu-ú*

---

(14) [.......................*te*$_9$*-ri-in-*]*na-ti-šu-nu at-ri-šu-nu*
(15) [..] *tam-lu-ú*

---

(16) 1 ŠU [*in-ṣa-bá-tu*$_4$ KÙ.GI *te*$_9$*-ri-in-na-ti*]*-šu-nu* NA$_4$.ZA.GÌN KUR *ù gu-ug-gu-bi-šu-nu* NA$_4$.NÍR KUR

---

(17) 1 ŠU *in-ṣa-b*[*á-tu*$_4$ KÙ.GI *te*$_9$*-ri-in-na-t*]*i-šu-nu* NA$_4$.NÍR KUR *gu-ug-gu-bi-šu-nu* NA$_4$.ZA.GÌN KUR

---

(18) 1 ŠU *in-ṣa-bá-tu*$_4$ KÙ.GI *t*[*e*$_9$*-ri-in*]*-na-ti-šu-nu* NA$_4$.NÍR KUR 4 TA.ÀM
(19) *gu-ug-gu-bi-šu-nu* NA$_4$.NÍR KUR

EA 25

TRANSLATION

COL. I

(1–5) [...]

---

(6) [........................]pure lapis lazuli·33 [...........]
(7) [........................ pure lapis lazuli· 20(?) [.........]

---

(8) [..........................]pure lapis lazuli·[............]

---

(9) [.........................].. [....................]

---

(10) [........................] and [their] con[es]
(11) [...]

---

(12) [...............................]their [co]nes of pure lapis lazuli
(13) [...] inlay

---

(14) [........................]their [co]nes, their extras
(15) [..] inlay

---

(16) 1 set [of earrings, of gold]; their [cones] of genuine lapis lazuli, their *guggubu* ornaments of genuine *ḫulalu*-stone.

---

(17) 1 set of ear[rings, of g]old; [cones] of genuine *ḫulalu*-stone, and their *guggubu* ornaments of genuine lapis lazuli.

---

(18) 1 set of earrings, of gold; their c[on]es of genuine lapis lazuli, 4 on each;
(19) their *guggubu* ornaments of genuine *ḫulalu*-stone.

---

(20) 1 ŠU *in-ṣa-bá-tu*$_4$ KÙ.GI *t*[*e*$_9$*-ri*]*-in-na-ti-šu-nu* NA$_4$.ZA.GÌN. KUR ša-sà-*tu*$_4$
(21) *gu-ug-gu-bi-šu-nu* NA$_4$.NÍR KUR

---

(22) 1 ŠU *du-dì-na-tu*$_4$ *tam-lu-ú tam-lu-ú-šu-nu* NA$_4$.ZA.GÌN KUR SAG-*sú-nu.*^{NA_4}*ḫi-li-bá*

---

(23) 1 ŠU *du-dì-na-tu*$_4$ *tam-lu-ú tam-lu-ú-šu-nu* NA$_4$.ZA.GÌN KUR SAG-*sú-nu* NA$_4$.NÍR KUR

---

(24) 1 ŠU *du-dì-na-tu*$_4$*.tam-lu-*⸢*ú*⸣ *tam-lu-ú-šu-nu* NA$_4$.ZA.GÌN KUR SAG-*sú-nu* NA$_4$.NÍR KUR

---

(25) 1 ŠU *du-dì-na-tu*$_4$ *tam-l*[*u-ú*] *tam-lu-ú-šu-nu* NA$_4$.ZA.GÌN KUR SAG-*sú-nu* NA$_4$.NÍR KUR

---

(26) 1 ŠU *du-dì-na-tu*$_4$ *tam-lu-ú tam-lu-ú-šu-nu* NA$_4$.ZA.GÌN KUR SAG-*sú-nu.*^{NA_4}*ḫi-li-bá*

---

(27) 1 ŠU *du-dì-na-tu*$_4$ KÙ.GI *ša da-ma šu-lu-ú ša pè-er-ʾ-a-zi* SAG-*sú* ^{NA_4}*ḫi-li-bá*

---

(28) 1 ŠU *du-dì-na-tu*$_4$ NA$_4$.N[Í]R KUR SAG-*sú-nu* ⸢NA$_4$.⸣[N]ÍR KUR

---

(29) 1 ŠU *du-dì-na-tu*$_4$ NA$_4$.N[ÍR] KUR SAG-*sú-nu* ^{NA_4}*ḫi-li-bá*

---

(30) [1] [Š]U *du-dì-na-tu*$_4$ N[A$_4$.][NÍR] KUR SAG-*sú-nu* ^{NA_4}*ḫi-li-bá*

---

(31) [1] [ŠU] *du-dì-na-tu*$_4$ KÙ.GI [*up-p*]*u-qù-tu*$_4$ SAG-*sú-nu* NA$_4$.ZA.GÌN KUR

---

(32) 1 ŠU *du-dì-na-tu*$_4$ KÙ.GI *up-pu-qù-tu*$_4$ SAG-*sú-nu* NA$_4$.NÍR KUR

---

(33) 1 *mi-iḫ-ṣú* 6 NA$_4$.ZA.GÌN KUR 7 ^{NA_4}*ḫi-li-bá* 14 *bi-ik-rù* KÙ.GI 72 *ma-ni-in-ni* NA$_4$.ZA.GÌN KUR
(34) 40 *ma-ni-i-in-nu* KÙ.GI

---

(20) 1 set of earrings, of gold; their c[o]nes of genuine lapis lazuli,
(21) their *guggubu* ornaments of genuine *ḫulalu*-stone.

(22) 1 set of toggle pins, (with) inlay; their inlay of genuine lapis lazuli; their top of genuine *ḫulalu*-stone.

(23) 1 set of toggle pins, (with) inlay; their inlay of genuine lapis lazuli; their top of genuine *ḫulalu*-stone.

(24) 1 set of toggle pins, (with) inlay; their inlay of genuine lapis lazuli; their top of genuine *ḫulalu*-stone.

(25) 1 set of toggle pins, (with) inlay; their inlay of genuine lapis lazuli; their top of genuine *ḫulalu*-stone.

(26) 1 set of toggle pins, (with) inlay; their inlay of genuine lapis lazuli; their top of *ḫiliba*-stone.

(27) 1 set of toggle pins, of gold with *a reddish tinge* (and) of *perʾāzi*, their top of *ḫiliba*-stone.

(28) 1 set of toggle pins, of genuine *ḫulalu*-stone. their top of genuine *ḫulalu*-stone.

(29) 1 set of toggle pins, of genuine *ḫulalu*-stone. their top of *ḫiliba*-stone.

(30) [1] [se]t of toggle pins, of genuine [...]; their top of *ḫiliba*-stone.

(31) 1 set of toggle pins, of solid gold; their top of genuine lapis lazuli

(32) [1] [se]t of toggle pins, of solid gold; their top of genuine *ḫulalu*-stone.

(33) 1 "weave": 6 genuine lapis lazuli beads, 7 *ḫiliba*-beads, 14 *bikru*-gems of gold, 72 strings of genuine lapis lazuli
(34) 40 strings of gold.

(35) [1] [*m*]*i-ḫi-ṣú* 9 NA$_4$.ZA.GÌN.KUR 10 ^{NA_4}*ḫi-li-bá* 20 *bi-ik-ri* KÙ.GI
(36) [x] *ma-ni-in-nu* NA$_4$.ZA.GÌN.KUR 38 *ma-ni-in-nu* KÙ.GI

---

(37) [1] [*mi-iḫ*]-*ṣú* KÙ.GI 1 ^{NA_4}*ḫi-li-bá* 4 NA$_4$.ZA.GÌN.KUR 4 *ḫi-in-du* KÙ.GI

---

(38) [1] [*ma-ni-i*]*n-nu ša* NA$_4$.KIŠIB NA$_4$.ZA.GÌN KUR 13 *i-na mi-nu-ti* KÙ.GI GAR

---

(39) [x] [*ma-ni-i*]*n-nu ša* NA$_4$.KIŠIB 13 [NA$_4$.KIŠI]B NA$_4$.ZA.GÌN KUR KÙ.GI GAR 2 NA$_4$.KIŠIB NÍR KUR KÙ.GI GAR

---

(40) [1] [*ma-ni-i*]*n-nu kab-bu-tu*$_4$ 28(?) NA$_4$.ZA.GÌN KUR 28 ^{NA_4}*ḫi-li-bá* MURUB$_4$ NA$_4$.NÍR KUR KÙ.GI GAR

---

(41) [1] [*ma-ni-i*]*n-nu šar-mu* 16(?) NA$_4$.ZA.GÌN KUR 25 KÙ.GI MURUB$_4$ NA$_4$.ZA.GÌN KUR KÙ.GI GAR

---

(42) [1] [*ma-ni-i*]*n-nu šar-mu* 26 NA$_4$.ZA.GÌN KUR 26 ^{NA_4}*ḫi-li-bá* MURUB$_4$ NA$_4$.ZA.GÌN KUR KÙ.GI GAR

---

(43) [1] *ma-ni-in-nu šar-mu* 37 NA$_4$.ZA.GÌN KUR 39 KÙ.GI *ša tù-ut-tù-ri* MURUB$_4$ NA$_4$.NÍR KUR KÙ.GI GAR

---

(44) 1 *ma-ni-in-nu šar-mu* 38 NA$_4$.ZA.GÌN KUR 38 KÙ.GI *ša tù-ut-tù-ri* MURUB$_4$ NA$_4$.NÍR KUR KÙ.GI GAR

---

(45) 1 *ma-ni-in-nu šar-mu* 26 N[A$_4$.Z]A.GÌN KUR 28 ^{NA_4}*ḫi-li-bá* MURUB$_4$ NA$_4$.ZA.GÍN KUR KÙ.GI GAR

---

(35) 1 "weave": 9 genuine lapis lazuli beads, 10 *ḫiliba*-beads, 20 *bikru*-gems of gold, [*x*] strings of lapis lazuli, 38 strings of gold,

(36) [*x*] strings of lapis lazuli, 38 strings of gold.

---

(37) [1] ["wea]ve," of gold: 1 *ḫiliba*-stone, 4 genuine lapis lazuli beads, 4…of gold.

---

(38) [1] [*mani*]*nnu*-necklace, of seal-shaped beads of lapis lazuli; 13 per string, mounted on gold.

---

(39) [1] [*mani*]*nnu*- necklace, of seal-shaped beads; 13 seal-shaped beads of genuine lapis lazuli; mounted on gold; 2 seal-shaped beads of genuine-*ḫulalu*-stone, mounted on gold.

---

(40) [1] [*mani*]*nnu*-necklace (with) a *counterweight*: 28 genuine lapis lazuli beads, 28 *ḫiliba*-beads; the centerpiece a genuine *ḫulalu*-stone mounted on gold.

---

(41) [1] [*man*]*innu*-necklace, cut: 16(?) genuine lapis lazuli beads, 25 of gold; the centerpiece a genuine lapis lazuli stone mounted on gold.

---

(42) [1] [*mani*]*nnu*-necklace, cut: 26 genuine lapis lazuli beads, 26 *ḫiliba*-beads; the centerpiece a genuine lapis lazuli stone mounted on gold.

---

(43) [1] *maninnu*-necklace, cut: 37 genuine lapis lazuli beads, 39 (*pieces of*) gold *leaf*; the centerpiece a genuine *ḫulalu*-stone mounted on gold.

---

(44) 1 *maninnu*-necklace, cut: 38 genuine lapis lazuli beads, 38 (*pieces of*) gold *leaf*; the centerpiece a genuine *ḫulalu*-stone mounted on gold.

---

(45) 1 *maninnu*-necklace, cut: 26 genuine lapis lazuli beads, 28 *ḫiliba*-beads; the centerpiece a genuine lapis lazuli stone mounted on gold.

---

(46) 1 *ma-ni-in-nu šar-mu* 38 N[A$_4$. ZA.GÌN KUR] 38 KÙ.GI *ša* [*tù-ut-tù-ri*] MURUB$_4$ NA$_4$.NÍR KUR KÙ.GI GAR

(47) [1] *ma-ni-in-nu šar-mu* 43 NA$_4$.[ZA.GÌN KUR ^{N}]$^{A}{}_{4}$*ḫi-li-bá* [MURUB$_4$] NA$_4$.SAG. KAL KÙ.GI GAR

(48) 1 *ma-ni-in-nu šar-mu* 32 NA$_4$.[ZA.GÌN KUR x $^{NA}{}_{4}$*ḫi-l*]*i-b*[*á* MURUB$_4$ NA$_4$.]NÍR KUR KÙ.GI GAR

(49) [1] [*m*]*a*-⸢*ni*⸣-⸢*in*⸣-*nu šar-mu* 30 NA$_4$.⸢ZA⸣.GÌN KUR 28 $^{NA}{}_{4}$*ḫi*-[*li-bá* MURUB$_4$ NA$_4$.NÍR KUR] KÙ.GI GAR

(50) 1 *ma-ni-in-nu šar*-⸢*mu*⸣ 34(?) NA$_4$.ZA.GÌN KUR 35 [........] MURUB$_4$ NA$_4$.NÍR KUR KÙ.GI GAR

(51) 1 *ma-ni-in-nu šar-mu* 17 NA$_4$.ZA.GÌN KUR 16 NA$_4$.SAG.KAL 35 KÙ.GI MURUB$_4$ NA$_4$.SAG.KAL KÙ.GI GAR

(52) 1 *ma-ni-in-nu šar-mu* 23 NA$_4$.ZA.GÌN KUR 25 $^{NA}{}_{4}$*mar-ḫa-lì*
(53) 48 KÙ.GI *ša tù-ut-tù-ri* MURUB$_4$ NA$_4$.ZA.GÌN KUR KÙ.GI GAR

(54) 1 *ma-ni-in-nu šar-mu* 34 NA$_4$.ZÚ 33 KÙ.GI MURUB$_4$ NA$_4$.ZA.GÌN.KUR KÙ.GI GAR

(55) ⸢1⸣ *ma-ni-in-nu kab-bu-tu*$_4$ 14(?)NA$_4$.ZA.GÌN KUR 25 NA$_4$.NÍR KUR 17 $^{NA}{}_{4}$*ḫi-li-bá*
(56) [MURUB$_4$] NA$_4$.ZA.GÌN KUR KÙ.GI GAR

(57) [1] [*ma-ni-i*]*n-nu* ⸢*kab*⸣-*b*[*u*]-*tu*$_4$ 14(?) [N]A$_4$.ZA.GÌN KUR 16 NA$_4$.NÍR KUR 30 KÙ.GI
(58) [*tù-ut-tù-ri*(?) MURUB$_4$......] KÙ.GI GAR

(46) [1] *maninnu*-necklace, cut: 38 [genuine lapis lazuli stone]s, 38 (*pieces of*) gold [*leaf*]; its centerpiece a genuine *ḫulalu*-stone mounted on gold.

---

(47) [1] *maninnu*-necklace, cut: 43 [genuine lapis lazuli] beads, [*x*] *ḫiliba*-[sto]nes; [the centerpiece] a SAG.KAL-stone mounted on gold.

---

(48) 1 *maninnu*-necklace, cut: 32 [genuine lapis lazuli beads, *x ḫil*]*iba*-beads; the centerpiece a genuine *ḫulalu*-stone mounted on gold.

---

(49) [1] *maninnu*-necklace, cut: 30 genuine lapis lazuli beads, 28 *ḫi*[*liba*-]beads; the centerpiece a [*ḫulalu* -stone] mounted on gold.

---

(50) 1 *maninnu*-necklace, cut: 34 genuine *ḫulalu*-beads, 35 [...beads]; the center[piece] a genuine *ḫulalu*-stone mounted on gold.

---

(51) 1 *maninnu*-necklace, cut: 17 genuine lapis lazuli beads, 16 SAG.KAL-beads, 35 gold (beads); the centerpiece a SAG.KAL-stone mounted on gold.

---

(52) 1 *maninnu*-necklace, cut: 23 genuine lapis lazuli beads, 25 carnelian (?) beads;

(53) 48 (*pieces of*) gold *leaf*; the centerpiece a genuine lapis lazuli stone mounted on gold.

---

(54) 1 *maninnu*-necklace, cut: 34 obsidian beads; 33 (*pieces of*); the centerpiece a genuine lapis lazuli stone mounted on gold.

---

(55) 1 *maninnu* necklace (with) *counterweight*: 14 genuine lapis lazuli beads, 25 genuine *ḫulalu*-beads, 17 *ḫulalu*-beads;

(56) [the centerpiece] a genuine lapis lazuli stone mounted on gold.

---

(57) [1] [*mani*]*nnu*-necklace (with) *counterweight*: 14 genuine lapis lazuli beads, 16 genuine *ḫulalu*-beads; 30 (*pieces of*) gold

(58) [*leaf*; the centerpiece a...] mounted on gold.

---

(59) [1] [*ma-ni-in-nu*.....N]A$_4$.NÍR KUR 24 KÙ.GI *ša tù-ut-tù-ri*
(60) [MURUB$_4$......] KÙ.GI GAR

---

(61) [1] [*ma-ni-in-nu*....x NA$_4$.NÍ]R KUR 26 KÙ.GI ⸢*ka*⸣-*ma-ru* MURUB$_4$ NA$_4$.NÍR.KUR KÙ.GI GAR

---

(62) [1] [*ma-ni-in-nu*............] 24 ⸢KÙ.GI⸣ ⸢*ka*⸣-⸢*ma*⸣-⸢*ru*⸣ MURUB$_4$ NA$_4$.ZA.GÌN KUR KÙ.GI GAR

---

(63) [1] [*ma-ni-in-nu*...............N]A$_4$.ZA.GÌN KUR 24 NA$_4$.NÍR KUR
(64) [MURUB$_4$...........N]A$_4$.ZA.GÌN KUR KÙ.GI GAR

---

(65) [1] [*ma-ni-in-nu*............] NA$_4$.SAG.KAL 16 NA$_4$.ZA.GUG
(66) [MURUB$_4$.............^{NA_4}NÍR K]UR KÙ.GI GAR

---

(67) [...]
(68) [....................................K]Ù.G[I GAR]

---

(69) [................. *ṭì-im-bu-ʾ*]-*ú* ⸢NA$_4$⸣.Z[A.GÌN KUR] 10 [*ṭì-im-bu*]-*ʾ-ú* ^{NA_4}*ḫi-li-bá*

---

(70) [...]x-*ir-ti*

---

(71) [......*qa-du na*]-*ak-ta-mi-šu-nu* KÙ.GI SAG[-*sú-nu*] NA$_4$.ZA.⸢GÌN⸣ KUR
(72) [...............] *gu$_5$-u-ḫa-aṣ-ṣí*.KÙ.GI *šu-uk-ku-ku*

COL. II

(1) [*x*] [SU *á*]*š-ki-ru-u-uš-ḫu q*[*a-d*]*u na-ak-ta-mi-šu-nu*[............]
(2) [.....-*š*]*u* ... *ṣa-bi-ti* [..........................]

---

(3) [*x*] [......] *ú-tu-pu* 1 *šu-ši* NA$_4$.ZA.GÌN KUR 1 *šu-ši* NA$_4$.NÍR KUR.⸢8⸣ ⸢NA$_4$.⸣ZA.[...............................]
(4) [x+]5 *du-ú-ul-ti* KÙ.GI 10 *lu-u-ri-me-ti* NA$_4$.GUG 5 NU.ÚR. ⸢MA⸣.A NA$_4$ SA[G.KAL]

---

(59) [1] [*maninnu*-necklace...*x*] genuine *ḫ̮ulalu*-beads; 24 (*pieces of*) gold *leaf*;
(60) [the centerpiece, a...-stone] mounted on gold.

---

(61) [1] [*maninnu* necklace...*x*] genuine *ḫ̮ulalu* beads; 26 gold ⸢*kama*⸣*ru*; the centerpiece a genuine lapis lazuli stone mounted on gold.

---

(62) [1] [*maninnu* necklace] 24 gold ⸢*kamaru*⸣; the centerpiece a genuine lapis lazuli stone mounted on gold.

---

(63) [...] genuine lapis lazuli beads; 24 genuine *ḫ̮ulalu*-beads;
(64) [...the centerpiece] a genuine lapis lazuli stone mounted on gold.

---

(65) [...]...SAG.KAL beads, 16 carnelian beads;
(66) [...the centerpiece ge]nuine [...-stone] mounted on gold

---

(67) [...],
(68) [...mounted on g]ol[d].

---

(69) [...“*cricket*]*s*,” of [genuine] l[apis lazuli]; 10 “*cr*[*icke*]*ts*,” of *ḫ̮iliba-stone*.

---

(70) [..]...

---

(71) [...along with] their [co]vers, of gold; their tops [...] of genuine lapis lazuli;
(72) [...] are strung [on] gold wire.

COL. II

(1) [*x*] [*a*]*škiruš*ḫ̮*u*-vessels, along with their covers
(2) [...]...gazelle [...].

---

(3) [*x*] *utuppu*: 60 genuine lapis lazuli beads, 63 genuine *ḫ̮ulalu*-beads, 8 *ḫ̮u*[*lalu*-beads...]
(4) [*x*+]5 “worms” of gold, 10 pomegranates of carnelian, 5 pome-granates of SA[G.KAL]-stone.

---

(5)	[*x*]	*ḫé-ri-iz-zi wu-uš-ru* 1 *me* 22 NA$_4$.ZA.GÌN KUR [x +]6 NA$_4$.NÍR KUR 1 *me* 80 *du-ul-[ti]*
(6)		[N]A$_4$.NÍR KUR *ra-aq-⸢qu⸣* KÙ.GI GAR 3 NA$_4$.KIŠIB NÍR KUR ⸢KÙ.GI⸣ [GAR]
(7)	[x]	U$_4$.SAKAR NA$_4$.NÍR.KUR 13 *i-na mi-nu-ti i-na* KÙ.GI [*ša*] ⸢*da*⸣*-ma šu-[l]u-ú*
(8)		[*uḫ-ḫu*]*-uz* 14 NA$_4$.KIŠIB NÍR KUR KÙ.GI GAR
(9)	[x]	[...*u*]*z(?)-za-ti* KÙ.GI GAL.MEŠ *ša da-ma šu-⸢lu⸣-ú* 11 *i-na mi-n[u]-ti*
(10)		[NA$_4$.ZA.]GÌN KUR GAR-*nu* 12 *bi-ik-ru* NA$_4$.KIŠIB N[ÍR] KUR
(11)	[x]	[..........]-*gu*(?) 1 U$_4$.SAKAR N[A$_4$.]⸢NÍR⸣ [KUR KÙ.]GI GAR 2 U$_4$.SAKAR NA$_4$.ZA.GÌN ⸢KUR⸣ KÙ.GI GAR
(12)	[x]	[..........] 3(?) NA$_4$.NÍR KUR *kab-b[u-ut-t]i* 4 *ḫi-in-t[e-n]a* KÙ.GI
(13)	1	ŠU [*a*]*-gàr-ḫu* GAL NA$_4$.ZA.GÌN KUR NA$_4$.NÍR KUR NA$_4$.ZÚ KUR NA$_4$.NÍR.M[UŠ.GÍR]
(14)		MURUB$_4$ NA$_4$.ZA.GÌN KUR KÙ.GI GAR *ul-lu-ri-šu-nu* ^{NA_4}*ḫi-li-bá* NU.GAR
(15)	3	ŠU *a-gàr-ḫu* TUR.MEŠ NA$_4$.ZA.GÌN KUR NA$_4$.NÍR KUR [......] NA$_4$.ZÚ KUR
(16)		NA$_4$.NÍR.MUŠ.GÍR MURUB$_4$-*šu-nu* NA$_4$.NÍR KUR KÙ.GI GAR 1 *ul-lu-ru* ^{NA_4}*ḫi-li-bá* ⸣
(17)		NU.GAR.RA 4 *bi-ik-ru* KÙ.GI
(18)	27	IGI.MEŠ NA$_4$.NÍR KUR KÙ.GI GAR *ša* ŠU
(19)	13	IGI.MEŠ NA$_4$.NÍR.MUŠ.GÍR KÙ.GI GAR *ša* ŠU
(20)	2	*me* 19 *ṭì-im-bu-ʾ-ú* NA$_4$.ZA.GÌN KUR GAR NU.GAR.RA *ša* ⸢ŠU⸣

(5) [*x*] *ḫerizzi* stones *wušru*: 122 genuine lapis lazuli beads, [*x*+]6 *ḫulalu*-beads, 180 worms
(6) of genuine *ḫulalu*-stone, a thin (*band*) overlaid with gold, 3 cylinder shaped beads of genuine *ḫulalu*-stone, mounted on gold.

---

(7) [*x*] new-moon crescents of genuine *ḫulalu*-stone, 13 per string, of gold *tinged with red*
(8) [moun]ted(?); 14 cylinder shaped beads of genuine *ḫulalu*-stone, mounted on gold.

---

(9) [*x*] large [...]...of gold *tinged with red*, 11 per string,
(10) set [in] genuine [lapis lazu]li, 12 *bikru*-gems and a seal-shaped stone of genuine *ḫulalu*-stone.

---

(11) [*x*] [...]...1 new-moon crescent of [genuine] ⸢*ḫulalu*⸣-stone, mounted on gold; 2 new-moon crescents of genuine lapis lazuli, mounted on gold.
(12) [*x*] [..........] 3 genuine *ḫulalu*-beads (*for a*) counter[weight]; 4 bea[d]s, ‹mounted› on gold.

---

(13) 1 set of large [*a*]*garḫu*-jewels, of genuine lapis lazuli, genuine *ḫulalu*-stone, genuine obsidian, *mu*[*ššaru*]-stone;
(14) the centerpiece a genuine lapis lazuli stone mounted on gold; their *ulluru* of *ḫiliba*-stone, not mounted.

---

(15) 3 sets of small *agarḫu*-jewels, of genuine lapis lazuli, genuine *ḫulalu*-stone, [........]genuine obsidian,
(16) serpentine; their centerpiece a genuine *ḫulalu*-stone mounted on gold; 1 *ulluru* of *ḫiliba*-stone,
(17) not mounted; 4 *bikru*-gems of gold.

---

(18) 2 "eye"-stones, of serpentine, of genuine *ḫulalu*-stone, mounted on gold, for the hand.

---

(19) 3 "eye"-stones, of serpentine, mounted on gold, for the hand.

---

(20) 219 "crickets," of genuine lapis lazuli, not mounted, for the hand.

---

(21) 3 ŠU(!).GUR NA$_4$.NÍR KUR 2 ŠU(!).GUR NA$_4$.ZA.GÌN KUR. 2 ŠU(!).GUR ^{NA_4}*ḫi-li-*[*bá*]

(22) 1 ŠU(!).GUR ^{NA_4}*iš-me-ek-ki* 2 ŠU(!).GUR *tam-lu-ú* 3 ŠU(!).GUR AN.[BAR]

(23) 5 ŠU(!).GUR KÙ.GI *up-pu-qù-*[*tu*$_4$]

---

(24) 14 ḪAR KÙ.GI ša ŠU *up-pu-qù-tu*$_4$.2 ḪAR KÙ.GI *ša*.GÌR *up-pu-*[*qù-tu*$_4$]

(25) 3 *me* 90.SU *i-na* KI.LÁ.[BI]

---

(26) 2 ḪAR KÙ.GI *ša* ŠU *ti*$_7$*-iṣ-bu-tù-tù ša me-sú-kí* ^{MEŠ} *me-sú-uk-*[*ki-šu-nu*]

(27) *tam-lu-ú* NA$_4$.ZA.GÌN KUR 30 SU *i-na* KI.LÁ.[BI]

---

(28) 10 ḪAR ŠU *ša* AN.BAR *ra-aq-qà-tu*$_4$ KÙ.GI GAR 30 SU KÙ.GI *i-na* ŠÀ-*š*[*u-n*]*u* [*na-di*]

---

(29) 1 *gu*$_5$*-u-ḫa-as-sú* TUR *ša ku*$_8$*-un-nu-ki* KÙ.GI 1 NA$_4$.KIŠIB ZA.GÌN KUR KÙ.GI [GAR]

(30) 1 ⌜ NA$_4$.⌝AN.GUG.ME KÙ.GI GAR 1 NA$_4$.KIŠIB ŠI.TIR KÙ.GI GAR 2 NA$_4$.ZA.GÌN KUR

(31) *kab-bu-ta-ti* KÙ.GI GAR 2 NA$_4$.N[Í]R KUR *kab-bu-ta-ti* KÙ.GI 4 *ḫi-i*[*n*]*-te-na* KÙ.GI [GAR]

---

(32) 2 *ki-ri-is-sú* NA$_4$.NÍR KUR SAG-*sú* NA$_4$.ZA.GÌN KUR KÙ.GI GAR 1 *ki-*[*ri*]*-is-sú*

(33) NA$_4$.NÍR KUR SAG-*sú* ^{NA_4}*ḫi-li-bá* KÙ.GI GAR 3 ½ SU KÙ.GI *i-na lì*[*b-b*]*i-šu n*[*a-di*]

---

(34) 1 *ḫa-ru-uš-ḫu* NA$_4$.NÍR KUR SAG-*sú* ^{NA_4}*ḫi-li-bá* KÙ.GI GAR 1 *ḫa-ru-uš-ḫu* [NA$_4$ x]

(35) KÙ.GI GAR 1 *ḫa-ru-uš-ḫu* ZÚ.SÚN KÙ.GI GAR 3 SU KÙ.GI *i-na lìb-bi-šu-nu na-*[*di*]

---

(21) 3 finger-rings, of genuine *ḫulalu*-stone; 2 finger-rings, of genuine lapis lazuli; 2 finger-rings of *ḫiliba*-stone;

(22) 1 finger-ring of malachite; 2 finger-rings, (with) inlay; 2 finger-rings, of *ir*[*on*];

(23) 5 finger-rings, of solid gold.

---

(24) 14 hand-bracelets, of solid gold; 2 anklets, of sol[id] gold.

(25) 390 shekels in weight.

---

(26) 2 hand-bracelets, of gold, one attached to the other, (with) *mesukku*-birds;

(27) the *mesukku*-birds (have) an inlay of genuine lapis lazuli. 30 shekels in weight.

---

(28) 10 thin bracelets, of iron, overlaid with gold; 30 shekels of gold [have been used] on them.

---

(29) 1 small torque, for a seal-shaped stone, of gold. 1 seal-shaped stone, of genuine lapis lazuli mounted on gold.

(30) 1 ...-stone mounted on gold. 1 seal-shaped stone of *pendu* mounted on gold. 2 genuine lapis lazuli stones,

(31) *counterweights*, mounted on gold. 2 genuine *ḫulalu*-stones (*to serve as*) *counterweights,* ‹mounted› on gold. 4. ...mo[unted on] gold.

---

(32) 1 pin, of genuine *ḫulalu*-stone; its top of genuine lapis lazuli. mounted on gold. 1 pin,

(33) of genuine *ḫulalu*-stone; its top of *ḫiliba*-stone mounted on gold. 3 shekels of gold have been u[sed] on them.

---

(34) 1 *ḫarušḫu* animal, of genuine *ḫulalu*-stone; its top of *ḫiliba*-stone mounted on gold. 1 *ḫarušḫu* animal [of...stone]

(35) overlaid with gold. 1 *ḫarušḫu* animal, overlaid with ivory and gold. 3 shekels of gold have been [used] on them.

---

(36) 1 [*i*]*š-ḫu-un-na-tu*$_4$ KÙ.GI 1 *pa-ra-ak-ka-ta-nu* KÙ.GI 1 *uz-za-a*[*p*]-*na-an-nu* [KÙ.GI]
(37) ⸢6⸣ [...-]*ra-an-nu* KÙ.GI 1 *ḫu-zu-nu* KÙ.GI 3 *ki-iz-zi wu-uš-ru* [KÙ.GI]
(38) 1 ⸢*ḫa*⸣-⸢*ru*⸣-⸢*uš*⸣-⸢*ḫu*⸣ KÙ.GI 7 NU.ÚR.MA TUR.MEŠ KÙ.GI 6 *mi-iḫ*-[*ṣ*]*ú* [KÙ.GI]
(39) 11 *tù-ul-ti* KÙ.GI 13 SU *i-na* KI.[L]Á.BI
(40) *šu-kut-tu*$_4$ *an-ni-tu*$_4$ *ša šu-ur-k*[*u*$_8$-*si*]

---

(41) 10 ŠU ^{KUŠ}*šu-ḫu-up-pát-tu*$_4$ *ù gu-dup-pí-a-na ša* KÙ.GI [...]
(42) ⸢*bu*⸣-*ti-in-na-šu-nu* $^{\text{NA}_4}$*ḫi-li-bá* 1 *me* SU KÙ.GI *i-na l*[*ìb-bi-šu na-di*]

---

(43) 1 *pí-iš-ša-tu*$_4$ *ri-it-ta-šu* NA$_4$.AN.GUG.ME [*ša*]-*kàr*-[*šu*]
(44) ALAM NA$_4$.GIŠ.NU$_{11}$.GAL [......*x*]

---

(45) 1 *pí-iš-ša-tu*$_4$ *ri-it-ta-šu* NA$_4$.GIŠ.NU$_{11}$.GAL *ša-kàr-šu*[...] [KÙ].G[I GAR]
(46) 2 NA$_4$.ZA.GÌN KUR *i-na lìb-bi-šu* [*na-du*]

---

(47) 1 *pí-iš-ša-tu*$_4$ *ri-it-ta-šu* $^{\text{NA}_4}$*a-bá-aš-mu-ú ša-kàr-šu s*[*i-nu*]-*un-t*[*u*$_4$] [KÙ.GI.GAR]
(48) 1-*en* NA$_4$.ZA.GÌN KUR *i-na lìb-bi-šu* [*na-di*]

---

(49) 1 *pí-iš-ša-tu*$_4$ *ri-it-ta-šu* $^{\text{NA}_4}$*mar-ḫal-lu ša-kàr-šu* [*ni-*]*im-ru* KÙ.G[I.GAR]
(50) NA$_4$.ZA.GÌN *ù* NA$_4$.GIŠ.NU$_{11}$.GAL [*ti*]-*ša-ak-ku*$_8$-[*un*]

---

(51) 1 *pí-iš-‹ša›-tu*$_4$ *ri-it-‹ta›-šu* KÙ.GI GAR *ša-kàr-šu a-bu-ú-bu* KÙ.G[I.GAR]

---

(52) 30 SU KÙ.GI *i-na lìb-bi-šu-nu u‹ḫ›-ḫu-u-*[*zu*]

---

(53) ⸢1⸣ ⸢NÍG⸣.⸢ŠU⸣.[LUḪ].⸢ḪA⸣ ⸢KÙ.GI⸣ 1 *me* 23 SU *i-na* KI.LÁ.BI
1 NÍG.ŠU.LUḪ.ḪA KÙ.⸢BABBAR] ⸢80⸣ SU *i-na* KI.LÁ.B[I]

---

(54) 1 *ša me-e šu-‹ú-li-i›* KÙ.GI 30 SU *i-na* KI.LÁ.BI
1 *ša ú-*⸢*ḫu*⸣-⸢*li*⸣ [KÙ].GI 14 *i-na*.KI.LÁ.B[I]
(55) 1 *ša ú-ḫu-li* KÙ.BABBAR 20 SU *i-na* KI.LÁ.B[I]

---

(36) 1 [bunc]h of grapes, of gold. 1 *parakkatanu*, of gold. 1 *uzzapnannu*, [of gold].
(37) 6 [...]..., of gold. 1 *ḫuzunu*, of gold. 3..., [of gold].
(38) 1 *ḫarušḫu* of gold. 7 small pomegranates of gold. 6 "weaves," of gold.
(39) 11 "worms," of gold. 13 shekels in weight.
(40) This jewelry is for atta[ch]ing.

---

(41) 10 pairs of boots and *guduppiāni* of gol[d...].
(42) Their b[ut]tons are of *ḫiliba*-stone. 100 shekels of gold ha[ve been used] o[n them].

---

(43) 1 ointment spoon; its "scoop" of...-stone; the handle a
(44) figure of alabaster. [...]

---

(45) 1 ointment spoon; its "scoop" of alabaster; its handle a [....] overlaid with g]ol[d];
(46) 2 genuine lapis lazuli stones [are set] in the center.

---

(47) 1 ointment spoon; its "scoop" of *abašmu*-stone; it s handle a s[wal]low overlaid with gold;
(48) 1 genuine lapis lazuli stone [is set] in the center.

---

(49) 1 ointment spoon; its "scoop" of *marḫallu*-stone; its handle [a pan]ther [overlaid with] gold.
(50) With alternating insets of lapis lazuli and alabaster.

---

(51) 1 oin‹t›ment spoon; its sco‹op›› overlaid with gold; its handle a deluge-monster overlaid with gold

---

(52) 30 shekels of silver ‹we›re overl[aid] on them.

---

(53) 1 wa[shba]sin, of gold; 123 shekels in weight. 1 washbasin of silver; 80 shekels in weight.

---

(54) 1 water-dip‹per›, of gold; 30 shekels in weight. 1 alkali container of [go]ld; 14 shekels in weight.
(55) 1 alkali container of silver; 20 shekels in weight.

---

(56) 1 *na-ma-ru ša* KÙ.BABBAR 40 SU *i-na* KI.LÁ.BI *ša-kàr-šu* AL[AM] MUNUS-tu_4 *ša* ZÚ.S[ÚN]
(57) 1 SU 3 *tù-mu-un-sal-‹li›* KÙ.GI *i-na lìb-bi-šú uḫ-ḫu-*[*zu*]

(58) 1 *na-ma-ru ša* KÙ.BABBAR 40 SU *i-na* KI.LÁ.BI *ša-kàr-šu* ALAM MUNUS-tu_4 *ša* GIŠ.E[SI]
(59) 1 SU 3 *tù-mu-un-sal-li* KÙ.GI *i-na lìb-bi-šú uḫ-ḫu-*[*zu*]

(60) 1 *ku-ni-nu ša* NA_4 ŠÀ-*šu ù i-ši-is-sú* KÙ.GI GAR 20 ⸢SU⸣ KÙ.GI *i-na lìb-bi-*[*šu*]
(61) *uḫ-ḫu-*zu_x!(SU) 1 NA_4.ZA.GÌN KUR *i-na lìb-bi-šu* GAR-⸢*in*⸣

(62) 1 *ku-ni-nu* KÙ.GI 20 SU *i-na* KI.LÁ.BI 1 GA. RÍG *ša* NA_4 *bu-u*[*š-lu*]

(63) 1 ŠÀ KÙ.GI *tam-lu-ú* NA_4.ZA.GÌN KUR 30 SU [*i-na*] KI.L[Á.BI]

(64) 30 ŠÀ KÙ.GI *tam-lu-ú* 9 *me* SU *i-*[*na* KI.LÁ.BI]

(65) 20 GA.RÍG KÙ.BABBAR.MEŠ [............]

(66) 10 GA.RÍG KÙ.BABBAR.MEŠ.10(?) [.................] ME[Š]

(67) 10 GA.RÍG KÙ.BABBAR.MEŠ.[.......................] ME[Š]

(68) 10 GA.RÍG KÙ.BABBAR.MEŠ.[.......................] ME[Š]

(69) 10 GA.RÍG KÙ.BABBAR.MEŠ.[.......................] ME[Š]

(70) [*x*] [GA.]RÍG KÙ.BABBAR.MEŠ [...........................]

(71) 10 GA.RÍG KÙ.BABBAR.MEŠ [...........................]

(72) 10 GA.RÍG KÙ.BABBAR.MEŠ [...........................]

(73) 10 GA.[RÍG KÙ.BABBAR.ME]Š [...........................]

(56) 1 mirror, of silver; 40 shekels in weight; its handle a figure of a woman, of ivory.
(57) 1 3/4 shekels of gold have been overlaid on them.

(58) 1 mirror, of silver; 40 shekels in weight; its handle a figure of a woman, of ebony.
(59) 1 3/4 shekels of gold have been overlaid on them.

(60) 1 *kuninnu*-bowl, of stone; its inside and its base have been overlaid with gold; 20 shekels gold are in it,
(61) plated; 1 genuine lapis lazuli stone is set in it.

(62) 1 *kuninnu*-bowl, of gold; 20 shekels in weight. 1 comb of mol[ten] glass.

(63) 1 heart, of gold; the inlay, genuine lapis lazuli; 30 shekels in weight.

(64) 30 hearts, of gold; (with) inlay; 900 shekels i[n weight].

(65) 20 combs of silver [................................].

(66) 10 combs of silver 10 [..............................].

(67) 10 combs of silver [.................................].

(68) 10 combs of silver [................................].

(69) 10 combs of silver [................................].

(70) [10] [co]mbs, of silver [......................................].

(71) 10 combs of silver [.....................................].

(72) 10 combs of silver [.....................................].

(73) 10 combs of silver [.....................................].

COL. III

(1–11) [..]

(12) ⸢1⸣ [.........KÙ.]BABBAR 2 *li-im* [.......................]

(13) [x] [.............] KÙ.BABBAR 1-*nu-tu*$_4$ *pa-ab-be*(?) [.......]

(14) [x] [........] KÙ.BABBAR 3 *me* SU [......................]

(15) 1 ŠU *an-gur-bi-in-nu* KÙ.BABBAR 1(?) [....................]

(16) 1 ŠU *mu-ša-lu qa-du na-ak-ta-a*[*m-mi-šu-nu*.........^{NA_4}N]ÍR [KUR...]
(17) *šu-uk-ku*$_8$*-ku*$_8$ 10 SU KÙ.GI 30 [SU KÙ.BABBAR.........
N]A$_4$.GIŠ.[NU$_{11}$.GAL]

(18) 25 ŠU *mu-ša-lu qa-du na-ak-t*[*a-*(*am*)*-mi-šu-nu*................]
(19) 42 SU 3 *tù-mu-un-sal-li* KÙ.G[I *i-na lìb-bi-šu*]*-nu* [*na-di*]

(20) 26 ŠU *mu-ša-‹lu› qa-du na-ak-*[*ta-*(*am*)*-mi-šu-nu* GIŠ.ES]IG [....]
(21) 42 SU 3 *tù-mu-un-sal-*[*li* KÙ.GI *i-na lìb-bi-šu*]*-nu*......[*na-di*]

(22) [x] ŠU *mu-*⸢*ša*⸣*-*[*lu qa-du na-ak-ta-mi-šu-nu š*]*a* 1-*en i-na lì*[*b-bi-šu-nu*]
(23) [..] N[A$_4$]

(24) [x] [......................] KÙ.GI GAR 30 [............]
(25) [..]

(26) [x] [..............................*š*]*a*(?).KUR(?) [x........]

(27) 25 ŠU *áš-ku-ru-*[*uš-ḫu qa-du na-ak-ta-am-mi-šu-nu*.............]
(28) 20 SU KÙ.GI [...]

(29) 25 ŠU *áš-ku-ru-*[*uš-ḫu qa-du na-ak-ta-am-mi-šu-nu*.............]

(30) [x] [..]
(31) [......................*i-na lì*]*b-*⸢*bi*⸣*-*⸢*šu*⸣*-nu* [............*na-di*]

COL. III

(1–11) [...]

(12) 1 [....of sil]ver, 2000 [...................................].

(13) [*x*] [.........], of silver. 1 set of...[........................].

(14) [*x*] [...], of silver. 300 shekels [.............................].

(15) 1 set of *angurbinnu*, of silver. 1 [...........................].

(16) 1 set of mirrors, along with their covers [...*ḫu*]*lalu*-stone [...]
(17) strung. 10 shekels of gold, 30 sh[ekels of silver............ ala]baster.

(18) 25 sets of mirrors, along with [their] co[vers [................].
(19) 42¾ shekels of gol[d have been used on the]m.

(20) 26 sets of mirr‹ors›, along with [their] c[overs...eb]ony [...].
(21) 42¾ shekels of silver [have been used] on the]m.

(22) . [*x*] sets of mirr[ors, along with their covers, of wh]ich 1 amo[ng them]
(23) [...] stone

(24) [x] [..................], overlaid with gold. 30 [...........].
(25) [..]

(26) [x] [............................o]f the *country* [..........].

(27) 25 sets of *aškuruš* [*ḫu*-vessels.with their covers...............].
(28) 20 shekels of gold [......................................]

(29) 25 sets of *aškuru*[*šḫu*-vessels with their covers...............].

(30) [*x*] [..]
(31) [..................have been used o]n them [..................]

(32)	[x]	[ŠU *áš-ku-ru-uš-*]*ḫu qa-du ‹na›-ak-ta-mi-*[*šu-nu*............]
(33)	1	ŠU [......]*-te-šu-nu ša* SI UDU.MEŠ [..................]
(34)		*i-na gu*$_5$*-*[*ḫa-az-zi šuk-k*]*u-ku* 16 SU KÙ.GI [*i-na lìb-bi-šu-nu na-di*]
(35)	25	S[I ZÚ.SÚN GAL.MEŠ] KÙ].GI GAR 12 SU [*i-na lìb-bi-šu-nu na-di*]
(36)	[x]	[SI ZÚ SÚN GAL.MEŠ] GAR 12 SU [*i-na lìb-bi-šu-nu na-di*]
(37)	[x]	[SI ZÚ SÚN GAL.MEŠ KÙ.]GI GAR 1 *mu-*[............]
(38)	4	[SU KÙ.GI *i-*]*na lìb-bi-*[*šu-nu na-di*]
(39)	5	SI Z[Ú SÚN GAL.MEŠ KÙ.]GI GAR 18 [SU] ⸢KÙ.GI⸣ ⸢*i*⸣-⸢*na*⸣ *l*[*ìb-bi-šu-nu na-di*]
(40)		*ša* 1*-en i-na* [*lìb-bi-šu-nu*..............................]
(41)	5	SI ZÚ SÚN TUR.MEŠ [......SAG]*-sú-nu* KÙ.GI GAR 16 SU K[Ù.GI GAR]
(42)	1	SI AM KÙ.GI GAR 3*-šu tam-lu-ú* [...*re-e-et-*]*ta-šu* ^{NA_4} [x....]
(43)	1	SI AM KÙ.GI GAR 2*-šu tam-lu-ú* NA$_4$. ZA.GÌ[N KUR *re-e-et-ta-*]*šu.*^{NA_4} *ḫ*[*i-li-bá*]
(44)	1	SI *ša* GU$_4$ KUR KÙ.GI GAR *ù i-ša-as-*[*sú*..........] *ti-ša-*[*ak-ku*$_8$*-un*]
(45)	1	SI AM KÙ.GI GAR 3*-šu tam-lu-ú ù re-*[*e-et-ta-šu*] NA$_4$.⸢GIŠ⸣.[NU$_{11}$].GAL
(46)	1	SI *lu-lu-tu* KÙ.GI GAR *re-e-et-ta-šu* GIŠ.ESI NA$_4$.ZA.GÌN KUR[....*ti-ša*]*-ak-ku*$_8$*-un*

(32) . [*x*] [sets of *aškuruš*]*ḫu*-vessels, along with [their] ‹c›overs,.....].

---

(33) 1 set of [...] their [...]...of ram-horn [...
(34) [st]rung on a w[ire of gold]. 16 shekels of gold [have been used on them].

---

(35) 25 [large] ivory wild cow-[rhytons] overlaid with gold. 12 shekels of [gold have been used on them].

---

(36) [*x*] [large ivory wild cow-rhytons...] overlaid [with gold]. 12 shekels of [gold have been used o]n t[hem].

---

(37) [*x*] [large ivory wild cow-rhytons] overlaid [with gol]d 1 [....]
(38) 4 [...have been used o]n t[hem].

---

(39) 5 [large] ivo[ry wild cow-rhytons] overlaid [with go]ld. 18 [shekels] of gold [have been used on them],
(40) among [which] 1 [of them.........................]

---

(41) 5 small ivory wild cow-rhytons, of ivory [...] their [top] overlaid with gold. 16 shekels [of gold overlaid].

---

(42) 1 auroch horn rhyton, overlaid with gold 3 times; inlay, [...]; its [han]dle of [...]-stone.

---

(43) 1 auroch horn-rhyton, overlaid with gold 2 times; inlay of [genuine] lapis [lazuli]; its handle of [...]-stone.

---

(44) 1 mountain-ox horn-rhyton, overlaid with gold, and [its] base *is se*[*t here and there with...*].

---

(45) 1 aurochs horn-rhyton, overlaid with gold 3 times; inlay, and [its] ha[ndle] of ala[bas]ter.

---

(46) 1 *lulutu* (animal) horn-rhyton, overlaid with gold; its *rettu* of ebony. It [is set] alternately with genuine lapis lazuli (and) [........]

---

(47) 1 SI *lu-lu-tu*$_4$ KÙ.GI GAR *re-e-et-ta-šu* ZÚ.SÚN NA$_4$.ZA.GÌN KUR [.........*ti-ša*]*-ak-ku*$_8$*-un*

(48) 90 SU KÙ.GI *i-na lìb-bi-šu-nu na-di*

(49) 20 SI *ai-gal-lu-ḫu*.MEŠ KÙ.GI GAR *re-et-ta-šu-nu* ZÚ.SÚN *ša* [1-*en i-n*]*a lìb-bi-šu-nu*
(50) *re-e-et-ta-šu* GIŠ.ESI 35 SU KÙ.GI *i-na lìb-bi-šu-nu* [*na-di*]

(51) 14 SI AM GAL.MEŠ KÙ.GI GAR *re-e-et-ta-šu-nu* ZÚ.SÚN 42 SU KÙ.GI *i-na* [*lìb-bi-šu-nu na-di*]

(52) 1 *ša* NIM *ku*$_8$*-uš-šu-dì* KÙ.GI GAR *re-et-ta-šu ù* ⌜KIN⌝-*šu a-na* [x-*šu*......]
(53) *pa-rat-ti-ti-na-šu* ^{NA_4}*ḫi-li-bá i-na gu*$_5$*-ḫa-az-zi* KÙ.GI *šu-uk-ku*[*-ku*]
(54) *ù gu*$_5$*-ḫa-az-za-šu* NA$_4$.NÍR KUR NA$_4$.ZA.GÌN KUR NA$_4$.GUG *šuk-ku-ku* 30 SU KÙ.GI *i-na lìb-*[*bi-šu na-di*]

(55) 2 ŠU *ka-pí-iz-zu-uḫ-ḫé* KÙ.GI 2 ŠU *in-ṣa-bá-t*[*u*$_4$] KÙ.GI *te*$_9$*-ri-in-na-a-ti-šu-nu* ^{NA_4}*ḫi-l*[*i-bá*]
(56) *gu-ug-gu-bi-šu-nu* NA$_4$.NÍR 2 ŠU *tù-dì-na-tu*$_4$ KÙ.GI SAG-*sú-nu* NA$_4$.ZA.GÌN 2 *mi-iḫ-ṣú* [...]
(57) *ù* ^{NA_4}*ḫi-*[*li-bá š*]*a ša-an-za-a-ti* 9 *ma-ni-in-na* NA$_4$.ZA.GÌN *ša it-ti* KÙ.GI *pu-un-*[*nu-gu*]
(58) 12 ḪAR ŠU KÙ.GI 8 ḪAR GÌR KÙ.GI *šu-kut-tu*$_4$ *an-ni-tu*$_4$ *ša* 2 MUNUS.EME.DA GAL 3 *me* 13 [SU......]

(59) 2 ŠU *in-ṣa-bá-tu*$_4$ KÙ.GI *te*$_9$*-ri-in-na-a-ti-šu-nu* ^{NA_4}*ḫi-li-bá gu-ug-gu-ub-šu-nu* NA$_4$.N[ÍR...]
(60) KÙ.GI SAG-*sú-nu* NA$_4$.NÍR 2 ŠU *mi-iḫ-ṣú* NA$_4$.ZA.GÌN *ù* ^{NA_4}*ḫi-li-bá ša-a-tu*$_4$ *ša*[x *ma-ni-in-nu*]
(61) NA$_4$.ZA.GÌN *ša it-ti* KÙ.GI *pu-un-nu-gu* 12 ḪAR ŠU KÙ.GI 8 ḪAR GÌR KÙ.GI *šu-k*[*ut-tu*$_4$ *an-ni-tu*$_4$]
(62) *ša* 2 MUNUS.EME.DA 2 *me* 8 SU KÙ.GI *ša i-na lìb-bi-*[*šu-nu na-du-ú*]

(63) 10 ḪAR ŠU KÙ.GI 10 ḪAR GÌR KÙ.GI *ša* 10 LÚ.TUR.MEŠ 74 SU *i-na* KI.[LÁ.BI]

(47) 1 *lulutu* (animal) horn-rhyton, overlaid with gold; its handle of ivory. [It *is se*]*t*] *here and there* with genuine lapis lazuli (and)... - stone [...].

---

(48) 90 shekels of gold have been used on them.

---

(49) 20 *ayigalluḫu* (animals) horn-rhytons, overlaid with gold; their handle of wild cow ivory; on one of which
(50) its handle is ebony. 35 shekels of gold [have been used] on them.

---

(51) 14 giant aurochs horn-rhytons, overlaid with gold; their handle of ivory. 42 shekels of gold [have been used] on [them].

---

(52) 1 fly-whisk, overlaid with gold; its handle and its work..[..]
(53) its [*p*]*arattatinu*, of *ḫiliba*-stone, strung on a wire of gold;
(54) and its wire strung with genuine *ḫulalu*-beads, genuine lapis . lazuli beads, carnelian beads 30 shekels of gold [were used] on [them].

---

(55) 2 sets of *kapissuḫḫu*-ornaments, of gold. 2 sets of earrin[gs], of gold; their cones, of *ḫiliba*-stone;
(56) their *guggubu*, of *ḫulalu*-stone. 2 sets of toggle pins, of gold; their top of lapis lazuli. 2 "weaves" [of...]
(57) and *ḫili*[*ba*]-stone[o]f šanzāti 9 *maninnu*-necklaces, of lapis lazuli, *with* a gold *knob*.
(58) 12 hand-bracelets, of gold. 8 anklets, of gold. This jewelry is for the 2 principal ladies-in-waiting. 313 [shekels of gold].

---

(59) 2 sets of earrings, of gold; their cones, of *ḫiliba*-stone; their *guggubu* of *ḫula*[*lu*]-stone...].
(60) of gold; their top of *ḫulalu*-stone. 2 sets of "weaves," of lapis lazuli and *ḫiliba*-stone. Those of [*x maninnu*-necklaces],
(61) of lapis lazuli, *with* a gold *knob*. 12 hand-bracelets, of gold. 8 anklets, of gold. [This] jewe[lry] is
(62) for the 2 principal ladies-in-waiting. It is 208 shekels of gold that [have been used] on [them].

---

(63) 10 hand-bracelets, of gold. 10 anklets, of gold, for 10 servant boys. 74 shekels in wei[ght].

---

(64) 4(?) *me* ḪAR.MEŠ GÌR KÙ.BABBAR *ša* MUNUS.MEŠ-*ti* 1 *me* ŠU *tù-dì-na-tu*$_4$ KÙ.BABBAR.MEŠ SAG-*sú*-[*nu........*]

(65) *ša* 1 *me* MUNUS.MEŠ *mu-lu-ú-gi*$_5$ 1 *li-im* 4 *me* 40 SU KÙ.BABBAR *i-na lìb-bi-š*[*u-nu na-di*]

(66) 30 ŠU *in-ṣa-*˹*bá*˺*-tu*$_4$ KÙ.GI *te*$_9$*-ri-in-na-a-ti-šu-nu* NA$_4$.ZA.GÌN [*ša*] 30 MUNUS.[MEŠ *mu-lu-ú-gi*$_5$]

(67) 1(?) *šu-ši* SU KÙ.GI AŠ ŠÀ-*šu-nu na-di* 30 ḪAR ŠU KÙ.[GI *ša* 30 LÚ.]˹MEŠ˺ 40 S[U KÙ.GI *i-na* ŠÀ-*šu-nu na-di*]

* * *

(68) [1] [^{GIŠ}*ṭup-pu ša*] ALAM.MEŠ *ka-zi-ri*^{MEŠ} KÙ.GI KÙ.BABBAR 10 SU K[Ù.GI KÙ.BABBAR *i-na*] *lìb-bi-šu-nu na-d*[*i*]

* * *

(69) [1] [^{GIŠ}*ṭup-pu*] *ša* ALAM.MEŠ *ša ka-zi-ri*[^{MEŠ} KÙ.GI]. KÙ.BABBAR 36 SU KÙ.BABBA *i-na lìb-bi-šu-nu na-d*[*i*]

* * *

(70) [x] [BAL.MEŠ KÙ.]GI 8 SU *i-na* KI.LÁ.BI 26 BAL.MEŠ KÙ.BABBAR 10 [SU] ˹*i*˺-˹*na*˺ KI.LÁ.BI

(71) [x] [BAL.MEŠ KÙ.GI] 10 BAL.MEŠ NA$_4$.ZA.GÌN 16 BAL.MEŠ NA$_4$. ˹GIŠ˺.[NU$_{11}$.]GAL

(72) [x] [BAL.MEŠ] 11 BAL.MEŠ $^{\text{NA}_4}$*ki-zi*-[x...........x] 33 BAL.MEŠ *ša* SI

* * *

(73) [x] [^{GIŠ}*ṭup-pu ša* ALAM.MEŠ *š*]*a*(?) *ap-sà-a-›ab‹-sà-ti*^{MEŠ} KÙ.[GI] GAR 1 *me* SU KÙ.GI *i-na* ŠÀ-*šu na-di*

(74) [...........] 15 *i-na* [*lìb-bi*]*-šu* *na-di*

(75) [.......................................] *ša ta-ki-il-ti*

* * *

(76) [.....................................M]EŠ-*šu ù ka-sí*^{MEŠ}*-š*[*u*]

(77) [........................K]Ù.GI 47 [.....................]

(78) [...]

COL. IV

(1) [x] [.........] *ša* NA$_4$.DU$_8$.ŠI.A K[Ù.GI KÙ.]BABBAR GAR

(2) [x] [....NA$_4$.DU$_8$.ŠI.]˹A˺.KÙ.GI KÙ.BABBAR GAR 15 SU KÙ.GI 38 SU KÙ.BABBAR [*i-na* KI.LÁ.BI

(3) [x] [..........] 1(?) ^{TÚG}*šu-ub-tu*$_4$ *ša ta-kíl-*˹*ti*˺

* * *

(64) 4[0]0 anklets, of silver, for women. 100 sets of toggle pins, of silver, their top [...],

(65) for 100 dowry-women. 1440 shekels of silver [have been used] on th[em].

(66) 30 sets of earrings, of gold; their cones of lapis lazuli, for 30 [dowry]-women.

(67) 160 shekels of gold have been used on them. 30 arm bracelets, of go[ld, for 3]0 [me]n. 40 she[kels of gold have been used on them].

---

(68) [1] [*plaque*], with *kaziru*-figures, of gold and silver. 10 shekels of go[ld and silver] have been used on them.

---

(69) [1] [*plaqu*]*e*, with *kaziru*-figures, of gold and silver. 36 shekels of silver have been us[ed] on them.

---

(70) [*x*] [libation bowls, of gol]d, 8 shekels in weight. 26 libation bowls, of silver, 10 [shekels] in weight.

(71) [x] [libation bowls of gold] 10 libation bowls, of lapis lazuli. 16 libation bowls, of al[abas]ter.

(72) [*x*] [libation bowls, of...] 11 libation bowls, of...[...]-stone. 33 libation bowls, of horn.

---

(73) [1] [plaque with figures o]f *apsasu*-animals, [ov]erlaid with gol[d]. 100 shekels of gold have been used on it.

(74) [...] 15 (shekels) have been used o[n it]

(75) [......................................] of blue-purple

---

(76) [......................................] and i[ts] goblets

(77) [...................], of gold. 47 [....................].

(78) [...]

COL. IV

(1) [*x*] [.............] of *dušu*-stone, overlaid with [sil]ver.

(2) [*x*] [...of *dušu*-sto]ne, overlaid with gold and silver. 15 shekels of gold, 38 shekels of silver [in weight].

(3) [*x*] [.........]. 1 *šubtu*-garment, of blue-purple wool.

---

(4) [1] [^{GIŠ}*ṭup-pu ša* ALAM.]MEŠ *ša a-bu-ú-be*^{MEŠ} KÙ.GI KÙ.BABBAR [G]AR

(5) [x SU KÙ.GI x SU KÙ.BABBAR *i-n*]*a lìb-bi-šu* *n*[*a-di*]

(6) [x] [.........D]UG.DAL.MEŠ KÙ.GI GAR 15 SU KÙ.[GI $^{\textit{i-na lìb-bi-šu na-di}}$]

(7) [x] [.............] ⌜SU⌝ ⌜KÙ.GI⌝ [......................]

(8) [x] [..]

(9) [x] [...................] 6? SU [KÙ.]⌜BABBAR⌝ [...........]

(10) [x] [......................................*i-na*] KI.LÁ.[BI]

(11) [x] [............................*i-na lìb-bi-šu-*(*nu*)] *na-di*

(12) [x] [.................................*n*]*u* GAR-*in pa-nu-šu*

(13) [x] [.................................] *i-na lìb-bi-šu-nu na-di*

(14) [x] [^{GIŠ}*ṭup-pu ša* ALAM. MEŠ *š*]*a* ⌜DÀRA⌝.MAŠ.MEŠ

(15) [.........................*š*]*a*.UR.[M]AḪ.MEŠ

(16) [x SU...............*i-na lìb-bi-šu-nu*] *na-di*

(17) [x] [.......................] KÙ.GI GAR 2 SU [KÙ.GI *i*]-*na lìb-bi-šu-nu* *n*[*a-di*]

(18) [x] [..................] *a-ma-ar-ti-šu* [.......] *bi* [.........]

(19) [...]

(20) [...]

(21) [1] [...] NA$_4$.ZA.GÌN *a-ma-ar-ti-šu* [......................]

(22) [......NA]$_4$. ZA.GÌN KÙ.GI KÙ.BABBAR GAR 6 SU KÙ.GI 26 SU KÙ.BABBAR [*i-n*]*a lìb-bi-*[*šu-nu na-di*]

(23) [x] [.......GI]Š.TÚG KÙ.GI KÙ.BABBAR GAR 12 SU KÙ.GI 30 SU KÙ. BABBAR *i-na lìb-bi-šu-nu na-di*

(24) [...] ZÚ.SÚN

(4) 1 [*plaque*, with figure]s of Deluge-monsters, overlaid with gold and silver.
(5) [*x* shekels of gold, *x* shekels of silver], hav[e been used o]n it.

(6) [*x*] ...] *tallu*-jars, overlaid with gold. 15 shekels of gold have been used on them.

(7) [*x*] [..........] shekels of gold [..........................]

(8) [*x*] [..]

(9) [*x*] [............] 6? shekels of silver [....................]

(10) [*x*] [.............................shekels of.....in] weight.
(11) [*x*] [..............shekels of....] have been us[ed on them].

(12) [*x*] [.......................................] is set. Its front
(13) [*x*] [..............*x* shekels of....] have been used on them.

(14) [*x*] [plaque(s) with figures o]f deer
(15) [*x*] [plaque(s) with figures o]f lions
(16) [*x* shekels of..........] have been used [on them].

(17) [*x*] [...], overlaid with gold. 2 shekels [of gold] hav[e been used o]n them.

(18) [*x*] [...............] its side-board [......................]
(19) [..]
(20) [..]

(21) [1] [...of] lapis lazuli, its side-board [of..................]
(22) [...]of lapis lazuli, overlaid with gold and silver. 6 shekels of gold, 26 shekels of silver, hav[e been used o]n [it].

(23) [*x*] [..., of bo]xwood, overlaid with gold and silver. 12 shekels of gold, 30 shekels of silver, have been used on them.
(24) [...] of ivory.

(25) [x] [.......] GIŠ.TÚG KÙ.BABBAR GAR 16 SU KÙ.BABBAR *i-na lìb-bi-šu-nu na-di*
(26) [...] ZÚ.SÚN

---

(27) [x] [.......KÙ.]BABBAR 3 *me* 80 SU *i-na* KI.LÁ.BI

---

(28) [x] [*al-tap-pí*]*-pu* ⌜*ša*⌝ [.....] ALAM-*šu-nu* ⌜ZÚ⌝.[SÚN] [.......]
(29) [............................GI]Š.⌜ESI⌝ *i*-⌜*ši*⌝-[*is-sú*]-⌜*nu*⌝
(30) KÙ.GI [GAR 1] *al-tap-*[*pí-pu*..........] ^{GIŠ}*e-lam*(*a*)*-ku* KÙ.GI KÙ.BABBAR GAR
(31) [x +] ⌜3⌝ S[U KÙ.]GI 1 *šu-ši* ⌜4⌝ ⌜SU⌝ [KÙ. BABBAR *i-na lìb-b*]*i-šu na-di*

---

(32) [x] [...*gu*$_5$-*ḫa*]*-aṣ-ṣí-i ra-ka-bi-*[............*i*]*-na* ŠÀ*-šu na-di*
(33) [...*ku-ur*]*-si-i-in-ni na-d*[*i*....................*x-*]*di-ni* GÌR
(34) [.....]ME[Š] *ša* ⌜*ku*⌝*-ḫi-iš* 25 [...................]*-ti-nu*
(35) [...]-⌜*an*⌝-⌜*na*⌝ [...]*-ip-pa-še pa-a-an-*[........*k*]*u-ḫi-iš* [...]
(36) [x SU KÙ.]BABBAR [*i-n*]*a lìb-bi-šu-nu* *na-*[*di*]

---

(37) [x] [.......] 3(?) AŠ KÙ.GI 14 AŠ (*ina*) *šar-*[...*x*] *ep-šu* 19 ŠU
(38) [..........$^{\text{NA}_4}$]*dú-šu li-tu*$_4$ *zi-*[...]*in-na-an-ni*
(39) [..]*-a-ta-an-ni*

---

(40) [x] [......*ḫ*]*a-*[*ṣ*]*u-*[*r*]*a* 2 TÚG.MEŠ [*ša ka-p*]*í-iz-zu-uḫ-ḫu*

---

(41) [x] [................] 1 TÚG [*š*]*a i-šu-uḫ-ḫu*

---

(42) [x] [.......] *a* [........]MEŠ ḪUŠ.A

---

(43) [x] [................................*u*]*z-zi-ḫat-sú-nu* KÙ.GI

---

(44) 10 *be-*[x...........]11 *me* 10 PA *šal-ši ur-ra-a-še-na*

---

(45) 4 ⌜TÚG⌝.⌜GÚ.MEŠ-*t*[*u*$_4$] GÙN.A 1 ⌜TÚG⌝ [*š*]*a Tuk*(*!*)*-ri-iš* GÙN.A

---

(46) 1 PA [*ša*]-⌜*al*⌝-*š*[*i*] *ur-ri* GÙN.A 11 $^{\text{TÚ[G]}}$*šu-ši-in-nu* GÙN.A

---

(25) [*x*] [..., of bo]xwood, overlaid with silver. 16 shekels of silver have been used on them.
(26) [...] of ivory.

---

(27) [*x*] [........of sil]ver, 380 shekels in weight.

---

(28) [*x*] [ches]ts, of [......]; their f[ig]ures, of iv[ory.............]
(29) [.................................. e]bony; [the]ir ba[se]
(30) with gold. [1] c]he[st....] of *elammakku*-wood, overlaid with gold and silver.
(31) [*x* +] 3 she[kels of go]ld, 64 [shekels of silver], have been used [on] it.

---

(32) [*x*] [...wi]res superimposed[......]have been used on it.
(33) [...an]kles use[d...............................]...foot
(34) [.....]..of....25 [..................................]...
(35) [......]....face[..........................].....[...]
(36) [*x* shekels of sil]ver have been used [o]n them

---

(37) [*x*] [.......] 3(?) in gold 14 in...[.......] worked 19 pair of
(38) [.........]*dušu*-stone.........[x -]....................
(39) [..].........

---

(40) [*x*] [......]Hazor (style) 2 garments[of...]..................

---

(41) [*x*] [................] 1 garment o[f] *iššuḫu* style

---

(42) [*x*] [, , , , , , , , , , ,.......].....red

---

(43) [*x*] [..............................]their...........of gold

---

(44) 10 [................]110...................desiderata

---

(45) 4 cloaks, of multi-colored cloth. 1 garment, *Tukriš*-style, of multi-colored cloth.

---

(46) 1 ...., of multi-colored cloth. [1]0 *šušinnu*-garments, of multi-colored cloth.

---

(47)	40	$^{\text{TÚ[G]}}$ [...]-⸢*it*⸣-⸢*za*⸣ ⸢GÙN⸣.⸢A⸣ *ša* MUNUS.MEŠ [x TÚG.MEŠ] GÙN.A *ša* TÚG.MEŠ *ša* MUNUS.MEŠ
(48)	41	TÚ[G].MEŠ [BAR].⸢SIG⸣? 10 [TÚ]G AN.TA KI.TA *ṭe*$_4$*-mu-tu*$_4$
(49)	30	⸢TÚG⸣.⸢SIG$_4$⸣.⸢ZA⸣.MEŠ GAL. MEŠ 4 TÚG GÍD.DA *ša* GIŠ.NÁ
(50)	2	TÚG LÚGUD!(⸢PÚ⸣).⸢DA⸣ *sú-nu-šu-nu* GÙN.A *ša* ⸢GIŠ⸣.NÁ 4 TÚG.SIG$_4$.ZA GÌR 4 TÚG.SIG$_4$.ZA SAG
(51)	1	$^{\text{NA}_4}$*ta-pa-tu*$_4$.Ì *mur-ri* [1] $^{\text{NA}_4}$*ta-pa-tu*$_4$.Ì ŠIM.GIG
(52)	2	⸢$^{\text{NA}_4}$⸣⸢*ta*⸣-⸢*pa*⸣-*tu*$_4$ Ì ZI.KÍL 1 $^{\text{NA}_4}$*ta-pa-tu*$_4$ Ì *sú-ʾa-a-dì*
(53)	2	$^{\text{NA}_4}$*ta-pa-tu*$_4$ Ì ŠIM.AZ ⸢1⸣ $^{\text{NA}_4}$*ta-pa-tu*$_4$.Ì *pè-er-ša-an-ti*
(54)	1	$^{\text{NA}_4}$*ta-pa-tu*$_4$ ⸢Ì⸣ ⸢*sú*⸣-*ʾa-a-dì* ‹1 $^{\text{NA}_4}$*ta-pa-tu*$_4$› Ì ŠIM.AZ
(55)	10	^{DUG}⸢*ki*⸣-*r*[*a-tu*$_4$ *ša*] Ì DÙG.GA DIR
(56)	1	*na*-⸢*ar*⸣-⸢*ma*⸣-⸢*ak*⸣-*tu*$_4$ ZA[BAR x] *du-ú-du* ZABAR
(57)	[x]	[*nam-ḫa*]*r* GAL.MEŠ ZABAR [x] [*n*]*am-ḫar*^{MEŠ} TUR Z[ABAR]
(58)	[x]	[........] ⸢ZABAR⸣ DUG[.......] MEŠ [...........]
(59)	[x]	[..........] ⸢ZABAR⸣ [...............................]
(60)	[x]	[...... *p*]*a*(?)*-al-ru* ZABAR 10 NÍG.ŠU.L[UḪ.ḪA]
(61)	[10]	[*š*]*a* IZI ZABAR 10 ŠU *an-gu*$_5$*-ri-i*[*n-nu* ZABAR]
(62)	1	[*ša me-e šu-l*]*i* ZABAR 1-*en ša ú-ḫu-li* ZABAR 20 GÍR.MEŠ [ZABAR]

(47) 40 […]…-garments, of multi-colored cloth, for women. [*x* garments], of multicolored cloth, for women.

(48) 41 *head scarves*(*?*)]. 10 garments, plaited above and below.

(49) 30 large blankets. 4 long spreads, for a bed.

(50) 2 sh[or]t spreads, of which the trimmings are multi-colored, for a bed. 4 wraps, for the feet. 4 wraps, for the head.

(51) 1 stone scent container, with myrrh-scented oil. 1 stone scent container, with *kanatku*-oil.

(52) 2 stone scent containers, with pure oil. 1 stone scent container, with *su'adi* oil.

(53) 2 stone scent containers, with oil of myrtle. 1 stone scent container, with *peršantu*-oil.

(54) 1 stone scent container, with *elder*-oil. 1 ‹stone scent container›, with oil of myrtle.

(55) 10 *kirru*-pots that are full of "sweet oil."

(56) 1 washbasin, of bronze. [1] kettle, of bronze.

(57) [*x*] large [jar]s, of bronze. [*x*] small [j]ars, of br[onze].

(58) [*x*] [..........], of bronze. [..........] pots [...........].

(59) [*x*] [..........] of bronze. [.............................].

(60) [*x*] […]…, of bronze. 10 wash[basins, of bronze].

(61) [*x*] [10 bra]ziers, of bronze. 10 sets of *angurin*[*nu*, of bronze].

(62) [1] [water-dip]per, of bronze. 1 container for alkali, of bronze. 20 knives, [of bronze].

(63) [x] [GIŠ.]BUGIN!(BÚGIN).TUR GIŠ.TÚG.MEŠ 20
GIŠ.BUGIN!(BÚGIN).TUR ^{GIŠ}e-*lam-ma-*[*ku..........*]

---

(64) [x] [GI]Š.DÍLIM.MEŠ ^{GIŠ}e-*lam-ma-ku* 2 *me* 70 MUNUS.MEŠ 30
LÚ.MEŠ *mu-lu-gu*$_5$ [......]

---

(65) [*qi-ša*]*-te-e*^{MEŠ} *mu-lu-gi*^{MEŠ} *an-nu-ti gáb-bá-šu-nu-m*[*a............*]
(66) [^{I}*Tù*]*-uš-rat-ta* LUGAL KUR ⸢*Mi*⸣-⸢*i*⸣-⸢*it*⸣-⸢*ta*⸣*-an-n*[*i..............*]
(67) [..................] *ša id-*[*di-nu............................*]

(63) [*x*] small boxes, of boxwood. 20 small boxes, of *elammakku*-wood.

---

(64) [20+*x*] [s]poons, of *elammakku*-wood. 270 women, 30 men, are the dowry-personnel.

---

(65) It is all these [gi]fts (and) dowry-personnel
(66) t[hat Tu]shratta, the king of Mittani, [.........................]
(67) [.................] ga[ve...................................]

EA 26

TRANSCRIPTION

Obv. 01) ⸢*a*⸣-*n*[*a*...^{MUNUS}*Te-i-e*] NIN KUR *Mi-i*[*ṣ-ri-i qí-bi-ma*]

02) *u*[*m-ma* ^{I}*Tù-uš*]*-rat-ta šàr* ⸢K⸣[UR *Mi-ta-an-ni a-na ia-ši*]

03) *š*[*ul-mu*]⸢*a*⸣*-na ka-a-ši lu-ú* ⸢*šul*⸣[*-mu a-na* É*-ka a-na*]

04) ⸢DUMU⸣-⸢*ka*⸣ *lu-ú šul-mu a-na* ^{MUNUS}*Ta-a-du*$_4$*-Ḫé-bá*

05) É.GI$_4$.A-*ka lu-ú šul-mu a-na* ⸢KUR⸣.⸢MEŠ⸣-*ka a*[*-na* ÉRIN.MEŠ-*ka*]

06) *ù mim-mu-ka dan-*⸢*níš*⸣ *dan-*⸢*níš*⸣ *lu-*⸢*ú*⸣ [*šul-mu*]

---

07) *at-ti-i-ma ti-i-dá-an-ni ki-i-me-*⸢*e*⸣[*a-na-ku it-ti*]

08) ^{I}*Mi-im-mu-re-ia mu-ti-i-ka ar*[*-ta-na-ʾa-a-mu*]

09) *ù* ^{I}*Mi-im-mu-re-ia ap-pu-na mu-u*[*t-ka*]

10) *ki-i-me-e it-ti-ia ir-ta-na-ʾa-am* [*ú a-na-ku*]

11) ⸢*a*⸣-⸢*na*⸣ ^{I}*Mi-im-mu-re-ia mu-ti-i-ki ša a-š*[*a-ap-pa-ru*]

12) ⸢*ù*⸣ ⸢*ša*⸣ *a-dáb-bu-bu ù* ^{I}*Mi-im-mu-*⸢*re*⸣[*-ia*]

13) [*ap-pu*]*-*⸢*na* ⸣ *mu-ti-i-ki a-ma-te*^{MEŠ} *a-na ia-š*[*i ša*]

14) [*il-ta-n*]*a-ap-pa-ru ù ša i-dáb-bu-bu at-ti-*[*i*]

15) [^{I}*Ké-li*]*-ia ù* ^{I}*Ma-né-e i-de*$_4$ *ù at-ti-i-m*[*a*]

16) [*ap-pu-n*]*a el gáb-bi-šu-nu-ma ti-i-de*$_4$ *a-ma-te*^{MEŠ}

17) [*ša it-t*]*i ḫa-mi-iš ni-id-bu-bu ma-am-ma*

18) [*ša-nu-u*]*m-ma la i-de*$_4$*-šu-nu*

---

19) [*ù a-nu*]*-um-ma at-ti-i-ma a-na* ^{I}*Ké-*⸢*li*⸣*-ia*

20) [*ta-aq-*]*ta-bi a-na be-li-i-ka qí-bi-i-m*[*ì*]

21) ^{I}*M*[*i-im-*]*mu-re-ia mu-ti it-ti a-bi-i-k*[*a*]

22) *ir*[*-t*]*a-na-ʾa-am-mì ù ak-ka-a-ša it-ta-ṣa-ar-k*[*a*]

23) *ù* [ ]*it-ti a-bi-i-ka ra-ʾa-mu-ut-ta-šu la im-š*[*e?*]

24) *ù ḫar-ra-na ša il-ta-na-ap-pa-ru la ip-r*[*u-us*]

25) *ù i-n*[*a-*]*an-na at-ta it-ti* ^{I}*Mi-im-mu*[*-re-ia*]

26) ŠEŠ-*ka*[*r*]*i-ʾi-mu-ut-ka la ta-ma-aš-ši i*[*t-ti*]

27) ^{I}*Na-ap-ḫur-*⸢*re*⸣*-*[*i*]*a ru-ub-bi ù ú-ṣú-ur-š*[*u*]

28) *ù ḫar-*⸢*ra*⸣*-na* ⸢*ša*⸣ [*i-na?*] *ḫi-du-ti ta-al-ta-na-a*[*p-pa-ru*]

29) *la ta-pa-*[ ]⸢*ar*⸣*-ra-as*

EA 26

TRANSLATION

(1–6) [Speak] to [Teye] the mistress of the land of Eg[ypt]: T[hus (says) Tush]ratta king of the l[and of Mitanni. With me] it is [well]; may it be we[ll]with you. May it be well [with your house, with] your son; may it be well with Tadu-Ḫeba your daughter-in-law. May it be very, very [well] with your lands, wi[th your troops] and your property.

(7–18) It is you who knows me, how [I myself]al[ways showed love towards Mimmureya your husband, and Mimmureya [your] husband, on the other hand, how he always showed love towards me. [And as for me], what I wo[uld write and] what I would say to Mimmureya your husband and as for Mimmure[ya, [on the other]hand, your husband, [what] words to me [he would always] write and would always say, you, [Kel]ia and Mane know and it is you, [on the other han]d, more than all of them, who knows the words [which] we said to one another. No one [els]e knows them.

(19–29) [And no]w, you [have sp]oken to Keliya, "Speak to your lord: M[im]mureya, my husband continually showed love to your father and for you he maintained it; and towards your father he did not forget his love and the [ca]ravans that he used to send, he did not cut o[ff]. And now you must not forget your [l]ove towards Mimmi[reya], your brother; w[ith] Napḫur-reya, increase and keep i[t], and the caravan which you joyfully(?) have been sen[ding], you must not cut off."

30) it-ti ^{I}Mi-im-mu-re-ia[ ] mu-ti-i-ki ra-ʾa-mu-ut-t[a la]
31) a-⸢ma⸣-⸢aš⸣-ši el ša pa-n[a-n]a-nu i-na-an-na-a-m[a]
32) it-ti ^{I}Na-ap-ḫur-re-i[a] ⸢DUMU⸣-ka a-na 10-š[u]
33) dan-níš dan-níš ar-ta[-na-ʾa]-⸢am⸣ ù a-ma-⸢a⸣-te^{M}[^{EŠ}]
34) ^{I}Mi-im-mu-re-ia m[u-ti-i-ki at-ti-i-ma ti-i-de$_{4}$ ù]
35) šul-ma-a-ni ša a-na[šu-bu-li mu-ut-ki iq-bu-ú]
Lo.ed. 36) mi-it-ḫa-ri-iš la tu-š[e-e-bi-li ù ALAM.MEŠ ša KÙ.GI.MEŠ]
37) ša-ap-ku$_{8}$-ú-ti ub-⸢bu⸣-[qú-ú-ti ša a-na mu-ti-i-ki]
38) e-te-ri!(TI)-iš um-ma Š[EŠ-ia ALAM.MEŠ ša KÙ.GI.MEŠ]
39) ù ša NA$_{4}$.ZA.GÌN KUR a-n[a ia-ši li-še-bi-la-ma]
Rev. 40) ù i-⸢na⸣-an-na ^{I}Na-ap[-ḫur-re-ia DUMU-ka ALAM.MEŠ]
41) ša GIŠ ù-te-eḫ-ḫi-iz-ma [uš-te-bi-il ù i-na KUR ša DUMU-ka]
42) KÙ.GI.MEŠ e-pé-ru šu-ú [am-]mi-i-ni i-na Š[À-šu]
43) ša DUMU-ka im-tar-⸢ṣú⸣-ma [l]a id-dì-na ù an-ni-t[a-ma]
44) ap-pu-na a-na ⸢ia⸣-[š]i ⸢a⸣[-n]a na-dá-a-ni i-te[-pu-uš]
45) ra-a-ʾa-mu-tu$_{4}$ an-nu-⸢ú⸣[ ]šu-ú um-ma a-n[a-ku-ma]
46) el a-bi-i-šu a-na 10[ ]-šu ^{I}Na-ap-ḫur-re[-ia DUMU-ka]
47) ù-ut-ta-ra-an-ni-⸢mi⸣[ ] ù a-nu-um-ma i-na[-an-na-a-ma]
48) ša a-bu-ú-šu-ú-ma [ ] i-na-an-dì-nu la[id-dì-na]

49) a-ma-a-te^{MEŠ} š[a at-ti]-i-ma i-na pí-i-ki a-[na ia-ši]
50) ta-aq-ta-⸢bi⸣[ ] ù a-na pa-ni ^{I}Na-ap-[ḫur-re-ia]
51) am-mi-⸢ni⸣[la-]a ta-at-ru-uṣ šum-ma[at-ti-i]
52) a-na ⸢pa⸣-[ni-š]u la ta-tar-ra-aṣ ù m[a-an-nu]
53) ša[-nu-ú] i-de$_{4}$ ALAM.MEŠ ša KÙ.GI up-pu[-qú-ú-ti]
54) [^{I}Na-a]p-ḫur-re-ia li-id-dì-na la mi-im-ma[...]
55) [lìb-]bi lu-ú la-a ú-ša-am-ra-aṣ-ma la-a[...]
56) ⸢el⸣ a-bi-šu 10-šu li-i-it-te-er-an[-ni-ma]
57) [i-n]a ra-a-ʾa-mu-ti ù i-na ku$_{8}$-ub-bu[-ti]

58) [ù] at-tù-ki LÚ.DUMU.MEŠ.KIN-ki it-ti LÚ[.DUMU.MEŠ. KIN.-šu]
59) [š]⸢a⸣ ^{I}Na-ap-ḫur-re-ia it-ti NÍ[G.BA]
60) [a-n]a ^{MUNUS}I-ú-ni DAM-ia li-i[l-li-ku]
61) [a-n]a ma-al-dá-ri-iš-ma ù LÚ.DUMU.[MEŠ-ša]
62) [š]a ^{MUNUS}I-ú-ni DAM-ia a-na [ka-a-ši]
63) [li]-il-⸢li⸣-⸢ku⸣ a-na ma-al-dá-[ri-iš]

(30–39) The love towards Mimmureya, your husband, I will not forget. More than formerly, even now I am [express]ing ten times much more love to Napḫurreya, your son. But as for the words of Mimmureya, [your] hus[band, it is you that knows (them), but] my greeting gift which [your husband said] to s[end], you do not s[end] accordingly, [and the] solid cast [statues of gold which] I requested [from your husband], saying "[My] br[other, statues of gold] and of real lapis lazuli [may he send] t[o me]."

(40–48) But now, as for Nap[ḫurreya your son], he has plated [statues of wood [and sent (them). But in the land of your son] gold is (like) dirt; [w]hy have they distressed the he[art] of your son so that he did not give (them) to me but rather, this, has he [had] given to me? Is this love? I said: "Ten times more than his father, Napḫurre[ia your son] will surpass for me, but now he [did not give me] even what his father used to give."

(49–57) As for the words whi[ch you yo]urself spoke, t[o me], then why don't you present to Nap[ḫurreia]? If [you] don't present (them) befo[re h]im, then who e[lse] knows? So[lid] statues of gold, may [Na]pḫurreya give me. May he not cause me any distress whatsoever! May [he not…]. Ten times more than his father may he surpass f[or me] in love and in respect.

(58–63) [And] may your own envoys c[ome] regularly with the a[mbassadors] of Napḫurreya, with a g[ift fo]r Yuni my wife; and [may] the envoy[s] [o]f Yuni my wife go to [you] regularly.

---

64) [*a-*]*nu-um-ma a-na šul-ma-ni-i-ka* [*uš-te-bi-la*]
65) ⸢1⸣ NA_4 *ta-pa-tu*$_4$ *ša* Ì *ṭá-a-bá* [*ma-lu-ú*]
66) ⸢1⸣-*nu-tu*$_4$ NA_4.MEŠ [KÙ.GI GAR.RA]

Hieratic: Two illegible lines on reverse, on left edge, more unreadable signs on BM 29794. On left edge of A 9356:

[*nb.t tꜣwy*] (*ḥm.t nswt*)

(64–66) [N]ow for your greeting gift, [I have sent] one scent container [full] of sweet oil; one set of stones [set in gold].

[Lady of the Two Lands] (Wife of the King)

EA 27

TRANSCRIPTION

Obv.

01) [*a-na* ^{I}*Na-ap-ḫur-re-ia šàr* KUR *Mi-iṣ-*]⸢*ri*⸣*-i* ⸢ŠEŠ⸣*-ia ḫa-ta-ni-ia ša* [*a-ra-ʾa-a-mu*]

02) [*ša i-ra-ʾa-a-ma-an-ni qí-bí-ma um-ma* ^{I}*T*]*ù-uš-*⸢*rat*⸣*-ta* LUGAL GAL LUGAL KUR *Mi-*[*i-ta-an-ni*]

03) [*e-mu-ka ša i-ra-ʾa-a-mu-ka* ŠEŠ*-ka-*]*ma a-na ia-*⸢*ši*⸣ *šul-mu a-na ka-a-ša l*[*u-ú šul-mu*]

04) [*a-na* ^{MUNUS}*Te-i-e* AMA*-ka a-na*]⸢É⸣*-ka lu-ú šul-*[*mu a-n*]*a* ^{MUNUS}*Ta-a-du-Ḫé-bá* DUM[U.MUNUS*-ia*]

05) [DAM*-ka a-na ri-ḫu-ú-ti* DAM.MEŠ*-ka*] *a-na* DUMU.MEŠ[*-ka a-na* LÚ.GAL.]MEŠ*-ka a-na* GIŠ.⸢GIGIR⸣*-ka*

06) [*a-na* ANŠE.KUR.]⸢RA⸣*-ka a*[*-na* ÉRIN.MEŠ*-ka a-na* KUR*-ka*] ⸢*ù*⸣ *a-na* [*mim-mu-k*]*a dan-níš lu-ú šul-mu*

---

07) [^{I}*Ma-*]⸢*né*⸣*-e* LÚ.DUMU.KIN*-šu ša* ŠÉŠ*-ia* [*it-tal-ka ù šu*]*l-ma-a-na š*[*a* ŠÉŠ*-ia*] *el-te-me-ma*

08) [*a*]*ḫ-tá-du dan-níš ù-nu-ta ša* ŠEŠ-⸢*ia*⸣ [*ú-še-e-*]⸢*bi*⸣-⸢*lu*⸣ *a-ta-mar-ma a*[*ḫ*]-⸢*tá*⸣*-du dan-níš*]

---

09) ŠEŠ*-ia a-ma-ta an-ni-ta iq-ta-bi* ⸢*ki*⸣-⸢*i*⸣*-me-e it-ti a-bi-i*[*a* ^{I}]*Mi-im-mu-re-ia*

10) *ta-ar-ta-na-ʾa-a-mu-ú-mi ù a-ka-an-na i-na-an-na ri-ta-ʾa-*[*ma-an-ni*] ⸢*ul*⸣*-tu*$_{4}$ ŠEŠ*-ia*

11) ⸢*it*⸣*-ti-ia ra-a-mu-ú-ta ḫaš-*⸢*ḫu*⸣ ⸢*ù*⸣ *a-na-ku it-ti* ŠEŠ*-ia*] *ra-a-m*[*u-ú-ta*] *ul ḫaš-ḫa-ku*

12) UGU *a-bi-ka i-na-an-na-ma* ⸢*it*⸣-⸢*ti*⸣-⸢*ka*⸣ *dan-níš a-na* 10*-šu ar-t*[*a-na-ʾa-*]*am*

EA 27

TRANSLATION

(1–6) [Speak to Napḫurreya, the king of the land of Eg]ypt, my brother, my son-in-law whom [I love and who loves me; thus T]ushratta, the great king, king of the land of Mi[ttanni, your father-in-law who loves you, your brother.] It is well with me. M[ay it be well] with you. May it be we[ll with Teye, your mother, with] your household. With Tadu-Ḫeba, [my] daugh[ter, your wife, with the rest of your wives,] with [your] sons, [with your senior official]s, with your chariotry, [with]your [hor]ses, w[ith your troops, with your land, and] with [yo]ur possessions, may it be exceedingly well.

(7–8) [Ma]ne, the envoy of my brother, [has come and] I have heard of the [we]lfare o[f my brother,] and [I] rejoiced greatly; the goods which my brother [se]nt have I seen and I re[j]oiced greatly.

(9–12) My brother said this: "Ju[st] as you continually expressed love to m[y] father, Mimmureya, so likewise now express love [to me] continuously." [Si]nce my brother desires a loving relationship with me, will I not desire a loving relationship with my brother? Even now, I am ex[pressing] exceeding [lo]ve for you, ten times more than for your father.

13) *ù a-bu-ka* ^{I}*Mi-im-mu-re-[i]a a-ma-ta an-ni-ta i-na ṭup-pí-šu i[q-ta-bi-mì u]n-tum*^{I} ⸢*Ma*⸣*-né-e*

14) *ter-ḫa-ta ub-lu ù a-*⸢*ka*⸣*-*⸢*an*⸣*-na* ŠEŠ-*ia* ^{I}*Mi-im-mu-ú-re-ia iq-ta-[b]i-mì an-nu-ú ú-nu-ta*

15) *ša i-na-an-na ú-še-e-bi-*⸢*lu*⸣ *la mi-im-ma-a-me ù* ŠEŠ-*ia* ⸢*la*⸣ *ut-ta-za-*⸢*am*⸣*-mì mi-im-ma*

16) *la ú-še-e-bíl-mì an-nu-ú ú-nu-ta ša i-na-an-na ú-še-e-*⸢*bí*⸣*-la-kum-mì ka-am-ma-me*

17) *ul-te-e-bíl-ak-*⸢*kum*⸣*-mì ù un-du* DAM-*ti ša e-ri-šu* ŠEŠ-*ia i-na-an-din-ma-a-mì*

18) *i-le-eq-qú-ú-*⸢*nim*⸣*-ma-mì a-am-ma-ru-me ù* 10-*šu ma-la an-ni-i ú-še-bél-ak*(!)*-kum-mì*

---

19) *ù* ALAM.⸢MEŠ⸣ *ša* KÙ.GI *ša-ap-ku*$_8$*-tu*$_4$ *up-pu-qu-ú-tu*$_4$ 1-*en* ALAM *a-na* [*i*]⸢*a*⸣*-ši ù ša-ni-tu*$_4$ ALAM

20) *a-na* ALAM ⸢^{MUNUS}⸣*Tá-a-du-Ḫé-e-bá* DUMU.MUNUS-*ia a-šar a-bi-ka-ma* ^{I}*Mi-im-mu-*⸢*re*⸣*-ia e-te-ri-iš*

21) *ù* ⸢*iq*⸣*-ta-bi a-bu-ka-ma muš-šèr a-na ša* KÙ.GI-*ma ša-pí-ik-ta up-pu-u[q]-ta na-dá-a-an-sú-nu-mì*

22) ⸢*ù*⸣ *ša* NA$_4$.ZA.GÌN KUR *a-na-an-din-ak-kum-mì ù* KÙ.GI *ap-pu-na ša-na-a* ⸢*ma*⸣*-ʾa-dá ú-nu-ta*

23) ⸢*ša*⸣ *pa-ṭá la i-šu-ú it-ti* ALAM.MEŠ *a-na-an-din-ak-kum-mì ù* KÙ.GI *ša* [A]LAM.MEŠ LÚ.DUMU.MEŠ KIN-*ia*

24) [*gá*]*b-bi-i-šu-nu-ma ša i-na* KUR *Mi-iṣ-ri-i aš-bu i-na* IGI.MEŠ-*šu-nu i-ta-am-*⸢*ru*⸣ *ù* ALAM.MEŠ *a-bu-*⸢*ka*⸣*-ma*

25) [*a-n*]*a pa-ni* LÚ.DUMU.MEŠ KIN-*ia a-na ši-ip-ki ut-te-e-er-šu-nu i-te-pu-us-sú-*⸢*nu*⸣ *ig-ta-mar-šu-nu*

26) ⸢*uz*⸣*-ze-ek-ki-šu-nu ù ki-i a-na ši-ip-*⸢*ki*⸣ *tù-ur-ru* LÚ.DUMU.MEŠ.KIN-[*i*]*a* ⸢*i*⸣-⸢*na*⸣ ⸢IGI⸣-⸢*šu*⸣*-nu i-tam-ru*

27) ⸢*ù*⸣ *ki-i gám-ru-ma za-ku*$_8$*-ú i-na* IGI.MEŠ-*šu-nu i-ta-am-ru*

---

28) *ù* KÙ.GI *ša-nu-ú ma-ʾa-du ša pa-ṭá la i-šu-ú ša a-na ia-ši ú-še-e-[e]b-bé-lu uk-te-li-im-ma*

29) *ù iq-ta-bi a-na* LÚ.DUMU.MEŠ KÙ.GI-*ia a-nu-um-ma* ALAM.MEŠ *ù a-nu-um-ma* KÙ.[GI] *ma-a-dá ù ú-nu-ta*

30) *ša-a pa-ṭá la-i-šu-ú ša a-na* ŠEŠ-*ia ú-še-bé-lu ù i-na* IGI.MEŠ-*ku*$_8$*-nu am-ra-a-mì*

31) ⸢*ù*⸣ LÚ.DUMU.MEŠ KIN-*ia i-na* IGI.MEŠ-*šu-nu i-ta-am-ru*

(13–15) And your father, Mimmureya, s[aid] this in his letter; when Mane brought the bride price, thus my brother, Mimmureya said: "These goods which I have sent now are nothing and my brother should not complain.

(16–18) I have sent nothing. These goods that I have sent to you now, thus have I sent to you but when my brother gives the wife that I have requested (and) they bring (her) hither, (and) I see (her), then ten times more than this will I send to you."

(19–27) And statues of solid cast gold one statue of me and another statue for a statue of Tadu-Ḫeba, my daughter, did I request from your father, Mimmureya. And your father said "Lay off of giving statues only of solid cast gold, and I will give you (statues) of lapis lazuli and other gold, moreover, (and) much goods without limit with the statues will I give to you." And as for the gold for the statues, all my envoys who were posted in Egypt saw with their own eyes, and as for the statues, it was your father, in the presence of my envoys, who recast them, fashioned them, finished them, purified them. And when the recasting took place, my envoys saw with their own eyes and when they were finished and they were purified, with their own eyes they saw.

(28–31) And he showed much other gold, without limit, which he was sending to me. And he said to my envoys, "Now the statues and now much gold and goods without limit am I sending to my brother, so see with your own eyes." So my envoys saw with their own eyes.

---

32) ⸢*ù*⸣ *i-na-an-na* ŠEŠ-*ia* ALAM.MEŠ *up-pu-qu-ú-tù ša a-*⸢*bu*⸣*-ka ú-še-e-eb-bé-*⸢*lu*⸣ *la tù-še-e-bi-la*
33) ⸢*ù*⸣ ⸢*ša*⸣ GIŠ.MEŠ *uḫ-ḫu-zu-tù tù-ul-te-e-bi-la ú-nu-*⸢*ta*⸣ *ša a-bu-ka a-na* ⸢*ia*⸣*-ši ú-še-e-eb-bé-lu*
34) [*l*]*a tù-še-e-bi-lam-ma ù tù-ul-te-e-mì-iṣ dan-níš-ma*

---

35) ⸢*ù*⸣ *a-ma-tù mi-im-ma ša i-du-ú ša a-na* ŠEŠ-*ia aḫ-ṭù-ú ia-nu-ú i-na* ⸢*a*⸣*-i-im-me-e u*$_4$*-mi ša* ŠEŠ-⸢*ia*⸣
36) ⸢*šul*⸣-⸢*ma*⸣*-an-sú el-te-me ù u*$_4$*-ma ša-a-šu bá-ni-ta e-te-pu-uš-sú*

---

37) *ù* [^{I}*Ḫ*]*a-*⸢*a*⸣*-maš-ši* LÚ.DUMU.KIN-*šu ša* ŠEŠ-*ia un-du a-na* UGU-*ia il-li-*⸢*ku*$_8$⸣ *ù un-du ša* ŠEŠ-*ia*
38) *a-ma-*⸢*te*⸣[^{M}]^{EŠ}*-šu iq-bu-ú-ma eš-mu-ú ù a-ka-an-na aq-ta-bi ki-i-*⸢*me*⸣*-e it-ti* ^{I}*Mi-mu-re-ia*
39) *a-bi-*⸢*ka*⸣ *ar-ta-na-ʾa-a-mu-mì ù i-na-an-*⸢*na*⸣ 10-*šu it-ti* ^{I}*Na-ap-ḫur-*⸢*re*⸣*-ia ar-ta-na-ʾa-am-mì*
40) *dan-níš* ⸢*ù*⸣ *a-ka-an-na a-*⸢*na*⸣ ^{I}*Ḫa-a-maš-ši* LÚ.DUMU.KIN-*ka aq-ta-bi*

---

41) *ù i-na-an-*⸢*na*⸣ ŠEŠ-*ia* ⸢ALAM⸣.MEŠ *ša* KÙ.GI *up-pu-*⸢*qu*⸣*-tù la ú-še-e-bi-*⸢*la*⸣ *ù ri-iḫ-ta ú-nu-ta*
42) *ša* ^{I}*a-bu-ka a-na šu-bu-li* ⸢*iq*⸣*-*[*bu*]*-ú mi-it-ḫa-*⸢*ri*⸣*-*⸢*iš*⸣ ŠEŠ-*ia la ú-še-*⸢*e*⸣*-bi-lam-ma*

---

43) *i-na-an-na* ŠEŠ-*ia* ⸢ALAM⸣.MEŠ *ša* KÙ.GI *up-pu-qu-ú-tù ša a-na a-*⸢*bi*⸣*-ka e-*⸢*ri*⸣*-*[*š*]*u*
44) *li-id-din-am-ma lu-*[*ú la-*]⸢*a*⸣ *i-kál-la-a-*[*šu-nu*]

---

45) KUR.KUR *gáb-bi-i-*[*šu-nu......................a-na*] *na-dá-a-ni i*[*q-bu-ú*]
46) *ù i-na-an-na šum-m*[*a................*] *gáb-bi-*⸢*i*⸣*-š*[*u-nu*]
47) *šum-ma it-til-tu*$_4$ [*.........................*] *ta a-*[...]
48) *a-na la ṭá-bu-ut-t*[*i................................*] ALAM.MEŠ [...*a-na*]
49) *na-da-ni iq-bu-*⸢*ú*⸣ [*.....................*] ⸢*ru*⸣ [.....]
50) *ù i-na* KUR *ša* ŠE[Š-*ia* KÙ.GI *ki-i e-pé-ri ma-a-dá-at am-mi-i-ni i-na* ŠÀ-*šu š*]*a* ŠEŠ[-*ia* ALAM.MEŠ]
51) *im-tar-ṣa-a-ma la* [*id-dì-na ki-i ša iq-bu-ú* ^{I}*Mi-im-mu-re-ia a-bu-k*]*a-ma a-na i*[*a-ši*]

(32–33) And now, my brother, the solid statues that your father was going to send, you have not sent. But you have sent plated ones of wood; the goods that your father was sending me,
you have not sent and you have reduced (them) greatly.

(35–36) And there is no matter that I know of in which I have been negligent towards my brother. On whatever day that I have heard of the welfare of my brother, I have made a festive occasion.

(37–40) As for [Ḫ]amashshi, the envoy of my brother, when he came to me and when he related my brother's words and I heard, then thus I said: "As with Mimmureya, your father, I continually showed love, so now ten times more will I continually show much love to Napḫurreya." So thus I spoke to Ḫamashshi, your envoy.

(41–42) But now my brother has not sent the solid gold statues, and the rest of the goods that your father ordered to be sent, likewise, my brother has not sent.

(43–44) Now, may my brother give me the solid gold statues that I requested from your father. May he [no]t withhold them.

(45–51) The territories, all [of them…]he s[aid to] give, and now if […] all o[f them.] If one time[…]for no good[…]he said [to] give the statues. But in the land of [my] broth[er, gold is plentiful like dirt; why have the statues] caused so much distress [in my] brother's [heart] that he has not [given them as was promised] to m[e by Mimmureya, yo]ur [father]?

52) ^{I}*Ḫa-a-maš-ši* ⸢LÚ⸣.[DUMU.KIN-*šu ša* ŠEŠ-*ia un-du a-na* UGU-*ia*] *it-ta-al-*⸢*ka*⸣[.........]

53) *mi-im-ma la* ⸢*ú*⸣[-*še-e-bi-la*...............*k*]*a* ⸢*ù*⸣[...............]

54) *ù a-ka-an*[-*na a-na mi-*]⸢*i*⸣-*ni* ŠEŠ[-*ia*] ⸢*lu*⸣-[*ú*] ⸢*la*⸣ [*id-dì-na*]

---

55) [^{I}*Ḫa-*]⸢*a*⸣-*m*[*aš-ši* LÚ.DUMU.KIN-*šu ša a-bi-ka*] ⸢*i*⸣-*na kál-le-*⸢*e*⸣ [*al-ta-ap-ra-aš-šu-m*]*a*

56) [*ù i-na ša-la-a-ša-a-at ar-ḫi i-n*]*a* ⸢*kál*⸣-⸢*le*⸣-⸢*e*⸣-⸢*em*⸣-⸢*ma*⸣ *ut-te-e-er-šu*

57) [*ù a-bu-ka* KÙ.GI *ma-a-dá-at*] *ul-te-*⸢*e*⸣-[*bi*]-*la ù er-be-e-et ma-aš-ku*$_{8}$

58) [*ša* KÙ.GI *ma-lu-ú ša ú-še-e-bi-lu*] *ù* [^{I}*Ḫa-a-*]⸢*maš*⸣-*ši-i-ma* ŠEŠ-*ia* LÚ.DUMU.KIN-*šu li-is-*⸢*al*⸣

Rev

59) [...........]*a ar-k*[*a*]-⸢*nu*⸣ *i*[-*n*]*a-*[*a*]*n-d*⸢*i*⸣-*nu-ma* ^{I}*Ké-li-ia i*[*l-la-ak*] ⸢*ù*⸣ *ki-i-me-*[*e*]

60) [.....]⸢*ù*⸣ *a-k*[*a*]-*a*[*n-n*]*a* [^{I}*Pi-ri-is-sí*]⸢*ù*⸣ ^{I}*Tu-lu-ub-*[*ri* LÚ DUMU.MEŠ.KIN-*ia al*]*ta-pár-šu-nu*

61) [*ù*] ⸢*mi*⸣(?)-*im-m*[*a*.......*li-š*]*a-*⸢*a*⸣-⸢*nu*⸣ ⸢*ša*⸣ KÙ.[GI ....] *ma-aš-k*[*a*](?)

62) ⸢*ša*⸣ ⸢*a*⸣-⸢*bu*⸣-⸢*ka*⸣[*iq-bu-ú a-na na-da-ni. ù*] ⸢KÙ.GI⸣(?) [................ŠEŠ]-⸢*i*⸣-⸢*a*⸣

---

63) ⸢*ù*⸣ ⸢*a*⸣-⸢*ka*⸣-⸢*an*⸣-[*na*] *i*[*q-t*]*a*[-*bi a-*]*b*[*u-ú*]-[*k*]*a* KÙ].GI.MEŠ *ša-*⸢*a*⸣-⸢*šu*⸣-⸢*nu*⸣[*ù an-n*]*u-*[*ú ú-nu-tu*]

64) ⸢*bá*⸣[.......]*i-na*[-*a*]*n-n*[*a a-na* ŠEŠ-]*ia-*⸢*ma*⸣ ⸢*ter*⸣-⸢*ḫat*⸣-⸢*ka*⸣ *ul-te-*⸢*e*⸣-⸢*bíl*⸣-*m*[*ì ù a-bu-ka r*]*a*[-*a-ma*]

65) ⸢*it*⸣-⸢*ti*⸣-⸢*ia*⸣ ⸢*a*⸣-⸢*na*⸣ ⸢*ra*⸣-[*a-mu-ú-ut-ti ú-t*]*e-*⸢*ti*⸣-*ir ù a-k*[*a-an-na ta-a-mu-*]*ur-t*[*u*.....]

66) ⸢*im*⸣-*ma-*⸢*ti*⸣-⸢*i*⸣-⸢*me*⸣ [................................] *nu*[.........]

67) [*ù*] ⸢*la*⸣ ⸢*ú*⸣-⸢*še*⸣[-*bi-la*.............ŠEŠ-*i*]*a li-t*[*u*$_{4}$.......]

68) [......]⸢*ša*⸣ ⸢*a*⸣[.........*š*]*u*(?) [.....................]

(52–54) As for Ḫamashshi, the [envoy of my brother, when] he came[to me…] he did not b[ring] anything […] and […] and thu[s wh]y [did my] brother ve[rily not give]?

(55–58) As for [Ḫa]ma[shshi, the envoy of your father, I sent him] with all haste [and in three months] with all haste, he sent him back. [And your father] sent [much gold,] and (it was) four sacks [full of gold that he sent.] So may my brother ask [Ḫa]mashshi, his envoy.

(59–62) […]afte[rw]ards he will let Keliya c[ome] and just as[…and] thus, [Perissi]and Tulubri, [my envoys,] did I send [and] the property[…] Now the go[ld was in…s]acks](?) which your father [commanded to give. But]the gold(?)[…..] my [brother.]

(63–68) And thus your father said: "Those [go]ld objects [and th]ese [goods…]. Now [to my brother,] have I sent your bride price." [And your father [re]turned love to me in a loving relationship. And th[us the audie]nce gift […] when […But] he did not se[nd….m]y [brother,] pow[er…..] which […..]

69) [ù a-ma-]tu$_4$ ša-a ⌜it⌝[-ti a-bi-i-ka a-dáb-b]u-bu ⌜ù⌝ ša ⌜a⌝-b]u-ú-⌜ka⌝[i-dáb-bu-bu it-t]i-⌜ia⌝

70) [.........]ma-am-ma ul ⌜i⌝-d[e$_9$ ^{MUNUS}Te-i-e AMA-ka i-de$_9$] ^{I}⌜Ké⌝-⌜li⌝-⌜i⌝a[ù ^{I}Ma-né-e ul i]-de$_9$

71) ⌜ù⌝ ⌜ma⌝-am-ma ša-nu-ú-um-ma ⌜ul⌝ ⌜i⌝-⌜de$_4$⌝-[šu-nu-ti]⌜ù⌝ AMA-šu [ša ŠEŠ-ia i-de$_4$ gáb-]⌜bá⌝-šu

72) ⌜ki⌝-⌜i⌝-me-e a-bu-ú-ka it-⌜ti⌝-ia [i-dáb-bu-bu ra-]mu-ú-ut[-ta-šu it-ti a-bi-ia la im-]⌜še⌝(?)

73) ki-i-me-e a-na-ku it-ti a-bi-i-⌜ka⌝ i-dáb-bu-bu ra-m[u-ú-ta-ia it-ti a-bi-ka la am-še]

---

74) ⌜ù⌝ ⌜i⌝-⌜na⌝-⌜an⌝-⌜na⌝ ŠEŠ-ia ⌜iq⌝-⌜ta⌝-[b]i k[i]-⌜i⌝-me-e ⌜it⌝-ti ⌜a⌝-[bi]-⌜i⌝a ta-[ar-ta-na-ʾa-a-mu-mì ù]

75) ⌜a⌝-⌜ka⌝-⌜na⌝ it[-ti-ia] ⌜ri⌝[-ta-ʾa-am-m]ì ⌜ù⌝ ŠEŠ-ia-ma ⌜i⌝-⌜mar⌝-an-ni ki[-i-me-e it-ti ŠEŠ-ia]

76) a[r-]t[a-n]a-[ʾa-a-mu-mì ù a-na]-⌜ku⌝ ⌜aq⌝-⌜ta⌝-bi ŠEŠ-ia AMA-šu l[i]-[i]š-[t]a-ʾa-[al-ši....]

77) [..........t]i [ŠEŠ-ia-ma] i-[ma]r-an-ni ki-i-me-e[.......ù]

78) [i-n]a-an-n[a.....] d[á-an-níš-ma a]ḫ[-ta-du-ma]

---

79) ^{I}⌜Ma⌝-⌜né⌝-e [LÚ.DUMU.KIN-šu š]a ⌜ŠEŠ⌝-[ia....]ki[-i-me-e] ⌜it⌝(?)-[t]al-⌜ka⌝ a[-na ia-ši]

80) a-š⌜a⌝-ar[..]

81) a-bi-[i]-šu [ša] ⌜ŠEŠ⌝-⌜ia⌝[.......................el-te-me]

82) a-ma-te-^{MEŠ}⌜šu⌝ [ša] ⌜ŠEŠ⌝-⌜ia⌝ ⌜ù⌝ aḫ-⌜ta⌝-[du] ⌜dá⌝[-an-níš-ma]

---

83) ù i-na-an-⌜na⌝ ⌜^{I}⌝⌜Ma⌝-⌜né⌝-⌜e⌝ [i-n]a ⌜MU⌝ ⌜an⌝[-ni-ti ú-maš-šar-šu-ma šum-ma LÚ.DUMU.MEŠ.KIN-ia ŠEŠ-ia la]

84) ik-ta-la-a-šu-nu [....................M]EŠ[.............]

85) ù aš-šum an-ni-ti [......................................]

86) ù ḫé-du-ú-tù dá-a[n]-⌜níš⌝-⌜ma⌝ [........................]

87) EZEN i-mar ^{d}IM ù ⌜^{d}⌝⌜A⌝-[ma]-⌜nu⌝[....................]

88) li-mèš-šèr-ma a-na-ku ù Š[EŠ-ia........................]

69–73) [The wor]ds that [I used to speak] t[o your father], and that [your fa]ther [used to speak to m]e, no one [knows. Teye, your mother, knows.] Keli[a and Mane don't k]now, and no one else knows [them] but [my brother's] mother [knows] it [al]l: how your father [would speak] with me and did not for]get his] lov[e for my father]. Likewise, I would speak with your father (and) [my] lo[ve for your father I would not forget.]

(74–78) [And n]ow, my brother has said, "As to my father, you [continually expressed love, so] likewise, t[o m]e, ex[press love continua]lly." And, my brother will see me, a[s to my brother, I will c[ontinually e]xpr[ess love and] ⸢I⸣ [sa]id, "My brother, m[ay he a]s[k]his mother [...my brother will se]e me, just as [...and n]ow [...] gr[eatly have I] re[joiced]."

(79–82) Mane [the envoy o]f [my] br[other], ju[st as] he came to [me] fr[om...] the father [of] my brother [...I heard] the words of my brother and I rejoiced gr[eatly].

(83–85) And now, as for Mane, [i]n th[is] year [will I let him go if my brother does not]hold back [my envoys...] and because of this [...]
and great rejoicing [...] he will see a festival day. May Teshub and Amo[n....] permit and I and you [....]

89) *a-nu-um-ma* ^{I}⸢*Pi*⸣-⸢*ri-is*-⸢*sí*⸣ ⸢*ù*⸣ [^{I}*Tu-lu-ub-ri it-ti* LÚ.DUMU.MEŠ.KIN-*šu* *ša* ŠEŠ-*ia*]

90) *a-na* ŠEŠ-*ia a-na* ⸢*kál*⸣-*le*-⸢*e*⸣-*e*[*m-ma al-ta-pár-šu ù a-na du-ul-lu-ḫi aq-ta-bá-a-šu-nu*]

91) *ù* ŠEŠ-*ia* ⸢*lu*⸣-⸢*ú*⸣ ⸢*la*⸣-⸢*a*⸣ [*ik-ta-la-šu-nu ḫa-mut-ta li-mèš-šèr-šu-nu-ma ṭe*$_4$*-e-ma*]

92) *li-te-er*-[*ru*]-*ú*-⸢*ni*⸣ ⸢*ša*⸣ ⸢ŠEŠ⸣[-*na šul-ma-an-šu lu-uš*-]*me-e-ma* [*lu-ú*]-⸢*uḫ*⸣-[*du*]

---

93) *ù* ⸢*ša*⸣-*a* ⸢ŠEŠ⸣-⸢*ia*⸣ [LÚ.DUMU.MEŠ.KIN-*šu it-t*]*i* ^{I}*Pi-ri-is-sí* ⸢*i*⸣-⸢*na*⸣ ÉRIN-*i*[*a*]

94) *a-na* [*du-lu-ḫi a-na ia-ši li-i*]*l-li-ku*$_8$*-ni a-na* ⸢*ša*⸣-⸢*a*⸣-[*šu*]-⸢*nu*⸣ *a-ta*-[*mar*]

95) *a*-⸢*dì*⸣ ⸢*ša*⸣-*a* [...............................] *ul-li-i is-sà-aḫ-ḫa-r*[*u*]

96) *ù a*-⸢*ka*⸣-*an-na* [^{I}*Ma-né-e* LÚ.DUMU.KIN-*šu ša* ŠE]Š-*ia ú*-⸢*maš*⸣-*šar-šu ù at-tù-ia*

97) LÚ.⸢DUMU⸣.⸢MEŠ⸣.⸢KIN⸣-[*ia* ŠEŠ-*ia li-mèš-šèr-šu-nu-ma ù* ^{I}] *Ma-né-e a-ša-ap-pár a-na ḫé-du-ú-ti*

98) ⸢*a*⸣-⸢*na*⸣ ⸢*ša*⸣(?) *er*[-*ṣé-ti*] *a-ḫi-i-a*

---

99) ⸢*ù*⸣ ⸢*un*⸣-*d*[*u i-ka-aš-ša-du* LÚ].DUMU.MEŠ.KIN-*šu ša a-ḫi-i-a*

100) ⸢*it*⸣-[*t*]*i* [^{I}*Pi-ri-is-sí ù* ^{I}*Tu-lu-ub-ri a-n*]*a i-sí-i-ni ra-bi-i a-na gi*$_5$*-im-ri*

101) *a-na*-[*ku e-ep-pu-us-sú-nu-ti ù i-na-an-n*]*a lu-ú ik-šu-du ù šum-ma a-ka-an*-⸢*na*⸣

102) *a*-[*na ia-ši i-ka-a*]*š*-⸢*ša*⸣-⸢*du*$_4$⸣[*ù m*]*i-i-na-a ep-pu-us-sú-nu-ti*

103) [*ù li-it*-]*ta-l*[*a-ku*$_8$*-ú*] ⸢*lik*⸣[....*a-na*] *i-sí-ni*

---

104) ⸢*ù*⸣ Š[EŠ]-⸢*ia*⸣ KÙ.GI *ma-a*-⸢*dá*⸣ ⸢*li*⸣-*še-e-bi*-⸢*la*⸣ [*a-na*] ⸢*i*⸣-⸢*si*⸣-*ni gi*$_5$*-im*-⸢*ri*⸣

105) *ù* ⸢*it*⸣-*ti* ⸢*ma*⸣-⸢*a*⸣-*dá-a*-⸢*ti*⸣ ⸢*ú*⸣-⸢*nu*⸣-*ú-ti* ŠEŠ-*i*[*a lu-ú-ka-ab-bá-ta-ni*]

106) [*i-na* KUR] ⸢*ša*⸣ ⸢ŠEŠ⸣-⸢*ia*⸣ ⸢KÙ.GI⸣ [*k*]*i*-⸢*i*⸣ *e-pé-ri ma*-⸢*a*⸣-[*dá-at*] ⸢ŠEŠ⸣-⸢*ia*⸣ *li*-⸢*ib*⸣-⸢*bi*⸣

107) [*lu-ú la-a ú-šá*]*m*-⸢*ra*⸣-*aṣ* K[Ù.GI *ma*-]*a-dá* ⸢*li*⸣-*še-e-bi-l*[*a ki*-]*me-e a*-‹*na*› ŠEŠ-*ia*

108) [*ù it-ti*] *ma*-⸢*a*⸣-*dá*-⸢*a*⸣-*ti* [*ú-nu-ú-t*]*i ú-ka*-⸢*ab*⸣-⸢*bá*⸣-⸢*ta*⸣-⸢*ni*⸣ [ŠEŠ]-*ia* ⸢UGU⸣ *a-bi*-⸢*i*⸣-*šu*

109) [.......] [........]-⸢*ta*⸣ *li*-⸢*i*⸣-⸢*it*⸣-*ter*-⸢*an*⸣-⸢*ni*⸣

(89–92) Now Pirissi and [Tulubri with the envoys of my brother, have I sent] to my brother with haste [I have commanded them to hurry] and [may] my brother not [detain them; with all haste may he release them; a message] may he return. [May I] hear [of the welfare] of my brother and may I [rejoice].

(93–98) And [may the envoys] of my brother come with [haste to me wi]th Pirissi by m[y]troop. For them have I been [looking] until [...] they will return. And thus, [Mane, the envoy of] my [brother] will I release and as for my envoys, [may my brother release them and] Mane will I dispatch with rejoicing to the l[and of] my brother.

(99–103) And whe[n] the envoy of my brother [arrives] with [Pirissi and Tulubri, it is t]o a great festival of completeness that I will [make for them. So no]w may they arrive. And if thus they [reach me,] then what shall I do for them? [So may they c]om[e....to] the feast.

(104–109) So may my brother send much gold for the feast of completion so [with]very many goods [may] my brother [honor me. In the land] of my brother, gold is plentiful [li]ke dirt. [May] my brother [not make] my heart grieve. May he send [as mu]ch g[old] as my brother has. [And with] much [good]s my [brother] will honor me more than his father. [...] may he exceed for me.

110) [*a-nu-um-ma a-na šul-ma-ni-k*]*a* [1] ⸢TÚG⸣.GÚ *Ḫur-ri* 1 TÚG. [G]Ú ⸢URU⸣ 1 TÚG.⸢BAR⸣.DUL 1 ^{NA_4}[........]
111) [..........1 ŠU] ⸢*ša*⸣ ⸢*qa*⸣-⸢*ti*⸣ ⸢IGI⸣.MEŠ-*tu*$_4$ NÍR KUR 5(?) *i-na* ŠID-*ti* KÙ.GI GAR

---

112) [1 ^{NA_4}*ta-pa-tu*$_4$ *š*]*a* ⸢Ì⸣.⸢DÙG⸣.⸢GA⸣ *ma*-[*lu-ú*] 1-*nu*-⸢*tu*$_4$⸣ ⸢NA$_4$⸣.MEŠ KÙ.GI [GAR] ⸢*a*⸣-⸢*na*⸣ ^{MUNUS}*Te-i-e* AMA-[*ka*]

---

113) [1 ^{NA_4}*ta-pa-tu*$_4$ *ša* Ì.DÙG.GA] [*ma*]-⸢*lu*⸣-*u* 1-*nu*-[*tu*$_4$] NA$_4$.MEŠ ⸢KÙ.GI⸣ [GAR *a-na*] ⸢^{MUNUS}⸣*Ta-a-du*$_4$-*ḫé-e-ba*!
114) [DUMU.MÍ-*ia*] D[AM-*k*]*a ul*-⸢*te*⸣-*bíl*

Lft. ed. (Hieratic colophon)
ḥꜣt sp 2 *ꜣbd 1 prt*, [*sw* 9](?) *ỉw.tw m nwt rsyt m pꜣ bḫn n ḥ*ʿ*-m-ꜣḫwt mỉtt n š*ʿ*t na-ha-*[*r*]*i-n*[*a*] *ỉn.n wpwty Pi-ri-si wp*[*wty Trbr*]

(110–111) [Now as yo]ur [greeting gift, one] Ḫurrian style shirt, one city style shirt, one robe, one [precious] stone, [one pair] for the hand with "eye"-stones of genuine *ḫulalu* stone, five(?) in number, set in gold.

---

(112) [One scent container] fil[led] with "sweet [oi]l"; one set of stones set in gold; for Teye, [your]mother.

(113–114) [One scent container, fil]led [with "sweet oil"]; one s[e]t of stones [mounted] in gold; for Tadu-Ḫeba, [my daughter,] [yo]ur w[ife], have I sent.

Left edge Hieratic colophon:

[Ye]ar 2, first month of winter, day [9?], when one (pharaoh) was in the southern city, in the castle of Ḫʿ-m-ꜣḫt ("Rejoicing in the Horizon"); copy of the Naharina letter that the envoy Pirissi and the envoy [Tulubri] brought.

EA 28

TRANSCRIPTION

Obv. 01) *a-na* ^{I}*Nap-ḫur-i-re-ia šàr* KUR *Mi-iṣ-ri-*[*i*]

02) ŠEŠ-*ia ḫa-ta-ni-ia ša i-ra-ʾ*[*a-am-an-ni*]

03) *ù ša a-ra-mu-uš qí-bi-*⸢*ma*⸣

04) *um-ma* ^{I}*Tù-uš-rat-ta šàr* KUR *Mi-it-ta-a-an*!-*n*[*i*]

05) *e-mu-ú-ka ša i-ra-ʾa-mu-ú-ka* ŠEŠ-*ka-ma*

06) *a-na ia-ši šul-mu a-na ka-a-ša lu-ú šul-mu*

07) ⸢*a*⸣-⸢*na*⸣ É.MEŠ-*ka a-na* ^{MUNUS}*Te-i-e* AMA-*ka* [N]IN KUR *Mi-iṣ-ri-i*

08) *a-na* ^{MUNUS}*Ta-a-du*$_{4}$-*Ḫe-e-bá* DUMU(!).MUNUS-*ia* DAM-*ka*

09) *a-na re-ḫu-ú-ti* DAM.MEŠ-*ka a-na* DUMU.MEŠ-*ka a-na* LÚ.GAL.MEŠ-*ka*

10) *a-na* GIŠ.GIGIR.MEŠ-*ka a-na* ANŠE.KUR.RA.MEŠ-*ka a-na* ÉRIN.MEŠ-*ka*

11) *a-na* KUR-*ka ù a-na mim-mu-ka dan-níš dan-níš lu-ú* ⸢*šul*⸣-*mu*

12) ^{I}*Pi-ri-is-sí ù* ^{I}*Tul-ub-ri* LÚ.DUMU.MEŠ.KIN-*ri-*[*i*]*a*

13) *a-na* ŠEŠ-*ia a-na kál-le-e al-ta-pár-šu-nu ù a-*[*na*]

14) *du-ul-lu-ḫi dan-níš dan-niš aq-ta-bá-a-šu-nu-t*[*i*]

15) *ù šu-nu mi-i-ṣú-ú-ta-am-ma al-ta-pár-šu-nu*

16) *ù a-ma-ta an-ni-ta i-na ma-aḫ-ri-i-im-*⸢*ma*⸣

17) *a-na* ŠEŠ-*ia aq-ta-bi* ^{I}*Ma-né-e* LÚ.DUMU.KIN-*šu ša* [ŠEŠ-*ia*]

18) *a-kál-la-a-šu-ú-mì a-dú* LÚ.DUMU.KIN-*ri-ia-mì* ŠEŠ[-*ia*]

19) *ú-maš-ša-ru-ú-ma-a-mì i-il-la-ku*$_{8}$-*ú-ni*[*m*]

20) *ù i-na-an-na* ŠEŠ-*ia a-na ga*$_{14}$-*am-ra-ti-im-ma*

21) *la ú-maš-šar-šu-nu-ti a-na a-la-ki ù ik-ta-la-a-šu-*⸢*nu*⸣-*ti*

22) *dan-níš dan-niš* LÚ.DUMU.MEŠ.KIN-*ri mi-nu-ú*

23) *ú-ul iṣ-ṣú-ru-ú ip-par-ra-šu-ú-ma i-il-la-ku*$_{8}$

24) ⸢ŠEŠ⸣-*ia aš-šum* LÚ.DUMU.MEŠ.KIN-*ri am-mi-ni* ŠÀ-*šu*

25) [*i-i*]*k-kál-šu am-mi-ni ul-lu-ú a-na pa-ni ul-l*[*i-i*]

26) [*né-šu*]-*ru la in-né-eš-šèr ù ul-lu-*[*ú*]

27) [*ša ul*]-*li-i šul-ma-an-sú la-a i-še-em-m*[*e*]

28) [*ù*]*ḫa-da-nu dan-niš dan-niš u*$_{4}$-*mi-šà*[*m-ma*]

EA 28

TRANSLATION

(1–11) Speak to Napḫurireya king of the land of Egypt, my brother, my son-in-law, who lo[ves me] and whom I love. Thus Tushratta, king of the land of Mittanni, your father-in-law, who loves you, your brother:
For me all is well; for you may all be well, for your household, for Teye, your mother, the [mis]tress of Egypt, for Tadu-Ḫeba, my daughter, your wife, for the rest of your wives, for your children, for your senior officials, for your chariotry, for your horses, for your troops, for your land, for your property, may it be very, very well.

(12–19) Pirissi and Tulubri, [m]y emissaries, have I sent posthaste to my brother and I told them to really make haste. And as for them, I sent them with a very small escort. And earlier I had sent this message to my brother: "Mane, the emissary of [my brother] am I detaining until [my] brother releases my emissary and he comes to me."

(20–28) And now my brother has absolutely refused to release them to go and he has put them under very strict detention! What are emissaries? They are not birds that they should fly away and come! My brother, why does he eat his heart out because of emissaries? Why can't each [sure]ly go directly to the other and each hear the greeting [of the ot]her [so that] we can rejoice exceedingly every day?

29) [ŠEŠ-]⌜*i*⌝*a* LÚ.⌜DUMU⌝ KIN-*ia ḫa*-⌜*mu*⌝-*ta li*-⌜*me*⌝-*eš-šèr*[-*šu-ma*]
30) [*ša* ŠE]Š-*ia šul-ma-an-sú* ⌜*lu*⌝-⌜*uš*⌝-⌜*me*⌝[-*ma*]
31) [...]⌜LÚ⌝.⌜DUMU⌝.⌜MEŠ⌝.⌜KIN⌝-⌜*ri*⌝ ⌜*ša*⌝ [Š]E[Š-*ia*]
32) [............] traces only [.................]
Rev. 33) [............] traces only [.................]
34) [..]
35) [..]
36) [............*g*]*i-ú-ti š*[*a*.....................]

37) [[I]*Ma-né-e l*]*u-meš-šèr-šu ù* LÚ.DUMU.MEŠ K[IN-*ri-ia*]
38) [*a-na* ŠEŠ-*i*]*a ki-i pá-ni-i-ti lu-uš-pur* ⌜*ù*⌝[*ki-ma ša*]
39) [*ul-li*-]⌜*i*⌝?-*ta pá-ni-i-ta ša* ŠEŠ-ia *lu-u*[*š-me-ma*]
40) ⌜*a*⌝-⌜*na*⌝ ŠEŠ-*ia il*-⌜*li*⌝-⌜*ik*⌝ *ù* ŠEŠ-*ia* ⌜*ša*⌝ *lìb-bi-i*[*a*]
41) *gáb-ba-šu-nu-ma* ⌜*li*⌝-*pu-uš ù lìb-bi lu la-a ú*[-*še-em-ri-iṣ*]

42) *ù a-ma-te*^{MEŠ} ⌜*gáb*⌝?-*ba-ši-na-ma ša it-ti a-bi-k*[*a*]
43) *ad-bu-bu* ^{MUNUS}*Te-i-e* AMA-*ka i-de-e-ši-na-a-ti*
44) *ma-am-ma ša-nu-ú-um-ma ú-ul i-de-e-ši-na-a-ti*
45) *ù a-šar* ^{MUNUS}*Te-i-e* AMA-*ka ti*-⌜*ša*⌝-*ʾa-al-šu-nu-ti-ma*
46) *li-id-bu-bá-ak-ku ki-i-me-e a-bu-ka it-ti-ia*
47) *ir-ta-na-ʾa-am ù a-ka-an-na* ŠEŠ-*ia i-na-an-na*
48) *it-ti-ia li-ir-ta-ʾa-am ù ša ša-ni-i ša ma-am-ma*
49) ŠEŠ-*ia lu la-a i-še-em-me*

(29–36) May my [brother] release my emissary promptly [and] let me hear the greeting [of] my [bro]ther.....

(37–41) [As for Mane,] I want to release him and I want to send [my] emissaries [to m]y [brother] as in the past and [as in tim]es past I w[ant to hear] (the greeting) of my brother. He has gone to my brother so, may my brother do all the things that I want and may he not cause me dis[tress].

(42–49) And as for all the words which I spoke to yo[ur] father, Teye, your mother, knows them. No one else knows them. Ask those things of Teye, your mother so she can tell you. Just as your father always showed love to me, so now may my brother always show love to me. And may my brother not listen to anything from anyone else.

EA 29

TRANSCRIPTION

Obv.

01) [*a-na* ^{I}*Nap-ḫu-u-re-ia šàr* KUR *Mi-iṣ-ri-i* ŠEŠ-*i*]*a ḫa-ta-ni-ia ša a*[*-ra-a*]*m-mu-ú-uš ù ša i-ra*[*-ʾa-ma-an-ni*]

02) [*qí-bí-ma um-ma* ^{I}*Tù-uš*]-⸢*rat*⸣-[*ta*] *š*[*àr* KUR *Mi-it-ta-an-n*]*i* ⸢ŠEŠ⸣-⸢*ka*⸣-*ma e-mi-ka* [*š*]*a i-ra-ʾa-*⸢*mu*⸣*-ka a-na ia-ši šul-m*[*u a-na ka-a-ša*]

03) [*lu-ú šul-mu a-na*] ⸢^{MUNUS}⸣⸢*Te*⸣-*i*-⸢*e*⸣ *l*[*u-ú š*]*ul-*[*mu a-n*]*a* ^{MUNUS}*Ta-*⸢*a*⸣*-du-ḫé-*⸢*e*⸣*-b*[*á*] DUMU.MUNUS-[*i*]*a* DAM-*ka lu-ú* [*šul-mu*]

04) [*a-na* DAM.MEŠ-*ka re-e-*]*ḫé-ti lu-ú* ⸢*šul*⸣*-mu a-na* DUMU.MEŠ-*ka a-na* LÚ.MEŠ ⸢GAL⸣.MEŠ-*ka* GIŠ.GIGIR.MEŠ-*ka a-na* AN[ŠE].KUR.[RA.MEŠ-*ka*]

05) [*a-na* ÉRIN.MEŠ-*ka a-na* KU]R-*ka ù a-na mim-mu-ka dan-níš dan-níš dan-níš lu-u* [*šul-mu*]

---

06) [*iš-tu re-eš šà*]*r-ru-ti-ia a-d*[*i*] ⸢^{I}⸣*Ni-im-mu-u-re-ia-ma a-bu-ka* [*a*]*-na ia-ši il-ta-nap-pa-ra el sú-lu-u*[*m*]*-me-*[*e*]

07) [*il-ta-nap-pár*] *mi-im-ma ša-n*[*u-ú*] *ša il-ta-nap-pa-ru ia-nu mi-nu-um-me-e a-ma-a-tu*$_4$ *gáb-bá-ši-n*[*a*]*-a*[*-ma*]

08) [*ša* ^{I}*Ni-im-mu-u-re-i*]*a a-bi-ka š*[*a a-na*] *ia-ši il-ta-nap-‹pa›-ru ù* ⸢^{MUNUS}⸣⸢*Te*⸣-[*i*]-*e* DAM-*at* ^{I}*Ni-im-mu-u-re-*⸢*ia*⸣ ⸢*ra*⸣*-bi-tu*$_4$

09) [*ra-im-tu*$_4$] AMA-*ka gáb-bá-*⸢*šu*⸣*-*⸢*nu*⸣ *i-de*$_4$*-šu-nu a-na* ^{MUNUS}*Te-i-e-ma* A[MA]-⸢*ka*⸣ *gáb-bá-šu-nu-ma ši-*⸢*ta*⸣*-*⸢*a*⸣*-*⸢*al*⸣*-šu-nu-ti*

10) [*ša il-ta-nap-pa-ru*] *a-bu-ú-ka a-ma-a-te*^{MEŠ} *ša it-ti-ia id-dá-na-am-bu-bu*

EA 29

TRANSLATION

(1–5) [Speak to Napḫureya, the king of the land of Egypt, m]y [brother], my son-in-law, whom I [lo]ve and who lo[ves me; the message of Tush]rat[ta,] the kin[g of the land of Mittan]i, your brother, your father-in-law, [wh]o loves you. It is we[ll]with me. [May it be well with you. With] Teye ma[y it all be w]el[l. Wi]th Tadu-Ḫeba, [m]y daughter, your wife, may [it be well. With the re]st [of your wives] may it be well. With your sons, with your senior officials, your chariotry, with [your] horse[s], [with your troops, with] your [lan]d, and with your possessions, may it all be very, very [well.]

(6–10) [From the beginning of my ki]ngship, while Nimmureya, your father, continually wrote to me, [he continually wrote] about peace. There was no oth[er] subject about which he continually used to write. Whatever were all the words [of Nimmurey]a, your father, that he continually wrote [to] me, Teye, the senior wife of Nimmureya, your [beloved] mother, knows all of them. It is to Teye, your mo[th]er, that you should make inquiry concerning all of them, [the things which] your father [used to continually write], the words that he was continually speaking with me.

11) [ra-ʾa-mu-ti ša it-ti ŠEŠ-]ia 10-šu dan-níš-⸢ma⸣ ša ⸢it⸣-ti ^{I}Ni-im-mu-u-r[e]-ia a-bi-i-ka ša ni-ir-⸢ta⸣-⸢na⸣-⸢ʾa⸣-a-m[u]

12) [ù mi-nu-um-me-e ša] ⸢^{I}⸣Ni-im-mu-u-re-ia a-bu-ka it-ti-ia id-⸢dá⸣-[na]b-bu-bu šu-ú ia-ši lìb-bi i-⸢na⸣ ⸢mi⸣-⸢ni⸣-⸢im⸣-m[a]

13) [a-ma-ti ú-ul ul-te]-em-ri-iṣ ù mi-⸢nu⸣-um-me-e a-ma-tu$_4$ ša ⸢a⸣-qáb-bu-ú-ma ù am-mi-tu$_4$ ⸢i⸣-⸢na⸣ u$_4$-mi ša-a-š[u]

14) [i-te-pu-uš ù a-na-ku] at-tù-šu ŠÀ-šu i-na mi-ni-im-ma a-ma-ti ú-ul ul-te-em-ri-iṣ ù mi-nu-um-me[-e]

15) [a-ma-tu$_4$ ša i-qáb-ba-]am-ma ù ⸢am⸣-⸢mi⸣-tu$_4$ i-na u$_4$-mi ša-a-šu-ma e-te-pu-u[š]

---

16) e-nu[-ma ^{I}(Mn-ḫprw-rʿ)] a-bu-šu ša ⸢^{I}⸣[Ni-i]m-mu-u-re-ia a-na ^{I}A[r]-⸢ta⸣-ta-a-ma a-bá a-bi-⸢ia⸣ ⸢iš⸣-⸢pu⸣-⸢ru⸣ ù ⸢DUMU⸣.MUNUS -[sú]

17) ša ⸢a⸣[-bá a-bi-ia a-ḫa-at] ⸢a⸣-bi-ia i-te-[ri]-is-sí 5-šu 6-šu i[l]-ta-pár ù ú-ul id-⸢di⸣-na-aš-⸢ši⸣ im-ma-ti-⸢i⸣-me-⸢e⸣

18) 7-šu [a-na a-bá a-bi-ia il-t]a-pár ù i-na e-mu-ú-qí-im-ma it-[ta]-din-ši un-du ^{I}Ni-im-⸢mu⸣-⸢u⸣-⸢re⸣-⸢i⸣a a-bu-ka a-na ^{I}Šut-t[ar-na]

19) a-bi-⸢i⸣[a ki-i iš-pu-ru] ù DUMU.MUNUS-⸢sú⸣ ša a-bi-ia a-ḫa-a-⸢ti⸣at-tù-ia ki-i ⸢i⸣-ri-šu 3-šu ù 4-šu ⸢il⸣-⸢ta⸣-[pár]

20) ù [ù-ul id-di-]⸢na⸣-⸢aš⸣-ši im-ma-ti-⸢i⸣-⸢me⸣-e 5-šu ù 6-šu ⸢il⸣-⸢ta⸣-pár ù i-na e-⸢mu⸣-ú-⸢qí⸣-im-ma i[t-ta-din-ši]

21) ⸢un⸣[-du] ^{I}Ni-⸢im⸣-mu-u-re-ia [a-bu-ka] a-na ia-ši ki-i ⸢iš⸣-[pu]-ru ù DUMU.MUNUS-ti ki-i [i-]⸢ri⸣-šu ⸢ù⸣ ⸢ú⸣[-ul-la]

22) [la -a] ⸢aq⸣-bi ⸢i⸣-⸢na⸣ ⸢ma⸣-aḫ-[ri-im-ma a-na LÚ.]DUMU. KIN-ri-šu aq-ta-bi ⸢um⸣-⸢ma⸣-a a-na-an-din-aš-ši-i-ma-a-ku DUMU.⸢KIN⸣-ka i-na ⸢ša⸣!-nu-ut-t[im]-m[a]

23) [ki-i] il-li-ka ù ⸢Í⸣.⸢MEŠ⸣ [a-na qa-]aq-qa-dì-ša it-tab-⸢ku⸣ ù [te]-⸢er⸣-ḫa-ti-i-ša ki-i il-qú-ú ù at-ta-di[n-ši]

24) [ù te-]er-ḫa-tu$_4$ ša [^{I}]Ni-⸢im⸣-⸢mu⸣-⸢re⸣[-ia a-bi-i-]ka ša [ú-še-b]i-lu ZAG.MEŠ la i-šu AN ù KI ⸢uš⸣-⸢te⸣-el-li la-a [aq-bi]

25) [ul-la] a-na-an-din-aš-⸢ši⸣ ù ^{I}Ḫa-a-⸢ma⸣-⸢aš⸣-š[i LÚ.DUMU. KIN-r]i ša ⸢ŠEŠ⸣-[i]a a-na kál-l[e-e a-n]a ^{I}Ni-im-⸢mu⸣-⸢re⸣-[i]a al-tap-⸢ra⸣-⸢aš⸣-[šu]

26) [ù i-n]a 3 ITI.ME[Š a-n]a ḫa-mut-ti dan-níš-ma [il-ta-pár-aš-šu] ù 4 K[UŠ.MEŠ K]Ù.[GI] ⸢ma⸣-⸢lu⸣-⸢ú⸣ ⸢ul⸣[-te-bíl]

27) [muš-š]èr šu-kut-tù [ša] ⸢a⸣-⸢bi⸣-[ka] ⸢a⸣-ḫe-én-na-a TA.ÀM ša ú-š[e-bi-lu]

(11–14) [My love for] my [brother] is tenfold more than what we always had with Nimmureya, your father. [And whatever] Nimmureya, your father, would continually discuss with me, he never caused me distress in any [matter]. And whatever word that I would say then on that very same day, [he did]that. [And as for me,] in no matter whatever did I cause him distress, and whatever [word that he would s]ay to me, then on that very same day, I would do that.

(16–20) When [Min-kheperu-Reʿ], the father of [Ni]mmureya, wrote to Artatama, my grandfather, and requested the daughter of [my] gr[andfather,] he wrote five times or six times but he did not give her. Only when [he wro]te [to my grandfather] the seventh time, then under such pressure did he give her. When Nimmureya, your father, [wrote] to Shut[arna], m[y] father, and requested the daughter of my father, my own sister, three times or four times he wro[te] but [he did not give] her. Only when he wrote the fifth time or the sixth time, then under such pressure d[id he give her.

(21–27) Wh[en] Nimmureya, [your father,] wrote to me and requested my daughter, then I did [not] say ["No."] The [very] first ti[me], I said [to] his envoy, "I will certainly give her." As for your envoy, on the second time [that] he came, they poured oil [on]her [he]ad and they brought her bride price, then I gav[e her]. [And the br]ide price of Nimmure[ya], your [father], which he [brou]ght was without limit; it surpassed heaven and earth. I did not [say,] "I will [no]t give her." I sent with all due speed Ḫaamašš[i], m[y] brother's [envoy, t]o Nimmureya. [And i]n three month[s wi]th great haste [he sen]t [him back] and he se[nt] four b[ags] filled with [go]ld, [not inclu]ding the jewelry [which your] father s[ent] separately.

28) [*im*]-*ma*-⸢*ti*⸣-⸢*i*⸣-⸢*me*⸣ [DUMU.]MUNUS -*ti at-ta*-⸢*din*⸣-*ši ù ki*-⸢*i*⸣ [*ub*]-*la-aš-ši ù* ^{I}*Ni*-⸢*im*⸣-*mu-u-re-ia a-bu-ka ki-i i-ta*-⸢*mar*⸣-⸢*ši*⸣ *i*[*ḫ-ta-du*]

29) [*mi-im-ma ú-u*]*l iḫ-du* [*ù*] *iḫ*-⸢*ta*⸣-*du* [*dan-níš*] *dan-níš-ma ù* ⸢*iq*⸣-*ta-bi* ŠEŠ-*ia um-ma-a i-na ku*$_8$-*ù-ul* ŠÀ-*š*[*u*]

30) [^{I}*Tù-uš-rat-ta* ŠEŠ-*ia i*]*t-ta-din-ši ù i-te-pu-u*[*š*] ⸢*u*$_4$⸣-*mu am-mi-tu*$_4$ *bá*-[*n*]*i-i-tu*$_4$ *it-ti* KUR-*šu-ma i-na muḫ-ḫi* DUMU.KIN-⸢*ia*⸣

31) [*ù a-bu-ka ki-*]*me-e* ⸢*a*⸣-*mi-lu-tu*$_4$ *me-ḫé-er-š*[*u*] *ki-i i-mu-ru ù ù-kab-bá-as-sú ù ka-an-na* ^{I}*Ni-im-mu-u-re*-⸢*ia*⸣

32) [LÚ.DUMU.MEŠ KIN-*ia ki-i*] *me-eḫ*-⸢*ru*⸣-*ti ù ki-i* ⸢*it*⸣-⸢*bá*⸣-⸢*ru*⸣-*ti uk-te-te*-⸢*eb*⸣-*bi-it ù i-na* ŠÀ É.MEŠ-*ti ša a-na* ^{MUNUS}*Ta-du-Ḫé-bá*

33) [*aš-bu* LÚ.DUMU.MEŠ KI]N-*ia gáb-bá-šu-nu-ma ša aš-bu* [*us*]-*sé-eḫ-ḫé-er ù i-na lìb-bi* LÚ.DUMU.MEŠ.KIN-*ia ša i-ru-bu*

34) [1-*en ša mi-im-ma la-a id-di-*]*nu ia-nu ša* ^{I}*Ké-li-ia* [*li*]-⸢*ša*⸣-⸢*a*⸣-⸢*an*⸣-⸢*šu*⸣ [*ša*] KÙ.GI *ša* 1 *li-im* SU *i-na* KI.LAL.BI *it-ta-din*

35) [x KUŠ.MEŠ KÙ.GI *ma-*]*lu-ú* ^{I}*Ni-im-mu-u-re-ia a-na* [^{MUNUS}*Ta-a-du-ḫe*]-*e-bá it-ta-din ù* ^{MUNUS}*Ta-a-du-ḫe-e-bá*

36) [*a-na muḫ-ḫi* LÚ.DUMU.MEŠ KIN-]*ia it-ta-tá*-⸢*ad*⸣-[*din*] *ù* ⸢*a*⸣-*n*[*a muḫ-ḫi* LÚ.DUMU.MEŠ K]IN-*ia* ^{I}*Ni-im-mu-u-re-ia i-na* ⸢*ra*⸣-*ʾa-a-mi*

37) [*ù i-na ku*$_8$-*ub-bu-ut-ti*] *uk-te-te-eb-bi-i*[*s-*]*s*[*ú-n*]*u* [*ù* ^{I}*Ni-im-mu-*]*u-re-ia* ^{I}*Ni-i-u* LÚ.DUMU.KIN-*šu il-ta-pár-šu*

38) [*it-ti* ^{I}*Ké-li-ia* LÚ.DUMU.KIN] *ša at-tù-ia* ⸢*ù*⸣ ⸢*it*-⸣⸢*ta*⸣-[*din-šu-nu a-la-ka a-n*]*a kál-le-e i-na ma-aḫ-ri-ia* 7(?) ⸢KUŠ⸣.MEŠ *ša* KÙ.GI.MEŠ

39) [*ki-i ú-bi-lu it-ti* 1 *li-*]⸢*ša*⸣-⸢*a*⸣-⸢*nu*⸣ ⸢*ša*⸣ KÙ.[GI] ⸢*ša*⸣ [1 *li-im* SU *i-na* KI.]LAL.BI *ša* ^{I}*Ké-li-ia ù* ⸢*a*⸣-⸢*ka*⸣-*an-na*

40) [^{I}*Ni-im-mu-u-re-ia ki-ma* AB.]⸢BA⸣.A.MEŠ-[*šu*] *i*[*t-ti-ia i-na ra*]-*a-ʾa-mi ú-te-te-et-ti-ir* ⸢*la*⸣-⸢*am*⸣ LÚ.DUMU.MEŠ KIN-⸢*i*⸣*a*

41) [*it-ta-aṣ-ṣú it-ta-la-ku a-n*]*a muš*-⸢*šu*⸣-[*r*]*i*-⸢*šu*⸣-*n*[*u*] ⸢*ú*⸣-[*ul iq-ta-*]⸢*bá*⸣-⸢*a*⸣ *ul-la-a ú-še-bi-la* ⸢*a*⸣-⸢*na*⸣ ⸢*kál*⸣-*le-e*

42) [*i-na ma-aḫ-ri-ia*] *ù* ⸢*ṭe*$_4$⸣-⸢*e*⸣-*ma il*-⸢*ták*⸣-*na-aš*-[*šu-nu*] ⸢*ki*⸣-⸢*me*⸣-[*e la-a*] ⸢*ta*⸣-*ak-ka-al-‹la› i-na kál-le-e i-na ša-pa-ri-šu*

43) [ALAM.MEŠ *ú-u*]*l ú-še-e-bíl-an-ni-ma* ⸢*ša*⸣ ⸢*mi*⸣-*i*[*m-ma*] ⸢*mi*⸣-[*nu-um-me-e š*]*a ú*-⸢*še*⸣-*bi-lu pa-ṭá la i-šu ù a-ka-an-na*

44) [^{I}*Ni-im-mu-u-*]*re-ia a-bu-ú-ka i-na* ⸢*mi*⸣-⸢*im*⸣[-*m*]*a a-ma*[*-ti a-di* 1]-*en pa-ṭi a-na šu-um-ru-ṣi ú-ul um-te-eš-šèr*

(28–30) [At that]very time when I gave my [daugh]ter and [I]sent her, and Nimmureya, your father, saw her, he re[joiced. Was there anything] he did [no]t rejoice about? He rejoiced ve[ry], very much! And my brother said, "With all h[is] heart, [Tushratta, my brother, has g]iven her," and he made that day a celebration for his land, in honor of my envoy.

(31–34) [And your father, just] as one views his peers, so he honored him and thus within the palace for Tadu-Ḫeba, my [envoys dwelled]. All of them who were there, he sent back and among my envoys that had entered in (to Egypt), there was not [one to whom he did not giv]e. He gave an ingot of gold to Keliya that was one thousand shekels in weight.

(35–39) Nimmureya gave [*X* bags fu]ll [of gold] to [Tadu-Ḫe]ba and Tadu-Ḫeba handed over [to] my [ambassad]ors. And to[wards] my [ambassado]rs Nimmureya always showed them honor in love [and in respect]. [And Nimm]ureya sent Niyu, his envoy, [with Keliya,] my own [envoy,] and he let [them go in h]aste to me. [He sent] seven bags of gold [with the one in]got of go[ld] of [one thousand sh]ekels [in wei]ght of Keliya. And thus

(40–42) [Nimmureya, like his fa]thers, always exceeded [in l]ove f[or me.] Before my envoys [would go forth and depart,] he did n[ot s]ay "No," [to] releasing them; he sent them with haste [to me]. And he gave [them] a command, "[Don't] be delay‹ed›!"

(42–44) In sending him posthaste, he did [no]t send [the statues;] of the pro[perty,] what[ever th]at he did send, it had no limit. And thus, [Nimmu]reya, your father, did not permit distress to be caused in an[y] matt[er, not even to the slight]est extent.

45) [*ù a-ma-te*^{MEŠ}]⌜*ša*⌝ *a-qáb-bu-ú gáb-bá-*⌜*šu*⌝*-*[*nu-m*]*a ma-am-*[*ma ša-na-*]⌜*am*⌝*-ma ši-i-bu-ú-ta ú-ul a-qáb-bi* ^{MUNUS}*Te-i-e-ma*

46) [AMA-*ka*] ⌜*ši*⌝*-i-it ša* [*a-q*]*áb-bu-ú ù* ^{MUNUS}*Te-*⌜*i*⌝*-*⌜*e*⌝[*-ma* AMA-]*ka ši-ta-a-al-ši šum-ma i-na a-*⌜*ma*⌝*-ti ša a-qáb-bu-ú*

47) [*a-di* 1]*-en* ⌜*a*⌝*-ma-tu*$_4$ *la* [*k*]*i-i-na-ti i-*⌜*bá*⌝*-aš-ši* [*šum-ma a-ma-*]*tu*$_4$ *ša la* ^{I}*Ni-im-mu-u-re-ia a-bi-i-ka šum-ma*

48) [^{I}*Ni-im-mu*]*u-*⌜*re*⌝*-ia a-bi-i-*⌜*ka*⌝ *it-ti-*⌜*i*⌝*a a-ḫa-*⌜*miš*⌝ [*ra-a-ma ú-ul*] ⌜*ú*⌝*-né-ep-pí-iš šum-ma* ^{I}*Ni-im-*⌜*mu*⌝*-u-re-ia a-bi-i-ka*

49) [*ú-u*]*l iq-*⌜*bi*⌝ *im-ma-ti-i-me-*⌜*e*⌝ KÙ.GI.⌜MEŠ⌝ *ša* [KUR *Mi-iṣ-*]⌜*ri*⌝*-*⌜*i*⌝ *i-na* KUR *Ḫa-ni-gal-bat ú-*⌜*še*⌝*-*⌜*em*⌝*-ṣi ù ša-ar-ru-um-ma*

50) [KÙ.GI.]MEŠ *ú-ul ú-še-eb-*⌜*bal*⌝ *e-te-*⌜*ri*⌜*-iš* ⌜2⌝ [ALAM.MEŠ *ša* KÙ.GI.]MEŠ *up-‹pu›-qú-ú-tu*$_4$ *muš-šu-*⌜*ru*⌝*-tu*$_4$ ⌜*a*⌝*-*⌜*šar*⌝ ^{I}*Ni-im-mu-u-re-ia*

51) [*a-bi-i-*]*ka ù iq-ta-*⌜*bi*⌝ ^{I}⌜*Ni*⌝*-*⌜*im*⌝*-mu-*⌜*u*⌝*-*⌜*re*⌝*-*⌜*i*⌝*a* ⌜*a*⌝*-b*[*u-ka*] ⌜*mi*⌝*-nu-ú* ALAM.MEŠ *ša* KÙ.GI.MEŠ ⌜*ša*⌝ *la mi-im-ma-ma*

52) [*ša* Š]EŠ-*ia i-ri-šu muš-*⌜*šèr*⌝ *ša* KÙ[.GI-*m*]*a ù* ⌜*ša*⌝ [$^{\text{NA}_4}$ZA.GÌ]N KUR *e-*⌜*ep*⌝*-pu-uš-ma ú-še-e-bél-ak-*⌜*ku*⌝

53) [*ù*] ⌜*a*⌝*-ka-an-na* ^{I}⌜*Ni*⌝*-im-mu-u-re-ia* ⌜*a*⌝*-*⌜*bu*⌝*-*⌜*ka*⌝ *i-na a-*[*m*]*a-ti a-i-im-ma a-ma-ti a-na la a-ma-ti la ut-te-e-*⌜*er*⌝

54) [*ù l*]*ìb-bi i-na a-ma-ti a-*⌜*i*⌝*-im-ma ú-ul ú-še-em-ri-iš*

---

55) [*ù* ŠEŠ-]⌜*ia*⌝ ⌜^{I}⌝⌜*Ni*⌝*-*⌜*im*⌝*-mu-u-*⌜*re*⌝*-ia a-na ši-i-im-ti-i-šu ki-i il-li-ku iq-ta-bu-uš ù* ⌜*ša*⌝ *iq-bu-ú*

56) [*el-te-me ù*]⌜*la*⌝ [*ma-ma-an*] *i-*⌜*na*⌝ *ru-uq-qí ul-te-eb-ši-il ù a-na-ku i-na u*$_4$*-mi ša-a-šu ab-ta-ki*

57) [*ù i-na qa-bal mu-ši at-t*]*a-ša-ab* ⌜NINDA⌝.MEŠ *ù* A.MEŠ *i-*⌜*na*⌝ ⌜*u*$_4$⌝*-mi ša-a-šu ú-ul el-*[*te-qé*]*-*⌜*e*⌝ *ù am-ta-ra-aṣ*

58) [*um-ma-a lu-ú mi-ta-ku a*]*-na-ku-ma* ⌜*ù*⌝ *lu-ú mi-i-it* [10,000] *i-na* KUR *at-tù-ia ù i-*⌜*na*⌝ [KUR ŠE]Š-⌜*i*⌝*a* 60 x SIG$_7$!(GAŠAN).MEŠ-*ma*

59) [*ù* ŠEŠ-*ia ša a-ra-am-mu-ú-u*]*š ù* ⌜*ša*⌝ *i-ra-ʾa-ma-an-ni* ⌜*lu*⌝*-ú bá-li-iṭ it-ti* AN *ù* K[I *ša*] *ni-ra-ʾa-a-mu*

60) [*ra-a-ʾa-mu-ú-tu*$_4$] *am-mi-*⌜*tu*$_4$⌝ *i-na lìb-bi-ni* ⌜*ù*⌝ *lu-ú nu-ú-ur-ri-ik*

(45–50) [As for] all [the things] that I say, I call no [oth]er witnesses. Teye, [your mother,] it is she that I call, so inquire of Teye, your [mother]: if among the words that I speak, there is [even on]e word not true; [if there is one wo]rd that is not of Nimmureya, your father; if [Nimm]ureya, your father, [did not] generate [love] mutually with me; if Nimmureya, your father, [did n]ot say: "When I have caused the gold of [the land of Eg]ypt to be sufficient in the land of Ḫanigalbat, then, for sure, I will not send [gol]d."

(50–54) I requested two [statues of] so‹l›id chased [gold] from Nimmureya, your [father], and Nimmureya, [your] fa[ther], said, "What are statues of gold without anything, [that] my [bro]ther requested? Leave it! Of go[ld] and of real [lapis lazu]li, will I make and I will send to you." [So] thus Nimmureya, your father, in no matter whatever, ever repudiated a matter as not important. [And] in no matter whatever did he cause me distress.

(55–60) [And] when my [brother], Nimmureya went to his fate, they reported it and [I heard] what they said; [and] n[o one] cooked in a pot; and I myself cried in that day. [And in the midst of the night, I] sat; I did not take bread or water in that day and I grieved, [saying "If only it were] I [that had died], or if only [sixty thousand] had died in my land or sixty thousand in [the land of] my [broth]er, [while my brother whom I lov]e and who loves me, could be alive, as heaven and earth. That [love which] we love is in our hearts and would we could make it last."

61) [*ù un-du iq-ta-bu-(uš) um-ma-a* ^{I}*Na*]*p*-[*ḫu-u-ri-i*]*a-mì* DUMU-*šu* [*r*]*a-bu-ú ša* ^{I}*Ni-im-mu-u-re-ia ša* ^{MUNUS}*Te-i-e* DAM-*šu*

62) [*ra-bi-ti i-na ma-aš-ka-ni-šu šàr*]*-ru-ta i-ip-pu-uš-*⸢*ši*⸣ *ù aq-ta-bi um-ma-a la mi-i-it* ^{I}*Ni-im-mu-u-re-ia*

63) [ŠEŠ-*ia* ^{I}*Nap-ḫur-re-*]*ia* DUM[U-*š*]*u ra-bu-*⸢*ú*⸣ ⸢*ša*⸣ ^{MUNUS}⸢*Te*⸣*-i-e* DAM-*šu ra-bi-ti i-na ma-aš-ka-ni-šu-ma*

64) [*šàr-ru-ta i-ip-pu-uš*] *la ú-*⸢*še*⸣*-*⸢*en*⸣*-nu-ú a-m*[*a-a-tu*$_4$ *a-i*]*-im-ma-ma iš-tu ma-aš-ka-ni-ši-na ki-i ša pa-na-a-nu*

---

65) [*ù i-na-an-na i-na lìb-bi-i*]*a a-qáb-*⸢*bi*⸣ *um-ma-a* ^{I}*N*[*a*]*p-ḫu-u-ri-ia-ma* ŠEŠ-*ia i-na lìb-bi-ni ša ni-ra-ʾa-a-mu*

66) [*am-mi-tu*$_4$ *i-na-an-na el*] ^{I}*Ni-im-mu-u-re-ia a-bi-i-šu* ⸢10⸣-⸢*šu*⸣ *i-*[*m*]*a-ʾi-id aš-šum* ^{MUNUS}*Te-i-e* AMA-*šu ša* DAM-*at*

67) [^{I}*Ni-im-mu-u-re-ia ra-bi-t*]*i ra-*⸢*im*⸣*-tu*$_4$ *bal-ṭá-at* ⸢*ù*⸣ *i-ta-ar-ra-aṣ a-ma-a-tu*$_4$ *a-na pa-ni* ^{I}*Nap-ḫu-u-re-ia*

68) [DUMU-*šu ša* ^{I}*Ni-im-mu*]*-u-re-ia mu-ti-šu* ⸢*ma*⸣*-a-dì-iš dan-níš dan-níš ša ni-ir-ta-na-ʾa-a-mu*

---

69) [*ù un-du* ŠEŠ-*ia-ma*] *i-na ma-a-aḫ-ri-im-ma a-na* [*ia-ši*] *ki-i iš-*⸢*pu*⸣*-ru un-du* ^{I}*Ké-*⸢*li*⸣*-ia ú-me-eš-še-ru-ma*

70) [*ù un-du* ŠEŠ-*ia-m*]*a* ⸢^{I}⸣⸢*Ma*⸣*-*⸢*né*⸣*-*⸢*e*⸣ ⸢*ki*⸣*-*⸢*i*⸣ *iš-pu-*[*ru*] *ù* ALAM.MEŠ *ša* GIŠ.MEŠ ŠEŠ-*ia ú-še-bi-la ù* KÙ.GI.MEŠ

71) [*ša* ^{I}*Ni-im-mu-u-re-*]⸢*ia*⸣*-ma* ⸢*iq*⸣*-*⸢*bu*⸣*-*[*šu*]*-*⸢*nu*⸣ ⸢*ki*⸣*-*[*i a-ta-ma*]*r-šu-n*[*u*] *ki-i la* KÙ.GI.MEŠ *ù ki-i la up*[*-pu-qú*]

72) [.......... KÙ.GI.M]EŠ-*šu ù am*[*-ta-ra-aṣ*] *ap-pu-na dan-níš-ma iš-tu pa-na-a-nu-u*[*m-m*]*a*

73) [..............*u-nu-te*^{ME}]^{Š} ⸢*ap*⸣*-pu-na* ^{I}*Ni-im-mu-*[*u-re-i*]*a* ⸢ŠEŠ⸣*-ia ša a-na ia-ši id-di-na* ŠEŠ-⸢*ia* ⸣

74) [*ú-ṣe-eḫ-ḫé-er-m*]*a ù* ⸢*ar*⸣*-ta-*⸢*ʾu*⸣*-ub*[*-ma*] *ki-*⸢*me*⸣*-*⸢*e*⸣*-ma ma-*⸢*a*⸣*-dì-iš* ⸢*dan*⸣*-níš a-na-ak-ké-e-er*

75) [.............] *ù* ⸢*a*⸣*-*⸢*na*⸣*-ku um-ma-a* [*a-qáb-bi-i-*]*ma-a* [^{I}]⸢*Ni*⸣*-*⸢*im*⸣*-*⸢*mu*⸣*-*⸢*u*⸣*-*⸢*re*⸣*-ia* ⸢ŠEŠ⸣*-*⸢*ia*⸣ *ta-a-mu-ur-*⸢*ti*⸣

76) [*a-na ia-ši ki-i ú-še-*]*bi-lu* ⸢*ša*⸣ ^{I}*Nap-ḫu-u-re-ia* ⸢ŠEŠ⸣*-*[*i*]a *ša-n*[*u-ti-m*]*a* ⸢*e*⸣*-li-*⸢*šu*⸣ *ú-ul ú-re-ed-dì*

77) [*ú-nu- te*^{MEŠ}] *a-bi-ka*! *ša ú-š*[*e*]*-bi-lu ù ki-*⸢*i*⸣ [*ú-nu-te*^{ME}]^{Š}-⸢*šu*⸣ *ip-*⸢*ṭù*⸣*-*⸢*ru*⸣ ⸢ŠÀ⸣*-*⸢*ia*⸣ ⸢*ul*⸣*-*⸢*te*⸣*-*⸢*em*⸣*-ri-iṣ*

78) [................]*-ma ù a-na pa-ni* ^{I}*Ma-né-e* [ŠÀ-*šu ú-ul*] ⸢*ul*⸣*-te-em-ri-iṣ*

79) [*mi*]*-im-*⸢*ma*⸣*-*⸢*a*⸣*-ma*

(61–64) [But when they announced, saying "Na]p[ḫurey]a, the senior son of Nimmureya (and) of Teye, his [senior] wife, is exercising [kin]gship [in his place,"] then I said, saying, "Nimmureya [my brother,] is not dead! [Napḫure]ya, [hi]s senior so[n], of Teye, his senior wife, in his place [is exercising kingship]. Noth[ing what]ever will change from the situation as it was before."

(65–68) [And now, in m]y [heart] I am saying, "N[ap]ḫureya is my brother. It is in our hearts that we love. [This, now, more than] Nimmureya, his father, will he increase ten fold because Teye, his mother, who is the beloved [senior] wife [of Nimmureya] is alive and she will confirm matters in the presence of Napḫureya, [the son of Nimmur]eya, her husband, that we have always loved (one another) very, very much."

(69–79) [But when my brother] wrote to [me for] the first time, when he released Keliya, [and when my brother] sen[t Ma]ne, and my brother sent statues of wood, but the golden ones [of which Nimmure]ya had said that I would see them, were not gold and were not so[lid,...]his [gol]d and I [was], moreover, much more [pained] than before. [...the object]s, moreover, which Nimm[urey]a, my brother, had given to me, my brother [has decreased] and I was angry and I became exceedingly antagonistic [...] and I thus [was saying,] "Nimmureya, my brother, [se]nt a present [to me]". As for that ot[he]r (gift) of Napḫureya, [m]y brother, he did not add anything to [the goods of] your father, which he sent, and when [they] un[packed] his [good]s, I caused my heart distress. [...] in the presence of Mane, I [did not] cause [his heart] distress at all.

80) [*ù un-du Ma-né-e ki-i ik-ta-ša-du it-ti*] ⸢*ú*⸣-⸢*nu*⸣-⸢*te*⸣$^{⸢MEŠ⸣}$ *ša* ŠEŠ-*ia id*-⸢*dì*⸣-⸢*na*⸣ *ú-še-e-el-li ù u*[*n-du*]

81) [*a-ta-mar ú-nu-te*^{MEŠ} *ša* ŠEŠ-*ia ú-še-bi-lu aq-ta-bi a-n*]*a* LÚ.MEŠ GAL.MEŠ-*ia* ⸢*um*⸣-*ma-a* ⸢*it*⸣-⸢*ti*⸣ ŠEŠ-*ia i-na k*[*u*$_{8}$-*u*]*l*

82) [*lìb-bi-ia ar-ta-ta-ʾa-a-am ù ki-me-e ša*] ⸢AB⸣.BA.A.MEŠ-*ia ap-pu*-⸢*na*⸣-⸢*ma*⸣ *it-ti* AB.BA.A.MEŠ-*šu*

83) [*ša* ŠEŠ-*ia ir-ta-ta-ʾa-a-mu ù*] *qí-i-ša-a-ti*^{MEŠ} *ša* ŠEŠ-*ia* ⸢*ul*⸣-⸢*te*⸣-*e-bi-la-am-ma*

84) [..................*lu-ú*] *ni-iḫ-du dan*-⸢*níš*⸣ *ù u*$_{4}$-*ma* ⸢*bá*⸣-⸢*na*⸣-*a lu-ú ni-i-pu-uš*

85) [........................]*it-ta-aṣ-ṣí-ma* [*ù i*]-*na qà-bal mu-ši at-ta-ša-am-ma*

86) [.......................]⸢*ša*⸣ ⸢*it*⸣-⸢*ta*⸣-⸢*aṣ*⸣-⸢*ṣí*⸣-[*m*]*a ù* ^{I}*Ma-né-e ú-nu-te* ^{MEŠ}

87) [.......................]-*ma ù iṭ-ṭe*$_{4}$-*ḫé ú-nu-te*^{MEŠ} *a-na pa-ni-i*[*a*]

88) [.......................]⸢*ú*⸣-*uḫ*-⸢*ḫa*⸣-⸢*ra*⸣-*a*[*m-m*]*a ù* ⸢*aḫ*⸣-⸢*ta*⸣-⸢*du*⸣ *i-na u*$_{4}$-*m*[*i*]

89) [*ša-a-šu*................]⸢*it*⸣-⸢*ti*⸣ ⸢NUN⸣.MEŠ [*ú*]-*bá-r*[*u*]-*ti* ^{I}⸢*Ma*⸣-⸢*né*⸣-⸢*e*⸣-*ma* LÚ.DUMU.⸢KIN⸣-[*šu*]

90) [*ša* ŠEŠ-*ia*................] ⸢*iḫ*⸣-⸢*ta*⸣-*du ù li-iq-bá*-[*ak-ku*]

---

91) [^{I}*Pi-ri-is-sí ù* ^{I}*Tul-up*]-*ri a*-⸢*na*⸣ *du-ul*-[*lu-ḫi*] ⸢*a*⸣-⸢*na*⸣ ⸢*kál*⸣-*le-e al-ta*-⸢*pár*⸣-*š*[*u-nu*]

92) [.........*al-t*]*a*-⸢*pár*⸣ ⸢*ù*!⸣ [...*ú*]-⸢*še*⸣-⸢*bíl*⸣-[*aš-šu*] *ù aš-pu*[-*ra*]

93) [..........] 3 *me-e* x[..............................]

Rev. 94) [..]

95) [..]

96) [..]

97) [..]

98) [..]

99) [....................................*um*]-⸢*te*⸣-⸢*eš*⸣-⸢*šèr*⸣

[.....................................]

100) [..................ŠE]Š-⸢*i*⸣[*a*.............]⸢*dan*⸣-⸢*niš*⸣

101) [....................]*a it-ti* [^{I}*Ni-im-mu-u-re*]-⸢*ia*⸣ ŠEŠ-⸢*i*⸣[*a*]

(80–85) [And when Mane arrived with] the goods that my brother had given, he brought (them) up and wh[en I saw the goods that my brother had sent, I spoke t]o my senior officials, saying, "With my brother in a[ll my heart have I continually shown love and just as] my fathers, moreover, with the fathers [of my brother, always showed love, so]gifts which my brother has sent [...May] we rejoice greatly, and may we make a celebration [...] will go forth [and i]n the midst of the night I sat down

(86–90) [...]which would come forth and Mane [...] the goods."
[...] and he brought the goods into my presence [...] he will delay. And I rejoiced in [that] day [...]with the foreign nobles, Mane, the envoy of [my brother...] rejoiced so let him tell [you].

(91–93) [Pirissi and Tulup]ri, with urgency and with all speed have I sent. [...] have I sent and [...I] have sent [to him], and I sent [...] three hundred [....]

ev. 94) [...]

95) [..]

96) [..]

97) [..]

98) [..]

99) [..he] sen[t]

100) [..................m]y bro[ther ....]greatly

101) [.....................]with [Nimmure]ya m[y] brother

102) [...................Ì]R-*du-ti ša t*[*a*...................]
103) [...................]-⸢*ú*⸣ *ù* x-*ar*-⸢*ka*⸣[...................]
104) [................*š*]*a* ⸢*i*⸣-⸢*na*⸣ ⸢*te*⸣-⸢*er*⸣-⸢*ṣi*⸣ ^{I}*Ni-im-mu-u*-⸢*re*⸣[*- ia a-bi-ka*]
105) [...................]*a* DUMU-*ia a-na* 10-*šu lu-ù* [........]
106) [............*ša a-bu*]-*ka i-te-né-ep-pu-šu ù an*-⸢*nu*⸣-*t*[u_4.....]
107) [...................]⸢*a*⸣-*du-šu-ú* ^{MUNUS}*Te-i-e* AMA-*ka a-na* ⸢*a*⸣-*b*[*i-ka*] ⸢ŠEŠ⸣-⸢*ia*⸣

---

108) [*ù am-ma-a*-tu_4 *a-ma-a*-tu_4 *ša ta-*]*aq-bá-a ù a-ni-*[*na*] *i-na-an-na a-ma-a*-tu_4 *ša* AMA-*ka ša a-na* ^{I}*Ké-li-*[*ia i*]*q*-[*ta*]-*bu*
109) [............ALAM.MEŠ *š*]*a* KÙ.GI.MEŠ ⸢*up*⸣[*pu-qú-*]tu_4 *muš-šu-ru*-tu_4 *e-te-ri-iš ù me*-⸢*e*⸣-*re-še*[*-ti-ia*]
110) [*ša a-na* ^{I}*Ni-im-mu-u-re-ia a-bi-ka e-te-ri-šu la a-d*]*a-ag-gal* ⸢*ù*⸣ [LÚ.]DUMU.MEŠ KIN-*ia* ŠEŠ-*ia la ú-maš-šar-šu-nu*-⸢*ma*⸣ *ù la* [*il-li-ku-ma*]
111) [*ù šul-ma-an-šu ša* ŠEŠ-*ia*] *ú-ul ut-te-er-r*[*a-aš-*]*šu ù* $ṭe_4$*-e-ma ul iš-ku-na-an-ni ù* ⸢ALAM⸣.MEŠ *š*[*a* KÙ.GI.MEŠ]
112) [*up-pu-qú*-tu_4 *muš-šu-ru*-tu_4 *ša a-na* ^{I}*Ni-im-mu-u-re-ia e-te-ri-š*]*u i-na-an-na* [*a-na*] ⸢*ka*⸣-*a-ša e-te-ri-iš-ma ul ta-ad-di-na* ⸢*ù*⸣ *me-re-*[*še-ti-ia*]
113) [*ša a-na ka-a-ša e-ri-šu ú-ul a-da-ag-gal ù* $ṭe_4$*-ma u*]*l ta-aš-ku*-⸢*na*⸣- [*ni ù*] ⸢LÚ⸣.⸢DUMU⸣.⸢MEŠ⸣ ⸢KIN⸣-*ia ul*-tu_4 4 MU.MEŠ-*ti* ⸢*ta*⸣[*-ak-ta-la-šu-nu*]
114) [................*ù* LÚ.DUMU.MEŠ KIN-*i*]*a ša i*-⸢*ta*⸣!-*la-ka* [*šul-ma-ni-ia it-tab-lu a-na* ŠEŠ-*i*]*a a-na ka*[*-a-ša id-di-nu ù*]
115) [LÚ.DUMU.MEŠ KIN-*šu ša* ŠEŠ-*i*]*a ki-i* ⸢*il*⸣-[*la*-ku_8-*ú*-ni_7 *šul-ma-ni-šu ša* ŠEŠ-*ia ub-ba-lu a-na ia-ši* LÚ.DUMU.MEŠ KIN-*šu ša* ŠEŠ-*ia*]
116) [*a-na a-la-ki ḫa-mut-t*]*a a-na-da-a*[*n-šu-nu ù la a-*]⸢*ka*⸣-*al*[*-la -šu-nu*....] *ša* [............]
117) [..........] ⸢^{MUNUS}⸣⸢*Te*⸣-⸢*i*⸣-*e* AMA-⸢*ka*⸣[..........]x *-ma* ⸢*šum*⸣-⸢*ma*⸣ ⸢*am*⸣-⸢*mi*⸣-⸢tu_4⸣ [......]x-*ma* [.......]
118) [.............] *ka-la-*[*ma*] *ḫa-mut-ta la* [*mu*]*š-šu*-⸢*ri*⸣-[*šu-nu*]

102) [...................ser]vants whom y[ou(?)[...........]

103) [...................]and afterwards(?)[...............]

104) [..................wh]ich was in the time of Nimmre[ya your father]
105) [...................]my son, ten fold may [.........]

106) [.........which]your[father] always did and thi[s......]

107) [...................]...him, Teye your mother concerning [your] fat[her,] my brother

---

(108–110) [and those are the words that you] spoke and right now the words of your mother that she [s]p[ok]e to Keli[ya.....statues o]f solid chased gold I requested and [my] reques[ts which I requested of Nimmureya, I do not] see and as for my envoys, my brother does not release them and [they] have not [come.

(111–114) And the greeting of my brother, he does not return and he has not made a decision in my behalf and the statues o[f solid chased gold which I requested from Nimmureya,] now I have requested from you and you have not given and [my] requ[ests which I have requested of you, I do not see and] you do not make a [decision] concerning me, and] since four years ago, my envoys have you [detained..and m]y [envoys who went forth [brought my greeting gift to m]y [brother;] to y[ou did they give (it).

(115–118) And the envoys of m]y [brother,]when they come[to me, will bring the greeting gift of my brother to me and the envoys of my brother,] I will permit [to travel with all has]te [and I will not] deta[in them...] Teye, your mother [...]if that [...]detain, swiftly not to [re]lease [them].

---

119) [*ù un-du il-li-ku* LÚ.DUMU.MEŠ KIN-*ia*]⸢*iḫ*⸣*-mu-ṭù a-an-nu-ú-*[*tu*$_4$ *ki-*]*i ša pa-na-a-nu iš-tu sí-*⸢*ma*⸣*-an* ⸢*a*⸣*-*[*bi-i-ka*]

120) [.............]⸢*ša*⸣ *a-na ma-am-ma* x[...]⸢*šu*⸣ ⸢*ù*⸣ *ša ni-ir-ta-na-*⸢*ʾa*⸣[*-a-m*]*u* ⸢*el*⸣ [*ša pa-na-a-nu*]

121) [........*i-na ter-*]*ṣi* AB.BA.A.MEŠ-*ni*[.........]*iš-tu lìb-bi-*⸢*i*⸣[*a* (?)........] ⸢1⸣-⸢*en*⸣ ⸢*ul*⸣

122) [...........*i-n*]*a lìb-bi-šu-nu ir-t*[*a-na-ʾa-a-mu ma-d*]*i-iš dan-níš ù* ŠEŠ-[*ia*] *it-ma-am-ma lu la* ⸢*i*⸣*-še-*⸢*em*⸣*-*⸢*me*⸣

123) [.........*ki-i ša pa-n*]*a-*⸢*a*⸣*-nu ú-bá-an pa-ti*[*iš-tu*] ⸢*sí*⸣*-*⸢*ma*⸣*-*⸢*an*⸣ *a-bi-i-ka* ⸢*lu*⸣*-ú la ú-*⸢*še*⸣*-*[...]

124) [.....^{MUNUS}*Te-*]⸢*i*⸣*-e* ⸢AMA⸣*-ka l*[*u-ú te-še-*]⸢*em*⸣*-me šum-*[*ma*] ^{MUNUS}⸢*Te*⸣*-*⸢*i*⸣*-e* ⸢*i*⸣*-n*[*a*]*-an-din-ka it-ti-ia* [......]

125) [.......ŠEŠ-*ia*] ⸢*i*⸣*-*⸢*qáb*⸣*-bi l*[*a ta-a*]*r-ta-na-ʾa-*⸢*am*⸣ *ù la ta-*[*ar*]*-*⸢*ta*⸣*-*⸢*na*⸣*-ʾa-am ù ki-i pí-*[*i*]

126) [......*ḫa-mut-*]*ta lu-*⸢*ú*⸣[*l*]*i-*⸢*it*⸣*-*⸢*te*⸣*-er ù* [*a-qáb-bi a-na-*]⸢*ku*⸣ *a-ma-*⸢*tu*$_4$⸣ *ša a-na muḫ-*⸢*ḫi*⸣

127) [ŠEŠ-*ia lu-û e-pu-šu ù am-mu*]*-tu*$_4$ *at-ta* [*i-n*]*a-an-na a-na muḫ-ḫi* [ŠEŠ-*ka lu-ú t*]*e-pu-uš ù mi-nu-um-me-e*

128) [*a-ma-tu*$_4$ *ša* ^{I}*Ni-im-mu-u-re-ia a-bi-ka š*]*a i-na muḫ-ḫi*[*-ia*] *ša in-né-ep-*⸢*pu*⸣*-šu* [*ù am-*]*m*[*u-t*]*u*$_4$ *i-na-an-na at-ta* 10-*šu*

129) [*a-na muḫ-ḫi* ŠEŠ-*ka lu-ú te-pu-uš*] ⸢*dan*⸣*-*⸢*níš*⸣ [*ul-lu-*]*ú ša ul-li-i a-ma-ti-šu lu-ú la u-na-*⸢*ak*⸣*-kàr*

130) [*mi-nu-um-me-e a-ma-tu*$_4$ *ša a-qáb-bu am-mu-*]⸢*tu*$_4$⸣ ŠEŠ-*ia* ⸢*lu*⸣*-*⸢*ú*⸣ ⸢*i*⸣*-*[*pu-uš*] *ù mi-nu-um-me-e a-ma-tu*$_4$ *ša* ŠEŠ-*ia*

131) [*i-qáb-bu lu-ú e-pu-uš*] *ul-lu-*⸢*ú*⸣ *ša ul-l*[*i-*]⸢*i*⸣ *i-*⸢*na*⸣ *mi-ni-im-ma a-ma-ti* ŠÀ-*šu*

132) [*lu-ú la ú-šàm-ra-aṣ*..........*lu-ú*] *ni-ir-ta-na-ʾa-am ù lu-ú ni-*⸢*ḫa*⸣*-ad-du* ⸢*a*⸣*-di ni-i-nu-ú-ma*

133) [*ù el* KUR.KUR.MEŠ-*ti gáb-ba-ši-na-ma* KUR.KUR.MEŠ-*tu*$_4$*-n*]*i la-le-e-ši-na ú-la-al-la ù i-qáb-bu-ú um-ma-a ki-i*

134) [*ir-ta-na-ʾa-mu* LUGAL.MEŠ KUR *Ḫa-ni-gal-bat ù* KUR *Mi-iṣ-r*]*i-i šum-ma ka-an-na el* KUR.KUR.MEŠ-*ti gáb-ba-ši-na-ma ma-*⸢*dì*⸣*-iš*

135) [*dan-níš* KUR.KUR.MEŠ-*tu*$_4$*-ni la-le-e-ši-na ú-la-al-la ù i-*]*qáb-bu-ú* KUR.KUR.MEŠ-*tu*$_4$ *gáb-ba-ši-na-ma i-na muḫ-ḫi-ni*

(119–129) [And when my envoys went,] they hastened. Thes[e were a]s in the period of [your] fa[ther…]which to whom *x*[…] it and which we always showed lo[ve] more than [previously…in the er]a of our fathers […]from m[y] heart […]Not a single one […i]n their hearts they sh[owed love ve]ry much and [my] brother swore an oath; may he verily not listen […as for]merly a narrow margin [from] the period of your father may he verily not…[…To Te]ye, your mother ve[rily you should] listen, i[f] Teye will give you, with me […My brother] is saying, "[You] are n[ot] showing love," but you are not showing love and according to the text [of the oath(?)…hasti]ly may he verily return and [I, myse]lf, [say,] a word that is for [my brother, verily will I carry it out and th]ese, you, now for [your brother, may y]ou carry out and whatever [word of Nimmureya, your father, th]at was for [me], which was always carried out, [then tho]se now, you ten times more [for your brother may you carry out] diligently. [On]e must not change the words of the other.

(130–134) [Whatever word that I may say, th]at may my brother verily ca[rry out] and whatever word that my brother [may say, I will verily carry out.] One [verily must not cause distress] to the other in any matter whatsoever[….May] we show love and may we rejoice as long as we live. [And more than all the other countries, o]ur [countries will] enrich their abundance and they will say thus, "How [the kings of the land of Ḫanigalbat and of the land of Egy]pt [show love for each other]." If it is thus, more than all the lands,

[our lands will flourish] very [much and] all the lands will speak of us.

136) [*ù a-nu-um-ma ap-pu-*]*na-ma* ⸢*lu*⸣-⸢*ú*⸣ [*a-na-ku*(?) ALAM.]MEŠ *ša* KÙ.GI.MEŠ ⸢*up*⸣-‹*pu*›-*qú-tu*$_4$ *muš-šu-ru-*⸢*tu*$_4$⸣ *iš-tu ma-ḫa-ar* ^{I}*Ni-*⸢*im*⸣-⸢*mu*⸣-*u-*⸢*re*⸣-*ia-ma*

137) [*a-bi-ka e-te-ri-iš ù* KÙ].GI.MEŠ *ma-a-at-ta* ⸢*ša*⸣ ⸢*ši*⸣-⸢*ip*⸣-*r*[*a la ep-*]⸢*šu*⸣ *dan-níš dan-níš e-*⸢*te*⸣-*ri-iš* ⸢*i*⸣-*na-an-na* ŠEŠ-*ia* AL[AM].⸢MEŠ⸣

138) [*ša* KÙ.GI.MEŠ *up-pu-qú-tu*$_4$] ⸢*muš-šu-ru-tu*$_4$ *li-id-*⸢*di*⸣-⸢*na*⸣ *ù* KÙ.GI.⸢MEŠ⸣ *ma-a-at-ta ša ši-ip-ra la* ⸢*ep*⸣-*šu dan-níš dan-níš* ⸢ŠEŠ⸣-⸢*ia*⸣

139) [*li-id-di-na* ALAM.ME]Š *ša* KÙ.GI.MEŠ ⸢*a*⸣-*bu-*⸢*ka*⸣-*ma a-na ia-ši i*[*d-di-n*]*a* ⸢*am*⸣-*mi-i-ni-im-ma i-na lìb-bi-*⸢*ka*⸣ *mar-ṣa ù* ⸢*la*⸣ *t*[*a-aš-al*] ⸢*šum*⸣-⸢*ma*⸣

140) [*a-na-ku a-šar a-bi-ka*] *ul e-te-ri-iš ù a-bu-ka ap-pu*[*-na-ma*] ⸢*a*⸣-⸢*na*⸣ ⸢*ia*⸣-⸢*ši*⸣ *ú-ul id-di-na ù* ⸢*i*⸣-⸢*na*⸣-⸢*an*⸣-⸢*na*⸣-⸢*ma*⸣ *a-šar* ŠEŠ-[*i*]⸢*a*⸣ ⸢*e*⸣-⸢*te*⸣-⸢*ri*⸣-⸢*iš*⸣

141) [*ù ki-na-a am-mu-tu*$_4$ *a-ma-a-t*]*u*$_4$ *ù la-*⸢*a*⸣ *ki-*⸢*na*⸣-*a ia-nu-um-ma-a ap-*[*pu-n*]*a a-šar a-bi-ka-ma* ALAM.MEŠ *ša* ⸢*e*⸣-*ri-šu it-ta-an-na* ⸢*ù*⸣ ⸢*i*⸣-⸢*na*⸣-⸢*an*⸣-⸢*na*⸣

142) [*a-šar* ŠEŠ-*ia ša-nu-ti-ma e-*]⸢*te*⸣-*ri-*⸢*iš*⸣ ⸢*ù*⸣ ⸢ŠEŠ⸣-⸢*i*⸣*a ša-nu-ti-m*[*a*] *la e-ep-pu-uš-ma-a la i-na-an-di-na-a lìb-bi-i ù-*⸢*šàm*⸣-⸢*ra*⸣-⸢*aṣ*⸣

143) [........]⸢*mu*⸣[.....]*ú ša a-ma-a-ti gáb-bi-im-*[*ma*] ⸢^{MUNUS}⸣*Te-i-*⸢*e*⸣-[*m*]*a* AMA-*ka ši-i-it ù* ^{MUNUS}*Te-i-e-ma* ⸢AMA⸣-⸢*ka*⸣ *ša-*⸢*a*⸣-*a*[*l*]-*ši*

144) [*šum-ma* ALAM.MEŠ *ša* KÙ].GI.MEŠ ⸢*ù*⸣ [KÙ.GI.M]EŠ *ma-a-at-ta a-šar a-bi-k*[*a ul e-te-ri-i*]*š ù a-bu-ka a-na* ⸢*ia*⸣-*ši ul id-di-na* ⸢*ù*⸣ ⸢ŠEŠ⸣-[*i*]⸢*a*⸣

145) [ALAM.MEŠ *ša* KÙ.GI.MEŠ] ⸢*up*⸣-⸢*pu*⸣-*qú-t*[*u*$_4$ *mu*]*š-šu-ru-tu*$_4$ *ù* KÙ.GI. MEŠ [*ma-at-ta* ŠEŠ]-⸢*i*⸣*a li-id-di-nam-ma ù* ŠEŠ-*ia lìb-bi lu la ú-šà*[*m*]-*r*[*a-aṣ*]

146) [*i-na* KUR ŠEŠ-*ia* KÙ.GI].MEŠ *ki-i* [*e-pé-*]*ri ma-a-dá-at ù* [*lìb-bi* ŠEŠ]-*ia lu-ú la ú-še-em-ri-iṣ šum-ma ka-ra-aš-ka*

147) [*a-na* AB.BA.A.MEŠ-*ia*] *la e-ep-pa-aš ù mi-na-a e-ep-pu-us-sú-nu*

(136–140) [And now more]over, verily [have I requested stat]ues of s‹o›lid chased gold from Nimmureya, [your father, and] I requested very, very much [go]ld which had [not been wo]rked. Now, may my brother, give statues [of solid] chased [gold] and [may] my brother [give] very, very much gold that has not been worked. It was your father who g[ave] to me [statu]es of gold. Why is it painful to your heart so that yo[u don't ask] whether [I] did not request [from your father] and your father mor[eover] did not give? And now I have requested from my brother.

(141–146) [And true are those wor]ds or not true? No? Moreover, the statues that I requested from your father, he gave. And now [from my brother it is others that I] have requested. So will my brother not make others and will he not give (and) cause me distress? [...]of all the words. Teye, she is your mother, so a[sk] your mother [if I did not reque]st [statues of go]ld and much [gol]d from your father, and (if) your father did not give to me. So, [m]y brother, may my [brother] give me [statues of] solid, chased [gold] and much gold. And may my brother not make my heart si[ck. In the land of my brother, go]ld is plentiful like d[ir]t. And verily I have never made my [brother's heart] sick. If I cannot make a mausoleum
[for my ancestors], what will I do for them?

148) [*ù aq-ta-bi um-ma-a*] ŠEŠ-[*ia*] ^{I}*Ké-li-ia-ma li-tú-*⸢*ur*⸣-⸢*ra*⸣-*aš-šu ša* ŠEŠ-[*ia*] ŠÀ-*šu-ú ú-šàm-ra-aṣ* ^{I}*Ké-li-ia ú-ta-ar-ra-aš-šu*

149) [*a-na* ŠEŠ-*ia a-*]*na-k*[*u*] ⸢*um*⸣-*ma-a* LÚ.DUMU.MEŠ KIN[-*šu ša*] ⸢ŠEŠ⸣-*ia a-na* ⸢*ḫa*⸣-⸢*mut*⸣-*ti* [*ú-*]*ta-a-ar-ra-ak-kum-ma-a-ku im-ma-ti-me-e* ŠEŠ-*ia-ma* DUMU.MEŠ KIN-*ia*

150) [*ú-ta-ḫi-is-sú-nu a-n*]*a-k*[*u a*]*n-nu-tu*$_4$ *an-ni-ka-a*[-*am*] ⸢*ú*⸣-*ta-ḫi-is-*⸢*sú*⸣-*nu u*[*m-ma*]*lu-ú a-na-ku-ma im-ma-ti-i-me-e* LÚ.DUMU.MEŠ KIN-*ia ú-maš-šar-ma*

151) [*il-li-ku*$_8$*-ni ù ki-i-me-*]⸢*e*⸣ *ṭe*$_4$*-e-ma i-ša-ak-*[*ka*]*-nu-ni ù* ^{I}*Ma*[*-né-*]⸢*e*⸣ *ú-maš-šar-šu-ma ù* ^{I}*Ké-li-ia a-na* ŠEŠ-[*ia*] *ki-i pa-ni-ti*

152) [*a-na-ku-ma ú-ta-a*]*r-*⸢*ra*⸣-[*aš-*]*šu im-ma-ti-me-e* ⸢ŠEŠ⸣-*ia* LÚ.DUMU.MEŠ KIN-*i*[*a k*]*i-i ma-*⸢*aš*⸣-⸢*ši*⸣-⸢*ti*⸣ *i-na-aḫ-ḫi-is-sú-nu ù a-na-ku ki-*⸢*i*⸣ ⸢*aḫ*⸣-⸢*sú*⸣-⸢*sú*⸣

153) [*e-ep-pu-uš i*]-⸢*na*⸣-⸢*an*⸣-⸢*na*⸣ *ap-pu-na a-ma-tu*$_4$ *ša* ⸢ŠEŠ⸣-*ia ša a-na k*[*a-ar-ṣ*]*í mi-*⸢*im*⸣*-ma i-bá-aš-ši aš-*⸢*šum*⸣ *mi-i-ni-i ša* ŠEŠ-*ia*

154) [AMA-*šu iq-ta-bi um-ma-a*] *eṭ-lu šu-ú ù a-na* ⸢GIŠ⸣.⸢GU⸣.ZA *a-bi-šu* ⸢DINGR⸣-⸢*lu*⸣-⸢*um*⸣-*ma* ⸢*it*⸣-⸢*ta*⸣-*ša-ab ù ša lìb-bi-šu* ŠEŠ-*ia* ⸢*lu*⸣ *i-pu-*⸢*uš*⸣

155) [*ù a-na-ku-ma*] *aq-ta-bi um-ma-a* ⸢ŠEŠ⸣-*ia* [LÚ].⸢DUMU⸣.MEŠ KIN-*ia ul ú-maš-šar-šu*[*-nu-*]*ti-ma-a-ku ù ma-a-dì-iš i-na-aḫ-ḫi-is-sú-nu-ti-i-ma-a-*[*ku-ma*]

156) [*ka-ar-ṣí-šu*] *ù* ŠEŠ-*ia lu-ú* ⸢*a*⸣!*-k*]*ál* ⸢*ak*⸣-⸢*kál*⸣-*ma-a-ku* ^{I}*Ma-sí-bá-a-ad-li* ⸢LÚ⸣.DUMU.KIN-*ia a-ḫa a-bi-šu ša* ^{I}*Ké-li-ia-ma a-n*[*a* ŠEŠ-*ia*]

157) [*al-ta-pár-šu*] *ù* ⸢*a*⸣-⸢*na*⸣⸢*ḫe*⸣-*d*[*u*]-*ti* ⸢*a*⸣-[*na* ŠEŠ-]*ia al-ta-pár-šu ù* ŠEŠ-*ia lu-ú la ut-ta-az-za-am ki-i-me-e* ^{I}*Ké-li-ia* ⸢*ul*⸣ *aš-pu*[*r-šu*]

158) [*ù a-na ḫe-du-t*]*i ú-*⸢*ul*⸣ *aš-*[*pu*]*r-šu ù* ⸢*ul*⸣-*lu-ú* LÚ.DUMU.KIN-*ia ša a-na* ŠEŠ-*ia aš-pu-ru* ŠEŠ-*šu-ma ša* ^{I}*Ké-li-ia* DUMU AMA-*šu-ma* [*šu-ut*]

159) [*ù a-na* ŠEŠ-*i*]*a a-na* ⸢*kál*⸣-*le-e aš-pur-šu ki-i* ŠEŠ-*ia la* ⸢*ú*⸣-⸢*mèš*⸣-*šèr-*[*š*]*u ḫa-mut-ta la i-tù-ur-ra ù* ŠEŠ-*ia a-*⸢*na*⸣ [*ia-ši*]

160) [*a-na a-ma-ti me-*]*e-re-še-ti-ia ša e-ri-šu ṭe*$_4$*-e-ma ú-ul iš-ku-na-an-ni ù aš-*⸢*šum*⸣ *an-ni-ti* ^{I}*Ké-li-ia* ⸢*ú*⸣*-ul aš-*[*pur-šu*]

161) [*ù* ŠEŠ-*ia*] *a-na ta-az-zi-i-im-ti ù a-*⸢*na*⸣ *mi-im-ma-*[*m*]*a lu-ú la ú-ta-a-*[*a*]*r*

(148–154) [And I said, “My] brother, may Keliya return to him. My brother should not get upset. Keliya will return to him.” [To my brother,] ⌜I⌝ (say): “The envoys of my brother [wil]l return to you speedily.” When my brother [holds on] to my envoys, ⌜I⌝ hold on to these here. I verily say: “When he releases my envoys and [they come to me and whe]n they give me a report, then I will release Ma[ne] and Keliya with him as formerly.” [It is I who will se]nd him back. When my brother delays them like a forgotten thing then [I will do] as I had planned. Now, moreover, it is the affair of my brother that is become something of a sc[and]al; why did my brother’s [mother say,] “He is a grown man, he has taken the throne of his deceased father,” and my brother verily does what he pleases.

(155–158) [And] I, [myself,] said: “My brother does not release my envoys and he detains them too long.” I ve[hemen]tly protest! [I sent] Masibadli, my envoy, the uncle of Keliya, and I sent him t[o] my [brother] joyfully, so my brother should not be angry because I did not send Keliya. Didn’t I send him [joyfull]y? And as for the other envoy that I sent to my brother, the brother of Keliya, the son of his mother [is he].

(159–161) [And] I sent him [to m]y [brother] with due haste. Since my brother has not released him; he does not return speedily. And my brother has not made a report to [me in the matter of] my [re]quests that I requested and because of this, I have not s[ent] Keliya. [And] may [my brother] not repeat the complaint or anything.

162) [*ù* ^{I}*Ma-sí-bá-a*]*d-li a-na* ŠEŠ-*ia ša aš-pu-ru a-ḫa a-bi-šu ša* ^{I}*Ké-*⸢*li*⸣*-ia-ma ù* ALAM.MEŠ *ša* KÙ.GI.MEŠ *up-pu-qú-tu*$_4$ ⸢*muš*⸣-⸢*šu*⸣-[*ru*]-⸢*tu*$_4$⸣

163) [ŠEŠ-*ia li-id-di-na*] *ù* KÙ.GI.MEŠ *ma-a-at-*⸢*ta*⸣ *ša ši-ip-ra la ep-šu ša* ⸢*ka*⸣-*r*[*a*]-*aš-ki ša a-na* ŠEŠ-*ia e-ri-šu* ŠEŠ-*ia li-id-*⸢*di*⸣-[*na-an-ni*]

164) [*ù* ŠEŠ-*ia líb-b*]*i* ⸢*lu*⸣ *l*[*a*] *ú-ša-am-ra-aṣ* ⸢*ù*⸣ *lu-ú* ⸢*la*⸣ *i-kál-la* ⸢*ù*⸣ *i-na* K[UR ŠE]Š-*ia* KÙ.GI.M[EŠ] *ki-i e-pé-ri ma-a-dá-*[*a*]*t*

165) [*ù a-na-ku lìb-b*]*i* [*š*]*a* ŠEŠ-*ia* [*lu-ú*] ⸢*la*⸣ ⸢*ú*⸣-[*ša-am-r*]*a-a*[*ṣ*]

166) [*ù* ŠEŠ-*ia*] ⸢*el*⸣ *a-bi-šu ra-ʾa-mu-ta* [*ù* Š]E[Š]-*u*[*t*]-*ta* 10-*šu li-te-et-te-er-an-*⸢*ni*⸣ *ù it-t*[*i*]-*ia ni-ir-t*[*a-na-ʾa-*]*am da*[*n-ní*]*š* ⸢*dan*⸣-*níš*-⸢*ma*⸣

167) [*ù* LÚ.]MEŠ DUMU.KIN-*ia* ŠEŠ-*ia* ⸢*ḫa*⸣-[*mut-t*]*a li-me-eš-šèr -šu-nu-ti-ma ù* ^{I}*Ma-né-e* ⸢*it*⸣-⸢*ti*⸣ ⸢LÚ⸣.[MEŠ] DUMU.KIN-*ia* ŠEŠ-*ia* [*l*]*i-iš-pur-šu-ma* ⸢*li*⸣-⸢*il*⸣[*-li-ku-ni-m*]*a*

168) [*ki-i*] ⸢*pu*⸣-*ú še-*⸢*ri*⸣*-ia i*[*q-ta-bu-ma*] ŠEŠ-*ia li-id-di-na ù* ^{I}*Ké-li-ia a-na* [ŠEŠ-]*ia* ⸢*lu*⸣-*uš-*⸢*pur*⸣-*ma ù ge-*[*er-ra ra*]-⸢*bá*⸣-*a a-na* [ŠE]Š-*ia*

169) [*lu-ú-še-bi-*]*il* ⸢*ù*⸣ [*mi-nu-*]*um-me-e a-ma-a-tu*$_4$ *gáb-bá-ši-na-a-ma ša* ŠEŠ-[*ia*] ⸢*i*⸣-*dáb-bu-bu ù am-mu-tu*$_4$ *lu-ú e-*⸢*pu*⸣-⸢*uš*⸣

170) [*am-mu-tu*$_4$] *lu-ú-pu-uš*[*-ma*] *lu ep-šu ù i-na-an-na a-na* ŠEŠ-*ia ki-*[*i*] *pa-ni-ti ú-ul aš-pur ka-a-am-ma ki-i-m*[*é-e*]

171) [*aš-pu-ru*] *ù* ŠEŠ-*ia* [*lu-ú*] *i-dá-an-ni* ŠEŠ-*ia lu-ú la ut-ta-az-*[*za-am*] *ù a-na* ŠEŠ-*ia ša-pa-a-ra ra-*⸢*ba*⸣-[*a*]

172) [*e-pu-uš-ma*] ^{I}*Ké-li-i*[*a a-ša-a*]*p-pár-ma ù ša-pa-a-ra ra-bá-a a-*⸢*na*⸣ [ŠE]Š-*ia a-ša-ap-*[*pár*]

(162–165) [And Masiba]dli, whom I sent to my brother, is the uncle of Keliya, so statues of solid chased gold, [may my brother give] and much gold that has not been worked for the mausoleum, which I requested of my brother, may my brother give [to me. And]may [my brother] not cause me [dist]ress and may he not hold back; for in the la[nd of] my [bro]ther gold is plentiful like dirt. [And may] I not [cause dis]tress to my brother.

166–172) [And] may [my brother] exceed in love and [broth]erhood ten times more than his father and with me we will con[tinually sh]ow love very, very much. [And] as for my envoys, may my brother release them speedily and [m]ay my brother send Mane with my envoys and may [they] come [to me]. [As] my very own mouth h[as spoken,] may my brother give and may I send Keliya to my [brother] and a large caravan [will I verily send] to my [brother] and [what]ever things, all of them, that [my] brother will say, then those will I verily do. [Those] may I do [and] let them be done! And now I have not written to my brother thus as before. As [I have written], then [may] my brother understand me. May my brother not be ang[ry]. And for my brother [I have prepared] a great shipment and Keliya [will I] send and a great shipment will I send to my [bro[ther].

173) [*ù* ŠEŠ-*ia aš-šum* ^{I}*Ar-*]*te-eš-šu-bá* ⸢*ù*⸣ ^{I}*A-sa-li iq-ta-bi-šu-nu um-ma šu-ú-* [*m*]*a i-na* ⸢KUR⸣ *ša* ŠEŠ-*ka iḫ-ta-ṭù-mì ul-te-r*[*i-bu*]

174) [*ki-la-al-la*]*-šu-nu ù ul-*⸢*te*⸣*-*⸢*ri*⸣*-bu* ÌR.MEŠ-*ia re-e-ḫu-tu*$_4$ *ša i-na* KUR *M*[*i-*]*iṣ-ri-i ú-ši-bu* ^{I}*Ma*[*-né-e*]

175) [LÚ.DUMI.KIN-*ka*] *a-*⸢*na*⸣ *pa-ni-ia* ⸢*i*⸣[*-te-*]⸢*ru*⸣*-ub ù ub-ti-i-ir-ru-ú-šu-nu a-na* ⸢*pa*⸣*-*[*ni-i*]*a ù i-dáb*[*-bu-bu-ma*]

176) [*ni-te-pu-uš-mì*] *ù aq-ta-bi a-na pa-ni-šu-nu šu-um-ku*$_8$*-nu am-mi-i-ni* [..........]*ma-mì* [*ù* ŠEŠ-*ia*]

177) [^{I}*Ma-né-e ša-a-*]⸢*al*⸣*-*⸢*šu*⸣ *ki-i-me-e e-te-pu-us-sú-nu i-na šèr-*⸢*šèr*⸣*-re-ti ù* ⸢*iz*⸣*-*⸢ŠU⸣ *a*[*l-ták-na-šu-nu*]

178) [*ù ki-la-al-la*]*-šu-nu* 1-*en a-na i-di* 1-*en a-na* URU-*ia ša qa-an-ni* KUR-*ti* ⸢*ul*⸣[*-te-bi*]*l ù ša-ni-*⸢*ta*⸣ [ŠEŠ-*ia*]

179) [*ul iq-ta-bi*] *ù* ⸢*aš*⸣*-šum an-ni-ti la a-du-uk-šu-nu* ŠEŠ-*i*⸢*a*⸣ ⸢*šu*⸣*-*⸢*nu*⸣ *ki-i i*[*ḫ-ta-ṭù*]

180) [*ù* ŠEŠ-*ia ú-*]⸢*ul*⸣ *iq-bi* ⸢*ù*⸣ ⸢ŠEŠ⸣*-ia ù-ul as-ʾa-al* ⸢*i*⸣*-*⸢*na*⸣*-an-na* ⸢ŠEŠ⸣*-ia né-e-pé-el-t*[*i*] *š*[*a*]

181) [*iḫ-ṭù*] *li-iš-*[*ku*]$_8$*-un ù k*[*i-i-me*]*-e* ŠEŠ-*ia ḫa-še-eḫ-šu-*[*n*]*u ù a-ka-*⸢*an*⸢*-na lu-ú-pu-*⸢*us*⸣*-*⸢*su*⸣*-*[*nu*]*-t*[*i*]

---

182) [*a-nu-um-ma a-n*]*a* ⸢*šul*⸣*-ma-ni ša* [ŠEŠ-*ia*] 1 GA.ZUM KÙ.GI *tam-lu-ú* KUR SAG *bu-ur-ḫi-iš* 1 GIŠ.TUKUL.SAG.NA$_4$

183) [..............]x-*uš* NA$_4$.ZA.GÌ[N.KUR.......M]EŠ 1 ŠU *ša* ŠU.MEŠ NA$_4$.KUR 1 ⸢*šu*⸣*-ru-uḫ-tu*$_4$ [KÙ].GI.GAR 3 TÚG.MEŠ 3 ŠU TÚG[........]

184) [............1 T]UG.⸢GÚ⸣ ⸢URU⸣ [...x GI]Š.BAN.MEŠ 3 KUŠ.É.AMAR.RU K[Ù.G]I.GAR. ⸢80⸣ [G]I.MEŠ UD.KA.BAR (= ZABAR) *šar-m*[*u-tu*$_4$]

185) [....................] *ti-a-an-nu dám-qù-ú-tu*$_4$ 3 GIŠ. [TU]KUL.⸢GÚ⸣(?).⸢MEŠ⸣ [*a-n*]*a šul-ma-ni* ŠEŠ-*ia u*[*l-te-bil*]

---

186) [..................*ša*] KÙ.GI.MEŠ 1 ŠU *ša* ŠU.MEŠ ^{NA_4}[.....x ŠU]*an-ṣa-bá-a-tu*$_4$ x[.................]

187) [..........................]2 TÚG.MEŠ *a-na šul-ma-*[*ni ša* ^{MUNUS}*Te*]*-*⸢*i*⸣*-e* ⸢AMA⸣*-ka u*[*l-te-bil*]

---

188) [..........................] 1 ŠU *ša* ŠU.MEŠ ⸢^{NA_4}⸣[.... ....x ŠU *an-ṣ*]*a-bá-*[*a-tu*$_4$.............]

189) [..........................x] TÚG.MEŠ *a-*[*n*]*a* ⸢*šul*⸣*-ma-n*[*i ša* ^{MUNUS}*Ta-a-du-ḫé-bá* DUMU.M]UNUS-*ia-ma* [*ul-te-bil*]

(173–181) [And my brother] spoke [concerning Ar]teššuba and Asali; he said, "They have committed a misdeed in your brother's country." They brought in [the two of] them and they brought in the rest of my servants who have been dwelling in Egypt. Ma[ne, your envoy,] came in to my presence and they convicted them in my presence, and they de[clared, "We did it."] So I said to them, "Why did you [disgrace(?) your name?" [My brother, as]k [Mane] how I treated them. I pu[t them] in chains and fetters. [And both of] them, one beside the other, I se[nt] to a town of mine on the frontier of the land. And furthermore, [my brother did not say,] and for this reason I did not slay them. My brother, they verily co[mmitted a misdeed, but my brother] did not say. So, my brother, I did not ask. Now, may my brother define the activity by which [they sinned] and ac[cording]to his desire for them, then thus will I do to th[e]m.

(182–185) [Now fo]r the greeting gift of [my brother,] one gold comb, inlaid, genuine, with the head of a buffalo; one mace [...genuine] lapis lazuli [...] one pair for the hands, of genuine stone; one *šuruḫtu* ornament, inlaid with [go]ld; three garments; three pairs of [...] garments; [one] city style shirt; [*x*] bows; three quivers overlaid with gold; 9[0 ar]rows of bronze, trimmed; [*x*......]*x* of high quality; three ma[ces; a]s the greeting gift of my brother [have] I [sent.]

(186–187) [...of] gold; one pair for the hands, of [...] stone; [*x* pairs of] earrings; [...]; two garments; as the greeting gif[t of Te]ye, your mother, [have] I [sent.]

(188–189) [...] one pair for the hands, of [...] stone [...*x* pairs of ear]rin[gs ;......*x*] garments; as the greeting gif[t of Taduḫeba,] my [daught]er, [have I sent.]

EA 30

TRANSCRIPTION

Obv. 01) *a-na* LUGAL.MEŠ *ša* KUR *Ki-na-a-aḫ*[*-ḫi*]
02) ÌR.MEŠ ŠEŠ-*ia um-ma* LUGAL-*ma*
03) *a-nu-um-ma* ᴵ*A-ki-ia* LÚ.DUMU ⸢KIN⸣-⸢*ia*⸣
04) *a-na* UGU ⸢*šàr*⸣ ⸢KUR⸣ *Mi-iṣ-ri-i* ŠEŠ-⸢*ia*⸣
05) *a-na du-*⸢*ul*⸣-⸢*lu*⸣*-ḫi a-na kál-le-e*
06) *al-ta-pár-šu ma-am-ma*
07) *lu-ú la i-na-aḫ-ḫi-is-sú*
08) *na-aṣ-ri-iš i-na* KUR *Mi-iṣ-ri-i*
09) *šu-ri-bá ù a-na* ŠU
10) ⸢LÚ⸣ *ḫal-zu-uḫ-li ša* KUR *Mi-iṣ-*⸢*ri*⸣*-i*
Lo.ed. 11) ⸢*id*⸣-⸢*na*⸣-⸢*šu*⸣(?) *ḫa-mut-ta* ⸢*li*⸣!*-il-*⸢*li*⸣!-⸢*ik*⸣!
Rev. 12) *ù kad‹-ru›-sú mi-im-ma*
13) *i-na muḫ-ḫi-šu lu-ú la ib-bá-aš-ši*

Impression of a cylinder seal

EA 30

TRANSLATION

(1–2) To the kings of Canaa[n], the servants of my brother, thus (says) the king:

(3–6) Now, as for Akiya, my envoy, I have dispatched him to hasten with all speed to the king of the land of Egypt, my brother.

(6–13) Let no one detain him. Provide him safe entry to the land of Egypt and hand him over to the fortress commander of the land of Egypt. Let him go quickly. And let there be no bri‹bes› demanded from him.

EA 31

TRANSCRIPTION

Obv. 01) [*u*]*m-ma* ^{I}*Ni-mu-wa*$^{!}$*-r*[*i-y*]*a* LUGAL.GAL LUGAL KUR *Mi-iṣ-ṣa-ri*
02) [*A-N*]*A* ^{I}*Tar-ḫu-un-da-ra-du* LUGAL KUR *Ar-za-wa QÍ-BÍ-MA*
03) *kat-ti-mi* SIG$_5$ *-in* É.ḪI.A*-mi* DAM.MEŠ*-mi* DUMU.MEŠ*-mi*
04) LÚ.MEŠ GAL.GAL*-aš* ÉRIN.MEŠ*-mi* ANŠE.KUR.RA. ḪI.A*-mi*
05) *pí-ip-pí-it-mi* KUR.KUR.ḪI.A*-mi-kán an-da*
06) *ḫu-u-ma-an* SIG$_5$*-in*

---

07) *du-uq-qa kat-ta ḫu-u-ma-an* SIG$_5$*-in e-eš-tu*
08) É.ḪI.A*-ti* DAM.MEŠ*-ti* DUMU.MEŠ*-ti* LÚ.MEŠ GAL.GAL*-aš*
09) ÉRIN.MEŠ*-ti* ANŠE.KUR.RA.ḪI.A*-ti pí-ip-pí-it-ti*
10) KUR.ḪI.A*-ti ḫu-u-ma-an* SIG$_5$*-in e-eš-tu*

---

11) *ka-a-aš-ma-at-ta u-i-e-nu-un* ^{I}*Ir-ša-ap-pa*
12) ^{LÚ}*ḫa-lu-ga-tal-la-an-mi-in a-ú-ma-ni* DUMU.MUNUS*-ti*
13) ^{d}UTU *-mi ku-in* DAM*-an-ni ú-wa-da-an-zi*
14) *nu-uš-ši li-il-ḫu-wa-i Ì-an* SAG.DU*-ši*
15) *ka-a-aš-ma-ta up-pa-aḫ-ḫu-un* 1 ^{KUŠ}*ḫa-la-li-ya* KÙ.GI*-aš*
16) SIG$_5$*-an-ta*

---

17) *a-ni-ya-at-ta-aš-ma-mu ku-e-da-aš ḫa-at-ra-a-*[*e*]*š*
18) *up-pí-wa-ra-at-mu ne-et-ta up-pa-aḫ-ḫi* EGIR*-an-da*
19) *na-aš-ta* ^{LÚ}*ḫa-lu-ga-tal-la-at-ti-in am-me-el-la*
20) ^{LÚ}*ḫa-lu-ga-tal-la-an* EGIR*-pa pa-ra-a ḫu-u-da-a-ak*
21) *na-i na-at ú-wa-an-du*

---

22) *nu-ut-ta ú-wa-an-zi ú-da-an-zi ku-ša-ta* DUMU.MUNUS^{TI}
23) ^{LÚ}*ḫa-lu-ga-tal-aš-mi-iš* ^{LÚ}*ḫa-lu-ga-tal-la-ša*
24) *ku-iš tu-el ú-it na-aš ag-ga-aš*
25) *nu-mu an-tu-uḫ-šu-uš Ga-aš-ga-aš* KUR*-ya-aš up-pí iš-ta-ma-aš-šu-un*
26) *zi-in-nu-uk ḫu-u-ma-an-da*

EA 31

TRANSLATION

(1–6) Thus (says) Nimuwariya, the Great King, king of Egypt: to Tarḫundarasu, king of Arzawa, (say) as follows: With me it is well. With my houses, my wives, my children, the senior officials, my troops, my chariots, my *possessions*, whatever is in my lands, all is well.

(7–10) May everything be well with you. With your houses, your wives, your children, the senior officials, your troops, your chariots, your *possessions*, your lands, may all be well.

(11–16) Behold, I have sent to you Iršappa, my messenger. Let us see the daughter whom they will bring to My Majesty in marriage. Let him pour oil on her head. Behold, I have sent to you one *ḫalaliya* of good-quality gold.

(17–21) As for the operation about which you wrote to me: "Send it to me," I will send it to you afterwards. (But first) send back promptly your messenger and my messenger and let them come (to me).

(22–26) (When) they return to you they will bring the bride-price for the daughter. My messenger and the messenger of yours, he came and...Send me people of the land of Gašga. I have heard that everything is *finished.*

---

27) *nu Ḫa-ad-du-ša-aš-ša* KUR-*e i-ga-it*
28) *nu-ut-ta ka-a-aš-ma pí-ip-pé-eš-šar up-pa-ḫu-un* [?] ŠU-x[...]
29) *ki-iš-ša-ri-iš-ši* ^{I}*Ir-ša-ap-pa* ^{LÚ}*ḫa-lu-*[*ga-tal-la-aš-mi-iš*]
30) $_{1}{}^{\text{EN KUŠ}}$*ḫa-la-li-ya* KÙ.GI KI.LÁ.BI
31) 20 MA.N[A] KÙ.GI 3 GADA.SIG 3 GADA.È.A S[IG$^{?}$]
Lo.ed. 32) 3 GADA *ḫu-uz-zi* 8 GADA *ku-ši-it-ti-in*
33) 1 ME GADA-*an*$^{!}$ *wa-al-ga-an* 1 ME GADA *ḫa-ap-p*[*a*(-)]
Rev. 34) 1 ME GADA *pu*$^{!}$*-tal-li-ya-aš-ša*[...]
35) 4 $^{\text{NA}_4}$KU-KU-BU GEŠTIN.DÙG.GA 6 $^{\text{NA}_4}$KU-[KU-BU]
36) *ŠA* Ì.DÙG.GA 3 ^{GIŠ}GU.ZA ^{GIŠ}ESI *šar-pa* BÁ-NA[-A KÙ.G]I GAR.RA
37) 10 ^{GIŠ}GU.ZA *ša* ^{GIŠ}ESI IŠ-TU ZU$_9$ *AM-S*[*I*]
38) *u-uḫ-ḫu-uz* 1 ME ^{GIŠ}ESI *aš-šu-li*

(27–38) And also the land of Ḫattuša is *frozen/paralyzed*. Behold, I have sent you a consignment...in the hand of Iršappa, [my] mess[enger]:
One *ḫalaliya* of gold weighing 20 minas of gold;
3 fine linens; 3 f[ine?] linen coats;
3 linen *ḫuzzi*;
8 linen *mantles*;
100 linen *walgan*;
100 linen *ḫapp*[*a*(-);
100 linen *sashes*; [...]
4 *kukkubu*(-vessels) for/with fine wine;
6 *ku*[*kkubu*(-vessels)] for/with fine oil;
3 chairs of ebony overlaid with exquisite *leather* [and gol]d;
10 chairs of ebony inlaid with ivory; 100 ebony (plates); as a greeting-gift.

EA 32

TRANSCRIPTION

Obv. 01) *[k]a-a-ša-mu ki-i ku-it* ^{I}*Kal-ba-ya-a[š]*

02) *[u]t-tar me-mi-iš-ta ma-an-wa-an-na-aš*

03) *iš-ḫa-ni-it-ta-ra-a-tar i-ya-u-e-ni*

---

04) *[nu(?)]*^{I}*Kal-ba-ya-an ú-ul ḫa-a-mi*

05) INIM-*ya-at me-mi-iš-ta a-na ṭup-pí-ma-at-ša-an*

06) *ú-ul ki-it-ta-at*

---

07) *nu ma-a-an ḫa-an-da-a-an am-me-el* DUMU.MUNUS-*ya*

08) *ša-an-ḫi-iš-ki-ši nu-ut-ta ú-ul im-ma*

09) *pí-iḫ-ḫi pí-iḫ-ḫi-it-ta*

---

10) *nu-mu-kán* ^{I}*Kal-ba-ya-an* EGIR-*pa pa-ra-a*

11) *iš-tu* ^{LÚ} ṬE-MI-YA *li-li-wa-aḫ-ḫu-u-an-zi*

12) *na-i ku-u-un-na-mu me-mi-an ṭup-pí-az*

13) EGIR-*pa ḫa-at-ra-a-i*

---

14) *ki-i-kán* TUP-PÍ *ku-iš* DUB.SAR-*a[š]*

Lo.ed. 15) *ḫal-za-a-i na-an* ^{d}É$^{!}$-A

16) *ḫa-at-ta-an-na-aš* LUGAL-*uš*

17) *ḫi-lam-na-aš-ša* ^{d}UTU-*uš*

Rev. 18) *aš-šu-ú-li pa-aḫ-ša-an-ta-ru*

19) *nu-ut-ta* ŠU.ḪI.A *-uš a-ra-aḫ-za-an-da*

20) *aš-šu-ú-li ḫar-kán-du*

---

21) *zi-ik-mu* DUB.SAR-*aš aš-šu-ú-li*

22) *ḫa-at-ra-a-i nam-ma-za* [Š]UM-*an* EGIR-*an*

23) *i-ya*

---

24) DUB.ḪI.A*[-ká]n ku-e ú-da-an-zi*

25) *nu ne-eš-[u]m$^{!}$-ni-li ḫa-at-ri-eš-ki*

EA 32

TRANSLATION

(1–6) Behold, with regard to this matter that Kalbaya said to me, "We should establish a blood-relationship between ourselves,"

(4–6) I do not trust Kalbaya. He said it, but it does not figure on the tablet.

(7–9) If you really want my daughter, would I not give her to you? I will give (her) to you.

(10–13) Send Kalbaya back to me promptly together with my envoy and write back to me (about) this matter on a tablet.

(14–20) The scribe who reads out this tablet, let Ea the king of wisdom, and the Sun-god of the gate house protect him in good will! Let them hold the(ir) hands in good will around you!

(21–23) You, scribe, write to me in good will and add (your) name thereafter.

(24–25) The tablets that are brought (here) keep writing (them) in Nešite (i.e. Hittite).

EA 33

TRANSCRIPTION

Obv. 01) ⸢*a*⸣*-na* LUGAL KUR *Mi-iṣ-ri* ŠEŠ-*i*⸢*a*⸣

02) *um-ma* LUGAL KUR *A-la-ši-ia* ŠEŠ-*ka*

03) *a-na ia-ši šul-mu*—————————

04) *a-na maḫ-ri-ka lu-ú šul‹-mu›*

05) *a-na* É-*ka* DAM-*ka*$_4$ DUMU-*ka*

06) ⸢ANŠE⸣.KUR.RA-*ka* GIŠ.GIGIR-*ka*

07) ⸢*ù*⸣ *a-na lìb-bi* KUR-*ka*

08) [*ma*]*-gal lu šul-mu*

---

09) [*ša-*]*ni-tam ù iš-te-mé a-na-ku*

10) [*i-n*]*u-ma aš-ba-ta* UGU-*li*

11) [GIŠ.G]U. ZA É *a-bi-ka*

12) [*ù u*]*š-te-bi-ir*!(RI)*-mi*

13) [NÍG.BA *š*]*a-la-mi*

14) [*ù iš*]*-te-mè šu-ul-ma-na*

15) [*ša* ŠEŠ-]*ia ù uš-ta-bar*[*-ra-*]*ku*

16) [*ši-ip*]*ra-ta* 2 *me* URUDU.MEŠ [*ù*]

17) [*u*]*š-te-bi-ra-ku-m*[*a*]

18) [1-*en* G]Ú 10 GÚ.UN [URUDU DÙG]

---

19) [*ù* DU]MU *ši-ip-r*[*i ša a-bi-ka*]

Lo.ed. 20) [*ša*]⸢*iš*⸣*-ta-n*[*a-pa-ar*]

21) [*a-*]*na mu-ḫi*[*-ia ki-ma*]

22) ⸢*ar*⸣*-ḫi-iš* ⸢*ú*⸣[*-wa-aš-ši-ir-*(*šu*)]

Rev. 23) ⸢*ù*⸣ *šu-pu-r*[*a-am-ma* (?)]

24) [L]Ú-*ia ša i*[*t-ti-ka*(?)]

25) [Š]EŠ-*ia la-a ú*[*-uḫ-ḫar-šu*(?)]

26) [*u*]*š-ši‹-ir-›šu ki-ma* [*ar-ḫi-iš*]

EA 33

TRANSLATION

(1–8) To the king of the land of Egypt, my brother, thus the king of the land of Alashia your brother. It is well with me; may it be we‹ll ›with you. To your house, your wife(s), your son(s) your horse(s), your chariot(s) and throughout your country, may it be [ve]ry well.

(9–18) [Fu]rthermore, then I myself have heard [th]at you are seated on the [th]rone of the house of your father [and I] have transported [a gift of p]eace. [And I] heard of the well being [of] my [brother and I transp[orted] to you [a sh]ipment of two hundred (talents) of copper [and I] transported to you [one lo]ad of ten talents of [fine copper].

(19–26) [And as for the am]bassado[r of your father which] he used [to send t]o me, [with] haste I [sent (him) back]. So send [hither(?)] my [m]an who is w[ith you(?)]. My brother, don't cause [him to delay], sen‹d› him with [haste].

---

27) ⸢*ù*⸣ MU.KAM^{V} *ù* MU[.KAM^{V}-*ma*]
28) [D]UMU *ši-ip-ri-ia-ma* [*a-na pa-ni-ka*]
29) ⸢*li*⸣-*li-ki*(sic!) *ù at-t*[*a-ma*]
30) [D]UMU *ši-ip-ri-ka-ma*!(IP)
31) ⸢MU⸣.KAM^{V} MU.KAM^{V}-*ma i‹-na› pa-ni-i*[*a*]
32) *li-li-ki*(sic!)-*ma*

(27–32) So year by yea[r] let my [a]mbassador go [to you] and as for yo[u], may your [a]mbassador come year by year t‹o› me.

EA 34

TRANSCRIPTION

Obv. 01) *um-ma* LUGAL KUR *A-la-ši-ia*
02) *a-na* LUGAL KUR *Mi-iṣ-ri* ŠEŠ-*ia-ma*
03) *li-ma-ad i-nu-ma šal-ma-ku ù*
04) *ša-lim* KUR-*ia ù iš-tu šul-mu-ka*$_4$
05) *ù šu-lum-ka*$_4$ *šu-lum* É-*ka*$_4$ DUMU.MEŠ-*ka*$_4$
06) DAM.MEŠ-‹*ka*$_4$› ANŠE.KUR.RA.MEŠ-‹*ka*$_4$› GIŠ.GIGIR-*ka*$_4^{\text{MEŠ}}$
07) KUR.KI-*ka*$_4$ *ma-gal lu-ú šal-mu a-mur at-‹ta›* ŠEŠ-⸢*i*⸣[*a*]
08) *i-nu-ma ta-aš-tap-ra a-na ia-a-*⸢*ši*⸣
09) *a-na mi-nim-mi la-a tu-wa-ši-ra*
10) LÚ.DUMU *ši-ip-ri-ka a-na maḫ-ri-ia*
11) *ša-ni-tam ù la-a iš-mé i-nu-ma*
12) *ti-na-qú ni-qa-am ù la-a ti-*⸢*ša*⸣*-*⸢*kán*⸣
13) *mi-ma a-na lìb-bi-ka*$_4$ *ù aš-šu-ú*
14) *iš-ma-am ù a-nu-ma ut-ta-šir*$_9$
15) LÚ.DUMU *ši-ip-ri-ia a-na maḫ-ri-ka*$_4$
16) *ù al-lu-ú ut-ta-šir*$_9$*-ka*
17) *i-na qa-ti* LÚ.DUMU *ši-ip‹-ri›-ia a-na ka-ta*$_5$
18) 1 *me* GÚ.UN URUDU.MEŠ *ša-ni-tam ù a-nu-ma*
19) *ú-nu-tu*^{MEŠ} *yu-ba-al* LÚ.DUMU *ši-ip-ri-ka*$_4$
20) 1-*en* ^{GIŠ}*er-šu* GIŠ.ESI KÙ.GI *šu-ḫa*!*-a*
21) *ù* GIŠ.GIGIR-*tu*$_4$ *šu-ḫi-tu i-na* KÙ.GI
22) *ù* 2 ANŠE.KUR.RA *ù* 42 GADA.MEŠ *ù*
23) 50 GÚ.GADA.MEŠ *ù* 2 *ku-ši-ti* GADA *ù*
24) 14 GIŠ.ESI.MEŠ *ù* 17 NA$_4$. *ḫa-ba-na-tu* Ì DÙG.GA
25) [*ù*] *iš-tu* GADA LUGAL ⸢4⸣ GADA *ù* 4 GÚ.GADA
26) [*ù iš*]*-tu ú-nu-te ša i-ia-nu*
27) [.......] *ù* KUŠ *i-ma-ru*
28) [........] *ša* ^{GIŠ}*er-ši ù*
29) [*iš-tu ḫa-b*]*a-na-tu ša i-ia-nu*
30) [.........] MEŠ *ut-ta-šir*$_9$
31) [*i-na qa-ti* LÚ.DUMU *š*]*i-ip-ri-ia*

EA 34

TRANSLATION

(1–7) Thus the king of the land of Alashia to the king of the land of Egypt, my brother: Be informed that I am well and my country is well. And *as to* your welfare, so your welfare, the welfare of your house, of your sons, of ‹your› wives, of ‹your› horses, of your chariots, of your land, may they be very well.

(7–15) Look, yo‹u› are ⸢my⸣ brother. In as much as you have written to me, "Why have you not sent your envoy to me?" moreover, then I had not heard that you were making a celebration. So don't take it to heart. So as soon as I heard, then I have sent now my envoy to you.

(16–25) And behold, I have sent by the hand of my ambas‹sador› to you one hundred talents of copper. Moreover, so now the vessels that your envoy should bring: One bed of ebony, gold overlaid and a chariot overlaid with gold and two horses and forty-two pieces of linen and fifty linen scarves and two linen robes; fourteen ebony trees and seventeen stone *ḫabannatu* vessels of fine oil [and] *as for* byssos: four pieces of linen and four linen scarves.

(26–31) [And *as*] *for* vessels which are not [...] and the hide of a donkey [...] of a bed and [*as for ḫab*]*annatu* vessels which are not [...] I have sent [in the hand of] my [amba]ssador

Lo.ed. 32) [...........] ŠE.MEŠ
Rev. 33) [...................]*na ù* [...]
34) [...LÚ.DUMU *ši-ip-*]*ri-ia qa*[*-du*]
35) [................*a*]*š-šu uš-ši-*[*ir*]
36) [*ki-ma ar-ḫi-iš*] *ù* DUMU *ši-ip*[*-ri-ka*$_4$]
37) [*uš-ši-ir a-na* KUR.]KI*-ia ù* x[...]
38) [*yi-li-ku*] *ki-ma ar-ḫi-iš*
39) [*a-na* KUR *A-*]*la-ši-ia* LÚ *tám-kà-ri*
\-*ia*
40) [*ù* 2]0 L[Ú.MEŠ *tám-*]*kà-ru-ka ù*
41) [x]*-i-it* [...] *ga-gi it-ti-šu-nu*
42) *ù lu-*[*ú te-né*]*-pu-uš ki-it-tu*
43) *i-na bi-*[*ri*]*-ku-ni ù*
44) LÚ.DUMU *ši-ip-‹ri›-ia a-na maḫ-ri-ka*$_4$
45) *yi-li-ku ù* LÚ.DUMU *ši-ip-ri-ka*
46) *a-na maḫ-ri-ia yi-*⸢*li*⸣*-ku ša-ni-tam*
47) Ì.MEŠ *ù* GADA.MEŠ *a-na mi-ni*$_7$ *la-a*
48) *tu-wa-ši-ru-ni a-na* TÚG[*-t*]*e ù ša*
49) *te-ri-šu at-ta ù a-*[*na-k*]*u id-di-nu*
50) *ù al-lu-ú ḫa-ba-na-at-*⸢*tu*⸣? [*ša*] Ì DÙG.GA
51) *ma-la-at a-na ta-bá-ki a-na* [*qa-qa*]*-di-ka*
52) *uš-ši-ir-ti i-nu-ma tu-ša-ab a-na* GIŠ.GU.ZA
53) *šàr-ru-*⸢*ta*⸣*-ka*

(32–41) […] grain […] So […] my [ambassa]dor wi[th…] his […] sen[d with haste] and as for [your] ambassa[dor, send to] my [lan]d and [may they come] with haste [to the land of A]lashia, my business agent [and tw]enty [busin]ess agents of yours and […] with them.

(42–46) So may a treaty [be ma]de between us and my ambassad‹or› will go to you and your envoy will come to me.

(46–48) Moreover, why haven't you sent to me oil and linen for garme[nt]s?

(48–53) And that which your request, ⸢I⸣ will give. And behold I have sent a *ḫabannatu* jar [that is] full of fine oil to pour on your [he]ad because you have sat on your royal throne.

EA 35

TRANSCRIPTION

Obv. 01) [*a-na š*]*àr-ri* KUR *Mi-iṣ-ri* ŠEŠ-*ia qí*[*-bí-ma*]

02) [*um-ma*] LUGAL KUR *A-la-ši-ia* ŠEŠ-*ka-ma*

03) [*a-na*] UGU-*ia šul-mu* É.MEŠ-*ia* DAM.‹MEŠ›-*ia* DUMU.MEŠ-*ia*

04) [LÚ].GAL.GAL.MEŠ-*ia* ANŠE.KUR.RA.MEŠ-*ia* GIŠ.GIGIR.MEŠ-*ia ù i-na*

05) ⸢*lìb*⸣*-bi* KUR.MEŠ-*ia dan-níš lu-ú šul-mu ù a-na* UGU ŠEŠ-*ia*

---

06) *lu-ú šul-mu a-na* É.MEŠ-*ka* DAM.MEŠ-*ka* DUMU.MEŠ-*ka* LÚ.GAL.GAL-*ka*

07) ANŠE.KUR.RA.MEŠ-*ka* GIŠ.GIGIR.MEŠ-*ka ù i-na lìb-bi* KUR.KUR.MEŠ-*ka*

08) *dan-níš lu-ú šul-mu a-ḫi a-nu-ma* LÚ.DUMU.KIN-*ia it-ti*

09) LÚ.DUMU.KIN-*ka a-na* UGU-*ka al-ta-pár i-na* KUR *Mi-iš-ri*

---

(10) *e-nu-ma a-na* UGU-*ka* 5 *me-at* URUDU *ul-te-bi-la-ak-ku*

(11) *a-na šu-ul-ma-ni ša* ŠEŠ-*ia ul-*⸢*te*⸣*-bi-la-ak-ku*

(12) *a-ḫi ki-i* ⸢*ṣe*⸣*-ḫé-er* URUDU *i-na lìb-bi-ka la-a i-*⸢*ša*⸣*-ki-in*

(13) *šum-ma i-na* KUR-*ia* ŠU-*ti* ^{d}MAŠ.MAŠ EN-*li-ia gáb-ba*

(14) LÚ.MEŠ *ša* KUR-*ia i-du-uk ù e-pí-*⸢*iš*⸣ URUDU *ia-*⸢*nu*⸣

(15) *ù* ŠEŠ-*ia i-na lìb-bi-ka la-a* ‹*i*›*-ša-ki-in*

---

(16) LÚ.DUMU.KIN-*ka it-ti* LÚ.DUMU.KIN-*ia ar-ḫi-iš*

(17) *uš-še-er ù mi-nu-um-me* URUDU *ša te-ri-iš-šu*

(18) ŠEŠ-*ia ù a-na-ku ul-te-bi-la-ak-ku*

---

(19) *a-ḫi at-ta a-na ia-ši* · KÙ.BABBAR *ma-a-ad* · *dan-níš*

(20) *ul-te-bi-la-an-ni* ŠEŠ-*ia* KÙ.BABBAR DINGIR.MEŠ *i-din-an-ni*

(21) *a-na-ku ù a-na* UGU *ša* ŠEŠ-*ia mi-nu-um-me-e*

(22) *ša te-ri-iš-šu* ŠEŠ-*ia ù a-na-ku ul-te-bi-la-*⸢*ak*⸣*-ku*

EA 35

TRANSLATION

(1–5) Sp[eak to the k]ing of the land of Egypt, my brother; [Thus] the king of the land of Alashia, your brother: It is well [wit]h me. For my palace, my wiv‹es›, my sons, my senior officials, my horses, my chariots and in my territories all is very well indeed.

(6–8) And with my brother may all be well. With your palace, your wives, yours sons, your senior officials, your horses, your chariots and within your territories may all be very well.

(8–9) My brother, now I have sent my envoy with your envoy to you to the land of Egypt.

(10–15) Now I have sent to you five hundred (talents) of copper. As my brother's greeting gift have I sent it to you. My brother, that the amount of copper is small, may it not be taken to your heart, because the hand of Nergal, my lord, is in my land. He has smitten all the men of my land and there is no copper worker. So, my brother, may it not be [t]aken to your heart.

(16–18) Send your envoy with my envoy quickly and whatever copper that you request, my brother, I will send it to you.

(19–22) You are my brother. (May) he send me a very great amount of silver. My brother, give me the finest ("divine") silver. As for me, then to my brother, whatever you should request, my brother, then I myself will send it to you.

---

(23) *ša-ni-tam a-ḫ̮i* GU$_4$ *ša te-ri-iš-šu* LÚ.DUMU.KIN-*i*⌜*a*⌝
(24) *ù i-din-an-ni* ŠEŠ-*ia ù* Ì.MEŠ *ša* DÙG.GA ŠEŠ-*ia*
(25) 2 DUG *ku-ku-bu uš-še-er-an-ni* ŠEŠ-*ia*
(26) *ù* 1 LÚ.MEŠ *ša-i-li* Á.MUŠEN.MEŠ *uš-še-ra-an-ni*

---

(27) *ša-ni-tam* ŠEŠ-*ia* LÚ.MEŠ *ša* KUR-*ia it-ti-*⌜*i*⌝[*a*]
(28) *i-dáb-bu-bu* GIŠ.MEŠ-*ia ša* LUGAL KUR *Mi-i*[*ṣ-ri*]
(29) ⌜*i*⌝*-le-qú-ni ù* ŠEŠ-*ia* ŠÀM.MEŠ *ši-*[*mi i-din*]
Rev. 30) *ša-ni-tam ki-ia-am* LÚ *ša* KUR ⌜*A*⌝[*-la-ši-ia*]
31) *i-na* KUR *Mi-iṣ-ri mi-it ù ú-nu-*⌜*tu*⌝-[*šu*]
32) *i-na* KUR-*ka ù* DUMU-*šu* DAM-*šu it-ti-i*⌜*a*⌝
33) *ù* ŠEŠ-*ia ú-nu-tu*$_4$ LÚ.MEŠ *A-la-ši-ia* MÁŠK[IM]
34) *ù i-na* ŠU-*ti* LÚ.DUMU.KIN-*ia i-din-šu* ŠEŠ-*ia*

---

35) *a-ḫ̮i i-na lìb-bi-ka la-a ‹i›-ša-ki-in ki-i*
36) LÚ.DUMU.KIN-*ka* 3 MU.MEŠ *aš-bu i-na* KUR-*ia*
37) *aš-šum* ŠU-*ti* ^{d}MAŠ.MAŠ *i-ba-aš-ši i-na* KUR-*ia*
38) *ù i-na* É-*ia* DAM-*ia* TUR *i-ba-aš-ši*
39) *ša-a mi-it i-na-an-na* ŠEŠ-*ia*

---

40) LÚ.DUMU.KIN-*ka it-ti* LÚ⌝.⌜DUMU⌝.KIN-*ia na-aṣ-ri-iš*
41) *ar-ḫ̮i-iš uš-še-er ù šu-ul-ma-na*
42) *ša* ŠEŠ-*ia ul-te-bi-la-ak-ku*

---

43) *ša-ni-tam* ŠEŠ-*ia* KÙ.BABBAR *ša e-ri-ša-ak-ku*
44) *ú-še-bi-la ma-ad dan-níš* ŠEŠ-*ia*
45) *ù ú-nu-tu*$_4$ *ša e-ri-ša-ak-ku* ŠEŠ-*ia uš-šèr*
46) *ù mi-nu-um-me-e a-ma-te*^{MEŠ} *gáb-ba* ŠEŠ-*ia*
47) *ip-pu-uš ù at-ta mi-nu-um-me-e a-ma-te*^{MEŠ}
48) *ša ta-qáb-bi a-na ia-ši ù a-na-ku ep-pu-uš*

---

49) *it-ti* LUGAL *Ḫ̮a-at-ti*$_7$ *ù it-ti* LUGAL *Ša-an-ḫ̮a-ar*
50) *it-ti-šu-nu la ta-ša-ki-in a-na-ku*
51) *mi-nu-um-me-e šu-ul-ma-nu ša ú-še-bi-lu*
52) *a-na ia-ši ù a-na-ku* 2-*šu a-na* UGU-*ka*
53) *ú-te-er-ru*

---

54) [LÚ.]DUMU.KIN-*ka il-lik it-ti-*⌜*ia*⌝ *qad-mi-i*[*š*]
55) [*ù*] LÚ.DUMU.K[I]N-*ia il-lik it-ti-ka qad-mi-i*[*š*]

(23–26) Furthermore, my brother, the ox which my envoy has ‹re›quested, give to me, my brother, and of the best oil, my brother, send me two *kukubu* jars, my brother, and send me one of the experts in vulture divination.

(27–29) Furthermore, my brother, the men of my country are talking about my lumber which they delivered to the king of the land of Eg[ypt], so, my brother, [pay] the sums that are due.

(30–34) Furthermore, thus a man of the land of A[lashia] died in the land of Egypt and [his] belongings are in your country but his son and his wife are with me. So, my brother, the possessions of the men of Alashia take in charge and hand them over to my envoy, my brother.

(35–39) My brother, don't let it be taken to heart that your envoy has been sitting in my country for three years, because the hand of Nergal is in my land and in my house there is a young wife of mine who died.

(39–42) Now, my brother, send your envoy with my envoy safely and quickly and I will send my brother's greeting gift.

(43–48) Furthermore, (may) my brother ship the silver which I requested of you, a very large amount, my brother, and the objects which I have requested of you, my brother, send. And as for whatever the things, my brother will do all (of them). And as for you, whatever the things that you say to me, then I, myself, will do.

(49–53) You have not been ranked with the king of Ḫatti or with the king of Shanhar. As for me, whatever greeting gift they send to me, then I send double the amount to you.

(54–55) (May) your envoy come to me as before [and] (may) my envoy come to you before.

EA 36

TRANSCRIPTION

Obv. -7) [*a-na* LUGAL KUR *Mi-iṣ-ri* ŠEŠ-*ia*]
-6) [*qí-bí-ma um-ma* LUGAL KUR *A-la-ši-ia*]
-5) [ŠEŠ-*ka-ma a-na ia-ši šu-ul-mu*]
-4) [*a-na* ŠEŠ-*ia lu-ú šu-ul-mu*]
-3) [*a-na* É-*i-šu a-na* DAM.MEŠ-*i-šu*]
-2) [*a-na* DUMU-*e-šu a-na* ANŠE.KUR.RA-*šu* GIŠ.GIGIR-*šu*]
-1) [*ù a-na lìb-bi* KUR-*i-šu dan-níš lu-ú šu-ul-mu*]
01) [......................]traces[...]
02) [....................] *mi na-ab* [...]
03) [................*mi-i*]-*iṣ*.......[...]
04) [....................] *i-pu-šu* [...]
05) [...*as-ḫ*]*u-ur* x [U]RUDU *ma-l*[*a i-*]*pu-šu ú-še-bi-*[*la ù*]
06) [*i-na-na a*]-*na* ŠEŠ-*ia ú-še-bi-lu* 12[0(+ X?) URU]DU *ri-ḫu* 70 URUDU AŠ G[Ú.UN]
07) [*ù* GÚ.U]N *mim-ma ta-aḫ-ba-ṣí* 30 +[AŠ G]Ú.UN URUDU TAR KUR *ta-ḫi*[...]
08) [*i-na-n*]*a* ŠEŠ-*ú-a ša tu-še-bi-la ma-ar ši-ip-ri-ka-m*[*a i-din*]
09) [*a-na-k*]*u ša ú-še-bi*[*-l*]*a-ku mi-i-iṣ i-na-na a*[*s*]-*ḫu*⸣-⸢*ur*⸣ [*ù*]
10) [*ma-l*]*a li-bi-ka* [*l*]*u-ú-še-‹bi›-la-ku* [...]
11) [*ù š*]*a-a e-ri-šu*[-*k*]*a šu-bi-la it-ti li-bi-k*[*a*...]
12) [*i-na-n*]*a a-na* ŠEŠ-*i*[*a*] URUDU *ma-ʾa-da e-pu-uš-m*[*a*...]
13) [GIŠ.]MÁ.MEŠ *lu-ú* [*ma-ʾ*]*a-da šu-up-ra-ma* URUDU [...]
14) [*ša-*]*a-ti ki-*⸢*i*⸣ ⸢*ma*⸣-[*a*]-[*d*]*a* URUDU *i-pu-šu* ŠE.BAR *i*[-*na*...]
15) [GIŠ.MÁ.MEŠ *iš-tu*] ⸢*pi*⸣-*ḫa-ti ša ki-na-ḫi* [*šu-bi-la*]
16) [*ki-ma i-na* UD.KAM.MEŠ *p*]*a-ni-ma a-ka-la lu* [*e-pu-uš*]
17) [..]

Rev. 18) [*i-na-na ma-ar ši-ip-r*]*i-ia* 2 *ša-na-ti ta*[-*ak-ta-la-šu*]
19) [*šu-ul-ma-na-ka*] *ša il-qa-a* ⸢*ù*⸣ *a-ma*[-*te*MEŠ *ša*]

EA 36

TRANSLATION

Obv.
(-7 – -1) [Speak to the king of the land of Egypt, my brother; the message of the king of the land of Alashia, your brother. It is well with me; may it be well with my brother. With his house, with his wives, with his sons, with his horses (and) his chariots and within his land, may it be very well indeed].

(1–4) [............] little [...]they processed[......]

(5–11) [I have sou]ght *x*[of co]pper, as much as [they have] prepared, I have sent, [and now] I have sent to my brother 120 (+ x) (talents of) copper; 70 talents remain; [among] some of the talents you may rejoice(?), 30+[1(?) among the tal]ents are multicolored (alloyed?) [...No]w, my brother, [cause] that you send your messenger. [As for m]e, what I sent to you is little; now I have sought [and as much] as you desire, I will [ve]rily se‹n›d to you [and w]hat I request of [yo]u, send. Your desire [...]

(12–17) [No]w, m[y] brother, I have prepared much copper [...]May the ships be many, send (them) here. The copper [...] Since they have prepared m[uc]h copper, grain [in ships from] the province of Canaan [send to me as in] former [days], [so that I] may [make] bread [........]

Rev.(?)
(18–19) [Now, as for] my [messenger], you [have detained him] two years. [Your welfare th]at he brought (will bring) to me and the th[ings that I requested of you, send to me].

20) [*e-ri-šu-ka šu-bi-la*] blank space [...]
21) [..............]*el pu-nu-k i*[........................]
22) [..]
23) [..]
24) [..]

Remainder broken off

(20–24) *Illegible. Further lines broken away.*

EA 37

TRANSCRIPTION

Obv.
01) [a-n]a L[UGA]L K[U]R [Mi-iṣ-ri ŠEŠ]-⌜ia⌝
02) [qí-]bí-ma ⌜um⌝-⌜ma⌝ [LUGAL K]UR ⌜A⌝-la-si-ia
03) [ŠE]Š-ka-ma a-na ia-⌜ši⌝ [šu]-⌜ul⌝-mu
04) [a]-na ŠEŠ-ia lu-ú ⌜šu⌝-⌜ul⌝-[m]u
05) ⌜a⌝-na É-i-šu a-na ⌜DAM⌝.⌜MEŠ⌝-i-šu
06) [a-n]a DUMU-e-šu a-na ANŠE.KUR.RA‹-šu› GIŠ.G[IGIR]-šu
07) ⌜ù⌝ a-na lìb-bi KUR-i-šu dan-‹níš› lu-ú [šu]-ul-mu
08) [šu-u]l-ma-nu ša ŠEŠ-ia
09) [NA$_4$ m]é-ku 5 GÚ.UN 5 ṣì-mi-it-⌜tu$_4$⌝ ⌜ANŠE⌝.⌜KUR⌝.⌜RA⌝
10) [šu]-ul-ma-nu ša ŠEŠ-ia
11) [DUM]U ši-ip-ri ša ŠEŠ-ia
12) ⌜ḫa⌝-mu-ta al-ta-ap-⌜ra⌝
13) ù e-né-en-na ŠEŠ-i⌜a⌝ ⌜DUMU⌝ [ši-ip-]r[i-i]a
14) ḫa-mu-ta li-iš-⌜te⌝-⌜ši⌝-⌜ra⌝-a[m-m]a
15) šu-ul-ma-na ša ⌜ŠEŠ⌝-[i]a
16) lu-uš-a-al ù ⌜ša⌝ ḫa[-á]š-ḫ[a-t]a ?
17) i-na ṭup-pi šu-ku-un-ma lu-še-bi-[l]a
18) KÙ.BABBAR ṣa-ar-pa šu-bi-la
19) ŠEŠ-ú-a DUMU ši-ip-ri-ia
20) la-a i-ka-al-la li-iš-[pu]r

Rev.
21) [^{I}]?Bá-áš-tum-me-e
22) ^{I}Ku-né-e-a
23) ^{I}E-til-lu-na
24) [^{I}x-]⌜ru⌝-⌜um⌝-ma
25) ^{I}Uš-bar-ra
26) ^{I}Be-e[l]-⌜ša⌝-a[m]-⌜ma⌝
27) ⌜ŠEŠ⌝-⌜ú⌝-a ⌜l[i⌝-[mé-]š[i-r]a-[š]u-⌜nu⌝[-t]i
28) š[a] i[t]-t[i-] [i]a....
29) a-r[u-]?

EA 37

TRANSLATION

Obv.

(1–7) Speak [t]o the k[in]g of the land [of Egypt,] my [brother], thus [the king of the l]and of Alasia, your [broth]er: It is well with me. [W]ith my brother may all be well. With his house, with his wives, [wit]h his sons, with ‹his› horses (and) his cha[riots] and throughout his territories may it be ve‹ry› [we]ll.

(8–12) As for [the greeti]ng gift for my brother, [ra]w glass, five talents, five teams of horses, are the [gre]eting gift for my brother. The envoy of my brother have I sent post haste.

(13–20) And now, my brother, may he dispatch [m]y ambass[ador] post haste, so that I may inquire about my brother's welfare. And whatever you ⸢desire⸣, put in a letter and I will verily sen[d] (it). Send refined silver. My brother, don't retain my envoy. May he send (him).

Rev.

(21–24) As for Baštummê, Kunêa, Etilluna, [–]r[u]mma, Ušbara, Bē[l]-šamma, my brother, may he release them.....

EA 38

TRANSCRIPTION

Obv. 01) *a-na šàr-ri* KUR *Mi-iṣ-ri* ŠEŠ-*ia qí-*⸢*bí*⸣-⸢*ma*⸣
02) *um-ma šàr-ri* KUR *A-la-*⸢*ši*⸣*-ia* ŠEŠ-*ka-ma*
03) *a-na ia-ši šul-mu ù a-na ka-ša lu-ú šul-*⸢*mu*⸣
04) *a-na* É-*ka* NITLAM$_4$.MEŠ-*ka* DUMU.MEŠ-*ka* ANŠE.KUR.RA.MEŠ-*ka*
05) GIŠ.⸢GIGIR⸣.MEŠ-*ka ù i-na ma-a-du* ÉRIN.MEŠ-*ka*
06) KUR.KUR-*ka* LÚ.MEŠ GAL.GAL-*ka dan-niš* ⸢*lu*⸣*-ú šul-mu*

---

07) *am-mi-ni* ŠEŠ-*ia a-wa-ta an-ni-ta*
08) *a-na ia-ši ta-qáb-bi šu-ú* ŠEŠ-*ia*
09) *la-a i-de*$_4$*-šu a-wa-‹ta›-ma an-ni-ta la-a i-pu-uš*
10) *a-na-ku e-nu-ma* LÚ.MEŠ *ša* KUR *Lu-uk-*⸢*ki*⸣
11) *ša-at-ta ša-ta-ma* ⸢*i*⸣-⸢*na*⸣ KUR-*i*⸢*a*⸣ ⸢URU⸣ ⸢*ṣ*⸣*é-eḫ-ra*
12) *i-lé-qè*

---

13) ŠEŠ-*ḫi at-ta ta-qáb-bi a-na ia-*⸢*ši*⸣
14) LÚ.MEŠ *ša* KUR-*ka it-ti-šu-nu i-ba-aš-ši*
15) *ù a-na-ku* ŠEŠ-*ia la-a i-de*$_4$*-mì ki-i it-ti-šu-nu*
16) *i-ba-aš-ši šum-ma i-ba-aš-ši* ⸢LÚ⸣.MEŠ *ša* KUR-*ia*
17) *ù at-ta a-na ia-ši šu-pur ù a-na-ku*
18) *ki-i* ⸢*lìb*⸣*-bi-ia e-pu-uš*

---

19) *at-ta-ma la-a ti-de*$_4$*-e* LÚ.MEŠ *ša* KUR-*i*[*a*]
20) *la-a e-*⸢*pu*⸣-⸢*uš*⸣ *a-ma-ta an-ni-ta šum-ma*
21) *i-pu-šu* LÚ.MEŠ *ša* KUR-*ia ù at-ta ki-i* ⸢*lìb*⸣*-b*[*i*]-⸢*ka*⸣
22) *e-pu-uš*

---

23) *e-nu-ma* ŠEŠ-*ia ki-i* LÚ.DUMU KIN-*ri-ia*
24) ⸢*la*⸣-⸢*a*⸣ *ta-aš-pur ṭup-pu an-ni-tu*$_4$ ŠEŠ *ša* LUGAL
25) ⸢*li*⸣*-iš-pur ša* ⸢*e*⸣*-pu-*⸢*uš*⸣ [L]Ú DUMU KIN-*ri-*⸢*ka*⸣
Lo.ed. 26) ⸢*i*⸣*-qáb-*⸢*bu*⸣-⸢*ni*⸣

EA 38

TRANSLATION

(1–6) Speak to the king of the land of Egypt, my brother; thus the king of the land of Alashia, your brother: It is well with me; may it be well with you. With your house, your spouses, your sons, your horses, your chariots and within your vast army, your territories, your senior officials, may it be very well.

(7–12) Why, my brother, do you say this thing to me? As for that, does my brother not know it? I did not do this thin‹g›! Now the men of the land of Lycia, year by year, are taking a small town in my land.

(13–18) My brother, you say to me, "Men of your country are with them." But I, my brother, did not know that they are with them. If there are men of my country with them, then you write to me and I will do what I will (with them).

(19–22) You don't know (that there are) men from m[y] country (with them). I did not do this thing! If men of my country did (it) then you do what you will.

(23–26) Now, my brother, since you did not send my envoy back, (here is) this tablet. It is the brother of the king, let him write. Your envoy will tell me what I am to do.

Rev. 27) *⸢ša⸣-ni-tam a-i-‹ú›-tu*$_4$ *a-ba-e-kà a-na*
28) *a-ba-e-ia i-na pá-na-ni e-pu-šu*
29) *a-ma-‹ta› an-ni-ta ù i-na-an-na* ŠEŠ-*ia*
30) *la-a ta-ša-kà-an i-na lìb-bi-ka*

(27–30) Furthermore, which of your fathers did this thing to my fathers in the past? So now, my brother, don't take it to heart.

EA 39

TRANSCRIPTION

Obv. 01) *a-na* LUGAL KUR *Mi-iṣ-ri* Š[E]Š-*ia*
02) *qí-bí-ma*
03) *um-ma* LUGAL KUR *A-la-ši-ia* ŠEŠ-*ka-ma*
04) *a-na ia-ši šul-mu*
05) *ù a-na* UGU-*ka lu-ú šul-mu*
06) *a-na* É-*ka* NITLAM_4.MEŠ-*ka* DUMU-*ka*
07) DAM.MEŠ-*ka* GIŠ.GIGIR.MEŠ-*ka ma-du* ANŠE.KUR.RA.MEŠ-*ka*
08) *ù i-na* KUR *Mi-iṣ-ri* KUR-*ka*
09) *ma-gal lu-ú šul-mu*

---

10) ŠEŠ-*ia* LÚ.DUMU.KIN-*ri-ia*
11) *ḫa-mu-ut-ta na-aṣ-ri-iš*
12) *uš-še-ra-šu-nu ù iš-mé*
13) *šu-lu-um-ka*

---

14) LÚ *an-nu-ú* DAM.GÀR-*ia* ŠEŠ-*ia*
15) *na-aṣ-ri-iš ḫa-mu-*[*ut-t*]*a*
16) *uš-še-ra-šu-nu*
17) LÚ.DAM.GÀR-*ia* GIŠ.MÁ-*ia*
18) ⸢LÚ⸣ *pa-qá-ri-ka ul*
19) *ia-qá-ar-ri-ib*
20) *it-ti-šu-nu*

Rev.

šʿt n wr n ʾÀ-la-śa

EA 39

TRANSLATION

Obv. (1–3) Speak to the king of Egypt, my brother, thus (says) the king of Alashia, your brother:

(4–9) It is well with me. May it be well with you. With your house, your spouses, your son(s), your wives, your chariotry, your many horses, and within Egypt, your country, may it be very well.

(10–13) My brother, as for my messengers send them quickly and safely so that I may hear of your welfare.

(14–16) These men are my merchants. My brother, send them safely (and) quick[l]y.

(17–20) As for my merchant(s) (and) my ship, may your customs' inspector not draw near to them.

Rev. In Hieratic in black ink:

Letter of the great one of Alashia

EA 40

TRANSLATION

Obv.

(01) [*a-na* M]ÁŠKIM *ša* KUR *Mi*[*-iṣ-ri* ŠEŠ*-ia*]
(02) *qí-bí*[*-ma*]
(03) *um-m*[*a* MÁŠKIM *š*]*a* KUR *A-la*[*-ši-ia* ŠEŠ*-ka-*]*ma*
(04) *a-na* ˹*ia*˺(!)-[*ši*] *šul-mu*
(05) *ù a-na* [UGU*-ka*] *lu-ú šul-mu*

---

(06) ŠEŠ-‹*ia*› *a-na* [*m*]*aḫ-r*[*i* ^{I}*Šu-m*]*i-it-ti*
(07) 9 URUDU 2 *ši-in*[*-nu š*]*a* [*p*]*í-ri*
(08) 1 GIŠ *ša* G[IŠ.M[Á] *aš-pu-ru-u*[*š-šu-nu*(?)]
(09) *ù š*[*u-ut mi*]*-im-ma l*[*a*]*-a i-din-n*[*a*]
(10) [*a-n*]*a* [*ia-š*]*i ù at-ta ši-in-n*[*u ša*] ˹*pí*˺-˹*ri*˺
(11) *t*[*a*]*-aš-pu-ra-am-ma* ŠEŠ*-ia*

---

(12) *i-nu-ma a-na šu-ul-ma-ni-ka*
(13) 5 URUDU 3 GÚ.UN URUDU D[Ù]G.G˹A˺
(14) 1 *ši-in-nu ša pí-ri* 1 GIŠ.TAŠKARIN
(15) 1 G[I]Š *ša* GIŠ.MÁ *ul-te-bíl*

---

(16) [*ša*]*-ni-tam* ŠEŠ*-ia* LÚ *an-nu-tu*$_4$
(17) [*ù*] ˹GIŠ˺.MÁ *an-nu-ú ša* LUGAL
(18) [*be-li-i*]*a ù at-ta* ‹GIŠ›.MÁ [*ša* LUGAL]
(19) [*be-li-ia*] *ḫa-mu-ut-ta*
(20) [*na-aṣ-r*]*i-iš šu-pu-ra*[*-am-ma*]

Rev.

(21) [*ù a*]*t-ta* ŠEŠ*-ia* ˹*mi*˺*-n*[*u*]*-u*[*m-me*]
(22) [*š*]*a te-ri-iš-šu ki-ma* [*li-bi-ka*]
(23) *ù a-na-ku i-dì-na-ak*[*-ku*]

---

(24) ˹LÚ˺ *an-nu-ú* ÌR *ša* LUGAL *be-*[*li-ia*]
(25) *ù* LÚ *p*[*a-*]*qá-ri-ka it-ti-*[*šu-*]*nu*
(26) *ul i-qè-ri-ib* UGU*-šu-nu*
(27) *ù at-ta* ŠEŠ*-ia na-aṣ-r*[*i-i*]*š*
(28) *ḫa-mu-ut-ta šu-pu-ra-am-ma*

EA 40

TRANSLATION

(1–5) [To the co]mmissioner of E[gypt, my brother speak; thu[s (says) the commissioner o]f Ala[shiya, your brother]: It is well with m[e]. May it be well with [you].

(6–11) ‹My› brother, to [Šum]itti,
9 (talents) of copper, 2 pieces of [el]ephant ivo[ry],
1 beam for [a ship] I was sending t[hem(?)],
but h[e] didn't giv[e an]ything [t]o [m]e, but you sent ⸢elephant⸣ ivor[y], my brother.

(12–15) Now, as your gift
5 (talents) of copper,
3 (talents) of fine copper,
1 piece of ivory, 1 (beam) of boxwood,
1 (beam) of a ship have I sent.

(16–20) [Mo]reover, my brother, these men [and] this ship belong to the king, [my lord]. So you, the ship [of the king, my lord] quickly (and) [saf]ely send [me] (back).

(21–23) [And y]ou, my brother, [wh]at[ever] that you request, then I will give it to y[ou].

(24–28) These ⸢men⸣ are the servants of the king, [my] lo[rd]. So may your customs' inspector not draw near to them. And you, my brother, safely (and) quickly send (them back to me).

EA 41

TRANSCRIPTION

Obv.

01) [*um-ma* ^{d}UTU-*ši*] ^{I}*Šu-up-pí-*⸢*lu*⸣*-li-u-ma* ⸢LUGAL⸣ G[AL]

02) [*šàr* KUR URU *Ḫ*]*a-*[*a*]*t-ti* ^{KI} *a-na* ^{I}*Ḫu-u-ri-i-*⸢*i*⸣[*a*]

03) [*šàr* KUR URU *Mi*]*-iṣ-ri-i* ^{KI} ŠEŠ-*ia qí-bí-*[*m*]*a*

---

04) [*a-na ia-ši šu*]*l-mu a-na maḫ-ri-ka lu-ú šul-*⸢*mu*⸣

05) [*a-na* DAM.MEŠ-*k*]a DUMU.MEŠ-*ka* É-*ka* ÉRIN.MEŠ-*ka* GIŠ.GIGIR.MEŠ-*ka*

06) [*ù i-*]*na* ⸢*lìb*⸣*-bi* KUR-*ka dan-níš lu-ú šul-mu*

---

07) [L]Ú.MEŠ DUMU.KIN-*ri-ia ša a-na a-bi-ka aš-pu-u-ru*

08) *ù* ⸢*mé*⸣*-re-eš*$_{15}$*-ta ša a-bu-ka e-ri-šu* [*i*]-⸢*na*⸣ *bé-*⸢*e*⸣*-r*[*i-*]*ni*

09) *at-te-ru-tam-*⸢*ma*⸣ *lu-ú ni-ip-pu-*[*u*]*š-mi* ⸢*ù*⸣ ⸢LUGAL⸣(?I.AŠ)

10) *la-a ak-t*[*a-l*]*a mi-nu-me-e ša a-bu-ka id-bu-*⸢*bá*⸣

11) LUGAL(?I.AŠ) *gáb-b*[*á-am-m*]*a lu-ú e-pu-uš ù mé-re-eš*$_{15}$*-ta-*⸢*ia*⸣

12) ⸢*ša*⸣ *a-na a-bi-ka e-ri-šu a-bu-ka mì-im-ma ú-ul*

13) ⸢*ik*⸣*-la gáb-bá-am-ma lu-ú id-dì-na*

---

14) *un-du a-bu-ka bal-*[*ṭ*]*ù šu-bi-la-a-te-*⸢*e*⸣

15) *ša ú-še-bi-la* ŠEŠ-*ia am-mì-ni ták-la-aš-šu-nu-ti*

---

16) *i-na-an-na* ŠEŠ-*ia a-na* GIŠ.GU.ZA *ša a-bi-ka*

17) [*t*]*e-e-te-li ù ki-me-e a-bu-ka ù a-na-ku*

18) *šul-ma-na i-na bé-e-ri-ni ḫa-aš-ḫa-a-nu-ma*

19) *ù i-na-an-na-ma* ⸢*at*⸣*-ta* ⸢*ù*⸣ *a-na-ku i-na be-ri-ni*

20) *ka-an-na lu-ú ṭa-a-bá-a-nu ù mé-re-eš*$_{15}$*-ta* ‹*ša*›

21) *a-*⸢*na*⸣*-*[*k*]*u a-na a-bi-ka aq-bu-ú a-na* ŠEŠ-*ia-ma*

22) [*a-qa-bi a-ḫ*]*u-uz-za-ta i-na bé-e-ri-ni i ni-ip-pu-uš*

EA 41

TRANSLATION

(1–3) [The message of the Sun,] Suppiluliuma, the gr[eat king, [the king of the land of Ḫ]atti; spea[k] to Ḫuriya, [the king of the land of E]gypt, my brother.

(4–6) [It is we]ll [with me; may it be well with you; [with yo]ur [wives], your sons, your household, your troops, your chariots, [and w]ithin your land may it be very well.

(7–13) As for my envoys that I sent to your father and the request that your father requested between us: "Let us establish friendly relations!" then *surely*(?) I did not hold back. Whatever your father said, *surely*(?) I verily carried out and my request that I requested of your father, he did not withhold anything, he verily granted everything.

(14–15) Why have you withheld the shipments that your father sent when your father was alive?

(16–22) Now, my brother, you have ascended the throne of your father, and just as your father and I desired greeting gifts between us, so now may you and I thus enjoy good relations between us, and the request ‹that› I made to your father, to my brother [will I make:] "May we make a [mar]riage agreement between us."

---

23) [mi-im-m]a ša a-na a-bi-ka e-ri-iš-ta
24) [at-ta ŠE]Š-ia la-a ta-kà-al-la-a-šu
25) [...2 ṣ]a-al-ma-a-ni ša KÙ.GI 1-en
26) [li-zi-iz] 1-en li-ši-ib ù 2 ALAM.MEŠ ša MUNUS.MEŠ
27) [ša KÙ.BABBA]R-ma ù NA$_4$.ZA.GÌN ra-bi-ta ù a-na
28) [...k]à-an-na-šu-nu ra-bu-ú ŠEŠ-ia [li-še-bi-la]

Rev. 29) [..........] i[...]⸢e⸣ a \ [.........]
30) [........ul-t]e-bi-la-[m]a ù [...........]
31) [......] ù šum-ma ŠEŠ-ia [ḫa-šeḫ a-na]
32) [na-dá-ni ŠE]Š-ia li-id-dì-in-šu-nu-[ti]
33) [ù šum-m]a ŠEŠ-ia a-na na-a-dá-ni-šu-nu[-ma]
34) [la-]⸢a⸣ ⸢ḫa⸣-šeḫ ki-me-e GIŠ.GIGIR.MEŠ-ia a-na
35) [na-š]e GADA ḫu-uz-zi(!) i-⸢gam⸣-ma-⸢ru⸣-ma a-na ŠEŠ-ia
36) ú-tá-a-ar-šu-nu-ti ù mi-ni-um-me-e
37) ša ŠEŠ-ia ḫa-aš-ḫa-ta ⸢šu⸣-⸢u⸣-⸢up⸣-ra-⸢am⸣-ma
38) lu-še-bíl-ak-ku

---

39) a-nu-um-ma a-na šul-ma-ni-ka 1 bi-ib-ru
40) KÙ.BABBAR UDU.‹A›.LUM 5 ma-na KI.LÁ.BÉ 1 bi-ib-ru
41) KÙ.BABBAR UDU.SIR$_4$ \ pu-u-ḫi-lu 3 ma-na KI.LÁ.BÉ
42) 2 [k]à-ak-kà-ru KÙ.BABBAR 10 ma-na KI.LÁ.BÉ-ma
43) 2 ^{GIŠ}ni-kip-tu$_4$ ra-a-bu-tì ul-te-bíl-ak-ku

(23–28) [As for whatev]er the request to your father, [you,]my [bro]ther, do not withhold. [...two s]tatues of gold: one [may it be standing], one may it be sitting; and two statues of women [of silve]r and much lapis lazuli and for [...] their large [s]tand, [may] my brother [send].

(29–32) I ha]ve sent and [.....] and if my brother [desires....to give...] may my [broth]er give the[m].

(33–38) [But if] my brother does [no]t desire to grant them; my chariots will finish [carr]ying linen *sheets*(?). I will return them to my brother. And whatever my brother desires, write to me that I may send to you.

(39–43) Now, for your greeting gift, one silver rhyton, a ram, five minas in weight, one silver rhyton, a breed ram, three minas in weight, two [ta]lents of silver, ten minas in weight, two large medicinal shrubs, have I sent to you.

EA 42

TRANSCRIPTION

Obv. 01) [*um-ma* ^{d}UTU-*ši* ^{I}*Šu-up-pí-lu-li-u-ma* LUGAL GAL]
02) [*šàr* KUR URU *Ḫa-at-ti*^{KI} *a-na* ^{I}*Ḫu-u-ri-i-ia*]
03) [*šàr* KUR URU *Mi-iṣ-ri-i*^{KI} ŠEŠ-*ia qí-bi-ma*]
[——————————————————————————————————]
04) [*a-na ia-ši šul-mu a-na maḫ-ri* ŠEŠ-*ia*]
05) *lu-*⸢*ú*⸣ ⸢*šul*⸣-⸢*mu*⸣ ⸢*a*⸣-⸢*na*⸣ D[AM.MEŠ-*ka* DUMU.MEŠ-*ka*]
06) LÚ.MEŠ GAL-*ka a-na* ÉRIN[.MEŠ-*ka* ANŠE.KUR.RA-*ka*]
07) GIŠ.GIGIR.MEŠ-*ka ù i-n*[*a lìb*⸣-*bi* KUR-*ka dan-niš lu-ú šul-mu*]
———————[————————]
08) ŠEŠ-*ia ki-a-am ši-mé*[..............................]
09) *a-ba a-bi-ni iš-tu* K[UR............................]
10) [*šum-*]*ma iš-tu* KUR URU *Ḫu*[*r-ri* ....]
11) [*šum-ma*] ⸢*iš*⸣-*tu* KUR-*tì* [...........................]
12) *i-la-k*[*am*[.......................................]
13) *a-na pá-ni* [......................]⸢*ša*⸣[...........]
14) *li-iš-al-ma*
——————————[—————]
15) *ù i-na-an-na ṭup-pá-ka ša* [*ta-aš-pu-ra-a*]
16) *šum-ka e-li šum-ia am-mi-*⸢*ni*⸣[*tù-ra-ab-bi*]
17) *ù ma-an-nu ša ba-a-na-a-ti* [*i-na bé-ri-ni*]
18) *uš-*⸢*bal*⸣*-kat-ma pár-ṣú ki-na-an*[*-na-ma*]
19) ŠEŠ-*ia aš-šum-ma sú-lum-me-e* [*i-na bé-ri-ni*]
20) *ta-aš-pu-u-ra-a ù šum-ma* [*ki-na-an-na-ma šum-ka*]
21) *am-mi-*ni_7 *tù-ra-ab-bi ù a-*[*na-ku ki-ma*]
22) [*n*]*a-pu-ul-tì ki-a-am ḫa-as*[*-sa-ku šu-mi ša*]
23) [*ṭu*]*p-šar* ^{I}*Ru-mi-in-*⸢*ta*⸣(?)[.......................]
24) [*aš*]*-ṭur ù šum-ka* [...............................]
25) [*a-pá-a*]*š-ši-iṭ ù* [.................................]
26) [.......]*na la-a la*[..............................]
[——]———[——————————]
Rev. 27) [*um-ma*]*-a* LÚ *ṭup-šar* ⸢*ša*⸣ [........................]
28) [*ki-a*]*-ma la-a ti-iz-z*[*i-iz-ma*]
[——]———[——————————]

EA 42

TRANSLATION

(1–3) [Thus (says) the Sun, Suppiluliuma, the great king, the king of the land of Ḫatti; speak to Ḫuria(?), king of the land of Egypt, my brother]

[——————————————————————————————]

(4–7) [It is well with me; with my brother] may it be well. [With your wives, your children,] your senior officials, with [your] troop[s, your horses], your chariotry and wi[thin your land may it be very well.]

(8–14) My brother, thus hear [...]the father of our father from the l[and of...I]f from the land of Ḫur[ri...If] from the land of [...]he shall com[e...] before the presence of [...]that[...] may he inquire.

(15–18) And now, as for your tablet that [you sent to me], why did [you magnify] your name over my name? And who nullified the good relations [between us]? Is the correct practice thu[s]?

(19–22) My brother, was it concerning peace [between us] that you wrote? And if [so, your name,] why did you exalt? And I] am consid[ered thus like] a corpse?

(22–26) [The name of] the scribe is Ruminta [....I have] written and your name [...I will blo]t out [...]no [...].

(27–28) [Thu]s (says) the scribe of [....Th]us do not stan[d....]

EA 43

TRANSCRIPTION

About three lines missing

Obv. 01) [..a-*n*]*a-ku a-na* UGU[…]
02) […*t*]*i*? *an-ni-ta*$_5$ DUMU[-*šu* GAL?]
03) […*ip*-]⸢*pu*⸣-*ša-aš-šu i-na* […]
04) […] LÚ.MEŠ *ṣa-ab-ru-tì*
05) […] *an-ni-ta*$_5$ *ša it-ti-šu*
06) […]*du-šu ù i-du-ku-šu*
07) […] *i-de a-na pa-ni* DINGIR.MEŠ

---

08) […]⸢*ti*$_7$⸣-*di-i ki-i a-bu-šu*
09) […]⸢*ip*⸣-*pu-uš ki-i* ⸢*a*⸣-⸢*bu*⸣-*šu*
10) […] *it*-⸢*ta*⸣-⸢*al*⸣-*la-ak*
11) […]*a-na-aṣ-ṣa-ar*-⸢*šu*⸣-*nu-ma*
12) […*gáb*-]*bá-šu-nu ù* DUMU-*šu* GAL
13) […]*tì ša a-bi-šu*
14) […]*dam-qí-iš ki-i* ⸢*ip*⸣-*pu-ša-aš-šu*
15) […]*la-a ti*$_7$-*di-i*
16) […] *at-ta la-a ti*$_7$-[*di-i*]
17) […]*ma ma-am-ma la-a* […]
18) […] *ù* ⸢*šu*⸣-⸢*ú*⸣ […]
19) […] traces? […]

Lo.ed. Uninscribed

Rev. 20) […] traces […]
21) […] traces ⸢*li*⸣[…]
22) [……………]
23) […]-⸢*ma*⸣?-⸢*a*⸣ L[UGAL?…]
24) […Ḫ]I.A *ba-n*[*a*…]
25) […] *bal i-n*[*a*…]
26) […x ⸢*an*⸣-*nu*-⸢*tim*⸣ […]
27) […]NA$_4$ ZA.GÌN *i-n*[*a*…]
28) […NA$_4$ Z]A.GÌN GAL SIG$_5$ *l*[*i*…]

EA 43

TRANSLATION

About three lines missing

(1–7) [...]⸢I⸣ to [...] this [...his elder?] son [...he] did to him in [...]malicious men [...] this which is with him [...]they ...him and they slew him [...] I know in the presence of the gods.

(8–19) [...] you know that his father [...] did as his father (had done) [...]he was going out [...]I will protect them [...a]ll of them and his elder son [...] of his father [...]it is well that he is doing to him [...]you do not know [...] you do not know [...] anything [...] not [...] and he [...]

ev. 20) [...] *traces* [...]
21) [...] *traces* ...[...]
22) [..............]
23) [...]...k[ing?...]
24) [...]...nic [e...]
25) [...]x i[n...]
26) [...]x these [...]
27) [...]*lapis lazuli* i[n...]
28) [...*la*]*piz lazuli* large and attractive [...]

29) [...*ša*] ŠEŠ-*ia ḫa-šiḫ*
30) [...] *a-na-* ⸢*ku*⸣?
31) [...] *šu* [...]

---

32) [*a-nu-um-ma a-na šu-*]*ul-m*[*a-ni-ka...*]
33) [ ] traces
34) [.................................]
35) [ ] traces

29) [...that] my brother desires
30) [...] ⸢I⸣?
31) [...] he [...]

---

32) [Now for your] greeting [gift...]
33) [ ] *traces*
34) [.................................]
35) [ ] *traces*

EA 44

TRANSCRIPTION

Obv. 01) *a-na be-lí šàr* KUR [UR]U *Mi-iṣ-ri-*⸢*i*⸣
02) *a-bi-ia qí-bí-*⸢*ma*⸣
03) *um-ma* ^{I}*Zi-*⸢*i*⸣*-*⸢*dan*⸣ DUMU LUGAL
04) DUMU-*ka-ma*

---

05) *a-na ma-ḫar be-lí a-bi-ia*
06) *gáb-ba lu-ú šul-mu*

---

07) *i-na maḫ-ri-i* KASKAL *a-i-ú-tì*
08) DUMU.MEŠ KIN-*ri-ka a-na* KUR URU *Ḫa-at-ti*
09) *it-tal-ku ù ki-i-me-e a-na muḫ-ḫi-ka*
10) *it-it-as-ḫa-ru ù a-na-ku-ma*
11) *a-na ak-ka-a-ša a-bi-ia*
12) ⸢*šul*⸣*-ma-na aš-pur ù šu-bi-il*$_5$*-ta*
13) [*a-n*]*a muḫ-ḫi-ka ul-te-*⸢*bíl*⸣

---

14) [………….. DUMU.]MEŠ KIN-*ka*
15) […………………*e*]*l*
16) […………………]*aš-p*[*ur*](*?*)

Lo.ed. 17) [……………………………………]

Rev. 18) […………]⸢*a*⸣-⸢*nu*⸣*-um-ma* DUMU.MEŠ KIN-⸢*ka*⸣
19) [*iš-tu* KU]R URU *Ḫa-at-ti a-na muḫ-ḫi-ka*
20) [*ú-ka-ši-is-*]*sú-nu-ti ù a-na-ku-ma*
21) [*i*]*t-ti* DUMU.MEŠ KIN-*ka at-tu-ia* DUMU.MEŠ KIN-*ia*
22) *a-na muḫ-ḫi a-bi-ia aš-pur-šu-nu-ti*
23) *ù šu-*⸢*bi*⸣*-il*$_5$*-ta* 16 LÚ.MEŠ
24) *a-na šul-ma-ni-ka ul-te-bíl-ak-ku*

---

25) *ù a-*⸢*na*⸣*-ku* [KÙ.]GI ⸢*ḫa*⸣*-aš-ḫa-ku*
26) *ù a-bu-*[*i*]*a* KÙ.GI *šu-bi-la*
27) *ù mi-nu-um-me-e be-lí a-bi-ia*
28) *ḫa-aš-ḫa-tá šu-up-ra-ma ú-*⸢*še*⸣*-bíl-ak-ku*

EA 44

TRANSLATION

(1–4) Speak to the lord, king of the land of the [ci]ty of Egypt, my father; thus Zidan, the son of the king, your son.

(5–6) May all be well with the lord, my father.

(7–13) With a previous caravan of any of your envoys, they came to the land of the city of Ḫatti, and when they returned to you, then it was I who sent a greeting gift to you, my father, and I had a shipment sent to you.

(14–17)[…………] your [ambass]adors […….] I sent(?) [……..]

(18–24) […………] Now, as for your envoys, [I am expediting] them on their way [from the la]nd of the city of Ḫatti to you and it is I who am sending [w]ith your own envoys, my envoys and a shipment of sixteen men have I had brought to you as a greeting gift.

(25–28) And I desire [go]ld, so, my father, send gold and whatever my lord, my father, you desire, write to me and I will have it brought to you

---

EA 45

TRANSCRIPTION

Obv. 01) [*a-na* LUGAL]⸢^{d}⸣UTU-*ši* [EN-*ia qí-bí-ma*]
02) [*um-ma* ^{I}*Am-m*]*i-is-tam-*[*ri* ÌR-*ka*]
03) [*a-na* UZU.GÌR.MEŠ]-*ka* 7[*ù* 7 *am-qut*]
04) [*lu-ú šul-mu a-na*] UG[U LUGAL ^{d}UTU-*ši*]
05) [EN-*ia a-na* É.]ḪI.A-*k*[*a* MUNUS.UŠ-*ka* DAM.MEŠ-*ka*]
06) [DUMU.MEŠ-*ka* ÉRIN.MEŠ *pí-ṭá-t*]*i-*[*ka ù mi-im-mu*]
07) [LUGAL ^{d}UTU-*ši* EN-*ia*] ⸢*lu*⸣[-*ú šul-mu*]

---

08) [..]
09) [..]
10) [..]
11) [..]
12) [..........]x-*ni-šu-nu* DUMU(?)[*ši-ip-ri-šu*.......]
13) [*ù a-k*]*án*^{an}-*na-am a-na-ku* [*aq-ta-bi*]
14) [*an-nu-*]*tu*$_{4}$ *šu-nu* LÚ.MEŠ [KUR *Mi-iṣ-ri*]
15) *am-mi-ni-im-ma a-na-a*[*n-din-šu-nu-ma*...]
16) *ù ú-še-šar an-n*[*u-tu*$_{4}$...]
17) *ù i-ra-aš-ši-š*[*u-nu ù*]
18) *ad-*⸢*din*⸣-*šu-nu-ma a*[-*na* ^{d}UTU-*ši* EN-*ia*]
19) *ù* ⸢DUMU⸣ *ši-ip-ri-*⸢*i*⸣[*a*...]
20) *a-na pa-ni* ^{d}UTU-*ši* [EN-*ia*...]
21) *i-*⸢*na*⸣-*an-na ad-d*[*in-šu-nu-ma*]

-----

22) [*ša*]-⸢*ni*⸣-*tam šàr* KUR[*Mi-iṣ-ri*...]
23) ⸢*am*⸣-*mi-ni-mi* D[UMU.MEŠ *ši-ip-ri-ia*]
24) *ta-ṣa-bat-mi* [*a-na ia-ši*]
Rev. 25) *iš-pur-ma* 2-*šu* [*iš-pur*]
26) *ù ki-ia-am iq*[-*ta-bi*]
27) *ù a-na* KUR *Mi-iš*-[*ri-mi.*]
28) *šum-ma-mi tu-še-bá*[-*al-šu-nu*]
29) *a-nu-um-*⸢*ma*⸣ ⸢ÌR⸣ ⸢*ša*⸣ ⸢LUGAL⸣ ⸢^{d}⸣[UTU-*ši* EN-*ia a-na-ku*]

EA 45

TRANSLATION

(1–7) [Speak to the king,] the sun god,[my lord; the message of ʿAmm]i-stam[ri, your servant. At] your [feet] seven (times) [and seven (times) have I fallen. May it be well] wi[th the king, the sun god, my lord, with] yo[ur pala]ce, [your chief wife, your (other) wives, your sons, your regular troo]ps, [and the possessions of the king, the sun god, my lord,] may [it be well].

(8–11) [...]

(12–21) [...] their [his(?)] ambas[sadors...and th]us I myself [said, "As for th]ese, they are men of [the land of Egypt(?)."] Why should I gi[ve them...] so I am preparing (their sendoff?). These...] and he will acquire th[em and] I have given them t[o the sun god, my lord,] and m[y] envoys [...] before the sun god, [my lord ...] have I now gr[anted them.]

(22–29) [Fu]rthermore, the king of the land of [Egypt(?)...] wrote [to me], "Why do you seize [my] am[bassadors?"] Two times [did he write] and thus he s[poke,] "And to the land of Egy[pt, if you will sen[d them."] Now [I] am the servant of the s[un god, my lord.]

---

30) *ša-ni-tam as-sú-ri-im-*[*ma* ^{d}UTU-*ši* EN-*ia*]
31) *it-ti-ia i-na-ki-ir-m*[*a* ^{d}UTU EN-*ia*]
32) TI.LA.MEŠ *ba-la-a-ṭá ša-a* U[ZU.ZI-*ia*]
33) *li-iq-bi* TI.LA.MEŠ UZU.⸢ZI⸣[-*ia*...]
34) lu-ú *i-*de_4*-mi šum-ma-mi* [ÌR *ki-it-ti*]
35) [*a-n*]*a* KUR URU ⸢*Ú*⸣-⸢*ga*⸣-⸢*ri*⸣-[*ta*....]
36) [.....]⸢*ú*⸣?-[*nu-te-šu-nu*..........]
37) [................................]
38) [................................]
39) [................................]
40) [................................]
41) [......*ú-n*]*u-te*[-*šu-nu*............]
42) [LÚ.ME]Š-*i*⸢*a*⸣[....................]
43) [.......] *a* [......................]
44) [.......]*ú-*[*nu-te-šu-nu*...........]
45) [.......] *ri*[......................]
46) [......] *a-na* [.....................]
47) [.....]ÌR-*š*[*u*......................]
Up.ed. 48) [.................................]

(30–35) Furthermore, god forbid that [the sun god, my lord] should become alienated from me! May [the sun god, my lord, pronounce the breath of life for my soul. The breath of life for my soul is [from him(?)] and he surely knows whether [there is a loyal servant i]n the land of Ugari[t...].

(36–48) [...their] eq[uipment........their equ]ipment[...] my [men...their] eq[uipment....] to [.....]hi[s] servant [...].

EA 46

TRANSCRIPTION

Obv. 01) ⸢LÚ⸣.⸢AB⸣.B[A-*e-ia*......................]
02) *ù* ^{d}U[TU-*ši be-li*........................]
03) *la tu-b*[*a*...............................]
04) *ša a-na pa*[*-ni*............................]
05) *kán-na-am-m*[*a*..........................]
06) *ša* ^{d}UTU-*ši* [............................]
07) *am-mi-ni*$_{7}$ *pa-n*[*i-šu*.......................]
08) *iš-tu muḫ-ḫi-i*⸢*a*⸣ [........................]
09) LÚ.AB.BA-*e-ia*[.........................]
10) ⸢*ù*⸣ *pa-nu-šu-nu ša* [......................]
11) *a-na muḫ-ḫi* LÚ.D[UMU.KIN-*ri*...........]
12) *ù ú-nu-t*[*e*.............................]
13) *ú-še-*[*bi-il*..............................]
14) 1-*šu*...................................]
15) SAG.D[U ....]

Lo.ed. 16) *be-li* [..................................]
17) *ù* K[UR..............................]

Rev. 18) *a-na* LÚ.[DUMU.KIN-*ri*.................]
19) *ša ir-te-*[*ḫu*..............................]
20) *ù a-na pa-ni* [..........................]
21) *ù* ^{d}UTU-*ši be-*[*li*.........................]

---

22) ^{d}UTU-*ši be-li k*[*i-ma pa-na-nu*.............]
23) LÚ.AB.BA-*e-ia* [.........................]
24) *ù* ^{d}UTU-*ši be-li* [*ù i-na-an-na*..............]
25) *a-na-ku* LÚ.ÌR ^{d}U[TU-*ši be-li-ia ù*...........]
26) ⸢*a*⸣-⸢*na*⸣ ⸢^{d}⸣⸢UTU⸣-*ši be-l*[*i*.................]

---

27) *ù* ^{d}UTU-*ši* [*be-li*.........................]
28) ⸢*li*⸣-*še-bi-i*[*l*.............................]
29) [......................................]

EA 46

TRANSLATION

bv. 01) [my] father[s............................]
02) and the su[n god, my lord,..............]
03) you did not se[ek.......................]
04) which is in the pre[sence of.............]
05) thus [.................................]
06) of the sun god [.........................]
07) why is [his] fa[ce.......................]
08) from me[..............................]
09) my fathers [...........................]
10) and their faces, viz. of [..................]
11) to the envoy(s) [..................
12) and the equipment [....................]
13) I have sent [...........................]
14) one time [.............................]
15) hea[d] (capital?)........................]

.ed. 16) [my] lord [.............................]
17) and the l[and of.........................]
ev. 18) to the am[bassador(s)....................]
19) that rema[in...........................]
20) and in the presence of [....................]
21) and the sun god [my] lord...............]

---

22) Oh sun god, my lord, jus[t as formerly.....]
23) my fathers [............................]
24) and the sun god, my lord,[*and now*........]
25) I am the servant of the su[n god, my lord, and]
26) to the sun god, [my] lord[................]

---

27) and the sun god, [my lord................]
28) may he sen[d...........................]
29) [.....................................]

EA 47

TRANSCRIPTION

Obv. 01) [....................................]
02) [....................................]
03) [....................................]
04) [....................................]
05) [....................................]
06) [....................................]⸢*ni*⸣
07) [........................KU]R.KI-*ka*
08) [..................*k*]*a* LÚ.AB.BA.MEŠ-*ia*
09) [*a-na* LÚ.AB.BA.]⸢MEŠ⸣-*ka* ÌR.MEŠ-*ta i-pu-šu*
10) [*ù i-n*]*a-an-na a-na-ku a-na* LUGAL ^{d}UTU-*ši*
11) [EN-*i*]*a lu-ú* ÌR.MEŠ-*ma*

---

12) [*ša-ni-tam*] LÚ.DUMU.KIN-*ri-ia a-na muḫ-ḫi* EN-*ia*
13) [*al-ta-*]⸢*pár*⸣ *ù* EN-*ia la iš-al-šu*
14) [*ù a-na g*]*áb-bi* LÚ.DUMU.KIN-*ri ša* LUGAL.E.NE
15) [*ta-n*]*a-an-din ṭup-pa-ka ta-šap-pár*
Lo.ed. 16) [LÚ.]DUMU.KIN-*ri-ka it-ti-šu-nu*
17) [*ta-ša-*]⸢*pár*⸣ *ù a-na ša ia-a-ši*
Rev. 18) [*ù a-na* LÚ.DU]MU.KIN-*ri-ia ṭup-p*[*a-k*]*a*
19) [*la-a ta-ad*]-⸢*din*⸣ ⸢*ù*⸣ LÚ.DUMU.KIN-*ri-ka*
20) [*it-ti-š*]*u la-*⸢*a*⸣ *ta-áš-pur*
21) [*ú-ul ki*]*-ma* ⸢*ki*⸣-*it* UZU *lìb-bi-ia*

---

22) [*ša-ni-tam am*]-⸢*mi*⸣-⸢*ni*⸣ *te*$_{9}$*-še-em-me*
23) [*a-na a-w*]*a-*⸢*te*⸣⸢^{MEŠ}⸣ ⸢*ša*⸣-⸢*a*⸣ ^{I}*Ḫa-an-ia*
24) [...] ⸢*ša*⸣-⸢*a*⸣ *al-li-i*ʾ
25) [LUGAL ^{d}UTU-*ši*] ⸢EN⸣-*ia be-li mi-*⸢*na*⸣-*a*
26) [*a-na ša-a* ^{I}*Ḫa-a*]*n-ia šul-ma-*⸢*an*⸣-*šu*
27) [................]⸢*ù*⸣ ⸢*šum*⸣-⸢*ma*⸣
28) [.................*a-n*]*u-ma*
29) [....................E]N-*ia*
30) [....................................]

EA 47

TRANSLATION

(1–6) [...

(7–11) [...]your [la]nd [...yo]ur [...] my fathers [were subservient [to] your [father]s. [And n]ow I am verily subservient to the king, the sun god, [my lord].

(12–21) [Furthermore, I se]nt my envoy to my lord, but my lord did not inquire of him. [But to a]ll the envoys of the kings [you g]ive and you send your tablet. Your envoy you send with them. [But to] my [am]bassador [you did not gi]ve your tablet and your envoy you did not send [with h]im. [This is not] in accor]dance with the loyalty of my heart.

(22–30) [Furthermore, w]hy do you listen [to the wor]ds of Ḫanya [...] which (?) [the king, the sun god,] my lord. My lord, why [to] the greeting gift of [Ḫa]nya [...] But if [...N]ow [...]

EA 48

TRANSCRIPTION

Obv.
01) [*a-na.........b*]*e-le-ti-ia*
02) [*um-ma........ḫ*]*é-bá* GÉME-*ki*
03) [*a-na* GÌR.MEŠ *be-le-t*]*i-ia am-qut*
04) [*a-na* UGU *be-le-ti-*]⌜*i*⌝*a lu-ú šul-mu*

---

05) [................*t*]*a-at-ta-ad-ni*
06) [..........*ù a-nu*]*-um-ma a-na-ku*
07) [...............*a-n*]*a be-le-ti-ia*
08) [.............]DUG.KAŠ *ri-qú*\\ *ṣú-ur-wa*

EA 48

TRANSLATION

(1–4) [To (woman's name)] my [l]ady, [the message of (…)-Ḫ]eba, your handmaiden. [At the feet of] my [lad]y have I fallen. [With] my [lady] may all be well.

(5–8) [……….y]ou have given to me [……and n]ow I [….t]o my lady […….] a beer jar of aromatics \\ balsam

---

EA 49

TRANSCRIPTION

Obv. 01) *a-na* LUGAL ^{d}UTU-*ši* EN-*ia*
02) *um-ma* ^{I}*Níq-ma-*^{d}IŠKUR ÌR-*ka-ma*
03) *a-na* UZU.GÌR.MEŠ LUGAL ^{d}UTU-*ši* EN-*ia am-qut*
04) *lu-ú šu*[*l*]*-mu a-na* ⌜UGU⌝ LUGAL! ^{d}UTU-*ši* EN-*ia*
05) É.[ḪI.A-*š*]*u* ⌜*a*⌝-⌜*na*⌝ NI[TLAM$_{4}$]-*šu a-na* DAM.MEŠ-*šu*
06) *a-na* [DUMU.MEŠ-*šu a-na* ANŠE.KUR.RA-*šu*] É[RIN].Ḫ[I].⌜A⌝ *pí-ṭá-ti*
07) *a-*[*n*]*a* [GIŠ.GIGIR.MEŠ-*šu*........ *ša* LUGAL] ⌜^{d}⌝UTU-*ši* EN-*ia*
08) [...]
09) [...]
10) [...]
11) [...]
12) [...]
Lo.ed. 13) [...]
14) [...]
Rev. 15) [...]
16) [...]
17) [...]
18) [.........................]⌜*ú*⌝(?) [...] ⌜*a*⌝*-bi-ia pa-na-n*⌜*u*⌝
19) [.........................] ⌜*ù*⌝ *be-li-ia* 2 *ṣú-ḫa-*[*ri*]
20) L[Ú].É.GAL ⌜*ša*⌝ KUR *Ka-ši*
21) *li-din-an-ni*
22) *ù* LÚ.DUMU É.GAL A.ZU-*a*
23) *id-na-an-ni*
24) *an-na-ka* LÚ.A.ZU-*ú*
25) *ia-nu a-n*[*u-*]*ma* [^{I}*Ḫa*]*-ra-ma-sa*
26) *sa-al* ⌜*ù*⌝ (erasure)
Lft.ed. 27) *ù a-nu-*⌜*ma*⌝ [...]
28) *ù* 1 *me-at* [...]
29) *a-na šul-m*[*a-ni-ka*]

EA 49

TRANSLATION

(1–3) To the king, the sun god, my lord, the message of Niqmaddu, your servant. At the feet of the king, my lord, have I fallen.

(4–7) May it be well with the king, the sun god, my lord, his household, with his consort, with his wives, with [his sons, with his horses,] the regular troops, with [his chariots,...of the king,] the sun god, my lord.

(8–17) (Entirely missing)

(18–21) [...] ⌜and⌝(?) [...] my father, formerly [...] and my lord. May he give to me two youths, palace personnel of the land of Cush.

(22–26) And give to me a palace retainer, a physician. There is no physician here. Now ask [Ḫa]ramassa ⌜and⌝ (erasure).

(27–29) And now [...] and one hundred [...] for [your] greeting [gift].

EA 50

TRANSCRIPTION

Obv.	01)	*a-na* ^{MUNUS}*T*[*a-ḫa-mu-un-šu* (?)]
	02)	^{MUNUS}NIN-*i*⸢*a*⸣ [*qí-bí-ma*]
	03)	*um-ma* DUMU.⸢MUNUS⸣ [LUGAL(?)]
	04)	MUNUS.GÉME *am-t*[*i-ki*]
	05)	*a-na* 2 GÌR.MEŠ-[*pí*(?) *ša*]⸢^{MUNUS}⸣⸢NIN⸣-*ia*
	06)	[7]-*šu* 7-*ta*-[*a-an*]
	07)	[*am*]-*qut al*[-*lu-ú-mi*]
	08)	slight traces
	09)	[.........................]
	10)	[.........................]
Rev.	11)	⸢*zu*⸣-⸢*ka*⸣-*ti*
	12)	^{MUNUS}NIN-*ia*

EA 50

TRANSLATION

(1–12) [Speak] to the [royal wife(?)], my lady, the message of the daughter of [the king(?) your] handmaiden. At the two feet [of] my lady, seven times and seven ti[mes] [have I fa]llen. Be[hold.......] the illness(?) of my lady.

EA 51

TRANSCRIPTION

Obv. 01) [*a-n*]*a* ^{d}UTU-*ši* LUGAL *be-lí-ia* LUGAL KUR *Mi-iṣ-ri*
02) [*u*]*m-ma* ^{Id}IŠKUR-*ni-ra-*⸢*ri*⸣ ÌR-*ka-ma*
03) [*a-n*]*a* GÌR.MEŠ *be-lí-*[*i*]*a am-qut*
04) [*a-*]⸢*mur*⸣ ⸢*e*⸣*-nu-ma* ^{I}*Ma-*⸢*an*⸣*-aḫ-pí-ia* LUGAL KUR *Mi-iṣ-ri a-bi a-b*[*i*]*-ka*
05) ⸢^{I}⸣[*T*]*a*[*-ku a-b*]⸢*i*⸣ ⸢*a*⸣*-b*[*i-*]*ia i-na* KUR *Nu-ḫa-aš-še*
06) *a-na šàr-ru-ta*$_5$ *i-ip-p*[*u-š*]*a-aš-šu ù* Í.MEŠ *a-na* SAG.⸢DU⸣-⸢*šu*⸣
07) *iš-ku-un-šu ù ki-a-a*[*m i*]*q-*⸢*ta*⸣*-bi ša* LUGAL ⸢KUR⸣ [*Mi-iṣ-r*]*i*
08) *a-na šàr-ru-ta*$_5$ *ša i-ip-pu-š*[*a-aš-šu ù* Í.MEŠ *a-na* SAG.DU-*šu*]
09) *ša iš-ku-un-šu ma-am-ma* [*la*..........................]
10) *it-ta-din-šu qa-d*[*u*..................................]
11) *a-nu-*⸢*um*⸣*-*[*ma*....................................]

Rev. 01) *ù* [..]
02) ^{I}*Ta-ku a-*⸢*bi*⸣[*a-bi-ia*..................................]
03) *ù i-na-an-na be-lí-ni ṭ*[*up-pa-te*^{MEŠ} *ù ri-ik-sa-te*............]
04) *ù* LUGAL KUR *Ḫa-at-ti*$_7$ *a-na m*[*uḫ-ḫi-ia*.................]
05) *be-lí ṭup-pa-te*^{MEŠ} *ù ri-ik-*[*sa-te*.........................]
06) *ù a-na ša* LUGAL KUR *Mi-iṣ-ri* [ÌR *ki-it-ti a-na-ku*........]

---

07) *ù i-na-an-na be-li-ni a-na mu*[*ḫ-ḫi-ni li-ṣa-an-ni*............]
08) *ù a-na* ŠU-⸢*ti*⸣-⸢*šu*⸣ ⸢*lu*⸣[*-ú ni-iṣ-bat* KUR.MEŠ]
09) *ù* ⸢*lu*⸣[*-ú nu-tar*] *a-na be-li-ni*
10) [*ù be*]*-lí-ia i-na* MU.KAM.MEŠ ⸢*li*⸣*-iz-zi*[*-za*]
11) *lu-ú la te-me-ek-e* ⸢*ki*⸣*-i-me-e a-na* ÌR-*du-ut-ti*
12) *a-na ša be-lí-ia lu-ú ki-it-tu*$_4$ *ta-mar-šu-*⸢*nu*⸣
13) *ù šum-ma be-lí-ia a-na a-ṣi-i-im la* ⸢*i*⸣*-ma-an-gur*$_{16}$
14) *ù be-lí-ia* 1-*en* ⸢LÚ⸣ *mi-il-kà-šu*

Up.ed. 15) [*q*]*a-du* ÉRIN.MEŠ-*šu ù* ⸢*qa*⸣*-du* GIŠ.GIGIR.MEŠ-*šu li-iš-pur*

Lft.ed. 16) [..........................ME]Š-*šu ša be-lí-i*[*a*]
17) [..........................]⸢*be*⸣*-lí-ia*

EA 51

TRANSLATION

(1–3) [T]o the Sun, the king, my lord, king of the land of Egypt, thus Adad-nirari, your servant: [A]t the feet of my lord have I fallen.

(4–11) [Lo]ok, when Manaḫpiya, king of the land of Egypt, the father of your father, would appoint [T]a[ku, the fath]er [of] my [fath]er to kingship in the land of Nuǵasse, then he poured oil on his head and thu[s] he said, "Whom the king of E[gypt] has app[ointed]to kingship [and] poured [oil on his head], [let not] anyone [.......] He gave [....] Now [.......]

Rev.
(1–6) And [...] Taku, the father of my fat[her...] And now, our lord, ta[blets and treaties...] And the king of the land of Ḫatti [*has sent*(?)] to [me], my lord, tablets and trea[ties]. My lord, [I *rejected*(?)] the tablets and tre[aty agreements] and [I am the loyal servant] of the king of Egypt [.......]

(7–17) And now [may] our lord [come forth] t[o us], and into [h]is power [*we will*] in[deed *seize the lands*] and indeed [we will return them] to our lord. [So] may our lord take a stand here this year. Do not be neglectful. You will see that they are loyal to the service of the king, my lord. And if my lord is not willing to come forth himself, may my lord send one of his advisors [to]gether with his troops and with his chariotry [...]of m[y] lord [...] my lord.

EA 52

TRANSCRIPTION

Obv. 01) ⸢*a*⸣*-na šàr* KUR *Mi-iṣ-ri* ^{KI}
02) *um-ma* ^{I}*A-ki-iz-zi* ÌR-*ka-ma*
03) *i-na* 7 *a-na* GÌR *b*[*e-l*]*-ia*
04) ^{d}IŠKUR-*ia am-qut*

---

05) *a-*⸢*mur*⸣ ⸢*be*⸣*-*⸢*li*⸣*-ia ṭup-pá-te-šu* [*li-im-mu*]*r*
06) É.⸢ḪI⸣.⸢A⸣ URU *Qa*[*t*]*-na*⸢^{KI}⸣ *ù a-na* ŠU
07) ⸢*be*⸣*-*⸢*li*⸣*-ia -m*[*a*]

---

08) [*a-nu-u*]*m-ma* [......................]*ka*
09) [...............................]
10) [...............................]
11) [......................*i*]*d-du-*[*u*]*k-ku*
12) [.......................] ⸢*ša*⸣ *be-*[*li*]*-ia*
13) [...............................]
14) [....................*š*]*a a*[*-na*.....]
15) [......................]⸢*i*⸣*-na-an-din*
16) [...................*i-na-*]*an-din-šu-nu*
17) [........................] *a-bu-tù-ni*
18) [........................*a-n*]*a* LUGAL
19) [...................*i-na-an-d*]*in-šu-nu*
20) [....................*a-bu-t*]*ù-*[*ni-ma*]
21) [...............................]
22) [...............................]
Lo.ed 23) [...............................]
24) [...............................]
Rev. 25) [...............................]
26) [..............]*šir*[..............]

EA 52

TRANSLATION

(1–4) To the king of the land of Egypt, the message of Akizzi, your servant. Sevenfold at the foot of my lord, my Storm God, have I fallen.

(5–7) Behold, my lord, [may he examine] his tablets, the palace of the city of Qatna, is in my lord's hand.

(8–24) [No]w [...]your [...........]they attacked [...] of my lord [.......... wh]ich to[......]he will give [....he will] give them [...]our fathers [...t]o the king [...he will gi]ve them [...our fa]th[ers]..
...........]

(25–26) [...]

---

27) [..........................]*a-li-k*[*a*]
28) [..........................*b*]*e-li-ia*
29) [.............................*n*]*u*
30) [...................KUR *Ḫa-a*]*t-te*^{KI}
31) [.....................]*ti iš-ri-iq-šu-nu*

---

32) [...........................]*ia i-na* 2-*šu*
33) [.........................]*ú uṣ-ṣú-n*[*im-ma*]
34) [.........................*i-n*]*a* DUB-*ia*
35) [.........*l*]*i*[.....................]

---

36) [*an-n*]*a-kám* 3 MU *be-li-ia*
37) *e-nu-ma a-n*[*a* E]*N-ia* ⸢*ú*⸣[-*u*]*t-ta-nam-*[*ma-aš*]
\\\\ [*bu*]-⸢*ša*⸣ ⸢*ù*⸣ LÚ.MEŠ DUMU K[IN]
38) *ù* KASKAL-*nu*
39) *la-a* ⸢*i*⸣-*de*$_4$ *a-*⸢*na*⸣ [E]N-[*i*]*a*
40) \\\\ *am-mu-li a-*[*na* EN-*ia*] *ù la i-de*$_4$
41) ⸢*i*⸣-⸢*na*⸣ ŠÀ KASKAL-*ni*⸣[-*ka*] [*li-*]*li-ku-ni*

---

42) *al-kám-mi* [EN]-*ia e-zi-*⸢*ba*⸣*-an-ni*
43) \\\\ *pu-ru-*[x-x-]-*nu la-aš-ti-na-an*

---

44) *a*[-*n*]*a* ⸢KA⸣! [*š*]*a be-li-ia*
45) *ù* ⸢*a*⸣-⸢*na*⸣ *ša* ^{I}*Bi-*⸢*ru*⸣*-a-za*
46) [*lu*]-⸢*ú*⸣ *la-a i-páṭ-ṭar*

(27–31) [....]I came [...]my lord [...the land of Ḫa]tte [...]he stole them.

(32–35) [...] for the second time [...]and they will come forth [...i]n my tablet [...]

(36–41) [He]re, it is three years, my lord, that I have been trying to dispatch to my lord [go]ods and envoys but as for the caravan, I did not know. To my lord \\ *am-mu-li* to [m]y [lo]rd, but I did not know. [Ma]y they come in [your] caravan.

(42–43) Come, my lord, spare me! \\ *pu-ru-*[x-x-]*-nu la-aš-ti-na-an*

(44–46) From the command of my lord and from that of Biryawaza, verily will I(sic!) not depart.

EA 53

TRANSCRIPTION

Obv. 01) ⸢a⸣-⸢na⸣ ^{I}N[am]-⸢ḫur⸣-⸢ia⸣ DUMU ^{d}UTU be-lí-ia /
02) ⸢um⸣-⸢ma⸣ [^{I}A]-⸢ki⸣-⸢iz⸣-⸢zi⸣ LÚ-ÌR-ka-ma
03) ⸢7⸣-⸢šu⸣ [7-šu a-n]a ⸢UZU⸣-GÌR-MEŠ be-lí-ia am-qut

---

04) ⸢be⸣-⸢lí⸣ ⸢LÚ⸣.⸢ÌR⸣-⸢ka⸣ a-na-ku-ma bá-li-iṭ ù la-a ÚŠ [: mi-it]
05) [a-na-ku] ⸢a⸣-⸢na⸣ ⸢ša⸣ be-lí-ia ⸢ù⸣ ⸢i⸣-⸢na⸣-⸢an⸣-[n]a ⸢be⸣-⸢lí⸣
06) [LÚ.Ì]R ⸢ša⸣ be-lí-ia-ma i-na ⸢aš⸣-⸢ri⸣ ⸢an⸣-⸢ni⸣-⸢im⸣
07) [ù] ⸢i⸣-⸢na⸣-an-na ⸢i⸣-⸢na⸣ aš-ri ⸢an⸣-⸢ni⸣?-[im] ⸢LÚ⸣ ⸢ÌR⸣-ka-ma
08) ⸢ša⸣ be-lí-ia ⸢a⸣-[na-ku-m]a ⸢ù⸣ [i-na]-⸢an⸣-⸢na⸣ ^{I}A-i-ṭu-kà-ma [qa-du]
09) LUGAL KUR Ḫa-⸢at⸣-⸢ti$_7$⸣ [a-na muḫ-]⸢ḫi⸣-ia ⸢ú⸣-uṣ!(IṢ)-ṣí
10) ù UZU.⸢SAG⸣.⸢DU⸣-⸢ia⸣ ⸢ú⸣-ba-ʾá-a-šu

---

11) ù i-na-an-na ⸢^{I}⸣[A-i-ṭu-kà-]⸢ma⸣ ⸢a⸣-[n]a ia-ši iš-ta-pár
12) ù iq-ta-[b]i [al-kám-mi] ⸢it⸣-ti ia-ši
13) a-na ša ⸢LUGAL⸣ ⸢KUR⸣ ⸢Ḫa⸣-a[t-ti$_7$ ù aq-ta]-bi ⸢a⸣-⸢na⸣-⸢ku⸣
14) ki-i a-⸢na⸣-⸢ku⸣ a[l-la-ak a-na]⸢ša⸣ ⸢LUGAL⸣ KUR Ḫa-⸢at⸣-ti$_7$
15) a-na-ku a-⸢na⸣ ⸢ša⸣ ⸢be⸣-[lí-ia LUGAL KUR Mi-]⸢iṣ⸣-⸢ri⸣^{KI}
16) aš-ta-pár ⸢ù⸣ ⸢aq⸣-[ta-bi ki-ia-a]m ⸢a⸣-⸢na⸣ ⸢ša⸣ ⸢šàr⸣ KUR Ḫa-⸢at⸣-ti$_7$

---

17) be-lí [.......................................]
18) ⸢ù⸣ KUR-tu$_4$ ⸢a⸣-⸢nu⸣-⸢ú⸣ [................] ⸢an⸣[...]
19) ù šum-ma [....................................]
20) ù be-lí-ia ⸢ki⸣-⸢ma⸣ [ar-ḫi-iš l]i-wa-aš-še-er-šu
21) ⸢ù⸣ li-il-⸢li⸣-⸢kám⸣ a-[na muḫ-ḫi ^{I}A-i-]⸢ṭu⸣-kà-ma
22) ki-i-me-⸢e⸣ be-lí [....]⸢pa⸣?-⸢nu⸣-ka
23) i-pal-la-⸢aḫ⸣ ⸢ù⸣ KUR ⸢Ú⸣?[-pè ib-bal-ka]t? [a-]n[a] ⸢ša⸣ be-lí-ia

---

EA 53

TRANSLATION

(1–3) To Namḫuria, son of the sun god, my lord, thus (speaks) Akizzi, your servant: Seven times (and) [seven times a]t the feet of my lord have I fallen.

(4–10) My lord, your servant am I, alive and not dead [: dead]. ⸢I⸣ belong to those of my lord [and] now, my lord, (I am) [the ser]vant of my lord in this place. [And] now in this place, your servant, of my lord, a[m] ⸢I⸣. But [n]ow Aiṭukama, [with] the king of the land of Ḫatti, is going forth [again]st me and he seeks my head.

(11–16) And now [Aiṭuka]ma has written to me and said, "[Come] with me to those of the king of the land of Ḫa[tti."] I [sai]d, "How could I [go to] those who belong to the king of the land of Ḫatti? I am one of those who belong to [my] lo[rd, the king of the land of Eg]ypt." I wrote and I sp[oke th]us to those who belong to the king of the land of Ḫatti.

(17–23) My lord [....] and this land [....] and if [....]. So, my lord, with [haste m]ay he send him (it) and may he come a[gainst Ai]ṭukama, as my lord [....] your presence(?), he is afraid. But the land of U[pe has rebell]ed(?) against my lord.

---

24) *be-lí* $^{⸢I⸣⸢d⸣}$⸢IŠKUR⸣-⸢*ni*⸣-⸢*ra*⸣-⸢*ri*⸣ [*šàr* KUR *Nu-ḫa-aš-še*]
25) ⸢*a*⸣-⸢*na*⸣ ⸢*ša*⸣ KUR *Ḫ*[*a-at-ti*$_7$ *qa-du* ^{I}*A-i-ṭu-kà-ma*] ⸢LÚ⸣ *nu-kúr-tu*$_4$
26) *ša be-lí-ia* [LÚ ÌR ^{Id}IŠKUR-*ni-ra-ri*]
27) *ù* KUR ⸢*Nu*⸣-[*ḫa-aš-še* KUR *ša*] *ab-bi-šu*
28) *be-lí* ⸢*il*⸣-⸢*li*⸣-*kam* ^{I}*A-i-ṭ*[*u-kà*]-⸢*ma*⸣ [*a-na* KUR *Ú-p*]*é*
29) KUR-KUR-*tu*$_4$ [*š*]*a be-lí*-⸢*ia*⸣ [*ù il-te-qè*]-⸢*šu*⸣-⸢*nu*⸣

---

30) *ù il-te-qè-šu* É-⸢*tu*$_4$⸣ [*ša Bir*$_5$-‹*ya*›-*wa-za*]
31) *ù il-te-qè-šu* 2 *me k*[*a*$_4$-*ak-ka*$_4$-*ru*.... KÙ.GI?]
32) *ù il-te-qè-šu* 3 ⸢*me*⸣ ⸢*ka*$_4$⸣-⸢*ak*⸣-⸢*ka*$_4$⸣-⸢*ru*⸣[KÙ-BABBAR?]
33) *ù il-te-qè-šu* ⸢1⸣ ⸢*me*⸣ ⸢*ka*$_4$⸣-⸢*ak*⸣-⸢*ka*$_4$⸣-⸢*ru*⸣ [ZABAR?]
34) *iš-tu* É-*tu*$_4$ ⸢*ša*⸣ $^{⸢I⸣}$*Bir*$_5$-‹*ya*›-*wa-za*

---

35) ⸢*be*⸣-*lí i-šak-kà*-⸢*nu*⸣ ^{I}*Te-ú*-⸢*wa*⸣-*at-ti* URU *L*[*a-bá-n*]*a*
36) *ù* $^{I⸢}$*Ar*⸣-*sà-ú-ia* URU *Ru-ḫi*-⸢*iṣ*⸣-*ṣí*
37) *a-na pa-ni* ^{I}*A-i-ṭu-kà-ma ù* KUR ⸢*Ú*⸣-⸢*pé*⸣
38) KUR-⸢KUR⸣-*tu*$_4$ *ša be-lí-ia*
39) *i-na* IZI.MEŠ *i-šar-ri-ip-šu*

Rev. 40) *be-lí ki-i-me-e a-na-ku a-na* LUGAL *be-lí*-⸢*ia*⸣
41) *a-ra-á*ʾ*-am ù ki-ia-am šàr* KUR *Nu-ḫa-aš-še*
42) *šàr* KUR *Ni-i šàr* KUR *Sí-in-za-ar*
43) *ù šàr* KUR *Tu-na-na-ab*!(AT) *ù an-nu-ut-ti*
44) *gáb-bá* LUGAL.MEŠ *a-na ša be-lí-ia* LÚ ÌR.MEŠ-⸢*šu*⸣

---

45) *ki-i-me-e i-le-é*ʾ*-e* LUGAL *be-lí-ia ù it-t*[*a-aṣ-ṣí*]
46) ⸢*ù*⸣ ⸢*šum*⸣-*ma-a* LUGAL ⸢*be*⸣-⸢*lí*⸣-⸢*ia*⸣ *la it-ta*-⸢*aṣ*⸣-⸢*ṣí*⸣
47) ⸢*ù*⸣ ⸢*be*⸣-⸢*lí*⸣-⸢*ia*⸣ ÉRIN.MEŠ ⸢*pí*⸣-⸢*iṭ*⸣-*ṭá-te li-wa-aš*-⸢*še*⸣-⸢*er*⸣
48) ⸢*ù*⸣ ⸢*li*⸣-⸢*il*⸣-⸢*li*⸣-⸢*kám*⸣ *iš-tu* KUR-*tu*$_4$ *an-nu-*[*ú*]
49) [*ki*]-⸢*i*⸣-⸢*me*⸣-*e be-lí* LUGAL.MEŠ *an-nu-ti* ⸢LÚ⸣ ⸢ÌR⸣.MEŠ-*šu*
50) ⸢LÚ⸣ GAL-*bi ša be-lí-ia ù mi-nu-um-me-e*
51) NÍG.BA.MEŠ-*šu-nu li-iq-bi ù li-id-dì-nu-ni*$_7$

---

52) *be-lí šum-ma* KUR-*tu*$_4$ *an-nu-ú iš-tu lìb-bi be-lí-ia*
53) *i-šak-kà-an ù* ÉRIN.MEŠ *pí-iṭ-ṭá-te be-lí-ia*
54) *li-wa-aš-še-er ù li-il-li-kám ù* LÚ.MEŠ DUMU.KIN-*šu*
55) *ša be-lí-ia ik-šu-du-ni*$_7$

(24–27) My lord, look, Adad-nirari, [king of the land of Nuǵasse], is the enemy of those who belong to the land of Ḫ[atti with Aiṭukama]. Of my lord, [the servant is Adad-nirari] and (so is) the land of Nu[ǵasse, the land of] his fathers.

(28–34) My lord, Ai[ṭukam]a has come [to the land of Up]e, territories [o]f my lord [and he has taken] them. And he took it, viz. the palace, and he took it, viz. two hundred t[alents of gold(?)], and he took it, viz. three hundred talents [of silver(?)], and he took it, viz. one hundred talents of [copper(?)] from the house of Bir‹ya›waza.

(35–39) My lord, Teuwatti of the town of L[aban]a and Arsawuya of Rôǵiṣi are at the disposition of Aiṭukama, and he is sending the land of Upe, the territories of my lord, up in flames.

(40–44) My lord, just as I am devoted to the king, my lord, so the king of the land of Nuǵassi, the king of the land of Niyi, the king of the land of Sinzar and the king of the land of Tunanab and all these kings of those who belong to my lord, are his servants.

(45–51) As far as the king, my lord, is able, then he should co[me forth], but if the king, my lord, does not come forth, then, may my lord send the regular army and may it come to this country, [si]nce, my lord, these kings are his servants. As for the official of my lord, may he specify whatever their gift should be and let them render them.

(52–55) My lord, if this land is of concern to my lord, then may my lord send the regular army and let it come. But (only) emissaries of my lord have come.

---

56) *be-lí šum-ma* ^{I}*Ar-sà-ù-ia* URU *Ru-ḫi-ṣí*

57) *ù* ^{I}*Te-ú-wa-at-ti* URU *La-bá-na i-na* ⸢KUR⸣ *Ú-pé aš-bu*

58) *ù* ^{I}⸢*Tá*⸣*-ša i-na* KUR *Am-qí aš-bu* ⸢*ù*⸣ *lu-ú i-de*$_{4}$*-šu-nu*

59) *be-lí-ia e-nu-ma* KUR *Ú-pé ša la be-lí-ia*

60) *i-na u*$_{4}$*-mi-ša-am-ma a-na* ^{I}*A-i-ṭu-kà-ma i-ša-*⸢*ap*⸣*-pa-ru-ni*$_{7}$

61) *ù ki-ia-am iq-bu-ni*$_{7}$ *al-kam-mi ù li-q*[*è-mi*]

62) KUR *Ú-pé gáb-bá-am-ma*

---

63) ⸢*be*⸣*-lí ki-i-me-e* URU *Dì-ma-aš-qì i-na* KUR *Ú-pé*

64) ⸢*a*⸣-⸢*na*⸣ ⸢^{UZU}⸣GÌR.MEŠ-*ka* \\ *ka*$_{4}$*-ti-ḫu ù ki-ia-am* URU *Qàt-na*

65) ⸢*a*⸣-⸢*na*⸣ ^{UZU}GÌR.MEŠ-*ka* \\ *ka*$_{4}$*-ti-ḫu-li-ìš ù be-lí-ia*

66) ⸢*a*⸣*-na pa-ni* LÚ.DUMU.KIN-*ia* NAM.TIL.LA *i-ir-ri-š*[*u ki-i-m*]*e-e*

67) *la pal-ḫa-ak-ku a-na pa-ni* ÉRIN.MEŠ *pí-iṭ-*⸢*ṭá*⸣-[*te ša be-*]*lí-*⸢*ia*⸣

68) *e-nu-ma* ÉRIN.MEŠ *pí-iṭ-ṭá-te ša be-lí-*[*ia*]

69) *ki-i-me-e ú-wa-aš-šar-an-ni ù i-*⸢*ru*⸣[*-bu*]

70) *i-na* URU *Qàt-na*

(56–62) My lord, if Arsawuya of the town of Rôǵiṣi and Teuwatti of the town of Labana remain in the land of Upe and Taššа remains in the land of ʿAmqi, then my lord should also be aware of them because the land of Upe does not belong to my lord. Daily they write to Aiṭukama and thus they say: "Come and ta[ke] all of the land of Upe."

(63–70) My lord, just as Damascus in the land of Upe is at your feet (Hurrian gloss), so the city of Qatna is at your feet (Hurrian gloss). And, my lord, in the presence of my emissary they are seeking life. [Th]us I do not fear from the regular troop[s of] my [lo]rd. When the regular troops of [my] lord thus he sends to me, then [they] will ent[er] into the city of Qatna.

EA 54

TRANSCRIPTION

Obv.

01) [*a-n*]*a* LUGAL *be-lí-ia*
02) *um-ma* ^{I}*A-ki-iz-zi* ÌR-*k*[*a*]
03) *a-na* GÌR.MEŠ *be-lí-ia* [*am-qut*]

---

04) *be-lí* [.....................................]
05) *ù aš*[*-ta-na-pár*..............................]
06) *i-na-an*[*-na*.................................]
07) *ù*[...]
– [...]
08) ⸢*ù*⸣[.......................................]
09) [..]
10) [..]
11) [..]
12) [..]
13) [..]*aš*
14) [...*a*]*k-ku*
15) [..]⸢*i*⸣*a*
16) [...*n*]*u*
17) [..]
18) [.......................................*aš-t*]*a-na-ap-pár*
19) [..]
20) [..]⸢*da-an-na*⸣
21) [..]⸢*ḫi*⸣
[..] –
22) [.........................*A-i-ṭu-ga-ma* L]Ú URU *Qí-in-sà*
23) [.......................................*a-š*]*i-ib*
24) ⸢*ù*⸣ *a-n*[*a*..................................]
25) [*i-k*]*à-aš*[*-ša-ad*.............*ma-mi-ta*(?)]
26) ⸢*id*⸣(?)-⸢*di*⸣(?)*-nu-*⸢*ni*$_7$⸣[^{I}*Ar-sà-ú-ia* LÚ *ša* U]RU *Ru-ḫi-ṣi*
27) ⸢*ù*⸣ ^{I}*Te-ú*[*-wa-at-ti* LÚ *ša*] URU *La-bá-na*
28) ⸢*it*⸣-⸢*ti*⸣ ^{I}*A*[*-i-ṭu-ga-ma* LÚ *ša*] URU *Qí-in-sà*
29) *ù it-ti* [*šàr* KUR *Ḫa-at-ti*$_7$] *iḫ-ḫa-zu-*⸢*ni*$_7$⸣

–––––[...............]–––––

EA 54

TRANSLATION

bv. 01) To the king, my lord,
02) the message of Akizzi yo[ur] servant
03) at the feet of my lord [have I fallen.]

---

04) My lord, [..................................]
05) And I [have been writing....................]
06) No[w....................................]
07) and[.......................................] —[.......................................]
08) ⸢and⸣[....................................]
09) [..]
10) [..]
11) [..]
12) [..]
13) [..]
14) [...t]o you
15) [..]my
16) [..]
17) [..]
18) [....................................I]kept on writing
19) [..]
20) [...]⸢strong⸣
21) [..] [..]—
22) [....................Aiṭugama, rul]er of the city of Kedesh
23) [......................................lo]cated
24) and t[o...................................]
25) [he] will[come..............................]
26) [..].......[Arsawia, the ruler of the ci]ty of Rôǵiṣi
27) ⸢and⸣ Teu[watti, the ruler of] the city of Labana
28) with A[iṭugama, the ruler of] city of Kedesh
29) and with [the king of the land of Ḫatti,] they are seizing.

-----[...............]-----

30) am-mi-ni$_7$ [.................................]
31) [^{I}]⸢Ar⸣[-za-ú-ia. LÚ ša URU Ru-ḫi-]ṣí
Lo.ed. 32) ⸢ù⸣ ^{I}⸢Te⸣[-ú-wa-at-ti LÚ ša URU] La-bá-na
33) ⸢ù⸣ š[àr KUR Ḫa-at-ti$_7$........................]
34) [it]-⸢ti⸣ [a-ḫa-miš a-na ša LUGAL]⸢be⸣-lí-ia
35) [.......................it-ta]l-ka [...]
Rev. 36) [i]-kà-aš[-ša-da-ni(?)...........................]
37) [ù] ⸢it⸣-⸢ti⸣[-šu-nu..............it-tal-k]a
[....]———————[............]—————
38) [ù] ⸢LÚ⸣.DUMU.KIN[-šu ša be-lí-ia]⸢a⸣-na UGU-ia
39) ⸢it⸣-tal-kam [ù ki-ia-am iq]-ta-bi
40) i-na KUR Mi-it-t[a-an-ni a-tal-l]a-ak
41) ⸢ù⸣ L[UGAL.ME]Š ⸢3⸣ [4..n]a-ak-ru
42) a-n[a ša šàr] ⸢KUR⸣ ⸢Ḫa⸣[at-ti$_7$ ša gáb-b]u-ú
43) ⸢i⸣-⸢na⸣ [pa-ni-]⸢ia⸣ [ša-ak-nu]
[...........]——[......]
44) [........]⸢ÉRIN⸣.⸢MEŠ⸣[-šu] ⸢ù⸣ GIŠ.GIGIR.MEŠ-šu
45) [........i]⸢a⸣ ⸢ù⸣[.....LÚ].DUMU.KIN-šu
46) [.........]⸢a⸣-⸢na⸣[a-ṣí] la e-le-éʾ-e
47) [..................] la i-na-aḫ-ḫi-is
[..................]———
48) [..................i]a ip-še-et-šu-nu
49) [.................n]im-mì
50) [..................a]n-ni
51) [..........URU Kàr-]ga-mi-iš
52) [..................]ša at-tù-ia
53) [..................i]k-šu-dú-ni$_7$
54) [..................]⸢šu⸣-⸢nu⸣
55) [...........i-ka-ša-]dú-ni$_7$
56) [..................]
57) [......................]traces

30) Why [................................]
31) Ar[*zauia*, ruler of the city of Rôĝi]ṣíi
).ed. 32) And Te[uwatti, the ruler of the city of] Labana
33) and the k[ing of the land of Ḫatti............]
34) all [together against the king,]my lord.
35) [.......................he went [...]
ev. 36) [he] will [come to me(?)................]
37) [and] with[them...............he wen]t. [....]-------[............]-----
38) [and the] envoy[of my lord]to me
39) *has come*[and thus he s]poke:
40) "In the land of Mitt[anni I wen]t around;
41) and three [or four k[ings] were hostile
42) to the k[ing of the land of Ḫat[ti. And a]ll
43) were cord[ial to]me." [...........]--[......]
44) [........his]troops and his chariots
45) [........m]y and[...] his envoy
46) [.........]to [come forth] I am not able.
47) [...................] he will not withdraw. [...................]----
48) [............mi]ne, their behavior
49) [...................]
50) [...................]
51) [..........the city of Car]kemish
52) [...................]which is mine
53) [................they] have come
54) [...................]theirs (or acusative "them")
55) [.............they will] come.
56) [...................]
57) [......................] *traces*

EA 55

TRANSCRIPTION

Obv. 01) ⸢*a*⸣-*na* ^{I}*Nam-ḫur-ia* DUMU ^{d}UTU *be-lí-ia qí-bí*-⸢*ma*⸣
02) *um-ma* ^{I}*A-ki-iz-zi* ÌR-*ka-ma*
03) 7 *a-na* UZU.GÌR.MEŠ *be-lí-ia am-qut*

---

04) *be-lí i-na aš-ri an-ni-im a-na-ku šu-ú-ut*
05) LÚ ÌR-*ka a-na* ⸢*ša*⸣ *be-lí-ia* ^{SILA}*ur-ḫu ub-ta-e*
06) *iš-tu ša be-lí*-⸢*ia*⸣ *la a-páṭ-ṭar-mì*

---

07) *e-nu-ma šu-ut-ma* LÚ.MEŠ *ab-bu-te*^{MEŠ}-*ia*
08) *a-na ša* LÚ.MEŠ.ÌR-*ti-ka-ma* KUR-*tu*$_4$ *an-nu-ú* KUR.ḪI.A-*ka*
09) URU *Qat*-⸢*na*⸣^{KI} URU-*ka a-na-ku a-na ša be-lí-ia*

---

10) *be-lí e-nu-ma* ÉRIN.MEŠ -*šu ù* GIŠ.GIGIR.MEŠ-⸢*šu*⸣
11) *ša be-lí il-li-kám* NINDA.ḪI.A KAŠ.ḪI.A GU$_4$.MEŠ
12) ÙZ.ḪI.A LÀL.ḪI.A *ù* Ì.GIŠ.MEŠ *a-na pa-ni*
13) ERÍN.MEŠ-*šu ù* GIŠ.GIGIR.MEŠ *ša be-lí-ia ú-uṣ-ṣa-ni*
14) *ù a-nu-um-ma* LÚ.MEŠ GAL-*tu*$_4^{MEŠ}$ *ša be-lí-ia*
15) *ù* ⸢*li*⸣-*iš-al-šu-nu be-lí-ia*

---

16) *be-lí a-na pa-ni* ÉRIN.MEŠ -*ka ù a-na pa-ni* GIŠ.GIGIR.MEŠ-*ka*
17) KUR.KUR-*tu*$_4$ *gáb-bá i-pal-la-aḫ*
18) *šum-ma be-lí-ia* KUR.⸢KUR⸣-*tu*$_4$ *an-nu-ú*
19) *a-na ša* KUR-*šu i-ṣa-ab-bat-šu ù i-na* MU *an*-⸢*ni*⸣-*i*[*m*]?
20) ⸢*be*⸣-*lí-ia* ÉRIN.MEŠ-*šu ù* GIŠ.GIGIR.MEŠ-*šu li-wa-aš*-⸢*šèr*⸣
21) *ù li-il-li-kám ki-i-me-e* KUR *Nu-ḫa-aš-še gáb-bá*-⸢*am*⸣-⸢*ma*⸣
22) *a-na ša be-lí-ia šum-ma be-lí* ⸢ÉRIN⸣.MEŠ ⸢*uṣ*⸣-⸢*ṣí*⸣-[*m*]*i*
23) *aš-šum* KAM 6 *u*$_4$-*mi i-zi-iz-mi i-na* KUR MAR.⸢TU⸣(?)
24) *ù lu-ú il-te-qè-šu-nu* ^{I}*A-zi-ra*

---

25) *ù šum-ma i-na* KAM.MU *an-ni-im* ÉRIN.MEŠ-*šu* [*ù* GIŠ.GIG]IR-*š*[*u*]
26) ⸢*ša*⸣ ⸢*be*⸣-⸢*lí*⸣-*ia la it-ta-ṣí ù la ik*-[*ta-aš-da*]
27) ⸢KUR⸣ [*a-na*] ⸢*pa*⸣-*ni* ^{I}*A-zi-ra i-pal-la-a*[*ḫ*]

EA 55

TRANSLATION

(1–3) To Namḫur(e)ya, son of the sun god, my lord, speak; Message of Akizzi, your servant: seven (times) at the feet of my lord have I fallen.

(4–6) My lord, in this place I am the one who is your servant; I have sought the way to my lord. I do not depart from my lord.

(7–9) From the time that my ancestors became your servants, this land has been your land; the city of Qatna is your city; I belong to my lord.

(10–15) My lord, when the infantry and the chariotry of my lord came hither, food and drink, large cattle, small cattle, honey and oil I was bringing forth for the infantry and chariotry of my lord. And now, there are my lord's senior officials, so may my lord ask them.

(16–24) My lord, the entire land is afraid in the face of your infantry and your chariotry. If my lord would take this country for his own country, then in this year, my lord, may he dispatch his infantry and his chariotry and let them come. Because the entire land of Nuǵasse belongs to my lord. If, my lord, the army had only come out, (and if) in six days, it had taken a stand in Amurru, then verily they would take Aziru.

(25–27) So if in this year, the infantry [and the chario]try of my lord do not sally forth and do not ge[t here], the land will be in fear of Aziru.

---

28) [...........*r*]*i i-pát-ṭar-ru* [..................]
29) [............]⸢LÚ⸣(?).⸢MEŠ⸣ [.................]
30) Broken off
Lo.ed. 31) Broken off
32) " "
33) " "
34) " "
Rev. 35) " "
36) LÚ.M[EŠ..*r*]*i*(?) ⸢LÚ⸣.⸢ERÍN⸣.MEŠ x[....]
37) *a-na ša be-lí-ia e-nu-*[*ma*.....................]

---

38) *be-lí i-de*$_4$*-šu be-lí-ia* [........................]
39) LÚ.MEŠ *ab-bu-te*^{MEŠ}*-šu ša* [*be-lí-ia*...........]
40) *ù i-na-an-na šàr* KUR *Ḫa-*[*at-ti*$_7$..............]
41) *i-na i-ša-ti i-šar-ri-ip-šu-nu*
42) DINGIR.MEŠ-*šu ù* LÚ.MEŠ *mu-de*$_4$^{MEŠ}*-šu ša* U[RU *Qat-*]⸢*na*⸣?
43) *šàr* KUR *Ḫa-at-ti*$_7$ *il-te-qè-šu-nu*

---

44) *be-lí* ⸢LÚ⸣.⸢MEŠ⸣ [URU] ⸢*Qàt*⸣*-na* LÚ.ÌR.MEŠ-*ia*
45) ^{I}*A-zi-r*[*u*] ⸢*šu*⸣? ⸢*il*⸣*-te-*⸢*qè*⸣*-šu-nu ù ip-qid*$_4$*-šu-nu*
46) *iš-tu* ⸢KUR⸣?-⸢*šu*⸣? ⸢*ša*⸣ ⸢*be*⸣-⸢*lí*⸣*-ia*
47) *ù* ⸢*i*⸣-⸢*na*⸣-⸢*an*⸣-⸢*na*⸣ *aš-*[*bu*]-⸢*ni*$_7$⸣ ⸢*iš*⸣-⸢*tu*⸣ KUR-*tu*$_4$ *ša be-lí-ia*
48) ^{UZU}⸢*lìb*⸣-⸢*ba*⸣?-⸢*am*⸣? ⸢*li*⸣?-⸢*im*⸣?-⸢*lik*⸣? *be-lí-ia*
49) *li-wa-aš-*[*šèr ip-ṭe*$_4$*-ra?*] ⸢*ša*⸣? LÙ.MEŠ URU *Qàt-na*
50) ⸢*be*⸣-⸢*lí*⸣-⸢*ia*⸣? [*ù*] ⸢*lu*⸣*-ú ip-ṭur-šu-nu*
51) ⸢*lik*⸣-[*šu?-du*]-⸢*ni*$_7$⸣ ⸢*be*⸣*-lí-ia* KÙ.⸢BABBAR⸣.MEŠ *ip-ṭe*$_4$*-re-šu-nu*
52) ⸢*ki*⸣-⸢*i*⸣*-me-e* ⸢*šu*⸣*-ú-ut ù lu-ud-din* KÙ.BABBAR.MEŠ

---

53) *be-lí* ^{d}UTU DINGIR *a-bi-ia* LÚ.MEŠ *ab-bu-te*^{MEŠ}*-ka*
54) *i-te-ep-pu-uš-šu-nu ù šu-mu*
55) *iš-tu muḫ-ḫi-šu i-ša-kán-šu-nu*
56) *ù i-na-an-*⸢*na*⸣ ^{d}UTU DINGIR *a-bi-ia*
57) *šàr* KUR *Ḫa-at-ti*$_7$ *il-te-qè-šu-nu*
58) *ù i-de*$_4$*-šu-nu be-lí-ia ip-še-et-šu-nu ša* DINGIR.MEŠ
59) *ki-i-me-e šu-ú-ut ù i-na-an-na* ^{d}UTU DINGIR *a-bi-ia*

(28–29) [..........] they will depart [...........] the men [.......]

(30–35) *The entire bottom of the tablet is broken off, approximately six lines; one at the bottom of the obverse, four on the lower edge and one more at the top of the reverse.*

(36–37) the me[n of......] the troop(s) [...] of the king, my lord wh[en......]

(38–43) My lord knows it. My lord [...] the ancestors of [my lord...] and now the king of the land of Ḫa[tti] has burned them with fire. As for the gods and the elite of the c[ity of Qat]na, the king of the land of Ḫatti has taken them away.

(44–52) My lord, the men of [the city of] Qatna are my servants. Aziru is the one who has taken them and transferred them away from the land of my lord and now they are lo[ca]ted away from the land of my lord. May my lord take counsel(?) in (his) heart; may my lord se[nd the ransom] for the men of Qatna [and] may he ransom them. Let them come hither, my lord. As for the money of their ransom, as much as it may be, and I will verily pay the money.

(53–59) My lord, a (statue of) the sun god, the god of my father, each of your ancestors made and the name (of each one) was placed before him. But now, as for the sun god‹s›, the god‹s› of my father, the king of the land of Ḫatti has taken them. And my lord knows them, viz. the manufacture of (those) gods, just as they are.

60) *a-na muḫ-ḫi-ia i-tu-ur* ^{UZU}*lìb-ba-am*
61) *be-lí-ia i-*⸢*di*⸣*-*⸢*in*⸣*?-šu ù li-id-din-šu*
62) GÍN(“ZU”) KÙ.GI.MEŠ *ki-i ma-aṣ-ṣí-im-ma*
63) *a-na* ^{d}UTU DINGIR *a-bi-ia ki-i-me-e*
64) *e-te-pu-šu-ni ù šu-mu*
Lo.ed. 65) *be-lí-ia aš-šum pa-na-nu-um-ma*
66) *iš-tu muḫ-ḫi* ^{d}UTU *i-šak-kán*

(60–66) And now, the sun god, the god of my father has returned to me. Take it under consideration, my lord, and may he furnish it, viz. the shekel(s) of gold as much as is needed for the sun god, the god of my father. As soon as he does thus for me, then the name of my lord will be (exalted) before the sun god, just as in the past.

EA 56 + EA 361

TRANSCRIPTION

Obv. 01) [*a-na* LUGAL *be-lí-ia qí-bí-ma*]
02) [*um-ma* ^{I}...........ÌR-*ka-ma*]
03) [*a-na* GÌR.MEŠ *be-lí-*]⸢*ia*⸣ [*am-qut*]

---

04) [*a-mur* LÚ *na-a*]*k-ru i-l*[*a*]*-an-ni*
05) [*ù aš-pu*]*r a-na be-*⸢*lí*⸣*-ia šàr* KUR [*Mi-iṣ-ri*]
06) [*ù be-l*]*í-ia iq-*⸢*ta*⸣*-bi i-na m*[*i-ni*]
07) [*a-na* UG]U-*ia la* ⸢*ta*⸣-⸢*aš*⸣*-pur*
08) [*ù be-*]*lí-ia la i*[*t*]*-t*[*a*]*-aṣ-ṣí*

---

09) [*ù a-n*]*a-ku* ÌR-*ka* ⸢*ù*⸣ *be-lí-ia*
10) [*iš-tu*] ŠU-*ti-šu lu-*⸢*ú*⸣ *la tu-wa-aš-š*[*ar-an-ni*]
11) [*ù a-na-k*]*u iš-tu* ⸢*ša*⸣ ⸢*be*⸣*-lí-ia la* [*a-paṭ-ṭar*]
12) [*ù a-na š*]*a be-lí-ia* ÉRIN.MEŠ-*šu*
13) [*ù a-na* GI]Š.GIGIR-*šu* [*ta*]*-ak-la-ak-k*[*u*]

---

14) [*a-mur-m*]*i be-*⸢*lí*⸣*-ia i-ḫa-aš-ša*$_{10}$-⸢*ša*⸣[*-an-ni*]
15) [.........]⸢*ù*⸣ [*a*]*-na lìb-bi be-lí-ia*
16) [............*a-*]*nu-um-ma* ^{I}*Ta-aš-šu*
17) [................]*a-na* UGU-*ia il*(!)-[*la-am*(?)]
18) [.................]⸢*ú*⸣*-ʾé-ir-šu*
19) [....................]*-lí ša al-*⸢*ta*⸣[*-pár*]
20) [.....................]⸢*qa*⸣*-ti-*⸢*i*⸣[*a....*]
21) [...................................]
22) [...............*tu-*]⸢*uṣ*⸣*-ṣa-a*[*n- ni...*]

---

23) [*a-mur-mi* ^{I}*A-tak*]*-ka*$_4$*-ma ṣab-t*[*u gáb-bi*]
24) [URU.MEŠ-*nu ù*]⸢*ni*⸣*-i-nu* ÌR.[MEŠ.....]
25) [..........]*ti* ÌR.MEŠ ⸢*ša*⸣ [*be-lí-ia....*]
26) [*š*]*a* URU.⸢KI⸣ *Ru-ḫi-ṣi* [...............]
27) *it-*⸢*ti*⸣ ^{I}*A-ta*[*k-ka*$_4$]-⸢*ma*⸣ x[...............]
28) *i*[*m*]*-ta-na-*⸢*aḫ*⸣*-ḫa-sú-n*[*i*$_7$.............]

EA 56 + EA 361

TRANSLATION

(1–3) [Speak to the king, my lord; the message of ---- (Akizzi?), your servant; at the feet of] my [lord, have I fallen].

(4–8) [Look, the en]emy has attacked (lit. come up against) me, [and I have wri]tten to my lord, the king of the land of [Egypt] [and] my [lo]rd said: "W[hy] did you not write [to]me?" [And] my [lo]rd did not c[om]e forth.

(9–13) [And] ⸢I⸣ am your servant, so may my lord not relea[se me from] his hand. [And] ⸢I⸣ will not [depart] from my lord. And I [t]rust [in] my lord's troops [and in] his chariotry

---

(14–22) [Look, my lord remembers [me…]and to my lord's heart (desire) […] now, Taššu […] against me has at[tacked (lit. come up) […] I dispatched him […] which I wro[te…] m[y] hand […you] will come forth t[o me].

(23–28) [Look Aitak]kama has seiz[ed all our towns and] and we are the ser-van[ts…]servants of [my lord…]of the town of Rôǵiṣi[…]with Aita[kkama…] have been constantly smiting him, namely [……..]

EA 57

TRANSCRIPTION

——

Obv.? 01) [.....................]⸢^{I}⸣⸢*Pu*⸣-⸢*ḫu-r*[*a*....]x

02) [.................*il-la-*]⸢*kám*⸣ ⸢^{I}⸣⸢*A*⸣-*ki-iz-*⸢*zi*⸣*šàr* ⸢*Qàṭ*⸣[*-na* ^{KI}]

03) [.....................]*ta šàr Bar-ga*

04) [.....................]*ù it-ta-ta-lak*(?)

05) [.....................]⸢ÉRIN.MEŠ⸣ ⸢*ḫu*⸣-⸢*ra*⸣-*te*

06) [..............*a-na mu*]*ḫ* -⸢*ḫi*⸣ ⸢^{I}⸣⸢*Pu*⸣-⸢*ḫu*⸣-*ru*

07) [.....................]*ni*

08) [.....................]⸢*iš*⸣-⸢*ša*⸣-⸢*an*⸣-*ni*

09) ›[.....................]‹

10) [..................*a-na*] *muḫ-ḫi* ^{I}*Pu-ḫ*[*u-ra*]

——

11) [...........*i*]-⸢*dab*⸣-⸢*bu*⸣-⸢*ub*⸣ LUGAL.MEŠ

12) [.........................*T*]*u-ni-*⸢*ip*⸣ ^{KI}

13) [..................................] ^{I}*Šu-mi-it-t*[a....]

Rev.? 01) [..................................*Tu-*]*ni-ip*

02) [..]

03) [..]

04) [..]

05) [..................................*ú-wa-aš-*]*šar*

06) [......................................]*gi-an-ni*

07) [..]⸢*šu*⸣

EA 57

TRANSLATION

——

Obv.? 01) [......................]Puḫur[a.........]
02) [.................he we]nt, Akizzi, king of Qaṭ[na]
03) [......................]*x* king of Barga
04) [......................]and he continually went
05) [......................]the elite troops
06) [......................t]o Puḫuru
07) [......................]*x*
08) [......................]he brought to me
09) ›[......................]‹
10) [......................t]o Puḫuru

——

11) [............he]will speak. The kings.....
12) [..........................T]unip
13) [...................................] Shumitt[a....]

Rev.? 01) [...................................Tu]nip
02) [..]
03) [..]
04) [..]
05) [.................................. he will se]nd
06) [......................................]*x* to me
07) [..]his/him

EA 58

TRANSCRIPTION

Obv. 01) [*a-na* LUGAL GA]L BAD-*ia qí*[*-bí-ma*]
02) [*um-ma* ^{I}]*Te*$_{9}$*-ḫ̮u-te*$_{9}$*-šu-bá* Ì[R-*ka-ma*]
03) [*a-na*] ⸢GÌR⸣.MEŠ EN-*ia am-qú-*[*ut*]
04) [*šá-*]*ni-tam li-*⸢*ma*⸣*-ad i-nu-m*[*a*]
05) ⸢*šàr*⸣ KUR *Mi-ta-an a-ṣí q*[*a-du* GIŠ.GIGIR]
06) ⸢*ù*⸣ *qa-du* ÉRIN.MEŠ KAL.KASKAL+[?.BAD]
07) [*n*]*i-iš-mé a-na mi-me-e*[*šum-šu*]
08) ⸢*ú*⸣*-la-a ù pal-ḫ̮*[*a-nu/ku*]
09) [*iš*]*-tu ša-šu* [..................]
10) [............................]

Rev. Lower part only

01) [...]*tu*$_{4}$-ni[..................]
02) [*tu-*]*ša-am-ru-ri* ⸢*ù*⸣ [...........]
03) [*ù* ^{I}]ÌR-*A-ši-ir-ti* ⸢*il*$_{5}$⸣*-te*$_{9}$[*-qú-šu*(*?*)]
04) [*ù*]*a-nu-ma ni-*⸢*pu*⸣*-*[*u*]*š an-n*[*i-ta ù*]
05) [*ni-ìl-q*]*é-ši a-na ma-ḫ̮ar* LUG[AL EN-*ia*]
06) [*šá-ni-ta*]*m Ḫ̮a-ia-ra*
07) [^{I}]⸢*ḫ̮a*⸣*-di ù* [............]
08) [........] *a-na* LUG[AL EN-*ia*]
09) [.........UR]U-*ni*^{MEŠ}
Up.ed. 10) [..............^{d}UTU DIN[GIR -*ia*]
11) [................*i*]*a-ši a*[*-na* [....]

EA 58

TRANSLATION

(1–3) Sp[eak to the gre]at [king], my lord, [the message of Teḫu-Teshup, [your] se[rvant; at]the feet of my lord have I fall[en].

(4–10) [Fur]thermore, know that the king of Mitanni came forth wi[th the chariotry] and with expeditionary troops. We have heard not[hing] at all and we/I are/am afraid of him [.......].

Rev.

(1–5) [....they] drove out(sic!) and [....] and as for ʿAbdi-Ashirti, [they] too[k him and now we have done th[is and we have taken it before the ki[ng. my lord].

(6–11) [Further]more, Ḫaya did not se[nd Rib]haddi and [...] to the ki[ng, my lord...the ci]ties [...]the sun god, [my] go[d...to] me to [...].

EA 59

TRANSCRIPTION

Obv. 01) *a-na šàr* KUR-*ti*$_4$ *Mi-iṣ-ri be-lí-n*[*i*]
02) *um-ma* DUMU.MEŠ URU *Tù-ni-ip*^{KI} LÚ ÌR-*ka-ma*
03) *a-na* UGU-*ka lu-ú šul-mu*
04) ⸢*ù*⸣ *a-na* GÌR.MEŠ *be-lí‹-ni›? ni-am-qut*

---

05) *be-lí um-ma* URU *Tù-ni-ip* LÚ.ÌR-*ka* ⸢*iq*⸣-*ta-bi*
06) URU *Tù-ni-ip*^{KI} *ma-an-nu* ⸢*i*⸣-*na pa-na-nu-um*
07) *ú-uš-ša*$_{10}$-*bu-šu la ú-uš-ša*$_{10}$-*bu-šu-ú*
08) ^{I}*Ma-na-aḫ-pí-ir-ia* \\ *am-ma-ti-wu-uš*

---

09) DINGIR.MEŠ-*šu ù* ⸢GIŠ⸣ ⸢*mu*⸣-*ta-aš-šu* \\ *na-ap-ri-il-la-an*
10) *ša šàr* KUR-*ti*$_4$ *Mi-iṣ-ri be-lí-ni i-na* URU *Tù-ni-ip*^{KI} *aš-bu-*⸢*ni*$_7$⸣
11) *ù li-iš-al-šu-nu be-lí-ni la-bi-ru-te-šu* \\ *am-ma-ti*
12) *ù i-nu-ma-mi ni-i-nu ša la be-lí-ni šàr* KUR *Mi-iš-ri*^{KI}

---

13) *ù i-na-an-*⸢*na*⸣ 20 MU.KAM.MEŠ *a-na* LUGAL *be-lí-ni ni-iš-tap-ru*
14) *ù* LÚ.MEŠ DUMU.KIN-*ri-ni a-na* LUGAL *be-lí-ni aš-bu-ni*$_7$
15) *ù i-na-an-na be-lí-ni* DUMU *A-*⸢*ki*⸣-^{d}IŠKUR
16) *a-na* LUGAL *be-lí-ni ni-ir-ri-iš-šu-ni*$_7$
17) *ù li-id-din-šu be-lí-ni*

---

18) *ù be-lí* DUMU *A-ki-*^{d}IŠKUR *šàr* KUR-*ti*$_4$ *Mi-iṣ-ri*^{KI}
19) *id-din ù a-na mi-ni*$_7$ *šàr-ru be-lí-ni*
20) *i-na* KASKAL-*ni i-ta-ar-ra-aš-šu*

---

21) *ù i-na-an-na* ^{I}*A-zi-ra* LÚ.ÌR-*ka*
22) LÚ NU.GIŠ.KIRI$_6$-*ka i-še-em-me-šu-nu*
23) *ù i-na* KUR-*ti*$_4$ *Ḫa-at-at*^{KI}
24) NAM *sar-ra-tu*$_4$ *ik-šu-ud-šu-nu*

EA 59

TRANSLATION

(1–4) To the king of the land of Egypt, ou[r] lord, thus (speak) the sons of the city of Tunip, your servant. May it be well with you. And at the feet of ‹our› lord, we have fallen.

(5–8) My lord, thus spoke the city of Tunip, your servant. As for the city of Tunip, in the past who occupied it? Did not Manaḫpirya occupy it, namely your ancestor?

(9–12) His deity and his *statue*(?) of the king of the land of Egypt, our lord, have been located in the city of Tunip. So may our lord ask them, namely his ancients, when did we not belong to our lord, king of the land of Egypt?

(13–17) And now, twenty years we have been writing to the king, our lord, and our envoys have been located with the king, our lord. But now, our lord, we have been requesting the son of Aki-Teššub of the king, our lord, so may our lord give him.

(18–20) And my lord gave the son of Aki-Teššub, so why is the king, our lord, holding him back from the way?

(21–24) And now, Aziru, your servant, your gardener, is heeding them and from the land of Ḫatti a criminal fate has overtaken them.

Lo.ed. 25) *ù i-nu-ma* ERÍN.MEŠ-*šu ù* GIŠ.GIGIR-*šu*
26) *uḫ-‹ḫi-›ru-*⸢*nim*⸣*-mi*
Rev. 27) *ù ni-i-nu* ^{I}*A-zi-ra*
28) *ki-i-ma* URU *Ni-i*^{KI} *i-ip-pu-uš-šu-nu*

---

29) *šum-ma ni-i-nu-ma qá-a-la-nu*
30) *ù šàr* KUR-*ti*$_{4}$ *Mi-iṣ-ri i-qá-al-mi*
31) *aš-šum a-wa-te*^{MEŠ} *an-ni-tu*$_{4}$ *ša i-ip-pu-šu-nu*
32) ^{I}*A-zi-ra i-nu-ma-mi* ^{UZU}*qa-ta*
33) *a-na muḫ-ḫi be-lí-ni li-wa-aš-šèr-ru*

---

34) *ù i-nu-ma-mi* ^{I}*A-zi-ra* URU *Ṣu-mu-ri*^{KI} *i-ru-bu*
35) *ù i-te-pu-uš-šu-nu* ^{I}*A-zi-ra*
36) *ša lìb-bi-šu i-na* É-*ti*
37) *ša šàr-ri be-lí-ni ù aš-šum a-wa-te*^{MEŠ}
38) *an-‹nu›-tu*$_{4}$ *be-lí-ni i-qá-al-mi*

---

39) *ù* ⸢*i*⸣*-na-an-na* URU *Tù-ni-ip*^{KI}
40) URU-*ka i-ba-ak-ki*
41) *ù dì-ma-te*^{MEŠ}*-šu i-la-ak*
42) *ù a-na ṣa-ba-ti-šu ša* UZU.ŠU-⸢*ti*⸣*-ni ia-nu-um*

---

43) *ni-i-nu-ma a-na* LUGAL *be-lí šàr* KUR-*ti*$_{4}$ *Mi-iṣ-ri*
44) *a-na* 20 MU.KAM.MEŠ *ni-iš-tap-ru*
45) *ù a-wa-at ša be-li-ni*
46) 1-*en a-na mu-uḫ-ḫi-ni la i-kaš-ša*$_{10}$-⸢*ad*⸣

Lo.ed. 29) *ù am-*[*m*]*i-ni*$_{7}$ ⸢*be*⸣-⸢*lí*⸣-⸢*ni*⸣[.......]
30) DUMU.MEŠ [URU] ⸢*Ṣú*⸣[........]
Rev. 31) *ù b*[*e-li-i*]*a* [....UR]U[..........]
32) *la iš-*⸢*te*⸣[*m*]*e* [..................]
33) *it-ti* ÌR[.......................]
34) *ša be-lí-ia ir-*⸢*ru*⸣(?)[*-ub*..........]
35) ÌR-*ka i-kaš-šad-an-ni* [...........]

(25–28) And since his infantry and his chariots have de‹l›ayed, then as for us, Aziru treats us like the city of Niyi.

(29–33) If we keep silent and the king of the land of Egypt keeps silent concerning these things that Aziru is doing, then he will surely turn his hand against our lord.

(34–38) And inasmuch as Aziru entered Ṣumur and did to them just as he pleased in the palace of the king, our lord, then concerning these things, our lord keeps silent

(39–42) So now, the city of Tunip, your city, is weeping and its tears are flowing and there is none to grasp our hand.

(43–46) We belong to the king of the land of Egypt and we have been writing twenty years but not a single word of our lord has reached us.

(29–35) And why, does our lord, the citizens of [the city of] Ṣu[...] and my lord [...]did not hear/he[ed...] with the servant [...of my lord enter [in...]your servant will come to me [.....]

36) *ù* LÚ.DUMU KIN-*ri-šu ša b*[*e-*]*l*[*í-ia*]
37) *a-*⌜*na*⌝ UGU-*ia it-tal-kam*
38) ⌜*ù*⌝ ⌜*ki*⌝*-ia-am iq-ta-b*[*i*]
39) *i-na* KUR *Mi-it-ta-a*[*n*]*-ni* ⌜*a*⌝*-t*[*a-la-ak*]
40) ⌜*ù*⌝ LUGAL.MEŠ 3 *ù* 4 *na-*⌜*ak*⌝*-*[*ru a-na*]
41) [*š*]*a* LUGAL KUR *Ḫa-at-ti*$_7$ *ša gáb-*[*bu?*]
42) [*a-na*]⌜*pa*⌝*-ni-ia ša-ak-nu*

---

43) [*ù b*]*e-lí-ia iq-ta-b*[*i....*]*-šu-nu*
44) [...]⌜KUR⌝ ⌜*Ḫur*⌝*-*⌜*ri*⌝ [..............]
45) [..........]⌜ḪI.A⌝ ⌜*ma*⌝*-*⌜*ti*$_7$⌝[.........]
46) [..........]⌜KUR⌝ ⌜URU⌝.⌜ḪI.A⌝ *a-l*[*i-ik*]
47) [........................]*be ša*[....]
48) [...........................]⌜*li*⌝*-šu-n*[*u*]
49) [................]⌜*a*⌝(?)*-*⌜*na*⌝(?) ⌜*be*⌝(?)[*-lí-ia*]
50) [.................]⌜*a*⌝(?)*-*⌜*na*⌝(?) ⌜UGU⌝*-*[*ia*]
51) [.........................]⌜*nim*⌝[.....]

(36–42) And the envoy of [my] lord came to me and thus he said, “I we[nt about] in the land of Mittanni and there were three or four kings hostile [to] the king of the land of Ḫatti of which al[l were] well disposed towards me.”

(43–51) [And] my [lo]rd sai[d...]them [...]the land of Ḫurri [...] the city states I [went...]their [cit]ies(?) [...]to(?) [my] lo[rd...]against/to [me........]

EA 60

TRANSCRIPTION

Obv. 01) [*a-n*]*a* ^{I}LUGAL ^{d}UTU EN-*ia*
02) ⸢*um*⸣-*ma* ^{I}ÌR-^{d}*Aš-ra-tu*$_{4}$
03) [Ì]R-*ka*$_{4}$ *ep-ri ša* GÌR.ḪI.A-[*k*]*a*$_{4}$
04) [*a-n*]*a* GÌR.ḪI.A LUGAL EN-[*ia*]
05) *7-šu ù 7-šu am-qut*
06) *a-mur a-na-ku* ÌR LUGAL *ù*
07) UR.GI$_{7}$ *ša* É-*šu ù*
08) KUR *A-mur-ri gáb-ba-šu*
09) *a-na* LUGAL EN-*ia a-na-ṣa-ar-šu*
10) *aq-bi aš-ta-ni a-na* ^{I}*Pa-ḫa-na-te*
11) LÚ.MÁŠKIM-*ia le-qa-mi*
12) ÉRIN.MEŠ *til-la-tì a-na na-ṣa-ri*
13) ⸢KUR⸣.⸢ḪI.A⸣ LUGAL *a-nu-ma gáb-bi*
14) LUGAL.[ḪI].A *ša* LUGAL ERÍN.MEŠ *Ḫur-ri*
15) *tu*-⸢*ba*⸣-*ú-ni*$_{7}$ KUR.[ḪI].A
16) ⸢*a*⸣-*na ḫa-ba-lì iš*-⸢*tu*⸣
17) [Š]U-⸢*i*⸣*a ù* ŠU [LÚ.MÁŠKIM]
Lo.ed. 18) [*š*]*a* LUGAL EN-[*ia ù*]
19) [*a-n*]*a-ṣa*-⸢*ar*⸣-*š*[*u-nu a-mur*]
20) [^{I}*Pa-ḫ*]*a-na*-⸢*te*⸣ *i*[*t-ti-ka*]
Rev. 21) ⸢*yi*⸣-⸢*iš*⸣-*al-šu* LUGAL ^{d}[UT]U-[*ia*]
22) *šum-ma la a-na-ṣa-ar*
23) URU *Ṣu-mu-ri* URU *Ul-la*-⸢*sà*⸣
24) *i-nu-ma* LÚ.MÁŠKIM-*ia*
25) *i-na ši-pir*$_{6}$-*ti* LUGAL ^{d}UTU
26) *ù a-na-ku* ŠE.KIN.KU$_{5}$ ŠE.ḪI.A
27) *ša* URU *Ṣu-mur ù gáb-bi*
28) KUR.ḪI.A *a-na* LUGAL ^{d}UTU-*ia*
29) EN-*ia a-na-ṣa-ar-šu*
30) *ù* LUGAL EN-[*i*]*a lu-ú yi-da-an-ni*
31) *ù yi-ip*-⸢*qí*⸣-*id-ni a-na* ŠU
32) ^{I}*Pa-ḫa-na-te* LÚ.MÁŠKIM-*ia*

EA 60

TRANSLATION

(1–5) [T]o the king, the sun god, my lord, the message of ʿAbdi-Ashratu your [ser]vant, the dirt under your feet: [a]t the feet of the king, my lord, seven times and seven times have I fallen.

(6–13) Look, I am the servant of the king and the hound of his household and I guard the land of Amurru in its entirety for the king, my lord. I have said repeatedly to Paḫa(m)nate, my commissioner, "Bring auxiliary troops to protect the lands of the king."

(13–19) Now all the kings of the king of the Hurrian host are seeking to confiscate the lands from my control and from the control of [the commissioner] of the king, [my] lord, [but I] am guarding th[em.]

(19–29) [Look, Paḫ]a(m)nate is w[ith you]; may the king, my sun god, ask him if I am not guarding the city of Ṣumur and the city of Ullassa while my commissioner is on a mission of the king, my lord. And I am guarding the barley harvest of the city of Ṣumur and all the territories of the king, my sun god, my lord.

(30–32) So may the king, my lord, recognize me (officially) and assign me to the jurisdiction of Paḫa(m)nate, my commissioner.

EA 61

TRANSCRIPTION

Obv.	01)	[*a-na* LU]GAL ^{d}UTU EN-*ia*
	02)	[*um-m*]*a* ⌜^{I}⌝ÌR-*A-ši-*⌜*ir*⌝*-ti*$_{7}$ ÌR[-*ka*$_{4}$]
	03)	[*ù*] *ṭi-iṭ* ⌜GÌR⌝.⌜ḪI⌝.⌜A⌝-*ka*$_{4}$ U[R. GI$_{7}$]
	04)	[*š*]*a* É LUGAL EN-*ia a-n*[*a*]
	05)	[GÌR.ḪI.A LU]G[AL EN-]⌜*i*⌝-⌜*a*⌝
	06)	[7-*šu ù* 7-*šu am-qut*]

Bottom half(?) of the text is missing

Rev.	01)	[...] traces [...]
	02)	[...............]L[Ú]
	03)	[URU]⌜*Ul*⌝-⌜*la*⌝-*sí*^{KI} *a-n*[*a*...]
	04)	[...] URU ⌜*Ṣu*⌝-*mu-r*[*i*^{KI}...]
	05)	[...*gá*]*b-bá* KUR MAR.T[U...]
Up.ed.	06)	[*a-na* LUGA]L ^{d}UTU ⌜EN⌝-⌜*ia*⌝[...]
	07)	[...] LUGAL ^{d}UTU EN-*ia*
	08)	[...] *ù a-*⌜*wa*⌝*-ta*$_{5}$ *li-*⌜*te*⌝[-*ra*]
	09)	*a-na* ÌR-*šu*

EA 61

TRANSLATION

(1–5) [To the ki]ng, the sun god, my lord; [the messa]ge of ʿAbdi-Ashirta, [your] servant [and] the mud on your feet, the ho[und o]f the king, my lord: a[t the feet of the ki]n[g, my [lord seven times and seven times have I fallen].

Rev. and Up.ed.
(1–9) […]the ru[ler of the city of] Ullasa, t[o…] the city of Ṣumur […a]ll the land of Amur[ru…to the kin]g, the sun god, my lord […] the king, the sun god, my lord […] so may he sen[d back] word to his servant.

EA 62

TRANSCRIPTION

Obv. 01) [*a-na* ^{I}]⸢*Pa*⸣-⸢*ḫa*⸣-⸢*na*⸣-*te* ⸢*be*⸣-⸢*lí*⸣-⸢*ia*⸣
02) [*um-ma*] ^{I}⸢ÌR⸣-⸢*A*⸣-⸢*ši*⸣-⸢*ir*⸣-⸢*te*⸣ ⸢ÌR⸣-[*ka-ma*]
03) [*a-na* GÌR.]⸢MEŠ⸣ *be-lí*-⸢*ia*⸣ [*am-qut*]
04) [*mi-*]⸢*i*⸣-*nu a-wa-te*$^{⸢MEŠ⸣}$-⸢*ka*⸣ ⸢*be*⸣-⸢*lí*⸣⸢*a*⸣!-⸢*na*⸣! ⸢*muḫ*⸣-⸢*ḫi*⸣-⸢*i*⸣[*a*]
05) [*ša ta-d*]*ab-bu-ub*-⸢*šu*⸣-⸢*nu*⸣ [*a-na m*]*i*-⸢ni_7⸣ ⸢*ki*⸣-⸢*ia*⸣-[*a*]*m*
06) [*ta-dab-bu*]-⸢*ub*⸣ ⸢*be*⸣-⸢*lí*⸣ ⸢*at*⸣-⸢*ta*⸣-⸢*mi*⸣ ⸢LÚ⸣.K[ÚR]
07) [*ša* KUR *Mi*]-*iṣ-ri*$^{⸢KI⸣}$ ⸢*ù*⸣ ⸢*te*⸣-⸢*ep*⸣-⸢*pu*⸣-⸢*uš*⸣ [*ar-na*]
08) [*a-na* LÚ.]⸢MEŠ⸣ KUR *M*[*i-*]⸢*iṣ*⸣-⸢*ri*⸣-*i*$^{⸢KI⸣}$ ⸢*li*⸣-[*i*]*š*-[*me*]
09) [*be-lí ia-*]⸢*nu*⸣ LÚ.⸢MEŠ⸣ ⸢*i*⸣-⸢*na*⸣ ⸢*lìb*⸣-*bi* ⸢URU⸣ ⸢*Ṣu*⸣-⸢*mu*⸣-*ri* ^{KI}
10) [*a-na na-ṣ*]*a-ri-ši* [*ki-ma qa*]-*be-šu* ⸢*ù*⸣
11) [URU *Ṣu-m*]*u-ri*$^{⸢KI⸣}$ ⸢ÉRIN⸣.⸢MEŠ⸣ URU *Š*[*e*]-⸢*eḫ*⸣-⸢*la*⸣-[*li*] ^{KI}
12) [*iṣ-ba-tu*] *ia-nu* ⸢LÚ⸣.⸢MEŠ⸣ ⸢*i*⸣-⸢*na*⸣ ⸢*lìb*⸣-*bi-ši* [*a-na na*]-⸢*ṣa*⸣-*ri-ši*
13) ⸢*ù*⸣[*in-n*]*é-ri*-⸢*ir*⸣ ⸢*a*⸣-⸢*na*⸣-⸢*ku*⸣ *iš-tu* ⸢URU⸣ ⸢*Ir*⸣-[*qat*]$^{⸢KI⸣}$
14) ⸢*ù*⸣ ⸢*ak*⸣-⸢*šu*⸣-[*ud*]-*ma* ⸢*a*⸣-⸢*na*⸣-⸢*ku*⸣ ⸢URU⸣ ⸢*Ṣu*⸣-*mu-ri*$^{⸢KI⸣}$
15) ⸢*ù*⸣ *u*!-*uš*[-*te-ṣí-*]*ka* ⸢*iš*⸣-⸢*tu*⸣ UZU.ŠU-*ti*
16) ÉRIN.MEŠ URU ⸢*Še*⸣-[*eḫ*]-⸢*la*⸣-[*li*]$^{⸢KI⸣}$ ⸢*šum*⸣-*ma ú-ul aš-bá-ku*
17) *a*-⸢*na*⸣-⸢*ku*⸣ ⸢*i*⸣-⸢*na*⸣ [URU *Ir-qat*]$^{⸢KI⸣}$ ⸢*šum*⸣-*ma i-na a-šar* É *né-eḫ*
18) *aš*-⸢*bá*⸣-⸢*ku*⸣ *ù* [*lu-ú i*]-⸢*šar*⸣-⸢*ra*⸣-*pu*-ni_7
19) ⸢*i*⸣-⸢*na*⸣ ⸢IZI⸣-*te*^{MEŠ} [URU] ⸢*Ṣu*⸣-*mu-ri*$^{⸢KI⸣}$
20) ⸢*ù*⸣ ⸢É⸣.⸢GAL⸣-*š*[*i*] ⸢ÉRIN⸣.⸢MEŠ⸣ ⸢URU⸣ *Še-eḫ-la-li*$^{⸢KI⸣}$
21) ⸢*ù*⸣ ⸢*i*⸣-*nu-ma in-né-ri-ir a-na-ku*
22) *iš-tu* URU *Ir-qat*$^{⸢KI⸣}$ *ù ak*-⸢*šu*⸣-⸢*ud*⸣-*m*[*i*] ⸢*a*⸣-*na-ku*
23) *i-na* URU *Ṣu-mu-ri*[^{KI}] *ù ia-nu* LÚ.MEŠ
Lo.ed. 24) ⸢*ša*⸣ *aš-bu i-na* É.GAL-*ši ù a-nu-um-ma*
25) ⸢LÚ⸣.MEŠ *ša aš-bu*-ni_7 *i-na* É.GAL-*ši*
Rev. 26) ^{I}*Ša-bi*-DINGIR ^{I}*Bi-ši-ta-nu* ^{I}*Ma-a-ia*
27) ^{I}*Ar-ṣa-yu a-nu*-⸢*um*⸣-*ma* 4 LÚ.MEŠ
28) *ša aš-bu*-ni_7 *i*-⸢*na*⸣ É.GAL-*ši*

EA 62

TRANSLATION

(1–3) [To] Paḫa(m)nate, my lord, [the message of ʿAbdi-Ashirte, [your] servant; [at the fee]t of my lord [have I fallen].

(4–8) [Wh]at are your words, my lord, to m[e, that you are sa]ying? [Wh]y [do you spe]ak [thu]s, my lord? "You [are an] ene[my of the land of E]gypt and you are com[mitting a crime against the me]n of the land of E[gy]pt."

(8–16) May [my lord] lis[ten!] There are [n]o men within Ṣumur [to pro]tect it [in accordance with] his (my lord's) command and the troops of the city of Sheḫlali [had seized] the city of Ṣumur. There were no men within it [to pro]tect it. But I was called out from the city of ʿIr[qat] and I reached the city of Ṣumur and I brou[ght] you out of the hand of the troops of the city of Sheḫlali.

(16–24) If I were not located in [ʿIrqat], if I had been located in a restful place, then the troops of the city of Sheḫlali would have burned [the city of] Ṣumur with fire and its palace. But when I was called out from the city of ʿIrqat and I reached the city of Ṣumur, there were no men that were dwelling in its palace.

(24–28) But now, the men that were dwelling in its palace were Šabi-ilu, Bishitanu, Maya (and) Arṣayu. Now the four men who dwelt in its palace

29) *ù iq-bu-ni*$_7$ *šu-nu a-na ia-ši*
30) *še-ez-zi-bá-an-na-ši-mi iš-tu* ŠU-*ti*
31) ÉRIN.MEŠ URU *Še-eḫ-la-li* KI *ù ú-še-ez-zi-*[*bá*]-⸢*šu*⸣
\\\\-*nu*
32) [*i*]*š-tu* ŠU-*ti* ÉRIN.MEŠ URU *Še-eḫ-la-li*
33) [4 Z]I.⸢MEŠ⸣ *ú-wi-i-mi* 25 *ša i-dú-ku-ni*$_7$
34) [ÉRIN.MEŠ URU *Še-e*]*ḫ-la-li* KI *ù i-nu-ma lìb*!-*bi*
35) [*be-lí-ia ù uš-ši-*]*ra* ÉRIN.MEŠ
36) [*a-na la-qí* 4 LÚ.ME]Š *an-nu-te*MEŠ
37) [*ù ša-a*]*l*-⸢*šu*⸣-⸢*nu*⸣ *iš-tu* URU *Ṣu-mu-ri* KI
38) [*šu-nu in-na-*]⸢*ab*⸣-*tu*$_4$-⸢*ma*⸣ *la-a aṭ-ru-ud-m*[*i*]
39) [*am-mi-*]*ni*$_7$ ⸢*i*⸣-⸢*ka*⸣-⸢*az*⸣-*zi-bu-ni*$_7$
40) [LÚ.MEŠ] ⸢*ḫa*⸣-*za-nu*-⸢*te*⸣⸢MEŠ⸣ *a-na pa-ni-ka*
41) [*ù t*]*e*-⸢*eš*⸣-⸢*te*⸣-⸢*nim*⸣-*me a-na ša-šu-nu*
42) [*ù* I]⸢*I*⸣-⸢*a*⸣-⸢*ma*⸣-⸢*a*⸣-*ia* ⸢*i*⸣-*nu-ma i-šap-pár*
43) [*a-na*] ⸢*muḫ*⸣-⸢*ḫi*⸣-⸢*ka*⸣ *ù i-ka-az-zi-ib*
44) [*a-na pa-n*]*i*-⸢*ka*⸣ *ù te*-⸢*eš*⸣-*te-nim-me*
45) [*a-na a-wa-*]⸢*te*⸣⸢MEŠ⸣-⸢*šu*⸣ I*Ia-ma-a-ia*
46) [*id-bu-ub i*]*t-ti* ⸢ÉRIN⸣.MEŠ URU *Še-eḫ-la-*
li⸢KI⸣
47) [*ù i-qa-bu-*]⸢*ni*$_7$⸣ *a-na ṣa-bá-at*
48) [URU *Ṣu-mu-*]⸢*ri*⸣⸢KI⸣ *ù il-te*-⸢*qè*⸣
49) [ÉRIN.MEŠ *a-na*] ⸢*ṣa*⸣-*bat* URU-*la-ma*
Up.ed. 50) [LÚ.]MEŠ *mar-ṣa-a a-ni-na*
51) *aš-ku-un i-na* URU ⸢*Ṣu*⸣-⸢*mu*⸣-[*ri* KI]
52) *an-na na-ṣa-ri-ši*

Lft.ed. 53) [.....................URU *Ṣu-m*]*u-ri* KI
54) [..............................]*be-lí*-⸢*i*⸣*a*
55) [......................*a-na la-ma-*]*di* LUGAL-*ma*

(29–34) and they (themselves) said to me: "Deliver us from the hand of the troops of the city of Sheḫlali." So I delivered them from the hand of the troops of the city of Sheḫlali. [Four liv]es I saved. There were twenty five that [the troops of the city of Sheḫ]lali slew.

(34–49) But when [my lord decides, then se]nd troops [to take] these [four men and interroga]te them. From the city of Ṣumur [they fl]ed; I did not expell (them). [Wh]y do the city rulers lie to your face? ⸢And [yo]u always listen to them. But Yamaia, when he writes [t]o you, then he lies [to] your [fac]e and you always listen [to] his [wor]ds. Yamaya [communicated wi]th the troops of the city of Sheḫlali [and th]ey [spok]e about capturing [the city of Ṣumu]r and he took [troops to] capture the city.

(50–52) These sick [men] have I placed in the city of Ṣumur to protect it.

(53–55) [...the city of Ṣum]ur [....] my lord [...for the informat]ion of the king.

EA 63

TRANSCRIPTION

Obv. 01) [*a-na*] ⸢^{I}⸣*šàr-ri* ⸢EN⸣-⸢*ia*⸣
02) ⸢*qí*⸣-*bí-ma*
03) *um-ma* ^{I}*Ab-di-Aš-ta-‹ar›-ti*
04) ÌR ^{I}*šàr-ri*
05) *a-na* 1 GÌR.MEŠ ^{I}*šàr-ri* ⸢EN⸣-⸢*ia*⸣
06) 7 *ù* 7 *ma-aq-ta-*⸢*ti*⸣ ⸢*a*⸣-⸢*na*⸣ ⸢GÌR⸣.MEŠ ⸢*ša*⸣ ⸢^{I}⸣⸢LUGAL⸣ ⸢EN⸣-⸢*ia*⸣⸢\⸣ ⸢*am*⸣-⸢*qú*⸣-*ut*
07) *ù a-wa-ti qa-ba šàr-*⸢*ri*⸣ ⸢EN⸣‹-*ia*›
08) [*a-*]⸢*na*⸣ ^{I}*ia-ši ù iš-te-*⸢*mu*⸣
09) [*a*]*-wa-ti* ^{I}*šàr-ri* E[N-*ia*]
10) [*iš*-]⸢*te*⸣*-mu ù*
11) [*li-*]⸢*iš*⸣*-te-mé* ^{I}L[UGAL EN-*ia*]

Rev. 12) [*a-wa-*]⸢*ti*⸣*-ia* [*i-nu-ma*]
13) [KÚ]R.NU ⸢*da*⸣-⸢*na*⸣*-at* U[GU-*ia*]
14) ⸢*li*⸣-⸢*de*⸣
15) ⸢*ù*⸣ ⸢*yi*⸣-⸢*il*$_5$⸣-⸢*ma*⸣-⸢*ad*⸣ (?)
16) ⸢^{I}⸣⸢*šàr*⸣-⸢*ri*⸣

EA 63

TRANSLATION

(1–6) Speak [to] the king, my lord, the message of ʿAbdi-Ashta‹r›t, the servant of the king: At the feet of the king, my lord, seven and seven (times) have I fallen; at the feet of the king, my lord, have I fallen.

(7–9) And the king, ‹my› lord, has spoken words to me and I am heeding the words of the king, [my] lo[rd].

(10–13) [I] am heeding so [may] the k[ing, my lord] heed my [wo]rds [because hos]tility is strong a[gainst me].

(14–16) May the king be apprised and may he be informed.

EA 64

TRANSCRIPTION

Obv. 01) *a-na šàr-ri* EN-*ia*
02) *qí-bí-ma*
03) *um-ma* ^{I}ÌR-^{d}INNIN ÌR *šàr-ri*
04) *a-na* ^{I}GÌR.MEŠ *šàr-ri* EN-*ia*
05) *ma-aq-ti-ti* 7 GÌR.MEŠ *šàr-ri* EN-*ia*
06) *ù* 7 *mi-la-an-na*
07) *ù ka-ba-tu-ma ù ṣú*!-*uḫ-ru-ma*
08) *ù yi-il*$_{5}$*-ma-ad šàr-ri* EN-ia
09) *ki-ma da-na-at* KÚR.NU UGU-*ia*
10) *ù yi-da-mi-iq*
11) *i-na pa-ni šàr-ri* EN-*ia*
12) *ù yu-wa-ši-ra*
13) 1 LÚ.GAL *a-na na-ṣa-ri-ia*

Rev. 14) *ša-ni-tam a-wa-ti*
15) *ša-pa-ar šàr-ri*
\ EN-*ia*
16) *a-na* ^{I}*ia-ši*
17) *ù iš-te-mu*
18) *gáb-bi a-wa-ti šàr-ri* EN-⸢*ia*⸣
19) *iš-te-mu*
20) *a-nu-ma*
21) 10 MUNUS.MEŠ

---

22) \ *mé-ki-*^{tu}

---

23) \ *ia-pa-aq-ti*

EA 64

TRANSLATION

(1–7) Speak to the king, my lord, the message of ʿAbdi-Ashtart, the servant of the king: At the feet of the king, my lord (feet of the king my lord), have I fallen seven (times) and seven times, on the stomach and on the back.

(8–13) And may the king, my lord, be informed that the hostility against me is strong so may it be pleasing to the king, my lord, and may he send a senior official to protect me.

(14–23) Furthermore, the king, my lord, wrote words to me and I have heeded. All the words of the king, my lord, have I heeded. Now
ten women,

---

viz. of glass,

---

have I produced.

EA 65

TRANSCRIPTION

Obv.
01) [*a-na šàr-ri* EN-*ia*]
02) [*qí- b*]*í-* ⌜*ma*⌝
03) [*um-ma*]⌜^{I}⌝⌜*Ab*⌝-⌜*di*⌝- ^{d}INNIN ÌR-*ka*
04) *a-na* ^{I}GÌR.MEŠ EN-*ia* 7 *ù* 7 *mi-la*
05) \\ *ma-aq-ta-ti ù ka-ba-tu-ma ù ṣú-ú*ʾ*-ru-*^{ma}
06) *a-na* ^{I}GÌR.MEŠ *šàr-ri* EN-*ia*
07) *ù ki-*⌜*ma*⌝ *a-wa-ti ša-pa-ra šàr-ri* EN-*ia*
08) ⌜*a*⌝*-na ia-ši iš-tu-mu* ⌜*gáb*⌝*-bi a-wa-ti šàr-ri* ‹EN›-⌜*ia*⌝
\\ *iš* [*-te-mu*](?)
09) *ù* URU.DIDLI.MEŠ *šàr-ri* ⌜*it*⌝*-ti-‹ia›*
10) *ù i-na-ṣa-ru*
11) *ù ‹i›-šu-ši-ru*
12) [*a*]-⌜*na*⌝ *pa-ni* ÉRIN.MEŠ *pí-ṭ*[*á-t*]*i*
13) [*šàr*]*-ri* EN-*ia*
14) ....traces......

EA 65

TRANSLATION

(1–6) [Spe]ak [to the king, my lord; the message] of ʿAbdi-Aštarti your servant. At the feet of my lord seven and seven times \\ have I fallen both on the stomach and on the back, at the feet of the king, my lord.

(7–13) And according to the words that the king, my lord wrote to me, I am heeding all the words of the king, and the towns of the king (that are) under ‹my› responsibility. And I am guarding and ‹I› am preparing for the coming of the regular tr[oo]ps of the [ki]ng, my lord.

(14) *traces*

EA 66

TRANSCRIPTION

Obv.

01) [*a-na* ^{I}*šàr-*]⸢*ri*⸣ E[N-*ia*]
02) [...........E]N-⸢*ia*⸣
03) [.........*iš*-]⸢*ta*⸣-⸢*pa*⸣-*a*[*r*]
04) [..........]⸢^{I}⸣⸢*Ḫa*⸣-⸢*ya*⸣
05) [..........]⸢*yi*⸣-⸢*na*⸣-⸢*di*⸣-[in_4]
06) [^{I}*šàr-*]⸢*ri*⸣ ⸢EN⸣-⸢*ia*⸣ ⸢*pa*⸣-⸢*ni*⸣[-*šu a-na*]
07) ⸢KUR⸣-⸢*ia*⸣ ⸢*da*⸣-⸢*na*⸣-⸢*at*⸣ ⸢KÚR⸣-⸢*ti*⸣
08) ⸢UGU⸣-⸢*ia*⸣ *ti*-⸢*di*⸣-⸢*in*⸣-⸢*ni*⸣
09) ⸢*i*⸣-⸢*na*⸣ ⸢*qa*⸣-⸢*ti*⸣-⸢*šu*⸣ ⸢*ù*⸣ ⸢*ti*⸣-[*din-šu*]
10) [*a*-]⸢*na*⸣ ⸢LÚ⸣.⸢MÁŠKIM⸣[.....]
11) [.......]⸢*ša*⸣ ⸢ÌR⸣ [.......]
12) [........]*uš*-[*ši-ir*........]
13) [........................]

EA 66

TRANSLATION

obv. 01) [To the ki]ng,[my] lo[rd]
02) [...........] my [lo]rd
03) [.........he w]rote
04) [..........]Ḫaya
05) [..........]may he giv[e]
06) [the ki]ng, my lord, [his]attention [to]
07) my land. Strong is the hostility
08) against me. May you give me
09) into his hand, and may you app[oint him]
10) as the commissioner [...........]
11) [.......]of the servant[......]
12) [........] se[*nd*............]
13) [............................]

EA 67

TRANSCRIPTION

Obv. 01) [*a-na* LUGAL ^{d}UTU-*ši be-lí-ia qí-bí-ma um-ma*]
02) [^{I}.................ÌR-*ka-ma a-n*]*a* G[ÌR.MEŠ LUGAL ^{d}UTU-*ši b*]*e-lí-i*[*a*]
03) [7 *ù* 7 *am-qú-ut*....
04) [*a-nu-um-ma li-de-mi* ^{d}UT]U-*ši be-lí-i*[*a a-na*]
05) [URU.KI ^{d}UTU-*ši be-lí-ia* URU]*Ṣu-mu-*⸢*ri*⸣^{K}[^{I}]
06) [*a-nu-um- ma i-na-an-na* ^{I}*A-zi-ru*] *a-ši-ib i-n*[*a*]
07) [URU *Ṣu-mu-ri*^{KI} *qa-du* ÉRIN.]MEŠ-*šu qa-du* GI[Š.GIGIR.MEŠ-*šu*]
08) [*ù* LUGAL ^{d}UTU-*ši be-lí li-iš*]-*a*[*l*-]*mi*
09) [*a-na* URU *Ṣ*]*u-*⸢*mu*⸣-⸢*ri*⸣[^{KI} UR]U.⸢KI⸣ ⸢^{d}⸣[UTU-*š*]*i be-*⸢*lí*⸣*-ia*
10) [*ù* ^{d}U]TU-*ši lu-ú i-*[*d*]*e-mi* SIG$_5$ *g*[*áb*]-*bu* LÚ.MEŠ KUR *M*[*i-iṣ-ri*]
11) [*ša a*]*š-bu-ni*$_7$ *i-na* [URU] *Ṣu-mu-*⸢*ri*⸣^{KI} URU.KI ^{d}U[TU-*ši be-lí-ia*]
12) [*it-t*]*a-ṣú-ni*$_7$ *ù i-na* KUR-*ti*$_4$*-ia aš-bu-ni*$_7$
13) [*be-l*]*í ù i*$_{15}$*-te-pu-uš ma-mi-ta*
14) [*it-*]*ti* LÚ [*š*]*a* URU *Gu*$_5$*-ub-li*^{KI} *ù it-ti* L[Ú *ša* URU....]
15) ⸢*ù*⸣ *gáb-bu* LÚ.MEŠ *ḫal-zu-uḫ-lu-ti ša* KUR-*ka* ⸢*ù*⸣(?)
16) ⸢*it*⸣*-ti-šu* DUG.GA-*ni*$_7$ *be-lí i-na-an-na šu-ú-ut k*[*i-ma*]
17) [LÚ] SA-⸢GAZ⸣.ZA.MEŠ UR.GI$_7$ *ḫal-qú ù iṣ-ba-at*
18) [URU *Ṣu*]-*m*[*u-*]*ri*^{KI} URU.KI ^{d}UTU-*ši be-lí-ia*
19) [.........................*lí* DINGIR-*lu*$_4$
20) [.........................]^{d}UTU-*ši be-lí-ia*
21) [.........................*u*]*b-*⸢*la*⸣*-mi*

Rev. 01') [...................................]
02') [...................................]
03') *ši*...................................]
04') *i*[*l*...................................]
05') [...................................]
06') *i*[*m*...................................]
07') *ša*[...................................]
08') *aš*[...................................]
09') *a* [...................................]
10') *ù* [...................................]
11') *ša*[...................................]
12') [...................................]

EA 67

TRANSLATION

(1–3) [Speak to the king, the sun god, my lord. Thus (says)…, your servant. A]t the fe[et of the king, the sun god,] my [l]ord, [seven (times) and seven (times) have I fallen.]

(4–5) [Now may the sun] god, my lord, [be apprised concerning the city of the sun god, my lord, the city of] Ṣumur.

(6–16) [Right now, Aziru (?)] is located in [the city of Ṣumur with his troo]ps, with [his] c[hariotry. So may the king, the sun god, my lord make in]quiry [concerning the city of Ṣ]umur, [the cit]y of the [sun go]d, my lord. [And] may [the su]n god be apprised: all the men of the land of E[gypt that we]re located in [the city of] Ṣumur, the city of the sun [god, my lord,] are all right; they [ca]me forth and are located in my territory, my [lo]rd. But he has made a treaty oath [wi]th the ruler of the city of Byblos and with the ru[ler of the city of…] and as for all of the fortress commanders of your land, now they are on good terms with him, my lord.

(16–21) Now, he is l[ike] the *ʿapîru* [man], a stray dog. And he has seized [the city of Ṣu]m[u]r, the city of the sun god, my lord. […]my [lor]d, the god […]the sungod, my lord […I] brought [………….]

Reverse: *Only signs at the beginning of the lines. Someone has scraped away the lines on the back to create a smooth surface, sunken into the backside of the tablet.*

EA 68

TRANSCRIPTION

Obv. 01) [^{I}*Ri*]-*ib-ḫa-ad-*⸢*da*⸣(?)
02) [*iq-*]*bi a-na* EN-*šu*
03) [*šàr*] KUR.KI.ḪI.A LUGAL GAL
04) [^{d}]NIN *ša* URU *Gu-ub-la*
05) *ti-id-di-in*$_{4}$ *du-na*
06) *a-na* LUGAL *be-li-ia*
07) *a-na* GÌR.MEŠ EN-*ia* ^{d}UTU-*ia*
08) 7-*šu* 7-*ta-a-an am-qut*
09) *lu-ú i-de* LUGAL EN-*ia*
10) *i-nu-ma šal-ma-at* URU *Gub-la*
11) GÉME *ki-it-ti ša* LUGAL
12) *ù* KAL.GA *ma-gal nu-kúr-tu*$_{4}$
13) ⸢*ša*⸣ ÉRIN.MEŠ SA.GAZ.MEŠ
14) [UG]U-*ia ù la-a* ‹*i*›*a-qúl-mì*
Lo.ed. 15) LUGAL EN-*ia iš-tu*
Rev. 16) [UR]U ⸢*Ṣu*⸣-*mu-ur* ^{KI}
17) [*l*]*a -a in*$_{4}$*-né-pu-uš gá*[*b-b*]*u*
18) ⸢*a*⸣-*na* ÉRIN.MEŠ SA.GAZ.MEŠ
19) *i-na* LÚ.MÁŠKIM *šàr-ri*
20) *ša i-šu-ú i-na* ⸢URU⸣ *Ṣu-mu-ur*
21) *ba-*⸢*al*⸣*-ṭá-at* URU ⸢*Gub*⸣*-la*
22) *a-nu-um-ma* ^{I}*Pa-ḫa-a*[*m*]-⸢*na*⸣-*ta*
23) LÚ.MÁŠKIM LUGAL *ša i-n*[*a*]
24) URU *Ṣu-mu-ur*^{KI} ⸢*i*⸣-⸢*de*⸣-*mì*
ma-gal!(NA-AŠ)
25) *pu-uš-qám*
26) *ša* UGU URU *Gub-la*
27) *iš-tu* KUR *Ia-ri-im-mu-ta*
28) *nu-bal-li-iṭ*
29) KAL.GA *ma-gal nu-*⸢*kúr*⸣-⸢*tu*$_{4}$⸣
30) [UG]U-*nu ù ú-ul*
Up.ed. 31) [*ia*]-*qúl-mì* LUGAL *iš-t*[*u*]
32) [UR]U. DIDLI.KI-*šu*

EA 68

TRANSLATION

(1–8) [R]ib-Hadda [sp]oke to his lord, [king] of the lands, the great king: May the Lady of the city of Byblos grant strength to the king, my lord; at the feet of my lord, my sun god, seven times and seven times have I fallen.

(9–21) May the king be apprised that it is well with the city of Byblos, the loyal handmaiden of the king but the hostility of the *ʿapîru* troops against me is very fierce. So may the king, my lord, not keep silent concerning [the ci]ty of Ṣumur lest ev[ery o]ne join the *ʿapîru* troops. It is through the commissioner of the king whom he has in the city of Ṣumur that the city of Byblos is sustained.

(22–32) Now, Paḫamnata, the king's commissioner who is in the city of Ṣumur, knows the great(!) pressure that is on the city of Byblos. It is from the land of Yarimuta that we got supplies. Very fierce is the hostility [aga]inst us so may the king not [ke]ep silent concerning his [ci]ties.

EA 69

TRANSCRIPTION

Obv. 01) [*a-na* ^{I}.........*a-bi-ia*]
02) [*qí-bí-ma*]
03) [*um-ma* ^{I}*Ri-ib-*^{d}IŠKUR DUMU-*ka*]
04) [*a-na* GÌR.MEŠ-*ka am-qú-ut*]
05) [^{d}NIN *ša* URU *Gub-la* DINGIR LUGAL]
06) [*be-li-ia ti-din* TÉŠ-*ka*]
07) ⸢*a*⸣-*na* ⸢*pa*⸣[-*ni* LUGAL *be-li-ia* DINGIR-*ia*]
08) ^{d}UTU-*ia* [..........]
09) ⸢*ù*⸣ *bi-ta-*⸢*ka*⸣ ⸢É⸣? ⸢x⸣[.......*ù*]
10) ⸢*a*⸣-*qa-bu ìl-te*$_{9}$*-qú-mi g*[*áb-bu a-wa-ti*]
11) ⸢*i*⸣-*na be-ri-šu-nu* ⸢UGU⸣[-*ia*]
12) [*ša*]-*ni-tam a-nu-ma i-na-an-na*
13) ⸢*i*⸣-*na-mu-šu ur-ra m*[*u-ša*]
14) ⸢*i*⸣-*na nu-kùr-ti*^{MEŠ} *ša* UGU-‹*ia*›
15) ⸢*ša*⸣-⸢*ni*⸣-⸢*tam*⸣ *at-ta ti-de-mi*
16) ⸢URU⸣.⸢KI⸣.⸢MEŠ⸣-*ia da-an-nu* UGU-*ia*
17) [*ù*] ⸢*ú*⸣-⸢*ul*⸣ ⸢*i*⸣-*le-‹i› i-pé-èš*
18) [SIG$_{5}$]-⸢*qa*⸣ ⸢*it*⸣-⸢*ti*⸣-⸢*šu*⸣[-*nu ša-ni-*]*tam*
Lo.ed. 19) ⸢ÉRIN⸣.⸢MEŠ⸣ *nu*-KÙR-⸢*ia*⸣ [*da-an-*]*nu-ta*$_{5}$
Rev. 20) ⸢*ša*⸣ ⸢URU⸣ *Ma-*⸢*ag*⸣-⸢*da*⸣-*lì*
21) ⸢*ù*⸣ ÉRIN.MEŠ URU *Ma*!-*aṣ-pat*^{KI}
22) ⸢*nu*⸣-*kúr-tu*$_{4}$ UGU-*ia ù a-nu-ma*
23) *ia-nu-um* LÚ-*lu*$_{4}$ *ša yi-ri-ṣú-ni*
24) *iš-tu qa-ti-šu-nu ša-ni-tam*
25) *i-na ka-‹ša›-ad* ^{I}*Ap-pí-ḫa a-na maḫ-ri-ia*
26) *ši-si-tu*$_{4}$ UGU-*ia ù gáb-bi*
27) KÁ.GAL.MEŠ-*ia ti-la*!-*qé* U[RUDU?]
28) \ *nu-ḫu-uš-tu*$_{4}$ *ša-*⸢*al*⸣[-*mi*]
29) ^{I}*Ap-pí-ḫa* LÚ-*ka ki g*[*áb-bi*]
30) *a-wa-ti ša-ni-tam qú-ru-*⸢*ud*⸣

EA 69

TRANSLATION

(1–8) [To…, my father, speak; message of Rib-Haddi, your son: At your feet I have fallen. May the Lady of the city of Byblos, *the goddess of the king, my lord*, give you honor] in the pres[ence of the king, my lord, my deity,] my sun god.

(9–11) […] and your house, Beth-[NIN.IB(?) and] I have been saying "They have a[ll] made an [agreement] against [me]."

(12–14) Furthermore, now I am in retreat day and night because of the hostility against ‹me›.

(15–18) Furthermore, you should know that my towns are stronger than I [and] I am unable to con[cilia]te the[m].

(18–24) [Further]more, the troops of my [str]ong enemie‹s› of the city of Magdal and the troops of Maṣpat(!) are hostile to me and now there is no man that can deliver me from their hand.

(24–30) Furthermore, upon Appiḫa's rea‹ch›ing me, there was an outcry against me, and as for all my gates, the bronze was taken. Ask Appiḫa, your man, about the wh[ole] affair.

31) *a-na* LUGAL *be-l*[*i-ka ù yu-ḫa-mi-iṭ*]
32) *a-*⌜*ṣi*⌝ É[RIN.MEŠ *pí-ṭá-ti*]

33–37) completely broken off

Lft.ed. 38) [.......*gá*]*b-b*[*u*...]
39) [........*i-pé-e*]$š_{15}$ ⌜SIG_5⌝-*q*[*a it-ti-šu-nu*]

(30–37) Furthermore, entreat the king, [your] lo[rd that he *hasten*] the coming forth of the re[gular troops...........].

(38–39) [...a]l[l...to conci]liat[e them].

EA 70

TRANSCRIPTION

Obv. 01) [^{I}*Ri-ib-*^{d}IŠKUR *iq-bi*]
02) [*a-na* EN-*šu* LUGAL KUR.KUR.KI.MEŠ]
03) [LUGAL GAL ^{d}NIN *ša* URU *Gub-la*]
04) [*ti-di-*in_4 KAL.GA *a-na* LUGAL-*ri*]
05) [EN-*ia a-n*]*a* G[ÌR.MEŠ]
06) [EN-*ia*] ⸢^{d}⸣UTU-*i*[*a* 7-*šu*]
07) [7-*ta-a*]*n am-qú-u*[*t a-mur*]
08) [URU.K]I.ḪI.A URU *Gub*[*-la*]
09) [*nu-kúr*]*-tu-nu* URU *Ma-*⸢*a*⸣[*g?-da-lì*]
10) [URU *ki-it-t*]*i-ka iš-tu*
11) [*da-ri-*]*ti li-ma-ad*
12) [*i-nu-ma*] *uš-ši-*[*i*]*r-ti*
13) [*mi-im-ma*]*-šu ù la-a*
14) [*ú-ka-li*] *na?-ad!-na-ti*
15) [KÙ.BABBAR] *a-na* DUMU-*šu*
16) [*tu?-pa?-*]*ra-*[*a*]*š? be-ri-ku-n*[*i*]
17) [*ù u*]*š-ši-ra-ni*

Lo.ed. 18) [x LÚ.MEŠ] KUR *Mi-iṣ-*[*r*]*i*
19) [*ù* x LÚ.ME]Š KUR *Me-l*[*u*]*-ḫa*

Rev. 20) [*ki-i-*]*ma* LUGAL.MEŠ
21) [*ša na-a*]*d-na-ta* GIŠ.
22) [GIGIR.MEŠ-*š*]*u-nu ù ti-n*[*a*]*-ṣa-‹ru›-*⸢*ni*⸣
23) [*a-di a-ṣ*]*í* ÉRIN.MEŠ *pí-ṭá-ti*
24) [*ù y*]*i-de* LUGAL EN-*ia*
25) [*i-nu-ma*] KUR *A-mur-ri ur-ra*
26) [*mu-ša*] *tu-ba-‹ú-na› a-ṣa* ‹ÉRIN.MEŠ› *pí-ṭá-ti*
27) [*i-na* U]D. KAM^{v}.MEŠ *ka-š*[*a-a*]*d*
28) [ÉRIN.MEŠ *pí-*]*ṭá-ti* KUR ⸢*A*⸣-[*mur-ri*]
29) [*lu-ú* in_4]*-né-ep-ša-*[*at*]
30) [*gáb-bu a-n*]*a šàr-r*[*i* EN-*ia*]
31) [x x x *š*]*u-*⸢*nu*⸣ x[...]

Remainder broken away

EA 70

TRANSLATION

(1–7) [Rīb-Haddi spoke to his lord, the king of all lands, the great king; may the Lady of Byblos grant strength to the king, my lord. A]t the fe[et of my lord], m[y] sun god, [seven times (and) seven time]s have I fall[en.]

(7–11) [Look, the tow]ns of the city of Bybl[os] are our [enem]ies. The town of Ma[gdali(?) was] your [loy]al [city from [of ol]d.

(11–16) Be apprised [that] I sent/released his [property] and I did not [withhold.] I gave [silver] to his son. [You may deci]de between us.

(17–23) [But s]end to me [*x* men of] the land of Egypt [and *x* me]n of the land of Meluḫ̮ḫ̮a [just a]s the kings [to whom] you [have gra]nted [t]heir [chariots], that they may prot‹ect› me [until the coming for]th of the regular troops.

(24–31) [And may] the king, my lord, [be] apprised [that] the land of Amurru day [(and) night] is seeki‹ng› the coming forth of the regular ‹troops›. [On the d]ay of the arrival of [the re]gular [troops] the land of Am[urru will verily go] over [entirely t]o the kin[g, my lord] [.....t]heir [...].

EA 71

TRANSCRIPTION

Obv. 01) [*a-na* ^{I}]*Ḫa-ia pa-sí-t*[*e*]
02) [*um*]-*ma* ^{I}*Ri-ib*-^{d}IŠKUR[ÌR-*ka*]
03) *a-na* GÌR.MEŠ-*ka am-qú*[-*ut*]
04) ^{d}*A-ma-na* DINGIR *ša* LU[GAL *be-li-k*]*a*
05) *ti-di-nu* TÉŠ-*ka i-na*
06) *pa-ni* LUGAL *be-li-ka*
07) *a-mur at-ta* LÚ *em-qú*
08) *i-de* LUGAL *ù i-na em-‹qú›-ti-ka*
09) *iš-ta-pár-ka šàr-ru*
10) *i-na* LÚ.MÁŠKIM *a-na mi-ni*$_{7}$
11) *qa-la-ta ù la-a*
12) *ti-iq-bu a-na šàr-ri*
13) *ù yu-wa-ši-ru-na*
14) ÉRIN.MEŠ *pí-ṭá-ti ù*
15) *ti-ìl-te*$_{9}$-*qú-na*
Lo.ed. 16) URU *Ṣu-mu-ra mi-nu*
17) ^{I}ÌR-*A-š*[*i-ir*]-*ta* ÌR
Rev. 18) UR.GI$_{7}$ *ù yi-ìl-qú*
19) KUR LUGAL *a-na ša-a-šu*
20) *mi-nu ti-la-at-šu*
21) *ù* KAL.GA *i-na* LÚ.GAZ GA.KAL
22) *til-la-at-šu ù*

EA 71

TRANSLATION

(1–6) [To] Ḫaya, the vizi[r], the [mes]sage of Rib-Hadda, [your servant]: At your feet have I fall[en]. May Amon, the god of the ki[ng, yo]ur [lord], give you honor in the presence of the king, your lord.

(7–16) Look, you are a wise man; the king knows (this) and because of your wis‹do›m, the king sent you as commissioner. Why have you kept silent and not spoken to the king that he should send regular troops that they should take the city of Ṣumur?

(16–22) What is ʿAbdi-Ash[ir]ta, the slave, the dog, that he should take the land of the king for himself? What is his militia that he is strong? By the *ʿapîru* men is his militia strong!

23) *uš-ši-ru-na-ni* 50 *ta-pal*
24) ANŠE.KUR.RA *ù* 2 *me* ÉRIN.MEŠ GÌR.MEŠ
25) *ù i-zi-za i-na* URU *Ši-ga-*
ta
26) *i-na pa-ni-šu a-di*
27) *a-ṣí* ÉRIN.MEŠ *pí-ṭá-ti*
28) *ú-ul yu-pa*!(BAR)-*ḫi-ra ka-li*
29) LÚ.MEŠ GAZ.MEŠ *ù*
30) ⸢*yi*⸣-*ìl-qa* URU *Ši-ga-t*[*a*]
31) ⸢*ù*⸣ URU *Am-pí* ⸢*ù*⸣ [*yi-iṣ-bat*]
32) [ḪUR].SAG *ša y*[*i-zi-za*]

Up.ed. 33) [*ù*] *mi-na i-pu-*[*šu-na*]
34) [*ù*] *ia-nu a-šar*
35) [*ir-r*]*u-bu a-na mu-ḫi-*[*šu*]

(22–32) So send me fifty pairs of horses and two hundred foot troops and I will take up a position against him in the town of Shigata until the regular army comes forth. Let him not assemble all the *ʿapîru* men and take the town of Shigata and the town of Ampi and seize the [hill co]untry where he can [take a stand.]

(33–35) Then what can I [do since] there is no place to which I can enter?

EA 72

TRANSCRIPTION

Obv. 01) [....................]⸢*i*⸣-⸢*de*⸣ *šàr-ru*
02) [*i-nu-ma* KAL.]⸢GA⸣ *nu-kúr-tu*$_4$
03) [UGU URU *Gub-la*]⸢*ù*⸣ UGU-*ia la-a*
04) [................]*ki-ma* URU *Ir-q*[*a-*]⸢*ta*⸣
05) [................]*ù* URU *Ar-*[*da*]-⸢*ta*⸣
06) [................]*a-na ša-a-šu*
07) [..........*yu-ba-*]⸢*ú*⸣ URU *Gub-la*
08) [.........URU *A*]*m-pí ù*
09) [..............*q*]*a-du* ÉRIN.MEŠ *p*[*í-ṭá-ti*]
10) [*ù mi-na i-pu-šu-na*]*a-na-ku i-*⸢*na*⸣
11) [*i-de-ni-ia*.........]-*ni-in*$_4$
12) [................]⸢*ša*⸣-*ni-tam*
13) [................] *ti-ìš*[*-me*.....]
14) [................]*ka*[..........]
15) [..............................]
16) [..............................]
Lo.ed. 17) [..............................]
Rev. 18) [..............................]
19) [..............................]
20) [..............................]
21) [..............................]
22) [..............................]
23) [..............................]
24) [..............................]
25) [...............]MEŠ [.........]
26) [...............]⸢*uš*⸣-⸢*ši*⸣-[*ra*.....]
27) [*šàr-ru* 30 *ta-pal* ANŠE.KU]R.RA.⸢MEŠ⸣[*ù* x]GIŠ.GIGIR
28) [...........URU *Ṣu-mu-*]*ra* ^{KI}[...]
29) [................]URU *Am-p*[*í*]
30) [..........ÉRIN.MEŠ *pí-ṭ*]*á-t*[*i*...]
31) [..........KUR *A-mu*]-*ri* ^{KI}
32) [.....................LÚ.M]EŠ GAZ.MEŠ

EA 72

TRANSLATION

bv. 01) [....................]may the king be apprised
02) [that stro]ng is the hostility
03) [against the city of Byblos] and against me. Let not
04) [................]like the town of ʿIrqata
05) [................]and the town of Ardata
06) [................]to himself
07) [..........he is seeki]ng the city of Byblos
08) [.........the town of A]mpi and
09) [...............wi]th regular t[roops]
10) [and what can I do,] myself, all
11) [alone........]???
12) [................]Furthermore
13) [................] may you lis[ten]
14) [................]you[.........]
15) [..............................]
16) [..............................]
o.ed. 17) [..............................]
ev. 18) [..............................]
19) [..............................]
20) [..............................]
21) [..............................]
22) [..............................]
23) [..............................]
24) [..............................]
25) [...............] ––– [.........]
26) [...............]sen[d.....]
27) [oh king, thirty teams of ho]rses[and *x*]chariots
28) [...........the town of Ṣumu]ra [...]
29) [................]the town of Amp[i]
30) [..........regular troo]ps [...]
31) [..........the land of Amur]ru
32) [......................]ʿ*apîru* [me]n.

EA 73

TRANSCRIPTION

Obv. 01) *⸢a⸣-⸢na⸣* ^{I}*⸢A⸣-ma-an-ap-pa a-bi-ia*
02) *um-ma* ^{I}*Ri-ib-ad-da* DUMU-*ka-⸢ma⸣*
03) *a-na* GÌR.MEŠ *a-bi-ia am-qú-ut*
04) ^{d}NIN *ša* URU *Gub-la ti-din*
05) *ba-aš-ta-ka i-na pa-ni*
06) *šàr-ri* EN-*ka a-na mi-ni*$_{7}$
07) *qa-la-ta ù la-a táq-bu*
08) *a-na šàr-ri* EN-*li-ka*
09) *ù tu-ṣa-na qa-du* ÉRIN.MEŠ
10) *pí-ṭá-ti ù ti-ma-qú-tu*
11) UGU KUR *A-mur-ri šum-ma*
12) *ti-iš-mu-na a-ṣí-mi* ÉRIN.MEŠ
13) *pí-ṭá-ti ù i-zi-bu* URU.MEŠ-*šu-nu*
14) *ù pa-aṭ-ru at-ta ú-ul*
15) *ti-i-de* KUR *A-mur-ri i-nu-ma*
16) *⸢a⸣- šar da-an-ni ti-la-ku-na*
17) *⸢ù⸣ an-nu-uš i-na-an-na*
18) *[ú]-ul i-ra-a-mu a-na* ^{I}ÌR-*A-ši-ir-ta*
19) *⸢mi⸣-na yi-pu-šu a-na ša-⸢šu⸣-⸢nu⸣*
Lo.ed. 20) *⸢ù⸣ tu-⸢ba⸣-ú-na ur-ra*
Rev. 21) *⸢ù⸣ mu-ša-am a-ṣí* ÉRIN.MEŠ
22) *⸢pí⸣-ṭá-ti ù ⸢i⸣-te*$_{9}$*-pu-uš*
23) *⸢a⸣-na ša-a-ši*$_{x}$(ŠE) *ù ka-li*
24) LÚ.MEŠ *ḫa-za-nu-te tu-ba-ú-na*
25) *i-pé-eš an-nu-tu*$_{4}$ *a-na* ^{I}ÌR-*A-ši-ir-ta*
26) *⸢i⸣-nu-ma yi-iš-ta-pár a-na* LÚ.MEŠ
27) URU *Am-mi-ia du-ku-mi* EN-*ku-nu*
28) *ù in-né-ep-⸢šu⸣ a-na*
29) LÚ.MEŠ GAZ *ki-na-⸢na⸣ ti-iq-bu-⸢na⸣*
30) LÚ.MEŠ *ḫa-⸢za⸣-nu-tu*$_{4}$ *ki-na-na*
31) *yi-pu-šu a-na ia-ši-nu*
32) *ù ti-né-pu-šu ka-li* KUR.MEŠ
33) *a-na* LÚ.MEŠ GAZ *ù qí-ba-mi*

EA 73

TRANSLATION

(1–6) To Amanappa my father, the message of Rib-Haddi your son: At the feet of my father I have fallen. May the Lady of the city of Byblos grant you honor before the king, your lord.

(6–11) Why do you keep silent and not speak to the king, your lord so that you may come forth with regular troops and pounce on Amurru?

(11–16) If they hear of the coming forth of the regular troops they will abandon their towns and desert. Don't you know Amurru, that they follow the strong one?

(17–28) And now they don't like ʿAbdi-Ashirta; what is he doing to them? And they seek day and night the coming forth of the regular army, and I will join it. And all the city rulers seek to do this thing to ʿAbdi-Ashirta because he wrote to the men of the city of Ammia, "Slay your lord and join the *ʿapîru*."

(29–33) Thus the city rulers are saying, "He will do the same to us," and all the territories will join the *ʿapîru*.

34) *a-wa-ta*$_5$ *an-ni-ta a-na* ⌜*pa*⌝*-ni*
35) *šàr-ri* EN-*li-ka i-nu-ma*
36) *a-bu ù be-lu at-ta-ma*
37) *a-na ia-ši ù a-na ka-ta*$_5$
38) *pa-ni-ia na-ad-na-ti*
39) *ti-i-de pa-ar-ṣa-ia*
40) ⌜*i*⌝*-nu-ma i-ba-ša-ta i-na*
Up.ed 41) ⌜URU⌝ ⌜*Ṣu*⌝*-mu-ra i-nu-*⌜*ma*⌝
42) ⌜ÌR⌝ ⌜*ki*⌝*-it-ti-ka a-na-ku*
Lft.ed. 43) *ù* ⌜*qí*⌝*-bi a-na* LUGAL *be-li*[*-ka*]
44) *ù tu-wa-ša-‹ar› til-la-tu* ⌜*a*⌝[*-na*]
45) ⌜*ia*⌝*-ši ki-ma ar-ḫi-iš*

(33–38) So relate this matter in the presence of the king, your lord, because you are father and master to me and to you have I turned.

(39–45) You know my conduct when you were in Ṣumur, that I am a loyal servant. So speak to the king, your lord so that an auxiliary force may be se‹nt› to me immediately.

EA 74

TRANSCRIPTION

Obv.

01) ^{I}*Ri-ib-ad-da iq-bi a-na* EN-*l*[*i-šu*]
02) *šàr* KUR.KUR LUGAL GAL *šàr ta-am-ḫa-ri* ^{d}[NIN]
03) *ša* URU *Gub-la ti-di-in* GA.KAL *a-na* [LUGAL]
04) EN-*ia a-na* GÌR.MEŠ EN-*li-ia* ^{d}UTU-*i*[*a*]
05) 7-*šu* 7-*a-an am-qú-ut lu-ú i-de šàr-ru*
06) EN-‹*li*› *i-nu-ma šal-ma-at* URU *Gub-la* GÉME
07) *ki-it-ti ša šàr-ri iš-tu* UD.KAM.MEŠ
08) *ša ab-bu-ti-šu ù* ⸢*an*⸣*-nu-uš i-na-an-na*
09) *i-te-zi-ib šàr-ru* URU *ki-it-ti-šu*
10) *iš-tu qa-ti-šu li-*⸢*da*⸣*-ga*l LUGAL *ṭup-*⸢*pí*⸣^{MEŠ}
11) *ša* É *a-bi-šu i-nu-*⸢*ma*⸣ ⸢*ú*⸣*-ul* ÌR *ki-ti*
12) LÚ.*lí* ⸢*ša*⸣ *i-ba-aš-ši* ⸢*i*⸣*-na* URU *Gub-la*
13) *ú-ul ta-qa-al-mi a-na* ÌR-*ka šum-ma*
14) [G]A.KAL *nu-kúr-tu*$_4$ *ša* ÉRIN.MEŠ GAZ UGU‹*-šu*› *ù*
15) DINGIR.MEŠ KUR-*k*[*a*]⸢TI⸣ *ga-am-ru* DUMU.MEŠ-*nu* MUNUS.DUMU.MUNUS.MEŠ‹*-nu*›
16) GIŠ.É-*nu i*[*-n*]*a na-da-ni*$_7$ *i-na* KUR *Ia-ri-mu-ta*
17) *i-na ba-l*[*a-*]*ṭá* ZI-*nu* A.ŠÀ-*ia aš-ša-ta*
18) *ša la m*[*u-*]*ta ma-ši-ìl* ⸢*aš*⸣*-šum ba-li*
19) ⸢*i*⸣*-re-ši*[*-i*]*m gáb*‹*-bi*› URU.MEŠ-*ia ša i-na*
20) ḪUR.SAG \ ⸢*ḫa*⸣*-ar-ri ù i-na a-ḫi a-ia-ab*
21) *i-ba-aš-šu in-né-ep-šu a-na* ÉRIN.MEŠ GAZ
22) URU *Gub-*‹*la*› *qa-du* 2 URU.MEŠ *ir-ti-ḫu a-na ia-ši*
23) *ù an-nu-uš i-na-an-na ìl-te*$_9$*-qé*
24) ^{I}ÌR-*A-ši-ir-ta* URU *Ši-ga-ta a-na ša-a-šu*
25) *ù iq-bi a-na* LÚ.MEŠ URU *Am-mi-ia du-ku-mi*
26) ⸢*eṭ*⸣*-la-ku-nu ù i-ba-ša-tu-nu ki-ma ia-ti-nu*
27) ⸢*ù*⸣ *pa-aš-ḫa-tu-nu ù ti-né-ep-šu ki-ma*
28) [*a-*]⸢*wa*⸣*-te*^{MEŠ}*-šu ù i-ba-aš-šu ki-ma*

EA 74

TRANSLATION

(1–5) Rib-Haddi said to [his] lord, king of the lands, the great king, the king of battle: May the [Lady] of the city of Byblos give strength to the [king], my lord. At the feet of my lord, m[y] sun god, seven times and seven times have I fallen.

(5–12) May the king, ‹my› lord be apprised that the city of Byblos, the faithful handmaiden of the king, has been at peace since the days of his fathers, but now the king has forsaken his loyal city. May the king examine the tablets of his fathers' palace whether the man who is in Byblos has not been a loyal servant.

(13–19) Do not be silent concerning your servant since [g]reat is the hostility of the *ʿapîru* troops against ‹him›. And as the gods of yo[ur] land live, used up are our sons and ‹our› daughters, (and) the wood of our houses f[or] payment to the land of Yarimuta to preserve our lives. My field is like a wife with no husband for lack of a cultivator.

(19–22) Al‹l› my towns which are in the hills and on the seacoast have joined the *ʿapîru* troops. The city of Bybl‹os› and two towns remain to me.

(23–29) And now ʿAbdi-Ashirta has taken over the town of Shigata and he has said to the men of the town of Ammiya, "Kill your 'lad' and become like us, and you will be at rest." And they have been won over in accordance with his [wo]rds and they are like the *ʿapîru* troops.

Lo.ed. 29) ⸢ÉRIN⸣.MEŠ GAZ ⸢*ù*⸣ *an-nu-uš i-na-*⸢*an*⸣*-na*
30) *iš-tap-pa-ar* ^{I}ÌR-*A-ši-ir-ta a-na* ÉRIN.MEŠ
31) AŠ É NIN.IB *pu-ḫu-ru-nim-mi ù*
Rev. 32) *ni-ma-qú-ut*!(WA?) ⸢UGU⸣ URU *Gub-la šum-ma ia-*[*nu*]
33) LÚ.*lí ša ú-še*$_{20}$*-zi-bu-*⸢*ši*$_{x}$⸣(⸢ŠE⸣) *iš-tu qa-ti-nu*
34) *ù nu-da-bir*$_{5}$ ⸢LÚ⸣.⸢MEŠ⸣ ⸢*ḫa*⸣*-za-nu-ta iš-tu*
35) *lìb-bi* KUR.KUR.KI *ù ti-né-pu-uš ka-li* KUR.KUR.MEŠ.KI
36) *a-na* LÚ.MEŠ ⸢GAZ⸣ ⸢*ù*⸣ ⸢*ki*⸣*-tu ti-in‹-né-pu-uš›-ma*
37) *a-na ka-li* KUR.KUR.⸢KI⸣ ⸢*ù*⸣ *pa-aš-ḫu* DUMU.MEŠ
38) *ù* MUNUS.DUMU.MUNUS.MEŠ *a‹-na› da-ri-ti* UD.KAM.MEŠ
39) *ù šum-ma ap-*⸢*pu*⸣*-na-ma yu-ṣa-na šàr-ru*
40) *ù ka-li* KUR.KUR.KI *nu-kúr-tu*$_{4}$ *a-na ša-šu*
41) *ù mi-na yi-pu-šu a-na ia-ši-nu*
42) *ki-na-na ti-ìš-ku-nu* NAM.‹NE›.RU *a-na be-ri-šu-nu*
43) *ù ki-na-na pa-al-ḫa-ti ma-gal ma-gal ›i-nu-ma‹*
44) [*i*]*-nu-ma ia-nu* LÚ *ša ú-še-zi-ba-an-ni*
45) [*iš*]*-tu qa-ti-šu-nu ki-ma* MUŠEN.MEŠ *ša*
46) ⸢*i*⸣-⸢*na*⸣ *lìb-bi ḫu-ḫa-ri* \ *ki-lu-bi*
47) ⸢*ša*⸣*-ak-na-at ki-šu-ma a-na-ku i-na*
48) ⸢URU⸣ ⸢*Gub*⸣-⸢*la*⸣ ⸢*am*⸣*-mi-ni ta-qa-al-mi a-na* KUR-*ka*
49) *a-nu-ma ki-a-ma aš-ta-pa-ar a-na* É.GAL
50) ⸢*ù*⸣ *ú-*⸢*ul*⸣ *ti-ìš-mu-na a-wa-tu-ia*
51) *a-nu-ma* ^{I}*A-ma-an-ap-pa it-ti-ka ša-*⸢*al*⸣*-šu*
52) *šu-ut yi-de ù ia-ta-mar pu-uš-*[*qa*]
53) *ša* UGU-*ia li-ìš-mé šàr-ru a-wa-te* ÌR-*šu*
54) *ù ia-di-na ba-la-ṭá* ÌR-*šu*
55) *ù yu-*⸢*ba*⸣*-li-iṭ* ÌR-*šu ù*
56) *a-na-ṣa-*⸢*ra*⸣ [URU] ⸢*ki*⸣*-it-ti-šu a-di* N[IN]-*nu*
57) DINGIR.MEŠ-*nu a*[*-na ka-ta*$_{5}$] ⸢*ù*⸣ *yi-da-*⸢*gal*⸣ [LUGAL]

Up.ed. 58) [K]U[R]-*šu ù* [ÌR-*šu ù yi-*]⸢*im*⸣*-lik a-na* KUR[-*šu*]
59) *ù šu-*⸢*up*⸣[*-ši-iḫ* URU-*š*]*u-ma li-iṭ-ri-*⸢*iṣ*⸣(!)
60) ⸢*i*⸣-⸢*na*⸣ *pa-ni* ⸢LUGAL⸣ ⸢EN⸣-*ia yu-wa-ši-*⸢*ra*⸣
Lft.ed. 61) ⸢LÚ⸣-⸢*šu*⸣ *ù yi-zi-iz i-na-an-na ù ak-*⸢*šu*⸣*-u*[*d*](?)
62) ⸢*a*⸣*-na-ku a-na ma-ḫar šàr-ri* EN‹-*ia*› *da-mi-iq it-*⸢*ti*⸣-⸢*ka*⸣
63) *a-na ia-ši mi-na i-pu-šu-na a-na-ku i-na*
64) [*i-*]*de-ni-ia a-nu-ma ki-*[*a*]-⸢*ma*⸣ *ú-ba-ú ur-ra*
65) *mu-*⸢*ša*⸣

(29–41) And now, ʿAbdi-Ashirta has written to the troops, "Assemble at the temple of Ninurta and let us fall upon the city of Byblos since there is no man who can deliver it from our hand. And let us drive the city rulers from the lands so that all the lands will join the *ʿapîru* men, and let an alliance be ‹made› for all the lands so that (our) sons and daughters will be at peace f[or]ever more. And if, moreover, the king comes forth and all the lands will be hostile to him, then what can he do to us?"

(42–48) Thus they have made an alliance among themselves and thus I am very much afraid because there is no man who can deliver me [fr]om their hand. Like birds that are sitting in a cage, thus am I in the city of Byblos. Why do you keep silent concerning your land?

(49–50) Now, thus I have written to the palace but my words are not heeded.

(51–57) Now Amanappa is with you, ask him. He knows and he has seen the pressu[re] against me. May the king heed the words of his servant and may he grant sustenance to his servant and may he keep his servant alive and I will guard his faithful [city] with our La[dy] (and) our deity, f[or you].

(57) And may [the king] see to
his [land] and [his servant and may he ta]ke counsel concerning [his] land and paci[fy] h[is city].

(59–62) May it be pleasing to the king, my lord that he send his man so that he may take up a post now and so that I, myself, may go to the presence of the king, ‹my› lord.

(62–65) It will be good for me to be with you. What can I do by my[se]lf? Now thus I am seeking day and night.

EA 75

TRANSCRIPTION

Obv.
01) [^{I}*R*]*i-ib-a*[*d-d*]*a* [*iq-bi*]
02) [*a-*]*na* EN-⸢*šu*⸣ *š*[*àr* KUR.KUR.(KI.MEŠ)]
03) ^{d}NIN *ša* U[RU *Gub-la*]
04) *ti-din* KAL.⸢GA⸣ ⸢*a*⸣[*-na* EN-*ia*]
05) *a-na* GÌR.MEŠ EN-*ia* ^{d}[UTU-*ia*]
06) [7-]⸢*šu*⸣ *7-a-an am-qú-*⸢*ut*⸣ [*lu-ú*]
07) *i-de* LUGAL EN-*li i-nu-*[*ma*]
08) *šal-ma-at* URU *Gub-la* ⸢GÉME⸣-[*ka*]
09) *›eš‹ iš-‹tu› da-ri-it* UD.KAM.MEŠ
10) *ša-*⸢*ni*⸣*-tam* GA.KAL *nu*-KÚR *ša* ÉRIN GAZ.MEŠ
11) U[GU]-*ia ga-am-ru* DUMU.MEŠ DUMU.MUNUS.MEŠ
12) GIŠ.[MEŠ] É.MEŠ *i-na* ⸢*na*⸣-⸢*da*⸣*-ni*
13) [*i-na*] KUR *Ia-ri-mu-ta i-na*
14) *›i-na‹ ba-la-aṭ* ZI-*n*[*u*]
15) ⸢A.ŠÀ⸣-*ia* DAM *ša la mu-*[*t*]*a*
16) *ma-ši-*il_5 *aš-šum ba-li*
17) *i-re-š*[*i-i*]*m aš-ta-pa-ar ù*
18) [*aš-*]*ta-ni a-na* É.GA[L] *aš-šum mur-ṣí-i* UGU-*ia*
19) [*ia-nu*] *ša i-da-gal a-wa-*[*te*]^{MEŠ} *š*[*a*]*-a*
20) [*ti-ik-šu*]*-du-na li-ìš-mé*
21) [LUGAL *a-na a*]*-wa-te*^{MEŠ} ⸢ÌR⸣-[*šu*]

Lo.ed.
22) [.....................................]
23) [.....................................]

Rev.
24) [.............*i-zi-b*]*u-n*[*i*] *ka*[*-li*]
25) [KUR.KUR.MEŠ] *š*[*à*]*r-ri* EN-*ia* ^{I}*A-d*[*u-na*]
26) [LÚ] URU *Ir-qa-*⸢*ta*⸣ *i-du-ku-*⸢*šu*⸣
27) [ÉRIN.]MEŠ GAZ.⸢MEŠ⸣ *ù ia-nu*
28) *ša ‹ia›-aq-bi mi-im-ma a-na*
29) ^{I}ÌR-*A-ši-ir-ta ù ti-ìl-q*[*ú*]
30) ^{I}*Mi-ya* LÚ UR[U] *A-ra-aš-ni*
31) *iṣ-ṣa-bat* URU *Ar-*⸢*da*⸣*-ta*

EA 75

TRANSLATION

(1–6) [R]ib-a[dd]a [spoke t]o his lord, the ki[ng of the lands; May the Lady of the ci[ty of Byblos] grant strength t[o my lord]. At the feet of my lord, [my sun] god, [seven] times and seven times have I fallen.

(6–9) [May] the king, my lord, know tha[t] the city of Byblos, [your] handmaiden, has been at peace from ancient times.

(10–14) Furthermore, intense is the hostility of the *ʿapîru* troops against me; exhausted are our sons, daughters, household furnishings in payment [in] the land of Yarimuta for preserving our lives.

(15–17) My field is like a woman without a husband due to lack of cultivation.

(17–23) I wrote repeatedly to the palace concerning the distress against me; [there is no one] that considered the word[s] that [were arri]ving. May the [king] listen [to the w]ords of his servant. [..........].

(24–31) [.....]a[ll the lands of] the king my lord [have aband]oned me. As for Ad[una, the ruler] of the city of ʿIrqata, *ʿapîru* [troop]s have slain him and there is no one who spoke to ʿAbdi-Ashirta. And th[ey] too[k] Miya, the ruler of the city of Arashni. The city of Ardata is taken.

32) *ù an-nu-uš* [*i*]-*na-an-na*
33) ⸢LÚ⸣.MEŠ URU *Am-mi-i‹a› ti-du-ku*
34) EN-⸢*šu*⸣ *ù p*[*a-*]*al-ḫa-ti a-na-ku*
35) *li-il*$_5$-[*m*]*a-ad* LUGAL *be-li*
36) *i-nu-ma iṣ-*[*ṣ*]*a-bat šàr Ḫa-ti*
37) *ka-li* KUR.KUR KU.TI.TI (= GÙ.[UN].DI$_6$.DI$_6$?)
38) *šàr* KUR *Mi-it-ta-ni-ma*
39) *šàr* KUR *Na-aḫ-‹ri›-ma*
40) KUR LUGAL.LUGAL *ra-bu-*[*te*]
41) ^{I}ÌR-*A-ši-ir-*⸢*ta*⸣ [ÌR]
42) UR.GI$_7$ *yi-ìl*[*-qú* KUR.KUR LUGAL *ù*]
43) *uš-ši-ra* É[RIN.MEŠ *pí-ṭá-ti*]
44) ⸢GA⸣.⸢KAL⸣ [....]
45) x-*m*[*a*...........]
46) x-*m*[*a*...........]
47) x-*t*[*a*............]
Lft.ed. 48) [*a-wa-tu-ia la-*]*a ti-ìš*[*-mu-na*]
49) [*ù uš-š*]*i-ra* LÚ *a-na* URU [*Gub-la*]
50) [*ù ú-t*]*a-ra a-na-ku a-w*[*a-te*^{MEŠ}*-ia*]

(32–34) And now the men of the city of Ammiy‹a› killed its lord and I myself am afraid.

(35–41) May the king, my lord, be apprised that the king of Ḫatti has taken all the lands, *tribute bearers*(?), of the king of the land of Mittani, the king of the land of Nah‹ri›na, the land of great kings.

(41–50) ʿAbdi-Ashirta, [the slave,] the dog, is taki[ng the lands of the king so] send a large [regular] f[orce......my words are not be[ing heard, so se]nd a man to the city [of Byblos and I,] myself, [will send ba]ck [my] wo[rds].

EA 76

TRANSCRIPTION

Obv.	01)	⸢^{I}⸣⸢*Ri*⸣-*ib*-^{d}IŠKUR *iq-bi a*-⸢*na*⸣
	02)	⸢LUGAL⸣ ⸢KUR⸣.KUR.KI.MEŠ *šàr-ri* GAL
	03)	LUGAL *ta-am-ḫa-ra* ^{d}NIN *ša*
	04)	URU *Gub-la ti-di-in*$_4$ KAL.GA
	05)	*a-na šàr-ri be-li-ia a-na* GÌR.MEŠ
	06)	EN-*ia* ^{d}UTU-*ia* 7-*šu* 7-*a-an am-qú-ut*
	07)	*lu*-⸢*ú*⸣ *i-de šàr-ru* EN-*li i-nu-ma*
	08)	KAL.GA *nu-kúr-tu*$_4$ *ša-a* ^{I}ÌR-*A-ši-ir-ta*
	09)	UGU-*ia a-nu*-⸢*ma*⸣ 2(?) URU *ša ir-ti-ḫu*
	10)	⸢*a*⸣-[*na*] ⸢*ia*⸣-*ši* ⸢*yu*⸣-*ba-ú la-qa*
	11)	[*a-na ša-a-šu*] ⸢*ša*⸣-*ni-tam mi-nu šu-ut*
	12)	[^{I}ÌR-*A*-]*ši*-⸢*ir*⸣-*ta* UR.GI$_7$ *ù yu-ba-ú*
	13)	[*l*]*a*-⸢*qa*⸣ *ka-li* URU.MEŠ *šàr-ru*(sic!) ^{d}UTU
	14)	[*a-n*]*a ša-a-šu* LUGAL KUR *Mi-ta-na*
	15)	[*ù*] LUGAL KUR *Ka-aš-še šu-ut i-nu-ma*
	16)	[*yu*]-*ba-ú la-qa* KUR LUGAL *a-na ša-a-šu*
	17)	[*a*]-⸢*nu*⸣-⸢*ma*⸣ ⸢*i*⸣-*na-an-na pu-ḫi-ir*
	18)	[*k*]*a*-⸢*li*⸣ LÚ.MEŠ GAZ UGU URU *Ši-ga-ta*
	19)	⸢*ú*⸣ URU *Am-pí ù la-qa-ma*
	20)	[*š*]*u-ut* 2 URU *an-ni*-⸢*ta*⸣ *ù*
	21)	[KAL.G]A *ia-a-nu a-šar er-ru-bu*
	22)	[URU *Ir-qa*-]*tu*$_4$ *a-na ša-a-šu ṣa-bat*
	23)	[ḪUR.S]AG \ *ša yi-par-sà*
	24)	[*ù u*]*š-ši-ra-ni* 4 *m*⸢*e*⸣
Lo.ed.	25)	[LÚ.MEŠ *ma-ṣa*-]*ar-ta* [*ù*]
	26)	[30 *ta-pal*] ANŠE.KUR.RA.⸢MEŠ⸣
Rev.	27)	[*ki-ma ar-ḫi-iš a*-]⸢*nu*⸣-*ma* ⸢*ki*⸣-[*a-ma*]
	28)	[*aš-tap-ru a-na* É.GA]L ⸢*ù*⸣ [*la-a*]
	29)	[*tu-te-ru-n*]*a* [*a*]-⸢*wa*⸣-⸢*ta*$_5$⸣ [*a-na ia*-]*ši*

EA 76

TRANSLATION

(1–6) Rib-Hadda spoke to the king of the lands, the great king, the King of Battle: May the Lady of Byblos grant strength to the king, my lord. At the feet of my lord, my sun god, seven times (and) seven times have I fallen.

(7–16) May the king, my lord, be apprised that strong is the hostility of ʿAbdi-Ashirta against me. Now the two towns that remain to me, he is seeking to take [for himself]. Furthermore, who is he, [ʿAbdi-A]shirta, the dog, that he seeks to take all the towns of the king, the sun god, [fo]r himself? Is he the king of Mittani or the king of Kašše that [he] is seeking to take the land of the king for himself?

(17–29) Now, he has assembled all the *ʿapîru* men against the town of Shigata [and] the town of Ampi. If [h]e takes these two towns, then [he will be stro]ng. There is nowhere that I can enter into. [The city of Irqa]tu belongs to him. He has seized [the hill co]untry \ which has been cut off. [So s]end to me four hundred [garri]son troops [and 30 pairs of] horses [in a hurry. N]ow, thus [have I written to the pala]ce, but [you do not return a [w]ord [to m]e.

30) [*ú-ul ki-ma pa-*]⸢*na*⸣*-nu ka-‹li›* KUR.KUR.MEŠ
31) [*šàr-*]*ri* MU.KAM.MEŠ *tu-ṣa-na*
32) [ERÍN.]⸢MEŠ⸣ *pí-ṭá-ti a-na da-gal*
33) [KUR.KU]R.⸢KI⸣.MEŠ *ù an-nu-uš*
34) ⸢*i*⸣*-na-an-na in*$_4$*-né-ep-ša-at*
35) KUR.KI LUGAL *ù* URU *Ṣu-mu-ra*
36) URU *ma-ṣa-ar-ti-ku-nu*
37) *a-na* LÚ.GAZ.MEŠ *ù qa-la-ta*
38) *uš-ši-ra* ÉRIN.MEŠ *pí-ṭá-ti*
39) *ra-ba ù tu-da-bi-ir*
40) *a-ia-bi* LUGAL *iš-tu*
41) *lìb-bi* KUR*-šu ù*
42) *ti-né-ep-šu ka-li*
43) KUR.KUR.MEŠ *a-na šàr-ri ša-ni-tam*
44) *at-ta* EN GAL *ú-ul*
45) *ta-qa-al-mi ìš-tu*
46) ⸢*ši*⸣*-ip-ri an-nu-ú*

(30–43) [Was it not in the p]ast, regarding al‹l› the lands of the king, that yearly the regular troops were coming forth to inspect [the lan]ds? But now the lands of the king and the city of Ṣumur, your (pl.) garrison city, have gone over to the *ʿapîru* men and you keep silent. Send a large regular army and you can drive out the enemies of the king from within his land and all the lands will be joined to the king.

(43–46) Furthermore, you are the great lord; you must not ignore this message.

EA 77

TRANSCRIPTION

Obv.
01) *[a-]na* ^{I}*A-⸢ma⸣-[an-ap-pa qí-bí-ma]*
02) *um-ma* ^{I}*Ri-i[b-*^{d}IŠKUR *a-na* GÌR.MEŠ*-ka]*
03) *am-qú-ut* ^{d}*[A-ma-na* DINGIR LUGAL]
04) EN*-ka* ⸢*ù*⸣ [^{d}NIN *ša* URU] ⸢*Gub*⸣*-* [*la*]
05) *ti-di-‹nu›-mi* T[ÉŠ*-ka*] *i-na*
06) *pa-ni* LUGAL E[N*-ka*] *i-nu-ma*
07) *ta-aš-pu-ra* ⸢*a*⸣[*-na*] URUDU.MEŠ *ù a-na*
08) *ší-in*$_{4}$*-ni-m[i ti-]*⸢*i*⸣*-de* ^{d}NIN
09) *ša* URU *Gub-l[a] šum-ma* ⸢*i*⸣*-šu*
10) URUDU.MEŠ *ù š[i-i]n*$_{4}$*-ni [pí-r]i*
11) *a-na ia-ši* ⸢*ù*⸣[URU].KI*-*⸢*li*⸣*-ši*$_{x}$(ŠE)
12) ⸢^{I}⸣*Mil-ka-yu* 1 ⸢NÁ⸣ *ma-[ḫ]a-aṣ*
13) ⸢*ù*⸣ *na-ad-n[a-t]i ši-*⸢*in*$_{4}$⸣*-na-šu*
14) *[a-n]a ba-la-ṭ[ì-ia] a-na*
15) [LUGAL] ⸢URU⸣ ⸢*Ṣur*⸣*-r[i] at-ta*

Lo.ed.
16) *[ú-ul] ti-i-de[pu-uš-]qa-ia*
17) *[qa-l]a-ta a[-na ia]-ši*

Rev.
18) *[a-nu-ma] a-na m[i-ni qa]-la-ta*
19) *[a-na] ub-ri* U[R.GI$_{7}$] *ša*
20) *[yi-]na-mu-ša [a-n]a* KUR.KI.MEŠ
21) *[ú]-ul ta-aq[-bu a-n]a* EN*-ka ù*
22) *yu-wa-ši-ru-n[a-]ka i-na*
23) *pa-ni* ÉRIN.MEŠ *pí[-ṭ]á-ti ù*
24) *tu-ša-am-ri-*⸢*ru*⸣ LÚ.MEŠ GAZ
25) *iš-tu* LÚ.MEŠ ⸢*ḫa*⸣*-za-nu-ti*
26) *šum-ma* MU.MEŠ *a[n-n]i-ta ú-ul*
27) *yu-ṣa-na* ÉRIN.ME[Š *pí-ṭ*]*á-ti*
28) *ù in-n[é-ep-ša-a]t ka-li*
29) KUR.KUR.KI.MEŠ ⸢*a*⸣[*na* LÚ.MEŠ GA]Z

EA 77

TRANSLATION

(1–6) [Speak t]o Ama[n-appa], the message of Ri[b-Hadda: at your feet] have I fallen. May [Amon the god of the king], your lord, and the La[dy of the city of] Byblos grant [your] hon[or] before the king, [your] lo[rd.

(6–15) Inasmuch as you have written con[cerning] copper and concerning ivory, the Lady of Byblos [kn]ows if I have (or: there is) copper or [elepha]nt ivory, either to me or to her [cit]y! Milkayu overlaid one ⸢bed⸣ but I gave its ivory [fo]r [my[sustenance to [the king] of the city of Tyre.

(15–18) Don't you know my [distr]ess? You [have ig]nored [m]e!

(18–25) [Now,] wh[y have] you [kept si]lent [concerning] the foreigner, the d[og(?)] who [is] attacking the territories? [W]on't you spea[k t]o your lord that he send you at the head of regular troops that you may drive off the *ʿapîru* men from the city rulers?

(26–29) If this year the regul[ar tro]ops do not come forth, then all the territories will join the [*ʿapîru* men].

30) *šum-ma qa-a*[*l-mi* LUGAL EN-*l*]*i*
31) *ù ia -nu*[ÉRIN.MEŠ *pí-ṭá-ti ù*]
32) GIŠ.MÁ LÚ.M[EŠ URU *Gub-la*]
Up.ed. 33) ⸢LÚ⸣.MEŠ-*ka* DIN[GIR.MEŠ *ti-ìl-qé*]
34) *a-di muḫ*[*-ḫi-ka ù i-te-zi-ib*]
35) ⸢URU⸣ [*Gub-la a-mur*]
Lft.ed. 36) *pal-ḫa-ti* LÚ.MEŠ *ḫu-u*[*p-ši-ia*]
37) *ul ti-ma-ḫa-ṣa-na-n*[*i*]

(30–35) If [the king,] my [lor]d keeps sile[nt] and there are no [regular troops, then may] ships [take] the men of [Byblos], your men, (and) the go[ds], to y[ou and I will leave] the city of [Byblos].

(35–37) [Look,] I am afraid of [my] yeoman [farmers], lest they smite me!

EA 78

TRANSCRIPTION

Obv. 01) [^{I}*Ri-i*]*b*-⸢^{d}⸣IŠKUR *iq-b*[*i*]

02) [*a-na* EN]-*šu* LUGAL KUR.KUR.Ḫ̮I.A.K[I]

03) [LUGAL GAL] ^{d}NIN *ša* URU [*Gub-la*]

04) [*ti-di-*]*in*$_4$ GA.KAL *a-na* [LUGAL EN-*ia*]

05) [^{d}U]TU-*ia a-na* GÌR.MEŠ E[N-*ia*]

06) [^{d}]UTU-*ia* 7-*šu* 7-*a-an am-*[*qut*]

07) [*lu-*]⸢*ú*⸣ *i-de šàr-ru* EN-*li* [*i-nu-ma*]

08) [KAL.G]A *nu-kúr-tu*$_4$ *ša-a*

09) [^{I}Ì]R-*A-ši-ir-*⸢*ta*⸣ UGU-*i*[*a*]

10) [*ìl-t*]*e*$_9$-*qé* ⸢*ka*⸣-*li* URU.K[I.MEŠ-*ia*]

11) [*a-nu-*]*ma* 2 URU.KI *ir-ti-*⸢*ḫu*⸣

12) [*a-n*]*a ia-ši ù šu-nu* ⸢*yu*⸣[*-ba-ú*]

13) [*la*]-*qa-a a-nu-ma ki-ma* MUŠ[EN]

14) [*ša*] *i-na lìb-bi ḫu-ḫa-r*[*i*]

15) [*ša*]-*ak-na-at ki-šu-*[*ma*]

16) [*a-na-k*]*u i-na lìb-bi* URU *Gub-l*[*a*]

17) [*ù*] *yi-ìš-me* EN-*li a-wa-*[*te*]

18) [ÌR]-*šu a-nu-ma i-na*

19) [URU] *Baṭ-*⸢*ru*⸣-*na i-ba-*⸢*ša*⸣-*ti*

20) [.........]⸢*ù*⸣(?)[...........]

21) [..........................]

22) [..........................]

23) [..........................]

Lo.ed. 24) [..........................]

Rev. 25) [..........................]

26) [..........................]

27) [..........................]

28) [..................*p*]*a-ni*[...]

29) [................]MEŠ *š*[*i*...]

EA 78

TRANSLATION

(1–6) [Ri]b-Hadda spo[ke to] his [lord], king of the lands, [the great king]: May the Lady of the city of [Byblos] [gra]nt strength to [the king, my lord,] my sun god. At the feet of [my] lo[rd], my sun god, seven times (and) seven times have I fal[len].

(7–13) [Ma]y the king, my lord be apprised [that] the hostility of [ʿAb]di-Ashirta against me is [sever]e. [He] has taken all [my] tow[ns]. Now (only) two towns remain [t]o me and these he [is seeking to t]ake.

(13–18) Now like a bird [that] is situated inside a cage, thus [am] I within the city of Byblos. [So] may my lord heed the wor[ds of] his [servant].

(18–19) Now I was in [the city of] Baṭrôna [.......]and[.......].

(20–29) [.............................]

30) [...........]⸢ŠE⸣.ZÍZ.Ḫ̮I.A [.]
31) [.......*iš-tu* KUR] *Ia-r*[*i-mu-ta*]
32) [..........]⸢*i*⸣?-*ma*-⸢*ḫ̮a*⸣?-*a*[*r* ?]
33) [.............] *ù* [.........]
34) [..........................]
35) [*i-n*]*a* ⸢*pa*⸣[-*ni*...............]
36) [*š*]*a-a* [.....................]
37) [..]x [..]-*i*[*a*..]⸢*uš*⸣-⸢*ši*⸣-⸢*ra*⸣[-*an-ni*]
38) [*ki-ma*] *ar*-⸢*ḫ̮i*⸣-*ìš* ⸢*ù*⸣[*uš-ši-ra*]
39) [LÚ.MEŠ] *ma*-⸢*ṣa*⸣-⸢*ar*⸣-*ta* ⸢*ki*⸣-[*ma*]
40) [....]⸢*ia*⸣[.......*i*-]*na* ⸢*qa*⸣[-*at*]
41) [..........................]
42) [..........................]
43) [..........................]
Up.ed. 44) [..........................]
45) [..........................]

(30–34) [...] emmer wheat [...from the country of] Yari[muta ....] I will receive [............]and [.......]

(35–40) [i]n the pre[sence of.......wh]ich [..........] send [to me [with] utmost haste and [send] garrison [troops], a[s....]my[...i]n the charge of [........]

(41–45) [...............]

EA 79

TRANSCRIPTION

Obv.	01)	[^{I}*Ri-i*]*b*-^{d}IŠKUR *iq-bi*
	02)	[*a-na* EN-]*šu šàr* KUR.KUR.KI LU[GAL GA]L
	03)	[*šàr ta*]*-am-ḫa-ra* ^{d}NIN
	04)	[*ša* U]RU *Gub-la ti-di-in*$_4$
	05)	[KAL.G]A *a-na šàr-ri* EN-*ia*
	06)	[*a-na* G]ÌR.MEŠ EN-*ia* ^{d}UTU-*ia*
	07)	⌜7⌝-⌜*šu*⌝ 7-*a-an am-qú-ut li-ma-ad*
	08)	*i-nu-ma iš-tu ka-ša-ad*
	09)	^{I}*A-ma-an-ap-pa a-na mu-ḫi-ia*
	10)	*ka-li* LÚ.MEŠ GAZ.MEŠ *na-*⌜*ad*⌝*-nu*
	11)	*pa-ni-šu-nu a-na ia-ši a-*[*na*]
	12)	KA \ *pí-i* ^{I}ÌR-*A-ši-ir*[*-ta*]
	13)	*ù yi-iš-me* EN-*li*
	14)	*a-wa-te*^{MEŠ} ÌR-*šu ù* [*uš-si-r*]*a-ni*
	15)	LÚ.MEŠ *ma-ṣa-ar-ta a-*[*na*]
	16)	⌜*na*⌝*-ṣa-ar* URU LUGAL *a-d*[*i*]
	17)	[*a-*]⌜*ṣa*⌝ ÉRIN.MEŠ *pí-ṭá-ti*
	18)	[*šum-m*]*a ia-nu* ÉRIN.MEŠ *pí* ‹*pí*›[*-ṭá-ti*]
Lo.ed.	19)	[*ù*] *in*$_4$*-né-*⌜*ep*⌝*-šu ka-*[*li*]
	20)	[KUR].MEŠ *a-na* LÚ.M[EŠ G]AZ.MEŠ *ši-me*
Rev.	21)	[*iš-*]⌜*tu*⌝ *ṣa-ba-at* URU ⌜É⌝*-ar-*[*ḫa*]
	22)	[*a-na*] *pí-i* ^{I}ÌR-*A-ši-ir-ta*
	23)	[*ù*] ⌜*ki*⌝*-na-na tu-ba-ú-na*
	24)	[*i-p*]*u-ša* URU *Gub-la ù*
	25)	URU *Baṭ-ru-na*^{KI} *ù in*$_4$*-*[*né-ep-šu*]
	26)	*ka-li* KUR.KUR.MEŠ *a-na* LÚ.MEŠ GAZ.MEŠ
	27)	2 URU.KI.MEŠ *ša ir-ti-ḫu a-*⌜*na*⌝ [*ia-ši*]
	28)	*ù tu-ba-ú-na la-*⌜*qa*⌝*-šu*[*-nu*]
	29)	*iš-tu qa-at šàr-ri yu-wa-š*[*i-ra*]
	30)	EN-*li* LÚ.MEŠ *ma-ṣa-ar-*⌜*ta*⌝
	31)	*a-na* 2 URU-*ni-šu a-di a-ṣí* É[RIN.MEŠ]
	32)	*pí-ṭá-ti* ⌜*ù mi-im-ma*⌝
	33)	*yu-da-na-ni a-na a-*⌜*ka*⌝*-li-šu-nu*

EA 79

TRANSLATION

(1–7) [Ri]b-Hadda spoke [to] his [lord, king of the lands, the gr[ea]t ki[ng, the king of ba]ttle: May the Lady [of the ci]ty of Byblos grant [stren]gth to the king, my lord. [At the fe]et of my lord, my sun god, seven times (and) seven times have I fallen.

(7–17) Be informed that since Amanappa reached me, all the *ʿapîru* men have concentrated their efforts on me at the instigation of ʿAbdi-Ashirta, so may my lord heed the words of his servant and [send] to me garrison troops t[o] protect the city of the king unt[il the coming] forth of the regular army.

(18–26) [I]f there are no reg[ular] troops, [then] a[ll the lan]ds will join the *ʿapîru* men. Listen! [Sin]ce the capture of the town of Bit-Ar[ḫa] at]the instigation of ʿAbdi-Ashirta, [then] they are striving to do likewise to the city of Byblos and the city of Baṭrôna so that all the territories will [join] the *ʿapîru* men.

(27–33) There are two cities that remain to me and they are seeking to take th[em] from the control of the king. May my lord send garrison troops to his two cities until the coming forth of the regular t[roop]s and may something be given me for their food.

34) *ia-nu mi-im-ma a-na ia-ši*
35) *ki-ma* MUŠEN *ša i-na lìb-b*[*i*]
36) [*ḫ*]*u-ḫa-ri* \ *ki-lu-bi ša-ak-na-at*
37) [*ki-*]⸢*šu*⸣*-ma a-na-ku i-na*
38) [URU] *Gub-la* ^{KI} *ša-ni-tam*
39) [*šum-m*]*a la-a i-le-e*
40) [*šàr-r*]*u la-qa-ia ìš-tu*
41) [*qa-at*] *na-ak-ri-šu*
Up.ed. 42) [*ù*] *in*$_4$*-né-ep-ša-at*
43) [*ka-l*]*i* KUR.KI.MEŠ
44) [*a-na* ^{I}ÌR-]*A-ši-ir-ta*
Lft.ed. 45) [*mi-nu š*]*u-ut* UR.GI$_7$ *ù*
46) [*yi-ìl-*]*qú* KUR.KUR.MEŠ *šàr-ri* ⸢*a*⸣[*-na*]
47) [*ša*]*-šu*

(34–38) I don't have anything. Like a bird sitting in the midst of a cage, thus am I in the [city] of Byblos.

(38–47) Furthermore, [i]f [the ki]ng is unable to deliver me from the [grip] of his enemies, [then al]l of the territories will join [ʿAbdi]-Ashirta. [What is h]e, the dog that [he tak]es the territories of the king f[or him]self?

EA 80

TRANSCRIPTION

Obv. 01) [..............................]
02) [..............................]
03) [..............................]
04) [..............................]
05) [..............................]
06) [..............................]
07) [..............................]
08) [..............................]
09) [..............................]
10) [..............................]
11) [..............................]
12) [...............]*ka ia-ši*[............]
13) [..........M]EŠ-*nu ù*[..............]
14) [..........*m*]*a i-na ṭu*[*p-pí*..........]
15) [*šap-ra-ti a-n*]*a ka-t*[*a*..................]
16) [.........]*ma-an ìš*[*-ta-pár*...........]
17) [.........]ÌR *ki-ti-šu* [................]
18) [.......*m*]*a-ti ù ti-*[*ìl-qú*.............]
19) [^{I}ÌR-*A-ši-i*]*r-ta ù š*[*ap-ra-ti*.............]
20) [*a-na ka-ta uš-*]*ši-ra* 1 *m*[*e*.............]
21) [LÚ.MEŠ *a-na ia-ši*] ⸢*ša*⸣[*-ni-tam*.......]

Lo.ed. 22) [..............................]
23) [..............................]

Rev. 24) [..............................]
25) [..............................]
26) [..............................]
27) [..............................]
28) [..............................]
29) [.............]*ma* ⸢*ù*⸣[..............]
30) [*le-q*]*é-ni a-na* ⸢*pa*⸣[*-ni-ka*...............]
31) [*at-t*]*a šàr-ru* ^{d}UTU E[N-*ia*...........]
32) [*ù*] *at-ta tu-ba-l*[*i-iṭ a-na*..............]

EA 80

TRANSLATION

)bv. 01) [..................................]
02) [..................................]
03) [..................................]
04) [..................................]
05) [..................................]
06) [..................................]
07) [..................................]
08) [..................................]
09) [..................................]
10) [..................................]
11) [..................................]
12) [...............]to me[.............]
13) [..........citi]es and[..............]
14) [...........] in a tab[let............]
15) [I wrote t]o you [.....................]
16) [.........]––– I had [written.........]
17) [.....]his loyal servant [.............]
18) [.......] ––– and they [took[.........]
19) [ʿAbdi-Ashi]rta so [I] w[rote...........]
20) [to you: "Se]nd one hu[ndred.....
21) [men to me. Furt[hermore............]
o.ed. 22) [..................................]
23) [..................................]
ev. 24) [..................................]
25) [..................................]
26) [..................................]
27) [..................................]
28) [..................................]
29) [..................................]
30) [tak]e me to [your] pre[sence.........]
31) [Yo]u are the king, the sun god, [my] lo[rd]
32) [and] you give li[fe to...............]

33) [ÌR *k*]*i-ti-ka* ⸢*ù*⸣ É[RIN.MEŠ............]
34) [*pí-ṭ*]*á-ti* [-*ka*]

33) your [loy]al [servant] and [your]
34) reg[ular tro]ops

EA 81

TRANSCRIPTION

Obv. 01) [^{I}*Ri-ib-*^{d}IŠKUR *iq-b*]*i a-na* EN-[*šu*]
02) [*šàr* KUR.KUR.KI LUGAL GAL *š*]*àr ta-am-ḫa-*[*ra*]
03) [^{d}NIN *ša* URU *Gub-la*] ⸢*ti*⸣*-di-in*$_4$ KA[L.G]A
04) [*a-na šàr*]-⸢*ri*⸣ [EN-*ia a-na* GÌR.MEŠ E]N-*ia*
05) [^{d}UTU]-*ia* ⸢*7*⸣*-šu 7-a-an a*[*m-q*]*ú-ut*
06) [*lu-ú*] ⸢*i*⸣*-de šàr-ru* EN-*li* ⸢*i*⸣*-nu-ma*
07) [KAL.]⸢GA⸣ ⸢*nu*⸣*-kúr-tu*$_4$ *ša* ÌR-*A-*⸢*ši*⸣*-ir-ta*
08) ⸢*ù*⸣ *ìl-te*$_9$*-qé ka-li* URU.K[I.M]EŠ-[*i*]⸢*a*⸣
09) [*a-na*] *ša-a-šu* URU *Gub-la ù* U[RU] ⸢*Baṭ*⸣*-ru-*[*na*]
10) [*ir-t*]*i-ḫa a-na ia-ši ù* 2 ⸢URU⸣ *y*[*u-ba-*]*ú*
11) [*la-q*]*a-a ù iq-bi a-na* LÚ.MEŠ [URU *Gub-l*]⸢*a*⸣
12) [*du-*]⸢*ku*⸣*-mi* EN-*ku-nu* ⸢*ù*⸣ *in*$_4$*-né-*[*ep-šu*]
13) [*a-na*] LÚ.MEŠ GAZ *ki-*⸢*ma*⸣ ⸢URU⸣ *Am-m*[*i-ia*]
14) [*ù*] *in*$_4$*-né-ep-*⸢*šu*⸣ *ar-‹nu› a-na* [*ia-ši*]
15) [*i*]-⸢*zi*⸣-⸢*iz*⸣ LÚ ZABAR!(UD![BAR].KA.BAR) GÍR \ ⸢*pat*⸣*-*[*r*]*a* UGU-*i*[*a*]
16) ⸢*ù*⸣ ⸢*da*⸣-⸢*ak*⸣*-ti-šu ù* L[Ú] ⸢*ši*⸣*-ir-da-nu*
17) [*š*]*a-a i-de p*[*a-ṭá-ar a-n*]*a ma-ḫar*
18) [^{I}]ÌR-*A-ši-ir-ta i-na pí-šu a-pí-ìš*
19) [*ip*]*-šu an-nu-ú a-na ia-ši a-nu-ma*
20) [*ki-a*]-⸢*ma*⸣ *aš-ba-ti ù qa-la-ti i-na*
21) [*lìb-bi* URU-*i*]⸢*a*⸣ *la-a i-le-e a-ṣa*
22) [*a-na* EDIN.MEŠ] ⸢*ù*⸣ *aš-ta-pár a-na* É.GAL
23) [*ù la-a tu*]*-te-ru-na a-wa-tu*
24) [*a-na ia-ši* 9-*t*]*a-an am-ma-ḫa-aṣ*[*-ni*]
25) [*ki-na-n*]*a* ZI-*ia pal*[*-ḫa-ti*]
26) [*ù aš-ta-pa-a*]*r ù aš-t*[*a-ni*]
Lo.ed. 27) [*a-na* É.GAL] *ú-ul ta-*[*qa-al-mi*]
28) [*a-na mi-ni*$_7$ *qa-*]*la-ta aš-*[*šum pu-uš-qí*]
Rev 29) [UGU-*ia šu*]*m-ma* 2 ITI *an*[*-nu-ú-ta*$_5$]
30) [*ia-nu* ÉRIN.ME]Š *pí-ṭá-ti* ⸢*ù*⸣[*yi-ìl-qú*]
31) [URU.MEŠ] ⸢*ú*⸣*-ul yi-ma-qú-ta* [UGU]
32) [URU-]*ia ù yi-ìl-qa-ni a*[*š-ta-pár a-na*]

EA 81

TRANSLATION

(1–5) [Rib-Hadda spo]ke to [his] lord, [king of the lands, the great king, the ki]ng of battle: May [the Lady of Byblos] grant str[ength to the ki]ng, [my lord. At the feet of] my [lo]rd, my [sun god,] seven times (and) seven times have I fallen.

(6–14) [May] the king, my lord, be apprised that the hostility of ʿAbdi-Ashirta is [sev]ere and he has taken all of my towns [for] himself. The city of Byblos and the ci[ty] of Baṭrô[na re]main to me and he [is seeking to ta]ke the two cities and he said to the men of [the city of Bybl]os, "[Ki]ll your lord and jo[in] the *ʿapîru* men like the city of ʿAmm[iya]." So they became trai[tors] to [me].

(15–29) A man attacked me with a bronze dagger but I slew him and the Sherdanu who knew (about it) r[an off t]o ʿAbdi-Ashirta. This deed was done to me at his command. Now, [thu]s I sat and kept silent in [m]y [city]. I was unable to go out [into the fields. So] I wrote to the palace, [but] words did not return [to me. Nine ti]mes was I smitten. [Thus, I fe]ared for my life. [So I wrote] repea[tedly to the palace.] Don't ke[ep silent]! [Why have] you [kept sil]ent be[cause of the pressure against me?]
(29) [against me]?

(29–32) [I]f in t[hese] two months [there are no regular] troops, then [he will take the cities]. Lest he pounce [upon] my [city] and take me, I [wrote to the pa]lace.

33) [É.]GAL *ù mi-na ‹a-qa-bu-na› a-na* LÚ.MEŠ *ḫ*[*u-u*]*b*-[*ši-ia*]
34) [*a*]*-nu-ma ki-ma* MUŠEN ša *i-na l*[*ìb-bi*]
35) [*ḫu*]*-ḫa-ri* \ *ki-lu-bi ša-ak-*[*na-at*]
36) [*ki-*]*šu-ma šu-nu i-na lìb-bi* U[RU *Gub-l*]*a*
37) [A.ŠÀ-]*šu-nu* DAM *ša la mu-ta* ⸢*ma*⸣-⸢*ši*⸣-*ìl*
38) [*aš-šu*]*m* ⸢*ba*⸣-⸢*li*⸣ *i-re-ši ga-am-ru*
39) [DUMU.MEŠ-*šu-nu* MUNUS.]D[UMU].M[UNUS-*šu-nu* GI]Š.MEŠ É.MEŠ-*šu-nu*
40) [*i-na*] ⸢*na*⸣-⸢*da*⸣-*ni* [*i-n*]*a* ⸢KUR⸣ ⸢*Ia*⸣*-ri-mu-ta*
41) [*i-na*] *ba-la-aṭ* ZI-*šu-nu a-nu-*⸢*ma*⸣
42) [*ki-a-ma*] *aq-bi a-na ša-a-šu-nu* DINGIR-⸢*ia*⸣
43) [TI.LA] ÉRIN.MEŠ *pí-ṭá-ti i-nu-ma ti-*⸢*du*⸣-[*ú*]
44) [*ù*] *ia-nu ù an-nu-ú na-ad-nu* [*pa-ni-šu-nu*]
45) [*a-na*] *ia-‹ši›-nu šum-ma* 2 ITI.MEŠ *la-a tu*[*-ṣa-na*]
46) [ÉRIN.M]EŠ *pí-ṭá-ti ù i-te*$_9$*-la*
47) [^{I}]⸢ÌR⸣-*A-ši-ir-ta ù ìl-te*$_9$*-qé* 2 U[RU]
48) [*pa-n*]*a-nu* ⸢URU⸣ ⸢*Ṣu*⸣*-mu-ra ù* LÚ.MEŠ [MÁŠKIM]
49) [*da*]*n-nu-tu*$_4$ ⸢*i*⸣*-ba-aš-šu ù* LÚ[.MEŠ]
50) [*ma-ṣ*]*a-ar-*⸢*tu*$_4$⸣ *it-ti-nu mi-*[*n*]*a*
51) [*i-pu-*]*šu-*⸢*na*⸣ [*a-na-*]*ku i-na i-*⸢*de*⸣-[*ni*]-*ia*
52) ⸢*ù*⸣ [........]⸢*da*⸣*-ga-lu* ⸢*it*⸣*-ta-ṣi*
53) [*a-na ia-ši-nu*]⸢*ù*⸣ *ìl-t*[*e*$_9$]-⸢*qú*⸣
54) [URU *Baṭ-ru-na a-na ša-a-šu*]
55) [..................]*ta*[....]
Up.ed. 56) [.................]*ù*[......]
57) [................] *ù ki-na-n*[*a*]
58) [^{I}ÌR-*A-ši-ir-ta*]*ìl-te*$_9$*-qú*
59) [URU *ša-a it*]*-ti-ia*

(32–41) And what ‹shall I say› to the yeo[man farmers]? Now, like a bird that is situated in the midst of a cage, [th]us are they in the midst of the ci[ty of Byblos]. Their [field] is like a woman without a husband [becau]se of a lack of cultivation; [their sons,] their [dau]gh[ters, the wood of] their houses are all used up to make payments to the land of Yarimuta [for] the provisions to keep them alive.

(41–47) Now, [thus], I said to them, "[By the life] of my god, (there will be) regular troops." When they found out [that] there are none, then, behold, the turned [their faces against] ‹u›s. If in two months the [regu]lar troops do not co[me forth] then ʿAbdi-Ashirta will come up and he will take the two c[ities].

(48–51) [For]merly, the city of Ṣumur and there were [st]rong [commissioners] and there were [garris]on troops with us. What [can] ⸢I⸣ do by mys[el]f?

(52–59) And [.......] seeing, he will come forth [against us] and he will take [the city of Baṭrôna for himself] [..................] and thus [ʿAbdi-Ashirta] will take [the city that is in] my charge.

EA 82

TRANSCRIPTION

Obv. 01) ⸢*a*⸣-*na* ^{I}⸢*A*⸣-⸢*ma*⸣-⸢*an*⸣-*ap-pa a-bi-i*⸢*a*⸣
02) *qí-bí-ma*
03) *um-ma* ^{I}*Ri-ib-*^{d}IŠKUR DUMU-*ka*
04) *a-na* GÌR.MEŠ *a-bi-ia am-qú-ut*
05) *aq-ta-bi ù aš-ta-ni*
06) *a-na ka-*ta_5 *ú-ul ti-le-ú-na*
07) *la-qa-ia iš-tu qa-at*
08) ^{I}ÌR-*A-ši-ir-ta ka-li*
09) LÚ.MEŠ GAZ.MEŠ *it-ti-šu*
10) *ù* LÚ.MEŠ *ḫa-za-nu-tu ú-ul*
11) *ti-ìš-mu-na mi-im-ma*
12) *ù šap-ru a-na ša-a-šu*
13) *ù ki-na-na* KAL.GA *ù*
14) *ta-aš-ta-na a-wa-*ta_5 *a-*⸢*na*⸣ *ia-ši*
15) *uš-ši-ra-mi* LÚ-*ka it-ti-ia*
16) *a-na* É.GAL *ù la-a ka-ši-id*
17) *i-re-šu ù uš-ši-ir-ti-šu*
18) *qa-du* ÉRIN.MEŠ *til-la-ti a-na ka-*ta_5
19) *a-di a-ṣí* ÉRIN.MEŠ *pí-ṭá-ti*
20) *a-na na-ṣa-ar* ZI-*ka* ⸢*ù*⸣
21) ⸢*aq*⸣-*bi a-na ka-*ta_5 *la-a*

Lo.ed. 22) *i-le-ú uš-ša-ar*[-*šu*]
23) *ú-ul yi-ìš-ma* ^{I}ÌR-*A-ši-i*[*r-ta*]
24) ⸢*ù*⸣ ⸢*ma*⸣-*an-nu ìl-*te_9*-qa-n*[*i*]

Rev. 25) ⸢*ìš*⸣-*tu qa-ti-šu ù ta-a*[*q?-bu*]
26) *a-na ia-ši ú-ul ta-pa-la-*[*aḫ*]
27) *ù ta-aš-ta-ni a-wa-*ta_5 *a-na ia-ši*
28) *uš-ši-ir-mi* GIŠ.MÁ *a-na*
29) KUR *Ia-ri-mu-ta ù ú-ṣa-ka*
30) KÙ.BABBAR.MEŠ *lu-bu-ši ìš-tu ša-šu*

EA 82

TRANSLATION

(1–4) Speak to Aman-appa, my father, the message of Rib-Haddi, your son: At the feet of my father I have fallen.

(3–13) I have repeatedly said to you, "Are you not able to rescue me from the hand of ʿAbdi-Ashirta? All of the *ʿapîru* men are with him and as for the city rulers, no sooner do they hear something but they write to him. So thus he is strong."

(13–20) But you kept replying to me, "Send your man to me, to the palace, and as soon as the request arrives and I will send him with an auxiliary force for you until the regular army comes forth to protect your life."

(20–25) But I said to you, "I am unable to send [him]. No sooner than ʿAbdi-Ashi[rta] hears, then who will rescue m[e] from his hand."

(25–30) But you s[ay] to me, "Don't be afra[id]," and you kept saying to me "Send a ship to the land of Yarimuta so that silver for clothing will be issued to you from it."

31) *a-nu-ma* LÚ.MEŠ *ša na-ad-na-ta*
32) *a-na ia-ši* in_4*-na-ab-tu gáb-bu*
33) *ḫa-ba-li-ia* UGU-*ka šum-*⸢*ma*⸣
34) *ta-*⸢*qú*⸣*-ú-ul a-na ia-ši a-nu-*⸢*ma*⸣
35) *ìš-*te_9*-mé ú-ul i-nu-ma*
36) *uš-ši-ir-ti* LÚ-*ia a-na* É.GAL
37) *ù iq-bi a-na* LÚ *ù iz-zi-iz*
38) GÍR ZABAR ⸢UGU⸣-⸢*ia*⸣ *ù am-ma-ḫa-aṣ-ni*(?)
39) 9-*ta-an a-nu-ma* GA.KAL *i-na*
40) *ar-ni an-nu-ú ù i-na ar-ni*
41) *ša-ni mi-nu ìl-*te_9*-qa-ni šum-ma*
42) 2 ITU *ia-nu* ÉRIN.MEŠ *pí-ṭá-ti*
43) *ù i-*te_9*-zi-ib* URU.KI
44) *ù pa-aṭ-ra-ti ù*
45) *bal-ṭá-at* ZI-*ia a-*⸢*di*⸣
46) *i-pé-šu i-pé-eš lìb-bi-i*⸢*a*⸣
Up.ed. 47) *ša-ni-tam ú-ul ti-i-de*
48) *at-ta* KUR *A-mur-ri ur-ra*
49) *mu-ša tu-ba-ú-na*
Lft.ed. 50) ÉRIN(!).MEŠ *pí-ṭá-ti ú-ul ta-ša-aš*
51) \ *na-aq-ṣa-pu ù qí-bi a-na* LUGAL
52) *ku-uš-da ki-ma ar-ḫi-ìš*

(31–34) Now the men whom you gave to me have all fled. My injury is your responsibility if you ignore me.

(34–36) Now I have obeyed. Is it not that I sent my man to the palace?

(37–41) And he (ʿAbdi-Ashirta) spoke to a man and he assaulted me with a bronze dagger so that I was hit nine times. Now he is resolute in this crime and from another criminal act, who will deliver me?

(41–46) If in two months there are no regular troops, then I will leave the city and I will go away so that I will stay alive while I do as I please.

(47–52) Furthermore, don't you yourself know the land of Amurru? Day and night they long for the regular army. Don't get angry! So speak to the king! Come here quickly!

EA 83

TRANSCRIPTION

Obv. 01) [^{I}*Ri-*]*ib*[-^{d}IŠKUR *i*]*q-*⸢*bi*⸣ ⸢*a*⸣[*-na*]
02) [EN-*š*]*u* LUGAL KUR.KUR.KI.MEŠ LUGAL GAL
03) [^{d}N]IN *ša* URU *Gub-la ti-di-in*$_4$
04) [KAL.G]A *a-na šàr-ri* EN-ia
05) *a-na* GÌR.MEŠ EN-*ia* ^{d}UTU-*ia*
06) 7-*šu* 7-*ta-an am-qú-ut*
07) *a-na mi-ni la-a tu-te-*⸢*ru*⸣-[*n*]*a*
08) *a-wa-ta*$_5$ *a-na ia-a-ši ù*
09) *i-de ip-ša ša i-pu-š*[*u*]
10) LÚ-*ia ut-ta-ši-ir a-na ma-*[*ḫa*]*r*
11) [E]N-*ia ù la-qú* 2 ANŠE.KUR.RA-*šu*
12) ⸢*ù*⸣ LÚ *ša-nu la-qí* LÚ-*šu*
13) ⸢*ù*⸣ *ṭup-pí* LUGAL *la-a na-di-*⸢*in*$_4$⸣
14) [*i-n*]*a qa-at* LÚ-*ia ši-*⸢*mé*⸣ ⸢*ia*⸣-*ši*
15) [*a-n*]*a mi-‹ni› qa-la-ta ù tu-*⸢*ul*⸣-⸢*qú*⸣
16) ⸢KUR⸣-*ka ú-ul yu-uq-ba i-na*
17) UD. KAM^{V}.MEŠ LÚ.MEŠ MÁŠKIM *la-qú* LÚ.MEŠ GAZ.MEŠ
18) *ka-li* KUR.KUR.ḪI.A *ú-ul ka-a-ma*
19) ⸢*yu*⸣-*uq-bu i-na* UD. KAM^{V}.MEŠ‹-*ka*›
20) *ù la-a ti-le-ú la-qa-ši*
21) ⸢*ša*⸣-*ni-tam aš-ta-pár a-na* LÚ.MEŠ *ma-ṣa-ar-ti*
22) *ù a-na* ANŠE.KUR.RA.MEŠ *ù la-a*
23) ⸢*tu*⸣-*da-nu-na šu-te-ra a-wa-ta*$_5$
24) *a-na ia-ši ù i-pu-ša a-na-ku*
25) *ki-ta it-ti* ^{I} ÌR-*A-ši-ir-ta*
26) ⸢*ki*⸣-*ma* ^{I}*Ia-pa-*^{d}IŠKUR *ù* ^{I}*Zi-*⸢*im*⸣-*re-*⸢*da*⸣
27) *ù* ⸢*bal*⸣-*ṭá-ti ša-ni-tam šum-ma*
Lo.ed. 28) *ap-pu-na-ma a-nu-ma pa-aṭ-ra*
29) ⸢URU⸣ *Ṣu-mu-ra ù* URU É-*Ar-*[*ḫ*]*a*(?)
Rev. 30) [*t*]*a-din-ni i-na qa-at*
31) ^{I}*Ia-an-ḫa-mi ù ia-dì-na*
32) ŠE.*IM*.ḪI.A *a-na a-ka-li-ia*
33) *a-na-ṣa-ra* URU LUGAL *a-na ša-a-šu*

EA 83

TRANSLATION

(1–6) [R]ib[-Haddi s]poke t[o h]is [lord,] king of all lands, the great king: May the [La]dy of the city of Byblos grant [stren]gth to the king, my lord; at the feet of my lord, my sun god, seven times and seven times, have I fallen.

(7–14) Why do you not send back word to me so that I may know the thing that I should do? I sent my man to my [lo]rd but they confiscated both his horses, then a second man had his man (squire) taken. And no letter of the king was delivered to my man.

(14–20) Listen to me: [W]hy do you keep silent so that your territory is being taken? Was it not said, in the days of the commissioners, "The *ʿapîru* men have taken all the territories"? Will they not speak thus in ‹your› days and you are unable to take it (them) back?

(21–27) Furthermore, I have been writing for garrison troops and for horses but they are not being given. Just send me the word and I myself will make a treaty with ʿAbdi-Ashirta like Yapaʿ-Haddi and Zimredda, and I will stay alive.

(27–33) Furthermore, if moreover now the town of Ṣumur and the town of Bêt-Arḫa have defected, assign me to Yanḫamu and allot grain for my sustenance so that I may guard the city of the king for him.

34) *ù ia-aq-bi* LUGAL *ù yu-wa-ši-*⸢*ra*⸣
35) LÚ-*ia* LÚ.MEŠ-*šu ti-ša-šu-na* UGU-*ia*
36) *ur-ra mu-ša at-ta-mi na-ad-*⸢*na*⸣-⸢*ta*⸣
37) DUMU-*nu a-na* LUGAL *ù uš-ši-ra-šu šu-ut*
38) 3! LÚ URU I-*bir*$_5$*-ta al-la-mi i-na*
39) É ^{I}*Ia-an-*⸢*ḫa*⸣*-mi ša-ni-tam qí-ba-mi*
40) *a-na* ^{I}*Ia-‹an›-ḫa-mi al-lu-mi* ^{I}*Ri-ib-*^{d}IŠKUR
41) *i-na qa-ti-ka ù mi-im-mu*
42) *ša ‹in*$_4$*›-né-ep-šu a-na ša-šu* ⸢UGU⸣-*ka*
43) *ú-*⸢*ul*⸣ *yi-ma-qú-ta* ÉRIN.MEŠ *ka-ra-*⸢*ši*⸣
44) UGU-*ia ù aš-pu-ru a-na ša-šu*
45) ⸢*šum*⸣-⸢*ma*⸣ *ki-a-ma la-a ti-iq-bi*
46) *ù i-ti-zi-ib* ⸢URU⸣ *ù*
47) *pa-aṭ-ra-ti ša-ni-tam šum-ma la-a*
48) *tu-te-ru-na a-wa-ta*$_5$ *a-na ia-ši*
49) *ù i-ti-zi-ib* URU *ù*
50) *pa-aṭ-ra-ti qa-du* LÚ.MEŠ
51) *ša i-ra-a-mu-ni ù*
52) *li-ma-ad al-li-mi*
53) $^{⸢MUNUS⸣}$*Um-ma-aḫ-nu ù* ^{I}*Mil-ku-ru*
54) *mu-ut-ši*$_x$(ŠE) GÉME *ša* ^{d}NIN
55) [*ša*] ⸢URU⸣⸢*Gub*⸣-⸢*la*⸣ ⸢*ù*⸣ ⸢KAL⸣.GA
Up.ed. 56) [*a-na* LUGAL EN-*ia ti-ka*]-⸢*ra*⸣-*b*[*u*]
57) [*a*]-⸢*na*⸣ ^{d}[NIN *ša* URU *Gub-la*]

(34–39) And may the king speak and may he release (send back) my man. His people are furious with me, (saying) day and night: "It was you who handed over our son to the king." So release him, especially him. As for the three men of ʿIbirta, behold they are in the house of Yanḥamu.

(39–51) Furthermore, speak to Ya‹n›ḫamu, "Behold, Rib-Haddi is in your charge and whatever [ha]ppens to him is your responsibility," lest the expeditionary force attack me. And I (will) write to him, "If thus, you don't speak, then I will abandon the city and I will depart. Furthermore, if you do not send back word to me then I will abandon the city and I will depart with the men who are loyal to me. So be apprised."

(52–57) Behold, Ummaḫnu, and Milkuru her husband, is the handmaiden of the Lady [of] the city Byblos and [she pra]ys to the L[ady of Byblos] for strength [for the king, my lord].

EA 84

TRANSCRIPTION

Obv. 01) [*a-n*]*a* LUGAL BAD-*ia* ^{d}UTU KUR.KI.DIDLI.ḪI.A
02) [*qí*]══════════ *bí*══════════*ma*
03) [*u*]*m-ma Ri-ib-ad-di* ÌR-*ka*
04) [GI]Š.GÌR.GUB GÌR.MEŠ-*ka a-na* GÌR.MEŠ ^{d}UTU
05) BAD-*ia* 7-*it-šu ù* 7-*ta-a-an*
06) *am-qú-ut šá-ni-tam da-mi-iq-mi*
07) *a-na pa-ni* LUGAL BAD-*ia i-pí-iš*
08) ^{I}ÌR-^{d}*A-ši-ir-ti* UR.GI$_7$ *i-nu-ma*
09) *in*$_4$*-né-ep-ša-at* KUR.KI.ḪI.A LUGAL
10) *a-na ša-šu ù qa-al a-na* KUR.KI-*šu*
11) *ù a-nu-um-ma i-na-an-na*
12) *in*$_4$*-né-ep-ša-at* URU ⌜*Ṣu*⌝*-mu-ur*
13) *tar-ba-aṣ* BAD-*ia ù* É ⌜*ur*⌝-*ši*-⌜*šu*⌝ ⌜*a*⌝-⌜*na*⌝ ⌜*ša*⌝-[*šu*]
14) *ù i-ṣa-lu-ul a-na* É *u*[*r-ši* BAD-]*ia*
15) *ù i-pé-ti a-šar ni-ṣí-*[*ir-ti*]
16) [BAD]-*ia ù qa-al mi-i*[*a-mi*]
17) [*šu-u*]*t* LÚ.LUL *ù* UR.GI$_7$
18) [*ù d*]*a-an šá-ni-tam i-nu-ma*
Lo.ed. 19) [*i-qa-bu-*]*ni*$_7$ LÚ.MEŠ *a-na pa-*[*ni* BAD-*i*]⌜*a*⌝
20) [*ṣa-ab-ta-a*]*t-mi* URU *Gub-la*
21) [LÚ-*šu ma-an-g*]*a i-de* ⌜BE⌝-*lí-ia*
Rev. 22) [*ú-ul il-*]*te*$_9$*-qú* URU *Gub-la*
23) [*ka-li* LÚ.MEŠ] *qí-ip-tu*$_4$
24) [*pa-aṭ-ru*] *ù ma-ri-iṣ ma-*[*gal*]
25) [*a-na* KUR.]KI.ḪI.A *be-li-ia*

EA 84

TRANSLATION

(1–6) [Sp]eak [to] the king, my lord, the sun god of the nations, t[he m]essage of Rib-haddi, your servant, the footstool of your feet, at the feet of the sun god, my lord seven times and seven times have I fallen.

(6–10) Furthermore, is it good in the sight of the king, my lord, viz. the deed of ʿAbdi-Ashirta, the dog, that the lands of the king have joined him, so that he keeps silent?

(11–18) And even now the city of Ṣumur, the court of my lord and his bed-chamber, has joined him! And he has slept in the bed[chamber of] my [lord] and he has opened the treas[ury of] my [lord], but he (Pharaoh) keeps silent. W[ho is h]e, the rebel and the dog, [that he is] strong?

(18–25) Furthermore, when men [sa]y in the pre[sence of m]y [lord], "The city of Byblos [has been] seized, [its ruler is in distr]ess," know, my lord, the city of Byblos [they have] not taken; [all the men,] the officials, [have departed] and the situation is very bitter [for the lan]ds of my lord.

26) *šá-ni-tam lu-wa-ší-ra-am* LUGAL [BAD-*lí-i*]⌜*a*⌝
27) LÚ.MÁŠKIM-*šu ša da-an qa-d*[*u* ÉRIN.MEŠ]
28) *ù li-iṣ-ṣur* URU.KI BAD-*ia*
29) *ù ip*-⌜*ṭù*⌝-⌜*ra*⌝ *a*-⌜*na*⌝-⌜*ku*⌝ ⌜*ù*⌝
30) ‹⌜*ù*⌝› ⌜*ur*⌝-⌜*ra*⌝-⌜*ad*⌝ BAD-*ia* ^{d}UTU
31) KUR.KI.ḪI.A *ù lu-wa-ši-ra be-li-ia*
32) LÚ.MEŠ *ú ti-ìl-qú mi-im-mi*^{MEŠ}
33) ^{d}DA.MU-*ia a-na ma-ḫar* BAD-*ia*
34) *ù ú-ul ìl-te*$_{9}$*-qa mi-im-ma*^{MEŠ}
35) ⌜*ša*⌝ DINGIR.MEŠ-*ka* LÚ.UR.GI$_{7}$ *šu-ut*
36) [*ù*] SIG$_{5}$-*mi i-nu-ma iṣ-bat* URU *Gub-la*
37) [*a-mur*]-*mi* URU *Gub-la ki-ma* URU *Ḫi-ku-up*-⌜*ta*⌝-*aḫ*
38) [*i*]-*ba-ša-at a-na šàr-ri šá-ni-tam*
39) [*a*-]-⌜*mur*⌝ ^{I}ÌR.NIN.IB LÚ *ša uš-šir*$_{4}$*-ti*

Up.ed. 40) ⌜*it*⌝-*ti* ^{I}*Pu-ḫe-ya* LÚ *kir*-⌜*dib*⌝
41) ⌜*ù*⌝ *uš-ši-ra-šu a-na* ÌR-*k*[*a*]

Lft.ed. 42) [*šá-ni-tam*] ⌜*a*⌝-⌜*mur*⌝ ^{MUNUS}⌜*Um*⌝-⌜*ma*⌝-*a*[*ḫ-nu*] GÉME ^{d}[NIN *ša*]
43) [URU *Gub-la*] ⌜LÚ⌝ ⌜*mu*⌝-*ut-ši* ^{I}*Mil-kur*
44) [*ù* x DUG] SAR *ye-ni uš-ši-i*[*r-ti*]

(26–38) Furthermore, may the king, [m]y [lord] send his commissioner who is strengthened with [troops] and let him protect the city of my lord so that I, myself, may depart and so that I may serve my lord, the sun god of the nations. So may my lord send men that they may take the possessions of my Adonis to my lord. But let not that dog take away the property of your god(s). But is it good that he take the city of Byblos? [Look]! The city of Byblos belongs to the king like Ḥikuptaḥ (Memphis).

(38–41) Furthermore, [lo]ok, as for ʿAbdi-NIN.IB whom I sent with Puḫeya, the groom, now send him to yo[ur] servant.

(42–44) [Furthermore,] look, Umma[ḫnu], the handmaiden of [the Lady of Byblos], her husband Milkur [and *x*] *šaḫarru* jar(s) of wine have [I] sent.

EA 85

TRANSCRIPTION

Obv. 01) [*a-na šàr-ri*] ⸢EN⸣-*ia* ^{d}UTU *qí-b*[*í-ma*]
02) [*um-ma* ^{I}*Ri-i*]*b*-^{d}⸢IŠKUR⸣ ⸢ÌR⸣-*ka-ma a-na* ⸢GÌR⸣.[MEŠ]
03) [EN-*ia*] ^{d}UTU 7-*šu* 7-*ta-an a*[*m-qú-ut*]
04) [^{d}NI]N *ša* URU *Gub-la ti-di*-⸢*in*$_{4}$⸣
05) [KAL.G]A *a-na šàr-ri* EN-*ia*
06) [*a-n*]*u-ma ki-a-ma-am iš-tap-ru a-na š*[*àr-ri*] ⸢EN⸣-*ia*
07) ⸢*ù*⸣ *la-a yi-iš-mu-na a-wa-te*-⸢*ia*⸣
08) *a-nu-ma* 3-*ta-an i-zi-iz* UGU-*ia* MU. KAM^{v}.MEŠ
09) *an-ni-ta ù* 2 MU *am-ma-ša-ʾu*$_{5}$
10) ŠE. IM.ḪI.A-*ia ia-nu* ŠE. IM.ḪI.A *a-na*
11) [*a*]-*ka-li a-na ia-ši-nu mi-na a-qa-bu-na*
12) ⸢*a*⸣-*na* LÚ.MEŠ *ḫu-up-ši-ia ga*-⸢*am*⸣-*ru*
13) DUMU.MEŠ-*šu-nu* MUNUS.DUMU.MUNUS-*šu-nu* GIŠ.MEŠ É-*šu-nu*
14) *i-na na-da-ni i*-⸢*na*⸣ KUR ‹*Ia*›-*ri-mu-ta*
15) *i-na bá-la-aṭ* ⸢ZI⸣-*nu ša-ni-tam*
16) *yi-iš-mé šàr-ru* ⸢EN⸣-*li a-wa-te*
17) ÌR *ki-ti-šu ù yu-wa-ši-ra*
18) ŠE.*IM*.ḪI.A *i-na lìb-bi* GIŠ.MÁ.MEŠ *ù yu-ba-li-iṭ*
19) ÌR-*šu ù* URU-*šu ù ia-di-na*
20) 4 *me* LÚ.MEŠ 30 *ta*-⸢*pal*⸣ ⸢ANŠE⸣.⸢KUR⸣.⸢RA⸣.MEŠ
21) *ki-ma na*-⸢*da*⸣-*ni a-na* ^{I}*Sú*-⸢*ra*⸣-⸢*ta*⸣
22) *ù ti-na-ṣa-ru* URU *a-na ka-ta*$_{5}$
23) ⸢*ša*⸣-*ni-tam i-nu-ma yi-iq-bi* ^{I}*Ia-an-ḫa-mu*
24) [*na-a*]*d-na-ti-mi* ŠE.*IM*.ḪI.A *a-na* ^{I}*Ri-ib*-^{d}IŠKUR
25) [*ù a*]*d-di-in*$_{4}$ *a-na ša-a-šu*
26) [……….]-*sú* \ *ḫu-ṭá-ri-ma*
27) [……….]ŠE.[*IM*].⸢ḪI.A⸣ 40 LÚ.MEŠ
28) ⸢*mi*⸣-[*na*] ⸢*na*⸣-*da-an* ⸢*šu*⸣-⸢*ut*⸣ [*a*]-[*n*]*a ia*-‹*ši*›
29) *ù an-nu-ú i-na* ‹ŠU› ^{I}*Ia-pa*-^{d}[IŠ]KU[R⸣
30) ⸢*ad*⸣-*di* KÙ.BABBAR.MEŠ-*šu-nu al-lu-mi*
31) ⸢^{I}⸣⸢*Pu*⸣-⸢*ḫé*⸣-*ya it*-‹*ti*›-*ka ša-al-šu*
32) ⸢*ù*⸣ *yi-iq-bi gáb-ba i-na pa-ni-ka*

EA 85

TRANSLATION

(1–5) Spe[ak to the king,] my lord, the sun god, [the message of Ri]b-Hadda, your servant: at the fe[et of my lord,] the sun god, seven times (and) seven times, have I [fallen.] May [the La]dy of the city of Byblos grant [streng]th to the king, my lord.

(6–15) [N]ow, thus I write to the k[ing,] my lord, but he does not heed my words. Now three times he has attacked me this year and for two years I have been robbed of my grain. There is no grain for us to [e]at. What shall I say to my yeoman farmers? Their sons and their daughters, the furnishings of their houses are gone as payment in the land of ‹Ya›rimuta to sustain our lives.

(15–22) Furthermore, may the king, my lord, heed the words of his loyal servant and may he send grain in the hold of ships that he may sustain his servant and his city and may he give four hundred troops and thirty pairs of horses just as he gave to Surata, and may they protect the city for you.

(23–32) Furthermore, inasmuch as Yanḫamu said, "I [ga]ve grain to Rib-Hadda," and I will give him [...] "the branches [...] grain for forty men," what did he give to me? But behold, I deposited their silver with Iapaʿ-Hadda. Behold, Puḫeya is with you, ask him and let him tell everything in your presence.

33) ⸢*ša*⸣*-ni-tam li-id-mì-iq i-na pa-ni*
34) ⸢*šàr*⸣*-ri* EN-*ia ù yu-da-na*$_{7}$
35) ⸢ŠE⸣.*IM*.ḪI.A *mu-*⸢*ú*⸣*-*⸢*ṣa*⸣(?) KUR *Ia-ri-mu-ta*
36) ⸢*ša*⸣*-a yu-*⸢*da*⸣*-*[*nu*] ⸢*pa*⸣*-na-nu i-na* URU ⸢*Ṣu*⸣*-*⸢*mu*⸣*-ra*
37) [*y*]*u-da-na*$_{7}$ ⸢*i*⸣*-na-na i-na* URU *Gub-la*
38) ⸢*ù*⸣ ⸢*nu*⸣*-ba-li-*⸢*iṭ*⸣ *a-di ti-š*[*a-i-l*]*u*
39) [*a-na*] URU-*li-ka* ⸢*ša*⸣*-ni-tam li-i*[*b-lu-uṭ*]
40) ⸢*šàr*⸣*-*⸢*ru*⸣ EN *a-*⸢*di*⸣ LÚ.MEŠ-*ia ra*[*-i-mu-ni*]
Lo.ed. 41) [^{I}ÌR-*A-ši-*]*ir-ta* ⸢*ù*⸣ ⸢LÚ⸣.⸢MEŠ⸣ ⸢GAZ⸣ [*al-ku*]
42) [*a-na ma-ḫa*]*r* ^{I}*Ia-pa-*^{d}IŠKUR *i-na* [URU]
43) [*Be-ru-t*]*a ù tu-pa-šu* [*ki-tu*]
Rev. 44) [*a-*]⸢*nu*⸣*-m*[*a*] *ia-nu* LÚ *i-na* ⸢URU⸣[*-ka ù*]
45) [*uš*]*-ši-ra* ⸢LÚ⸣.⸢MEŠ⸣ ⸢*ma*⸣*-ṣa-ar-*⸢*ta*⸣ [*a-na*]
46) [*na-ṣ*]*a-ar* ⸢KUR⸣-⸢*ia*⸣ ⸢*ú*⸣*-ul tu-ṣa-bat*
47) [KUR]-*ka ša-*⸢*ni*⸣*-tam ši-mé ia-a-ši*
48) [*qí-*]*ba-mi a-na* ⸢^{I}⸣⸢*Ia*⸣*-an-ḫa-mi ù*
49) [*y*]*i-*[*ìl*]*-qé* KÙ.BABBAR.M[EŠ *a-ka-*]⸢*lì*⸣ *a-na* ⸢LÚ⸣.⸢MEŠ⸣
50) [UR]U ⸢*Gub*⸣*-la i-*⸢*na*⸣ ⸢KUR⸣ ⸢*Ia*⸣*-ri-mu-*⸢*ta*⸣
51) *ša-ni-tam* LUGAL ⸢KUR⸣ ‹*Mi*›*-ta-na* ⸢*a*⸣*-ṣé*
52) *a-di* U[RU] *Ṣu-*⸢*mu*⸣*-*⸢*ra*⸣ *ù yu-ba-*⸢*ú*⸣
53) *a-la-k*[*a*$_{13}$] ⸢*a*⸣*-di* URU *Gub-la ù* ⸢*i*⸣[*a*]*-nu*
54) A-*u a-na* ⸢*ša*⸣*-te-*⸢*šu*⸣ *ù ta-ra*
55) *a-*⸢*na*⸣ KUR-⸢*šu*⸣ ⸢*a*⸣*-nu-ma ki-a-ma ìš-tap-ru*
56) ⸢*a*⸣*-*⸢*na*⸣ ⸢É⸣.GAL *a-na i-re-eš-ti-*⸢*i*⸣⸢*a*⸣
57) [*a-na mi-*]*ni* ⸢*la*⸣*-*[*a*] ⸢*tu*⸣*-te-ru-*⸢*na*⸣
58) [*a-wa-ta*$_{5}$] ⸢*i*⸣*-ba-ši-mi ù i-ia-nu*
59) [*i-*]⸢*re*⸣*-eš-*⸢*ti*⸣ ÌR-*ia ù i-de*
60) ⸢*ip*⸣*-ša* ⸢*ša*⸣ ⸢*i*⸣*-pu-šu*
61) ⸢*a*⸣*-*⸢*di*⸣ *yi-*[*ik*]*-*⸢*ta*⸣*-aš-du-na šàr-ru*
62) ⸢*ù*⸣ *yi-*⸢*da*⸣*-ga-lu šàr-ru*
63) ⸢ÌR⸣ *ki-ti-šu mi-ia-mi*
64) ^{I}⸢ÌR⸣-⸢*A*⸣*-*⸢*ši*⸣*-*⸢*ir*⸣*-*⸢*ta*⸣ ⸢ÌR⸣ ⸢UR⸣.⸢GI$_{7}$⸣ ⸢*ù*⸣
65) ›⸢*ù*⸣‹ [*yu*]*-qa-bu šum-šu i-na*
66) [*pa-*]⸢*ni*⸣ LUGAL ^{d}UTU *i-nu-ma* 1 *ḫa-za-nu*
67) *lìb-bu-šu it-ti lìb-bi-ia*

(33–39) Furthermore, may it please the king that grain, the produce of the land of Yarimuta be given. What was given formerly to the city of Ṣumur, may it be given now to the city of Byblos, and we may be sustained until you [investigate concerning your city.

(39–47) Furthermore, as the king, my lord, l[ives], my people are still lo[yal to me. ʿAbdi-Ash]irta and the *ʿapîru* men [went to vis]it Yapaʿ-Hadda in [the city of Beiru]t and [a treaty] was made. [N]ow there is no man in [your] city, [so se]nd garrison troops [to pro]tect your territory lest your [country] be captured.

(47–50) Furthermore, listen to me, [sp]eak to Yanḥamu that he take silver for the [foo]d for the men of [the city of] Byblos in the land of Yarimuta.

(51–55) Furthermore, the king of the land of ‹Mi›tanni came forth as far as the c[ity] of Ṣumur and he was seeking to come [as far] as the city of Byblos but there was no water for him to drink so he returned to his land.

(55–63) Now, thus have I been writing to the palace concerning my needs. [Wh]y don't you send back [word], to wit, "My servant's request is available," or "is not available," and I will know the thing that [I] must do until the king will come and the king will see to his loyal servant.

(64–69) Who is ʿAbdi-Ashirta, the slave, the dog, that his name should be mentioned in the [pre]sence of the king, the sun god? If (there were) one city ruler whose heart were one with my heart,

68) *ù ú-da-bi-ra* ^{I}ÌR-*A-ši-ir-ta*
69) *iš-tu* KUR *A-mur-*⌜*ri*⌝ *ša-ni-tam* ⌜*iš*⌝*-tu*
70) *ta-ri a-bi-ka ìs-tu*
71) URU *Ṣí-du-na iš-tu* UD. KAM^{v}.MEŠ
72) *šu-wa-at in*$_{4}$*-né-ep-ša-at*
73) KUR.MEŠ *a-na* LÚ.MEŠ GAZ.MEŠ *ki-na-na*
74) *ia-nu mi-*[*a*]*m-ma a-na ia-ši*
75) [*y*]*i-ìš-mé šàr-ru a-wa-te* ÌR-*šu*
76) [*i*]⌜*a*⌝*-di-na* LÚ.MEŠ *a-na na-ṣa-ar*
77) [URU]*-šu ú-ul yu-pa-ḫi-ra ka-li*
78) [LÚ].MEŠ GAZ.MEŠ *ù* DI-*ab-tu*
79) [URU] *ù i-na* UD. KAM^{v}.MEŠ
80) [*an-nu-*]*ti uš-ši-ra* ÉRIN.MEŠ [*pí-ṭá-*]⌜*ti*⌝
Up.ed. 81) [*ù tu*]*-da-bi-ra-šu i*[*š-tu*]
82) [KUR *A-mur-*]*ri i-nu-ma* LÚ.MÁŠKIM *š*[*àr-ri*]
83) [*it-*]*ti-*⌜*nu*⌝ *ù a-na* ⌜*ša*⌝*-*⌜*šu*⌝
Lft.ed. 84) [*nu-uš-pu-*]*ru ù nu-*⌜*uš*⌝*-pu-ru a-*[*na ka-*]*ta*$_{5}$ ^{MUNUS}⌜*Um*⌝*-m*[*a-aḫ-nu*]
85) [*ù mu-u*]*t-ši* ^{I}*Mil-ku-*⌜*ru*⌝ GÉME ^{d}N[IN *ša*] URU *Gub*[*-la ù*]
86) [*li-ib-lu-*]*uṭ šàr-ru a-di* GÉME ⌜^{d}⌝[NI]N *i-na* [.......*ù*]
87) [*uš-ši-ra-*]*na i-na qa-at* LÚ.GAL [*a-na*] ^{d}NIN[*ša* URU *Gub-la*]

(68–82) then I would drive ʿAbdi-Ashirta from the land of Amurru. Furthermore, since your father's return from the city of Ṣidon, from that very time, the land has joined the *ʿapîru* men. Thus, I have no supplies. [M]ay the king heed the words of his servant; [m]ay he give men to protect his [city], lest he (ʿAbdi-Ashirta) assemble all the *ʿapîru* men and seize [the city]. So in [the]se days, send the regul[ar ar]my [that they] may expell him f[rom] [the land of Amur]ru.

(82–87) If the k[ing's] commissioner be [wi]th us, then to him [will we wri]te. And we are sending t[o yo]u the lady Umm[aḫnu and] her [husban]d, Milkuru, the handmaiden of the L[ady of] the city of Byb[os and as] the king [liv]es, the handmaiden of the [La]dy is still in [...so sen]d (her) in the charge of a senior official [to] the Lady [of the city of Byblos.]

EA 86

TRANSCRIPTION

Obv. 01) [*a-na*] *A-ma-a*[*n-ap-pa qí-bí-ma*]

02) ⸢*um*⸣-*ma* ^{I}*Ri-ib*-⸢^{d}⸣[IŠKUR *a-na* GÌR.MEŠ-*ka*]

03) *am-qú-ut* ^{d}*A-ma*[*-na* DINGIR *ša* LUGAL]

04) EN-*ka ti-di-nu* TÉŠ-*ka* [*i-na pa-ni*]

05) *šàr-ri* EN-*ka ši-mé i*[*a-ši nu-kúr-tu*$_{4}$]

06) KAL.GA *ù ku-uš-da q*[*a-du*]

07) ÉRIN.MEŠ *pí-ṭá-ti ù* [*ti-ìl-qé*]

08) KUR *A-mu-ri ur-ra m*[*u-ša*]

09) [*ti-*]⸢*ša*⸣*-si*$_{17}$ *a-na ka-ta*$_{5}$ [*ù*]

10) [*ti-i*]*q-ta-bu ma-ad m*[*a-gal*]

11) [*mi-i*]*m-mu ša yu-ul-*⸢*qú*⸣ *ì*[*š-tu*]

12) [*ša-*]*šu-nu a-na* KUR *Mi-ta-n*[*a ù*]

13) [*a-nu-m*]*a i-na-na la-a ta*[*-aq-bu*]

14) [*ù*] *a-mi-ni tu-ṣa-na* É[RIN.MEŠ]

15) [*a-nu*]*-ma taq-bi* ^{I}*Ia-an-ḫa*[*-mu*]

16) [*u*]*š-ši-ir* ‹I›M.ŠE.ḪI.A *a-na k*[*a-ta*$_{5}$]

17) ⸢*la*⸣*-a ti-iš-mé* ÌR *šu-u*[*t…*]

18) [*a-n*]*a ša-a-šu ù d*[*a -an-nu*]

19) [KU]Š \ *ma-aš-ka a-n*[*a…*]

20) [*ša-a-*]*šu la ra-b*[*u*]

21) [*…*]*a ù la y*[*u-da-an*]

22) [*…*K]Ù.BABBAR.MEŠ *iš-*⸢*tu*⸣ [*…*]

23) [*ù*] *li-ma*[*-ad al-li-mi*]

Lo.ed. 24) [^{MUNUS}*Um*]*-ma-aḫ*[*-nu ù mu-ut-ši*$_{x}$(ŠE)]

Rev. 25) [^{I}*Mil-ku*]*-ra* G[ÉME ^{d}NIN]

26) [*ša-a*] URU *Gub*[*-la…*]

27) [*qí-b*]*i a-na* I*a-r*[*i-mu-ta*]

28) ⸢*ù*⸣ *qí-bi a-na* LUGAL [*ù*]

29) [*t*]*u-da-na a-na* ^{d}[NIN]

30) [*ú-*]*ul ti-ka-li m*[*i-im-ma*(?)]

EA 86

TRANSLATION

(1–5) [Speak to] Ama[n-appa], the message of Rib-[Haddi; at your feet] have I fallen. May Amo[n, the god of the king,] your lord, bestow honor upon you [in the presence of] the king, your lord.

(5–22) Listen to m[e! The hostility] is severe, so com[e with] regular troops [so that you may] take the land of Amurru. Day and ni[ght it has cr]ied to you [and it s]ays the property that was taken f[rom th]em for Mittan[i] is very much. [But n]ow you do not speak [so] why should the a[rmy] come forth? [No]w you have said, "Yanḥamu [s]ent grain to y[ou]." Have you not heard? Tha[t] slave [...t]o them and he is s[trong]. The leather [h]e has is not ext[ensive...] and much silver from [Mittani] has not [been given].

(23–30) [So] be appr[ised. Behold, Um]maḫ[nu and her husband, Milku]ra, is the ha[ndmaiden of the Lady of the city Byblos. So speak to Ya[rmuta] and speak to the king [that] there be given for the L[ady]. Do not withhold an[ything]!

31) ⸢*ša*⸣*-ni-tam qí-ba-mi a-na*[LUGAL]
32) *ù yu-da-na a-*[*na* ÌR-*šu*]
33) ⸢*mu*⸣*-ú-ṣa ša* KUR *Ia-a*[*r-mu-ta*]
34) ⸢*ki*⸣*-ma na-da-ni-šu* [*pa-na-nu*]
35) ⸢*a*⸣*-na* URU *Ṣu-mu-*⸢*ra*⸣ [*ù*]
36) *ni-ub!-lu-uṭ a-di na*[*-da-an-šu*?]
37) *šàr-ru a-na* URU-*šu* [*ù*]
38) [*a*]*-nu-ma* 3 MU. KAM^{v}.MEŠ *a*[*m-ma-ša-ʾu*$_5$]
39) ŠE.*IM*.ḪI.A-*nu ia-nu m*[*i-im-ma*]
40) *a-na na-da-ni a-na* A[NŠE.KUR.RA]
41) *ù a-na mi-ni ia-*[*di-na*]
42) *šàr-ru* 30 *ta-pal* [ANŠE.KUR.RA]
43) *ù ti-ìl-qa at*[*-ta-ma*]
44) 10 *ta-pal šum-ma t*[*i-ìl-qu*]
45) *ù li-qa gáb*[*-ba*]
46) *ù iš-tu* KUR *I*[*a-ar-mu-ta*]
47) *yu-da-na* ŠE.[*IM*.ḪI.A]
48) ⸢*a*⸣*-*⸢*na*⸣ *a-ka-*⸢*li*⸣[*-nu*(?)]
Up.ed 49) ⸢*ù*⸣ ⸢*uš*⸣*-ši-*⸢*ir*⸣ [GIŠ.MÁ.(MEŠ)? *ù*]
50) [*nu*]*-ṣa*

(31–34) Furthermore, speak to [the king] that produce of the land of Ya[rmuta] be given t[o his servant].

(35–50) as [formerly] to Ṣumur, [and] we will stay alive until the king [has given it?] to his city. [And n]ow for three years I have [been plundered] of our grain. There is n[othing] to pay for the h[orses]. And why should the king allot thirty pairs of [horses] and you yourself take ten pair? If you're [going to take], then take al[l]! But from the land of Ya[rmuta] let grai[n] be given for [us] to eat, or send [ships? and] we will go out.

EA 87

TRANSCRIPTION

Obv.	01)	[*a-na A-m*]*a-an-ap-pí* E[N-*ia*]
	02)	⌜*qí*⌝-*bí-ma*
	03)	*um-ma Ri-ib-*^{d}IŠKUR ÌR[-*ka*]-ma
	04)	*a-na* GÌR.MEŠ EN-*ia am-qú-ut*
	05)	^{d}*A-ma-na ù* ^{d}NIN
	06)	*ša* URU *Gub-la ti-di-nu*
	07)	TÉŠ-*ka a-na pa-ni* LUGAL BAD-*ia*
	08)	*šá-ni-tam a-na mi-nim-mi tu-uš-te*$_{9}$*-ti*$_{7}$*-iq-ni*
	09)	*uš-ši-ra-am-mi* LÚ.DUMU KIN-⌜*ka*⌝
	10)	*it-ti-ia a-na ma-ḫar*
	11)	LUGAL BAD-*ka ù lu-ú*
	12)	*li-di-na-ku* ÉRIN.MEŠ *ù* GIŠ [GIG]IR.⌜MEŠ⌝
	13)	⌜*i*⌝-*zi-ir-ta*$_{5}$ *a-na ka-ta*$_{5}$
Lo.ed.	14)	⌜*ù*⌝ *ti-ṣú-ru* URU
Rev.	15)	⌜*ù*⌝ ⌜*an*⌝-⌜*nu*⌝-*ú i-še*$_{20}$*-me a-na*
	16)	⌜*a*⌝-*wa-te*^{MEŠ}-*ka ù ú-wa-ši*[*r*$_{4}$]‹-*šu*›
	17)	*ù uṣ-ṣa-am ri-qú-tám*
	18)	*ù i-še*$_{20}$*-me-e ú ia-nu-um* ⌜ÉRIN⌝.MEŠ
	19)	*it-ti-šu ù te-né-pu-*⌜*uš*⌝
	20)	URU *Baṭ-ru-na a-na ša-šu*
	21)	*ù* ÉRIN.MEŠ SA.GAZ.MEŠ *ù* GIŠ.GIGIR.MEŠ
	22)	*ša-ki-in*$_{4}$ *i-na* ⌜*lìb*⌝-*bi*
	23)	*ù la*!(AD) *i-nam-mu-šu-ni*$_{7}$
	24)	[*i*]*š-tu pí* KÁ.GAL URU *Gub*‹-*la*›^{KI}
	25)	[*a-mu*]*r qú-ru-ud-mi a-na* LUGAL BAD-*ia*
	26)	[*tu-ṣa-a*]*m it-ti-ka* ÉRIN.MEŠ *ša* SIG$_{5}$
	27)	[*qa-du* GI]Š.GIGIR.MEŠ *ù ú-uš-*⌜*še*⌝[-*er*]
	28)	[ÉRIN.]MEŠ *it-ti-šu*
Up.ed.	29)	[*ù ú-*]*ṣa-am ù ú-ṣú-u*[*r* URU]
	30)	[*šum-ma*] *at-ta mi-*⌜*ta*⌝-*t*[*a ù*]
Lft.ed.	31)	[*a-na-ku*] BA.ÚŠ-*at*

EA 87

TRANSLATION

(1–7) Speak [to] Amanapa,[my] lo[rd], the message of Rib-Haddi, [your] servant: At the feet of my lord have I fallen. May Amon (and) the Lady of Byblos grant your honor before the king, my lord.

(8–14) Furthermore, why did you stall me? (saying) "Send your envoy to me to the presence of the king, your lord, so that verily he will give you troops and [cha]riots, support for you, so that they will guard the city."

(15–24) And behold, I heeded your words and I sen[t] ‹him› but he came forth empty handed. And he (ʿAbdi-Ashirta) heard that there were no troops with him then the town of Baṭrôna went over to him and he stationed *ʿapîru* troops and chariots within (it). And they do not depart from the entrance to the city gate of the city of Byb‹los›.

(25–28) [Loo]k, beseech the king, my lord, (and) [let] an elite force [come] forth with you, [with] chariots and I will send [troop]s with it.

(29–31) [and I will] come forth. So protect [the city]; [if] you die, [then I] will die.

EA 88

TRANSCRIPTION

Obv. 01) [^{I}*Ri-i*]*b*-[^{d}IŠ]KU[R *i*]*q-b*[*i a-na* BAD-*šu*]

02) [*a-na*] *maḫ-ri šàr* KUR[.KI.ḪI.A LUGAL GAL]

03) [7]-*it* 7-*ta-a-an* ⸢*a*⸣[-*na* GÌR.MEŠ BAD-*ia*]

04) ^{d}UTU-*ia am-qú-*⸢*ut*⸣ *a*[*š-tap-pár*]

05) *ù aš-ta-ni a-na* [*ka-ta*$_5$ *nu*-KÚR UGU URU] ⸢*Ar*⸣-*da-at*

06) UGU URU *Ir-qat ù* U[GU URU *Ṣu-mu-ra*]

07) ⸢*ù*⸣ UGU URU *Am‹-mi›-*⸢*ia*⸣ [*ù* URU *Ši-ga-t*]*a*

08) [URU.]KI.ḪI.A *ki-it-ti* LUGA[L *ù qa-al*]

09) [LUGAL] BAD-*ia šá-ni-tan mi-nu-*⸢*um*⸣-⸢*mi*⸣ [*šu-ut*]

10) [^{I}]⸢ÌR⸣-*Aš-ra-ti* ÌR UR.GI$_7$ *ú i*[*p-pu-u*]*š*

11) [*ki-m*]*a lìb-bi-šu i-na* KUR.KI.ḪI.A BAD-⸢*ia*⸣

12) [*ù*] *qa-al* LUGAL BAD-*ia a-na* ÌR[-*šu*]

13) [*šá-ni-*]⸢*tam*⸣ *aš-tap-pár* LÚ.DUMU.KIN-*ia i-nu-ma*

14) [*ìl-*]⸢*qé*⸣ URU.KI.ḪI.A-*ia ù i-te*$_9$-*la-a*[*m*]

15) [*a-na*] *ṣe-ri-ia ù a-nu-um-ma*

16) [*i-n*]*a-an-na ìl-qé* URU *Baṭ-ru-na*

17) [*ù*] *i-te-la-am a-na ṣe-ri-ia*

18) [*a-*]⸢*mur*⸣ URU.KI! ⸢*ù*⸣ *pí* KÁ.GAL ›*u*‹?

19) [UR]U *Gub-la ma-ni* UD. KAM^{v}.MEŠ-*ti la yi-na-mu-uš*

20) *iš-tu* KÁ.GAL *ù ú-ul ni-le-ú*

21) *a-ṣa-am a-na* EDIN.MEŠ *šá-ni-tam šum-*[*ma*]

22) ⸢URU⸣ *Gub-la ú-ba-ú ṣa-*⸢*ba*⸣-*ta-am*[....]

23) ⸢*ù*⸣ *li-iš-me* LUGAL BAD-*ia a*[-*na a-wa-te* Ì]R-*šu*

24) [*lu-ú*]-*ḫa-mu-ṭám* GIŠ.GIGIR.MEŠ ⸢*ù*⸣ [ÉRIN.MEŠ]

25) [*ki-ma*] *ar-ḫi-iš ù ti*[-*ṣú-ru*]

26) [URU.KI] BAD-⸢*ia*⸣ ⸢*ù*⸣ [ÌR-*šu*]

Lo.ed. 27) [*a-di*] ⸢*ka*⸣-⸢*ša*⸣-⸢*ad*⸣ ⸢LUGAL⸣[BAD-*ia*]

Rev. 28) [*ù*] *a-na-ku a-wa-at* BAD-[*ia*]

EA 88

TRANSLATION

(1–4) [Ri]b-Had[da s]ai[d to his lord; be]fore the king of the lan[ds, the great king: seven] times, seven times a[t the feet of my lord,] my sun god, have I fallen.

(5–9) I [have written] repeatedly to [you, "There is hostility against the city of] Ardat, against the city of ʿIrqat and ag[ainst the city of Ṣumur] and against the city of Am‹mi›y[a and the city of Šigat]a, loyal [cit]ies of the kin[g but the king], my lord [has kept silent.]"

(9–12) Furthermore, who is [he, ʿA]bdi-Ašarti, the slave, the dog, that he [should do as] he pleases in the lands of my lord [that] the king, my lord has kept silent concerning [his] servant?

(13–17) [Further]more, I sent my envoy every time he [too]k my towns and came up [against] me and now he has taken Baṭrôna [and] he has come up against me.

(18–21) [L]ook, as for the city and the entrance to the city gate of [the cit]y of Byblos, how many days has he not departed from the city gate so that we are unable to go out to the countryside?

(21–28) Furthermore, sin[ce] he is seeking to capture the city of Byblos [...], may the king my lord heed t[he words of] his [ser]vant; [may he ha]sten chariots and [troops with] all speed so that t[hey may guard the city of] my lord and [his servant].
[until] the arrival of the king, [my lord.]

29) [*ú-u*]*l iz-zi-ib ù šu*[*m-ma la yi-iš-mu*]
30) ⸢LUGAL⸣ BAD-*ia a-na a-wa-te* Ì[R-*šu*]
31) ⸢*ù*⸣ *in*$_4$*-né-ep-ša‹-at›* URU *Gub*[*-la*]
32) *a-na ša-šu ù gáb-bi* KUR.KI.ḪI.A L[UGAL]
33) *a-di* KUR *Mi-iṣ-ri ti-né-ep-šu*
34) *a-na* LÚ.MEŠ SA.GAZ.MEŠ *šá-ni-tam a-wa-*[*te*]
35) *la yu-šé-bi-la be-li a-na* ÌR!-⸢*šu*⸣
36) *ki-ma ar-ḫi-iš a-na ṭup-pí ù na-‹ṣa›-*⸢*ri*⸣*-*⸢*šu*⸣
37) URU.KI *a-na ša-šu ù er-ri-*⸢*iš*⸣
38) ⸢URU⸣.KI *iš-tu ša-šu*
39) [*a*]-⸢*na*⸣ *a-ša-bi-ia ú bal-‹ṭá›-ti*
40) ⸢*šá*⸣-⸢*ni*⸣-⸢*tam*⸣ ⸢*lu*⸣*-ḫa-mu-ṭám* LUGAL BAD-*ia*
41) [ÉR]IN.MEŠ GIŠ.GIGIR.MEŠ *ù ti-ṣú-ru*
42) URU.KI LUGAL BAD-*ia a-mur*
43) URU *Gub-la la ki-*⸢*ma*⸣ URU.KI.ḪI.A *š*[*u-nu*]
44) URU *Gub-la* URU *ki-it-ti* LUGAL B[AD-*ia*]
45) *iš-tu da-ri-ti šá-ni-tam*
46) LÚ.DUMU.⸢KIN⸣ *šàr* URU *Ak-ka*
47) *ka*$_4$*-bi-it iš-tu* LÚ.DUMU *ši-ip-r*[*i-ia*]
48) *k*[*i-i*] ⸢*na*⸣*-ad-nu* ANŠE.KUR.RA *šap-li*[*-šu*]
49) [*ù la-*]*qú* 2 ANŠE.KUR.RA
50) [*ša* LÚ*-i*]⸢*a*⸣ *iš-tu šap-li-šu*
51) [*i-na ri-qú-*]⸢*ti*⸣ ⸢*la*⸣ *uṣ-ṣa-am*

(28–34) [And] as for me, I do [no]t abandon the word of my lord, but i[f] the king, my lord, [does not heed] the words of [his] ser[vant], then the city of Byb[los] will join him (i.e. ʿAbdi-Ashrata) and all the cities of the k[ing] as far as the land of Egypt with join the *ʿapîru* men.

(34–39) Furthermore, should my lord not have brought word[s], to his servant with all speed, by a tablet, and pro‹te›ct the city for himself, then I will request from him a city for me to dwell in so that I may l‹iv›e.

(40–42) Furthermore, may the king, my lord, hasten [tro]ops (and) chariots that they may guard the city of the king, my lord.

(42–45) Look, the city of Byblos is not like t[hose] cities, the city of Byblos is a loyal city of the king [my] l[ord] from of old.

(45–51) Furthermore, the envoy of the king of ʿAkkô was honored more than [my] ambassa[dor] because they supplied him with a horse, [but] they [too]k two horses [of m]y [man]. May he not come forth [empty hand]ed.

EA 89

TRANSCRIPTION

Obv. 01) [^{I}*Ri-ib-*]^{d}IŠKUR *iq-b*[*i a-na*]

02) [EN-*šu š*]*àr* KUR.MEŠ LUGAL GA[L]

03) [^{d}NIN] ⸢*ša*⸣ URU *Gub-l*[*a ti-di-in*$_4$]

04) [KAL.GA *a-n*]*a šàr-ri* ⸢EN⸣[*-ia*]

05) [*a-na* GÌR.M]EŠ ⸢EN⸣*-ia* ^{d}UT[U*-i*]*a*

06) [7*-šu*]⸢7⸣*-ta-an am-*⸢*qú*⸣*-ut*

07) [*a-nu-ma*] *ki-a-ma aš-ta-pa-ru*

08) [*a-na* É.]GAL *a-wa-tu-ia ú-ul*

09) [*tu-ul*$_{11}$*-qú*]*-na ù ša-ma ú-ul*

10) [*tu-u*]*š-*⸢*mu*⸣*-na a-mur i-pé-eš*

11) U[RU] *Ṣur-ri ki-na-na pal-ḫa-ti*

12) *i-na-na la-a yi-ša-a-lu šàr-ru*

13) *a-na ḫa-za-ni-šu a-na a-ḫi-ia yi‹iš-me›* LUGAL \ *a-wa-te-ia*

14) *ú-ul ki-*⸢*na*⸣ *a-wa*!(NA)*-ti-šu-nu*

15) *šum-ma šàr-ru yi-ša-i-lu*

16) *ù na-ad-na pa-ni-nu a-na*

17) *a-ra-di-ka a-na-ku-mì ep-ša-ti*

18) *i-mu-*⸢*ta*⸣ ⸢*a*⸣*-*⸢*na*⸣ URU *Ṣur-ri*

19) *i-ba-šu* ⸢*i*⸣*-na pa-ni-ia*

20) *al-lu-ú ḫa-za-na-šu-nu da-ku*

21) *qa-du a-ḫa-ti-ia ù* DUMU.MEŠ*-ši*$_x$(ŠE)

22) NUMUN.DUMU.MUNUS.MEŠ *a-ḫa-‹ti›-ia uš-ši-ir-ti*

23) *a-na* URU [*Ṣu*]*r-*[*ri*] ⸢*iš*⸣*-tu pa-ni*

24) ^{I}ÌR-⸢*A*⸣[*-ši-ir-ta ù da-ku*]*-šu*

25) *qa*[*-du a-ḫa-ti-ia ù* É]*-šu*

26) *m*[*a*..................................]

27) [..................................]

28) [..................................]

29) [..................................]

Lo.ed. 30) [*šum-ma a-na a-ḫi-ia yi-ša-i-lu*]

Rev. 31) *šàr-ru* [*ù ti-né-ep-šu*]

32) *ka-li* KUR.MEŠ [*a-na šàr-ri* EN*-ia*]

EA 89

TRANSLATION

(1–6) [Rib]-Hadda spo[ke to his lord, the ki]ng of the lands, the grea[t] king: [May the Lady] of Byblos [grant strength t]o the kin, [my] lord. [At the fe]et of my lord, [m]y sun [god], [seven times (and) seven times have I fallen.

(7–14) [Now] thus I have been writing [to the pa]lace; my words are not [accep]ted, and they go utterly unheeded. Behold the deed of the ci[ty] of Tyre, thus I became afraid. Now, the king does not investigate concerning the city ruler, concerning my brother! May the king h‹eed› my words. Their word is not trustworthy!

(15–19) If the king will inquire, then ‹we› will devote ourselves to serving you. I made a marriage alliance with the city of Tyre; they were in good relations with me.

(20–26) Behold, they killed their city ruler with my sister and her children. I had sent the daughters of my sister to Tyre away from ʿAbdi-A[shirta and they killed] him wi[th my sister and] his [house.

(27–29) [..]

(30–32) [If] the king [will investigate concerning my brother, then] all the lands [will be joined to the king, my lord].

33) šum-ma a-na a-ḫi-i[a la-a]
34) yi-ša-i-lu šàr-ru [ù]
35) GUR i-na ba-li-i[ṭ a-ḫi-ia]
36) ya-aš-pu-ru a-na šàr-r[i ù]
37) la-a tu-uš-mu-na a-⸢wa⸣-⸢tu⸣-šu
38) ù ma-ti-ma šu-ut a-nu-‹ú›
39) i-de-šu ù šum-ma a-na a-ḫi-ia
40) ti-ša-i-lu ù ta-aq-bu
41) URU an-nu-ú la-a ḫa-za-nu ša-al
42) šàr-ru UGU-šu ú-ul ni-le-ú
43) ⸢i⸣-pé-eš mi-im-mi ù pal-ḫu-ni
44) šum-ma a-na ḫa-za-ni URU Ṣur-ri
45) la-a yi-ša-i-lu šàr-ru
46) i-nu-ma ma-id mi-mu-šu ki-ma
47) a-ia-ab a-na-ku i-de-šu
48) a-mur É URU Ṣur-ri
49) ia-nu É-ti ḫa-za-ni [ki-]ma
50) ‹[ki-]ma› šu-a-ta ki-ma É
51) [UR]U Ú-ga-ri-ta i-ba-ši
52) [ma-i]d ma-gal mi-mu
53) [i-na] lìb-bi-šu yi-ìš-me šàr-ru
54) [a-wa-t]e ÌR‹-šu› yu-wa-ši-ra
55) [^{I}....-u]š-da ù yi-zi-iz
56) [i-na e]r-ṣé-ti ù
57) [yi-de] a-na ḫa-za-nu-ti ù
58) [la-a y]u-da-an ⸢mi⸣-⸢mu⸣ [a-na]
Up.ed. 59) [qa-ti]-šu-nu ⸢ù⸣ m[i-lik a-na]
60) [LÚ.MEŠ] ⸢MÁŠKIM⸣ šàr-ri ⸢i⸣-[le-qú]
61) [iš-tu] qa-ti šàr-ri k[a-li]
62) KUR.MEŠ
Lft.ed. 63) [a-na-ku lu] i-de i-ra-am šàr-ru
64) [i-nu-ma ^{I}ÌR-A-]ši-ir-ta la-qa a-ia-⸢ab⸣ š[a]
65) [i-n]a pa-ni-šu-nu ù pa-aš-ḫu
66) [yu-pa-l]i-iḫ-šu-nu šàr-ru ú-ul aš-pu-r[u]
67) ar-na-‹šu›-nu ⸢a⸣-⸢na⸣ ⸢LUGAL⸣

(33–35) If concerning m[y] brother, the king [does not] make inquiry, [then] he will do it again(?).

(35–39) During the life of [my brother] he was writing to the king [but] his words were not heeded and thus he died. Behold, I know it!

(39–43) But if concerning my brother you make inquiry, then the city will say "Behold, there is no city ruler." Inquire, oh king, concerning him. We are unable to do anything because they are afraid.

(44–47) If concerning the city ruler of the city of Tyre the king does not make inquiry, then great is his property, like the sea. I know it.

(48–53) Look, as for the palace of the city of Tyre, there is no city ruler's house like that one. It is like the palace of the city of Ugarit, [ve]ry great is the property [in] it.

(53–59) May the king heed [the word]s of ‹his› servant; may he send [...u]šda that he may take a stand [in the l]and so that [he may become knowledgeable] of the city rulers. So [let not] the riches [be] given [into] their [hand].

(59–62) So ta[ke care for the commi]ssioners of the king. [They are ta]king [from] the hand of the king a[ll] the lands.

(63–67) [I want] to know: Does the king like it [that Abdi-A]shirta has taken the sea wh[ich] [is be]fore them so that they are at peace. [May] the king [terri]fy them! Do I not write to the king about ‹th›eir crime?

EA 90

TRANSCRIPTION

Obv. 01) [*a-na*] LUGAL EN-*ia* [^{d}UTU-*ia*]
02) [*qí*] *bí-* [*ma*]
03) ⸢*um*⸣-*ma* ^{I}⸢*Ri*⸣-*ib*-^{d}IŠKUR Ì[R-*ka*]
04) *a-na* GÌR.⸢MEŠ⸣ EN-*ia* ^{d}UTU-[*ia 7-šu 7-a-an*]
05) *am*-⸢*qú*⸣-*ut li-ma-ad* [*i-nu-ma*]
06) KAL.GA *nu-kúr-tu*$_{4}$ UGU-[*ia ìl-qé*]
07) *ka-li* URU.MEŠ-*ia* UR[U *Gub-la*]
08) *i-na e-de-ni-ši*$_{x}$(ŠE) *ir*-⸢*ti*⸣[-*ḫa-at*]
09) *a-na ia-ši i-na* URU *Ši-g*[*a-ta*]
10) *i-ba-ša-ti ù aš*-⸢*ta*⸣-[*pár*]
11) ⸢*a*⸣-[*n*]*a* ⸢*ka*⸣-⸢*ta*$_{5}$⸣ *mi-lik-mi a-na* UR[U-*ka*]
12) [*ú-u*]*l* ⸢*yi*⸣-*ìl-qé-ši* ^{I}ÌR[-*A-ši-ir-ta*]
13) [*ù*] ⸢*la*⸣ *ti-ìš-me* ⸢*a*⸣-⸢*na*⸣ ⸢*ia*⸣-*š*[*i ù*]
14) [*iš*]-⸢*tu*⸣ ⸢URU⸣ *Baṭ-ru*-⸢*na*⸣ *iš-t*[*a-pár a-na ka-ta*$_{5}$]
15) [*u*]*š*-⸢*ši*⸣-*ra-mi* LÚ.MEŠ *ti*[-*na-ṣa-ru*]
16) [UR]U ⸢*a*⸣-⸢*na*⸣ ⸢*ka*⸣-*ta*$_{5}$ *a-wa-tu*[-*ia*]
17) [*ú*]-⸢*ul*⸣ ⸢*tu*⸣-*uš-mu-na* ⸢*ù*⸣[*la-*]⸢*qa*⸣
18) [*ú*]-⸢*ul*⸣ ⸢*tu*⸣-*ul-qú-na a-nu-ma*
19) [*yi-ìl*]-⸢*qú*⸣ URU.MEŠ-*ia ša-ni-tam a-nu-*[*ma*]
20) [*a-*]⸢*na* ⸣ ⸢KUR⸣ *Mi-ta-na i-ba-aš-ši*
21) [U]R.⸢GI$_{7}$⸣ *šu-ut ù pa-nu-šu* ⸢*i*⸣-⸢*na*⸣
22) [URU] ⸢*Gub*⸣-*la ù mi-na i-pu-šu-*[*na*]
23) [*a-na-ku*] ⸢*i*⸣-*na i-de-ni-ia at-t*[*a*]
24) ⸢*qa*⸣-*la-ta a-na* URU.MEŠ-*ka i-nu-m*[*a*]
25) [*yi-*]⸢*ìl*⸣-*te*$_{9}$-*qú-šu-nu* LÚ.GAZ.MEŠ
26) [UR.GI$_{7}$] *ù a-na ka-ta na-ad*-⸢*na*⸣-⸢*ti*⸣
27) [*pa-ni-i*]*a* ⸢*ša*⸣-*ni-tam ka-li* ⸢LÚ⸣.M[EŠ]
28) [*ḫa-za-nu-tu*] *šal-mu a-na* ^{I}ÌR-*A*-[*ši-ir-ta*]
Lo.ed. 29) [……….]⸢LÚ⸣.MÁ[ŠKIM]-⸢*šu*⸣ [….]
30) [……….] ? ? ? ? […………..]

EA 90

TRANSLATION

(1–5) [Sp]eak [to] the king, my lord, [my sun god;] the message of Rib-Hadda, [your servant,] at the feet of my lord, [my] sun god, [seven times (and) seven times] have I fallen.

(5–19) Be informed [that] the hostility against [me] is severe. [He has taken] all of my towns. The tow[n of Byblos] alone remai[ns] to me. I was in the town of Shig[ata] and I wro[te] to you: "Take counsel concerning [your] ci[ty], [les]t ʿAbdi-[Ashirta] take it." [But] you did not listen to me [and] [fr]om the town of Baṭrôna I wr[ote to you,] "Send people that t[hey may guard [the to]wn for you." [My] words were never heeded and [veri]ly not accepted. Now [he is tak]ing my towns.

(19–27) Furthermore, now that dog belongs [to] Mittani and his intent is on [the town of] Byblos. What can [I] do by myself? You keep silent while the *ʿapîru* [dog] is taking them. But it is to you that I have turned.

(27–30) Furthermore, all of the [city rulers] are at peace with ʿAbdi-A[shirta...] his comm[issioner......]

Rev. 31) [...URU] ⸢*Ṣu*⸣-⸢*mu*⸣-⸢*ra*⸣ [............]
32) [......]⸢*i*⸣-⸢*la*⸣-⸢*ka*⸣ ⸢*a*⸣-⸢*na*⸣ ⸢URU⸣ *Ṣu*-⸢*mu*⸣-*ra*]
33) [*gáb-bu a*-][*na*] ⸢*ša*⸣-⸢*šu*⸣ ⸢*iš*⸣-⸢*tu*⸣ ⸢URU⸣.⸢KI⸣ [...]
34) [*a-di*.....................................]
35) [G]A.⸢KAL⸣..............................]
36) [*ù*]⸢*ga*⸣[-*am*]-⸢*ru*⸣ [DUMU.MEŠ]-⸢*nu*⸣ [DUMU.MUNUS]-*nu*
37) [GIŠ].⸢MEŠ⸣ [É].M[EŠ] ⸢*i*⸣-⸢*na*⸣ ⸢*na*⸣-⸢*da*⸣-[*n*]*i*
38) [*a-na*] ⸢KUR⸣ ⸢*Ia*⸣-⸢*ri*⸣-⸢*mu*⸣-[*t*]*a* ›⸢*i*⸣-⸢*na*⸣‹
39) [*i-n*]*a* ⸢*ba*⸣-⸢*la*⸣-⸢*at*⸣ ⸢ZI⸣-[*n*]*u k*[*i-ma*]
40) [MUŠEN *š*]*a* ⸢*i*⸣-⸢*na*⸣ ⸢*lìb*⸣-⸢*bi*⸣ ⸢*ḫu*⸣-[*ḫa*]-⸢*ri*⸣
41) [*ša-a*]*k*-⸢*na*⸣-⸢*at*⸣ *ki*-⸢*šu*⸣-⸢*ma*⸣ [*a-na-ku i-n*]*a*
42) [URU *Gub*-]*la* ⸢A⸣.[Š]À-*ia* ⸢DAM⸣ ⸢*ša*⸣ ⸢*la*⸣-⸢*a*⸣
43) [*mu-t*]*a* ⸢*ma*⸣-⸢*ši*⸣-*ìl* ⸢*aš*⸣-⸢*šum*⸣ ⸢*ba*⸣-⸢*li*⸣
44) [*i*-]⸢*re*⸣-⸢*ši*⸣ ⸢*ša*⸣-⸢*ni*⸣-⸢*tam*⸣ ⸢*yi*⸣-⸢*iš*⸣-⸢*me*⸣
45) [LUGAL EN-*i*]*a* ⸢ÌR⸣ ⸢*ki*⸣-⸢*ti*⸣-*šu* ⸢*ù*⸣ ⸢*uš*⸣-⸢*ši*⸣-⸢*ru*⸣
46) [x] ⸢*me*⸣ [ÉRIN].MEŠ ⸢*ù*⸣ 30 ⸢*ta*⸣-⸢*pal*⸣ ⸢ANŠE⸣.⸢KUR⸣.⸢RA⸣
47) ⸢*ù*⸣ ⸢*i*⸣-⸢*na*⸣-⸢*ṣa*⸣-⸢*ra*⸣ ⸢URU⸣ ⸢*a*⸣-⸢*na*⸣ ⸢*ka*⸣-⸢*ta*$_5$⸣
48) ⸢*ù*⸣ ⸢LÚ⸣.MEŠ ⸢DUMU⸣ ⸢*ši*⸣-⸢*ip*⸣-⸢*ri*⸣-⸢*ka*⸣
49) ⸢*uš*⸣-⸢*ši*⸣-*ra-aš*-⸢*šu*⸣-⸢*nu*⸣? ⸢*ù*⸣ *i-re-ši*
50) ⸢*ù*⸣ ⸢*šum*⸣-[*m*]*a* ⸢*la*⸣-⸢*a*⸣ ⸢*tu*⸣-⸢*wa*⸣-⸢*ši*⸣-[*ru*]
51) [L]Ú.MEŠ *ma-ṣa-ar*-⸢*ta*⸣ ⸢*ù*⸣
52) ⸢*ul*⸣ *ti*-⸢*bal*⸣-⸢*li*⸣?-⸢*iṭ*⸣ URU ⸢*ù*⸣
53) ⸢*pal*⸣-⸢*ḫa*⸣-⸢*ti*⸣ ⸢ZI⸣-*ia*
54) ⸢LÚ⸣.MEŠ ⸢DUMU⸣ ⸢*ši*⸣-⸢*ip*⸣-⸢*ri*⸣ ⸢*gáb*⸣-*b*[*u ša*]
55) ⸢ḪAR⸣-*šu* ⸢*šu*⸣-*nu ut-ta*-[*ši-ra*]
56) [*š*]*a*-[*ni*]-⸢*tam*⸣ [*at*]-*ta* E[N-*ia*]
57) [*ú*]-⸢*ul*⸣ ⸢*ta*⸣-*qa*-⸢*al*⸣[-*mi a-na* ÌR-*ka*]
58) [*u*]*š-ši*-⸢*ra*⸣ ⸢*ma*⸣-*ṣa-a*[*r-ta a-na*]
Up.ed. 59) [*n*]*a*-⸢*ṣa*⸣?-⸢*ri*⸣ ⸢URU⸣.KI-*k*[*a*]
60) [*u*]*š*-⸢*ši*⸣-⸢*ra*⸣ ÉRIN.MEŠ *p*[*í-ṭá-ti*]
61) [*ù ti*]-⸢*il*$_5$⸣-*qé* KUR [*A-mur-ri*]

Lft.ed. 62) [*ur*-]*ra mu*-⸢*ša*⸣ *p*[*a-nu ka-li a-na a-ṣí* ÉRIN.MEŠ *pí-ṭ*]*á*-[*ti*]
63) [*ù*] ⸢*am*⸣-*ma-ša-aḫ* [ŠE.*IM*.ḪI.A-*ia ù a-na ka-ta*$_5$]
64) [*na*]-⸢*ad*⸣-*na-ti* [*pa-ni-ia*]

(31–35) [...the town of] Ṣumur [...] he will come to the town of Ṣumura [....It all] belongs to him from [......to.....so he is st]rong [.....].

(36–44) [And] our [sons], our [daughters], the [furnishings] of the [hous]es are all used up in pay[ment to] the land of Yarimuta for sustaining our lives. L[ike a bird th]at is placed inside a cage, th[us am I i]n [the city of Gub]la; my field resembles a wife without a [hu]sband through lack of a cultivator (or: cultivation).

(44–49) Furthermore, may [the king, m]y [lord] heed his servant and send [*x*] hundred [troop]s and thirty teams of horses and I will protect the city for you. And as for your envoys, send them and my request.

(50–55) But i[f] you don't send garrison troops and you don't provision the city, then I am afraid for my life. Every envoy [that] has his bracelet, them have I sent away.

(56–61) [F]ur[ther]more, [yo]u are [my] lo[rd. Don't keep silent [concerning your servant]. Send a garrison [to] protect(?) yo[ur] city. Send regular tr[oops that] they may take the land of [Amurru].

(62–64) [D]ay and night, [everyone is expecting the coming forth of the regular tr]oo[ps]. I have been plundered [of my grain, so to you] have I tur[ned.]

EA 91

TRANSCRIPTION

Obv. 01) [^{I}*Ri-ib*-^{d}IŠKUR *iq-bi a-na*] ⸢EN⸣-*š*[*u a-na* GÌR.MEŠ]

02) [EN-*ia* 7-*šu* 7-*ta-an a*]*m-qú-ut* [*aš-ta-pár a-na*]

03) [*ka-ta*$_5$ *a-n*]*a m*[*i-ni*] ⸢*aš*⸣?-⸢*ba*⸣?-*ta*

04) [*ù*] *qa*-⸢*la*⸣-⸢*ta*⸣ ⸢*ù*⸣ *yi-ìl*-⸢*qú*⸣

05) [URU.MEŠ-*k*]*a* ⸢LÚ⸣.⸢GAZ⸣.⸢MEŠ⸣ UR.GI$_7$

06) [*i-nu-ma* UR]U *Ṣu-mu-ra yi-ìl-qa*

07) [*ù aš-t*]*a-pár* ⸢*a*⸣-⸢*na*⸣ ⸢*ka*⸣-*ta*$_5$ *a-na mi-ni*

08) [*qa-la-t*]*a* ⸢*ù*⸣ ⸢*tu*⸣-*ul-qé*

09) [URU É] *Ar*-⸢*qa*⸣ ⸢*i*⸣-⸢*nu*⸣-*ma yi*-⸢*da*⸣-*gal*

10) [*ù*] ⸢*ia*⸣-⸢*nu*⸣ ⸢*ša*⸣ *yi-iq-bi* ⸢*mi*⸣-*am-ma*

11) [*a-na ša-š*]*u* UGU URU *Ṣu-mu-ra*

12) [*ù*] ⸢*yu*⸣-⸢*dan*⸣-*ni-in*$_4$ *lìb-bu-šu*

13) [*ù*] ⸢*yu*⸣-⸢*ba*⸣-⸢*ú*⸣ *la-qa* URU *Gub-la*

14) [*ù*] ⸢*yi*⸣-⸢*im*⸣-⸢*ma*⸣-⸢*qú*⸣-*ut* UGU-*ia* GIŠ.KIRI$_6$.MEŠ-*ia*

15) [*ù* A.ŠÀ.]MEŠ-*ia in*$_4$-*na-ka-às*

16) [ŠE.Ḫ]I.A-*ia am-ma-ša-ʾa ù*

17) [*ú*]-⸢*ul*⸣ [*ta*]-*di-in*$_4$ *li-im* KÙ.BABBAR.MEŠ

18) ⸢*ù*⸣ 1 *me* KÙ.GI.MEŠ *ù ip-ta-ṭú-ur*

19) [*iš*-]*tu mu-ḫi-ia ù ìl-qé*

20) [*k*]*a-li* URU.MEŠ-*ia* URU *Gub-la*

21) [*a*-]*na i-de-ni-ši ir-ti-ḫa-at*

22) [*a*]-*na ia-ši ù yu-ba-ú*

23) ⸢*la*⸣-*qa-ši a-nu-ma eš-mé pu-ḫi-ir-mi*

24) [*k*]*a-li* LÚ.MEŠ GAZ.MEŠ

Lo.ed. 25) [*a*]-⸢*na*⸣ *ma-qa-ti* UGU-*ia mi-n*[*a*]

26) [*i*]-*pu-šu-na a-na-ku a-na i-de*-[*ni*-]-⸢*ia*⸣

Rev. 27) [*a*]-⸢*nu*⸣-*ma* ⸢*ki*⸣-⸢*a*⸣-⸢*ma*⸣ *aš-pu-ru a*-⸢*na*⸣

28) ⸢ÉRIN.MEŠ⸣ *pí-ṭá-ti ù*

29) ⸢ÉRIN⸣.MEŠ *til-la-ti ù ú-ul tu-*
uš-mu-n[*a*]

30) [*a*]-*wa-tu-ia*

31) [*ša-ni-t*]*am mi*-[*li-ik at*]-*t*[*a a-n*]*a* KUR.MEŠ-*ka*

32) [*ù mi-nu*] *i*[-*pu-šu a-na*-]*ku ša*-[*ni*]-*tam*

EA 91

TRANSLATION

(1–2) [Rib-Hadda spoke to] h[is] lord: [at the feet of my lord, seven times and seven times] have [I] fallen.

(2–9) [I wrote to you, "Why] do you sit idly [and] keep silent and the man of the *ʿapîrû*, the dog, is taking [yo]ur [cities]?" [When] he took over [the to]wn of Ṣumur, [then I w]rote to you, "Why [are yo]u [keeping silent?"] Then the town of Bīt] ʿArqa was taken.

(9–19) When he saw [that] there was no one who said any[thing] [to hi]m concerning Ṣumur, [then] he became obstinate in his heart [and] he began seeking to take the town of Byblos [and] he pounced on me. My orchards [and] my [field]s were cut down. I am plundered of my [gra]in. But you could [not] give one thousand (shekels) of silver [or] one hundred (shekels of) gold that he should depart from me.

(19–23) So he has taken [a]ll of my towns. The town of Byblos alone remains to me and he is seeking to take it.

(23–26) Now I have heard, "He has assembled [a]ll of the *ʿapîru* men" [in order] to pounce on me. What can I do by myself?

(27–30) [N]ow, I keep writing for regular troops or auxiliary troops but my words are not heeded.

(31–32) [Furtherm]ore, ta[ke counsel yo]u[rself concern]ing your lands [for what can I do mys]elf?.

33) [*ši-mé a-na ia-ši ù šum-m*]*a ia-nu*
34) [ÉRIN.MEŠ *pí-ṭá-ti*] *ù* ⸢*til*⸣-*la-ta*
35) [*ù ia-nu ba-la-ṭá a*]-⸢*na*⸣ URU *Gub-la*
36) [*ù a-na* LÚ.MEŠ GAZ.MEŠ *ti-né*]-⸢*ep*⸣-*šu* LU[GAL]
37) [*ši-mé a-na ia-ši ù uš*-]⸢*ši*⸣-*ra* ÉRIN.ME[Š]
38) [*pí-ṭá-ti ù t*]*i-ìl-qé* KUR *A-mur-*[*r*]*i*
39) [*a-nu-ma i-na-an-na*] *pa-nu ka-li*
40) [*ur-ra ù mu-*]*ša*
41) [*a-na a-ṣí* ÉRIN.MEŠ *pí-ṭ*]*á-ti*
42) [*ù yi-im-lik-*]*m*[*i*] *šàr-ru* EN-*li*
43) [*a-na* ÌR *ki-ti-šu*] *ù*
44) [*uš-ši-ra šàr-ru* ÉRIN.]MEŠ *pí-*⸢*ṭá*⸣-*ti*
45) [*ù til-la-ti ù ti-*]*ìl-qé*
46) [KUR *A-mu-ur-ri*] *ù*
47) [*a-na-ṣa-ru* URU EN-]⸢*ia*⸣ *a-di*
48) [*ka-ša-*]⸢*di*⸣ ⸢ÉRIN⸣[ḪI.]⸢A⸣.MEŠ
49) [*pí-ṭá-ti šàr-r*]*i* [EN-*ia*]

(32–36) Fur[ther]more, [listen to me, but i]f there are no [regular troops] or auxiliary troops [and there are no supplies] for Byblos, [then it will] go over [to the ʿ*apîru* men].

(36–38) Oh king, [listen to me and se]nd [regular] troops [that they] take the land of Amur[ru].

(39–49) [Right now] everyone is looking [day and night] [for the coming forth of the regu]lar [troops, so may] the king, my lord, [take counsel concerning his faithful servant], so [send, oh king,] the regular [tro]ops [or auxiliaries that they may] take [the land of Amurru].

(46–49) So [I will guard the city of] my [lord] until the [arriva]l of the [regular] troops of the kin]g [my lord].

EA 92

TRANSCRIPTION

Obv. 01) [^{I}]⸢*Ri*⸣-⸢*ib*⸣-⸢*ad*⸣-⸢*di*⸣ ⸢*iq*⸣-⸢*bi*⸣
02) [*a*]-*na* ⸢LUGAL⸣ *be-li-šu* ^{d}⸢UTU⸣ KU[R.MEŠ]
03) ⸢*a*⸣-*na* ⸢GÌR⸣.⸢MEŠ⸣ LUGAL BAD -*ia* ⸢^{d}⸣⸢UTU⸣-[*i*]*a*
04) 7-*šu* ⸢7⸣-*ta-a-an am*-[*q*]*ú-u*[*t*]
05) ^{d}NIN *ša* URU *Gub*^{ub}-⸢*la*⸣ *t*[*i*-]-*d*[*in*]
06) [G]A.KAL *a-na* LUGAL ⸢EN⸣-*i*[*a*] ⸢^{d}⸣[UTU-]⸢*i*⸣*a*
07) [*ša-ni-*]*tam* ^{d}ÌR-*a*[*š-r*]*a*-⸢*ti*⸣ ⸢LÚ⸣.⸢UR⸣.⸢GI$_{7}$ ⸢*gáb*⸣-⸢*ba*⸣
08) ⸢LÚ⸣.⸢MEŠ⸣-⸢*i*⸣*a* ⸢GAZ⸣(?) [ÌR.MEŠ]LUGAL URU-*šu* [*la-qa a-na*]
09) *ša*-[*šu*] ⸢*šum*⸣-*ma ša-al* ⸢UGU⸣ ⸢*ip*⸣-⸢*ši*⸣ ⸢*a*⸣-⸢*ni*⸣-⸢*i*⸣(?)
10) *a-na* [*lì*]*b-bi-ši-na a-ša-b*[*a l*]*u a-ši*-⸢*ib*⸣ *ù* ⸢*i*⸣-⸢*na*⸣-*an-na*
11) ⸢*nu*⸣-*kùr-tu*$_{4}$^{MEŠ} *maš-ši-ik-tu*$_{4}$ *it-ti*-[*i*]*a* [*i*]*n*$_{4}$-*né-pu*-⸢*uš*⸣
12) *ù aš-tap-pár ṭup-pí-ia ù* ⸢LÚ⸣ [KIN]-⸢*ia*⸣
13) *a-na ma-ḫar* LUGAL BAD-*ia ù* L[UGAL]
14) *a-wa-te*^{MEŠ} *ṭup-pí-ia ù* ⸢LÚ⸣ [KIN-*ia*]
15) *la yi-iš-mé ù mi-na ip*-⸢*pu*⸣-⸢*šu*⸣-[*na*]
16) *ù aš-tap-pár* LÚ.KIN-*ia a-n*[*a*] LUGAL BAD-[*ia*]
17) ⸢UGU⸣ URU.KI.ḪI.A-*ia ša ìl-qé*
18) ^{I}ÌR-^{d}*Aš-ra-ti ù iš*-[*te*$_{9}$-*mé*]
19) ^{I}ÌR-*Aš-ra-tu*$_{4}$ *i-nu-ma ka-ši*-⸢*id*⸣
20) LÚ-*ia iš-tu ma-ḫar* LUGAL BAD-⸢*ia*⸣
21) *ù i-še*$_{20}$-*mé* ⸢*ù*⸣ *ia-nu-um* ⸢*mi*⸣-[*im*]-*ma*
22) *ù i-nu-ma ia-nu-um* LÚ.MEŠ *ti-la-ta*$_{5}$ *ša a*-[*ṣa*]-⸢*at*⸣
23) ⸢*a*⸣-⸢*na*⸣ *ia-a-ši ù a-nu-ú i-te*$_{9}$-⸢*el*⸣-⸢*lu*⸣
24) [*i*]-*na-an-na a-na ṣe-ri-ia*
25) [*ù*] ⸢*a*⸣-*nu-ú* UGU-*ia* ⸢*iš*⸣-⸢*te*⸣-*mé*

Lo.ed. 26) ⸢*i*⸣-*nu-ma* LÚ.[KIN-*ia*.........]
27) [..]
28) [..]

Rev. 29) *in*$_{4}$-*na-an-n*[*a*]⸢*ù*⸣ ⸢*mi*⸣-*na*-⸢*am*⸣
30) ⸢*a*⸣-*qa*-⸢*bu*⸣-⸢*na*⸣ *a*[-*na-k*]*u* ⸢*ša*⸣-⸢*ni*⸣-⸢*tam*⸣ ⸢SIG$_{5}$⸣-*mi*

EA 92

TRANSLATION

(1–6) Rib-Hadda spoke to the king, his lord, the sun god of the nati[ons]: At the feet of the king, my lord, my sun god, seven times and seven times have I fallen. May the Lady of Byblos grant strength to the king, m[y] lord, [m]y [sun] god.

(7–15) [Further]more, ʿAbdi-Ashrati, the cur, all of my men(?) he has slain,(?) [servants of] the king. His city [has he taken for] him[self]. If he (the king) had inquired concerning this deed, within them, he is verily dwelling. And now vicious aggression has been perpetrated against me. So I sent my tablet and my amba[ssador] to the king, my lord, but the k[ing] did not heed my tablet or [my] amba[ssador]. What am I to do?

(16–28) So I sent my envoy to the king, [my] lord, concerning my cities which ʿAbdi-Ashrati took and ʿAbdi-Ashrati he[ard] that my man had come from the king, my lord, and he heard that there were no supplies and that there were no auxiliary troops that came forth to me so behold, he has risen up now against me. [And] behold, concerning me he heard that [my] am[bassador....]

(29–30) Now, and what could I say myself?

31) ⸢*i*⸣-*pé-eš*$_{15}$ ⸢LUGAL⸣ ⸢BAD⸣-*ia* ⸢*i*⸣-*nu-ú*
32) ⸢*ša*⸣-*pár* ⸢LUGAL⸣ *a-na šàr* URU PÚ.⸢ḪI.A⸣.⸢KI⸣
33) ⸢*ù*⸣ ⸢*a*⸣-⸢*na*⸣ ⸢*šàr*⸣ ⸢URU⸣ ⸢*Ṣi*⸣-*du-na*
34) ⸢*ù*⸣ ⸢*a*⸣-⸢*na*⸣ ⸢*šàr*⸣ ⸢URU⸣ ⸢*Ṣur*⸣-⸢*ri*⸣
35) [*al*]-⸢*lu*⸣-⸢*mi*⸣ *iš-tap-ru* ^I^*Ri-ib-ad-*[*da*]
36) [*a*]-⸢*na*⸣ *ka-tu-nu a-na ti-la-ti*
37) ⸢*ù*⸣ ⸢*at*⸣-[*la*]-*ku gáb*-⸢*bu*⸣-⸢*ku*⸣-*nu ù an-nu*-⸢*ú*⸣ ⸢DÙG⸣.[GA]
38) ⸢UGU⸣-⸢*ia*⸣ ⸢*ù*⸣ *aš-tap-pár* LÚ [DUMU].KIN-*ia*
39) *ù* [*ú*]-⸢*ul*⸣ *il-la-ku* ⸢*ù*⸣ ⸢*la*⸣ ⸢*iš*⸣-⸢*ta*⸣-⸢*pa*⸣-*ru*
40) ⸢LÚ⸣.DUMU.[KIN]-*šu-nu a-na ša*-⸢*al*⸣ ⸢*šul*⸣-*m*[*i*]-*nu*
41) ⸢*ša*⸣-*ni-tam* ⸢*mi*⸣-⸢*ia*⸣-⸢*mi*⸣ *šu-ut i-nu-ma il*-[*qé*]
42) ⸢*ka*⸣-*li* LÚ.MEŠ *a*-[*di*] GU$_4$.⸢MEŠ⸣ *it-ti-š*[*u*]
43) ⸢*mi*⸣-⸢*na*⸣-[*a*]*m id*-⸢*din*⸣ ⸢*a*⸣-*na* ⸢*ša*⸣-*šu-nu*
44) *ù* 3 ŠEŠ *ni-nu-um ù aš*-⸢*tap*⸣-⸢*pár*⸣
45) *a-na ša-šu-nu a-na re-ṣí*-⸢*ia*⸣
46) *ù li*-⸢*it*⸣-*ri-iṣ*
47) *a-na pa-ni* LUGAL BAD-*ia ù* [*tu-wa-*]⸢*ši*⸣-⸢*ru*⸣
48) ÉRIN.MEŠ KAL.BA[D].KASKAL MAḪ(?) ⸢*ša*⸣ [LUGAL BAD-*ia*]
49) ⸢*ù*⸣ ÌR-*šu ù ip*-⸢*pu*⸣-⸢*uš*⸣ [*a-na-ku nu-kùr-ta*$_5$]
50) [*iš-t*]*u* KUR.KI LUGAL BAD-*ia* DÙG.G[A *i-nu-ma*]
51) [LUGAL] BA[D-*i*]*a* ⸢*i*⸣-*de šum-ma la i-le*-[*ú*]
52) [.........]*uk-šu* ⸢*šum*⸣-⸢*ma*⸣ ⸢*la*⸣ *ú-w*[*a-ši-ru*]
53) [LUGAL] ⸢BAD⸣- *ia* ÉRIN.MEŠ.⸢KAL⸣.[BAD.KASKAL]
Up.ed. 54) [*ù ti-la-ta*$_5$] *ù a-na-ku*
55) [*iz-zi-ib*]⸢URU⸣ BAD-[*i*]*a*
Lft.ed. 56) [.....................]*ia* [..............]
57) [.........]LÚ.MEŠ *ḫa*(?)-*za-nu*-[*ti*]

(30–40) Furthermore, the deed of the king, my lord, was good when he wrote to the king of Beirut and to the king of Sidon and to the king of Tyre, "Behold, Rib-Hadda has written to you for auxiliary troops so go out, all of you." So, behold, it was good for me. So I sent my [amba]ssador but they did not come and they did not send their envoy to inquire of our well being.

(41–43) Furthermore, who is he that he to[ok] with him all the men wi[th] the cattle? What did he pay for them?

(44–50) But the three of us are brothers (colleagues) so I wrote to them for help. So may it please the king, my lord that [the]y may send the expeditionary force of [the king, my lord,] and his servant and I will make [war fr]om the land of the king, my lord.

(50–57) It is we[ll], (that) [the king,] my lord know since I am una[ble…], if [the king,] my lord does not se[nd] the expedi[tionary force or auxiliaries,] then I [will abandon]the city of the king, [m]y lord [.....] my [.....] the city rulers [......]

EA 93

TRANSCRIPTION

Obv. 01) [*a-na* ^{I}*A-m*]*a-an-ap-*⸢*pa*⸣
02) [*um-ma* ^{I}*R*]*i-ib-*^{d}IŠKUR
03) [*a-na* G]ÌR.MEŠ-*ka am-qú-ut*
04) [*a-mur a*]-*ta-ša-aš a-na-ku*
05) [\ *na-*]*aq-ṣa-ap-ti*
06) [*i-na*] *a-wa-te-ka a-*⸢*nu*⸣-⸢*ma*⸣
07) [*ka*]-*aš-da-ti a-na ka-*⸢*ta*$_5$⸣
08) [*ki*]-*a-ma ti-ša-pa-ru*
09) [*a-n*]*a ia-ši ši-mé i*⸢*a*⸣-⸢*ši*⸣
10) *qí-ba-mi a-na šàr-ri*
11) *ù yi-di-na a-na* ⸢*ka*⸣-*ta*$_5$
12) 3 *me* LÚ.MEŠ *ù ni-*[*d*]*a-gal*
13) ⸢URU⸣ ⸢*ù*⸣ *ni-pu-uš*
Lo.ed. 14) [*a-na* LUGAL] ⸢*ú*⸣-⸢*ul*⸣
15) ⸢*ti*⸣-*b*[*a-ú-na*] ⸢LÚ⸣.MEŠ
Rev. 16) ⸢MÁŠKIM⸣.MEŠ *a-ṣa* ÉRIN.MEŠ
17) *pí-ṭá-ti* KAL.GA ⸢*nu*⸣!-KÚ[R!]
18) UGU LUGAL *ša-ni-tam*
19) ⸢*ù*⸣ *šum-ma ni-le-*⸢*ú*⸣
20) [*ṣa*]-*ba-at* URU *Baṭ-ru-*⸢*na*⸣
21) [*a-*]*na ka-ta*$_5$ *ša-ni-tam*
22) *i-te*$_9$*-zi-bu* LÚ.MEŠ
23) ⸢^{I}⸣ÌR-*A-ši-ir*!(NI)-*ta*
24) [*ú*]-*ul ki-ma pa-na-nu*
25) [*šu*]*m-ma* MU.KAM^{v} *an-ni-ta*
26) [*i*]*a-nu* ÉRIN.MEŠ *pí-ṭá-*⸢*ta*⸣
27) ⸢*ù*⸣ GA.KAL *a-di*
28) [*da-r*]*i-ti*

EA 93

TRANSLATION

(1–3) [To Am]anappa, the message of Rib-Hadda; [at] your [fe]et have I fallen.

(4–9) [Look, I] got angry myself, (I [ra]ged) [at] your words, "Now I am [co]ming to you." [Th]us you write [t]o me.

(9–14) Listen to me, speak to the king that he give you three hundred men so that we can look after the city and we may restore (it) [to the king.]

(14–18) Aren't the commissioners se[eking] the coming forth of the regular army? There is strong hostility(!) against the king.

(18–24) On the one hand then, if we are able to [t]ake Baṭrôna [f]or you, on the other hand the men of ʿAbdi-Ashirta will desert. It is not like it was before.

(25–28) [I]f this year there are [n]o regular troops then he will be [permane]ntly strong.

EA 94

TRANSCRIPTION

Obv.

01) [[I]*R*]*i*-[*ib*]-*ad*-[*d*]*i* [*iš*-*t*]*a*-⸢*pár*⸣ *a-na* [*š*]*à*[*r*]-[*r*]*i*

02) [LUG]AL [KU]R.⸢KUR⸣.⸢KI⸣ LU[GAL] *be*-[*l*]*í*-[*šu* DINGIR]-*šu*

03) *a*-[*n*]*a* GÌR.MEŠ *be-l*[*í-i*]*a* 7 *ù* 7 *a*[*m*]-*qut*

04) *a*-[*n*]*a mi-ni la-a yi-iš-mé be-l*[*í*]

05) *a*-⸢*wa*⸣-[*t*]*e* ÌR-*šu yi-de be-lí i-nu-ma*

06) [*i*]*a-a-nu-mi le-em-na i-n*[*a a*]-*w*[*a*-]*te* ⸢ÌR⸣-*šu*

07) [*ú*]-*u*[*l*] *i*[*q*]-*bu a-wa-ta*$_5$ *ša-ru*-⸢*ta*$_5$⸣ *m*[*i-i*]*m-ma*

08) *a-na* LUGAL *b*[*e-lí*]-*ia a-wa-te i-d*[*a-g*]*al*

09) *ù a-wa*-[*t*]*e da*!(*iš*)-*mi-iq* LUGAL *be-li*

10) ⸢*qa*⸣-*bi*$_4$-*ti*$_7$ *a-na* LUGAL *be-lí*[-*i*]*a* ⸢*uš*⸣-*ši-ra-mi*

11) ⸢ÉRIN⸣.⸢MEŠ⸣ *pí-ṭá-ti ù ti-il*$_5$-⸢*qé*⸣ [I]ÌR-*Aš-ra-ta*

12) *mi-ia-mi yi-ma-lik i-zi-za* [*i*]-*na* ⸢*pa*⸣-*ni*

13) ÉRIN.MEŠ *pí-ṭá-at* LUGAL *be-lí-ia*

14) ⸢*ša*⸣(?)-⸢*ni*⸣(?)-⸢*tam*⸣ *ti*$_7$-*iq-bu-na* L[Ú.M]EŠ *ša-ru-tu*

15) [*a-wa-te ša*]-*r*[*u-t*]*e a*-[*na* LUGAL] *be-lí-ia*

16) [..............] ÉRIN.MEŠ *pí*-[*ṭá*]-*ti*

17) [.................]ÉRIN.MEŠ *pí-ṭá-at*

18) [LUGAL *be-lí-ia*.................]

19–58) [...............................]

The lower half (or more) of the tablet is broken away.

EA 94

TRANSLATION

(1–3) [R]i[b]-Haddi [has w]ritten to the king, [the kin]g of [the la]nds, the king, [his] lord, his [god,]: at the feet of [m]y lord, seven (times) and seven (times) have I fallen.

(4–8) Why has [my] lord not heard the words of his servant? May my lord be apprised that there is no evil in [the w]ords of his servant. I do not speak lying words whatever to the king, my l[ord].

(8–9) May the king, my lord, examine the words and may the words be well pleasing.

(10–13) I said to the king, [m]y lord, "send regular troops that they may take ʿAbdi-Ashirta. Who would advise to stand up to the regular troops of the king, my lord?"

(14–18) Furthermore, lying men are speaking [fa]lse [words] t[o the king,] my lord. [....] the regular troops [....] regular troops of [the king, my lord....]

(19–58) *The lower half (or more) of the tablet is broken away.*

EA 95

TRANSCRIPTION

Obv. 01) [a-na] ⸢LÚ⸣.⸢GAL⸣ qí-bí-ma
02) [um]-⸢ma⸣ ^{I}Ri-ib-⸢^{d}⸣IŠKUR a-⸢na⸣ ⸢GÌR⸣.[MEŠ]-⸢ka⸣
03) [am-qú]-ut ^{d}A-ma-na ù
04) ›⸢›ù⸣‹ ^{d}NIN ša URU Gub-⸢la⸣
05) ⸢ti⸣-di-nu TÉŠ-ka ⸢i⸣-⸢na⸣ ⸢pa⸣-⸢ni⸣
06) ⸢šàr⸣-ri EN-⸢li⸣-⸢ka⸣-⸢ma⸣
07) ⸢i⸣-⸢nu⸣-ma t[a]-⸢aš⸣-⸢pu⸣-⸢ra⸣ ⸢a⸣-na ia-ši
08) ib[............]be-⸢e⸣?- lí-ka
09) i[b............................]
10) [..............................]
11) [............................]qa
12) [...........]na ⸢a⸣-na [LÚ.MEŠ] ⸢ÉRIN⸣.MEŠ
13) a[....................]⸢ma⸣ ⸢ar⸣-⸢ṣí⸣
14) ⸢ù⸣ [...................]pa-ra
15) ⸢ù⸣[a-na] ⸢ia-ši⸣ ⸢ku⸣-uš-di
16) ⸢ù⸣ [.............]⸢ÉRIN⸣.MEŠ pí-⸢ṭá⸣-⸢ti⸣
17) ⸢ù⸣ ⸢ku⸣-⸢uš⸣-⸢da⸣ ⸢i⸣-na ⸢ÉRIN⸣.⸢MEŠ⸣
18) ⸢pí⸣-⸢ṭá⸣-⸢ti⸣-⸢šu⸣ ⸢ù⸣ ⸢ti⸣-⸢ìl⸣-⸢qé⸣ [URU]
19) ⸢a⸣-⸢ni⸣-⸢ka⸣-⸢am⸣? ⸢ù⸣ ⸢yi⸣-⸢de⸣
20) ⸢ki⸣ ⸢la⸣ ⸢ú⸣-⸢še$_{20}$⸣-⸢ru⸣-⸢bu⸣-ka
21) [a]-⸢na⸣ ⸢KUR⸣ ⸢A⸣-mur-⸢ri⸣ ⸢ši⸣-⸢mé⸣
22) ⸢ia⸣-⸢ši⸣ ⸢ù⸣ [...................]
Lo.ed 23) [a]-⸢ni⸣-ka-ma ⸢ù⸣! ⸢ú⸣-ul
24) [k]i ⸢pa⸣-na-⸢nu⸣ ^{I}⸢ÌR⸣-⸢A⸣-[ši-ir-ta]
Rev. 25) x-nu i-ru-⸢ub⸣-⸢ma⸣
26) [....a]-⸢na⸣ ⸢ma⸣-⸢ni⸣ ⸢i⸣-la[-ak?]
27) [a-na-ku] ⸢šàr⸣ ⸢KUR⸣ ⸢Mi⸣-t[a-ni]
28) ⸢KUR⸣ A-mur-⸢ri⸣ ⸢ù⸣ ⸢yi⸣-da-g[al?]
29) ⸢ù⸣ ⸢yi⸣-⸢iq⸣-⸢bi⸣ mi-nu
30) ⸢KUR⸣ ⸢an⸣-⸢ni⸣-⸢tu⸣ ⸢ma⸣-⸢á'⸣-⸢da⸣-a[t]
31) ⸢KUR⸣ -⸢ka⸣ ⸢a⸣-⸢na⸣ ⸢ia⸣-⸢ši⸣ ⸢yu⸣-wa-⸢ši⸣-[r]a
32) ⸢šàr⸣ KUR ⸢Mi⸣-⸢iṣ⸣-⸢ri⸣ ⸢LÚ⸣.⸢MÁŠKIM⸣-⸢šu⸣
33) ⸢ù⸣ ⸢yi⸣-⸢ìl⸣-⸢qé⸣-⸢ši⸣ a-na ša-⸢šu⸣

EA 95

TRANSLATION

(1–6) Speak [to] the senior official; [mes]sage of Rib-Hadda; at your fee[t] have [I fa]llen. May Amon and ›and‹ the Lady of the city Byblos grant your honor before the king, your lord.

(7–24) Now you have written to me [...] your lord(?) [...] for troops...[for] distress(?) and [...] I have written and [...] arrive(?) and [...] regular troops, so come with regular troops and take [the city] here and may he know that I will not get you into the land of Amurru. Listen to me and [...h]ere and not [a]s formerly, ʿAbdi-A[shirta].

(25–33) [...]? I entered [...t]o whom will I g[o, myself]? (To) the king of the land of Mit[anni] ? (To) the land of Amurru? But let him loo[k] and let him say, "What is this land? Your land is extensive," to me. May the king of the land of Egypt send his commissioner and let him take it for himself.

34) *[š]a-⸢ni⸣?-⸢tam⸣ ⸢ku⸣-⸢uš⸣-⸢da⸣ ⸢at⸣-[t]a*
35) *⸢ki⸣-⸢ma⸣ ⸢ar⸣-⸢ḫi⸣-⸢iš⸣ ù ⸢li⸣-[q]a*
36) *gáb-ba ⸢ù⸣ ⸢tu⸣-ur*
37) *⸢ù⸣ ⸢li⸣-⸢qa⸣* ⸢ÉRIN⸣.⸢MEŠ⸣ *pí-ṭá-[ti]*
38) *⸢ar⸣-⸢ka⸣-⸢nu⸣ [ša]-⸢ni⸣-⸢tam⸣ ⸢li⸣-⸢qa⸣*
39) *[........ù] ⸢li⸣?-⸢qa⸣* 2(?) *me* [LÚ.MEŠ]
40) ⸢KUR⸣ *⸢Mé⸣-lu-ḫa ù [ti-de i-nu-ma]*
41) ⸢I⸣⸢ÌR⸣-*⸢A⸣-⸢ši⸣-⸢ir⸣-⸢ta⸣ ma-ri-⸢iṣ⸣ [ma]-⸢gal⸣*
42) *m[i]-nu ⸢i⸣-⸢de⸣ ⸢i⸣-⸢nu⸣-⸢ma⸣* BA.ÚŠ
43) *⸢i⸣-⸢nu⸣-⸢ma⸣ ⸢dan⸣-⸢na⸣ ⸢ù⸣ ⸢tu⸣-⸢ur⸣-⸢ra⸣*
44) ⸢URU⸣ *⸢Ši⸣-⸢ga⸣-⸢ta⸣ ⸢ù⸣* ⸢URU⸣ *⸢Am⸣[-pí]*
45) *[ù]* ⸢URU⸣ *⸢Am⸣-⸢mi⸣-⸢ia⸣*
46) *[ù]* ⸢URU⸣ *⸢Baṭ⸣-r[u-na] ⸢ar⸣?-⸢ki⸣*
47) *[....]ak[....................]*
48) [...........................]
49) [...........................]
50) [...........................]
Lft. ed. 51) *[.............]qa[...........]*
52) *[...]ul[.....................]*
53) *[......]a[...................]*

Rev.

59) *[š]a-n[i-tam....................]*
60) LÚ *na-a-ru[....................]*
61) *ša-ki-in* U[GU..................]
62) *ù al-lu-ú [......................]*
63) *ù al-li* U[RU...........LÚ] *na-a-ri*
64) *šu-ut yi-de* [LUGAL *be-]lí ša-na*
65) *ù* A *mé-e i-[n]a-š[a]-šu-nu-ma*
66) *šu-ut yu*-TIL.LA-*aṭ-šu-nu*
67) *i-nu-ma i-ka-ši-iš a-na-ku*
68) LÚ.MEŠ GAZ *nu-kùr-tu i-na ia-ši*
69) *ù šu-ut* TE.LA-*šu-nu-ma*
70) *ù li-im-lik* LUGAL ‹*a-na*› ÌR-*šu*
71) *li-ši-ra* LUGAL LÚ *ra-bi-ṣa-šu*
72) *[l]i-[m]a-lik i-na aš-ri šu-ut*
73) *[l]a-⸢a⸣-mi ⸢yi⸣-iš-ta-ḫi-iṭ*

(34–38) [F]urthermore, come yourself with all due haste and take it all and return and take the regular army afterwards.

(38–43) [F]urthermore, bring [...and] bring two(?) hundred [men of] the land of Meluḫḫa and [be apprised that] ʿAbdi-Ashirta is [ve]ry sick and who knows if he will die (or) if he will recover and return.

(44–53) As for the town of Shigata and the town of Am[pi and] the town of Ammiya [and] the town of Baṭr[ôna] after(?) [.....................].

(59–69) [F]urth[ermore....] the murderer [....] is placed ag[ainst....] and behold [....] and behold the ci[ty of...] may the [king] my [lo]rd be apprised of that other murderer, and give them water. And it is he who must supply them because I am destitute. The *ʿapîru* men are hostile to me and he furnishes them supplies.

(70–73) So may the king take counsel concerning his servant; may the king send his commissioner and [ma]y he tak[e cou]nsel in this place lest he attack.

74) [*pa-n*]*a-n*[*u*]-*ma* [*i-n*]*a* ANŠE.MEŠ *yi-iq-bi*
75) LUGAL *a-*[*n*]*a n*[*a-d*]*a-ni a-na* ÌR
Lft.ed. 76) [*ki-it-ti-šu ù a-nu-ma i-na-an-na*] *ia-nu mi-ma a-na* [*š*]*u-u*[*t*]
77) [..............]*ši i-*[*n*]*a* [*n*]*a-š*[*u*]-[*n*]*i a-na*
78) [..................] *lu*[..............]

(74–78) [Form]erly the king spoke [abo]ut asses to furnish to his [loyal] servant [and now] he has nothing [....]

EA 96

TRANSCRIPTION

Obv.	01)	[*a*]-⸢*na*⸣ ^{I}*Ri-ib-*^{d}IŠKUR
	02)	⸢DUMU⸣-*ia qí-bí-ma*
	03)	*um-ma* ^{I}LÚ.GAL ÉRIN.[MEŠ A]D-*ka-*⸢*ma*⸣
	04)	*a-bi-ka* DINGER.MEŠ-⸢*nu*⸣
	05)	*šu-lum-ka šu-lum* É-*ka*
	06)	*li-iš-al i-*⸢*nu*⸣*-ma*
	07)	*taq-bu-ú la-a-mi*
	08)	*an-ti-in-nu e-re-eb*
	09)	LÚ.MEŠ *ša* URU *Ṣu-mu-ri*^{KI}
	10)	[*a-na*] URU.KI-*ia mu-ta-nu-mi*
	11)	⸢*i*⸣*-na* URU *Ṣu-mu-ri-*[^{KI}]
	12)	*mu-ta-nu-ú m*[*uḫ-ḫi*]
	13)	⸢LÚ⸣.MEŠ-*ú ù i-na* [*muḫ-ḫ*]*i*
	14)	ANŠE.MEŠ *ma-an-nu mu-*[*ta*]*-nu*
	15)	*muḫ-ḫi* ANŠU.MEŠ [*i*]*-nu-*[*ma*]
Lo.ed.	16)	*la-a ta-la-ku-*[*na*]
Rev.	17)	ANŠE.MEŠ *ù ú-ṣ*[*ú-ur*]
	18)	[A]NŠE.MEŠ *šàr-ri*
	19)	*ù ú-ul la-a*
	20)	*ḫal-qú mi-im-mi*
	21)	LUGAL *a-di ú-ba-a-šu-nu*
	22)	*be-lu-šu-nu šum-ma*
	23)	*šàr-ru* EN-*lì* ANŠE.MEŠ
	24)	*bu-a-mi* ANŠE.MEŠ
	25)	LUGAL *am-mi-nim-mi*
	26)	*te-ep-pu-šu ki-šu-ma*
	27)	*a-na* ÌR.MEŠ-*e* LUGAL
	28)	*uš-ši-ra-am-mi* LÚ.MEŠ
	29)	[*a-n*]*a na-ṣa-ar* URU.KI
	30)	[*ù*] *al-lu-ú ša-ap-ra-ti*
Up.ed.	31)	[*a-n*]*a* LUGAL *muḫ-ḫi-ku-nu*
	32)	[*l*]*i-te-ra-*⸢*an*⸣*-ni i-na*
Lft.ed.	33)	[*ṭu*]*p-pí muḫ-ḫi gáb-b*[*i*]

EA 96

TRANSLATION

(1–6) Speak to Rib-Hadda, my son, the message of the general, your [fa]ther (your father): May the deity seek after your welfare and the welfare of your household.

(7–17) Inasmuch as you say "I will not permit the men of the town Ṣumur to enter [into] my city; there is a plague in the town of Ṣumur," Is it a plague against men or against asses? What is the plague against asses [th]a[t] the asses cannot walk?

(17–25) So gu[ard] the asses of the king, or not? May the property of the king not be lost until their owner looks for them. If the king is the owner of the asses, search for the asses of the king!

25–29) Why do you behave thus towards the servants of the king? Send men [t]o protect the city.

(30–33) [And] behold, I have written [t]o the king concerning you. [Let] him reply to me in a [let]ter concerning everything.

EA 97

TRANSCRIPTION

Obv. 01) [*a*-]*na* ^{I}*Šu-mu-ḫa*-⸢*di*⸣ [*qí-bí-ma*]

02) [*u*]*m-ma* ^{I}*Ia*-⸢*ap*⸣-⸢*pa*⸣-⸢*aḫ*⸣-[^{d}IŠKUR]

03) [DINGIR.]⸢MEŠ⸣ *šu-lum-ka li*-[*iš-al*]

04) [*i*-]⸢*de*$_{9}$⸣ *ki-i-ma*

05) ⸢*la*⸣-*mi-in šum-ka*

06) *a-na pa-ni* LUGAL *ù*

07) ⸢*la*⸣-*a ti-ta-ṣa-am*

08) [*i*]*š-tu* KUR *Mi-iṣ-ri*

09) [*la*]-*a* ⸢*tu*⸣-*ḫal-li-iq-mi*

Lo.ed. 10) [KUR.MEŠ LUGAL] ⸢*yu*⸣-*ḫal-li-iq*

Rev. 11) [^{I}ÌR-*A-ši-ir-t*]*a*

12) [KUR.MEŠ LUGAL.......]

13) [.....................]⸢*te*⸣

14) [........................]

15) [.......................]*ša*

16) [.....................]⸢*li*⸣-*de*$_{4}$

17) [........................]

18) [........................]

19) [........................]

Up.ed. 20) [*ù*]⸢*na*⸣-*ad-na-ma*

21) [*a-na* DUMU.MEŠ ^{I}]⸢ÌR⸣-*A-ši*-⸢*ir*⸣-⸢*ta*⸣

EA 97

TRANSLATION

(1–3) [Speak t]o Shumu-Haddi, [the mes]sage of Yappaʿ-[Baʿlu]. May [the deity seek] your welfare.

(4–15) ⸢I⸣ know that your reputation with the king is bad and you can't come forth [fr]om the land of Egypt. You did not cause the loss of [the lands of the king. [ʿAbdi-Ashirta] caused the loss [of the lands of the king.....]

(16)-17) [..............] may he be apprised [............]

(18–21) [..........and] he gave [to the sons of]ʿAbdi-Ashirta

EA 98

TRANSCRIPTION

Obv. 01) [*a-na*] ^{I}*Ia-an-ḫa-mi*
02) [*qí*]*-bí-ma um-ma* ^{I}*Ia-pa-*⸢*aḫ*⸣-^{d}IŠKUR
03) *am-mi-ni-mi qa-la-ta*
04) *iš-tu* URU *Ṣu-mu-ra i-nu-ma*
05) *na-ak-ra-at-mi*
06) *gáb-bi* KUR.⸢MEŠ⸣ *ar-ki*
07) ⸢^{I}⸣*A-zi-ri iš-tu*
08) URU *Gu-ub-li* ^{KI}
09) *a-di* URU *Ú-ga-ri-ti*
10) *ù na-ak-ra-at-mì*
11) URU *Ši-ga-ti* ^{KI} *ù*
12) ⸢URU⸣ *Am-pí* ^{KI} *u a-nu-*[*m*]*a*
Lo.ed. 13) [*š*]*a-ka-an* GIŠ.MÁ.MEŠ
13a) (traces of erased signs)
Rev. 14) [URU] ⸢*Ar*⸣*-wa-*⸢*da*⸣
15) [*i-n*]*a* URU *Am-pí*^{KI} *ù*
16) *i-na* URU *Ši-ga-ti* ^{KI}
17) *ù!* (*a-na*) *ba-li šu-ri-bi*
18) ⸢ŠE⸣.MEŠ *a-na* URU *Ṣu-mu-ri*
19) *u la-a ni-le-ú*
20) *e-re-ba a-na* URU *Ṣu-mu-ri*
21) *u mi-na-am-mi* ⸢*ni*⸣*-*⸢*pu*⸣*-šu-na*
22) *ni-nu ù šu-pu-ur-mì*
23) *a-na* É.GAL UGU
24) ⸢*a*⸣*-wa-ti an-ni-ta*$_{5}$
25) [*ù da-*]*mi-iq*
26) [*i-nu-m*]*a lum-da-ta*

EA 98

TRANSLATION

(1–2) [Sp]eak [to] Yanḫamu; the message of Yapaʿ-Hadda:

(3–12) Why have you kept silent concerning the city of Ṣumur when all the states have revolted following Aziru, from the city of Byblos to the city of Ugarit? And the city of Shigata and the city of Ampi revolted?

(12–20) And now he has [pl]aced the ships of [the city of] Arvad [i]n the city of Ampi and in the city of Shigata and it is impossible to deliver grain to the city of Ṣumur and we are unable to enter into the city of Ṣumur.

(21–22) So what can we do ourselves?

(22–26) So write to the palace concerning this matter. [And it is]well [tha]t you learn about it.

EA 99

TRANSCRIPTION

Obv. 01) [*a-na* ^{I}X-X-*a*]*ṣ*-⸢*ma*⸣-⸢*a*⸣-⸢*nu*⸣

02) [LÚ UR]U *Am-mi-ia*

03) [*q*]*í-bí-ma u*[*m*]*-ma*

04) LUGAL-*ma* ⸢*a*⸣-*nu-u*[*m-m*]*a*

05) *ṭup-pa* ⸢*a*⸣-[*n*]*a*-⸢*a*⸣ *uš*!-*te-bi*!-*la-ku*

06) *qá-bé-e* [*a-n*]*a k*[*a*]*-a-ša*

07) *ù uṣ-ṣu*[*r*] *lu-ú*

08) *na-ṣa-ra-ta aš-ru*

09) LUGAL *ša it-ti-ka*

10) *šu-ši-ir* DUMU.MUNUS-*ka*

11) ⸢*a*⸣-*na* LUGAL EN-*ka*

12) *ù šu-ši‹-ir›* IGI.DU$_{8}$.ḪI.A

Lo.ed. 13) [2]0 ÌR.MEŠ SIG$_{5}$-*tì*

14) ⸢KÙ⸣.BABBAR GIŠ.GIGIR.MEŠ

Rev. 15) ANŠE.KUR.RA.ḪI.A SIG$_{5}$-*tì*

16) *ù li-iq-bá-ku*

17) LUGAL EN-*ka ši-ia-tù b*[*a*]*-a*[*n-t*]*ù*

18) *ša tá-ad-din-šu*

19) IGI.DU$_{8}$ *a-na* LUGAL

20) EGIR DUMU.MUNUS-*ka*

21) *ù lu-ú ti-i-de*$_{9}$

22) *i-nu-ma ša-lim* LUGAL

23) *ki-ma* ^{d}UTU

24) *i-na ša-me-e*

25) [É]RIN.MEŠ‹*šu*› GIŠ.GIGIR.MEŠ-*šu*

26) *ma-a-du ma-gal šul-mu*

EA 99

TRANSLATION

(1–4) [Sp]eak [to…a]ṣmānu, [the ruler of the ci]ty of ʿAmmiya: T[hu]s the king:

(5–20) T[hi]s tablet have I sent to you (to) speak to you, so guard! Be on guard in the place of the king that is in your charge. Prepare your daughter for the king, your lord and prep‹are› contributions: [Twe]nty able bodied slaves, silver, chariots, healthy horses. So may the king, your lord, say to you, "This is g[oo]d that you have given it, viz. a contribution to the king to accompany your daughter."

(21–26) And may you be apprised that the king is well like the sun god in heaven. To (his) [tr]oops (and) his massive chariotry it is exceedingly well.

EA 100

TRANSCRIPTION

Obv. 01) *ṭup-pí an-nu ṭup-pí*
02) URU *Ir-qa-ta a-*⸢*na*⸣ *šàr-*⸢*ri*⸣
03) EN-*nu um-ma* URU *Ir-qa-ta*
04) *ù* $^{\mathrm{LÚ.MEŠ}}$*ši-bu*!(ŠE)*-ti-ši*
05) *a-na* GÌR.MEŠ *šàr-ri* EN-*nu*
06) 7-*šu* 7-*ta-an ni-am-qú-ut*
07) *a-na* EN-*nu* ^{d}⸢UTU⸣ ⸢*um*⸣*-ma*
08) ⸢URU⸣ *Ir-qa-ta i-de lìb-bi*
09) ⸢LUGAL⸣ EN‹-*nu*› *i-*⸢*nu*⸣*-ma ni-na-ṣa-*⸢*ru*⸣
10) URU ⸢*Ir*⸣-⸢*qa*⸣-⸢*ta*⸣ *a-na ša-*[*š*]*u*
11) *i-nu-ma y*[*u*]-⸢*wa*⸣*-ši-r*[*a* L]UGAL
12) EN-*nu* ^{I}⸢DUMU⸣*-pí-ḫa-a* [*ù*]
13) *yi-iq-bi a-na ia-*[*ši-n*]*u*
14) *um-ma* ⸢LUGAL⸣ ⸢*ú*⸣*-ṣa-ru-m*[*i*]
15) URU *Ir-qa-*⸢*ta*⸣ DUMU.M[EŠ]
16) ^{LÚ}*ša-ri šàr-*⸢*ri*⸣
17) *tu-ba-ú-na nu*[-KÚR]
18) URU *Ir-qa-ta tu-b*[*a-ú*]
19) ⸢*ki*⸣*-ta a-na šàr-r*[*i*]
20) ⸢*i*⸣-⸢*nu*⸣*-ma na-ad-nu* [KÙ.BABBAR *a-na*]?
21) ⸢KUR⸣ ⸢*Su*⸣*-ba-ri q*[*a-du*]
Lo.ed. 22) ⸢30⸣(?) ⸢ANŠE⸣.KUR.⸢RA⸣.MEŠ GIŠ.G[IGIR.MEŠ]
Rev. 23) ⸢*ti*⸣*-de lìb-bi* URU *Ir*[*-qa-ta*]
24) *i-nu-ma ka-ši-*⸢*id*⸣
25) *ṭup-pí* LUGAL *a-na ša-š*[*i*]
26) KUR *ša ìl-qú* LÚ.MEŠ *š*[*a-ru-tu*]
27) *šàr-ri i-te*$_9$*-ep-š*[*u*]
28) *nu*-KÚR *it-ti-nu a-na* L[UGAL]
29) EN-*nu* LÚ *ša ti-ìš-ta-*[*kán-šu*]
30) UGU-*nu a-di ni-na-ṣa-ru-š*[*u*]

EA 100

TRANSLATION

(1–10) This tablet is the tablet of the city of ʿIrqata to the king, our lord. The message of the city of Irqata and of its el[de]rs: At the feet of the king, our lord, seven times (and) seven times we have fallen. To our lord, the sun god, the message of the city of ʿIrqata: The heart of the king, ‹our› lord, knows that we are guarding the city of ʿIrqata for him.
(11–19) Inasmuch as the king, our lord, sent DUMU-piḫā [and] he said to us, "Message of the king: 'Guard the city of ʿIrqata,'" the sons of the traitor to the king are seeking ho[stility]; the city of ʿIrqata see[ks] loyalty to the king.

(20–30) Inasmuch as they gave [silver(?) to] the land of Subaru wi[th] thirty horses and chariots,

(23–29) you should know the heart of the city of ʿIr[qata]. When the tablet of the king reached h[er], the land which the [traitors] to the king had taken became hostile to us because of [the king], our lord.

(29–30) As for the man which you pla[ced] over us, we are still guarding hi[m].

31) *yi-ìš-mé šàr-ru* EN-*nu*
32) *a-wa-te* ÌR.MEŠ *ki-ti-šu*
33) *ù ia-di-na* NÍG.BA
34) *a-na* ÌR.‹MEŠ›-*šu ù ti-da-ga-lu*
35) LÚ.MEŠ *a-ia-bu-nu ù*
36) *ti-ka-lu ep-ra ša-ri*
37) *šàr-ri ú-ul ti-na-mu-uš*
38) *iš-tu mu-ḫ̮i-nu*
39) *a-bu-la-nu ú-du-lu a-di*
40) *ka-ša-di ša-ri*
41) [LUG]AL *a-na ia-ši-nu*
Up.ed. 42) [G]A.KAL *nu*-KÚR UGU-*nu*
43) [*m*]*a-gal ma-gal*

(31–36) May the king, our lord, heed the words of his loyal servants and may he bestow a gift on his servant‹s› so that our enemies will see and eat dirt.

(36–38) May the breath of the king not depart from us.

(39–42) Our gate is closed until the breath of [the ki]ng reaches us.

Up.ed.
(42–43) The hostility against us is exceedingly great.

EA 101

TRANSCRIPTION

Obv. 01) [*ša-n*]*i-tam mi-nu nu-kúr-*⸢*tu*$_4$⸣
02) [UGU] LUGAL *ú-ul* ^{I}*Ḫa-ya-a*
03) [*i-nu-m*]*a la-a ti-ru-bu-na*
04) ⸢GIŠ⸣.MÁ.MEŠ LÚ.MEŠ *mi-ši a-na*
05) KUR *A-mur-ri ú da-ku*
06) ^{I}ÌR-*A-ši-ir-ta i-nu-ma*
07) ⸢*i*⸣*a-nu* SÍG *a-na ša-šu-nu*
08) *ù ia-nu* GADA ZA.GÌN NA$_4$.MAR \ *bu-bu-mar*
09) *a-na ša-šu a-na na-da-ni*
10) GÚ.UN *a-na* KUR *Mi-ta-na*
11) *ša-ni-tam* GIŠ.MÁ.MEŠ *ša ma-ni*
12) *i-zi-zu* UGU-*ia ú-ul*
13) LÚ.MEŠ URU *Ar-wa-da*
14) *ù a-la* ⸢*šu*⸣*-nu i-na-na*
15) *it-ti-ka ṣa-bat* GIŠ.MÁ.MEŠ
16) LÚ.MEŠ URU *Ar-wa-da*
17) *ša-a i-ba-šu i-na*
18) ⸢KUR⸣ *Mi-iṣ-ri ša-ni-tam* ⸢*i*⸣*-nu-ma*
19) [*i*]*a-aq-bu* ^{I}*Ḫa-ya-a*
Lo.ed. 20) [*a-na šà*]*r-ri šum-ma la*
21) [*a-ṣé*] ⸢*ni*⸣*-nu a-na* KUR *A-mur-*[*r*]*i*
Rev. 22) [*ù t*]*u-ba-lu-na*
23) [LÚ.MEŠ U]RU ⸢*Ṣur*⸣*-ri ù* LÚ.MEŠ
24) [URU] *Ṣí-du-na ù* LÚ.MEŠ
25) [UR]U *Be-ru-ta a-na ma-an-ni*
26) URU.MEŠ *an-nu-tu ù-ul a-na* LUGAL
27) *šu-ku-un* 1 LÚ 1 LÚ *i-na lìb-bi*
28) URU *ù la yi-di-in*$_4$ GIŠ.MÁ
29) KUR *A-mur-ri ù da-ku*
30) ^{I}ÌR-*A-ši-ir-ta* LUGAL *ìš-ta-kán-šu*
31) UGU ⸢*šu*⸣*-nu ú-ul šu-nu*
32) *ia-*⸢*aq*⸣*-bi* LUGAL *a-na* 3 URU.MEŠ
33) *ù* GIŠ.MÁ.‹MEŠ› LÚ.MEŠ *mi-ši*

EA 101

TRANSLATION

(1–10) [Further]more, who is hostile[to] the king? Is it not Ḫaya? [Becau]se, the ships of the navy do not enter the land of Amurru, and kill ʿAbdi-Ashirta, because they do not have wool and he does not have garments of lapiz lazuli or *mar*-stone color to give as payment to the land of Mittani.

(11–18) Moreover, whose ships have been hostile to me, is it not the men of the city of Arwad? Behold, they are with you now; seize the ships of the men of the city of Arwad which are in the land of Egypt.

(18–33) Moreover, inasmuch as Ḫaya says [to the ki]ng, "If we don't [go forth], then [the men of the ci]ty of Tyre and the men of [the city] of Sidon and the men of the [ci]ty of Beirut will bring (him)," whose cities are these? Not the king's? Place one man in each city and let him not permit the ships of the land of Amurru (to go forth), so that they will kill ʿAbdi-Ashirta. The king placed him over them, not they themselves. May the king speak to the three cities and to the ships of the navy,

34) *ú la-*⸢*a*⸣ *ti-la-ku a-na*
35) KUR *A-mur-ri ù ṣa-bat* ᴵÌR-*A-‹ši›-*⸢*ir*⸣-[*t*]*a*
36) *ù yi-di-in*$_4$ *a-na*
37) *ka-ta*$_5$ *ù li-ma-ad*
38) *a-wa-te* ÌR *ki-ti-ka*

(34–38) and no sooner will they go to the land of Amurru than he (Ḫaya) will capture ʿAbdi-Ashirta and he will hand him over to you. So learn the words of your servant.

EA 102

TRANSCRIPTION

Obv. 01) [*a-na* ^{I}*Ia-an-ḫa-*]⌜*mi*⌝?[...]
02) [*qí*]*-bí-ma*
03) ⌜*um*⌝*-ma* ^{I}*Ri-ib-*^{d}IŠKUR
04) *a-na* GÌR.MEŠ*-ka am-qú-ut*
05) ⌜^{d}⌝NIN *ša* URU *Gub-la*
06) DINGIR LUGAL BAD*-ia li-din*
07) TÉŠ^{ba}*-ka a-na pa-ni* LUGAL *be-li-ku*
08) ^{d}UTU KUR.DIDLI.MEŠ.KI *šá-ni-tam ti-de-mi*
09) *i-nu-ma lam-da-ta uḫ-ḫu-ra-ta*
10) *a-ṣa a-na mi-ni*$_{7}$ *ta-šap-pár-ta*
11) *ù an-nu-ú i-na-an-na ti-ir-bu*
12) *a-na* É*-ti re-qí ga-mi-ir gáb-bu*
13) *ti-iḫ-ta-ti gáb-ba šá-ni-tam*
14) *i-nu-ma ta-aš-tap-ra a-na ia-ši*
15) *a-lik-mi i-zi-iz a-na* URU *Ṣu-mu-ur*
16) ⌜*a*⌝*-di ka-ša-*⌜*di*⌝*-ia*

Lo.ed. 17) ⌜*ti*⌝*-de i-*⌜*nu*⌝*-ma nu-kúr-tu*$_{4}^{\text{MEŠ}}$
18) ⌜KAL⌝.GA *ma-gal* UGU-⌜*ia*⌝

Rev. 19) *ù ú-ul i-le-*⌜*ḫé*⌝! *a-la-*[*ka*]*m*^{V}
20) *ù a-nu-ma* URU *Am-bi nu-kùr-tu*$_{4}$
21) *it-ti-ia ti-de i-‹nu-ma›*
22) LÚ GAL *ù* LÚ.MEŠ *be-li* URU
23) *šal-mu it-*⌜*ti*⌝⌜DUMU⌝.MEŠ ^{I}ÌR*-Aš-ra-ta*
24) *ù ki-na-an-na la i-le-*⌜*ú*⌝(?)
25) *a-la-kam ti-de i-*[*nu*]*-*⌜*ma*⌝ *gáb-bu*
26) *ša-ru ù* ⌜*la*⌝*-*⌜*mi*⌝(?) ⌜*ti*⌝*-ša-lu-ni*
27) *a-na* LÚ *ʾa*$_{4}$*-ia-*⌜*bi*⌝*-*⌜*ia*⌝ *ù* ⌜*i*⌝*-*⌜*na*⌝*-*⌜*an*⌝*-*⌜*na*⌝
28) *ki-na-an-na pal-ḫa-ku* ⌜*šá*⌝*-ni-tam*
29) *ši-me-e ia-ši ḫu-mi-ṭa*$_{9}$ *ki-ma*
30) *ar-ḫi-iš ka-ša-da ù*
31) *i-ru-ub aš-ra-nu ti-de i-nu-ma* LÚ.MEŠ
32) ⌜*ša*⌝*-ru-tu*$_{4}$ *šu-nu šá-ni-tam la-mi*
33) [*tu-uḫ-ḫ*]*i*(?)*-ra ka-ša-da*

EA 102

TRANSLATION

(1–7) [To Yanḫa]mi(?) speak; Message of Rib-Haddi: At your feet I have fallen. May the Lady of Byblos, the goddess of the king, my lord, grant you honor before the king your lord, the sun god of the lands.

(8–13) Furthermore, know that, though informed, you have delayed in coming forth. Why did you write? And behold now, you will enter into an empty house. Everything is finished. I am completely devastated(?).

(13–19) Furthermore, inasmuch as you have written to me, "Go and stay in Ṣumur until my arrival," know that there is very much hostility against me. I was unable to go.

(20–28) And now the town of Ampi is hostile to me. Know th‹at› the senior official and the lords of the city are at peace with the sons of ʿAbdi-Ashirta so thus I am unable to go. Know that all of them are traitors, so don't ask me about my enemies! So now, thus, I am fearful.

(28–33) Furthermore, Don't [del]ay coming

34) [*ù uš-ši-ra*] ⸢ÉRIN ⸣.MEŠ *pí-ṭá-*[*ti*]
35) [*a-na ša-bat* URU EN-*k*]*a*
Lft.ed. 36) [*i-r*]*u-*⸢*ub*⸣ ⸢*la*⸣ *tu-pal-la-aḫ*
37) [*ú ir-*]*ba-ta a-na* URU-*lì ù*
38) ⸢*iš*⸣]-*tu* ŠÀ-*ši ta-šap-pár a-*⸢*na*⸣ [*ia-ši*]

(34–38) [and send] regular troo[ps in order to (re)take the city of yo]ur[lord]. [En]ter, don't be afraid! [And (after) you have en]tered into the city, then you can write to [me] from within it.

EA 103

TRANSCRIPTION

Obv. 01) [*a-n*]*a šàr-ri* EN-*ia*
02) ^{d}UTU-*ia um-ma* ^{I}*Ri-ib*-^{d}⸢IŠKUR⸣
03) ÌR-*ka-ma a-na* GÌR.MEŠ EN-*ia*
04) ^{d}UTU-*ia 7-šu 7-ta-an*
05) *am-qú-ut yi-ìš-me šàr-ru*
06) EN-*li a-*⸢*wa*⸣*-te* ÌR
07) *ki-ti-šu ma-ri-iṣ ma-gal*
08) *a-na ia-ši* GA.KAL *nu-kúr-tu*$_{4}$
09) ^{I}DUMU.MEŠ ÌR-*A-ši-ir-ta i-ru-bu*
10) *i-na* KUR *A-mur-ra a-‹na› ša-šu-*⸢*nu*⸣
11) *ka-li* KUR.KI URU *Ṣu-mu-ra*
12) *ù* URU *Ir-qa-ta ir-ti-ḫu*
13) *a-na* LÚ.GAL *ù a-nu-ma i-na*
14) URU *Ṣu-mu-ra i-zi-za-ti*
15) *i-nu-ma ma-ri-iṣ* LÚ.GAL
16) UGU *nu-kúr-ti i-te*$_{9}$-⸢*zi*⸣-⸢*ib*⸣
17) URU *Gub-la ù ia-*[*nu*]
18) ^{I}*Zi-im-re-*⸢*da*⸣ ⸢*ù*⸣
19) ^{I}*Ia-pa-*^{d}IŠKUR [*i*]*t-ti-ia*
20) *a-nu-ma ki-*[*a-m*]*a yi-ìš-*⸢*ta*⸣*-pár-ru*
21) LÚ.⸢GAL⸣ *a-na ša-šu-nu ù*
22) *l*[*a-a*] *ti-ìš-ma-na a-na ša-šu*
23) ⸢*ù*⸣ *yi-ìš-mé šàr-ru* EN-*li*
24) [*a*]*-wa-te* ÌR *ki-ti-šu*
25) [*u*]*š-ši-ra til-la-ta*
Lo.ed. 26) [*k*]*i-ma ar-ḫi-iš a-na*
27) [U]RU *Ṣu-mu-ra a-na na-ṣa-*⸢*ri*⸣-⸢*ši*$_{x}$⸣(⸢ŠE⸣)
Rev. 28) [*a-d*]*i ka-ša-ad* ÉRIN.MEŠ
29) [*pí*]*-ṭá-at šàr-ri* ^{d}UTU
30) *ù yu-ša-am-ri-ir šàr-ru*
31) ^{d}UTU LÚ.MEŠ *ša-ru-ta ìš-tu*
32) ⸢*lìb*⸣*-bi* KUR-*šu ša-ni-tam yi-ìš-mé*

EA 103

TRANSLATION

(1–5) [T]o the king, my lord, my sun god, message of Rib-Hadda, your servant: At the feet of my lord, my sun god seven times and seven times have I fallen.

(5–22) May the king, my lord, hear the words of his loyal servant. It is very distressful for me. The hostility of the sons of ʿAbdi-Ashirta is severe. They have entered into the land of Amurru. All the territories are theirs. The city of Ṣumur and the city of ʿIrqata remain to the senior official. And now I am stationed in Ṣumur because the senior official is distressed because of the hostility. I left Byblos, but Zimredda [and] Yapaʿ-Hadda are not with me. And now the senior official keeps writing to them but they do not listen to him.

(23–27) So may the king, my lord hear the words of his faithful servant. Send an auxiliary force with all speed to the city of Ṣumur to protect it.

(28–32) [un]til the arrival of the regular army of the king, the sun god, and so may the king, the sun god, expel the rebels from his land.

33) *šàr-ru* EN‹*-li*› *a-wa-te* ÌR-*šu*
34) *ù uš-ši-*‹*ra*› LÚ.MEŠ *ma-ṣa-ar-ta*
35) *a-na* URU *Ṣu-mu-ra ù*
36) *a-na* URU ⸢*Ir*⸣*-qa-ta šum-ma*
37) *in*$_4$*-na-a*[*b*]*-tu ka-li*
38) LÚ.MEŠ *ma-*[*ṣa*]*-*⸢*ar*⸣*-ti iš-tu*
39) URU *Ṣu-*⸢*mu*⸣*-*[*r*]*a ù*
40) *yi-it-ru-*⸢*uṣ*⸣ ⸢*i*⸣*-*⸢*na*⸣ ⸢*pa*⸣*-*⸢*ni*⸣
41) ⸢EN⸣ ^{d}UTU KUR.ḪI.A *ù*
42) ⸢*id*⸣*-na-ni* 20 *ta-pal*
43) ANŠE.KUR.RA.MEŠ *a-na ia-ši*
44) *ù uš-ši-ra til-la-ta*
45) *ki-ma ar-ḫi-ìš*
46) *a-na* URU *Ṣu-mu-ra a-na*
47) *na-ṣa-ri-ši*$_x$(ŠE) *ka-li*
48) LÚ.MEŠ *ma-ṣa-ar-ti*
49) *ša-a ir-ti-ḫu mar-ṣa*
50) ⸢*ù*⸣ *ṣé-eḫ-ru* LÚ.MEŠ
Up.ed. 51) ⸢*i*⸣*-*⸢*na*⸣ *lìb-bi* URU ⸢*šum*⸣*-*⸢*ma*⸣
52) *la-a* ⸢ÉRIN⸣.⸢MEŠ⸣ *pí-ṭá-*‹*ta*› *la-a*
53) ⸢*tu*⸣*-wa-*‹*ši*›*-ru-na ù*
Lft.ed. 54) *ia-nu* URU *ša-a ti-ir-ti-ḫu*
55) *a-na ka-ta*$_5$ *ù šum-ma* ÉRIN.MEŠ *pí-ṭ*[*á-ti*]
56) ⸢*i*⸣*-*⸢*ba*⸣*ša-at ka-li* KUR.MEŠ
57) *ni-ìl-qú* ⸢*a*⸣*-*⸢*na*⸣ *šàr-ri*

(32–51) Furthermore, may the king heed the words of his servant. Send garrison troops to the city of Ṣumur and to the city of ʿIrqata since all of the garrison troops have fled from the city of Ṣumur. And may it please the lord, the sun god of the lands and give me twenty pairs of horses and send an auxiliary force with all speed to the city of Ṣumur to protect it. All the garrison troops that remain are sick and few are the men who are in the city.

(51–57) If you do not send the regular army, then there is no city that will remain to you. But if the regular ar[my] will be (here), we will take all the lands for the king

EA 104

TRANSCRIPTION

Obv. 01) *a-na šàr-ri* EN-*ia* ^{d}UTU-*ia*
02) *qí-bí-ma*
03) *um-ma* ^{I}*Ri-ib-*^{d}IŠKUR ÌR-*ka*
04) *a-na* GÌR.MEŠ EN-*ia* ^{d}UTU-*ia*
05) 7-*šu* 7-*ta-an am-qú-ut*
06) *yi-de šàr-ru* EN-*li*
07) *i-nu-ma* ^{I}*Pu-ḫa-á*ʾ*-la*
08) ^{I}DUMU ÌR-*A-ši-ir-ta*
09) *i-te*$_{9}$*-ru-ub a-na* URU *Ul-la-sà*
10) *a-na ša-šu-nu* URU *Ar-da-ta*
11) URU *Ya-á*ʾ*-li-ia* URU *Am-pí*
12) URU *Ši-ga-ta ka-li*
13) URU.MEŠ *a-na ša-šu-nu*
14) *ù yu-ši-ra šàr-ru*
15) *til-la-ta a-na* URU *Ṣu-mu-ra*
16) *a-di yi-ma-li-ku*
17) *šàr-ru a-na* KUR-*šu mi-ia-mi*
18) DUMU.MEŠ ^{I}ÌR-*A-ši-ir-ta*
19) ÌR UR.GI$_{7}$ *šàr*
20) KUR *Ka-aš-ši ù šàr*
21) KUR *Mi-ta-ni šu-nu*
22) *ù ti-ìl-qú-na*
23) KUR *šàr-ri a-na*
Lo.ed. 24) *ša-šu-nu pa-na-nu*
Rev. 25) ⌜*ti*⌝*-ì*[*l-q*]*ú*[*-n*]*a* URU.MEŠ
26) *ḫa-za-ni-ka ù qa-la-ta*
27) *an-nu-ú i-na-na du-bi-r*[*u*]
28) LÚ.MAŠKIM-*ka ù la-qú*
29) URU.MEŠ-*šu a-na ša-šu-nu*
30) *a-nu-ma la-qú* URU *Ul-la-sà*

EA 104

TRANSLATION

(1–5) Speak to the king, my lord, my sun god; the message of Rib-Haddi, your servant: at the feet of my lord, my sun god, seven times (and) seven times have I fallen.

(6–13) May the king, my lord, be apprised that Pu-Baʿla, the son of ʿAbdi-Ashirta, has entered into the city of Ullasa. The city of Ardata, the city of Yaʿliya, the city of Ampi, the city of Shigata are theirs. All the cities are theirs.

(14–17) So may the king send support troops to the city of Ṣumur until the king can take council concerning his territory.

(17–26) Who are the sons of ʿAbdi-Ashirta, the slave, the dog? Are they the king of the Cassite land or the king of the land of Mittani that they should take the territory of the king to themselves? Formerly, they were taking the towns of your city rulers and you kept silent.

(27–30) Behold, now they have expelled your commissioner and they have taken his towns for themselves. Now they have taken the city of Ullasa.

31) *šum-ma ki-a-ma qa-la-ta*
32) *a-di ti-ìl-qú-na*
33) URU *Ṣu-mu-ra ù*
34) *›ù‹ ti-du-ku-na* LÚ.MAŠKIM
35) *ù* ÉRIN.MEŠ *til*!(BI)*-la-ti*
36) *ša i-na Ṣu-mu-ra mi-na*
37) *i-pu-šu-na ù a-na-ku*
38) *la-a i-le-ú a-la-k*[a_{13}]
39) *a-na Ṣu-mu-ra*
40) URU.URU *Am-pí*
41) URU *Ši-ga-ta* URU *Ul-la-sà*
42) URU *Er*$_{4}$*-wa-da nu-*KÚR
43) *a-na ia-ši ša-ma-ma šu-nu*
44) *›šu-nu‹ i-nu-ma i-te*$_{9}$*-ru-bu*
45) *i-na* URU *Ṣu-mu-ra*
46) URU.MEŠ *an-nu-tu* GIŠ.MÁ.MEŠ
47) *ù* DUMU.MEŠ ^{I}ÌR-*A-ši-i*[*r*]-
ta
48) *i-na ṣé-ri ù*
49) [*i*]*z-*[*z*]*i-za* UGU‹*-šu-nu*› *ù*
50) *la-a i-le-ú*
Lft.ed. 51) *a-ṣa ù ep-ša-at* URU *Gub-la*
52) [*a*]*-na* LÚ.MEŠ GAZ.MEŠ *a-na* URU *I-bir*$_{5}$*-ta*
53) *al-‹li›-ka ù b*[*u*]*-ú en-ni-ip-ša*
54) *a-na* LÚ.MEŠ GAZ.MEŠ

(31–39) If thus you keep quiet until they take the city of Ṣumur and kill the commissioner and the support troops that are in Ṣumur, what can I do while I am unable to go to Ṣumur?

(40–52) The cities Ampi, the city of Shigata, the city of Ullasa (and) the city of Arvad are hostile to me. If they should hear that I have entered into the city of Ṣumur, these cities (will be in) ships and the sons of ʿAbdi-Ashirta (will be) in the field and [I] will have to confront ‹them› and I will be unable to come forth and the city of Byblos will go over to the *ʿapîru* men.

(52–54) To the town of ʿIbirta I went and they sought to join the *ʿapîru* men.

EA 105

TRANSCRIPTION

Obv. 01) [^{I}*Ri*]-*ib*-^{d}IŠKUR *iq-bi a-na* EN[-*šu*]
02) [LUGAL] GAL *šàr* KUR.⌜KI⌝.MEŠ *šàr* [*t*]*a-am-ḫ*[*a-ra*]
03) ⌜^{d}⌝NIN *ša* URU *Gub-la ti-di-in*$_4$ K[AL.GA]
04) *a-na šàr-ri* EN-*ia a-na* GÌR.MEŠ EN-*ia*
05) ^{d}UTU-*ia* 7-*šu* 7-*ta-an am-qú-ut*
06) *ša-ni-tam ya*-⌜*am*⌝-*li-ik šàr-ru*
07) *a-na* URU *Ṣu*-⌜*mu*⌝-*ra a-mu-ur*
08) URU ⌜*Ṣu*⌝-*mu-ra ki-ma* MUŠEN *ša lìb-bi*
09) *ḫu*-[*ḫ*]*a-ri* [\] *ki-lu-bi ša-ak-na-at*
10) *ki-na-na* ⌜*i*⌝-*ba-ša-at* URU *Ṣu-mu*[-*ra*]
11) ⌜^{I}⌝DUMU.MEŠ ÌR-⌜*A*⌝-*ši-ir*-⌜*ta*⌝ *iš-tu qa-qa*-⌜*ri*⌝
12) *ù* LÚ.MEŠ ⌜URU⌝ ⌜*Ar*⌝-*wa-da iš-tu*
13) ⌜*a*⌝-*ia-ba* ⌜*ur*⌝-⌜*ra*⌝ *mu-ša* U[GU-*ši*]
14) *ù uš*-‹*ši*›-*ir*-⌜*ti*⌝ 3 G[IŠ].M[Á].M[EŠ *a-na*]
15) *ma-ḫar* ^{I}*Ia*-[*an-ḫa*-]*mi* [*ù* GIŠ.MÁ.MEŠ]
16) LÚ.MEŠ ⌜URU⌝ ⌜*Ar*⌝-*wa-d*[*a*] ⌜*a*⌝-⌜*na*⌝ *ṣa-ba-ti-š*[*i-na*]
17) *ù a*-⌜*ṣa*⌝-*ú a-mu-ur* ⌜LÚ⌝.MEŠ
18) ⌜URU⌝ ⌜*Ar*⌝-*wa-da* ⌜*i*⌝-*na a-ṣí* ÉRIN.MEŠ
19) ⌜*pí*⌝-*ṭá-ti ka-li* ⌜*mi*⌝(?)-*am* ^{I}ÌR-*A-ši-ir-t*[*a*]
20) *it-ti-šu-nu la-a la-qí ù* ⌜GIŠ⌝.⌜MÁ⌝.⌜MEŠ⌝-*šu*-⌜*nu*⌝
21) *a-ṣa ki-ma ki-ti iš-tu* KUR *Mi-iṣ-ri*
22) *ki-na-na la-a ti-pa*-⌜*li*⌝-*ḫu-na*
23) ⌜*a*⌝-*nu-ma la*-⌜*qú*⌝ ⌜URU⌝ *Ul*-⌜*la*⌝-*sà ù*
24) URU *Ṣu-mu*-⌜*ra*⌝ *tu-ba-ú-na la*-⌜*qa*⌝
25) ⌜*ù*⌝ ⌜*ka*⌝-⌜*li*⌝ ⌜*mi*⌝-*im-mi* ^{I}ÌR-*A-ši-ir*-[*ta*]
26) ⌜*na*⌝-⌜*ad*⌝-*nu a*-⌜*na*⌝ [DU]MU.MEŠ *ù* ⌜*i*⌝-*na-na*
27) ⌜*da*⌝-*an-nu ù* GIŠ.MÁ.MEŠ LÚ.MEŠ *mi-ši*
28) ⌜*la*⌝-*qú qa-du mi-im-mi-šu-nu*
29) ⌜*ù*⌝ *a-na*-⌜*ku*⌝ *la-a i-le-ú*
30) *a-la- ka*$_{13}$ *a-na til-la-ti*
31) *a-na* ⌜URU⌝ *Ṣu-mu*-⌜*ra*⌝ ^{I}⌜*I*⌝*a-pa*- ^{d}IŠKUR
32) *nu*-KUR *it-ti-ia* ⌜UGU⌝ *mi*-⌜*im*⌝-*mi*[-*ia*]
33) *ša-a it-ta-šu ni-te*-⌜*pu*⌝-⌜*uš*⌝

EA 105

TRANSLATION

(1–5) [Ri]b-Hadda spoke to [his] lord, the great [king], king of he lands, the king of batt[le; may the Lady of Byblos grant s[trength] to the king, my lord; at the feet of my lord, my sun god, seven times (and) seven times have I fallen.

(6–13) Furthermore, may the king take council concerning the city of Ṣumur. Look, as for the city of Ṣumur, like a bird put inside a cage, thus is the city of Ṣumur. The sons of ʿAbdi-Ashirta from the land and the men of the city of Arvad from the sea, day and night they are against it.

(14–22) So I sent three ships [to] Ya[nḫa]mu [and the ships of] the men of the city of Arvad were (there) to capture th[em] and they came forth. Look, as for the men of the city of Arvad, with the withdrawal of the regular army troops, all the property of ʿAbdi-Ashirta was not taken from them so their ships came forth from Egypt by consent. Thus they are not afraid.

(23–31) Now they have taken the city of Ullasa and they are trying to take the city of Ṣumur and all the property of ʿAbdi-Ashirta was given to the sons so now they are strong and they even took the ships of the expeditionary force with their supplies. So I am unable to go to the aid of the city of Ṣumur.

(31–33) Yapʿ-Hadda is hostile to me because of [my] property that is with him. Let us put the

34) *di-na a-na pa-ni* ^{I}*A-*⸢*ma*⸣*-an-*[*ma-š*]*a*
35) *ù* ^{I}DUMU-*Pí-ḫa-a ù a-*[*na*] ⸢*pa*⸣*-*⸢*ni*⸣
36) ^{I}⸢*Ia*⸣*-an-ḫa-mi ù ti-du*
37) ⸢*šu*⸣*-nu ki-ti-ia* UGU *mi*(?)*-*⸢*im*⸣*-*⸢*mi*⸣*-*⸢*ia*⸣
38) UGU *ma-id* ⸢*mi*⸣*-im-mi-ia*
39) ⸢*it*⸣*-ta-šu* ⸢*ki*⸣*-*[*na*]*-na i-te-pu-*[*u*]*š*
Lo.ed. 40) [*nu*]-KÚR *a-*⸢*na*⸣ *ia-ši ù i-nu-ma eš-me*
41) [*ṣa-bat*] URU *Ul-la-sà ù aš-ta-pár*
42) x-*mi a-na ša-a-šu* ⸢*ù*⸣
Rev. 43) ⸢*yi*⸣*-*⸢*iš*⸣*-*⸢*ta*⸣*-*⸢*ḫa*⸣*-*⸢*at*⸣ [*iš*]*-*⸢*tu*⸣ ⸢2⸣ ⸢DUMU⸣.⸢MEŠ⸣(?)
44) ⸢*ù*⸣ *la-*⸢*qa*⸣ [*................it-ti*] ⸢*ša*⸣*-šu-ni*
45) ⸢*i*⸣*-*⸢*te*⸣*-*⸢*pu*⸣*-*⸢*uš*⸣ [*nu*-KUR *it-*]*ti-ia*
46) UGU *m*[*i-im-mi-ia............a-*]*ia-ba-ši*$_x$(*ŠE*)
47) ⸢*a*⸣*-*⸢*na*⸣ *la-*⸢*qí*⸣ [ŠE-*IM a-na a-ka-li i*]*š-tu*
48) ⸢KUR⸣ ⸢*Ia*⸣*-*[*ri-mu-ta ù la-a a-*]*mu-tu*

(34–48) case before Aman-[mašš]a and Bin-Piḫa and before Yanḥamu and so that they will know my rights concerning my property. Because my property that is with him is considerable, thus he became hostile to me. And when I heard about [the capture] of Ullasa I wrote [...] to him but he was intimidated(?) by the two sons so he took [...with] the two of them and he became [hostile t]o me because of [my] p[roperty...]its[e]nemy to take [grain for consumption fr]om the land of [Yarimuta so that I would not d]ie.

49) [……………………URU *Ṣu-mu-*]*ra*
50) [……………………………………]
51) [……………………………………]
52) [……………………………………]*ši-ia*
53) [……………………………………]*nu*
54) [……………………………………]
55) [……………………………………]
56) [……………………………*uš-ši*]*ir-ti*
57) [……………………………………]
58) [……………………………………]
59) […………………………………*r*]*u-ti-ia*
60) [……………………………………]˹A˺ ˹*me*˺
61) […………………………………*r*]*u-t*[*i-i*]*a*
62) [……………………………………]*a-na* ˹*ša*˺*-šu*
63) [……………………………………]
64) [……………………………………]
65) [……………………………………]
66) [……………………………………*it-ti-šu-nu*
67) [……………………………………]
68) [……………………………………]
69) [……………………………………]
70) [……………………………………]
71) [……………………………………]*ia*
72) U[GU……………………………………]
73) [……………………………………]
74) [……………………L]Ú.MEŠ GAZ.MEŠ
75) […………………………^{I}*Ia-*]*pa-*^{d}IŠKUR
76) [……………………………………]*im-mi-ia*(!)
77) [……………………………URU *I-b*]*ir*$_{5}$*-ta.*
78) [……………………………………]
Up.ed. 79) [*lu-wa-š*]*i-r*[*a*……………………………]
80) [*ù n*]*i-pu-uš di-*˹*na*˺ *i-na* [*pa-ni-šu-nu*]
81) [*ka-*]*li mi-im-mi-*[*i*]*a ša-*[*a*]
82) [*it-*]*ta-šu yu-ul-qé a-*[*na*] LU[GAL]

(49–78) (*Impossible to read; some signs at the ends of lines but no connected text.*)

(79–82) [May he se]nd [.........that w]e may present the case be[fore them. Let a]ll [m]y property that is [wi]th him be taken for the ki[ng].

Lft.ed. 83) ˹*ù*˺ *yi-ib-lu-uṭ* ÌR *ki-t*[*i*] ˹*a*˺-*na šàr-ri* ˹LÚ˺.MEŠ KUR *Mi-iṣ-*˹*ri*˺

84) [*š*]*a a-ṣa iš-tu* URU *Ul-la-sà* [*a*]-*nu-ma it-ti-ia šu-nu ù* ˹*i*˺*a-n*[*u*]

85) [ŠE-*I*]*M a-na a-ka-li-šu-nu* ^{I}*I*[*a*]-*pa*-^{d}IŠKUR *la-a* ˹*i*˺*a-di-nu* GIŠ.MÁ.MEŠ-*ia*

86) [*a-n*]*a* KUR *Ia-ri-mu-ta* ˹*ù*˺ *uš-ša-ar-šu-nu a-na* URU ˹*Ṣu*˺-*mu-r*[*a*]

87) ˹*la*˺-*a i-le-*˹*ú*˺ [*aš-š*]*um* GIŠ.MÁ.˹MEŠ˺ URU *Ar-*˹*wa*˺-˹*da*˺ ˹*al*˺-*lu-ú*

88) *ia-aq-bu a*[-*na ša-šu* ^{I}*R*]*i-ib*[-^{d}IŠKUR] ˹*la*˺-˹*qa*˺-˹*šu*˺ ˹*ki*˺-[*na-na* UGU-*ia*

89) [……………]traces [………………]

(83–88) and let the faithful servant live for the king. The men of the land of Egypt who came forth from the city of Ullasa [n]ow are with me but there is no [grai]n for them to eat. Yapaʿ-Hadda does not let my ships (go) to the land of Yarimuta and to send them to Ṣumur I am not able [bec]ause of the ships of the city of Arvad. Behold, he says t[o him] "[R]ib-[Hadda] has taken it. Th]us he is against me." [....].

EA 106

TRANSCRIPTION

Obv. 01) ^{I}*Ri-ib*-^{d}IŠKUR *iq-bi* ⸢*a*⸣-[*na*]
02) *šàr-ri* KUR.KI.ḪI.A *a-na* GÌR.ME[Š BAD-*ia šàr-r*]*i*
03) 7-*šu ù* 7-*ta-a-an am*-[*qú-ut iš-tu*] *da-ri-ti*
04) [*a*]-*mur* URU *Gub-la* URU *ki-it-t*[*i ša*]
05) [*b*]*e-li-ia* ^{d}UTU KUR.KUR.KI.DIDLI ⸢*ù*⸣
06) [*a*]-*mur a-na-ku* GIŠ.GÌR.GUB *ša* GÌR.MEŠ-⸢*pí*⸣
07) LUGAL BAD-*ia a-na-ku ù* ÌR *ki-it-ti-šu*
08) *a-nu-ma* URU *Ṣu-mu-ur nu-kùr-tu*$_4$^{MEŠ} *ma-gal*
09) KAL.GA UGU-*ši ù* UGU-*ia* KAL.GA-*at*
10) *ù a-nu-ma i-na-an-na ši-iḫ-ṭá-at*
11) URU *Ṣu-mu-ur a-di a-bu-li-ši*
12) *ša-ḫa-aṭ-ši i-le-ú ù ṣa-bat-ši*
13) *la i-le-ú šá-ni-tam a-na mi-ni*$_7$
14) *yi-iš-tap-ru* ^{I}*Ri-ib*-^{d}IŠKUR *ki-na-an-na-ma*
15) *ṭup-pa a-na* É.GAL *ma-an-ga iš-tu a-ḫi-šu*^{MEŠ}
16) UGU URU *Ṣu-mu-ur a-mur a-na-ku*
17) *nu-kúr-tu*$_4$ UGU-*ia* 5 MU.MEŠ *ù ki-na-an-na*
18) ⸢*iš*⸣-[*tap*]-*ru a-na* BAD-*ia a-mur a-na-ku ú-u*[*l*]
19) *k*[*i-ma*] ⸢^{I}⸣*Ia-pa-á*ʾ-^{d}IŠKUR *ù ú-ul k*[*i-ma*]
20) [^{I}*Zi-i*]*m-re-da gáb-bi* ŠEŠ.MEŠ *pa-a*[*ṭ-ru*]
21) [UG]U-*ia nu-kùr-tu*$_4$ UGU URU *Ṣu-mu*-[*ur*]
22) ⸢*ù*⸣ *a-nu-ma i-na-an-na mi-it* LÚ MÁ[ŠKI]M-*ši*
23) ⸢*ù*⸣*a-nu-ma a-na-ku i-na-an-na* ⸢*mar*⸣-⸢*ṣa*⸣-⸢*ku*⸣
24) ⸢*ù*⸣ *i-ba-ša-ti i-n*[*a* URU *Ṣu-mu-ur*]

Lo.ed. 25) [*ù gá*]*b-bi* LÚ.MEŠ-*ši in*$_4$-[*na-bi-tu*]
26) [*ù lu-*]*wa-ši-ra be-li* [LÚ.MÁŠKIM]
27) [*ù* ERÍN.]MEŠ *it-ti-šu ki*[-*ma ar-ḫi-iš*]

EA 106

TRANSLATION

(1–7) Rib-Hadda spoke t[o] the king of the lands: at the feet [of my lord the kin]g, seven times and seven times have I [fallen. From] of old, behold, the city of Byblos is the loyal city [of] my [lo]rd, the sun god of the lands and [be]hold, as for me, the footstool of the feet of the king, my lord, am I, and his loyal servant.

(8–13) Now, as for Ṣumur, the hostility is very strong against it and against me is it strong. And right now Ṣumur is besieged up to its city gate. They are able to besiege it but they are unable to conquer it.

(13–27) Furthermore, "Why does Rib-Hadda keep sending a tablet to the palace in this manner? He is more distraught (stressed out) over Ṣumur than his colleagues (brothers)!" Look, as for me, there has been hostility against me for five years so thus I keep writing to my lord. Look, I am not li[ke] Yapaʿ-Hadda and not l[ike Zi]mredda; all the colleagues have dese[rted]. Against me there is hostility because of the city of Ṣumur and just now its com[miss]ioner has died and even now ⌜I am sick⌝. But I was in [the city of Ṣumur and a]ll its personnel fl[ed. So may] my lord send [a commissioner and troop]s with him with ut[most haste].

Rev. 28) [*ù li-iṣ*]-⸢*ṣur*⸣-*ši ù a-na-ku la* ⸢*iṣ*⸣[-*ṣu-ru-ši*]
29) [*i*]-⸢*na*⸣-*mu-uš-mi bi-ri-šu-ni ša* [UGU-*ia*]
30) *ù ki-i i-qa-bu* LUGAL *a-na mi-ni*$_{7}$ *iš-tap-r*[*u*]
31) ^{I}*Ri-ib*-^{d}IŠKUR *ṭup-pa a-na ma-ḫar be-li-š*[*u*]
32) UGU *lu-um-ni ša pa-na-nu-um i-né-p*[*u-uš*]
33) *ù a-nu-ma i-na-an-na la i-né-pu*-[*šu*]
34) *ki-šu-ma i-na-an-na a-na ia-a-ši*
35) *šá-ni-tam li-it-ri-iṣ a-na pa-ni be-l*[*i-ia*]
36) *ù lu-wa-ši-ra* ^{I}*Ia-an-ḫa-ma*
37) *i-na* LÚ.MÁŠKIM-*ši* ^{I}*Ia -an-ḫa-ma*
38) *mu-ṣa-li-ìl* LUGAL *be-li-ia i-še*$_{20}$-*mé*
39) *iš-tu* UZU.KA LÚ.MEŠ-*tu*$_{4}$ LÚ *em-qú šu-ut*
40) *ù gáb-bi* LÚ.MEŠ *i-ra-ʾa* $_{4}$-*mu-šu*
41) *šá-ni-tam li-it*-‹*ri*›-*iṣ a-na be*-EN-*ia*
42) *ù lu-wa-ši-ra* 20 *tap-pal ša* SIG$_{5}$-*qú*
43) ANŠE.KUR.RA *a-na* ÌR-*šu ma-du* LÚ.MEŠ
44) *it-ti-ia aš-šum-ma a-la-ki-ia*
45) *a-na nu-kúr-ti*^{MEŠ} LUGAL BAD-*ia šá-ni-tam*
46) *gáb-bi* URU.KI.ḪI.A-*ia ša i-qa-bi a-na pa-ni* BAD-*ia*
47) *i-de be-li šum-ma ta-ru i-na u*$_{4}$-*m*[*i*]
48) *pa-ṭá-ar* ÉRIN.MEŠ KI.KAL.KASKAL.KUR! *be-li*-[*ia*]
49) *na-ak-ru gáb-bu*

(28–34) and [may he] protect it. But I am not pro[tecting it]. I got out from between the two of them (the brothers) who were [against me]. So why does the king say, "Why does Rib-Hadda keep send[ing] a tablet to his lord about some evil that was do[ne] in the past?" But right now isn't the same thing being done, now, to me?

(35–40) Furthermore, may it please [my] lo[rd] that he send Yanḫamu as its commissioner, Yanḫamu the parasol bearer of the king, my lord. I have heard it said by the men that he is a wise man and that everyone loves him.

(41–45) Furthermore, may it pl[ea]se my lord and may he send twenty pairs of horses to his servant—many are the men with me—in order that I may go forth to the battles of the king, my lord.

(45–49) Furthermore, as for all of my towns of which I spoke to my lord, my lord knows if they have returned. On the day that the expeditionary force of [my] lord withdrew, they all became hostile.

EA 107

TRANSCRIPTION

Obv. 01) [^{I}]*Ri-ib-*^{d}IŠKUR *iq-b*[*i*]
02) *a-na* EN-*li šàr* KUR.KUR.KI.MEŠ
03) LUGAL.GAL *šàr ta-am-ḫa-ra*
04) ^{d}NIN *ša* ⸢URU⸣ *Gub-*⸢*la*⸣
05) *ti-di-in*$_{4}$ GA.KAL *a-na* LU[GAL]
06) EN-*ia a-na* GÌR.MEŠ EN-*ia*
07) ^{d}UTU-*ia 7-šu 7-ta-an*
08) *am-qú-ut a-mur* ⸢*a*⸣*-na-ku*
09) ÌR *ki-ti šàr-ri* ^{d}UTU
10) *ù pu-ia a-wa-te*^{MEŠ} *aq-bu*
11) *a-na šàr-ri ki-ta-ma yi-ìš-me*
12) *šàr-ru* EN-*li a-wa-te*^{MEŠ}
13) ÌR *ki-ti-šu ù*
14) *yi-zi-iz* ^{I}*iḫ-ri-pí*
15) *i-na* URU *Ṣu-mu-ra*
16) *ù li-qé* ^{I}*Ḫa-ip*
17) *a-na mu-ḫi-ka ù*
18) *da-gal-šu ù*
19) ⸢*li*⸣*-ma-ad a-wa-*[*te*^{MEŠ}*-šu*]
Lo.ed. 20) ⸢*ù*⸣ *šum-*⸢*ma*⸣ ⸢*da*⸣*-mi-i*[*q*]
21) *i-na pa-ni-ka ù*
Rev. 22) ⸢*šu*⸣*-ku-un i-na*
23) LÚ.MÁŠKIM-*ši* DUGUD *i-*[*na*]
24) ⸢*pa*⸣*-ni* LÚ.MEŠ *ḫa-za-nu-ti* LU[GAL]

EA 107

TRANSLATION

(1–8) Rib-Hadda spoke to the lord, king of the lands, the great king, the king of battle: May the Lady of Byblos grant strength to the ki[ng], my lord; at the feet of my lord, my sun god, seven times (and) seven times have I fallen.

(8–24) Look, I am a loyal servant of the king, the sun god, and as for my mouth I always speak words of truth to the king. May the king, my lord, heed the words of his loyal servant in order that an army commander may take up his post in the town of Ṣumur, and bring Ḥaʿpi to you and interrogate him and learn what he has to say. And if it is pleasing in your sight, then appoint a commissioner respected by the city rulers of the ki[ng].

25) *ù yi-iš me* EN‹*-li*› *a-wa-*[*te-ia*]
26) *a-nu-ma* ^{I}*A-zi-ru* DUMU
27) ^{I}ÌR-*A-ši-ir-ta qa-du*
28) ŠEŠ.MEŠ-*šu i-na* URU *Du-ma-aš-qa*
29) *ù uš-ši-ra* ÉRIN.MEŠ
30) *pí-ṭá-ti ù ti-ìl-qé-šu*
31) *ù ta-ap-šu-uḫ* KUR LUGAL
32) *ù šum-ma ki-a-ma i-*⸢*ba*⸣*-šu*
33) *ù la-a ti-zi-za*
34) URU ⸢*Ṣu*⸣*-mu-ra ša-ni-tam*
35) *yi-ìš-mé šàr-ru* EN-*li*
36) *a-wa-te* ÌR *ki-ti-šu*
37) *ia-nu* KÙ.BABBAR.MEŠ *a-na na-da-ni*
38) *a-na* ANŠE.KUR.RA *ga-mi-ir*
39) *gáb-bu i-na* ZI-*nu ù*
40) ⸢*id*⸣*-na-ni* 30 *ta-pal*
41) [A]NŠE.KUR.RA *qa-du* GIŠ.GIGIR.M[EŠ]
Up.ed. 42) [*i-*]*ba-šu*⸢LÚ⸣.MEŠ ⸢KEŠDA⸣
43) [\]⸢*mar*⸣*-ia-nu-ma a-na i-a-ši*
44) ⸢*ù*⸣ *ia-nu* AN[ŠE].KUR.RA
Lft.ed 45) [*a-na*] *ia-ši a-*⸢*na*⸣ *a-*⸢*la*⸣*-ki a-na*
46) ⸢*a*⸣-⸢*na*⸣ *nu-*KÚR LUGAL *ki-na-na-ma*
47) ⸢*pal*⸣*-*⸢*ḫa*⸣*-ti ù ki-na-na* ⸢*la*⸣*-*⸢*a*⸣
48) ⸢*al*⸣*-*⸢*ka*⸣*-ti a-na* URU ⸢*Ṣu*⸣*-*⸢*mu*⸣*-*⸢*ra*⸣

(25–34) And may the ‹my› lord heed [my] wor[ds]: Now ʿAziru son of ʿAbdi-ʾAshirta, with his brothers, is in Damascus! So send the regular army in order that it may capture him so that the land of the king may be at peace. But if thus they remain, then Ṣumur will not be able to stand.

(34–48) Furthermore, may the king heed the words of his loyal servant: There is no silver to pay for horses. Everything is used up for our sustenance! So give me 30 teams of horses with chariots. I have warriors (*mariannu*), but I don't have horses in order to go to the king's war. So therefore, I was afraid and therefore I did not go to Ṣumur.

EA 108

TRANSCRIPTION

Obv. 01) ⸢{I}⸣⸢*Ri*⸣-*ib*-{d}IŠKUR *iš-ta-pár*
02) *a-na* EN-*šu šàr* KUR.KUR.MEŠ.KI
03) LUGAL GAL *šàr ta-am-ḫa-ra*
04) {d}⸢NIN⸣ *ša* URU *Gub-la ti-di-in*$_4$
05) KAL.GA *a-na šàr-ri* EN-*ia*
06) *a-na* GÌR.MEŠ EN-*ia* {d}UTU-*ia*
07) 7-*šu* 7-*ta-an am-qú-ut*
08) *ša-ni-tam da*-⸢*mi*⸣-⸢*iq*⸣ *i-na pa-ni*
09) *šàr-ri ša ki-ma* {d}IŠKUR
10) ⸢*ù*⸣ {d}UTU *i-na ša-me i-ba-ši*
11) ⸢*ù*⸣ *ti-pu-šu-na* DUMU.MEŠ
12) {I}ÌR-*A-ši-ir-ta ki*-⸢*ma*⸣
13) ⸢*lìb*⸣-*bi-šu*-⸢*nu*⸣ *la -qú* ANŠE.KUR.RA.MEŠ
14) ⸢*šàr*⸣-*ri ù* GIŠ.GIGIR.MEŠ *ù*
15) *na-ad-nu* LÚ.MEŠ KEŠDA \ ši-ir-*ma*
16) *ù* LÚ.MEŠ *wi-i-ma a-na*
17) ›*a-na*‹ KUR *Su-‹ba›-ri i-na lu-qi*
18) *i-na* UD. KAM{v}.MEŠ *ša-a ma-ni*
19) *a-pí-ìš ip-šu an-nu-ú*
20) *i-na-na yu-qa-bu a-wa-tu*
21) *ša-ru-tu i-na pa-ni šàr-ri*
22) {d}UTU *a-na-ku* ÌR *ki-ti-ka*
23) *ù a-wa-ta ša-a i-de*
24) *ù ša-a eš-te-me aš-pu-r*[*u*]
25) *a-na šàr-ri* EN-*ia mi*-⸢*i*⸣[*a-mi*]
26) *šu-nu* UR.GI$_7$ *ù ti-z*[*i-zu-na*]
27) *i-na pa-ni* ÉRIN.MEŠ *pí-ṭ*[*á-ti*]
28) *šàr-ri* {d}UTU *aš-ta-pár* ›*a*[-*na*]‹
29) *a-na a-bi-ka ù yi*-[*iš-me*]
30) ⸢*a*⸣-⸢*wa*⸣-⸢*te*⸣-*ia ù*

Lo.ed. 31) *yu*[-*wa-ši*-]*ra* ⸢ÉRIN.MEŠ⸣.MEŠ
32) *pí-ṭ*[*á-t*]*i ú-ul la-qí*

Rev. 33) ⸢{I}⸣ÌR-⸢*A*⸣-*ši-ir-ta a-na š*[*a-šu*]

EA 108

TRANSLATION

(1–7) Rib-Hadda wrote to his lord, king of the lands, the great king, king of battle. May the Lady of Byblos grant strength to the king, my lord. At the feet of my lord, my sun god, seven times and seven times have I fallen.

(8–19) Furthermore, is it good in the sight of the king, who is like Baal and the sun god in heaven, that the sons of ʿAbdi-Ashirta are doing whatever they please? They have taken the horses of the king and the chariots and they have given chariot warriors and soldiers to the land of Su‹ba›ru as *hostages*(?). In whose days has a deed like this been done?

(20–28) Now a false message is being spoken in the presence of the king, the sun god. I am your loyal servant and the word that I know and which I have heard, I write to the king, my lord. Wh[o] are they, the dog(s) that they could st[and up]to the regular tr[oops] of the king, the sun god?

(28–33) I wrote to your father and he he[eded] my words and he se[nt] regular troops. Did he not take ʿAbdi-Ashirta for hi[mself]?

34) *ša-ni-tam šum-ma* LÚ.MEŠ
35) *ḫa-za-nu-tu*$_4$ *la-a na-a*[*d-nu*]
36) *pa-ni-šu-nu a-na mu-ḫi-š*[*u-nu*]
37) *ù ki-na-na da-an-n*[*u*]
38) *šu-nu ù* LÚ.MEŠ *mi-ši*
39) *tu-ba-lu-na ḫi-ši-iḫ-t*[*a-šu-nu*]
40) *ki-na-na la-a pal-ḫ*[*u*]
41) LÚ.GAL *i-nu-ma la-qú* ANŠE.[KUR.RA.MEŠ]
42) *ù* KAL.GA *i-na pa-ni-šu-nu*
43) *i-nu-ma ni-de ù* KAL.GA *ù*
44) *ni-iq-‹bi› a-na* LUGAL KAL.GA-*mì*
45) *al-lu-ú la-a ti-le-ú-na*
46) *i-nu-ma uš-ši-ir-ti* 2 LÚ
47) DUMU *ši-ip-ri a-na* URU *Ṣu-mu-*⌜*ra*⌝
48) *ù ú-ka-li* LÚ.*lí*
49) *an-nu-ú a-na šu-te-er*
50) ⌜*a*⌝*-wa-ti a-na šàr-ri ša-ni-tam*
51) *a-na mi-ni ti-ìš-mu-na*
52) LÚ.MEŠ *ša-nu-tu mu-*⌜*ša*⌝
53) *tu-ba-lu-na ù mu-šå*
54) *tu-te-ru-na* LÚ.MEŠ
55) DUMU *ši-ip-ri ša-a šàr-ri*
56) *iš-tu pa-ni* UR.GI$_7$ *šum-ma*
57) *lìb-bi šà*[*r-r*]*i* ^{d}UTU *i-na*
58) UD. KAM^{v}.MEŠ ⌜*tu*⌝*-ul-qú-na*
59) *ša-ni-tam* ⌜*ú*⌝-⌜*ul*⌝ ⌜*ia*⌝*-aš-ku-un*
60) *lum-ni-*[*ia i-*]*na lìb-bi-k*[*a*] ›⌜*ka*⌝‹
61) *ù pa*[*-ṭá-*]⌜*ar*⌝⌜*ù*⌝ LÚ *an*[*-nu-ú*]
Up.ed. 62) *al-ku* LÚ.MEŠ ⌜SA⌝.GAZ.MEŠ
63) *iš-tu* URU *Ṣu-mu-r*[*a*]
64) *a-na ṣa-ba-ti-šu*
Lft.ed 65) *ù la-a na-ad-na-ti-šu ù yi-ì*[*š-me*]
66) *šàr-ru a-wa-te* ÌR-*šu ù uš-ši-ra*
67) ⌜20⌝ LÚ.MEŠ KUR *Mé-lu-ḫa* 20 LÚ.MEŠ KUR *Mi-iṣ-ri-*⌜*i*⌝
68) *a-na na-ṣa-*⌜*ri*⌝ URU *a-na šà*[*r-r*]*i*
69) ^{d}UTU ⌜EN⌝-*ia* ⌜ÌR⌝ *ki-ti-*⌜*ka*⌝

(34–45) Furthermore, since the city rulers did not tu[rn] their faces against them, thus, they are strong. And the expeditionary force was bringing them all [their] needs. Thus they did not fear the senior official when they took the hor[ses]. And they are bold. When we became aware that they were strong, then we sp[oke] to the king, "They are strong." Behold, they are not really able.

(46–58) When I sent two diplomats to the city of Ṣumur, then I kept this man back in order to send a reply to the king.

(50–58) Furthermore, Why are other men listened to? (or: Why do you listen to other men?). At night they bring and at night they return the emissaries of the king, because of the dog(s). If the k[in]g, the sun god, wants to, in a day they can be taken.

(59–69) Furthermore, may he (the king) not harbor evil thoughts in your heart about me. Then he de[par]ted; and as for th[is] man, the *ʿapîru* men came from the city of Ṣumur in order to seize him but I did not give him over. So may the king he[ed] the words of his servant and send twenty men from the country of Meluḫḫa (and) twenty men of the land of Egypt to guard the city for the king, the sun god, my lord, (and) your loyal servant.

EA 109

TRANSCRIPTION

Obv. 01) [^{I}]⸢*Ri*⸣-*ib*-^{d}IŠKUR [*iq-bi a-na*] ⸢LUGAL⸣ ⸢EN⸣-⸢*šu*⸣
02) *šàr* KUR.MEŠ LUGAL [GAL] ^{d}NIN *ša* URU *Gub*-⸢*la*⸣
03) *ti-di-in*$_{4}$ K[A]L.GA *a-na* LUGAL EN-*ia*
04) *a-na* GÌR.MEŠ EN-*ia* ^{d}UTU-*ia* 7-*šu*
05) 7-*ta-an* ⸢*am*⸣-*qú-ut pa-na-nu*
06) [*šà*]*r* KUR *Mi*-⸢*ta*⸣-*na nu*-KÚR *a-na a-bu-ti-ka*
07) ⸢*ù*⸣ *la-a yi-na-mu-šu*-⸢*na*⸣
08) [*a*]-*bu-tu*-⸢*ka*⸣ *iš-tu* ⸢*a*⸣-*b*[*u-ti-ia*]
09) ⸢*ù*⸣ *an-nu-ú* ⸢DUMU⸣.MEŠ [Ì]R-*A-ši-ir-ta*
10) [Ì]R UR.GI$_{7}$ [*la-qú*] URU.MEŠ *šàr-ri ù*
11) [URU.]⸢KI⸣.MEŠ ⸢*ḫa*⸣-[*za*]-*ni-šu ki-ma lì-bi-šu-nu*
12) [URU *Ir-qa-*]*ta a-na ša-šu-nu*
13) [*la-qé*] *šu-nu ù qa-la-ta*
14) [*a-na ip-ši-š*]*u-nu i-nu-ma ti-iš-me*
15) [*ù* URU *Ú-l*]*a-sà la-qù a-na-ku aq-bu*
16) [*šum-ma* UD.K]AM^{v}.MEŠ *yi-iš-mu šàr-ru*
17) [*ù* UD].KAM^{v}.MEŠ *yi-ìl-te*$_{9}$-*qú-šu-nu*
18) [*ù šum-*]*ma mu-ša yi-iš*-⸢*mu*⸣ *ù*
19) [*mu-š*]*a yi-ìl-te*$_{9}$-*qú-šu-nu ki-na-*[*na*]
20) [*aq-b*]*u a-na-ku i-na lìb-bi-ia la-q*[*ú*]
21) [KAL.G]A LÚ.MEŠ *ḫa-za-ni-ka ù* L[Ú.MEŠ KEŠDA]
22) [GIŠ.GIGI]R.MEŠ-*ka ù* LÚ.MEŠ *we-e-*[*ma la-q*]*ú*
23) ⸢*ù*⸣ *qa-la-ta ki-na-na ka-y*[*a-nu i-na*]
24) [*lì*]*b-bi-šu-nu ù ar-na a*[*r-na-ma*]
25) [*t*]*u-ba*-⸢*ú*⸣-*na ù an-nu-ú nu*-[KÚR]
26) [*i*]*t-ti-ia ù ṣa-ab-t*[*u* 12 LÚ.MEŠ-*ia*]
27) ⸢*ù*⸣ *ra-ak-šu*-‹*šu*›-*nu i-na* ⸢É⸣ [*ki-li-*]
28) *šu-nu ù ša-ak-nu i*[*p-ṭe*$_{6}$-*ra*]
29) [*be*]-*ri-nu* 50 KÙ.BABBAR.MEŠ *ù* [...]
30) [*ù*] ⸢*la*⸣-⸢*qí*⸣-⸢*ti*⸣ *iš-tu* ⸢É⸣[^{d}NIN *ša* URU]
31) [*Gub-l*]*a* ⸢*ù*⸣ [12 LÚ].⸢MEŠ⸣

Lo.ed. 32) [*pa-aṭ-ra-ti*..................................]
33) [..]

EA 109

TRANSLATION

(1–5) Rib-Hadda [spoke to] the king, his lord, the king of the lands, the [great] king. May the Lady of the city of Byblos grant str[en]gth to the king, my lord. At the feet of my lord, my sun god, seven times (and) seven times have I fallen

(5–15) Formerly, the [ki]ng of the land of Mitanni was hostile to your fathers but your fathers did not desert [my] fath[ers]. But behold, the sons of ʿAbdi-Ashirta, the [sl]ave, the dog, [have taken] the cities of he king and [the ci]ties of his city ruler, as they please. [The city of ʿIrqa]ta belongs to them. They [took] (it) and you kept silent [about th]eir [deeds], when you heard. [So] they took [the city of Ul]lasa.

(15–25) As for me, I keep saying, "[If in a da]y the king will listen, [then in a d]ay he will take them. [And i]f] in a night, he heeds, then [in a nigh]t he will take them." Thu[s] I [have been say]ing in my heart. Th[ey] have taken the [for]ces of the city rulers and the [*maryannu*] me[n], your [chario]ts, and [they have tak]en the foot soldie[rs], but you have kept silent. Thus, they are firm in their resolve, so they are seeking to commit crime after crime.

(25–32) And behold, (they) are hos[tile t]o me and [they] seized [twelve of my men] and they bound ‹th›em in their pri[son] and they set a red[emption price be]tween us of fifty (shekels) of silver and [...so] I took from the temple of [the Lady of the city of Byblos and [I ransomed the twelve me]n. [...]

Rev. 34) [*ù qa-la-*]*t*[*a*] ⸢*a*⸣-[*na ip-ši-*]
35) [*šu-n*]*u ti-la-qú* ⸢URU⸣ *Ši-g*[*a-ta* ^{KI}]
36) ⸢*šu*⸣*-nu ša-ra-qú-ma ù* [*an-nu-ú*]
37) *i-de* ^{I}*Ia-an-ḫa-mu* LÚ [*ša uš-ši-ir*]
38) *šàr-ru ša-ak-nu-šu i-na* [KISLAḪ]
39) \ *tu-uḫ-nu ù* LÚ *we-a ti-d*[*i-nu*]
40) *i-na* KUR *Su-ba-ri i-na lu-qi*
41) *a-na a-ka-*⸢*li*⸣*-šu-nu a-mur*
42) *a-na-ku* ÌR ⸢*ki*⸣*-ti a-na šàr-ri* ⸢*ù*⸣
43) *ia-nu ki-*⸢*ma*⸣ *ia-ti-ia* ÌR *a-*[*na*]
44) *šàr-ri pa-na-nu da-ga-li-ma*
45) LÚ KUR ⸢*Mi*⸣*-*⸢*iṣ*⸣*-ri ù in*$_4$*-ab-tu*
46) [LUGAL.]MEŠ ⸢KUR⸣ *Ki-na-aḫ-ni iš-tu pa-*[*ni-šu*]
47) [*ù*] ⸢*an*⸣*-nu-ú* DUMU.MEŠ ^{I}ÌR-*A-ši-i*[*r-ta*]
48) [*ti-*]*da-‹ga›-lu-na* LÚ.MEŠ KUR *Mi-iṣ-ri* [*ki-ma*]
49) [UR.]GI$_7$.MEŠ *da-mi-iq mu-tu a-*[*na ia-*]⸢*ši*⸣
50) [*ù*] *iš-mu lum-‹na› a-na* EN-*ia ù*
51) [TI.LA] ⸢ZI⸣*-ia ka-li* DINGIR.MEŠ-*nu*
52) ⸢*ù*⸣ [^{d}NIN *š*]a URU *Gub-la* ^{KI}
53) ⸢TI⸣.LA *m*[*u-tu a-n*]*a* LÚ *ša-a yu-ba-ú*
54) *lum-na a-n*[*a*] E[N-*š*]*u šum-ma du-na du-na-ma*
55) *ú-ba-ú a-na-ku* ⸢*a*⸣*-*[*na*] ⸢EN⸣*-ia*
56) *ša-ni-tam la-a i-le-*⸢*ú*⸣ ⸢*šu*⸣*-*⸢*ri*⸣*-ib*
57) LÚ-*ka an-nu-ú a-na* URU ⸢*Ṣu*⸣*-*[*mu-r*]*a*
58) *ka-li* URU.MEŠ-*ia nu-*⸢KÚR⸣ *a-na* ⸢*ia*⸣*-*[*ši*]
59) *it-ti* DUMU.MEŠ ^{I}ÌR-*A-ši-ir-ta*
60) *ki-na-na da-nu ù* LÚ.MEŠ
61) ⸢*ḫa*⸣*-*⸢*za*⸣*-nu-tu* ⸢*ú*⸣*-*⸢*ul*⸣ ⸢*tar-ṣa it-ti-ia*

Up.ed. 62) ⸢*a*⸣*-*⸢*nu*⸣*-ma* ^{I}*Ḫa-*[*ya ù* ^{I}]⸢*A*⸣*-ma-an-ap-*[*pa*]
63) [*a*]*-ṣí iš-t*[*u* URU *Ṣu-*]*mu-ra*
64) ⸢*qa*⸣*-du* URUDU[.MEŠ *ù* KÙ.BABBAR.]MEŠ-*šu*
65) [.......................] traces [.........]

Lft.ed. 66) [..]
67) [..]
68) [............................*t*]*i-iq-t*[*a-bu-na*]
69) [............ÌR]*ki*[*-it-ti-šu a-*]*na-ku*

(34–41) [but] y[ou kept silent] re[garding the]ir [deeds]. They took the town of Shig[ata]. They are thieves! And [behold] Yanḫamu knows. The king [sent] a man; they put him in the [granary]: for millet. And they ga[ve] a foot soldier to the land of Subaru as a hostage for their food

(41–49) Look, I am a loyal servant of the king and there is no servant of the king like me. Formerly, on seeing a man of Egypt, [the king]s of the land of Canaan fled from bef[ore him]. [But] behold, the sons of ʿAbdi-Ashirt[a] loo‹k› at men of Egypt [as d]ogs.

(49–55) Death is better f[or m]e [than that] I should hear ev‹il› about my lord! And [as] my soul [lives, as our gods and [the Lady o]f the city of Byblos live, de[ath t]o the man that seeks evil fo[r hi]s lo[rd], since I myself seek more and more power f[or] my lord.

(56–61) Furthermore, I am unable to get your man into the city of Ṣu[mu]r. All of my cities are hos[tile] to me with the sons of ʿAbdi-Ashirta. Thus they are strong and the city rulers are not correct towards me.

(62–64) Now Ḫa[ya and] Amanappa [we]nt out fro[m the city of Ṣu]mur with the copper [and] its [silver(?)..................................]

(68–69) [......................t]hey are sa[ying..........a]lo[yal servant am] I.

EA 110

TRANSCRIPTION

Obv. 01) [*a-na* LUGAL EN]-⌜*ia*⌝ ⌜^{d}⌝[UTU-*ia*]
02) [*qí-bí-ma*]*um-ma* ^{I}*Ri*[-*ib*-^{d}IŠKUR]
03) [ÌR-*ka* ^{d}NIN] *ša-a* URU[*Gub-la*]
04) [*ti-di-in*$_{4}$ KA]L.GA *a-na* LU[GAL EN-*ia*]
05) [^{d}UTU-*ia a-n*]*a* GÌR.MEŠ ‹EN›-*ia*
06) [^{d}UTU-*ia* 7-]⌜*šu*⌝ ⌜7⌝-⌜*ta*⌝-⌜*an*⌝ *a*[*m-qut*]
07) [*a-na mi-ni qa-la*]-*ta* [*ù*]
08) [DUMU ^{I}ÌR-*A-ši*-]*ir-ta* [*ki-ma*]
09) [*lìb-bi-šu-nu ti-p*]*u-šu-na* [*ù la-qú*]
10) [URU.MEŠ-*ka gáb*-]⌜*bi*⌝-*šu*[-*nu*...]
11) [............*k*]*i-a*-[*ma*]
12) [...]
13) [...]
14) [...]
15) [...]
16) [...]
17) [...]
18) [...]
19) [...]
20) [.............................]DIŠ[.......]
21) [...........................ME]Š *k*[*i*.......]
22) [...........................*m*]*i-ma*[......]
23) [...............................]*ki-nu*[*a-na*]
24) [..............................*yu-k*]*al*-⌜*šu*⌝
25) [.....................................]-*ia*
26) [..............................*qa-la*]-*ta*
27) [...]
28) [...]
29) [...]
30) [...]
Lo.ed. 31) [...]

EA 110

TRANSLATION

(1–6) [Speak to the king, m]y[lord, my]s[un god;] the message of Ri[b-Hadda, your servant: may the lady] of the city of [Byblos grant str]ength to the ki[ng, my lord, my sun god; a]t the feet of my ‹lord›, [my sun god, seven] times (and) seven times have I [fallen].

(7–11) [Why do] you [keep silent while the sons of ʿAbdi-Ash]irta are doing [what they want? And they have taken all] your [cities…thus […].

(12–31) [……]property[….he with]holds it […] my [……]you [keep silent [……….]

Rev.
32) [..............................]
33) [...............................]
34) [........................] ᴵ*A*[-*zi-ru*]
35) [.................]-*na-da* L[UGAL]
36) [.........*la-a*(?) *i-r*]*a-a-mu-šu-n*[*u*]
37) [................*š*]*u-nu i-na ša-*[..]
38) [................*yi-*]*pu-šu ša aq-b*[*i*]
39) [.............]˹*šu*˺-*nu i-na er-ṣé-*˹*ti*˺
40) [................*m*]*i-na la-a yu-ṣú*
41) [...................*a-n*]*a* SAG.[DU]-*šu-nu*
42) [..........*la-a*(?) *i-r*]*a-am-šu-*[*nu*]
43) [...................]*i-na er-ṣé-*[*ti*]
44) [....*m*]*a*[.............] ᴵ*A-zi-r*[*u*]
45) [........................]˹*ù*˺ *la-a*
46) [....................]*šu um*[-*ma*]
47) [.........LÚ.MEŠ *mi-*]*ši-*˹*šu*˺-*n*[*u*]
48) [GIŠ.]˹MÁ˺ L[Ú.MEŠ *mi-*]*ši* ˹*la*˺[-*a*]
49) [*tu-*]*ṣa-n*[*a iš-t*]*u* KUR *Ki-n*[*a-aḫ-ḫi*]
50) [*a-na*] *mi-ni la ia-*˹*di*˺-*n*[*u*]
51) [*mi-i*]*m-mi* LUGAL *ša tu*[*-ba-lu-na*]
52) [GIŠ.MA.]MEŠ LÚ.MEŠ *mi-š*[*i*]
53) [LÚ.MEŠ] *ḫa-za-nu-tu* ˹*ù*˺[...]
54) [*tu-b*]*a-lu-na a-na* [..........]
55) [.............*lu-ú*]*yi-*˹*de*˺
56) [LUGAL EN-*ia*]˹*a*˺-˹*na*˺[......]
57) [............................]
58) [..........]˹*ša*˺[............]

(32–58) [.....]A[ziru.....] the k[ing.....]they (don't)? [lo]ve them[....] them in [.....he] is doing what I sai[d......]them in the land [...w]hy does he not come forth? [....o]n their he[ad...]they [(don't)? l]ove them [...] in the land [...]Azir[u...]and not[...] his, say[ing...the men of]their [fl]eet [a sh]ip of the [men of the fl]eet does no[t go] forth [fro]m the land of Cana[an. W]hy does he not give the king's [pro]perty which [the ship]s of the men of the fleet are br[inging]? [The] city rulers and [...] they are [br]inging [...so may the king, my lord] be apprised concerning [...]of[...]

EA 111

TRANSCRIPTION

Obv.	01)	[*a-na šàr*]-⸢*ri*⸣ ⸢EN⸣-⸢*ia*⸣ [^{d}UTU-*ia*]
	02)	[*qí-*]⸢*bí*⸣[*-ma*]
	03)	[*um-ma* ^{I}]⸢*Ri*⸣-⸢*ib*⸣-⸢^{d}⸣⸢IŠKUR⸣ [ÌR-*ka-ma*]
	04)	[*a-na* GÌR.MEŠ EN-*ia* ^{d}UTU-*ia*]
	05)	⸢7⸣-⸢*šu*⸣ ⸢7⸣-⸢*ta*⸣-⸢*an*⸣ [*am-qutI*]
	06)	⸢*a*⸣-⸢*nu*⸣-⸢*ma*⸣ ⸢*iš*⸣-[*ta-pa-ru*]
	07)	[*a-na*] ⸢É⸣(?).⸢GAL⸣(?) [*a*]-⸢*na*⸣ ⸢LÚ⸣(?).M[EŠ(?)]
	08)	[*ma*]-⸢*ṣa*⸣(?)-⸢*ar*⸣-⸢*ti*⸣ ⸢*ù*⸣[....]
	09)	[......................*ù*]
	10)	[*uš*]-⸢*ši*⸣-⸢*ra*⸣-⸢*ni*⸣-[*ma*]
	11)	[*x ta-pal*] ⸢ANŠE⸣.⸢KUR⸣.⸢RA⸣.[MEŠ]
	12)	[*ù* y ÉRIN.MEŠ GÌR.MEŠ....]
Lo.ed.	13)	[.........................]
	14)	[....................*a-na*]
Rev.	15)	⸢*na*⸣-⸢*ṣa*⸣-[*ri*] ⸢URU⸣(?) [LUGAL]
	16)	*a-na-ku ú*-⸢*ra*⸣-*d*[*a-am* LUGAL EN-*ia*]
	17)	\ *ba-lu* ⸢*ma*⸣-*nu*[...*šum-ma* MU. KAM^{v}]
	18)	⸢*an*⸣-⸢*ni*⸣-*ta ia-n*[*u* ÉRIN.MEŠ]
	19)	⸢*pí*⸣-*ṭá-ti ù* [*in*$_4$*-né-ep-šu*]
	20)	[*ka*]-*li* KUR.MEŠ *a-na* [LÚ.MEŠ]
	21)	[GA]Z.MEŠ *a*-⸢*mur*⸣ LÚ.MEŠ *m*[*i-ši*]
	22)	[*er*]-*bu i-na* URU *Ak*-[*ka*]
	23)	[*aš-šum*] *ba-li* ⸢*me*⸣-*e*[*m*]
	24)	⸢*ḫi*⸣-⸢*ši*⸣-⸢*iḫ*⸣-*ti* LUGAL [....]
	25)	[........] ⸢*a*⸣-⸢*na*⸣ ⸢*mi*⸣-⸢*ni*⸣(?)[....]
	26)	[....]⸢*lìb*⸣-*bu-ia* [.......]
	27)	[.....] ⸢*ú*⸣-⸢*ul*⸣[........]
	28)	[.....................]

EA 111

TRANSLATION

(1–5) [Sp]ea[k to the ki]ng, my lord, [my sun god; the message of] Rib-Hadda, [your servant. At the feet of my lord, my sun god,] seven times (and) seven times [have I fallen].

(6–17) Now, I have been w[riting to the] ⸢palace⸣(?) [con]cerning [ga]rrison troo[ps], but [..........so se]nd me [*x* teams of] horses [and *y* foot troops [..........to] protect the city [of the king.(?)]. I serve [the king, my lord] \ without? [...].

(17–21) [If] this [year] there are n[o] regular [troops], then [a]ll the lands [will join] the *'apîru* [men].

(21–27) Look, the men of the exped[tionary force] have [ent]ered into the city of Ac[co......] for lack of wa[ter.] The request of the king [...] Why [...] my heart [...] lest [...]

EA 112

TRANSCRIPTION

Obv. 01) [^{I}]⸢*Ri*⸣-⸢*ib*⸣[-^{d}IŠKUR *iš-ta-pár*]
02) [*a-n*]*a* EN-⸢*li*⸣-⸢*šu*⸣ *š*[*àr* KUR.KUR.MEŠ]
03) [LU]GAL GAL ^{d}NIN *ša* [URU *Gub-la*]
04) [*ti*]-*di-in*$_{4}$ KAL.GA *a-n*[*a* LUGAL]
05) [EN]-*ia a-na* GÌR.MEŠ E[N-*ia*]
06) [^{d}]UTU-*ia* 7-*šu* 7-*ta-an*
07) [*am*]-*qú-ut a-na mi-ni yi-iš*-⸢*ta*⸣-*pa-ru*
08) [*š*]*àr-ru* EN-*li a-na ia-ši*
09) *ú-ṣur-mi lu-ù na-ṣir-ta*
10) *iš-tu ma-an-ni i-na-ṣa-ru-na*
11) *iš-tu na-ak-ri-ia*
12) *ù iš-tu* LÚ.MEŠ *ḫu-up-ši-ia*
13) *mi-nu yi-na-ṣí-ra-an-ni*
14) *šum-ma* LUGAL ⸢*yi*⸣-⸢*na*⸣-⸢*ṣí*⸣-*ru*
15) ÌR-⸢*šu*⸣ [*ù ba-al-ṭá-*]*ti*
16) ⸢*ù*⸣ [*šum-m*]*a* [*š*]*à*[*r*]-⸢*ru*⸣ ⸢*la*⸣-⸢*a*⸣
17) [*yi*]-⸢*na*⸣-*ṣa-ru-ni mi-nu*
18) *yi-na-ṣí-ru-ni šum-ma*
19) *šàr-ru yu-wa-ši-ru-na* LÚ.MEŠ
20) KUR *Mi-iṣ-ri ù* KUR *Mi-lu-ḫa*
21) *ù* ANŠE.KUR.RA.MEŠ *a-na qa-at*
22) LÚ-*ia an-nu-ú* ⸢*ki*⸣-*ma*
23) *ar-ḫi-iš* ⸢*ù*⸣ *bal-ṭá-ti*
24) ⸢*a*⸣-*na a-ra-ad šàr-ri* EN-*ia*
25) [*š*]*um-ma ia-nu mi-im-ma*
26) [*a-n*]*a ia-ši a-na la-qé*

Lo.ed. 27) ⸢ANŠE⸣.KUR.RA.⸢MEŠ⸣ [*ga-m*]*i*-⸢*ir*⸣ *gá*[*b-b*]*i*
28) ⸢*i*⸣-⸢*na*⸣ *na-da*-⸢*ni*⸣ ⸢*i*⸣-⸢*na*⸣

Rev. 29) KUR *Ia-ri-mu*-⸢*ta*⸣ *i*-⸢*na*⸣
30) *ba-la*-⸢*aṭ*⸣ ZI-*ia šum*[-*ma*]

EA 112

TRANSLATION

(1–7) Rib-[Hadda wrote t]o his lord, k[ing of the lands], the great [ki]ng. May the lady of [the city of Byblos g]rant strength t[o the king], my [lord]. At the feet of [my] lo[rd,] my sun god, seven times (and) seven times have [I] fallen.

(7–13) Why does the [ki]ng, my lord, write to me: "Guard! May you be on guard!" From whom should I guard, from my enemies? And from my own yeomen farmers what (who) will protect me?

(14–30) If the king will protect his servant, [then will] I [live,] but [i]f the [k]ing will not protect me what (who) will protect me? If the king will send with utmost haste men of the land of Egypt and of the land of Meluḫḫa and horses (chariotry) in the charge of this man of mine, then I will live to serve the king, my lord. I do not [ha]ve anything to requisition horses (chariotry), (it is because) ev[eryth]ing is [used] up in paying to the land of Yarimuta for the sustenance of my life.

31) *lìb-bi ›bi‹ šàr-ri a-na*
32) *ba-la-aṭ* ÌR-*šu ù*
33) URU-*li-šu uš-ši-ra* ‹LÚ.MEŠ›
34) ⸢*ma*⸣-*ṣa-ar-ta ù*
35) ⸢*ti*⸣-*na-ṣa-ru* ⸢URU⸣-*ka ù*
36) ⸢ÌR⸣-*ka a-di* ⸢*yi*⸣-*du šàr-ru*
37) ⸢*a*⸣-⸢*na*⸣ KUR.MEŠ-*šu ù yu-wa-ši-ru*
38) ÉRIN.MEŠ ⸢*pí*⸣-⸢*ṭá*⸣-*ti-šu ù*
39) *yu-ša-ap-ši-*⸢*ḫu*⸣ KUR.⸢MEŠ⸣-*šu*
40) *da-mi-iq ki-a-ma* ⸢*pa*⸣-⸢*ni*⸣ ⸢LUGAL⸣
41) *i-na ša-pa-ri-ka a-*⸢*na*⸣ [Ì]R-*k*[*a*]
42) *šu-ri-ib-mi* ᴵ*Ḫa-ia a-na*
43) URU *Ṣu-mu-ra* 13 KÙ.BABBAR.MEŠ
44) 1 *ta-pal na-al-ba-ši*
45) *na-ad-na-ti ag-ru-ut*
46) LÚ GAZ *i-nu-ma šu-‹ri›-ib ṭup-pí*
47) *a-na* URU *Ṣu-mu-ra al-lu-mì*
48) ᴵ*Ḫa-ia ša-al-šu a-di*
49) *mu-ša šu-ri-ib a-na*
50) ›*a-na*‹ URU *Ṣu-mu-ra pa-na-nu*
51) *ba-lu-aṭ* LUGAL *i-ba-ši* ⸢UGU⸣-[*i*]*a*
52) *ù ni-di-nu ag-‹ru›-ut* LÚ
53) *ša ni-iš-pu-ru ù*
54) [*a-*]*nu-ú i-na-na ia-*[*nu*]
55) [*ba*]-⸢*la*⸣-*aṭ* LUGAL ⸢*ù*⸣ [*ia-nu*]
Up.ed. 56) [LÚ.MEŠ *ma-ṣa-a*]*r-ta* U[GU-*ia*]
57) [*ki-ma*] ⸢*a*⸣-⸢*bu*⸣[*ti-ia*]
Lft.ed 58) [...*an-n*]*u-ú ia-*[*nu*...] *ki-ma*
59) [...]*ši i-n*[*a*...]

(30–39) If the king desires the life of his servant and of his city, send garrison ‹troops› that they may protect your city and your servant until the king is apprised concerning his lands and sends his regular troops and pacifies his lands.

(40–50) It thus pleased the king when you wrote to yo[ur ser]vant, "Get Ḫaya into the city of Ṣumur." Thirteen (shekels) of silver and one pair of cloaks did I pay as the hire of an *ʿapîru* man when he brou‹gh›t my tablet into the city of Ṣumur. Here is Ḫaya, ask him. It was still night when he got him into ›into‹ the city of Ṣumur.

(50–59) Formerly, the king's logistic support was at [m]y disposal and we would pay the hire of the man whom we would send. But [be]hold, now there is [no] royal [logis]tic support and [there are no [garris]on [troops] at [my disposal as with my] fath[ers.…Beh]old, there is [no…]as [with…]

EA 113

TRANSCRIPTION

Obv. 01) ˹*ša*˺-*ni-ta*$_5$ [.........]
02) *la-a ti*-[*le-ú*..........]
03) *ù* LÚ *ḫa-za-na*-[*šu*...]
04) *ša-a-la aš-šum ḫa-z*[*a-ni*...]
05) *ša-ni ù ú-ul y*[*i-pu-šu*]
06) *ar-na ù ia-aš-ku*[-*n*]*u*
07) *i-na lìb-bi-šu al-lu-mi*
08) ^{I}*Ia-pa*-^{d}IŠKUR *i-t*[*e*$_9$-*p*]*u*-[*uš*]
09) *ar-na li-ma-ad* [*mi*]-[*na*]
10) *a-pa-aš šàr-ru a-na ša-a*-[*šu*]
11) *ša-ni-tam mi-na ip-ša-ti a*-[*na*]
12) ^{I}*Ia-pa*-^{d}IŠKUR *i-nu-ma yu-l*[*a-mi-nu*]
13) *lum-na lum-na-ma a-na ia*-[*ši*]
14) *a-nu-ma* 2 GIŠ.MÁ-*ia ḫa*-˹*ba*˺-˹*ta*˺ [GU$_4$.MEŠ]
15) ˹*ù*˺ ÙZ.MEŠ-*ia ù mi-im-mi-ia*
16) [*ma-i*]*d ma-gal it-ti-šu*
17) [*yu-wa*]-*ši-ra šàr-ru* LÚ.MÁŠKIM-*šu*
18) [*ù yu*-]*pa-ra-aš be-ri-ku*-[*n*]*i*
19) [*ka-li*] *mi-im-mi ša-a*
20) [*yu-ul*-]*qú iš-tu ša-a-šu* [LUGAL]
21) [*yi-ìl-qé*] UGU *m*[*i*-]*im-mi*-[*ia*]
22) [*ša-a*] *it-ti*-[*šu yi-ša-al* LUGAL]
Rev. 23) [*a-na* LÚ.]MEŠ-*ia* ˹*ka*˺-*l*[*i ša*]
24) [*iš-t*]*u* ^{I}*Ri-ib*-^{d}IŠKUR [*yu-ul-qa*]
25) [*ù*] *a-na* LÚ.MEŠ GAZ.MEŠ *n*[*a-din*]
26) [*gáb-b*]*a ù ia-nu ša-a*
27) [*yi-ìl*-]*qú mi-im-ma-šu iš-tu*
28) [GIŠ.MÁ]-*ia a-na mi-ni la-a*

EA 113

TRANSLATION

(1–7) Furthermore [...] they are not [able to ...]. And he asked his city ruler concerning another city ru[ler] and is he not [committing] a crime and schem[in]g in his heart?

(7–16) Behold, Yapaʿ-Haddi has co[mmi]tted a crime. Be apprised! [What] has the king done to him?

(11–13) Furthermore, what have I done t[o] Yapaʿ-Haddi that he pl[ots] evil upon evil against m[e]?

(14–28) Now two of my ships he robbed, [the cattle] and the small cattle; so my property that is with him is very [extens]ive. May the king [se]nd his commissioner [and] may [he adj]udicate between us. [All] the property that [will be ta]ken from him, may [the king take!] Concerning [my] pro[per]ty [that] is with [him, may the king inquire of] my [m]en. Al[l that was taken fr]om Rib-Haddi [now] is all [given] to the *ʿapîru* men and there is no one that [can ta]ke his property from my [ship].

29) [*i*]-*le-ú uš-ša-ar* LÚ-*lì*
30) [*a-n*]*a* É.GAL *ki-ma tap-pí-ia*
31) URU.MEŠ-*šu-nu a-na ša-šu-nu* [*ù*]
32) *pa-aš-ḫu yi-di-*in_4 ^{d}UTU TÉ[Š-*ia*]
33) *i-na pa-ni-ka ù šu-up-ši-i*[*ḫ* ÌR-*ka*]
34) *ù la-a yi-na-mu-šu*
35) *iš-tu mu-ḫi-ka ù* [*al-lu-mi*]
36) ^{I}*A-ma-an-ma-ša qí-ba*[*-mi a-na*]
37) *ša-a-šu ù yi-zi*[*-za*]
38) *it-ti-ia aš-šum a-ba*[*-li*]
39) *ṭup-pí-ia a-na mu-ḫi-k*[*a ù*]
40) *pa-ṭá-ri-ma šu-ut* [*ù*]
41) *ia-nu ša-a yu-ba-lu* [*ṭup-pí-ia*]
42) *a-na mu-ḫi-ka ù i*[*-de*]
43) [*šà*]*r-ru a-na* ^{I}*A-*[*ma-an-ma-ša*]
44) [*ù*] *yi-z*[*i-za it-ti-ia*]
45) [........traces.......]
46) [traces...............]
Lft.ed. 47) *ù* ^{I}*Ia-pa-*^{d}IŠKUR [*yi-ìl-qú*]
48) TIL.LA *a-na* URU.MEŠ *š*[*a la-a*]
49) *na-ak-ru iš*[*-tu mu-ḫi-ka*]

(28–35) Why am [I] not able to send my man [t]o the palace like my colleagues? They have their cities [and] they are at peace. May the sun god grant [me] fav[or] in your sight and bring peac[e to your servant] and he will not depart

(35–44) from you. And [behold], Aman-maša, spea[k to] him that he prese[nt himself] to me in order to car[ry] my tablet to y[ou. So] when he departed [then] there was no one that could deliver [my tablet] to you. So may [the ki]ng be appri[sed] concerning A[m]a[n-maša and] may he pres[ent himself to me].

(45–46) [.................]

(47–49) And Yapʿ-Haddi [is taking] the supplies belonging to the cities th[at are not] alienated fr[om you].

EA 114

TRANSCRIPTION

Obv. 01) [^{I}*Ri-ib-*^{d}IŠKUR *iš-ta-pár*] *a-na* EN[*-šu*]

02) ⸢*šàr*⸣ [KUR.MEŠ LUGAL GAL *šàr*]*ta-am-ḫa-a*[*r*]

03) ^{d}⸢NIN⸣ ⸢*ša*⸣ ⸢URU⸣ ⸢*Gub*⸣*-la ti-di-in*$_4$

04) KAL.GA *a-na* ⸢LUGAL⸣ ⸢EN⸣*-ia a-*⸢*na*⸣ GÌR.⸢MEŠ⸣

05) EN*-ia* ^{d}UTU*-ia* 7*-šu* 7*-*⸢*ta*⸣*-*⸢*an*⸣

06) *am-qú-ut lu-ú i-de* LUGAL EN*-ia*

07) *i-nu-ma nu-*KÚR ^{I}*A-zi-ru* ⸢*it*⸣*‹-ti›-ia*

08) *ù ṣa-bat* 12 LÚ.MEŠ*-ia ù ša-ka-an*

09) ⸢*ip*⸣*-ṭe*$_6$*-ra be-ri-nu* 50 KÙ.BABBAR.MEŠ *ù*

10) ⸢LÚ⸣.MEŠ *ša-a* ⸢*uš*⸣*-ši-ir-ti a-na*

11) ⸢URU⸣ *Ṣu-mu-ra ṣa-ab-bat i-na*

12) ⸢URU⸣ *Ya-aḫ-li-ia* GIŠ.MÁ.MEŠ LÚ.MEŠ

13) URU ⸢*Ṣur*⸣*-ri* URU *Be-ru-ta* URU *Ṣí-du-na*

14) ⸢*gáb*⸣*-bu i-na* KUR *A-mu-*⸢*ri*⸣ *šal-mu šu-nu*

15) *a-na-ku-mi* ⸢*nu*⸣*-*KÚR *ù an-nu-ú i-na-na*

16) *nu-*KÚR ^{I}*Ia-pa-*^{d}IŠKUR *it-ti* ^{I}*A-zi-ri*

17) *a-na ia-ši ù al-lu-ú ṣa-bat* GIŠ.MÁ*-ia*

18) *ù al-*⸢*lu*⸣*-*⸢*ú*⸣ *ki-na-na-ma yi-te*$_9$*-lu*

19) *i-na* ⸢*lìb*⸣*-bi a-ia-ba aš-šum ṣa-ba-at*

20) GIŠ.MÁ.MEŠ*-ia ù ya-am-lik* LUGAL

21) *a-na* URU*-šu ù* ÌR*-šu ù* ⸢LÚ⸣.⸢MEŠ⸣

22) *ḫu-‹up›-ši-ia pa-ṭá-ra-ma tu-ba-ú-na*

23) *šum-ma la-a ti-le-ú la-qa-i*[*a*]

24) *iš-tu qa-at na-ak-ri-ia* ⸢*ù*⸣

25) *te-ra-ni a-wa-ta*$_5$ *ù i-de*

26) *ip-ša ša i-pu-šu a-nu-ma*

27) *ki-‹a›-ma iš-*⸢*tap*⸣*-ru a-na ka-ta*$_5$ UGU

28) URU *Ṣu-mu-ra a-nu-ma i-ti-lik*

29) ⸢*ù*⸣ ⸢*aḫ*⸣(?)*-ta-ni* ⸢ÉRIN⸣.⸢MEŠ⸣ *a-na*

30) [*na-ṣa-ri-š*]*i ù a-nu-‹ma› i-ti-zi-ib-ši ù*

Lo.ed. 31) [*ka-li* LÚ.MEŠ] UN*-tù*

32) [*ù* LÚ.MÁŠKIM *pa-aṭ-*]*ru a-nu-ma*

Rev. 33) [PN LÚ.D]UMU *ši-ip-ri-*[*ia*]

EA 114

TRANSLATION

(1–6) [Rib-Hadda wrote] to [his] lord, king of [the lands, great king, king of] battl[e]: May the Lady of Byblos grant strength to the king, my lord. At the feet of my lord, my sungod, seven times and seven times have I fallen.

(6–12) May the king be apprised that Aziru is hostile to me and he has seized twelve of my men and he has set a ransom between us, fifty (shekels of) silver; and it was the men whom I sent to the town of Ṣumur that he seized in the town of Yaʿlia.

(12–15) The ships of the men of the town of Tyre, the town of Beirut, the town of Sidon, are all in Amurru. They are at peace; I am at war.

(15–20) Behold now Yapaʿ-Haddi is hostile to me along with Aziru. And behold, he has seized my ship and behold now he is likewise going out in the high sea to seize my ships.

(20–26) So may the king take counsel concerning his city and his servant. And my yeo‹ma›n farmers seek to depart. If you are not able to rescue me from the hand on my enemy then send word back to me and I will know the thing that I should do.

(26–33) Now thus I have been writing to you concerning the town of Ṣumur. Now I went and I urged the troops to [guard i]t. But now I have abandoned it and [all the men of] the garrison troops [and the commissioner have de]parted. Now,

34) [*u*]*š-ši-ir-ti-šu ù aš-ta-ni*
35) [*ma*]*-ni* UD. KAM^{v}.MEŠ *ú-wa-ši-ru-šu*
36) *ù la-a yi-le-*⸢*ú*⸣
37) ⸢*i*⸣*-re-ba a-na* URU *Ṣu-mu-ra ṣa-ab-\tu*
38) ⸢*ka*⸣*-li* KASKAL.MEŠ *a-na ša-a-šu*
39) *a-na nu-*KÚR *ša-a* UGU*-ia ù* UGU
40) URU *Ṣu-mu-ra šu-ut i-da-gal*
41) 2 ITI *a-ši-ib it-ti-ia* UGU
42) *ša* [*m*]*a-an-ni yu-pa-šu ki-a-ma*
43) ÌR *ki-ti-ka* UGU *a-ra-di-ka*
44) *šum-ma la-a ti-le-ú la-qa* ÌR*-ka*
45) *ù uš-ši-ra* ÉRIN.MEŠ *pí-ṭá-ti*
46) *ti-ìl-qé-ni da-mi-iq it-ta-ka*
47) ⸢*a*⸣*-ia-bu* LUGAL *nu-*KÚR *it-‹ti›-ia ù* LÚ.MEŠ
48) ⸢*ḫa*⸣*-za-nu-‹tu›-šu ša-a yi-ma-*⸢*li*⸣*-*⸢*ku*⸣
49) *a-na ša-a-šu-nu ki-na-na-ma*
50) ⸢*ma*⸣*-ri-iṣ ma-gal a-na ia-ši*
51) *al-lu* ^{I}*A-ma-an-ma-ša ša-nu*
52) *ša-al-šu šum-ma la-a* KUR ⸢*A*⸣*-la-ši-ia*
53) *uš-ši-ir-ti-*⸢*šu*⸣ *ana mu-ḫi-ka*
54) *mi-lik a-na* ÌR *ki-ti-*⸢*ka*⸣ ⸢*pa*⸣*-*⸢*na*⸣*-*⸢*nu*⸣
55) *iš-tu* KUR *Ia-ri-mu-ta*
56) *tu-ba-li-ṭú-na* LÚ.MEŠ
57) *ḫu-up-ši-ia ù an-nu-ú*
58) *an-nu-ú la-a ia-di-nu-šu-nu*
59) ⸢^{I}⸣*Ia-pa-*^{d}IŠKUR *a-la-ka*$_{13}$ *a-n*[*a*]
60) [*mi-ni qa-l*]*a-ta* LÚ.MEŠ *ma-ṣa-ar-*[*ta*]
61) [*šàr-ru yu-*]*wa-ši-ru-na*
62) [*a-na na-ṣa-ri* ÌR *ki-t*]*i-ka*
Up.ed 63) [.....................]⸢*ti*⸣/*ši*(?)
64) [...........................]
Lft.ed. 65) *a-ia-*⸢*bi*⸣ ⸢LUGAL⸣ *ù ti-da-‹ga›-lu-na*
66) ⸢*ḫa*⸣*-za-*⸢*na*⸣ ⸢*ša*⸣ *yu-ra-du-ka i-na*
67) *ki-ti ša-ni-tam mi-lik a-na ia-*⸢*ši*⸣
68) ⸢*mi*⸣*-*⸢*ia*⸣ *i-ra-mu ù* ⸢*a*⸣*-mu-*⸢*ta*⸣(?)
69) *al-lu* ^{I}*Ia-pa-*^{d}IŠKUR *it-ti* ^{I}*A-zi-r*[*i*]

(33–43) [as for PN, my am]bassador, I sent him repeatedly. [Ho]w many days have I sent him and he was unable to enter the town of Ṣumur! They have seized all of the roads to it because of the war against me and against the town of Ṣumur. He has been waiting two months sitting with me. For what reason is your loyal servant being treated thus? Because of serving you?

(44–50) If you are unable to fetch your servant then send the regular army that it may fetch me. It is good with you. The enemies of the king are hostile to me and the city rulers about whom you are so concerned. Thus it is very grievous for me.

(51–53) Behold the other Aman-massa; ask him if it was not by way of Alashia that I sent him to you.

(54–62) Take counsel concerning your loyal servant. Formerly, they furnished sustenance for my yeoman farmers but behold, behold, Yapaʿ-Haddi does not permit (us) to go. W[hy are you sil]ent? [The king should se]nd garrison troops [to protect] your [loya]l [servant]

(63–67) [....] the enemie(s) of the king and they inti‹mid›ate the city ruler who serves you loyally.

(67–69) Moreover, take counsel concerning me. Who will be devoted if I die? Behold Yapaʿ-Haddi is allied with Aziru.

EA 115

TRANSCRIPTION

Obv. 01) [...............] ma[................]
02) [................] le-qú[................]
03) [..............]i-re-bi [..............]
04) [..............]a-[na] n[u-KÚ]R ⸢KAL⸣.⸢GA⸣ U[GU-ia]
05) [.........]⸢ir⸣-⸢bu⸣ [i]-⸢na⸣-⸢ṣí⸣-r[a............]
06) [.....]a ⸢uš⸣-⸢ši⸣-ra ki-[ma]
07) [ar-ḫi-iš šu]m-ma i-ia-nu š[a-a]
08) [i-na-ṣí-ru UR]U i-na qa-ti[-ia ù]
09) [......i-ia-n]u lìb-ba a-na UR[U.......]
10) [mi-na i-pu-]šu-na a-na-ku š[um-ma]
11) [........lìb-]bi ⸢LUGAL⸣ i-na [........]
12) [...........] ù [.................]
Lo.ed. 13) [....uš-ši-i]r ki-[ma ar-ḫi-iš]
14) [ù-ul ti-ìl-]qú URU Ṣ[u-mu-ra ù]
Rev. 15) [.......]aḫ-šu ^{I}A-zi[-ru.......]
16) [........U]RU Ṣu-mu-r[a.......]
17) [.......K]UR A-mur-ra i[t-ti-šu]
18) [......r]a a-na LUGAL ⸢ù⸣[........]
19) [a-mur i-na UD.]MEŠ a-bu-ti-i[a....]
20) [LÚ.MEŠ ma-]ṣa-ar-ti [............]
21) [it-ti-šu-nu] ⸢ù⸣ an-nu-ú[.........]
22) [..........UR]U Ṣu-[mu-ra....]

EA 115

TRANSLATION

(1–22) [......]take[....to]enter[....] for intense ho[stility] ag[ainst me...I] will protect [......]send wi[th utmost haste. I]f there is none [who can protect the ci]ty in [my] charge? [...] the cit[y of...] has no heart [...What shall I]do myself? I[f...the inte]ntion of the king[...]and[..sen]d wit[h utmost haste. Let them not ta]ke the city of Ṣ[umur and...] his [...] Aziru [...the ci]ty of Ṣumur [...the la]nd of Amurru is wi[th him...] to the king and [...Look, in the day]s of m[y] fathers[...there were garr]ison troops [with them] and behold [...the ci]ty of Ṣu[mur].

EA 116

TRANSCRIPTION

Obv. 01) [^{I}*Ri-ib*-^{d}IŠKUR] *iš-ta-pár a-n*[*a*]
02) [EN-*šu* LUG]AL GAL *šàr* KUR.KUR.KI *šàr*
03) [*ta-*]*am-ḫa-ar* ^{d}NIN *ša* URU *Gub-*[*la*]
04) [*ti-*]*di-in*$_{4}$ KAL.GA *a-na šàr-*⸢*ri*⸣
05) [EN-]*ia a-na* GÌR.MEŠ EN-[*i*]*a* ^{d}UTU‹*-ia*›
06) [7-*šu*] 7-*ta-an am-qú-ut lu-ú i-de*
07) [*šàr-*]*ru* EN-*li i-nu-ma* KAL.GA *ma-gal nu*-KÚR
08) [U]GU-*nu i-nu-ma yu-qa-bu-na i-na*
09) [*pa-*]*ni-ka i-ba-ša-at-mi*
10) [UR]U *Ṣu-mu-ra a-na šàr-ri yi-de*
11) [LU]GAL *i-nu-ma ma-qa-ti-ma a-‹na›* UN-*nu*
12) ⸢*ù*⸣ *ṣa-ab-tu-ši*$_{x}$(ŠE) DUMU.MEŠ ^{I}ÌR-*A-ši-ir-*[*t*]*a*
13) *ù ia-nu ša-a yu-ba-lu a-wa-t*[*a*]$_{5}$
14) [*a*]*-na šàr-ri ù mi-lik i-nu-ma*
15) ⸢ÌR⸣ *ki-ti-ka a-na-ku ù ka-l*[*i*]
16) *ša-a eš-mu aš-pu-ru a-na* EN-[*ia*]
17) *ša-ni-tam mi-lik a-na* URU *Ṣu-mu-*[*ra*]
18) *ki-ma* MUŠEN *ša i-na lìb-bi ḫu*[*-ḫa-ri*] \ *ki-lu*[*-bi*]
19) ⸢*ša*⸣*-ak-na-at ki-na-na*
20) *i-ba-ša-at* KAL.GA *ma-gal* [*nu*-KÚR]
21) *ù* LÚ.MEŠ DUMU *ši-ip-ri š*[*a tu-ṣu-na*]
22) *iš-tu* E.GAL [*l*]*a-a ti*[*-l*]*e*[*-ú*]
23) *i-re-ba* [*a*]*-na* URU *Ṣu-mu-ra*
24) *mu-š*[*a*] *š*[*u-*]*ri-ib-ti-šu-nu*

EA 116

TRANSLATION

(1–6) [Rīb-Haddi] wrote t[o his lord, the] great [ki]ng, king of the lands, the king of [ba]ttle. May the Lady of the city of Byblos [gr]ant strength to the king, my [lord; at the feet of [m]y lord, ‹my› sun god, [seven times] (and) seven times have I fallen.

(6–13) So may [the ki]ng, my lord, be apprised that very great is the hostility [a]gainst us. Inasmuch as it is said in your [pre]sence, "[The c]ity of Ṣumur belongs to the king," may the [ki]ng be apprised that the sons of ʿAbdi-Ashirta have fallen up‹on› our garrison and they have seized it and there is no one that can bring wor[d t]o the king.

(14–16) So take counsel, because your loyal servant am I and al[l] that I hear I write to [my] lord.

(17–24) Furthermore, take counsel concerning the city of Ṣumu[r]; it is like a bird that is placed in a cage. Thus [hostility] is exceedingly great. And the envoys th[at come forth] from the palace are [un]able to enter [in]to the city of Ṣumur. At night I in[s]erted them.

25) *ù* ^{I}*Ia*[*-pa-*]^{d}IŠKUR *ki-na-na-ma*
26) *ú-ul* [*ta*]-[*r*]*i-iṣ it-it-ia*
27) *ka-š*[*a-d*]*i-ma* LÚ-*ia ù*
28) *ra-ak-*[*š*]*a-šu ù* [*na*]*-ad*!*-na*
29) *ki-ti-ia ma-id ma-gal ù*
30) *an-nu-ú* LÚ.MEŠ MÁŠKIM *šàr-ri*
31) *yu-wa-ši-ru-na š*[*à*]*r-ru ù*
32) *ia-aq-bi šàr-ru a-na ša-šu-nu*
33) *ù tu-pa-ri-šu be-ri-ku-ni*
34) *šum-ma ia-di-nu šàr-ru a-na* ÌR-*šu*
35) *ù i-di-*in_4 *ù šum-ma ap-pu-*[*n*]*a-ma*
36) *yi-ìl-qé* LUGAL *gáb-ba a-na ša-*[*š*]*u*
37) *ša-ni-tam ka-li* URU.MEŠ-*ia*
38) ⌜in_4⌝-*né-ep-šu a-na* LÚ.MEŠ G[AZ.MEŠ]
39) *ù ka-li-šu-nu* [*ma-gal nu-*KÚR]
40) *it-ti-ia ù* [^{I}*Ia-pa*]-^{d}⌜IŠKUR⌝
Rev. 41) *lum-na lum-na-ma* [*yu-la-mi-nu*]
42) UGU-*ia ia-nu mi-i*[*m-m*]*a a-na*
43) *ša-šu-nu ša-a* 2 *ša-a* 3 *a-pí-ì*[*l*]
44) KÙ.BABBAR.MEŠ *ip-ṭì-ri ù yi-ìš-mé šà*[*r-*]*ru*
45) *a-wa-te* ÌR *ki-ti-šu ù*
46) *ia-di-*in_4 *ba-la-ṭá a-na* ÌR-*šu*
47) *ù* GÉME-*šu* URU *Gub-la ša-ni-tam*
48) *da-mi-iq a-na ia-ši ù*
49) *i-ba-ša-ti it-ti-ka ù*
50) *pa-aš-ḫa-ti al-lu-ú* ^{I}*A-zi-ru ù*
51) ^{I}*Ia-pa-*^{d}IŠKUR *la-qú a-wa-ta* [*b*]*e-ri-šu-nu*
52) UGU-*ia ù la-a i-le-ú* [*i-p*]*é-eš*
53) *mi-im-mi ù ip-šu-šu-nu* [*nu-kúr-t*]u_4
54) *it-ti-ia ki-na-na ma-r*[*i-iṣ ma-*]*gal*
55) *a-na ia-ši ša-ni-tam a-mur ni-*[*nu* ÌR.MEŠ] *ki-ti*

(25–34) And Ya[paʿ]-Haddi therefore, is not [stra]ight with me. When my man arrived, then he bound him and [ga]ve away (sold?) my rightful due, it being very extensive. So, behold, the king is sending the king's commissioners. So may he speak to them that they should adjudicate between you (or: us). If the king would give (it) to his servant,

(35–36) then give. But if, on the other hand, let the king take it all for himse[lf].

(37–42) Furthermore, all of my towns have joined the *ʿap*[*îru*] men and all of them are e[xtremely hostile] towards me. And [Yapaʿ]-Haddi [plots] evil upon evil against me.

(42–47) They have no[thi]ng, having paid ransom money some twice, some three times. So may the ki[n]g heed the words of his loyal servant and may he give sustenance to his servant and to his handmaiden, the city of Byblos.

(47–55) Furthermore, it would be good for me if I were with you and I were at peace. Behold, Aziru and Yapaʿ-Haddi have made a league between them against me and I am unable [to d]o anything. And their deeds are [hostili]ty against me. Thus, it is sorely grievous to me

56) *šàr-ri iš-tu da-ri-t*[*i* UD.]MEŠ
57) *ša-ni-tam a-na-ku* ÌR *ki-t*[*i-ka*]
58) *ù mur-ṣa-ma a-na ia-ši a*[*-mur*]
59) *a-wa-ta an-ni-ta a-mur a-n*[*a-ku*]
60) *ep-ru ša-a* GÌR.MEŠ-*ka šà*[*r-ru*]
61) *a-mur a-bu-ka la-a a-ṣí* [*ù*]
62) *la-a i-da-gal* KUR.KUR.KI.MEŠ [*ù*]
63) *ḫa-za-ni-šu ù an-nu-ú na-a*[*d-nu-ka*]
64) DINGIR.MEŠ *ù* ^{d}UTU *ù* ^{d}N[IN]
65) *ša* URU *Gub-la ù aš*-[*b*]*a*[*-ta*]
66) *a-na* GIŠ.GU.ZA É *a-bi-ka*
67) *a-na* KUR-*ka mi-ia-mi šu-n*[*u*]
68) DUMU.MEŠ ^{I}ÌR-*A-ši-ir-ta ù*
69) ˹*la*˺-*qú* KUR LUGAL *a-na ša-šu-nu*
70) *šàr* KUR *Mi-ta-na šu-nu ù šàr*
71) [K]UR *Ka-ši ù šàr* KUR *Ḫa-ta*
72) ˹*yu*˺-*wa-ši-ra* LUGAL ÉRIN.MEŠ
73) *pí-ṭá-ti* ^{I}*Ia-an-ḫa-‹ma› qa-du*
74) [*qí-pa-*]*ni* KUR *Ia-ri-mu-ta*
75) [*ù*] MÁŠKIM URU *Ku-mi-di*
76) [*it-ti-*]*šu ù la-qú* [*gáb-bi*]
77) [LÚ.MEŠ SA.GA]Z.MEŠ ˹*ù*˺[
78) [.................]*du* L[UGAL(?)]
Lft.ed. 79) [.........................UR]U *Gub-la*
80) [...........................] *a-na* ÌR *ki-ti-*[*šu*]

(55–67) Look, w[e are] loyal [servants]of the king from olde[n day]s. Furthermore, I am [your] lo[yal] servant and it is grievous to me. Note this word. Look, ⌜I⌝ am the dirt under your feet, O ki[ng]. Look, your father did not come forth [and] he did not inspect the lands [or] his city rulers. But behold, the gods and the sun god and the La[dy] of the city of Byblos have gran[ted you] that you should si[t] on the throne of the house of your father for your land.

(67–69) Who are they, the sons of ʿAbdi-Ashirta that they take the land of the king for themselves?

(70–71) The king of the land of Mittani? or the king of the [l]and of Cush? or the king of the land of Ḫatti?

(72–80) May the king send regular troops, Yanḥamu, with [the overseer]er of the land of Yarimuta [and] the commissioner of the city of Kômidi [with]him that they may take [all the *ʿapîr*]*u* [men] and [.....] the k[ing.....the ci]ty of Byblos [.......] to [his] loyal servant.

EA 117

TRANSCRIPTION

Obv.
01) [^{I}]*Ri-ib* ^{d}IŠKUR [*iš-ta-pár a-na* EN-*šu*]
02) [*šàr-*]*ri* GAL ⸢*šàr*⸣ [*ta-am-ḫa-ra*]
03) [^{d}]NIN *ša* URU *G*[*ub-la*] *t*[*i-di-in*$_{4}$]
04) [GA.K]AL *a-na šàr-ri* ⸢EN⸣-*ia* [^{d}UTU-*ia*]
05) [*a-n*]*a* ⸢GÌR⸣.MEŠ EN-*ia* ^{d}UTU-*i*[*a*]
06) [7]-*šu* 7-*ta-an am-qú-ut a*[*l-lu-*]⸢*me*⸣
07) ⸢*i*⸣*a-aq-bu šàr-ru* EN-*li* ⸢*a*⸣-[*n*]*a*
08) *mi-ni at-ta-ma ti-ìš-tap-ru-na*
09) *a-na ia-ši a-mur a-na-ku ya-nu*
10) *ḫa-za-na i-na ar-ki-ti-ia*
11) *ìš-tu* URU *Ṣu-mu-ra ù al-lu*
12) *pa-nu gáb-bi a-na ia-ši ù* 2 LÚ
13) KUR *Mi-iṣ-ri ša-a ša-ap-ra-*⸢*ti*⸣
14) *a-na* É.⸢GAL⸣ *ú-ul a-ṣa ú-ul*
15) *ša-ap-*⸢*ra*⸣-⸢*ti*⸣ *a-na šàr-ri ia-nu*
16) LÚ *ša-a* [*y*]*u-ba-lu ṭup-pí-ia*
17) *a-na* ⸢É⸣.GA[L] *a-nu-ma* 2 LÚ *an-nu-tu*
18) *tu-ba-lu-na* ⸢*ṭup*⸣-*pí a-na šàr-ri*
19) *ù* ‹*i-na*›-*an-na ú-ul a-ṣa ki-na-na*
20) *pal-ḫa-ti ù* ⸢*na*⸣-⸢*ad*⸣-*na-ti pa-ni-ia*
21) ⸢*a*⸣-⸢*na*⸣ ⸢*ma*⸣-⸢*ḫar*⸣ EN-*ia* ⸢*ša*⸣-⸢*ni*⸣-*tam* ⸢LÚ⸣ *ša-ap-ra-ti*
22) [*a-n*]*a d*[*a-ga-*]⸢*li*⸣-⸢*ma*⸣ ⸢*a*⸣-⸢*na*⸣ ⸢*a*⸣-⸢*bi*⸣-*ka*
23) *i-nu-ma yi-la-*[*kam*^{v}] ⸢^{I}⸣⸢*A*⸣-⸢*ma*⸣-⸢*an*⸣-*ap-pa*
24) *i-na* ÉRIN.MEŠ *ṣé-*⸢*eḫ*⸣-[*ri*] ⸢*ù*⸣ *aš-ta-pár*
25) *a-na* É.GAL *ù* ⸢*yu*⸣-⸢*wa*⸣-[*ša*]-⸢*ra*⸣
26) ›*ù yu-wa-ša-ra*‹ *šàr-ru* ⸢ÉRIN⸣.⸢MEŠ⸣
27) *ra-ba ú-ul la-qí* ⸢^{I}⸣ÌR-*A-ši-ir-*⸢*ta*⸣
28) *qa-du mi-im-mi-šu ki-ma qa-bi-ia*
29) *a-wa-te ša-ru-ta aš-ta-pa-ru*
30) *a-na* EN-*ia ù ti-qa-bu a-na mi-ni*
31) *ti-ìš-ta-pa-ru a-wa-te ša-ru-ta*

EA 117

TRANSLATION

(1–6) Rib-Hadda [wrote to his lord], the great [ki]ng, the king of [battle]: May the Lady of the city of By[blos] g[rant] [stren]gth to the king, my lord, [my sun god]; at the feet of my lord, m[y] sun god, [seven] times (and) seven times have I fallen.

(6–21) Be[hold,] the king, my lord, says, "Why do you keep on writing to me?" Look, as for me, there is no city ruler behind me, from Ṣumur and indeed, everyone is antagonistic to me. And two Egyptians that I sent to the palace did not come forth. Did I not write to the king, "There is no one that can bring my tablet to the palace"? Now, these two men will bring my tablet to the king. But ‹n›ow have they not come forth? Thus I feared and I have turned to my lord.

(21–31) Furthermore, I sent a ⸢man⸣ for an au[dien]ce with your father when Amanappa ca[me] with a small force, so I wrote to the palace and the king sent a large army. Did he not take ʿAbdi-Ashirta with his property just as I had said? Had I been writing lying words to my lord? But you say, "Why do you write lying words?"

32) *šum-ma a-wa-te-ia tu-uš-mu-*[*na*]
33) *a-di yu-ú-ul-qú* ^{I}*A-za-ru ki-ma* ⸢*a*⸣-[*bi-š*]*u*
34) *a-*⸢*mur*⸣ *a-na-ku* KAL.GA *šàr-ri* E[N-*ia*]
35) *ša-ni-tam mi-ia-mi šu-nu* ⸢DUMU⸣.⸢MEŠ⸣
36) ^{I}ÌR-*A-ši-ir-ta* ÌR UR.G[I$_7$ *ù la*]-*qú*
37) URU.MEŠ *ḫa-za-nu-ti* LUGAL *a-na* [*ša-šu-nu*]
38) *šu-nu it-ti-ka* URU.MEŠ-*š*[*u-nu a-na*]
39) ^{I}*A-zi-ri ú-ul yi-te-r*[*u-bu*]
40) LUGAL *a-na* URU.MEŠ-*šu-nu ú-ul š*[*ul-mu*]
41) *a-na ša-šu-nu iš-tu* URU *Ṣ*[*u-mu-ra a-di*]
42) URU *Ul-la-sà* URU *ša yu-w*[*a-ši-ru*]
43) GIŠ.GIGIR.MEŠ *pa-na-nu ú-b*[*a-ú*]
44) ⸢*uš*⸣-⸢*ša*⸣-*ar* LÚ.D[UMU *ši-ip-ri*]
Lo.ed. 45) [*a-d*]*i* ÉRIN.MEŠ ⸢*ù*⸣ [GIŠ.GIGIR.MEŠ]
46) [*a-na*] URU *Ṣu-mu-*⸢*ra*⸣ ⸢*ù*⸣
47) [^{I}*Pa*]-*wu-ra A-zi-r*[*u da-ak*]
Rev. 48) ⸢*ù*⸣ ÉRIN! *a-na-ku* LÚ.[MEŠ *uš-ši-ir-ti*]
49) [*a-n*]*a* KUR *Mi-iṣ-ri* ⸢*ù*⸣
50) ›⸢*ù*⸣‹ *uš-ši-ra-at* [*ma*]-⸢*ṣa*⸣-[*ar-tu*]
51) *i-na qa-ti-šu-nu a-na ia-ši*
52) *ki-na-na uš-ši-ir-ti* LÚ *an-nu-ú*
53) *ša-ni-tam ú-ul aš-ta-pár a-na šàr-*⸢*ri*⸣
54) *a-nu-ma* 2 LÚ KUR *Mi-iṣ-ri šu-nu*
55) *tu-ṣa-na ša-ri a-na ia-ši*
56) *ù la-a a-ṣa šum-ma* MU. KAM^{v} *an-ni-*[*ta*]
57) *ia-nu* ÉRIN.MEŠ *pí-*⸢*ṭá*⸣*-ti ù k*[*a-li*]
58) KUR.MEŠ *a-na* ⸢LÚ⸣.MEŠ GAZ.MEŠ *ù*
59) *šum-ma lìb-bi* LUGAL *ba-li uš-ša-*[*ar*]
60) LÚ.MEŠ *pí-ṭá-ti ia-aš-pu-ur a-na*
61) ^{I}*Ia-an-ḫa-mì ù a-na* ^{I}*Pí-*⸢*ḫu*⸣-[*r*]*a*
62) *al-ku-mi qa-du* LÚ.MEŠ *ḫa-za-ni-ku-nu*
63) *le-qú-na* KUR *A-mur-ri i-na* UD.KAM^{v}
64) *ti-ìl-*⸢*qú*⸣*-na-ši*$_{x}$(ŠE) *ša-ni-tam di-nu a-na ia-ši*
65) *it-*⸢*ti*⸣ [^{I}]*Ia-pa-*^{d}IŠKUR *ù it-ti* ^{I}*Ḫa-‹ip›*
66) *ù* ⸢*yu*⸣*-wa-ši-ra* LUGAL ⸢LÚ⸣.⸢MÁŠKIM⸣
67) [*ù*] ⸢*yu*⸣-⸢*pa*⸣-⸢*ri*⸣-⸢*iš*⸣ ⸢*be*⸣*-ri-nu* ⸢*ka*⸣-⸢*li*⸣
68) *mi-im-mì ša-a yu-ú-ul-qú-na*
69) *ìš-tu ša-šu-nu a-na* LUGAL *ú-ul*
70) *yi-ìl-qé-šu* LÚ *ša-nu a-na ša-šu*
71) ⸢*da*⸣*-mi-iq a-*⸢*na*⸣ *šàr-ri ša-ni-tam*

(32–34) If my words will be heeded, then Aziru can be taken like [h]is fa[ther]. Behold, I am the strength of the king, my lo[rd].

(35–52) Furthermore, who are they, the sons of ʿAbdi-Ashirta, the slave, the do[g, that they ta]ke the cities of the city rulers of the king for [themselves]? They are with you? Th[eir] cities [belong to] Aziru! The king cannot ent[er] into their cities. They are not at [peace] with you from the city of Ṣ[umur as far as] the city of Ullasa, the city where he has be[en sending] chariots. Formerly, I was se[eking] to send an emi[ssary wi]th troops and [chariots to] the city of Ṣumur, but Azir[u kille]d [Pa]wura. As for troop‹s›, [I sent] me[n] to the land of Egypt and a garrison was sent to me in their charge. Likewise, have I sent this man.

(53–64) Furthermore, did I not write to the king, "Now the two men are Egyptians; may my (life) breath come forth to me"? But they did not come. If this year there are no regular troops, then a[ll] the lands will belong to the *ʿapîru* men. But if the king does not desire to send the regular army, may he write to Yanḫamu and to Piḫuru, "Go with your city rulers; take the land of Amurru." In one day will they take it.

(64–66) Furthermore, I have a litigation with Yapaʿ-Hadda and Ḥa‹ʿip›. So may the king send a commissioner

(67–71) [and] let him decide between us. All the property that will be taken from them goes to the king. Let not another man take it for himself. May it be pleasing to the king.

72) *yu-wa-ši-ra šàr-ru* ANŠE.KUR.RA *a-na*
73) ›*a-na*‹ ÌR-*šu ù a-na-ṣa-ra* URU.KI
74) LUGAL *ia-nu mi-im-ma a-na ia-ši*
75) *ga-mi-ir gáb-bu i-na na-da-ni*
76) *i-na ba-la-aṭ* ZI-*ia ù* LÚ-*ia*
77) *an-nu-ú yu-wa-ši-ra-šu šàr-ru*
78) ⸢*ki*⸣-⸢*ma*⸣ *ar-ḫi-ìš ù ia-di-na*
79) ⸢LÚ⸣.MEŠ *ma-ṣa-ar-ra a-na* ›⸢*na*⸣-⸢*ṣa*⸣‹
80) *na-ṣa-ar* ÌR *ki-ti-šu ù* URU.⸢KI⸣
81) *ù* LÚ.MEŠ KUR *Me-lu-ḫa it-ti-šu-nu*
82) *ki-ma pár-ṣí ša-a a-bu-ti*-⸢*ka*⸣
83) *ša-ni-tam i-nu-ma yi-qa-bu*
84) *šàr-ru ú-ṣ*[*ur-mì*] ⸢*lu*⸣ ⸢*na*⸣-⸢*ṣa*⸣-*ra-t*[*a*]
85) ⸢*mi*⸣-*nu yi*-[*na-ṣí-ra-ni a-mur i-na*]

Up.ed. 86) [UD.]MEŠ *a-b*[*u*]-⸢*ti*⸣-[*ia ba-laṭ šàr-ri* UGU-*šu-nu*]
87) [*ù*] *ma-ṣa-ar*[*-ti šàr-ri*]
88) [*it-*]*ti-šu*-⸢*nu*⸣ ⸢*ù*⸣ [*šul-mu a-na ša-šu-n*]*u*
89) [*ù*] *a-na-ku nu-k*[*úr-tu*$_4$ GA.KAL *a-na*]

Lft.ed. 90) [UG]U-*ia ḫu-up-ši-ia a*[*-pa-l*]*a-aḫ a-na-ku ki-a-ma aš-pu-r*[*u*]
91) [*a-na*] ⸢É⸣.GAL *a*-[*na*] *ma-ṣa-ar* ⸢*ù*⸣ LÚ.MEŠ KUR *Mé-lu-ḫa ù la-a*
92) [*na-ad-na-*]*ta* 1 ⸢*da*⸣-[*a*]*n*]-*na* ⸢*mi*⸣-⸢*na*⸣ ⸢*i*⸣-[*p*]*u-šu-na yu-wa-*‹*ši*›*-ra šàr-ru*
93) ⸢LÚ⸣.MEŠ *ma-*[*ṣa*]*-ar ù* L[Ú.MEŠ] KUR *Mé-lu-ḫa a-na na-ṣa-ri-ia*
94) *ú-ul ti*-⸢*né*⸣-*pu-u*[*š*] URU *a-na* GAZ.MEŠ

(71–82) Furthermore, may the king send horse(s) to his servant so that I may guard the city of the king. I don't have anything; it has all been used up to buy subsistence for my life. And as for this man of mine, may the king send him with utmost haste and may he give garrison troops to guard his loyal servant and the city and men of the land of Meluḫḫa with them like the practice of your fathers.

(83–94) Furthermore, when the king says, "Guard! May you be on guard!" Who will [protect me? Look, in] the days of [my] fathers, [they had the king's sustenance and] a garrison unit of the [king] was [wi]th them and [they had peace]. [But] as for me, there is [fierce] hos[tility agains]t me. My yeoman farmers I [fe]ar myself. Thus I kept wri[ting to] the palace for a garrison and men of the land of Meluḫḫa but you did not [give] even one strong one (one unit?). What can I do? May the king send garrison men and men of the land of Meluḫḫa to protect me. Let not the city join the *ʿapîru*!

EA 118

TRANSCRIPTION

Obv. 01) [*a*]-*na* ^{I}*šàr-ri* EN-*ia*
02) ^{d}UTU *qí-bí-ma*
03) *um-ma* ^{I}*Ri-ib-*^{d}IŠKUR ÌR-*ka-ma*
04) *a-*⌜*na*⌝ GÌR.MEŠ EN-*ia* ^{d}UTU
05) 7-*šu* 7-*ta-an am-qú-ut*
06) ^{d}NIN *ša* URU *Gub-la*
07) *ti-di-*in_4 KAL.GA *a-na* LUGAL
08) EN-*ia a-nu-ma ki-a-ma*
09) *aš-ta-pa-ru a-*⌜*na*⌝ ⌜É⌝.⌜GAL [KA]L.[GA]
10) ⌜*ma*⌝!-[*gal nu*]-KÚR *ša-a* UGU-*ia*
11) *ù ia-di-na* LUGAL
12) LÚ.MEŠ *ma-ṣa-ar-ta*
13) *a-na* ÌR-*šu ša-ni-tam di-nu*
14) *a-na ia-ši uš-ši-ra*
15) LÚ.MAŠKIM *yi-ìš-me a-wa-te-ia*
16) *ù ia-di-na* ⌜*ki*⌝-*ti-*⌜*ia*⌝
17) *i-na qa-ti-ia* ⌜*ù*⌝
18) *šum-ma ap-pu-na-ma yi-ìl-qé*
19) LUGAL *mi-im-mi-ia iš-tu*
20) LÚ.MEŠ *ḫa-za-nu-ti a-na ša-a-šu*
21) ⌜*ša*⌝-*ni-tam nu-*KÚR KAL.GA
22) [*a-na*] *ia-ši ù ba-la-*⌜*ṭá*⌝
23) [*a-na*] LÚ.MEŠ *ḫu-*⌜*up*⌝-⌜*ši*⌝ [*ia-nu*]
Lo.ed. 24) ⌜*ù*⌝ *al-*⌜*lu*⌝-*m*[*i*] ⌜*pa*⌝-*ṭ*[*á*]-⌜*ri*⌝!
25) [*a-n*]*a ma-ḫar* DUMU.MEŠ
Rev. 26) $^{⌜I⌝}$ÌR-*A-ši-ir-ta ù*
27) [*a-*]*na* URU *Ṣí-‹du›-na ù*
28) URU *Be-ru-ta al-lu-mi*
29) DUMU.MEŠ ^{I}ÌR-*A-ši-ir-ta* [*nu*]-KÚR
30) ⌜*a*⌝-*na* LUGAL *ù* URU *Ṣí-*⌜*du*⌝-⌜*na*⌝
31) *ù*!(ŠI) URU *Be-ru-ta ú-ul*
32) *a-na* LUGAL *uš-ši-ra*

EA 118

TRANSLATION

(1–8) Speak [t]o the King, my lord, the sun god; the message of Rib-Hadda, your servant. At the feet of my lord, the sun god, seven times (and) seven times have I fallen. May the Lady of the city of Byblos grant strength to the king, my lord.

(8–13) Now, thus I have been writing to the palace, "The hostility which is against me is ve[ry stro]n[g]. So may the king grant garrison troops to his servant."

(13–20) Furthermore, I have a case; send a commissioner that he may hear my words and that he may give my just due into my hand. Or, on the other hand, let the king take my property from the city rulers for himself.

(21–32) Furthermore, the hostility is strong [against] me and [there are no] rations for my yeomen farmers, and behold, if they depart [t]o the sons of ʿAbdi-Ashirta or to the city of Si‹do›n or the city of Beirut, behold the sons of ʿAbdi-Ashirta are [ho]stile to the king and the city of Sidon and(!) the city of Beirut will not belong to the king.

33) LÚ.MÁŠKIM *yi-ìl-qa-šu-nu*
34) *ú-ul* ›DIŠ‹ *i-te*$_9$*-zi-ib* ⸢URU⸣-*lì*
35) *ù* ⸢*i*⸣-*pa-ṭá-ra*
36) *a-na mu-ḫi-ka al-lu*
37) *pa-ṭá-ri-*^{ma} LÚ.MEŠ *ḫu-up-ši ù*
38) *ṣa-ab-tu* LÚ.MEŠ GAZ.MEŠ
39) URU *a-mur a-*⸢*na*⸣*-ku pa-nu-ia-ma*
40) [*a-n*]*a* ⸢*a*⸣*-ra-ad* LUGAL *ki-a pár-ṣí*
41) *ša a-bu-*⸢*ti*⸣*-*⸢*ia*⸣ ⸢*ù*⸣
42) *yu-wa-ši-ra šàr-ru*É[RIN.MEŠ]
43) *pí-ṭá-ti-*⸢*šu*⸣
44) *ù yu-ša-ap-ši-iḫ* KUR-*šu*
45) *a-*⸢*mur*⸣! LÚ.MEŠ *ḫa-za-nu-tu* URU.MEŠ
46) *a-na ša-šu-nu ù pa-aš-ḫu*
47) *ù la-a ti-ìš-pu-ru-na*
48) *a-na šàr-ri* UGU-*ia-ma*
49) *ù* UGU ^{I}*Ia-an-ḫa-*⸢*mì*⸣
Up.ed. 50) NU.KÚR *a-*›*na*‹*-*⸢*mur*⸣ *pa-na-nu*
51) LÚ.MEŠ ⸢MÁŠKIM⸣ *ša-a*
52) ⸢URU⸣ *Ṣu-mu-*[*ra*]
Lft.ed. 53) [*tu*]-⸢*pa*⸣*-ri-šu* ⸢*be*⸣*-ri-nu ù an-nu-*[*ù*]
54) [*l*]*a-a yi-ìš-*⸢*mu*⸣ *ḫa-za-nu a-na ša-*[*šu*]
55) ⸢*i*⸣*a-nu* ÌR ⸢*ki*⸣*-*⸢*ma*⸣ ^{I}*Ia-an-ḫa-mi*
56) *a-na* L[UGA]L ÌR *ki-ti*

(32–36) Send a commissioner that he may take them,

(34–36) lest I leave my(?) city and depart to you.

(36–39) Behold, if the yeomen farmers depart, the *ʿapîru* men will take the city.

(39–44) Look, as for me, it is my intent [t]o serve the king according to the manner of my fathers, so may the king send his regular troops and may he pacify his land.

(45–50) Look, the city rulers have cities and they are at peace and they don't write to the king. It is against me and against Yanḫamu that there is hostility.

(50–56) Look(!), formerly the commissioners of Ṣumur would [se]ttle cases between us but behold, no city ruler listens to hi[m]. The k[in]g has no servant like Yanḫamu, a loyal servant.

EA 119

TRANSCRIPTION

Obv. 01) [^{I}]*Ri-ib-*^{d}IŠKUR ⸢*iš*⸣-[*ta-pár*]
02) ⸢*a*⸣-*na* EN-*šu šàr-ri* G[AL]
03) *šàr ta-am-ḫa‹-ra›* ^{d}NIN *š*[*a*]
04) URU *Gub-la ti-di-in*$_{4}$ GA.[KAL]
05) *a-na šàr-ri* EN-*ia*
06) *a-na* GÌR.MEŠ EN-*ia* ^{d}UTU-*ia*
07) 7-*šu* 7-*ta-an am-qú-ut*
08) *i-nu-ma yi-ìš-ta-pa-ru šàr-ru*
09) EN-*li ú-ṣur-mì ra-ma-an-ka*
10) ⸢*mi*⸣-*nu yi-na-ṣa-ra-ni*!(IR) *a-nu-ma*
11) *k*[*i*]-⸢*a*⸣-*ma aš*-⸢*ta*⸣-*pa-ru a-na* É.GAL ‹*a-na*›
12) LÚ.MEŠ ⸢*ma*⸣-⸢*ṣa*⸣-*a*[*r*]-*ti ù a*-⸢*na*⸣
13) ANŠE.KUR.RA.MEŠ ⸢*ù*⸣ [*i-na*-]⸢*ṣa*⸣[-*ru* URU-]⸢*šu*⸣
14) *mi-na i-pu-šu*-⸢*na*⸣ *a-na-ku*
15) *i-na ba-la-ṭì-ia i-na*-⸢*ṣí*⸣-*ru*
16) URU LUGAL *a-na ša-a-šu ù*
17) *šum-ma mi-ta-ti mi-na*
18) *i-pu-‹šu›-na i-nu-ma qa-bi a-na*
19) *pa-ni šàr-ri* ^{I}*Ri-ib-*^{d}IŠKUR
20) *šu-mi-it* ÉRIN.MEŠ *pí-ṭá-at*
21) *šàr-ri i-nu-ma ba-al-ṭù*
22) LÚ.MEŠ MÁŠKIM.MEŠ *ù*
23) *a-da-bu-ba ka-li ip-ši-šu-nu*
24) *ù yi*-⸢*du*⸣ *šàr-ru i-nu-ma*
25) ⸢ÌR⸣ *ki-ti a-na-ku a*-⸢*na*⸣ *ša-šu*
26) [*ú*]-*ul yi-iš-me* LUGAL *kar*$_{5}$-*ṣí*
27) [ÌR] *ki-ti-šu ša-a*
28) [*ta*-]⸢*aq*⸣-*bu a-na pa-n*[*i*]
29) [*šàr-ri* EN]-⸢*i*⸣-⸢*a*⸣ L[Ú.MEŠ]

Lo.ed. 30) [*ša-ru-tu* broken off........]
31) [.........broken off........]
32) [.........broken off........]

Rev. 33) [.........traces.........]

EA 119

TRANSLATION

(1–7) Rib-Hadda wr[ote] to his lord, the great king, the king of batt‹le›. May the Lady of Byblos grant str[ength] to the king, my lord. At the feet of my lord, my sun god, seven times (and) seven times have I fallen.

(8–10) Inasmuch as the king, my lord, writes "Guard yourself," who will guard me?

(10–18) Now thus have I been writing to the palace ‹for› garrison troops and for horses so that I [can] guard his [city]. What can I do myself? While alive I can guard the city of the king for him, but if I am dead, what can I [d]o?

(18–30) Inasmuch as it is said in the presence of the king, "Rib-Hadda caused the death of regular troops of the king," as the commissioners live, then I will report all their deeds. And the king knows that his loyal servant am I. May the king not listen to the slander of his loyal servant that the [evil] men are speaking in the presence of [the king,] my [lord].

(30–32) [............]

(33) *Broken away*

34) [^{I}*R*]*i-ib-*^{d}IŠKUR *i-na*
35) [*i-d*]*e-ni-šu* ÌR *a-na šà*[*r-ri*]
36) [*ia-*]*nu* ⸢LÚ⸣ *ša ia-aq-b*[*u*]
37) *ki-ti-i*⸢*a*⸣ ⸢*a*⸣*-na pa-ni šàr-*⸢*ri*⸣
38) EN-*ia ki-ti-ia yi-du*
39) *yi-du* LUGAL *ma-ni* UD. KAM^{v}
40) *yi-pu-šu du-um-qa*
41) *a-na ia-ši i-nu-ma*
42) *ia-nu lìb-bi ša-na* ⸢*a*⸣-⸢*na*⸣ *ia-ši*
43) *pa-nu-ia-ma a-na a-ra-ad*
44) *šàr-ri* EN-*ia a-nu-ma*
45) *di-nu an-nu-ú di-in*$_{4}$ *ki-ti-*[*i*]⸢*a*⸣
46) *ša-a qa-bi-ti ka-li*
47) *mi-im-mi yi-ìl-qé-šu*
48) *šàr-ru* EN-*l*[*i gáb-ba*]
49) ⸢*a*⸣*-na* ⸢*ša*⸣-⸢*a*⸣-[*šu ù*]
50) [*ú-nu-ta*] ⸢*ṣé*⸣*-ḫe-ru-ta*
51) *ia-di-nu* EN-*li a-na* ⸢ÌR⸣-^{d}[IŠKUR?]
52) *ù an-nu la-a la-qí*
53) *mi-na a-qa-bu-na*
54) *ap-pu-na-ma*
55) *a-nu-ma ṭup-pí ša-nu*
56) *ù ka-li ú-nu-tu-ia*
57) *ša* ⸢*it*⸣*-ti* ^{I}*Ia-pa-*^{d}⸢IŠKUR⸣
58) *šu-ut yi-ša-kan*
59) *i-na* ⸢*pa*⸣*-ni šàr-ri*

(34–44) [R]ib-Hadda, by himself, is the servant of the ki[ng]. [There is] no man who will confirm my loyalty before the king, my lord. He knows my loyalty. The king knows how long he has treated me favorably because I have no other mind; my committal is to serve the king, my lord.

(44–54) Now this case is a case about my loyalty. What I have said is, "As for all the property, may the king take it [all] for himself. [And] the small [objects], my lord may give to ʿAbdi-[Hadda]." This may not be acceptable. What more can I say?

(55–59) Now, there is a second tablet and all my possessions that are with Yapaʿ-Hadda. May it be placed before the king.

EA 120

TRANSCRIPTION

Obv. 01) [*ṭup-pí*] ⸢*ú*⸣*-nu-te* ⸢*ša*⸣ *it-*[*ti*]
02) [^{I}*Ia-pa-*]^{d}IŠKUR 10 ⸢*a*⸣*-ša-l*[*u*]
03) [x…]*ma* 2 *li-im* ⸢2⸣ *l*[*i-*]*im*
04) [..KI.LA]L.BI 10 KUŠ SUG? ⸢*ze*⸣*-ru-*⸢*tu*⸣
05) [1] *li-im* 1 *li-*⸢*im*⸣ ⸢KI⸣.LAL.BI
06) 1 *me* GÍR.GAL 1 *me* ⸢GÍR⸣.[TUR 8]0 ⸢*šu*⸣*-bu-bu*
07) 1 KUŠ SUG? ⸢*zi*⸣*-*⸢*ru*⸣ ⸢4⸣ [……]*me*
08) 1 GI *ma-*[…]⸢*tu*⸣ 4 [GI………]⸢*me*⸣
09) 1 GI *ku-*⸢*ku*⸣*-*⸢*tu*⸣ 4 ⸢GI⸣[…………]
10) 1 GI *ir-ta*$_{5}$ 4 […………………]
11) [1] *ma-qí-*⸢*bu*⸣ [1………………]
12) [1] *nam-ši-ti* [………………*t*]*i-*⸢*ma*⸣*-*⸢*me*⸣
13) [1]*me aš-qú-ma* ⸢*il*⸣(?)-[…]⸢MEŠ⸣[…..]⸢*šu*⸣*-nu*
14) [1]*me* 1 *li-*⸢*im*⸣ ⸢KUR⸣[…………]
15) [.....] 40 […………………]
16) ⸢*aš*⸣*-*⸢*šar*⸣*-ru-*⸢*ti*⸣ [………………]
17) [1] NÁ 2 KÙ.GI *uḫ-ḫi-*⸢*za*⸣
18) 1 [G]U.⸢ZA⸣ *ka-aḫ-šu* KÙ.GI *u*[*ḫ-ḫi-za*]
19) ⸢*ka*⸣*-*⸢*li*⸣*-*⸢*ši*⸣*-na ša* 1*-en*(?)
20) ⸢10⸣ *ki-p*[*a*]*-l*[*al*]*-l*[*u*] GIŠ.TASKARIN 1 *me* GU.Z[A] 1 *me* GAL*-ma*
21) 15 *ša-ba-tu* 15 ⸢*ma*⸣*-*⸢*ar*⸣*-*[*b*]*a-d*[*u*]
22) 90 *me* GÉME.MEŠ ÌR.MEŠ
23) ⸢*ia*⸣*-nu* ⸢*i*⸣*-*⸢*na*⸣ *bá-nu-*⸢*te*⸣ TÉŠ*-ši-*⸢*na*⸣
24) ⸢GAL⸣.TE*-ni* ⸢*yi*⸣*-*⸢*tu*⸣*-*⸢*ra*⸣*-*⸢*na*⸣*-*⸢*ši*⸣*-*⸢*na*⸣
25) ⸢*ù*⸣ ⸢*li*⸣*-*⸢*qá*⸣*-*⸢*a*⸣ ⸢NITA⸣.⸢MEŠ⸣
26) [1] *me* KÙ.[GI…⸢*la*⸣*-*⸢*qa*⸣[….]
27) ⸢*ḫa*⸣*-*⸢*ba*⸣*-*⸢*lu*⸣*-*⸢*ma*⸣ ⸢*zi*⸣[……….]

Lo.ed. 28) *a-ḫu-ši*$_{x}$(ŠE) [………………]
29) ⸢*dan*⸣*-na* ⸢*ù*⸣ ⸢*ia*⸣*-*⸢*nu*⸣

Rev. 30) ⸢*ša*⸣*-*⸢*a*⸣ *yi-pu-šu d*[*i-na*]
31) ⸢*it*⸣*-ta-šu* ^{I}ÌR-^{d}IŠ[KUR *ù*]

EA 120

TRANSLATION

(1–2) [Tablet of] the belongings that are with [Yapaʿ]-Hadda:
(2) 10 *ašallu* bowls
(3–4) [*x*...] two thousand each their weight.
(4–5) 10 leather ..., braided, one thousand each, their weight.

(6) 100 swords, 100 dag[gers], 80 *šububu.*
(7) 1 leather [...], braided, 4 [......]
(8) 1 reed *ma*[.....]*tu*, 4 [reed....]
(9) 1 reed *kukutu*, 4 reed [...]
(10) 1 reed breast plate, 4 [...]
(11) [1] hammer [1..........]
(12) [1] washbasin [.........]
(13) [1] hundred *ašquna* [....] *their* [....]
(14) [1] hundred 1 thousand [......]
(15) [......] 40 [.................]
(16) *aššarruti* [...................]
(17) [1] bed, 2 (ends?) overlaid with gold.
(18) 1 *kaḫšu*-[th]rone overlaid with gold.
(19) All of them of one (batch/person?)
(20) [10 *k*]*ipa*[*l*]*allu* of boxwood(?). 1 hundred chairs, 1 hundred [....]
(21) 15 *šabattu* garments, 15 blank[ets].
(22) 90–100 maidservants (and) man servants.
(23–25) There is none (like them) in the beauty of their persons (dignity), they are courtiers. May he return ⸢them⸣. But take the males.

(26–31) [1] hundred (shekels) of gold [...] he took [...] the debt [...] her brother [...] He is strong and there is no [...] who can take legal action against him.

32) ^{I}DUMU-*a-ṣí-mi* ⸢*uš*⸣-*ši-i*[*r*]
33) *šàr-ru a-na la-qí-ši-m*[*a*]
34) *ti-da-ga-lu pa-na*
35) *ù a-na* ^{I}ÌR-^{d}IŠKUR ⸢*qa*⸣-⸢*ba*⸣
36) *šàr-ru uš-ši-ir ú-n*[*u*]-⸢*te*⸣-⸢*ši*$_x$⸣(⸢ŠE⸣)
37) *a-na ša-ši*$_x$*(ŠE)*⸣ *ù* [...........]
38) *šàr-ru i-na ša-me*[.......]
39) *la-a ú-ṣí di-nu* [.........]
40) *a-nu-ma ka-li ú-nu-*⸢*te*⸣
41) *a-na ma-*⸢*ḫar*⸣ ⸢LUGAL⸣ ⸢*uš*⸣-⸢*ši*⸣-⸢*ir*⸣-*ti*
42) [*i-n*]*a* [*lì*]*b-bi* ⸢*ṭup*⸣-⸢*pí*⸣
43) [*šàr*]-*ru a-*⸢*na*⸣ *ša-a-šu* ⸤*yi-ìl-qé*⸥
44) ⸢*a*⸣-⸢*na*⸣ EN-*ia ú-da-mì-i*[*q ù*]
45) *a-*⸢*na*⸣ ^{LÚ}*tap-pí-ia*

(31–39) ʿAbdi-Had[da and] Bin-aṣimi the king has sent to fetch her; may they attend (to her). And to ʿAbdi-Hadda the king spoke, "Send her possessions to her." And the king [...] on hearing [the message]. The legal case was not pursued [...].

(40–45) Now I sent all the belongings to the king in a tablet. May the king [take] it all for himself. I wish to act favorably towards my lord [and] towards my associate.

EA 121

TRANSCRIPTION

Obv. 01) [^{I}]⸢*Ri*⸣-[*ib*]-^{d}⸢IŠKUR⸣ *i*[*š-tap-p*]*ár a-*[*na*]
02) EN-⸢*šu*⸣ LUGAL KUR.⸢MEŠ⸣ LUGAL GA[L]
03) ⸢^{d}⸣NIN *ša* URU *Gub-l*[*a*]
04) *ti-di-*⸢*in*$_4$⸣ ⸢KAL⸣.⸢GA⸣ *a-*[*na šàr-*]*ri*
05) EN-*ia* ⸢*a*⸣-[*n*]*a* [GÌR].MEŠ ⸢EN⸣-*ia*
06) ^{d}UTU-*ia* ⸢7⸣-⸢*šu*⸣ 7-*ta-a*[*n*]
07) *am-qú-ut i-nu-ma yi-ì*[*š-t*]*ap-ru-na*
08) *šàr-ru* EN-⸢*i*⸣*a* ⸢*a*⸣-*na i*⸢*a*⸣-[*š*]*i*
09) *ú-ṣur-mì* ⸢*ra*⸣-*m*[*a-a*]*n-k*[*a*]
10) *mi-nu yi-n*[*a-ṣí-*]*ra*[*-an-ni*]
11) *a-mur* LÚ.MEŠ *a-*[*bu-t*]*i-*⸢*i*⸣[*a*]
12) ⸢LÚ⸣.MEŠ *ma-ṣa-a*[*r*]-⸢*ti*⸣
13) *it-ti-šu-nu* ⸢*ù*⸣ [*ba-la-aṭ*]
14) ⸢*šàr*⸣-*ri* ⸢UGU⸣-[*šu-nu*]
15) [*a-mur*] ⸢*a*⸣-⸢*na*⸣-⸢*ku*⸣ [*ú-ul*]
16) [*ba-*]⸢*la*⸣-⸢*ṭu*⸣ ⸢LÚ⸣.⸢MEŠ⸣ *ma-*[*ṣa-ar-ti*]
17) [*i*]*š-tu šàr-*⸢*ri*⸣ *a-na* ⸢*i*⸣[*a-ši*]
18) [*ù*] *an-nu-ú* ⸢*i*⸣-⸢*na*⸣-*na nu*[*-kúr-tu*$_4$]
19) [KAL.G]A ⸢UGU⸣‹-*ia*› *qa-*⸢*bu*⸣ DUMU.MEŠ
20) [^{I}ÌR-]⸢*A*⸣-*ši-ir-*⸢*ta*⸣ *a-na*
21) [LÚ.MEŠ] GAZ.MEŠ ⸢*ù*⸣ LÚ.MEŠ
22) [*ša i-*]*te*$_9$*-ep-šu mi-nu-*[*um*]
23) [*a-n*]*a* ^{I}*Ri-*⸢*ib*⸣-^{d}IŠKUR
24) [*ù mi-li*]*k a-*[*na*] ⸢ÌR⸣-*ka*
25) [*ù a-na* URU-]⸢*ka*⸣ *aq-ba*
26) [..........]⸢*ma*⸣-*ti*[...]
Lo.ed. 27) [....................]
28) [....................]

EA 121

TRANSLATION

(1–7) Ri[b]-Hadda has w[ritt]n t[o] his lord, king of the lands, the gre[at] king; may the Lady of the city of Byblos grant strength t[o the ki]ng, my lord; at the feet of my lord, my sun god, seven times (and) seven times have I fallen.

(7–10) Inasmuch as the king, my lord, keeps writing to m[e], "Protect yourself," who will pro[tec]t [me]?

(11–17) Look, as for my fa[ther]s, garrison troops were with them and royal [provisions] were in their charge. [Look,] as for me, I have no [pro]visions, no garr[ision] troops from the king.

(18–23) [And] behold now, there is [seve]re ho[stility] against ‹me›. The sons of [ʿAbdi-]Ashirta have said to the *ʿapîru* [men] and (to) the men [who] have [jo]ined, "Who/what [do]es Rib-Hadda have?"

(24–28) [So take counsel co[ncerning] your servant [and concerning] your [city]. I said [....].

Rev. 29) [....................]
30) [....................]
31) [....................]
32) [....................]
33) [....................]
34) [....................]
35) [....................]
36) [....................]
37) [....................]
38) [.................]⸢*i*⸣-*a*
39) [.................]x ⸢*ša*⸣-*a*
40) [...]⸢*ti*⸣-⸢*ri*⸣[..........]
41) [*aš*-]*tap-pár a*-⸢*na*⸣ [É.GAL]
42) [*uš*]-*ši-ir* ⸢ÉRIN⸣.[MEŠ *pí-ṭá-ti*]
43) [*ú-u*]*l la-qú* [*i-na* UD. KAM^{v}]
44) [KUR.M]EŠ *a-na š*[*àr-ri ù*]
45) [*an-n*]*u-ú i-n*[*a-na yi-ìš-me*]
46) [*šàr*-]*ru a-wa*-⸢*te*⸣ Ì[R-*šu*]
47) *ù yu-wa*-⸢*ši*⸣-⸢*ra*⸣[-*an-ni*]
48) ÉRIN.MEŠ *pí-ṭá*-⸢*ti*⸣ ⸢*yi*⸣[-*ìl-qé*]
49) KUR *šàr*-⸢*ri*⸣ *a*-⸢*na*⸣ *šàr*-⸢*ri*⸣
50) *ù* ⸢*šu*⸣-[*up*]-⸢*ši*⸣-*iḫ* LÚ.MEŠ
51) *ḫa-za-n*[*i* LUGAL] *i-na* KUR.MEŠ
52) *ú-ul t*[*u*]-⸢*da*⸣-*ku*
53) *ki-ma* ⸢UR⸣.⸢GI_7⸣ *ù qa-la*-⸢*ta*⸣
54) ⸢*ša*⸣-⸢*ni*⸣-⸢*tam*⸣ [...*ki*]-*a-ma*
55) [*nu-kúr-*tu_4 *ma*-]*gal* UGU-[*i*]*a*
56) ⸢*di*⸣-⸢*ni*⸣[...........]*te mim*-⸢*ma*⸣
Up.ed. 57) [.....................]*ti*
58) ⸢LÚ⸣(?).⸢MEŠ⸣(?) [........]*la*
59) ⸢*ù*⸣(?) [..............]*t*[*i*]
Lft.ed. 60) [*uš*]-*ši*-⸢*ra*⸣ LÚ[..........]
61) ⸢*šum*⸣-⸢*ma*⸣ *i-ra-a*[*m*.......]
62) ⸢*a*⸣-⸢*na*⸣ ⸢ÌR⸣-*šu* ⸢*ù*⸣ [.......]
63) *a-na ša-a*-⸢*šu*⸣[...........]

(29–40) [...]

(41–53) [I] wrote to [the palace], "Send [regular army] troops." Did they [no]t take [the land]s for the k[ing in one day]? Behold no[w, may the ki]ng [heed] the words of [his] ser[vant] and may he send [to me] regular army troops that [they may] ta[ke] the land of the king, for the king. So pacify the city rulers [of the king] in the lands. Were they not [s]lain like dogs and you kept silent?

(54–59) Furthermore, [...Th]us there is se[vere hostility] against [m]e. My case [...]property [...] men [...] and [...]

(60–63) [...]send [...] If he loves [...] to his servant and[...] to him [...]

EA 122

TRANSCRIPTION

Obv.	01)	[^{I}]*Ri-ib*-^{d}IŠKUR *iš-tap*-⸢*pár*⸣
	02)	[*a-n*]*a* EN-*šu šàr* KUR.KI.‹MEŠ› LU[GAL GAL]
	03)	⸢*šàr*⸣ *ta-am-ḫa-ar*
	04)	^{d}NIN *ša* URU *Gub-la*
	05)	*ti-di-in*$_{4}$ KAL.GA *a-na*
	06)	*šàr-ri* EN-*ia a-na*
	07)	GÌR.MEŠ EN-*ia* ^{d}UTU-*ia*
	08)	7-⸢*šu*⸣ 7-*ta-an am-qú*-⸢*ut*⸣
	09)	⸢*i*⸣-⸢*nu*⸣-⸢*ma*⸣ *yi-qa-bu* ⸢*šàr*⸣-⸢*ru*⸣
	10)	⸢*ú*⸣-[*ṣu*]*r-mi ra-ma-an*-⸢*ka*⸣
	11)	*a-m*[*ur*] ⸢*pa*⸣-*na-nu i-na*
	12)	⸢UD⸣. K[AM^{v}].⸢MEŠ⸣ *a-bu-ti*-⸢*ia*⸣
	13)	LÚ.[MEŠ *m*]*a-ṣa-ar-‹ti›* LUGAL
	14)	⸢*it*⸣-⸢*ti*⸣-*šu-nu ù mi-im-mì*
	15)	LUGAL ⸢UGU⸣-*šu-nu ù an-nu-ú*
	16)	*a-na-ku ia-nu* ⸢*ba*⸣-*la*-⸢*aṭ*⸣
	17)	*šàr-ri i*-[*na*] ⸢ŠU⸣-*ia ù*
	18)	*ia-nu* LÚ.⸢MEŠ⸣ ⸢*ma*⸣-*ṣa-ar-ti*
	19)	⸢*šàr*⸣-⸢*ri*⸣ ⸢*it*⸣-*ti-ia a-na-ku*
	20)	⸢*i*⸣-⸢*na*⸣ ⸢*i*⸣-⸢*de*⸣-*ni-ia*
	21)	⸢*i*⸣-*na-ṣa*-[*ru ra-m*]*a-ni-ia*
	22)	[*a-mu*]*r* ⸢*a*⸣-[*bu-ia* URU *Gub-l*]*a*
	23)	⸢*a*⸣-*na ša*-[*šu ù*]
Lo.ed.	24)	LÚ.MEŠ *ma-ṣa-a*[*r-ti*]
Rev.	25)	⸢LÚ⸣-⸢*ti*⸣ *šàr-ri*
	26)	*it-ta-šu ù ba*-[*la*]-*aṭ*
	27)	*šàr-ri* UGU-*šu ù*
	28)	*an-nu-ú a-na-ku ú-ul*
	29)	*ma-ṣa-ar-tu ù ú-ul*
	30)	*ba-la-aṭ* LUGAL *a-na*
	31)	*ia-ši ù* ^{I}*Pa-ḫu-ra*

EA 122

TRANSLATION

(1–8) Rib-Hadda has written [t]o his lord, the king of the land‹s›, the [great] ki[ng], the king of battle; may the Lady of the city of Byblos grant strength to the king, my lord; at the feet of my lord, my sun god, seven times (and) seven times have I fallen.

(9–21) Inasmuch as the king says, "Protect yourself," look, formerly in the days of my fathers, garrison troops of the king were with them and property of the king was entrusted to them. But behold, as for me, there are no royal supplies i[n] my hand and there are none of the king's garrison troops with me. I, by myself, must prote[ct m]yself.

(22–31) [Loo]k, as for [my] fa[ther], he had [the city of Bybl]os [and] garrison troops, the king's men, were with him and royal provisions were entrusted to him. But behold, as for me, I have neither garrison troops nor royal provisions.

32) *a-pa-aš ip-ša ra-ba*
33) *a-na ia-ši uš-ši-ir*
34) LÚ.MEŠ KUR *Su-te ù*
35) *da-ku* LÚ *Še-er-da-*
\ *ni*
36) *ù* 3 LÚ.MEŠ
37) *šu-ri-ib a-na* KUR *Mi-iṣ-ri*
38) *ù* ⸢*ma*⸣*-ni* UD. KAM^{v}.MEŠ
39) *ti-ša-šu* URU UGU-*i*⸢*a*⸣
40) *ù al-le-e*
41) *ta-aq-bu* URU *ip-šu*
42) *ša la a-pí-ìš iš-tu*
43) *da-ri-ti a-pí-ìs*
44) *a-na ia-ši-nu ù yi-ìš-me*
45) *šàr-ru a-wa-te* ÌR-*šu*
46) ⸢*ù*⸣ *yu-wa-ši-ra*
47) [L]Ú.MEŠ *ú-ul ti-pu-uš*
48) [U]RU *ar-na mi-na*
Up.ed. 49) *i-pu-šu-na a-na-*⸢*ku*⸣
50) *ši-mé ia-‹ši›* UGU-*‹šu-nu›*
51) *ú-ul ti-im-i*
Lft.ed. 52) [*šum-ma*] ⸢LÚ⸣.MEŠ *i-na* [*p*]*a-ni šàr-ri* ⸢*ù*⸣
53) [*ia-*]*nu ši-mé ia-ši a-nu-ma*
54) [*k*]*i-a-ma aš-pu-ru a-na* É.GAL
55) *ù a-‹wa-tu-ia ú-ul› tu-uš-mu-na*

(31–35) And Paḫuru perpetrated a great misdeed against me. He sent Sutean men and

(35–49) they killed a Sherdanu and (they) took three men into the land of Egypt. And how many days has the city been enraged at me! And behold, the city is saying, "A deed that has never been done since time immemorial has been done to us!" So send the men lest the city commit rebellion. What could I do?

(50–55) Listen to m‹e›; do not refuse concerning ‹them›. [If] the men are in the king's presence or [no]t, listen to me. Now, thus I have been writing to the palace but ‹my words are not› being heeded.

EA 123

TRANSCRIPTION

Obv. 01) ^{I}*Ri-ib*-^{d}IŠKUR *iš-ta-pár*
02) *a-na* EN-*šu šàr-ri* GAL
03) *šàr-ri* KUR.KUR.KI *šàr-ri*
04) *ta-am-ḫa*-⸢*ar*⸣ ^{d}NIN
05) *ša* URU ⸢*Gub*⸣-*la ti-di-in*$_{4}$
06) KAL.GA *a-na* ⸢*šàr*⸣-*ri*
07) ⸢EN⸣-*ia a-na* ⸢GÌR⸣.MEŠ
08) ⸢EN⸣-*ia* ^{d}UTU ⸢7⸣-*šu*
09) 7-*ta-an am-‹qú-ut› ip-šu*
10) *ša-a la a-pí-ìš*
11) ⸢*iš*⸣-*tu da-ri-ti*
12) [*a*-]*pí-ìš a-na* URU *Gub-la*
13) [*u*]*š-ši-ir* ^{I}*Pí-ḫu*-⸢*ra*⸣
14) [LÚ].MEŠ KUR *Su-te d*[*a-ku*]
15) [LÚ] *Še-er-da-ni* [*ù*]
16) [*l*]*a-qú* 3 LÚ.‹MEŠ› ⸢*ù*⸣
17) [*š*]*u-ri-bu* ⸢ÌR⸣[.MEŠ-*ia a-na*]
18) ⸢KUR⸣ *Mi-iṣ*-⸢*ri*⸣ [*šum-ma*]
Lo.ed. 19) *la-a yu-wa*-[*ši-ru*-]
20) *šu-nu šàr-ru* E[N-*li*(?)]
Rev. 21) [*a*]-*di ti-pu-šu* [URU]
22) ⸢*ar*⸣-*na* UGU-*i*[*a*]
23) [*šum*]-*ma i-ra-am šà*[*r-ru*]
24) [EN]-*li* ÌR *ki-t*[*i-šu*]
25) [*ù*] *uš-ši-ra*
26) [3] LÚ.‹MEŠ› *ù ib-lu*-⸢*ṭá*⸣
27) ⸢*ù*⸣ *i-na-ṣí-ra*
28) URU *a-na šàr-ri*

EA 123

TRANSLATION

(1–9) Rib-Haddi has written to his lord, the Great King, king of ‹all› countries, the King of Battle: May the Lady of the city of Byblos grant power to the king, my lord; at the feet of my lord, ‹my› Sun, seven times and seven times I have fa‹llen›.

(9–21) A deed which has not been done from time immemorial [has] been done to the city of Byblos. Piḫura [s]ent Suteans; they sm[ote] a Sherdani [man and] they [t]ook three m‹en› and delivered [my] ser[vants to] the land of Egypt. [If] the king, [my] lo[rd,] does not rel[ease] them, [the city] will [y]et revolt against m[e].

(23–28) [I]f the ki[ng], my lord, loves [his] faith[ful] servant, [then] send the [three] m‹en› that I may live and that I may guard the city for the king.

29) *i-nu-ma i-ša-pa-ru*
30) *šàr-ru ú-ṣur-mi*
31) *ra-ma-an-ka iš-tu* \ *ma-ni*
32) *i-na-ṣí-ru-na*
33) 3 LÚ.‹MEŠ› *ša-a šu-ri-ib*
34) ^{I}*Pí-ḫu-ra uš-*⌜*ši*⌝*-ra*
35) *ù bal-ṭá-ti*
36) ^{I}ÌR-*i-ra-ma*
37) ^{I}SÌ.^{d}IŠKUR ^{I}⌜ÌR⌝.LUGAL
38) [*m*]*i-nu* ^{I}DUMU.MEŠ ^{I}ÌR-*A-ši*
Up.ed. 39) ⌜*ù*⌝ *la-qú* KUR \\-*ir-ta*
40) ⌜*šàr*⌝-⌜*ri*⌝ ⌜*a*⌝*-na ša-**šu-nu*

Lft.ed. 41) *yu-wa-ši-r*[*a* LUGAL ÉRIN.MEŠ]
42) *pí-ṭá-ti* ⌜*ù*⌝ [*ti-ìl-qé-*]
43) ⌜*šu*⌝⌜*-nu*⌝ [*a-na* EN-]⌜*li*⌝[*-ia*](?)

(29–37) Since the king writes, "Guard yourself!" with what shall I guard? Send the three m‹en› whom Piḫura brought in and I will survive: ʿAbdi-Râma, Yattin-Haddi, ʿAbdi-Milki

(38–43) [W]ho are the sons of ʿAbdi-Ashirta that they take the territory of the king for themselves? May [the king] send regular [troops] [that they may capture] them [for my lor]d.

EA 124

TRANSCRIPTION

Obv.
01) [*a-na šà*]*r-ri* EN-*i*[*a* ^{d}UTU-*ia*]
02) [*um-m*]*a* ^{I}*Ri-ib*-^{d}IŠKUR Ì[R-*ka-ma*]
03) [^{d}N]IN *ša-a* URU *Gu*[*b-la ti-di-in*$_4$]
04) [KAL.]GA *a-na šàr-ri* EN-[*ia a-na*]
05) [GÌ]R.MEŠ EN-*ia* ^{d}UTU-*ia* [7-*šu*]
06) [7-]*ta-an am-qú-ut* ^{I}*Ri-i*[*b*-^{d}IŠKUR]
07) [*i*]*š-ta-pár a-na* EN-*šu la-q*[*a-mi*]
08) [^{I}]*A-zi-ru ka-li* URU.MEŠ[-*ni-ia*]
09) URU *Gub-la i-na i-de-ni-ši*$_x$(ŠE)
10) *ir-te*$_9$-*ḫa-at a-na ia-ši* ⸢*ù*⸣
11) *mi-lik a-na* ÌR *ki-ti-ia*
12) *a-nu-ma i-te*$_9$-*li* ÉRIN.MEŠ *i-na*
13) URU *Gub-la ù la-qa-ši*$_x$(ŠE)
14) *i-na-na a-di yu-pa-ḫi-ru ka*[-*li*]
15) URU.MEŠ *ù yi-ìl-qú-ši*$_x$(ŠE) *a-ia*[-*mi*]
16) *i-zi-zu-na a-na-ku al*-[*lu-ú*]
17) *ki-a-ma yi-qa-bu la-qé*-[*mi*]
18) URU.MEŠ ^{I}*Ri-i*[*b* ^{d}IŠKU]R [*ù*]
19) URU *Ṣu-mu*[-*ra*..........]
20) *mi-ia*-[*mi*] *š*[*u-ut* ÌR UR.GI$_7$]
21) *ù la-qa* U[RU.MEŠ LUGAL *a-na ša-šu*]
22) *ù ḫa-za-nu*[-*ti da-ak*]
23) *yi-ša-al* [LUGAL...........]
24) *a-di ki-na-an*[-*na*............]
25) LUGAL *a-na na-ṣa*-[*ar* URU-*šu la-a*]
26) [*ìl*-]*te*$_9$[-*qé-ši*$_x$(ŠE) ^{I}*A-zi-ru*]

From the bottom of the obverse and the lower edge five lines must be missing.

Rev.
32') [^{I}*A-zi-ru*] ⸢*uš*⸣-*ši-ir* É[RIN.MEŠ *a-na*]
33') [*ṣa-b*]*a-at* URU *Gub-la* [*ù a-na*]
34') [*ṣa*-]*ba-at* URU *Baṭ-ru-na a*[*l-lu-ú*]

EA 124

TRANSLATION

(1–6) [To the ki]ng, m[y] lord, [my sun god; the messa]ge of Rīb-Haddi [your] se[rvant. May the La]dy of the city of By[blos grant stren]gth to the king, [my] lord. [At the fe]et of my lord, my sun god, [seven times (and) seven] times have I fallen.

(6–11) Rī[b-Haddi has] written to his lord: Aziru has ta[ken] all of [my] citi[es]. The city of Byblos, alone, remains to me. So take counsel concerning your loyal servant.

(12–22) Now, should an army come against the city of Byblos then it will take it. Even now, he is assembling al[l] the cities and he will take it. Whe[re] will I take a stand? Be[hold] thus he is saying, "Taken are the cities of Rī[b-Hadd] [and] the city of Ṣumu[r.....]." Wh[o] is h[e, a slave, a dog,] that he has taken the ci[ties of the king for himself] and [has slain] the city ruler[s]?

(23–26) May [the king] ask [...] still likewise [...] the king to prote[ct his city lest Aziru ta]k[e it].

(32'–34') [Aziru] has sent troops to [se]ize the city of Byblos [and to se]ize the city of Baṭrōna.

35’) [*k*]*i-a-ma ti-qa-bu at-‹ta›-m*[*a*

36’) [*t*]*i-ìš-tap-ru a-na ia-ši iš-t*[*u*]

37’) [*k*]*a-li* LÚ.MEŠ *ḫa-za-nu-ti a-*[*na*]

38’) [*m*]*i-ni ti-iš-ta-pa-ru-na š*[*u-nu*]

39’) [*a-n*]*a ka-ta*$_5$ URU.MEŠ-*nu a-na š*[*a-šu-nu*]

40’) [URU.]MEŠ-*ni-ia la-qa* ^{I}*A-z*[*i-ru*]

41’) [*ù a*]*n-nu-ú ta-ra a-na*

42’) [*ṣa-ba-a*]*t* URU *Gub-la a-n*[*a*]

43’) *di-*[*ni* ^{I}ÌR-*A-*]*ši-ir-ta* [*ù*]

44’) ^{I}*Pa-w*[*u-ra i-na*]*-na y*[*i-qa-bu*]

45’) *a-na ia-ši a-nu-*[*ma la-a*]

46’) *yu-ṣa* LUGAL *ù* [*lu tu-ṣa*]

47’) *ki-ma a-bu-ti-ka* [*na-ak-ru*]

48’) LÚ.MEŠ *ša-ru-tu iš-t*[*u* LUGAL]

49’) *a-mur a-na-ku ú-ul* 1 GU$_4$.MEŠ

50’) *ù la-a* ÙZ.MEŠ *ù a-na*

51’) [*m*]*i-ni uš-ši-ir* LUGAL ÉRIN.MEŠ ⌜KEŠDA⌝-*ma*

52’) [*p*]*í-ṭá-ti a-na la-qí* URU[.MEŠ]

53’) [*l*]*a-a yi-le-ú la-qa*[*-ši*$_x$(ŠE)*-na*]

54’) [*ù*] *la-qa-ma* URU *Gub-*[*la*]

55’) [*iš-t*]*u qa-ti-ka la-a-*[*mi*]

56’) [*ti-ìl-q*]*u-ši*$_x$(ŠE) *a-di da-r*[*i-ti*]

57’) [*šum-ma*] *lìb-bi* LUGAL *a-na ‹na›-ṣ*[*a-ar* URU-*šu*]

58’) [*id*]*-na ù uš-š*[*i-ra* LÚ.MEŠ]

59’) [*ma-ṣa-*]*ar-ta* [*ki-ma*]

60’) [*ar-*]*ḫi-iš i-n*[*a ḫa-mu-ti-iš* (?)]

61’) [*al-lu-*]*ú* 3 LÚ.MEŠ-[*ia ša*]

62’) [*šu-ri-bu* LÚ.]MEŠ KUR!(ŠE) *Su*[*-tu*]

Lft.ed. 63’) [.........................]

64’) [.........................]

65’) [.........................]

66’) [.........................]

67’) [...........] U[RU.......]

(34'–48') B[ehold th]us you say, "It is yo‹u› always writing to me mo[re than a]ll the city rulers." W[h]y should they write [t]o you? [They] have cities. [It is my citi]es Az[iru] has taken. [And b]ehold, he has turned to [sei]ze the city of Byblos. In [the] ca[se of 'Abdi-A]shirta [and] Paw[ura, he s[ays n]ow to me, "No[w] the king [did not] come forth." But [may you come forth] like your forefathers. Rebellious men [have become openly hostile] again[st the king].

(49'–56') Look, as for me, there is not one of the oxen or of the goats. [W]hy did the king send regular troops (chariot warriors and [a]rchers) to take the cities? He was [n]ot able to take [them?]. If (Aziru) should take the city of Bybl[os fr]om your hand, [you will not ta]ke it ev[er].

(57'–60') [If] it is the king's will to ‹pro›te[ct his city, gr]ant and se[nd garri]son [troops right] away,] in [a hurry(?)].

(61'–67') [Beho]ld the three men [that the me]n of the land(!) of the Su[teans took to (Egypt)........].

EA 125

TRANSLATION

Obv. 01) *a-na* ⸢*šàr*⸣*-ri* E[N-*ia*]
02) ⸢*um*⸣*-ma* ^{I}*Ri-ib-*⸢^{d}⸣⸢IŠKUR⸣ Ì[R-*k*]*a-*⸢*ma*⸣
03) *a-na* GÌR.MEŠ EN-*ia* ^{d}U[TU]-⸢*ia*⸣
04) 7-*šu* 7-*ta-*⸢*an*⸣ *am-qú-ut*
05) ^{d}NIN *ša* URU *Gub-la*
06) *ti-di-in*$_{4}$ GA.KAL *a-na*
07) *šàr-ri* EN-*ia i-nu-ma*
08) *i-qa-bu šàr-ru* EN-*ia*
09) *ú-ṣur-mì ra-ma-an-ka*
10) *ù ú-ṣur* URU *šàr-ri*
11) *ša it-ti-ka iš-*⸢*tu*⸣
12) *ma-ni i-na-ṣa-ru-na*
13) *ra-ma-ni-ia* ⸢*ù*⸣ URU [LUGAL]
14) ⸢*pa*⸣*-na-nu* LÚ.MEŠ *ma-ṣa-ar-*⸢*ti*⸣
15) *šàr-ri it-ti-ia ù*
16) *šàr-ru ia-di-*⸢*nu*⸣ ŠE.*IM*.ḪI.A
17) *iš-tu* KUR *Ia-ri-mu-ta*
18) *a-na a-ka-li-šu-nu ù*
19) *an-nu-ú i-na-na*
20) *iš-ta-ḫa-aṭ-ni* ^{I}*A-zi-ru*
21) *ù iš-ta-ni ú-ul*
22) GU$_{4}$.MEŠ *ù la-a* ÙZ.[MEŠ]
23) *a-na ia-ši la-qa-a*
24) ^{I}*A-zi-ru gáb-ba*

Lo.ed. 25) *ù ia-nu* ŠE.*IM*.ḪI.A
26) *a-*⸢*na*⸣ *a-ka-*⸢*li*⸣*-ia*

Rev. 27) *ù* LÚ.MEŠ [*ḫu*]*-up-ši*
28) *pa-aṭ-ru a-*[*na*] URU.MEŠ
29) *a-šar i-ba-*⸢*ši*⸣ ŠE.*IM*.[ḪI.A]
30) *a-na a-ka-li-šu-nu*

EA 125

TRANSLATION

(1–7) To the king, my lord, the message of Rib-Haddi [yo]ur ser[vant]: At the feet of my lord, my s[un god,] seven times (and) seven times have I fallen. May the Lady of the city of Byblos grant power to the king, my lord.

(7–13) As to the king, my lord, saying, "Guard yourself and guard the city of the king which is in your charge," with whom will I guard myself and the city [of the king]?

(14–18) Formerly garrison troops of the king were with me and the king would furnish grain from the land of Yarimuta for their sustenance.

(18–30) But behold now, Aziru has repeatedly raided me. I have no oxen and no goats. Aziru has taken all, and there is no grain for my sustenance. And my yeoman farmers have departed t[o] towns where there is grain for their sustenance.

31) *ša-ni-tam a-mi-ni yi-ìš-ta-*⸢*ka*⸣*-nu-ni*
32) *šàr-ru ki-ma* LÚ.MEŠ ⸢*ḫa*⸣*-za-*⸢*nu*⸣*-*⸢*ti*⸣
33) LÚ.MEŠ *ḫa-za-nu-tu* URU-*šu-*⸢*nu*⸣
34) *a-na ša-šu-nu* LÚ.MEŠ
35) *ḫu-‹up›-šu-šu-nu i-na* [erasure]
36) *šap-li-šu-nu ù*
37) *a-na-ku* URU.MEŠ-*ia a-na* ^{I}*A-zi-ri*
38) *ù ia-ti yu-ba-ú*
39) *a-na ma-ni i-pu-šu ki-ta*
40) *it-ti-šu mi-nu* UR.G[I_7.MEŠ]
41) ^{I}DUMU.MEŠ ^{I}ÌR-*A-ši-ir-t*[*a*]
42) *ù ›ù‹ ti-pu-šu-*⸢*na*⸣
43) *ki-ma lìb-bi-šu-nu ù*
44) *tu-wa-ši-ru-na* URU.MEŠ
45) *šàr-ri i-na* ^{d}IZI

(31–45) Moreover, why does the king rank me like the city rulers? As for the city rulers, they have their towns;

(35–45) their ye‹om›an farmers are subject to them. But, as for me, my towns belong to Aziru and he is seeking (to kill) me. Why should I make an alliance with him? Who are the do[gs], the sons of ʿAbdi-Ashirt[a] that they should do as they please and send the cities of the king up in flames?

EA 126

TRANSCRIPTION

Obv. 01) ^{I}*Ri-ib-ed-di qí-bí*-[*ma*]
02) *a-na* LUGAL *be-li-ia a-na* KI.⸢TA⸣
03) GÌR.MEŠ BAD-*ia* 7 *u* 7 *am-qut*^{ut}
04) *i-nu-ma ša-pár be-li a-na* GIŠ.⸢TASKARIN⸣-*ma*
05) *iš-tu* KUR.MEŠ *Sà-al-ḫi ù iš-t*[*u*]
06) URU.KI *Ú-ga-ri-ti*$_{7}$ *tu-ul*$_{11}$*-qú*-⸢*na*⸣
07) *la-a-mi i-le-ú uš-šar*
08) GIŠ.MÁ.MEŠ-*ia a-na aš-ra-nu*
09) *i-nu-ma nu-kúr-tu*$_{4}$ ^{I}*A-zi-ru*
10) *it-ti-ia ù gáb-bi* LÚ.MEŠ ⸢*ḫa*⸣-*za-nu*-
tu$_{4}$
11) *šal-mu-šu ki lìb-bi-šu-nu*
12) *ti*$_{7}$*-la-ku-na* GIŠ.MÁ.MEŠ-*šu-nu*
13) *ù* ⸢*ti*$_{7}$⸣-*ìl-qú-na ḫi-ši-iḫ-ta-šu-nu*
14) *ša-ni-tam mi-nu-um ia-di-nu*
15) ⸢*mi*⸣-⸢*im*⸣-*ma ù ba-la-ṭá*(*m*)
16) LUGAL *a-na* ^{LÚ}*ḫa-za-nu-ti ib-ri-ia*
17) *ù a-na ya-ši la-a-mi*
18) *ia*-⸢*di*⸣-*nu mi-im-ma ù pa*-⸢*na*⸣-*nu*
19) *a-na* ^{LÚ}*a-bu-ti-ia yu-ša-ru*
20) *iš-tu* É.GAL.MEŠ KÙ.BABBAR.MEŠ
21) *ú mi-im-mu a-na ba-la-ṭì-šu*-‹*nu*›
22) *ù yu-ši-ru be-li* ÉRIN.MEŠ
23) *a-na ša-a-šu-nu ù a-nu-ma*
24) *a-na-ku aš-pu-ru a-na be-li-ia*
25) *a-na* ÉRIN.MEŠ *ù* ⸢ÉRIN⸣.⸢MEŠ⸣ *ma-ṣa-ar-tu*
26) *la-a tu*-[*ša-ru-na*] *ù*
27) *mi-im-mu* [*la-a-*]*mi*
28) *yu*-⸢*da*⸣-⸢*nu*⸣ [*a-na i*]*a-a-ši*
29) ⸢*ù*⸣(!) ⸢*a*⸣(!)-⸢*ya*⸣(!) *a*[*l-la-ka*]*-am*
Lo.ed. 30) ⸢*a*⸣-*na-ku i*-⸢*nu*⸣-[*ma qa-bi*]-*m*[*i*]
31) ⸢LUGAL⸣ *be-li ú*[*-ṣur ra-ma-an-ka*]

EA 126

TRANSLATION

(1–3) Rib-Hadda: Speak to the king, my lord: Beneath the feet of my lord seven (times) and seven (times) have I fallen.

(4–13) Inasmuch as my lord has written for boxwood, it is from the mountains of Salḫu and from the city of Ugarit that they are brought. I am unable to send my ships there because Aziru is at war with me and all the city rulers are at peace with him. Their ships go about as they please and they bring whatever they need.

(14–30) Furthermore, why does he (the king) give royal supplies and rations to the city rulers, my fellows, while to me he does not give anything? But formerly, to my fathers, silver was sent from the palace, and supplies for their sustenance and my lord sent troops to them. But now, I write to my lord but troops and garrison troops are not s[en]t and supplies are not issued [to] me. ⸢So⸣(!) ⸢where](!) [can] I [g]o myself?

(30–31) Inasmuch as the king, my lord [has said:] "G[uard yourself]

Rev. 32) *ù ú-ṣ*[*ur* URU LUGAL *ša it-ti-ka*]
33) *ki a-na-ṣa*[*-ru ra-ma-ni-ia*]
34) *ša-pár-ti* ⸢*a*⸣-[*na* LUGAL *be-li-ia*]
35) *la-qú-mi* [*gáb-bi* URU.MEŠ-*ia*]
36) DUMU ^{I}ÌR[-*A-ši-ir-ta* EN?-]⸢*šu*⸣-⸢*nu*⸣
37) URU.KI *Gu-u*[*b-la* 1-*en ir-ti-ḫa-at*]
38) *a-na ia-a-ši ù a*[*l-lu ú-ši-ir-*]*ti*
39) LÚ.DUMU *ši-‹ip›-ri-ia a-*[*na* LUGAL E]N-*li-ia*
40) ÉRIN.MEŠ *la-a yu-ša-r*[*u*]
41) *ù* LÚ.DUMU *ši-ip-r*[*i-ia*]
42) *la-a tu-ša-ṣú-na-*[*šu*]
43) *ù uš-ši-ra-šu qa-*⸢*du*⸣*-mi*
44) ÉRIN.MEŠ *re-ṣú-ti šum-ma* LUGAL
45) *za-ir* URU.KI-*šu ù i-*⸢*zi*⸣*-ba-ši*
46) *ù šum-ma ia-ti-ia* ⸢*ù*⸣
47) ⸢*i*⸣*-pa-ṭá-ra-ni-mi* ⸢*ù*⸣
48) *uš-ši-ra* LÚ-*ka yi-n*[*a-ṣa-a*]*r-ši*
49) *mi-nu-mi la-a yu-da-n*[*u*]
50) *iš-tu* ⸢É⸣.GAL *mi-im-*[*m*]*u*
51) *a-na ia-ši ù*!(LA) ÉRIN.MEŠ ⸢*Ḫa*⸣-[*t*]*i*
52) *ù i-ša-ra-pu* KUR.M[EŠ *a-n*]*a* IZI
53) *aš-tap-pár aš-ta-ni la-*[*a*]
54) *ia-tu-ru-na a-wa-tu*
55) *a-na ia-a-ši ṣa-ab-tu*
56) *ka-li* KUR.MEŠ LUGAL BAD-*ia*
57) *ù qa-al be-li iš*!(TU)-*tu-šu-nu*
58) *ù a-nu-ma i-na-na tu-*
59) [*b*]*a-lu-na* ÉRIN.MEŠ KUR.MEŠ *Ḫa-ti*
Up.ed. 60) ⸢*a*⸣-[*n*]*a ṣa-*⸢*ba*⸣*-ti* URU.KI *Gub*[*-la*]
61) *ù mi-lik a-na* URU.⸢KI⸣-[*ka*]
62) ⸢*ù*⸣ *la-a-mi yi-*⸢*iš*⸣*-me*
Lft.ed. 63) [LU]GAL *a-na* LÚ.MEŠ *mi-ši gáb-*⸢*bi*⸣ [K]Ù.BABBAR *u* ⸢KÙ⸣.⸢GI⸣ LUGAL
64) *ta-di-nu-ni a-na* DUMU.MEŠ ÌR-*A-ši-*⸢*ir*⸣*-ti*
65) *ù šu*(!)*-a-ti ta-di-nu-ni* DUMU.MEŠ ÌR-*A-ši-*⸢*ir*⸣*-ti*
66) *a-na šàr-ri* ⸢*da*⸣*-an-ni ù ki-na-na da-nu*

(32–44) and gua[rd the city of the king that is in your charge]," how can I pro[tect myself]? I wrote [to the king, my lord,] "[All my towns] are taken! The son of ʿAbdi-[Ashirta is] their [master]. Only the city of Byb[los remains] to me," and be[hold,] I [sent] my emissary t[o the king,] my [lo]rd; troops were not sent and as for [my] emissary, they are not sending [him] forth. So send him wi[th] rescue forces.

(44–51) If the king hates his city, then I will abandon it, but if it is me (he hates) then I will absent myself, then send your man, let him g[uard] it. Why are supplies not issued to me from the palace?

(51–58) And(!) as for the Hittite army, thus it is setting fire to the territories. I have written over and over; word does not come back to me. All the territories of the king, my lord, are seized, but my lord keeps silent concerning them.

(58–66) And even now, they are bringing the Hittite army to capture the city of Byblos, so take counsel concerning [your] city and don't listen to the men of the expeditionary force. They were transferring all the king's silver and gold to the sons of ʿAbdi-Ashirta and the sons of ʿAbdi-Ashirta are transfering that (silver and gold) to the strong king (i.e. of Ḫatti) and thus they are strong.

EA 127

TRANSCRIPTION

Obv. 01) [.........................]trace
02) [^{I}*Ri-ib-*^{d}IŠKUR *iš-tap-*]*pár*
03) [*a-na* LUGAL] ⌜EN⌝-[*šu*]
04) [*um-ma* ^{I}*Ri-ib-*^{d}IŠKUR]⌜ÌR⌝ *ki-ti-šu*
05) [*a-na* LUGAL EN-*ia*] *qi*(?)-*bí-mi*
06) [*a-nu-ma la-qí* URU] ⌜*Ṣu*⌝-⌜*mu*⌝-⌜*ur*⌝
07) [^{I}*Pa-wu-ra la na-da-*]⌜*an*⌝ ⌜URU⌝ *Ṣu-mu-ur*
08) *a*[*-na* LÙ.MEŠ SA.GAZ.MEŠ] *ù qé-bi-ir qa-al*
09) [LUGAL EN-*ia ù la-qú*] *gáb-bi*
10) [URU.MEŠ-*ia ú*]*an-nu-ú i-qa-bu-ni*$_{7}$
11) [*uṣ-ṣur lu na-aṣ-ra-ta* URU.]KI
12) [*Gub-la a-nu-ma* ^{I}*Ia-ab-ni-*]^{d}IŠKUR *uṣ-ṣí*
13) [ÉRIN.]⌜MEŠ⌝ ⌜*pí*⌝[*-ṭá-ti*] ⌜*ù*⌝ *ìl-qé-nu ši-*⌜*si*⌝*-mi*
14) *p*[*a-n*]*i-nu* UGU U[RU] *Gub-la ù ma-an-nu*
15) *ù a-nu-ma gáb-‹bi›-mi a-na m*[*u-ḫ*]*i-ia*
16) [*ù*] ⌜*ma*⌝-⌜*an*⌝-[*n*]*u i-re-*⌜*ṣa*⌝*-an-ni*
17) [*al-l*]*u-mi la-*⌜*qí*⌝ URU *Gub-la* ^{KI}
18) ⌜*ù*⌝ *ia-nu-um* LÚ.MEŠ KUR *Mi-iṣ-ri*
19) [*ša*] ⌜*i*⌝*-ri-bu-ni*$_{7}$ ⌜*an*⌝*-na- kam*^{V}
20) [*ti-né-*]⌜*ep*⌝*-ša-mi* ⌜URU⌝ ⌜*Gub*⌝*-la*
Lo.ed. 21) [*a-na* LÚ S]A.⌜GAZ⌝.⌜MEŠ⌝ *ù ia-*⌜*nu*⌝-⌜*um*⌝
22) [ÉRIN.MEŠ *Ka-š*]*a ša* ⌜*ir*⌝*-‹ri›-bu-*⌜*ni*$_{7}$⌝
Rev. 23) [*ù al-*]*lu-mi* ^{I}*Ia-an-ḫa-*⌜*mu*⌝
24) [*it-ti*] LUGAL *i-*⌜*ša*⌝*-al-šu*
25) [*a-na ka-*]*ar-ṣí* URU *Gub-la* URU ⌜*ki*⌝*-ti-mi*
26) ⌜*šum*⌝*-ma lìb-*⌜*bi*⌝ ⌜LUGAL⌝ *be-li-ia*
27) *a-*[*na*] *na-ṣa-*[*a*]*r* URU-*šu ù yi-di-na*$_{7}$
28) BAD-*ia* LÚ.MEŠ *ma-ṣa-ar*$^{M⌜EŠ⌝}$*-šu*(?)
29) ⌜*ù*⌝ *na-*⌜*aṣ*⌝*-ra-at*

EA 127

TRANSLATION

(1–14) [....Rib-Hadda wro]te [to the king, [his] ⌜lord⌝; [the message of Rib-Haddi,] his loyal servant: speak [to the king, my lord], [Now taken is the town of] Ṣumur. [Pawura did not giv]e the town of Ṣumur t[o the *ʿapîru* men] and he was buried; [the king] kept silent [and they have taken]all[my towns, and] behold, he is saying to me, ["Guard, may you guard the cit]y [of Byblos; now, Iabni]-Baʿlu, has come forth (with) the [regul]ar tro[ops] come forth and he will take us." Cry: "Our concern is with the ci[ty] of Byblos!" And who?

(15–22) And now, all are against me and who will help me? Behold, the city of Byblos is taken and there will be no Egyptian personnel [who] can enter there. (If) the city of Byblos [joi]ns [the *ʿa*]*pîru* men then there will be no [Cush]ite [troops] who can enter in.

(23–29) [And be]hold, Yanḫamu is [with] the king; may he ask him [concerning the sla]nder of the city of Byblos, the faithful city. If it is the king's desire to protect his city, then may my lord give of his(?) garrison troops and it will be protected.

30) *ù a-nu-ú i-qa-bu* BAD-*ia*
31) *ki-ma pa-na-nu-um i-te*$_{9}$*-lu* ^{I}ÌR-*Aš*-⸢*ra*⸣-*tu*$_{4}$
32) *a-na ṣé-ri-ia da-*[*n*]*a-ku*
33) ⸢*ù*⸣ *a-nu-*⸢*ú*⸣ *re-ḫi-iṣ-mi* LÚ.MEŠ-⸢*ia*⸣
34) ⸢*ù*⸣ ⸢*ša*⸣-⸢*ni*⸣-⸢*tam*⸣ ⸢*la*⸣ ⸢*ma*⸣-*ṣa-ku* \ *ṣí-ir-ti*
35) ⸢*ù*⸣ *li-di-na*$_{7}$ *be-li-ia*
36) [x]*me* LÚ.MEŠ *ù* 1 *me* ⸢ÉRIN.MEŠ⸣ KUR *Ka-ši*
37) ⸢*ù*⸣ 30 GIŠ.GIGIR.MEŠ ⸢*ù*⸣ *lu-ú a-na-ṣa-ar*
38) [KUR].KI *be-li-ia a-di a-ṣí*
39) [ÉRIN.ME]Š *pí-ṭá-ti ra-bi-ti*
40) [*ù i*]*l-qú* BAD-[*i*]⸢*a*⸣ KUR *A-mur-ri*
41) [*a-na*] ⸢*ša*⸣-⸢*šu*⸣ ⸢*ù*⸣ ⸢*pa*⸣-*aš-ḫa-at*
Up.ed. 42) [KUR.KI-*šu*] ⸢*ù*⸣ [URU.]KI-*ia*
43) [...]
Lft.ed. 44) [............LU]⸢GAL⸣ *ša* [.................]
45) [..........URU *Gu*]*b-la*^{K}[^{I}].................]
46) [.........LÚ S]A.GAZ.MEŠ......*ù*]*mi-ta-*[*ti*]

(30–42) And, behold, I say: My lord, as in the past ʿAbdi-Ashrata was attacking me (and) I was strong, but behold, my personnel are crushed and furthermore, I am not adequate (I am hard pressed), so may my lord give [*x*] hundred men (of Egypt) and one hundred Cushite warriors and thirty chariots and I will verily protect [the lan]d of my lord until the coming forth of a large [re]gular army [that] my lord [may ta]ke the land of Amurru [for] himself so that [his land] will be pacified and my [cit]y.

(42–46) […the kin]g of […the city of Byb]los […the *ʿa*]*pîru* men [….and I] will be dead.

EA 128

TRANSCRIPTION

Not Collated

Obv. 01) [..]
02) [..]
03) [..]
04) [..]
05) [..]
06) [..]
07) [..]
08) [..............M]ÁŠKI[M..........................]
09) [................]LUG[AL........................]
10) [................] ^{I}*A-z*[*i-ru*........................]
11) [..............*gá*]*b-b*[*i*..........................]
12) [.................] trace [.........................]
13) [..]
14) [..]
15) [..]
16) [..]
Lo ed. 17) [..]
18) [..]
Rev. 19) [..........*g*]*áb-bi* [................................]
20) [URU *Gu-u*]*b-la* ^{KI}.................................]
21) [..........]^{I}*I-li-ra-*[*pí-í*?...........................]
22) [*a-na* KI.]TA GÌR.MEŠ LUGAL E[N-*ia*]
23) [^{d}UTU-*ia* 7-*šu* 7-*ta-an- am*]-*qut* ^{ut}-⌜*ma*⌝
24) [*ù yi-i*]*š-mé* LUGAL *be-l*[*i*.............................]
25) [*i-pí-iš*] LÚ *ar-ni-šu*
26) [.......................*a*-]*mur šu-ut*
27) [..........................]*yi-iq-b*[*u-*...]
28) [..........................] *mi-im-m*[*a*]
29) [..........................]*a-mur-m*[*i*]
30) [..........................]*a-na* LÚ.ME[Š]-*k*[*a*]
31) [................] trace [..........................]

EA 128

TRANSLATION

This fragmentary tablet is noted in the records as missing since 1963.

(1–7) [––––].

(8–11) [...co]missio[ner....] the kin[g...]Az[iru...a]ll[...].

(19–30) [...] a]ll [....the city of By]blos [....] Ilu-ra[piʾ...under]neath the feet of the king, [my] l[ord, my sun god, seven times (and) seven times have I] fallen [so may] the king, my lord, [lis]ten t[o the deed] of his transgressor [...L]ook he [...] he is sayi[ng...] look, [...] to ⸢your⸣ men [....].

EA 129

TRANSCRIPTION

Obv. 01) *[^{I}Ri-i]b-⸢ad⸣-⸢di⸣ [qi-bí-mi]*
02) *[a-n]a* ⸢LUGAL⸣ *be-⸢li⸣-[šu* LUGAL GAL *a-na* KI.TA]
03) [GÌR.]⸢MEŠ⸣*‹-ka›* 7 *ù* ⸢7⸣[*am-qut^{ut}*]
04) *⸢yi⸣-‹iš›-al* ⸢LUGAL⸣ *be-l[i a-na]* ⸢DUMU⸣.⸢MEŠ⸣
05) ⸢^{I}⸣⸢ÌR⸣*-A-ši-ir-⸢ti⸣ ⸢i⸣-⸢nu⸣-⸢ma⸣*
06) *[k]i-⸢i⸣ ⸢lìb⸣-bi-⸢šu⸣-⸢nu⸣ ⸢ti⸣-⸢pu⸣-[šu-na]*
07) *⸢mi⸣-⸢i⸣a šu-nu* UR.⸢MEŠ⸣ *⸢ka⸣-‹al›-b[u]*
08) *⸢i⸣-⸢nu⸣-ma ti-pu-šu-⸢na⸣ ⸢a⸣[-na ša-šu-nu]*
09) *⸢ki⸣!-⸢am⸣-ma gu$_5$-mi-ru gáb!-b[i]*
10) [KUR].MEŠ LUGAL *a-na* UZ[U.M]EŠ *qa-[ti-šu-nu]*
11) L[Ú].⸢MEŠ⸣ *ḫa-za-ni* LUGAL *⸢da⸣-[ku]* ⸢ÉRIN⸣.⸢MEŠ⸣*-⸢ka⸣*
12) *⸢ù⸣* LÚ.MEŠ *we-ʾì ⸢ù⸣* ⸢LÚ⸣.⸢MEŠ⸣ ⸢LUGAL⸣
13) *⸢i⸣-na-an-na ša ìl-⸢qú⸣ ⸢a⸣-⸢na⸣ ⸢qa⸣[-at]*
14) LÚ.MEŠ MÁŠKIM .MEŠ ^{I}LUGAL *be-⸢li⸣-[ia]*
15) *ù ra-b[i]-ṣú* LÚ *⸢em⸣[-qú šu-ut]*
16) *ša ka-bu-ut ma-gal ⸢ù⸣ ⸢da⸣-[ku-šu]*
17) *gáb-‹bi›* URU.⸢MEŠ⸣*-ia a-⸢na⸣ ⸢šu⸣-⸢nu⸣ [ù]*
18) URU.⸢KI⸣ *Baṭ-ru-na ⸢ir⸣-⸢ti⸣-⸢ḫa⸣-[at a-na ia-ši]*
19) *⸢ù⸣ ti-ba-⸢ú⸣-na-ši la-q[a-a]*
20) *[l]a-qí-mi ši-a-ti ⸢ù⸣* [URU.KI *Gub-la*]
21) *[ti-]⸢ìl⸣-⸢qú⸣-na ⸢i⸣-nu-ma* [...........]
22) [......]*qa-ti* [...]UZU[.MEŠ *qa-ti*]
23) [.......]⸢ŠÀ⸣?[................]
24) *ù l[a?*........................]
25) UGU*-šu* [....................]
26) *⸢ma⸣-gal a-di ti-qa-b[u-na ar-na]*
27) [GA]L *i-⸢pé⸣-ša ù i-⸢nu⸣-[ma* LUGAL]
28) *l[a uš-]⸢šer$_9$⸣ ṭup-⸢pa⸣*$^{⸣MEŠ}$ *a-na* LÚ.MEŠ *⸢ḫa⸣[-za-ni]*
29) *⸢ù⸣ ⸢ti⸣-⸢ba⸣-ú-na i-pé-eš$_{15}$ [ar-na]*
30) *⸢šum⸣-⸢ma⸣ ia-nu* ÉRIN.MEŠ *pí-ṭá-⸢ta$_5$⸣[ù]*
31) *[pa-]⸢nu⸣-šu-nu a-na ṣa-ba-ti* URU.K[I *Gub-la*]
32) *⸢ù⸣ ti-⸢iq⸣-bu-na ṣa-bat-mi ⸢ni⸣[-nu]*
33) URU.⸢KI⸣.⸢MEŠ⸣ *Gub^{ub}-li ù mi-[na]*

EA 129

TRANSLATION

(1–3) [Ri]b-Eddi: [Speak t]o the king, [his] lord, [the great king: Beneath]‹your›[fee]t, seven and seven (times) [have I fallen].

(4–12) May the king, [my] lord in‹qu›ire [concerning] the sons of ʿAbdi-Ashirti because they are do[ing] as they please. Who are they, the dogs, that they are doing f[or themselves] thus? They have completely taken all the lands into [their] grasp. They have kil[led] the city rulers of the king, your troops and your soldiers and the king's men.

(13–25) Now what they took was under the ch[arge] of the king's commissioners and as for the commissioner, [he] was a wi[se] man who was very honorable but [they] kil[led him]. They are in possession of all my towns, but the town of Baṭrôna remai[ns to me] and they are seeking to take it. If it be taken, then they will [ta]ke [the city of Byblos] because [...] hand [...hand...]heart [...] and no[t...] against him [...].

(26–29) [...] very much, they are still talk[ing] about committing [grea]t [treason] and sin[ce the king has n[ot se]nt letters to the city [rulers], then they are seeking to commit [treason].

(30–31) If there are no regular troops [then] their intention is to seize the city of [Byblos].

(32–33) And they are saying: "If w[e] seize the cities of Byblos then wh[at] will the regular troops do?"

34) [*t*]*i*-⸢*pu*⸣-*šu* ÉRIN.MEŠ *pí-ṭá-tu a*[-*mur-mi*]
35) ⸢*i*⸣-⸢*nu*⸣-⸢*ma*⸣ *ša-pár-mi* LUGAL *be-l*[*i*]
36) *a-nu-ma* ÉRIN.MEŠ *a-ṣa-at u ti-i*[*q-bu-na*]
\ *ka-ma-m*[*i*]
37) ⸢*ka*⸣-*az-bu-tu*
38) *ia-nu-mi* ÉRIN.MEŠ *pí-ṭá-ta*$_5$ *la*[-*a*]
39) ⸢*tu*⸣-*ṣú u da-nu* UGU-*nu*
40) [*a-mur-m*]*i ba-li a-ṣí* ÉRIN.MEŠ *pí-ṭ*[*á-ti*]
41) [*i-na* MU *š*]*a*-⸢*an*⸣-⸢*ti*⸣ *an-ni-ti*
Lo.ed. 42) [*ù la-q*]*ú-mi* U[RU.MEŠ] *G*[*ub*]^{ub}!-*la*
43) [*šum-ma la-qú-m*]*i* URU.MEŠ *Gub*^{ub}-*li*
44) [*ti-iq-bu-na m*]*i-na ti-pu-šu* ÉRIN.MEŠ
45) [*pí-ṭá-ti ù* ^{I}]*Ri-ib-ad-di*
Rev. 46) ⸢*a*⸣-*n*[*a a-bu-ti-i*]*a* LUGAL.MEŠ *pa-nu*-⸢*ú*⸣
47) *ti-n*[*a-ṣa-ru-na* UR]U.KI *Gub-li*
48) *ù at*-⸢*ta*⸣ *la-a ti-zi-ib-ši*$_x$(ŠE)
49) *šum-ma ia-nu* ÉRIN.MEŠ *pí-ṭá-ta*$_5$ MU ⸢*an*⸣-*nu*
50) *ù uš-ši-ra* GIŠ.MÁ *ti-ìl-qú-ni*
51) *qa-du* DINGIR.MEŠ *ba-al-ṭì a-na be-lí-ia*
52) *la-a-mi yi-iq-ba* LUGAL *be-lí*-[*ia*]
53) *mi-de la ṣa-ab-ta-at pa*[-*aš-ḫa-at*]
54) *u i-na-an-na* ⸢*tu*⸣-*iṣ*?-*ba -t*[*u-na*]
55) LÚ.MEŠ DUMU.M[EŠ *ši-ip-ri* LUGAL]
56) LUGAL.M[EŠ.................]
57) ÉRIN.MEŠ [*pí-ṭá-ti*..............]
58) *ù* [............................]

(34–39) L[ook], inasmuch as the king, [my] lord wrote: "Now the regular troops have gone out," then th[ey are saying thus: "Lies! There are no regular troops. They have not come forth that they should overpower us."

(40–45) [Loo]k, without the coming forth of the reg[lar] troops [in] this [y]ear, [then] they [will ta]ke the ci[ties of B[yb]los. [If they take] the cities of Byblos, [they will say, "Wh]at can [the regular] troops [and] Rib-Hadda do?"

(46–53) For [m]y [ancestors] the former kings used to g[uard the ci]ty of Byblos and you must not abandon it. If there are no regular troops this year, then send a ship that you may take me with the deities, my life, to my lord. May the king, my lord not say, "Perhaps, it is not captured, it is at p[eace]."

(54–58) But now the amba[ssadors of the king] are bei[ng] seized. The kings [...] the [regular] troops [....] and [...].

59) *i* [..............................]
60) [..............................]
61) [..............................]
62) [..............................]
63) [..............................]
64) [..............................]
65) [..............................]
66) [..............................]
67) [.............................]
68) [.............................]
69) [.............................]
70) [.............................]
71) [.............................]
72) [.............................]
73) ⸢*a*⸣[............................]
74) URU[.MEŠ *Gub*^{ub}*-li mi-ia-mi šu-nu*]
75) *šàr* ⸢KUR⸣[*Mi-ta-ni šu-nu šàr* KUR *Ka-ši ù*]
76) *šàr* KUR.M[EŠ *Ḫa-ti i-nu-ma* KUR .MEŠ LUGAL]
77) *a-na* DUMU.MEŠ ÌR.⸢MEŠ⸣ ⸢UR⸣.⸢MEŠ⸣ *ki-n*[*a-na*]
78) *yu-ḫa-mi-ṭá uš-šar* ÉRIN.MEŠ *pí-ṭá-*$_{ti}$
79) LUGAL *ù yi-ìl-qé-šu-nu* ⸢*ù*⸣
80) *ti-né-pu-uš* KUR.MEŠ *a-na* LUGAL ⸢*be*⸣-⸢*lí*⸣-⸢*i*⸣[*a*]
81) *mi-ia šu-nu* UR.MEŠ *ka-‹al›-bu šum-ma*
82) ^{I}⸢*Bir*$_5$⸣*-ya-wa-zi pal-ḫa ‹iš›-tu* LUGAL
83) *la-a la-qé-šu-nu šum-ma* LUGAL *b*[*e-lí-ia*]
84) *yi-iq-bu a-na* LÚ.GAL URU.KI *A*[*z-za-ti ù*]
85) [*a-n*]*a* LÚ.GAL URU.KI *Ku-mi-di li*[*-qú-šu-nu*]
86) [*u l*]*a-a-mi la-qú-šu-nu* ⸢*ar*⸣[*-na*]
87) [*ep-šu*] ⸢*a*⸣*-na ia-ši pa-nu-šu-nu*
88) [*na-ad*]*-nu-ma te*$_9$*-e-te-*⸢*pu*⸣*-š*[*u*]
89) [KUR.MEŠ] ⸢*a*⸣-⸢*na*⸣ LÚ.MEŠ SA.⸢GAZ⸣.[MEŠ *ù*]
Up.ed. 90) [URU.MEŠ]*-ia ša* [.................]
91) [...]*aš pu-ḫi-ir* [...................]
92) [................................]

(59–73) [...]

(74–81) The city of [Byblos. (?) Who are they]? The king of the land of [Mitanni? The king of the land of the Cassites? Or] the king of the lands of [Ḫatti? That the lands of the king] should belong to the sons of ‹ʿAbdi-Ashirta›, slaves, dogs? Thus, may he hasten to send the regular troops of the king that they may capture them and the lands will be joined to the king, my lord. Who are they? Dogs!

(81–92) If Biryawaza was afraid ‹o›f the king, he did not capture them. If the king [my] l[ord], will speak to the senior official of the city of G[aza and t]o the senior official of the city of Kumidi, "Ca[pture them,"] but they did [n]ot capture them. They [have committed] a cr[ime] against me. Their intention is that [the lands] should join the *ʿapîru*-men. My cities which [...] *x* he assembled [....].

Lft.ed. 93) [......................]⌜*tu*⌝ *a-n*[*a*.....] ⌜*ki*⌝-⌜*ti*⌝ ⌜*ù*⌝ ⌜*a*⌝-⌜*na*⌝-⌜*ku*⌝
[*ù* UR]U.MEŠ[-*ia*]

94) [.........]*nu*[.........]*lìb-bi*[-*šu-nu mi-ia-*]*mi* ⌜*šu*⌝-*nu i-*⌜*nu*⌝-[*ma*]
ia[-*nu*......]

95) [ÉRIN.MEŠ *pí*-]⌜*ṭá*⌝-*ta*$_5$ *ù* [...]*nu a*[..........]*nu la-qú-mi* [I]*Pí-wu-r*[*i*]

96) [*ù*] ⌜*da*⌝-⌜*ku*⌝-⌜*šu*⌝ ⌜*ù*⌝ *na-ad-n*[*u pa-ni-šu-nu a-na ia-ši ù*] *la-qú-mi*
KUR.KI URU Ṣ[*u-mu-*]
\ *ri*

97) [*a-n*]*a ša-šu-nu ù* [.......]⌜*ù*⌝ [I]*Pí-wu-ri šum-*⌜*ma*⌝ *a*[*r-na*]

98) *la-a yi-iš-m*[*u* LUGAL *a-na ia-ši ù uš-ši-r*]*a* GIŠ.MÁ.MEŠ

(93–98) [...]t[o...]loyal and I [and my cit]ies [...]heart[...who] are they that there are no [...re]gular [troops] and [...]they took Piwuri [and] they killed him and [they] turned [their attention to me and] they took the land of the city of Ṣ[umu]r [fo]r themselves and [...]and Piwuru. If [the king] will not listen [to me then sen]d ships.

EA 130

TRANSCRIPTION

Obv. 01) [*a-n*]*a šàr-ri* EN-*ia*
02) [*qí*]-*bí-ma um-ma*
03) ^{I}*Ri-ib*-^{d}IŠKUR ÌR-*k*[*a*]-ma
04) ^{d}NIN *ša-a* URU *Gub-la*
05) *ti-di-in*$_4$ KAL.GA *a-na*
06) *šàr-ri* EN-*ia a-na*
07) GÌR.MEŠ EN-*ia* ^{d}UTU-*ia*
08) 7-*šu* 7-*ta-an am-qú-ut*
09) *i-nu-ma yi-iš-tap-pa-ra*
10) *šàr-ru a-na ia-ši a-nu-ma*
11) ^{I}*I-ri-ma-ia-aš-ša*
12) *ia-ak-šu-du-na a-na*
13) *mu-ḫi-ka ú-ul ka-ši-id*
14) *a-na mu-ḫi-ia i-nu-ma*
15) *yi-ìš-ta-pa-ra šàr-ru*
16) *a-na ia-ši ú-ṣur-mì*
17) ⸢*ra*⸣-*ma-an-ka ù*
18) ⸢*ú*⸣-⸢*ṣur*⸣ URU *šàr-ri ša-a*
19) *it-ti-ka ma-an-nu*
20) *yi-na-ṣí-ra-ni*
21) [*a*]-⸢*mur*⸣ *pa-na-nu* LÚ.MEŠ *a-bu-ti-ia*
22) [*d*]*a-nu nu-kúr*-‹*tu*$_4$› *a-na ša*-⸢*šu*⸣-[nu]
23) [*ù*] *ma-ṣa-ar-ti*
24) [LUGAL] *it*-‹*ti*›-*šu-nu ba-l*[*a-aṭ*]
25) [LUGAL] ⸢UGU⸣-*šu-nu* ⸢*ù*⸣
Lo.ed. 26) [*i-na-na*] KAL.G[A *nu-kúr*-‹*tu*$_4$›]
27) [*a-na muḫ-ḫi-ia ù*]
Rev. 28) [*ba-la-a*]*ṭ* ⸢*šàr*⸣[-*ri*]
29) [*ù ma-ṣa-*]*a*[*r-ti* LUGAL]

EA 130

TRANSLATION

(1–8) [Sp]eak [t]o the king, my lord, the message of Rib-Hadda, yo[ur] servant: May the Lady of Byblos grant strength to the king, my lord; at the feet of my lord, my sun god, seven times (and) seven times have I fallen.

(9–14) Inasmuch as the king has written to me "Now, Irimayašša is coming to you," he has not come to me.

(15–20) Inasmuch as the king has written unto me, "Protect yourself and protect the city of the king that is in your charge," who will protect me?

(21–29) [L]ook, formerly, my ancestors were strong; hostility was against them [but] they had [royal] garrison troops with them, [royal] supp[lies] were issued to them; but [now] ho[stility is str]ong [against me but]

30) [*i*]*a-nu* ⸢*a*⸣-[*na*] *ia-ši m*[*i-na*]
31) ⸢*i*⸣-*pu-šu-na a-nu-ma*
32) [^{I}]*ḫa-za-nu-tu ti-du-ku-*[*na-šu*]-⸢*nu*⸣(?)
33) URU-*la-nu-šu-nu ki-ma*
34) UR.GI$_7$ *ù ia-nu*
35) *ša-a yu-ba-ú ar-ki-šu-nu*
36) *mi-na i-pu-šu-na*
37) *a-na-ku ša-a aš-ba-ti*
38) *i-na lìb-bi* LÚ.MEŠ ⸢GAZ⸣.MEŠ
39) *šum-ma i-na-na ia-*[*nu*]
40) *ba-la-aṭ šàr-ri*
41) *a-na ia-ši ù* ⸢*ul*⸣-⸢*ta*⸣-*ma-*⸢*nu*⸣
42) LÚ.MEŠ *ḫu-up-ši-ia*
43) *ka-‹li›* KUR.MEŠ *nu-kúr-‹tu$_4$›* *a-na ia-ši*
44) *šum-ma lìb-bi šàr-ri* [*a-n*]*a*
45) *na-ṣa-ar* URU-*šu ù*
46) ÌR-*šu uš-ši-ra*
47) LÚ.MEŠ *ma-ṣa-ar-ta*
48) *ù ti-na-ṣí-ru* URU
49) [*i*]-*na-ṣí-ru i-na*
50) [*b*]*a-la-ṭì-ia i-nu-*⸢*ma*⸣
51) [*a*]-*mu-ta mi-nu*

Up.ed. 52) ⸢*yi*⸣-*na-ṣa-ru-ši$_x$*(ŠE)

(30–31) I do not have ro[yal suppli]es [and royal garri]s[on troops. What can I do?

(31–38) Now, as for the city rulers, their own cities are killing them like dogs! And there is none who will call them to account. What can I, who is living among *ʿapîru* men, do?

(39–43) If now there are no royal supplies for me, then I will become embroiled in dispute with my yeoman farmers. Al‹l› of the countries are hostile to me.

(44–48) If it is the king's desire [t]o protect his city and his servant, send garrison troops that they may guard the city.

(49–52) [I] will guard while I'm alive; when [I] die, who will guard it?

EA 131

TRANSCRIPTION

Obv. 01) [*a-na* LUGAL EN-*ia* UTU-*ia qí-bi-ma*]
02) [*um-ma* ^{I}*Ri-ib*-^{d}IŠKUR ÌR-*ka-ma*]
03) [^{d}NIN *ša-a* URU *Gub-la ti-di-in*$_{4}$ KAL.GA]
04) [*a-na šàr-ri* EN-*ia a-na* GÌR.MEŠ]
05) [EN-*ia* ^{d}UTU]-*ia* [7-*šu* 7-*ta-an am-qú-ut*]
06) [*yu-š*]*i*-⸢*ru*⸣ ⸢*be*⸣-*li* ⸢ÉRIN ⸣.⸢MEŠ⸣ *ma-ṣa*-⸢*ar*⸣[-*ta*]
07) *a-na* URU *Gub-li ù i-na-an*[-*na*]
08) *ṣa-ab-ta-at* URU.KI *Ṣu-mu*-⸢*ri*⸣
09) ÉRIN.MEŠ URU *Gub*^{ub}-*li di-ku*
10) *šum-ma lìb-bi* LUGAL *be*-⸢*li*⸣-*ia*
11) *a-na* URU.KI *Gub*^{ub}-*la ù*
12) *yu-ši-ra be-li* 3 *me* ÉRIN.MEŠ 30 GIŠ.GIGIR.⸢MEŠ⸣
13) *me* ⸢LÚ⸣.⸢MEŠ⸣ KUR.MEŠ *Ka-ši ù ti-na-ṣa-ru*
14) URU.⸢KI⸣ ⸢*Gub*⸣^{ub}-*li* URU *be-li-ia*
15) ⸢*šum*⸣-⸢*ma*⸣ ⸢ŠE⸣.⸢MEŠ⸣ ⸢*qè*⸣-*e-ṣí la-a yu-ši-r*[*u*]
16) LUGAL ⸢ÉRIN⸣.⸢MEŠ⸣ ⸢*pí*⸣-⸢*ṭá*⸣-⸢*ta*$_{5}$⸣ *a-na* URU.KI *Gub-l*[*a*]
17) *ù la*-⸢*qé*⸣-⸢*mi*⸣ *ti-ìl-qú-na-ši*
18) *ù ia*-⸢*a*⸣-⸢*ti*⸣ [ÌR-*ka*] ⸢*ti*⸣-*du-ku-na*
19) *ù gu*$_{5}$-⸢*mi*⸣-⸢*ru*⸣ [*yu-ši-ru-*]*na* LUGAL ›AŠ‹
20) *be-li-ia* ⸢LÚ⸣.⸢MEŠ⸣ ⸢*ma*⸣-⸢*ṣa*⸣-⸢*ar*⸣-*ti ù*
21) *qa-ar-bu a-na* ⸢LÚ⸣.⸢MEŠ⸣ MÁŠKIM(!) \ *ma-lik*^{MEŠ}
22) LUGAL *i-nu-ma di-ki* ^{I}*Pí-wu-ri*
23) LÚ ⸢*ma*⸣-*lik* LUGAL *ù* ⸢*ša*⸣(?)-*ki-in*
24) ⸢*a*⸣-⸢*na*⸣[-*ku*] ⸢ÌR⸣ ⸢*ki*⸣-⸢*ti*⸣ *ù* ⸢*Pí*⸣-*ḫu-ri*
Lo.ed. 25) *ù* ⸢*ni*⸣-*nu* ÌR.MEŠ ⸢LUGAL⸣ *ù*
26) *ma-ri-iṣ a-na* IGI.MEŠ-⸢*nu*⸣ *i-nu-ma*
27) *ni-dám-mì-qú ù* ⸢*pal*⸣-*ḫa-ti a*-⸢*na*⸣-⸢*ku*⸣

EA 131

TRANSLATION

(1–5) [Speak to the king, my lord, my sun god, the message of Rib-Haddi your servant: May the Lady of Byblos give strength to the king, my lord; at the feet of my lord,]my[sun god, seven times and seven times have I fallen.]

(6–14) My lord used to s[end] a garrison to Byblos, but now Ṣumur has been seized and the troops of Byblos have been killed. If the king cares about Byblos, then may my lord send three hundred troops, thirty chariots and one hundred Cushite men that they may guard the city of Gubla, the city of my lord.

(15–19) If by the time of the summer grain the king does not send regular troops to Byblos, then verily they will take it and me, [your servant] they will kill so that they will have gained full control.

(19–23) The king should [send] garrison troops that they should be near to the commissioners because Piwuri has been slain, the counselor of the king and commissioner.

(24–27) I am a loyal servant and (so is) Piḫuri and we are servants of the king and it is distressing for us since we are behaving properly. And I myself am afraid

Rev. 28) *la-a-mi ú-da-a-k*[*a* LÚ Ú]Š(?)
29) *yu-na-*⌜*da*⌝ LÚ KI[.SÌ.GA-]*pí*
30) ⌜*ia*⌝*-nu a-na ša-a-*⌜*šu*⌝ [*ù a-*]*nu-ma*
31) *ti-pu-*[*š*]*u-na ki-*⌜*am*⌝-⌜*mi*⌝ ⌜*ù*⌝
32) *yu-šir*$_9$*-mi* LUGAL AD-*bu*[*-ka*]
33) ÉRIN.MEŠ *pí-*⌜*ṭá*⌝*-ta*$_5$ TUR *ù* ⌜*yi*⌝-⌜*ìl*⌝-⌜*qé*⌝
34) *gáb-ba ù la-a yi-iš-*⌜*mu*⌝
35) *a-na ia-a-ši* [I]*Pa-ḫa-am-na-*⌜*ta*⌝
36) *ù yi-pu-šu ip-ša-ta*$_5$ *ša-r*[*u-t*]*a*$_5$
37) *ù an-nu* DUMU *mar-šu yu-ḫa-*[*liq*]
38) URU *Ṣu-mur-ri ù yi-iš*[*-mé* LUGAL]
39) *a-wa-at* ÌR-*šu ù* ⌜*yu*⌝[*-ši-ra*]
40) ÉRIN.MEŠ ⌜*pí*⌝*-ṭá-ta*$_5$ GAL-*ta*$_5$ *yi*[*-ìl-qa gáb-b*]*a*
41) *mi-nu-ma yi-qa-bu a-na* [*pa-ni*]
42) LUGAL *ia-nu-mi* ŠE.MEŠ NÍG.MEŠ
43) *a-ka-al* ÉRIN.MEŠ *pí-ṭá-ti a-*⌜*ia*⌝*-mi*
44) *gáb-bi* DIDLI.URU.KI-*ni* LUGAL *be-li-*⌜*ia*⌝
45) ⌜*iš*⌝*-tu* ⌜*lìb*⌝-⌜*bi*⌝-⌜*šu*⌝*-nu* ⌜NÍG⌝.MEŠ *u* ŠE.MEŠ
46) [..............................Š]E.MEŠ
47) [......................................]
48) [......................................]
49) [......................................]
50) [......................................]
51) [......................................]
52) [......................................]
53) [......................................]
54) [......................................]
55) [......................................]
56) [......................................]

Lft.ed. 57) [ÉRIN.MEŠ *pí-ṭ*]*á-ti ù* ÉRIN.MEŠ *ti-la-t*[*i*.....]
58) [*a-na na-ṣa-ar*] URU.KI *Gub-la la-a-mi* [*yi-m*]*a-a*[*k*]
-ki
59) [LUGAL URU.KI-*šu šum-ma*] *la-a yu-wa-*⌜*ša*⌝*-ru-na*
60) [*a-na* URU.KI *Gub-l*]*a ù la-qú-ši ù*
61) [*ya-ti*] ⌜*ù*⌝ *ia-nu* KUR.MEŠ *Ki-na-aḫ-*⌜*ni*⌝
\\ *a-na* LUGAL
62) [*ù yi-ša-al* [I]]*Ia-an-ḫa-ma a-na a-‹wa›-te*[MEŠ] *a‹-nu›-te*

(28–36) lest I be killed, a corpse cast away having no one to care for its funerary offerings and [n]ow they are doing th[us. But] the king, your father sent a small regular force and they took all. But Paḫamnata would not listen and he continued to commit rebellious acts.

(37–40) And behold, his son has caused the [loss] of Ṣumur. So may [the king] he[ed] the word of his servant and may he se[nd] a large regular force that [he may take everythi]ng.

(41–45) Who is saying in [the presence of] the king, "There is no grain or bread as food for the regular troops"? Where are all the cities of the king my lord? From their midst bread and grain [can be found(?)].

(46–56) [..]

(57–62) [regular tr]oops and support troops [...to guard] the city of Byblos. [The king] must not [negle]ct [his city. If] he does not send [to the city of Byb]los then they will take it [and me] and the territories of Canaan will not belong to the king. [So may he ask] Yanḫamu about th‹es›e th‹in›gs

EA 132

TRANSCRIPTION

Obv.	01)	[*a-na*] LUGAL EN-*ia* ^{d}UTU-⸢*i*⸣[*a*]
	02)	[*qí*]-*bi-ma um-ma* ^{I}*Ri-ib*-⸢^{d}⸣⸢IŠKUR⸣
	03)	[Ì]R-*ka-ma* ^{d}NIN *ša-a*
	04)	[UR]U *Gub-la ti-di-in*$_{4}$ KAL.GA
	05)	*a-na šàr-ri* EN-*ia a-na*
	06)	GÌR.MEŠ EN-*ia* ^{d}UTU-*ia*
	07)	7-*šu* 7-*ta-an am-qú-ut*
	08)	*ša-ni-tam mi-li-ik ‹a-na›*
	09)	URU *Gub-la* URU *ki-ti-ka*
	10)	*pa-na-nu yi*-⸢*zi*⸣-*iz-mi*
	11)	^{I}ÌR-*A-ši*-⸢*ir*⸣-*ta* UGU-*ia*
	12)	*ù aš-ta-pa-ar a-na*
	13)	*a-bi-ka uš-ši-ra-mi*
	14)	ÉRIN.MEŠ *pí*-⸢*ṭá*⸣-*ti* ⸢*šàr*⸣-*ri*
	15)	*ù tu-ul-qú ka-li*
	16)	KUR *i-na* UD. KAM^{v}.MEŠ *ú-ul*
	17)	*la-qí* ^{I}ÌR-*A-ši-ir-t*[*a*]
	18)	*qa-du mi*-⸢*am*⸣-*mi-šu a-na* [*ša-šu*]
	19)	*ù an-nu-ú i-na-na*
	20)	*pu-ḫi-ir* ^{I}*A-zi-ru ka*-[*li*]
	21)	LÚ.MEŠ GAZ.MEŠ *ù q*[*a-bi*]
	22)	*a-na ša-šu-nu šum-ma*
	23)	URU *Gub-la la-a ir-t*[*i-ḫa-at*]
	24)	[*š*]*u-ut* ⸢*yu*⸣-⸢*ṣa*⸣[..........]
	25)	[......................]
Lo.ed.	26)	[......................]
	27)	[......................]
Rev.	28)	[*ša*] ⸢ÌR⸣(?)-⸢*ka*⸣[..........]
	29)	⸢*al*⸣-*lu-mi* ^{I}*Ia-an-ḫ*[*a-mu*]

EA 132

TRANSLATION

(1–7) Speak [to] the king, my lord, my sun god, the message of Rib-Haddi your [ser]vant: May the Lady of Byblos give strength to the king, my lord; at the feet of my lord, my sun god, seven times and seven times have I fallen.

(8–18) Furthermore, give thought to Byblos, your loyal city. Formerly, ʿAbdi-Ashirta attacked me and I wrote to your father, "Send regular troops of the king and the entire land will be taken in a day." Was not ʿAbdi-Ashirta taken with his property for [him (the king)]?

(19–27) And now Aziru has assembled all the *ʿapîru* men and sa[id] to them, "If the city of Byblos does not rem[ain,] [h]e will go forth [.........](3 lines missing).

(28–29) [...of] your servant [...]. Behold Yanḫ[amu] is

30) *it-ti-ka ù* ⸢*ša*⸣[*-al-šu*]
31) *šum-ma la-a qa-bi-ti*
32) *a-na ša-a-šu a-pa-ši-m*[*ì*]
33) *at-ta ki-ta it*[*-ti* DUMU.M]EŠ
34) ^{I}ÌR-*A-ši-ir-ta* ⸢*ù*⸣
35) *la-qú-ka ša-ma a-*⸢*na*⸣ [*ia-ši*]
36) *ù na-ṣa-ar* URU.[MEŠ]
37) LUGAL EN-*šu qa-bi-ti*
38) *ki-na-na a-na* ^{I}*Pa-wu-*[*ra*]
39) *ù la-a yi-iš-mu* [*a-na ia-ši*]
40) *i-na a-wa-te*^{MEŠ} ^{I}*Ḫa-i*[*p*]
41) *a-*⸢*bu*⸣*-šu nu-ki-ir* URU.M[EŠ]
42) *an-*⸢*nu*⸣*-ú* ^{I}*Ḫa-ip na-*⸢*da*⸣[*-an*]
43) URU *Ṣu-mu-ra ú-ul*
44) *ia-qú-ul* LUGAL *a-na i-*[*pé*]*-*⸢*ši*⸣
45) *an-nu-ú i-*⸢*nu*⸣*-ma di-ka*
46) LÚ.MÁŠKIM *šum-ma i-na-*⸢*na*⸣
47) *qa-la-ta ù* ^{I}*Pí-ḫu-ra*
48) *la-a yi-zi-za i-na*
49) URU *Ku-mì-di u ka-li* ⸢LÚ⸣.MEŠ
50) ⸢*ḫa*⸣*-za-ni-ka tù-da-*⸢*ku*⸣*-*⸢*na*⸣
51) [*a*]*-nu-ma ki-*⸢*a*⸣*-ma ‹aš›-pu-ru a-na* ⸢É⸣.⸢GAL⸣
52) ⸢*ù*⸣ *la-a yu-uš-mu*

Up.ed. 53) [*a-n*]*a ia-ši uš-ši-ra*
54) [GIŠ].⸢MÁ⸣.MEŠ *ti-ìl-qú mi-im-*[*ma*]
55) [^{d}]NIN *ù ia-*⸢*ti*⸣

Lft.ed. 56) [*uš-ši-*]*ra* 50 ⸢*me*⸣ LÚ.MEŠ *u* 30 ⸢*me*⸣ [LÚ.MEŠ] *š*[*a*]
57) [KUR *Me-lu-*]*ḫa* 50 GIŠ.GIGIR ⸢*ù*⸣ [*ti-n*]*a-ṣí-r*[*u*]
58) [URU]⸢*a*⸣*-na ka-ta*$_{5}$ *uš-š*[*i-ra*] ÉRIN.MEŠ
59) *pí-ṭá-ti ù šu-up-*⸢*ši*⸣*-iḫ* KUR

(30–50) with you, so a[sk him] if I did not say to him, "You make a treaty wi[th the son]s of ʿAbdi-Ashirta and they will capture you." He listened to [me] and protected the cit[ies] of the king, his lord. I spoke thus to Pawu[ra] but he would not listen [to me] because of the words of Ḫaʿip. His (Ḫaʿip's) father alienated the cities. Behold Ḫaʿip handed [over] the city of Ṣumur! May the king not keep silent concerning this deed since the commissioner was slain. If now you keep silent and Piḫura does not stand fast in the city of Kômidi, all of your city rulers will be slain.

(51–59) [N]ow thus have I been writing to the palace but no attention is paid [t]o me. Send ships! Let them take the property of the Lady and me. [Se]nd 50–100 men and 30–100 [men] o[f the land of Meluḫ]ḫa, 50 chariots that they may [gua]rd [the city] for you. Se[nd] regular troops and pacify the land.

EA 133

TRANSCRIPTION

Obv.

01) [LUGA]L ⸢EN⸣-[*ia*....]
02) [*ša-ni-*]⸢*tam*⸣ *mi-lik at*[*-ta*]
03) [*a-n*]*a* ÌR-*ka* ⸢*ù*⸣
04) ⸢*a*⸣*-na* URU *Gub-la* ^{K}[^{I}]
05) ⸢URU⸣ *Ṣu-mu-ra i*[*ṣ-bat*]
06) ⸢*ka*⸣*-li* URU.MEŠ[*-ka la-qú*]
07) ⸢DUMU⸣.MEŠ ^{I}ÌR-*A-ši-i*[*r-ta*]
08) [*e*]*p-šu nu*-KÚR *it-*[*ti-ia*]
09) [*a*]*-nu-ma* ^{I}*Ḫa-ip* [*it-ti-ka*]
10) [*š*]*a-al-šu* ⸢*ù*⸣ [*li-it-ri-iṣ*]
11) ⸢*i*⸣*-na pa-ni-ka* [*ù*]
12) *uš-ši-ra* LÚ.⸢MEŠ⸣ [*ma-ṣa-ar-ta*]
13) [*a*]*-na* URU.MEŠ-⸢*ka*⸣ [*a-na*]
14) ⸢*ar*⸣*-ḫi-ìš a-nu-ma k*[*i-a-ma*]
15) [*ìš-tap*]*-ru a-na šàr-ri* [EN-*ia*]
16) [*uš-ši-*]*ra-an-ni* L[Ú.MEŠ]
17) [*Me-lu-*]*ḫa* \ *Ka*[*-ši ù*]
18) [*a-na-ṣa-*]*ar* [URU.........]
19) [........................]

EA 133

TRANSLATION

(1) [The kin]g, [my] lord.

(2–8) [Further]more, take counsel yourself [concern]ing your servant and concerning the city of Byblos. The city of Ṣumur is taken. The sons of ʿAbdi-Ashirta [have taken] all [your] cities. They are at war wi[th me].

(9–14) Now Ḫaʿip is [with you], ask him and [may it be pleasing] in your sight [and] send [garrison] troops [t]o your cities [with]all due haste.

(14–18) Now th[us have I been wri]ting to the king, [my lord,] “Send to me m[en of Meluḫ]ḫa \ Cush[ites, and I will gua]rd [the city....”]

EA 134

TRANSCRIPTION

Obv. 01’) [.........] *mi*[*-lik*]

02’) [*a-na* URU *Gu*]*b-la ú-u*[*l*]

03’) [*yi-ìl-*]*qé-ši* ^{I}*A-z*[*i-ru*]

04’) *a-mur iš-tu da-r*[*i-ti*]

05’) *la-a i-te*$_{9}$*-li-y*[*u*]

06’) *i-na* URU *Gub-la* DINGIR.M[EŠ]

07’) [*i*]*-na-an-na uš-ši*[*-ir*]

08’) [^{I}]*A-zi-ru* ÉRIN.MEŠ *a-n*[*a*]

09’) [*ṣa-*]*ba-ti-ìš i-nu-ma*

10’) [*n*]*a-ad-nu* DINGIR.MEŠ*-nu* [*ù*]

11’) [*a-ṣ*]*a-ú ù ia-nu* [ÉRIN.MEŠ]

12’) [*i-*]*na* URU *a-na da-k*[*i*]

13’) [ÌR L]Ú.UR.RI *lim-*⸢*ni*⸣ [*ù*]

14’) [*ú-u*]*l ti-tu-ru-na*

15’) [*mi-*]*na i-pu-šu-na* [*a-na-ku*]

16’) [*i-*]*na i-de-ni-ia* [LÚ.MEŠ]

17’) [*ša-*]*a i-ba-šu i*[*-na*]

18’) [URU]*-lì pa-aṭ-ru g*[*áb-bu*]

19’) [*la-*]*qí ba-la-ṭ*[*ì-šu-nu*]

20’) [*a-n*]*a š*[*a-šu-nu*.......]

21’) [.....] traces [.......]

Rev. 22’) [......................]

23’) [*ù u*]*š-ši-ru* [LÚ.MEŠ]

24’) [*ma-ṣa-*]*ar a-na* U[RU*-ka*]

25’) [*a-na-*]*ku ù* UR[U *Gub-la*]

26’) [ÌR.MEŠ] *ki-ti šàr-r*[*i ù*]

EA 134

TRANSLATION

(1'–3') [...] take coun[sel concerning the city of By]blos. Let not Az[iru take]it.

(4'–14') Look, nev[er] have the gods gone up from the city of Byblos. [N]ow Aziru has sent troops t[o ca]pture it because the gods have granted (it) [and] they have [go]ne out and there are no [troops i]n the city to attac[k the slave,] the evil dog(?), [and] they (the gods) will [no]t return.

(15'–20') [Wh]at can [I] do [b]y myself? [The men wh]o were i[n the cit]y have departed. A[ll to]ok [their supp]lies [fo]r t[hemselves....]

(22'–26') [....so s]end (pl.) [garris]on [troops] to [your] ci[ty]. ⸢I⸣ and the c[ity of Byblos are] loyal [servants] of the ki[ng].

27') [L]Ú-*ia an-nu-ú uš-š*[*i-ir-ti*]
28') *a-na* É.GAL *a-na mi-n*[*i*]
29') *la-a ìš-tap-pa-ar* LU[GAL]
30') [*p*]*a-na-ni a-na ka-tu*[*-nu*]
31') *ù ìš-tap-pa-ar i-n*[*a-na*]
32') *nu*-KÚR KAL.GA UGU-*i*[*a*]
33') *ù pal-ḫa-ti al*[*-lu-ú*]
34') *la-qa-a* URU *Ṣu-mu-r*[*a*]
35') *mi-nu qa-ba mi-im-ma*
36') *a-na ša-a-šu ki-na-‹na›-*⸢*ma*⸣
37') [*n*]*a-da-an pa-ni-šu a-n*[*a*]
38') [URU *Gub-l*]*a yi-ìš-ta-*[…]
39') [.....*k*]*a-ra-š*[*u*.....]
40') [................]-*lu*
41') [................] *t*[*u*…]

(26'–39') [And] this [m]an have [I] se[nt] to the palace. Why did the ki[ng] not write? My [f]ace is towards you (pl.) so I have written. No[w] there is intense hostility against m[e] and I am afraid. Be[hold,] he (Aziru) has taken the city of Ṣumu[r]. Who said anything to him? Thu‹s›, he has [s]et his face towa[rds the city of Bybl]os. May (the king) give hee[d] [...] h[is a]rmy [........].

EA 135

TRANSCRIPTION

(**Not Collated**)

Obv. 01) (traces) [...]

02) *a-na* [...]

03) URU *Ṣ*[*u-mu-ra* ....]

04) *ù* LÚ.MEŠ M[ÁŠKIM ....]

05) *ù a-ṣí-i*[*t* ....]

06) *ù* 2 (3?) *me* GIŠ.GIG[IR.MEŠ ....]

07) *ù* [1-*e*]*n* ....]

08) [...]

09) [...]

Lo.ed. 10) [...]

Rev. 11) [*l*]*a-qú* [...]

12) *ù l*[*i-im-li-ik* LUGAL EN-*ia*]

13) *a-na* ÌR *k*[*i-it-ti-šu ù a-na* URU]

14) *ki*(?)-*it*(?)-*ti ša* [LUGAL EN-*ia la-a-mi*]

15) [*ì*]*l-qé* URU *ki*[*-it-ti-šu*...................................]

16) *ù iq-bi* [...]

17) *ir-tam-mi* UG[U ....]

18) LÚ.MEŠ KUR *Mi-i*[*ṣ-ri* ....]

19) *ù aq-bi* [...]

20) *ù* [...]

21) ⌜URU⌝ [...]

Rest of reverse broken

Lft. ed. 22) [...............]*i*[*t*] *a-na* LÚ[...........................]

23) [.............] LUGAL BE-*ia* [........................]

24) [..........*n*]*u-kùr-*ta_5 *a-na* BE-*ia*[......................]

25) [........*uš*-]*ši-ir-ti a-na mu-ḫi* LÚ[.....................]

EA 135

TRANSLATION

(*Tablet melted by rainwater*)

(1–7) (traces) [...] to [...] the town of Ṣ[umur...] and the co[missioners...]and the coming out [....] and two (three?) hundred char[iots...] and o[ne....].

(11–21) they took [....] so ma[y the king, my lord, take counsel] concerning [his] f[aithful] servant [and concerning the faithful [city] of [the king, my lord, lest h]e take [his] fa[ithful] city [...] and I spoke [...] I have always loved(?) [....] the men of the land of E[gypt...] and [...] the city [....].

(22–25) [....] to the [commissioner(?)...] the king, my lord [....ho]stility against my lord [....] I [se]nt to the commissioner(?)....].

EA 136

TRANSCRIPTION

Obv. 01) [*a*]-*na* LUGAL EN-*ia*
02) *um-ma Ri-ib*-^{d}IŠKUR ÌR-*ka*
03) SAḪAR \ *e-pé-ri ša* 2 GÌR.MEŠ-*ka*
04) *a-na* GÌR.MEŠ LUGAL EN-*ia*
05) 7 *u* 7-*ta-an am-qú-ut*
06) *ù lu-ú yi-iš-me* LUGAL EN-*ia*
07) *a-wa-te* ÌR-*šu*
08) LÚ.MEŠ URU *Gub-la ù* É-*ia*
09) *ù* MUNUS.DAM-*ia*
10) *ti*$_{7}$-*iq-bu-na a-na ia-ši-ia*
11) *a-li-ik-mi* EGIR
12) ^{I}DUMU ÌR-*A-ši-ir-ta*
13) *ù ni-pu-uš šal-ma be-ri-nu*
14) *ù i*$_{15}$-*ma-i*$_{15}$ *a*-⸢*na*⸣-*ku*
15) *la-a iš-me a-na ša-šu-nu*

---

16) *šá-ni-tam šap-ra-ti a-na* LUGAL ⸢EN⸣-*ia*
17) *ù iš-ta-ni uš-ši-ra*-⸢*am*⸣
18) LÚ.MEŠ UN \ *ma-ṣa-ar-ta*
19) *a-na* ÌR-*ka ù lu-ú*
20) ⸢*ti*⸣-*na-ṣa-ru* URU.KI
Lo.ed. 21) ⸢*a*⸣-⸢*na*⸣ LUGAL EN‹-*ia*› *ù la-a*
22) ⸢*ka*⸣-*ši-id a-wa-tu*
23) LUGAL EN-*ia a-na* ÌR-*šu*

EA 136

TRANSLATION

(1–5) [T]o the king, my lord, the message of Rib-Haddi your servant, the dirt at your feet: At the feet of the king, my lord, seven times and seven times have I fallen.

(5–15) So may the king, my lord, heed the words of his servant. The men of the city of Byblos and my house and my wife kept saying to me, "Follow the son of ʿAbdi-Ashirta so we can make peace between us." But I refused; I did not listen to them.

(16–23) Furthermore, I wrote repeatedly to the king, my lord, "Send me garrison troops to your servant that they may protect the city for the king, ‹my› lord." But a word from the king, my lord, has not reached his servant.

Rev. 24) *šá-ni-tam ù in-du-um*
25) *yu-ṣa-ḫi-ra-am a-na ia-ši*
26) *ù im-lu-uk iš-tu*
27) ŠÀ-*ia a-li-ik-mi a-na-ku*
28) *i-pu-ša*!(MA)-*am* DÙG.GA \ tu-ka
29) *it-ti-šu ša* ^{I}*Am-mu-ni-ra*
30) *ù al-ka-ti*
31) *a-na* É-*šu aš-šum*
32) *e-pu-uš* DÙG.GA *bi-ri‹-nu›*
33) *ù a-na-ku a-tu-ur a-na* É-⸢*i*⸣*a*
34) *ù id-du-ul* É *iš-tu*
35) ⸢*pa*⸣*-ni-ia ù* ⸢LUGAL⸣ EN-*ia*
36) *yi-im-lu-uk a-na* ÌR-*šu*

---

37) *a-nu-um*!(IM)-*ma* UD.KAM^{v} *ù mu-ša*
38) *ú-qa-mu* ÉRIN.MEŠ *pí-ṭá-at*
39) LUGAL EN-*ia ù* LUGAL EN-*ia*
40) *yi-im-lu-uk a-na* ÌR-*šu*
41) *šum-ma i-ia-nu* ŠÀ *ša-na-*⸢*am*⸣
42) ⸢UGU⸣ LUGAL EN-*ia* BA.ÚŠ *a-na-ku*
Up.ed 43) *ù* LUGAL EN-*ia* ⸢TI⸣.⸢LA⸣ ÌR‹-*šu*›
44) ⸢*šá*⸣*-ni-tam* 2 DUMU-*ia ù* ⸢2⸣ ⸢MUNUS⸣.DAM
45) *na-ad-nu a-na* LÚ *ar-ni*
Lft.ed 46) ⸢*ša*⸣ ⸢LUGAL⸣

(24–32) Furthermore, when the pressure got too tough for me, then I thought to myself, "Come, let me make a treaty with him, namely ʿAmmunīra." So I went to his house in order that I could make a treaty between ‹us›.

(33–36) Then I returned to my house but he (my brother) had locked me out of the house. So may the king, my lord, take counsel concerning his servant.

(37–43) Now, day and night I wait for the regular army of the king, my lord. So may the king, my lord, take counsel concerning his servant, because I have no other attitude. For the king, my lord, I would die! So may the king, my lord, give life to ‹his› servant.

(44–46) Furthermore, my two sons and two wives have been handed over to the rebel against the king.

EA 137

TRANSCRIPTION

Obv.

01) ^{I}*Ri-ib-ad*[*-di qí-bi-mi*]
02) *a-na* LUGAL *be-l*[*i-ia* ^{d}UTU KUR.MEŠ]
03) *a-na* KI.TA GÌR-*p*[*í* LUGAL *be-li-ia*]
04) 7-*ta-an ù* 7-*ta*[*-an ma-aq-ta-ti*$_{7}$]
05) *aš-tap-pár aš-ta-ni a-n*[*a* ÉRIN.MEŠ *ma-ṣa-ar-ti*]
06) *ù la-a tu-da-nu* ⸢*ù*⸣ [*la-a*]
07) *yi-iš-mé* LUGAL *be-li a-wa-t*[*e* ÌR-*šu*]
08) *ù i-wa-ši-ir* LÚ.DUMU ^{I}*š*[*ìp-ri-ia*]
09) *a-na* É-*ti* É.GAL *ù* ⸢*i*⸣[*a-tu-ur*]
10) *ri-qú-tam i-ia-nu* ÉRIN.MEŠ *ma-ṣa-a*[*r-ta*$_{5}$]
11) *a-na ša-a-šu ù ti-mu-ru* L[Ú.MEŠ URU!-]*ia*
12) *i-nu-ma la-a na-di-in* KÙ.BABBAR *ti-iš-la\ḫu*
13) *a-na ia-ši ki-ma* LÚ.MEŠ *ḫa*^{MEŠ}*-za-ni* ŠEŠ.‹MEŠ›-*ia*
14) *ù ti-na-i-ṣú-ni šá-ni-tam a-na-ku-mé-e*
15) *al-ka-ti a-na ma-ḫar-ri* ^{I}*Ḫa-mu-ni-ri*
16) *ù* ŠEŠ-*ia* TUR *iš-tu ia-ti*
17) *i-na-kar*$_{5}$*-mi* URU *Gub-la*^{KI}
18) *a-na na-da-ni* URU.KI-*li*
19) *a-na* DUMU.MEŠ ÌR-^{I}*A-ši-ir-ti*
20) *i-nu-ma yi-mur* ⸢LÚ⸣.ŠEŠ-*ia i-nu-ma*
21) *a-ṣí* LÚ.DUMU *šìp-‹ri›-ia ri-qa-mi*
22) *i-ia-nu* ÉRIN.MEŠ *ma-ṣa-ar-ta*$_{5}$ *it-ti-šu*
23) *ù ia-an-aṣ-ni ù ki-na-an-na*
24) *yi-pu-uš ar-na ù yu-ṭá-ri-id-ni*
25) *iš-tu* URU-*li*^{KI} *ú-ul ia-qú-ul-mi*
26) LUGAL *be-li a-na ip-ši* UR *an-nu-ú*
27) *a-nu-ma a-na-ku la-a e-la-ú-mi*
28) *i-re-ba a-na* KUR.MEŠ *Mi-iṣ-ri-i*$_{15}$
29) *ši-ba-ti ù mur-ṣú dan-nu*
30) *a-na* UZU *ra-ma-ni-ia ù i-de-mi*
31) LUGAL *be-li i-nu-ma* DINGIR.MEŠ URU *Gub-la*
32) *qa-di-šu ù mur-ṣu-ú ma-gal*
33) *ù ḫi-i*$_{15}$*-ṭí ep-‹ša›-ti a-na* DINGIR.MEŠ

EA 137

TRANSLATION

(1–4) (For) Rib-Ha[ddi speak] to the king, [my] lord, [the sun god of the lands]. Under the fee[t of the king, my lord] seven times and seven ti[mes have I fallen].

(5–7) I have repeatedly written fo[r garrison troops] but they have not been given and the king, my lord, has [not] heeded the word[s of his servant].

(8–14) So I sent [my] ambas[sador] to the royal palace but he re[turned] empty handed; he had no garri[son] troops. And the men of my [city] saw that silver was not sent (you did ‹not› send) to me like the city rulers, my colleague‹s› and they reviled me.

(14–26) Furthermore, I myself went to ʿAmmunīra and my brother, younger than me, alienated the city of Byblos in order to give the city to the sons of ʿAbdi-Ashirta because my brother saw that my amba‹ss›ador came forth empty handed, there being no garrison troops with him, and he reviled me. And thus treason was committed and he expelled me from the city. May the king, my lord, not keep silence concerning the deeds of this dog!

(27–33) Now I am unable to enter into the lands of Egypt. I have grown old and the disease is strong in my own body. And the king, my lord, knows that the gods of the city of Byblos are holy and the illness is strong and I have com‹mit›ted my sin against the gods.

34) *ki-na-an-na la-a* ⸢*i*⸣*-ri-bu*
35) *a-na ma-ḫar* LUGAL *be-*⸢*li*⸣*-ia*
36) *ù a-nu-ma* DUMU-*ia* ÌR LUGAL BAD-*ia*
37) *uš-ši-ir-ti a-na ma-ḫar* LUGAL *be-li-ia*
38) *ù yi-iš-mé* LUGAL *a-‹wa›-te* ÌR-*di-šu*
39) *ù ia-di-na* LUGAL *be-li*
40) [ÉRIN.]MEŠ *pí-ṭá-ta*$_{5}$ *ù* [*t*]*i*$_{7}$*-iṣ-*[*ba-tu*]
Lo.ed. 41) [U]RU *Gub*^{ub}*-*⸢*li*⸣^{KI} *ù la-*⸢*a*⸣
42) [*ti-r*]*i-bu-mi* ÉRIN.MEŠ *ša-ra-‹tu›*
43) *ù* [DUMU⸣.MEŠ Ì[R-!*A*]*-*⸢*ši*⸣*-*⸢*ir*⸣*-ti*
Rev. 44) ⸢*a*⸣*-*⸢*na*⸣ *lìb-bi-ši* ⸢*ù*⸣ *ti-i*[*m*]*-*⸢*ta*⸣*-ṭi*
45) ÉRIN.MEŠ *pí-ṭá-at* LUGAL *be-li-i*[*a*]
46) *a-na la-qí-ši a-mur ma-ʾa-du*
47) LÚ.MEŠ *ra-i-mu-ia a-na lìb-bi* URU.KI
48) TUR LÚ.MEŠ *ša-ru-tu a-na lìb-bi-ši*
49) *a-ṣí-mi* ÉRIN.MEŠ *pí-ṭá-tu ù ša-mu*
50) *a-na ú-mi ka-ša-di-ši ù*
51) *ta-ra-at* URU.KI *a-na* LUGAL *be-li-ia*
52) *ù yi-de be-li i-nu-ma* UGU-*šu a-mu-tu*
53) *i-nu-ma a-na-ku a-na* URU-*li* ^{KI} *a-na-ṣa-ar-/ši*
54) *a-na be-li-ia ù*!(ŠI) *ta-ri-iṣ lìb-bi*
55) UGU LUGAL *be-li-ia la-a na-din-mi*
56) URU.KI *a-na* DUMU.MEŠ ÌR-*Aš*!(ḪAL)*-ra-ti*
57) *ki-na-an-na nu-*KÚR*-mi* ŠEŠ-*ia* URU.KI
58) *a-na na-da-ni-ši a-na* DUMU.MEŠ ÌR-*Aš-ra-ti*
59) *ú-ul ia-qú-ul*$_{11}$*-mi* LUGAL *be-li iš-tu*
60) URU-*li* ^{KI} *šum-ma ma-gal ma-ad*
61) KÙ.BABBAR KÙ.GI *a-na lìb-bi-ši a-na* É DINGIR.MEŠ-*ši*
62) *ma-ad mi-im-mu šum-ma yi-iṣ-ba-*⸢*tu*⸣*-ši*
63) LUGAL *be-li ki-ma yi-pu-šu a-na* ÌR-*šu*
64) *yi-pu-uš ù ia-di-‹na›* URU-*la Bu-ru-zi-lì*
65) *a-na a-ša-bi-ia a-nu-ma a-na ma-ḫar*
66) ^{I}*Ḫa-mu-ni-ri i-ba-ša-ti i-nu-ma*
67) *na-kar*$_{5}$*-ra-at* URU.KI.DIDLI URU *Bu-ru-zi-lì*
Rev. 68) *na-*KÚR*-ru pal-ḫa-tu* DUMU.MEŠ ÌR-*Aš-ra-ti*

(34–35) Thus, I do not enter to the presence of the king, my lord.

(36–46) So now my son, the servant of the king, my lord, have I sent to the presence of the king, my lord, so that the king may hear the w‹or›ds of his servant. Then may the king, my lord, grant regular [troop]s that they may sei[ze] the [ci]ty of Byblos so that reb[el] troops and the sons of ʿAb[di-A]shirta may not enter into it, and the regular troops of the king, my lord will be too few to take it.

(46–51) Look, many are the men that support me within the city; few are the rebellious men within it. When the regular troops come forth and they hear (it), on the day of their arrival then the city will return to the king, my lord.

(52–58) And may my lord know that I will die for him; when I was in the city, I guarded it for my lord and(!) my heart was devoted to the king, my lord; it (my heart) did not give the city to the sons of ʿAbdi-Ashirta. Thus my brother alienated the city to hand it over to the sons of ʿAbdi-Ashirta.

(59–65) May the king, my lord, not turn away from his city since very great is the silver (and) gold within it; there is much property belonging to the temple of its gods. If the king, my lord, seizes it, he may do to his servant whatever he will. May he gra‹nt› the city of Buruzili for my dwelling.

(65–67) Now, I am in the presence of ʿAmmunīra because the cities are hostile. The city of Buruzili

(68) became hostile, fearing the sons of ʿAbdi-Ashirta.

69) *i-nu-ma al-ka-ti a-na ma-ḫar* ^{I}*Ḫa-mu-\ni-ri*
70) *aš-šum* DUMU.MEŠ ÌR-*A-ši-ir-ti i-nu-ma*
71) *da-nu* UGU-*ia ù i-ia-nu ša-ri*
72) ^{KA}*pí* LUGAL *a-na ia-ši ù qí-bi*$_4$*-ti*
73) *a-na be-li-ia a-mur* URU *Gub-li* URU-*lu* ^{KI} *ši-na*
74) *ma-ad mi-im* LUGAL *a-na lìb-bi-ši mar-ši-te*^{MEŠ}
75) LÚ.MEŠ *ab-‹bu›-ti-nu pa-na-nu šum-ma qa-al* LUGAL *a-na* URU.KI
76) *gáb-bi* DIDLI.URU.KI.KUR *Ki-na-aḫ-ni ia-nu a-*[*n*]*a \ ša-šu*
77) *la-a ia-qú-ul*$_{11}$ LUGAL *a-na ip-ši an-nu*
78) *a-nu-ma* ÌR-*ka* DUMU-*ia uš-ši-ir-ti a-na*
79) *ma-ḫar* LUGAL BAD-*ia ù yu-ši-ra-šu ḫa-mi-*[*i*]*t*?-*t*[*a*$_5$]?
80) LUGAL *qa-du* ÉRIN.MEŠ *ti-*⌜*ìl*⌝*-qú* URU-*la* ^{KI}
81) *šum-ma* LUGAL *be-li yi-iḫ-na-nu-ni ù*
82) *yu-te-ru-ni a-na* URU.KI *ù a-na-ṣár-š*[*i*] *ki-*[*na-na*]
83) *ki pa-na a-na* LUGAL *be-li-ia šu*[*m-ma la yu-te-ru-ni*]
84) LUGAL *be-li a-na lìb-bi-ši ù* ⌜*i*⌝[*a-di-na*(?)]
85) URU-*la iš-tu Bu*[*-r*]*u-z*[*i-lì a-na a-ša-bi-ia*(?)]
86) *ki-ma yi-p*[*u-šu* LUGAL *a-na* ÌR-*šu yi-pu-šu ù la-a*]
87) *i-zi*[*-ba*..............................]
88) ^{I}*Ḫa-mu-*[*ni-ri*........................]
89) *a-di ma-t*[*i i-zi-za it-ti-šu ù*]
90) *yi-iš-mé* [L]U[GAL *be-li a-wa-te*^{MEŠ}]
91) ÌR-*šu k*[*i-ma ar-ḫi-iš ù yu-uš-ši-ra*]
Lft.ed. 92) ÉRIN.MEŠ *ki-ma ḫa-*⌜*mu*⌝*-ti-iš*
93) *ù ti-ìl-qú* URU-⌜*la*⌝ ^{KI}
94) *la-a ia-qú-ul-mi* LUGAL *be-li*
95) *a-na ip-ši mar-ṣí an-nu-ú*
96) *ša yu-pa-aš-mi a-na* KUR.MEŠ L[UGAL BAD-*ia*]
97) *ù ya-ar-ḫi-ša* LUGAL *be-li*
98) ÉRIN.MEŠ *pí-ṭá*[*-ṭ*]*a*$_5$ *ù ti-iṣ-ba-tu*
99) URU.KI *ki-ma ar-ḫi-iš*
100) *i-nu-ma qa-bi*$_4$*-mi a-na pa-ni* LUGAL
101) *a-n*[*a* U]RU.KI URU-*lu-mi dan-na-tu*
102) *la dan-na-at a-na pa-ni*
103) ÉRIN.MEŠ LUGAL *be-li-ia*

(69–75) When I went to the presence of ʿAmmunīra due to the sons of ʿAbdi-Ashirta, because they are stronger than I and I did not have the breath of the mouth of the king, then I spoke to my lord, "Look, as for the city of Byblos, (if it became) the city of those two, great is the property of the king within it, the acquisitions of our forefa‹th›ers."

(75–77) If the king keeps silent concerning the city, he will not have any cities in the land of Canaan. May the king not keep silent concerning this deed.

(78–80) Now, your servant, my son, have I sent to the presence of the king, my lord, so may the king send him with haste together with troops that they take the city.

(81–89) If the king, my lord, shows me favor and returns me to the city then I will protect it, th[us] as formerly, for the king, my lord. I[f] the king, my lord, [will not reinstate me] within it, then may h[e grant] a city from Burus[ili for my dwelling]. Whatever [the king] would [do to his servant, let him do but] I will [not] aban[don….] ʿAmmu[nīri….]. How long [should I remain with him?]

(89–93) [So] may the [k]i[ng, my lord,] heed [the words of] his servant qu[ickly and may he send] troops with haste that they may take the city.

(94–99) May the king, my lord not keep silent concerning this grievous deed that has been done in the territories of the king, [my lord,] and may the king, my lord hasten the regular troops that they should take the city quickly.

(101–103) If it be said concerning the city in the presence of the king, "It is a strong city," it is not strong before the troops of the king, my lord.

EA 138

TRANSCRIPTION

Obv. 01) *⸢a⸣-na* LUGAL *⸢be⸣-⸢li⸣-⸢ia⸣* $^{⸢d⸣}$⸢UTU⸣ ⸢KUR⸣.⸢MEŠ⸣
02) *um-ma* ^{I}*Ri-ib-⸢ad⸣-⸢di⸣* ÌR-*⸢ka⸣*
03) *a-na* KI.TA ⸢GÌR⸣.⸢MEŠ⸣ ⸢LUGAL⸣ ⸢EN⸣-*⸢li⸣-⸢ia⸣*
04) 7-*tam ù* ⸢7⸣ *⸢ma⸣-⸢aq⸣-ta-⸢ti*$_7$⸣
05) *i-nu-ma qa-bi-mi ⸢a⸣-na pa-ni* ⸢LUGAL⸣
06) *a-na* URU *Ia-⸢a⸣-pu* ^{KI} *šu-ut*
07) *ga-[am]-[r]u ⸢da⸣-an-na ù ki-i ⸢šu⸣-⸢nu⸣-⸢ti⸣*
08) *ú-⸢ul⸣ [a]l-⸢ka⸣-ti ⸢a⸣-⸢na⸣ ma-ḫar* ^{I}*A-⸢ya⸣*
09) *ù a-⸢nu⸣-⸢ma⸣ i-na-an-na ša-ap-ru-mi*
10) LÚ.⸢MEŠ⸣ *⸢ša⸣* ⸢URU⸣ *Gub*$^{⸢ub⸣}$*-la a-na ia-ši*
11) *la-a-mi ti-⸢pa⸣-⸢ṭe*$_6$⸣*-⸢er⸣ iš-tu* URU A.PÚ.KI.MEŠ
12) *aš-šum-⸢ma⸣ ni-⸢i⸣-ṣú ù ni-ri-bu-ka*
13) *[a]-⸢mur⸣* ⸢LÚ⸣.⸢MEŠ⸣ *šu-nu ša-a-ru-tu*
14) *id-na šu-⸢te⸣-⸢ši⸣-⸢ir⸣ i-na-mu-šu*
15) *ša-⸢ru⸣-⸢ta⸣ [la-a aq-bu] ⸢pí⸣-⸢ia⸣*
16) [..................................]
17) [................] MEŠ ÌR [.........]
18) [...............] LÚ.MEŠ URU *G[ub*^{ub}*-la]*
19) *a-na i-re-[b]i-ia a-na* ⸢URU⸣.KI ⸢A⸣.[PÚ.MEŠ]
20) *iš-tu* DÙG.⸢GA⸣ *⸢ri⸣-⸢iṣ⸣-ia ⸢iš⸣-⸢tu⸣* ⸢12⸣ ⸢ITI⸣
21) *ú-ul aš-ba-⸢ti⸣ ⸢i⸣-⸢na⸣* URU A.⸢PÚ⸣.⸢MEŠ⸣.⸢KI⸣ *mi-ia-mi*
22) *‹a-na-ku› ù uš-ši-ir-⸢ti⸣ ⸢ṭup⸣-⸢pí⸣ [a-na* É.GA]L LUGAL
23) *ù a-nu-ma A-zi-[ru nu-kúr-tu*$_4$] ⸢4⸣? ITI-*ḫi*^{MEŠ}
24) *a-na ia-a-ši ki-a-ma ⸢li⸣-i-[de] be-li*
25) *a-na* ÌR-*⸢di⸣-šu a-mur-⸢mi⸣ ⸢a⸣-na-k[u]* ⸢ÌR⸣ LUGAL
26) *i-ia-nu* LÚ.MEŠ *ḫa-za-na* LU[GAL]*ki-[ma i]a-ši*
27) *a-na* LUGAL *ša-a ia-mu-tu* [UGU *be-l]i-ia*
28) *i-nu-ma yi-iṣ-bat* URU *Ṣu-⸢mu⸣-ri*
29) ^{I}ÌR-*Aš-ra-ti ù a-na-[ṣa-a]r-mi*
30) URU-*la*^{KI} *a-na i-de-‹ni›-ia i-ia-nu*
31) LÚ.MEŠ *ma-ṣa-ra-ta*$_5$ *it-ti-‹ia› ù aš-pu-ur*!
32) *[a]-na* LUGAL *be-li-ia ⸢ù⸣ tu-ṣa*!(A) ERÍN.MEŠ
33) *[ù] ti-il-qé* URU *⸢Ṣu⸣-⸢mu⸣-ri ù*

EA 138

TRANSLATION

(1–4) To the king, my lord, the sun god of the lands, the message of Rib-Hadda your servant: beneath the feet of the king, my lord, seven times and seven (times) have I fallen.

(5–22) Inasmuch as it has been said in the king's presence, "He (has gone) to the town of Yapô (Joppa); he has run out of strength." Because of those (people) I did not go to Aya. And even now men of Byblos have written to me, "Don't depart from Beirut in order that we may come forth and we will come in to you." Behold, these men are liars. Grant that arrangements be made (and) I will depart. (With) my mouth [I do not speak] treachery. [........] men of B[yblos] for my entering in to the city of Be[irut] for the benefit of helping me. Since twelve months have I not been sitting in Beirut? Who ‹am I› that I should send a letter [to the] royal [pala]ce?

(23–33) And now Azi[ru has been hostile] for four months against me. Thus, may my lord be appri[sed] concerning his servant. Look, I am the servant of the king; the king has no city ruler like me, who will die [for] my [lo]rd. When ʿAbdi-Ashirta seized the town of Ṣumur, then I protected the city (Byblos) by myse‹l›f; there was no garrison unit with ‹me›. And I wrote to the king my lord and an army came forth [and] it took the town of Ṣumur.

34) [^{I}ÌR-*A-ši-*]*ir-ti ù a*[*-nu-ma*] *i-na-an-na*
35) [*la-qa* URU] ⸢*Ṣu*⸣-⸢*mu*⸣-[*ri* ^{I}]*A-zi-ru*
36) *ù ti-mu-*⸢*ru*⸣ ⸢LÚ⸣.⸢MEŠ⸣ ⸢URU⸣ ⸢*Gub*⸣$^{⸢ub⸣}$-⸢*li*⸣
37) *a-di ma-ti ni-ka-ši-šu* DUMU ^{I}ÌR[*-A-ši-ir-ti*]
38) *ga-mi-ir* KÙ.BABBAR-*pu* ›*na*‹ *a-na nu-kúr-ti*
39) *ù ti-na-mu-šu* UGU-*ia ù a-du-uk-*
šu-nu
40) *ù ti-iq-bu a-di ma-ti ti*$_7$*-du-*
41) *ku-nu* ⸢*a*⸣*-ya-mi ti-ìl-qú* LÚ.MEŠ *a-na a-ša-bi*
42) ⸢a⸣-*na* URU.KI *ù aš-pu-ur a-na* É.GAL
43) *a-na* ⸢ÉRIN⸣.⸢MEŠ⸣ *ù ú-ul tu-*⸢*da*⸣*-nu* ÉRIN.MEŠ *ia-*
ši
44) *ù* ⸢*ti*⸣*-iq-bi* URU.⸢KI⸣ *i-*⸢*zi*⸣*-bu-šu*
45) *ni-te-pu-uš-mi a-na* ^{I}*A-zi-ri ù*
46) *aq-bi ki-i i-te*$_9$*-pu-šu a-na ša-šu*
47) *ù i-zi-bu* LUGAL *be-li ù yi-iq-bi*
48) ŠEŠ-*ia* ⸢*ù*⸣ ⸢*yi*⸣-⸢*it*⸣*-mi a-na* URU.KI
49) *ù ti-dáb-bi-bu ù* LÚ.MEŠ BAD‹*-li*› URU.KI
50) [*ti-t*]*e-pu-šu-mi a-na* DUMU.MEŠ ^{I}ÌR-*Aš-ra-*[*ti*]
51) ⸢*ù*⸣ [*al*]*-la-ak-mi a-na-‹ku› a-na* URU A.PÚ.M[EŠ]
52) *a-na da*[*-ba-b*]*i a-na ma-ḫar* ^{I}*Ḫa-mu-ni*[*-ri*]
53) *ù ni-pu-*[*uš*] ⸢*ki*⸣*-ta aš-šum-ma* ^{I}*Ḫ*[*a-mu-ni-ri*]
54) *i-nu-*⸢*ma*⸣ ⸢*ti*⸣ [......]*nu ù* [..............]
55) *iš-tu aš*[*-ra-nu*...........................]
56) URU.KI UG[U-*ia ù*] ⸢*ni*⸣[*-la-a*]*k-mi*
57) *a-na-ku ù* ^{I}⸢*A*⸣-[*ya*] U[GU URU.]KI
58) *ú-ul na-*⸢*ad*⸣*-nu-ni* [*i-r*]*e-ba*
59) *la-qí* LÚ *ar-*⸢*ni*⸣ ⸢LUGAL⸣ L[Ú.ÉRIN.M]EŠ ^{I}*A-zi-ri*
60) *ša-ka-an a-na l*[*ìb-bi* U]RU.[KI] *ù*
61) *ti-mu-ru* URU.K[I] ⸢*i*⸣*-nu-m*[*a* ÉR]IN.MEŠ *ša-nu*
[\\] *a-ša-bu*
62) *a-na* URU.KI *ù t*[*i-m*]*a-ga-r*[*u*]
63) *i-re-bi a-na* U[RU.]KI *ù t*[*i*]*-iq-bu*
64) ⸢*a*⸣*-na ša-a-šu a*[*l*]*-lu-ú-mi* BA.ÚŠ
Lo.ed. 65) *be*!*-èl-nu ki-i ta-aq-bu mi-it*
66) ^{I}*Ri-ib-ad-di ki-ka-nu iš-tu*
67) ŠU.MEŠ *qa-*⸢*ti*⸣*-šu la-a-mi* [*ia*]-⸢*aš*⸣*-pu-ra*
Rev. 68) *a-na* KUR.MEŠ *Mi-iṣ-ri* ⸢*ù*⸣ *yi-ìl-qa-nu*
69) *qa-du* DUMU.MEŠ*-nu ù ti-*[*dá*]*-bi-ru*
70) ÉRIN.MEŠ ^{I}*A-zi-*⸢*ri*⸣ *iš-*⸢*tu*⸣URU.KI

(34–35) and [ʿAbdi-Ash]irta. But right now, Aziru [has taken the town of] Ṣumur

(36–64) and the men of the city of Byblos saw (and said) "How long will we be impoverished (by) the son of ʿAbdi-[Ashirti]? The silver has been used up for the war." So they rejected me and I smote them, but they said "How long will you smite us? Where will you get men to inhabit the city?" So I wrote to the palace for troops but troops were not given to me. And the city said, "Leave him, let us join Aziru!" But I said, "How can I join him and abandon the king, my lord?" Then my brother spoke and swore to the city and they conferred and the men, the lor‹ds› of the city, [jo]ined the sons of ʿAbdi-Ashra[ti] and I went myse‹lf› to the city of Beirut to consult with ʿAmmunira and we made a pact because of ʿA[mmunira]. When [.....] from t[here........] the city aga[inst me, then] I and A[ya] went t[o the cit]y; they did not permit me to enter. The rebel against the king took [troop]s of Aziru (and) he placed them wi[thin] the [ci]ty. Then the city saw that there were foreign troops dwelling in the city and they agreed to the entering of the city and they said to him, "Behold, dead is

(65–70) our lord," because you said, 'Dead is Rib-Hadda'; thus we are no longer under his authority. Let him not write to the land of Egypt so that he will take us with our children, "and they will expel the troops of Aziru from the city."

71) *a-nu-ma* URU.KI *mi-ši-*[*ìl-š*]*i ra-im*
72) *a-na* DUMU.MEŠ ÌR-*A-ši-ir-*⸢*ti*⸣ *ù mi-ši-ìl-ši*
73) *a-na be-li-ia* ⸢*ù*⸣ *k*[*i-i*] *i-pí-iš*
74) *yu-pa-šu a-na* ⸢LÚ⸣-⸢*li*⸣ *ša a-ši-ib a-na* URU.KI-*šu*
75) *yu-pa-šu ia-a-ši i-nu-ma iš-tu*
76) 10 *še-ti ka-ša-di-*[*i*]*a* ⸢*a*⸣-*na* URU A.PÚ.MEŠ
77) *uš-ši-ir-ti* DUMU-*ia* ⸢*a*⸣-*na* É.GAL NUN
78) *iš-tu* 4 ITI ⸢*ú*⸣-*ul* ⸢*yi*⸣-*mur-mi pa-ni* LUGAL
79) *um-ma* LÙ-*ia a-na* URU *Ta-aḫ-da* ^{KI}
80) *ka-ša-ad-ti-šu a-*⸢*na*⸣ *mi-ni ḫa-ṣí-*⸢*ri*⸣
81) LÚ-*li ša-a uš-ši*[*-ir-ti*]⸢*a*⸣-[*na* É.]⸢GAL⸣ [LUGAL]
82) *a-na-ku aq-bu-*⸢*na*⸣ ⸢*a*⸣-[*na*................]
83) ⸢*ù*⸣ ⸢*ti*-⸢*na*⸣-⸢*mu*⸣-[*šu-na*..................]
84) *a-na mi-ni ti-ka*[*-al-lu-šu i-na*]
85) KUR.MEŠ *Ia-pu a-na m*[*i-ni la uš-šir-ta*]
86) *a-na ia-ši i-nu-ma* [*aš-ba-ti i-na*]
87) URU *ki-it* ⸢*ù*⸣ *a*[*l-lu-ú-mi*...]
88) *i-nu-ma* ⸢*aš*⸣-⸢*ba*⸣-*ti a-na* [URU A.PÚ.MEŠ]
89) *i-ia-nu* LÚ LUGAL *be-li ša y*[*i-lik a-na* MAḪ-*ia*]
90) *ù ti-iq-bu* URU.KI *al-lu-mi* [I][*Ri-ib-ad-di*]
91) *a-ši-ib a-na* URU A.⸢PÚ⸣.‹MEŠ› *a-ya-mi* LÚ-*lu*
92) *ša a-lik iš-tu* KUR.MEŠ *Mi-iṣ-ri a-na maḫ-‹ri›-šu*
93) *ù ti*$_{7}$*-né-pu-šu-na a-na* [I]*A-zi-ri*
94) *pa-na-nu aš-pu-ru a-na* LUGAL *ú-ul yi-iš-mu*
95) *a-wa-ti a-nu-ma i-na-na a-na* URU A.PÚ.‹MEŠ›
96) *aš-ba-ti ki-i*$_{15}$ UR.GI$_{5}$ *la-a tu-uš-mu*
97) *a-wa-ti šum-ma* ⸢*ša*⸣-*mi* LUGAL *a-na* ÌR-*šu*
98) ⸢*ù*⸣ *na-ad-na-at* ÉRIN.MEŠ *ia-ši*
99) [*ù na-aṣ-ra-a*]*t* URU.KI *a-na* LUGAL
100) *ù* ⸢*yi*⸣-⸢*di*⸣-*in*$_{4}$ [LUGAL ÉRIN].⸢MEŠ⸣ ⸢*ù*⸣
101) *ni-iṣ-bat* ⸢URU⸣.⸢KI⸣ *l*[*a-a ti-ìl-qé-ši*]
102) ÉRIN.MEŠ DUMU.MEŠ [I]ÌR-*aš*-⸢*ra*⸣-*ti* ⸢*a*⸣-⸢*na*⸣ [*ša-šu-nu*]
103) *ù* ⸢*ti*⸣-⸢*bal*⸣-⸢*ki*⸣-⸢*tu*⸣ LÚ.MEŠ-*ši ù a-m*[*ur*]

(71–93) Now, as for the city, hal[f of i]t prefers the sons of ʿAbdi-Ashirti and half of it prefers my lord. Just as is done for a ruler who is residing in his city, thus should be done for me because within ten minutes after my arrival in Beirut, I sent my son to the palace of the ruler(ship). Four months he has not seen the face of the king. My man reported, "To the city of Taḫda, I have reached it." Why is the man whom I se[nt] to the royal [pal]ace detained? I say to [.....] and [they will] depart [.......]. Why are they [holding him in] the territory of Yapô (Joppa)? Wh[y did you not send] to me when [I was dwelling in] the faithful city? B[ehold,....] while I am dwelling in [the city of Beirut] there is no man of the king, my lord, who will [come to me]. And the city said, "Behold [Rib-Hadda] is dwelling in Beirut. Where is the man who went to him from the land of Egypt?" So they joined Aziru.

(94–100) Formerly, I wrote to the king; he did not listen to my word. Right now, I am dwelling in Beirut like a dog (and) my word is not heeded. If the king had listened to his servant and troops had been given to me, [then] the city [would have been guarded] for the king. So may the king grant that

(101–103) we will seize the city. L[et not] the troops of the sons of ʿAbdi-Ashrati [take it] for [themselves], and its people rebel.

104) LÚ-*lu ar-nu a-*⸢*na*⸣ *na-*⸢*da*⸣-›*na*‹-⸢*ni*⸣ *a-na*
105) ›*a-na*‹ ᴵ*A-zi-ri* ⸢*yi*⸣-⸢*pu*⸣-⸢*uš*⸣ ⸢*ip*⸣-*ša* G[A]L
106) *ù la-qí* ‹NÍG›.GA.MEŠ ⸢*ù*⸣ ⸢*yu*⸣-⸢*dáb*⸣-⸢*bi*⸣-⸢*ra*⸣-[*an-ni*]
107) [*ù*] ⸢*ṭá*⸣-*pí-ìl* ᴵ*A-pí q*[*a-du…*]
108) [*ù y*]*u-ba-ú* [*na-da-na* URU.KI]
109) *a-na* ᴵ*A-zi-*⸢*ri*⸣ ⸢*ù*⸣ [*ú-ul i*]*a-*⸢*qú*⸣-⸢*ul*⸣
110) LUGAL *be-li* [*iš*]-⸢*tu*⸣ [UR]U-*šu ù*
111) *ta-aq-bi* [URU.K]I ᴵ[*Ri-i*]*b*[-*a*]*d-*⸢*di*⸣
112) BA.ÚŠ *ki*[-*ka-nu iš-tu* ŠU]-*šu a-na*
113) ᴵ*A-zi-ri* [*ni-te-pu-uš*] ⸢*ù*⸣
114) *ú-ul ya-*[*qú-u*]*l* [LUGAL *be-li*] ⸢*a*⸣-⸢*na*⸣ URU.⸢KI⸣
115) ⸢*a*⸣-⸢*na*⸣ [LÚ.]⸢MEŠ⸣ *ša-*⸢*ru*⸣-*ta*₅ [*e-p*]*u-*[*u*]*š*
116) *a-na pí-i* ⸢DUMU⸣.MEŠ ᴵÌR-⸢*Aš*⸣-⸢*ra*⸣-*t*⸢*i*⸣
117) *yi-pu-*⸢*uš*⸣ ⸢*ar*⸣-*na* [*an-ni-ta*₅] ⸢*ù*⸣?
118) *a-mur-mi* ⸢*a*⸣-*n*[*a-ku*] ⸢*ú*⸣-⸢*ul*⸣ [*aq-ta-b*]*i*
119) *ka-az-*⸢*bu*⸣-[*ta*₅] ⸢*a*⸣-⸢*na*⸣ L[UGAL *be-li-ia*]
120) *pal-ḫa-tu* [.......................]
121) URU.KI LÚ-⸢*la*⸣ ⸢*ar*⸣-‹*ni*› LUGAL ⸢*ù*⸣ *a*[*l-lu-ú-mi*]
122) *ta-aš-pu-ru-na* LÚ.MEŠ URU *Gub-*⸢*la*⸣
123) *a-ya-mi i-nu-ma ia-aš-pu-ru*
124) LUGAL *be-èl-ka* [*a-na*] *maḫ-*‹*ri*›*-ka*
125) *a-ya-mi* ÉRIN.MEŠ [*i-n*]*u-ma uš-ši-ra-at*
126) *a-na ka-a-ta*₅ *ù* [*i*]⸢*a*⸣-*pu* \ *ḫa-mu-du*
127) *ša-a ša-pí-ir* ⸢*iš*⸣-*tu*
128) LUGAL *be-li la-a na-di-in*
129) *ia-a-ši a-na* URU-*ia* ŠE-⸢*IM*⸣
Uped 130) *i-ka-al* \ *ḫa-ṣí-ri*
131) *ù mi-nu-um yi-iq-*⸢*ta*⸣-⸢*bu*⸣
132) ⸢ᴵ⸣⸢*Ḫa*⸣-⸢*mu*⸣-⸢*ni*⸣-*ri*
Lft.ed. 133) *a-di ma-ti i-zi-*[*za*]-*ti*₇ *it-ti-šu ù yi-*[*di*]-*na* LUGAL ÉRIN.MEŠ *la-a-mi*
134) *ti-*⸢*ri*⸣-*bu* DUMU.MEŠ [ᴵÌR-*a*]*š-ra-tu*₄ *a-na* URU.KI *ù* [UR]U A.PÚ *ti-iṣ-ba-tu-na*
135) *ù ia-nu* KUR.MEŠ *a-n*[*a*] LUGAL *be-li-ia ša-ni-tam a-*‹*na*› ⸢*i*⸣-[*a*]-*ši yu-pa-šu ki-š*[*u-ma*] *ša-a*
136) *yi-de-ni* LUGAL *be-*⸢*li*⸣ *ù mi-nu-um ni-dá-*⸢*an*⸣ LÚ *ša-na ù a-na-*⸢*ku*⸣-*ma*
137) *mi-ta-ti*!(UD) *ù* DUMU.[ME]Š-*ia* ÌR.MEŠ ⸢LUGAL⸣ *ba-*⸢*al*⸣-⸢*ṭú*⸣ *ù ti-iš-pu-ru-*⸢*na*⸣ *a-na* LUGAL
138) *i ti-ir-nu-mi* U[RU].⸢KI⸣-*nu mi-nu*[-*um*] *qa-al be-*⸢*li*⸣ *iš-*‹*tu*› *ia-ši-ia*

(103–121) And l[ook], the rebellious man did a very (bad) deed in order to give the city to Aziru, and he took the ‹pro›perty and he expell[ed me] [and] he insulted Api w[ith....]. [And] he is seeking [to give the city] to Aziru, so may the king, my lord, [not] keep silent [con]cerning his [ci[ty] so that the city will say, "Rib-Hadda is dead, th[us we are free from] h[is authority; let us join] Aziru." May the [king, my lord] not ke[ep silent] concerning the city; [a]ct against the treacherous me[n]. At the command of the sons of ʿAbdi-Ashrati he has done [this] crime. So look, as for me, I [have not spoke]n lies to the k[ing, my lord]. Fearing [.........] the city, the rebel of the king.

(121–130) And be[hold, the men of the city of Byblos write, "Where? That the king, your lord, would write to you? Where are the troops [th]at have been sent to you?" And the favor which is sent from the king, the lord, is not given to me. Grain is withheld from the city.

(131–135) Why does ʿAmmunira keep saying, "How long will I be located with him." May the king give troops lest the sons of [ʿAbdi]-Ashrati enter the city and they will take the city of Beirut and the king, my lord, will have no territories.

(135–138) Furthermore, thu[s] has been done to me, whom the king, my lord, knows well, and what *will be done* (?) to another man? And it is I who am dead and my sons, the servants of the king, are alive, and they shall write to the king, "Return us to our city." Why should my lord keep silent conce[rning] me?

EA 139

TRANSCRIPTION

Obv. 01) *a-na* LUGAL E[N-*ia* ^{d}UTU-*ia*]
02) *um-ma* DINGIR-*ra*[*-pí-iḫ* ÌR-*ka*]
03) *um-ma Gu-‹ub›-la*[^{KI} GÉME-*ka a-na*]
04) GÌR.MEŠ EN ^{d}UTU ⸢7⸣[7 *am-qut*]
05) *la-a ta-qú-ul* L[UGAL *a-na Gu-‹ub›-la*^{KI}]
06) URU-*ka ù* URU *a-bu-t*[*i-ka*]
07) *iš-tu da-ri-ti ša-ni*⸢*-tam*⸣ *a-*⸢*mur*⸣
08) URU *Gu-‹ub›-la ki-ma Ḫi*(!)*-ku-‹up›-ta-aḫ ki-*⸢*na*⸣*-na*
09) URU *Gu-‹ub›-la a-*⸢*na*⸣ ⸢LUGAL⸣ EN-*ia*
10) *la-a ta-qú-ul a-na A-zi*!(ME.ZU)*-ri* ⸢ÌR⸣
11) *ù yi-pu-iš ki-ma* ŠÀ-*šu i-na*
12) KUR.KUR.MEŠ *šàr-ri a-mur ar-na ša*
13) *a-*⸢*pá*⸣*-aš* ^{I}*A-zi-ru i-na šàr-ri*
14) [*da-a*]*k* LUGAL KUR *Am-mi-ia ù*
15) [LUGAL KUR *A*]*r*(?)*-da-ta ù* LUGAL KUR *Ir-*
16) [*qa-ta ù* M]ÁŠKIM LUGAL EN-*ia ù*
17) [URU *Ṣu-m*]*u-ra pa-la-ša*

---

18) [*ù a-nu-ma*] *i-na-an-na yu-ba-ú*
19) [*i-pé-eš*$_{15}$] *ar-‹ni› i-na* LUGAL *ša-ni-tam*

EA 139

TRANSLATION

(1–4) To the king, [my] lo[rd, my sun god], message of ʾIlî-rā[piʾ, your servant], message of By‹b›los [your handmaiden: At] the feet of the lord, the sun god, seven (times and) [seven times, I have fallen].

(5–7) Do not keep silent, (O) k[ing, concerning Byblos], your city and the city of [your] ancest[ors] from of old.

(7–10) Furthermore, behold, as for the city of Byblos, as does Ḥikuptaḥ (Memphis), thus does the city of Byblos belong to the king, my lord.

(10–12) Do not keep silent concerning Aziru(!), the slave, that he has done as he pleased in the territories of the king.

(12–17) Behold the crime which Aziru has committed against the king: [he has sla]in the king of the land of Ammiya and [the king of the land of A]rdata and the king of the land of ʿIr[qata and the com]missioner of the king, my lord, and he has forced his way into [the city of Ṣumu]r.

(18–19) [And even] now he seeks [to commit] a cri‹me› against the king.

20) [^{I}*Pí-ḫ*]*u-ru yi-qa-bu*
21) [*a-na* LÚ.MEŠ *ša*] ⌜URU⌝ *Gu-‹ub›-la*
22) [*ù a-na* LÚ.MEŠ URU A.PÚ]UGU *i-*⌜*pé*⌝*-*⌜*eš*$_{15}$⌝
23) [*nu-kúr-ti it-ti* ^{I}*A-zi-ri ù*] *yi-*⌜*de*⌝
Lo.ed. 24) [*i-nu-ma la i-le-ú na-ṣ*]*a-ar*
Rev. 25) [URU *Gub-la a-na* LUGAL] ⌜EN⌝-⌜*ia*⌝
26) [....................]*tu ka-la-at*
27) [*yi-qa-bu*] ⌜*ša*⌝*-ra-qí ù la-a*
28) [*yi-qa-bu ki-t*]*i mi-im-ma i-na ša-šu-nu*
29) [*ša-ra-*]*qú ù yi-de* LUGAL EN
30) [*a-na-k*]*u* ⌜ÌR⌝ *ki-ti-šu ù yi-*
31) ⌜*iš*⌝*-ši-ra ma-ṣa-ar-ta i-na*
32) URU-*šu* 30 LÚ.MEŠ *ù* 50 LÚ.MEŠ *a-di*
33) ⌜URU⌝ *Gub-la ‹la›-a ia-aš-ku-un* ⌜LUGAL⌝ ŠÀ-*šu*
34) *i-na mi-im-mi ša yi-iš-ši-ru*
35) ^{I}*A-zi-ru a-na ša-šu mi-im-mu*
36) *ša yi-iš-ši-ru a-wa-ti Ṣu-mu-*
ru
37) *ù mi-im-‹mu›* ^{I}*ḫa-za-ni* LUGAL
38) ⌜*ša*⌝ *da-ak yi-iš-ši-ru*
39) *a-na ka-ta a-mur* ^{I}*A-zi-ru*
40) *ar-‹nu›* LUGAL EN-*ia*

(19–33) Furthermore, [Piḫ]uru keeps saying [to the men of] the city of Byblos [...] concerning waging [war with Aziru and] he knows [that I am unable to guard the city of the king,] my lord. [...He is speaking] lies and he does not [speak tru]th at all to them. [He is a li]ar but the king, the lord, knows (that) ⌜I⌝ am his true servant so may he send a garrison contingent to his city, thirty men or fifty men as far as Byblos. May the king ‹not› pay attention

(34–40) to the property which Aziru is sending to him. The property that he is sending is things of Ṣumur and the property of the city ruler of the king whom he slew. Behold, Aziru is a trai[tor] to the king my lord.

EA 140

TRANSCRIPTION

Obv. 01) [*a-na* LU]GAL EN-‹*ia*› ^{d}UTU-*ia um-ma*
02) ⸢URU⸣ ⸢*Gub*⸣-*la* GÉME-*ka um-ma*
03) ⸢^{I}⸣DINGIR-*ra-pí-i*ʾ ÌR-*ka a*-⸢*na*⸣
04) ⸢GÌR⸣.MEŠ EN-*ia* ^{d}UTU-‹*ia*› 7 ⸢7⸣ ⸢*am*⸣-*qut*
05) *la-a yi-qú-lu* LUGAL EN-*ia*
06) *i-na* URU *Gub-la* GÉME-*šu*
07) URU *šàr-ri iš-tu da-ri-ti*
08) *ša-ni-tam a-na mi-ni iš-ši-ir šàr-ru*
09) *i-na* ^{I}*A-zi-ri ù yi-pu-šu*
10) *ki-ma* ŠÀ-*šu a*-⸢*mur*⸣ ^{I}*A-zi-ru* ^{I}*A-du-na šàr* KUR *Ir-qa-ta*
11) *da-ak šàr* KUR *Am-mi-ia*
12) *ù šàr* KUR *Ar-da-ta*
13) *ù* LÚ GAL *da-ak ù la-qa*
14) URU.MEŠ-*šu-nu a-na ša-šu*
15) URU *Ṣu-mu-ra a-na ša-šu*
16) URU.MEŠ *šàr-ri* 1-*en* URU *Gub-la*
17) *is-sí-la-at šàr-ri*
18) *ša-ni-tam* ⸢*a*⸣-*mur* URU *Ṣu-mu-ra*
19) ⸢*ù*⸣ ⸢URU⸣ *Ul-la-às-sà pa-la-ša*
20) [*š*]*a-ni-tam a*-⸢*mur*⸣ *ar-na š*[*a*]
21) [*yi*]-*pu-iš* ^{I}*A-zi-ru*
22) [*i-n*]*a ur-ru-bi-šu*
Lo.ed. 23) [*a-na*] *mu-ḫi-ka ar-nu*
Rev. 24) [*a-na mu-ḫi-n*]*u iš-ši-ir* LÚ.ME[Š]-
25) [*šu a-na*] *maḫ-‹ri›* ^{I}*I-ta-ka-ma*
26) [*ù*] ⸢*da*⸣-*ak ka-li*
27) [KUR.]KUR.MEŠ *Am-qí* KUR.MEŠ *šàr*-⸢*ri*⸣
28) *ù i-na-an-na iš-ši-ir*
29) LÚ.MEŠ-*šu i-na ṣa-ba-at* KUR.KUR.MEŠ
30) *Am-qí ù* KI.KI *ša-ni-tam la-*
31) *a yi-pu-šu šàr* KUR *Ḫa-at-\ta*
32) *ù šàr* KUR *Na-ri-ma*
33) *ù*

EA 140

TRANSLATION

(1–4) [To the ki]ng, ‹my› lord, my sun god, the message of the city of Byblos, your handmaiden (and) the message of ʾIlu-rapiʾ, your servant; at the feet of my lord,‹my› sun god, seven (times and) seven (times) have I fallen.

(5–7) The king, my lord, should not keep silent concerning the city of Byblos, his handmaiden, a royal city from of old.

(8–17) Furthermore, why did the king send to Aziru so that he might do as he pleases? Look, Aziru slew Aduna, the king of the land of ʿIrqata; the king of the land of Ammiya, the king of the land of Ardata and the senior official, he slew and he took their towns for himself. The city of Ṣumur belongs to him, the cities of the king. Only, the city of Byblos, is a (stone) vessel of the king.

(18–19) Furthermore, look, he broke into the city of Ṣumur and the city of Ulassa.

(20–30) Furthermore, look, the crime which Aziru committed [wh]en he entered in to you. It was a crime [against] us; he sent [his] men [to] Itakama [and] he attacked all [the lan]ds of ʿAmqi, lands of the king. And now he has sent his men to seize the lands of ʿAmqi and their territories.

(30–33) Furthermore, the king of Ḫatti did not do, or the king of Na(h)rîma or....

EA 141

TRANSCRIPTION

Obv. 01) *a-na ša* LUGAL EN-*ia* ^{d}UTU-⸢*i*⸣[*a*]
02) DINGIR.MEŠ-*ia ša-ri* TIL.LA-*ia*
03) *qí-bí-ma um-ma Am-mu-ni-ra*
04) LÚ URU PÚ.ḪI.A ÌR-*ka ù* SAḪAR-*ra* \ *a-pa-ru*
05) *ša* GÌR.MEŠ-*ka* ––––––––––

---

06) *a-na* GÌR.MEŠ LUGAL EN-*ia* ^{d}UTU-*ia* DINGIR.MEŠ-$_{\backslash ia}$
07) *ša-ri* TIL.LA-*ia* 7 *u* 7 *ta-a-an*
08) *am-qú-ut šá-ni-tam iš-te-me*
09) *a*-⸢*wa*⸣-*te*^{MEŠ} ⸢DUB⸣ *ša šàr-ri* ⸢EN⸣-*ia*
10) ^{d}UTU-*ia* DINGIR.MEŠ-*ia ša-ri ba-la-ṭì-ia*
11) *ù ḫa-di* ŠÀ ÌR-*ka ù*
12) *i-pí-ri ša* GÌR.MEŠ LUGAL EN-*ia*
13) ^{d}UTU-*ia ù* DINGIR.MEŠ-*ia ša-ri* TIL.LA‹-*ia*›
14) *ma-gal ma-gal i-nu-ma a-ṣa-at*
15) *ša-ru ša* LUGAL EN-*ia*
16) ^{d}UTU-*ia* DINGIR.MEŠ-*ia*
17) *a-na* ÌR-*šu ù i-pí-ri ša* GÌR.MEŠ-*šu*

---

18) *šá-ni-tam i-nu-ma ša-pa-ar šàr-ru*
19) EN-*ia* ^{d}UTU-*ia a-na* ÌR-*šu*
20) *ù i-pí-ri ša* GÌR.MEŠ-*šu*
21) *šu-ši-ir-mi a-na* ⸢*pa*⸣-*ni*
22) ÉRIN.ḪI.A *pí-ṭá-at ša* LUGAL EN-⸢*ka*$_4$⸣
23) *iš-te-mé ma-gal ma-gal*
Lo.ed. 24) *ù a-›na‹-nu-um-ma šu-ši-ra*-⸢*ku*⸣
25) *qa-du* ANŠE.KUR.RA-*ia* ḪI.A *ù*
Rev. 26) *qa-du* GIŠ.GIGIR.⸢ḪI.A⸣-*ia ù qa-du*
27) *gáb-bi mi*-⸢*im*⸣-*mi-ia*$^{\text{ḪI.A}}$
28) *ša i-ba-aš-ša it-ti*
29) ÌR *ša* LUGAL EN-*ia a-na*
30) *pa-ni* ÉRIN.ḪI.A *pí-ṭá-at ša* LUGAL ⸢EN⸣‹-*ia*›

EA 141

TRANSLATION

(1–5) Speak to the king, my lord, m[y] sun god, my deity, the breath of my life, the message of ʿAmmunīra, the ruler of the city of Beirut, your servant, the dirt at your feet.

(6–8) At the feet of the king, my lord, my sun god, my deity, the breath of my life, seven and seven times have I fallen.

(8–17) Furthermore, I have heard the words of the tablet of the king, my lord, my sun god, my deity, the breath of my life, and the heart of your servant, the dirt at the feet of the king, my lord, my sun god, my deity, the breath of ‹my› life rejoiced very much, because the breath of the king, my lord, my sun god, my deity, has come forth to his servant and the dirt at his feet.

(18–23) Furthermore, when the king, my lord, my sun god wrote to his servant and the dirt at his feet, "Make ready for the regular army of the king, your lord," I heeded very carefully.

(24–30) And now, I am ready with my horses and with my chariots and with all my possessions that are with the servant of the king, my lord, for the coming of the regular army of the king, ‹my› lord.

31) *ù lu-ú ti-ra-ḫa-aṣ* ÉRIN.ḪI.A *pí-ṭá‹-at›-šu*
32) *ša* LUGAL EN-*ia* ᵈUTU-*ia* DINGIR.MEŠ-*ia*
33) UZU.SAG.DU ⸢LÚ⸣.MEŠ *a-ia-bi-šu*
34) *ù lu-ú ti-mu-ru* 2 IGI ÌR-*ka*
35) *i-na* TIL.LA *ša* LUGAL EN-*ia*
36) *šá-ni-tam ù a!-mur* ‹ÉRIN.ḪI.A *pí-ṭá-at*› *ša* LUGAL EN‹-ia›
37) ᵈUTU-*ia* DINGIR.MEŠ-*ia ša-ri* TIL.LA-*ia*
38) *tu-ti-ru* ⸢*gi*⸣-*mi-li* ÌR-*šu*
39) *a-nu-um-ma a-na-ku* ÌR *ša* LUGAL EN‹-*ia*›
40) *ù* GIŠ.GÌR.GUB *ša* GÌR.MEŠ-*šu*
41) *a-nu-um-ma uṣ!-ṣú-ru*
42) URU *ša* LUGAL EN-*ia* ᵈUTU-*ia*
43) *ša-ri ba-la-ṭì-ia*
44) *ù* BÀD-*ši* \ *ḫu-mi-tu*
45) *a-di i-*⸢*mu*⸣-⸢*ru*⸣ ⸢2⸣ ⸢IGI⸣.ḪI.A‹-*ia*›
46) ÉRIN.ḪI.A *pí-ṭ*[*á-at ša* L]UGAL EN-*ia*
Up.ed. 47) *ù* [*a-nu-um-ma a-na-ku*]ÌR *ša* LUGAL
48) [*a-n*]*a a-*⸢*ra*⸣-⸢*di*⸣-[*šu*]

(31–32) So may the regular army of the king, my lord, my sun god, my deity,

(33–35) smash the head of his enemies; and may the eyes of your servant behold the life of the king, my lord.

(36–38) Furthermore, behold may ‹the regular army› of the king, ‹my› lord, my sun god, my deity, the breath of my life, bring recompense to his servant.

(39–40) Now, I am the servant of the king, ‹my› lord, and the footstool of his feet.

(41–48) Now, I am guarding the city of the king, my lord, my sun god, the breath of my life, and its wall until I see the eyes of the re[gular army of the k]ing, my lord, and [now I am] the servant of the king [in] order to serve him.

EA 142

TRANSCRIPTION

Obv. 01) [*a-na* LUGAL EN-*ia ša-ri*] TIL.LA-⸢*ia*⸣

02) [*um-ma Am-mu-ni-*]*ra* ÌR-*ka*

03) [*ù i-pí-ri*] *ša* 2 GÌR.MEŠ-*ka*

04) [*a-na* GÌR.MEŠ] LUGAL EN-*ia* 7 *u* 7 *ta-a-an*

– – – – – – – – –

05) [*am-qú-ut š*]*á-ni-tam*

---

06) [*is-te-m*]*e a-wa-te*^{MEŠ} DUB *ša uš-te*$_{9}$-⸢*bil*⸣!-⸢*la*⸣-

07) [*an-n*]*i* LUGAL EN-*ia ù en-du-um*

08) [*iš*]-*te-me a-wa-te*^{MEŠ} DUB LUGAL EN-*ia*

09) ⸢*ù*⸣ *yi-iḫ-di* ŠÀ-*ia ù* ––––––––––

10) [*i*]*n*$_{4}$-*nam-mu-ru* 2 IGI.MEŠ-*ia ma-gal*

---

11) [*šá*]-*ni-tam a-nu-um-ma na-aṣ-ra-ku ma-gal*

12) ⸢*ù*⸣ *uṣ*-⸢*ṣú*⸣-*ru* URU.KI PÚ.ḪI.A

13) ⸢*a*⸣-*na* LUGAL EN-*ia a-di ka-ša-di*

14) ÉRIN.MEŠ *pí-ṭá-ti* LUGAL EN-*ia*

---

15) *šá-ni-tam a-na* LÚ URU *Gub-la ša i*$_{15}$-*ba-aš-ša*

16) *it-ti-ia a-nu-um-ma i-na-ṣa-ru-šu*

17) *a-di yi-im-lu-ku* LUGAL *a-na* ÌR-*šu*

18) *šá-ni-tam yi-il*$_{5}$-*ma-ad* LUGAL EN-*ia*

19) *i*$_{15}$-*pí-iš* ŠEŠ-*šu ša i*$_{15}$-*ba-aš*-⸢*ša*⸣

20) *i-na* URU *Gub-la i-nu-ma na*-⸢*da*⸣-[*an*]

21) DUMU.DUMU.MEŠ *ša* ^{I}*Ri*-⸢*ib*⸣-⸢^{d}⸣⸢IŠKUR⸣

Lo.ed. 22) ⸢*ša*⸣ *i*$_{15}$-*ba-aš-šu it-ti*-⸢*šu*⸣!

23) [*a*]-*na* ⸢LÚ⸣.⸢MEŠ⸣ ⸢*ar*⸣-*nu*-⸢*ti*⸣ ⸢*ša*⸣

Rev. 24) *šàr-ri ša i-na* KUR *A*-⸢*mur*⸣?-⸢*ri*⸣

EA 142

TRANSLATION

(1–5) [To the king, my lord the breath of] my life, [the message of ʿAmmu-nī]ra, your servant [and the dirt] at your feet. [At the feet of] the king, my lord, seven (times) and seven times [have I fallen.]

(5–10) [Fu]rthermore,

[I have hear]d the words of the tablet which the king, my lord, sent [to me], and when [I h]eard the words of the tablet of the king, my lord, my heart rejoiced and my eyes brightened up greatly.

(11–14) Furthermore, now I am very much on guard and I am guarding the town of Beirut for the king, my lord, until the arrival of the regular army of the king, my lord.

(15–17) Furthermore, as to the ruler of Byblos who is with me, I am guarding him until the king takes counsel concerning his servant.

(18–24) Furthermore, may the king, my lord, be apprised of the deed of his brother who is in the city of Byblos, when he handed over the sons of Rib-Haddi who were with him to the rebels against the king who are in the land of Amurru.

---

25) ⸢*šá*⸣-*ni-tam a-nu-um-ma* ⸢*šu-ši*-⸢*ra*⸣-⸢*ku*⸣
26) *qa-du* ANŠE.KUR.RA.ḪI.A-⸢*ia*⸣ ›⸢*ù*⸣‹
27) *ù qa-du* GIŠ.GIGIR.ḪI.A-*ia ù* ⸢*qa*⸣-⸢*du*⸣
28) *gáb-bi mi-im-mi*$^{\text{ḪI.A}}$
29) *ša* i_{15}-*ba-aš-ša it-ti-ia*
30) *a-na pa-ni* ÉRIN.MEŠ *pí-ṭá-at*
31) LUGAL EN-*ia*

---

32) *šá-ni-tam a-na* GÌR.MEŠ LUGAL EN-*ia*
33) [7] *u* 7-*ta-a-an am-qú-ut*

(25–31) Furthermore, now I am prepared with my horses and with my chariots and with all the possessions that are with me, for the coming of the regular army of the king, my lord.

(32–33) Furthermore, at the feet of the king, my lord, [seven (times)] and seven times have I fallen.

EA 143

TRANSCRIPTION

Obv. 01) *a-na* LUGAL EN-*ia š*[*a-ri*
02) TIL.LA-*ia* [*qí-bi-ma*]
03) ⸢*um*⸣-*ma Am-mu-ni*-⸢*ra*⸣ [ÌR-*ka*]
04) [*ù*] SAḪAR.RA *ša* G[ÌR.MEŠ-*ka*]
05) [*a-na* GÌR.]MEŠ LUGAL E[N-*ia*]
06) [7 *ù* 7-*ta-a-an am-qú-ut*]
07) [..............................]
08) [..............................]
09') [LUGAL EN-*ia ša-ri* TIL.L]A-*ia*

10') [*iš-pu-ur* LUGA]L EN-*ia*
11') *a-na* ÌR-*šu ù a-na* SAḪAR.RA\ *ḫa-pa-ru*
12') *ša* GÌR.MEŠ-*šu a-na* ⸢*ši*⸣-*pí-ir-ti-šu*
13') *a-šar i-ba-ša-at*
14') *ši-pí-ir-ti* LUGAL EN-*ia*
15') *ša-ri* TIL.LA-*ia ù ú-ba*-⸢*ú*⸣-⸢*n*⸣*a-ši*
16') *ù uš-ši-ru-na-ši*
17') *a-na* LUGAL EN-*ia ša-ri* TIL.LA!-*ia*

18') ⸢*šá*⸣-⸢*ni*⸣-⸢*tam*⸣ *a-nu-um-ma i-na i-re-bi*
19') ⸢GIŠ⸣.MÁ.ḪI.A *ša* LUGAL EN-*ia*
20') ⸢*ša*⸣ *sí-ki-pu*
Rev. 21') *i-na* URU PÚ.ḪI.A *uš-ši-ru*-⸢*na*⸣
22') [MU]NUS.GÉME *ša* LUGAL EN-*ia*
23') *ki-ma tu*(?)-*la-*
24') *iš-tu........e-......ṣa-ta*
25') *ki-na*-⸢*an*⸣-⸢*na*⸣ URU PÚ.ḪI.A
26') *a-na* LUGAL EN‹-*ia*›
27') *ù a-na-ku ki-ma* LÚ *ta-a*[*ṣ-r*]*a-ḫi*
28') ANŠE.KUR.RA.ḪI.A *ša*
29') LU[GAL] ⸢EN⸣-[*i*]*a i*$_{15}$-*ba-ša-ku*
30') [*a-na* LUGAL EN-*i*]*a ù*
31') [..................*k*]*i a-na* LUGAL EN-*ia*

EA 143

TRANSLATION

(1–6) [Speak] to the king, my lord, the br[eath] of my life, the message of 'Ammunira, [your servant and] the dirt under [your] f[eet]: [at the fee]t of the king, [my] lo[rd, seven and seven times have I fallen]

(7–8) *Missing due to a break in the tablet; approximately two lines.*

(9) [the king, my lord, the breath of] my [lif]e.

(10'–17') [The kin]g, my lord [has written] to his servant and the dirt under his feet concerning his requisition. Wherever the requisition of the king, my lord, the breath of my life, is located, I will seek it out and I will send it to the king, my lord, the breath of my life.

(18'–31') Furthermore, now with the arrival of the ships of the king, my lord, which are anchored at Beirut, the handmaiden of the king, my lord, I will send off. Like the....from....thus is Beirut for the king, ‹my› lord. And as for me, like the warmer of the horses of the ki[ng], my lord, am I [for the king, m]y [lord] and [....................] to the king, my lord.

32’) [..................LUGAL EN-]*ia*
33’) [*ša-ri*] ⸢TIL⸣.L[A-*ia*...........]
34’) [*i-n*]*a lìb-bi* G[IŠ.MA.ḪI.A *ša*]
35’) [LUG]AL EN-*ia* ⸢*uš*⸣[*-ši-ru-na-ši*]

36’) [*šá*]*-ni-tam yi-il*$_5$*-m*[*a-ad* LUGAL EN-*ia*]
37’) ⸢*i*⸣*-nu-ma ga-ma-r*[*u*...........................]
38’) [*š*]*a*-LUGAL EN-*ia* [..........................]

39’) *šá-ni-tam yi-il*$_5$*-ma-*[*ad* LUGAL EN-*ia*]
40’) *i-nu-ma da-at-nu* [....................]
41’) [*a-n*]*a* ÌR-*šu*

(32'–35') [...........the king,] my [lord], [the breath of my] life, [i]n the hold of the [ships of the ki]ng, my lord [will I send it]

(36'–38') [Fu]rthermore, may [the king, my lord] be informe[d] that [all the...] of the king my lord, is used up [..............].

(39'–41') Furthermore, may [the king, my lord,] be informed that our gift.....(?) [fo]r his servant.

EA 144

TRANSCRIPTION

Obv. 01) *a-*⌜*na*⌝ *šàr-ri* EN-*ia*
02) DINGIR.MEŠ-*ia* ^{d}UTU-⌜*ia*⌝ *ša-ri* TIL.LA-⌜*i*⌝*a*
03) *qí-* *bí-* *-ma*
04) *um-*⌜*ma*⌝ ^{I}*Zi-im-re-ed-di*
05) ^{LÚ}*ḫa-za-nu ša* URU *Ṣí-du-na* ^{KI}
06) *a-na* GÌR.MEŠ EN-*ia* DINGIR.MEŠ ^{d}UTU *ša-ri*
07) *ša* TIL.LA-*ia a-na* GÌR.MEŠ EN-*ia*
08) DINGIR.MEŠ-*ia* ^{d}UTU-*ia ša-*⌜*ri*⌝ TIL.LA-*ia*
09) 7-*šu ù* 7-*ta-a-an am-qú-ut*
10) *lu-ú i-de* LUGAL EN-*ia i-nu-ma*
11) *šal-ma-at* URU *Ṣí-du-na*^{KI} GÉME-*ti*
12) LUGAL EN-*ia ša i-din i-na qa-ti-ia*
13) *ù i-nu-ma iš-te-mé a-wa-at*
14) LUGAL EN-*ia i-nu-ma iš-tap-pár a-na* ÌR-*šu*
15) *ù yi-iḫ-di lìb-bi-ia ù*
16) *yi-*⌜*ša*⌝*-qí* SAG-*ia ù in*$_{4}$*-nam-ru*

Lo.ed. 17) 2 IGI-*ia* \ *ḫe-na-ia i-na ša-me*
18) *a-wa-at* LUGAL EN-*ia ù i-de*

Rev. 19) LUGAL *i-nu-ma* ⌜*šu*⌝*-ši*$_{x}$(ŠE)*-ra-ku i-na*
20) *pa-*⌜*ni*⌝ ⌜ÉRIN⌝.MEŠ *pí-ṭá-ti* LUGAL EN-*ia*
21) *šu-*⌜*ši*$_{x}$⌝(⌜ŠE⌝)*-ra-ku gáb-ba ki-ma qa-bi* LUGAL
22) *ù i-de* LUGAL EN-*ia i-nu-ma* \EN-*ia*
23) *da-na-at nu-*⌜*kúr*⌝*-tu*$_{4}$ *ma-gal* UGU-*ia*
24) *gáb-bi* ⌜URU⌝.⌜DIDLI⌝.⌜KI⌝.⌜ḪI⌝.A *ša i-din* LUGAL
25) *i-na* ⌜*qa*⌝-⌜*ti*⌝-[*i*]⌜*a*⌝ *in*$_{4}$*-né-ep-šu*
26) [*a*]*-na* ⌜LÚ⌝.⌜MEŠ⌝ S[A.G]AZ.MEŠ *ù yi-din-ni*
27) ⌜LUGAL⌝ *i-*[*na*] ⌜*qa*⌝-⌜*at*⌝ LÚ-*lì ša yi-la-ak*
28) *i-na pa-*⌜*ni*⌝ ÉRIN.MEŠ *pí-ṭá-at* LUGAL
29) *a-na ša-al* URU.DIDLI.KI.[ḪI].A *ša in*$_{4}$*-né-ep*
30) *a-na* LÚ.MEŠ SA.GAZ.MEŠ *šu*

EA 144

TRANSLATION

(1–9) Speak to the king, my lord, my deity, my sun god, the breath of my life; thus (says) Zimreddi, the ruler of the city of Ṣidon: At the feet of my lord, the deity, the sun god, the breath of my life at the feet of my lord, my deity, my sun god, the breath of my life, seven times and seven times have I fallen.

(10–12) May the king, my lord, be apprised that the city of Ṣidon, the handmaiden of the king, my lord, which he placed in my charge, is well.

(13–18) And when I heard the word of the king, my lord, when he wrote to his servant, then my heart rejoiced and my head was lifted up and my eyes shone at hearing the word of the king, my lord.

(18–21) So may the king be apprised that I have prepared in anticipation of the regular troops of the king, my lord. I have prepared it all according to the command of the king, my lord.

(22–30) And may the king, my lord be apprised that hostility is very strong against me. All the towns which the king entrusted to me have joined the *ʿapîru* men. So may the king put me in the charge of the man that will lead the regular troops of the king in order to call to account the cities that have gone over to the *ʿapîru* men.

31) *ù tú-*⸢*ta*⸣*-ar*!(RI)*-ši-na i-na*
32) *qa-ti-ia* ⸢*ù*⸣ ⸢*i*⸣*-*⸢*le*⸣*-i a-ra-ad*
33) LUGAL EN-*ia ki-*⸢*i*⸣*-ma* LÚ.MEŠ *a-*⸢*bu*⸣*-ti-nu*
34) *pa-na-nu-um*

(31–34) so you can return them to my charge, and I will be able to serve the king, my lord like our ancestors before.

EA 145

TRANSCRIPTION

Obv. 01) [*a-na* ^{I}*Šu-mi-*]⸢*it*⸣-⸢*ti*⸣ [EN-*ia*]
02) [*qí-*]⸢*bí*⸣-[*ma*]
03) [*um-ma* ^{I}*Zi-*]⸢*im*⸣-⸢*ri*⸣-[*da* ÌR-]⸢*ka*⸣
04) [*a-na* GÌR.MEŠ]-⸢*ka*⸣ ⸢*am*⸣-*qú-ut*
05) [*lu-*]⸢*ú*⸣ ⸢*ti*⸣-⸢*i*⸣-⸢*de*⸣ *i-nu-ma*
06) ⸢*šal*⸣-⸢*ma*⸣-*ku ù* ⸢*at*⸣-*ta iš-tu*
07) ⸢*šul*⸣-*mi-k*[*a*] ⸢*iš*⸣-⸢*tu*⸣
08) *ma-ḫar šàr-ri* [EN]-*i*⸢*a*⸣
09) *ša-a-ri* UZU.[K]A ⸢\⸣⸢*pí*⸣-⸢*ka*⸣
10) *tú-ti-ra-an-*⸢*ni*⸣
11) ⸢*iš*⸣-*te-*⸢*mé*⸣ *a-wa-te*$^{M[EŠ]}$-*k*[*a*]
12) ⸢*ša*⸣ ⸢*a*⸣-⸢*na*⸣ *qa-at* ^{I}⸢*A*⸣-⸢*pí*⸣
13) ⸢*ti*⸣-⸢*iš*⸣-*tap-ra-an-*⸢*ni*⸣
14) *d*[*a-an-*]⸢*na*⸣-*at nu-kúr-*⸢*tu*⸣ *ma-gal*

Lo.ed. 15) [*ù*] ⸢*ti*⸣-⸢*ka*⸣-⸢*aš*⸣-*ša-da* ⸢*ša*⸣-*r*[*i* LUGAL]
16) [*a*]-⸢*na*⸣ ⸢ŠU⸣(?) LÚ.MEŠ MÁ[ŠKIM LUGAL]

Rev. 17) ⸢*ù*⸣ ⸢*a*⸣-⸢*nu*⸣-[*um*]-⸢*ma*⸣ ⸢*ù*⸣ *šàr-*[*ru*]
18) ⸢EN⸣-⸢*nu*⸣ *u*[*m*]-[*te-*]⸢*ek*⸣-⸢*kí*⸣ *iš-t*[*u*]
19) KUR.ḪI.A-*šu* ⸢*ù*⸣ *la-a ti-ik-*⸢*šu*⸣-
du-na
20) *ša-a-ri pí-i-*⸢*šu*⸣
21) ⸢*a*⸣-⸢*na*⸣ *ma-*⸢*ḫar*⸣ ⸢ÌR⸣.MEŠ-*šu ša i-šu-*⸢*ú*⸣
22) *i-na* KUR.ḪI.A *ṣú-uḫ-ri šá-ni-tam*
23) ⸢*ù*⸣ ⸢*i*⸣-*nu-ma táq-bu*
24) *a-na* KUR.ḪI.A *A-mur-ri a-wa-at-mi*
25) ⸢*ti*⸣-⸢*iš*⸣-*te*$_9$-*mé iš-tu aš-ra-*⸢*nu*⸣-*u*[*m*]
26) ⸢*tú*⸣-*te-ra-am* ⸢*a*⸣-*na ia-a-ti*
27) [*ù*] ⸢*iš*⸣-*te-mé gáb-bu-um-mi*
28) [ÌR.MEŠ]-⸢*ka*⸣ \ *ia-aq-wu-*⸢*un*⸣-⸢*ka*⸣
29) [*ù a-da-g*]*a-*⸢*al*⸣ ⸢2⸣ IGI.⸢MEŠ⸣-⸢*ka*⸣

EA 145

TRANSLATION

(1–4) [Sp]ea[k to Paḫa(m)]nati, [my lord. The message of Zi]mre[dda,] your [servant. At] your [feet] have I fallen.

(5–10) [May] you be apprised that I am well and as for you, may you send back to me concerning your welfare from the presence of the king, my [lord], the breath of his!(your) mouth.

(11–16) I have heard your words that you sent by the hand of Api. Very s[tro]ng is the hostility [so] may the breat[h of the king] arrive [b]y the hand of [the king's] commiss[ioners].

(17–22) But now then, the ki[ng], our lord, is being neglectful of his lands and the breath of his mouth does not reach his servants in his hinterlands(?). Furthermore…

(23–29) (Furthermore), and inasmuch as you say "Concerning the lands of Amurru, the word which you have heard from there, may you send back to me," [and] I have heard: "All your [servants] are expecting you" [and I would (like to) see your two eyes.

30) [*a-nu-um-ma iš-t*]*u* KUR.ḪI.A *a-lik*(?)-*mi*!(IGI)
31) [.....................]*us-sú a-n*[*a*]
32) [..........]⸢*gu*⸣[..............]
Lft.ed. 33) [............*ṭup*]-*pí*^{MEŠ} *ù aš-šum-m*[*a*]
34) [...............]-*ia* [.............]
35) [..............*i*]*t-ti-k*[*a*] *i-ba-aš*[-*ši*]
36) [...............]IGI.⸢2⸣ *mi-it*-[........]
37) [...............Ì]R-⸢*ka*⸣ ⸢*a*⸣-[*na-k*]*u* [.......]

(30–37) [Now] go [fr]om the lands [...] to [....tabl]ets, and on account of [...that] are [w]ith you [...]eyes [...]your [ser]vant am ⌜I⌝.

EA 146

TRANSCRIPTION

Obv. 01) [*a-na* LUGAL *b*]*e*[*-i-ia* ^{d}UTU-*ia*]

02) [*um-ma A-*]*bi-m*[*il-ki* ÌR-*ka*]

03) [7 *u* 7 *a-n*]*a* GÌR.ME[Š LUGAL *be-li-ia am-qut*]

04) [*a-na-ku ep*]*-ru iš-t*[*u*]

05) [*šu-pa-al*] GÌR.MEŠ ^{KUŠ}*še*[*-ni*]

06) [LUGAL *be-l*]*í-ia at-ta* [^{d}UTU-*ia*]

07) [*iš-me* ^{I}]^{M}*še-ḫu* DÙG.GA [*ša i-ta-ṣí*]

08) [*i-na-n*]*a be-*⸢*li*⸣*-ia* [*at-ta-ma*]

09) [*ù a-na-ku*] ÌR-⸢*ka*⸣ *i-ṣ*[*ur-ru*]

10) [URU *Ṣur-r*]*i* URU LUGAL *be-l*[*i-ia*]

11) [*ú-qa-am*]*-ma ša-*⸢*a*⸣*-ri* [LUGAL *be-li-ia*]

12) [*a-na ia-*]⸢*ši*⸣ *a-di i-kà-š*[*a-ad*]

13) [*ša-ru*] LUGAL *dan-níš a-na ia-*[*ši nu-*KÚR]

14) [*i-na-n*]*a an-nu-ú* ⸢LÚ⸣ URU[*Ṣí-du-na*]

15) [*Zi-*]*im-re-*⸢*da*⸣ \ *i*[*-na-ki-ir*]

16) [*a-na*] *ia-ši i-na* u_4-⸢*mi*⸣[*-ša-ma la-qé*]

17) [A \ *m*]*i-ma la-a i-*[*n*]*a-*[*din-ni*]

18) [*a-ša-a*]*s-sí* LÚ [*ar*]*-*⸢*na*⸣ [LUGAL]

19) [*ù*] ⸢*li*⸣*-qé-ni* [*iš-t*]*u* ⸢*še*⸣[.........]

20) [....] *ù* A \ ⸢*mi*⸣-⸢*ma*⸣ [*ia-nu*]

21) [*a-na ša-t*]*i-šu-nu iš-t*[*a*.......]

22) [.......LÚ.MEŠ] ⸢SA⸣.⸢GAZ⸣ ⸢*su*⸣[...]

23) [...............................]

24) [...............................]

25) [...............................]

26) [...............................]

27) [...............................]

Rev. 28) [...............................]

29) [........*be-l*]*í-*⸢*i*⸣[*a*...............]

30) [*šàr-*]*ru l*[*i-qé-ni*..................]

31) [....]*id-d*[*in-ni*..................]

32) [....*š*]*u ù li*[*-qé-ni*................]

33) [......]*a-na ia-*[*ši*................]

EA 146

TRANSLATION

(1–7) [To the king, my] lo[rd, my sun god; the message of A]bim[ilki, your servant. Seven (times) and seven (times) a]t the feet[t of the king, my lord, have I fallen. I am the du]st un[der] the feet (and) sa[ndals of the king,] my [lo]rd. You [are my sun god. I have heard] the good breath [that has come forth.]

(8–13) [No]w, my lord [are you, and I,] your servant, am [guarding the city of Tyr]e, the city of the king, [my] lo[rd. And I am wai]ting for the breath [of the king, my lord]. Until [the breath] of the king rea[ches m]e, [hostility] is very strong against me.

(14–22) [No]w, behold, the ruler of the city of [Sidon, Zi]mredda, is [hostile to] me. Daily, he does not per[mit me to take] water. [I cry o]ut, "[Trai]tor [to the king!" So] take me [fro]m [....]but [there is no] water [for] them [to dri]nk [...] the *ʿapîru* [men...]

(23–27) [...]

v. 28) [................................]
29) [........]m[y lor]d...............]
30) [Ki]ng t[ake me...................]
31) [....g]iv[e to me..................]
32) [....h]im and ta[ke me.............]
33) [.......]to m[e...................]

34) [......]*ti a-mur* [..................]
35) [......]\\ *ia-a-p*[*u*................]
36) [......]-*šu* UGU [.................]
37) [......]*a-na* [......................]
38) [..................................]

34) [……]Look[…………………]
35) [……]\\ beauti[ful…………..]
36) [……]him against[……………]
37) [……]to[……………………]
38) [……………………………]

EA 147

TRANSCRIPTION

Obv. 01) *a-na* LUGAL EN-*lí-ia* DINGIR.MEŠ-⸢*ia*⸣ ⸢^{d}⸣⸢UTU⸣-*ia*
02) *um-ma A-bi*-LUGAL ÌR-*ka*
03) 7 *u* 7 *a-na* GÌR.MEŠ LUGAL EN-*lí-ia am-qut*
04) *a-na-ku ep-ru iš-tu šu-pa-li*
05) *ši-ni* LUGAL EN-*lí-ia be-li*
06) ^{d}UTU *ša it-ta-ṣí i-na muḫ-ḫi*
07) KUR *ma-ta-ti i-na* u_4*-mi ù* u_4*-mi-ma*
08) *ki-ma ši-ma-at* ^{d}UTU *a-bu-šu* SIG_5
09) *ša i-ba-li-iṭ i-na še-ḫi-šu* DÙG!(U).GA
10) *ù i-sà-ḫur i-na ṣa-pa-ni-šu*
11) *ša it-ta-ṣa-ab gáb-bi* KUR-*ti*
12) *i-na pa-ša-ḫi i-na du-ni* ZAG \\ *ḫa-ap-ši*
13) *ša id-din ri-ig-ma-šu i-na sa-me*
14) *ki-ma* ^{d}IŠKUR *ù* ⸢*tar*⸣*-gu*$_5$*-ub gáb-bi*
15) KUR-*ti* ⸢*iš*⸣*-tu ri-ig-mi-šu*
16) *an-nu-ú iš-pu-ur* ÌR-*du a-na be-li-šu*
17) *e-nu-ma iš-me* DUMU KIN-*ri* SIG_5
18) *ša* LUGAL *ša i-kà-ša-ad a-na* ÌR-*šu*
19) *ù še-ḫu* DÙG.GA *ša it-ta-ṣí*
20) *iš-tu* ^{UZU}*pí*^{MEŠ} LUGAL *be-li-ia*
21) *a-na* ÌR-*šu ù i-sà-ḫur še-ḫu-šu*
22) *la-am kà-ša-ad* LÚ.KIN-*ri* LUGAL *be-*⸢*li*⸣*-ia*
23) *la-a i-sà-ḫur še-ḫu i-sà-kir*
24) KA.MEŠ *ap-pí-ia a-mur i-*⸢*na*⸣*-an-*⸢*na*⸣
25) *e-nu-ma it-ta-*⸢*ṣí*⸣
26) *še-ḫu* LUGAL *a-na muḫ-*⸢*ḫi*⸣*-*⸢*ia*⸣
Lo.ed. 27) *ù ḫa-ad-ia-ti ma-gal*
28) *ù* \\ *a-ru-ú i-na* u_4*-mi u* ⸢u_4⸣[*-mi-*]*ma*

EA 147

TRANSLATION

(1–5) To the king, my lord, my deity, my sun god, the message of Abi-Milku, your servant: seven (times) and seven times I have fallen at the feet of the king, my lord. I am the dirt beneath the sandals of the king, my lord.

(5–15) My lord is the sun god who has come forth over all lands day by day according to the manner of the sun god, his gracious father, who has given life by his sweet breath and returns with his north wind; of whom all the land is established in peace by the power of (his) arm; who has given his voice in the sky like Baʿal, and all the land was frightened at his cry.

(16–21) Behold, the servant has written to his lord since he has heard the gracious envoy of the king who comes to his servant and the sweet breath which has come forth from the mouth of the king, my lord, to his servant—and his breath returns!

(22–24) Before the arrival of the emissary of the king, my lord, breath was not coming back; my nose was blocked!

(24–28) Look! now, when the breath of the king came forth to ⸢me⸣, then I rejoiced greatly and daily, day by day.

29) *aš-šum ḫa-dì-ia-ti la-a ti-*⸢*ši*⸣*-*⸢*ir*⸣

Rev. 30) *er-ṣé-tu*$_4$ *e-nu-ma iš-me*

31) ⸢DUMU⸣.⸢KIN⸣*-ri* SIG$_5$ *ša iš-tu be-*⸢*li*⸣*-*⸢*ia*⸣

32) *ù gáb-bi* KUR*-ti pal-ḫa-at*

33) *iš-tu pa-ni be-li-ia e-nu-ma*

34) *iš-me še-ḫu* DÙG.GA *ù* DUMU.KIN*-ri* SIG$_5$

35) *ša i-kà-ša-dá-ni e-nu-ma*

36) *iq-bi* LUGAL *be-li-ia* \\ *ku-na*

37) *a-na pa-ni* ÉRIN.MEŠ GAL *ù iq-bi*

38) ÌR*-du a-na be-li-šu* \\ *ia-a-ia-ia*

39) *a-na muḫ-ḫi ga-bi-dì-ia muḫ-ḫi* \\ *ṣú-ri-ia*

40) *ú-bal a-ma-ta*$_5$ LUGAL *be-li-ia*

41) *ša iš-mé* ⸢*a*⸣*-na* LUGAL *be-li-šu ù*

42) *ú-ra-ad-šu i-na aš-ra-ni-šu*

43) *ù it-‹ta›-ṣí* ^{d}UTU *i-na muḫ-ḫi-šu*

44) *ù i-sà-ḫur še-ḫu* DÙG.GA *iš-tu* ^{UZU}*pí be-li-šu*

45) *ù la-a iš-te-mé a-ma-ta*$_5$ LUGAL *be-*⸢*li*⸣*-šu*

46) *ḫal-qá-*⸢*at*⸣ URU*-šu ḫa-li-iq* É*-šu*

47) *ia-nu šu-um-šu i-na gáb-bi*

48) KUR*-ti i-na da-ri-ti a-mur*

49) ÌR*-da ša iš-me a-na ›a-na‹ be-li-šu*

50) *šul-mu* URU*-šu šul-mu* É*-šu*

51) *šu-um-šu a-*⸢*na*⸣ ⸢*da*⸣*-ri-ti*

52) *at-ta* ^{d}UTU *ša* ⸢*it*⸣*-ta-ṣí i-na muḫ-ḫi-šu*!(WA)

53) *ù du-ú-ri* ZABAR(UD.KA.BAR) *ša iz-qú-pu*

54) *a-na ša-a-šu ù aš-šum* ZAG LUGAL

55) *be-li-ia da-na-ti*

56) \\ *nu-uḫ-ti* \\ *ba-ṭì-i-ti*

57) *an-nu-ú iq-bi*

58) *a-na* ^{d}UTU *a-bi* LUGAL *be-li-ia*

59) *ma-ti-mi i-mur*

60) *pa-ni* LUGAL *be-li-ia*

Up.ed. 61) *ù a-nu-um-ma a-na-an-ṣur*

62) URU *Ṣur-ri* URU *ra-bi-tu*

63) *a-na* LUGAL *be-li-ia a-di*

Lft.ed. 64) *i-wa-ṣí* ZAG LUGAL *da-na-tu i-na muḫ-ḫi-ia*

65) *a-na na-da-an me-e a-na šu-ta-ia*

66) *ù* GIŠ.MEŠ *a-na šu-ḫu-ni-ia ša-ni-tam* ^{I}*Zi-im-re-da*

(29–35) Because I rejoiced, the land did not attack, since I heard the gracious envoy who is from my lord, then the entire land feared before my lord, when I heard the sweet breath and the gracious envoy who came to me.

(35–40) When the king, my lord said: "Be ready for the arrival of the great army," then the servant said: "Yea, yea, yea!" On my stomach and on my back I carry the word of the king, my lord.

(41–48) Whoever has obeyed the king, his lord and serves him in his places, then the sun god comes forth over him and the sweet breath returns from the mouth of his lord; but whoever has not heeded the word of the king his lord, his city is destroyed and his house is destroyed, his name does not exist in all the land forever.

(48–51) Behold, the servant who has heeded his lord, his city is prosperous, his house prospers, his name is eternal.

(52–56) You are the sun god who has come forth over him(!), and a brazen wall set up for him; and because of the mighty arm of the king, my lord, I am at rest, I am confident.

(57–60) Behold, I have said to the sun god the father of the king, my lord, "When will I see the face of the king, my lord?"

(61–66) So now I am guarding the city of Tyre, the great city of the king, my lord, until the mighty arm of the king comes forth to me to provide water for my drinking and wood for my warming.

67) LÚ URU *Ṣí-du-na iš-pu-ur i-na u*$_4$*-mi ù u*$_4$*-mi-ma*
68) [L]Ú *ar-ni* ^{I}*A-zi-ri* DUMU ÌR-^{d}*Aš-ra-tu*$_4$
69) *aš-šum gáb-bi a-ma-ta*$_5$ *ša iš-te-mé iš-tu* KUR *Mi-iṣ-*⸢*ri*⸣
70) *a-nu-um-ma iš-pu-ur a-na be-li-ia ù* SIG$_5$
71) *e-nu-ma i-de*$_4$

(66–69) Furthermore, Zimredda, the ruler of the city of Sidon, has written daily to the rebel Aziru son of ʿAbdi-Ashirtu concerning every word that he has heard from the land of Egypt.

(70–71) Now, I have written to my lord and it is good that he know.

EA 148

TRANSCRIPTION

Obv.
01) *a-na* LUGAL EN-*lí-ia* DINGIR-*ia* ^{d}UTU-*ya*
02) *um-ma A-bi*-LUGAL ÌR-*ka*
03) 7 *u* 7 *a-na* GÌR.MEŠ LUGAL *be-li-ia am-qut*
04) LUGAL *be-li-ia iš-ta-pár*
05) *aš-šum* ^{NA_4}*me-ku ša i-bá-aš-ši*
06) *it-ti-ia at-ta-din*
07) *a-na* LUGAL *be*-⸢*li*⸣-*ia*
08) ⸢1⸣ *me-at* KI.LÁ *ù*
09) *li-it-ta-din* LUGAL *be-li-ia*
10) *pa-ni-šu a-na* ÌR-*šu*
11) *ù li-id-din* URU *Ú-sú* ^{KI}
12) *a-na* ÌR-*šu* DUG*a-ku-ni**mé-ma*
13) *a-na ši-te-šu li-it-ta-din*
14) LUGAL *be-li-ia* 10 LÚ.GÌR
15) *a-na na-ṣa-ri*
16) URU-*šu ù li-ru-ub*
17) *ù li-mur pa-ni* LU[GAL] *be-li-ia*
18) ⸢SIG$_5$⸣ *pa-nu-ia a-na*

Rev.
19) *muḫ-ḫi* LUGAL *be-li-ia*
20) *ki-i-me e-nu-ma*
21) *ip-qí-id-ni* LUGAL *be-li-ya*
22) *a-na na-ṣa-ri* URU-*šu*
23) *ù aš-ta-pár a-na* LUGAL *be-li-*
ya
24) *e-nu-ma* u_4-*mi-ša-ma*
25) *il-qè šàr* URU *Ṣí-du-na*
26) LÚ.GÌR-*ia li-it-ta-din*

EA 148

TRANSLATION

(1–3) To the king, my lord, my deity, my sun god, the message of Abi-milki, your servant: Seven times and seven times at the feet of the king, my lord, have I fallen.

(4–8) The king, my lord, has written concerning raw glass that I have. I have given to the king, my lord, one hundred shekels worth.

(8–13) So may the king, my lord, always give his attention to his servant and may the city of Usû give his servant a jar of water for him to drink.

(13–17) May the king, my lord, continue to grant ten soldiers to guard his city and may I enter and may I see the face of the ki[ng,] my lord,

(18–22) My face will be pleasing to the king, my lord, as when the king, my lord, appointed me to protect his city.

(23–26) And I wrote to the king, my lord, because daily the king of Sidon has taken one of my soldiers.

27) *pa-ni-šu* LUGAL *a-na* ÌR-*šu*
28) *ù li-ip-qí-id*
29) *a-na* LÚ.MÁŠKIM-*šu ù*
30) *li-id-din* URU *Ú-sú* KI
31) *a-na* A.MEŠ *mé-e-ma*
32) *a-na* ÌR-*šu a-na la-q*[*í*]
33) GIŠ.MEŠ *a-na* IN *ti-ib-nu*
34) *a-na ṭì-i-ṭì e-nu-ma*
35) *i-pu-uš nu-kúr-tu*$_4$
36) *la-a it-te-er*
37) *ma-mi-ta*
Up.ed. 38) *ia-nu* LÚ.[GÌ]R *ša*$_{10}$*-nu*
39) *ša iš-ḫa-*[*a*]*t* KUR LUGA[L]
40) *šàr* URU *Ṣí-du-n*[*a*]
41) *šàr* URU *Ḫa-ṣú-ra*
Lft.ed. 42) *i-te-zi-ib* É-*šu ù it-ta-ṣa-*[*a*]*b*
43) *it-ti* LÚ.SA-GAZ *li-i-de*$_4$
44) LUGAL *a-na* LÚ.GÌR *sa-ru-ti ša*!*-nu-ta*$_5$ *ù*
45) *i-pu-uš* KUR LUGAL *a-na* LÚ.SA.GAZ
46) *li-í-al* LUGAL LÚ.MÁŠKIM-*šu ša i-de*$_4$
47) KUR *Ki-na-á*ʾ*-na*

(26–34) May the king continue to give his attention to his servant and may he command his commissioner that he give the city of Usû for water for his servant, for taking lumber, for straw, for clay.

(34–38) Because he made war, he did not return an oath (of peace). Not another [sold]ier is left.

(39–40) The one who has raided the land of the king is the king of Sidon.

(41–45) The king of Hazor has abandoned his palace and he has taken up a position with the *ʿapîru*. So may the king be apprised concerning that other wicked man. And he has joined the land of the king to the *ʿapîru*.

(46–47) May the king ask his commissioner who knows the land of Canaan.

EA 149

TRANSCRIPTION

Obv.

01) ⸢*a*⸣*-na* LUGAL EN-*lí-ia* ^{d}UTU-*ia* DINGIR.MEŠ-*ya*
02) *um-ma* ^{I}*A-bi*-LUGAL ÌR-*k*[*a*]
03) 7 *u* 7 *a-na* GÌR.MEŠ LUGAL *be*-[*lí-y*]*a* ⸢*am*⸣*-qut*
04) *a-na-ku ep-ru iš-tu šu-pa-al* GÌR.MEŠ
05) ^{KUŠ}*še-ni* LUGAL *be-li-ia*
06) LUGAL *be-li-ia ki-i-ma* ^{d}UTU
07) *ki-ma* ^{d}IŠKUR *i-na sa-me at-ta*
08) *li-im-li-ik* LUGAL *a-na* ÌR-*šu*
09) LUGAL *be-li-ia ip-qí-id-ni*
10) *a-na ‹na›-ṣa-ar* URU *Ṣur-ri* GÉME LUGAL
11) *ù aš-ta-pár ṭup-pa ḫu*!(Ú)*-mu-ṭa*
12) *a-na* LUGAL EN-*lí-ia ù la-a*
13) *it-te-er a-ma-ta*$_5$ *a-na ia-ši*
14) *a-na-ku* LÚ.MÁŠKIM LUGAL *be-li-ia*
15) *ù a-na-ku ša ú-bal a-ma-ta*$_5$
16) DÙG.GA *ù a-na-a-ma li-im-na*
17) *a-na* LUGAL *be-li-ia li-wa-aš-šèr*
18) LUGAL 20 LÚ GÌR *a-na ‹na›-ṣa-ar*
19) URU-*šu ù le-ru-ub a-na muḫ-ḫi*
20) LUGAL *be-li-ia ù li-mur pa-ni-šu*
21) *ma-an-nu ba-la-aṭ* LÚ GÌR
22) *e-nu-ma la-a it-ta-ṣí*
23) *ša-a-ru iš-tu* ^{UZU}*pí* LUGAL *be-li-šu*
24) ⸢*ù*⸣ *ba-li-iṭ šum-ma* LUGAL *iš-ta-pár*
25) [*a-n*]*a* ÌR-*šu ù ba-li-iṭ*
26) [*a-na*] ⸢*da*⸣*-ri-ti a-na-ku*
27) [*iš-t*]*u ša-an-ti-qá-dì-ma*
28) [*pa-nu-ia*] *a-na i-re-bi*
29) [*a-na da-g*]*a-li pa-ni* LUGAL *be-li-ia*

EA 149

TRANSLATION

(1–5) To the king, my lord, my sun god, my deity: Message of Abimilki, yo[ur] servant: seven and seven (times) at the feet of the king [m]y lo[rd] have I fallen. I am the dirt from under the feet (and) sandals of the king, my lord.

(6–20) O king, my lord, you are like the sun god, like the storm god in heaven! May the king take counsel concerning his servant. The king, my lord, assigned me to ‹gu›ard the city of Tyre, the handmaiden of the king, and I sent an urgent tablet to the king, my lord, but he has not sent word back to me. I am the commissioner of the king, my lord, and it is I who brings good news and likewise bad to the king, my lord. May the king send twenty foot soldiers to ‹gu›ard his city so that I may enter in to the king, my lord, and that I may see his face.

(21–26) What is the life of a foot soldier when breath has not come forth from the mouth of the king, his lord, that he may live? If the king wrote [t]o his servant, then he would live [for] ever.

(26–29) As for me, [sin]ce last year, [my intention has been] to enter in [in order to behold the face of the king, my lord.

30) [^{I}*Zi-im-re-da p*]*a-wu-ra*
31) [*iš-te-mé-n*]*i it-te-er-mi*
32) [GIŠ.MÁ-*ia iš-t*]*u* LUGAL *be-li-ia*
33) [*ma-an-nu-mi*] ⸢*i*⸣-*še-ri-ib-ka*
34) [*a-na muḫ-ḫi* LUGAL *ši-*]*ma be-li*
Lo.ed. 35) [*il-qè* URU *Ṣu-mu-*]*ra* ^{I}*A-zi-ra*
36) [DUMU ^{I}ÌR-^{d}]*Aš-ra-tu*$_{4}$
37) [LÚ] ⸢*ar*⸣-⸢*ni*⸣ LUGAL ^{I}*Ḫa-a-pí*
38) [*ú-š*]*e*$_{20}$*-e-li ša -ri* LÚ.⸢MEŠ⸣ ⸢KÚR⸣-[*i*]*a*
Rev. 39) [*it-*]*ta-din* URU *Ṣu-mu-ra*
40) [*a-n*]*a* ^{I}*A-zi-ra ù la-a*
41) ⸢*i*⸣-*qú-ul* LUGAL *iš-tu* URU-*šu ù*(?)
42) *iš-tu* KUR-*šu e-nu-ma aš-te-mu*
43) *šu-um* LUGAL ⸢*ù*⸣ *šu-um um-ma-ni-šu*
44) *ù pal-ḫu ma-gal ù gáb-bi*
45) KUR-*ti pal-*⸢*ḫa*⸣-*at ù ša-a la-a*
46) *i-la-ak a-*⸢*na*⸣ EGIR LUGAL *be-li-ia*
47) LUGAL *i-de*$_{4}$-*šu* ⸢*e*⸣-⸢*nu*⸣-*ma ša-ak-na-ta-ni*
48) *i-na* LÚ.MÁŠKIM *i-na* URU *Ṣur-ri*
49) *il-qè* ^{I}*Zi-*⸢*im*⸣-*re-da* URU *Ú-sú*
50) *iš-tu* ÌR-*dì*‹-*šu*› *i-ta-zi-ib-šu*
51) *ù ia-nu* A.MEŠ *ia-nu* GIŠ.MEŠ *a-na ia-ši-nu*
52) *ù ia-nu a-ia-ka*$_{4}$*-mi ni-ša*!(IŠ)-*kán*
53) LÚ BA.UG$_{7}$ *ù* ⸢LUGAL⸣ *be-li-ia*
54) *li-*⸢*im*⸣-*li-ik a-na* ÌR-*šu* LUGAL *be-li-ia*
55) *i-na ṭup-pí iš-ta-pár a-na ia-ši*
56) *mi-nu-um-mi ta-aš-te-me ù šu-pur*
57) *a-na* LUGAL ^{I}*Zi-im-re-da* URU *Ṣí-du-na*
58) *ù* ^{I}*A-zi-ra* LÚ *ar-ni* LUGAL
59) *ù* LÚ.MEŠ URU ⸢*Ar*⸣-⸢*wa*⸣-*da it-mu-ni*
60) *ù iš-ta-ni ma-mi-ta i-na be-ri-šu-nu*
61) *ù ip-ḫu-ru-ni*$_{7}$ GIŠ.MÁ.MEŠ-*šu-nu*
62) GIŠ.GIGIR.MEŠ-*šu-nu* ÉRIN.MEŠ GÌR.MEŠ-*šu-nu*
63) *a-na ṣa-ba-ti* URU *Ṣur-ri* GÉME LUGAL

(30–40) [Zimredda, t]he prince [heard about m]e; he turned back [my ship fr]om (going to) the king, my lord, ["Who] will cause you to enter [to the king?" Lis]ten, my lord, Aziru the son of ʿAbdi-Aširata, the traitor to the king, [has taken the city of Ṣumu]r. Ḫaʿpi, [has in]stalled the traitors, my enemies; [he has] given the city of Ṣumur [t]o Aziru. So may the king not keep silent concerning his city and his land.

(42–54) When I hear the name of the king and the name of his army then they will be very afraid and the entire land will be afraid. As for he who does not follow the king, the king knows him, because he installed me as the commissioner in the city of Tyre. Zimredda has taken the town of Usû from ‹his› servant; I have abandoned it and we have no water, no wood, and there is nowhere that we can place (bury) the dead. So may the king, my lord, take counsel concerning his servant.

(54–55) The king, my lord, wrote to me in a tablet,

(56–63) "Whatever you have heard, then send to the king." Zimredda (of) Sidon and Aziru, the traitor to the king, and the men of Arvad have sworn and rep‹ea›ted an oath between them and they have gathered their ships, their chariots (and) their infantry in order to capture the city of Tyre, the handmaiden of the king.

64) *kà-aš-dá-at qa-ti* LUGAL *da-an-na-tu*$_4$
65) *ù da-kà-at-šu-*⸢*nu*⸣ URU *Ṣur-ri*
66) *la-a i-lé-ú-ni*$_7$ *a-na ṣa-bat*
67) *ù* URU *Ṣu-mu-ra ṣa-ab-tù-ni*$_7$
68) *i-na* ^{UZU}*pí* ⸢^{I}⸣*Zi-im-re-da*
69) *ša ù-ba-lu*$_4$ *a-ma-ta*$_5$ LUGAL
70) *a-na* ^{I}*A-zi-ra ù aš-ta-pár*
71) *ṭup-pa a-na* LUGAL *be-li-ia*
72) *ù la-a it-te-er-ni*
73) ⸢*a*⸣*-ma-ta*$_5$ *a-na* ÌR-*šu*
Up.ed. 74) [*i*]*š-tu* MU-*qá-dì nu-kúr-tu*$_4$!(incomplete sign)
75) ⸢*i*⸣*-na muḫ-ḫi-ia ia-nu* A.MEŠ
76) *ia-nu* GIŠ.MEŠ *li-wa-aš-šèr*
77) *ṭup-pa a-na* ÌR-*šu*
Lft.ed. 78) *ù le-ru-ub ù li-mur pa-ni-šu ù* LUGAL [*li-im-li-ik*]
79) *a-na* ÌR-*šu a-na* URU-*šu ù la-a* ⸢*i*⸣[*-te-zi-ib*]
80) URU-*šu* KUR-*šu am-mi-ni*$_7$ *i-nam-mu-*[*uš* LÚ.MÁŠKIM *ša*]
81) ⸢LUGAL⸣ *be-li-nu iš-tu* KUR-*ti ù i-*⸢*de*$_4$⸣ [^{I}*Zi-im-re-da*]
82) *ù i-de*$_4$ *ša-a-i-ru* Á LUGAL *ša ia-nu a-nu-*⸢*um*⸣-[*ma ú-bal*]
83) *ṭup-pí-ia* LÚ GÌR *a-na muḫ-ḫi* LUGAL ^{d}UTU EN-[*ia*]
84) *ù* LUGAL *li-it-te-er a-na* ÌR-*šu*

(64–73) No sooner than the powerful arm of the king arrives, then it will smite them. They are not able to capture the city of Tyre, but they have captured the city of Ṣumur at the behest of Zimredda, the one who delivers the king's message to Aziru. So I sent a tablet to the king, my lord, but he has not sent back word to his servant.

(74–84) [S]ince last year, there has been hostility against me. There is no water and there is no wood. May he send a tablet to his servant, so that I may enter in and that I may see his face. So may the king [take counsel] concerning his servant and concerning his city. Why should [the commissioner of] the king, my lord, have to withdr[aw] from the land? [Zimreda] knows and the traitor knows that the arm of the king is absent. No[w], a foot soldier [is bringing] my tablet to the king, the sun god, [my] lord, so may the king reply to his servant.

EA 150

TRANSCRIPTION

Obv. 01) [*a-na*] LUGAL *be*[*-li-ia*]
02) [*u*]*m-ma* ^{I}*A-bi-mil-k*[*i* ÌR-*ka*]
03) 7 *u* 7 *a-na* GÌR.MEŠ L[UGA]L E[N-*ia am-qut*]
04) *na-da-an* LUGAL *pa-ni-šu*
05) *a-na* ÌR-*šu ù na-d*[*a-a*]*n*
06) LÚ.MEŠ *w*[*e*]*-i-ma a-n*[*a*]
07) *na-ṣa-ri* URU LUGA[L EN-*i*]a
08) *ù a-na-ku ki-ma* ⌜LÚ⌝(?)
\⌜LÚ⌝ *we-ú*
09) *šu-*[*ú-u*]*t i-na-an-ṣár*
10) URU LUGAL EN-*ia ù*
11) *a-n*[*a-k*]*u i-ra-ab*
12) *a-na da-ga-li*
13) *pa-ni* LUGAL *be-li-ia*
14) *ù li-id-din*
15) LUGAL *pa-ni-šu*
Rev. 16) [*a*]*-na* ÌR-*dì-šu*
17) *ù li-id-din-šu*
18) URU *Ú-sú aš-šum*
19) *ba-la-ṭì-šu*
20) *ù aš-šum* ›⌜*iš*⌝‹(?) ⌜*ša*⌝-⌜*ti*⌝
21) ⌜A⌝.⌜MEŠ⌝ [*me-e-*]*ma*
22) ⌜*a*⌝*-n*[*a*...] \\ *a-*[*b*]*u-tù*
23) *aš*[*-šum be-l*]*í-ia* GÌR.MEŠ-*š*[*u*]
24) [......................]*ù*
25) *qa*[*-al-mi* LU]GAL EN[*-ia*]
26) [......................]*ku*
27) [......................]
28) [......................]
29) [......................]
30) [......................]
31) [......................]
32) [......................]

EA 150

TRANSLATION

(1–3) [To] the king, [my] lo[rd]; the [me]ssage of Abimilk[i, your servant], seven (times) and seven (times) at the feet of the k[in]g [my] lo[rd have I fallen.]

(4–13) The king gave his attention to his servant and he g[av]e troopers to protect the city of the kin[g, m]y [lord] and I, as that man \ trooper, am guarding the city of the king, my lord. I would enter in to behold the face of the king, my lord.

(14–16) So may the king give his attention [t]o his servant.

(17–26) And may the king grant him the city of Usu for his sustenance and in order to drink water fo[r..] \\ the fathers, in [behalf of] my [lor]d, h[is] feet [....] and [the ki]ng, [my] lord kept [silent] [....]

(27–32) [*About six lines completely broken off*]

Lft.ed. 33) [*i*]-*na* SIL[A *i-n*]*a-bu* [*a-n*]*a-an-din*
34) GIŠ.MEŠ-*ma* GEŠTIN LUGAL EN-*li*
35) [*i*]*d*!-*din*[*a*]-*na a-bu-ti-ia*
36) ⸢*a*⸣-⸢*na*⸣ *a-bu-ti-ia* DINGIR.[ME]Š
37) UGU LUGAL EN-*ia* ⸢*iš*⸣-⸢*tap*⸣-*p*[*ár*]

(33–37) [I]n the stre[et I will pro]claim. I will give lumber and wine. The king, my lord, [g]ave to my fathers, to my fathers (and) the gods. To the king, my lord, have I sent.

EA 151

TRANSCRIPTION

Obv. 01) [*a*]-*na* LUGAL ^{d}UTU-*ia* DINGIR-⸢*ia*⸣ ⸢DINGIR⸣.⸢MEŠ⸣-*ia*

02) *um-ma* ^{I}*A-bi*-LUGAL ÌR-*ka*

03) 7 *u* 7 *a-na* GÌR.MEŠ LUGAL EN-*lí-ya am-qut*

04) *a-na-ku ep-ru iš-tu šu-pa-li*

05) ^{KUŠ}*še-ni* LUGAL EN-*lí-ia*

06) *an-nu-ú a-na-an-ṣár* URU LUGAL

07) *ša ip-qí-id i-na qa-ti-ia ma-gal*

08) *pa-nu-ia a-na a-la-ki*

09) *a-na a-ma-ri pa-ni* LUGAL *be*-⸢*li*⸣?-⸢*ia*⸣

10) *ù la-a i-lé-e iš-tu*

11) *qa-ti* ^{I}*Zi-im-re-da* URU *Ṣí-du-na*^{KI}

12) *iš-mé-ni-ma* ⸢*e*⸣-*nu-ma*

13) *i-ra-bu ù i-pu-uš*

14) *nu-kúr*-⸢*tu*$_4$⸣ *it-ti-ia li-id-din-ni*

15) LUGAL ⸢EN⸣-⸢*lí*⸣-⸢*ia*⸣ 20 LÚ.MEŠ *a-na*

16) ⸢*na-ṣa-ri*⸣ URU LUGAL *be-li-ia*

17) *ù le*-⸢*ru*⸣-⸢*ub*⸣ *a-na maḫ-ri*[*-ti*]

18) LUGAL *be*-⸢*li*⸣-⸢*ia*⸣ *a-na da-ga-l*[*i*]

19) *pa-ni*-⸢*šu*⸣ ⸢SIG$_5$⸣-⸢*ta*⸣ *at-ta-din*

20) *pa*-⸢*ni*⸣-⸢*ia*⸣ ⸢*a*⸣-*na* ⸢*mi*⸣-*ru-ti* \\ *ú-pu-ti*

21) ⸢LUGAL⸣ ⸢EN⸣-⸢*lí*⸣-⸢*ia*⸣ *li-iš-al*

22) L[UGAL] ⸢*be*⸣-⸢*li*⸣-*ia* LÚ.MÁŠKIM-*šu*

23) *e*-[*nu*]-*ma at*-⸢*ta*⸣-*din pa-ni*-⸢*ia*⸣

24) ⸢*a*⸣-⸢*na*⸣ ⸢*maḫ*⸣-⸢*ri*⸣-⸢*ti*⸣ LUGAL *be-li*-⸢*ia*⸣

25) ⸢*a*⸣-*nu-um-ma* LÚ KIN-⸢*ri*⸣-[*ia*]

26) ⸢*uš*⸣-*še-er-ti a-na* [*maḫ-ri-ti*]

27) [LUGAL] *be-li-ia* ⸢*ù*⸣ *l*[*i-wa-aš-šèr*]

28) [LUGAL] *be-li-ia* LÚ [KIN-*ri-šu*]

29) [*ù*] ⸢*ṭup*⸣-*pa-šu a*-⸢*na*⸣ [*ia-ši*]

EA 151

TRANSLATION

(1–5) To the king, my sun god, my god, my deity: Message of Abimilki, your servant: seven and seven (times) at the feet of the king, my lord, have I fallen. I am the dirt under the sandals of the king my lord.

(6–24) Behold, I am guarding very diligently the city of the king that he entrusted to me. My intention is to go in order to see the face of the king, my lord but I am not able because of the hand of Zimredda (of) Sidon. He heard concerning me that I would go in (to Egypt) so he committed aggression against me. May the king give 20 men to guard the city of the king, my lord, that I may enter the presence of the king, my lord, in order to behold his gracious face. I have turned my face to the beauty of the king, my lord. May the k[ing], my lord, ask his commissioner whether I have turned my face to the presence of the king, my lord.

(25–29) Now, my envoy have I sent to [the presence of] the [king], my lord, so ma[y the king], my lord, [send his] mes[senger and] his tablet to [me],

Lo.ed. 30) ⸢*ù*⸣ ⸢*le*⸣-⸢*ru*⸣-⸢*ub*⸣ *a-na* [*maḫ-ri-ti*]
31) LUGAL EN-*lí-ia ma*-[*gal ma-gal*]
Rev. 32) [*a*]*t-ta-din pa*-⸢*ni*⸣-*ia*[*a-na* LUGAL *be-li-ia*]
33) *a-na* ⸢*maḫ*⸣-*ri*-⸢*ti*⸣ L[UGAL *a-na a-ma-ri*]
34) *pa-ni* LUGAL EN-*lí*[-*ia ù*]
35) *la-a i-te-zi-ib* L[UGAL *be-li*]
36) ÌR-*šu iš-tu qa-t*[*i-šu*]
37) ⸢*li*⸣-*it-ta-din pa-n*[*i-šu*]
38) LUGAL *be*-⸢*li*⸣-*ia ù i*[*d-din*]
39) A.⸢MEŠ⸣ *a-na ši-it-yi* [ÌR-*šu*]
40) ⸢*ù*⸣ ⸢GIŠ⸣.⸢MEŠ⸣ *a-na* ÌR-*šu*[*ù*]
41) *i-de*$_4$ ⸢LUGAL⸣ *be-li e-nu-ma*
42) *i*-⸢*na*⸣ ⸢ŠÀ⸣ ^{d}AB.BA *ni-ta*-⸢*ṣa*⸣-*ab*
43) *ia*-⸢*nu*⸣ ⸢A⸣.⸢MEŠ⸣ *ù ia-nu* GIŠ.MEŠ
44) *a-na ia-ši-nu a-nu-um-ma*
45) *uš-še-er‹-ti›* ^{I}DINGIR.LUGAL LÚ KIN-*ri‹-ia›*
46) *a-na maḫ-ri* LUGAL *be-li-ia*
47) *ù at-ta-din* 5 GUN ZABAR
48) ^{GIŠ}*ma-‹qí›-bu-ma* 1 ^{GIŠ}ÙŠAN \\ *qì-na-zu*
49) LUGAL *be-li-ia iš-ta-pár a-na ia*-⸢*ši*⸣-*nu*
50) *ša ta-aš-me iš-tu* KUR *Ki-na-aḫ-na*
51) *ù šu-pur a-na ia-ši*
52) LUGAL KUR *Da-nu-na* BA.ÚŠ
53) *ù ša-ar-ra* ŠEŠ-*šu*
54) *a-na* EGIR-*šu ù pa-aš-ḫa-at*
55) KUR-*šu ù* É LUGAL URU *Ú-ga-ri-it*^{KI}
56) *i-ku-ul i-ša-tu*$_4$ *mi-ši*-⸢*il*⸣-*šu*
57) *i-kúl ù mi-ši-‹il›-šu ia-nu*
58) *ù* LÚ.MEŠ ÉRIN *Ḫa-at-ti ia-nu*

(30–36) that I may enter into [the presence of] the king, my lord. [I] have made a very [strong] commitment [to the king, my lord], to the presence of the k[ing, in order to see] the face of the king, [my] lord. [So] may [the king, my lord] not abandon his servant.

(37–44) May the king give [his] attention, and g[ive] water for [your servant] to drink and wood for your servant. [And] may the king, my lord, be apprised that we are situated in the midst of the sea. We have no water and no wood.

(44–48) Now, ‹I› have sent Ili-milku, ‹my› envoy to the king, my lord, and I have given five talents of copper, ha‹mm›ers and one whip.

(49–58) The king, my lord, wrote to me, "What you hear from (there in) Canaan, then write to me." The king of the land of Dannuna is dead and his brother reigns in his stead and his land is pacified. And fire destroyed the royal palace of the city of Ugarit; half of it is destroyed and ha‹l›f not. But the troops of the land of Ḫatti are not (there).

59) ^{I}*E-ta-ga-ma pa-wu-ri*
60) URU *Qí-id-ši ù*
61) ^{I}*A-zi-ra nu-kúr-tu*$_4$
62) *it-ti* ^{I}*Bir*$_5$*-ia-wa-zi*
63) *nu-kúr-tu*$_4$
Up.ed. 64) *a-ta-mur ḫa-ba-li*
65) ^{I}*Zi-im-re-da*
66) *e-nu-ma ip-ḫu-*⸢*ur*⸣
Lft. ed. 67) GIŠ.MÁ.MEŠ ÉRIN.MEŠ *iš-tu* URU.DIDLI.ḪI.A ^{I}*A-zi-ra*
68) ⸢*a*⸣*-na muḫ-ḫi-ia ù da-mi-iq e-nu-ma i-*⸢*kal*⸣*-l*[*i*]
69) LÚ GÌR *be-li-ia ù ip-li-ḫu gáb-bu* ⸢*li*⸣*-id-*⸢*din*⸣
70) *pa-ni-šu* LUGAL ⸢*a*⸣*-na* ÌR*-šu ù* ⸢*li*⸣*-sà-ḫir* \\ *yu-ṣa* ⸢*a*⸣*-*⸢*na*⸣ ⸢*ia*⸣*-š*[*i*]

(59–70) Etagama, the prince of Qidši, and Aziru are at war; it is with Biryawaza that they are at war. I have suffered the aggression of Zimredda when he assembled ships (and) troops from the towns of Aziru against me. So is it good that the soldier of my lord should hold back? And all are in fear. May the king give his attention to his servant and may he return (come forth) ⸢to me⸣.

EA 152

TRANSCRIPTION

Obv. 01) [*a-n*]*a* ⸢LUGAL⸣ ⸢*be*⸣-⸢*lí*⸣-⸢*ia*⸣ DIN[GIR.MEŠ-*ia* ^{d}UTU-*ia*]
02) [*u*]*m-ma A-*⸢*bi*⸣*-mi*[*l-k*]*i* ÌR-*k*[*a-m*]*a*
03) [*ù ep-ru iš-tu*] ⸢*šu*⸣-⸢*pa*⸣-⸢*li*⸣ ⸢^{KUŠ}⸣*še-ni* GÌR.MEŠ [*be-lí-ia*]
04) ⸢*a*⸣-[*na* GÌR.MEŠ LUGAL] E[N]-*lí-ia* DINGIR.MEŠ-*ia* ^{d}⸢UTU⸣-⸢*ia*⸣
05) [7 *u* 7 *am-qut*] *l*[*i-i-*]⸢*de*$_4$⸣ *šàr-*⸢*ri*⸣ be-[li-ia]
06) [DINGIR.MEŠ-*ia* ^{d}UTU-*ia a-n*]*a* URU-*šu* GÉ[ME-*šu*]
07) [*a-nu-ma nu-*KÚR] ⸢^{I}⸣⸢*Zi*⸣*-im-re-*[*da*] L[Ú]
08) [URU *Ṣí-du-na* ^{KI}] *a-na* UGU-[*ia*]
09) ⸢*ù*⸣[............]⸢LUGAL⸣ ⸢*be*⸣*-li-*[*ia-m*]*a*
10) [...............]⸢*ur*⸣ LÚ.MEŠ[....]
11) [................]*ù*[................]
12) [..........................*it-*]*ti-šu*
13) [............URU] *Gub-l*[*a* ^{KI}.......]
14) [.....................................]
15) [.....................................]
16) [.........]*zu*[.......................]
17) [.....................................]
18) *i*[*q*..................................]
19) *a-na* [................................]
20) *iš-*⸢*tu*⸣[...............................]
21) ⸢*la*⸣*-a a-na* [............................]
22) [.]⸢GÉME⸣-*k*[*a*.........................]
23) [.....................................]
24) [......]*te* [............................]
25) [.....................................]
26) [.....................................]
27) [.....................................]
Lo.ed. 28) [.....................................]
29) [.....................................]
Rev. 30) [.....................................]

EA 152

TRANSLATION

(1–6) [T]o the king, my lord, [my] dei[ty, my sun god; me]ssage of Abimilki, your servant [and the dirt from]under the sandals of the feet of [my lord]; at the [feet of the king,] my lord, my deity, [my sun god, seven (times) and 7 (times) have I fallen]. M[ay] the king, [my lord, my deity, my sun god,] be apprised [con]cerning his city, [his] hand[maiden].

(7–19) [Now hostile is] Zimredda, the ruler of [the city of Ṣidon] towards [me]. And [....] the king, [my] lord [..............]

(10–30) [.........*scattered words only*...........]

31) [......................................]
32) [......................................]
33) [......................................]
34) [......................................]
35) [......................................]
36) [.........*i*]*t-ti* [........................]
37) [*uš-ši-r*]*a-šu* LUGAL *be-l*[*i-ia*..............]
38) [*a-n*]*a* ÌR-⸢*šu*⸣ *ù* [.........................]
39) [....]LUGAL ⸢^{d}⸣⸢UTU⸣ *b*[*e-li-ia*.........]
40) [...........]*mar ša*[...................]
41) [.......]*bal*...*am-ma*[...................]
42) L[UGAL] *be-l*[*í-ia yi-iš-*]*ta-p*[*a-ar*..........]
43) *a*[*-na i*]*a-ši ù né- e*[........................]
44) [*a-na*] ⸢LUGAL⸣ ⸢*be*⸣-⸢*li*⸣-⸢*ia*⸣...............]
45) [...*it*]-*ti-*[*i*]*a* ⸢*li*⸣-⸢*id*⸣-*din*[*-ni*............]
46) [.....]*a-na da-ri-ti a-na.*[ÌR-*šu*...........]
47) [*ù*] *li-id-din-ni* 80 LÚ.M[EŠ..................]
48) *a*[*-n*]*a na-*[*ṣa-ar*] *ti-e-ti* [..................]
49) ⸢*nu*⸣-⸢*kúr*⸣-*t*[u_4 *da*]*-na-at* [.................]
50) [*i*]-*na* ⸢*muḫ*⸣-[*ḫi-ia*] ⸢*qa*⸣-*du* LÚ.MEŠ *w*[*i-i-m*]*a*
51) ⸢*a*⸣-*wa-sú*..............................]
52) *i-zi-za* [...............................]
53) *ù i-bá-al-li-*[*iṭ*] *i-*^{de4}[.............................]
54) LUGAL ^{d}UTU EN-⸢*li*⸣ *ša* ÌR [*ki-ti*]
55) *ù* ^{I}*A-bu-*LUGAL [..]*ù id-*[*din* LUGAL]
56) [*pa-ni-*]*šu a-na* \\ *ú-pu-ut* L[UGAL *be-li-ia*]
57) [...].LUGAL ^{d}UTU ⸢*be*⸣-⸢*li*⸣-⸢*ia*⸣ [..............]
58) [......................................]
59) [......................................]
60) [......................................]
61) [......................................]
Lft.ed. 62) [..........]^{d}UTU ⸢*be*⸣-*li-*[*ia*............]
63) [......................................]
64) [......................................]
65) [......................................]
66) [......................................]
67) [......................................]

(31–36) [.......................................]

(37–41) [sen]d him, oh king, [my] l[ord, to]his servant [...] the king, my s[un god], [my] l[ord......]

(42–57) The k[ing, my] lo[rd wro[te] t[o m]e and [....to] the king, my lord [...wi]th [m]e. May he grant [to me....] forever, to [his servant...] and may he grant to me tr[oops] t[o] pro[te]ct *ti-e-ti* [......]The hostility is strong against [me] along with the *w*[*īma*] troops [....]I took a stand [....] and I will live [...]The king, the sun god, my lord knows that the [loyal] servant is Abu-milki [...] so gi[ve, oh king,]his[attention to the mission of the k[ing, my lord ...]the king, my sun god, my lord [...]

(58–61) [....]

(62–67) [...] the sun god, [my] lord [..............................]

EA 153

TRANSCRIPTION

Obv. 01) [*a-na*] LUGAL EN-*lí-ia*
02) [*u*]*m-ma* ^{I}*Ia-bi*-LUGAL ⸢ÌR⸣-*ka*
03) 7 *u* 7 *a-na* GÌR.MEŠ-*ka am-qut*
04) *ša i*[*q-b*]*i* LUGAL *be-li-ia*
05) *šu-*[*ut*] *e-te-pu-uš*
06) *pal-ḫa-at gáb-bi*
07) KUR-*ti iš-tu pa-ni*
08) ÉRIN.MEŠ LUGAL EN-*lí-ia*
09) *su-ḫi-iz-ti* LÚ.MEŠ-*ia*
10) GIŠ.MÁ.MEŠ *a-na pa-ni*
11) ÉRIN.MEŠ LUGAL *be-li-ia*
12) *ù ša la iš-te-mé*
13) *ia-nu* É-*šu ia-nu*
14) *bal-ṭá-šu an-nu-ú*
15) *a-na-an-ṣ*[*ár* UR]U(?)
16) LUGAL *be-*[*li-ia*]
Lo.ed. 17) ⸢*ù*⸣ ⸢*šu*⸣-⸢*ul*⸣-*m*[*i a-na??*]
18) *mu-ḫi* LUGAL *li-*[de_4 LUGAL]
Rev. 19) *a-na* ÌR-*šu ša*
20) *it-ti-šu*

EA 153

TRANSLATION

(1–2) [To] the king, my lord: [Mes]sage of Abi-milku, your servant:

(3–5) At your feet seven (times) and seven times I have fallen. What the king my lord ha[s sai]d, that I have done.

(6–8) All the land is in fear of the troops of the king, my lord.

(9–11) I have manned my ships in view of (the coming) of the troops of the king, my lord.

(12–14) And the one who has disobeyed has no house and has nothing alive.

(14–20) Behold, I am guarding the [cit]y of the king, my lord and [my] welf[are] is the responsibility of the king. May [the king] be app[rised] concerning his servant who is with him.

EA 154

TRANSCRIPTION

Obv. 01) *a-na* LUGAL EN-*lí-ia*

02) *um-ma* ^{I}*A-bi-mil-ki* Ì[R-*ka*]

03) 7 *u* 7 *a-na* GÌR.MEŠ LUGAL *be-*⸢*lí*⸣-[*i*]⸢*a*⸣ *am-qut*

04) ⸢*a*⸣-*na-ku ep-ru iš-tu* ^{KUŠ}*še-ni*

05) LUGAL *be-*⸢*li*⸣-*ia* ⸢*aš*⸣-*te-me*

06) *ša* ⸢*iš*⸣-⸢*ta*⸣-*pár* LUGAL *a-na*

07) ÌR-*šu* ⸢\⸣ ⸢*ia*⸣-*ku-‹un› e-mu-qí*

08) ⸢*muḫ*⸣-⸢*ḫi*⸣ *Ia-wi ša iq-bi*

09) ⸢LUGAL⸣ *šu-ut e-te-pu-uš*

10) *ḫa-di-ia-ku ma-gal ma-gal*

11) *ša-ni-tam* ⸢*iš*⸣-*tu pa-ṭá-ri*

12) ÉRIN.MEŠ LUGAL EN-*lí-ia*

13) *muḫ-*⸢*ḫi*⸣-*ia* ⸢*la*⸣-*a i-na-an-din-ni*

14) LÚ URU *Ṣí-du-na*

15) LÚ.⸢MEŠ⸣-*ia a-ra-da*

16) *a-na er-ṣé-ti*

17) *a-na la-qí* GIŠ.MEŠ

18) *la-qí* A.MEŠ *a-na ši-*⸢*ti*⸣

19) LÚ ‹1›-*en da-a-kà*

20) *ù* LÚ ^{en}1 *la-*[*qí* (or: *qa* ?)

21) ⸢UŠ⸣+U+U *ṣí-bá-a*[*t*]

Lo.ed. 22) ⸢LÚ⸣.[M]EŠ-*ia il-*[*te-qú*]

23) ⸢^{I}⸣*Z*[*i-im-re-da*]

Rev. 24) [LÚ URU *Ṣí-du-na ù*]

25) [L]Ú [*ar-nu* ^{I}*A-zi-ru*]

26) *ù* [ÌR *ša is-me a-na* EN-*šu*]

27) *šu*[*l-mu* URU-*šu šul-mu* É-*šu*]

28) *ù* ⸢*li*⸣-⸢*i*⸣-*de*$_{4}$ ⸢LUGAL⸣ ⸢*a*⸣-[*n*]*a*

29) ÌR-*šu*

EA 154

TRANSLATION

(1–5) To the king, my lord, the message of Abimilki, [your] se[rvant]: seven (times) and seven (times) at the feet of the king, [m]y lord have I fallen. I am the dirt from the sandals of the king, my lord.

(5–10) I have heard what the king has written to his servant, "May my forces be rea‹dy› for (or: against) Yawi." What the king has said, that I have done. I rejoiced exceedingly (or: I am exceedingly happy).

(11–25) Furthermore, since the departure of the troops of the king, my lord, from me, the ruler of the city Sidon does not let me or my men go down to the land to take wood supplies (or) to take water for drinking. He killed one man and he took another one. Eighty (shekels), tax for my men, Zi[mredda, the ruler of the city of Sidon and the criminal, Aziru] have ta[ken].

(25–29) But [as for the servant that listened to his lord, his city is at] pe[ace, his house is at peace.] So may the king be apprised con[ce]rning his servant.

EA 155

TRANSCRIPTION

Obv. 01) ⸢*a*⸣-*na* LUGAL ^{d}[UTU *be-li-ia*]
02) *um-ma A-bi-m*[*il-ki* ÌR-*ka*]
03) 7 *u* 7 *a-na* GÌR.MEŠ L[UGAL *be-li-ia am-qut*]
04) *a-na-ku ep-ru iš-*[*tu*]
05) *šu-pa-li* ^{KUŠ}*še-ni* L[UGAL *be-li-ia*]
06) *ù* LUGAL ^{d}UTU *da-ri*[-*tu*$_{4}$]
07) LUGAL *iq-bi a-na* ÌR-*šu* [*ù*]
08) *a-na* ÌR ^{MUNUS}*Ma-ia-a-ti*
09) *a-na* ⸢*na*⸣-*da-ni še-ḫu ù a-na* [*n*]*a-*⸢*da*⸣-⸢*ni*⸣?
10) A.MEŠ \ *mé-ma a-na ši-te-šu*
11) *ù la-a i-pu-uš-šu-ni*$_{7}$
12) *ki-ma qa-bi* LUGAL *be-li-ia*
13) *la-a i-na-an-din-nu-ni*$_{7}$
14) *ù li-im-li-ik* LUGAL
15) *a-na* ÌR $^{I.MUNUS}$*Ma-*⸢*ya*⸣-*a-ti*
16) *a-na na-da-ni* A.MEŠ
17) *aš-šum ba-la-ṭì-šu ša-ni-tam*
18) *be-li* LUGAL *e-nu-ma ia-nu*
19) GIŠ.[MEŠ *i*]*a-‹nu›* A.MEŠ *ia-nu* IN$_{4}$.NU
20) *ia-nu i*[*p*]*-ru ia-nu ša-mu*
21) *a-na ba*[*-la-ṭì*]*-ma li-de*$_{4}$ LUGAL *be-li*
22) *a-na* ÌR $^{⸢I⸣.⸢MUNUS⸣}$*Ma-ya-a-ti*
23) *a-na na-d*[*a-n*]*i ba-la-ṭì a-na ša-šu*
24) *e-nu-ma it*[*-t*]*a-din*
25) LUGAL *be-li-ia* A.M[EŠ] ⸢*a*⸣-*na ši-ti*
26) ÌR ^{MUNUS}*Ma-ia-a-*⸢*ti*⸣
27) *ù id-din pa-ni-ia* VAT 1872
28) *a-na ur-da-ti-šu* [*ù*]
29) $^{I.MUNUS}$*Ma-ia-a-ti* BAD-*ti-*[*i*]*a*
30) *mu-šu ù ur-ra* [*ù*]

Lo.ed. 31) *e-nu-ma i-te-r*[*u-ub*]
32) *i-na pa-ni* LUGAL *be*[*-li-ia*]
33) ⸢*ù*⸣ *pal-ḫa-ku* \\ *ir-t*[*a-*]

EA 155

TRANSLATION

(1–6) To the king, the [sun god, my lord,] message of Abi-m[ilki, your servant:] Seven (times) and seven (times) at the feet of the k[ing, my lord, have I fallen.] I am the dirt fr[om] beneath the sandal(s) of the k[ing, my lord], and the king is the etern[al] sun god.

(7–17) The king said to give the breath of life to his servant [and] the servant of Mayati and to ⸢give⸣? water for him to drink, but they have not done for me as the king, my lord, commanded; they are not providing for me. So may the king take counsel concerning the servant of Mayati to give water for his sustenance.

(17–23) Furthermore, my lord, O king, because here is no woo[d], there is n[o] water, there is no straw, there is no ration (or: dirt), there are no plants for sus[tenance](?), may the king, my lord, be apprised concerning the servant of Mayati to furnish sustenance for him.

(24–33) When the king, my lord, g[a]ve water for the servant of Mayati to drink, then I set my face to the service of him [and] of Mayati, my lady, night and day. [But] when I ent[ered] into the presence of the king, [my] lo[rd], [then] I was afraid,

Rev. 34) ⸢*ù*⸣ *la-a e-lé-ú* [*qa-ba* (?)]
35) *e-nu-ma i-mur* LUGAL ^{d}U[TU]
36) *ù la-a i-pu-*⸢*uš*⸣
37) LÚ.⸢MÁŠKIM⸣ [*ki-ma qa-bi*](?)
38) LUGA[L *la-*]⸢*a*⸣ *id-din* G[IŠ.MEŠ *ù*] BM 29814
39) [A.MEŠ *ki-*]*ma qa-bi* LUG[AL]
40) *ù* ⸢*li*⸣*-de*$_{9}$ LUGAL *a-na* ÌR-*šu*
41) *ù a-na* URU *Ṣur-ri*
42) URU $^{I.MUNUS}$*Ma-ya-a-ti*
43) *ù ša it-ta-ṣí a-ma-ta*$_{5}$
44) ⸢*iš*⸣*-tu* ^{UZU}*pí*^{MEŠ} LUGAL
45) *a-na* ÌR-*šu šu-ut i-*⸢*pu*⸣*-uš*
46) ⸢*ù*⸣ ⸢*a*⸣-⸢*na*⸣ LUGAL *di!-ni-mu* [*i-*]*la-*⸢*ak*⸣
47) LUGAL ⸢^{d}⸣UTU *da-ri-*⸢*tu*$_{4}$⸣
48) *ù a-na-‹ku›* ÌR *ki-it-*⸢*ti*⸣
49) ⸢LUGAL⸣ *be-li-i*[*a*] ⸢LUGAL⸣ ⸢*ip*⸣-⸢*qí*⸣*-i*[*d-ni*]
50) *a-na na-*⸢*ṣa*⸣-⸢*ri*⸣ ⸢URU⸣ $^{⸢I.⸣⸢MUNUS⸣}$⸢*M*⸣*a-*⸢*ya*⸣-⸢*a*⸣*-ti*
51) BAD-*ti-ia* ⸢*a*⸣-⸢*nu*⸣-⸢*um*⸣-⸢*ma*⸣ ⸢*a*⸣-[*na*]-⸢*an*⸣*-ṣur!-r*[*u*]
52) *ša-ni-tam be-li* ⸢*iš*⸣-[*tu pa-ṭá-*]⸢*ri*⸣?
53) ÉRIN.MEŠ *muḫ-*⸢*ḫi*⸣-⸢*ia*⸣ *l*[*a-a i-le-e*]
54) *a-na er-*⸢*ṣé*⸣*-ti* [*a-la- kam*^{V}]
55) *e-nu-ma ik-*⸢*šu*⸣*-ud* ⸢*ṭup*⸣-⸢*pu*⸣ [*ša*]
56) LUGAL *be-li-ia ù i-qá-*⸢*rib*⸣-⸢*bu*⸣
57) *i-na er-ṣé-ti ù*
58) LUGAL *be-li-ia lìb-bi gáb-*[*bi*]
59) KUR-*ti i-de*$_{9}$ *ù li-id*[*-din*]
60) *pa-ni-šu* LUGAL *a-na* Ì[R-*šu*]
61) *ù* URU *Ṣur-ri*
62) URU $^{⸢I.⸣MUNUS}$*Ma-ia-*[*a-ti*]
63) ⸢*a*⸣-⸢*na*⸣ *na-da-a*[*n* GIŠ.MEŠ]
Up.Ed. 64) ⸢*ù*⸣ A.MEŠ *a-na ba-l*[*a-ṭì-šu*]
65) ⸢*ša*⸣*-ni-tam be-l*[*i*...]
Lft.ed. 66) [*li-*]*ša-al* LUGAL LÚ.MÁŠKIM *e-nu-ma* [*a*]*š-bu-ni*$_{7}$
67) [*i*]*-na* URU *Ṣu-mu-ri a-mur* LÚ.MEŠ URU ⸢PÚ⸣-⸢*ru*⸣*-ti i-na*
68) [x] GIŠ.MÁ *a-li-ik ù* LÚ URU *Ṣí-du-*[*n*]*a i-na* 2 GIŠ.M[Á]
69) [*i*]*-la-ak ù a-na-ku i-la-ak qa-du gáb-*[*b*]*i* GIŠ.MÁ-*k*[*a*]
70) *ù li-im-li-ik* LUGAL *a-na* ÌR-*šu* \\ *gáb-bi* ⸢URU⸣*-ia*
71) ⸢*ù*⸣ *ú-ṣur* GIŠ.M[Á L]UGAL *i-na*

(34–35) [and] I was not able [to speak(?)] when I saw the king, the su[n god].

(36–42) But the commissioner has not done [as]the kin[g] [commanded]; he has [not] given w[ood and water a]s the ki[ng] commanded. So may the king, be apprised concerning his servant and concerning the city of Tyre, the city of Mayati.

(43–51) And the thing that comes forth from the mouth of the king to his servant, he will do and for the king, he would die! The king is the eternal sun god and ˹I˺ am the loyal servant of the king, m[y] lord. The king appoint[ed me] to guard the city of Mayati, my lady; now, I am guarding.

(52–64) Furthermore, my lord, si[nce] the troops [withdr]ew from me, [I am unable to go] to the mainland. No sooner than the tablet of the king, my lord, arrives, then I will approach the mainland. And the king, my lord, knows the heart (sentiments) of the whole land. So may the king turn his attention to [his] ser[vant] and to the city of Tyre, the city of Maya[ti], to provide [wood] and water for [his] sus[tenance].

(65–68) Furthermore, my lord, [...]? [May] the king ask the commissioner if they are occupying the city of Ṣumur. Behold, the men of Beirut went in [*x*] ship(s) and the man of Ṣid[o]n in 2 ships.

(69–71) but I will go with all *your*(?) ships. So may the king take counsel concerning his servants and guard the sh[ip(s)] of the [k]ing in all my town(s).

EA 156

TRANSCRIPTION

Obv. 01) *a-na* LUGAL EN-*ia* DINGIR-*ia* ^{d}UTU-*ia*

02) *um-ma* ^{I}*A-zi-ri* ÌR-*ka-ma*

03) 7-*šu u* 7-*šu a-na* GÌR.MEŠ EN-*ia am-qut*

---

04) *a-nu-um-ma mé-re-eš*$_{15}$-*tu*$_{4}$

05) *ša e-te-er-ri-iš*

06) ^{d}UTU EN-*ia a-na-ku* ÌR-⸢*ka*⸣

07) *a-di dá-ri-i-ti*

08) *ù* DUMU.MEŠ-*ia* ÌR.M[EŠ-*ka*]

---

09) *a-nu-um-ma* 2 LÚ T[UR.MEŠ]

10) *at-ta-din* DUMU.MEŠ[-*ia*]

11) *ù li-ip-pu-š*[*u gáb-ba*]

12) *ša i-qáb-bi* E[N-*ia*]

13) *ù li-wa-aš-šar*[-*an-ni* EN-*ia*]

Lo.ed. 14) *i-na* KUR *A-mur-r*[*i*]

EA 156

TRANSLATION

(1–3) To the king, my lord, my god, my sun god; the message of Aziru, your servant: seven times and seven times at the feet of my lord have I fallen.

(4–8) Now, as for the request that the king, my lord, has been making, I am ⌜your⌝ servant for ever and my sons are [your] servant[s].

(9–14) Now, two lads have I given, viz. my sons. So may th[ey] carry out [everything] that my lord shall command. But may [my lord] leave me in the land of Amurru.

EA 157

TRANSCRIPTION

Obv. 01) [*a-na*] *šàr-r*[*i* EN-*ia* DINGIR-*ia ù* ^{d}UTU-*ia*]
02) [*qí*]–––*b*[*í- ma*]
03) *um-ma* ^{I}*A-z*[*i-ri* ÌR-*ka-ma*]
04) 7-*šu ù* ⸢7⸣-⸢*šu*⸣ ⸢*a*⸣-⸢*na*⸣ [GÌR.MEŠ EN-*ia*]
05) DINGIR-*ia ù* ^{d}UTU-*ia a*[*m-qut*]

---

06) ⸢*i*⸣-⸢*na*⸣-*an-na lu-ú i-de*$_{4}$-*an-n*[*i*]
07) LUGAL EN-*ia i-nu-ma* LÚ.ÌR-[*ka*]
08) *a-na-ku a-di dá-ri-*⸢*ti*⸣ *iš-tu a-ma-te* EN-*ia* ⸢*la*⸣ *a-pa-aṭ-ṭar*

---

09) EN-*ia iš-tu pa-*⸢*na*⸣-*nu-um-ma*
10) *a-ra-á*ʾ-*a-am a-na* LÚ.ÌR.MEŠ
11) LUGAL EN-*ia ù* LÚ.MEŠ GAL-*bu-te*^{MEŠ}
12) *ša* URU *Ṣu-mu-ri la-a ú-wa-aš-ša-ru-ú-ni-ni*
13) *ù i-na-an-na la-a ḫi-iṭ-ṭám*
14) *la mi-im-ma-an a-na* LUGAL EN-[*i*]*a*
15) *la e-te-pu-uš šàr-*⸢*ru*⸣ ⸢EN⸣-*ia*
16) *i-de*$_{4}$ LÚ.MEŠ *be-el ar-ni-š*[*u*]

---

17) *ù mi-i-nu-um-me*
18) *mé-*⸢*re*⸣-⸢*eš*$_{15}$⸣-*ta-š*[*u ša* LUGAL EN-*ia*]
19) *a-na-*⸢*ku*⸣ ⸢*lu*⸣-⸢ú⸣ ⸢*ad*⸣-[*din*]

---

20) *ù* [..................................]
Lo.ed. 21) *a-na* [................................]
22) *ù* [..................................]
23) ⸢*ù*⸣ [................................]
24) [...................................]

EA 157

TRANSLATION

(1–5) [Sp]eak [to] the king, [my lord, my god and my sun god], the message of Az[iru, your servant:] Seven times and seven times at [the feet of my lord,] my god and my sun god, [have] I [fallen].

(6–8) Now may the king, my lord, take cognizance of me, that [your] servant am I forever. From the words of my lord I will not depart.

(9–16) My lord, from before I have desired to serve the king, my lord, but the senior officials of Ṣumur have not been permitting me. And now, I have not committed any dereliction or anything else against the king, [m]y lord. The king, my lord, knows the (real) rebels.

(17–19) And whatever the request [of the king, my lord], verily will I give it.

(20–24) And [...] to [....] and [...] and [........................]

Rev. 25) *ù ki-a-am* [..............................]
26) *a-na* ^{d}UTU *i-*⸢*na*⸣[*-an-na*..................]
27) *ù bá-la-aṭ*[...............................]
28) *šum-ma* LUGAL KUR *Ḫa*[*-at-ti*$_7$............]
29) ⸢*a*⸣-⸢*na*⸣ *nu-kúr-ta*$_5$ UGU-*ia* [*il-la-ak* (?)]
30) ⸢*ù*⸣ *šàr-ru* EN-*ia* ÉRIN.⸢MEŠ⸣ ⸢*ṣa*⸣*-b*[*i pí-ṭá-te*]
31) ⸢*ù*⸣ GIŠ.GIGIR.ḪI.A *id-din-an-ni*
32) [*a*]-⸢*na*⸣ *i-*⸢*re*⸣*-eṣ-ṣú-ti-ia*
33) *ù* KUR-*šu ša* LUGAL EN-*ia* ⸢*aṣ*⸣-⸢*ṣur*⸣

---

34) *ša-ni-tam i-na ḫa-mut-iš*
35) [*uš*]*-še-ra-am* LÚ.⸢DUMU⸣.⸢KIN⸣-*ia*
36) ⸢*ù*⸣ ⸢*lu*⸣-⸢*ú*⸣ *il*$_5$(?)-⸢*kà*⸣[*-am*]

---

37) ⸢*ù*⸣ *mi-i-na-am-me-e ša id-din-‹nu›-ni*$_7$
38) LÚ.MEŠ ⸢*Ḫa*⸣*-za-an-nu-ú-tu*$_4$
39) *ù a-na-ku lu-ú ad-din*
40) ⸢*ù*⸣ ⸢LUGAL⸣ EN-*ia* DINGIR-*ia ù* ^{d}UTU-*ia*
41) [*lu-ú*] *ad-din a-di dá-ri-ti*

(25–33) So thus [.....] for the sun god, no[w...] and sustenance [...] If the king of the land of Ḫa[tti...should come(?) against me in a hostile manner, then (may) the king, my lord, grant to me the [regular] troops and the chariotry, for my assistance. Then will I protect the land of the king, my lord.

(34–36) Furthermore, with all due haste release my envoy so that he may ⸢come hither.⸣

(37–41) And whatever the city rulers have been giving, thus I will verily give. So, O king, my lord, my god and my sun god, [veri]ly will I give.

EA 158

TRANSCRIPTION

Obv.

01) *a-na* ^{I}*Tù-ú-tù* EN-*ia a-bi-i*[*a*]
02) *um-ma* ^{I}*A-zi-ri* DUMU-*ka* ÌR-*ka*[*-ma*]
03) *a-na* GÌR.MEŠ *a-bi-ia am-qut*
04) *a-na muḫ-ḫi a-bi-ia lu-ú šul-mu*

---

05) ^{I}*Tù-ú-tù a-nu-um-m*[*a a*]*t-*[*t*]*a-din*
06) *e*[*-ri-iš*]*-ti* LU[GAL] EN[*-i*]*a*
07) *ù mi-nu-um-ma e-ri-iš-tù-*⸢*šú*⸣
08) *ša* LUGAL EN-*ia li-iš-pur*
09) *ù a-na-ku a-*[*n*]*a-an-din*

---

10) *ša-ni-tam a-m*[*u*]*r at-ta i-na aš-ra-nu*
11) *a-bi-ia ù mi-nu-um-me e-ri-iš-ti*
12) ^{I}*Tù-ú-tù a-bi-ia šu-pur*
13) *ù a-na-ku lu-ú ad*!(⸢*id*⸣?)*-din*

---

14) [*a*]*-mur at-ta a-bi-ia ù* EN-*ia*
15) [*ù*] *a-na-ku* DUMU-*ka* KUR.MEŠ *A-mur-ri*
16) [KUR.ME]Š-*ka ù* É-*ia* É-*ka*
17) [*ù*]*mi-nu-um-ma e-ri-iš-tù-ka*
18) [*šu-up*]*-ra-am ù a-na-ku*
19) [*gáb-b*]*á e-ri-iš-ti-ka lu-ú ad-din*

---

20) [*ù a-m*]*ur at-ta a-na pa-ni*
21) [LUGAL EN]*-ia aš-bá-ta*
22) [*as-su*]r_x([AMA]R)*-ri* LÚ.MEŠ *sa-ru-tù*
23) [*a-wa-t*]*a ṣa-bu-ur-ta*
24) [*a-na muḫ-ḫ*]*i-ia a-na pa-ni*

Lo.ed.

25) [LUGAL EN*-i*]*a* ⸢*iq*⸣*-*⸢*bu*⸣*-nim*
26) [*ù*]*at-ta la tù-wa-aš-šar-šu-nu*

EA 158

TRANSLATION

(1–4) To Tutu, my lord, my father; the message of Aziru, your son, your servant: At the feet of my lord have I fallen. May it be well with my father.

(5–9) Tutu, now I have furnished the re[que]st of the ki[ng] [m]y lord, and whatever the request of the king, my lord, let him write and I will furnish (it).

(10–13) Furthermore, look, you are my father there and whatever the request of Tutu, my father, write and I verily will furnish (it).

(14–19) [L]ook, you are my father and my lord [and] I am your son. The territories of Amurru are your [territori]es and my house is your house. [And] whatever your request, [wr]ite to me and I will verily furnish [al]l of your requests.

(20–26) [And lo]ok, you abide in the presence of [the king,] my [lord. Sur]ely lying men would speak a false [wor]d [concern]ing me in the presence of [the king, m]y [lord. But] you must not permit them.

Rev. 27) [*ù a-*]*mur at-ta a-na pa-ni*
28) [LUGAL] EN-*ia* [*ki-i-m*]*a a-ia-ši*
29) [...] *aš-ba?-ta* [...]
30) [*ù*] *a-wa-te*^{MEŠ} *ṣa-bu-ur-ta*
31) [*a-n*]*a muḫ-ḫi-ia la tù-wa-aš-šar*

---

32) ⸢*ù*⸣ *a-na-ku* ÌR-*du ša* LUGAL EN-*ia*
33) [*ù*] *iš-tu a-wa-te*^{MEŠ} LUGAL EN-*ia*
34) [*ù*] *iš-tu a-wa-te*^{MEŠ} ^{I}*Tù-ú-tù a-bi-ia*
35) [*l*]*a a-pa-aṭ-ṭá-ar a-di dá-ri-iš*

---

36) *ù* ⸢*šum*⸣-⸢*ma*⸣ ⸢LUGAL⸣ ⸢EN⸣-*ia la i-ra-am-*⸢*an*⸣*-ni*
37) *ù i-zé-i-ra-an-ni*
38) *ù a-na-ku mi-na-am lu-ú aq-bi*

(27–31) [So lo]ok, you [...] are [...] in the presence of [the king,] my lord [representi]ng me [so] you should not permit lying words [ag]ainst me.

(32–35) And I am the servant of the king, my lord, [and] from the words of the king, my lord [and] from the words of Tutu, my father, I will [n]ot depart, ever.

(36–38) So if the king does not love but hates me, what can I say?

EA 159

TRANSCRIPTION

Obv. 01) [*a-na*] LUGAL EN-*ia* DINGIR-*ia* ^{d}UTU!(ÉRIN)-*ia*
02) [*um-m*]*a* ^{I}*A-zi-ri* LÚ.ÌR-*ka-ma*
03) [7-*š*]*u ù* 7-*šu a-na* GÌR.MEŠ EN-*ia*
04) [DINGIR-*i*]*a ù* ^{d}⌜UTU⌝!(⌜ÉRIN⌝)-*ia am-qú-ut*

---

05) [*iš-tu*]*a-ma*[-*te*^{MEŠ} L]UGAL EN-*ia* DINGIR-*i*[*a*]
06) [*ù* ^{d}UT]U!([ÉRI]N)-*ia la a-pa-aṭ-ṭar*
07) [EN-*ia*] ⌜*at*⌝-⌜*ta*⌝ *ki-i-ma* ^{d}I[ŠKUR]
08) [*ù at-*]*ta* ⌜*ki*⌝-*i-ma* ^{d}UTU!(ÉRIN)
09) [*ù k*]*i-i ú-kà-az-zi-*[*bu-ni*$_{7}$]
10) [LÚ.ÌR.]MEŠ *a-na pa-ni* EN-*ia* [DINGIR-*ia*]

---

11) [*a-mu*]*r a-na-ku ú-bá-an-*⌜*ni*⌝
12) [URU Ṣ]*u-mu-ri i-na-a*[*n-na*]
13) [.........]*ú*[...................................]
14) [*i-na šu*]*l-mi-i*[*š*...................................]
15) [URU Ṣ]*u-mu-ri ki-i-*[*me-e*]
16) [*i-bá-a*]*š-ši ki-i-me-e*[.............................]

---

17) [*a-na-ku*] UR.GI$_{7}$ *ša* LUGAL [EN-*ia*]
18) [*i-na*] KUR-*šu ša* EN-*ia* [DINGIR-*ia*]
19) [................] ⌜UGU⌝-⌜*ia*⌝ [......]
20) [...]
21) [...]
22) [...]
23) [...]
24) [...]

Rev. 25) [.........*šàr-*]*ru*[..............................]
26) [..........]⌜*bá*⌝-*nu-ta* [.........................]
27) [*šàr-*]*ru* EN-*ia* [..................................]
28) [*a-ma*]-*te*^{MEŠ}-*š* [*u*..............................]

EA 159

TRANSLATION

(1–4) [To] the king, my lord, my god, my sun god, the [messa]ge of Aziru, your servant. [Seven ti]mes and seven times at the feet of my lord, [m]y [god] and my sun god, have I fallen.

(5–10) [From] the wor[ds of the k]ing, my lord, m[y] god [and] my [sun go]d, I do not depart. [My lord,] you are like the st[orm god and yo]u are like the sun god, [so h]ow could [the serv]ants lie in the presence of my lord, [my god]?

(11–16) [Loo]k, I will build [the city of Ṣ]umur now [....] and [...in p]eace [...The city of Ṣ]umur is li[ke...], like [....]

(17–24) [I am] the dog of the king, [my lord, in] the land of my lord, [my god....]against me [..]

(25–28) [....the ki]ng [....] beautiful/good[......the ki]ng, my lord [...] h[is wor]ds [...................]

---

29) [..........]⌜*uš*⌝-*še*-[*ra-am*......................]
30) [..........*i*]*l-l*[*i*..............................]
31) [...........] x [..............................]
32) [...........] *ù* [..............................]
33) [........] GIŠ.Ì.MEŠ [..........................]
34) [x *ma*-]*na as-sí m*[*i*..............................]
35) [..........]MEŠ *ù* GIŠ[........................]
36) [x KUŠ.MEŠ] SÚN.MEŠ *ši*-[......................]
37) [...........] *ša i*-⌜*bá*⌝-*aš*-⌜*ši*⌝
38) [..............] *a-na* EN-*ia ú*-[*še-bíl*]

---

39) [*aš-š*]*um* LÚ.MEŠ *ḫa-za-an-nu-ú*[-*te*^{MEŠ}]
40) [.........]*bi gáb-bi-šu-nu*
41) [LÚ.MEŠ *sa*]-*ar-ru-u*-tu_4 EN-*ia-ma*
42) [*li-mu-u*]*r-šu-nu*

---

43) [EN-*i*]*a* URU *Ṣu-mu-ri i-na-an-na-ma*
44) [*i-na*] *ḫa-mut-iš ú-bá-an-ni-ši*
Up.ed 45) [*i-na*-]*an-na li-qí-pa-an-ni*
46) [*i-n*]*u-ma ú-bá-an-ni* URU *Ṣu-mu-ri*

(29–38) [....]sen[d....]and[....] oil [....*x* mi]nas of myrtle [...]and [...] wood[...*x* skins of] wild cows [.....] that are [...] to my lord have I [sent].

(39–42) [con]cerning the city rule[rs...] all of them [are li]ars. [May] my lord [exam]ine them.

(43–46) [M]y [lord], as for the city of Ṣumur, [with] haste will I build it. [No]w, may he trust me, [th]at I will build the city of Ṣumur.

EA 160

TRANSCRIPTION

Obv. 01) [*a-na*]*šàr-ri* GAL-*bi* E[N-*ia* DINGIR-*ia* ^{d}UTU-*ia*]
02) [*um-m*]*a* ^{I}*A-zi-ri* LÚ.ÌR[-*ka-ma*]
03) ⸢7⸣-*šu ù* 7-*šu a-na* GÌ[R.MEŠ EN-*ia*]
04) DINGIR-*ia ù* ^{d}UTU-*ia am-q*[*ut*]

---

05) EN-*ia* DINGIR-*ia* ^{d}UTU-*ia*
06) *a-na-ku* LÚ.ÌR-*ka ù* DUMU.MEŠ-*ia*
07) *ù* ŠEŠ.MEŠ-*ia* LÚ.MEŠ.ÌR-*tu*$_{4}$
08) *ša* LUGAL-*ri* EN-*ia a-di dá-ri-ti*

---

09) *a-nu-um-ma gáb-bi mé-re-eš*$_{15}$*-te*^{MEŠ}
10) *ša* LUGAL EN-*ia ú-še-eš-še-er*
11) *ù ša it-ta-aṣ-ṣí*
12) [*i*]*š-tu* UZU.KA *pí-i*
13) LU[GAL] ⸢EN⸣-⸢*ia*⸣ *ú-še-eš-še-er*

---

14) *a-nu-um-ma* ⸢8⸣ GIŠ.MÁ.M⸢EŠ⸣ ⸢*ù*⸣ [GI]Š?.TÚG-*nu*^{MEŠ}
15) *ù* GIŠ.MEŠ GAL-*bu-t*[*u*$_{4}$.....*b*]*e?*[-]*nu*
16) *gáb-bi ša it-*⸢*ta*⸣[*-ṣí*]
17) *iš-tu* UZU.K[A *pí-i*]
18) ⸢LUGAL⸣-*ri* EN-*i*[*a* DINGIR-*ia* (*ù*) ^{d}UTU-*ia*]
19) [*a-n*]*a-ku lu-ú* [*ú-še-ši-ir(?)*]

Lo.ed. 20) [*ù*]? LUGAL-*ri* [EN-*ia aš-šum* URU *Ṣu-mu-ri*]
Rev. 21) [*ša*]*i-qá-ab*[*-bi a-na muḫ-ḫi-ia*]
22) [*ma-ti t*]*a-bá-an-n*⸢*i*⸣ [URU *mu-ša ù*]
23) [*ú-r*]*a-am ša* E[N-*ia i-qá-ab-bi e-še-em-me*]
24) *ù* LUGAL.MEŠ KUR *Nu-ḫa*[*-aš-še*]
25) *n*[*a*]*-ak-ru-ni*$_{7}$ *it-*⸢*ti*⸣-⸢*i*⸣[*a*]
26) ⸢*ù*⸣ *la ú-bá-an-ni-ši*
27) URU *Ṣu-mu-ri i-na* MU.K[A]M^{v}-*ma*
28) *a-bá-an-*[*n*]*i* URU *Ṣú-mu-ri*
29) EN-*ia a-na-ku* LÚ.ÌR-*ka a-di dá-ri-ti*

EA 160

TRANSLATION

(1–4) [To] the great king, [my] lo[rd, my god, my sun god], [the mes]sage of Aziru [your] servant. Seven times and seven times at the fe[et of my lord,] my deity and my sun god, have I fall[en].

(5–8) My lord, my god, my sun god, I am your servant and my sons and my brothers are servants of the king, my lord forever.

(9–13) Now I am preparing all the requests of the king, my lord, and whatever comes forth [f]rom the mouth of the ki[ng], m[y] lord, [my god, my sun god, I will prepare.

(14–19) Now eight boats and [*taš*]*karinu* logs and large logs [...] all that came [forth] from the m[outh] of the king, m[y] lord, my god (and) my sun god] have ⸢I⸣ verily [prepared(?)].

(20–23) [And] my king, [my lord concerning the city of Ṣumur that] he spok[e to me, "When will yo]u buil[d the city?" Night and da]y, what my lord says, I pay heed.]

(24–29) But the kings of Nuǵa[sse] are at war with m[e] and I have not rebuilt it, viz. the city of Ṣumur. In a year I will build the city of Ṣumur. My lord, I am your servant forever.

30) *ù* LUGAL *a-na* LÚ.[ME]Š *sa-ar-ru-ti*
31) [*š*]*a* ⸢*i*⸣-⸢*k*⸣*ál-lu-ú-nim kàr-ṣi-ia*
32) ⸢*a*⸣[*-na pa-n*]*i* EN-*ia la te-še-em-mé*

---

33) *ù šàr-ru* EN-*ia* DINGIR-*ia ù* ^{d}UTU-*ia*
34) LÚ.DUMU.⸢KIN⸣-*ri-šu li-iš-pur-ra-am*
35) *it-ti* LÚ.DUMU.⸢KIN⸣-⸢*ri*⸣-*ia*
36) *ù li-il-*⸢*qá*⸣-⸢*a*⸣ *gáb-b*⸢*i*⸣
37) *ša i-qá-ab-*⸢*bi*⸣ L[UGAL[EN?-*ia*?]

---

38) EN-*ia i-na-an-na* [*i-na* MU.]K[AM^{v}-*ma*]
39) [*ki*]-*i-me-e ú-bá*[*-an-ni* URU? *ša*?]
40) [LUGAL] EN-*ia* DINGIR-*i*[*a* (*ù*) ^{d}UTU-*ia*]
Up.ed. 41) [*ù š*]*àr-ru* EN-*ia*[LÚ.DUMU.KIN-*ri-ka*?]
42) [*it-*]*ti* LÚ.DUMU.KIN-[*ri-ia*?]
Lft.ed. 43) [*i-na*] *ḫa-mut-iš uš-še-ra-am*
44) [*ù*]*bi-il-ta-šu ša* LUGAL EN-*ia ú-ba*[*l*]

(30–32) But may the king not listen to the treacherous men [th]at are slandering me before my lord.

(33–37) So may the king, my lord, my god, my son god, send his envoy with my envoy and may he take away everything of which the king, [my lord,] will say.

(38–40) My lord, now [it is in a year(?), w]hen I re[build the city of the king,] my lord, m[y] god [(and) my sun god.]

(41–44) [And O k]ing, my lord, send [with] all haste [your envoy wi]th [my] envoy, [and] the tribute of the king, my lord, will I deliver.

EA 161

TRANSCRIPTION

Obv. 01) *a-na* LUGAL GAL-*bi* EN-*ia* DINGIR-*ia* ⸢^{d}⸣[UTU-*ia*]
02) *um-ma* ^{I}*A-zi-ri* ⸢LÚ⸣ ÌR-*ka-ma*
03) 7-*šu ù* 7-*šu* ⸢*a*⸣-⸢*na*⸣ ⸢GÌR.MEŠ EN-*ia* ⸢DINGIR⸣-[*i*]⸢*a*⸣ ^{d}UTU!(ÉRIN)-*ia am-qut*

---

04) EN-*ia a-na-ku* LÚ ÌR-*ka ù i-na kà-ša-dì-ia*
05) *a-na pa-ni* LUGAL EN-*ia ù aq-ta-bi*
06) *gáb-bi a-ma-te*^{MEŠ}-*ia a*-⸢*na*⸣ *pa-ni* EN-*ia*
07) EN-*li-mi a-na* LÚ.MEŠ *sa-ar-ru-ti*
08) *ša i-kà-lu-ú-ni*$_7$ *kàr-ṣi-ia*
09) *a-na pa-ni* LUGAL EN-*ia la-a te-še-em-me-e*
10) *a-na-ku-mi* LÚ ÌR-*ka a-di dá-ri-ti*

---

11) *ù aš-šum* ^{I}*Ḫa-an-i* LUGAL EN-*ia iq-ta-bi*
12) EN-*ia i-na* URU *Tu-ni-ip aš-bá-ku*
13) *ù la i-de*$_4$ *i-nu-ma kà-ši-id*
14) *im-ma-ti*-⸢*i*⸣-*me-e i-še-em-mé*
15) *ù e-te-él-li i-na ar-ki-šu*
16) *ù la-a a-kà-ša-ad-šu*
17) *ù li-ik-šu-ú-ud* ^{I}*Ḫa-an-i*
18) *i-na šul-mi ù li-iš-al-šu*
19) LUGAL EN-*ia ki-i-me-e ú-ta*-⸢*na*⸣-*bal-šu*
20) ŠEŠ.MEŠ-*ia ù* ^{I}*Be-ti*-DINGIR *iz-za-zu-ni*$_7$
21) *a-na pa-ni-šu* GU$_4$.MEŠ ÙZ.MEŠ *ù* MUŠEN.MEŠ
22) NINDA-*šu* KAŠ.MEŠ-*šu i-din-nu-ni*$_7$

---

23) ⸢ANŠE⸣.KUR.RA.MEŠ ANŠE.MEŠ *at-ta-din*
24) [*a*]-⸢*na*⸣ KASKAL-*ni-šu ù* LUGAL EN-*ia*

Lo.ed. 25) ⸢*a*⸣-⸢*ma*⸣-⸢*te*^{MEŠ}⸣-*ia* ⸢*li*⸣-*iš-mé*
26) ⸢*i*⸣-⸢*na*⸣ *a-la-ki-i-ia a-na mu-ḫi* LUGAL EN-*ia*

EA 161

TRANSLATION

(1–3) To the Great King, my lord, my god, [my sun god]; Message of Aziru, your servant: Seven times and seven times at the feet of my lord, my god, my sun god, have I fallen.

(4–10) My lord, I am your servant, and on my arrival before the king, my lord, I spoke of all my affairs in the presence of the king, my lord. My lord! Do not listen to the treacherous men who are slandering me before the king, my lord. I am your servant forever!

(11–22) And concerning Ḫan'i has the king, my lord, spoken. My lord, I was in the city of Tunip and I did not know that he had arrived. As soon as I heard, then I went up after him but I did not overtake him. So may Ḫan'i arrive safely so that the king, my lord, may question him about how I entertained him. My brothers and Bêt-'ili put themselves at his service. Cattle, small cattle, and fowl, his food (and) his drink did they furnish (him).

(23–26) I provided horses and asses for his journey. So may the king, my lord, heed my words. When I come to the king, my lord,

Rev. 27) ^{I}*Ḫa-an-i i-la-*⸢*ak*⸣ ⸢*a*⸣-⸢*na*⸣ *pa-ni-ia*
28) *ú-ut-ta-na-ab-bal-ni ki-i-ma*
29) ^{MUNUS}*um-mi ki-i-ma a-bi*
30) *ù i-na-an-‹na› i-qá-ab-bi* EN-*ia*
31) *iš-tu-mi pa-ni* ^{I}*Ḫa-an-i*
32) *ti-ir-ta-qí-i-mi* DINGIR.MEŠ-*nu-ka*
33) *ù* ^{d}UTU!(ÉRIN) *lu-ú i-du-ú-ni*$_7$
34) *šum-ma la i-na* URU *Tu-ni-ip aš-bá-ku*

---

35) *ša-ni-tam aš-šum bá-na-i-šu ša* URU *Ṣu-mur*
36) *šàr-ru* EN-*ia iq-ta-bi* LUGAL.MEŠ KUR *Nu-ḫa-aš-še*
37) *na-ak-ru it-ti-ia ù* URU.ḪI.A-*ia*
38) *i-le-*⸢*eq*⸣*-qú-ni*$_7$ *i-na* ^{UZU}*pí-i* ^{I}*Ḫa-ti-ip*
39) *ù la* ⸢*ú*⸣*-bá-an-ni-ši i-na-an-na*
40) *i-na ḫa-mut-iš ú-bá-an-ni-še*

---

41) *ù* EN-*ia lu-ú i-de*$_4$ *i-nu-ma*
42) BAR-*šu-nu ša ú-nu-te*^{MEŠ} *ša id-din*
43) LUGAL EN-*ia* ^{I}*Ḫa-ti-ip i-le-*⸢*eq*⸣*-qè*
44) *ù* KÙ.GI.MEŠ *ù* KÙ.BABBAR-*pa ša* LUGAL
45) EN-*ia id-din-an-ni gáb-bá i-le-eq-qè*
46) ^{I}*Ḫa-ti-ip ù* EN-*ia lu-ú i-de*$_4$

---

47) *ša-ni-tam ap-pu-na-ma* LUGAL EN-*ia*
48) *iq-bi am-mi-i-ni-mi tu*$_4$*-ta-na-bal*
49) LÚ.DUMU.KIN-*ri* LUGAL KUR *Ḫa-at-ti*$_7$
50) ⸢*ù*⸣ LÚ.DUMU.KIN-*ri-ia la tu*$_4$*-ta-na-bal*
51) *u an-nu-ú* KUR EN-*ia ù šàr-r*[*u*]
52) EN-*ia iš-ku-na-*⸢*an*⸣*-ni*

Up.ed. 53) ⸢*i*⸣*-na* LÚ.MEŠ *ḫa-za-nu-ti*

Lft.ed. 54) *li-il-li-kà-am* LÚ.DUMU.KIN-*ri be-li-ia*
55) *ù gáb-bi ša aq-ta-bi a-na pa-ni be-li-ia lu-ú-din*
56) ⸢TIN!⸣.ZI.MEŠ GIŠ.MÁ.MEŠ Ì.MEŠ GIŠ.TUKUL.MEŠ *ù* GIŠ.MEŠ *li-*⸢*din*⸣

(27–34) Ḫan'i came out to meet me and he was taking care of me like a mother and like a father. But now my lord says: "You hid yourself from Ḫan'i." May your gods and the sun god be witnesses whether I was in Tunip.

(35–40) Furthermore, concerning the rebuilding of the city of Ṣumur, the king, my lord, has spoken. The kings of Nuǵasse are hostile to me and they are taking my cities at the command of Ḥatip so I have not rebuilt it. Now I will rebuild it in all haste.

(41–46) And may my lord be apprised that Ḥatip is taking half of the things that the king, my lord has given (to me). And Ḥatip is taking all the gold and the silver that the king, my lord, gave to me. So may my lord be apprised.

(47–53) Furthermore, moreover, the king, my lord, said: "Why do you entertain the envoy of the land of Ḫatti but my envoy you do not entertain?" But this is the land of my lord, and the king, my lord placed me among the city rulers.

(54–56) May the envoy of my lord come, and all that I said before the king, my lord, will I surely do. Let him (the envoy) furnish provisions, ships, oil, weapons and wood.

EA 162

TRANSCRIPTION

Obv.

01) [*a-na* ^{I}*A-zi-ri*] ⸢LÚ⸣ ⸢URU⸣ ⸢*A*⸣*-mu-ur-ra qí-bí-m*[*a*]
02) [*um-ma-a-m*]*i* LUGAL EN-*ka um-ma-a* LÚ URU *Gub*^{ub}*-la*
03) [*iq-ba-a*]*k-ku ša a-ḫu-šu i-na ba-a-bi it-ta-*⸢*sú*⸣*-uk-šu*
04) [*um-ma-a l*]*i-qá-an-ni ù šu-ri-ba-an-ni i-na* URU.KI-*ia*
05) [*ma-ad* KÙ.BABBA]R *ù lu-*⸢*ud*⸣*-dì-na-ak-ku an-nu-ù mi-im-ma ma-ad*
06) [*ù i-*]⸢*i*⸣*a-nu it-ti-ia šu-ú ki-na-an-na iq-ba-ak-ku*

---

07) [*ú-u*]*l at-tá tá-ša-pa-ar a-na* LUGAL EN-*ka*
08) [*um-m*]*a-a* ÌR-*ka a-na-ku ki-i gáb-bi* LÚ.MEŠ ⸢*ḫa*⸣-⸢*za*⸣-⸢*nu*⸣-*te*⸢^{MEŠ}⸣ *bá-nu-ti*
09) [*ša*] *i-na lìb-bi* URU.KI-*šu* ⸢*ù*⸣ *te-ep-pu-uš ḫe-e-ṭa*
10) [*a-n*]*a la-qé-e* LÚ *ḫa-za-an-na ša* ŠEŠ-*šu i-na* ⸢*bá*⸣-⸢*a*⸣-*bi*
11) *iš-tu* URU.KI-*šu it-ta-sú-uk-šu*

---

12) *ù i-na* URU *Ṣí-dú-na a-ši-ib ù* ⸢*tá*⸣*-at-tá-dì-in-šu*
13) *a-na* LÚ.MEŠ *ḫa-za-nu-ú-ti ki-i ṭe*$_4$*-e-mi-ka*
14) *ú-ul ti-i-de*$_9$ *sà-ar-ru-ut-tá ša* LÚ.MEŠ

---

15) ⸢*šum*⸣*-ma* ÌR *ša* LUGAL *at-tá ki-i ki-i-it-ti*
16) *am-mì-ni la-a tá-a-ku-ul kar-ṣí-i-šu a-na pa-ni* ⸢LUGAL⸣ EN-*ka*
17) *um-ma-a* LÚ *ḫa-za-an-nu an-nu-ú il-tap-ra-an-ni um-ma-a*
18) *li-qá-an-*⸢*ni*⸣ *a-na ka-a-ša ù šu-ri-ba-an-ni i-na* URU.KI-*ia*

---

19) *ù šum-ma te-*⸢*te*⸣*-*⸢*pu*⸣*-*⸢*uš*⸣ ⸢*ki*⸣*-i ki-it-ti ù-ul ki-i-na*
20) *gáb-bi a-wa-te*^{MEŠ} *ša tàš-pur* UGU-*ši-na šar-ru-um-ma* LUGAL
21) *iḫ-sú-us um-ma-a la-a šal-mu gáb-bu ša táq-bu-ú*

---

22) *ù a-nu-ma* LUGAL!(LÚ) *iš-mé um-ma-a šal-ma-a-tá it-ti* LÚ URU *Qí-id-ša*
23) NINDA.ḪÁ KAŠ.M‹EŠ› ⸢*it*⸣*-ti a-ḫa-mi-iš tá-ak-kà-a-la ù* ⸢*ki*⸣*-i-na*
24) *am-mì-ni te-*⸢*ep*⸣*-*⸢*pu*⸣*-uš ki-na-an-na am-mi-ni šal-ma-a-tá*
25) *it-ti* LÚ *ša* LUGAL *iṣ-ṣé-él it-ti-šu ù šum-ma*
26) *te-te-pu-uš ki-i ki-it-ti ù tá-am-mar ṭe*$_4$*-em-ka* ⸢*ù*⸣ *ṭe*$_4$*-em-šu*

EA 162

TRANSLATION

(1–6) Speak[to Aziru] the ruler of the city of Amurru, [Thus says] the king, your lord, as follows: The ruler of the city of Byblos [has spoken] to you, he whom his brother threw out of the gate, [saying, "T]ake me and get me back into my city. [There is much silver] and I will verily give it to you. Behold the property is great, [but there]is none with me." He spoke to you thus.

(7–11) [Haven't you] been writing to the king, your lord, [sayin]g, "Your servant am I, like all the good city rulers [each] in his city"? But you are committing a crime [in ta]king a city ruler whom his brother cast out of the gate, from his city.

(12–14) And he is sitting in the city of Sidon, and you gave him over to the city rulers according to your command. Don't you know the evil of men?

(15–18) If you are in truth the servant of the king, why did you not denounce him before the king, your lord, saying, "This city ruler has written to me, saying 'Take me to yourself and reinstate me into my city' "?

(19–21) But if you have truly done (this thing), all the words of which you wrote to me concerning them are not true. Forthwith, the king thought, saying, "All that you say is not amicable."

(22–26) And now the king has heard, saying: "You are on good terms with the ruler of Qidšu." Food and strong drink have you been taking in fellowship with him? So is it true? Why are you doing thus? Why are you on good terms with the man at whom the king is angry? Also, if you have behaved trustworthily, then you will see that your relationship (with me) and his relationship (with me)

27) *i-ia-nu la-a ták-la-tá a-na a-ma-te*^{MEŠ} *ša te-ep-pu-*⸢*uš*⸣ ⸢*ul*⸣*-tu pa-na-nu*
28) *mi-nu-ú in-né-*⸢*pu*⸣*-ša-ak-ku i-na lìb-bi-*⸢*šu*⸣*-nu*
29) ⸢*ù*⸣ *ú-ul* ⸢*it*⸣*-*⸢*ti*⸣ ⸢LUGAL⸣ EN-*ka at-tá*

---

30) ⸢*a*⸣*-*⸢*mur*⸣ *an-nu-ut-ti ša* [*ú*]*-la-am-ma-du-*⸢*ka*⸣ *a-na ša-šu-nu*
31) ⸢*a*⸣*-*⸢*na*⸣ *lìb-bi i-ša-ti a-na na-sà-*⸢*ki*⸣ *ú-ba-ú-ka ù qá-lu*
32) *ù at-tá mi-im-ma tá-ra-am dan-níš*

---

33) *ù šum-ma te-ep-pu-uš* ÌR-*tá a-na* LUGAL EN-*ka*
34) *ù mi-na-a ša ú-ul ip-pu-ša-ak-ku* LUGAL *a-na kà-a-ša*
35) ⸢*šum*⸣*-*⸢*ma*⸣ *aš-šum* ⸢*mi*⸣*-im-ma tá-ra-am e-pé-ši an-mu-ut-ti*
36) *ù šum-ma tá-ša-ak-kà-an an-mu-ut-ti a-*⸢*wa*⸣*-*⸢*te*⸣^{MEŠ}
37) *sà-ar-ru-ut-ti i-na lib-bi-ka ù i-na ḫa-*⸢*aṣ*⸣*-*⸢*ṣí*⸣*-in-ni*
38) ⸢*ša*⸣ LUGAL *tá-ma-at qa-du gáb-b*[*i k*]*i-im-ti-ka*

---

39) *ù e-pu-uš* ÌR-*tá a-na* LUGAL EN-*ka* ⸢*ù*⸣ *bal-ṭa-tá*
40) *ù ti*$_{7}$*-i-de*$_{9}$ *at-tá ki-i* LUGAL *la-a ḫa-ši-iḫ*
41) *a-na* KUR *Ki-na-aḫ-ḫi gáb-bá-ša ki-i i-ra-ú-ub*

---

42) *ù ki-i tàš-pur um-ma-a lu-ma-šer*$_{9}$*-an-ni* LUGAL EN-*ia*
43) MU.KAM^{v} *ša-at-tá an-ni-tá ù lu-ul-l*[*i-kà*]
44) *i-na ša-at-ti ša-ni-ti a-na ma-ḫar* LUGAL E[N-*ia*]
45) *ia-nu-um-ma* DUMU-*ia ma-ri-ia a-*[*na* LUGAL *li-il-li-k*]*à*(?)
Rev. 46) ⸢*ù*⸣ *a-nu-ma* ⸢LUGAL⸣ ⸢EN⸣-*ka i-te-ez-bá-*⸢*ak*⸣*-*⸢*ku*⸣ [*i-na*]
47) MU. KAM^{v}-*ti ša-at-ti an-ni-ti ki-i ša táq-bu-ú*
48) ⸢*al*⸣*-kà at-tá šum-ma* DUMU-*ka šu-pur*
49) *ù tá-mar* LUGAL *ša gáb-bi* ⸢KUR⸣.⸢KUR⸣.⸢ḪÁ⸣ ⸢*i*⸣*-*⸢*bal*⸣*-lu-ṭù*
50) *a-na a-ma-ri-šu ù la-a tá-qáb-b*[*i u*]*m-ma-a*
51) *lu-ma- šer*$_{9}$ MU.KAM^{v} *ša-at-tá an-ni-tá ap-pu-na-na*
52) *a-na a-la-ki a-na ma-ḫar* LUGAL EN-*ka i-ia-nu-um-ma*
53) DUMU-*ka uš-še-er a-na* LUGAL EN-*ka ki-i-mu-*⸢*u*⸣*-ka*
54) *i-ia-nu li-il-li-kà*

---

55) *ù a-nu-ma* LUGAL EN-*ka iš-mé* ⸢*ki*⸣*-*⸢*i*⸣ ⸢*tàš*⸣*-pur a-na* LUGAL
56) *um-ma-a lu-ma-šer*$_{9}$*-an-ni* LUGAL EN-⸢*ia*⸣ ^{I}*Ḫa-an-ni*
57) LÚ.DUMU.KIN *ša* LUGAL *ša-ni-ia-nu*
58) *ù lu-še-bi-il* LÚ.MEŠ *a-*[*i*]*a-bé-e* ⸢*ša*⸣ LUGAL *a-na* ŠU-*ti-šu*
59) *a-nu-ma it-ta-al-kà-ak-ku ki-i ša táq-bu-ú*

(27–29) are incompatible. You are not trusting in the things you used to do formerly. What happened to you among them that you are not on the side of the king?

(30–32) Look at these about whom [I] must inform you: They are seeking to cast you into the flames but they are burnt. But you love property too much.

(33–38) But if you accept servitude to the king, your lord, what will the king not do for you? If because of riches, you prefer these deeds and if you harbor these treacherous things in your heart, then by the king's battleaxe you will die, with all your kin.

(39–41) But render service to the king, your lord, and you will live. And you know that the king does not desire (to come) to the whole land of Canaan when he is angry.

(42–54) And inasmuch as you have written, saying: "May the king, my lord, give me leave this year and really I will c[ome] in the second year to the presence of the king, [my] lo[rd]; if not, my son [verily will co]me [to the king]." So now, the king, your lord has released you [in] this year according to what you have said. Come yourself or send your son, and you will see the king at whose sight all the lands live. But don't say, saying, "Give me leave this year also." Moreover, if it is not possible to come before the king; send your son to the king, your lord, in your stead. If it is not possible, let him come.

(55–59) And now, the king has heard that you have written to the king, saying, "May the king, my lord, send to me Ḫanni, the envoy of the king, once again and I will verily deliver the enemies of the king into his charge."

60) *ù šu-bi-la-aš-šu-nu-ti ù* 1*-en la-a te-ez-zi-ib*
61) *i-na lìb-bi-šu-nu a-nu-ma* LUGAL ⸢EN⸣*-ka ul-te-bi-la-ak-ku*
62) *šu-mu ša* LÚ.MEŠ *a-ia-‹bé›-e ša* LUGAL *i-na lìb-bi ṭup-pí*
63) *a-na* ŠU*-ti* ^{I}*Ḫa-an-*⸢*ni*⸣ ⸢LÚ⸣ DUMU.⸢KIN⸣ *ša* LUGAL
64) *ù šu-bi-la-aš-*⸢*šu*⸣*-*⸢*nu*⸣*-*[*ti*] *a-na* LUGAL EN*-ka*
65) *ù* 1*-en la-a te-ez-zi-ib i-na* ⸢*lìb*⸣*-bi-šu-nu*
66) *ù* ŠÈR.ŠÈR URUDU *lu-ú ša-ak-nu i-na* NUNUZ GÌR.MEŠ*-šu-nu*
67) *a-mur* LÚ.MEŠ *ša tu-še-eb-bé-él a-na* LUGAL EN*-lí-ka*
68) ^{I}*Ša-ar-ru qa-du gáb-bi* DUMU.MEŠ*-šu*
69) ^{I}*Tu-u-ia*
70) ^{I}*Le-e-ia qa-du gáb-bi* DUMU.MEŠ*-šu*
71) ^{I}*Pi-iš-ia-ri qa-du gáb-bi* DUMU.MEŠ*-šu*
72) LÚ *ḫa-at-nu ša* ^{I}*Ma-an-ia qa-du* DUMU.MEŠ-⸢*šu*⸣
73) *qa-du* DAM.MEŠ*-ti-šu aš-ša-te-e-šu*
74) LÚ *Pa-ma-ḫa-a ša ḫa-an-ni-pa i-de*$_{4}$*-e-i-ú*
75) *ša-šu ‹ša› u-bá-a-ra il-tá-na-aṣ*
76) ^{I}*Da-a-šar-ti-i* ^{I}*Bá-a-lu-ú-ma*
77) ^{I}*Ni-im-ma-ḫe-e* LÚ *ḫa-bá-tú i-na* KUR *A-mu-rišu-ú*

---

78) *ù lu-ú ti-i-de*$_{9}$ *i-nu-ma ša-lim* LUGAL *ki-ma* ^{d}UTU*-aš*
79) *i-na* AN *sa-me-e* ÉRIN.MEŠ*-šu* GIŠ.GIGIR.MEŠ*-šu ma-a-du*
80) *i-na* KUR UGU*-tì a-di* KUR GAM*-ti ṣi-it* ^{d}UTU*-aš*
81) [*a-d*]*i e-re-bi* ^{d}UTU*-ši ma-gal šul-mu*

(59–64) Now he has come to you in accordance with what you said. So deliver them and don't leave out even one from among them. Now the king, your lord, has sent to you the names of the ene‹m›ies of the king, in a tablet, in the charge of Ḫanni, the ambassador of the king, so send them to the king, your lord.

(65–77) And don't leave out even one from among them. May bronze fetters be put on the ankles(?) of their feet. Look, the men whom you are to deliver to the king, your lord:

Sharru with all his sons,
Tûya,
Lêya with all his sons,
Pishiari with all his sons,
the son in law of Manya with his sons, (and) with his wives,
the warrior who knows sacrilege, him who always insults the foreigner,
Dāshartî,
Baʿluma,
Nimmaḫê, the robber in the land of Amurru.

(78–81) And may you be apprised that it is well with the king, like the sun god in heaven; his troops and his chariots being many; from the Upper Land to the Lower Land, the coming forth of the sun [t]o the entering in of the sun, it is all very well.

EA 163

TRANSCRIPTION

Obv. 00) [..................................]

––––

01) [.......................]*pa-na* ⸢SIG$_5$⸣.⸢GA⸣

02) [.......................*gá*]*b-bi*

03) [.......................*a-n*]*a a-ma-ri-šu*

04) [.......................*a-šu*]*m be-lu-ti*

05) [.......................(traces)]

Rev.

01) [*ù lu-ú ti-i-de*$_4$ *i-nu-ma ša-lim* LUGAL]

02) [*ki-ma* ^{d}UTU-*aš i-na* AN] ⸢*sa*⸣-⸢*me*⸣ [ÉRIN.MEŠ-*šu*]

03) [GIŠ.GIGIR.MEŠ-*šu ma-a-d*]*u i-*[*na*] KUR ⸢UGU⸣-⸢*tim*⸣

04) [*a-di* KUR GAM-*tim ṣi-i*]*t* ^{d}UTU-*aš*

05) [*a-di e-re-bi* ^{d}UTU-]*ši ma-gal šul-mu*

––––––

EA 163

TRANSLATION

Obv. 00) [.................................]

----

01) [.......................]pleasant face
02) [........................a]ll
03) [........................t]o see him
04) [........................because] of lordship
05) [........................(*traces*)]

Rev.
01) [And may you be apprised that the king is well]
02) [like the sun in] heaven; [his troops, (and)]
03) [and his chariots being vas]t fr[om] the Upper Land
04) [to the Lower Land, the going for]th of the Sun
05) [to the entering in of the Su]n it is all very well

EA 164

TRANSCRIPTION

Obv. 01) ⸢*a*⸣*-na* ^{I}*Tù-u-tù* EN-*ia a-bi-*⸢*ia*⸣
02) *um-ma* ^{I}*A-zi-ri* ÌR-*ka-ma*
03) *a-na* GÌR.MEŠ EN-*ia am-qut*

---

04) ^{I}*Ḫa-ti-ip i-il-la-kà-am*
05) *ù ú-ub-bá-*⸢*la*⸣*-am a-ma-te*^{MEŠ}
06) LUGAL EN-*ia bá-*⸢*nu*⸣*-*⸢*ta*$_{5}$⸣ *ù* DUG.GA-*ta*
07) *ù ḫa-ad-ia-ku ma-gal ma-gal*
08) *ù* KUR-*ia* ⸢*ù*⸣ ŠEŠ.MEŠ-*ia*
09) LÚ.MEŠ ÌR *ša* LUGAL EN-*ia*
10) *ù* LÚ.MEŠ ⸢ÌR⸣ ^{I}*Tù-u-tù* EN-*ia*
11) *ḫa-du*$_{4}$*-*⸢*ni*$_{7}$⸣ ⸢*ma*⸣*-*⸢*gal*⸣ *ma-gal*
12) *i-nu-ma i-*⸢*il*⸣*-la-kà-am*
13) *ša-ar-ru ša* LUGAL EN-*ia*
14) UGU-*ia iš-*⸢*tu*⸣ *a-ma-te*^{MEŠ}
15) EN-*ia* DINGIR-*ia* ^{d}⸢UTU⸣-*ia*
16) *ù iš-tu* ⸢*a*⸣*-ma-*⸢*te*⸣[^{MEŠ}] ^{I}*Tù-u-tù*
17) EN-*ia* ⸢*la*⸣ *a-pa-aṭ-ṭar*

---

18) EN-*ia* ⸢a⸣*-nu-um-ma* ^{I}*Ḫa-ti-ip*
19) *iz-za-az it-ti-ia*
20) *a-na-ku ù šu-ú-ut ni-il-la-ak*
21) EN-*ia šàr* KUR *Ḫa-at-ti*$_{7}$
Lo.ed. 22) *i-il-la-kà-am i-na* KUR *Nu-*⸢*ḫa*⸣-⸢aš⸣-⸢*še*⸣
23) ⸢*ù*⸣ *la i-le-eʾ-e a-la-*⸢*kà*⸣
24) [*l*]*i-ip-tu*$_{4}$*-ur šàr* KUR *Ḫa-*⸢*at*⸣*-ti*$_{7}$
Rev. 25) *ù a-nu-um-ma i-il-la-*⸢*ak*⸣
26) *a-na-ku ù* ^{I}*Ḫa-ti-ip*

EA 164

TRANSLATION

(1–3) To Tutu, my lord, my father: the message of Aziru, your servant. At the feet of my lord have I fallen.

(4–17) Ḥatip has come, and he has brought the lovely, sweet words of the king, my lord, and I have rejoiced very greatly. Also, my land and my colleagues (brothers), the servants of the king, my lord and the servants of Tutu, my lord, rejoiced very greatly. Since the breath of the king, my lord has come to me. From the words of my lord, my deity, my sun god, and from the words of Tutu, my lord, I do not deviate.

(18–20) My lord, now Ḥatip is staying with me. He and I will come (together).

(21–26) My lord, the king of the land of Ḫatti, has come to the land of Nuǵasse and I am unable to come. Let the king of the land of Ḫatti depart, and then I will come and also Ḥatip.

---

27) LUGAL EN-*ia a-ma-te*^{MEŠ}*-ia*
28) *li-iš-me-e* EN-*ia pal-ḫa-ku*
29) *iš-tu pa-ni* LUGAL EN-*ia*
30) *ù iš-tu pa-ni* ^{I}*Tù-u-tù*
31) *ù a-nu-um-ma* DINGIR.MEŠ-*ia*
32) *ù* LÚ.DUMU.KIN-*ri-ia ù lu-ú-*⸢*ta*$_5$⸣-⸢*am*⸣-⸢*mi*⸣
33) ^{I}*Tù-u-tù ù* LÚ.MEŠ GAL-*bu-te*⸢^{MEŠ}⸣
34) *ša* LUGAL EN-*ia ù lu-ú a-al-*⸢*la*⸣*-ak*

---

35) *ù ki-i-ia-am* ^{I}*Tù-u-tù*
36) *ù* LUGAL EN-*ia ù* LÚ.MEŠ GAL-*bu-te*^{MEŠ}
37) *šum-ma-mi ni-iš-ku-un*!(UK?) *mi-im-ma*
38) UGU ^{I}*A-zi-ri ša la* SIG$_5$-*iq*
39) *ù ki-i-ia-am tu*$_4$*-ut-ta-mi*
40) *a-na* DINGIR.MEŠ-*ia ù a-na* ^{d}A
41) *ù a-nu-um-ma a-na-ku*
42) *ù* ^{I}*Ḫa-ti-ip* ^{LÚ}ÌR LUGAL *bá-nu*

---

43) ^{I}*Tù-u-tù lu-ú ti-i-de*$_4$
44) ⸢*i*⸣*-nu-ma a-la-kà-ak-ku*

(27–34) May the king, my lord, heed my words. My lord, I fear before the presence of the king, my lord and before the presence of Tutu. And now, my deities and my envoys, I verily swear. Tutu and the senior officials of the king, my lord, I will verily come.

(35–42) So thus, Tutu and the king, my lord, and the senior officials (must swear): "If we have imputed anything that is unseemly to Aziru." So thus you must swear by my deities and by Aten. And then I and Ḥatip the servant of the king are guiltless.

(43–44) Tutu, may you be apprised that I will come to you.

EA 165

TRANSCRIPTION

Obv. 01) [*a-n*]*a* L[UGAL EN-*ia* DINGIR-*ia* ^{d}UTU-*ia*]
02) *um-ma* ⸢^{I}⸣[*A-zi-ri* ÌR-*ka-ma*]
03) 7-*šu u* ⸢7⸣[-*šu a-na* GÌR.MEŠ EN-*ia am-qut*]

---

04) EN-*ia* DINGIR-*i*[*a* ^{d}UTU-*ia*]
05) *mi-i-na-am a*[*p-pu-na-ma ú-bá-ʾa-i*]
06) *pa-ni* LUGAL EN-*i*[*a* ^{d}UTU-*ia*]
07) *bá-nu-ta ú-bá-ʾa*[-*i a-ma-ra*]
08) *a-di dá-ri-ti ù* [*a-na-ku*]
09) ⸢*ù*⸣ ^{I}*Bá-a-lu-ia* ⸢LÚ⸣.⸢MEŠ⸣ [ÌR-*ka*]

---

10) KUR LUGAL EN-*ia a-na-aṣ-ṣú-ur*
11) *ù pa-ni-ia a-na* LÚ.MEŠ ÌR-*tu*$_{4}$
12) *ša* LUGAL EN-*ia i-na šul-mi*
13) ⸢*pa*⸣-⸢*ni*⸣ LUGAL EN-*ia bá-nu-ti lu-ú a*-[*mur*]

---

14) ⸢EN⸣-*ia a-nu-um-ma a-na-ku*
15) ⸢*ù*⸣ ^{I}*Ḫa-ti-ip ni-il-la*-⸢*ak*⸣
16) ⸢*ù*⸣ *li-i-de*$_{4}$ ⸢EN⸣-*ia i-nu-ma*
17) [*kà*]-*aš-dá-ku* ⸢*i*⸣-⸢*na*⸣ *ḫa-mu*[*t-i*]*š*

---

18) ⸢LUGAL⸣ ⸢KUR⸣ ⸢*Ḫa*⸣-⸢*at*⸣-⸢*ti*$_{7}$⸣ [*i-na* KUR *Nu-ḫa-aš-še*]
19) *a-ši-ib ù pal*[-*ḫa-ku iš-tu pa-ni-šu*]
20) *as-sur*$_{x}$(ṢUR)-*r*[*i-m*]*i* [*i-na* KUR MAR.TU]
21) [*i*]-*na* KUR-[*š*]*u š*[*a* LUGAL EN-*ia i-la-kà-am*]

Lo.ed. 22) [*ù*] UGU *a-ma*-[*ti an-ni-ti*]
23) ⸢*iz*⸣-⸢*za*⸣-⸢*az*⸣ *l*[*i-ip-ṭu*$_{4}$-*ur*]
Rev. 24) ⸢*ù*⸣ *li-tu*$_{4}$-*ur* ⸢*i*⸣-⸢*na*⸣ [KUR-*šu*]
25) ⸢*ù*⸣ *a-nu-um-ma a-al*-[*la-kà-am*]
26) ⸢*a*⸣-[*na*]-⸢*ku*⸣ ⸢*ù*⸣ ^{I}⸢*Ḫa*⸣-⸢*ti*⸣-⸢*ip*⸣ [*a-na-ku*]
27) ⸢LÚ⸣.⸢ÌR⸣ ⸢LUGAL⸣ *bá-ni* ⸢*ma*⸣-⸢*gal*⸣ ⸢*ma*⸣-[*gal*]

EA 165

TRANSLATION

(1–3) [T]o the k[ing, my lord, my god, my sun god]; the message of [Aziru, your servant: Seven times and seven [times have I fallen at the feet of my lord.]

(4–9) My lord, [m]y god, [my sun god,] what, m[oreover, do I seek?] The beautiful face of the king, m[y] lord, [my sun god] do I seek [to behold] forever and [I] and Baʿluya are [your] ser[vants].

(10–13) I protect the land of the king, my lord, and my intention (face) is to the service of the king, my lord. In safety would I l[ook] on the beautiful [f]ac[e] of the king, my lord.

(14–17) My lord, now, I and Ḥatip will come so may the my lord be apprised that I will arrive with all due alacr[ity].

(18–21) The king of the land of Ḫatti is situated [in the land of Nuǵasse,] and [I am] af[raid of him], lest [he come to the land of Amurru, t]o the land [of the king, my lord].

(22–27) [So] because of [this] matter, I am standing pat. L[et him depart,] and let him return to [his own country] and then I will [come], I and Ḥatip. [I] am a [ser]vant of the most gracious king.

---

28) [EN-*ia*] ⸢*mi*⸣-⸢*im*⸣-⸢*ma*⸣ ⸢*i*⸣-⸢*na*⸣ ⸢^{UZU}⸣⸢ŠÀ⸣ ⸢EN⸣[-*ia*]
29) [*la ta-ša-kà*]-*an* ⸢*kà*⸣-*aš*-⸢*dá*⸣-*ku*
30) ⸢*pa*⸣-⸢*ni*⸣-⸢*ia*⸣-⸢*ma*⸣ ⸢*a*⸣-⸢*na*⸣ ⸢LUGAL⸣ KUR *Ḫa-at*-⸢*ti*$_7$⸣
31) ⸢*ù*⸣ [*a-n*]*u*[-*um-m*]*a kà-aš-dá*-⸢*ku*⸣
32) ⸢*a*⸣-⸢*na*⸣ ⸢*a*⸣-[*ma-ri pa*-]*ni* ^{d}UTU ⸢EN⸣-⸢*ia*⸣
33) ⸢EN⸣-⸢*ia*⸣ [*a-na-ku i*]-*na* [URU *Tu*$_4$-*ni*]-*ip*
34) *aš-bá-ku* ⸢*ù*⸣ *i-la-kà*-[*am* LUGAL] KUR *Ḫa-a*[*t-t*]*i*$_7$
35) *i-na* KUR MAR.TU KUR LU[GA]L EN-*ia*
36) *ki*-⸢*i*⸣ *la ú*-⸢*wa*⸣-*aš-šar*-⸢*an*⸣-⸢*ni*⸣
37) LUGAL EN-*ia a-na na-ṣa-ar* KUR-⸢*šu*⸣
38) *ù* ⸢*i*⸣-⸢*na*⸣-*an-na i-na* KUR *Nu-ḫa-aš-še*
39) *a-ši-ib* 2 1-*tì* KASKAL-*nu* ⸢*i*⸣-*na* URU *Tu*$_4$-*ni*-⸢*ip*⸣
40) *ù pal-ḫa-ku iš-tu ša-ḫa-ṭì-šu*
41) URU *Tu*$_4$-*ni-ip li-ip-ṭu*$_4$-*ur*

---

42) ⸢*ša*⸣-⸢*ni*⸣-⸢*tam*⸣ EN-*ia a-na* ⸢LÚ⸣.MEŠ ⸢*sa*⸣[-*ar-ru-ti*]
43) *la* ⸢*te*⸣-*še-em-me-e a*-⸢*na*⸣[-*ku ù* ŠEŠ.MEŠ-*ia*]
44) ⸢*ù*⸣ DUMU.MEŠ-*ia* ⸢LÚ⸣.⸢MEŠ⸣ [ÌR *ša* LUGAL EN-*ia*]
45) *a-di dá-ri*-[*ti*]

(28–41) [My lord, don't ta]ke anything to heart. I am coming. My concern is the king of the land of Ḫatti, but now I am coming to s[ee the fa]ce of the sun god, my lord. My lord, [I] am located in [the city of Tun]ip and [the king] of the land of Ḫatti is coming to the land of Amurru, the land of the king, my lord. If only the king, my lord, would permit me to guard his land. But now he (the king of Ḫatti) is located in Nuǵasse, two one day marches from Tunip and I am afraid of his attacking the city of Tunip. May he depart!

(42–45) Furthermore, my lord, don't listen to the tr[aitorous] men. I [and my brothers] and my sons are ser[vants of the king, my lord,] forever!

EA 166

TRANSCRIPTION

Obv. 01) [*a-*]⸢*na*⸣ ^{I}*Ḫa-*⸢*a*⸣*-i* ŠEŠ-*ia*
02) *um-ma* ^{I}*A-zi-ri* ŠEŠ-*ka-ma*
03) *a-na* UGU-*ka lu-ú šul-mu*
04) *ù iš-tu* ÉRIN.MEŠ *ṣa-bi pí-ṭá-ti*$_{7}$
05) *ša* LUGAL EN-*ia ma-gal lu-ú šul-mu*

---

06) *mi-i-na-am ap-pu-na-ma*
07) *ú-bá-ʾi-i pa-ni* LUGAL EN-*ia*
08) *bá-nu-ta ú-bá-ʾi-i*
09) *a-na-ku ù* DUMU.MEŠ-*ia*
10) *ù* ŠEŠ.MEŠ-*ia gáb-bu* LÚ.MEŠ ÌR
11) *ša* LUGAL EN-*ia bá-ni*

---

12) *a-nu-um-ma a-na-ku ù* ^{I}*Ḫa-ti-ip*
13) *ni-il-la-kà-am i-na-an-na-ma*
14) *i-na ḫa-mut-iš* ^{I}*Ḫa-a-i*
15) ^{UZU}*lìb-bá-ku-nu lu-ú i-de*$_{4}$
16) *i-nu-ma kà-aš-dá-ku*

---

17) [*i*]*š-tu a-ma-te*^{MEŠ} EN-*ia*
Lo.ed. 18) ⸢*la*⸣ *a-pa-aṭ-ṭar*
19) *ù iš-tu a-ma-te*^{MEŠ}*-ku-nu*
Rev. 20) ⸢*a*⸣-⸢*na*⸣-*ku* LÚ.ÌR *ša* EN-*ia*

---

21) LUGAL KUR *Ḫa-at-ti*$_{7}$ *i-na* KUR *N*[*u*]-⸢*ḫa*⸣-*aš-še*
22) *a-ši-ib ù pal-ḫa-ku*
23) *iš-tu pa-ni-šu as-sur*$_{\text{x}}$(ṢUR)-*ri-mi*
24) *i-na* KUR MAR.TU *i-la-‹kà›-am*
25) *ù šum-ma* URU *Tù-ni-ip*
26) *iš-ḫi-iṭ-ma* 2 1-*tì* KASKAL-*nu i-na a-šar a-ši-ib*
27) *ù pal-ḫa-ku iš-tu pa-ni-šu*
28) *ù* UGU *a-ma-ti šu-wa-ti*
29) *iz-za-az a-di pa-ṭá-ri-šu*

EA 166

TRANSLATION

(1–5) [T]o Ḫaʿi, my brother, the message of Aziru, your brother: May it be well with you and with the troops of the regular army of the king, my lord, may it be very well indeed.

(6–11) What, moreover, do I seek? It is the beneficent face (presence) of the king, my lord that I seek. I and my sons and my brothers, all are servants of the king, my beneficent lord.

(12–16) Now I and Ḥatip are coming immediately, with haste. Ḫaʿi, may your heart know that I am coming.

(17–20) [F]rom the words of my lord I do not depart and from your (pl.) words. I am the servant of my lord.

(21–29) The king of the land of Ḫatti is located in the land of N[u]ǵasse and I am afraid of him in case he might ‹co›me to the land of Amurru. And if he attacked the city of Tunip, it is only two day-marches from the place where he is located. So I am afraid of him and because of that matter, I am standing pat until his departure.

---

30) *ù a-nu-um-ma i-il-la-kà-am*
31) *i-na ḫa-⸢mut⸣-iš-ma*
32) *a-na-ku ù* ᴵ⸢*Ḫa*⸣*-ti-ip*

(30–32) And then I am coming quickly, I and Ḥatip.

EA 167

TRANSCRIPTION

Obv. 01) [*a-na* ^{I}*Tù-u-tù* EN-*ia a-bi-ia*]
02) [*um-ma* ^{I}*A-zi-ri* ÌR-*ka-ma*]
03) [*a-na* GÌR.MEŠ EN-*ia am-qut*]
04) [*a-na muḫ-ḫi* EN-*ia lu-ú-šul-mu*]

[————————————————————————]

05) [*iš-tu a-ma-te*^{MEŠ} LUGAL EN-*ia*]
06) [*la a-pa-*]⸢*aṭ*⸣-*ṭar*[*ù iš-tu a-ma-te*^{MEŠ}-*ka*]
07) [*la a-pa-*]*aṭ-ṭar*[*a-di dáß-ri-ti*]

---

08) [*mi-i-n*]*a-am ap-*⸢*pu*⸣-[*na-m*]*a* [*ú-bá-ʾa-i*]
09) [*pa-ni* LU]GAL *bá-nu-*⸢*ta*⸣ ⸢*ú*⸣[*-bá-ʾa-i a-ma-ra*]
10) [*a-na-ku* ÌR-]⸢*ka*⸣ ⸢*ù*⸣ [DUMU-*ka*]

---

11) [LUGAL] KUR *Ḫa-at-ti*$_7$ [*i-na* KUR *Nu-ḫa-aš-*]*še*
12) [*a-š*]*i-ib ù l*[*i-ip-tu*$_4$*-u*]*r*
13) ⸢*ù*⸣ *a-nu-um-ma* ⸢*i*⸣-⸢*na*⸣-[*an-na-ma*]
14) *a-na-ku ù* ^{I}[*Ḫa-ti*]-⸢*ip*⸣
15) *ni-il-la-*⸢*kà*⸣-⸢*am*⸣ [*i-na ḫa-mut-i*]*š*

---

16) *mi-im-ma-a*[*m-ma i-na* ^{UZU}*lìb -bi-ka*]
Lo.ed. 17) ⸢*la*⸣ *ta-ša-*⸢*kà*⸣-⸢*an*⸣ ⸢*kà*⸣-⸢*aš*⸣-⸢*dá*⸣-[*ku*]
18) ⸢*i*⸣-*na šul-mi ù pa-ni* E[N-*ia*]
19) [*l*]*u-ú a-mur bá-nu-ta*$_5$*-am*

Rev. 20) [*i-*]*na* ⸢KUR⸣*Nu-ḫa-aš-še* LUGAL KUR *Ḫa-at-*[*ti*$_7$]
21) ⸢*a*⸣-⸢*ši*⸣-⸢*ib*⸣ *ù pal-ḫa-ku iš-tu pa-ni-š*[*u*]
22) 2 1-⸢*en*⸣ ⸢KASKAL⸣-*nu i-na a-šar a-ši-ib*
23) ⸢*iš*⸣-⸢*tu*⸣ ⸢URU⸣ ⸢*Tu*$_4$⸣-*ni-ip ù pal-ḫa-ku*
24) ⸢*ù*⸣ ⸢*li*⸣-*ip-tu*$_4$*-ur ù kà-aš-dá-ku*

---

25) ⸢*as*⸣-*sur*$_{\text{x}}$(ṢUR)-*ri an-na-*⸢*kà*⸣-*am i-na* KUR MAR.TU
26) ⸢KUR⸣ ⸢EN⸣-⸢*ia*⸣ ⸢*i*⸣-⸢*il*⸣-*la-kà-am-ma*
27) ⸢*ù*⸣ ⸢*pal*⸣-⸢*ḫa*⸣-⸢*ku*⸣ ⸢*iš*⸣-*tu* KUR EN-*ia*

EA 167

TRANSLATION

(1–4) [To Tutu, my lord, my father; the message of Aziru your servant: At the feet of my lord have I fallen. May it be well with my lord.]

(5–7) [From the words of the king, my lord, I do not de]part[and from your words I do not de]part [forever].

(8–10) [Wh]at, more[ove]r, [do I seek?] [To see] the beautiful [face of the ki]ng [do] I [seek]. [I am] your [servant] and [your son].

(11–15) [The king of] the land of Ḫatti [is loc]ated [in the land of Nuǵas]se. Let him [depar]t and then [verily(?)] I and [Ḥat]ip will co[me with alacri]ty.

16–19) Don't take anythi[ng to heart]. I am coming. In safety may I see the beautiful face of [my] lo[rd].

(20–24) In the land of Nuǵasse, the king of the land of Ḫat[ti] is located and I am afraid of him. In the place where he is located it is two day marches from the city of Tunip so I am afraid. Let him depart and I will come.

(25–27) Let him surely not come here to the land of Amurru, the land of my lord. So I am afraid for the land of my lord.

---

28) ^{I}⸢*Tù*⸣-*u*-⸢*tù*⸣ ⸢*i*⸣-⸢*na*⸣-⸢*an*⸣-⸢*na*⸣ *a-mur*
29) ⸢^{UZU}⸣⸢*lìb*⸣-⸢*bi*⸣-⸢*ia*⸣ *ù a-ma-*⸢*te*⸣*-ia*
30) ⸢*am*⸣-⸢*ma*⸣-*la* ⸢*i*⸣-⸢*na*⸣ *ti-*⸢*ir*⸣*-ṣí* ⸢^{UZU}⸣⸢*lìb*⸣[*-bi-ka*]
31) [*ik-ta-*]*aš-*⸢*du*⸣ ⸢*it*⸣-⸢*ti*⸣ ^{I}*Tù-u-tù* ⸢EN⸣[*-ia*]
32) [EN-*ia*] ⸢*lu*⸣-⸢*ú*⸣ ⸢*ḫa*⸣-⸢*dì*⸣-*ia-ta*
33) [*i-nu-ma*] *kà-aš-*⸢*dá*⸣*-ku a-na-ku*
34) [*a-na a-ma-a-*]*ri pa-ni* ⸢LUGAL⸣ [EN-*ia*].

(28–34) Tutu, now look: My intention and my words in accordance with the indication of [your] hea[rt, have rea]ched Tutu, [my] lord. My lord, may you rejoice [because] I am coming myself [to see] the face of the king, [my lord.]

EA 168

TRANSCRIPTION

Obv. 01) [*a-na*] ⸢LUGAL⸣ ⸢EN⸣-⸢*ia*⸣ ⸢DINGIR⸣-⸢*ia*⸣ ^{d}[UTU-*ia*]
02) ⸢*um*⸣-⸢*ma*⸣ ^{I}*A*-⸢*zi*⸣-⸢*ri*⸣ ⸢ÌR⸣-⸢*ka*⸣-[*ma*]
03) 7-*šu u* ⸢7⸣-⸢*šu*⸣ ⸢*a*⸣-⸢*na*⸣ GÌR.MEŠ [EN-*ia* DINGIR-*ia*] ⸢^{d}⸣UTU-⸢*ia*⸣ ⸢*am*⸣-⸢*qut*⸣

---

04) ⸢^{d}⸣UTU EN-*ia* ⸢DINGIR⸣-⸢*ia*⸣
05) [*kà-aš-*]⸢*dá*⸣-⸢*ku*⸣ ⸢*i*⸣-⸢*na*⸣ ⸢*šul*⸣-⸢*mi*⸣
06) [*a-na a-ma*]-⸢*a*⸣[-*ri*]⸢*pa*⸣[-*ni*]
07) [LUGAL EN-*i*]*a* ⸢*ù*⸣ LÚ ⸢DUMU⸣ ⸢KIN⸣-[*ia*]
08) [*ù* ^{I}*Ḫa*-]*ti*-⸢*ip*⸣ ⸢*i*⸣-*kà*-⸢*aš*-⸣[*ša-du*$_{4}$-*ni*$_{7}$]
09) [*i-na š*]*ul-mi* ⸢*ù*⸣ ⸢*ú*⸣-⸢*nu*⸣-⸢*tu*$_{4}$⸣[^{MEŠ} *ša* LUGAL] EN-*ia*
10) [*i-na* GI]Š.⸢MÁ⸣.⸢MEŠ⸣ ⸢*kà*⸣-⸢*aš*⸣-*du*$_{4}$-*ni*$_{7}$
11) [*i-na*]⸢*šul*⸣-⸢*mi*⸣-⸢*iš*⸣ ⸢*i*⸣-⸢*na*⸣ ⸢KUR⸣ [LUGAL EN-*ia*]
12) [...*š*]*i*-⸢*id*⸣ *ù* [..............]

Rev. 01) [............................*š*]*u-n*[*u*]
02) [..........................]⸢*ep*⸣-*pu-š*[*a*]
03) [..............*a-na ia-*]*ši iq*[-*bi*]
04) [..........................]*il-l*[*a-ak*]
05) [................] (l. 9 from obverse)
06) [..................................]
07) [............................*a-na-ku*]
08) [*ù* ŠEŠ.MEŠ-*ia ù*] ⸢DUMU⸣.M[EŠ-]⸢*ia*⸣
09) [LÚ.MEŠ] ⸢ÌR⸣(?) [*ša* LUGAL] EN-*ia*
10) [DINGIR]-⸢*ia*⸣?[..........] LUGAL EN-[*ia*]
11) [................] (l. 3 from obverse)
12) [...EN-*i*]*a* ⸢DINGIR⸣-*ia* ⸢*ip*⸣[........*ù*]

Up.ed. 13) ⸢*li*⸣-*ma-lik-ku pí i-pu*-⸢*ša*⸣[....]

---

14) [*a*]-⸢*di*⸣ *kà-ša-di-ia a-na* ⸢*pa*⸣-⸢*ni*⸣[-*ka*]

Lft.ed. 15) [*t*]*ù-bal*-[*li-iṭ*...................................]
16) *ù* LÚ.D[UMU.KIN-*ia*............................]

EA 168

TRANSLATION

Obv.

(1–3) [To] the king, my lord, my god, [my sun god]; the message of Aziru, your servant: Seven times and seven times at the feet of [my lord, my god], my sun god, have I fallen.

(4–12) O sun god, my lord, my god, I will [arri]ve safely [to beho]ld the fa[ce of the king, m]y[lord], and my envoy [and Ḫa]tip will arri[ve sa]fely and the assets [of the king,] my lord, will arrive [sa]fely [by s]hips in the land [of the king, my lord…] and […].

Rev.

(1–6)) […t]hem […] I will do […to m]e he sa[id…]he will [go…]

(7–16) […I and my brothers and] my son[s] are [se]rvants of the king, [my] lord […m]y [lord, my god has d[one…so] may they take counsel (and) I will declare […]

[un]til my arrival before [you]

(15–16) [Y]ou gi[ve life…and [my] am[bassador…………………]

EA 169

TRANSCRIPTION

Obv. 00) [*a-na* LUGAL EN-*ia* DINGIR-*ia* ^{d}UTU-*ia*]
01) [*um-ma* (...) ÌR-*ka-ma*]
02) [*a-na muḫ-ḫi* EN-*ia lu-ú š*]*ul-mu*
03) [7-*šu ù* 7-*šu a-na* GÌR.MEŠ EN-*ia am-qut*]

---

04) [..................]*sa-a-nu ia-nu*
05) [............LUGAL]⸢EN⸣-*ni*
06) [*a-na pa-ni* LUGAL *n*]*i-dag-gal*
07) [*at*-]⸢*ta*⸣ ⸢*tù*⸣[-*bal*-]*la-ṭá-an*-⸢*ni*⸣
08) [*ù*] *at-ta tù-uš-mi*-⸢*it*⸣-⸢*an*⸣-⸢*ni*⸣
09) ⸢*a*⸣-⸢*na*⸣ *pa-ni-ka-ma a-dag-gal*
10) ⸢*ù*⸣ *at-ta-ma* EN-*ia*
11) *ù* EN-*ia li-iš-mé-mì*
12) *a-na* LÚ.MEŠ ÌR-*šu* ^{I}*A-zi-ri* LÚ.ÌR-*ka*
13) *i-na aš-ra-nu la tù-wa-aḫ-ḫi-ir-šu*
14) *ar-ḫi-iš uš-še-ra-aš-šu*
15) *ù* KUR.MEŠ *ša* LUGAL EN-*ni li-na-aṣ*-⸢*ṣár*⸣

---

16) *ša-ni-tam a-na* ^{I}*Tù-ut-tù* EN-*ia*
17) *ši-me a-ma-te*^{MEŠ} LÚ.MEŠ KUR *Nu-ḫa-aš-še*
18) *a-na ia-ši iq-bu-ni*$_{7}$
Lo.ed. 19) ⸢*a*⸣-*bu-ka-mi i-na* KÙ.GI.MEŠ
20) ⸢*ta*⸣-*ap-šur-šu*
21) ⸢*a*⸣-⸢*na*⸣ LUGAL KUR *Mi-iṣ-ri*

EA 169

TRANSLATION

(1–3) [To the king (?), my lord, my god, my sun god; message of (...), your servant. With my lord may it be well. Seven times and seven times at the feet of my lord, have I fallen.]

(4–10) [............] there is no [......the king(?)], our lord. [It is to the king that w]e look. [Y]ou can keep me alive [and] you can put me to death. It is to you that I look and it is you who are my lord.

(11–15) So, may my lord give heed to his servants. As for Aziru, your servant, do not delay him there; send him swiftly and may he protect the lands of he king, our lord.

(16–21) Furthermore, to Tutu, my lord: Hear the words of the men of Nuǵasse; they said to me, "As for your father, you ransomed him for gold to the king of the land of Egypt.

Rev. 22) *ù ma-te*$_9$-⸢*e*⸣-*mi ú-wa-šar-šu*
23) *iš*-⸢*tu*⸣ ⸢KUR⸣ *Mi*-⸢*iṣ*⸣-*ri*
24) ⸢*ù*⸣ ⸢*gáb*⸣-*bá* KUR.KUR.MEŠ *ù gáb-bá*
25) ⸢LÚ⸣.MEŠ ÉRIN.MEŠ *Sú-u-tù*
26) ⸢*ki*⸣-⸢*a*⸣-⸢am⸣-⸢*ma*⸣ ⸢*iq*⸣-*bu-ni*$_7$
27) ⸢*la*⸣-⸢*a*⸣-*mi* [*ú*]*uṣ-ṣí-mi*
28) ⸢^{I}⸣⸢*A*⸣-⸢*zi*⸣-⸢*ri*⸣ ⸢*iš*⸣-⸢*tu*⸣ KUR *Mi*-⸢*iṣ*⸣-⸢*ri*⸣
29) ⸢*ù*⸣ ⸢*i*⸣-*na-an-na* LÚ.MEŠ *Sú-u-tù*
30) ⸢*iš*⸣-⸢*tu*⸣ KUR.MEŠ ⸢*i*⸣-*pa*-⸢*ṭá*⸣-*ru*-⸢*ni*$_7$⸣
31) ⸢*ù*⸣ ⸢*ut*⸣-⸢*ta*⸣-*na-á*ʾ-*i*-⸢*du*⸣-*ni*$_7$
32) *a*-⸢*na*⸣ ⸢*muḫ*⸣-⸢*ḫi*⸣-*ia* ⸢*a*⸣-⸢*bu*⸣-⸢*ka*⸣-⸢*mi*⸣
33) [*i*]-⸢*na*⸣ KUR ⸢*Mi*⸣-⸢*iṣ*⸣-⸢*ri*⸣ *a-ši*-⸢*ib*⸣
34) [*ù*] *ni*-⸢*ip*⸣-⸢*pu*⸣-⸢*uš*⸣ ⸢*nu*⸣-⸢*kúr*⸣-⸢*ta*⸣ *it-ti*-⸢*ka*⸣
35) [..........]⸢*ma*⸣ ⸢LÚ⸣.⸢MEŠ⸣ *šu-nu ù ši-me*
36) [*ia-ši* ^{I}*Tù-ut-t*]*ù* EN-*ia* ^{I}*A-zi-ri*
37) [*ar-ḫi-iš uš-š*]*e-ra-am*
38) [.........LÚ MÁŠK]IM.MEŠ
39) [........KUR]⸢*Nu*⸣-*ḫa-aš-še*
40) [...............................]
41) [...............................]
42) [...............................]
43) [...............................]
44) [...............................]

Lft.ed. 45) [.................]*li-iz-zi-iz*
46) [................*nu*-]KÚR ⸢*it*⸣-⸢*ti*⸣-⸢*ka*⸣
47) [.............]⸢*ip*⸣[...]x[...*gá*]*b-bi*

(22–43) so when will he release him from the land of Egypt?" And all the countries and all the Sutu warriors spoke thus: "Aziru will never come forth from the land of Egypt!" And now the Sutu men are leaving the territories and they are continually informing me: "Your father is staying in Egypt [so] we will wage war against you." [....] those men. So listen [to me (?), Tut]u, my lord, [re]lease Aziru [in a hurry...the commi]ssioners [...] the land of Nuǵasse [.........................].

(45–47) [.........]let him take a stand [......hosti]lity against you [....a]ll.

EA 170

TRANSCRIPTION

Obv. 01) *a-na* LUGAL EN-*ni*
02) *um-ma* ^{Id}IŠKUR-*lu-ia ù um-ma*
03) ^{I}*Be-ti*-DINGIR *a-na* GÌR.MEŠ EN-*ni ni-am-qut*
04) *a-na muḫ-ḫi* EN-*ni lu-ú šul-mu*
05) *ù an-na- kam*^{V} *iš-tu* KUR.MEŠ-*šu*
06) *ša* EN-*ni dan-níš šul-mu*

---

07) EN-*ni mi-im-ma-am-ma*
08) *i-na lìb-bi-ka la ta-ša-kán*
09) *lìb-bá-ka la tù-uš-ma-ra-aṣ*
10) EN-*ni ki-i-me-e te-le-é*ʾ*-e-mi*
11) *ù pa-ni-šu-nu ṣa-bat* \\ *zu-zi-la-ma-an*
12) *ki-i-me-e i-na aš-ra-nu*
13) *la ú-wa-aḫ-ḫé-ru-ka*

---

14) *ša-ni-tam* ÉRIN.MEŠ KUR *Ḫa-at-ti*$_{7}$
15) ^{I}*Lu-pa-ak-ku il*$_{5}$*-te-qú-nim*
16) URU.ḪI.A KUR *Am-qí ù iš-tu*
17) ^{I}*A-ad-du-mi il*$_{5}$*-te-qú-nim-mi*
Lo.ed. 18) *ù be-lí-ni li-i-de*$_{4}$

---

19) *ša-ni-tam ki-a-am ni-ìš-te-mé*
Rev. 20) ^{I}*Zi-dá-na*
21) *il*$_{5}$*-li- kam*^{V}*-mi*
22) *ù* 9 x 10,000(SIG$_{7}^{V}$).MEŠ ÉRIN.MEŠ GÌR
23) *it-ti-šu ša il*$_{5}$*-li-kam*^{V}
24) *ù a-ma-ta la nu-tar-ri-iṣ*
25) *šum-ma i-na ki-it-ti i-bá-aš-šu-nim*
26) *ù i-kà-ša*$_{10}$*-du-nim*
27) *i-na* KUR *Nu-ḫa-aš-še*
28) *ù* ^{I}*Be-ti*-DINGIR
29) *a-šap-pár a-na pa-ni-šu*

EA 170

TRANSLATION

(1–6) To the king, our lord, the message of Baʿluya and the message of Beti-ili: at the feet of our lord, have we fallen. May it be well with our lord. And here from the lands of our lord, it is very well.

(7–13) Our lord, don't take anything to heart; don't make your heart sick. Our lord, whenever you are able, meet with them so that they do not delay you there.

(14–18) Furthermore, the troops of the land of Ḫatti (and) Lupakku have taken the cities of the land of ʿAmqi and they have taken from Addumi and may our lord be apprised.

19–29) Furthermore, we have heard, "Zidana has come and 90,000 foot troops are with him which have come." But that word, we have not confirmed, whether in truth they really are.

But if/when they arrive in the land of Nuǵasse, then I will send Beti-ilu to meet him.

30) *ki-i-me-e pa-ni-šu-nu*
31) *ni-ṣa-ab-bat ù* LÚ.DUMU.KIN-*ip-ri-ia*
32) *ar-ḫi-iš a-na muḫ-ḫi-ka*
33) *a-ša*$_{10}$*-ap-pár ki-i-me-e a-ma-tam*
34) *ut-te-er-ka šum-ma i-bá-aš-ši*
35) *ù šum-ma ia-nu*

---

36) *a-na* ^{I}GAL.DINGIR *ù* ^{I}ÌR-^{d}URAŠ
37) *a-na* ^{I}DUMU-*a-na ù* ^{I}GAL-*ṣí-id-*⸢*qí*⸣
Up.ed. 38) *um-ma* ^{I}*A-mur-*^{d}IŠKUR
39) *a-na muḫ-ḫi-ku-nu lu-ú šul-mu*
40) *lìb-ba-ku-nu la tù-uš-ma-ra*
\\ *ṣa-nim*
Lft.ed. 41) *ù mi-im-ma i-na* ŠÀ-*ku-nu la ta-ša-kán-*
\\ *nu-nim*
42) *ù an-na- kam*^{V} *iš-tu* É.MEŠ-*ku-nu*
43) *dan-níš šul-mu ù a-na* ^{I}*A-na-ti*
44) *šul-ma qí-bi*

(30–35) When we establish contact with them, then I will send my envoy immediately to you, so that he may give a reply to you whether it really is or whether it isn't.

(36–44) To Rabi-ʾilu and ʿAbdi-URAŠ, to Binana and Rabiṣidqi, the message of Amur-Baʿalu: May it be well with you. Do not make your hearts sick and don't take anything to heart. And here with your households it is very well. And say "hello" to ʿAnatu.

EA 171

TRANSCRIPTION

Obv.

01) [*a-na* LUGAL ^{d}UTU-*ia be-lí-ia*]

02) [*um-ma* ^{I}*A-zi-ri* ÌR]-⸢*ka*⸣-⸢*ma*⸣ ⸢*a*⸣-*n*[*a* GÌR.M]EŠ LUGAL ⸢^{d}⸣⸢UTU⸣ [*be-lí*]-⸢*ia*⸣ ›TAB‹ *am-qut*

03) [*iš-tu pa-na-nu-um-ma*]*i-ra-am* ⸢*a*⸣-⸢*na*⸣ *i-re*-⸢*bi*⸣

04) [*i-na* LÚ.ÌR-*d*]*u*$_{4}$-*ti ša* LU[GAL ^{d}UTU] *be*-⸢*lí*⸣-*ia*

05) [*ù* ^{I}*Ia*-]⸢*an*⸣-*ḫa*-⸢*mu*⸣ *la ú*-⸢*wa*⸣-⸢*aš*⸣-*šar-an*-⸢*ni*⸣

06) [*ù aš-t*]*a*-⸢*pár*⸣-⸢*šu*⸣-⸢*nu*⸣ [LÚ.MEŠ] ⸢DUMU⸣.⸢KIN⸣-⸢*ri*⸣-⸢*ia*⸣

07) [*a-n*]*a* ⸢LUGAL⸣ ⸢*be*⸣-⸢*lí*⸣-⸢*ia*⸣ [*ù ik-ta-la-šu-n*]*u* ^{I}*Ia-an-ḫa-mu*

08) [*i*]-⸢*na*⸣ ⸢KASKAL⸣-⸢*ni*⸣ *ù* [*la it-ta-aṣ-ṣú-nim*]

09) [*ù*] *id-di-nu* ⸢DINGIR⸣.[MEŠ] ⸢*ša*⸣ ⸢LUGAL⸣ ⸢*be*⸣-⸢*lí*⸣-*ia*

10) [*ù*] *it-ta*-⸢*aṣ*⸣-⸢*ṣú*⸣-⸢*nim*⸣ ⸢LÚ⸣.⸢MEŠ⸣ ⸢DUMU⸣.⸢KIN⸣-*ri-ia*

11) [*iš-t*]*u* ⸢ŠU⸣-⸢*ti*⸣ ⸢^{I}⸣⸢*Ia*⸣-*an-ḫa*-⸢*mu*⸣

12) ⸢*a*⸣-⸢*na*⸣-⸢*ku*⸣ *i-te*-⸢*ru*⸣-⸢*ub*⸣ *i-na* ⸢LÚ⸣.ÌR-*du*$_{4}$-*ti*

13) ⸢*ša*⸣ ⸢LUGAL⸣ DINGIR ⸢^{d}⸣UTU ⸢*be*⸣-⸢*lí*⸣-*ia* ⸢*ù*⸣ ^{I}*Ia-an-ḫa*-⸢*mu*⸣ *la ú-wa-aš-ši-ra-an-ni*

14) [*ù*] ⸢*i*⸣-*na-an-na* ⸢LUGAL⸣ *be-lí* ⸢*ik*⸣-[*š*]*u-ud-ni*

15) ⸢^{I}⸣⸢*Pu*⸣-*ú-wu-ru* [LÚ *iḫ-r*]*i-pí*-[*ṭá* LUGAL *be-lí-ia* ^{I}*Pu*]-*wu-ru*

16) ⸢*ki*⸣-⸢*it*⸣-*ti-ia* [*i-de*] *ù* [*li-it-ri-iṣ i-na pa-ni* (?)]

17) ⸢^{d}⸣⸢UTU⸣ ⸢LUGAL⸣ *be-lí*-[*ia ù*] *li-i*[*l-li-ká-am ù*] *li-qáb-bi-šu-nu*

18) ⸢*ù*⸣ ⸢*a*⸣-⸢*na*⸣-⸢*ku*⸣ LÚ.ÌR ⸢^{d}⸣[UTU LUGAL *be-lí-ia ù*]

19) ⸢*mi*⸣-⸢*im*⸣-*ma* ⸢*e*⸣[-*ri-iš-ti ša* ^{d}UTU LUGAL *be-lí-ia*]

20) ⸢*ù*⸣ ⸢*a*⸣-⸢*na*⸣-*ku e*[-*pu-uš ù*…]

21) ^{d}UTU LUGAL *be-lí*-⸢*ia*⸣ [*a-na-ku* LÚ.ÌR] *ša* LUGAL *be-lí-ia*

EA 171

TRANSLATION

(1–2) [To the king, the sun god, my lord; the message of Aziru,] your [servant]; at t[he fe]et of the king, the sun god, my [lord], have I fallen.

(3–13) [Formerly, I wanted to enter [into servit]ude for the ki[ng, the sun god], my lord, [but Y]anḫamu would not permit me. [So I s]ent them, my envoys, [t]o the king, my lord, [but] Yanḫamu [detained the]m [o]n the road and [they could not go forth. Then] the god[s] of the king, my lord, granted [that] my envoys should come forth [fr]om the hand of Yanḫamu. I entered into the servitude of the king, the god, the sun god, my lord but Yanḫamu did not permit me.

(14–21) [And] now, O king, my lord, Puwuru, [the army] commander [of the king, my lord] has come to me; [he knows] my loyalty, so [may it be pleasing (?) to] the sun god, the king, [my] lord, [that] he may c[ome and] he may report them. And I am the servant of the s[un god, the king, my lord, and] whatever the re[quest of the sun god, the king, my lord], then I will d[o (it) and I will send(?) it to] the sun god, the king, my lord, [I am the servant] of the king, my lord

22) *ša-ni-tam be-lí* [....................^{I}*Ia*]-*an-ḫa-mu*
23) *i-nu-ma i-za-za* [.....................]
24) ⸢*iš*⸣-⸢*tu*⸣ KUR.ḪI.A ⸢MAR⸣.[TU.........]
25) [.....]⸢*ḫi*⸣-⸢*ir*⸣ [.....................]
26) [LUGAL *be*-]⸢*lí*⸣-*ia* [...]*mi i*[.........]*nu*
27) [...........]*ru ma-nu-mi* [..........]
28) [...........]⸢*a*⸣-⸢*na*⸣-*ku a-na* [......^{I}*Ia-an-ḫ*]*a-mu*
29) [.......]⸢*lu*⸣-[*wa*-]*aš-šar-šu* [.............]
30) [.................]*nu-kúr*[...........]
Lo.ed. 31) [........]⸢*a*⸣-*wa-te*$^{\ulcorner\text{MEŠ}\urcorner}$ *an-nu-t*[*am*......]
32) [*ša*] ^{d}UTU LUGAL *be-lí-ia*[...............]
Rev. 33) [*a-wa*-]⸢*te*$^{\urcorner\text{MEŠ}}$ *an-nu-tam* [...............]
34) ⸢*ù*⸣ *a-na-ku iš-tu a-wa*-[*te*^{MEŠ}-*šu*]
35) *ù iš-tu* LÚ.ÌR-⸢*šu*⸣
36) *ša* ^{d}UTU LUGAL *be-lí*-⸢*ia*⸣
37) *la a-pa-aṭ-ṭar*

(22–33) Furthermore, my lord, [.......Ya]nḫamu, when he stood [...] from the lands of Amur[ru..........the king,] my [lo]rd [.....] who [....] I to [.....Yanḫ]amu [...]may he release him [......]hostili[ties...] the[se] words [.....of] the sun god, the king, my lord [.....] these [wo]rds.

(34–37) And I will not depart from the word[s] or from the servitude to the sun god, the king, my lord.

EA 172

TRANSCRIPTION

Obv. 01’) [...............*š*]*a* [...............]
02’) [............]*te*^{MEŠ} GI[Š............]
03’) [...........]*me* SIG_7 GI[Š...........]
04’) [............]*te*^{MEŠ} GI[Š...........]
05’) [............*š*]*a mi*[.................]

EA 172

TRANSLATION

Too fragmentary for translation. Reverse completely destroyed.

EA 173

TRANSCRIPTION

Obv.	01)	[*ù* GI]Š.⸢GIGIR⸣.⸢MEŠ [*a-na*]
	02)	[KUR] *Am-qí i-ma-qú-u*[*t*]

---

	03)	⸢*ù*⸣ *in-né-ri-ri* ⸢*ù*⸣ [...]
	04)	[...]⸢LÚ⸣.⸢MEŠ⸣ *ḫa-za-ni šà*[*r-ri ù*]
	05)	[ÉRIN.]M[EŠ] ⸢*pí*⸣-⸢*ṭá*⸣-⸢*ti*⸣ 2 UR[U.MEŠ]
	06)	[...]⸢*ta*⸣-⸢*aḫ*⸣-⸢*ḫa*⸣-⸢*zi*⸣ ⸢^{d}⸣U[TU]
	07)	[...]*me* [*a*]-⸢*na*⸣ ⸢KASKAL⸣-⸢*ni*⸣
	08)	[.......]⸢*ia*⸣ ⸢DUMU⸣.⸢KIN⸣[-*ia*..........]
	09)	[........*a*]-⸢*nu*⸣-*u*[*m-ma*.......]
Lo.ed.	10)	[*e-te-*]*lì a-na e*[*r*]-*ṣ*[*é-ti*]
	11)	[*šàr-r*]*i be-li-i*[*a a-na*]
Rev	12)	[*da-*]*a-ki-šu-nu*
	13)	[*a*]-*nu-um-ma* 10 LÚ.MEŠ *a*-[*sí-ri*]
	14)	[*ut-t*]*a-še-er a-na* LUGAL *be-l*[*i-ia*]
	15)	[*yi-de*] *šàr-ru bé-li a*-⸢*na*⸣
	16)	[LÚ.]⸢MEŠ⸣ *a-ia-bi-šu*

EA 173

TRANSLATION

(1–2) [and] chariotry [against] the [land of] ʿAmqi he make an attack.

(3–8) And I went to the rescue and [...] the city rulers of the k[ing and the regular [troops]. Two to[wns...] the onslaught of the sun god [...] to the caravan [...] my [...my] envoy [...]

(9–12) [...] no[w...he has come] up against the la[n]d of [the ki]ng, m[y] lord, [in order to] attack them.

(13–16) [N]ow, ten pr[isoners] [have I] sent to the king, [my] lo[rd]. [May] the king, my lord, [be apprised] concerning his enemies.

EA 174

TRANSCRIPTION

Obv. 01) [*a*]-*na* LUGAL E[N-*ia* DINGIR-*ia* ^{d}UTU-*i*]*a*
02) ⸢*qí*⸣-*bí*-*m*[*a*]
03) *um-ma Bi-i*$_{15}$-*ri* [ÌR-*k*]*a*
04) LÚ URU *Ḫa-ša-bu*
05) *a-na šu-pa-li up*-⸢*ri*⸣
06) GÌR.MEŠ LUGAL EN-*ia*
07) 7 *ù* 7 *am-qú-ut*
08) *a-mur-mi ni-i*$_{15}$-*nu i*$_{15}$-*ba-ša-nu*
09) *a-na* KUR *Am-qí* ⸢URU⸣.⸢DIDLI⸣.Ḫ[I.A]
10) LUGAL EN-*i*⸢*a* ⸣
11) ⸢*ù*⸣ *a-li*-⸢*uk*⸣ ⸢I⸣*I*$_{15}$-[*tá-kà-ma*]
12) [LÚ UR]U *Qí-in-sà*
13) [*a-na*] *pa-ni* ÉRIN.MEŠ
14) [KUR *Ḫ*]*a*-⸢*at*⸣-*t*[*i*$_{7}$]
Lo.ed. 15) ⸢*ù*⸣ *ša- ka*$_{4}$-⸢*an*⸣ [URU.DIDLI.ḪI.A]
Rev. 16) [LU]GAL EN-*ia*
17) *a-na i*$_{15}$-*ša-t*[*i*]
18) *ù li-de-mi*
19) LUGAL EN-*ia*
20) *ù li-di-na* LUGAL ⸣EN⸣[-*ia*]
21) ÉRIN.MEŠ *pí-ṭá-a-ti*$_{7}$
22) *ù ni-pu-uš* URU.DI[DLI.ḪI.A]
23) LUGAL EN-*ia*
24) *ù ni-ša-ab*
25) *a-na* URU.DIDLI.ḪI.A
26) LUGAL EN-*ia* DINGIR.MEŠ-*ia*
\ ^{d}UTU-*ia*

EA 174

TRANSLATION

(1–7) Speak [t]o the king [my] lo[rd, my god, m]y [sun god], the message of Bi'ri, [yo]ur [servant,] the ruler of Ḫashabu: beneath the dirt of the feet of the king, my lord, seven (times) and seven (times) have I fallen.

(8–26) Look, as for us, we are in the land of ʿAmqi, the cities of the king, my lord, and I[takama], [the ruler of the ci]ty of Qinsa (Qidši) came [at] the head of troops of [the land of Ḫ]atti and he set [the cities if the ki]ng, my lord, on fire. So may the king, my lord, be apprised and may the king, my lord, give regular troops that we may regain the cit[ies] of the king, my lord and so that we may dwell in the cities of the king, my lord, my god and my sun god.

EA 175

TRANSCRIPTION

Obv. 01) [*a-na*] LUGAL EN-*ia* DINGER[-*ia* ᵈUTU]-*ia*
02) [*qí*]-*bí-ma*
03) [*um-m*]*a* DINGIR-*da-a-ya-n*[*i* ÌR-*ka*]
04) ⸢LÚ⸣ URU *Ḫa-sí a-na šu-pa-*⸢*li*⸣
05) *up-ri* GÌR-*pí* LUGAL EN-*ia*
06) 7 *ù* 7 *am-*⸢*qú*⸣*-ut*
07) *a-mur-mi ni-i*$_{15}$*-nu i*$_{15}$*-ba-š* [*a*]-⸢*nu*⸣
08) *a-na* KUR *Am-qí* URU.DIDLI.ḪI.A L[UGAL] ⸢EN⸣-⸢*ia*⸣
09) ⸢*ù*⸣ ⸢*a*⸣*-li-uk* ᴵ*I*$_{15}$-[*tá-kà-m*]*a*
10) ⸢LÚ⸣ KUR *Qí-in-sà* ⸢*a*⸣[*-na pa-ni*]
11) ⸢ÉRIN⸣.MEŠ KUR *Ḫa-at-*[*ti*$_{7}$]
12) [*ù š*]*a-*⸢*ka*$_{4}$⸣*-a*[*n* URU.DIDLI.ḪI.A]
13) [LUGAL EN-*ia a-na i*$_{15}$*-ša-ti*]
14) [*ù li-de-mi* LUGAL EN-*ia*]
15) [*ù li-di-na* LUGAL EN-*ia*]
Lo.ed. 16) [ÉRIN.MEŠ *pí-ṭá-ti*$_{7}$]
17) ⸢*ù*⸣ [*ni-pu-uš* URU.DIDLI.ḪI.A]
Rev. 18) ⸢LUGAL⸣ [EN-*ia*]
19) ⸢*ù*⸣ [*ni-ša-a*]*b* ‹*a-na* URU.DIDLI.ḪI.A›
20) *a-na* LUGAL ⸢EN⸣-*ia*

EA 175

TRANSLATION

(1–6) [Sp]eak [to] the king, my lord, [my] god, my [sun god]; [the mess]age of Ilu-Dayyān[i], [yo]ur [servant], the ruler of the town of Ḫasi: beneath the dirt of the feet of the king, my lord, seven (times) and seven (times) have I fallen.

(7–20) Look, as for us, [we] are in the land of ʿAmqi, the cities of the ki[ng], my lord and I[takam]a, the ruler of the land of Qinsa (Qidši) has come at [the head] of troops of the land of Ḫat[ti] and [s]et [the cities of the king, my lord on fire. So may the king, my lord, be apprised and may the king, my lord give regular troops]th[at we may (re)gain the cities] of the ki[ng, my lord] and [so that we may dwel]l in ‹the cities of› the king, my lord.

EA 176

TRANSCRIPTION

Obv. 01) [*a-na* LUGAL EN-*ia* DINGIR-*ia* ^{d}UTU-*ia*]
02) [*qí-bí-ma*]
03) [*um-ma*....ÌR-*ka*]
04) [LÚ URU....*a-na šu-pa-li*]
05) [*up*-]⌜*ri*⌝ GÌR-*pí* LUGAL EN-⌜*ia*⌝
06) 7 *ù* 7 *am-qú-ut*
07) *a-mur-mi ni-*i_{15}*-nu* i_{15}*-ba-š*[*a-nu*]
08) *a-na* KUR *Am-qí* URU.DIDLI.ḪI.A L[UGAL EN-]*ia*
09) *ù a-li-uk* ^{I}*E-tá-*[*kà-ma*]
10) ⌜LÚ⌝ KUR *Qí-in-sà a-na pa-ni*
11) ⌜ÉRIN⌝.⌜MEŠ⌝ KUR ⌜*Ḫa*⌝-[*a*]*t-ta*
12) [*ù š*]*a-*ka_4-⌜*an*⌝ URU.DIDLI.ḪI.A LU[GAL E]N-*ia*
13) [*a-n*]*a* [i_{15}]-*š*[*a-t*]*i*
14) [*ù li-de-mi* LUGAL EN-*ia*] (traces)

Rev. 15) [*ù li-di-na* LUGAL EN-*ia*]
16) [ÉRIN.MEŠ] ⌜*pí*⌝-⌜*ṭá*⌝-⌜*a*⌝-*t*[$ṭi_7$]
17) ⌜*ù*⌝ *ni-pu-uš* URU.DIDLI.Ḫ[I.A]
18) LUGAL EN-*ia* DINGIR-*ia* ⌜^{d}⌝U[TU-*ia*]
19) *ù ni-ša-ab*
20) *a-na* URU.DIDLI.ḪI.A LUGAL EN-^{ia}

EA 176

TRANSLATION

(1–6) *[Speak to the king, my lord. my god, my sun god; the message of…, your servant, the ruler of.…Beneath the di]rt under the feet of the king, my lord, seven (times) and seven (times) have I fallen.

(7–13) Look, we were in the land of ʿAmqi, the cities of the k[ing,] my [lord], and Eta[kama,] the ruler of Qinsa (Qidši), came at the head of the troops of the land of Ḫatta and he [s]et the cities of the ki[ng, my lord, o]n [fi[re].

(14–20) [So may the king, my lord, be apprised. And may the king, my lord, grant] regular army [troops] that we may (re)gain the cities of the king, my lord, my god, [my] s[un god] and we may dwell in the cities of the king, my lord.

---

*The tablet has been shaved with a sharp instrument; the first four lines are completely gone.

EA 177

TRANSCRIPTION

Obv. 01) *a-na* LUGAL EN-*ia* ⸢DINGIR⸣-*ia* ^{d}UTU-*ia*
02) *um-ma* ^{I}*Ya-mi-ú-ta* LÚ URU *Gud-da-šu-na*
03) ÌR LUGAL EN-*ia*
04) *a-na up-ri* GÌR-*pí* LUGAL EN-*ia*
05) 7 *ù* 7 *am-*⸢*qú*⸣*-ut*
06) *li-*⸢*de*⸣*-mi* ⸢LUGAL⸣ [EN-*i*]*a*
07) *a-na* KUR.MEŠ-*šu*
08) *ù* LÚ.MEŠ [.......]
09) *ù* [...............]
Lo.ed. 10) ⸢KUR⸣(?) [.........]

EA 177

TRANSLATION

(1–5) To the king, my lord, my god, my sun god: The message of Yami'uta, the ruler of Guddashuna, the servant of the king, my lord. At the dust under the feet of the king, my lord, seven (times) and seven (times) have I fallen.

(6–10) May the king, [m]y [lord] be apprised concerning his lands and the personnel [...] and [....] ⸢land⸣[..........].

EA 178

TRANSCRIPTION

Obv. 01) [*a-na* L]Ú GAL EN-*ia*
02) [*um-ma*] ᴵ*Ḫi-bi-ya* ÌR-*ka*
03) [*a-n*]*a* GÌR-*pí* EN-*ia am-qú-ut*
04) ⸢*ù*⸣ *a-nu-ma ni-i*$_{15}$*-ta-lí*
\ *i-na* KUR.MEŠ
05) ⸢*ù*⸣ *yi-ta-lí*
06) [*ù*] *i*$_{15}$*-na-ṣa-ar-šu*
07) [*a*]-*d*[*i*] *ka*$_{4}$*-ša-du*
08) LÚ GAL EN-*ia*
09) *ù a-nu-ma da-na-at*
10) *nu-kúr-tu*$_{4}$ UGU URU.DIDLI.ḪI.A
11) LÚ GAL EN-*ia*
12) ⸢*ša*⸣-*ni-tam a-wa-ta*$_{5}$
13) [*iš*]-*te-mé ki-m*[*a*]
Lo.ed. 14) [*ša qa-bi*] [L]Ú [EN-*i*]*a*
Rev. 15) [..............................]
16) [..............................]
17) [..............................]
18) [............................] x
19) [........................]⸢*še*⸣-⸢*ú*⸣
20) [*ú*]-⸢*ra*⸣-⸢*ad*⸣ *iš-tu*
21) ⸢KUR⸣ *A-mur-ri ù yi-qa*
\ *bu*
22) *a-na ia-ši*
23) *ma-a-di* ⸢ŠE⸣.MEŠ-*mi*
24) *a*!(2)-*na* [KUR *A-mu*]*r-ri*
25) [*a-di ka*$_{4}$*-ša*]-*ad* ⸢LÚ⸣ GAL
26) [............]⸢\⸣ EN-*ia*

EA 178

TRANSLATION

(1–3) [To the Seni]or official (= Great King?), my lord; [the message] of Ḫibiya, your servant: at the feet of my lord have I fallen.

(4–8) And now, we have gone up into the hills(? or lands) and when he comes up, then I will protect him until the arrival of the senior official (great king?), my lord.

(9–11) And now, great is the hostility against the cities of the senior official (great king?).

(12–14) Furthermore, [I] have heeded the word as [the m]an (king?), [my lord has commanded].

(15–18) [....................................]

(19–26) [...is] seeking to go down from the land of Amurru and he commands me, "Much grain for Amurru [until the arri]val of the senior official (great king?), my lord [......]"

NOTE: Perhaps LÚ GAL is an error for LUGAL GAL, cf. EA 317:1, 7, 11.

EA 179

TRANSCRIPTION

Obv. 01) [...]
02) [...]
03) [...]
04) [...]
05) [...]
06) [...]
07) [...]
08) [...]
09) [...]
10) [...]
11) ⸢*ù*⸣ ⸢*li*⸣-⸢*te*⸣-⸢*ra*⸣-⸢*mi*⸣ [LUGAL EN-*ia* DINGIR]-⸢*ia*⸣ ⸢^{d}⸣⸢UTU⸣-*ia*
12) *a-wa-ta*$_{5}$ *ù up*-⸢*ša*⸣ [*a-na*]
13) ÌR ⸢LUGAL⸣ ⸢EN⸣-*ia* DINGIR-⸢*ia*⸣ [^{d}UTU-*ia*]
14) ⸢*ù*⸣ ⸢*a*⸣-⸢*mur*⸣-⸢*mi*⸣ ŠEŠ-*ia*
15) *ša i*$_{15}$*-ba-aš-ši*$_{x}$(ŠE) *a-na* URU *Ṭú-bi-ḫi*
16) ⸢LÚ⸣ *sú-ú-ru* ⸢*ù*⸣ *yi-la-ku*
17) [*a*]*-na e-pé-šu* URU.DIDLI.ḪI.A
18) [LU]GAL EN-*ia* ⸢DINGIR⸣-*ia* ⸢^{d}⸣U[TU-*ia ki-ma*]
Lo.ed. 19) [U]RU KUR.MEŠ ⸢*A*⸣*-mur-ri* ⸢*ù*⸣
Rev. 20) [*yu*]*-ga-mi-ir* LÚ.MEŠ *š*[*a*]
21) [*i*]*-na* URU.DIDLI.ḪI.A LUGAL EN-*ia* ⸢^{d}⸣U[TU-*ia*]
22) ⸢*a*⸣*-na* LÚ.MEŠ GAZ ⸢*ù*⸣ *a-na-an-na* (sic!)
23) *i*$_{15}$*-din* DINGIR LUGAL EN-*ia* DINGIR-*ia* ^{d}UTU-*ia*
24) *ù ṣa-ab-ta* URU ⸢*Ṭú*⸣*-bi-ḫi*
25) *ù i*$_{15}$*-ra-ar* ⸢ŠEŠ⸣-*ia*
26) *ù i*$_{15}$*-na-ṣa-ar* ⸢URU⸣ *Ṭú-bi-ḫi*
27) *a-na* LUGAL EN-*ia* DINGIR-*ia* ⸢^{d}⸣[UTU-*ia*]
28) *ù a-mur-mi* URU *Ṭú*[*-bi-ḫi*]
29) URU É-*ti a-bi-ia*

EA 179

TRANSLATION

(1–10) [...]

(11–13) So may [the king, my lord,] my [god], my sun god, send word back (to me) and breathe [on] the servant of the king, my lord, my god, [my sun god].

(14–27) And look, my brother who is in the city of Ṭôbiḫi is a traitor and he was going to make the cities if the [ki]ng, my lord, my god, [my] su[n god like] [a c]ity of the lands of Amurru and [he] recruited the men that were [i]n the cities of the king, my lord, [my] sun god, for *ʿapîru* men and now (may) the god of the king, my lord, my god, my sun god, grant that the city of Ṭôbiḫi be captured and I will curse my brother and I will guard the city of Ṭôbiḫi for the king, my lord, my god, [my sun] god.

(28–29) And look, the city of Ṭô[biḫi] is the city of my father's house.

EA 180

TRANSCRIPTION

Obv. 01’) [*a-mur-mi a-n*]*a-k*[*u* ÌR *ki-it-ti*]
02’) [LUGAL EN-*i*]*a* DINGIR[-*ia* ^{d}UTU-*ia*]
03’) ⸢*i*⸣-⸢*na*⸣ ⸢*aš*⸣-*ri an*-⸢*nu*⸣-*t*[*u*$_4$ *ù a-mur-mi*]
04’) ^{I}DUMU-*ia uš-ši-ir*-⸢*ti*$_7$⸣-*š*[*u a-na*]
05’) LUGAL EN-*ia* DINGIR-*ia* ^{d}UTU-*ia*
06’) *ù yu-uš-ši-ra* GIS.GIGIR.MEŠ
07’) LUGAL EN-*ia* DINGIR-*ia* ^{d}UTU-*ia*
08’) *it-ti* ^{I}DUMU-*ia ù ti*$_7$*-na-ṣa-ru*
09’) URU.DIDLI.ḪI.A LUGAL EN-*ia* DINGIR-*ia* ^{d}UTU-*ia*
10’) *ù uš-ši*-⸢*ra*⸣ GIŠ.GIGIR.MEŠ
11’) LUGAL EN-⸢*ia*⸣ [DIN]GIR-*ia* ^{d}UT[U]-*ia*
12’) *ù ti-ìl-qú-n*[*i*] *a-na mu-ḫi*
Lo.ed. 13’) LUGAL EN-*ia* DINGIR-*ia* ^{d}UTU-*ia*
Rev. 14’) ⸢*ù*⸣ *i*$_{15}$*-ri-ub a-na pa-ni*
15’) LUGAL EN-*ia* DINGIR-*ia* ^{d}UTU-*ia*
16’) *ù lu-ú i*$_{15}$*-qa-bi ša e-pu-iš*
17’) UGU KUR.MEŠ *ù a-mur-mi a-na-ku*
18’) ÌR *ki-it-ti* LUGAL EN-*ia* DINGIR-*ia* ^{d}UTU-*ia*
19’) *ù al*-⸢*lu*⸣*-mi ši-ir*!(NI)-*ti*$_7$ *a-na pa-ni*
20’) LUGAL EN-*ia* DINGIR-*ia* ^{d}UTU-*ia*
21’) ⸢*ù*⸣ *uš-ši-ra* GIŠ.GIGIR.MEŠ
22’) [*ù*] ⸢*ti*$_7$⸣-*ìl-qú-ni a-na mu-ḫi*
23’) [LUGAL EN]-⸢*ia*⸣ DINGIR-*ia* ^{d}[UTU-*ia*]
24’) [.................................]

EA 180

TRANSLATION

(1'–3') [Look,] I [am the loyal servant of the king, m]y [lord, my] god, [my sun god], in the[se]places.

(3'–9') [And look,] as for my son, I have sent hi[m to] the king, my lord, my god, my sun god. So may he send the chariotry of the king, my lord, my god, my sun god, with my son so that they may protect the cities of the king, my lord, my god, my sun god.

(10'–17') And send chariots of the king, my lord, my [go]d, my sun god, that they may take me to the king, my lord, my god, my sun god and I can enter into the presence of the king, my lord, my god, my sun god and I may verily recount what has been done against the lands.

(17'–23') And look, I am the loyal servant of the king, my lord, my god, my sun god. And behold, I am maligned(!) in the presence of the king, my lord, my god, my sun god, so send chariots [that] they may take me to [the king,] my [lord,] my god, [my] s[un god....].

The rest of the reverse is broken away. Gordon suggested that this fragment is the continuation of EA 183. Cf. EA 183 below for the combined text.

EA 181

TRANSCRIPTION

Obv. 01) [...]

02) [...]

03) [.............] traces [.....................]

04) [.............*k*]*u* [.........................]

05) [LUGAL EN-*ia* DINGIR-*ia*] ^{d}UTU-*ia*

06) [..................LÚ.]MEŠ-*šu*

07) [................]*li uš-ši-r*[*a*]

08) [LUGAL EN-*ia* DINGIR-*ia*] ^{d}UTU-*ia*

09) [.............] *ù ni-na-ṣa-*⸢*ar*⸣

10) [URU.MEŠ LUGAL EN-*ia*]DINGIR-*ia* ^{d}UTU-*i*[*a*]

11) [*a-na* LUGAL E]N-*ia* DINGIR-*ia* ^{d}[UTU-*ia*]

12) [.............*m*]*a-ab ú-d*[*i*]

13) [LUGAL EN-*ia* DINGIR]-*ia* ^{d}UTU-[*i*]*a*

Lo.ed. 14) [.............] traces [......................]

Rev. 15) [...]

16) [...]

17) [.............] traces [......................]

18) [...............................*i*]*š*

19) [...............................*i*]*a*

20) [...............................]⸢*ia*⸣

21) [...............................]*ia*

22) [LUGAL EN-*ia* DINGIR-*ia*] ^{d}UTU[-*ia*]

23) [...............................]*ab*

24) [LUGAL EN-*ia* DINGIR-*i*]*a* ^{d}U[TU-*ia*]

25) [.............] *lu-*⸢*wa*⸣*-a*[*š-ši-ir*]

26) [..............................]

EA 181

TRANSLATION

(1–22) […the king, my lord, my god], my sun god, […]his [m]en […]…Sen[d, O king, my lord, m]y [god], my sun god, […] that we may protect [the cities of the king, my lord], my god, m[y] sun god [for the king,] my [lo]rd, my god, [my sun god]…

(22–23) [the king, my lord, my god, my] sun god…

(24–26) [the king, my lord, m]y [god, my] sun [god]…

EA 182

TRANSCRIPTION

Obv. 01) [*a-na* ^{I}LUGAL] EN-*i*[*a* DINGIR-*ia*]⸢^{d}⸣UTU-*ia*
02) ⸢*um*⸣-⸢*ma*⸣ *Šu-tar-na* ⸢ÌR⸣[-*ka*] ⸢LÚ⸣ URU *Mu-ši-ḫu-na*
03) *a-na up-ri ša* GÌR-⸢*pí*⸣
04) LUGAL EN-*ia* DINGIR-*ia* ^{d}UTU-*ia*
05) 7 *ù* 7 *am-qú-ut*
06) *ù li-de-mi* LUGAL EN-*ia*
07) *a-na* KUR.MEŠ-*šu*
08) *ù yu-uš-ši-ra*
09) LUGAL EN-*ia*
10) LÚ.MEŠ *ma-ṣa-ar-ta*
11) *ù ni-lik* ⸢*a*⸣-⸢*na*⸣

Lo.ed. 12) URU.MEŠ LUGAL EN-*ia*

Rev. 13) DINGIR-*ia* ^{d}UTU-*ia*
14) *a-di yi-du* LUGAL EN-*i*⸢*a* ⸣
15) *a-na* KUR.MEŠ-*šu*

EA 182

TRANSLATION

(1–5) [To the king], m[y] lord, [my god], my sun god; the message of Shutarna, [your] servant, ruler of the city of Mushiḫuna: At the dirt (under) the feet of the king, my lord, my god, my sun god, seven (times) and seven (times) have I fallen.

(6–15) So may the king be apprised concerning his lands and may the king, my lord, send garrison troops so that we may go to the cities of the king, my lord, my god, my sun god, until the king, my lord takes cognizance of his lands.

EA 183 + EA 180

TRANSCRIPTION

Obv. 01) ⸢*a*⸣-⸢*na*⸣ LUGAL EN-*i*[*a* DINGIR-*ia*]⸢^{d}⸣UTU-*ia* **EA 183**
02) *qí-bí-ma*
03) *um-ma Šu-tar-na* ⸢LÚ⸣
04) \ URU *Mu-ši-ḫu-n*[*a*]
05) ÌR LUGAL EN-*ia*
06) ⸢*iš*⸣-⸢*tu*⸣ *ša šu-p*[*a-li*]
07) [*u*]*p-ri ša* GÌR-[*pí*]
08) LUGAL EN-*ia* [DINGIR-*ia* ^{d}UTU-*ia*]
09) [7 *ù* 7 *am-qú-ut*]

Obv. 01') [*a-mur-mi a-n*]*a-k*[*u* ÌR *ki-it-ti*] **EA 180**
02') [LUGAL EN-*i*]*a* DINGIR[-*ia* ^{d}UTU-*ia*]
03') ⸢*i*⸣-⸢*na*⸣ ⸢*aš*⸣-*ri an*-⸢*nu*⸣-*t*[u_4 *ù a-mur-mi*]
04') ^{I}DUMU-*ia uš-ši-ir*-⸢ti_7⸣-*š*[*u a-na*]
05') LUGAL EN-*ia* DINGIR-*ia* ^{d}UTU-*ia*
06') *ù yu-uš-ši-ra* GIS.GIGIR.MEŠ
07') LUGAL EN-*ia* DINGIR-*ia* ^{d}UTU-*ia*
08') *it-ti* ^{I}DUMU-*ia ù* ti_7*-na-ṣa-ru*
09') URU.DIDLI.ḪI.A LUGAL EN-*ia* DINGIR-*ia* ^{d}UTU-*ia*
10') *ù uš-ši*-⸢*ra*⸣ GIŠ.GIGIR.MEŠ
11') LUGAL EN-⸢*ia*⸣ [DIN]GIR-*ia* ^{d}UT[U]-*ia*
12') *ù ti-ìl-qú-n*[*i*] *a-na mu-ḫi*

Lo.ed. 13') LUGAL EN-*ia* DINGIR-*ia* ^{d}UTU-*ia*

Rev. 14') ⸢*ù*⸣ i_{15}*-ri-ub a-na pa-ni*
15') LUGAL EN-*ia* DINGIR-*ia* ^{d}UTU-*ia*
16') *ù lu-ú* i_{15}*-qa-bi ša e-pu-iš*
17') UGU KUR.MEŠ *ù a-mur-mi a-na-ku*
18') ÌR *ki-it-ti* LUGAL EN-*ia* DINGIR-*ia* ^{d}UTU-*ia*
19') *ù al*-⸢*lu*⸣*-mi ši-ir*!(NI)-ti_7 *a-na pa-ni*
20') LUGAL EN-*ia* DINGIR-*ia* ^{d}UTU-*ia*
21') ⸢*ù*⸣ *uš-ši-ra* GIŠ.GIGIR.MEŠ
22') [*ù*] ⸢ti_7⸣*-ìl-qú-ni a-na mu-ḫi*
23') [LUGAL EN]-⸢*ia*⸣ DINGIR-*ia* ^{d}[UTU-*ia*]
24') [...................................]

EA 183 + EA 180

TRANSLATION

EA 183

(1–5) Speak to the king, m[y] lord, [my god,]my sun god; the message of Shutarna, ruler of the city of Mushiḫuna, the servant of the king, my lord: From beneath the dirt under the feet of the king, my lord, [my god, my sun god seven (times) and seven (times) have I fallen].

EA 180

(1'–3') [Look] ⌜I⌝ [am the loyal servant of the king, m]y [lord, [my] god, [my sun god], in the[se]places.

(3'–9') [And look,] as for my son, I have sent hi[m to] the king, my lord, my god, my sun god. So may he send the chariotry of the king, my lord, my god, my sun god, with my son so that they may protect the cities of the king, my lord, my god, my sun god.

(10'–17') And send chariots of the king, my lord, my [go]d, my sun god, that they may take me to the king, my lord, my god, my sun god and I can enter into the presence of the king, my lord, my god, my sun god and I may verily recount what has been done against the lands.

(17'–23') And look, I am the loyal servant of the king, my lord, my god, my sun god. And behold, I am maligned(!) in the presence of the king, my lord, my god, my sun god, so send chariots [that] they may take me to [the king,] my [lord,] my god, [my] s[un god....].

The rest of the reverse is broken away.

EA 184

TRANSCRIPTION

Obv. 01) [*a-na* LUGAL EN-]*ia*
02) [DINGIR-*ia* ᵈUTU-*i*]*a*
03) [*qí-bi-ma u*]*m-ma*
04) [*Šu-ta*]*r-na* LÚ URU *Mu-ši-ḫu-ni*
05) [*a-na* GÌR.MEŠ LUG]AL EN-*ia am-*[*qú*]⸢*qut*⸣
06) [...]*ia*
07) [7 *ù* 7] *a-na* GÌR-*pí* LUGAL EN-*ia am-*[*qú*]*qut*
08) [...] GÌR-⸢*pí*⸣ L[UGAL] ⸢EN⸣-*ia*

EA 184

TRANSLATION

(1–8) [Speak to the king,] my [lord, my god, m]y [sun god; the me]ssage of [Shuta]rna, ruler of the city of Mushiḫuna: [At the feet of the ki]ng, my lord, have I fallen. My [...seven (times) and seven (times)] at the feet of the king, my lord, have I fallen.

EA 185

TRANSCRIPTION

Obv. 01) ⸢a⸣-na šàr-ri EN-ia DINGIR-ia ^{d}UTU-[i]⸢a⸣
02) qí————————bí————————ma
03) ⸢um⸣-ma ⸢Ma⸣-ya-ar-za-na LÚ URU Ḫa-sí ^{KI}
04) ÌR-⸢ka⸣ ⸢ep⸣-ri šu-pa-al GÌR.MEŠ-pí
05) [^{I}]⸢šàr⸣-⸢ri⸣ ⸢EN⸣-⸢ia⸣ ⸢DINGIR⸣-⸢ia⸣ ^{d}UTU-i⸢a⸣
06) qa-q[a]-⸢ri⸣ ⸢ša⸣ ⸢ka⸣-⸢bá⸣-⸢ši⸣-⸢šu⸣ a-na GÌR.MEŠ-pí
07) [^{I}šàr-r]i ⸢EN⸣-⸢ia⸣ ⸢DINGIR⸣-⸢ia⸣ ⸢^{d}⸣UTU-ia
08) [7-šu] ù ⸢7⸣-⸢šu⸣ ⸢am⸣-⸢qú⸣-ut

---

09) [ù] ⸢li⸣-⸢i⸣-⸢de$_9$⸣ ^{I}⸢šàr⸣-⸢ru⸣ EN-ia
10) ⸢DINGIR⸣-⸢ia⸣ ⸢^{d}⸣⸢UTU⸣-⸢ia⸣ ⸢ip⸣-⸢ši⸣ i-⸢pu⸣-uš
11) ^{I}⸢A⸣-⸢ma⸣-⸢an⸣-⸢ḫa⸣-⸢at⸣-⸢pé⸣ ⸢LÚ⸣ ⸢URU⸣ ⸢Tu⸣-⸢šu⸣-⸢ul⸣-⸢ti⸣⸢^{KI}⸣
12) UGU ⸢URU⸣.⸢DIDLI⸣.⸢ḪI.A⸣.⸢KI⸣ ^{I}šàr-ri EN-ia
13) i-⸢nu⸣-ma ⸢i⸣-⸢pu⸣-⸢šu⸣-⸢mi⸣ ⸢ÉRIN⸣.MEŠ LÚ.SA.GAZ.MEŠ
14) ⸢nu⸣-kúr-ta UGU-⸢ia⸣ ù ⸢ṣa⸣-⸢ab⸣-⸢tu⸣-mi
15) URU.DIDLI.ḪI.A.KI ^{I}⸢šàr⸣-⸢ri⸣ EN-ia ⸢DINGIR⸣-⸢ia⸣ ⸢^{d}⸣UTU-ia

---

16) ù ṣa-ab-tu-⸢mi⸣ ⸢LÚ⸣.MEŠ ⸢SA⸣.⸢GAZ⸣.MEŠ
17) URU Ma-aḫ-ṣí-⸢ib⸣-ti ^{KI} URU.KI ^{I}⸢šàr⸣-⸢ri⸣ EN-ia
18) ù i-⸢ša⸣-⸢la⸣-lu-mi ù ⸢uš⸣-ši-⸢ru⸣-ši-mi
19) i-⸢na⸣ ⸢IZI⸣ \ i-ša-ti ù ⸢a⸣-na mu-ḫi
20) ^{I}A-ma-⸢an⸣-[ḫa-at-p]é i-ri-bu-ni LÚ.SA.GAZ.MEŠ
21) ⸢ù⸣ ṣa-⸢ab⸣-⸢tu⸣-mi LÚ.SA.GAZ.MEŠ ›URU.KI‹
22) URU ⸢Gi⸣-⸢lu⸣-⸢ni⸣⸢^{KI}⸣ URU.KI ^{I}šàr-⸢ri⸣ EN-ia
23) ⸢ù⸣ i-ša-la-lu-ši ù ⸢uš⸣-ši-ru-ši-mi
24) i-na IZI ù É 1-⸢en⸣ qá-rib
25) bá-li-iṭ-mi iš-tu ⸢URU⸣ Gi-lu-ni ^{KI}
26) ù a-na ma-ḫar ^{I}A-ma-an-⸢ḫa⸣-⸢at⸣-pé i-‹ri›-bu-mi
27) LÚ.SA.GAZ.MEŠ

EA 185

TRANSLATION

(1–8) Speak to the king, my lord, my god, [m]y sun god; the message of Mayarzana, the ruler of Ḫasi, your servant, the dirt under the feet of the king, my lord, my god, my sun god, (and) the ground of his treading: at the feet of [the kin]g, my lord, my god, my sun god, [seven times] and seven times have I fallen.

(9–15) [And] may the king, my lord, my god, my sun god, be apprised of the deeds which Amanḥatpe, the ruler of Tushulti, has done, when the troops of the *ʿapîrû* made war on me and seized the towns of the king, my lord, my god, my sun god.

(16–27) And the *ʿapîrû* seized the city of Maḫṣibti, the city of the king, my lord, and they thoroughly plundered and they sent it up in flames and the *ʿapîrû* entered in to Aman[ḥatp]e. And the *ʿapîrû* seized the city of Gilôni, the city of the king, my lord, and they thoroughly plundered and they sent it up in flames and scarcely one household survived from the city of Gilôni and the *ʿapîrû* re‹p›orted in to Amanḥatpe.

---

28) ⸢*ù*⸣ *i-ṣa-‹ab›-tu-mi* LÚ.SA.GAZ.MEŠ
29) [UR]U ⸢*Ma*⸣*-ag-*⸢*da*⸣*-li* {KI} ⸢URU⸣.⸢KI⸣ ›{I}‹LUGAL›
Lo.ed. 30) ⸢*šàr*⸣*-*⸢*ri*⸣ ⸢EN⸣*-ia* ⸢DINGIR⸣*-ia* {d}UTU-⸢*ia*⸣
31) ⸢*ù*⸣ ⸢*i*⸣*-ša-la-lu-ši-mi ù uš-‹ši›-*⸢*ru*⸣*-ši*
32) *i-na* IZI \ *i-*⸢*ša*⸣*-*⸢*ti*⸣
Rev. 33) ⸢*ù*⸣ ⸢É⸣ 1-⸢*en*⸣ ⸢*qá*⸣*-*⸢*rib*⸣ ⸢*bá*⸣*-li-iṭ-m*[*i*]
34) *iš-tu* URU *Ma-*⸢*ag*⸣*-*[*da*]*-li* {KI}
35) ⸢*ù*⸣ ⸢*a*⸣*-*⸢*na*⸣ *mu-ḫi* {I}*A-ma*[*-an*]*-*⸢*ḫa*⸣*-at-pé*
36) *i-*⸢*ri*⸣*-*⸢*bu*⸣*-na* LÚ.S[A.G]AZ.MEŠ
37) *ù* URU ⸢*Uš*⸣*-te* {KI} [UR]U.[KI {I}]⸢*šàr*⸣*-*⸢*ri*⸣ EN-*ia*
38) *ṣa-ab-tu-mi* LÚ.⸢SA⸣.⸢GAZ⸣.MEŠ *ù* ⸢*i*⸣*-*⸢*ša*⸣*-la-l*[*u-š*]*i*
39) *ù uš-ši-ru-ši i-na* I[ZI] ⸢*ù*⸣ [*a-n*]*a*
40) *ma-ḫar* {I}*A-*⸢*ma*⸣*-*⸢*an*⸣*-ḫa-a*[*t-p*]*é* ⸢*i*⸣*-*⸢*ri*⸣*-*⸢*bu*⸣*-na*
41) LÚ.SA.GAZ.MEŠ

---

42) *ù a-mu-*⸢*ur*⸣*-mi* LÚ.SA.⸢GAZ⸣.MEŠ
43) *iš-ḫi-ṭú* ⸢URU⸣.⸢KI⸣ *Ḫa-sí* {KI} ⸢URU⸣.⸢KI⸣
44) {I}*šàr-ri* EN-*ia ù ni-pu-*⸢*uš*⸣*-mi*
45) *ta-*⸢*ḫa*⸣*-za* ⸢*i*⸣*-*⸢*na*⸣ LÚ.SA.GAZ.MEŠ ⸢*ù*⸣
46) ⸢*ni*⸣*-*⸢*da*⸣*-ak-*⸢*šu*⸣*-nu ù* ⸢i_{15}⸣*-*[*ri-bu-m*]*i*
47) 40 ⸢LÚ⸣.⸢SA⸣.⸢GAZ⸣.⸢MEŠ⸣ *a-*⸢*na*⸣ *mu-ḫi* {I}[*A-ma-an-ḫa-a*]*t-pé*
48) *ù ìl-*⸢*qé*⸣*-mi* [*ša*] *a-ṣa* ⸢*ù*⸣ [*i-n*]*a* URU *pa-aḫ-‹ru›-mi*
49) *ù* LÚ.⸢SA⸣.G[AZ {I}*A-ma-a*]*n-*⸢*ḫa*⸣*-at-pé*
50) *ù ni-*⸢*iš*⸣*-m*[*é i-nu-m*]*a* ⸢i_{15}⸣*-ba-šu-mi*
51) LÚ.SA.⸢GAZ⸣.[MEŠ *it*]*-ti* {I}*A-ma-an-ḫa-at-pé*
52) *ù t*[*i-na-am*]*-mi-šu* GIŠ.GIGIR.MEŠ-*ta*
53) ⸢ŠEŠ⸣.[MEŠ-*i*]*a* ⸢DUMU⸣.⸢MEŠ⸣*-ia* ÌR.MEŠ-*ka*
54) *a*[*-na m*]*a-ḫar* ⸢{I}⸣⸢*A*⸣*-*⸢*ma*⸣*-*⸢*an*⸣*-ḫa-at-pé ù*
55) *ti-*[*i*]*q-bu-mi* ŠEŠ.MEŠ-*ia a-na* {I}*A-ma-an-ḫa-at-pé*
56) *id-*[*n*]*a-mi* LÚ.SA.GAZ.MEŠ {LÚ}*ša-ri*{MEŠ}
57) {I}*šàr-*⸢*ri*⸣ *be-li-nu* ⸢*ni*⸣*-ša-al-šu-nu-mi*
58) ⸢*ša*⸣ ⸢*i*⸣[*-ri*]*-bu-mi it-ti-ka* LÚ.SA.GAZ.MEŠ
59) *pu-*⸢*ḫa*⸣*-a*[*t*] ⸢*i*⸣*-ṣa-ba-tu* URU.DIDLI.ḪI.A.KI {I}⸢*šàr*⸣*-ri* EN-*ia*
60) *ù* ⸢*i*⸣*-š*[*a-*]*r*[*a*]*-*⸢*pu*⸣*-ni-na i-na* IZI
61) *ù* ⸢*i*⸣*-ma-*⸢*gar*⸣ ⸢*na*⸣*-da-*⸢*an*⸣
62) LÚ.SA.GAZ.MEŠ *ù ìl-qé-šu-nu-mi* ⸢*a*⸣*-na mu-ši-mi*(!)
63) ⸢*ù*⸣ *in-na-bi-*⸢*it*⸣*-mi a-na* LÚ.SA.GAZ.MEŠ
64) ⸢*ù*⸣ *a-mu-ur-m*[*i*] ⸢{I}⸣⸢*A*⸣*-ma-an-ḫa-a*[*t*]*-pé* LÚ *ša-* *ru*

(28–41) And the *ʿapîrû* seized the [cit]y of Magdal, the city of the king, my lord, my god, my sun god, and they thoroughly plundered it and they sent it up in flames and scarcely one household survived from the city of Mag[da]l. And the *ʿapîrû* entered in to Am[an]ḫatpe. And the *ʿapîrû* seized the city of Ushte, the [cit]y of the king, my lord, and they thoroughly plundered it and they sent it up in flames and the *ʿapîrû* entered in to Amanḫatpe.

(42–60) And look, the *ʿapîrû* attacked the city of Ḫasi, the city of the king, my lord, and we made an assault on the *ʿapîrû* and we smote them but forty *ʿapîrû* fo[und refu]ge with [Amanḫa]tpe and he received [those who] escaped and [they] were assme‹bl›ed in the city, and Ama]nḫatpe is an *ʿapî*[*ru*]. And we heard [tha]t the *ʿapîrû* were with Amanḫatpe. So [m]y colleagu[es], my sons, your servants, dis[patch]ed the chariotry to [the prese]nce of Amanḫatpe and my colleagues said to Amanḫatpe, "Hand over the *ʿapîrû*, the traitors to the king, our lord; we want to demand a reckoning of them, those *ʿapîrû* who have sought refuge with you, because they have been capturing the cities of the king, my lord, and they have been burning them in fire."

(61–64) And he agreed to hand over the *ʿapîrû* but he took them by night and he fled to the *ʿapîrû*.

Up.ed. (65) [*ù*] ⸢*li*⸣-⸢*iš*⸣-⸢*al*⸣-⸢*šu*⸣-*mi*
(66) [^{I}]⸢*šàr*⸣-⸢*ru*⸣ ⸢EN⸣-*ia im-ru-ur*-⸢*mi*⸣
67) ⸢*iš*⸣-*tu ša*-⸢*šu*⸣ *la -a i-qa-al* ^{I}*šàr-ru*
68) ⸢EN⸣-*ia* ⸢*ba*⸣-*lu ša-a-al* ⸢^{I}⸣*A-ma-an-ḫa-at-*[*pé*]
Lft.ed. 69) LÚ *ša-nu ù la-*⸢*a*⸣ ‹*ú*›-*še*$_{20}$-*re-eb*(!)
70) LÚ *ša-ru-ta*^{MEŠ}
71) *a-na* KUR *ki-ti* ^{I}*šàr-ri* EN-*ia*
Lft.ed. 72) ⸢*ù*⸣ *ša-a-lu-*[*mi* ^{I}*šàr-*]*ru* ⸢EN⸣-*ia*
73) ⸢^{I}⸣⸢*A*⸣-*ma-an-ḫa-at*[-*pé* L]Ú *ša*-⸢*ra*⸣
74) ⸢*ù*⸣ *šu-um-r*[*i-ir i*]*š-tu*
75) *ša-a-šu* ⸢*ù*⸣ [*ni*]-*iš-m*[*u-m*]*i ù a-mu-ur a-na-ku* ⸢ÌR⸣ *ki*-⸢*ti*⸣
76) ^{I}⸢*šàr*⸣-⸢*ri*⸣ EN-*ia*

(64–68) So look, Amanḫatpe is a traitor, [so] may the king, my lord demand a reckoning of him. He has deserted from him. May the king, my lord, not keep silent without investigating Amanḫat[pe.]

(69–76) Another man; may he not put traitors(!) in the loyal territory of the king, my lord. Amanḫat[pe] is a traitor and he caused apostasy from him but we were obeying. So look, I am a loyal servant of the king, my lord.

EA 186

TRANSCRIPTION

Obv.

01) [*a-na šàr-ri* BAD-*ia* DINGIR-*ia* ^{d}UTU-*i*]⸢*a*⸣
02) [*qí--------bí--------ma*]
03) [*um-ma Ma-ya-ar-za-na* LÚ URU *Ḫa-sí* ^{KI} ÌR-*k*]*a*
04) [*ep-ri šu-pa-al* GÌR.MEŠ-*ka a-na* GÌR.MEŠ ^{I}*šàr-ri* BAD-*ia*] ^{d}UTU-⸢*i*⸣[*a*]
05) [DINGIR-*ia* 7-*šu ù* 7-*šu am-qú-u*]*t*
06) [*a-mu-ur-*]⸢*mi*⸣ *a-*⸢*na*⸣-[*ku*] ⸢ÌR⸣ ⸢*ki*⸣-⸢*ti*⸣ [^{I}*šàr-ri*] BAD-*ia*
07) [DINGIR-*ia*] ⸢^{d}⸣UTU-⸢*ia*⸣ ⸢*ù*⸣ ⸢*i*⸣-*ri-du* [^{I}]*š*[*àr*]-*ra*
08) [BAD-*ia* DINGIR-*ia* ^{d}UT]U-⸢*ia*⸣ ⸢*qa*⸣-⸢*du*⸣ [ŠE]Š.[ME]Š ⸢*ù*⸣ DUMU.MEŠ-
⸢*i*⸣[*a*]
09) [ÌR.M]EŠ ⸢*ki*⸣-[*ti* ^{I}*šàr-ri* BAD-*i*]*a* DINGIR-*ia* ^{d}⸢UTU⸣-[*i*]*a*
10) ⸢*ù*⸣ BA.UG$_{7}$ [*ni-mu-ut*] ⸢*a*⸣-⸢*na*⸣ *šu-pal* GÌR.MEŠ
11) ^{I}*šàr-ri* B[AD-*ia* ^{d}UTU-]*ia* DINGIR-*ia*
----[ ]----
12) *ù a-*⸢*mu*⸣-⸢*ur*⸣-*m*[*i* ^{I}*A-m*]*a-*⸢*an*⸣-*ḫa-*⸢*at*⸣-⸢*pé*⸣
13) LÚ [UR]U ⸢*Tu*⸣-*šu-*⸢*ul*⸣-[*ti* ^{KI} *i-nu-*]⸢*ma*⸣ ⸢*i*⸣-*ṣa-*⸢*ba*⸣-⸢*tu*⸣-*m*[*i*]
14) LÚ.⸢SA⸣.⸢GAZ⸣.MEŠ ⸢URU⸣.K[I *Ma-aḫ-ṣi-ib-*]⸢*ti*⸣ ^{KI} URU.KI
15) ⸢*ki*⸣-⸢*ti*⸣ ^{I}*š*[*àr-ri*] ⸢BAD⸣-[*ia* DINGIR-*ia*]⸢^{d}⸣UTU-*ia*
16) ⸢*ù*⸣ [*i-ša-la-lu-ši ù i-na* IZ]I.⸢MEŠ⸣
17) [*i-ša-ra-pu-ši ù a-na ma-ḫa*]*r* ^{I}[*A-ma-*]⸢*an*⸣-*ḫa-at-pé*
18) L[Ú URU *Tu-šu-ul-ti* ^{KI} *il-l*]*i*[*-k*]*u*
19) [*ù* ^{I}*A-ma-an-ḫa-at-pé* LÚ URU *Tu-šu-ul-*]*ti* ^{KI}
20) [*i-di-nu-mi* NÍG.MEŠ *qa-du* Ì.MEŠ *a-na* LÚ.]SA.GA[Z.]MEŠ
21) [*ù a-mu-ur-mi*]⸢URU⸣ [*Gi-lu-na*]⸢URU⸣.KI *ki-*[*ti*]
22) ^{I}[*šàr-ri* BAD-*ia* DINGI]R-[*i*]*a* [^{d}UTU-*ia i*]-⸢*ṣa*⸣-⸢*ba*⸣-*t*[*u*]-⸢*mi*⸣
23) [LÚ.SA.GAZ.]⸢MEŠ⸣ [*ù i-ša-la-lu-š*]*i* [*ù*]
24) [*i-šar-ra-*]⸢*pu*⸣-⸢*ši*⸣[*i-na* IZI *i-*]⸢*ša*⸣-[*ti*]
25) ⸢*ù*⸣ [*a-na ma-ḫ*]*ar* ^{I}⸢*A*⸣[*-ma-an-ḫa-at-pé*] ⸢LÚ⸣ URU *Tu-*[*šu-ul-ti*^{KI}]
26) *i-*⸢*ri*⸣-[*bu*]-*na ù* [^{I}*A-ma-an-ḫa-at-*]⸢*pé*⸣ ⸢LÚ⸣ ⸢URU⸣ *T*[*u-šu-ul-ti* ^{KI}]
27) *i-di-nu-mi* NÍG.MEŠ [*qa-du* Ì.MEŠ *a*]-*na* ⸢LÚ⸣.SA.GA[Z.MEŠ]

EA 186

TRANSLATION

(1–5) [Speak to the king, my lord, my god, m]y [sun god; the message of Mayarzana, the ruler of Ḫasi, yo]ur [servant, the dirt under your feet: At the feet of the king, my lord,] m[y] sun god, [my god, seven times and seven times have I falle]n.

(6–11) [Look,] I am the loyal servant of [the king,] my lord, [my god,] my sun god, and I serve the k[in]g, [my lord, my god, my sun god, with ‹my› [bro]thers and my sons, loy[al serv]ants [of the king, m]y [lord], my god, [m]y sun god, and we would die under the feet of the king, [my] lo[rd,] my [sun god,] my god.

(12–20) And lo[ok], as for [Am]anḫatpe, the ruler of the [ci]ty of Tushul[ti, whe]n the *ʿapîrû* seized the city of [Maḫṣib]ti, the loyal city of the k[ing, my] lord, [my god,] my sun god, and they [plundered it and with fi]re [they burned it and w]e[n]t [to Ama]nḫatpe, the ru[ler of the city of Tushulti, then Amanḫatpe, the ruler of the city of Tushul]ti kept furnishing food w[ith oil to] the *ʿapîrû*.

(21–26) [And look, the *ʿapîrû* [se]ized the city of [Gilôna,] the loyal city of [the king, my lord, [m]y [go]d, [my sun god, and they plundered i]t [and they burn]ed it [with fi]re and they en[te]red in to A[manḫatpe], the ruler of the city of Tu[shulti,] and [Amanḫat]pe, the ruler of the city of T[ushulti,]

(27) kept furnishing food [with oil t]o the *ʿapî*[*rû*].

---

28) *ù a-mu-ur-mi* UR[U *Ma-ag-d*]*a-li* URU.[KI *ki-ti*]

29) ^{I}*šàr-ri* B[AD-*ia*] ⸢DINGIR⸣-⸢*i*⸣[*a* ^{d}UTU-*ia*] ⸢*i*⸣-*ṣa-ba-*[*tu-mi*]

30) LÚ.SA.G[AZ.MEŠ *ù i-ša-l*]*a-lu-ši* ⸢*ù*⸣ [*i-šar-ra-pu-ši*]

31) *i-na* I[ZI *i-ša-ti ù a-na m*]*a-*⸢*ḫar*⸣ ⸢I⸣[*A-ma-an-ḫa-at-pé*]

32) LÚ URU[*Tu-šu-ul-ti* ^{KI}] ⸢*i*⸣[*-ri-bu-na*]

33) *ù* ^{I}[*A-ma-an-ḫa-at-pé* LÚ URU *Tu-šu-ul-ti* ^{KI}]

34) *i-*[*di-nu-mi* NÍG.MEŠ *qa-du* Ì.MEŠ *a-na* LÚ.SA.GAZ.MEŠ]

[————————————————————]

35) [*ù a-mu-ur-mi* URU *Uš-te*^{KI} URU.KI *ki-ti*]

36) [^{I}*šàr-ri* BAD-*ia* DINGIR-*ia* ^{d}UTU-*ia i-ṣa-ba-tu-mi*]

37) [LÚ.SA.GAZ.MEŠ *ù i-ša-la-lu-ši ù*]

38) [*i-šar-ra-pu-ši i-na* IZI *i-ša-ti*]

Rev. 39) [*ù a-*]⸢*na*⸣[*ma-ḫar* ^{I}*A-ma-an-ḫa-at-pé*]

40) [LÚ URU] ⸢*Tu*⸣[*-šu-ul-ti* ^{KI} *i-ri-bu-na*]

41) [*ù* ^{I}]⸢*A*⸣[*-m*]*a-an*[*-ḫa-at-pé* LÚ URU *Tu-šu-ul-ti*^{KI}]

42) ⸢*i*⸣-⸢*di*⸣-*nu-m*[*i* NÍG.MEŠ *qa-du* Ì.MEŠ *a-na* ⸢LÚ⸣.SA.GAZ.MEŠ]

---

43) ⸢*ù*⸣ *a-mu-ur*[*-mi* URU.KI *Ḫa-sí*^{KI} URU.KI *ki-ti* ^{I}*šàr-ri* BAD-*ia*]

44) ⸢LÚ⸣.⸢SA⸣.⸢GAZ⸣.MEŠ [*iš-ḫi-ṭú* URU.KI *Ḫa-sí*^{KI} URU.KI]

45) ^{I}⸢*šàr*⸣-⸢*ri*⸣ BAD-*ia* DINGIR-⸢*ia*⸣ ⸢^{d}⸣[UTU-*ia ù*]

46) *i-*[*du*]*-ku-mi* LÚ.ÌR.MEŠ *ki-ti* [^{I}*šàr-ri*]

47) ⸢BAD⸣-⸢*i*⸣[*a* DINGIR]*-ia* ^{d}UTU-*ia ù i-k*[*a-ša-da*]

48) ⸢LÚ⸣.[SA.G]AZ.M[EŠ] *qa-te*^{MEŠ} LÚ.MEŠ ÌR.[MEŠ *ki-ti*]

49) ^{I}*šà*[*r-ri*] ⸢BAD⸣-*ia* DINGIR-*ia* ^{d}UTU-*i*[*a ù*]

50) ⸢*i*⸣-⸢*ri*⸣-⸢*bu*⸣-⸢*mi*⸣ 40 ⸢LÚ⸣.MEŠ S[A.GAZ.MEŠ]

51) ›⸢LÚ⸣.⸢SA⸣.G[AZ].MEŠ‹ *a-na* ⸢*ma*⸣-*ḫar* ⸢I⸣⸢*A*⸣[*-ma-an-ḫa-at-pé*]

52) L[Ú URU *Tu-šu-ul-*]*ti* ^{KI} ⸢*ù*⸣ ⸢*ni*⸣-[*iš-mé*]

53) *i-*[*nu-ma* i_{15}*-ba-šu-m*]*i* 40 LÚ.⸢SA⸣.[GAZ.MEŠ]

54) ⸢*it*⸣-[*ti* ^{I}*A-ma-an-ḫa-at-p*]*é* LÚ URU *Tu*[*-šu-ul-ti* ^{KI}]

55) ⸢*ù*⸣ ⸢*ti*⸣-[*na-mi-*]⸢*šu*⸣*-mi* GIŠ.GIGIR.MEŠ-*šu-nu* ⸢ŠEŠ⸣-*ia*

56) ⸢*ù*⸣ ⸢DUMU⸣-[*ia*] ⸢ÌR⸣.MEŠ ^{I}*šàr-ri* BAD-*ia* D[INGIR-*ia*] ⸢^{d}⸣⸢UTU⸣-*ia*

57) *ti-*[*li-ku a*]*-na ma-ḫar* ⸢^{I}⸣⸢*A*⸣-⸢*ma*⸣-⸢*an*⸣-*ḫa-at-pé* L[Ú URU *Tu-š*]*u-*⸢*ul*⸣-⸢*ti*⸣^{K}[^{I}]

(28–34) And look, the *'apî*[*rû*] seiz[ed] the cit[y of Magda]lu, a [loyal] city of the king, [my] lo[rd, m[y] god, [my sun god, and] they [plun]dered it and [they burned it] with f[ire and they entered in t]o [Amanḫatpe] the ruler of the city of [Tushulti] and [Amanḫatpe, the ruler of the city of Tushulti] ke[pt furnishing food with oil to the *'apîrû*].

(35–42) [And look, the *'apîrû* seized the city of Ushte, the loyal city of the king, my lord, my god, my sun god, and they plundered it and they burned it with fire and they entered in t]o [Amanḫatpe, ruler of the city of] Tu[shulti, and] A[m]an[ḫatpe, the ruler of the city of Tushulti] kept furnishi[ng food with oil to the *'apîrû*.]

(43–57) And look, the *'apîrû* [attacked the city of Ḫasi, the loyal city of the king, my lord. The city of Ḫasi is the city of] the king, my lord, my god, [my sun god, and] they at[tac]ked the loyal servants of [the king], m[y] lord, my [god, my sun god. And the hand of the [loyal] servants of the king, my lord, my god, m[y] sun god, overpo[wered] the[*'a*]*pî*[*rû*] [but] forty men of the '[*apîrû*] ›*'apîrû*‹ entered in to A[manḫatpe] the ru[ler of the city of Tushul]ti. And we h[eard] th[at] forty *'ap*[*îrû*] were wi[th Amanḫatp]e, the ruler of the city of Tu[shulti] and my brothers and my sons, loyal servants of the king, my lord, [my] g[od,] my [sun god,] dis[pat]ched their chariots.

58) ⸢*ù*⸣ ⸢*ti*⸣-]*iq-bu-mi a-na* ⸢^{I}⸣⸢*A*⸣-⸢*ma*⸣-⸢*an*⸣-⸢*ḫa*⸣-⸢*at*⸣-*pé* [*id-na-mi*]
59) LÚ.[SA.]GAZ.MEŠ LÚ *ša*-⸢*ri*⸣⸢^{MEŠ}⸣ *ša* ^{I}⸢*šàr*⸣-⸢*ri*⸣ [BAD]-⸢*ia*⸣
60) ⸢DINGIR⸣-[*i*]*a* ^{d}UTU-[*i*]*a ni-ša-al-šu*-⸢*nu*⸣ *pu*-[*ḫa-at*]
61) [*i-ṣa-*]⸢*ba*⸣-⸢*tu*⸣-*mi* ⸢URU⸣.⸢DIDLI⸣.⸢ḪI.A⸣.⸢KI⸣ ^{I}*šàr*-⸢*ri*⸣⸢BAD⸣-[*ia*]
62) ⸢DINGIR⸣-[*i*]*a* ⸢^{d}⸣⸢UTU⸣-*ia ù* [*pu-ḫ*]*a-at iš*-⸢*ḫi*⸣-⸢*ṭú*⸣ U[RU *Ḫa*-]*sí* ^{K}[^{I}]
63) [URU.KI ^{I}*šàr-r*]*i* BAD-*ia* ⸢DINGIR⸣-⸢*i*⸣*u* ^{d}UTU-⸢*i*⸣[*a*]
64) [*ù i-ma-*]⸢*gar*⸣ *na-da-an* LÚ.SA.⸢GAZ⸣.⸢MEŠ⸣
65) [*ù*] ⸢*ìl*⸣-⸢*qé*⸣ [LÚ.SA.GA]Z.MEŠ ⸢*ù*⸣ ⸢*ìl*⸣-[*qé-mi*]
66) [ÌR.]MEŠ-*šu* ⸢*ù*⸣ ⸢*iḫ*⸣-[*l*]*i-iq a-na* LÚ.⸢SA⸣.[GAZ.MEŠ]
67) [*ia-n*]*u a-na* ⸢*ia*⸣-*ši* ÉRIN 1-⸢*en*⸣ ⸢*iš*⸣-⸢*tu*⸣ URU.[KI]
68) [*ù*] ⸢*i*⸣-⸢*de*⸣ ⸢*ar*⸣(?)-⸢*na*⸣(?)-⸢*šu*⸣ ⸢*ù*⸣ *iḫ-li-i*[*q*]
69) [*a-n*]*a* [LÚ.SA.GAZ.MEŠ *ù mi-na*] ⸢*i*⸣-*pu-šu-na*
70) [*a-na-ku ù uš*]-⸢*ši*⸣-*ir*-⸢*ti*⸣
71) [.....*a-na* ^{I}*šàr-ri*] ⸢BAD⸣-⸢*ia*⸣ ⸢DINGIR⸣-⸢*ia*⸣ [^{d}][U]TU[-*ia*]
72) [..........*a-na*]⸢*ia*⸣-⸢*ši*⸣[....................]
73) [..............]⸢*na*⸣[.......................]
74) [..]
75) [..]
Lft.ed. 76) *ki-i-ma* ⸢*il*⸣-*lí* ⸢*ù*⸣[*qa-at-šu*]
77) *ia-ri-im* [UGU ^{I}*šàr-ri* BAD-*ia*]
78) [DINGIR]-*ia* ^{d}UTU-[*ia ù*]
79) ⸢UGU⸣ KUR ⸢*ki*⸣-*t*[*i-šu ù*]
80) *ni-iš-mu a-w*[*a-te*^{MEŠ}]
81) [^{I}*šàr-ri* BAD-*ia* DING]IR-*ia* ⸢^{d}⸣⸢UTU⸣-*ia*
82) [.........]⸢*ù*⸣ ⸢*i*⸣-⸢*nu*⸣-*ma* ⸢*yi*⸣-⸢*iq*⸣-*bi*
83) [^{I}*šàr-ri* BAD-*i*]⸢*a*⸣ ⸢DINGIR⸣-*i*⸢*a*⸣ ⸢^{d}⸣UTU-*i*[*a*]
84) [.........]⸢*ù*⸣ ⸢*ti*⸣-[*i*]*l-qú-n*[*a*]
85) [.........]*ma-li* UGU-⸢*nu*⸣

(57–75) They w[ent t]o Amanḫatpe, the ruler of the city of Tushulti. [And th]ey spoke to Amanḫatpe: "[Hand over] the *ʿapîrû*, the traitors of the king, my [lord], [m]y god, m[y] sun god. We would demand a reckoning of th[em] be[cause] they [have] seized the cities of the king, [my] lord, [m]y god, my sun god, and because they atta[ck]ed the ci[ty of Ḫa]si, [the city of the kin]g, my lord, my god, m[y] sun god." [And he agr]eed to give over the *ʿapîrû*, [but] he took [the *ʿapîr*]*û* and he to[ok] his [servants and] he ran away to the *ʿapî*[*rû*.] I do [not] have one soldier from the city. [And] I know his crime but he esca[ped t]o [the *ʿapîrû* and what] can I do, [myself? So] I [se]nt [....to the king,] my lord, my god, [my s]un god [...to] me [...].

(76–85) As he rose up and rebelled [against the king my lord,] my [god, my] sun god [and] against [his] loy[al] land [but] we heed the wor[ds of the king, my lord,] my [go]d, my sun god [...] and when [the king, m]y [lord], my sun god, spoke [...] then they took [...] against us.

EA 187

TRANSCRIPTION

Obv. 01) [*a-na* ^{I}*šàr-*]⸢*ri*⸣ BAD-⸢*ia*⸣[DINGIR-*ia* ^{d}UTU-*ia*]
02) [*qí*]- *bí*- [*ma*]

---

03) [*um-*]*ma Ša-de*$_{9}$*-ya* LÚ U[RU............]
04) [Ì]R-*ka ep-ri šu-pa-a*[*l*]
05) ⸢GÌR⸣.⸢MEŠ⸣-⸢*pí*⸣ ^{I}*šàr-ri* BAD-*ia*
06) [*a*]-⸢*na*⸣ GÌR.MEŠ-*pí šàr-ri* BAD-⸢*i*⸣[*a*]
07) ⸢DINGIR⸣-⸢*ia*⸣ ^{d}UTU-*ia* 7-*šu ù* 7-[*šu*]

- - - - - - - - - -

08) [*am*]-*qú-ut*

---

09) ⸢*a*⸣-⸢*mu*⸣-*ur-mi a-na-ku* ÌR *ki*-⸢*ti*⸣
10) ^{I}*šàr-ri* BAD-*ia* DINGIR-*ia* ^{d}⸢UTU⸣-⸢*i*⸣[*a*]
11) ⸢*i*⸣-*na aš-ri an-ni-im*
12) *ù* URU *E-ni-ša-si*$_{20}$[^{KI}]
13) URU.KI *šàr-ri* BAD-*ia* DINGIR[-*ia* ^{d}UTU]-⸢*ia*⸣
14) ⸢*ù*⸣ ⸢*a*⸣-⸢*nu*⸣-⸢*ma*⸣ ⸢*i*$_{15}$⸣-⸢*na*⸣-⸢*ṣa*⸣-⸢*ru*⸣
15) [*a-š*]*ar* ⸢*šàr*⸣-⸢*ri*⸣ [BAD-*i*]*a* [DINGIR-*ia* ^{d}UTU-*ia*]
Lo.ed. 16) [.................................]
Rev. 17) [.................................]
18) [.................................]
19) [.................................]
20) [.................................]
21) [.................................]
22) ⸢*ù*⸣ ⸢*a*⸣-⸢*nu*⸣-⸢*ma*⸣ ⸢*uš*⸣-⸢*ši*⸣-⸢*ir*⸣-*t*[*i*]
23) DUMU.MUNUS-*ia* ⸢*a*⸣-*na* ⸢É⸣.⸢GAL⸣
24) [*a*]-*na šàr-ri* BAD-*ia* DINGIR-⸢*ia*⸣
25) ^{d}UTU-*ia*

EA 187

TRANSLATION

(1–8) [To the ki]ng, my lord, [my deity, my sun god, sp]eak: [Mess]age of Šadêya, ruler of the city of [....], your [ser]vant, the dirt under the feet of the king, my lord, [a]t the feet of the king, my lord, my god, my sun god, seven times and seven [times] have I fallen.

(9–13) Behold, I am the loyal servant of the king, my lord, my deity, [my] s[un god] in this place and the city of ʿÊni-šâsi [is?] the city of the king, my lord, [my] go[d], my [sun god]

(14–15) [And] now I am guarding the [pl]ace of the king my [lord, my god, my sun god].

(16–21) *Almost completely effaced*

(22–25) And now I have sent my daughter to the palace to the king, my lord, my god, my sun god.

EA 188

TRANSCRIPTION

Obv.
01') [*a-na* GÌR-*p*]*í š*[*àr-ri*]
02') [EN-*i*]*a* ^{d}UTU-*i*[*a*]
03') [7-*šu*] *ù* 7-⸢*šu*⸣ [*am-qú-ut*]
04') [*a-m*]*u-ur* ⸢*a*⸣-⸢*na*⸣-*ku* L[Ú.....]
05') ⸢*ù*⸣ *a-n*[*a-k*]*u* ÌR *k*[*i-it-ti*]
06') *šà*[*r-ri*] E[N-*ia*] DI[NGIR-*ia* ^{d}UTU-*ia*]
07') ⸢*ù*⸣ [....................]
08') ⸢x⸣ [....................]

EA 188

TRANSLATION

(1'–3') [...at the fe]et of the k[ing, m[y] [lord, m[y] sun god, [seven times] and seven times h[ave I fallen].

(4'–8') [Lo]ok, I am the [...] and I am the lo[yal] servant of]the ki[ng, my] lo[rd,] my] g[od, my sun god] and [...] *x* [.....]

EA 189

TRANSCRIPTION

Obv. 01) *a-na* LUGAL EN-*ia*
02) *um-ma* ^{I}*I*$_{15}$*-ták-ka-ma* ÌR-*ka*
03) *a-na* GÌR.MEŠ EN-*ia* ^{d}UTU-*ia*
04) 7-*šu a-na pa-ni* 7-*ta-an am-qut*
05) EN-*ia a-na-ku* ÌR-*ka*
06) *ù yi-la-mu-nu-ni* ^{I}*Bir*$_5$*-ia-wa-za*
07) *lam-nu-um a-na pa-ni-ka* EN-*ia*
08) *ù i-nu-ma yi-la-mu-nu-ni*
09) *a-na pa-ni-ka i-nu-ma la-qa-am*
10) *gáb-bi* É *a-bi-ia iš-tu*
11) KUR *Qì-id-ši ù* URU.ḪI.A-*ia*
12) *uš-ši-ir a-na* ^{d}IZI.MEŠ *i*$_{15}$*-ša-ti*$_7$
13) *ù al-lu-ú-mì* LÚ.MEŠ MAŠKÍM
14) LUGAL EN-*ia ù* LÚ.MEŠ GAL.MEŠ-*šu*
15) *i-du-mì ki-it-ti*$_7$*-ia*
16) *i-nu-ma aq-bi a-na* LÚ.GAL
17) ^{I}*Pu-ḫu-ri li-de-mì*
18) LÚ.GAL ⸢I⸣⸢*Pu*⸣-⸢*ḫu*⸣-⸢*ru*⸣ *i-nu-ma*
19) [..............]⸢É⸣ *l*[*i*.......]
20) [..............] x [.........]

Rev. 01) [................]⸢*du*⸣ *k*[*a*....]
02) [I]⸢*Bir*$_5$⸣*-ia-wa-za ki-na-an-n*[*a*]
03) *ur-ru-du-ka a-na-ku qa-*⸢*du*⸣*-m*[*ì*]
04) *gáb-bi* ŠEŠ.MEŠ-*ia ù a-šar*
05) *nu-kùr-tu*$_4$ *a-na* LUGAL EN-*ia*
06) *a-na-ku al-la-ak-mì qa-du*
07) ÉRIN.MEŠ-*ia ù qa-du* GIŠ.GIGIR.MEŠ-*ia*
08) *ù qa-du gáb-bi* ŠEŠ-*ia*

EA 189

TRANSLATION

(1–4) To the king, my lord; the message of Etakkama, your servant: At the feet of my lord, my son god, seven times on the face and seven times have I fallen.

(5–12) My lord, I am your servant but the evil Biryawaza as been slandering me before the king, my lord, and while he has been slandering me before you, then he took away all my patrimony from the territory of Qidšu and my cities he has sent up in flames.

(13–20) And behold, the commissioners of the king, my lord and his senior officials know my loyalty when I spoke to the senior official, Puḫuru. May the senior official, Puḫuru be apprised that [....................]

Rev. (1–8) [....]....Biryawaza. Thus I am serving you with all my colleagues and wherever there is hostility to the king, my lord, I go with my troops and with my chariotry and with all my colleagues.

09) *ù a-mur-mì* ^{I}*Bir*$_{5}$*-ya-wa-za*
10) *uš-ši-ir gáb-bi* URU.ḪI.A LUGAL
11) EN-*ia a-na* LÚ.MEŠ SA.GAZ.MEŠ
12) *i-na* KUR *Taḫ-ši ù i-na* KUR *Ú-pí*
13) *ù ka-aš-da-ti*$_{7}$ *ù il*$_{5}$*-la-ak*
14) DINGIR.MEŠ-*nu-ka ù* ^{d}UTU-*ku*
15) *a-na pa-ni-ia ù* URU.ḪI.A *ut-te-er*
16) *a-na* LUGAL EN-*ia iš-tu*
17) LÚ.MEŠ SA.GAZ.MEŠ *aš-šum ur-ru-di-šu*
18) *ù ú-pa-ṭír* LÚ.MEŠ SA.GAZ.MEŠ
19) *ù lu-uḫ-di* LUGAL EN-*ia*
20) *a-na I-ták-ka-ma* ÌR-*šu*
Up.ed. 21) *ù ur-ru-du-mì*
22) LUGAL EN-*ia qa-du*
23) *gáb-bi* ŠEŠ.MEŠ-*ia*
Lft.ed. 24) *ur-ru-du* LUGAL EN-*ia ù gáb-bi* KUR.[MEŠ-*ka*]
25) *ú-ša-aḫ-li-iq* ^{I}*Bir*$_{5}$*-ia-wa-za p*[*a-nu-šu*]
26) *a-na ḫa-ba-li-lum-ma ù a-na-ku* [ÌR-*ka*]
27) *a-di da-ri-t*[*i*]

(9–18) But look, Biryawaza had released all the cities of the king, my lord, to the *ʿapîru* men in the land of Taḫsi and in the land of ʾÔpi. But I came and your deity and your sun god were going before me and I returned the cities to the king, my lord, from the *ʿapîru* men in order to serve you. So I expelled the *ʿapîru* men,

(19–23) So may the king, my lord, rejoice in Itakkama, his servant and I will serve the king, my lord, with all my colleagues.

(24–27) I am serving the king, my lord, but Biryawaza caused the loss of all of [your] lands. [He is] com[mitted] to violence, but I am [your servant,] forever.

EA 190

TRANSCRIPTION

Obv. 01’) [...] KUR LUGAL ⌜EN⌝[-*ka*]
02’) [*ù uṣ-ṣur* ᴵ]⌜*Pu*⌝-*ḫu-ri* ⌜LÚ⌝ M[ÁŠKIM-*ka*]???
03’) [*lu na-a*]*ṣ-ra-ta ù uṣ-ṣ*[*ur*]
04’) [URU *Qi-id-*]*ši*ᴷᴵ *ù* ⌜*uṣ*⌝-*ṣur*
05’) [URU *Ku-mì-*]*dì*ᴷᴵ URU *ma-ṣa-ar*[*-ti* LUGAL]
06’) [*ša-ni-ta*$_5$] *ši-mu a-na a-wa-ti* L[UGAL]
07’) [*i-nu-*]*ma al-la-ka -ku-*⌜*um*⌝?
08’) [*qa-du*] GIŠ.GIGIR.MEŠ-*ia ù* [*qa-du*]
09’) [ÉRIN.MEŠ LU]GAL-*mì ù*(!) *qí-bá* UG[U]
10’) [ŠEŠ.MEŠ-*ka ù*] ⌜ÉRIN⌝!⌜MEŠ⌝! *Ka-ši-*⌜*i*⌝(!) [*ù*]
11’) [LÚ *Su-*]*te*ᴹᴱŠ-*ši qa-du* L[Ú.MEŠ]
12’) [SA.GAZ].MEŠ-*ši qa-du* [...]

EA 190

TRANSLATION

(1'–5') [...] the land of the king, [your] lord, [and guard] Puḫuru, [your] com[missioner; may] you [be on[guard] and gua[rd the city of Qede]sh and guard [the city of Kômi]di, the [king's] garris[on] city.

(6'–12') [Furthermore,] heed(pl) the words of the ki[ng, because] I am coming to you [with] my chariotry and [with the troops of the ki]ng, so command [your brothers] and the Cushite troops [and] its [Su]tû with its [*ʿapîru*] m[en] with [...]

EA 191

TRANSCRIPTION

Obv. 01) ⸢*a*⸣-⸢*na*⸣ ^{I}LUGAL-*ma* EN-*ia*
02) *um-ma* ^{I}*Ar-sà-wu-ya* LÚ URU ⸢*Ru*⸣-*ḫi-ṣa*
03) *a-na* GÌR.MEŠ EN-*ia am-qut*
04) LUGAL EN-*ia iš-pur-mi*
05) *a-na šu-ši-ri a-na pa-ni*
06) ÉRIN.MEŠ *pí-ṭá-at* LUGAL EN-*ia*
07) ⸢*ù*⸣ *a-na pa-ni* MÁŠKIM.MEŠ-*šu*
08) *ma-á*ʾ*-du-te*

---

09) *ù i-ma-la-ku ba-li-mì*
10) *ur-ru-ud* LUGAL EN-*ia*

---

11) *lu-uk-šu-da-am-mì*
12) ÉRIN.MEŠ *pí-ṭá-at* LUGAL
13) *ù* MÁŠKIM.MEŠ-*šu ù* ⸢*a*⸣-*na*-⸢*ku*⸣
14) *šu-ši-ra-ku gáb-bá*
15) ⸢*ù*⸣ *ar-ki-šu-nu*
Lo.ed. 16) ⸢*a*⸣-⸢*al*⸣-*la-ak-mì*
Rev. 17) *a-šar na-ak*-⸢*ru*⸣
18) LUGAL EN-*ia*
19) *ù ni*-il_5-*qé-šu-nu*
20) *i-na qa-at* LUGAL EN-*nu n*[*i*-]*din-mì*
21) ⸢*a*⸣-*ia-bi-šu*

EA 191

TRANSLATION

(1–3) To the king, my lord. the message of Arzawuya. the ruler of the city of Rōǵiṣi: At the feet of my lord, I have fallen.

(4–8) The king my lord has written to prepare for the arrival of the regular troops of the king, my lord and for the arrival of his many commissioners.

(9–10) And would I consider not serving the king, my lord?

(11–21) May the regular troops of the king and his commissioners arrive and I will have prepared everything and after them I will go wherever they oppose the king, my lord, and we will take them. We will hand his enemies over to the king, our lord.

EA 192

TRANSCRIPTION

Obv. 01) [*a-n*]*a* ⸢LUGAL⸣ EN-*ia*

02) [*u*]^{d}UTU *u* DINGIR.MEŠ-*ia*

03) [*qí*]-*bí-ma um-ma*

04) [^{I}]⸢*Ar*⸣-*sà-wu-ya* ÌR *ki-it-ti*

05) [*ša*] LUGAL EN-*ia*

06) ⸢*ep*⸣-*ri* GÌR.MEŠ LUGAL EN-*ia*

07) ⸢*a*⸣-⸢*na*⸣ GÌR.MEŠ LUGAL EN-*ia*

08) *u* ^{d}UTU *u* DINGIR.MEŠ-*ia*

09) ⸢7⸣-*šu ù* 7-*ta-a-an am-qut*

---

10) [*iš*]-*te-me a-wa-at*^{MEŠ}

11) [LUGAL] EN-*ia u* DINGIR.MEŠ-⸢*ia*⸣

12) [*u a-n*]*u-um-ma*

13) [*i-n*]*a-na l*[*i-iš-me*]

Lo.ed. 14) [*a-wa-te*^{MEŠ}-]*i*[*a*]

15) [LUGAL] EN‹-*ia*› *ù* [*la-a*]

Rev. 16) [*yi*]-*mé-ki* LUGAL EN-⸢*i*⸣[*a*]

17) [*iš*]-⸢*tu*⸣ KUR.KI-*šu*

EA 192

TRANSLATION

(1–9) [Sp]eak [t]o the king, my lord [and] the sun god and my deity; the message of Arsawuya, the loyal servant [of]the king, my lord, the dirt under the feet of the king, my lord: At the feet of the king, my lord and the sun god and my deity, seven times and seven times have I fallen.

(10–17) [I have] heard the words of [the king], my lord and my deity [and n]ow m[ay the king,] ‹my› lord, [heed] m[y words] and may the king, my lord, [not ne]glect his land.

EA 193

TRANSCRIPTION

Obv. 01) ⸢*a*⸣-*na* ^{I}LUGAL-*ma* EN-*ia*
02) *um-ma* ^{I}*Ti*$_{4}$-*wa-ti*$_{7}$
03) *a-na* GÌR.MEŠ LUGAL EN-*ia*
04) 7-*šu a-na pa-ni* 7-*an am-qut*

---

05) *a-nu-um-ma i-na* URU.KI
06) *i*$_{15}$-*ba-ša-ku-mì*
07) *lu-ú na-aṣ-ra-ku ma-gal*
08) *ù a-nu-um-ma*
09) ⸢ANŠE⸣.KUR.RA-⸢*ia*⸣
10) ⸢*ù*⸣ É[RIN.MEŠ-*ia*]
11) [*ù* GIŠ.GIGIR.MEŠ-*ia a-na*]
Rev. 12) ⸢*ur*⸣[-*ru-ud* LUGAL]
13) *ù* ⸢*a*⸣[-*na pa-ni*]
14) ÉRIN.MEŠ ⸢*pí*⸣-⸢*ṭá*⸣-[*ti*]
15) *a-na-ku it-ti*$_{7}$-⸢*ši*⸣(?)
16) *il*$_{5}$-*la-ku-mì*
17) *ù* LÚ *la yu-ra-du*
18) LUGAL *yi-ra-ru-šu*
19) *a-nu-um-ma*
20) GU$_{4}$.MEŠ UDU.MEŠ
21) *šu-uš-ši-ra-ti*$_{7}$
22) [*ki-m*]*a qa-bé-ka*
Up.ed. 23) [*i-n*]*a* ŠÀ *ṭup-pí*
24) ⸢*a*⸣-*na ia-ši*

EA 193

TRANSLATION

(1–4) To the king, my lord; the message of Tiwati: At the feet of the king, my lord, seven times on the face, have I fallen.

(5–7) Now, I am indeed in the city and verily I am diligently on my guard.

(8–18) And now my horses and [my] t[roops and my chariots are for] the ser[vice of the king], and at [the head] of the regular troo[ps] I, myself, will go with them. But the man who does not serve, the king will curse him.

(19–24) Now, I have prepared oxen and sheep [in accordance wi]th your command in the tablet to me.

EA 194

TRANSCRIPTION

Obv. 01) *a-na* ^{I}*šàr-ri* EN-*ia*
02) *um-ma* ^{I}*Bir*$_{5}$*-ia-wa-za* ÌR-⸢*ka*⸣
03) *a-na* GÌR.MEŠ-*pí* ^{I}*šàr-ri*
04) *be-li-ia* 7 *ù* 7-*ta*-⸢*an*⸣
05) *am*-⸢*qut*⸣ *a-mur ni-i-nu*
06) ⸢ÌR⸣.⸢MEŠ⸣ *a-ra-du*
07) ⸢^{I}⸣*šàr-ri iš-tu*
08) ⸢*da*⸣*-ri-ti*$_{7}$ *ki-ma*
09) ^{I}*Šu*-⸢*tar*⸣-*na a-bi-ia*
10) *ki-ma* ^{I}*Up*(?)-[..]-*tar* ⸢*a*⸣-*bi* [*a-bi-ia*]
11) [*a*-]⸢*mur* [.....]⸢*ni*⸣-*nu*
12) [..........] traces [..........]
Lo.ed. 13) [...........................]
Rev. 14) [...........................]
15) [...........................]
16) [...........................]
17) *m*[*a* [.......................]
18) DU[MU....................]
19) ⸢*aš*⸣-⸢*šum*⸣ [..................]
20) *a-na* ⸢*na*⸣-[*ṣa*-]⸢*ar*⸣
21) URU.⸢DIDLI⸣.⸢ḪI.A⸣-*ni ù*
22) KASKAL-⸢*ra*⸣-*na ša uš-ši-ir-ta*
23) [*a*]-⸢*na*⸣ ⸢KUR⸣ ⸢*Na*⸣-⸢*aḫ*⸣-*ri-mi*
24) [*l*]*i*-⸢*ta*⸣(?)-*ṣi*
25) [..........]⸢*ú*⸣-⸢*wa*⸣(?)
26) [...........................]
Up.ed 27) [....................]⸢*i*⸣*a*
28) [....*pa*-⸢*al*⸣-*ḫa-at*
29) *ma-gal*
Lft.ed. 30) [...]⸢*a*⸣-*nu-ma* ⸢ŠEŠ⸣-*ia*
31) [*ú*]-⸢*wa*⸣-⸢*aš*⸣-⸢*šer*$_{9}$⸣ ⸢*a*⸣-⸢*na*⸣
32) UGU-⸢*ka*⸣

EA 194

TRANSLATION

(1–5) To the king, my lord; the message of Biryawaza, your servant: At the feet of the king, my lord seven (times) and seven times have I fallen.

(5–10) Look, we are servants, serving the king from of old like my father, Sutarna, like Up[..]tar, [my father's] father.

(11–21) Look [...]are we [..........]s[on [...] in order to [....] to pro[te]ct the cities.

(21–24) And as for the caravan which you sent to the land of Nahrîmi, may it go forth.

(25–29) [..........it] is very much afraid.

(30–32) [And] now my brother have I sent to you.

EA195

TRANSCRIPTION

Obv. 01) *a-na* ^{I}*šàr-ri*
02) *be-li-ia*
03) *qí-bí-ma*
04) *um-ma* ^{I}*Bir*$_{5}$*-ia-wa-za*
05) ÌR-*ka* SAḪAR.MEŠ \ *ep-ri*
06) *ša* GÌR.MEŠ-*ka ù*
07) KI.MEŠ *ša ka-bá-sí-ka*
08) GIŠ.GU.ZA *ša a-ša-bi-ka*
09) *ù* GIŠ.GÌR.GUB \ *gi-iš-tap-pí*
10) *ša* GÌR.MEŠ-*ka*
11) *a-na* GÌR.MEŠ ^{I}LUGAL EN-*ia*
12) ^{d}UTU KIN.‹NIM› *še-ri*^{MEŠ}
13) \ *li-mì-ma*
Lo.ed. 14) 7-*šu a-na pa-ni*
Rev. 15) 7-*ta-an-ni am-qut*
16) *be-li-mi* ^{d}UTU
17) *i-na* AN *ša-me ù*
18) *ki-ma a-ṣa-i* ^{d}UTU.⸢M⸣EŠ
19) *iš-tu ša-me ki-na-an-na*
20) *tu-qa-ú-na* ÌR.MEŠ
21) ⸢*a*⸣*-ṣa-i a-wa-te*^{MEŠ}
22) *iš-tu* UZU.KA
23) \ *pí-i be-li-šu-**nu*
24) *a-nu-ma a-na-ku qa-du*
25) ÉRIN.MEŠ-*ia ù* GIŠ.GIGIR.MEŠ-*ia*
26) ⸢*ù*⸣ *qa-du* ŠEŠ.MEŠ-*ia*
27) *ù qa-du* LÚ.MEŠ SA.GAZ.MEŠ-*ia*
28) *ù qa-du*
Up.ed. 29) LÚ.MEŠ *Su-te-ia*
30) *a-na pa-ni* ÉRIN.MEŠ *pí-ṭá-ti*$_{7}$
Lft. ed. 31) *a-di a-šar yi-qa-bu*
32) ^{I}LUGAL *be-li-ia*

EA 195

TRANSLATION

(1–15) Speak to the king, my lord; the message of Biryawaza, your servant, the dirt under your feet and the ground of your treading, the chair of your sitting and the footstool of your feet; at the feet of the king, my lord, the sun god of the dawning \ of the nations, seven times on the face, (and) seven times have I fallen.

(16–23) My lord is the sun god in heaven and like the coming forth of the sun god from heaven, thus the servants await the coming forth of the words from the mouth of their lord.

(24–32) Now, I with my troops and my chariotry and with my colleagues (brothers) and with my *ʿapîru* men and with my Sutû men am anticipating the regular troops to wherever the king, my lord, commands.

EA 196

TRANSCRIPTION

Obv. 01) [*a-na* LUGAL EN-*i*]*a*[*q*]*í-b*[*í-ma*

02) [*um-ma* ^{I}*Bir*$_5$*-i*]*a-*⸢*wa*⸣*-*⸢*za*⸣ ⸢ÌR⸣[*-ka*]

03) [*a*]*-na* ⸢GÌR⸣.⸢MEŠ⸣ ⸢LUGAL⸣ ⸢EN⸣‹*-ia*› ⸢7⸣ *a-*⸢*na*⸣ [*pa-ni*]

04) *ši-bi-*⸢*ta*⸣*-*⸢*a*⸣*-an am-*⸢*qut*⸣

05) ⸢*ù*⸣ *i*[*š*]*-*⸢*te*⸣*-me* ⸢*i*⸣*-*⸢*nu*⸣*-*[*m*]*a ša-pár* L[UGAL]

06) E[N-*ia* ^{I}...]*sa-ia* [*ù*] [*n*]*a-a*[*ṣ*]*-r*[*a-k*]*u*

07) *ù* [*ur-ru-u*]*d a-na-*⸢*ku*⸣ [L]UG[AL] E[N-*i*]*a*

08) *i-n*[*a aš-r*]*i an-ni* ⸢*ti*⸣*-*[*i*]*k-šu*[*-da-a*]*m-mi*

09) [*ar-ḫi-iš* ÉRIN GA]L ⸢LUGAL⸣ ⸢EN⸣*-ia*

10) ⸢*a*⸣*-*⸢*na*⸣ *m*[*a-ḫar* LUGAL KUR *Ḫa-*]*at-*[*ti*$_7$ ^{KI}]

11) ⸢*ma*⸣*-*⸢*ṣar*⸣ [LU]G[AL EN-*ia paṭ-ru*]

12) *i*[*š-t*]*u m*[*u*]*-ḫi-ia* ⸢*a*⸣*-*⸢*na*⸣*-*⸢*ku*⸣ [1*-en* ÌR]

13) ⸢LUGAL⸣ ⸢*ša*⸣ ⸢*ir*⸣*-ti*$_7$*-ḫa-ti*$_7$ ⸢*a*⸣*-n*[*a ša-šu*]

14) [*ù l*]*i-*⸢*de*⸣ LUGAL EN-*ia* ⸢*ù*⸣

15) [*gáb-b*]*i* ÌR.MEŠ LUGAL EN-*ia*

16) [*i*]*t-ta-al-ku* EGIR!

17) [LUGAL] KUR *Ḫa-at-ti*$_7$^{KI} *ù*

18) [*ka-aš-*]*du gáb-bi* MÁŠKIM.⸢MEŠ⸣

19) [LUGAL E]N-*ia ša* ⸢*uṣ*⸣*-ṣ*[*u-ni*]

20) [.......................]

21) [.......................]

22) [.......................]

Lo.ed. 23) [.......................]

24) [.......................]

Rev. 25) [.......................]

26) [.........*i*]*a*[............]*i*[*a*]

27) [...........]DAM.MEŠ-*ia*

28) [*ù*] ⸢É⸣.GI.IA *ù*

29) [*ša-k*]*a-an i-na* ÚR \\ *su-ni-*[*šu*]

30) [*š*]*a-ni-tam i-nu-ma la-ma-ad*

31) [LUGAL] EN-*ia a-wa-ta*$_5$ *a-ni-ta*$_5$

32) *la-a i-pa-aš ip-*‹*ša*› *an-na* LÚ *iš-tu*

33) ⸢*da*⸣*-ri-ti*$_7$ *ša-ni-tam*

EA 196

TRANSLATION

(1–4) [Sp]ea[k to the king, m]y [lord; the message of Biry]awaza, [your] servant: [A]t the feet of the k[in]g, ‹my› l[ord], 7 times on [the face] (and) seven times, have I fallen.

(5–13) And I have heeded when the k[ing, my] l[ord,] sent [...]saya [and] I am on guard. And I [have serv]ed the [k]in[g], [m]y lo[rd] in this [plac]e. May [the gre]at [army] of the king, my lord, arrive [quickly] bef[ore the king of the land of Ḫa]t[ti]. The garrison of the [ki]n[g, my lord, departed from me. I am [the one servant of] the king that remains to [him].

(14–20) [So may] the king, my lord, be apprised that [al]l of the servants of the king, my lord, have gone away after(!) [the king] of the land of Ḫatti and all the commissioners [of the king,] my [lo]rd, that came forth [have arriv]ed [...].

(21–26) [..............................]

(27–29) [.....] my wives [and] my daughters in law and [he p]ut (them) in his lap (= had intercourse with them).

(30–33) [F]urthermore, inasmuch as [the king], my lord, learned of this matter, never has a man done such a de‹ed›.

34) ⌜*yu*⌝-*wa-ša-ra-ni-mì* LUGAL EN[-*ia*]
35) ⌜1⌝ *me-tì* LÚ.MEŠ *a-na* ⌜*na*⌝-*ṣa*-⌜*ri*⌝ Ì[R-*ka ù*]
36) [*a-n*]*a na-ṣa*-⌜*ri*⌝ ⌜URU⌝.DIDLI.ḪI.A LUGAL EN-[*ia*]
37) [*a-d*]*i* ⌜*i*⌝-*ma-ru* ÉRIN.MEŠ *pí-ṭá-ti*$_7$
38) [LUGA]L EN-*ia ù la-a*
39) [*y*]*i-qù-ul* LUGAL EN-*ia*
40) [*iš*-]*tu ip-ši an-ni ša*
41) [*i*]-*pa-aš* [I]⌜*Bi*⌝-*ri-da-aš-wa*
42) [*i-nu*-]*ma yi-na-ma-aš* KUR.KI
43) [LUGAL] EN-*ia ù* URU.DIDLI.[ḪI.A-*šu*]

(33–38) Furthermore, may the king, [my] lord, send me one (or two?) hundred men to protect [your servant and] to protect the cities of the king, [my] lord, until I see the regular troops of [the kin]g, my lord.

(38–43) And may the king, my lord, not [ke]ep silent [conce]rning this deed that Biridashwa [has] done [whe]n he caused (?) the land of [the king], my lord, and [his] citi[es] to desert.

EA 197

TRANSCRIPTION

Obv. -04) [*a-na* LUGAL EN-*ia qí-bí-ma*]
-03) [*um-ma* [I]*Bir*$_{5}$*-ia-wa-za* ÌR-*ka*]
-02) [*a-na* GÌR.MEŠ LUGAL EN-*ia* 7 *a-na pa-ni*]
01) [7-*ta-an-ni am-qut*]
00) [*a-mur* [I]*Ar-sà-wu-ya*]
01) [*yi-i*]*q-bi a-*[*na* [I]..............]
02) ⸢ÌR⸣-*ka i-na* URU *A*-[*ra-ri ? a-na*]
03) ANŠE.KUR.RA.MEŠ-*šu ù* GIŠ.GIGIR-*šu* [*i-di-in*$_{4}$*-šu-ni*]
04) *a-na* LÚ.MEŠ SA.GAZ *ù la-a ta*[*-di-in*$_{4}$*-šu-ni*]
05) *a-na* LUGAL EN-*ia u mì-ia-ti*$_{7}$ *a-*⸢*na*⸣*-ku* ›⸢*ù*⸣‹
06) ÌR *a-na ia-ši-ia a-na-mì* LUGAL *gáb-bu*
07) *yi-mur-ma* [I]*Bi-ri-da-aš-wa ip-ša an-na*
08) *ù yi-*‹MAŠ›*-na-mu-uš* URU *Ya-nu-am-ma* UGU-*ia*
09) *u yi-du-ul* KÁ.GAL *a-na* EGIR-*ia*
10) *ù yi-il*$_{5}$*-qé* GIŠ.GIGIR.MEŠ *i-na* URU *Aš-tar-ti*$_{7}$
11) *ù ya-di-in*$_{4}$*-šu-ni a-na* LÚ.MEŠ SA.GAZ
12) *ù la-a ya-di-in*$_{4}$*-šu-*⸢*ni*⸣ *a-na* LUGAL EN-*ia*
13) *yi-mur-ma šàr* URU *Bu-uṣ-ru-na*
14) *ù šàr* URU *Ḫa-lu-un-ni u ti*$_{7}$*-pa-šu*
15) *nu-kúr-ta it-ti* [I]*Bi-ri-da-aš-wa*
16) *a-na mu-ḫi-ia u ti*$_{7}$*-iq-bu-na*
17) *al-ka-am-mi nu-du-uk* [I]*Bir*$_{5}$*-ia-wa-za*
18) ⸢*ù*⸣ *la-a ni-wa-aš-ši-ru-šu a-na*
19) [KUR *Ta*]*ḫ-ši*$_{x}$(ŠE) *ù i-pa-ṭar a-na-ku iš-tu*
20) [*qa-ti-š*]*u-nu ù iz-zi-iz i-na*

Lo.ed. 21) [KUR *A-pí ù*] ⸢URU⸣ *Di-maš-qa i-nu-ma*
22) [*ti*$_{7}$*-mu-ru k*]*i-i ur-ru-*⸢*du*⸣

Rev. 23) [LUGAL EN-*ia ti*$_{7}$]*-iq-bu-n*[*a*]
24) [ÌR.MEŠ *šàr* KUR *Ḫa-a*]*t-ti*$_{7}$ *ni-nu*
25) *ù a-na-ku iq-bu* ÌR *šàr* KUR *Mi-iṣ-r*[*i*]
26) *a-na-ku ù yi-la-ak* [I]*Ar-sà-wu-ya*

EA 197

TRANSLATION

(-4–0) [Speak to the king, my lord; the message of Biryawaza, your servant: at the feet of the king, my lord, seven (times) on the face and seven times have I fallen. Look, Arsawuya]

(1–5) [sp]oke t[o PN,] your servant in the city of A[raru(?)] concerning his horses (and) his chariots, "[Hand them over] to the *ʿapîru* men but do not h[and them over] to the king, my lord."

(5–6) Who am I? A servant! It is to the king that everything of mine belongs.

(7–12) Biridashwa saw this deed and incited the town of Yanuʿam against me and he barred the gate behind me and he took the chariots from the town of Ashtartu and he handed them over to the *ʿapîru* men and did not hand them over to the king, my lord.

(13–19) The king of the town of Buṣruna and the king of the town of ʿAllônu saw (this) and they made war on me with Biridashwa, and they were saying, "Come on! Lets kill Biryawaza and not let him get away to [the land of Ta]ḫsi."

(19–21) But I escaped from their [grip] and I took a stand in the [land of Api and] the city of Damascus.

(21–26) When [they saw t]hat I serve [the king, my lord, they] kept sayin[g], "We are [servants of the land of Ḫa]tti." But I kept saying "I am the servant of the king of the land of Egyp[t]." And Arsawuya went

27) *a-na* URU *Qì-i*[*s-sà*] ⸢*ù*⸣ *yi-il*$_{5}$*-qa*
28) ÉRIN.MEŠ [I]*A*-⸢*zi*⸣-[*ri*] ⸢*ù*⸣ *iṣ-ba-at*
29) URU *Ša-ad-du u ya-di-in*$_{4}$*-ši a-na*
30) LÚ.MEŠ SA.GAZ *u la-a ia-di-in*$_{4}$*-ši*
31) *a-na* LUGAL EN-*ia ù a-mur* [I]*I-ta-at-ka*
-*ma*
32) *ḫu-li-iq* KUR *Qì-is-sà u an-nu-ú*
33) [I]*Ar-sà-wu-ya qa-du* [I]*Bi-ri-da-*
aš-wa
34) *yu-ḫa-li-qú* KUR *A-pí*
35) *ù lì-pa-qa-ad* KUR.KI-*šu* LUGAL *la-a-mì*
36) *til-qú-ši* LÚ.MEŠ *na-ak-ru-tu*
37) *i-nu-ma* ŠEŠ.MEŠ-*ia nu-kúr-tu a-na ia-ši-ia*
38) *a-na-ku i-na-ṣa-ru* URU *Ku-mì-di* URU LUGAL
39) ⸢EN⸣-*ia ù lu-ú yu*!(UD)-*ša-lim* LUGAL *a-na* ÌR-
\\⸢*šu*⸣
40) [*la-a y*]*i-zi-ib* ÌR-*šu* LUGAL
41) [*ù lu-ú*] *ti*$_{7}$*-da-ga-lu* LUGAL.MEŠ [KUR *Qì-is-sà*]?
42) [*ù*]⸢LUGAL⸣.MEŠ KUR *A-pí š*[*um-ma*]
....
Lft.ed. 43) ...*a-ta-mar* ÉRIN.MEŠ *pí-ṭá-ti*$_{7}$

(27–31) to the town of Qi[ssa] (Qedesh) and he took the troops of Azi[ru] and he seized the town of Shaddu and he handed it over to the *ʿapîru* men and did not hand it over to the king, my lord.

(31–34) Look! Itatkama has caused the loss of Qissa (Qedesh) and behold Arsawuya with Biridashwa is causing the loss of the land of Api.

(35–42) So may the king attend to his land lest the enemies take it. While my associates (brothers) are hostile to me, I am guarding the city of Kômidi, the city of the king, my lord. So may the king bring peace to his servant; may the king [not a]bandon his servant [and may] the kings of [the land of Qissa? and] the kings of the land of Api see wh[ether.…]

(43) [........] I beheld the regular troops

EA 198

TRANSCRIPTION

Obv. 01) [*a-na*]⸢LUGAL⸣ ⸢EN⸣-[*ia*]
02) DINGIR.MEŠ *ša* SAG.D[U-*ia*]
03) *qí-bí*-⸢*ma*⸣
04) *um-ma* ᴵ*A-ra*-[*aš*]-⸢*ša*⸣
05) LÚ URU *Ku-mi-di* ⸢ÌR⸣-*k*[*a*$_4$]
06) *ep-ri ša* G[ÌR].⸢MEŠ⸣-*k*[*a*$_4$]
07) *qa-qa-ri ka*$_4$-*bá*-⸢*si*⸣-*ka*$_4$
08) *a-na* GÌR.MEŠ LUGAL EN-*ia*
09) 7-*šu* 7-*ta-a-an am*-⸢*qut*⸣
10) *a-mur-mi a-na-ku* ÌR *ki-it-ti-ka*$_4$
11) *li-íš-al*$_x$(AN)-*mì* LUGAL EN-*ia*
12) *ka*$_4$-*li* LÚ.MEŠ MÁŠKIM-*šu*
13) *a-di a-na-ku* ÌR *ki-it-ti*
14) LUGAL EN-*ia li-ìš-al*$_x$(AN)-*mì*
15) LUGAL EN-*ia* ᴵ*Ḫa-ma-aš-š*[*e*]

Lo.ed. 16) ⸢*a*⸣-*di a*-[*n*]*a-ku* ÌR *ki-it-ti*

Rev. 17) LUGAL EN-*ia ù*
18) ⸢*li*⸣-*im-ḫu-ur-mì*
19) LUGAL EN-*ia ù*
20) *li-ba-lu-uṭ-ni*
21) *ù i-ia-nu-mì*
22) ANŠE.KUR.RA *ù i-ia-nu*
23) GIŠ.GIGIR *a-na ia-ši*
24) *ù li- it*! (UT)-*r*[*u*]-*uṣ*$_4$-*mì*
25) *i-na pa-ni* LUGAL EN-*ia*
26) *ù li-ba*-⸢*lu*⸣-*uṭ* ›*aš*‹
27) ÌR-*šu ù al*$_x$(AN)-*lu-ú-mì*
28) DUMU-*ia uš-ši-ir*-⸢*ti*⸣
29) *a-na ma-ḫar* LUGAL EN-*ia*
30) *ù li-ba-lu-uṭ-ni*
31) LUGA[L] ⸢EN⸣-*ia*

EA 198

TRANSLATION

(1–9) Speak [to] the king, [my] lord, my personal deity. The message of Ara[š]ša, the ruler of the city of Kômidi, yo[ur] servant, the dirt under your f[ee]t, the ground of yo[ur] treading: At the feet of the king, my lord, seven times (and) seven times have I fallen.

(10–17) Look, I am your loyal servant. May the king, my lord, ask his commissioners whether I am a loyal servant of the king, my lord. May the king, my lord, ask Ḫamašš[e] whether I am a loyal servant of the king, my lord.

(17–27) And may the king, my lord, accept (me) and may he grant me life since I do not have horse or chariot. So may it please the king, my lord and may he grant life to his servant.

(27–31) And behold, I have sent my son to the presence of the king, my lord, so may the king, my lord, grant me life.

EA 199

TRANSCRIPTION

Obv. 01) [*a-na* LUGAL EN-*ia* ^{d}UTU-*ia*]
02) [*qí-bi-ma um-ma* ^{I}......]
03) [ÌR-*ka-ma a-n*]*a* GÌR.MEŠ-*pí*
04) [EN-*i*]⸢*a*⸣ *a*[*m*]-*qut*
05) *a*-⸢*mur*⸣ [*ša-pár*] LUGAL ^{d}UTU-*ia*
06) *a-na ia*-⸢*ši*⸣ *ù*
07) *iš-te-mé an-n*[*a*] [*ša*]
08) LUGAL EN-*li-ia* [*ù*]
09) [*u*]*š-šu-ur*-⸢*ti*$_{7}$⸣ [*gáb-bi*]
10) [*ma-*]*gal ù* [*ú-wa-ši-ra*]

Rev. 11) [*gá*]*b-bi* KASKAL.ME[Š]
12) LUGAL EN *a-di*
13) URU *Bu-uṣ-ru-*[*n*]*i*
14) *ù iš-te-mé* [*ma-gal*]
15) *a-mur-mi a-*[*na*]-⸢*ku*⸣
16) [Ì]R-*ka* [...]
17) [*ù*] *qa-ba-t*[*i a-na*]
18) [DUMU KIN-*r*]*i-ka*
19) [..]*te*$^{ḪI.A}$
20) [.......]$^{⸢ḪI.A⸣}$
21) [...no traces!...]

EA 199

TRANSLATION

(1–4) [Speak to the king, my lord, my sun god. The message of [PN] your servant. A]t the feet of [m]y lord, have I fallen.

(5–14) Look, the king, my lord, [wrote] to me and I heard the "affirmative" [of] the king, my lord [and] I have diligently expedited [everything] and [I will expedite a]ll of the caravans of the king, my lord, as far as the city of Buṣurni. And I have heeded [diligently.]

(15–21) Look, I am your [ser]vant [...and] I spoke [to] your [envoy........].

EA 200

TRANSCRIPTION

Obv.	01)	[*a-na šàr-ri* EN-*ia*]
	02)	[DINGIR.MEŠ-*ia* ᵈUTU-*ia*]
	03)	⸢*qí*⸣-⸢*bi*⸣-[*ma*]
	04)	[*u*]*m*-⸢*ma*⸣ ᴵÌR.MEŠ[-*ka*]
	05)	7-*šu ù* 7-*šu n*[*i-im*(?)-*q*]*u-ut*
	06)	[*a-n*]*a* GÌR.MEŠ LUGAL *be-li-ia*
	07)	[*a-m*]*ur ša ni-iš-mu-ú*
	08)	[UGU D]UMU LÚ *Aḫ-la-ma-i*
	09)	[.....]⸢*a*⸣ LUGAL *ša Ka-ra-du-ni-aš*
	10)	[...........]*ù* LÚ *Aḫ*-⸢*la*⸣-*ma-ú*
	11)	[.........*a-n*]*a a-ka-li*
Lo.ed.	12)	[........LUGAL] ⸢*be*⸣-*li*
	13)	[...............]⸢*ú*⸣ *ki-i*
Rev.	14)	[..........]⸢*la*⸣ *ú-ṣú-ú*
	15)	[*ù la ša-a*]*p-ru-ni*
	16)	[....]-*at*

EA 200

TRANSLATION

(1–6) Speak [to the king, my lord, my deity, my sun god; the m]essage of [your] servants: Seven times and seven times have we [fall]en [a]t the feet of the king, my lord.

(7–16) [Lo]ok, what we have been hearing (are hearing/have heard) [concerning the so]n(s) of the Aḫlamu, [...]the king of Karaduniash [...] and the Aḫlamu [...t]o eat [...the king] my lord [.....] because/when [....] they did not come forth [and they did not wr]ite us [...].

EA 201

TRANSCRIPTION

Obv. 01) *a-na* ^{I}LUGAL EN-*ia*
02) *qí-bí-ma*
03) *um-ma* ^{I}*Ar-ta-ma-an-ya*
04) ^{I}LÚ URU *Ṣí-ri-Ba-ša-ni*
05) ÌR-*ka a-na* GÌR.MEŠ
06) ^{I}LUGAL *be-li-ia*
07) 7-*šu a-na pa-ni* 7-
08) *ta-an-ni am-qut*
09) *a-nu-ma*
Lo.ed. 10) *a-na ia-ši*
Rev. 11) *ša-ap-ra-ta*
12) *a-na šu-ši-ri*
13) *a-na pa-ni* ÉRIN.MEŠ *pí-ṭá-ti*$_{7}$
14) *ù mi-ia-mì a-na-ku*
15) UR.GI$_{7}$ 1-*en ù*
16) *la-a al*$_{x}$(AN)-*la-ku*
17) *a-nu-ma a-na-ku*
18) *qa-du* ÉRIN.MEŠ-*ia*
19) *ù* GIŠ.GIGIR.MEŠ-*ia*
20) *a-na pa-ni* ÉRIN.MEŠ
Up.ed. 21) *pí-ṭá-ti*$_{7}$
22) *a-di a-šar*
Lft.ed 23) *yi-qa-bu* ^{I}LUGAL
24) *be-li-ia*

EA 201

TRANSLATION

(1–8) Speak to the king, my lord, the message of Artamanya, ruler of Ṣiri-Bashani, your servant: At the feet of the king, my lord, seven times on the face (and) seven times have I fallen.

(9–16) Now you have written to me to make preparations towards the arrival of the regular troops and who am I, a dog, that I would not go.

(17–24) Now I, with my troops and with my chariotry, am in the vanguard of the troops of the king, my lord, to wherever they may go.

EA 202

TRANSCRIPTION

Obv.	01)	*a-na* [I]LUGAL EN-*ia*
	02)	*qí-bí-ma*
	03)	*um-ma* [I]*A-ma-ya-še*
	04)	ÌR-*ka a-na* GÌR.MEŠ
	05)	[I]LUGAL *be-li-ia*
	06)	⌜7⌝-*šu ù* 7-*šu am-qut*
	07)	⌜*a*⌝-*na ia-ši-ia*
Lo.ed.	08)	⌜*ša*⌝-*ap-ra*-⌜*ta*⌝
Rev.	09)	[*a-n*]*a* ⌜*a*⌝-⌜*la*⌝-*ki*
	10)	[*a-n*]*a pa-ni* ÉRIN.MEŠ
	11)	*pí-ṭá-ti*$_7$*ù*
	12)	*mi-ia-mi*
	13)	*a-na-ku* UR.GI$_7$ 1-*en*
	14)	⌜*ù*⌝ *la-a al*$_x$(AN)-*la-ku*
	15)	⌜*an*⌝-*nu*-⌜*ú*⌝ *a-na-ku*
	16)	*qa-du* ÉRIN.MEŠ-*ia*
Up.ed	17)	GIŠ.GIGIR.MEŠ-*ia*
	18)	*a-na pa-ni* ÉRIN.MEŠ
	19)	*pí-ṭá-te*

EA 202

TRANSLATION

(1–6) Speak to the king, my lord, the message of Amayashe, your servant: At the feet of the king, my lord, seven times and seven times have I fallen.

(7–14) To me you have written [t]o go before the regular troops and who am I, a dog, that I would not go?

(15–19) Now I, with my troops and with my chariotry, am in the vanguard of the troops of the king, my lord.

EA 203

TRANSCRIPTION

Obv. 01) *a-na* ^{I}LUGAL EN-*ia*
02) *qí-bí-ma*
03) *um-ma* ^{I}ÌR.LUGAL
04) LÚ URU *Ša-as-ḫ̮i-mi*
05) ÌR-*ka a-na* GÌR.MEŠ
06) ^{I}LUGAL *be-li-ia*
07) 7-*šu a-na pa-ni*
08) 7-*ta-ni am-qut*
09) *at-ta*
Lo.ed. 10) *ša-ap-ra-*
\ ⸢*ta*⸣
Rev. 11) ⸢*a*⸣-*na šu-ši-*⸢*ri*⸣
12) [*a-*]*na pa-ni* ÉRIN.MEŠ *pí-ṭá-ti*$_7$
13) ⸢*ù*⸣ *a-nu-ma a-na-ku*
14) *qa-du* ÉRIN.⸢MEŠ⸣-*ia*
15) *ù* GIŠ.GIGIR.MEŠ-*ia*
16) *a-na pa-ni* ÉRIN.MEŠ
17) *ša* ^{I}LUGAL
18) *be-li-ia a-di*
19) *a-šar ti*$_7$*-la-ku*

EA 203

TRANSLATION

(1–8) Speak to the king, my lord; the message of ʿAbdi-Milki, the ruler of Shasḫ̮ʿimi, your servant. At the feet of the king, my lord, seven times on the face and seven times, have I fallen.

(9–19) You wrote to make preparations in anticipation of the regular troops and now I, with my troops and with my chariotry, am in the vanguard of the troops of the king, my lord, to wherever they may go.

EA 204

TRANSCRIPTION

Obv. 01) *a-na* ^{I}LUGAL
02) *be-li-ia*
03) *qí-bí-ma*
04) *um-ma* ^{I}LÚ URU *Qa-nu-ú*
05) ÌR-*ka a-na* GÌR.MEŠ
06) ^{I}LUGAL *be-li-ia*
07) 7-*šu a-na pa-ni*
08) 7-*ta-ni am-qut*
Lo.ed. 09) ⸢*at*⸣-⸢*ta*⸣
10) ⸢*ša*⸣-⸢*ap*⸣-⸢*ra*⸣-⸢*ta*⸣
Rev. 11) ⸢*a*⸣-⸢*na*⸣ ⸢*ia*⸣-*ši*
12) *a-na šu-ši-ri*
13) *a-na pa-ni* ÉRIN.⸢MEŠ⸣
14) *pí-ṭá-ti*$_{7}$ *ù*
15) *a-nu-ma a-na-ku qa-du*
16) ÉRIN.MEŠ-*ia ù qa-du*
17) GIŠ.GIGIR.MEŠ-*ia* ⸢*a*⸣-[*na*] ⸢*pa*⸣-*ni*
18) ÉRIN.MEŠ ^{I}LUGAL *be-li-ia*
19) ⸢*a*⸣-⸢*di*⸣ ⸢*a*⸣-⸢*šar*⸣
20) ⸢*ti*$_{7}$⸣-⸢*la*⸣-⸢*ku*⸣

EA 204

TRANSLATION

(1–8) Speak to the king my lord; the message of the man of Qanû, your servant: At the feet of the king, my lord, seven times on the face and seven times (on the back) have I fallen.

(9–14) You have written to me to make preparations for the arrival of the regular troops.

(14–20) And now I, with my troops and with my chariotry, am in the vanguard of the troops of the king, my lord, to wherever they may go.

EA 205

TRANSCRIPTION

Obv.	01)	*a-na* ^{I}LUGAL EN-*ia*
	02)	*qí-bí-ma*
	03)	*um-ma* ^{I}LÚ URU *Ṭù-bu*
	04)	ÌR-*ka a-na* GÌR.MEŠ
	05)	^{I}LUGAL *be-li-ia*
	06)	^{d}UTU *li-mi-ma*
	07)	7-*šu a-na pa-ni*
	08)	7-*ta-ni am-qut*
	09)	*at-ta ša-ap-ra-ta*
Lo.ed.	10)	⸢*a*⸣-*na šu-ši-ri*
Rev.	11)	*a-na pa-ni*
	12)	ÉRIN.MEŠ *pí-ṭá-ti*$_{7}$
	13)	*ù a-nu-ma*
	14)	*a-na-ku qa-du* ÉRIN.MEŠ-*ia*
	15)	*ù* GIŠ.GIGIR.MEŠ-*ia*
	16)	*a-na pa-ni* ÉRIN.MEŠ
	17)	*ša* ^{I}LUGAL EN-*ia*
	18)	*a-di a-šar ti*$_{7}$-*la-ku*

EA 205

TRANSLATION

(1–8) Speak to the king, my lord, the message of the ruler of the city of Ṭôbu, your servant: At the feet of the king, my lord, the sun god of the nations, seven times forward and seven times have I fallen.

(9–12) You have written to prepare for the coming of the regular army.

(13–18) And now I, with my troops and with my chariotry, am in the vanguard of the troops of the king, my lord, to wherever they may go.

EA 206

TRANSCRIPTION

Obv.	01)	*a-na* ^{I}LUGAL
	02)	*be-li-ia*
	03)	*qí-bí-ma*
	04)	*um-ma* ^{I}LÚ URU *Na-ṣi-ba*
	05)	ÌR-*ka a-na* GÌR.MEŠ
	06)	^{I}LUGAL *be-li-ia*
	07)	7-*šu a-na pa-ni*
	08)	7-*ta-ni am-qut*
	09)	*at-ta*
Lo.ed.	10)	*ša-a[p-r]a-*
		\⸢*ta*⸣
Rev.	11)	⸢*a*⸣*-na šu-ši-ri*
	12)	*a-*⸢*na*⸣ *pa-ni* ÉRIN.MEŠ *pí-ṭá-ti*$_7$
	13)	*ù* ⸢*a*⸣*-nu-ma*
	14)	⸢*a*⸣*-na-ku qa-du* ÉRIN.MEŠ-*ia*
	15)	⸢*ù*⸣ GIŠ.GIGIR.[ME]Š-*ia*
	16)	*a-na pa-ni* [ÉR]IN.MEŠ
	17)	*pí-ṭá-ti*$_7$

EA 206

TRANSLATION

(1–8) Speak to the king, my lord, the message of the ruler of Naṣība, your servant: At the feet of the king, my lord, seven times on the face (and) seven times have I fallen.

(9–17) You wrote to prepare in anticipation of the regular troops. And now I, with my troops and with my chariotry, am in the vanguard of the troops of the king, my lord, to wherever they may go.

EA 207

TRANSCRIPTION

Obv. 01) [*a-n*]*a* LUGAL ⸢EN⸣-*ia* [^{d}UTU-*ia*]
02) [*qí-*]⸢*bi*⸣-*ma* ^{I}⸢*Ip*⸣-⸢*te*⸣(?)[........ÌR]-*ka*
03) [*a-n*]*a* ⸢GÌR⸣.MEŠ ⸢EN⸣-*i*[*a am-qut*]
04) ⸢*iš*⸣-⸢*te*⸣-⸢*me*⸣ *k*[*a-li a-wa-te* LUG]AL
05) ⸢*i*⸣-⸢*na*⸣ ⸢*lìb*⸣-⸢*bi*⸣ [*ṭup-pí*]
06) ⸢*a*⸣-⸢*mur*⸣ *a-na-ku* ⸢ÌR⸣ [*ki-it-ti*]
07) [*ša-a*] *yu-ra-ad* [LUGAL]
08) [*ia-a-*]⸢*nu*⸣ *ki-ma i*[*a-ši* ÌR]
09) [*ki-it-ti*] ⸢*ù*⸣ ⸢*i*⸣-*nu-ma* [*ta-a*]*q-bu*
10) [*mi-nu-*]⸢*mi*⸣ 2-*šu* ⸢*a*⸣-*wa-a*[*t* LUGAL]
11) [*yi-*]⸢*iq*⸣-*bu* ⸢LÚ⸣ *ra-*[*bi-iṣ*] LUGAL
12) [*a-na ka-*]⸢*ta*⸣ ⸢*a*⸣-⸢*mur*⸣ [*a-na-*]⸢*ku*⸣

Lo.ed. 13) [ÌR] ⸢*ša*⸣-[*a*] L[UGAL EN-*ia*]
14) ⸢*ù*⸣ *i-nu-*[*ma*] ⸢LUGAL⸣ ⸢*yi*⸣-[*iš*]-*al*

Rev. 15) [LÚ *ra-*]*bi-sú* [*a-na*] ⸢ÌR⸣-⸢*šu*⸣
16) ⸢*ki*⸣-⸢*ma*⸣ ^{d}UTU ⸢*ù*⸣ *ki-ma*
17) $^{⸢d⸣}$[IŠKUR] ⸢*al*⸣-⸢*lu*⸣-*mi* ^{I}*Pu-ḫu-ur*
18) *la-*⸢*a*⸣-[*mi yi-*]⸢*na*⸣-*ṣa-ar-ni*
19) *ḫa-*⸢*li*⸣-⸢*iq*⸣-*mì gáb-bi*
20) URU.K[I.ME]Š LUGAL *iš-tu qa-ti*[-*ia*]
21) [*a-na*]⸢LÚ⸣ GAZ.MEŠ \\ *ḫa-*⸢*pí*⸣(?)-⸢*ri*⸣(?)

EA 207

TRANSLATION

(1–3) [Sp]eak [t]o the king, my lord, [my sun god]; ‹Message of› Ipte- [...] your [servant, A]t the feet of m[y] lord [have I fallen].

(4–9) I have heeded a[ll the words of the kin]g in the [tablet]. Look, I am a [loyal] servant [who has]served [the king]. [There is n]one like m[e, a loyal servant].

(9–17) And inasmuch as [you s]ay, "[Why] does the comm[issioner] of the king have to say the words of the king twice [to yo]u?" Look, ⸢I⸣ am [the servant] of the ki[ng, my lord]. And if [the king] had asked his [commissioner] concerning his servant, "Like Shamash and like [Baʿal]!"

(17–21) Behold, Puḫur did not protect me. All the cities of the king are lost from [my] grip [to] the *ʿapîru* men!

EA 208

TRANSCRIPTION

Obv. 01) [............................]
02) [............................]
03) [............................]
04) [............................]
05) [............................]
06) [............................]
07) [........] slight traces [.......]
08) *a-na mu-ḫi-ia* ⸢*ù*⸣ *ma-*⸢x⸣[........]
09) *ù* ⸢*uš*⸣-⸢*ši*⸣-⸢*ir*⸣-ti_7*-šu ki-ma a*[*r-ḫi-iš*]
10) *ù al-lu-ú-mi*
11) ^{I}*Pu-ḫu-ru ša-al-šu*
12) [*a-n*]*a* URU.DIDLI.ḪI.A *šàr-ri* EN-*ia*
13) [*i*]-⸢*nu*⸣-*ma ša-al-mu*
Lo.ed. 14) [UR]U.DIDLI.⸢ḪI.A⸣ *šàr-ri* EN-*ia*

EA 208

TRANSLATION

(1–7) [..]

(8–14) to me and [......] and I sent him with all due [haste]. And behold, Puḫuru, ask him [abou]t the cities of the king, my lord, [i]f the [cit]ies of the king, my lord, are at peace.

EA 209

TRANSCRIPTION

Obv. 01) [*a-na*] ⸢*šàr*⸣-⸢*ri*⸣ ⸢*bé*⸣-*li*-⸢*i*⸣[*a*]
02) ⸢*qí*⸣-*bí-ma*
03) *um-ma* ⸢*Zi*⸣-*ša*-⸢*mi*⸣-*mi* ⸢ÌR⸣-⸢*ka*⸣-*m*[*a*]
04) *a-na* GÌR!(ANŠE).MEŠ-*pí*-⸢*ka*⸣ ⸢*am*⸣-*qú*⸣-⸢*ut*⸣
05) 7 *ù* 7 ⸢*am*⸣-⸢*qú*⸣-*ut a-na*
06) *pa-ni šàr-ri* ⸢*bé*⸣-*li-i*⸢*a*⸣
07) *ḫa-di* URU.MEŠ *a-la-nu*-⸢*ka*⸣
08) *ša it-ti*$_7$*-ia ù a*-⸢*mur*⸣
09) *a-na-ku* ÌR-*ka a*-⸢*di*⸣
10) *da-ri-ti*$_7$ ⸢*ù*⸣ ⸢*a*⸣-⸢*mur*⸣ ⸢*a*⸣-⸢*na*⸣-‹*ku*› ⸢ÌR⸣-*ka*
11) *ù* DUMU-*ka ù a-mur* ⸢URU⸣.⸢MEŠ⸣-[*k*]*a*
12) *ša it-ti*$_7$*-ia* URU ⸢*šàr*⸣-⸢*ri*⸣
13) ⸢*bé*⸣-*li-ia ù šu-ma*
14) ⸢*la*⸣ ⸢*ú*⸣-⸢*uṣ*⸣-*ra-ti*$_7$ URU.M[EŠ]-*k*[*a*]
15) ⸢*ù*⸣ ⸢DINGIR⸣.ME[Š]-*nu ša it*-‹*ti*$_7$›-*ka*
Lo.ed. 16) ⸢SAG⸣-⸢*qà*⸣-*di li-mu*-⸢*ḫu*⸣[-*ṣú*?]

EA 209

TRANSLATION

(1–6) Speak to the king, m[y] lord; the message of Zishamimi, your servant: at your feet have I fallen. Seven (times) and seven (times) have I fallen before the king, my lord.

(7–16) The cities that are in my charge rejoice. And look, I am your servant forever. And look, ⌜I⌝ am your servant and your son. And look, [yo]ur cities that are in my charge are cit‹ies› of the king, my [lord] and if I do [n]ot guard yo[ur] citi[es], then may the gods that are wi[th] you smite(?) my head.

EA 210

TRANSCRIPTION

Obv. 01) [*a-na* ^I^*Ni-í*]*b-ḫu-ri*[*-ia*]
02) [*qí-b*]*í-ma*
03) [*um-ma* ^I^]*Zi-ša-*⌜*mi*⌝[*-mi*...]
04) [.............]*lu-ka*
05) [.............]
06) [............*ú-nu*]*-ú-te a-*⌜*na*⌝ LUG[AL]

EA 210

TRANSLATION

Obv. 01) [To Ni]bḫuri[ia]
02) [Spe]ak;
03) [The message of] Zišami[mi]
04) your [................]
05) [.....................]
06) [............the chat]tels for the king

EA 211

TRANSCRIPTION

Obv.	01)	⸢*a*⸣-⸢*na*⸣ ⸢*šàr*⸣-*ri* EN-⸢*ia*⸣
	02)	*qí-bí*-⸢*ma*⸣
	03)	*um-ma* ^{I}*Zi*-⸢*it*⸣-⸢*ri*⸣-*ya*-⸢*ra*⸣
	04)	ÌR-*ka* 7 *ù ši*-⸢*ib*⸣-⸢*i*⸣-⸢*ta*⸣-*an*
	05)	*ù* ^{UZU}*ša-ša-lu-ma ù*
	06)	UZU.UR$_5$ *a-na* GÌR.MEŠ *šàr-ri*
	07)	EN-*ia* ⸢*am*⸣-⸢*qut*⸣ *a*-⸢*mur*⸣-*mi*
	08)	[*a-na*]-*ku* ÌR *ša-a šàr-ri*
	09)	⸢EN⸣-*ia a-na-ku ù*
	10)	[*a*]-⸢*ba*⸣-*at ša-a*
	11)	⸢*ša*⸣-*pár* L[UGAL EN-*ia*]
Lo.ed.	12)	[*a-n*]*a* ÌR-⸢*šu*⸣
Rev.	13)	⸢*yi*⸣-*ìš-te-mé* [ÌR-*šu*]
	14)	ÌR *šàr-ri a-na*-⸢*ku*⸣
	15)	EN-*ia a-mur* ⸢LUGAL⸣
	16)	*ki-i-ma* ^{d}UTU *iš*-*tu*$_4$
	17)	AN.ḪI.A \\ *ša-mu-ma ù*
	18)	*la-a ni-la-ú*
	19)	*e-ze-eb a-ba-at*
	20)	*šàr-ri* EN-*ia*
	21)	*ù* LÚ.MÁŠKIM
	22)	*ša-a ša-ak-na-t*[*a*]
Up.ed.	23)	⸢UGU⸣-*ia*
Lft.ed.	24)	*ni-ìš-mu a-na*
	25)	*ša-a-šu*

EA 211

TRANSLATION

(1–7) Speak to the king, my lord, the message of Zitriyara, your servant. Seven (times) and seven times both on the back and on the stomach, at the feet of the king, my lord have I fallen.

(7–13) Look, ⌜I⌝ am the servant of the king, my lord, and the word that the k[ing, my lord,] has written [t]o his servant, [his servant] has heeded.

(14–25) The servant of the king am I. My lord, look, the king is like the sun god from the heavens and we are unable to abandon the word of the king, my lord. And as for the commissioner that he has placed over me, we are obeying him.

EA 212

TRANSCRIPTION

Obv. 01) *a-na* LUGAL *be-li-i*[*a*]
02) *um-ma* ^{I}*Zi-it-ri-ya-*⸢*ra*⸣
03) ÌR-⸢*di*⸣-*ka a-na* GÌR.‹MEŠ›
04) *be-li-*⸢*i*⸣*a am-qa-ut*
05) 7 *ù* 7 *ta-na*
06) *ki-i ni-pu-šu* ⸢*iš*⸣-[*t*]*u*
07) *da-ri-ti*$_7$
08) *ki-i ka-li* LÚ *ḫa-za-nu-ti*$_7$
09) *ki íp-pu-šu a-na* LUGAL
10) *bé-li-ia* ÌR LUGAL
11) [*bé*]-*li-*⸢*ia*⸣ *a-na-ku*
Rev. 12) *ka-*⸢*li*⸣ *a-wa-ta*$_5$
13) LUGAL *bé-li-i*‹*a*›
14) *iš-te-mu*

EA 212

TRANSLATION

(1–5) To the king, my lord, message of Zitriyara, your servant, at the fe‹et› of my lord have I fallen, seven (times) and seven times.

(6–14) Just as we have always done, as all the city rulers (have done), thus I will do for the king, my lord. A servant of the king, my [lo]rd am I. All the words of the king, my lord, I obey.

EA 213

TRANSCRIPTION

Obv. 01) *a-na* ^{I}LUGAL EN-⸢*ia*⸣ ^{d}UTU-*ia*
02) DINGIR.MEŠ-*ia qí-bí-ma*
03) *um-ma* ^{I}*Zi-it-ta-ya-ra*
04) ÌR-*ka ep-ri ša* GÌR.MEŠ-*ka*
05) *ù ṭi*$_4$*-iṭ ša ka-bá-ši-ka*
06) *a-na* GÌR.MEŠ ^{I}LUGAL EN-*ia*
07) ^{d}UTU-*ia* DINGIR.MEŠ-*ia* 7-*šu*
08) *ù* 7-*ta-an am-qú-ut*
09) *ù ka-ba-tu-ma ù ṣe-ru-*[*m*]*a*
10) *iš-te-mé ša-pár* ^{I}*šàr-*⸢*ri*⸣
11) EN-*ia* ^{d}UTU-*ia* DINGIR.MEŠ-*ia*
12) ⸢*a*⸣-⸢*na*⸣ ÌR-*šu a-nu-ma*
13) [*š*]*u-še-er-ti ki-ma*

Lo.ed. 14) [*š*]*a qa-bi* ^{I}*šàr-ru*

Rev. 15) EN-*ia* ^{d}UTU-*ia* DINGIR.M[EŠ-*i*]*a*

EA 213

TRANSLATION

(1–9) Speak to the king, my lord, my sun god, my deity, the message of Zittayara, your servant, the dirt at your feet, the mud on which you tread: At the feet of the king, my lord, my sun god, my deity, seven times and seven times, have I fallen on the belly and on the back.

(10–12) I have heard the message of the king, my lord, my sun god, my deity, to his servant.

(12–15) Now, I have made preparations according to [wh]at the king, my lord, my sun god, [m]y dei[ty] has said.

EA 214

TRANSCRIPTION

Obv. 01) [*a-na* LUGAL EN-*ia* DINGIR.MEŠ-*ia*]
02) [^{d}UTU-*ia um-ma*]
03) [^{I}.................ÌR-*ka*]
04) [*a-na*] ⌜GÌR⌝.⌜MEŠ⌝ [*be-li-ia* DINGIR.MEŠ-*ia*]
05) ⌜^{d}⌝⌜UTU⌝-*ia* 7-*e-t*[*a-an ù* 7-*ta-an*?]
06) ⌜*uš*⌝(?)-*ḫe-ḫi-in*$_{4}$ ⌜LÚ⌝.[MÁŠKIM-*ka*]
07) [*ka*]-*ši-id a*-⌜*na*⌝ [*ia-a-ši*]
08) [*i-na-an-*]*na* UD. KAM^{v} [*ù mu-ša*]
09) ⌜*i*⌝-[*ba*]-⌜*ša*⌝-*at* URU.K[I *a-na pa-ni*]
10) ⌜ÉRIN⌝.M[EŠ EN]-*ia yu*[-*wa-ši-ir*]
11) [^{I}Z]*i*-⌜*it*⌝-⌜*ra*⌝-⌜*ya*⌝-[*ra*]
12) [...]-*ta*-[..................................]
13) [...]
14) [...]
15) [...]
16) [...]
17) [...]
18) [...]
Lo.ed. 19) [...]
20) [...]
21) [...]
22) [...]
23) [...]
24) [...]
Rev. 25) [...] *a* [..................................]
26) ⌜*mi*⌝-⌜*im*⌝-⌜*mi*⌝[-*ia ù*]
27) ⌜*mi*⌝-⌜*im*⌝-⌜*mi*⌝ [LUGAL EN-*ia*]
28) ⌜*a*⌝-⌜*na*⌝ ⌜*ša*⌝-⌜*šu*⌝-⌜*nu*⌝ ⌜*a*⌝-*n*[*u-m*]*a*
29) ⌜*ni*⌝-⌜*da*⌝-⌜*bi*⌝-⌜*ir*⌝
30) ⌜LÚ⌝.⌜*lí*⌝ ⌜*ša*⌝ [*l*]*a* [*yi-iš*-]⌜*mu*⌝
31) ⌜*a*⌝-⌜*wa*⌝-⌜*ti*⌝⌜^{MEŠ}⌝ ⌜LUGAL⌝ [EN-*ia*]
32) ⌜LÚ⌝ ⌜*ar*⌝-⌜*ni*⌝ ⌜*iš*⌝-*t*[*u*]
33) KUR-⌜*ka*$_{4}$⌝

EA 214

TRANSLATION

(1–6) [To the king, my lord, my deity, my sun god, the message of […], your servant: At] the feet of [my lord, my deity,] my sun god, seven times have I prostrated.

(6–11) [Your commisioner] has reached me. [No]w day [and night,] the city is [waiting for]the troo[ps of]my [lord]. [Z]itraya[ra] has [sent.....]

(12–25) [..]

(26–33) [my] property [and] the property of [the king, my lord, for himself. ⸢Now⸣, we will expel the man who [do]es [no]t [ob]ey the words of the king, [my lord,] the criminal, from your land.

EA 215

TRANSCRIPTION

Obv. 01) *a-na šàr-ri* EN-*ia*

02) ^{d}UTU-⸢*ia*⸣ DINGIR.MEŠ-*ia*

03) *um-ma* ^{I}*Ba-ia-wa*

04) ÌR-*ka* \ ⸢*ka*⸣-*ab-tum-ma*

05) *ù ša-ša-lu-ma*

06) 7 *ù ši-ib-e-ta-an*

07) *a-na* GÌR.MEŠ ⸢*šàr*⸣-*ri be-li-ia*

08) ^{d}UTU-*ia* DINGIR.MEŠ-*ia*

09) ⸢*am*⸣-*qú-ut lu-ú*

10) ^{I}*Ia-an-ḫa-ma*
11) ⸢*i*⸣-*ia-a-nu i*-⸢*na*⸣
Lo.ed. 12) [MU]-*ti an-ni-ti*$_{7}$
Rev. 13) [*ḫa*-]*al-qa-at*-⸢*ma*⸣

14) [*gáb*-]*bi* KUR.ḪI.A-*ti*
15) ⸢*i*⸣-*na* LÚ.MEŠ SA.G⸢AZ⸣.[K]I
16) *ù bu-li-iṭ*
17) KUR.ḪI.A-*ka*————

EA 215

TRANSLATION

(1–8) To the king, my lord, my sun god, my deity, the message of Bayawa, your servant: On the belly and on the back, seven (times) and seven times at the feet of the king, my lord, have I fallen.

(10–17) Should Yanḫamu not be here within this [yea]r, [al]l the territories will be lost to the *ʿapîru* men. So grant life to your lands.

EA 216

TRANSCRIPTION

Obv. 01) *a-n*[*a* ^{I}]*š*[*à*]*r-ri* EN-*ia*
02) *q*[*í*]-⸢*bí*⸣-*ma*
03) *um-ma* $^{⸢I⸣}$⸢*Ba*⸣-*ia-wa* ÌR-*ka*
04) *a-na* GÌR.[M]E[Š] *šàr-ri* E[N-*i*]*a*
05) ^{d}U[T]U-⸢*i*⸣*a* 7 *ù* 7-⸢*ta*⸣-*an*
06) ⸢*am*⸣-*qut iš-te*$_9$-*mé ša-pár*
07) [*š*]*àr-ri* EN-*ia a-na* ÌR-*šu*
08) ⸢*a*⸣-*na* ⸢*šu*⸣-⸢*ši*⸣-⸢*ri*⸣ *i-na pa-ni*
09) ÉRIN.MEŠ *pí*-⸢*ṭá*⸣-*ti*
10) ⸢*a*⸣-*nu-ma* ⸢*i*⸣-*šu-ši-ru*
11) ⸢*ki*⸣-*ma qa*-⸢*bi*⸣ LUGAL EN-*ia*
12) ⸢*ù*⸣ *iš-te*$_9$-*mu ma-gal ma-gal*
13) ⸢*a*⸣-⸢*na*⸣ ⸢*a*⸣-*wa-ti* ^{I}*Ma-ia*
14) L[Ú].MÁŠKIM *šàr-ri* EN-*ia*

Lo.ed. 15) ⸢*ù*⸣ *yu-ši-ra* LUGAL
16) EN-*ia* ÉRIN.MEŠ \ *pí*-⸢*ṭá*⸣-
\[*ti*]

Rev. 17) [*a*]-*na* ÌR.MEŠ-*šu*
18) ⸢LÚ⸣.MEŠ *ša la-a ti-iš-te*$_9$-⸢*mu*⸣-*na*
19) *a-na* LUGAL LUGAL EN-*ia*
20) *yi-im-lu-ku a-na ša-šu-nu*

EA 216

TRANSLATION

(1–6) Speak t[o the] king, my lord; the message of Bayawa, your servant: At the feet of the king, my lord, my sun god, seven and seven times have I fallen.

(6–9) I have heard the message of the [k]ing, my lord to his servant to prepare in anticipation of the regular troops.

(10–14) Now I am preparing according to the command of the king, my lord and I am heeding most diligently the words of Maya, the commissioner of the king, my lord.

(15–17) So may the king, my lord, send the regular troops to his servants.

(18–20) As for the men who do not obey the king, the king, my lord, will take counsel concerning them.

EA 217

TRANSCRIPTION

Obv. 01) ⸢*a*⸣-⸢*na*⸣ ⸢LUGAL⸣ ⸢EN⸣-⸢*ia* ⸣
02) ⸢*qí*⸣-⸢*bí*⸣-⸢*ma*⸣
03) ⸢*um*⸣-⸢*ma*⸣ ⸢I⸣⸢*Aḫ*⸣-[.........]
04) ⸢ÌR⸣-⸢*ka*⸣ *a*[-*n*]*a* ⸢GÌR⸣.⸢MEŠ⸣
05) ⸢LUGAL⸣ E[N-*ia* ^{d}UT]U-[*ia*]
06) ⸢7⸣ ⸢*ù*⸣ [7-*ta*]-*a*[*n*]
07) ⸢*am*⸣-⸢*qut*⸣ ⸢*iš*⸣-⸢*te*$_{9}$⸣-*mé*
08) *gáb*-⸢*bi*⸣ ⸢*a*⸣-⸢*wa*⸣-⸢*ti*⸣
09) ⸢LUGAL⸣ ⸢EN⸣[-*ia*] ⸢*ù*⸣
10) *a*-⸢*nu*⸣-[*ma šu-ši*-]⸢*ra*⸣-⸢*ti*⸣
Lo.ed. 11) [*gáb-ba a*]-⸢*di*⸣(?) ⸢*ka*⸣(?)-[*ša-di*]
Rev. 12) ⸢LUGAL⸣ E[N-*ia*]
13) *ù* ⸢*mi*⸣-⸢*i*⸣[*a-mi*]
14) [U]R.⸢GI$_{7}$⸣ [*ù la-a*]
15) ⸢*yi*⸣-⸢*iš*⸣-⸢*te*$_{9}$⸣-[*mu a-na*]
16) ⸢I⸣⸢*Ma*⸣-*y*[*a* LÚ.MÁŠKIM]
17) ⸢LUGAL⸣ E[N-*ia*]
18) ⸢*ù*⸣ *y*[*u-ši*-]⸢*ra*⸣-*m*[*i*]
19) ⸢LUGAL⸣ ⸢EN⸣-⸢*i*⸣[*a*] ⸢ÉRIN⸣.[MEŠ]
20) ⸢*a*⸣-⸢*na*⸣ ⸢KUR⸣-⸢*šu*⸣ ⸢*ki*⸣-⸢*ma*⸣ ⸢*ar*⸣-⸢*ḫi*⸣-⸢*iš*⸣
21) ⸢LÚ⸣.⸢MEŠ⸣ ⸢*ša*⸣ ⸢*la*⸣-⸢*a*⸣ ⸢*ti*⸣-[*iš-m*]u
22) ⸢*a*⸣-⸢*na*⸣ I*Ma-ya šu-nu ti-m*[*u*]-*t*[*u*]-⸢*na*⸣
23) ⸢*gáb*⸣-⸢*ba*⸣-‹*šu*›-*nu*

EA 217

TRANSLATION

(1–7) Speak to the king, my lord; the message of Aḫ[…], your servant. At the feet of the king, [my] lo[rd], [my sun g]od, seven (times) and [seven ti]m[es] have I fallen.

(7–12) I have heeded all the words of the king, [my] lord. And no[w] I [have pre]pared [everything un]til the ar[rival] of the king, [my] lo[rd].

(13–17) And who is [the d]og [that] he would [not] ob[ey] May[a, the commissioner] of the king, [my] lo[rd]?

(18–20) So, may the king, m[y] lord s[en]d troo[ps] to his land with utmost haste.

(21–23) As for the men who would not o[be]y Maya, they will die, all of ‹th›em.

EA 218

TRANSCRIPTION

Obv. 01) [*a-*]*na* [LUGAL EN-*ia*]
02) [*qí-bí-ma*]
03) [*um-ma* ^{I}........]
04) ⌜LÚ⌝ [URU......]
05) [*a-na* GÌR.MEŠ EN-*ia*]
06) [7] ⌜*ù*⌝ [7-*ta-an*]
07) [*am-*]⌜*qut*⌝ *e*[*š-te*$_9$*-me*]
08) ⌜*gáb*⌝*-bi a*[*-wa-ti*]
09) ⌜LUGAL⌝ ⌜EN⌝-⌜*i*⌝[*a*]
10) [*a*]-⌜*nu*⌝*-ma i*$_{15}$*-š*[*u-ši-ru*]
11) *k*[*i*]-⌜*ma*⌝ ⌜*qa*⌝-[*bi*]
12) L[UGAL E]N-*i*[*a ù*]
Lo.ed. 13) ⌜*iš*⌝*-te*$_9$*-mu a-w*[*a-ti*]
Rev. 14) ^{I}*Ma-*⌜*ya*⌝ ⌜*ma*⌝-⌜*gal*⌝ *m*[*a-gal*]
15) *ù yu-*⌜*ši*⌝*-ra-mì*
16) LUG[AL] EN-*ia* ÉRIN.MEŠ
17) *a-na* KUR.MEŠ-*šu*

EA 218

TRANSLATION

(1–7) [Speak t]o [the king, my lord; the message of…., the ruler of [the town of….; at the feet of my lord, seven (times)] and [seven times have I fa]llen.

(7–14) I [have heard all the wo[rds] of the king, m[y] lord. [N]ow I am p[reparing] just as the k[ing,] m[y lo]rd com[manded. And] I am obeying the wo[rds] of Maya very dil[igently].

(15–17) So may the ki[ng], my lord, send troops to his lands.

EA 219

TRANSCRIPTION

Obv. 01) [*a-na*] ⸢*šàr*⸣-⸢*ri*⸣ ⸢EN⸣[-*ia*.....]
02) [*qí*]⸢*bí*⸣-[*ma*]
03) *u*[*m-ma*............ÌR-*ka*]
04) 7 ⸢*ù*⸣ [7 *a-na* GÌR.MEŠ EN-*ia am-qú-u*]*t*
05) [...........................]
06) [...........................]
07) [...........................]
08) [...........................]
09) [...........................]
10) [...........................]
11) [...........................]
12) [...........................]
13) [...........................]
14) [...........................]
15) [...........................]
16) [...........................]
Rev. 17) [...........................]
18) [...........................]
19) [...........................]
20) [...........] *a* [..............]
21) [.........*a-n*]*a* ⸢*ka*⸣-*ta*$_5$ [.......]
22) [.....] *a* [..................]*mi*
23) ⸢*yi*⸣-⸢*ip*⸣[..................]*mu*-⸢*da*⸣
24) *la-a* [......................]*yi-pu-?*
25) 30 GAL [.................]KÙ.GI
26) *a-na* ⸢*mu*⸣-[.......DÙ]G.G[A......]
27) *li*-[*it-r*]*i-iṣ* [*a-na pa-ni-ka*]
28) *a*-⸢*na*⸣ [........................]
29) ⸢*ù*⸣(?) [..............]⸢*yu*⸣-[*uš-ši-ra*]
Up.ed. 30) [ÉR]IN.MEŠ \ ⸢*pí*⸣-[*ṭá-ti*]
31) [*a-n*]*a* KUR-[*šu*.................]
32) UGU [........................]
Lft.ed. 33) [...]⸢*ka*⸣(?) [.........................]
34) [..............................]

EA 219

TRANSLATION

(1–4) [Sp]ea[k to]the king, [my] lord; the me[ssage of....., your servant]: Seven (times and) [seven (times) at the feet of my lord have I falle]n.

(5–20) [...]

(21–34) [...t]o you [......]he will d[o (?)......]not [...]he will do(?). Thirty cups [......]of gold [.....for [....]sweet[wine?...].

May be ple[as]ing [n your sight....]and (?) [...] may he [send regu]lar troops [t]o the land of [...] against [................................]

EA 220

TRANSCRIPTION

Obv. 01) *a-na* ^{I}*šàr-ri* EN-*ia* [^{d}UTU-*ia*]
02) *qí-bí-*[*-ma*]
03) *um-ma* ^{I}KÚR-*ur-tu-wa* ⌜LÚ⌝ ⌜URU⌝ ⌜*Ṣú*⌝(?)-*nu*
04) ÌR-*ka* SAḪAR.MEŠ *ša* GÌR.MEŠ
05) *šàr-ri* EN-*ia* ^{d}UTU-*ia*
06) *ù* IM.MEŠ *ša ka-bá-ši-*[*k*]*a*(?)
07) *a-na* GÌR.MEŠ *šàr-ri* EN-*i*[*a*]
08) ^{d}UTU-*ia* 7 *ù* 7-*ta-an*
09) *am-qut iš-te*$_{9}$*-mé gáb-bi*
10) *a-wa-ti* L[U]GAL EN-*ia* ^{d}UTU-*ia*
11) *mi-ia-*⌜*ti*⌝ *a-na-ku ù la*
12) *iš-te*$_{9}$*-mu a-na* MÁŠKIM LUGAL EN‹-*ia*›
13) [^{d}UT]U-*ia ki-ma qa-bi*
14) [*šàr-*]*ri* EN-*ia* ^{d}UTU-*ia*
15) [*a-n*]*u-ma iṣ-ṣú-ru*

Rev. 16) [UR]U.KI LUGAL EN-*ia* ^{d}U[TU]-*ia*
17) *a-di ka-ša-di*
18) LÚ.MÁŠKIM *šàr-ri* EN-*ia*
19) ^{d}UTU-*ia ù li-de* LUGAL EN-⌜*ia*⌝
20) ^{d}UTU *iš-tu* AN *ša*$_{10}$*-me*
21) *i-nu-ma ša-aḫ-ṭá-at-mì*
22) URU.KI *ša šàr-ri* EN-*ia*
23) ^{d}UTU-*ia ša it-ti-ia*
24) *ù mi-ḫi-iṣ-mì a-bi-ia*
25) *ù a-nu-ma i*$_{15}$*-na-ṣa-ru*
26) URU.KI *ša šàr-ri* EN-*ia*
27) ^{d}UTU-*ia ša it-ti-ia*
28) *a-di ka-ša-di*
29) LÚ.MÁŠKIM LUGAL EN-*ia*
30) ^{d}UTU-*ia a-na la-ma-*⌜*di*⌝

Up.ed. 31) [K]U[R]-*ti*^{MEŠ} LUGAL EN-*ia* ⌜^{d}⌝U[TU-*ia*]

EA 220

TRANSLATION

(1–9) Speak to the king, my lord, [my sun god]. The message of Nukurtuwa, the ruler of ⸢Ṣunu⸣(?), your servant, the dirt under the feet of the king, my lord, my sun god, and the clay of your(?) treading: At the feet of the king, m[y] lord, my sun god, seven (times) and seven times have I fallen.

(9–14) I have heard all the words of the king, my lord, my sun god. Who am I that I should not heed the commissioner of the king ‹my› lord, my [sun] god, according to the command of [the ki]ng, my lord, my sun god?

(15–19) [No]w I am guarding [the ci]ty of the king, my lord, my sun [god], until the arrival of the commissioner of the king, my lord, my sun god.

(19–24) So may the king, my lord, the sun god from heaven be apprised that the city of the king, my lord, my sun god, that is in my charge was attacked and my father was smitten.

(25–31) And now I am guarding the city of the king, my lord, my sun god, that is in my charge until the arrival of the commissioner of the king, my lord, my sun god, to learn about the [l]a[n]ds of the king, my lord, [my] sun [god].

EA 221

TRANSCRIPTION

Obv. 01) *a-na šàr-ri* EN-[*i*]*a*
02) ^{d}UTU *iš-tu ša*$_{10}$*-me-*⸢*ma*⸣
03) *qí-bí-ma*
04) *um-ma* ^{I}*Yi-iq-dá-sú*
05) ÌR-*ka a-na* GÌR.MEŠ *šàr-ri*
06) EN-*ia* 7-*šu ši-bi-ta-an*
07) *uš-ḫé-ḫi-in*

---

08) *iš-te*$_{9}$*-me ša-pa-ar*
09) *šàr-ri* EN-*ia*
10) ⸢*a*⸣*-na ia-a-ši*

Rev. 11) *a-nu-ma*
12) *a-na-ṣa-ru*
13) URU *šàr-ri* EN-*ia*
14) *a-di ti-ik-šu-du*
15) *a-wa-at šàr-ri*
16) EN *a-na ia-ši*

EA 221

TRANSLATION

(1–7) Speak to the king, my lord, the sun from heaven, the message of Yiqdasu, your servant: At the feet of the king, my lord, seven times (and) seven times have I prostrated.

(8–10) I have heard the message of the king, my lord, to me.

(11–16) Now, I am guarding the city of the king, my lord, until the word of the king, my lord, comes to me.

EA 222

TRANSCRIPTION

Obv. 01) *a-na* ^I⌜*šàr*⌝[-*ri* EN-*ia*]
02) *qí-bí*-[*ma*]
03) *um-ma* ^I*Yi-iq*[-*dá-sú*]
04) *a-na* GÌR.MEŠ *šàr*-⌜*ri*⌝ [EN-*ia*]
05) *7-šu 7*-⌜*ta*⌝-*an*
06) *uš-ḫe-ḫi-in*$_4$ ⌜*i*⌝-[*nu*]-*ma*
07) *ša-pár* LUGAL EN-[*ia*]
08) *a-na ia-ši* ⌜*a*⌝-[*nu-ma*]
09) *ša i-ba*-[*ši it-ti-i*]*a*
10) *na-ad-na*-[*ti*]
11) *a-na* LUGAL E[N-*ia*]

EA 222

TRANSLATION

(1–6) Speak to the kin[g, my lord,] the message of Yiq[dasu;] at the feet of the king, [my lord,] seven times (and) seven times, have I prostrated.

(6–11) Inas[much] as the king, [my] lord, has written to me, n[ow,] what wa[s in m]y [possession, I] have given to the king, [my] lo[rd].

EA 223

TRANSCRIPTION

Obv.
01) *a-na* ^{I}[*šàr-r*]*i* EN-*ia* ^{d}UTU
02) *iš-t*[*u*] ⸢*ša*$_{10}$⸣-⸢*me*⸣-*ma*
03) *qí*-⸢*bí*⸣-*ma*
04) *um-ma* ⸢^{I}⸣⸢*In*$_{4}$⸣-⸢*tar*⸣-⸢*ú*⸣-*ta* ÌR-*ka*
05) *a-na* GÌR.MEŠ *šàr*-⸢*ri*⸣ ⸢*be*⸣-⸢*lí*⸣-*ia*
06) 7-*šu* 7-*ta-an* ⸢*uš*⸣-*ḫé-ḫi-in*$_{4}$
07) *gáb-bi* ⸢*mi*⸣-⸢*im*⸣-*mi*
08) *ša yi-qa*-⸢*bu*⸣
09) *šàr-ru be-lí*
10) ⸢*ú*⸣-*še-ši-ru-mi*

EA 223

TRANSLATION

(1–6) Speak to the [kin]g, my lord, the sun god fr[om] heaven; the message of Intaruta, your servant: At the feet of the king, my lord, seven times (and) seven times have I prostrated.

(7–10) All the goods that the king my lord commands, I will prepare.

EA 224

TRANSCRIPTION

Obv. 01) ⌜*a*⌝-*na* ^{I}LU[GAL] E[N-*ia* ^{d}UTU DINGER.MEŠ]-*ia*

02) *qí-bí*-[*ma*]

03) *um-ma* ^{I}*Šum-ad-d*[*a* ÌR *š*]*a* LUGAL EN-*ia*

04) *a-na* GÌR.MEŠ *šàr-ri* EN-*ia*

05) *am-qú-ut-mì*

06) 7-*šu* ⌜*ù*⌝ 7-*ta-a-an*

07) *i-nu-ma* ⌜*ša*⌝-*pár-mi*

08) LUGAL EN-⌜*ia*⌝ *a-na* ŠE.ḪI.A.MEŠ ⌜*duḫ*⌝-*ni*

09) \ *mu-ḫu-ṣu*

10) *ia-aš-al-mì*

11) LUGAL EN-*ia*

12) [L]Ú.MEŠ MÁŠKIM-*šu*

13) ⌜*šum*⌝-⌜*ma*⌝

Rev. 14) [*t*]*u*-⌜*ub*⌝-⌜*ba*⌝-*lu-na*

15) LÚ.MEŠ *a-bu-tu-nu*

16) *aš-šum* UD. KAM^{v}.MEŠ

17) ^{I}*Ku-sú-na*

18) LÚ *a-bi-nu*

19) ⌜*ù*⌝ ⌜*šum*⌝-⌜*ma*⌝ (erased)

EA 224

TRANSLATION

(1–6) Speak to the ki[ng], [my] lo[rd, ‹my› sun god], my [deity], the message of Shum-Hadd[a, the servant o]f the king, my lord: at the feet of the king, my lord, have I fallen, seven times and seven times.

(7–9) Inasmuch as the king, my lord, has written for cereal grain, it has been destroyed.

(10–18) May the king, my lord ask his commissioners whether our ancestors always shipped (grain) since the days of Kusuna, our father,

(19) ⸢and⸣ ⸢whether⸣....(*erased*).

EA 225

TRANSCRIPTION

Obv. 01) *a-na* ^{I}*šàr-ri* EN-*ia*
02) *qí-bí-ma um-ma*
03) ^{I}*Ša-mu-*^{d}IŠKUR LÚ.*lí*
04) URU *Ša-am-ḫu-na*
05) *a-na* ›PA‹GÌR (ANŠE) ^{I}*šàr-ri-ia* (‹EN›-*ia*?)
06) 7 *ù* 7 *mi-lí*
07) *am-qut gáb-bi*
08) *a-wa-te*^{MEŠ} *šàr-ri-ia* (‹EN›-*ia*?)
09) *iš-te-mu ù*
10) MÁŠKIM ‹*ša*› *ya-di-nu*
11) ^{I}*šàr-ri-ia* (‹EN›-*ia*?)
Rev. 12) UGU-‹*ia*› *iš-te-mu*
13) *gáb-bi a-wa-te-šu*
(Hieratic sign)

EA 225

TRANSLATION

(1–6) Speak to the king, my lord; the message of Shamu-Haddi, the ruler of the city of Sham‘ôna: At the feet(!) of my king (or: the king, my ‹lord›?), seven (times) and seven *times*(?) have I fallen.

(7–13) I am heeding all the words of my king (or: the king, my ‹lord›?) and as for the commissioner ‹whom› my king (or: the king, my ‹lord›?) will appoint over me, I will heed all of his words.

EA 226

TRANSCRIPTION

Obv. 01) *a-*⸢*na*⸣ ⸢I⸣*šàr-ri* E[N-*ia*]
02) ⸢*qí*⸣-⸢*bí*⸣*-ma um-*[*ma*]
03) ⸢I⸣*Ši-ip-ṭú-ri*[...ÌR-*ka*]
04) ⸢*ù*⸣ *ep-ri* ⸢*ša*⸣ [GÌR.MEŠ]-⸢*ka*⸣
05) *a-na* GÌR.‹MEŠ› *šàr-ri* ⸢7⸣ ⸢*ù*⸣ 7 *am-qut*
06) *yi-*⸢*de*⸣*-mi šàr-ru* EN-*ia*
07) *i-nu-ma šal-ma-at* URU.KI-⸢*šu*⸣
08) ⸢*ù*⸣ ⸢*gáb*⸣*-bi a-wa-te*^{MEŠ}
09) ‹*ša*› *ša-pár šàr-r*[*u*] EN‹-*ia*› *a-na* ÌR-*šu*
10) *iš-te-mu a-nu-ma*
11) ⸢*i*⸣*-ri-šu* \ *aḫ-*⸢*ri*⸣-[*šu*]
Lo.ed. 12) ⸢*ù*⸣ *i-ba-*⸢*qa*⸣*-m*[*a ù*]
Rev. 13) [*ú*]*-uṣ*$_4$*-ṣú-m*[*i*]
14) [*i*]-⸢*na*⸣ URU-*ia* [*ù*]
15) ⸢*i*⸣*-šu-ši-r*[*u*]
16) [Ì.MEŠ] *ù* NÍG.MEŠ ⸢*ù*⸣ [KAŠ.ME]Š
17) [*a-na*] *pa-ni* KASKAL.MEŠ
18) ⸢*šàr*⸣*-ri* EN-*ia*
19) ⸢*ù*⸣ *iš-te-mu*
20) *gáb-bi a-wa-te*^{MEŠ}
Up.ed. 21) ^{I}*šàr-ri* EN-*ia*

EA 226

TRANSLATION

(1–5) Speak to the king, [my] lo[rd], the message of Shipṭuri[...your servant], and the dirt beneath your [feet]: At the f‹ee›t of the king, seven (times) and seven (times) have I fallen.

(6–10) May the king, my lord, be apprised that it is well with his city, and I am obeying all the words (which) the king, ‹my› lord, wrote to his servant.

(10–21) Now I am cultivating and I am plucking [so I] keep going out [fr]om my city [and] I am preparing [oil] and food and [beer] in anticipation of the caravans of the king, my lord and I am obeying all of the words of the king, my lord.

EA 227

TRANSCRIPTION

Obv. 01) [*a*]-⸢*na*⸣ ⸢LUGAL⸣ EN-*ia*————

02) *qí*————*bí*————*ma*—

03) *um-ma* LUGAL URU *Ḫa-ṣú-ri*^{KI}

04) *a-na* GÌR.‹Ḫ›I.A EN-*ia am-qú-ut*

05) ⸢*a*⸣-*mur-mì a-na-ku na-aṣ-ra-ti* U[RU]

06) DIDLI.ḪI.A-*ni* LUGAL EN-*i*[*a*]

07) *a-di ka-ša-di* EN-*ia* DINGIR-*i*[*a*]

08) *u i*$_{15}$-*nu-ma iš-te-me a-wa-te*^{MEŠ}-*ka*

09) *an-nu-ta*$_{5}$ *u a-ṣé* TI ^{d}UTU EN-⸢*ia*⸣ *an*(*a*) ⸢*i*⸣*a-š*[*i*]

10) *u ki yi-ša-ma-aḫ* TI *am-tal*[-*li-ik*]

11) *u il*$_{5}$-*la-ti-ya ia-ṣa-at ša-*
\ *li-m*[*u*]

12) *u* DINGIR.MEŠ-*nu íp-pal-šu*

13) *an*(*a*) *ia-ši u a-nu-ma šu-ši-ra-ti*

14) *gáb-ba a-di ka-ša-di* LUGAL EN[-*ia*]

15) *a-mur-mì i-nu-ma yi-ik-šu-du*

16) [^{I}*Ḫa-n*]*i* DUMU *ši-íp-ri-ka*

17) [*u yi-iḫ-d*]*u*? ŠÀ‹-*ia*› *ma-gal*

18) [*il*$_{5}$-*la-ti-*]*ia ri-iš-ti*$_{7}$

Lo.ed. 19) [*yu-ṣu*] *i-nu-ma la yi-*[…]

Rev. 20) [*a*]*n-ni ú-*[.....]

21) URU *Ḫa-ṣú-*[*ra*^{KI}..]

22) *u ni-nu ni*[....]

23) *aš-šum* KUR[....]

24) *u gáb-*⸢*ba*⸣[....]

25) *i-nu-ma ka-*⸢*ša*⸣?[…]

26) *ša-ni-tam* ⸢*a*⸣-*m*[*ur*..]

27) *u ki-ia-*⸢*am*⸣? […]

28) *qa-du* ÉRIN.MEŠ[…]

Rest of reverse uninscribed

EA 227

TRANSLATION

(1–4) Speak to the king, my lord, the message of the king of the city of Ḫaṣôra (Hazor): at the feet of my lord have I fallen.

(5–7) Behold, I guard the cities of the king, my lord, until my lord's coming to m[e].

(8–13) And when I heard these your words then the life of the sun god, my god and [my sun god, came forth to me and when it was heard, I took [counsel]; and my elation came forth completely and the gods looked upon me.

(13–14) And now, I have prepared all until the arrival of the king, [my] lord.

(15–19) Behold, whenever [Ḫan]i, your envoy, arrives, [then] ‹my› heart [rejoi]ces greatly; my [elation,] exaltation, [goes forth].

(19–21) When [...] did not [...] Ḫaṣô[ra (Hazor)...].

(22–25) And we will [...] because of the land of [...] and all [...] when [...] arri[ves].

(26–28) Furthermore, beho[ld ---] and thus [---] with the [regular?] troops.

EA 228

TRANSCRIPTION

Obv. 01) [*a*]-⌜*na*⌝ ^{I}*šàr-ri* EN-*ia*
02) *qí-bí-ma*
03) *um-ma* ^{I}ÌR-*Šul-lim*
04) LÚ URU *Ḫa-ṣú-ra* ⌜ÌR⌝-⌜*ka*⌝
05) *a-na* I‹I›GÌR.ḪI.A-*pí*
06) ^{I}*šàr-ri* EN-*ia*
07) 7 *ù* 7-*ta-a-an*
08) *a-na* ⌜GÌR⌝.ḪI.A-*pí* ^{I}*šàr-rù*(sic!) EN-*ia*
09) *am-qú-ut-mi*
10) *a-mur-mi a-na-ku* ⌜ÌR⌝-[*d*]*i*(?)
11) *ša ki-it-ti*
12) ^{I}*šàr-ri* EN-*i*⌜*a*⌝ *ù*
13) *a-nu-um-ma-mi*
14) *i-na-ṣa-ru-um-mi*
15) URU *Ḫa-ṣú-ra*⌜^{KI}⌝
16) ⌜*qa*⌝-*du* URU.DIDLI.ḪI.A-*ni-ši*
17) [*a-n*]*a* ^{I}*šàr-ri* EN-*ia*
18) [*ù*] *li-iḫ-šu-uš*-⌜*mi*⌝
Lo.ed. 19) ⌜\⌝ *ya-az-ku-ur-mi*
Rev. 20) ⌜^{I}⌝*šàr-ri* EN-*ia*
21) *mi-im-ma ša*
22) in_4-*né-pu-uš-mi*
23) UGU URU *Ḫa-ṣú-ra*^{KI}
24) URU.KI-*ka ù*
25) UGU ÌR-*ka*

EA 228

TRANSLATION

(1–9) [Sp]eak to the king, my lord, the message of ʿAbdi-Shullim, ruler of the city of Ḥaṣôra (Hazor), your servant: at the t‹wo› feet of the king, my lord, seven (times) and seven times, at the feet of the king, my lord, have I fallen.

(10–17) Behold, I am the loyal servant of the king, my lord, and now I am guarding the city of Ḥaṣôra (Hazor) with her towns [fo]r the king, my lord.

(18–25) [So] may the king, my lord, give thought to what is being done against the city of Ḥaṣôra (Hazor), your city, and against your servant.

EA 229

TRANSCRIPTION

Obv. 01) *a-na* ^{I}LUGAL EN-*ia*
02) *qí-bí-m*[*a*]
03) *um-ma* ^{I}ÌR-*na*[...]
04) ⸢ÌR⸣-*ka* ÌR [*ki-ti* ^{I}LUGAL]
05) ⸢EN⸣-*ia* SAḪAR .M[EŠ *ša* GÌR.MEŠ
06) ⸢^{I}⸣⸢*šàr*⸣-*ri* ⸢EN⸣[-*ia* ^{d}UTU-*ia*]
07) [*a-na*]⸢GÌR⸣[.MEŠ ^{I}LUGAL EN-*ia*]

EA 229

TRANSLATION

(1–7) Speak to the king, my lord, the message of ʿAbdi-na[...], your servant, the [loyal] servant of [the king], my lord, the dirt [under the feet] of the king, [my] lord, [my sun god]: [at] the fee[t of the king, my lord...]

EA 230

TRANSCRIPTION

Obv. 01) [*a*]-*na* LUGAL BAD-*ia qí-bi*
02) *um-ma* ᴵ*Ia-ma* ÌR-*ka*
03) *a-na* GÌR.MEŠ-*ka am-qut*
04) *a*-⸢*mur*⸣-*mi a-na-ku* ÌR-*ka*
05) *i-na aš-ri ša i-ba-ša-ti*$_7$
06) *a*-⸢*mur*⸣ *aš-ra-nu ša i-ba-ša-ti*$_7$
07) URU.DIDLI.ḪI.A-*ka gáb-bu*
08) *a-na-ku* ÌR ‹*ki*›-*ti*$_7$-*ka*
09) [LÚ.ME]Š *ḫa-za-nu-te-ku*(sic!)
10) *lu-ú na-aṣ-ra-ku*
11) *šum-ma* LÚ ⸢*we*⸣-⸢*ʾu*$_5$⸣-*ka*
12) *il-la*-⸢*ak*⸣ ⸢*a*⸣-⸢*na*⸣ ⸢*mu*⸣-*ḫi-ia*
13) *ù* ⸢*uṣ*⸣-⸢*ṣur*⸣-⸢*šu*⸣
14) *ù* URU.DIDLI.⸢ḪI.A⸣ ⸢*ša*⸣ ⸢*i*⸣-*ba-ša-ti*$_7$
15) ⸢*lu*⸣-*ú na*-⸢*aṣ*⸣-*ru*
16) *gáb-bu* ⸢*á*⸣-⸢*na*⸣ *ka-ta*$_5$
Rev. 17) ⸢*ù*⸣ ⸢LÚ⸣.⸢MEŠ⸣ ⸢*ḫa*⸣-⸢*za*⸣-*nu-te*
18) *ša-al-šu*-⸢*nu*⸣
19) *šum-ma* ⸢*lu*⸣-*ú na-àṣ*(AŠ)-*ru*
20) ⸢*ù*⸣ ⸢*lu*⸣-*ú ti*$_7$-*de*
21) *i*$_{15}$-*nu*-‹*ma*› *ša-al-mu*
22) URU.DIDLI.ḪI.A *gáb-bu*

EA 230

TRANSLATION

(1–3) Speak to the king, my lord, the message of Yama, your servant: At your feet have I fallen.

(4–10) Behold, I am your servant in the place where I am. Look, the places where I am are all your cities; I am your [lo]yal servant; I indeed protect your city rulers.

(11–13) If a soldier of yours comes to me, then I will guard him.

(14–16) And the towns where I am are all verily protected for you.

(17–19) And as for the city rulers, ask them whether they are verily protected.

(20–22) So may you be apprised that it is well with all your cities.

EA 231

TRANSCRIPTION

Obv. 01) [*a-na šàr-ri* EN-*ia*]
02) [^{d}UTU *iš-tu* AN *ša*$_{10}$*-me-e*]
03) [*qí-bí-ma*]
04) [*um-ma* ^{I}..........]
05) [LÚ URU..........]
06) [Ì]R *š*[*a šàr-ri ep-ru*]
07) *ša* 2 GÌR.M[EŠ-*šu qa-qa-ru ša*]
08) *ka-ba-ši-š*[*u a-na* GÌR.MEŠ]
09) LUGAL EN-*ia* ⸢^{d}⸣[UTU *iš-tu*]
10) AN *ša*$_{10}$*-me-e* 7-[*šu* 7*-ta-an am-qut*]
11) *ki-ma ša yi-i*[*š-pu-ur*]
12) *šàr-ru* EN-⸢*ia*⸣ [^{d}UTU]
13) [*i*]*š-tu* AN *ša*$_{10}$*-m*[*e-e*]
Lo.ed. 14) [*ú*]-⸢*ṣur*⸣-⸢*mì*⸣ URU.KI *š*[*a*]
15) [LU]GAL [*ša it*]*-ka*[*ù*]
Rev. 16) [*a-*]*na-ṣa-r*[*u*] ⸢URU⸣.[KI]
17) ⸢*ki*⸣*-ma ša* ⸢*yi*⸣[*-iš-pu-ur*]
18) ⸢*šàr*⸣-⸢*ru*⸣ E[N-*ia* DINGIR.MEŠ-*ia*]
19) ^{d}UTU-*ia* [*iš-tu* AN *ša*$_{10}$*-me-e*]

EA 231

TRANSLATION

(1–10) [Speak to the king, my lord, the sun from heaven; the message of [..., the ruler of...] the [ser]vant o[f the king, the dirt] under [his] two feet, [the ground on which] h[e] walks: [At the feet] of the king, my lord, the [sun god from] heaven, seven [times (and) seven times I have fallen].

(11–19) As the king, my lord, [the sun god fr]om heaven, has w[ritten], "[Gu]ard the city o[f the ki]ng [which is in] your [charge," so I] am guarding the city just as the king, my lord, [my deity], my sun god [from heaven,] has w[ritten].

EA 232

TRANSCRIPTION

Obv. 01) *a-na šàr-ri* EN-*ia* ^{d}UTU *iš-tu ša*$_{10}$*-me-e*
02) *qí-bí-ma*
03) *um-ma* ^{I}*Sú-ra-ta*
04) LÚ URU *Ak-ka* ÌR *ša šàr-ri*
05) *ep-ru ša* GÌR.MEŠ-*šu ù qa-qa-ru ša ka-ba-ši-šu*
06) *a-na* GÌR.MEŠ LUGAL EN-*ia*
07) ^{d}UTU *iš-tu ša-me-e*
08) 7-*šu* 7-*ta-a-an*
09) *uš-ḫé-ḫi-in*
10) *i-na pa-an-te-e* \ *ba-aṭ-nu-ma*
11) *ù ṣe-ru-ma* \ *ṣú-uḫ-ru-ma*
12) *ma-an-nu* LÚ-*lu*$_{4}$
Lo.ed. 13) *ù ša-pár* ⸢LUGAL⸣
Rev. 14) EN-*šu a-na ša-*[*šu*]
15) *ù la-a yi-iš-*⸢*mu*⸣*-mi*
16) *ki-ma ša yu-uṣ-ṣí*
17) *iš-tu pí-i*
18) ^{d}UTU *iš-tu*
19) *ša*$_{10}$*-me-e* ⸢*ki*⸣-⸢*na*⸣*-an-na*
20) *yu-up-pa-*⸢*šu*⸣*-mi*

EA 232

TRANSLATION

(1–11) Speak to the king, my lord, the sun god from heaven; thus Surata, the ruler of the city of Acco, the servant of the king, the dirt under his feet, the ground of his tread: At the feet of the king, my lord, the sun god from heaven, seven times (and) seven times have I prostrated on the stomach and on the back.

(12–20) Who is the ruler to whom the king, his lord, has written, that he would not heed? Just as it has issued from the mouth of the sun god from heaven, thus it shall be done.

EA 233

TRANSCRIPTION

Obv. 01) *a-na* ^{I}*šàr-r*[*i* EN-*i*]*a*
02) ^{d}UTU *iš-tu* A[N *ša*$_{10}$*-m*]*e*
03) *qí-bí-ma*
04) *um-ma* ^{I}*Sà-ta-at-na*
05) LÚ URU *Ak-ka* ^{KI} ÌR-*ka*
06) ÌR *ša šàr-ri*
07) *ù* SAḪAR.MEŠ *ša* 2 GÌR.MEŠ-*šu*
08) KI.MEŠ *ša ka-bá-ši-šu*
Lo.ed. 09) *a-na* GÌR.MEŠ *šàr-ri*
10) EN-*ia* DINGIR.MEŠ-*ia*
Rev. 11) ^{d}UTU *iš-tu* AN *ša*$_{10}$*-me*
12) 7-*šu* 7-*ta-a-an*
13) *uš-ḫé-ḫi-in ù*
14) *ka-ba-tu-ma*
15) *ù ṣe-ru-ma*

---

16) *ša ia-aš-tap-pár* LUGAL
17) *be-li-ia a-na* ÌR-*šu*
18) *yi-iš-te*$_{9}$*-mu ù*
19) *gáb-bi ša yi-*⸢*qa*⸣*-*[*bi*]
20) EN-*ia ú-še-š*[*i-ru*]

EA 233

TRANSLATION

(1–3) Speak to the kin[g. m]y [lord], the sun god from h[eave]n.

(4–15) Thus Satatna, ruler of the city of Acco, your servant, the servant of the king and the dirt under his two feet, the ground of his treading: At the feet of the king, my lord, my deity, the sun god from heaven, seven times (and) seven times have I prostrated myself, both on the stomach and on the back.

(16–20) What the king, my lord, has written to his servant, I am heeding. Everything that my lord has commanded, I am prepa[ring].

EA 234

TRANSCRIPTION

Obv. 01) ⸢*a*⸣*-na* ^{I}*šàr-ri* EN-*i*[*a*]
02) ^{d}UTU *iš-tu* AN *ša*$_{10}$*-me-e*
03) *um-ma* ^{I}*Sà-ta-at-na* LÚ URU *Ak-ka*^{KI}
04) ÌR-*ka* ÌR ^{I}*šàr-ri ù*
05) SAḪAR.MEŠ *ša-a* 2 GÌR.MEŠ-*šu ù* KI.MEŠ
06) *ša ka-*⸢*ba*⸣*-ši-šu a-na* 2 GÌR.MEŠ
07) *šàr-ri* EN-*ia* ^{d}UTU *iš-tu*
08) AN *ša*$_{10}$*-me* 7-*šu* 7-*ta-a-an*
09) ⸢*uš*⸣*-ḫé-ḫi-in ù ka-bat-tu-ma*
\ *ù ṣe-ru-ma*

---

10) *yi-iš-me šàr-ru* EN-[*i*]*a*
11) *a-wa-at* ÌR-*šu* [^{I}*Zi-ir-*]*dam-ia-*[*aš*]*-da*
12) ⸢*pa*⸣*-ṭá-ar iš-t*[*u*]
13) ^{I}*Bir*$_{5}$*-ia- wa-za i*[*-ba-ši*]
14) ⸢*it*⸣*-ti* ^{I}*Šu-ta* [ÌR]
Lo.ed. 15) *šàr-ri i-na* URU ⸢UN⸣
16) [*l*]*a-a yi-qa-bi mi-im-*⸢*ma*⸣
Rev. 17) [*a-n*]*a ša-šu tu-uṣ-ṣa*
18) ÉRIN.MEŠ *šàr-ri* EN-*ia i-ba-*[*ši*]
19) *it-ti-ši i-na* URU *Ma-gíd-d*[*a* ^{KI}]
20) *la-a qa-bi mi-mu a-na ša-*⸢*šu*⸣
21) *ù yi-ip-ṭú-ra a-na mu-ḫi-ia*
22) *ù a-nu-ma*
23) *ia-aš-pu-ra* ^{I}*Šu-ta*
24) *a-na ia-ši i-din-mì*
25) ^{I}*Zi-ir-dam-ia-aš-da*
26) *a-na* ^{I}*Bir*$_{5}$*-ia-wa-za ù la-a*
27) *i-ma-gur* ⸢*na*⸣*-da-an-šu*

EA 234

TRANSLATION

(1–9) To the king, m[y] lord, the sun god from heaven, the message of Satatna, the ruler of the city of Acco, your servant, the servant of the king and the dirt under his two feet and the ground of his treading: At the two feet of the king, my lord, the sun god from heaven, seven times (and) seven times have I prostrated both on the stomach and on the back

---

(10–21) May the king, [m]y lord, hear the word of his servant: [Zir]damyashda deserted from Biriawaza. He w[as] with Shuta, the servant of the king, in the garrison town; he said nothing to him. The army of the king, my lord, came forth, he was with it in the city of Megiddo; nothing was said to him. He deserted to me.

(22–27) And now Shuta has written to me, "Hand over Zirdamyashda to Biryawaza," but I refused to hand him over.

28) *a-mur-mì* URU *Ak-ka*^{KI}
29) *ki-ma* URU *Ma-ag-da-lí* ^{KI}
30) *i-na* KUR *Mi-iṣ-ri ù la-a*
31) [*yi-*]⸢*iš*⸣*-te*$_{9}$*-ma šàr-ru*
32) [EN-*ia*] *ù yi-né-pu-*⸢*ša*⸣
Up.ed. 33) [^{I}*Šu-t*]*a* UGU-*ia ù lu-*⸢*ú*⸣
34) [*yu-uš-ši-*]*ra* LUGAL EN-*ia*
Lft.ed. 35) [LÚ].MÁŠKIM-*šu ù li-il-q*[*é-*]
\ *šu*

(28–35) Look, the city of Acco is like the city of Migdol in the land of Egypt. And the king, [my lord] has not heard that [Shut]a has turned against me. So [ma]y the king, my lord [sen]d his commissioner and may he take him.

EA 235 + EA 327

TRANSCRIPTION

EA 235

Obv. 01) *a-na* ^{I}*šàr-ri* EN-*ia*
02) ^{d}UTU-*ia* DINGIR.MEŠ-*ia*
03) ^{d}UTU *iš-tu* AN *ša*$_{10}$-*me-e*
04) *qí-bí-ma*
05) *um-ma* ^{I}*Sí-ta-at-na* ÌR-*ka*
06) SAḪAR.MEŠ GÌR.MEŠ-*ka a-na* GÌR.MEŠ
07) ^{I}*šàr-ri* EN-*ia* ^{d}UTU-*ia*
08) DINGIR.MEŠ-*ia* 7-*it ù*
09) 7-*it-ta-na* ‹*iš*›-*ḫé-ḫi*-⸢*in*$_{4}$⸣
10) *a-na* GÌR.MEŠ ⸢*šàr*⸣-⸢*ri*⸣ [EN-*ia*]

EA 327

11) ⸢*iš*⸣-*te-mé* [*a*]-*wa-ti* MÁŠ[KIM]
12) ^{I}LUGAL *a*-⸢*na*⸣ *ia-ši*
13) *a-na na*-⸢*ṣár*⸣ URU.DIDLI.KI.ḪI[.A *a-n*]*a*
14) ^{I}*šàr-ri* BAD-*ia* [*ù*]
15) *ú-na-ṣár ma-gal š*[*a-ni-ta*$_{5}$]
16) [^{I}]*šàr-ru* BAD-*ia* ⸢*ša*⸣[-*pár*]
Lo.ed. 17) ⸢*a*⸣-*na ia-ši a-na*
Rev. 18) ⸢NA$_{4}$⸣ ⸢*eḫ*⸣-*li*!(TU)-*pá-ak-ku*
19) ⸢*a*⸣-*nu-um-ma ú-ba-a*[*l*]
20) 50 MEŠ NI LAL \ *maš-qa-al*[-*šu-nu* (?)]
21) *a-na* ^{I}LUGAL EN-*ia*

EA 235 + 327

TRANSLATION

EA 235

(1–10) To the king, my lord, my sun god, my deity, the sun god from heaven, speak: Message of Sitatna, your servant, the dirt at your feet, at the feet of the king, my lord, my sun god, my deity, seven (times) and seven times ‹I have pro›strated myself at the feet of the king, my lord.

EA 327

(11–15) ⸢I⸣ have heeded the [wo]rds of the king's com[missioner] to me to guard the cities [fo]r the king, my lord, [and] I have guarded diligently.

(15–21) Fu[rthermore] the king, my lord has wr[itten] to me about raw glass. Now I have sent 50 (units), [their] weight, to the king, my lord.

EA 236

TRANSCRIPTION

Rev. 01) [……]⌜*a*⌝?-⌜*nu*⌝?-⌜*um*⌝?-⌜*ma*⌝?
02) [LÚ URU*A*]*k-ka* LÚ *nu-kù*[*r-ti*]
03) [*…lu-*]*ú il-qa-an-n*[*i…*]
04) [*…*]^{d}EŠDAR? *lu-ú*[*…*]
05) [*…n*]*a-ti lu-ú i*[*…*]
06) [*…a-n*]*a* LUGAL E[N-*ia*]
07) […] traces […]

EA 236

TRANSLATION

Rev.

(1–7) [……]Now(?) [the ruler of the city of A]cco is [hostile…ma]y he take[me […] Ishtar? May[…]? May[…t]o the king, [my] lo[rd.] […] traces […]

EA 237

TRANSCRIPTION

Obv. 01) […]⸢*ia*⸣[…………]
02) [*i*]*l*$_5$*-te*$_9$*-qú-ú* ^{I}⸢*La*⸣*-a*[*b-a-yu*]
03) *ù iz-za-az-zu* UGU UR[U.MEŠ]
04) *ša* ^{I}*šàr-ri* EN*-ia*
05) *ù il*$_5$*-te*$_9$*-qú* URU.ḪI.A
06) *ša* ^{I}LUGAL EN*-ia ša* NU(!)*-i*[*d*]
07) ^{I}*šàr-ru* ⸢EN⸣*-ia* ⸢*i*⸣*-na qa-t*[*i-ia*]
08) *a-na na-ṣa-ar*
09) *ù li-il-ma-ad*
10) ⸢^{I}⸣*šàr-ru* EN*-i*⸢*a*⸣
11) *i*$_{15}$*-nu-ma il*$_5$*-te*$_9$*-*⸢*qú*⸣*-ú*
Lo.ed. 12) ⸢URU⸣.⸢DIDLI⸣.ḪI.A ⸢*ša*⸣ ^{I}LUGAL EN*-i*[*a*]
13) [*ù*] URU.KI *ša i*$_{15}$*-ba-aš-*⸢*ša*⸣*-*⸢*ti*⸣
Rev. 14) [*i-n*]*a lìb-bi-ši a-nu-um-ma*
15) ⸢*na*⸣*-aṣ-ra-ti-ši*
16) *a-di a-ta-*⸢*mar*⸣ UZU 2 IGI
17) LÚ *ḫa-za-an* ⸢*ša*⸣ ^{I}*šàr-*⸢*ri*⸣
18) EN*-ia ù a-nu-um-ma*
19) *iš-tu u*$_4$*-mi uš-ši-*[*ir-ti*]
20) *ṭup-pa an-na-*⸢*am*⸣
21) *i-na* É.GAL ⸢^{I}⸣[LUGAL EN*-ia*]
22) *iz-za-zu* U[GU*-ia*]
23) *ù pu*[*-ḫi-ir*…………]
24) (traces)

EA 237

TRANSLATION

(1–8) [....]my[....] La[b'ayu] has taken and he is attacking the towns of the king, my lord and he is taking the towns of the king, my lord, which the king, my lord, has entrust[ed] to [my] char[ge] to protect.

(9–18) So may the king, my lord, be informed that he is taking the towns of the king, my lord. [But] as for the city that I am in, now I guard it until I see the two eyes of the official of the king, my lord.

(18–24) And now, from the day [I] sent this tablet to the palace of [the king, my lord], he is attack[ing me] and he has ass[embled.....]

EA 238

TRANSCRIPTION

Obv. 01) [*a-na*] ⸢LÚ⸣.GAL ⸢EN⸣-[*ia*]
02) [*um-m*]*a* ^{I}*Ba-ya-di* ÌR[-*ka*]
03) [*a-n*]*a* GÌR.MEŠ LÚ GAL EN-*ia* [*am-q*]*ut*
04) ⸢URU⸣.DIDLI.ḪI.A *ša* NU-*id* LÚ.G[AL]
05) EN-*ia i-na qa-ti-ia*
06) *il*$_5$*-te*$_9$*-qú-ú gáb-bi* URU.MEŠ
07) *ù* URU.KI *ša i*$_{15}$*-ba-aš-ša-ti*
08) *i-na lìb-bi-ši la-a e-le-é'-e*
09) *na-ṣa-ar-ši ù lu-*⸢*wa*⸣-[*aš*]-*ši-ra-an-ni-mi*
10) LÚ.GAL EN-*ia*
11) 50 LÚ.MEŠ *ma-an-*⸢*ṣa*⸣-*a*[*r-ta*]
12) *a-na na-ṣa-a*[*r* URU.KI]
13) *a-di ka*[*-ša-di*]
14) LÚ.GAL [EN-*ia*]
15) *ù* [.................................]
16) ⸢LÚ⸣.[GAL EN-*ia*....................]
17) [.................................]
18) [.................................]
Lo.ed. 19) [.................................]
Rev. 20) [.................................]
21) [.................................]
22) ⸢UGU⸣ [............................]
23) *ù* DUMU ^{I}Z[*a*.......................]
24) *ù* ^{I}*Ḫa-*⸢*gur*⸣*-r*[*u*.......................]
25) *ù il*$_5$*-te*$_9$*-qú-ú* [.......................]
26) *ù iz-za-zu* ⸢UGU⸣-*i*[*a*...................]
27) *ù il*$_5$*-te*$_9$*-qú-ú* ⸢URU⸣.⸢DIDLI⸣.[ḪI.A]
28) *ša* LÚ.GAL EN-*ia*
29) *ù* ⸢*li*⸣-⸢*il*$_5$⸣-*ma-ad*
30) LÚ.GAL EN-*ia*
31) *at-tu-nu tu-ša-ab-li-* \\ *ṭú-na-nu*
32) *ù at-tu-nu*
33) \\ *ti-mi-tu-na-nu*

EA 238

TRANSLATION

(1–3) [To] the senior official, [my] lord; [the mes]sage of Bayadi, your servant: [A]t the feet of the senior official, my lord, [have I fa]llen.

(4–6) As for the towns which the senior of[ficial], my lord, entrusted to my authority, they have taken all the towns.

(7–16) And as for the city in which I am located, I am unable to protect it so may the senior official, my lord, send to me fifty garrison troops to protec[t the city] until the ar[rival of the senior official, [my lord,] and [...]the [senior] official, [my lord....].

(17–21) [............]

(22–28) against [........] and the son of Za[...] and Ḫagurru [...] and they have taken [...] and they have attacked m[e...] and they have taken the towns of the senior official, my lord.

(29–33) So may the senior official, my lord, be informed. It is you (pl.) who can give us life and it is you (pl.) who can put us to death.

EA 239

TRANSCRIPTION

Obv. 01) [*a-na š*]*àr*[*-ri*]
02) [E]N-*ia qí*[*-bí-ma*]
03) *um-ma* ^{I}*Ba-du-za-n*[*a* Ì]R-⸢*ka*⸣
04) *a-na* GÌR.MEŠ-*pí*
05) ^{I}*šàr-ri* EN-*ia*
06) 7 *ù* 7-*ta-an*
07) *am-qut-mi*
08) *gáb-bi a-wa-te*^{MEŠ}
09) *šàr-ri* EN-*ia*
10) *i-ba-aš-ši*
11) *a-di it-ta-ṣí*
12) LÚ.GAL *ù*
Lo.ed. 13) *yi-*il_5*-te-qé*
Rev. 14) *mi-im-ma*
15) *ša iq-bi*
16) ^{I}*šàr-ru*
17) *be-li-ia*
18) *a-mur ni-i-nu*
19) ÌR.MEŠ *šàr-ri*
20) *ù li-it-ta-ṣí*
21) LÚ.GAL *ù*
22) *li-de-mi*
23) *ar-na-nu* ⸢*i*⸣*-nu-ma*
24) *li-im-ni*
25) ÌR.MEŠ-*ka*
26) *i-na pa-ni-*⸢*ka*⸣
27) [*y*]*i-iq*[*-bu*]

EA 239

TRANSLATION

(1–7) Spe[ak to the k]ing, my [lo]rd, the message of Baduzan[a], your [ser]vant: At the feet of the king, my lord, seven (times) and seven times have I fallen.

(8–17) All the things of the king, my lord, are ready until the coming forth of the senior official that he should take everything which the king, my lord, has said.

(18–27) Look, we are servants of the king so may the senior official come forth and may he know our crime because [h]e [has been] spea[king] evil of your servants in your presence.

EA 240

TRANSCRIPTION

Obv. 01) [*a*]-*n*[*a pa-ni* ÉRIN.MEŠ]
02) *pí-ṭ*[*á-ti ša* LUGAL BAD-*ka*]
03) *ù* GI[Š.GIGIR.MEŠ-*šu*]
04) *a-nu-u*[*m-ma šu-ši-ra-ti gáb-bi*]
05) *a-na pa-ni* É[RIN.MEŠ *pí-ṭá-ti ù*]
06) *a-na pa-‹ni›* GIŠ.GIGIR.M[EŠ *ša*]
07) LUGAL BAD-*ia* ⌜*ù*⌝ [......]
08) ⌜LÚ⌝ [*a-na p*]*a-ni* [........]

EA 240

TRANSLATION

(1–8) [To]wards the (coming of) the re[gular troops…] and the ch[ariotry of the king your lord]. No[w I have prepared everything] for the (coming of) the re[gular troops and] for the (coming of) the char[iotry of] the king, my lord and […] the man, for the (coming of) […]

EA 241

TRANSCRIPTION

Obv. 01) *a-na* ^{I}*šàr-ri* EN-*ia*
02) [DI]NGIR.MEŠ-⸢*nu*⸣-*ia* ^{d}UTU *qí-bí-*⸢*ma*⸣
03) *um-ma* ^{I}*Ru-uṣ-ma-an-ia* ⸢ÌR⸣-⸢*ka*⸣ (these two signs effaced)
04) LÚ URU *Ša-ru-na* ^{KI} ÌR-⸢*ka*⸣
05) SAḪAR.MEŠ *ša* GÌR.MEŠ-*ka*
06) *ṭe*$_{4}$-*ṭi ša ka-bá-ši-ka*
07) GIŠ.GÌR.‹GUB› *ša* GÌR.MEŠ EN-*ia* ‹*a-na* GÌR.MEŠ EN-*ia* ›
08) 7-*šu* 7-*ta-a-an* ‹*am-qut*›
09) *a-mur-mi a-na-ku* ÌR LUGAL
10) *iš-tu* ⸢*da*⸣-⸢*ri*⸣-*ti*
11) *šàr-*⸢*ri*⸣ EN-*ia ur-*⸢*ru*⸣-*du*
12) *ù a-nu-*⸢*um*⸣-⸢*ma*⸣ *i-na-*⸢*an*⸣-*na*
13) *šàr-*⸢*ra*⸣ EN-*ia*
Lo.ed. 14) [DINGIR]-⸢*i*⸣*a* [.............]
Rev. 15) [..........................]
16) [*ša*] ⸢*šà*⸣*r*-⸢*ri*⸣ ⸢EN⸣-⸢*ia*⸣
17) *ša-nu* ⸢*da*⸣-⸢*ki*⸣-*mi*
18) *i-n*[*a*] ⸢*qa*⸣-⸢*ti*⸣-*ia*
19) *ù a-*⸢*na*⸣-⸢*ku*⸣ ÌR *ki-it-*⸢*ti*⸣
20) *ša šàr-*⸢*ri*⸣ EN-*ia*

EA 241

TRANSLATION

(1–8) Speak to the king, my lord, my [d]eity, the sun god; the message of Ruṣmanya, ‹your servant›, the ruler of the city of Sharôna, your servant, the dust of your feet, the clay of your treading, the foot‹stool› of the feet of my lord: ‹At the feet of my lord› seven times (and) seven times ‹have I fallen›.

(9–11) Look, I am the servant of the king; from of old I have been serving my king, my lord.

(12–20) And just now the king, my lord, my [deity (I serve?)] of the king, my lord, another has been called up(?) in my authority and I am a loyal servant of the king, my lord.

EA 242

TRANSCRIPTION

Obv. 01) *a-na* ^{I}*šàr-ri* EN-*ia*

02) *u* ^{d}UTU-*ia qí-bí-ma*

03) *um-ma* ^{I}*Bi-ri-di-ya*

04) LÚ URU *Ma-gíd-da*^{KI}

05) ÌR *ki-ti šàr-ri*

06) ⸢*a*⸣-⸢*na*⸣ GÌR.MEŠ *šàr-ri* ⸢EN⸣-*ia*

07) *u* ^{d}UTU-*ia* 7-*šu u*

08) 7-*ta-a-an uš-ḫé-ḫi-in*$_{4}$

09) *al-lu-ú-mì na-ad-na-ku*

10) ⸢ŠU⸣. KAM^{v}.MI *šàr-ri*

11) [EN]-*ia* ⸢30⸣ ⸢GU$_{4}$⸣.MEŠ

12) [x ÙZ.MEŠ x *iṣ-ṣu*]-*ra-te*

Lo.ed. 13) [...............]x

Rev. 14) [...*a*]*l-lu-ú-mì*

15) [*gáb-bi* URU.ME]Š.KI

16) *šal-mu u a-na-ku*

17) *nu-kúr-tu*$_{4}$

EA 242

TRANSLATION

(1–8) Speak to the king, my lord and my sun god, the message of Biridiya, the ruler of Megiddo, your loyal servant: At the feet of the king, my lord and my sun god, have I prostrated myself.

(9–13) Behold, I have given the request of the king, my [lord]: 30 oxen, [*x* sheep and goats, *x* fo]wl [....].

(14–17) [...Be]hold, [all of the citi]es are at peace but I am at war.

EA 243

TRANSCRIPTION

Obv. 01) ⸢*a*⸣-⸢*na*⸣ *šàr-ri* E[N-*ia*]
02) *ù* ^{d}UTU-*ia u* D[INGIR.MEŠ-*ia qí-b*]*í-ma*
03) *um-ma* ^{I}*Bi-ri-di-*[*yu*]
04) ÌR *ki-it-ti* ⸢*ša*⸣ [*šàr-ri*]
05) *a-na* GÌR.MEŠ *šàr-ri* E[N-*ia*]
06) *u* ^{d}UTU-*ia u* DINGIR.MEŠ-*ia*
07) 7-*šu ù* 7-*ta-a-an a*[*m-qu*]*t*

---

08) *iš-te-me a-wa-te*^{MEŠ}
09) *šàr-ri* EN-*ia u* ^{d}UTU-*ia*
10) *ù a-nu-um-ma i-na-ṣa-*⸢*ru*⸣
11) URU *Ma-gi*$_5$*-da*^{KI}
12) URU.KI *šàr-ri* EN-*ia*
13) ⸢UD⸣.KAM^{v} *ù* GI$_6$-*ša* \ *l*[*e-l*]*a*
Lo.ed. 14) UD.KAM^{v} *i-na-ṣa-*⸢*ru*⸣
15) [*i*]*š-tu* A.ŠÀ.MEŠ
Rev. 16) ⸢*i*⸣-⸢*na*⸣ GIGIR.MEŠ *ù* ⸢*le*⸣-*l*[*a*]
17) *i-na-ṣa-*⸢*ru*⸣ ⸢BÀD⸣.⸢MEŠ⸣ [URU.KI]
18) *šàr-ri* EN-*ia*
19) *ù a-nu-um-*⸢*ma*⸣ ⸢*da*⸣-*a*[*n-na-a*]*t*
20) *nu-kúr-te* LÚ.MEŠ ⸢SA⸣.⸢GAZ⸣
21) *i-na* KUR.KI ⸢*ù*⸣ ⸢*lu*⸣-⸢*ú*⸣ *yi-de*
22) *šàr-ru* EN-*ia a-na* KUR.KI-*šu*

EA 243

TRANSLATION

(1–7) [Spe]ak to the king, [my] lo[rd] and my sun god, and [my] d[eity], the message of Biridi[ya], the loyal servant of [the king]: At the feet of the king, [my] lo[rd] and my sun god and my deity, seven times and seven times [have] I f[alle]n.

(8–18) I have heard the words of the king, my lord and my sun god. And now I am guarding the city of Megiddo, the city of the king, my lord, day and night. By day I am guarding [f]rom the open fields in chariots and [by] n[ight] I am guarding the walls of [the city of] the king my lord.

(19–22) But now the hostility of the *ʿapîru* men is in[tense] in the land so may the king, my lord be apprised concerning his land.

EA 244

TRANSCRIPTION

Obv. 01) ⸢*a*⸣*-na šàr-ri* EN-*ia*
02) *ù* ^{d}UTU-*ia qí-bí-ma*
03) *um-ma* ^{I}*Bi-ri-di-yi*
04) ÌR *ša ki-it-ti ša*
05) *šàr-ri a-na* 2 GÌR.MEŠ *šàr-ri*
06) EN-*ia ù* ^{d}UTU-*ia*
07) ⸢7⸣-*šu ù* 7-*ta-a-an*
08) *am-qú-ut-mì li-de-mì*
09) *šàr-ru* EN-*ia i-nu-ma*
10) *iš-tu i-re-bi* ÉRIN.MEŠ *pí-ṭá-ti*
11) *i-te*$_{9}$*-pu-uš-mì* ^{I}*La-ab-a-yu*
12) *nu-kúr-ta*$_{5}$ *i-na mu-uḫ-ḫi-ia*
13) *ù la-a-mi ni-le-ú*
14) ZÚ.SI.GA *ba-qa-ni* \ *qà-*⸢*ṣí*⸣*-ra*
15) *ù la-a-mì ni-le-ú*
16) *a-ṣí* KÁ *a-bu-ul-lí* \ *ša-aḫ-ri*
17) *iš-tu pa-ni* ^{I}*La-ab-a-yi*
18) *i-nu-ma la-ma-ad-mì*
19) *ù l*[*a*]*-a-mì ti-it*[*-ta-ṣ*]*ú-na*
Lo.ed. 20) ÉRIN.MEŠ *pí-ṭá-tu*$_{4}$
21) ⸢*ù*⸣ *a-nu-u*[*m-m*]*a*
Rev. 22) ⸢*ta*⸣*-ri-iṣ pa-ni*[*-šu*]
23) *a-na la-qí-i*
24) URU *Ma-gi-id*
\-⸢*da*⸣^{KI}
25) *ù lu-ú-mi*
26) *li-ik-ki-im-mi*
27) *šàr-ru* URU.KI-*šu la-a-mì*
28) *yi-iṣ-bat-ši*
29) ^{I}*La-ab-a-yu*

EA 244

TRANSLATION

(1–8) Speak to the king, my lord and my sun god. Thus says Biridiya, the loyal servant of the king: At the two feet of the king, my lord and my sun god, seven times and seven times have I fallen.

(8–20) May the king, my lord, be apprised that since the regular army went back (to Egypt), Lab'ayu has made war against me so that we are unable to pluck the sheep (or) complete the harvest. We can't even go out the city gate because of Lab'ayu since he found out that regular troops are not c[oming fo]rth.

(21–29) And no[w] he is determin[ed] to take Megiddo. So may the king please rescue his city; let not Lab'ayu seize it!

30) *šum-ma-mì* ⸢*ga*⸣-*am-ra*-⸢*at*⸣-*mì*
31) URU.KI *i-na* BA.ÚŠ
32) *i-na mu-ta-a-an*
33) *i-na* ⸢*dáb*⸣-⸢*ri*⸣ *ù lu-ú*
34) *li-di-nam-mi šàr-ru*
35) 1 *me* LÚ.MEŠ *ma-an-ṣa-ar-la*$_5$
36) *a-na na-ṣa-ri* URU.KI-*šu*
37) *la-a-mì yi-iṣ-bat-ši*
38) $^{⸢I⸣}$*La-ab-a-yu šum-ma-mì*
39) *i-ia-nu pa-ni-ma*
Up.ed. 40) *ša-nu-ta*$_5$ *i-na*
41) ^{I}*La-ab-a-yi*
Lft.ed. 42) ⸢*ṣa*⸣-*ba-at-mì* URU *Ma-gid*$_6$-⸢*da*⸣$^{⸢KI⸣}$
43) *yu-ba-á*ʾ-*ú*

(30–38) Since the city is ruined by an epidemic and by pestilence(?). So may the king please grant (us) one hundred garrison troops to guard his city; let not Lab'ayu seize it!

(38–43) Since Lab'ayu has no other intention. He seeks the destruction of Megiddo.

EA 245

TRANSCRIPTION

Obv. 01) *ša-ni-tam du-ub-bu-ba-ku-mi*
02) UGU ŠEŠ.ḪI.A-*ia*
03) *šum-ma-mi yi-pu-šu-mi*
04) DINGIR.MEŠ-*nu ša šàr-ri* EN-*nu*
05) *ù ni-ik-šu-du-um-mi*
06) ^{I}*La-ab-a-ia ù* TIL.LA-*nu-um-ma* \ *ḫa-ia-ma*
07) *nu-ub-ba-lu-uš-šu a-na šàr-ri* EN-*nu*
08) *ù tu-sà-aḫ-mì* \ *tu-ra*
09) MUNUS.ANŠE.KUR.RA-*ia ù iz-zi-iz-mì*
10) EGIR-*šu* \ *aḫ-ru-un-ú*
11) *ù ir-ka-ab-mi*
12) *it-ti* ^{I}*Ya-aš-da-ta*
13) *ù a-di ka-ša-di-ia*
14) *ù da-ku-šu* \ *ma-aḫ-ṣú-ú*
15) *ù al-lu-ú-mì* ^{I}*Ya-aš-da-ta*
16) ÌR-*ka ù šu-ú-ut*!(TE)
17) *yi-ru-ub-mi it-*⸢*ti*⸣-⸢*ia*⸣
18) *i-na* MÈ *ta-ḫa-z*[*i*]
19) *ù lu-ú yi-*⸢*na*⸣-⸢*an*⸣-⸢*di*⸣-⸢*in*⸣-[*šu*](?)
20) TI.LA-*aṭ šà*[*r*]-*r*[*i* EN-*i*]*a*
21) ⸢*ù*⸣ *li-pa-a*[*l-li-is*]
22) [*ṭ*]*a-ba i-na* ⸢*pa*⸣[*-ni*]

Lo.ed. 23) *šàr-ri* EN[*-ia…*]

EA 245

TRANSLATION

(1–14) Furthermore, I exhorted my associates, "If the deity of the king, our lord, cause that we overtake Lab'ayu, then we must bring him alive to the king, our lord." But my mare was shot and I got up after that and I mounted up with Yashdata but by the time I arrived, they had smitten him.

(15–23) And behold, Yashdata is your servant and he entered with me into the fray, so may the life of the ki[ng, m]y [lord] be granted (him) and may he (Yashdata) behold [go]od in [the presence of] the king, [my] lord [...].

24) *ù* ^{I}*Sú-ra-t*[*a*]
Rev. 25) *yi-il*$_{5}$*-qé-mì* ^{I}*La-*[*ab-a-ia*]
26) *iš-tu* URU *Ma-gid*$_{6}$-⸢*da*⸣[^{KI}]
27) *ù yi-iq-bi a-na ia-*⸢*a*⸣*-š*[*i*]
28) *i-na-mì* ŠÀ GIŠ.MÁ \ *a-na-*⸢*yi*⸣
29) *ú-ta-aš-ša-ru-uš-šu*
30) *a-na šàr-ri ù yi-ìl-qé-šu*
31) ^{I}*Sú-ra-ta ù yu-ta-šir*$_{9}$*-šu*
32) *iš-tu* URU *Ḫi-na-tu-na*^{KI}
33) *a-na* É*-šu ù* ^{I}*Sú-ra-*⸢*ta*⸣
34) *la-qí-mi* KÙ.BABBAR.ḪI.A *ip-ṭì-ir-*
ri-šu
35) *i-na* ŠU*-ti-šu* \ *ba-di-ú*
36) *ša-ni-tam mi-na-am-mi ep-ša-ku-mi*
37) *a-na šàr-ri* EN*-ia*
38) *i-nu-ma* SIG*-ia* \ *yi-qí-ìl-li-ni*
39) *ù* DUGUD \ *yu-ka-bi-id*
40) ŠEŠ.ḪI.A*-ia ṣé-eḫ-ru-ta*$_{5}$
41) *ù* ^{I}*Sú-ra-ta*
42) *yu-ta-šir*$_{9}$
43) ^{I}*La-ab-a-ia ù* ^{I}*Sú-ra-ta*
44) *yu-ta-šir*$_{9}$*-mì* ^{Id}IŠKUR*-me-ḫer*
45) *a-na* É*-šu-ni*
46) ⸢*ù*⸣ *lu-ú yi-de-mi*
Up.ed. 47) *šàr-ru* EN*-ia*

(24–35) But Surata took La[ba'aya] from the city of Megiddo and he said to me, "In a ship I will send him to the king." So Surata took him but he released him to his home from the town of Hannathon, and Surata took his ransom money from his hand.

(36–40) Furthermore, what have I done to the king, my lord, that he belittles me and honors my younger associates?

(41–47) But Surata released Lab'ayu and Surata released Baʿlu-meher to their house(s). So may the king, my lord, be apprised.

EA 246

TRANSCRIPTION

Obv. 01) [*a-na šà*]*r-ri* E[N-*ia*]
02) [*ù*] ⸢^{d}⸣UTU-*ia qí-b*[*í-*]*m*[*a*]
03) [*um-*]⸢*ma*⸣ ^{I}*Bi-ri-di-yu*
04) ÌR *ša ki-it-ti-*⸢*ka*⸣
05) *a-na* GÌR.MEŠ *šàr-ri* EN-*i*[*a*]
06) *ù* ^{d}UTU-*ia* 7-*šu*
07) *ù* 7-*ta-a-an am-*⸢*qut*⸣

---

08) *iš-te-mé-mì ši-*⸢*pí*⸣[*-ir-ta*]
09) ⸢*ša*⸣ ⸢*šàr*⸣-⸢*ri*⸣ [............]

Bottom half of tablet broken

Rev. 01) *ù nu*[*-kúr-tu*............]
02) *ù a-nu-um-*⸢*ma*⸣[.........]
03) *i-ba-aš-ša-tu-*[*nu*.........]
04) *li-de-mi šàr-ru* E[N-*ia*]
05) *ù a-nu-um-ma* 2 DUMU[.MEŠ]
06) ^{I}*La-ab-a-yi ti*$_{7}$*-i*[*d-di-n*]*u-na*
07) KÙ.BABBAR.MEŠ-*šu-ni a-na* LÚ.MEŠ.⸢SA⸣.⸢GAZ⸣
08) ⸢*u*⸣ *a-na* LÚ.MEŠ KUR *S*[*u-te*]
09) [*a-n*]*a i-pé-e*[*š nu-kúr-ta*]
10) [UG]U-*ia*[..*ù li-de-mi*]
Up.ed. 11) [*šàr*]*-ru a-na* [KUR.KI-*šu*]

EA 246

TRANSLATION

(1–7) Spea[k to the ki]ng, [my] lo[rd and] my sun god; the message of Biridiyu, your faithful servant. At the feet of the king, m[y] lord, and my sun god, seven times and seven times have I fallen.

(8–9) I have heard the mes[sage] which the king [......]

Rev.

(1–11) And ho[stilities...] And now [......] yo[u] are [....]. May the king, [my] lo[rd] be apprised. And now the two son[s] of Labʿayu are gi[ving] their silver to the *ʿapîru* men and to the men of the land of the S[utû, t]o mak[e war ag]ainst m[e. So may the ki]ng [be apprised] concerning [his land.]

EA 247

TRANSCRIPTION

Obv. 01) [*a-na šàr-ri* EN-*ia*]
02) [*ù* ^{d}UTU-*ia qí-bi-ma*]
03) [*um-ma* ^{I}*Bi-ri-di-yu*]
04) [ÌR *ša ki-it-ti-ka*]
05) [*a-na* GÌR.MEŠ *šàr-ri* EN-*ia*]
06) [*ù* ^{d}UTU-*ia* 7-*šu ù*]
07) 7-*t*[*a-a-an am-qut*]
08) *aš-šum š*[*i-pí-ir-ti ša*]
09) *ia-aš-pu*[*-ur šàr-ru*]
10) EN-*ia a-n*[*a ia-ši*]
11) *iš-te-me*[*a-wa-at*]
Lo.ed. 12) *šàr-ri*[EN-*ia*]
13) *ma-gal* [*ma-gal*]
Rev. 14) *ù mi-i*[*a-mì*]
15) [*a*]*-na-ku* UR[.GI$_7$ 1-*en*]
16) ⸢*ù*⸣ *la-a* [*iš-mu a-na*]
17) [*i*]*-ri-iš*[*-ti šàr-ri*]
18) EN-*ia a*[*-nu-um-ma*]
19) *ú-še-ši*[*-ru a-na*]
20) *šàr-r*[*i* EN-*ia gáb-bi*]
21) [*ša*] *q*[*a-bi šàr-ru*]
22) [*a-na* ÌR-*šu*]

Remainder of reverse broken away

EA 247

TRANSLATION

(1–7) [Speak to the king, my lord and my sun god; thus (says) Biridiyu, your faithful servant. At the feet of the king, my lord, and my sun god, seven times and] seven ti[mes have I fallen.]

(8–13) Regarding the me[ssage that the king], my lord, wro[te] t[o me,] I have heeded [the word of] the king, [my lord,] very [carefully].

(14–18) And wh[o am] I, [a] d[og], that [I would] not [listen to the re]ques[t of the king], my lord?

(18–22) N[ow] I am pre[paring for] the kin[g, my lord, all that the king] [com]man[ded his servant.......]

EA 248

TRANSCRIPTION

Obv. 01) [*a-na*] ^{I}*šàr-ri* ⸢EN⸣-⸢*ia*⸣
02) *u* ^{d}UTU‹-*ia*› *u* DINGIR.MEŠ-*ia*
03) *qí-bí-ma um-ma* ^{I}*Ya-a*[*š*]-⸢*da*⸣-*ta*
04) ⸢ÌR⸣ *ki-it-ti šàr-ri*
05) *ù ep-ri* GÌR.MEŠ *šàr-ri*
06) *a-na* GÌR.MEŠ *šàr-ri*
07) EN-*ia u* ^{d}UTU-‹*ia*› *u* DINGIR.MEŠ-*ia*
08) 7-⸢*šu*⸣ *u* 7-*ta-a-an am-qut*

---

09) *li-de-mi šàr-ru* EN-*ia*
10) *i-nu-ma gáb-bi mi-im-me*
11) *ša yi-id-din šàr-*[*r*]*u*
12) [EN]-*i*⸢*a*⸣ ⸢*a*⸣-⸢*na*⸣ ÌR-*š*[*u*]
Lo.ed. 13) *n*[*a*]*m-šu-mi*
14) ⸢LÚ⸣.MEŠ URU *Ta-á*ʾ-[*n*]*a*-⸢*ka*⸣
Rev. 15) ⸢*na*⸣-*ak-šu-mì*
16) GU$_{4}$.MEŠ-*ia ù*
17) *du-ub-bu-ru-ni*
18) *u a-nu-um-ma it-ti*
19) ^{I}*Bi-ri-di-yi*
20) *i-ba-aš-ša*$_{10}$-*ku ù*
21) *li-de-mi šàr-ru*
22) EN-*ia a-na* ÌR-*šu*

EA 248

TRANSLATION

(1–8) Speak [to] the king, my lord and ‹my› sun god and my deity; the message of Yashdata, the loyal servant of the king and the dirt under the feet of the king: At the feet of the king, my lord and ‹my› sun god and my deity, seven times and seven times have I fallen.

(9–17) May the king, my lord, be apprised that all the possessions that the king, my [lord], had given to h[is] servant have been expropriated; the men of the city of Taa⸢nach⸣ have slaughtered my cattle and they have driven me out.

(18–22) And now I am with Biridiyu. So may the king, my lord, be apprised concerning his servant

EA 249

TRANSCRIPTION

Obv.

01) [a-na] ⸢^{I}⸣šàr-ri be-l[í-ia]
02) [qí-b]i-ma um-ma ^{Id}IŠK[UR.UR.SAG(?)]
03) ⸢ÌR⸣-ka a-na GÌR.MEŠ ⸢EN⸣-⸢i⸣[a]
04) [a]m-qú-ut a-na LUGAL be-lí-⸢ia⸣
05) ⸢ù⸣ lí-de i-nu-ma ti$_7$-la-⸢ku⸣-⸢na⸣ L[Ú.MEŠ]-ia ‹a›-na!(UD) ^{I}Mi[-íl-ki-lí]
06) ⸢mi⸣-na ip-ša-ti$_7$ a-na ^{I}Mi-ìl-ki-lí
07) ⸢i⸣-nu-ma yi-ḫa-ba-tu LÚ.MEŠ-⸢ia⸣
08) UGU ÌR.MEŠ-šu a-na ^{I}Ta-gi
09) LÚ i-mi-šu na-da-an
10) ÌR.MEŠ-šu ⸢ù⸣ mi-na ip-pu-šu-na
11) ⸢a⸣-⸢na⸣-⸢ku⸣⸢i⸣-nu!-⸢ma⸣ ⸢ul⸣ ^{I}ÌR-⸢di⸣
12) [k]i-ti$_7$ šàr-ri ⸢a⸣-⸢na⸣-ku ù
13) [la-a]⸢mì⸣ ti$_7$-lé-ú-na LÚ.MEŠ-⸢tu$_4$⸣
14) [da-]⸢ga⸣-la i-na mu-ḫi-⸢ia⸣
15) [ù ti-]tu-ra-ni LUGAL a-wa-⸢tu⸣
16) [la-a yi-i]š-mé ^{I}Mil-ki-lu
17) [ù ^{I}La-a]b-⸢a⸣-yu ù
18) [an-nu-ma i-na-a]n-na yi-⸢ip⸣-[pu-šu]
19) [nu-kúr-ta$_5$ (?) ù yi-i]š-a[l]
20) [LUGAL be-lí-ia ^{I}Ia-an-ḫa-ma]

Rev.

21) [..................................]
22) [..................................]
23) [..................................]
24) [............................]te-⸢ia⸣
25) [...................yi-iš-ta-]⸢pa⸣-⸢ar⸣
26) [LUGAL a-na]⸢ia⸣-⸢ši⸣[ù u]š-še-⸢ir⸣-⸢ti$_7$⸣
27) [..........]⸢ti$_7$⸣[..........ù la-a]
28) [t]u-uḫ[-ḫa-ar (?) ù]la-a
29) ⸢yi⸣-⸢iš⸣(?)[-mé ^{I}Mil-ki-lu] ù
30) ⸢^{I}⸣[La-ab-a-yu]

EA 249

TRANSLATION

(1–4) [Spea]k [to] the king, [my] lor[d], the message of Baʿ[lu-meher(?)], your servant: At the feet of m[y] lord, have [I] fallen.

(4–17) To the king, my lord: and may he be apprised that my [men] are serving Milkilu. What have I done to Milkilu that he should commandeer my men for(?) his servants? To Tagi, his father-in-law, he gave his (own) men. So what can I do myself, because am I not a loyal servant of the king? But my men are [no]t able to [se]rve me? [So] may a word, O king, [come] back to me, [lest] Milkilu [he]ar, and Lab'ayu.

(17–20) And [no]w he is ma[king war(?). So may the king, my lord, a]s[k Yanḥamu(?)].

(21–25) *Broken away*

(25–30) [The king wro]te [to] me [and] I [s]ent [...so don't d]el[ay] and may [Milkilu not] he[ar], and [Lab'ayu]

EA 250

TRANSCRIPTION

Obv. 01) [*a-n*]*a* ^{I}LUGAL EN-*ia* ⌜*qí*⌝-*bí-ma*
02) *um-ma* ^{I}IŠKUR.UR.SAG ÌR-*ka-ma*
03) *a-na* GÌR.MEŠ LUGAL EN-⌜*i*⌝*a* 7-⌜*šu*⌝ *ù* 7-*ta-a-an am-qut*
04) *yi-de-mi šàr*-⌜*ru*⌝ ⌜EN⌝-*ia* ⌜*i*⌝-*n*[*u*-]⌜*ma*⌝
05) *tu-ur-ri-ṣú-m*[*ì*] ⌜2⌝ DUMU ^{LÚ}*ar*-⌜*ni*⌝ ⌜LUGAL⌝ [*b*]*e-lí-ia*
06) 2 DUMU *La-ab-a*[*-y*]*i pa*-⌜*ni*⌝-*šu-ni*
07) *a-na ḫal-lí-iq* KUR ⌜*šàr*⌝-⌜*ri*⌝ EN-*ia*
08) EGIR-*ki ša ḫu-l*[*í*-]*i*[*q*] ^{LÚ}*a-bu-šu*[*-ni*]
09) *ù yi-de-mi šàr*-⌜*ru*⌝ EN-⌜*i*⌝*a i-nu-ma*
10) *ma-ni* UD!(ÉRIN). KA[M^{v}.ME]Š *tu*-⌜*ba*⌝-⌜*ʾu*$_5$⌝-*na* UGU-*ia*
11) 2 DUMU *La-ab-a-yi am-mi-nim-mì*
12) ⌜*na*⌝-*ad-na-ta* URU *Gi-ti*-⌜*pa*⌝-*da-al-la*
13) [*i-n*]*a* ŠU *šàr-ri* EN-*ka* URU.KI
14) *ša la-qí-mi* ^{I}⌜*La*⌝-*ab-a-yu* ^{LÚ}*a-bu-nu*
15) ⌜*ù*⌝ *ki-a-am ti-iq-bu-na*
16) ⌜2⌝ DUMU *La-ab-a-yi a-na ia-ši i-pu-uš-mì*
17) *nu-kúr-ta*$_5$ *i-na* LÚ.MEŠ KUR *Gi-na* UGU *da-ku-mì*
18) ^{LÚ}*a-ba-nu ù šum-ma nu-kúr-ta*$_5$ *la-a ti-pu-šu*
19) *ù* ⌜*nu*⌝-*kúr-tu*$_4$-*ka ni-nu-u*$_{16}$ *ù* ⌜*ip*⌝-⌜*pal*⌝-*šu-ni*
20) *yi-ki-im-ni-mi* DINGIR-*lim ša* LUGAL E[N-*i*]a
21) *aš-šum i-pé-eš*$_{15}$ *nu-kúr*-⌜*ti*⌝ ⌜*i*⌝-*na* L[Ú.M]EŠ K[UR *G*]*i-na*
22) ÌR.MEŠ LUGAL EN-*ia* ⌜*ù*⌝ *yi*-⌜*it*⌝-*r*[*u-u*]*ṣ*
23) *i-na pa-ni* LUGAL EN-*ia ù lu*-[*ú*] ⌜*ia*⌝-*aš-p*[*ur-m*]*ì*
24) 1-*en* LÚ.MEŠ GAL-*šu a-na* ^{I}*Bir*$_5$-*ia-wa-za*
25) ⌜*ù*⌝ [*yi*-]*iq-bi a-na ša-a-šu*
26) ⌜*til*⌝-*la*-⌜*ku*⌝-*na-mì a-na mu-ḫi* 2 DUMU *La-ab-a-yi*
27) *ù* ^{LÚ}*ar-ni šàr-ri a*[*t*]-⌜*ta*⌝
28) *ù* EGIR-*šu a-di* ⌜*ia*⌝-*a*[*š*-]⌜*pu*⌝-⌜*ra*⌝ *šàr*-⌜*ru*⌝ EN-*ia*
Lo.ed. 29) *a-n*[*a ia*-]*ši* [*aš-šum*] *ip-ši*
30) [*ša yi-pu-š*]*u* [ÌR]-*ka* UGU 2 [D]UM[U *L*]*a-ab-a-yi*
31) [.....]⌜*ya*⌝ *š*[*a-ni-ta*]*m*

EA 250

TRANSLATION

(1–3) Speak [t]o the king, my lord; the message of Baʿl-meher, your servant: At the feet of the king, my lord, seven times and seven times have I fallen.

(4–8) May the king, my lord, be apprised [t]hat the two sons of the traitor to the king, my [l]ord, the two sons of Lab'ayu, have set their faces to cause the loss of the territory of the king, my lord, after the[ir] father caused its loss.

(9–14) And may the king, my lord, be apprised that for how many days the two sons of Lab'ayu have been badgering me: "Why did you give the city of Gath-padalla [in]to the hand of the king, your lord, the city which Lab'ayu, our father had taken over?"

(15–22) And thus the two sons of Lab'ayu are saying to me: "Make war against the men of the land of Gina because they slew our father. But if you do not make war, we are your enemies." And I answered them, "May the god of the king, [m]y lord, deliver me from making war with the men of Gina, servants of the king, my lord."

(22–31) So may it please the king, my lord, and may he dispatch one of his senior officials to Biryawaza and may he say to him, "You will march against the two sons of Lab'ayu or you are a traitor to the king." Afterwards, again may the king, my lord, write t[o m]e [concerning] the action [that] your [servant should tak]e against the two son[s of L]ab'ayu [...].

Rev. 32) *[ù ki-a-am] ⌜i⌝-⌜ri⌝-⌜ba⌝* ^{I}*Mil-ki-lì*
33) *[a-n]a m[u-ḫ]i-[š]u-ni yi-i[n*$_4$*]-na-pí-il*
34) *[šu-ul]-⌜ma⌝-⌜nu⌝-um i-⌜na⌝ lìb-bi-šu-ni*
35) *[ù] k[i-a-a]m a-ṣí-i[t]* UZU.ZI
36) ^{I}*Mi[l]-⌜ki⌝-⌜lì⌝ a-na [i-r]e-eb* 2 DUMU *La-ab-a-yi*
37) ⌜EGIR⌝ *⌜La⌝-⌜ab⌝-⌜a⌝-⌜yi⌝ u-n[a] ḫa-lí i[q]* ›EGIR-*ki*‹
38) KU[R] L[UGAL] ⌜EN⌝-*[i]a i[t]-t[i-š]u-ni* ⌜EGIR⌝-⌜*ki*⌝
39) *ša ḫu-lí-iq Mi[l-k]i-lu*$_4$ *⌜ù⌝* ^{I}*La-ab-a-y[u]*
40) *ù ki-ia-am ti-⌜iq⌝-bu-na* 2 [DU]M[U *L*]*a-a[b]-a-⌜ya⌝*
41) *i-pu-uš-mi nu-kúr-ta*$_5$ *ki-ma* ^{LÚ}*a-bi-nu*
42) *i-na* LUGAL EN-*ka i-nu-ma yi-iz-zi-iz*
43) UGU URU *Šu-na-ma ù* ⌜UGU⌝ URU *Bur-⌜qú⌝-⌜na⌝*
44) *ù* UGU URU *Ḫa-ra-bu ù*
45) *yi-is-sú-uḫ-ši-ni* \ *⌜ia⌝-[a]n-šu-ke-en-n[i]*
46) *ù yi-iṣ-bat-mi* URU *⌜Gi⌝-⌜ti⌝-ri-mu-ni-ma*
47) *ù yu-pa-at-ti* \ *ú-[gà]r-ri* LUGAL EN-*ka*$_4$
48) *ù ip-pal-šu-ni yi-i[k-k]i-im-ni-⌜mì⌝*
49) DINGIR-*lim ša* LUGAL EN-*ia a[š-]šu[m] i-pé-eš*$_{15}$
50) *nu-kúr-ti i-na* LUGAL EN-*ia šàr-ra* EN-*ia*
51) *i-ru-du a-na-ku ù* ŠEŠ.MEŠ-*ia*
52) *ša ti-iš-te*$_9$*-mu-na a-⌜na⌝ ⌜ia⌝-ši*
53) *⌜ù⌝ ⌜la⌝-a yi-nam-mu-šu* LÚ.DUMU *ši-ip-r[i ša]*
54) ^{I}*Mil-ki-lì iš-tu[*$_4$*] ⌜mu⌝-ḫi* 2 DUMU *La-ab-a-y[i]*
55) *u*$_4$*-ma a[n]-nu-um a-⌜na⌝ ⌜ḫal⌝-lí-iq*
56) KUR LUGAL EN-*ia yu-ba-á'-ú* ^{I}*⌜Mil⌝-[k]i-⌜lì⌝*
57) *ù i-ia-nu-um pa-nu-ta*$_5$ *ša-n[u-]ta*$_5$
58) *a-na ia-ši šàr-ra* EN-*ia*
59) *i-ru-du ù a-wa-at yi-qa-bu*
60) *[šà]r-ru* EN-*ia iš-te*$_9$*-mu*

(31–46) F[urthermo]re, [so thus] Milkilu entered in [t]o them; a [gree]ting gift was agreed upon between them [and] t[hu]s Milkilu acquiesced to the entering in of the two sons of Lab'ayu, after Lab'ayu, to cause the loss of the territo[ry of the]k[ing m]y lord, with them, after Milkilu and Lab'ayu caused the loss.

(40–47) And thus the two [so]n[s of L]ab['a]yu are saying, "Make war like our father did against the king, your lord, when he attacked the town of Shunama and against the town of Burquna and against the town of ʿArabu and he uprooted them (gloss: he ejected them). And he seized the town of Gath-Rimmon and he developed the agricultural lands of the king, your lord."

(48–52) But I answered them, "May the god of the king, my lord, deliver me from making war on the king, my lord. The king, my lord, do I serve with my colleagues that obey me."

(53–56) But the envoy of Milkilu does not depart from the two sons of Lab'ayu at this time. Milkilu seeks to cause the loss of the territory of the king, my lord.

(57–60) But I have no other intention; the king, my lord, I serve and the word that the [ki]ng, my lord, speaks, I obey.

EA 251

TRANSCRIPTION

Obv.	01)	*li-iš-al-⸢šu⸣-nu*
	02)	*šàr-ru šum-ma la ki-ti*$_7$
	03)	*mi-im-ma aš-šum* LÚ.*ḫa-za-ni*
	04)	*ù li-iq-bi*
	05)	*i-na pa-ni šàr-ri ù*
	06)	*šàr-ru be-lí-ia la-aš-al-ni*
	07)	*a-nu-ma ki-i-ia-am*
	08)	*qa-la-⸢ta⸣ a-di-mi*
	09)	*yi-ìl-ma-du šàr-ru*
Lo.ed.	10)	*be-lí-ia a-wa-ta*$_5$
Rev.	11)	*an-ni-ta*$_5$ *ù yu-te-⸢ru⸣-*
	12)	*na-ni šàr-ru be-lì-ia*
	13)	*a-wa-at yu-te-ru-na*
	14)	*ù a-na a-wa-at*
	15)	*⸢šàr⸣-ri iš-mu*
Up.ed	16)	erased signs
Lft. ed.	17)	*⸢ù⸣ i-ma-gu-⸢ru⸣ ⸢i⸣-⸢na⸣*
	18)	*⸢ip⸣-ša a-na ⸢ia⸣-⸢ši⸣*

EA 251

TRANSLATION

(1–6) May the king interrogate them if something is not true concerning the city ruler and may he speak before the king but let not the king, my lord, call me to account.

(7–11) Now, thus have you kept silent? The king, my lord, will yet understand this matter.

(11–15) And the king may reply to me whatever word he will and I will heed the word of the king.

(16) *erased*

(17–18) And I will agree in the deed (done) to me.

EA 252

TRANSCRIPTION

Obv. 01) *a-na* ^{I}LUGAL-*ma bé-lí-ia*

---

02) *qí -bí -ma*

---

03) *um-ma* ^{I}*La-ab-a-yu* ÌR-*ka*

---

04) *a-na* GÌR.MEŠ-⸢*pí*⸣ *be-lí-ia am-qú-ut*

---

05) *i-nu-ma šap-ra-ta*

---

06) *a-na ia-a-ši ú-ṣur-mì*

---

07) LÚ.MEŠ *ša ṣa-ab-tu* URU

---

08) *ki-i uṣ-ṣur-ru-*⸢*na*⸣ LÚ.MEŠ

---

09) *i-na nu-kúr-ti*$_{7}$ *ṣa-ab-ta-at-mì* URU

---

10) *ki it-mì ša-li-mì ù ki it-mì it-*⸢*ta*⸣*-mì*

---

11) ^{I}LÚ.GAL *it-ti-ia*

---

12) *ṣa-ab-ta-at-mì* URU

---

13) *ù i-li qa-bi*
14) *qa-ar-ṣí-ia* \ *ši-ir-ti*

---

15) *i-na pa-ni* ^{I}LUGAL-*ma be-lí-ia*
Lo.ed. 16) ⸢*ša*⸣*-ni-tam ki-i na-am-lu*
17) *tu-um-ḫa-ṣú la-a*
Rev. 18) *ti-ka-pí-lu ù ta-an-*⸢*šu*⸣*-*⸢*ku*⸣
19) *qa-ti* LÚ-*lì ša yi-ma-ḫa-aš-ši*

EA 252

TRANSLATION

(1–4) Speak to the king, my lord, the message of Lab'ayu, your servant: At the feet of my lord have I fallen.

(5–9) As to your having written to me, "Keep watch on the men who seized the town," how can I keep watch on the men? By violence was the city seized.

(10–13) When I swore my oath of peace—and when I swore, the senior official swore with me—the town was seized and my god.

(13–15) My slander has been expressed (I have been slandered) before the king, my lord.

(16–19) Furthermore, when ants are smitten, they do not just curl up, but they bite the hand of the man who smote them.

20) *ki-i a-na-ku i-ša-ḫa-ṭú*

---

21) *ú-ma a-nu-ta*$_5$ *ù*
22) *ṣa-ab-ta-at-mì* 2 URU-*ia*
23) *ša-ni-tam šum-ma ti-qa-bu*
24) *ap-pu-na-ma*
25) *nu-pu-ul-mì*
26) *ta-aḫ-ta-mu ù*
27) *ti-ma-ḫa-ṣú-ka*
28) *i-bi ú-ṣur-ru-na*
29) LÚ.MEŠ *ša ṣa-ab-tu*$_4$ URU ‹*ù*›
30) *i-li šu-sú-mì a-bi-ia*
31) *ù ú-ṣur-ru-šu-nu*

(20–22) How I am being pressed at this time! And two of my towns have been seized.

(23–31) Furthermore, if you further command, “Fall down beneath them so they can smite you,” I will verily keep watch on my enemy, the men who seized the town ‹and› my god, the plunderers of my father! And I will certainly keep watch on them!

EA 253

TRANSCRIPTION

Obv. 01) [a-na ^{I}šà]r-ri [EN-ia] ⸢ù⸣
02) [^{d}UTU]-⸢ia⸣ um-ma [^{I}La-a]b-a-ya
03) [ÌR]-ka ù e[p-ru]
04) [ša] ka-bá-⸢ši$_{x}$(ŠE)⸣-[ka]
05) [a-n]a GÌR.MEŠ š[àr-r]i ⸢EN⸣-ia
06) ⸢7⸣-⸢šu⸣ 7-ta-a-an am-qut
07) [iš-]te-me a-wa-te^{MEŠ}
08) [ša] ⸢šàr⸣-ru EN-ia
09) [i-]na lìb-[bi] ṭup-pí
10) ⸢iš⸣-tap-ra-⸢an⸣-⸢ni⸣
11) [a-mur a-n]a-⸢ku⸣ ÌR šàr-ri
12) [ki-ma a-b]i-⸢ia⸣ ù
13) [a-]b[i]⸢a⸣-⸢bi⸣-ia ÌR-du
14) ⸢ša⸣ ⸢šàr⸣-⸢ri⸣ iš-tu
15) ⸢pa⸣-⸢na⸣-⸢nu⸣-⸢um⸣ ù
Lo.ed. 16) [l]a[-a] ⸢ar⸣-⸢na⸣-⸢ku⸣
17) ⸢ù⸣ ⸢la⸣-⸢a⸣ ⸢ḫa⸣-ṭá-ku
18) ⸢an⸣-⸢nu⸣-⸢ú⸣ ⸢ar⸣-nu-ia
Rev. 19) ⸢ù⸣ ⸢an⸣-nu-ú
20) [ḫ]i-ṭú-ia i-⸢nu⸣-ma
21) ir(?)-ru-ba-⸢ti⸣ i(?)-na
22) URU Gaz-ri ^{KI}
23) um-ma a-⸢na⸣-⸢ku⸣-mi
24) yi-in$_{4}$-ni-nu-nu-mi
25) šàr-ru ù a-nu-ma
26) i$_{15}$-na-an-na ia-nu
27) pa-ni ša-⸢nu⸣-ta$_{5}$ iš-tu
28) ur-ru-ud šàr-ri
29) ⸢ù⸣ mi-⸢im⸣-ma ša
30) ⸢yi⸣-iq-ta-bu
31) ⸢šàr⸣-⸢ru⸣ ⸢iš⸣-⸢te⸣-mu

EA 253

TRANSLATION

(1–6) [To the ki]ng, [my lord] and my [sun god], Thus (spoke) [La]b'ayu, your [servant] and the di[rt of your] treading; [A]t the feet of the k[in]g, my lord, sev[en] times (and) seven times have I fallen.

(7–17) [I have he]ard the words [which] the king, my lord, wrote to me [i]n a tablet. [Look], ⌜I⌝ am the servant of the king [like] my [fath]er and [the fa]th[er of] my father was a servant of the king from of old and I have not rebelled and I have not been delinquent.

(18–31) Behold my crime and behold my delinquency that I entered into the city of Gezer, (and) I spoke thus: “The king is punishing us!” Even now there is no other intention than to serve the king. And whatever the king shall say, I will heed.

32) [*l*]*i-ip*-⌜*qí*⌝-*id-ni-mì*
33) ⌜*šàr*⌝-*ru i-na*
Up.ed. 34) [Š]U LÚ.MÁŠKIM-⌜*ia*⌝
35) [*a-na*] *na-ṣa-ri* U[RU LUGAL]

(32–35) May the king assign me to the [char]ge of my commissioner [in order to] protect the ci[ty of the king].

EA 254

TRANSCRIPTION

Obv. 01) *a-na šàr-ri* EN-*ia ù* ^{d}UTU-*ia*
02) *um-ma La-ab-a-yu* ÌR-*ka*
03) *ù ep-ru ša ka-bá-ši-ka*
04) *a-na* GÌR.MEŠ *šàr-ri* EN-*ia*
05) *ù* ^{d}UTU-*ia 7-šu 7-ta-a-an*
06) ⸢*am*⸣-*qut iš-te-me a-wa-te*^{MEŠ}
07) ⸢*ša*⸣ *šàr-ru iš-tap-ra-an-ni*
08) ⸢*ù*⸣ *mi-ia-ti a-na-ku ù*
09) ⸢*ya*⸣-*aḫ*!(ḪÉ)-*li-qú šàr-ru* KUR.KI-*šu*
10) ⸢UGU⸣-*ia a-mur a-na-ku* ÌR *ki-ti*
11) *šàr-ri ù la-a ar-na-ku*
12) *ù la-a ḫa-ṭá-ku ù*
13) *la-a a-kal-li* GÚ.UN.ḪI.A-*ia*
14) *ù la-a a-kal-li*
15) *e-ri-iš-ti*$_{7}$ LÚ *ra-bi-ṣí-ia*
16) *a-nu-ma yi-ka-lu ka-ar-ṣí-ia*
17) *ḫa-ba-lu-ma ù la-a*
18) *yu-sà-an-ni-qú šàr-ru* EN-*ia*
19) *ar-ni-ia ša-ni-tam*
20) *i*$_{15}$-*ba-aš-ši ar-ni-ia*
Lo.ed. 21) *i-nu-ma er-ru-ba-ti*
22) *a-na* URU *Gaz-ri*
Rev. 23) *ù aq-ta-bu*
24) *pu-uḫ*!(ḪÉ)-*ri-iš-mi*
25) *yi-il-te-qú šàr-ru*
26) *mim-mi-ia ù mim-mì*
27) ^{I}*Mil-ki-lì a-ia-ka-am*
28) *i*$_{15}$-*de ep-še-et-šu ša*
29) ^{I}*Mil-ki-li* UGU

\-*ia*

EA 254

TRANSLATION

(1–5) To the king, my lord and my sun god, thus says Lab'ayu, your servant and the dust on which you tread: At the feet of the king, my lord and my sun god, seven times (and) seven times I have fallen.

(6–10) I have heard the words that the king has sent to me. And who am I that the king lose his land because of me?

(10–15) Look, I am the loyal servant of the king and I am not a wrongdoer nor am I a criminal and I have not withheld my tribute nor have I withheld the request of my commissioner.

(16–29) Now I have been viciously maligned and the king, my lord, is not even investigating whether I'm guilty! Moreover, my wrongdoing is simply that I entered into Gezer and was saying: "Altogether the king takes my possessions but where are the possessions of Milkilu? I know the deeds of Milkilu against me."

30) *ša-ni-tam*
31) *a-na* ^{I}DUMU.MU-*ia ša-pár šàr-ru*
32) *ú-ul* i_{15}*-de i-nu-ma*
33) ^{I}DUMU.MU-*ia it-ti*
34) LÚ.MEŠ SA.GAZ
35) *it-ta-na-la-ku*
36) *ù al-lu-ú na-ad-na-*
ti-šu
37) *i-na* ŠU ^{I}*Ad-*⸢*da*⸣*-*[*i*]*a*
38) *ša-ni-tam ki-*i_{15} *šum-m*[*a*]
39) *a-na* DAM-*ia ša-pár šàr-rù*
40) *ki-*i_{15} *a-kal-lu-ši ki-*i_{15}
41) *šum-ma a-na ia-ši*
42) *ša-pár* ⸢*šàr*⸣*-ru*
Up.ed 43) *šu-ku-*⸢*un*⸣ GÍR ZABAR
44) *i-na lìb-bi-ka ù*
45) BA.ÚŠ *ki-*i_{15} *la-a*
Lft.ed. 46) *ep-pu-šu ši-pí-ir-ti šàr-ri*

ḥ3t sp 10 + 2 [+ *x*?]

30–37) Furthermore, concerning my son the king has written. I did not know that my son has been associating with the *ʿApiru*, but behold, have I not turned him over to Addaya?

38–46) In addition, if the king had written for my wife, how could I withhold her? Because if the king had written to me, "Stick a bronze dagger into your heart and die!" how could I not carry out the king's instruction?

Year 10 + 2(+*x*?)

EA 255

TRANSCRIPTION

Obv. 01) [*a*-]⸢*na*⸣ *šàr-ri* EN-⸢*i*⸣[*a*]
02) *ù* ^{d}UTU-*ia qí-bí*[-*ma*]
03) *um-ma* ^{I}*Mu-ut-ba-ʾa-l*[*i*]
04) ÌR-*ka* SAḪAR ⸢*ša*⸣ 2 GÌR.MEŠ[-*ka*]
05) *ṭi-ṭù ša ka-*⸢*bá*⸣*-ši-*⸢*ka*⸣
06) *a-na* GÌR.MEŠ *šàr-*⸢*ri*⸣ EN-*ia*
07) 7-*šu* 7-*ta-a-an am-qut*
08) LUGAL EN-*li ša-pár a-na muḫ-ḫi-*⸢*i*⸣*a* ^{I}*Ḫa-a-ia*
09) *a-na qa-bi* KASKAL-*ra-ni*$^{ḪI.A}$
10) KUR *Ḫa-na-gal*$_{9}$*-bat an-nu-ú*
11) *ú-wa-še-ru-na ù uš-še-ru-ši*
12) *mi-ia-ti a-na-ku ù* ⸢*la*⸣*-a*
13) *ú-wa-še-ru* KASKAL-*ra-ni*$^{ḪI.A}$
14) *šàr-ri* EN-*ia a-mur*
15) [^{I}*La-*]⸢*ab*⸣*-a-ia a-bi-ia*
16) [*yu-ra-d*]*u šàr-ra* EN-*šu*
17) [*ù šu-ut*] *yu-wa-še-ru*

Lo.ed. 18) [*ka-li* KASKAL-]⸢*ra*⸣-⸢*ni*⸣⸢$^{ḪI.A}$⸣
19) [*ša yu-wa-*]⸢*še*⸣*-ru šàr-ru*

Rev. 20) *a-na* KUR *Ḫa-na-gal-bat* ⸢*ù*⸣
21) *a-na* KUR *Ka-ra-du-ni-ia-aš*
22) *li-wa-še-ra šàr-ru*
23) EN-*ia* ⸢KASKAL⸣*-ra-na*$^{ḪI.A}$
24) *a-na-ku ub-ba-lu-ši*
25) *ki-ma ma-diš na-aṣ-ra-at*

EA 255

TRANSLATION

(1–7) Speak [t]o the king, m[y] lord, my son god, the message of Mut-Baʿlu, your servant, the dirt at [your] feet, the mud of your treading: At the feet of my lord, seven times (and) seven times, have I fallen.

(8–11) The king, my lord, has sent to me Ḫaʿya, to say: "Caravans to Ḫanigalbat, behold I am sending; so expedite (pl.) them!"

(12–14) Who am I that I would not expedite the caravans of the king, my lord?

(14–21) Look, [La]bʾayu, my father, [always serv]ed the king, his lord, [and he] always expedited [all the cara]vans [that] the king [would] send to the land of Ḫanigalbat and to the land of Karaduniyash.

(22–25) May the king, my lord, send caravans! I will transport them under heavy guard.

EA 256

TRANSCRIPTION

Obv. 01) *ana* ^{I}*Ia-an-ḫa-mì* EN-*ia*
02) *qí-bí-ma um-ma* ^{I}*Mu-ut-*^{d}IŠKUR
03) ÌR-*ka a-na* 2 GÌR.MEŠ EN-*ia*
04) *am-qut ki-i qa-bi-mì*
05) *i-na pa-ni-ka* ^{I}*Mu-ut-*^{d}IŠKUR-*mì*
06) *in-né-bi-it* ^{I}*A-ia-ab*
07) \ *ḫi-iḫ-bi-e ki-i in*$_{4}$*-né-bi-tu*
08) *šàr* URU *Pí-ḫi-lì iš-tu*
09) *pa-ni* LÚ.MEŠ *ra-bi-ṣí* \ *sú-ki-ni*
10) *šàr-ri* EN-*šu li-ib-lu-uṭ*
11) *šàr-ru* EN-*ia li-ib-lu-uṭ*
12) *šàr-ru* EN-*ia šum-ma i*$_{15}$*-ba-ši*
13) ^{I}*A-ia-ab i-na* URU *Pí-*˹*ḫi*˺*-lì*
14) *an-nu-ú* ˹2˺ ˹ITI˺.˹ḪI˺.˹A˺ *ia-*˹*nu*˺-[*u*]*m-*˹*ma*˺
Lo.ed. 15) *al-lu-ú* ^{I}*Bi-in*$_{4}$*-i*$_{15}$*-lí-ma*
Rev. 16) [*š*]*a-al al-lu-ú*
17) [^{I}*T*]*a-du-a ša-al*
18) ˹*al*˺*-lu-ú* ^{I}*Ya-šu-ia*
19) *ša-al a-di iš-tu*
20) GÁN.BA ^{I}DI.^{d}AMAR.UTU
21) URU *Aš-tar-ti in*$_{4}$*-né-ri-ir*
22) *i-nu-ma na-ak-ru gáb-bi*
23) URU.DIDLI.ḪI.A KUR *Ga-ri*
24) URU *Ú-du-mu* URU *A-du-ri*
25) URU *A-ra-ru* URU *Mì-iš-ta*$_{5}$
26) URU *Ma-ag-da-lì* URU *Ḫe-ni-a-na-bi*
27) URU *Za-ar-qí ṣa-ab-ta-at*
28) URU *Ḫa-yu-ni* URU *Yu-bi-lì-ma*

EA 256

TRANSLATION

(1–4) Speak to Yanḫamu, my lord, the message of Mut-Baʿlu, your servant: At the feet of my lord have I fallen.

(4–10) How is it said in your presence, "Mut-Baʿlu has fled; he has hidden Ayyâb"? How could the ruler of the city of Piḫilu flee from the commissioner of the king, his lord?

(10–14) As the king, my lord, lives, as the king, my lord, lives, (I swear) if Ayyâb is in Piḫil, behold, not for two months!

(15–19) Behold, Bin-ʾilîma, ask (him)! Behold [T]adu, ask (him)! Behold Yashuya, ask (him)!

(19–28) Further, from the emporium of Shullum-Marduk, I went to the aid of Ashtartu when all the cities of Garu became hostile: the city of Udumu, the city of Aduru, the city of Araru, the city of Mishta, the city of Magdal, the city of ʿÊni-ʿanabi, the city of Zarqu. The city of ʿAyyônu and the city of Yôbilu were seized.

29) *ša-ni-tam an-nu-ú iš-tu*
30) *ša-pa-ri-ka ṭup-pa a-na mu-ḫi-ia*
Up.ed. 31) *ša-pár-ti a-na ša-šu*
32) *a-di ku-ša-*⸢*di*⸣*-k*[*a*]
Lft.ed. 33) *iš-tu* KASKAL-*ra-ni-ka ù an-nu-*[*ú*]
34) *ka-ši-id a-na* URU *Pí-ḫi-lì*
35) *ù iš-te-mu-na a-w*[*a-*]*-t*[*e*]*-k*[*a*]

(29–35) Furthermore, behold, after your sending a tablet to me, I wrote to him. Before your arrival from your journey, then behold, he will have come to Piḫil, and I will surely obey your orders.

EA 257

TRANSCRIPTION

Obv. 01) [*a-na* ^{I}LUGAL E]N-*ia*
02) [*qí-b*]*í-ma*
03) [*um-m*]*a* ^{Id}IŠKUR-*mé-ḫe-er*
04) [Ì]R-*ka-ma*
05) *a-*⸢*na*⸣ 2! GÌR.MEŠ LUGAL EN-*ia*
06) 7 *u* 7 *am-qú-ut*
07) ⸢*a*⸣*-mur a-na-ku* ÌR ⸢*ki*⸣-⸢*ti*⸣
08) ⸢*ša*⸣ LUGAL *ù li-de*
09) [L]UGAL EN-*ia*
10) [*i-n*]*u-ma šal-ma-at*
Lo.ed. 11) [URU-*š*]*u ù* ÌR-*š*[*u*]
12) [*ù*] ⸢*a*⸣*-nu-ma*
Rev. 13) [*ša*]*-ak-na-ti*$_{7}$
14) [*ki-*]*ša-di-ia*
15) ⸢*i*⸣*-na ḫu-li*
16) *ša ú-ub*!*-ba-lu*
17) *ù li-de* ^{I}LUGAL EN-⸢*ia*⸣
18) ⸢*i*⸣*-nu-ma ú-ra-du-šu*
19) [*ma-*]*gal ma-gal*
20) [*ù t*]*u-ra-du-šu*
21) [URU-*šu a*]-⸢*na*⸣ *l*[*a*]?*-ma-di*
22) [^{I}LUGAL EN-*ia*] ⸢*ma*⸣-⸢*gal*⸣

EA 257

TRANSLATION

(1–6) [Spea]k [to the king], my [lo]rd, [messag]e of Baʿl-meher, your [se]rvant: At the feet of the king, my lord, seven (times) and seven (times) have I fallen.

(7–11) Look, I am the loyal servant of the king, so may the [k]ing, my lord, be apprised [th]at [h]is [city] is well and (also) h[is] servant.

(12–16) [And] now I have [pl]aced my [n]eck in the yoke which I carry, so may the king, my lord, be apprised that I am serving him [ve]ry diligently [and his city] is serving him. [F]or the information of [the king, my lord,] very well.

EA 258

TRANSCRIPTION

Obv. 01) *a-na* LUGAL EN-*ia*
02) *um-ma* [Id]IŠKUR-*me-ḫ̮ér*
03) ÌR *ki-it-ti*$_7$
04) LUGAL *a-na* GÌR.MEŠ LUGAL EN-*ia*
05) 7-*šu ù* 7-*ta-a-an am-qut*

---

06) *gáb-bi mi-im-mì*
07) *ša yi-te-pu-uš*
08) LUGAL EN-*ia*!(EN) *a-na* KUR-*šu*
09) SIG$_5$.GA *ma-gal*

Note hieratic sign in ink on back of tablet

EA 258

TRANSLATION

(1–5) To the king, my lord, the message of Baʿl-meher, the loyal servant of the king: At the feet of the king, my lord, seven times and seven times have I fallen.

(6–9) Everything that the king, my(!) lord, has done for his land is very good.

EA 259

TRANSCRIPTION

Obv.
01) *a-na* L[UGAL EN]-⸢*ia*⸣
02) ⸢*um*⸣-⸢*ma*⸣ ⸢I⸣[dIŠKUR-*mé-ḫ*]*e-e*[*r*]
03) [Ì]R ⸢*ki*⸣-⸢*it*⸣-*ti*₇ *š*[*àr*-]*ri*
04) ⸢*a*⸣-⸢*na*⸣ GÌR.⸢MEŠ⸣ LUGAL EN-*ia*
05) 7-⸢*šu*⸣ ⸢*ù*⸣ ⸢7⸣-⸢*ta*⸣-⸢*a*⸣-⸢*an*⸣ *am*-[*qut*]

---

06) *gáb-bi mi-im-mì*
07) [*ša iš-m*]*e qa-ba-ku*
08) [*a-na* LUGAL E]N-*ia*

EA 259

TRANSLATION

(1–5) To the k[ing,] my [lord], the message of [Baʿl-meh]e[r], the loyal [ser]vant of the k[in]g: At the feet of the king, my lord, seven times and seven times have I fallen.

(6–9) Everything [that I have he]ard, I have spoken [to the king], my [lo]rd.

EA 260

TRANSCRIPTION

Obv. 01) *a-na* LUGAL GAL *be-li-ia*
02) ^{I}*Ba-lu-mé-‹ḫe›-er iq-bi*
03) 7-*šu ù* 7-*šu-ma*
04) *a-na* 2 GÌR LUGAL GAL
05) ^{d}UTU *a-na* *ša*$_{10}$*-me im-qú-ut*
06) *a-na-ku ki-i*$_{15}$ *i-qa-bi*
07) LUGAL GAL *be-li*
08) *a-na-‹ku› iš-me a-wa-ti*
09) *ša* LUGAL GAL *be-li-ia*
10) ^{d}UTU *a-na* *ša*$_{10}$*-me*
11) LUGAL GAL *i-de*$_{4}$
12) *a-na* ÌR-*šu*
Rev. 13) *ù a-na-ku a-na* URU!.KI
14) *Ti-in*$_{4}$*-ni ú-ša-ab*
15) *ù* LUGAL GAL *be-li-ia*
16) *li-i-de*$_{4}$ *a-na* ÌR-*šu*

EA 260

TRANSLATION

(1–5) Baʿlu-me‹h›er has spoken to the great king, my lord: seven times and seven times at the feet of the great king, the sun god from heaven, have I fallen.

(6–10) As for me, when the great king, my lord, spoke, ⸢I⸣ heeded the words of the great king, my lord, the sun god from heaven.

(11–16) The great king knows his servant, and I am residing in the town of Tinni, so may the great king, my lord, be apprised concerning his servant.

EA 261

TRANSCRIPTION

Obv. 01) *a-na* ^{I}LUGAL EN-*ia*
02) ^{d}UTU-*ia qí-bí-ma*
03) *um-ma* ^{I}*Da-aš-ru*
04) ÌR *ki-it-ti*$_{7}$ LUGAL
05) *a-na* GÌR.MEŠ LUGAL EN-*ia*
06) *u* ^{d}UTU 7-*šu u* 7-*ta-a-an am-q*[*ú-ut*]
07) *gáb-bi mi-im-mì*
08) *ša yi-iq-bu*
09) LUGAL EN-*ia*
Lo.ed. 10) *iš-te-nem-mu*

EA 261

TRANSLATION

(1–6) Speak to the king, my lord, my sun god, the message of Dashru, the loyal servant of the king: At the feet of the king, my lord and sun god, seven times and seven times [have] I fal[len].

(7–9) Everything that the king, my lord, has said, I am continually obeying.

EA 262

TRANSCRIPTION

Obv. 01) *a-na* LUGAL EN-*ia*
02) *qí-bí-ma*
03) *um-ma* [I]*Da-aš-ru*
04) ÌR *ki-it-ti*$_7$ LUGAL
05) *a-na* GÌR.MEŠ LUGAL EN-*ia*
06) 7-*šu ù* 7-*ta-a-an am-qut*

---

07) *gáb-bi mi-im-mì*
08) *ša yi-pu-šu*
09) LUGAL EN-*ia a-na* KUR-*šu*
10) *gáb-bu* ⸢SIG$_5$⸣.GA
11) *ma-gal ma-gal*

EA 262

TRANSLATION

(1–6) Speak to the king, my lord; the message of Dashru, the loyal servant of the king: At the feet of the king, my lord, seven times and seven times have I fallen.

(7–11) Everything that the king, my lord, does concerning his land is very, very good.

EA 263

TRANSCRIPTION

Obv. 01) [*a-na* LUGAL *be-li-ia*]
02) [*qí-bí-ma*]
03) [*u*]*m-m*[*a*.........ÌR-*ka*]
04) *a-na* GÌR.[MEŠ *be-li-ia*]
05) *am-*⸢*qú*⸣-⸢*ut*⸣ 7 *ù* 7 [...]
06) *li-iš-mé be-li-ia*
07) *a-*[*wa*]*-te*^{MEŠ} ÌR-*šu i-nu-ma*
08) *i-*[*r*]*i-*[*i*]*b-*⸢*ti*⸣ *a-na* É-*ti*
09) *be-*[*li-i*]*a la-qí-i*
10) *gáb-bu iš-tu* É-*ti* ÌR-*ka*
11) *la-qí-i* KÙ.BABBAR.MEŠ *la-qí-i*
12) LÚ.MEŠ *la-qí-i* UDU.UDU.MEŠ \ *ṣú-ú-nu*
13) \ *ḫa-sí-lu* URU.MEŠ-*nu be-li-ia*
14) ⸢*ù*⸣ *mi-*⸢*im*⸣*-mu ša na-*⸢*da*⸣*-an*
Lo.ed. 15) ⸢*be*⸣-*li-ia a-na*
Rev. 16) ⸢ÌR⸣-*šu ù šu-ut*
17) *la-qí-i ù*
18) ⸢*li*⸣-*im-li-ik*
19) ⸢*be*⸣-*li-ia a-na*
20) ÌR-*šu ù qa-bi-ti*
21) *i-na qa-ti* ^{I}⸢*Pa*⸣-*wu-ra*
22) *a-wa-ta*$_5$ *an-ni-ta*$_5$ *ù*
23) ⸢*lu*⸣-*wa-ši-ra-ni be-li-ia*
24) LÚ.MEŠ \ *ma-ṣa-ar-ta*
25) *ù* ANŠE.KUR.‹RA.›MEŠ \ ⸢*sú*⸣-⸢*ú*⸣[-*sí-ma*]
26) *qa-ba be-*[*li-ia*]
27) *a-na* ÌR-[*šu a-na* ANŠE.KUR.MEŠ]
28) \ *s*[*ú-ú-sí-ma*]
29) [...]
30) [...]
31) [...]
32) [...]

EA 263

TRANSLATION

(1–5) [Speak to the king, my lord, the me]ssa[ge of……, your servant;] at the fe[et of my lord] have I fallen, seven (times) and seven [times?].

(6–17) May my lord hear the words of his servant: When I entered into the house of my lord, everything was taken from the house of your servant. The silver was taken; the men were taken; the small cattle were taken. The cities of my lord have been wiped out and as for the property that my lord gave to his servant, that was taken.

(18–22) May my lord take counsel concerning his servant. And I have spoken this word by means of Pawura, so

(23–28) may my lord send to me garrison troops and horses (i.e. chariotry). [My] lo[rd] had spoken to his servant about h[orses?].

(29–32) [……………………………………………]

Lft.ed. 33) [..................] ⌜I⌝*Ta-a-gi*
34) [..................] ⌜*ù*⌝ *i-na La-ab-a-*
35) \ *a-*⌜*ya*⌝

(33–35) [.......] Tagi [.......] and by Lab'aya.

EA 264

TRANSCRIPTION

Obv. 01) [*a*]-*na* ^{I}*šàr-ri* EN-⸢*i*⸣[*a*]
02) *um-ma* ^{I}*Ta-gi* ÌR-*k*[*a*]
03) *a-na* GÌR.MEŠ ^{I}*šàr-ri* ⸢EN⸣-*ia*
04) 7-*šu ù* 7-*ta-an am-qut*
05) *a-mur-mì a-na-ku* ÌR *ša* ^{I}*šàr-ri*
06) *ù bu-i-ti*$_7$ *pu-ḫi-ir*
07) KASKAL.ḪI.A *i-na qa-at* LÚ-*ia*
08) *ù ú-ba-an la-a mì-ḫi-iṣ*
09) *la-a i-le-ú uš-šir*$_4$
10) KASKAL.ḪI.A-*ia a-na* ^{I}*šàr-ri* EN-*ia*
11) *ù ša-al* LÚ.MEŠ MÁŠKIM-*ka*
12) *šum-ma la ú-ba-an la-a mì-ḫi-iṣ*
13) ŠEŠ-*ia ša-ni-tam*

Rev. 14) *a-mur ni-nu a-na* ⸢*mu*⸣-⸢*ḫi*⸣-*ka*$_4$
15) 2 IGI-*ia šum-ma ni-tel-lí*
16) *a-na* AN \ *ša-mì-ma šum-ma*
17) *nu-ra-ad i-na er-ṣé-ti*$_7$
18) *ù* SAG.DU-*nu* \ *ru-šu-nu*
19) *i-na qa-te-ka ù an-nu-ú*
20) *i-na-an-na bu-i-ti*$_7$ *uš-šir*$_4$
21) KASKAL.ḪI.A-*ia i-na qa-at*
22) LÚ *tap-pí-ia a-na* ^{I}*šàr-ri*
23) \ EN-*ia ù yi-ìl-ma-ad*
24) ^{I}*šàr-ru* EN-‹*ia*› *i-nu-ma ur-ru-du*
25) ^{I}*šàr-ra ù i-na-ṣa-ru*

EA 264

TRANSLATION

(1–4) [T]o the king m[y] lord, message of Tagi, yo[ur] servant: At the feet of the king, my lord, seven times and seven times, have I fallen.

(5–13) Look, I am the servant of the king and I sought to assemble a caravan in the charge of my man but he came within an inch of being smitten. I am unable to send my caravan to the king, my lord. So ask your commissioners whether my associate was not within an inch of being smitten.

(13–19) Furthermore, look, as for us, my eyes are towards you.

> If we should go up to heaven,
> If we should go down to the underworld,
> Then our head is in your hands.
>
> And behold now, I sought to send my caravan to the king, my lord, in the charge of my colleague. So may the king, ‹my› lord be aware that I am serving the king and I am guarding.

EA 265

TRANSCRIPTION

Obv. 01) [*a-n*]*a* ^{I}*šàr-ri* EN-*ia*
02) *um-ma* ^{I}*Ta-gi* ÌR-*k*[*a*]
03) *a-na* GÌR.MEŠ LUGAL EN-*ia*
04) [*am-*]⸢*qut*⸣ LÚ-*ia uš-šir-ti*$_{7}$
05) *q*[*a*]-⸢*du*⸣ ⸢LÚ⸣.MEŠ *a-na da-gal*
06) *p*[*a*]-⸢*ni*⸣ ⸢^{I}⸣⸢*šàr*⸣-*ri* EN-*ia*
07) [*ù uš*]-*ši-ir* ^{I}*šàr-ru*
08) EN-*ia šu-lu-uḫ-ta*
09) *i-na qa-at* ^{I}*Ta-aḫ-ma*-⸢*ia*⸣
10) [*a*]-*na ia-ši ù na-da*-⸢*an*⸣
Rev. 11) ⸢^{I}⸣⸢*Ta*⸣-*aḫ-ma-ya*
12) GAL 1-*en* KÙ.GI
13) *ù* 1[2] *ta-pal* TÚG.GADA.M[EŠ]
14) [*ù*] ⸢*a*⸣-[*n*]*a la-ma-ad*
15) [^{I}*šàr-r*]*i* EN-*ia*

EA 265

TRANSLATION

(1–4) [T]o the king, my lord, message of Tagi, yo[ur] servant: At the feet of the king, my lord [have I fal]len.

(4–6) My man have I sent with the men to behold the face of the king, my lord.

(7–15) [And] the king, my lord, [se]nt a shipment to me in the charge of Taḫmaya and Taḫmaya gave (me) one gold cup and tw[elve] pairs of linen garments [and] for the information of [the king], my lord.

EA 266

TRANSCRIPTION

Obv. 01) [*a-na*] ^{I}LUGAL E[N-*ia*]
02) [DINGIR.]MEŠ-*ia* ^{d}[UTU-*ia*]
03) [*q*]*í-bí-m*[*a*]
04) [*u*]*m-ma* ^{I}*Ta-a-g*[*i* ÌR-*ka*]
05) ⸢*ep*⸣-*ri* ⸢*ša*⸣ GÌ[R.MEŠ-*ka*]
06) ⸢*a*⸣-*na* GÌR.MEŠ LUGAL E[N-*ia*]
07) DINGIR.MEŠ-*ia* ^{d}UTU-*ia*
08) ⸢7⸣-*šu* 7-*tá-a-an* [*am-qut*]
09) ⸢*da*⸣-*ag-la-ti*
10) [*k*]*i-ia-am ù da*[-*ag-la-*]*ti*
11) [*ki*]-*ia-am ù* ⸢*la*⸣-[*a*]
12) [*na*]-*mu-ur* ⸢*ù*⸣
13) [*d*]*a-ag-la-t*[*i*]
14) [*a-na*] *mu-ḫi* LUGAL [EN-*ia*]
15) [*ù n*]*a-mur* ⸢*ù*⸣
Lo.ed. 16) [*a-nu-*]*ma ša-ak*[-*na-ti*]
Rev. 17) [*pa-n*]*i-ia a-na u*[*r-ru-*]
18) [LUGA]L EN-*ia* *u*[*d*]
19) ⸢*ù*⸣ *ti-na-ma-šu* [SIG$_{4}$-]
20) [*t*]*u* \\ *la-bi-tu*
21) [*i*]*š-tu ša-pal* [*tap-pa-te-ši*]
22) ⸢*ù*⸣ *a-na-ku la-a*
23) ⸢*i*⸣-⸢*na*⸣-*ma-šu iš-t*[*u*]
24) [*š*]*a-pal* GÌR.MEŠ
25) [LUGA]L EN-*ia*
26) [*ù*] *a-nu-ma uš-ši*[-*ir-ti*]
27) [KUŠ].MEŠ *a-ši-ti*
28) [*ša t*]*a-pal* ANŠE.[KUR.RA]
29) [*ù* G]IŠ.BAN ⸢*ù*⸣
30) [KUŠ] É.MA[R.URU$_{5}$]
31) [GIŠ] *i-mi-*[*it-ta*]
32) [TÚG] \\ *sà-dì-*[*in-ni*]
Up.ed. 33) [*a-n*]*a* LUGAL E[N-*ia*]

EA 266

TRANSLATION

(1–8) [S]peak [to] the king, [my] lo[rd, my [dei]ty, [my sun god], [the me]ssage of Tag[i, your servant], the dirt under [your] fe[et]: At the feet of the king, [my] lo[rd], my deity, my sun god, seven times (and) seven times [have I fallen].

(8–15) I looked this way and I lo[oked th]at way, but there was no [li]ght; then I [l]ooked [to]wards the king, [my lord, and there was [li]ght!

(15–25) So [no]w [I have] set my [fac]e to se[rv]e [the kin]g, my lord. And a brick may slip out [fr]om under [its mate] but I will not depart fro[m u]nder the feet of [the kin]g, my lord.

(26–33) [And] now, [I have] se[nt leather] harness [for a t]eam of hor[ses and a b]ow and [a qu]ive[r], [a s]pea[r, (horse) blankets, [t]o the king, [my] lo[rd].

EA 267

TRANSCRIPTION

Obv. 01) [*a*]-⸢*na*⸣ ^{I}LUGAL EN-*ia*
02) [DINGIR].MES-*ia* ^{d}UTU-*ia*
03) ⸢*qí*⸣-*bí-ma*
04) *um-ma* ^{I}*Mil-ki-li* ÌR-*ka-ma*
05) *ep-ri* ⸢*ša*⸣ GÌR.MEŠ-*ka*
06) *a-na* GÌR.MEŠ LUGAL EN-*ia*
07) DINGIR.MEŠ-*ia* ^{d}UTU-*ia*
08) 7-*šu* 7-*tá-a-an am-qú-ut*
09) *a-*⸢*wa*⸣*-at ul-te-bi-la*
10) LUGAL EN-*ia* DINGIR.MEŠ-*ia*
11) ^{d}UTU-⸢*ia*⸣ ⸢*a*⸣-[*na*] *ia-ši*
12) *a-nu-*⸢*um*⸣*-ma i-šu-ši-ru-šu*
13) *a-na* LU[GA]L EN-*ia*
14) ^{d}UTU *iš-tu* AN *ša*$_{10}$*-mì*
Lo.ed. 15) *ù lu-ú yi-i-de*$_{9}$
Rev. 16) LUGAL EN-*ia* DINGIR.MEŠ-*ia*
17) ^{d}UTU-*ia i-nu-ma*
18) *ša-lim a-šar*
19) LUGAL EN-*ia ša*
20) *it-ti*$_{7}$*-ia*

EA 267

TRANSLATION

(1–8) Speak [t]o the king, my lord, my [dei]ty, my sun god; the message of Milkilu your servant, the dirt under your feet: At the feet of the king, my lord, my deity, my sun god, seven times (and) seven times have I fallen.

(9–14) As for the word that the king, my lord, my deity, my sun god, sent t[o] me, now I am preparing it for the k[in]g, my lord, the sun god from heaven.

(15–20) And may the king, my lord, my deity, my sun god, be apprised that it is well with the place of the king, my lord, that is in my charge.

EA 268

TRANSCRIPTION

Obv. 01) [*a-na* ^{I}]⸢LUGAL⸣ [EN]-*ia* DING[IR.MEŠ-*i*]⸢*a*⸣
02) [^{d}UT]U-*ia qí-bí-ma*
03) [*um-m*]*a* ^{I}*Mil-ki-li* ÌR-*ka*
04) [*e*]*p*-⸢*ri*⸣ *ša* GÌR.MEŠ-*ka*
05) ⸢*a*⸣-*na* GÌR.MEŠ LUGAL EN-*ia*
06) DINGIR.MEŠ-*ia* ^{d}UTU-*ia*
07) 7-⸢*šu*⸣ 7-*tá-a-an* [*a*]*m*-⸢*qú*⸣-*ut*
08) *yi-de* [LUGAL EN-]*li* ⸢*i*⸣-*nu-ma*
09) *šal-ma-*[*at* URU] LUGAL ⸢EN⸣-*ia*
10) *ša* [*ip-qí-id*] *i-n*[*a*]
11) *qa-*[*ti-ia ù*] *a-w*[*a*]-⸢*at*⸣
12) [*ul-te-bi-la* LUGAL EN-*l*]*i*
13) [DINGIR.MEŠ-*ia* ^{d}UTU-*ia*]
14) [*šu-ši-ra-ti-šu-*]*nu*
15) [*ù a-nu-um-ma*]
Lo.ed. 16) [*uš- ši-ir-*]⸢*ti*⸣ [*i-na*]
Rev. 17) [*qa-a*]*t* ^{I}*Ḫa-y*[*a*]
18) ⸢46⸣ ^{MUNUS}*ar-d*[*i*]
19) *ù* 5 LÚ.MEŠ TUR
20) *ù* 5 LÚ.⸢MEŠ⸣ *a-ši-ru*
ma
21) *a-na* LUGAL EN-*ia*

EA 268

TRANSLATION

(1–7) Speak [to] the king, my [lord], [my] dei[ty], my [sun g[od], [the mess]age of Milkilu, your servant, [the di]rt under your feet: At the feet of the king, my lord, my deity, my sun god, seven times (and) seven times, have I fallen.

(8–10) May [the king,] my [lord], be apprised that [the city] of the king, my lord, which [he entrusted] to [my] auth[ority], is well.

(10–14) [And] the thing [which the king,] my [lord, my deity, my sun god, sent, I have prepared th]em.

(15–21) [And now,] I [have sent under the authori]ty of Ḫay[a]: forty six serving women and five servitors and five *ašîrûma* to the king, my lord.

EA 269

TRANSCRIPTION

Obv. 01) [*a*]-⸢*na*⸣ ^{I}LUGAL EN-*ia*
02) ⸢DINGIR⸣.⸢MEŠ⸣-⸢*i*⸣*a* ⸢^{d}⸣UTU-⸢*i*⸣*a*
03) ⸢*qí*⸣-*bi-ma*
04) ⸢*um*⸣-⸢*ma*⸣ ^{I}⸢*Mil*⸣-*ki-li* ÌR-*ka*
05) ⸢*ep*⸣-⸢*ri*⸣ *ša* GÌR.MEŠ-*ka*
06) ⸢*a*⸣-⸢*na*⸣ ⸢GÌR⸣.⸢MEŠ⸣ ⸢LUGAL⸣ EN-*ia*
07) ⸢DINGIR⸣.⸢MEŠ⸣-*i*⸢*a*⸣ ⸢^{d}⸣UTU-*ia*
08) 7-⸢*šu*⸣ ⸢7⸣-⸢*ta*⸣-*a-an am-qut*
09) *iš*-⸢*te*⸣-*mé* ⸢*ša*⸣-⸢*pár*⸣
10) LUGAL EN-*ia* ⸢*a*⸣-⸢*na*⸣ *ia-ši*
11) *ù yu-uš*-⸢*ši*⸣-⸢*ra*⸣
12) LUGAL *be-li* ÉRIN.MEŠ *pí*-⸢*ṭá*⸣-⸢*ta*⸣
13) *a-na* ÌR.MEŠ-*šu* ⸢*ù*⸣
14) *yu-uš-ši-ra*
15) LUGAL *be-li*
16) [I]Š+BI (= [Š]IM).ZAR.MEŠ \ *mu*-⸢*ur*⸣-*ra*
Lo.ed. 17) ⸢*a*⸣-⸢*na*⸣ *ri-pu-ú-ti*

EA 269

TRANSLATION

(1–8) Speak [t]o the king, my lord, my deity, my sun god, the message of Milkilu, your servant, the dirt at your feet: At the feet of the king, my lord, my deity, my sun god, seven times (and) seven times have I fallen.

(9–17) I have heard what the king, my lord, has written to me. So may the king, my lord, send regular troops to his servant and may the king, my lord, send myrrh for healing.

EA 270

TRANSCRIPTION

Obv. 01) *a-na* ^{I}LUGAL EN-*i*⸢*a*⸣
02) DINGIR.MEŠ-*ia* ^{d}UTU-*ia*
03) *qí-----bí-ma*
04) *um-ma* ^{I}*Mil-ki-li* ÌR-*ka*
05) *ep-ri ša* GÌR.MEŠ-*ka*
06) *a-na* GÌR.MEŠ LUGAL EN-*ia*
07) DINGIR.MEŠ-*ia* ^{d}UTU-*ia*
08) 7-*šu* 7-*tá-a-an am-qut*
09) *yi-de* LUGAL *be-li*
10) *ip-ši ša yi-pu-šu-ni*
11) ^{I}*Ya-an-ḫa-mu*
12) *iš-tu a-ṣí-ia*
13) [*i*]*š-tu mu-ḫi* LUGAL EN-*ia*
14) [*i*]*-nu-ma yu-ba-*[*ú*](?)
Lo.ed. 15) ⸢3⸣(?) *li-im* ⸢KÙ⸣.BABBAR.⸢MEŠ⸣
Rev. 16) *iš-tu qa-ti-i*⸢*a*⸣
17) *ù yi-iq-bu*
18) *a-na ia-ši id-na-m*[*i*](*?*)
19) DAM-*ka ù*
20) DUMU.MEŠ-*ka ù lu-ú*
21) *i-ma-ḫa-ṣa ù lu-ú*
22) *yi-de* LUGAL
23) *ip-ša an-na-am*
24) *ù lu-ú yu-uš-ši-*
\ *ra*
25) LUGAL *be-li*
26) GIŠ.GIGIR.MEŠ *ù lu-ú*
27) *yi-il-te-qé-ni*
28) ⸢*a*⸣*-na mu-ḫi-šu la-a*
29) *iḫ-la-aq*

EA 270

TRANSLATION

(1–8) Speak to the king, my lord, my deity, my sun god, the message of Milkilu, your servant, the dirt at your feet: At the feet of the king, my lord, my deity, my sun god, seven times (and) seven times, have I fallen.

(9–13) May the king, my lord, be apprised of the deeds that Yanḫamu is doing to me since my coming forth from the presence of the king, my lord,

(14–21) that he is demand[ing] three thousand (shekels of) silver from my hand and he is saying to me, "Give me your wife and your sons or else I will smite (you)."

(21–29) So may the king be apprised of this deed and may the king, my lord, send chariots and may he take me to his presence lest I perish.

EA 271

TRANSCRIPTION

Obv. 01) *a-na* ^{I}LUGAL EN-*ia*
02) DINGIR.MEŠ-*ia* ^{d}UTU-*ia*
03) *qí-bí-ma*
04) *um-ma Mil-ki-li* ÌR-⸢*ka*⸣
05) *ep-ri ša* GÌR.MEŠ-*ka*
06) *a-na* GÌR.MEŠ LUGAL EN-⸢*ia*⸣
07) DINGIR.MEŠ-*ia* ^{d}UTU-*ia*
08) 7-*šu* 7-*ta-a*-⸢*an*⸣ *am-qut*
09) *yi-de* LUGAL *be-li*
10) *i-nu-ma da-na*-⸢*at*⸣
11) *nu-kúr-tu* UGU-*ia*
12) *ù* UGU ^{I}*Šu-wa*-⸢*ar*⸣-⸢*da*⸣-⸢*ta*⸣
13) *ù yi-ki-im*
14) LUGAL *be-li* KUR-*šu*
15) ⸢*iš*⸣-*tu qa-at*
Lo.ed. 16) ⸢LÚ⸣.MEŠ SA.GAZ.MEŠ
17) [*šu*]*m-ma i-ia-nu*
Rev. 18) ⸢*ù*⸣ *uš-ši-ra*
19) LUGAL *be-li* GIŠ.GIGIR.MEŠ
20) *a-na* ⸢*la*⸣-*qí*-⸢*nu*⸣ [*l*]*a-a*
21) *ti*$_{7}$-*ma-ḫa-ṣú*-⸢*nu*⸣ ÌR.MEŠ-⸢*nu*⸣
22) ⸢*ù*⸣ ⸢*ša*⸣-*ni-tam*
23) ⸢*yi*⸣-⸢*ša*⸣-⸢*al*⸣
24) ⸢LUGAL⸣ ⸢*be*⸣-⸢*li*⸣
25) $^{⸢I⸣}$[*I*]*a*-⸢*an*⸣-*ḫa-ma* ⸢ÌR⸣-*šu*
26) ⸢*a*⸣-⸢*na*⸣ *ša yu*-⸢*pa*⸣-*šu*
27) *i-na* ⸢KUR⸣-*šu*

EA 271

TRANSLATION

(1–8) Speak to the king, my lord, my deity, my sun god, the message of Milkili, your servant, the dirt under your feet: At the feet of the king, my lord, my deity, my sun god, seven times and seven times have I fallen.

(9–21) May the king, my lord, be apprised that hostility is strong against me and against Shuwardata, so may the king, my lord, deliver his land from the hand of the *ʿapîru* men. But if not, then send, O king, my lord, chariots to take us lest our own servants should smite us.

(22–27) And furthermore, may the king, my lord, ask [Y]anḫamu, his servant, concerning what is being done in his land.

EA 272

TRANSCRIPTION

Obv. 01) [*a*-]⸢*na*⸣ ^{I}⸢LUGAL⸣ [EN-*ia* DINGIR.MEŠ-*ia*]
02) ⸢^{d}⸣⸢UTU⸣-⸢*ia*⸣ *q*[*í-bí-ma*]
03) ⸢*um*⸣-⸢*ma*⸣ ^{I}⸢^{d}⸣⸢IŠKUR⸣.⸢DI⸣.⸢KU$_5$⸣ [ÌR-*ka*]
04) ⸢*ep*⸣-⸢*ri*⸣ ⸢*ša*⸣ ⸢GÌR⸣.⸢MEŠ⸣-*k*[*a*]
05) [*a-n*]*a* ⸢GÌR⸣ [ME]Š ⸢LUGAL⸣ ⸢EN⸣-⸢*ia*⸣
06) ⸢DINGIR⸣.⸢MEŠ⸣-⸢*ia*⸣ ⸢^{d}⸣⸢UTU⸣-⸢*ia*⸣
07) ⸢7⸣-⸢*šu*⸣ ⸢7⸣-⸢*ta*⸣?-⸢*a*⸣-⸢*an*⸣ ⸢*am*⸣-⸢*qú*⸣-⸢*ut*⸣
08) ⸢ÌR⸣? [*k*]*i*-⸢*ti*⸣-⸢*šu*⸣ ⸢*ša*⸣
09) ⸢LUGAL⸣ ⸢EN⸣-*ia a-na*-⸢*ku*⸣-[*m*]*a* [*ù*]?
10) [*yi*-]⸢*de*⸣ ⸢LUGAL⸣ *be-li*
11) [*i*]-⸢*nu*⸣-⸢*ma*⸣ *ga-am-ru*
12) [LÚ.MEŠ *ḫ*]*a-za-nu-te*
13) [*ša-a*]*i-na ma-ḫa*-⸢*zi*⸣
14) [*ù p*]*a-aṭ-ra-at*

Lo.ed. 15) [*ka*-]⸢*li*⸣ ⸢KUR⸣ ⸢LUGAL⸣

Rev. 16) [E]N-⸢*ia* ⸣ *i-na*
17) [LÚ].MEŠ SA.GAZ
18) *ù yi-ša*-⸢*al*⸣
19) LUGAL *be-li*
20) LÚ *ra-bi-ṣa*-⸢*šu*⸣
21) *a-na ša* ⸢*yu*⸣-[*p*]*a*-⸢*šu*⸣
22) ⸢*i*⸣-⸢*na*⸣ KUR L[UGAL] ⸢EN⸣-⸢*ia*⸣
23) *ù yu-la-mi-dá*
24) ⸢LUGAL⸣ *be*-⸢*li*⸣ ÉRIN.MEŠ *pí*-⸢*ṭá*⸣-[*ti*]-

\ *šu*

25) ⸢*a*⸣-⸢*na* ⸣*ia*-⸢*ši*⸣

EA 272

TRANSLATION

(1–7) [T]o the king, [my lord, my deity], my sun god, [speak]: The message of Baʿlu-dāni, [your servant,] the ⸢dirt⸣ at [your] feet: [A]t the ⸢feet⸣ of the king, my lord, my deity, my sun god, seven times (and) seven times have I fall]en.

(8–9) A loyal servant of [the king,] my lord, am I.

(10–17) May the king, my lord, [be] apprised [th]at the city rulers [who were] in the strong point(s) are finished [and a]ll the land of the king, my lo[rd] has fallen away to the *ʿapîru*-men.

(18–25) So may the king, my lord, ask his commissioner concerning what is being done in the land of the k[ing], my lord, and may the king, my lord, direct the regular troops to me.

EA 273

TRANSCRIPTION

Obv. 01) *a-na* ^{I}LUGAL EN-*ia*
02) DINGER.MEŠ-*ia* ^{d}UTU-*ia*
03) ⸢*qí*⸣-*bí-ma*
04) *um-ma* ^{MUNUS}NIN.UR.MAḪ.MEŠ
05) GÉME-*ka a-na* GÌR.MEŠ LUGAL
06) EN-*ia* DINGIR.MEŠ-*ia* ^{d}UTU-*ia*
07) 7-*šu* 7-*tá-a-an am-qú-ut*
08) *yi-de* LUGAL *be-li*
09) *i-nu-ma nu-kúr-tu*
10) *i-pu-ša*-⸢*at*⸣ *i-na*
11) KUR *ù* ⸢*ga*⸣-⸢*am*⸣-*ra-at*
12) KUR LUGAL EN-⸢*ia* ⸣
13) *i-na pa-ṭá*-⸢*ri*⸣ *i-na*
14) LÚ.MEŠ SA.⸢GAZ⸣.MEŠ
15) ⸢*ù*⸣ *yi-de* LUGAL *be*-⸢*li*⸣

Lo.ed. 16) ⸢*a*⸣-*na* KUR-*šu ù yi*-[*de*]
17) ⸢LUGAL⸣ *be-li i-nu-ma*

Rev. 18) *ša-ap-ru*
19) LÚ.MEŠ SA.GAZ.MEŠ
20) *a-na* URU *A-ia-lu-na*
21) ⸢*ù*⸣ *a-na* URU *Ṣa-ar-ḫa*
22) ⸢*ù*⸣ ⸢*ú*⸣-*ba-an la-a*
23) *m*[*i*]-*iḫ-ṣú* 2 DUMU.ME[Š]
24) ⸢I⸣*Mil*-⸢*ki*⸣-*li* ⸢*ù*⸣
25) *y*[*i*]-*de* LUGAL ⸢*be*⸣-⸢*li*⸣
26) ⸢*ip*⸣-*ša an*-⸢*na*⸣

EA 273

TRANSLATION

(1–7) Speak to the king, my lord, my deity, my sun god; the message of "Lady of the Lions," your handmaid: At the feet of the king, my lord, my deity, my sun god, seven times (and) seven times have I fallen.

(8–16) May the king, my lord, be apprised that war is being conducted in the land and the land of the king, my lord, is finished off by desertion to (or by means of) the *ʿapîru* men. So may the king, my lord be apprised concerning his land.

(16–26) And may the king, my lord, be apprised that the *ʿapîru* men wrote (sent) to the town of Ayalon and to the town of Zorah and by an inch the two sons of Milkilu were not smitten. So may the king, my lord, be apprised concerning this deed.

EA 274

TRANSCRIPTION

Obv.	01)	*a-na* ^{I}LUGAL EN-*i*⸢*a*⸣
	02)	DINGIR.MEŠ-⸢*ia*⸣ ^{d}UTU-⸢*i*⸣*a*
	03)	⸢*qí*⸣-⸢*bí*⸣-⸢*ma*⸣
	04)	⸢*um*⸣-⸢*ma*⸣ $^{\ulcorner\text{MUNUS}\urcorner}$.NIN.⸢UR⸣.⸢MAḪ⸣.MEŠ
	05)	GÉME-*ka ep*-⸢*ri*⸣
	06)	*ša* GÌR.MEŠ-*ka*
	07)	*a-na* GÌR.MEŠ LUGAL ⸢EN⸣-⸢*ia*⸣
	08)	DINGIR.MEŠ-*ia* ^{d}UTU-*ia*
	09)	7-*šu* 7-*tá-a-an* ⸢*am*⸣-*qut*
	10)	*yi-ki-im* LUGAL
	11)	*be-li* KUR-*šu*
	12)	*iš-tu qa-te*
	13)	LÚ.MEŠ SA.GAZ.⸢MEŠ⸣
Lo.ed.	14)	*la-a* ti_7-*iḫ*-⸢*la*⸣-⸢*aq*⸣
Rev.	15)	*la-qí-ta*
	16)	URU *Ṣa-pu-ma*^{KI}
	17)	⸢*ù*⸣ *a-na* ⸢*la*⸣-*ma*-⸢*di*⸣
	18)	[L]UGAL EN-*ia*

EA 274

TRANSLATION

(1–9) Speak to the king, my lord, my deity, my sun god; the message of "Lady of the Lions," your handmaiden, the dirt under your feet: At the feet of the king, my lord, my deity, my sun god, seven times (and) seven times have I fallen.

(10–14) May the king, my lord, rescue his land from the hand of the *ʿapîru* men lest it be lost.

(15–16) Seized is the city of Ṣapuma.

(17–18) And (this is) for the information of the [k]ing, my lord.

EA 275

TRANSCRIPTION

Obv. 01) [*a-na* LUGAL EN-*ia*]
02) [DINGIR.ME]Š-˹*i*˺[*a* ^{d}UTU-*ia*]
03) ˹*qí*˺-*b*[*í-ma*]
04) *um-ma* ^{I}*Ia*-˹*aḫ*˺-˹*zi*˺-*ba*-˹*da*˺
05) ÌR-*ka ep-ri*
06) *ša* GÌR.MEŠ-*ka a-na* GÌR.MEŠ
07) LUGAL EN-*ia* DINGIR.MEŠ-*ia*
08) ^{d}UTU-*ia* 7-*šu* 7-*tá*-˹*a*˺-*an am-qut*
09) *a-wa-at iq-ta*!-*bi*
10) LUGAL EN-*ia*
11) [DINGIR].MEŠ-*ia* ^{d}˹UTU˺-*ia*
12) [*a-n*]*a ia-ši šu ru-*
Lo.ed. 13) [*a*]-*nu-ma* ˹*i*˺-*šu-še-ru-šu*
Rev. 14) [*a-na*] LUGAL EN-*ia*

EA 275

TRANSLATION

(1–8) Spe[ak to the ling, my lord,] m[y deit]y, [my sun god]; message of Yaʿzib-Hadda, your servant, the dirt under your feet: At the feet of the king, my lord, my deity, my sun god, seven times (and) seven times have I fallen.

(9–14) As for the word that the king, my lord, my [deity], my sun god, spoke to me, now I am preparing it [for] the king, my lord.

EA 276

TRANSCRIPTION

Obv.	01)	[*a-na* LUGAL EN-*ia*]
	02)	[DINGER.MEŠ-*ia* ^{d}UTU-*ia*]
	03)	[*qí-bí-ma*]
	04)	*um-ma* ^{I}[*I*]*a-a*[*ḫ-zi-ba-da*]
	05)	ÌR-*ka ep-ri* [*ša*]
	06)	GÌR.MEŠ-*ka a-na* GÌR.M[EŠ LUGAL EN-*ia*]
	07)	DINGIR.MEŠ-*ia* ^{d}UTU-*ia*
	08)	7-*šu* 7-*tá-a-an* ˹*am*˺-˹*qut*˺
	09)	*a-wa-at iš-tap-pár*
	10)	LUGAL EN-*ia* DINGIR.MEŠ-*ia*
	11)	[^{d}]UTU-*ia a-na ia-ši*
	12)	[*a-nu*]-*ma i-šu-ši-*˹*ru*˺-*šu*
Lo.ed.	13)	[*a-n*]*a* LUGAL EN-*ia*
Rev.	14)	[^{d}]˹UTU˺ *iš-tu*
	15)	AN *sa-mì*

EA 276

TRANSLATION

(1–3) [Speak to the king, my lord, my deity, my sun god:]

(4–8) Message of [Y]aʿ[zibadda,] your servant, the dirt [under] your feet: At the fee[t of the king, my lord,] my deity, my sun god, seven times (and) seven times have I fallen.

(9–15) As for the word that the king, my lord, my deity, my sun god, wrote to me, [no]w I am preparing it [fo]r the king, my lord, the sun [god] from heaven.

EA 277

TRANSCRIPTION

Obv. 01) [*a-na* LUGAL EN-*ia*]
02) [DINGIR.MEŠ ^{d}UTU-*ia*]
03) [*um-ma* ^{I}............]
04) [Ì]R-*k*[*a ep-ri ša* GÌR.ME]Š-*ka*
05) [*a-*]*na* ⸢GÌR⸣[.MEŠ LUGAL EN-*ia*]
06) ⸢DINGIR⸣.MEŠ-⸢*ia*⸣ ⸢^{d}⸣[UTU-*ia*]
07) 7-*šu* 7-*t*[*á-a-an am-*]*qú-ut*
08) *a-wa-at iš-*⸢*ta*⸣-⸢*pár*⸣
09) LUGAL EN-*ia* DINGIR.MEŠ-*ia*
10) ^{d}UTU-*ia a-na ia-ši*
11) *a-nu-ma i-šu-ši-*⸢*ru*⸣*-šu*
12) *a-na* LUGAL EN-*ia*

Lo.ed ———————————————

EA 277

TRANSLATION

(1–7) [To the king, my lord, my deity, my sun god, message of …] ⌜your servant⌝, [the dirt at] your [fee]t, [a]t the fee[t] of the king, my lord], my deity, [my sun] god, seven times and seven ti[mes have I f]allen.

(8–12) As for the word that the king, my lord, my deity, my sun god, has written to me, now I am preparing it for the king my lord.

EA 278

TRANSCRIPTION

Obv. 01) *a-na* LUGAL EN-*ia*
02) DINGIR.MEŠ-*ia* ^{d}UTU-*ia*
03) *qí-----bí ma*
04) *um-ma* ^{I}*Šu-wa-ar-da-ta*
05) ÌR-*ka ep-ri ša*
06) GÌR.MEŠ-*ka a-na* GÌR.MEŠ LUGAL
07) EN-*ia* DINGIR.MEŠ-*ia* ^{d}UTU-*ia*
08) 7-*šu* 7-*tá-a-an am-qut*
09) [*a*]-*wa-at ša iš-tap-pár*
10) [LUGAL] ⸢EN⸣-*ia* ^{d}UTU
11) [*iš-t*]*u* AN *ša*$_{10}$-*me a-na ia-ši*
12) [*a-nu-m*]*a i-šu-ši-ru-šu*
13) [*a-na* LUGAL] EN-*ia*
Lo.ed. 14) [^{d}UTU *i*]*š-tu*
Rev. 15) [AN] *ša*$_{10}$-*me*

EA 278

TRANSLATION

(1–8) Speak to the king, my lord, my deity, my sun god, the message of Shuwardata, your servant, the dirt at your feet: At the feet of the king, my lord, my deity, my sun god, seven times (and) seven times, have I fallen.

(9–15) As for the [w]ord that [the king,] my lord, the sun god [fr]om heaven, wrote to me, [no]w I am preparing it [for the king], my lord, [the sun god f]rom heaven.

EA 279

TRANSCRIPTION

Obv. 01) [*a-na*] LUGAL EN-*ia*
02) [DINGIR.MEŠ]-⌜*i*⌝*a* ^{d}UTU-*ia*
03) [*qí-b*]*í-ma*
04) [*um-ma* ^{I}]⌜*Šu*⌝-*wa-ar-da*-⌜*ta*⌝
05) ⌜ÌR⌝-⌜*ka*⌝ *ep-ri ša* GÌR.MEŠ-*ka*
06) ⌜*a*⌝-⌜*na*⌝ GÌR.MEŠ LUGAL EN-*ia*
07) DINGIR.MEŠ-*ia* ^{d}UTU-*ia*
08) 7-*šu* 7-*tá-a-an am*-⌜*qú*⌝-*ut*
09) *yi-de* LUGAL *bé-li i-nu-ma*
10) [*ga-am*]-*ra*-⌜*at*⌝ KUR LUGAL
11) [EN]-*ia i*-⌜*na*⌝ *it*-⌜*ta*⌝-⌜*ṣí*⌝
12) [*š*]*a* URU *Qí-il*$_5$-[*ti*]
13) [*a-n*]*a mu-ḫi* LÚ.MEŠ *š*[*a-ru-te*]
14) ⌜*ù*⌝ ⌜*yu*⌝-*uš-ši*-[*ra* LUGAL]

Lo.ed. 15) [ÉRIN.MEŠ] *pí*-[*ṭá*]-⌜*ta*$_5$⌝ ⌜*ù*⌝
16) [*yi*-]⌜*iš*⌝-⌜*mé*⌝ [LUGAL *a-na*]

Rev. 17) [LÚ].⌜MEŠ⌝ *ḫa-za-nu*-⌜*te*⌝(?)-[*šu*]
18) ⌜*ù*⌝ ⌜*lu*⌝-⌜*ú*⌝ *ni-zi*-⌜*iz*⌝
19) UGU-⌜*šu*⌝-*nu ù* ⌜*lu*⌝-[*ú*]
20) *ni-du-pu-ur*
21) LÚ.MEŠ *ša-ru-ta*
22) *iš-tu* KUR *šàr-ri*
23) EN-*ia*

EA 279

TRANSLATION

(1–8) [Sp]eak [to] the king, my lord, my [deity], my sun god, the message of Shuwardata, your servant, the dirt under your feet: At the feet of the king, my lord, my deity, my sun god, seven times (and) seven times have I fallen.

(9–13) May the king be apprised that the land of the king is [ru]ined by the going out of the town of Qilti [t]o the tr[aitors].

(14–23) So may [the king] send regular [troops] and may the king [lis]ten [to] his city rulers that we may take a stand against them and that we may expel the rebellious men from the land of the king, my lord.

EA 280

TRANSCRIPTION

Obv. 01) *a-n*[*a* ^{I}]LUGAL EN-*ia*
02) D[INGIR.MEŠ-*i*]*a* ^{d}UTU-*ia*
03) *q*[*í-*]*bí-ma*
04) *u*[*m-ma* ^{I}]*Šu-wa-ar-da-ta*
05) ÌR[-*k*]*a ep-ri ša* GÌR.MEŠ-*ka*
06) *a-na* [GÌR.]MEŠ LUGAL EN-*ia*
07) DINGIR.MEŠ-⸢*ia*⸣ ^{d}UTU-*ia*
08) 7-⸢*šu*⸣ ⸢7⸣-*tá-a-an am-qú-ut*
09) LUGAL *b*[*e*]-*li yu-uš-ši-ir-ni*
10) *a-na* [*e*]-*pu-uš nu-kúr-ti*$_7$
11) *i-na* UR[U] *Qí-il*$_5$*-ti*$_7$
12) *ip-pu-uš-ti nu-kúr-ta*
13) *šal-ma-at a-na ia-ti-ia*
14) *šu-te-ra-at* URU.KI-*ia*
15) *a-na ia-ti-ia*
16) UGU *ma-an-ni*
Lo.ed. 17) ⸢*iš*⸣-*tap-pár* ^{I}ÌR-*ḫe*-[*b*]*a*
Rev. 18) ⸢*a*⸣-*na* LÚ.MEŠ URU *Qí-il*$_5$*-ti*$_7$
19) ⸢*le*⸣-*qa-mi* KÙ.BABBAR.MEŠ *ù*
20) [*a*]*l-ku-ni a-na ar-ki-ia*
21) *ù yi-de* LUGAL *be-li*
22) *i-*⸢*nu*⸣-[*m*]*a il*$_5$*-te-qé*
23) URU.KI-*ia* ^{I}ÌR-*ḫe-ba*
24) *iš-tu qa-ti-ia ša-ni-tam*
25) *yi-iš-ta-al* LUGAL *be-li*
26) *šum-ma el-te*$_9$*-qé* LÚ
27) *ù šum-ma* 1-*en* GUD
28) *ù šum-ma* ANŠE *iš-tu*
29) *mu-ḫi-šu ù ki-it-tu šu*

EA 280

TRANSLATION

(1–8) S[p]eak t[o] the king, my lord, [m]y de[ity,] my sun god; the me[ssage] of Shuwardata [yo]ur servant, the dirt under your feet: At the [fee]t of the king, my lord, my deity, my sun god, seven times (and) seven times I have fallen.

(9–15) The king, my lo[rd], gave permission for me to conduct hostilities in the tow[n] of Qilti. I conducted hostilities; all is well with me; my town has been returned to me.

(16–20) For what reason did ʿAbdi-Ḫeba write to the men of the town of Qīlti, "Take silver and [f]ollow after me"?

(21–24) But may the king, my lord, be apprised that ʿAbdi-Ḫeba had taken my town from my control.

(24–29) Furthermore, may the king, my lord, investigate as to whether I have taken a man, or an ox, or an ass away from him. And that's the truth!

30) *ša-ni-tam* ^{I}*La-ab-a-yu*
31) BA.UG$_7$ *ša yi-il*$_5$*-te-qú*
32) URU.DIDLI.⸢ḪI⸣.⸢A⸣-*ni-nu ù*
33) ⸢*a*⸣-⸢*nu*⸣-⸢*ma*⸣ ^{I}*La-ab-a-yu*
34) ⸢*ša*⸣-⸢*nu*⸣ ^{I}ÌR-*ḫe-ba*
35) [*ù*] *yi-il*$_5$*-te-*[*q*]*ú* URU.DIDLI.ḪI.A-*nu*
36) [*ù*] *yi-de* ⸢LUGAL⸣ *a-na* ÌR-[*š*]*u*
Lft.ed. 37) UGU *ep-ši an-ni ù la-a*
38) *ep-pu-šu mi-im-ma a-*⸢*di*⸣
39) *yu-šu-*⸢*te*⸣*-ru* LUGAL *a-wa-ta*$_5$
40) *a-na* ÌR-*šu*

(30–35) Furthermore, Lab'ayu is dead, who used to take our towns, but now ʿAbdi-Ḫeba is another Lab'ayu! [And] he is tak[i]ng our towns.

(36–40) [So] may the king be apprised concerning [h]is servant with regard to this deed. But I am not doing anything until the king sends word back to his servant.

EA 281

TRANSCRIPTION

Obv. 01) ⸢*a*⸣-*na* ^{I}LUGAL EN-⸢*i*⸣[*a*]
02) DINGIR.MEŠ-⸢*nu*⸣-*ia* ⸢*ù*⸣ ^{d}UTU.M[EŠ]
03) [*ù*] *ša-ri-ia*
04) [*qí*]-*bí-ma*
05) [*u*]*m-ma* ^{I}⸢*Šu*⸣-⸢*wa*⸣-⸢*ar*⸣-⸢*da*⸣-⸢*ta*⸣ ÌR-*ka-ma*
06) ⸢*a*⸣-*na* GÌR.MEŠ EN-*ia* ⸢7⸣ *ù* 7 *am-qú-ut*
07) ⸢*ù*⸣ ⸢*ka*⸣-[*ba- t*]*u* ⸢*ù*⸣ *ṣè*(SI)-*ru-ma*
08) ⸢*ù*⸣ *yi*[-*il*$_5$-*ma-ad*] *šàr-ri*
09) E[N]-⸢*i*⸣[*a i*]-*nu*-[*ma gá*]*b-b*[*i*]
10) ⸢URU⸣.⸢DIDLI⸣.MEŠ-*ia nu*-KÚR.MEŠ
11) *a-na ia*-⸢*ši*⸣ ⸢*ù*⸣ *yu-ši-ra*
12) *šàr-ri* EN-*ia* ⸢ÉRIN⸣.MEŠ *pí-ṭá-ta*
13) ⸢*ù*⸣ ⸢*tu*⸣-⸢*ul*⸣-⸢*qu*⸣! *ki-ma* ⸢KA⸣ *ra-bu-*
ti!
14) [*a*]-⸢*na*⸣ [*ša*]-⸢*šu*⸣-⸢*nu*⸣ ⸢*ù*⸣ *yi*-⸢*il*$_5$⸣-*qé*-⸢*šu*⸣-⸢*nu*⸣
15) ^{I}L[UGAL] EN-*ia* LÚ.⸢MEŠ⸣ *re-di-ʾu*$_5$
16) ⸢*ti*⸣-⸢*na*⸣-⸢*an*⸣-⸢*ṣa*⸣-*ar ù*

Lo.ed. 17) ⸢*tu*⸣-⸢*ul*⸣-*qu* ⸢*an*⸣-⸢*nu*⸣-⸢*tu*⸣

Rev. 18) ⸢*ù*⸣ ⸢*ti*⸣-*ḫi-lu* [*a-na pa-*]*ni*
19) ^{I}⸢*šàr*⸣-*ri* EN-[*ia*]
20) ⸢*ù*⸣ ⸢*pa*⸣-*na*-⸢*ia*⸣ *it-tì*
21) ^{I}*šàr-ri* ⸢EN⸣-*ia* ⸢*ù*⸣
22) ^{I}LUGAL *yi*-[*de-mi*] ⸢*nu*⸣-KÚR.M[EŠ]
23) [UG]U-⸢*ia*⸣ [*mi-i*]*a-mi*
24) ⸢*yi*⸣-*pu-šu* [*ar-na*] ⸢*a*⸣-[*n*]*a* ^{I}LUGAL
25) ⸢*ù*⸣ UR.[GI$_7$.MEŠ] ⸢*an*⸣-⸢*nu*⸣-⸢*tu*⸣
26) ⸢*ù*⸣ ⸢*ti*⸣-*pu*-⸢*šu*⸣ *a*[*r-na*] ⸢*a*⸣-*na* LUGAL
27) *ù yu-ši-ra* [^{I}*šàr*]-⸢*ri*⸣
28) ÉRIN.MEŠ *pí*-⸢*ṭá*⸣-[*ta*]
29) *ù yi-i*[*l*$_5$-*qé*]-⸢*šu*⸣-⸢*nu*⸣
30) *ù yi*-⸢*il*$_5$⸣[-*ma*]-⸢*ad*⸣
31) ^{I}*šàr-ri* EN-*ia*

———

EA 281

TRANSLATION

(1–7) [Sp]eak to the king, my lord, my deity and sun god [and] my life breath; message of Shuwardata, your servant: At the feet of my lord, seven (times) and seven (times) have I fallen, both on the sto[ma]ch and on the back.

(8–14) So may the king, my lord be [apprised that al]l of my towns are hostile to me. So may my king, my lord, send the regular troops that they may be taken in accordance with the advice of the senior officials concerning them.

(14–19) So may the k[ing], my lord, take them. May the soldiers guard and may these be taken and may they writhe [befo]re the king, [my] lord.

(20–26) But my face is towards the king, my lord. So may the king be a[ware] of the hostility a[gainst m]e. Who is committing [a crime] against the king? And these are do[gs] and they have committed a cr[ime] against the king,

(27–31) So may the [ki]ng send the regular troo[ps] and may he t[ake] them. So may the king, my lord, be app[rised].

EA 282

TRANSCRIPTION

Obv. 01) *a-na* ^{I}*šàr-ri* EN-*ia*

---

02) DINGIR.MEŠ-*nu ù* ^{d}UTU-*ia*

---

03) *um-ma* ^{I}*Šu-wa-ar-da-ta* ÌR‹-*ka*›-*ma*
04) 7 *ù* 7 *mi-la ma-aq-ta-ti*
05) *a-na* GÌR.MEŠ ^{I}*šàr-ri* EN-*ia*
06) *ù ka-ba-tu-ma*
07) *ù ṣú-uḫ-ru-ma*
08) *li-il*$_5$*-ma-ad* ^{I}*šàr-ri*
09) EN-*ia a-na-ku* 1-*en i-ba-ša-ti*
10) *yu-uš-ši-ra* ^{I}*šàr-ri*
11) EN-*ia* ÉRIN.MEŠ *pí-ṭá-ti*

Rev. 12) *ma-á*ʾ-⸢*da*⸣ *ma*-⸢*gal*⸣
13) *ù yi-ki-im-ni*
14) \ *ya-ṣí-ni*
15) *ù yi*-‹*il*$_5$›-*ma-ad* ^{I}*šàr-ri*
16) EN-*ia*

EA 282

TRANSLATION

(1–8) To the king, my lord, ‹my› deity and my sun god, message of Shuwar-data, ‹your› servant, seven (times) and seven times have I fallen at the feet of the king, my lord, both on the stomach and on the back.

(8–14) May the king, my lord, be informed: I am alone. May the king, my lord, send very many regular troops that he may deliver me (bring me out).

(15–16) So may the king, my lord be in‹fo›rmed.

EA 283

TRANSCRIPTION

Obv. 01) *a-na* ^{I}*šàr-ri* EN-*ia*

---

02) DINGIR.MEŠ-*nu-ia ù* ^{d}UTU-*ia*

03) *um-ma* ^{I}*Šu-wa-ar-da-ta* ÌR-⌜*ka*⌝

04) *a-na* GÌR.MEŠ ^{I}*šàr-ri* EN-*i*⌜ a⌝ *am-qut*

05) 7 *ù* 7 *mi-la-an-na*

06) *ma-aq-ta-ti a-na* GÌR.MEŠ ⌜*šàr*⌝-⌜*ri*⌝ EN-*ia*

07) ⌜*ù*⌝⌜*ša*⌝-*ap*-⌜*ra*⌝ ^{I}*šàr-ri* ⌜EN⌝-⌜*ia*⌝

08) *a-na* ⌜*ia*⌝-⌜*ši*⌝ ⌜*ur*⌝-⌜*ru*⌝-*b*[*a*] ⌜*it*⌝(?)[-*ti*]

09) *du-gu-la lé-qé* ^{I}⌜*šàr*⌝-⌜*ri*⌝ ⌜EN⌝-⌜*ka*⌝(?)

10) *mi-ia-mi yi-ma-gi-ir*

11) *ur-ru-ba it-ti* ^{I}*šàr-ri* EN-*ia*

12) *le-qé-ma* KÙ.GI!.MEŠ! *ù* KÙ.GI!.MEŠ! GÙN

13) ^{I}*šàr-ri* EN-*ia a-nu-ma* ^{I}*Ia-an-ḫa*-⌜*mu*⌝

14) ⌜*it*⌝-‹*ti*›-*ka ù qí-bi it-ti-šu*

15) *šum-ma mi-la-an-na i-ia-nu*

16) ÉRIN.MEŠ *pí-ṭá-ti yi-ik-ki-mi-ni*

Rev. 17) ^{I}*šàr-ri* EN-*ia*

18) *yi-il*$_{5}$*-ma-ad* ^{I}*šàr-ri* EN-⌜*ia*⌝

19) *ki-ma* 30 URU.DIDLI.MEŠ *ip-pu-uš*

20) KÚR.NU *a-na ia-ši*

21) *a-na-ku* 1-*en i-ba-ša-ti*

22) *da-na-at* KÚR.NU UGU-*i*⌜*a*⌝

23) *nu-di-ni* ^{I}*šàr-ri* EN-⌜*ia*⌝

24) *iš-tu qa-ti-šu*

EA 283

TRANSLATION

(1–6) To the king, my lord, my deity and my sun god, the message of Shuwardata, your servant: At the feet of the king, my lord, seven (times) and seven times have I fallen at the feet of the king, my lord.

(7–13) And the king, my lord, wrote to me, "Enter in [to] the king, ⸢your⸣(?) lord, behold, take!" Who will grant to enter (that I enter) into the presence of the king, my lord, to take the gold and the red gold of the king, my lord?

(14–17) Now Yanḫamu is wi‹th› you, so speak with him. If at this time, there are no regular troops, may the king, my lord, deliver me!

(18–24) May the king, my lord, be informed that thirty towns are at war with me. I am alone. The hostility against me is strong. The king, my lord, has cast me from his hand.

25) *yu-uš-ši-ra* ^{I}*šàr-ri* EN-*ia*
26) ⌜ÉRIN⌝.⌜MEŠ⌝ ⌜*pí*⌝-⌜*ṭá*⌝-⌜*ti*⌝ *yi-ik-ki‹-mi-›ni*
27) ^{I}*šàr-ri* EN-*ia a-nu-ma*
28) ^{I}*Ia-an-ḫa-mu ù ra-bi-ṣi*
29) ^{I}*šàr-ri* EN-*ia yi-iq-*⌜*bi*⌝
30) ^{I}*šàr-ri* EN-*ia* ⌜*it*⌝*-ti-šu*
31) *da-na-at-mi* KÚR.NU
32) ⌜UGU⌝ $^{⌜I⌝}$*Šu-wa-ar-da-*⌜*ta*⌝
Up.ed. 33) *ù i-ia-nu*

(25–27) May the king, my lord, send the regular army; may the king, my lord deli‹ver› me.

(27–33) Now as for Yanḫamu, and (namely) the commissioner of the king, my lord, may the king speak with him, "Is the hostility against Shuwardata strong or not?"

EA 284

TRANSCRIPTION

Obv- 01) ⌜a⌝-⌜na⌝ ⌜^{I}⌝⌜šàr⌝-ri ⌜EN⌝-i[a]

02) ⌜um⌝-⌜ma⌝ ⌜^{I}⌝Šu-wa-ar-da-ta Ì[R-ka]

03) ⌜a⌝-na ⌜GÌR⌝.MEŠ ^{I}šàr-ri EN-i⌜a⌝

04) ⌜ma⌝-aq-ti-ti 7 ù 7 mi-⌜la⌝

05) ⌜ma⌝-⌜aq⌝-ti-ti ù ka-ba-tu-ma ⌜ù⌝ ⌜ṣú⌝-⌜ú’⌝-⌜ru⌝-⌜ma⌝

06) ⌜lì⌝-⌜ma⌝-⌜ad⌝ ^{I}šàr-ri EN-ia

07) ù la-qí-ta gáb-bi

08) ⌜KUR⌝.MEŠ ⌜^{I}⌝⌜šàr⌝-⌜ri⌝ ⌜EN⌝-ia i-ba-šu-ti

09) ⌜1⌝-⌜en⌝ ⌜ù⌝ ⌜a⌝-⌜nu⌝-⌜ma⌝ ^{I}Ra-⌜aḫ⌝-ma-nu ⌜ša⌝

10) ⌜da⌝-ga!(GÉME)-al KUR.MEŠ ^{I}šàr-ri ⌜EN⌝-⌜ia⌝

11) ⌜pa⌝-⌜aṭ⌝-ra-ma ⌜ia⌝-nu a-na ^{I}⌜šàr⌝-⌜ri⌝

12) lì-⌜il$_{5}$⌝-⌜qé⌝-⌜ni⌝ ^{I}⌜šàr⌝-⌜ri⌝

13) ⌜ša⌝-ap-⌜ra⌝-⌜ti⌝ ⌜a⌝-⌜na⌝ ^{I}⌜šàr⌝-⌜ri⌝ ⌜EN⌝-⌜ia⌝

14) ⌜i⌝-⌜de⌝-⌜mi⌝ UGU(?)-⌜ia⌝ ⌜mi⌝-nu-⌜mi⌝

15) ⌜ŠEŠ⌝(?)-ia na-⌜ra⌝(?)-⌜am⌝ a-na ^{I}šàr-ri

16) ⌜yu⌝-⌜uš⌝[-ši-]⌜ra⌝ ^{I}⌜šàr⌝-⌜ri⌝ ⌜EN⌝-⌜ia⌝

17) ⌜DUMU⌝(?).⌜KIN⌝(?).MEŠ(?)-⌜ri⌝ ⌜ù⌝ ⌜yi⌝-⌜il$_{5}$⌝-⌜qú⌝-⌜ni⌝ (around edge)

Rev- 18) mi-la ⌜an⌝-⌜na⌝ ⌜yu⌝-⌜uš⌝-ši-r[u]

19) ^{I}⌜šàr⌝-⌜ri⌝ ⌜EN⌝-⌜ia⌝ ⌜qa⌝-⌜ti⌝-⌜ḫu⌝

20) ⌜da⌝-⌜an⌝-⌜na⌝-⌜ta⌝

21) ⌜ù⌝!(ŠI) ⌜a⌝-⌜na⌝ ⌜GÌR⌝ ^{I}⌜šàr⌝-⌜ri⌝ ⌜EN⌝-⌜ia⌝

22) ⌜7⌝ ù 7 ma-aq-ti-⌜ti⌝

23) ⌜li⌝-ma-⌜ad⌝ ⌜SAG⌝(?) ⌜qa⌝-qa-di-⌜ia⌝(traces)[i-na]

24) ⌜^{I}⌝⌜šàr⌝-⌜ri⌝ ⌜EN⌝-⌜ia⌝ qa-⌜ti⌝(?) ⌜ša⌝(?)

25) ⌜le⌝(?)-qú-šu mu-⌜ta⌝-šu

26) ù ⌜É⌝-⌜te⌝-šu ⌜i⌝-ga!(GÉME)-mu-⌜ru⌝

27) [ḫa-za](?)-⌜nu⌝-⌜ti⌝ ù ⌜LÚ⌝.⌜GAL⌝ ›ù‹

28) ⌜ù⌝(?) ⌜ÉRIN⌝.⌜MEŠ⌝ ⌜pí⌝-⌜ṭá⌝-⌜ti⌝ ⌜ša⌝(?) ^{I}šàr-⌜ri⌝ ⌜EN⌝-[ia]

29) [..........^{I}]šàr-⌜ri⌝ ⌜EN⌝-[ia]

EA 284

TRANSLATION

(1–5) To the king, my lord; the message of Shuwardata [your] ser[vant]: At the feet of the king, my lord, I have fallen down, seven (times) and seven times, I have fallen on the stomach and on the back.

(6–12) May the king, my lord, be apprised that all the lands of the king, my lord, are taken. I am alone and now Raḫmānu who oversaw the land of the king, my lord, has departed. The king has none. May the king take me away!

(13–17) I wrote to the king, my lord, "(May he) know concerning me!" Why is my brother favored by the king? May the king, my lord, send emissaries that they may take me.

(18–22) At this time, (if) the king, my lord, will send *his* strong hand then at the feet of the king, my lord seven (times) and seven (times) I fall down.

(23–26) Be aware: [my] head is [in] the hand of the king, my lord. They took him. His men and his house they have "finished."

(27–29) [The city ru]lers and the senior official and the regular troops of the king my lord [.............] the king, my lord,

30) [............................]
31) ⸢URU⸣(?).⸢DIDLI⸣.KI. ⸢ḪI⸣.⸢A⸣ *ù* ⸢*a*⸣-⸢*nu*⸣-⸢*ma*⸣(?)
32) [*da*]-⸢*ga*⸣!(G[É]ME)-⸢*al*⸣(?)-⸢*ši*⸣ ⸢*ù*⸣ ⸢*a*⸣-[*nu*]-⸢*ma*⸣(?)
33) I⸢*Γ*⸣[*a*]-*a*[*n*]-*ḫ*[*a*(?)-*mu* LÚ(?) M]ÁŠKIM
34) [I*šàr*-]⸢*ri*⸣ ⸢*it*-⸢*ti*⸣-⸢*ka*⸣ *yu-w*[*a-ši*-]
\ *ra-š*[*u*]
Up.ed. 35) [I*šàr*-]⸢*ri*⸣ ⸢EN⸣-⸢*ia*

30–35) [......] the cities. And now see to it and now Yanḫ[amu, the comm]issioner, is there with you; may the king, my lord, send him!

EA 285

TRANSCRIPTION

Obv. 01) [*a-na šàr-ri* EN-*ia qí-bi-ma*]
02) [*um-ma* ^{I}]⸢ÌR⸣-*Ḫ*[*e-ba* ÌR-*ka-ma*]
03) [*a-n*]*a* ⸢2⸣ GÌR.MEŠ[*šàr-ri* EN-*ia*]
04) ⸢7⸣-*ta-a-an ù* 7-*t*[*a-a-an am-qut-mi*]
05) *a-mur a-na-ku la-a* LÚ [*ḫa-zi-a-nu*]
06) ⸢LÚ⸣ *ú-i-ú a-na-ku* ⸢*a*⸣-*n*[*a šàr-ri* EN-*ia*]
07) ⸢*am*⸣-*mi-ni*$_7$ DUMU LÚ.KIN-⸢*i*⸣[*a*]
08) ⸢*la*⸣-⸢*a*⸣ ⸢*ú*⸣-*ma-še-ra š*[*àr-ru* EN-*ia*]
09) [*ki-n*]*a-a*[*n-n*]*a ú-ma-š*[*e-ra*]
10) [^{I}*E-en-ḫa-*]*mu e-m*[*u-qa*]
11) [*ù it-t*]*i-ṣi* ⸢*ú*⸣-⸢*pa*⸣-⸢*ṭar*⸣-*šu a-na-ku*
12) [*ki-na-a*]*n-na*
13) [*li-iš-m*]*e šàr-ru*
14) [*a-na* ^{I}ÌR-*ḫ*]*e-ba* ÌR-*šu*
Lo.ed. 15) [*šum-ma i*]*a-a-nu-mi*
16) [ÉRIN.MEŠ] *pi-ṭa-tu*
Rev. 17) [*lu-ma-še-*]⸢*ra*⸣ ⸢*šàr*⸣-*ru* EN-*ia*
18) [LÚ.MÁSKIM] ⸢*ù*⸣ *li-il-qé*
19) [LÚ.MEŠ *ḫa-zi-a-*]*nu-ti it-ti-šu*
20) [*iš-tu gáb-bi* K]UR.ḪI.A *šàr-ru*
21) [*li-de*$_4$ *e-nu-ma pa-aṭ-*]*ru-ma*
22) [*iš-tu muḫ*]-⸢*ḫi*⸣-*ni ù* LÚ.MEŠ
23) [*ma-ṣar-tu*] ⸢*ša*⸣ *i-ba-šu-ú*
24) [*a-na* ^{I}*Ad-da-i*]*a* LÚ.MÁSKIM *šàr-*[*ri*]
25) *ra-šu* É-*šu-nu*
26) ⸢*ù*⸣ *li-is-ki-in šà*[*r-ru*]
27) [*a-*]*na ša-šu-nu*
28) ⸢*ù*⸣ *lu-ma-še-ra* DUMU ⸢LÚ⸣.[KIN-*ia*]
29) [*ḫ*]*a-mu-tam e-nu-*[*ma……*]
30) ⸢*e*⸣-⸢*mu*⸣-⸢*qa*⸣ [*…………*]
31) [*……………………*]

EA 285

TRANSLATION

(1–4) [Speak to the king, my lord, thus] ʿAbdi-Ḫ[eba, your servant: At] the feet [of the king, my lord,] seven times (and) seven t[imes have I fallen].

(5–6) Look, I am not [a city ruler;] I am a soldier of [the king, my lord].

(7–8) Why does the k[ing, my lord], not send back ⌜my⌝ envoy?

(9–14) [Th]u[s, Enḫa]mu sent a fo[rce, but it we]nt out; I, myself, sent it away. [Th]us, [may] the king [listen to ʿAbdi-Ḫ]eba, his servant.

(15–19) [If there] are no regular troops, [may] the king, my lord, [se]nd [a commissioner] and let him take [the city] rulers to him [from all the] lands.

(20–25) [May] the king [be apprised that they have depa]rted [from] us. And the men of [the garrison] that belong [to Adday]a, the commissioner of the ki[ng], have taken possession of their house.

(26–31) So may the ki[ng] pay attention [t]o them; and may he send [my] envoy [qu]ickly, when [...] the force [........................]

EA 286

TRANSCRIPTION

Obv. 01) [*a*]-*na* ^{I}⸢LUGAL⸣EN-*ia* ⸢*qí*⸣-⸢*bí*⸣-⸢*ma*⸣

02) *um-ma* ^{I}ÌR-*ḫé-ba* ÌR-*ka-ma*

03) *a-na* 2 GÌR.MEŠ EN-*ia šàr-ri*

04) 7-*ta-a-an ù* 7-*ta-a-an am-qut-mi*

05) *ma-an-na ep-ša-ti a-na* LUGAL EN-*ia*

06) *i-ka-lu ka-ar-ṣi*!(MURUB$_4$)-*ya* \ *ú-ša-a-ru*

07) ⸢*i*⸣-⸢*na*⸣ *pa-ni* LUGAL EN-*ri* ^{I}ÌR-*ḫé-ba*

08) *pa-ṭa-ar-mi a-na šàr-ri* EN-*šu*

09) *a-mur a-na-ku la-a* ^{LÚ}*a-bi-ia*

10) *ù la-a* ^{MUNUS}*ú-mi-ia* \ *ša-ak-na-ni*

11) *i-na aš-ri an-ni-e*

12) ⸢*zu*⸣-*ru-uḫ šàr-ri* KAL.GA

13) ⸢*ú*⸣-*še-ri-ba-an-ni a-na* É ^{LÚ}*a-bi-ia*

14) ⸢*am*⸣-*mi-nim-mi a-na‹-ku› e*-⸢*pu*⸣-*uš*

15) \ *ar-na a-na* LUGAL EN-*ri*

16) *a-di* LUGAL EN-*ia* TI.LA

17) *a-qa-bi a-na* LÚ.MÁŠKIM LUGAL ⸢EN⸣-[*ia*]

18) *am-mi-nim-mi ta-ra-ia-m*[*u*]

19) LÚ *ḫa-pí-ri ù* LÚ.MEŠ *ḫa-z*[*i-a-nu-ti*]

20) ⸢*ta*⸣-*za-ia-ru ù ki-na-an-na*

21) *ú-ša-à-ru i-na pa-ni* LUGAL EN-*ia*

22) *e-nu-ma à-qa-bi ḫal-qa-at*!(AB)-*mi*

23) KUR.ḪI.A LUGAL EN-*ia ki-na-an-na*

24) *ú-ša-à-ru a-na* LUGAL EN-*ia*

25) *ù li-de$_4$-mi* ^{I}LUGAL EN-*ia*

26) *e-nu-ma ša-ka-an* LUGAL EN-*ia*

27) [L]Ú.MEŠ *ma-ṣar-ta la-qí-mi*

28) [*gáb*]-⸢*ba*⸣-*š*[*a*] ^{I}*E-en-ḫa-mu*

29) [*ù ša-ka-an i-na* É]-⸢*šu*⸣ [*ù*] ⸢30⸣

Lo.ed. 30) [LÚ.MEŠ *ú-ma-še-er*]

31) [*a-na*]⸢KUR⸣ *M*[*i*]-*iṣ-ri*$^{\text{⸢KI⸣}}$ [*ù*]

EA 286

TRANSLATION

(1–4) Speak [t]o the king, my lord; thus ʿAbdi-Ḫeba, your servant: at the feet of my lord, the king, seven times and seven times have I fallen.

(5–8) What have I done to the king, my lord? They are maligning me; I am being maligned before the king, my lord: "ʿAbdi-Ḫeba has deserted the king, his lord."

(9–15) Look, as for me, neither my father nor my mother put me in this place. The strong arm of the king installed me in the house of my father. Why would I (of all people) commit a crime against the king, ‹my› lord?

(16–24) As (long as) the king, my lord, lives, I will say to the commissioner of the king, my lord, "Why do you love the *ʿapîru* and hate the city [rulers]?" Thus I am maligned in the presence of the king, my lord, because I am saying, "Lost are the lands of the king, my lord," thus am I slandered to the king, my lord.

(25–31) So may the king, my lord, be apprised that the king, my lord, placed a garrison (here) (but) Yenḫamu took [al]l of it. [He installed them in his house and] 30 [men he sent to] the land of Egypt
[So]

Rev. 32) [*li-de*$_4$*-mi*] ⸢LUGAL⸣ ⸢EN⸣-⸢*ri*⸣
33) [*ia-a-*]⸢*nu*⸣*-mi* ⸢LÚ⸣.⸢MEŠ⸣ *ma-ṣar-*⸢*ta*⸣
34) [*ù*] *l*[*i-iš-*]*ki-in*$_4$ LUGAL *a-na* KUR-*šu*
35) [*li-d*]*e*$_4$*-m*[*i*] ⸢LUGAL⸣ *a-na* KUR-*šu pa-ṭa-*⸢*ra*⸣-⸢*at*⸣
36) ⸢KUR⸣.⸢ḪI⸣.⸢A⸣ LUGAL EN *gáb‹-ba›-ša* ᴵ*I-li-mil-ku*
37) *i-ḫal-li-iq gáb-bi* KUR *šàr-ri*
38) *ù li-is-kín* LUGAL EN *a-na* KUR-*šu*
39) *a-na-ku a-qa-bi e-ru-ub-mi*
40) *it-ti šàr-ri* EN-*ia ù la-mur-mi*
41) 2 IGI.MEŠ LUGAL EN-*ia ù nu-kúr-tú*ᴹᴱŠ
42) KAL.GA *a-na mu-ḫi-ia* ⸢*ù*⸣ *la a-la-*⸢*á*ʾ⸣*-e*
43) *e-ra-ba iš-tu* LUGAL EN-*ia*
44) *ù li-it-ru-uṣ i-na pa-ni* LUGAL [*ù*]
45) *lu-ma-še-ra* LÚ.MEŠ *ma-ṣar-ta*
46) *ù le-ru*!(LU)*-ub ù la-mu-ur* 2 [IGI.MEŠ]
47) LUGAL EN-*ia* \ *e-nu-ma* LUGAL E[N-*ia*]
48) [T]I.LA ⸢*e*⸣-⸢*nu*⸣*-ma it-ta-ṣú-ú* LÚ.M[ÁŠKIM.MEŠ]
49) ⸢*a*⸣*-qa-bi* ⸢*ḫal*⸣*-qa-at-mi* KUR.ḪI.A LUGAL E[N-*ia ù*]
50) *la ta-ša-mé-ú a-na ia-a-ši*
51) *ḫal-qu-mi* ⸢*gáb*⸣*-bi* LÚ.MEŠ *ḫa-zi-a-nu-ti*
52) *ia-a-nu-mi* LÚ *ḫa-zi-a-nu a-na* LUGAL EN‹-*ia*›
53) *li-din* LUGAL *pa-ni-šu a-na* LÚ.MEŠ *pi-ṭa-ti*
54) *ù lu-ṣi-mi* LÚ.MEŠ ÉRIN *pi-ṭa-ti*
55) LUGAL EN-*ia ia-a-nu-mi* KUR.ḪI.A *a-na* LUGAL
56) LÚ.MEŠ *ḫa-pí-ru ḫa-bat gáb-bi* KUR.ḪI.A LUGAL
57) *šum-ma i-ba-aš-ši* LÚ ÉRIN.MEŠ *pi-ṭa-ti*
58) *i-na* MU *an-ni-ti i-ba-aš-ši* KUR.ḪI.A
59) LUGAL EN‹-*ia*› *ù šum-ma ia-a-nu-mi* LÚ ÉRIN *pi-*⸢*ṭa*⸣*-ti*
60) ⸢*ḫal*⸣*-qa-at* KUR.ḪI.A LUGAL EN-*ia*
61) [*a-n*]*a* ⸢*ṭup*⸣*-šar* ⸢LUGAL⸣ EN-*ia um-ma* ᴵ⸢ÌR⸣-⸢*ḫé*⸣-⸢*ba*⸣
Up.ed. 62) [Ì]R-*ka-ma* \ *še-ri-ib a-wa-ti*⸢ᴹᴱŠ⸣
63) ⸢*ba*⸣*-na-ta a-na* LUGAL EN-*ia ḫal-qa-at*
64) ⸢*gáb*⸣*-bi* KUR.ḪI.A LUGAL EN-*ia*

(32–34) [may] the kin[g], my lord, [be apprised]: [There are] no garrison troops. [So] may the king show concern for his land.

(35–38) [May] the king be apprised concerning his land: The lands of the king, (my) lord, have deserted, all of them. Ilimilku is causing the loss of all the king's land. So may the king, (my) lord, show concern for his land.

39–47) I keep saying, "I will go in to the king, my lord, so that I may behold the two eyes of the king, my lord." But the hostility against me is strong and I am unable to go in to the king, my lord. So may it be pleasing in the sight of the king [so that] he may send a garrison troop that I may enter(!) and that I may behold the two [eyes] of the king, my lord.

(47–52) As the king, [my] lo[rd], lives, whenever the com[missioners] come forth, I say, "Lost are the lands of the king, [my] lo[rd," but] they do not listen to me. All of the city rulers are lost. The king, ‹my› lord, has no city ruler.

(53–60) May the king turn his attention to the regular troops so that the regular troops of the king, my lord, may come forth. The king has no lands! The *ʿapîru* men have plundered all the lands of the king. If there are regular troops in this year, there will still be lands of the king, ‹my› lord. But if there are no regular troops, the lands of the king, my lord, are lost.

(61–64) [T]o the scribe of the king, my lord, thus ʿAbdi-Ḫeba, your [ser]vant: "Present eloquent words to the king, my lord; [al]l of the lands of the king, my lord, are lost!"

EA 287

TRANSCRIPTION

Obv. 01) [*a-na* ^{I}*šàr*]*-ri* EN-⌜*ia*⌝ [*qí-*]*b*[*i-ma*]
02) [*um-ma* ^{I}Ì]R-*ḫe-ba* ÌR-*k*[*a a-na* GÌR.MEŠ]
03) [LUGAL E]N-*ia* 7-*t*[*a-a-an ù* 7-*ta-a-an am-qut*]
04) [*a-mur gá*]*b‹-bi› a-wa-ta*$_5$[^{MEŠ} *ša šàr-ri* EN-*ia*]
05) [*ú-še-*]*ru-bu-ni a-na* [*ia-a-ši* LÚ.MÁŠKIM.MEŠ]
06) [*a-mur*] *ip-ša* \ ⌜*ša*⌝ *e*[*-pa-aš* ^{I}*Mil-ki-*DINGIR GIŠ.PAN.M]EŠ
07) ⌜URUDU⌝.GAG.Ú.TAG.GA \ [*i-din a-na* LÚ.MEŠ]
08) [DUMU.MEŠ *La-a*]*b-*⌜*a*⌝*-ya* [..................]
09) [...]
10) [...]
11) ⌜*a*⌝-⌜*na*⌝ [URU *Qí-il*$_5$*-t*]*i*^{KI} *ú-še-ru-bu li-de*$_4$ [*šàr*]-⌜*ri*⌝
12) *gáb-bi* KUR.⌜ḪI⌝.⌜A⌝ ⌜*ša*⌝*-li-mu a-na ia-a-ši nu-kúr-tú*
13) *ù li-is-kín šàr-ri a-na* KUR-*šu*
14) *a-mur* KUR [UR]U *Gaz-ri*^{KI} KUR URU *Aš-qa-lu-na* ^{KI}
15) *ù* URU *L*[*a-ki-s*]*i* ^{KI} *i-din-nu a-na ša-šu-nu*
16) NÍG.ḪI.A Ì.ḪI.A *ù mi-im-ma* \ *ma-aḫ-sí-ra-mu*
17) *ù li-is-kín šàr-ri a-na* ÉRIN.MEŠ *pi-ṭa-ti ú*
18) *lu-ma-še-ra* ÉRIN.MEŠ *pi-*⌜*ṭa*⌝*-ti a-na* LÚ.MEŠ
19) *ša ep-pu-šu ar-na* ⌜*a*⌝*-na šàr-ri* EN-*ia*
20) *šum-ma i-ba-aš-ši i-na* MU *an-ni-ti*
21) ÉRIN.MEŠ *pi-ṭa-tu*$_4$ *ù i-ba-aš-ši* KUR.ḪI.A
22) [*ù*] LÚ *ḫa-*⌜*zi*⌝*-a-nu a-na šàr-ri* EN-*ia*
23) [*ù š*]*um-ma* ⌜*ia*⌝-⌜*a*⌝-⌜*nu*⌝ ÉRIN.MEŠ *pi-ṭa-tu*$_4$ *ia-*⌜*a*⌝*-nu-*[*m*]*i*
24) [KUR.ḪI.]A *ù* LÚ.M[EŠ *ḫ*]*a-*⌜*zi*⌝-⌜*a*⌝-⌜*nu*⌝-⌜*ti*⌝ *a-na š*[*àr-ri*]
25) [*a*]*-mur* KUR URU *Ú-ru-sa-lim* ⌜*an*⌝-⌜*ni*⌝-⌜*ta*⌝
26) [*l*]*a-a* LÚ AD.DA.A.NI *la-a ú-mi-i*[*a*]
27) [*n*]*a-ad-na-an-ni* \ŠU\ *zu-ru-uḫ* [*šàr-ri* KAL].GA
28) [*n*]*a-ad-na-an-ni a-na ia-a-ši*
29) [*a*]*-mur ip-ša an-ni-ú ip-ši* ^{I}*Mil-ki-*⌜DINGIR⌝
30) *ù ip-ši* DUMU.MEŠ *La-ab-a-ya*
31) *ša na-ad-nu* KUR *šàr-ri ‹a-na›* LÚ.MEŠ *ḫa-pí-ri*

EA 287

TRANSLATION

(1–3) [Speak to the ki]ng, my lord; thus [ʿAb]di-Ḫeba, your servant: [At the feet of the king], my [lo]rd, seven [times and seven times have I fallen.]

(4–5) [Look, al]l the word[s of the king, my lord, the commissioner]s have brought in to [me].

(6–13) [Look,] the deed which [Milkilu] has [committed, he has furnished bows (and)] bronze arrows to the [men of the sons of La]bʾayu [.......and] they are bringing (them) in to [the town of Qilt]i. May the [kin]g be apprised, all the territories are at peace; against me there is hostility. So may the king give attention to his land.

(14–24) Look, the [cit]y state of Gezer, the city state of Ashkelon and the city of L[achi]sh have given to them bread, oil and whatever they need. So may the king give his attention to the regular troops and may he dispatch the regular troops against those who are committing treason against the king, my lord. If in this year there are regular troops then the king, my lord, will have territories and a city ruler, [but] if there are no regular troops, the king will have no [territorie]s or city rulers.

(25–28) [L]ook, neither my father nor my mother gave me this city state of Jerusalem. It was the [mig]hty arm of [the king] that gave it to me.

(29–31) Look, this deed is the deed of Milkili and the deed of the sons of Lab'ayu, that they have given over the land of the king to the *ʿapîru* men.

32) *a-mur* LUGAL EN-*ia ṣa-du-uq a-na ia-a-ši*
33) *aš-šum* LÚ.MEŠ *Ka-ši-yi li-iš-al-mi*
34) *šàr-ri* LÚ.MÁŠKIM.MEŠ *e-nu-ma* É GA.KAL *ma-gal*
35) ⌜*ù*⌝ *ú-ba-á*ʾ*-ú ar-na kab-tu* GAL
36) [*la*]*-qa-ḫu ú-nu-ta*$_5$*-šu-nu ù páṭ-*⌜*ru*⌝*-*⌜*ú*⌝
37) [*ṣ*]*a-*⌜*bat*⌝ *ú-re-e* \ *ga-ag-gi-m*[*i*]
Lo.ed. 38) ⌜*a*⌝*-*⌜*mur*⌝ *ú-ma-še-ru i-na* KUR [URU *Ḫa-za-ti*]
39) [LÚ.]MEŠ *ti-ta-lu it-t*[*i* x LÚ.MEŠ]
40) ⌜ÌR⌝.MEŠ *li-is-*⌜*kín*⌝ [*šàr-ri*]
Rev. 41) ⌜*a*⌝*-*⌜*na*⌝ *ša-šu-nu* \ *ta-za-qa-*⌜*pu*⌝ [*gáb-bi*]
42) KUR.ḪI.A *i-na qa-ti-šu-n*[*u ù*]
43) *li-iš-al-mi šàr-ri a-na ša-šu-*[*nu ù lu*]
44) *ma-ad* NÍG.ḪI.A *ma-ad* Ì.ḪI.A *ma-*⌜*ad*⌝ TÚG.⌜ḪI⌝.A-*t*[*i*]
45) ⌜*a*⌝*-di e-tel-li* ^{I}*Pa-ú-ru* LÚ.MÁ[ŠKIM] *šàr-ri*
46) ⌜*a*⌝*-*⌜*na*⌝ KUR URU *Ú-ru-sa-lim* ^{KI} *pa-*⌜*ṭa*⌝*-*⌜*ar*⌝
47) [^{I}]⌜*A*⌝*-da-ya a-di* LÚ.MEŠ *ma-*⌜*ṣar*⌝*-*⌜*ti*⌝ LÚ *ú-e-*⌜*ú*⌝
48) [*ša*] ⌜*i*⌝*-din šàr-ri li-de*$_4$*-mi šàr-ri*
49) [*iq-*]*bi a-na ia-a-ši* ^{I}*A-da-ya*
50) [*a-mu*]*r pa-aṭ-ra-an-ni la* ⌜*ti*⌝*-zi-ib-ši*
51) [MU] *an-ni-ta mu-še-ra-an-ni* LÚ *ma-ṣar-ta*
52) [*ù* LÚ].MÁŠKIM *šàr-ri mu-še-ra* *an-ni-ka-nu*
53) [KASKAL.Ḫ]I.A *mu-še-er-ti a-na šàr-ri* EN-[*i*]*a*
54) [x L]Ú.MEŠ *a-si-ru* 5 *li-im* [KÙ.BABBAR]
55) [*ù*] 8 LÚ.MEŠ *ù-bi-li-mi* [KA]SKAL.ḪI.A *šà*[*r-ri*]
56) ⌜*la*⌝*-qí-*⌜*ḫu*⌝ ⌜*i*⌝*-*⌜*na*⌝ ⌜*ú*⌝*-*⌜*ga*⌝*-ri* \ *ša-de*$_4$*-e*
57) URU *Ia-lu-na* ^{KI} *li-de*$_4$*-mi šàr-ri* EN-*ia*
58) *la-a a-la-á*ʾ*-e* \ *mu-še-ra* KASKAL
59) *a-na šàr-ri* EN-*ia aš-šum la-ma-de*$_4$*-ka*
60) *a-mur šàr-ri ša-ka-an* MU-*šu*
61) *i-na* KUR *Ú-ru-sa-lim* ^{KI} *a-na da-ri-iš*
62) *ù la-a i-le-é*ʾ*-e e-za-bi-ša*
63) KUR.ḪI.A URU *Ú-ru-sa-lim* ^{KI}

(32–37) Look, O king, my lord, I am in the right (I have righteousness) concerning the Cushite men! May the king inquire of his commissioners whether the palace is very strongly fortified. But they (the Cushites) sought to commit a very serious crime. They took their implements and mutinied to [se]ize the roof!

(38–52) Look, they sent from the [city] state of [Gaza(?)] support(!) troops with [*x* number of]slaves. May [the king] give his attention to them. [All] the territories are rising (in rebellion)] (or: "are being aroused to rebellion") at their doing. [So] may the king inquire concerning the[m and may] there be much bread, much oil, much clothing, until Pawuru, the commiss[ioner] of the king, comes up to the city state of Jerusalem. Addaya departed with the garrison troops, the soldier [that] the king had assigned. May the king be apprised: Addaya [sa]id to me: "[Lo]ok, he (the king) has dismissed me." Don't abandon it! This [year] send me a garrison [and] a royal commissioner send here.

(53–59) I have dispatched [a caravan (or: caravans)] to the king, [m]y lord, viz. *x* number of prisoners and five thousand [(shekels) of silver and] eight caravaniers of the king. They were taken in the open territory of the city of (A)yalon. May the king be apprised; I am unable to send a caravan to the king, my lord. For your information!

(60–63) Look, the king has established his name in the land of Jerusalem forever and he simply cannot abandon it, viz. the city state of Jerusalem.

64) *a-na ṭup-šar šàr-ri* EN-*ia*
65) *qí-bi-ma um-ma* ^{I}ÌR-*ḫe-ba* ÌR-*ka-ma*
66) *a-na* 2 GÌR.MEŠ-‹*ka*› *am-qut-mi* ÌR-*ka a-nu-ki*
67) *še-ri-ib a-wa-ta*$_5$^{MEŠ} *ba-na-ta*
68) *a-na šàr-ri* EN-*ia*
69) ⸢LÚ⸣ ⸢*ú*⸣-⸢*e*⸣-⸢*é*⸣ ⸢*šàr*⸣-⸢*ri*⸣ *a* ⸢*nu*⸣-⸢*ki*⸣
70) *ma-at-ti a-na ka-ta*$_5$!(WA)

---

71) *ù ti-ip-pa-ša ip-ša la-am-na*
72) *a-na muḫ-ḫi* LÚ.MEŠ ⸢KUR⸣ *Ka-ší*
73) ⸢*ú*⸣-*ba-na la-a* GAZ \ *de*$_4$-⸢*ka*⸣-⸢*ti*⸣
74) [*i-n*]*a* ŠU LÚ.MEŠ KUR *Ka-ši*
75) [*i-na*] *lìb-bi* É-*ia* \ ⸢*li*⸣[-*iš-al*]
76) *šàr-ru a-na ša*-⸢*šu*⸣[-*nu*]
Up.ed. 77) [7-*t*]*a-a-an ù* 7-*ta-a-an* [*am-qut*]
78) [*li-is-kín šàr*]-⸢*ru*⸣ EN-*ia a-na i*[*a-a-ši*]

(64–70) Speak to the scribe of the king, my lord; thus ʿAbdi-Ḫeba, your servant: At ‹your› feet have I fallen. Your servant am I. Present eloquent words to the king, my lord. I am a soldier of the king. I am ready to die for you!

(71–76) And you should do something really bad to the men of the land of Cush. I came within an inch of being slain by the hand of the men of the land of Cush [in]side my own palace! May the king make in[quiry] concerning the[m].

(77–78) [Seven t]imes and seven times [have I fallen]. May the king, my lord, [give his attention] to m[e].

EA 288

TRANSCRIPTION

Obv. 01) *[a-n]a* ^{I}*šàr-ri* EN-*ia* ⸢^{d}⸣⸢UTU⸣-⸢*ia*⸣ ⸢*qí*⸣-[*bi-ma*]
02) [*u*]*m-ma* ^{I}ÌR-*ḫe-ba* ÌR-⸢*ka*⸣-*ma*
03) ⸢*a*⸣-*na* 2 GÌR.MEŠ LUGAL EN-*ia* 7-*ta-a-an*
04) *ù* 7-*ta-a-an am-qut-mi*
05) *a-mur šàr-ri* EN-*ia ša-ka-an*
06) *šùm-šu a-na mu-ṣi* ^{d}UTU-*ši*
07) *ù er-bi* ^{d}UTU-*ši* ‹*a-mur*› *ḫa-an-pa*
08) *ša iḫ-nu-pu a-na mu*-⸢*ḫi*⸣-*ia*
09) *a-mur a-na-ku la-a* LÚ.*ḫa-zi-a-nu*
10) LÚ *ú-e-ú a-na šàr-ri* EN-*ia*
11) *a-mur a-na-ku* LÚ *ru-ʾi šàr-ri*
12) *ù ú-bi-il* GUN *šàr-ri a-na-ku*
13) *ia-a-nu-mi* LÚ.AD.DA.A.NI *ia-a-nu-mi*
14) ⸢^{MUNUS}⸣*um-mi-ia* ⸢*zu*⸣-*ru-uḫ šàr-ri* KAL.GA
15) ⸢*ša*⸣-⸢*ak*⸣-⸢*na*⸣-[*an-ni*] ⸢*i*⸣-⸢*na*⸣ É LÚ.⸢AD⸣.⸢DA⸣.[A-NI]
16) [.................................]
17) [*k*]*a-ša-ad a-na mu-ḫi-ia* [erasure]⸢^{I}⸣⸢*A*⸣-*d*[*a-ya*]
18) [*n*]*a-ad-na-ti* 10 LÚ ÌR.ME[Š] ⸢*a*⸣-⸢*na*⸣ ⸢*qa*⸣[-*t*]*i*-[*šu*]
19) [^{I}]*Šu-ú-ta* LÚ.MÁŠKIM *šàr-ri ka*-[*ša-ad*]
20) [*a*]-*na mu-ḫi-ia* 21 MUNUS.TUR.MUNUS.MEŠ
21) [8]0 LÚ.MEŠ *a-si-ri na-ad-na*-⸢*ti*⸣
22) [*a*-]*na qa-ti* ^{I}*Šu-ú*-⸢*ta*⸣ NÍG.BA *šàr-ri* EN-*ia*
23) *li-im-li-ik-mi* ⸢*šàr*⸣-*ri a-na* KUR-*šu*
24) *ḫal-qa*-⸢*at*⸣ KUR *šàr-ri gáb-ba-ša*
25) *ṣa-ba-ta-ni nu-kúr-tú a-na ia-a-ši*
26) *a-di* KUR.ḪI.A *Še-e-ri* ^{KI} *a-di* URU *Gin*$_{8}$-*ti-ki-ir*-⸢*mi*⸣-⸢*il*⸣
27) *šal-mu a-na gáb-bi* ⸢LÚ⸣.MEŠ *ḫa-zi-a-nu-ti*
28) *ù nu-kúr-tú a-na ia-a-ši*
29) *ep-ša-ti e-nu-ma* LÚ *ḫa-pí-ri*

Lo.ed. 30) ⸢*ù*⸣ *la-a a-mar* 2 IGI.MEŠ LUGAL
31) EN-*ia ki-i nu-kúr-tú*

Rev. 32) ⸢*a*⸣-*na muḫ-ḫi-ia ša-ak-na-ti*
33) *e-nu-ma* GIŠ.MÁ *i-na lìb-bi* A.AB.BA

EA 288

TRANSLATION

(1–4) Sp[eak t]o the king, my lord, my sun god; thus ʿAbdi-Ḫeba, your servant: At the two feet of the king, my lord, seven times and seven times have I fallen.

(4–7) Look, the king, my lord, has placed his name at the coming forth of the sun and at the going in of the sun.

(7–15) ‹Look›, it is infamy what they have done to me! Look, as for me, I am not a city ruler, (but rather) a soldier of the king, my lord. Look, as for me, a "companion" of the king and a bringer of the king's tribute am I. Neither my father nor my mother, (but rather) the strong arm of the king has placed me in my father's house.

(16–22) Add[aya] came to me; I handed over [to his]cha[rge] ten slaves. Shuta, the commissioner of the king, ca[me] to me; I handed over to the charge of Shuta twenty one girls and [ei]ghty prisoners, a gift for the king, my lord.

(23–31) May the king take counsel concerning his land. Lost is the land of the king, all of it. I am trapped! There is open hostility against me. From the mountains of Seir(?) to the city Gath-Carmel, all the city rulers are at peace, but there is war against me. I have become like an *ʿapîru* man and I cannot behold the two eyes of the king, my lord, because of the hostility

(32–33) against me. I am situated like a ship in the midst of the sea.

34) ŠU *zu-ru-uḫ* LUGAL KAL.GA
35) *ti-le-eq-*⸢*qé*⸣ KUR *Na-*⸢*aḫ*⸣*-ri-ma*^{KI}
36) ⸢*ù*⸣ KUR ⸢*Ka*⸣*-áš*!(PA)*-ší*^{KI} ⸢*ù*⸣ ⸢*i*⸣*-na-an-na*
37) ⸢URU⸣.DIDLI.ḪI.A *šàr-*⸢*ri*⸣
38) *ti-le-qé-ú* ⸢LÚ⸣.⸢MEŠ⸣ ⸢*ḫa*⸣*-pí-ru*
39) *ia-a-nu-mi* 1 ⸢LÚ⸣ ⸢*ḫa*⸣-⸢*zi*⸣-⸢*a*⸣*-nu*
40) *a-na šàr-ri* EN-*ia* ⸢*ḫal*⸣*-qu* ⸢*gáb*⸣*-bu*
41) *a-mur* ^{I}*Tu-ur-ba-ṣú* ⸢GAZ⸣ ⸢*de*$_4$⸣-⸢*ka*⸣
42) *i-na* KÁ.GAL ⸢URU⸣ *Sí-lu-ú*⸢^{KI}⸣ *qa-*⸢*al*⸣ *šàr-ru*
43) *a-mur* ^{I}*Zi-im-*⸢*re*⸣-⸢*da*⸣ ‹LÚ› URU ⸢*La*⸣-⸢*ki*⸣-⸢*si*⸣^{KI}
44) *ig-gi-ú-šu* ÌR.MEŠ *ep-šu* ⸢*a*⸣-⸢*na*⸣ ⸢LÚ⸣.⸢MEŠ⸣ ⸢*ḫa*⸣*-pí-*⸢*ri*⸣
45) ⸢^{I}⸣*Ia-ap-ti-iḫ-*^{d}⸢IŠKUR⸣ ⸢GAZ⸣ ⸢*de*$_4$⸣-⸢*ka*⸣
46) [*i-na*] ⸢KÁ⸣.GAL URU *Sí-lu-ú qa-al* [*šàr-ru*]
47) [*am-m*]*i-*⸢*ni*$_7$⸣ ⸢*la*⸣-⸢*a*⸣ *iš-al-*⸢*šu*⸣-[*nu šàr-ru*]
48) [*ù li-*]*is-kín šàr-*[*ru*]⸢*a*⸣[*-na* KUR-*šu*]
49) [*ù li-*]*din šàr-ru pa-ni-šu* ⸢*ù*⸣ [*lu-ṣí-m*]*i*
50) [LÚ.MEŠ] ÉRIN.MEŠ *pi-ṭa-ti a-na* KUR-*š*[*u*]
51) [*ù*] ⸢*šum*⸣*-ma ia-a-nu-mi* ÉRIN.MEŠ *pi-*⸢*ṭa*⸣*-tu*$_4$
52) ⸢*i*⸣-⸢*na*⸣ MU *an-ni-ti ḫal-qa-at a-ba-da-at*
53) \ *gáb-bi* KUR.ḪI.A *šàr-ri* EN-*ia*
54) *la-a i-qa-bi-ú a-na pa-ni* LUGAL EN-*ia*
55) *e-nu-ma ḫal-qa-at* KUR LUGAL EN-*ia*
56) *ù ḫal-qu gáb-bi* LÚ.MEŠ *ḫa-zi-*⸢*a*⸣*-nu-ti*
57) *šum-ma ia-a-nu-mi* ÉRIN.MEŠ *pi-ṭa-tu*$_4$
58) ⸢*i*⸣*-na* MU *an-ni-ti lu-ma-še-er*
59) *šàr-ru* LÚ.MÁŠKIM *ù li-il-qé-a-ni*
60) *a-na ia-a-ši a-di* ŠEŠ.MEŠ-‹*ia*› *ù* BA.ÚŠ
61) ⸢*ni*⸣-⸢*mu*⸣*-tu*$_4$ *it-ti šàr-ru* EN-*nu*
62) [*a-na*] ⸢LÚ⸣ *ṭup-šar šàr-ri* EN-*ia*
Up.ed. 63) [*um-ma*] ⸢^{I}⸣⸢ÌR⸣*-ḫe-ba* ÌR-*ma a-na* 2 GÌR.MEŠ
64) [*am-qut-*]*mi še-ri-ib a-wa-ta*$_5$^{M}[^{EŠ}]
65) *ba-na-ti a-na šàr-r*[*i*]
Lft.ed. 66) [*e-nu-ma* LÚ] ÌR[*-ka ù* LÚ.]⸢DUMU⸣*-ka a-na-ku*

(34–47) The strong arm of the king takes the land of Nahrîma and the land of Cush. But now the *ʿapîru* men are taking the cities of the king. There is not one city ruler left to the king, my lord. All are lost! Look, as for Turbaṣu, he was killed at the gate of the city of Sillô; the king kept silent. Look, as for Zimredda ‹ruler of› the city of Lachish, they smote him, viz. servants who joined the *ʿapîru* men! Iaptiḥ-Hadda was killed [at] the gate of the city of Sillô; [the king] kept silent. [Why] has [the king] not inquired about th[em]?

(48–61) [So may] the ki[ng] show concern f[or his land and may] the king [tu]rn his attention and [may] the regular troops [come fort]h to h[is] land. [But] if there are no regular troops during this current year, lost, lost are all the territories of the king, my lord. Have they not been reporting to the king, my lord, that the land of the king, my lord, is lost, and all the city rulers are lost? If there are no regular troops in this current year, may the king dispatch a commissioner and let him take me to *you*(!; written "me" by mistake), with ‹my› colleagues; then we may die with the king, our lord.

(62–66) [To] the scribe of the king, my lord, [thus]ʿAbdi-Ḫeba, ‹your› servant: At ‹your› two feet hav[e I fallen]. Present nice words to the king [because] I am [your] servant [and] your son.

EA 289

TRANSCRIPTION

Obv. 01) [*a*]-⸢*na*⸣ *šàr-ri* EN-*ia* [*qí-bi-ma*]
02) ⸢*um*⸣-⸢*ma*⸣ ^{I}ÌR-*ḫe-ba* ^{I}ÌR-*k*[*a-ma*]
03) *a-na* 2 GÌR.MEŠ EN-*ia š*[*àr-ri*]
04) 7-*ta-a-an ù* 7-*ta-a-an a*[*m-qut-mi*]
05) ⸢*a*⸣-⸢*mur*⸣ ^{I}*Mil-ki-lì la-a i-pa-aṭ-*[*ṭa-ar*]
06) *iš-tu* DUMU.MEŠ *La-ab-a-ya ù*
07) DUMU.MEŠ *Ar-ṣa-ya a-na e-re-š*[*i*]
08) KUR *šàr-ri a-na ša-šu-nu*
09) LÚ *ḫa-zi-a-nu ša e-pa-aš ip-*⸢*ša*⸣ *an-ni-à*
10) *am-mi-ni*$_7$ *šàr-ri la-a ša-al-šu*
11) *a-mur* ^{I}*Mil-ki-lì ù* ^{I}*Ta-gi*
12) *ip-šu* ⸢*ša*⸣ *e-pu-šu an-ni-yu*
13) ⸢*e*⸣-*nu-ma la-qí-ši* URU *Ru-bu-tá*(!)^{KI}
14) ⸢*ù*⸣ ⸢*i*⸣-⸢*na*⸣-⸢*an*⸣-⸢*na*⸣ ⸢URU⸣ ⸢*Ú*⸣-⸢*ru*⸣-⸢*sa*⸣-⸢*lim*⸣^{KI}
15) *šum-ma i-ba-aš-ši* KUR *an-ni-tu*
16) *a-na šàr-ri am-mi-ni*$_7$ *e-nu-ma*
17) URU *Ḫa-za-ti*^{KI} *a-na šàr-ri ša-ak-na-at*
18) *a-mur* KUR URU *Gin*$_8$*-ti-ki-ir-mi-il*^{KI}
19) *a-na* ^{I}*Ta-gi ù* LÚ.MEŠ URU *Gin*$_8$*-ti*^{KI}
20) *ma-ṣar-tú i-na* É-*sa-a-ni i-ba-aš-ši*
21) *ù lu ni-pu-uš-mi e-nu-ma*
22) ^{I}*La-ab-a-ya*
Lo.ed. 23) *ù* KUR *Ša-ak-mi i-*⸢*din*⸣*-nu*
24) *a-na* LÚ.MEŠ *ḫa-pí-ri*^{KI}
Rev. 25) ^{I}*Mil-ki-lì ša-pár a-na Ta-g*[*i*]
26) *ù* DUMU.MEŠ *lu-ú a-mi-la-tu-nu*
27) *id-nu-mi gáb-bi e-ri-iš-ti-šu-*⸢*nu*⸣
28) *a-na* LÚ.MEŠ *Qí-il*$_5$*-ti*^{KI}
29) *ù lu-ú ni-ip-ṭú-ur* URU *Ú-ru-sa-lim*^{KI}

EA 289

TRANSLATION

(1–4) [Speak t]o the king, my lord, thus ʿAbdi-Ḫeba, yo[ur] servant: At the feet of my lord, the k[ing], seven times and seven times [have] I [fallen].

(5–10) Look, Milkilu does not de[part] from the sons of Lab'ayu and the sons of Arṣayu, to seek the land of the king for themselves. As for the city ruler that does this deed, why has the king not questioned him?

(11–13) Look, as for Milkilu and Tagi, this is the deed which they have done when they took it, namely the town of Rubbôta.

(14–17) [And] now as for the city of Jerusalem, if this land belongs to the king, why, as the city of Gaza belongs to the king, is it just sitting (isolated)?

(18–24) Look, the territory of the city of Gath-carmel belongs to Tagi and the men of Gath are the garrison in Beth-shean, "So let us do like Lab'ayu!" And they have given the territory of Shechem to the *ʿapîru* men!

(25–29) Milkilu wrote to Tagi and to the sons (of Arṣaya/Lab'ayu), "Be ye men! Grant their every request to the men of Qilti (Keilah) and let us desert Jerusalem."

30) LÚ.MEŠ *ma-ṣar-ta*$_5$^{MEŠ} *ša tu-ma-še-er*
31) *i-na* ŠU ^{I}*Ḫa-ya* DUMU *Mi-ia-re-e*
32) ⸢*la*⸣*-qí-mi* ^{I}*Ad-da-ya ša-ka-an*
33) *i-na* É*-šu i-na* URU *Ḫa-za-ti* ^{KI}
34) ⸢*ù*⸣ ⸢20⸣ ⸢LÚ⸣.⸢MEŠ⸣ *a-na* KUR *Mi-iṣ-ri*^{KI}
35) *ú-ma-*⸢*še*⸣*-e*[*r l*]*u-*⸢*ú*⸣ ⸢*i*⸣*-*⸢*de*$_4$⸣*-mi* ⸢*šàr*⸣*-*⸢*ri*⸣
36) *ia-a-nu-mi* LÚ.MEŠ *ma-ṣar-tu*$_4$ *šàr-ri*
\ *it-ti-ia*
37) *ki-na-an-na li-ib-lu-uṭ šàr-ri*
38) *lu-ú ir-pí-šu* ^{I}*Pu-ú-ru*
39) *pa-ṭa-ar i-na ma-aḫ-ri-ia*
40) *i-na* URU *Ḫa-za-ti i-ba-aš-ši*
41) *ù li-iz-kur šàr-ri i-na pa-ni-šu*
42) *ù lu-ma-še-er* LUGAL 50 LÚ.MEŠ
43) *ma-ṣar-ta a-na na-ṣa-ar* KUR-[*šu*]
44) *gáb-bi* KUR *šàr-ri pa-ṭa-r*[*a-at*]
45) *mu-še-ra* ^{I}*Yi-ʾí-in*$_4$*-ḫa-m*[*u*]
46) *ù li-de*$_4$ KUR *šàr-ri*
47) ⸢*a*⸣*-*⸢*na*⸣ LÚ *ṭup-šar šàr-r*[*i* EN*-ia*]
Up.ed. 48) [*um*]*-ma* ^{I}ÌR-*Ḫe-ba* ÌR[*-ka*]
49) *a-wa-ta*$_5$^{MEŠ} *ba-n*[*a-ta*]
Lft.ed. 50) *i-din-mi a-na* ⸢*šàr*⸣*-ri ma-at-ti ma-gal*
51) ⸢*a*⸣*-na ka-ta*$_5$ ÌR*-ka a-na-ku*

(30–40) The garrison troops whom you sent in the charge of Ḫaya son of Miyare, Addaya took (and) placed in his house in the city of Gaza and twenty men he sent to Egypt. May the king be apprised: There are no royal garrison troops with me. Likewise, as the king lives! Verily his nobleman (*irpi*), Pawuru, has left me; he is in the city of Gaza.

(41–46) So may the king take thought and may the king send fifty garrison troops to protect [his] land. All the land of the king has deser[ted]. Send Yinḥamu that he may be apprised about the king's land.

(47–51) To the scribe of the king, [my lord,] thus ʿAbdi-Ḫeba, [your] ser[vant]. Present to the king many elo[quent] words. I would sincerely die for you! I am your servant!

EA 290

TRANSCRIPTION

Obv. 01) *[a-n]a* ^{I}*šàr-ri* EN-⸢*ia*⸣

02) *[qí]*-⸢*bí*⸣-*ma um-ma*

03) [^{I}ÌR-*ḫe-*]⸢*ba*⸣ ÌR-*ka-ma a-na* 2 GÌR.MEŠ

04) [^{I}*šàr-*]⸢*ri*⸣ ⸢EN⸣-⸢*ia*⸣ 7-*ta-a-an ù* 7-*ta-a-an am-qut*

05) *[a-m]ur* ⸢*ip*⸣-⸢*ša*⸣\ ⸢*ša*⸣ *e-pu-šu-ni*

06) ^{I}*Mil-*⸢*ki*⸣-⸢*lu*⸣ ⸢*ù*⸣ ^{I}*Šu-ar-da-tu*$_4$

07) *a-na* KUR ⸢*šàr*⸣-⸢*ri*⸣ EN-*ia*

08) *pu*!(MU)-*ḫi-ru* ⸢ÉRIN⸣.⸢MEŠ⸣ URU *Ga-az-ri* ^{KI}

09) ÉRIN.MEŠ URU *Gi-im-ti* ^{KI}

10) *ù* ÉRIN.MEŠ URU *Qí-il*$_5$*-ti* ^{KI}

11) *ṣa-ab-tu*$_4$ KUR URU *Ru-bu-te* ^{KI}

12) *pa-ṭa-ra-at* KUR *šàr-ri*

13) *a-na* LÚ.MEŠ *ḫa-pí-ri*

Lo.ed. 14) *ù i-na-an-na ap-pu-na-ma*

Rev. 15) URU KUR *Ú-ru-sa-lim*^{KI}

16) URU É-^{d}NIN.IB \ *šu-mu-ša*

17) URU *šàr-ri pa-ṭa-ra-at*

18) ⸢*a*⸣-*šar* LÚ.MEŠ URU *Qí-il*$_5$*-ti* ^{KI}

19) ⸢*li*⸣-*iš-me šàr-ri a-na* ^{I}ÌR-*ḫe-ba* ÌR-*ka*

20) *ù lu-ma-šer*$_9$ ÉRIN.MEŠ *pi-ṭa-ti*

21) *ù lu-ti-*⸢*ra*⸣ KUR *šàr-ri* ⸢*a*⸣-⸢*na*⸣ *šàr-ri*

22) *ù šum-ma ia-a-nu* ÉRIN.MEŠ *pi-ṭa-tu*$_4$

23) *pa-ṭa-ra-at* KUR *šàr-*⸢*ri*⸣ *a-*⸢*na*⸣ LÚ.MEŠ

24) \ *ḫa-pí-ri*

25) *ip-šu* \(!) *an-ni-ú*

26) ⸢*a*⸣-*[na]* ⸢KA⸣-⸢*i*⸣ ^{I}*Mil-ki-[li]*

27) *[ù a]*-⸢*na*⸣ ⸢KA⸣-⸢*i*⸣ ⸢^{I}⸣⸢*Šu*⸣-*[ar-d]a-ti*

Up.ed. 28) *[ù* L]Ú! ⸢URU⸣ ⸢*Gin*$_8$⸣-*t[i*^{KI}]

Lft.ed. 29) *ù li-is-ki-i[n]*

30) ⸢*šàr*⸣-*ri a-na* KUR-⸢*šu*⸣

EA 290

TRANSLATION

(1–4) [Sp]eak [to] the king, my lord, thus [ʿAbdi-Ḫe]ba, your servant: at the feet of [the ki]ng, my lord, seven times and seven times have I fallen.

(5–13) [Lo]ok, as for the deed which Milkilu and Shuwardata have done to the land of the king, my lord, they assembled(!) the troops of the city of Gezer, the troops of the city of Gath and the troops of the city of Qilti (Keilah) (and) they seized the town of Rubbôte. The land of the king has departed to the *ʿapîru* men.

(14–18) And now, moreover, a town of the land of Jerusalem, its name being Bit-NIN.IB, a city of the king, has deserted [in] the wake of the men of the city of Qilti (Keilah).

(19–21) May the king listen to ʿAbdi-Ḫeba, your servant, and may he send the regular army and may he return the land of the king to the king.

(22–28) But if there is no regular army, the land of the king is deserting to the *ʿapîru* men. This deed is a[t] the command of Milkilu [and a]t the command of [Shuward]ata, [and (?) the rul]er(!) of the ⸢city⸣ of Ga[th].

(29–30) So may the king show concern for his land.

EA 291

TRANSCRIPTION

Obv. 01) [.....................]
02) [.....................]
03) [.....................]
04) [.....................]
05) [.....................]
06) [.....................]
07) ⸢*ù*⸣[...................]
08) ⸢ÉRIN⸣(?).⸢MEŠ⸣ (?)[...]
09) [*a*]-⸢*na*⸣[..............]
10) ⸢*ù*⸣ [..................]
11) ⸢*ù*⸣ ⸢*a*⸣-⸢*na*⸣ ⸢LÚ⸣ [ÉRIN. MEŠ]
Lo.ed. 12) [*l*]*i*-[*i*]*m*-⸢*lik*⸣ ⸢LUGAL⸣
Rev. 13) ⸢*a*⸣-⸢*na*⸣ ⸢KUR⸣.[ḪI].⸢A⸣-⸢*šu*⸣
14) ⸢*ù*⸣⸢ÌR⸣.⸢ḪI⸣.⸢A⸣-[*šu*]

----

15) *a*-⸢*na*⸣⸢ÉRIN⸣.[MEŠ]-⸢*ka*⸣
16) ⸢*ti*⸣-⸢*ba*⸣-⸢*á'*⸣(?)-[*ú-na*...]
17) ⸢*ga*⸣-*a*[*m-ru gáb-bi*]
18) ⸢LÚ⸣.⸢MEŠ⸣ ⸢*šàr*⸣-⸢*ri*⸣
19) *šum*-⸢*ma*⸣ [...........]
20) ⸢*a*⸣-⸢*na*⸣ ⸢*bé*⸣[-*li-ia*]
21) ⸢*qa*⸣-⸢*bi*⸣[..............]
22) [.....................]
23) [................*a-na*]
Lft.ed. 24) [*l*]*a-ma*-⸢*di*⸣ [LUGAL]
25) [*be-li-ia*..........]

EA 291

TRANSLATION

Obv. 01) [.....................]
02) [.....................]
03) [.....................]
04) [.....................]
05) [.....................]
06) [.....................]
07) and⌝ [.................]
08) troops(?)[.............]
09) to [..................]
10) ⌜and⌝ [................]
11) ⌜and⌝ ⌜for⌝ [troops]
Lo.ed. 12) [ma]y the ⌜king⌝ attend
Rev. 13) to ⌜his⌝ land⌜s⌝
14) and [his] servants

––––

15) For your troops
16) they are see[king (?)...]
17) Fini[shed are all [(?) ...]
18) the king's men.
19) If [...................]
20) to [my] lo[rd..........]
21) it has been said [......]
22) [.....................]
23) [..................for]
Left.ed. 24) [the i]nformation [of the king,]
25) [my lord.............]

EA 292

TRANSCRIPTION

Obv. 01) *a-na* LUGAL EN-*ia* ⌜DINGIR⌝.⌜MEŠ⌝[-*ia*]
02) ^{d}UTU-*ia qí-bí*-⌜*ma*⌝
03) *um-ma* ^{Id}IŠKUR.DI.KUD ⌜ÌR⌝-⌜*ka*⌝
04) *ep-ri ša* 2 GÌR. M[EŠ]-⌜*ka*⌝
05) *a-na* GÌR.MEŠ LUGAL ⌜EN⌝-⌜*ia*⌝
06) DINGIR.MEŠ-*ia* ^{d}UTU-*ia* 7-*šu*
07) 7-*ta-a-an am-qú-ut*
08) *da-ag-la-ti*$_{7}$ *ki-ia*-⌜*am*⌝
09) *ù da-ag-la-ti*$_{7}$ *ki-ia-am*
10) *ù la-a na-mi-ir ù*
11) *da-ag-la-ti*$_{7}$ *a-na mu*-⌜*ḫi*⌝
12) LUGAL EN-*ia ù na-mi*-⌜*ir*⌝
13) *ù ti*$_{7}$*-na-mu-šu* SIG$_{4}$-⌜*tu*⌝
14) *iš-tu šu-pal tap-pa*-⌜*te*⌝-*ši*
15) *ù a-na-ku la-a i-na-mu-šu*
16) *iš-tu šu-pal* 2 GÌR.⌜MEŠ⌝
17) LUGAL EN-*ia* ⌜*iš*⌝-*te-mé*
18) *a-wa-te*$^{⌜MEŠ⌝}$ *ša iš-pu-ur*
19) LUGAL EN-*ia a-na* ÌR-*šu*
20) *ú-ṣur-mi* ⌜LÚ⌝.⌜MÁŠKIM⌝-⌜*ka*⌝
21) *ù ú-ṣur* URU.⌜DIDLI⌝.⌜ḪI⌝.⌜A⌝ *ša*
22) LUGAL EN-*ka a-nu-ma*
23) ⌜*iṣ*⌝-*ṣú-ru ù a*-⌜*nu*⌝-⌜*ma*⌝
Lo.ed. 24) [*i*]*š-te*-⌜*mu*⌝ UD. KAM^{v}-⌜*ma*⌝
Rev. 25) *ù mu*-⌜*ša*⌝ *a-wa-te*^{MEŠ} ⌜*ša*⌝
26) LUGAL EN-*ia ù yi-il-m*[*a-ad*]
27) LUGAL EN-*ia a-na* ÌR-*šu*
28) *nu-kúr-tu*$_{4}$ *iš-tu* ḪUR.SAG
29) *a-na ia-ši ù* ⌜*ra*⌝-*aṣ-pa-ti*$_{7}$ \ ⌜*ba*⌝-⌜*ni*⌝-⌜*ti*⌝ ?
30) É 1-*en* URU *Ma-an-ḫa-ti*$_{7}$ *šum*-⌜*ši*⌝
31) *a-na šu-ši-ri a-na pa-ni*
32) ÉRIN.MEŠ *pí-ṭá-at* LUGAL EN-*ia*
33) *ù al*-⌜*lu*⌝-⌜*ú*⌝ *il*$_{5}$*-qe-ši* ^{I}*Ma-a*-⌜*ia*⌝

EA 292

TRANSLATION

(1–7) Speak to the king, my lord, [my] deity, my sun god, the message of Baʿlu-dāni your servant, the dirt under your feet: At the feet of the king, my lord, my deity, my sun god, seven times and seven times I have fallen.

(8–17) I looked this way and I looked that way, but there was no light. Then I looked towards the king, my lord, and there was light. And a brick may fall out from under its partner but I will not depart from under the feet of the king, my lord.

(17–22) I have heard the words that the king, my lord, sent to his servant, "Protect your commissioner and protect the towns of the king, your lord."

(22–26) Now [I] am guarding and now I am obeying day and night the words of the king, my lord.

(26–33) And may the king, my lord be appr[ised] concerning his servant. There is hostility from the hill country against me so I refortified (rebuilt) a building, Manḫatu is its name, to prepare for the regular troops of the king, my lord. But behold, Maya has removed it

34) *iš-tu qa-te-ia ù ša-kán*
35) LÚ.MÁŠKIM-*šu i-na lìb-bi-ši*
36) *ù* NU-*id a-na* ^{I}*Re-a-na-ap*
37) LÚ.MÁŠKIM-*ia ù yu-šu-te-er*
38) URU.KI *i-na qa-te-ia ù*
39) *ú-še*$_{20}$*-šu-ru a-na pa-ni*
40) ÉRIN.MEŠ *pí-ṭá-at* LUGAL EN-*ia*
41) *ša-ni-tam a-mur ip-ši*
42) ^{I}*Pé-e-ia* DUMU ^{MUNUS}*Gu-la-t*[*i*$_{7}$]
43) *a-na* URU *Gaz-ri* MUNUS.GÉME-*ti*$_{7}$
44) *ša* LUGAL EN-*ia ma-ni*
45) UD. KAM^{v}.MEŠ-*ti yi-šal-la-l*[*u*]-⸢*ši*⸣
46) *ù in*$_{4}$*-né-ep-ša-a*[*t ki-ma*]
47) ⸢*ri*⸣-*qí ḫu-bu-l*[*i*]
Up.ed. 48) ⸢*a*⸣-*na ša-šu* ⸢*iš*⸣-⸢*tu*⸣
49) ⸢ḪUR⸣.⸢SAG⸣
Lft.ed. 50) *ip-pa-ṭá-ru* LÚ.MEŠ *i-na* 30 KÙ.BABBAR.MEŠ *ù iš-tu*
51) ^{I}*Pé-e-ia i-na* 1 *me* KÙ.BABBAR.MEŠ *ù li-ma-ad*
52) *a-wa-te*^{MEŠ} ÌR-*ka an-nu-ti*

(34–35) from my jurisdiction and placed his commissioner in it.

(36–40) So command Reʿ-anap, my commissioner, that he should return the town to my control and I will make preparation for the regular troops of the king, my lord.

(41–52) Furthermore, behold the deeds of Peʾya son of Gulat[i] against the town of Gezer, the handmaiden of the king, my lord. How long has he been plundering it so that it has become like a damaged pot because of him. From the hill country men are ransomed for thirty (shekels of) silver but from Peʾya for one hundred (shekels of) silver. So learn these words of your servant!

EA 293

TRANSCRIPTION

Obv. 01) [*a-na* LUGAL EN]-*ia*
02) D[INGE]R.⸢MEŠ⸣-[*i*]*a* [^{d}U]T[U-]*ia* ⸢*qí*⸣[-*bí-ma*]
03) *u*[*m*]-[*m*]*a* ⸢^{I}⸣⸢^{d}⸣⸢IŠKUR⸣.DI.KUD ⸢ÌR⸣-[*ka*]
04) ⸢*ep*⸣-⸢*ri*⸣ *ša* GÌR.MEŠ-*ka*
05) [*a-na*] GÌR.MEŠ LUGAL EN-*ia*
06) [DI]NGIR.MEŠ-*ia* ^{d}UTU-*ia* 7-*šu*
07) [7]-*ta-a-an am-qú-ut*
08) [*i*]*š-te-mé a-wa-at*
09) ⸢*ša*⸣ *iš-pu-ur* LUGAL EN-⸢*ia*⸣
10) ⸢*a*⸣-*na* ÌR-*šu ù-ṣur-mi*
11) *aš-ri* LUGAL *ša it*-⸢*ti*$_{7}$⸣-⸢*ka*⸣
12) ⸢*a*⸣-*nu-ma iṣ-ṣú-ru*
13) UD. KAM^{v}-*ma ù* ›UD‹ ⸢*mu*⸣-⸢*ša*⸣

Lo.ed. 14) *i-nu-ma*

Rev. 15) ⸢LÚ⸣.⸢KÚR⸣.‹MEŠ› L[UGA]L ⸢EN⸣-*ia*
16) ⸢LÚ⸣.⸢MEŠ⸣ [GA]Z.MEŠ *u* ⸢ÌR⸣! ⸢*ki*⸣-⸢*ti*$_{7}$⸣
17) ⸢LÚ⸣.MÁŠKIM-*šu a-nu-ma*
18) [..]⸢*tu*⸣-*ši a*-⸢*šar*⸣
19) [*yi-ka*]-⸢*aš*⸣-*ša-ad*
20) [...]*uš-ša* ⸢*it*⸣-⸢*ti*⸣-⸢*šu*⸣-⸢*nu*⸣
21) [*a-na* LUGAL] EN-*ia*
22) [*a-di*] ⸢*ka*⸣(?)-*ši-id*
23) [LUGAL EN-*ia*]

EA 293

TRANSLATION

(1–7) Sp[eak to the king,] my [lord,] [m]y d[ei]ty, my [su]n god; the me[ssa]ge of Baʿlu-dāni, [your] servant, the dirt under your feet: [At] the feet of the king, my lord, my deity, my sun god, seven times (and) [seven] times have I fallen.

(8–11) [I] have heard the word that the king, my lord, has written to his servant, "Guard the places of the king which are in your charge."

(12–17) Now I am guarding day and night because the enem‹ies› of the k[in]g, my lord, are the *ʿapîru* men but a loyal servant is his commissioner.

(17–23) Now [...] wherever [he shall] arrive [...] with them [for the king] my lord [until the king my lord] arrives.

EA 294

TRANSCRIPTION

Obv. 01) *a-na* ^{I}LUGAL EN-*ia* DINGIR.MEŠ-*i*⸢*a*⸣
02) ⸢^{d}⸣⸢UTU⸣-⸢*ia*⸣ ⸢*qí*⸣-⸢*bí*⸣-⸢*ma*⸣
03) ⸢*um*⸣-⸢*ma*⸣ ⸢^{I}⸣⸢*Zí*⸣-⸢*im*⸣-⸢*re*⸣-⸢*da*⸣ ÌR-*ka*
04) *a*-⸢*na*⸣ ⸢GÌR⸢.⸢ḪI⸣.⸢A⸣ ⸢LUGAL⸣ ⸢EN⸣-*ia* ⸢DINGIR⸣.⸢MEŠ⸣-*ia*
05) ^{d}UTU-⸢*ia*⸣ ⸢7⸣-⸢*šu*⸣ 7-*ta-a-an*
06) *am-qú-ut iš-te-mé a-wa-te*^{MEŠ}
07) *ša* LUGAL EN-*ia ša iš-pu-ur*
08) *a-na* ÌR-*šu ši-mé-mi a-na*
09) ›*a-na*‹ LÚ.MÁŠKIM-*ka ù ú-ṣur*
10) URU.DIDLI.ḪI.A ⸢*ša*⸣ LUGAL EN-*ka*
11) ⸢*ša*⸣ ⸢*it*⸣-*ti-ka a-nu-ma*
12) ⸢*iṣ*⸣-⸢*ṣú*⸣-⸢*ru*⸣ *a-wa-at ša*
13) ⸢*qa*⸣-⸢*ba*⸣ L[UGAL] EN-*ia a-na ia-ši*
14) [*ù*] *yi-il*$_5$-⸢*ma*⸣-*ad*
15) [LUGAL] EN-*ia a-na* ÌR-*šu*
Lo.ed. 16) [*a*]-⸢*mur*⸣ ⸢*ip*⸣-*ši* ^{I}*Pí-i-ia*
17) [DUM]U ^{MUNUS}*Gu-la-ti*$_7$
Rev. 18) [*a-na*]⸢*ia*⸣-⸢*ši*⸣ LÚ.MEŠ-*ia*
19) *š*[*a*] ⸢*uš*⸣-*ši-ir-ti a-na*
20) *ur-ra-di i-na* URU *Ia-pu*
21) *ù a-na na-ṣa-ri*
22) É-*ti* \ *šu-nu-ti* LUGAL EN-*ia*
23) *ù al-lu-ú il*$_5$-*qé-šu-nu*
24) ^{I}*Pí-i-ia* DUMU *Gu-la-ti*
25) *ù yi-il*$_5$-*ma-ad* LUGAL EN-*ia*
26) *a-wa-at* ÌR-*šu an-nu-ta*$_5$

EA 294

TRANSLATION

(1–6) Speak to the king, my lord, my deity, my sun god, the message of Zimredda(!), your servant: At the feet of the king, my lord, my deity, my sun god, seven times and seven times have I fallen.

(6–11) I have heard the words of the king, my lord, which he wrote to his servant, "Listen to your commissioner and guard the cities of the king, your lord, that are with you."

(11–15) Now I am keeping the word that the k[ing], my lord, spoke to me, [so] may [the king], my lord be informed concerning his servant.

(16–26) [Be]hold, the deeds of Piya, [so]n of Gulati [against] me. As for my men, whom I sent to serve in Yapô (Joppa) and to guard the storehouse of the king, my lord, then, behold, Piya son of Gulati took them. So may the king, my lord, be informed of this word of his servant.

27) *šum-ma* ⸢*ki*⸣-*ia-am yi-iq-bu*
28) LUGAL EN-*ia a-na ia-ši*
29) *iz-zi-ib-mi* URU.KI-*ka*
30) *iš-tu pa-ni* ^{I}*Pí-i-ia*
31) *ù lu-ú iz-zi-ba ù*
Up.ed. 32) ⸢*il*$_5$⸣-*la-ka ù lu-ú*
33) ⸢*ur*⸣-*ra-da* LUGAL EN-*ia*
Lft.ed. 34) UD.⸢KAM^{v}⸣-*ma ù mu-ša a-di*
35) ⸢*da*⸣-*ri-ia-ta*

(27–35) If thus the king, my lord, should say to me, "Abandon your city in favor of Piya," I would verily leave and I would come and I would truly serve the king, my lord, day and night, forever.

EA 295

TRANSCRIPTION

Obv.

01) [*a-na* ^{I}*šàr-ri* E]N-*ia* ⸢^{d}⸣UTU-*ia* DIN[GIR.MEŠ-*ia*]
02) [*qí* -*b*]*í* -*ma*
03) [*um-ma* ^{d}IŠKUR.]DI.KU$_5$ ÌR-*ka* ÌR *ki*[-*ti*]
04) [SAḪAR *iš-tu*] *šap-li* 2 KUŠ.E.SÍ[R]
05) [^{I}*šà*]*r-ri* EN-*ia a-na* GÌR.MEŠ ^{I}*šàr*[-*ri*]
06) EN-*ia* ^{d}UTU-*ia* DINGIR.MEŠ-*ia* 7-*š*[*u*]
07) *ù* 7-*it-ta-a-an am-qú*-⸢*ut*⸣
08) *a-mur-mì a-na-ku* ÌR ^{I}*šàr-ri* E[N-*ia*]
09) ⸢*ša*⸣ *ur-ru-du* ^{I}*šàr-ri* EN-*ia* [*iš-tu*]
10) [S]AG.DU-*ia a-di* GÌR.MEŠ-*ia ki*[-*ma*]
11) [*a-bu-*]*ti-ia iš-tu da-ri-t*[*i*]
12) *ù l*[*i-ìl-ma-a*]*d* ^{I}*šàr-ru* E[N-*ia*]
13) *a-na i-pé*[-*ši ša yi-p*]*u-uš-mi*
14) ^{I}*Ia-ab-n*[*i*-DINGIR LÚ URU *Ṣí*-]*du-na*
15) *a-na ia-ši m*[*a*...............]
16) ḪUL.GÁL \ *l*[*um-na* ?.......]
17) *ù yi-im-qú-ut* [*a-na*..........]
18) *qa-du* ^{I}*Ka-a*[*l-bi* LÚ URU......]
19) *qa-du* ŠEŠ.MEŠ-*š*[*u ù*.........]
20) *qa-du* LÚ.MEŠ K[UR.........]
21) *ù pu-ḫi*-[*ru*.................]
22) [*ša-ni-*]*tam i*⸢*a*⸣[..............]

Lower part of tablet is missing entirely, including reverse of the small fragment and thus also the beginning of the reverse.

Rev.

01) (traces)
02) [..........................]*ša*
03) [*e-p*]*í*-⸢*iš*⸣ ⸢ḪUL⸣.⸢GÁL⸣ ⸢*a*⸣-⸢*na*⸣ *tap-pí*[-*ia*]
04) *ù li-ìl-ma-ad* ^{I}⸢*šàr*⸣-*ru ki*[-*ti-ia*]
05) ⸢*ù*⸣ *li-di-in*$_4$-*mì* ^{I}⸢*šàr*⸣-*ru* EN[-*ia*]
06) 50 LÚ.MEŠ *qa-du* 1 LÚ IGI.KÁR EN.[NUN]
07) *a-na na-ṣa-ri* URU.KI \ *ti-e-ti* x[

EA 295

TRANSLATION

(1–7) [Spe]ak [to the king,] my [lo]rd, my sun god, [my] de[ity], [the message of Baʿlu-]dāni, your servant, the lo[yal] servant, [the dirt ben]eath the sanda[ls] of [the ki]ng, my lord: At the feet of the ki[ng], my lord, my sun god, my deity, seven ti[mes] and seven times, have I fallen.

(8–11) Look, I am the servant of the king, [my] lo[rd], who serves the king, my lord, [from] my [h]ead to my feet, li[ke] my [fath]ers from of old.

(12–21) So m[ay] the king, [my] lo[rd] be [informe]d of the de[ed that] Yabni[-ilu(?) the ruler of Ṣi]don (?) [com]mitted against me [...] evil [...] and he fell [on...] with Kal[bi ruler of...](?) with his brothers [and] with the men of the l[and of...] and they assem[bled....].

(22) [Furthermo]re,...[...]

(Rev. 1–3) [........] who [d]id evil to [my] partner.

(4–7) So may the king be informed of [my] lo[yalty] and may the king, [my] lord give fifty men with one garr[ison] commander to guard the city...

08) *ù a-nu-um-ma ḫar-ra-ni-ia ú-š*[*e-er-ti*](?)
09) *ù pa-nu-ia a-na i-re-bi*
10) *a-na ur-ru-ud* [I]*šàr-ri* EN-*ia* [

(8–10) And now [I] have s[ent] my caravan, and my intention is to enter (into Egypt) to serve the king, my lord.

EA 296

TRANSCRIPTION

Obv. 01) ⌜*a*⌝-⌜*na*⌝ ^{I}⌜*šàr*⌝-⌜*ri*⌝ ⌜EN⌝-⌜*ia*⌝
02) DINGIR.MEŠ-*ia* ⌜^{d}⌝⌜UTU⌝.⌜MEŠ⌝-⌜*ia*⌝
03) *qí-bí-ma*
04) *um-ma* ^{I}*I*⌜*a*⌝-⌜*aḫ*⌝-*ṭì*-⌜*ri*⌝ ÌR-*k*[*a*]
05) *ep-ri ša* GÌR.MEŠ-*ka*
06) *a-na* GÌR.MEŠ LUGAL EN-*ia*
07) DINGIR.MEŠ-*ia* ⌜^{d}⌝⌜UTU⌝.⌜MEŠ⌝-*ia* 7-*šu*
08) *ù* 7-⌜*it*⌝-⌜*ta*⌝-*a-an am-qú-ut*
09) *ša-ni-tam a*-⌜*mur*⌝ *a-na-ku* ÌR-*di*
10) *ša ki-it*-⌜*ti*⌝ LUGAL EN-*ia*
11) *da-ag-la-ti ki-ia*-⌜*am*⌝
12) *ù da-ag-la-ti*
13) *ki-ia-am ù la-a*
14) *na-mi-ir ù da-ag-la-ti*
15) *a-na mu-uḫ-ḫi* LUGAL EN-*ia*
16) *ù na-mi-ir ù*
17) *ti-na-mu-šu* SIG$_4$

Lo.ed. 18) \ *la-bi-tu iš-tu*

Rev. 19) ⌜*šu*⌝-*pal tap-pa-ti-ši*
20) *ù a-na-ku la-a i-na-mu-šu*
21) *iš-tu šu-pal* GÌR.MEŠ
22) *šàr-ri be-li-ia ù*
23) *yi-ša-al* LUGAL *be-li*
24) ^{I}*Ia-an-ḫa-ma* LÚ.MÁŠKIM-*šu*
25) *i-nu-ma* TUR *a-na-ku ù*
26) *šu-ri-ba-ni a-na* KUR *Mi-iṣ-ri*
27) *ù ur-ra-ad-ti* LUGAL
28) *be-li-ia ù iz-zi-iz-ti*
29) *i-na* KÁ.GAL LUGAL *be-li-ia*

EA 296

TRANSLATION

(1–8) Speak to the king, my lord, my deity, my sun god, the message of Yaʿṭiri yo[ur] servant, the dirt under your feet: At the feet of the king, my lord, my deity, my sun god, seven times and seven times have I fallen.

(9–22) Furthermore, look, I am the loyal servant of the king, my lord. I looked this way and I looked that way, but there was no light. Then I looked towards the king, my lord, and there was light. And a brick may fall out from under its partners, but I will not depart from under the feet of the king, my lord.

(22–29) So may the king, my lord ask Yanḥamu, his commissioner. When I was young, then he brought me into the land of Egypt and I served the king, my lord, and I was posted at the gate of the king, my lord.

30) *ù yi-ša-al* LUGAL EN-*ia*
31) LÚ.MÁŠKIM-*šu i-nu-ma a-na-ku a-*⸢*na*⸣-*ṣa-ru*
32) KÁ.GAL URU *Az-za-*⸢*ti*⸣ *ù* ⸢KÁ⸣.⸢GAL⸣
33) URU *Ya-pu ù a-na-ku it-*⸢*ti*⸣
34) ÉRIN.MEŠ *pí-ṭá-at* LUGAL *be-*⸢*li*⸣-[*ia*]
35) ⸢*a*⸣-*šar ti-la-ku a-na-ku it-*[*ti-šu-nu*](?)
36) ⸢*ù*⸣ *a-nu-ma ù i-na-*⸢*na*⸣
Up.ed. 37) ⸢*ša*⸣-⸢*ak*⸣?-⸢*na*⸣?-⸢*ti*⸣? ⸢*pa*⸣-⸢*an*⸣
Lft.ed. 38) ^{GIŠ}*ni-ri* \ *ḫu-ul-lu* LUGAL EN-*ia a-*⸢*na*⸣
39) $^{\text{⸢UZU⸣}}$GÙ-*ia ù ub-ba-lu-na*

(30–35) So may the king, my lord, ask his commissioner whether I am guarding the gate of the city of Gaza and the gate of the city of Yapô (Joppa) and I am with the regular troops of the king, [my] lord wherever they go, I am wi[th them].

(36–39) And now I have placed the yoke of the king, my lord, on my neck and I am carrying (it).

EA 297

TRANSCRIPTION

Obv. 01) ⸢*a*⸣-⸢*na*⸣ ^{I}LUGAL EN-*ia* DINGIR.MEŠ-⸢*ia*⸣
02) ^{d}UTU-*ia qí-bí-ma*
03) *um-ma* ^{I}*Ia-pa-ḫi* ÌR-⸢*ka*⸣-⸢*ma*⸣
04) *ep-ri ša* 2 GÌR.⸢MEŠ⸣-⸢*ka*⸣
05) *a-na* GÌR.MEŠ LUGAL EN-*ia*
06) DINGIR.MEŠ-*ia* ^{d}UTU-*ia* 7-*šu*
07) 7-*ta-a-an am-qú-ut*
08) *mi-im-ma ša qa-*⸢*ba*⸣
09) LUGAL EN-*ia a-na ia-ši*
10) *iš-te-mé-šu ma-gal*
11) SIG$_5$-*iš ša-ni-tam ù*
12) *in*$_4$*-né-ep-ša-ti*$_7$
13) *ki-ma ri-qí* URUDU \ $^{\textit{sí-ri}}$
14) *ḫu-bu-ul-li*
Lo.ed. 15) ⸢*iš*⸣-*tu qa-at*
Rev. 16) ⸢LÚ⸣.MEŠ KUR ⸢*Su*⸣-*te*^{MEŠ}
17) *ù a-nu-ma iš-te-mé*
18) *sa-ri ša* LUGAL DÙG.GA-*ta*
19) *ù it-ta-ṣa-at*
20) *a-na ia-ši ù pa-ši-iḫ*
21) *lìb-bi-ia ma-gal*

EA 297

TRANSLATION

(1–7) Speak to the king, my lord, my deity, my sun god, the message of Yapaʿi, your servant, the dirt at your two feet: At the feet of the king, my lord, my deity, my sun god, seven times (and) seven times have I fallen.

(8–11) Everything that the king, my lord said to me, I have heeded very carefully.

(11–16) Furthermore, so I have become like a damaged copper pot because of the men of the Sutû land.

(17–21) But now I have heard the sweet breath of the king, and it has come forth to me and my heart is very tranquil.

EA 298

TRANSCRIPTION

Obv. 01) [*a-n*]*a* ⸢LUGAL⸣ ⸢EN⸣-⸢*ia*⸣ DINGIR.MEŠ-⸢*ia*⸣
02) [^{d}UTU]-⸢*ia*⸣ ^{d}UTU ⸢*ša*⸣
03) ⸢*iš*⸣-⸢*tu*⸣ AN ⸢*ša*$_{10}$⸣-*mì-i*
04) ⸢*um*⸣-⸢*ma*⸣ $^{⸢I⸣}$*Ia-pa-ḫi* ⸢LÚ⸣ ⸢*ša*⸣
05) URU *Ga-az-ri*^{KI}
06) ⸢ÌR⸣-⸢*ka*⸣ ⸢*ep*⸣-⸢*ri*⸣ ⸢*ša*⸣
07) ⸢2⸣ GÌR.MEŠ-⸢*ka*⸣ LÚ *kàr-tap-pí*
08) *ša* ANŠE.KUR.⸢RA⸣-*ka*
09) ⸢*a*⸣-⸢*na*⸣ 2 GÌR.MEŠ LUGAL EN-*ia*
10) $^{⸢d⸣}$⸢UTU⸣ *ša iš*-⸢*tu*⸣ ⸢*ša*$_{10}$⸣-*mì*-⸢*i*⸣!
11) 7-*šu u* 7-*ta*-⸢*a*⸣-*an*
12) *lu-ú iš-ta*-⸢*ḫa*⸣-⸢*ḫi*⸣-⸢*in*⸣
13) *ka-bat-tum-ma u*
14) ⸢*ṣe*⸣-⸢*ru*⸣-*ma u mì-ma*
15) ⸢*ša*⸣ ⸢*i*⸣-*qa-ab-bi*
16) ⸢LUGAL⸣ ⸢EN⸣-⸢*ia*⸣ *a*-⸢*na*⸣ *ia-š*[*i*]
17) [*i*]*š*-⸢*te*$_{9}$⸣-⸢*me*⸣ ⸢*ma*⸣-*gal ma*-[*gal*]

Lo.ed. 18) ⸢ÌR⸣ ⸢LUGAL⸣ *a-na-ku*

Rev. 19) ⸢*u*⸣ ⸢*ep*⸣-*ri ša* 2 G[ÌR.MEŠ]-⸢*ka*⸣
20) ⸢*li*⸣-*il-ma-ad* ⸢LUGAL⸣
21) EN-*ia i-nu-ma*
22) LÚ ŠEŠ-*ia* TUR.⸢TUR⸣
23) *na-ka-ar* ⸢*iš*⸣-⸢*tu*⸣
24) *ia-ši u i-ru-ub*
25) *a-na* URU *Mu-ú*[ʾ]-*ḫa*-⸢*zi*⸣
26) *u na*-⸢*da*⸣-*an* 2 *qa*-‹*ti*›-*šu*
27) *a-na* LÚ ⸢SA⸣.⸢GAZ⸣.KI
28) ⸢*u*⸣ *a-nu*-⸢*ma*⸣ [*i*]-⸢*na*⸣-*an-na*
29) *nu-kùr*-⸢*tu*$_{4}$⸣ ⸢UGU⸣-*ia*
30) *u mi-lik a-na* KUR-*ka*
31) ⸢*li*⸣-*iš*-⸢*pu*⸣-*ra* EN-*ia*
32) *a-na* LÚ ⸢*ra*⸣-*bi-ṣí-šu*
33) UGU ⸢*ip*⸣‹-*ši*› ⸢*an*⸣-⸢*nu*⸣-*ú*

EA 298

TRANSLATION

(1–14) [T]o the king, my lord, my deity, my [sun god], the sun god from heaven, the message of Yapaʿi, the ruler of the city of Gezer, your servant, the dirt at your feet, the groom of your horse: At the feet of the king, my lord, the sun from heaven, seven times and seven times have I verily prostrated myself on the stomach and on the back.

(14–17) Everything that the king, my lord has said to me, I have heeded very care[fully].

(18–19) The servant of the king am I, and the dirt at your two fe[et].

(20–29) May the king, my lord, be informed that my younger brother has become hostile to me and he has entered into the city of Môʾḫazi and he has pl‹edg›ed himself to the *ʿapîru*. And now he is making war on me.

(30–33) So take counsel concerning your land. May my lord write to his commissioner concerning this mat‹ter›.

EA 299

TRANSCRIPTION

Obv. 01) *a-na* ^{I}LUGAL [EN]-*ia* ⸢DINGIR⸣.⸢MEŠ⸣-⸢*ia*⸣
02) ^{d}UTU-⸢*ia*⸣ ⸢^{d}⸣UTU ⸢*ša*⸣ ⸢*iš*⸣-*tu*
03) AN *ša*$_{10}$-*me um-ma* ^{I}*Ia*-⸢*pa*⸣-⸢*ḫi*⸣
04) LÚ *ša* URU *Gaz*-⸢*ri*⸣$^{⸢KI⸣}$
05) ÌR-*ka ep-ri* ⸢*ša*⸣ ⸢GÌR⸣-⸢*ka*⸣
06) LÚ *ku*$_{8}$-*sí* ANŠE.KUR.RA.MEŠ-⸢*ka*⸣
07) *a-na* 2 GÌR.MEŠ LUGAL EN-⸢*ia*⸣
08) DINGIR.MEŠ-*ia* ^{d}UTU-*ia* ⸢^{d}⸣⸢UTU⸣
09) *ša iš-tu* AN *ša*$_{10}$-*me* ⸢7⸣-*šu*
10) *u* 7-*ta-a-an lu-ú am-qut-ma*
11) *ka-bat-tum u ṣe-ru-ma*
12) *iš-te*$_{9}$-*me a-wa-te*^{MEŠ}
13) LÚ.DUMU *ši-ip-ri ša* LUGAL
14) ⸢EN⸣-*ia ma*-⸢*gal*⸣ *ma-gal*
15) *u li-im-li-ik* LUGAL EN-*ia*
16) ⸢^{d}⸣UTU *ša iš-tu* AN ⸢*ša*$_{10}$⸣-*mì*
17) ⸢*a*⸣-*na* KUR.KI-*šu a-nu*-⸢*ma*⸣
18) *da-an-nu* LÚ.SA.GAZ.MEŠ
19) UGU-*nu u* ‹*yu*›-*uš-ši-ra*
Lo.ed. 20) / *qa-at-šu* LUGAL ⸢EN⸣-*ia*
21) ⸢*it*⸣-*ti-ia u lu-ú*
Rev. 22) *yi-iṭ-ra*-⸢*ni*⸣? ⸢LUGAL⸣! EN-*i*[*a*]
23) *iš-tu qa-at*
24) LÚ.SA.GAZ.MEŠ *la-a*
25) *tu-ga-me-ru-nu*
26) LÚ.SA.GAZ.MEŠ-*tu*$_{4}$

EA 299

TRANSLATION

(1–11) [T]o the king, my lord, my deity, my sun god, the sun god from heaven, the message of Yapaʿi, the ruler of the city of Gezer, your servant, the dirt at your feet, the groom of your horses: At the two feet of the king, my lord, my deity, my sun god, the sun god from heaven, seven times, seven times have I verily fallen on the stomach and on the back.

(12–14) I have heeded very carefully the words of the emissary of the king, my lord.

(15–17) So may the king, my lord, the sun god from heaven, take counsel concerning his land.

(17–26) Now the *ʿapîru* men are stronger than we, so may the king, my lord, send forth his hand to me and may he deliver me from the hand of the *ʿapîru* men lest the *ʿapîru* men wipe us out.

EA 300

TRANSCRIPTION

Obv. 01) [*a-na* LUGAL E]N-*ia* [DI]NG[IR.MEŠ-*ia*]

02) [^{d}UTU-*ia*] ^{d}[UT]U ⸢*ša*⸣ ⸢*iš*⸣-*t*[*u*]

03) [AN *ša*$_{10}$-*mì*] ⸢*qí*⸣-[*b*]*í*-⸢*ma*⸣ [*um-ma*]

04) [^{I}*Ia-pa-ḫi* LÚ *š*]a

05) [URU] ⸢*Gaz*⸣-⸢*ri*⸣⸢^{KI}⸣ ⸢ÌR⸣-*ka*$_4$

06) ⸢*ù*⸣ ⸢*ep*⸣-⸢*ri*⸣ ⸢*ša*⸣ 2 ⸢GÌR⸣.⸢MEŠ⸣- *ka*$_4$

07) ⸢LÚ⸣ ⸢*kàr*⸣-⸢*tap*⸣-⸢*pí*⸣ ⸢*ša*⸣ ⸢ANŠE.⸢KUR⸣.⸢RA⸣.MEŠ-*ka*$_4$

08) ⸢*a*⸣-[*na*] 2 ⸢GÌR⸣.M[EŠ] ⸢LUGAL⸣ ⸢EN⸣-[*i*]*a*

09) ⸢7⸣-⸢*šu*⸣ ⸢*u*⸣ ⸢7⸣-⸢*ta*⸣-⸢*a*⸣-⸢*an*⸣

10) ⸢*am*⸣-⸢*qut*⸣ ⸢*li*⸣-⸢*de*⸣-⸢*mi*⸣ ⸢LUGAL⸣

11) ⸢EN⸣-⸢*ia*⸣ *a*-⸢*na*⸣ ⸢ÌR⸣-⸢*šu*⸣

12) ⸢TI⸣.L[A] ⸢*ḫal*⸣-⸢*qa*⸣ ⸢*iš*⸣-⸢*tu*⸣

13) ⸢KUR⸣-⸢*ia*⸣ *u a-‹nu›-ma ia-nu*

14) ⸢*mi*⸣-⸢*im*⸣-⸢*ma*⸣ ⸢*a*⸣-⸢*na*⸣ ⸢*ia*⸣-⸢*ši*⸣

15) [*u*] ⸢*lu*⸣-⸢*ú* ⸣ ⸢*yu*⸣-⸢*wa*⸣-⸢*ša*⸣-⸢*a*⸣*r* ⸢LUGAL⸣

16) ⸢ÉRIN⸣.⸢MEŠ⸣ ⸢*pí*⸣-⸢*ṭá*⸣-⸢*ta*⸣-⸢*šu*⸣

17) *šu-nu* ⸢*ia*⸣-⸢*a*⸣-⸢*ti*⸣

Lo.ed 18) *tu-šu-ra!-ba-ni*

Rev. 19) *a-na* URU.DIDLI.KI-*ni*-[*i*]*a*

20) *u lu*-⸢*ú*⸣ *i-ru-da-am*

21) LUGAL EN-*ia ki-ma ša*

22) A.A-*ia u* ⸢AB⸣!.⸢BA⸣-*ti*[-*ia*(?)]

---

23) *u ša-ni*-⸢*tam*⸣ ⸢*él*⸣-⸢*te*$_9$⸣-⸢*né*⸣-⸢*mé*⸣

24) ⸢*a*⸣-⸢*na*⸣ *a*-⸢*wa*⸣-⸢*te*⸣⸢^{MEŠ}⸣ ⸢LUGAL⸣ EN-*ia*

25) ⸢*u*⸣ *iš-te*$_9$-*mu* [*a-na*] ⸢*a*⸣-*wa*-⸢*te*⸣⸢MEŠ⸣

26) ⸢^{I}⸣*Ma-i*[*a*] ⸢MÁŠKIM⸣ ⸢LUGAL⸣

27) EN-*ia* ^{d}[UTU] *iš-tu*

28) AN *ša*$_{10}$-*mì* DU[MU] ⸢^{d}⸣UTU(!)

EA 300

TRANSLATION

(1–10) Sp[ea]k [to the king,] my [lo]rd, [my de]ity, [my sun god, the [sun god fro[m heaven; the message of Yapaʿi, the ruler o]f [the city of] Gezer, your servant and the dirt under your feet, the groom of your ho[r]ses: A[t] the feet of [the king, m]y lord seven times and seven times have I fallen.

(10–14) May the king, my lord, be apprised concerning his servant. Lost are the provis[ions] from my land and n‹o›w I don't have anything.

(15–22) So may the king send his regular troops. They can restore me to my cities and I will verily serve the king, my lord like my father and [my(?)] ancestors.

(23–28) And furthermore, I am constantly obeying the words of the king, my lord, and I am obeying the words of Maya, the commissioner of the king, my lord, [the sun god] from heaven, the s[on] of the sun god.

EA 301

TRANSCRIPTION

Obv. 01) ⸢*a*⸣-⸢*na*⸣ ⸢^{I}⸣[LU]GAL EN-*ia* ⸢^{d}⸣[UTU]
02) *ša iš*[-*t*]*u* AN ⸢*ša*$_{10}$⸣-*mì*-⸢*i*⸣
03) *um-ma* ^{I}*Šu-ba-an-di*
04) ÌR-*ka-ma e*[*p*]-*r*[*i*] *ša*
05) 2 GÌR.MEŠ-*ka a-na* 2 GÌR.MEŠ
06) LUGAL EN-*ia* DINGIR.MEŠ-*ia*
07) ^{d}UTU-*ia* ^{d}UTU *ša*
08) ⸢*iš*⸣-*tu* AN ⸢*ša*$_{10}$⸣-*mì*-⸢*i*⸣
09) ⸢7⸣-*šu ù* 7-*ta-a-an*
10) *iš-ti-ḫa-ḫi-in ka-bat-tum-ma*
11) *ù ṣe-ru*-⸢*ma*⸣
12) ^{I}*Ḫa-an-ia ša-pár*
13) *šàr-ru* EN-*ia* ^{d}UTU
14) *iš-tu* AN *ša*$_{10}$-*mì a-na ia-ši*
15) *ù a-nu-ma iš-te*$_{9}$-*me*
16) ⸢*a*⸣-*wa-at* LUGAL EN-*ia*
Rev. 17) [*ma*]-*gal ma-gal*
18) ⸢*ù*⸣ *a-nu-ma na-ad*[-*na*]-⸢*ti*⸣
19) 3? *me* GU$_{4}$.MEŠ *ù*
20) ⸢20⸣ DUMU.MUNUS.MEŠ *ù*
21) *aš-šum la-ma-ad*
22) LUGAL EN-*ia* ^{d}UTU
23) *ša* ⸢*iš*⸣-*tu* [AN *š*]*a*$_{10}$-*mì*

EA 301

TRANSLATION

(1–11) To the [ki]ng, my lord, the [sun] god that is from heaven; the message of Shubandu, your servant, the dirt under your two feet: At the two feet of the king, my lord, my deity, my sun god, the sun god from heaven, seven times and seven times have I prostrated myself on the stomach and on the back.

(12–17) The king, my lord, the sun god from heaven, has sent Ḫanya to me and now I have heeded the word of the king, my lord, [ve]ry explicitly.

(18–20) And now I have giv[en] three(?) hundred head of cattle and twenty daughters.

(20–23) So in order to inform the king, my lord, the sun god who is from [he]aven.

EA 302

TRANSCRIPTION

Obv.	01)	⸢*a*⸣-*na* ^{I}LUGAL ⸢EN⸣-*ia*
	02)	DINGER.MEŠ-*ia* ^{d}UTU-⸢*i*⸣*a*
	03)	^{d}UTU *iš-tu* ⸢*ša*$_{10}$⸣-⸢*mì*⸣-⸢*i*⸣
	04)	⸢*um*⸣-⸢*ma*⸣ ^{I}*Šu-ba-*⸢*an*⸣-⸢*di*⸣
	05)	ÌR-*ka ep-ri ša*
	06)	GÌR.MEŠ-*ka a-na* GÌR.MEŠ-⸢*pí*⸣
	07)	LUGAL EN-*ia* ^{d}UTU
	08)	*iš-tu* AN *ša*$_{10}$-*mì-i*
	09)	7-*šu ù* 7-*ta-*⸢*a*⸣-*an*
	10)	*iš-ti-ḫe-ḫi-in*
	11)	LÚ.DUMU *ši-ip-ri*
	12)	*ša iš-tap-pár šàr-ri* EN-*ia*
	13)	⸢*a*⸣-⸢*na*⸣ *ia-a-ši*
	14)	⸢*iš*⸣-*te-me a-wa-te*^{MEŠ}-*šu*
	15)	[*ma*]-⸢*gal*⸣ [*m*]*a-gal*
Lo.ed.	16)	⸢*ù*⸣ *a-nu-ma*
Rev.	17)	[*ú*]-⸢*še*⸣-⸢*ši*⸣-*ru-mì* ⸢*šu*⸣
	18)	⸢*ki*⸣-[*ma ša*] ⸢*qa*⸣-*bi-*

EA 302

TRANSLATION

(1–10) To the king, my lord, my deity, my sun god, the sun god from heaven, the message of Shubandu, your servant, the dirt of your feet: At the feet of the king, my lord, the sun god from heaven, seven times and seven times have I prostrated myself.

(11–18) As for the envoy whom the king, my lord, has sent to me, I have heeded his words very diligently and now [I] have prepared in accord[ance with what] he said.

EA 303

TRANSCRIPTION

Obv. 01) ⸢*a*⸣-⸢*na*⸣ ^{I}LUGAL EN-*ia* DINGIR.MEŠ-*i*⸢*a*⸣
02) ^{d}UTU-*ia* ^{d}UTU *ša iš-tu*
03) AN *ša*$_{10}$*-mì-i um-ma*
04) ^{I}*Šu-ba-an-di* ÌR-*ka*
05) *ep-ri ša* 2 ^{UZU}GÌR.MEŠ-*ka*
06) LÚ *ku-sí* ⸢*ša*⸣ ANŠE.KUR.RA-*ka*
07) *a-na* 2 ^{UZU}⸢GÌR⸣.MEŠ *šàr*-⸢*ri*⸣
08) EN-*ia* ^{d}⸢UTU⸣ ⸢*ša*⸣ ⸢*iš*⸣-⸢*tu*⸣
09) AN *ša*$_{10}$*-mì-i* ⸢7⸣-⸢*šu*⸣
10) *ù* 7-*ta*-⸢*a*⸣-⸢*an*⸣ ⸢*iš*⸣-⸢*te*$_{9}$⸣-⸢*ḫa*⸣-*ḫi-in*
11) ^{UZU}*ka-bat*-⸢*tu*⸣-⸢*ma*⸣
12) *ù* ^{UZU}*ṣe-ru-ma*
13) [*i*]*š-te*$_{9}$*-me a-wa-te*^{MEŠ}
14) [*gá*]*b-bi ša šàr-ri*
15) [EN]-*ia* ^{d}UTU *iš-tu*
16) [AN] *ša*$_{10}$*-mì*-⸢*i*⸣ *ù a-nu-ma*
Lo.ed. 17) [*i-n*]*a-ṣa-ru a*-⸢*šar*⸣
18) [*šàr-*]*ri ša* ⸢*it*⸣-*ti-i*[*a*]
Rev. 19) [*ù*] *iš-te*$_{9}$*-me*
20) [*a-n*]*a* ^{I}*Táḫ-ma-aš-ši*
21) [*m*]*a*-⸢*gal*⸣ *ma-gal*

EA 303

TRANSLATION

(1–12) To the king, my lord, my deity, my sun god, the sun god from heaven, the message of Shubandu, your servant, the dirt at your two feet, the groom of your horses: At the two feet of the king, my lord, the sun god from heaven, seven times and seven times have I prostrated on the stomach and on the back.

(13–16) I have heeded all the words of the king, my lord, the sun god from heaven,

(16–21) And now [I am] guarding the place of the [ki]ng that is in m[y] charge [and] I am obeying Taḫmašši [v]ery diligently.

EA 304

TRANSCRIPTION

Obv. 01) *a-na* ^{I}⸢LUGAL⸣ [EN-*ia*]

02) ^{d}⸢UTU⸣-⸢*i*⸣*a* ^{d}⸢UTU⸣ ⸢*ša*⸣

03) *iš-tu* AN *ša*$_{10}$*-mì-*⸢*i*⸣

04) *um-ma* ^{I}*Šu-*⸢*ba*⸣*-an-*⸢*di*⸣

05) ÌR-*ka* ⸢*ep*⸣-⸢*ri*⸣

06) ⸢*ša*⸣ ^{UZU}⸢GÌR⸣.⸢MEŠ⸣-⸢*ka*⸣

07) ⸢LÚ⸣ *ku*$_{8}$*-sí* ⸢*ša*⸣ A[NŠE.KUR.RA.]MEŠ-*ka*

08) *a-*⸢*na*⸣ $^{⸢\mathrm{UZU}⸣}$⸢GÌR⸣.⸢MEŠ⸣ [LUGAL]

09) ⸢EN⸣-⸢*i*⸣*a* $^{⸢\mathrm{d}⸣}$⸢UTU⸣ [*ša iš-*]⸢*tu*⸣

10) ⸢AN⸣ *ša*$_{10}$*-mì-*⸢*i*⸣ [7-*šu*]

11) ⸢*ù*⸣ 7-⸢*ta*⸣-⸢*a*⸣-⸢*an*⸣

12) ⸢*iš*⸣-⸢*ta*⸣-⸢*ḫa*⸣-⸢*ḫi*⸣-⸢*in*⸣

13) $^{⸢\mathrm{UZU}⸣}$[*ka*]-⸢*bat*⸣*-tu-ma*

14) *ù* $^{⸢\mathrm{UZU}⸣}$⸢*ṣe*⸣*-ru-*⸢*ma*⸣

15) ⸢*iš*⸣*-te-me a-*⸢*w*⸣*a-*⸢*te*⸣$^{⸢\mathrm{MEŠ}⸣}$

16) ⸢*ša*⸣ ⸢*ṭup*⸣-⸢*pí*⸣ $^{⸢\mathrm{I}⸣}$⸢LUGAL⸣ ⸢EN⸣-⸢*ia*⸣

17) ⸢*ša*⸣ ⸢*iš*⸣*-t*[*ap*]-⸢*ra*⸣-⸢*an*⸣-⸢*ni*⸣

Lo.ed. 18) *ù a-nu-ma*

19) ⸢*i*⸣*-na-ṣa-ru-mì*

Rev. 20) ⸢*a*⸣-⸢*šar*⸣ *šàr-ri*

21) EN-*ia ša it-*⸢*ti*⸣-⸢*ia*⸣

22) *ù šàr-ru i-*⸢*de*⸣-⸢*ma*⸣

23) ⸢*a*⸣-⸢*na*⸣ KUR.KI.MEŠ-*šu*

———————

EA 304

TRANSLATION

(1–14) To the king, [my lord], my sun god, the sun god from heaven, the message of Shubandu, your servant, the dirt at [your] feet, the groom of your [horse]s: At the feet of the [king], my lord, the sun god [fro]m heaven, [seven times] and seven times have I prostrated on the stomach and on the back.

(15–16) I have heard the words of the tablet of the king, my lord, which he sent to me.

(18–21) And now I am guarding the place of the king, my lord, which is in my charge.

(22–23) So may the king be apprised concerning his territories.

EA 305

TRANSCRIPTION

Obv. 01) *a-na* ^{I}LUGAL EN-*ia* ^{d}UTU
02) *ša iš-tu* AN *ša*$_{10}$*-mì-i*
03) DINGIR.MEŠ-*ia* ^{d}UTU-*ia*
04) *um-ma* ^{I}*Šu-ba-an-du*
05) ÌR-*ka-ma ep-ri*
06) *ša* UZU.GÌR.MEŠ-*ka*
07) LÚ *ku*$_{8}$-sí ANŠE.KUR.RA.MEŠ-*ka*
08) *a-na* 2 UZU.GÌR.MEŠ
09) LUGAL *be-lí-ia* ^{d}UTU
10) ⸢*ša*⸣ ⸢*iš*⸣-*tu* AN *ša*$_{10}$*-mì-i*
11) ⸢7⸣-⸢*šu*⸣ *ù* 7-*ta-a-an*
12) *lu-ú iš-ta-*⸢*ḫa*⸣*-ḫi-in*
13) UZU *ka-bat-tum-ma*
Lo.ed. 14) ⸢*ù*⸣ UZU *ṣe-ru-*⸢*ma*⸣
Rev. 15) ⸢*iš*⸣*-te*$_{9}$*-né-me*
16) *a-wa-at* LUGAL EN-*ia*
17) *ša iš-tap-pa-ra-ni*
18) *ù a-nu-ma a-na-ṣa-ru*
19) *a-šar* ⸢LUGAL⸣ *ša*
20) ⸢*it*⸣-*t*[*i*-]⸢*ia*⸣
21) *a-nu*[*-m*]*a d*[*a*]*-an-nu*
22) LÚ.SA.GAZ.MEŠ UGU-*nu*
23) ⸢*ù*⸣ ⸢LUGAL⸣ *i-de*
24) *a-*⸢*na*⸣ ⸢KUR⸣.KI.MEŠ-*šu*

EA 305

TRANSLATION

(1–14) To the king, my lord, the sun god who is from heaven, my deity, my sun god; the message of Shubandu, your servant, the dirt under your feet, the groom of your horses: At the two feet of the king, my lord, the sun god who is from heaven, seven times and seven times have I verily prostrated myself, on the stomach and on the back.

(15–20) I have been heeding the word of the king, my lord, which he has been sending to me and now I am guarding the place of the king that is in my charge.

(21–24) No[w], s[t]rong are the *ʿapîru* against us so may the king be apprised concerning his land.

EA 306

TRANSCRIPTION

Obv. 01) [*a-na* ^{I}LUGAL EN-*ia* DINGIR.MEŠ-*ia*]
02) [^{d}UTU]-[*i*]*a* ^{d}[UTU *ša iš-tu* AN *ša*$_{10}$*-mì-i*]
03) [*um-*]⸢*ma*⸣ ^{I}⸢*Šu*⸣-⸢*ba*⸣-*an*-[*di* ÌR-*ka*]
04) [*e*]*p*-⸢*ri*⸣ ⸢*ša*⸣ ⸢2⸣ G[ÌR.MEŠ-*ka*]
05) [LÚ] ⸢*ku*$_{8}$⸣-⸢*sí*⸣ *ša* [ANŠE.KUR.RA.MEŠ-*ka*]
06) [*a*]-⸢*na*⸣ 2 G[ÌR].MEŠ LUGAL ⸢EN⸣- ⸢*ia*⸣
07) ⸢^{d}⸣⸢UTU⸣ *ša* ⸢*iš*⸣-*tu* ⸢AN⸣ ⸢*ša*$_{10}$⸣- ⸢*mì*⸣- ⸢*i*⸣
08) ⸢7⸣-*šu* ⸢*ù*⸣ ⸢7⸣-⸢*ta*⸣-⸢*a*⸣- ⸢*an*⸣
09) ⸢*lu*⸣-*ú iš*-⸢*ta*⸣-⸢*ḫa*⸣- ⸢*ḫi*⸣- ⸢*in*⸣
10) ⸢^{UZU}⸣*ka-bat-tu*-⸢*ma*⸣
11) ⸢*ù*⸣ ⸢^{UZU}⸣⸢*ṣú*⸣- ⸢*uḫ*⸣- ⸢*ru*⸣- ⸢*ma*⸣ ⸢*ù*⸣(?)
12) [*i*]-*nu-ma* ⸢*ša*⸣-*pár* ⸢LUGAL⸣ E[N-*ia*]
13) ⸢*al*⸣-⸢*ka*⸣-⸢*mì*⸣ ⸢*ù*⸣ [*du-gu-ul pa-ni*]
14) ⸢LUGAL⸣ *be*-⸢*lí*⸣-⸢*ka*⸣ [*a-na*]
15) ⸢*ma*⸣-⸢*an*⸣-⸢*ni*⸣ ⸢*e*⸣[*-zi-bu* URU LUGAL]
16) ⸢*da*⸣-⸢*na*⸣-⸢*at*⸣-*mì* KÚR.*NU* [UGU-*ia*]
17) ÌR LUGAL *ša yi*-⸢*de*⸣ ⸢KUR⸣
18) LUGAL *be-lí-ia a-na*-[*ku*]
19) [*a*]-*nu-ma i-tan*-⸢*ḫu*⸣
Lo.ed. 20) *a-na na-ṣa-ar*
Rev. 21) KUR LUGAL ⸢*i*⸣-*nu*-⸢*ma*⸣
22) *mar-ṣa-ku ma*-⸢*gal*⸣ ⸢*ù*⸣
23) ⸢*al*⸣-*lu-ú uš-ši*-⸢*ir*⸣-*t*[*i*]
24) ÌR LUGAL ⸢*ša*⸣- ⸢*na*⸣- ⸢*am*⸣
25) ⸢*a*⸣- ⸢*na*⸣ *šu*-⸢*ta*⸣- *ši*-⸢*ri*⸣
26) ⸢*ù*⸣ *a-na* ⸢*da*⸣-⸢*ga*⸣-*al*
27) [*pa-ni*] LUGAL ^{d}UTU *i*[*š-tu ša*$_{10}$*-mì-i*]
28) ⸢*ù*⸣ ⸢*lu*⸣-*ú ti-de be*-⸢*lí*⸣
29) ⸢*i*⸣-*nu-ma ša-ar-p*[*u*]
30) URU.DIDLI.KI.MEŠ-*ka ù*
31) ⸢KISLAḪ⸣ \ *ma-aš-ka*-⸢*na*⸣-[*ti*]-⸢*ka*⸣
32) [*i-na* IZI.]MEŠ *i*-⸢*ša*⸣-⸢*ti*⸣

EA 306

TRANSLATION

(1–11) [To the king, my lord, my deity, m]y [sun god, the sun from heaven, the mes]sage of Shuban[du your servant] the [d]irt at [your feet], the groom of [your horses]: At the fe[e]t if the king, my lord, the sun god from heaven, seven times and seven times I have verily prostrated myself on the stomach and on the back.

(11–16) But(?) inasmuch as the king, [my] lo[rd], has written, “Come and [view the face] of the king, your lord,” [to] whom should I [leave the city of the king]? The hostility [against me] is great.

(17–18) A servant of the king who knows the [la]nd of the king, his lord, am I.

(19–22) Now, I am weary from guarding the king’s territory because I am very ill.

(23–27) And behold, I have sent another servant of the king to proceed directly and to see [the face] of the king, the sun god f[rom heaven].

(28–32) And may you know, my lord, that your cities and your storehouses are burned [with] fire.

33) [*a-nu-*]⌜*ma*⌝
34) [..........]⌜*a*⌝?-*na-ki-*[*am*?]
35) [..............]*ù*[............]
36) [.............................]
37) [.............................]
38) [..............................]
39) [..............................]
40) [..............................]
Left 41) [...........*r*]*a-b*[*i-*]*ṣa* ⌜*šum*⌝-*ma*
side 42) [.............*r*]*a* ⌜*be*⌝[...]*is*
43) [........................]*ḫi*

(33–43) [No]w [...h]ere [...com]missioner if [...(too broken for translation)].

EA 307

TRANSCRIPTION

Obv.	01’)	⌊7-*šu ù*] 7-[*ta-a-an*]
	02’)	[*iš*]-⸢*ti*⸣-*ḫa-ḫi-in*
	03’)	*a-nu-ma a-na-ṣa-ru*
	04’)	URU.KI *ša* LUGAL
	05’)	⸢*ša*⸣ *it-ti-ia*
	06’)	⸢*ù*⸣ *lu-ú yi-de-*⸢*mì*⸣
Lo.ed.	07’)	L[UGAL] *be-lí-ia*
Rev.	08’)	[*i-nu-*]*ma* ⸢*da*⸣-*an-nu*
	09’)	[LÚ.MEŠ SA.]G[AZ].MEŠ
	10’)	⸢UGU⸣-*nu ù*
	11’)	[*lu-*]⸢*ú*⸣ *yi-de-mì*
	12’)	[LUGAL] *a-na* KUR.K[I-*šu*]

EA 307

TRANSLATION

(1'–2') [seven times and]seven [times] have [I] prostrated myself.

(3'–12') Now I am guarding the city of the king which is in my charge and may my lord be apprised [th]at the *ʿap*[*îru* men] are strong against us so may [the king] be apprised concerning [his] land.

EA 308

TRANSCRIPTION

Obv. 00) [.....................]
01) [*ep-ri ša*] ⸢GÌR⸣.[MEŠ]-[*k*]*a*$_4$
02) [LÚ *kàr-tap-p*]*í* ⸢*ša*⸣ ANŠE.KUR.⸢RA⸣.⸢MEŠ⸣-*ka*$_4$
03) [*a-na* G]ÌR.⸢MEŠ⸣ ⸢LUGAL⸣ E[N]-*ia*
04) [DINGIR.MEŠ]-⸢*ia*⸣ [^{d}UTU]-⸢*ia*⸣ ^{d}U[TU]
05) [*ša*] ⸢*iš*⸣-[*tu* AN] *ša*$_{10}$-*mì-i*
06) [7]-*šu* [*ù* 7-]⸢*ta*⸣-⸢*a*⸣-⸢*an*⸣
07) [*l*]*u-ú iš-t*[*a-ḫa-*]⸢*ḫi*⸣-⸢*in*⸣
08) [.....] traces [........]

Rev. 01) [.....] traces [........]
02) *aš-šum la-ma-*⸢*ad*⸣
03) [LUGAL] EN-*ia* ⸢^{d}⸣⸢UTU⸣-[*ia*]
04) ⸢*aš*⸣-⸢*šum*⸣ *na-da-*⸢*an*⸣
05) ANŠE.KUR.RA.MEŠ *a-*⸢*na*⸣ ÌR-⸢*ka*$_4$⸣
06) ⸢*a*⸣-⸢*na*⸣ *na-ṣa-ri* [*ma-ṣ*]*a-a*[*r-ti*]
07) [LUG]AL EN-*ia* ⸢^{d}⸣[UTU]
08) *ša iš-*⸢*tu*⸣ ⸢AN⸣ [*š*]*a*$_{10}$-⸢*mì*⸣-⸢*i*⸣
09) *u a-na* ⸢*iz*⸣*-ze-e*[*b*]

EA 308

TRANSLATION

(0) [Speak to the king, my lord, my deity, my sun god, the sun god from heaven, the message of…your servant,]

(1–7) [the dirt under] your fe[et], [the groo]m of your horses: [At the fe]et of the king, my lo[rd, my [deity], my [sun god], the su[n god who] is fro[m he]aven, [seven] times [and seven] times, have I [v]erily pro[str]ated.

(1–9) […]in order that [the king], my lord, [my] sun god, may learn, in order to give horses to your servant to protect the [garr]ison of [the ki]ng, my lord, the sun god from [h]eaven, in order to "save"(?) [the city of the king, my lord…]

EA 309

TRANSCRIPTION

Obv. 01) ⌜*a*⌝-⌜*na*⌝ ^{I}LU[GA]L [EN-*ia*]
02) DINGIR.MEŠ-*ia*[^{d}UTU-*ia*]
03) ^{d}UTU ⌜*ša*⌝ [*iš-tu* AN *ša*$_{10}$-*mì*]
04) *um-ma* ^{I}[.................]
05) ⌜*ša*⌝[....................]
06) [.......................]
07) [.......................]
08) [.......................]
09) [.......................]
10) [.......................]
11) [.......................]
12) [.......................]
13) [.......................]
14) [.......................]
15) [.......................]
Rev. 16) [.......................]
17) [.......................]
18) [..] *be-l*[*í-ia*............]
19) [—*k*]*i ša* [................]
20) [*a-n*]*a* ÌR.MEŠ TUR [......]
21) ⌜*ù*⌝ 1 *m*[*e*] KÙ.BABB[AR.MEŠ]
22) [*a-n*]*a* LUGAL EN-*i*[*a*]
23) 10 ÌR.⌜MEŠ⌝ ⌜*ù*⌝
24) 10 MUNUS.GÉME.MEŠ [....]
25) *ù aš-šum-*⌜*ma*⌝
26) *la-ma-ad* LU[GAL]
27) EN-*ia* ^{d}UTU *š*[*a*]
28) *iš-tu* A[N] *š*[*a*$_{10}$-*mì*]

———

EA 309

TRANSLATION

(1–4) To the ki[n]g, [my lord,] my deity, [my sun god], the sun god who [is from heaven]; the message of [......]

(5–17) [*About nine or ten lines missing from the obverse and the lower edge; two lines missing from the reverse*]

(18–24) [...my] lo[rd...]which[...fo]r young slaves [...]and one hund[red] shekels of silv[er fo]r the king, m[y] lord. Ten slaves and ten handmaidens [...].

(25–28) So for the information of the ki[ng], my lord, the sun god w[ho] is from he[aven].

EA 310

TRANSCRIPTION

Obv. 01) [..................]⸢*in*⸣
02) [................*r*]*i*(?)
03) [...............*a*-]*nu-ma*
04) [*a-na-ṣa-ru* URU.K]I
05) [LUGAL EN-*ia ša*]⸢*it*⸣-⸢*ti*⸣-⸢*ia*⸣
06) [..................]*mi*
07) [*ù yu-uš-ši-ra-a*]*m*(?) LUGAL
08) [EN-*ia a-na*] ⸢*ia-ši*⸣
Lo.ed. 09) [..............]*mì*
Rev. 10) ⸢*ù*⸣[...] ⸢*a*⸣-[*nu-ma*]
11) [....]*a*-⸢*wa*⸣-⸢*te*⸣^{MEŠ}
12) [LUGAL EN-*ia*] ^{d}[UTU]
13) [*iš-t*]*u* AN [*ša*$_{10}$]-⸢*mì*⸣-⸢*i*⸣
14) [......]⸢*mì*⸣
15) [.....*i-la-k*]*a-am*
16) [........ [traces
17) [........]traces

EA 310

TRANSLATION

Obv. (01) [……………………]?
(02) [………………]?
(03) […………..n]ow
(04) [I am guarding the cit]y
(05) [of the king, my lord that is] in my charge
(06) [………………]?
(07–08) [So may] the king, [my lord, sen]d [to] me

Lo.ed. (09) […………..]?
Rev. (10) and n[ow]
(11) [….]the words of
(12) [the king, my lord, the] s[un god]
(13) [from] heaven
(14) [……]?
(15) [shall I g]o(?)
(16) [……..]*traces*
(17) [……..]*traces*

EA 311

TRANSCRIPTION

Obv. 01) [*a-na* LUGAL EN-*ia*]
02) ^{d}UTU[-*ia*............]
03) [....................]
04) [....................]
05) [....................]
06) [.................*ep-r*]*i*
07) [*ša* 2 GÌR.]⸢MEŠ⸣-*ka*
08) [LÚ *ku*$_{8}$-*sí*] ⸢ANŠE⸣.⸢KUR⸣.⸢RA⸣.[MEŠ-*ka*]
09) [*a-na* 2 GÌR.MEŠ] LUGAL
10) [EN-*i*]*a* ⸢^{d}⸣⸢UTU⸣ *ša*
11) [*iš*-]⸢*tu*⸣ ⸢AN⸣ [*ša*$_{10}$-]-*mì*
12) [7]-⸢*šu*⸣ ⸢*ù*⸣ ⸢7⸣-⸢*ta*⸣-⸢*a*⸣-⸢*an*⸣
13) [*iš-ta-ḫ*]*a-ḫ*[*i*-]*i*[*n*]
14) [*iš-te-*]⸢*me a*-⸢*wa*⸣[-*ti*]
15) [.................] x M[EŠ]
Rev. 16) [....................]
17) *a-na-ṣa-ru* U[RU.KI]
18) [LUGAL] ⸢*ša*⸣ *it-t*[*i-ia*]
19) [....................]

EA 311

TRANSLATION

(1–13) [To the king, my lord, my] sun god [...the di]rt[beneath] your [two feet, the groom of your] hors[es. I have prostr]a[ted myself at the feet] of the king, [my] lord, the Sun fr]o[m heaven, [seven ti]mes and seven times. [I have heard] the wor[ds...].

(14–19) [.......] I am guarding the city [of the king] that is in [my] charge.

EA 312

TRANSCRIPTION

Obv. 01) [*a-na* LUGAL EN-*ia*]
02) [*um-ma*...........]
03) [ÌR-*ka*...*ep*-]*ri*[*ša*]
04) [GÌR.]⌜MEŠ⌝-*k*[*a*]
05) ⌜*ù*⌝ LÚ*k*[*u-sí*]
06) [*ša* ANŠE.KUR.]RA.MEŠ-*k*[a]
07) [*a-na* GÌR.]MEŠ ⌜LU[GA]L [EN-*ia*]
08) [..............................]
09) [..............................]
10) [*ù li-i*]*l-ma-ad*
11) [LUGAL EN-*ia*] ⌜*i*⌝-*nu-ma*
12) [*ṣa-ab-t*]*a-at*
13) [URU EN]-*ia*
14) [URU.....]⌜*nu*⌝-*na*[KI]

Lo.ed. [..........]...*u*

Rev. 15) [.............]-ka_4
16) [.....] *u aš-šum*
17) [*la-ma-d*]*i* L[UG]AL
18) [*be-lí-*]*ia* ⌜*li*⌝-⌜*di*⌝-⌜*na*⌝
19) [...*š*]*a*-[*r*]*a*-[*š*]*u*]
20) [.........]*a ù*
21) [..............................]
22) [..............................]
23) [..............................]
24) [..............................]
25) [..............................]
26) [..............................]
27) [..............................]

EA 312

TRANSLATION

Obv. (01) [To the king, my lord]
(02) [The message of..........]
(03) [your servant and the di]rt[of]
(04) [your feet,] and the g[room(?)]
(05) [of]y[our hor]ses
(06) [At the feet] the ki[ng, [my lord]
(07) [..............................]
(08) [..............................]
(09) [..............................]
(10) [So may] be informed
(11) [the king, my lord] that
(12) [seiz]ed
(13) [is the city of] my [lord]
(14) [the city of...]nuna
Lo.ed. [..........]...and
Rev. (15) [............]of yours
(16) [.....] and in order
(17) t[o infor]m the k[in]g,
(18) my [lord]. May he grant
(19) [...]his breath [...]
(20) [.........]and
(21) [..............................]
(22) [..............................]
(23) [..............................]
(24) [..............................]
(25) [..............................]
(26) [..............................]
(27) [..............................]

EA 313

TRANSCRIPTION

Obv. 01') [.........]*ka*
02') 13 LÚ.MEŠ DA[M.GÀR.MEŠ]
03') *ša* KUR *Mi-iṣ-*⸢*ri*⸣^{KI}
04') *ša mì-iḫ-ṣú-mì*
05') *i-na na-ma-aš*
06') LÚ.SA.GAZ.MEŠ
07') *at-ta-din* 4 *me* KÙ.BABBAR.MEŠ
08') UGU 1 *li-mì*^{MEŠ}
09') *a-na qa-ti ša*
Lo.ed. 10') ^{LÚ}*ra-bi-ṣí* ⸢LUGAL⸣
Rev. 11') *ša* UGU-*ia* ›*ù*‹
12') *ù* LÚ.MEŠ *ša ip-pu-šu*
13') *ip-*⸢*ša*⸣*-*⸢*am*⸣ *an-nu-ú*
14') *id-din-*⸢*šu*⸣*-*⸢*nu*⸣ ^{d}UTU
15') *i-*⸢*na*⸣ ⸢*ša!*⸣*-*⸢*ri*⸣ *ša*
16') LU[G]AL ⸢*da*⸣*-na-ti*
17') ⸢*ù*⸣ *lu-*⸢*ú*⸣*-mì* 2 ÌR.MEŠ
18') [*ša* LUG]AL *la-a*
19') [..] *mì-iḫ-*⸢*ṣú*⸣*-*⸢*mì*⸣
20') traces

Lft.ed. [.............]*ti*

EA 313

TRANSLATION

(1'–11') [.....] your [...] thirteen mer[chants] of the land of Egypt who were smitten in the attack of the *'apîru*, I have given four hundred shekels over and above the thousand, into the hand of the commissioner of the king who is over me.

(12'–19') And as for the men who did this deed, may the sun god give them to the mighty breath of the king and may the two servants [of the ki]ng not [...] they were smitten [...]

EA 314

TRANSCRIPTION

Obv. 01) *a-na* ^{I}LUGAL EN-*ia* DINGIR.MEŠ-*ia*
02) ^{d}UTU-*ia* ^{d}UTU *ša iš-tu*
03) AN *ša*$_{10}$-*mì um-ma* ^{I}*Pu*-^{d}IŠKUR
04) ÌR-*ka* LÚ *ša* URU *Yu-ur-za*^{KI}
05) *a-na* 2 GÌR.MEŠ LUGAL EN-*ia*
06) DINGIR.MEŠ-*ia* ^{d}UTU-*ia* ^{d}UTU
07) *ša iš-tu* AN *ša*$_{10}$-*mì lu-ú*
08) *iš-ta-ḫa-ḫi-in* 7-*šu*
09) *ù* 7-*ta-na ṣe-ru-ma*
10) *ù ka-ba-tu-na*
11) *a-nu-ma i-na-ṣa-ru a-šar*
12) [L]UGAL ⌜EN⌝-‹*ia*› ^{d}UTU-*ia* ^{d}UTU
13) [*š*]*a iš-tu* AN.MEŠ *ša*$_{10}$-*mì*
14) [*mì-i*]*a-mì* LÚ.UR.G[U]
15) [*ù la y*]*i*[-*i*]*š*-[*te-mu*]
Lo.ed. 16) [*a-wa-te* LUGAL ^{d}]U[TU *ša* AN *ša*$_{10}$]-*mì*
17) [*i-nu-ma iq-t*]*a*[-*bi*]
Rev. 18) [LUGAL EN-*ia*]
19) [*a-na* N]A$_{4}$.[M]EŠ *eḫ-li*-⌜*pa*⌝

\-*ak-ku*

20) [*u*]*š-ši-ir-ti*
21) *a-na* LUGAL EN-*ia* DINGIR.MEŠ-*ia*
22) ^{d}UTU *ša* AN.ME[Š] *ša*$_{10}$-[*mì*]

EA 314

TRANSLATION

(1–10) To the king, my lord, my deity, my sun god, the sun god from heaven; the message of Pu-Baʿlu, your servant, the ruler of Yurza: at the two feet of the king, my lord, my deity, my sun god, the sun god who is from heaven, I have verily prostrated myself seven times and seven times, on the back and on the stomach.

(11–13) Now I am guarding the place of the [k]ing, ‹my› lord, my sun god, the sun god [w]ho is from heaven.

(14–16) [Wh]o is the do[g] that he [would] not [he]ed [the words of the king,] the s[un god of hea]ven.

(17–22) [Inasmuch as the king, my lord sp]o[ke about st]ones of raw glass, I have sent to the king, my lord, my deity, the sun god of heav[en].

EA 315

TRANSCRIPTION

Obv. 01) [*a-na* LUGA]L ⸢EN⸣-*ia* DINGIR.MEŠ -*ia*
02) ^{d}⸢UTU⸣ *ša iš-tu* AN *ša*$_{10}$-*mí*
03) *um-ma* ^{I}*Pu*-^{d}IŠKUR LÚ *ša* URU *Yu-ur-za* ^{KI}
04) ÌR-*ka ep-ri ša* 2 GÌR.MEŠ-*ka*
05) ⸢*a*⸣-⸢*na*⸣ 2 GÌR.⸢MEŠ⸣ LUGAL EN-*ia lu-ú*
06) *iš-ta-ḫa-*⸢*ḫi*⸣-*in* 7-*it-šu*
07) *ù* 7-*ta-na ṣe-ru-ma u ka-*⸢*ba*⸣-⸢*tu*⸣-⸢*ma*⸣

---

08) *a-nu-ma i-na-ṣa-ru* URU.KI *ša* LUGAL ⸢EN⸣-⸢*ia*⸣
09) *u a-šar* LUGAL EN-⸢*ia*⸣ ^{d}UTU *ša iš-*⸢*tu*⸣ ⸢AN⸣ ⸢ *ša*$_{10}$⸣-⸢*mì*⸣
10) *mi-im-ma ša qa-ba* LUGAL EN-*ia*
11) *a-nu-ma i-na-*⸢*ṣa*⸣-*ru* KAM^{v}.UD
12) *u mu-*⸢*ša*⸣ *a-wa-ta*$_{5}$ LUGAL EN-*i*⸢*a*⸣ (*ta*$_{5}$ error for *te*)

---

13) ^{I}⸢*Re*⸣-*a-na-pa* LÚ.MÁŠKIM *ša*
14) [LUGA]L⸢EN⸣‹-*ia*› *ša qa-ba* LUGAL EN-*ia*
15) [*da*]*m-qá ki-ma* ^{d}UTU *i-na* AN *ša*$_{10}$-*mí*
16) [*mi-i*]*a-mi* LÚ UR!(UŠ).GI$_{7}$!(GU) *u la-a*
17) [*yi-n*]*a-ṣa-ru a-wa-te* LUGAL EN-*ia*
18) [^{d}UTU *š*]*a* ⸢*iš*⸣-⸢*tu*⸣ AN *ša*$_{10}$-*mì*

EA 315

TRANSLATION

(1–7) [To the kin]g, my lord, my deity, the sun god from heaven, the message of Pu-Baʿlu, the ruler of the city of Yurza, your servant, the dirt at your two feet: At the two feet of the king, my lord, have I verily prostrated seven times and seven times on the back and on the stomach.

(8–12) Now, I am guarding the city of the king, my lord and the place (shrine?) of the king, my lord, the sun god from heaven. As for everything which the king, my lord, said, I am keeping day and night the words(!) of the king, my lord.

(13–18) Reʿanapa, the commissioner of [the kin]g, ‹my› lord, whom the king, my lord, commanded, is [fi]ne like the sun god in heaven. [Wh]o is the dog that would not [ke]ep the words of the king, my lord, [the sun] from heaven?

EA 316

TRANSCRIPTION

Obv. 01) [*a-na* LUGA]L ⌜EN⌝-⌜*ia*⌝ ⌜DINGIR⌝.⌜MEŠ⌝[-*ia*]

02) [^{d}]UTU-*ia iš*[-*t*]*u* AN *š*[*a*$_{10}$-*mi*]

03) [*um*]-*ma* ^{I}*Pu*-⌜^{d}⌝⌜IŠKUR⌝ ÌR-[*ka*]

04) [*u* SAHA]R ⌜*ép*⌝-⌜*ri*⌝ ⌜*ša*⌝ 2 GÌR.⌜MEŠ⌝-⌜*ka*⌝

05) ⌜LÚ⌝ \ [*ku*]$_{8}$-sí ⌜*ša*⌝ ANŠE.KUR.RA.⌜MEŠ⌝.⌜KUR⌝.⌜RI⌝-⌜*ka*⌝

06) *a*[-*n*]*a* ⌜2⌝ ⌜GÌR⌝.MEŠ LUGAL ⌜EN⌝-*ia* DINGIR.⌜MEŠ⌝-⌜*ia*⌝

07) ⌜^{d}⌝⌜UTU⌝-⌜*ia*⌝ ⌜*iš*⌝-⌜*tu*⌝ AN *ša*$_{10}$-*mi*

08) ⌜7⌝-*šu u* ⌜7⌝-*ta* ⌜*am*⌝-*qú-ut*

09) ⌜*ṣe*⌝-*ru*-⌜*ma*⌝ \ *u ka-íb-tù*-⌜*ma*⌝

10) [*a*]-⌜*nu*⌝-⌜*ma*⌝ ⌜*i*⌝-⌜*na*⌝-*ṣa-ru a*[-*šar*]

11) *š*[*àr-r*]*i* ⌜*ma*⌝-⌜*gal*⌝ ⌜*u*⌝ ⌜*mi*⌝-*ia-mi*

12) [LÚ] ⌜UR⌝.GU ⌜*ša*⌝ ⌜*yi*⌝-⌜*im*⌝-*ta-ku*$_{8}$

13) ⌜DUG$_{4}$⌝.⌜GAR⌝.⌜RA⌝ ⌜LUGAL⌝ *a*-⌜*nu*⌝-*ma*

14) ⌜*iš*⌝[-*te*-]⌜*mu*⌝ *a-wa-te*⌜^{MEŠ}⌝?

15) [^{I}*Ta*]*ḫ-m*[*a-i*]*a* ⌜LÚ⌝ ⌜GIR$_{5}$⌝+PA ⌜*ša*⌝ ⌜LUGAL⌝

——— ————

Rev. 16) [*a-n*]*a* ^{I}*ša-aḫ-ši-ḫa-ši*-⌜*ḫa*⌝ [EN-*ia*] (**Kn.**)

17) *um-ma* ^{I}*Pu*-⌜^{d}⌝⌜IŠKUR⌝ ⌜*a*⌝-⌜*na*⌝ ⌜2⌝ ⌜GÌR⌝.⌜MEŠ⌝-*ka* ⌜*am*⌝[-*qú-ut*]

18) ⌜*i*⌝-*ia*-⌜*nu*⌝ ⌜*mi*⌝-⌜*im*⌝-⌜*ma*⌝

19) ⌜*i*⌝-[*n*]*a* ⌜É⌝-*ia i-n*[*a*]

20) [*i*]-*re*[-*bi*-]⌜*i*⌝*a a*-[*na*] ⌜*ša*⌝-⌜*šu*⌝

21) ⌜*u*⌝ ⌜*ki*⌝-*na-na la*-[*a*] *uš-ši-ir*-[*t*]*i*$_{7}$

22) KASKAL-*ra*-⌜*na*⌝ *a-na k*[*a-ta*]$_{5}$

23) *a-nu-ma i*-⌜*šu*⌝[-*ši*-]*ru*

24) KASKAL-*ra-na dam*-⌜*qá*⌝-*ta*

25) ⌜*a*⌝-⌜*na*⌝ *ka-ta*$_{5}$

EA 316

TRANSLATION

(1–9) [To the kin]g, my lord, [my] deity, the sun fr[o]m hea[ven], the [mess]age of Pu-Baʿlu, [your] servant, [and the d]irt at your feet, the [gr]oom of your horses. [A]t the feet of the king, my lord, my deity, my sun god from heaven, seven times and seven times have I fallen on the back and on the stomach.

(10–13) [N]ow, I am guarding carefully the pl[ace] of th[e ki]ng, my lord. And who is the dog that would neglect the command(?) of the king?

(13–15) Now, I am o[be]ying the words of [Ta]ḫm[ay]a, the commissioner(!) of the king.

(16–25) [T]o the scribe of letters [of my lord], the message of Pu-Baʿlu: At your feet have I fa[llen]. There was nothing i[n] my house upo[n] my [e]nt[ering] it and therefore I did not send a caravan to y[ou]. Now I am preparing a nice caravan for you.

EA 317

TRANSCRIPTION

Obv. 01) ⸢*a*⸣-*na* LUGAL GAL *be-li-i*⸢*a*⸣
02) ^{Id}*Da-ga-an-ta-ka-la*
03) ÌR-*ka iq-bi*
04) 7-*šu ù* 7-*šu*-⸢*ma*⸣
05) ⸢*a*⸣-⸢*na*⸣ 2 GÌR LUGAL GAL *be-li-ia*
06) ⸢*im*⸣-*qú-ut*

---

07) *ú i-na-na a-na* LUGAL GAL
08) *be-li-ia*
09) $^{⸢I⸣}$⸢*Da*⸣-⸢*ga*⸣-⸢*an*⸣-⸢*ta*⸣-*ka-l*[*a*]
10) ÌR-*ka a*[*-nu-m*]*a a-wa-ti*
11) LUGAL GAL *be-li-ia*
12) *iš-mé da-ni-iš*
13) $^{⸢I⸣}$⸢*Da*⸣-*ga-an-ta-ka-la*
14) [*i*]*q-bi ki-ma a-bi-ia*
15) [*ú a-b*]*i a-bi-ia-ma*

Lo. ed.

Rev. 16) [*ti*]-*pu-šu a-na* LUGAL GAL
17) ⸢*a*⸣-*na-ku a-na* LUGAL GAL
18) *be-li-ia i-p*[*u*]-⸢*uš*⸣
19) *ú* LUGAL GAL *be-li-ia*
20) *iq-bi a-na ia-ši*
21) *ši-mé-ma a-na* LÚ.⸢MÁŠKIM⸣ ⸢*ḫa*⸣-*za-ni-ka*
22) *a*-⸢*na*⸣-[*k*]*u* ⸢*iš*⸣-*mé*-⸢*ma*⸣ *da-ni-iš*
23) *ù šum*-⸢*ma*⸣ *la*-⸢*a*⸣
24) *iš-mé a-na* LÚ *ḫa*-⸢*za*⸣-⸢*ni*⸣
25) *ú šu-ut i-de*$_4$*-ma*

EA 317

TRANSLATION

(1–6) Dagantakala, your servant, spoke to the great king, my lord: Seven times and seven times at the feet of the great king, my lord, have I fallen.

(7–10) And now, Dagantakala, your servant, belongs to the great king, my lord.

(10–12) N[ow], I have listened carefully to the words of the great king, my lord.

(13–18) Dagantakala spoke: "As my father [and the fath]er of my father [a]cted towards the great king, I will act towards the great king, my lord."

(19–22) And the great king, my lord, said to me, "Listen to your commissioner." I listened carefully.

(23–25) And if I did not listen to the commissioner then he will know it.

EA 318

TRANSCRIPTION

Obv. 01) *a-na* LUGAL GAL *be-li-*[*ia*]
02) ^{d}UTU *a-na ša-mi*
03) ^{Id}*Da-ga-an-ta-k*[*a-la*]
04) ÌR-*ka iq-bi*
05) 7-*šu ù* 7-*šu-ma*
06) *a-na* 2 GÌR LUGAL GAL
07) *be-li-ia im-qú-ut*
08) *še-zi-ba-an-ni*
09) *iš-tu* KÚR.MEŠ *da-a*[*n*]-⸢*nu*⸣-⸢*ti*⸣-⸢*ia*⸣
10) *iš-tu* ŠU *qa-ti*
11) LÚ.MEŠ.SA.GA.⸢AZ⸣.⸢MEŠ⸣
12) LÚ.MEŠ *ḫa-ba-ti*
13) *ù* LÚ.MEŠ *Šu-ti-i*
14) *ù še-zi-ba-*⸢*an*⸣-⸢*ni*⸣
15) ⸢LUGAL⸣ GAL *be-*⸢*li*⸣-⸢*ia*⸣
Rev. 16) ⸢*ù*⸣ *a-*⸢*mu*⸣-⸢*ur*⸣-⸢*mi*⸣
17) *al-tap-ra* ⸢*a*⸣-⸢*na*⸣ ⸢KÚR⸣.⸢MEŠ⸣-⸢*ia*⸣
18) ⸢*ù*⸣ ⸢*at*⸣-⸢*ta*⸣ ⸢LUGAL⸣ ⸢GAL⸣
19) ⸢*be*⸣-⸢*li*⸣-⸢*ia*⸣
20) ⸢*tu*⸣-⸢*še*⸣-⸢*ze*⸣-⸢*ba*⸣-⸢*an*⸣-⸢*ni*⸣
21) ⸢*ù*⸣ ⸢*i*⸣-⸢*na*⸣-⸢*ma*⸣-⸢*a*⸣-⸢*šu*⸣!
22) ⸢*a*⸣-⸢*na*⸣ ⸢LUGAL⸣ ⸢GAL⸣ *be-*⸢*li*⸣-⸢*ia*⸣

EA 318

TRANSLATION

(1–7) Dagantak[ala] your servant said to the great king, [my] lord, the sun god from heaven: Seven times and seven times at the feet of the great king, my lord, have I fallen.

(8–15) Deliver me from my powerful enemies, from the hand of the *ʿapîru* men, the robbers and the Sutû; so deliver me, oh great king, my lord!

(16–22) And look, I have written about ⌜my⌝ enemies. So you, oh great king, my lord, can deliver me so that I can depart to the great king, my lord.

EA 319

TRANSCRIPTION

Obv. 01) [*a-na* LUGAL] *be-lí-*⸢*ia*⸣ D[INGI]R.[ME]Š-⸢*i*⸣*a*
02) ^{d}[UTU-*ia*] ^{d}UTU *ša iš-tu*
03) AN [*ša*$_{10}$*-mì*]*-i um-ma*
04) ^{I}*Sú-*⸢*ra*⸣*-šar*
05) LÚ *ša* URU ⸢*Gin*$_{8}$⸣*-ti-aš-na*
06) ÌR-*ka-ma ep-ri ša*
07) UZU.GÌR.MEŠ-*ka* LÚ
08) *kàr-tap-pí* ⸢*ša*⸣ ANŠE.KUR.RA.⸢MEŠ⸣-*ka*$_{4}$
09) *a-na* 2 GÌR.MEŠ LUGAL EN-*ia*
10) DINGIR.MEŠ-*ia* ^{d}UTU-*ia* ^{d}UTU
11) *ša iš-tu* AN *ša*$_{10}$*-mì-i*
12) 7-⸢*šu*⸣ ⸢*u*⸣ ⸢7⸣*-ta-*⸢*a*⸣*-an*
13) *lu-ú iš-*⸢*ta*⸣*-*⸢*ḫa*⸣*-ḫi-in*
14) *ka-bat-*⸢*tu*$_{4}$⸣ ⸢*u*⸣ *ṣé-ru-ma*
15) ⸢*a*⸣*-*⸢*nu*⸣*-ma iš-te*$_{9}$*-me*
16) ⸢*a*⸣*-*⸢*na*⸣ *a-wa-te*^{MEŠ}

Lo.ed. 17) [LÚ].⸢MÁŠKIM⸣ *ša* LUGAL
18) ⸢EN⸣-*ia ma-gal ma-gal*

Rev. 19) ⸢*u*⸣ *ma-an-*⸢*nu*⸣*-me* ⸢LÚ⸣ ⸢*kal*⸣*-*⸢*bu*⸣
20) *ša la-a yi-iš-*⸢*mu*⸣
21) *a-na a-wa-te*^{MEŠ} LUGAL
22) EN-*šu* ^{d}UTU *ša iš-*⸢*tu*⸣
23) AN *ša*$_{10}$*-mì-i* DUMU ^{d}UTU

EA 319

TRANSLATION

(1–14) [To the king,] my lord, my d[eit]y, my sun god, the sun god from [heav]en; the message of Surashar, the ruler of the town of Ginti-Ashna, your servant, the dirt under your feet, the squire of your horses: At the feet of the king, my lord, my deity, my sun god, the sun god from heaven, seven times and seven times have I verily prostrated, on the belly and on the back.

(15–23) Now I have listened to the words of the commissioner of the king, my lord, very diligently. And who is the dog that would not listen to the words of the king, his lord, the sun god from heaven, the son of the sun god?

EA 320

TRANSCRIPTION

Obv.
01) [*a*]-*na* ^{I}LUGAL EN-*ia*
02) DINGIR.MEŠ-*ia* ^{d}UTU-*ia*
03) ^{d}UTU *ša* ⌜*iš*⌝-*tu*
04) AN *ša*$_{10}$-*me*-⌜*e*⌝ *um-ma*
05) ^{I}*Yi-id-ia* LÚ
06) *ša* URU *Aš-qa-lu-na*^{KI}
07) ÌR-*ka*$_{4}$ *ep-ri ša*
08) UZU.GÌR.MEŠ-*ka*$_{4}$ LÚ
09) *kàr-tap-pí ša* ANSE.KUR.RA-*ka*$_{4}$
10) *a-na* UZU.GÌR.MEŠ LUGAL
11) *be-lí-ia* 7-*šu u*
12) 7-*ta-a-an lu-ú*
13) *iš-ta-ḫa-ḫi-in*
14) *ka*-[*ba*]*t-tum-ma u*
15) ⌜*ṣe*⌝-*ru-ma*
16) ⌜*a*⌝-*nu-ma a-na-ṣa-r*[*u*]

Rev.
17) *a-šar* LUGAL *ša it-t*[*i-i*]*a*
18) *u mi-im-ma ša ša-pár*
19) L[UGAL] EN-*ia a-na ia-ši*
20) ⌜*iš*⌝-*te*$_{9}$-*mu-uš-šu*
21) ⌜*ma*⌝-*gal ma-gal*
22) *mi-ia-mì* LÚ *kal-bu*
23) *u la-a yi-iš-mu*
24) *a-na a-wa-te* LUGAL ⌜EN⌝-*šu*
25) DUMU ^{d}UTU

EA 320

TRANSLATION

(1–15) [T]o the king, my lord, my deity, my sun god, the sun god who is from heaven; the message of Yidia, the ruler of the city of Ashkelon, your servant, the dirt under your feet, the groom of your horse: At the feet of the king, my lord, seven times and seven times I have verily prostrated myself, on the stomach and on the back.

(16–21) Now I am guarding the place of the king that is in my charge. And as for everything that the king, my lord, has written to me, I am heeding it very diligently.

(22–25) Who is the dog that would not listen to the words of the king, his lord, the son of the sun god?

EA 321

TRANSCRIPTION

Obv. 01) [*a-n*]*a* ^{I}LUGAL EN-*ia*
02) DINGIR.M[EŠ]-⸢*i*⸣*a* ^{d}UTU-*ia*
03) ^{d}UTU ⸢*ša*⸣ *iš-tu*
04) AN *ša*$_{10}$-*mì* ⸢*um*⸣-*ma*
05) ^{I}*Yi-id*-⸢*ia*⸣ LÚ
06) *ša* ⸢URU⸣ ⸢*Aš*⸣-*qa-lu-na*
07) ÌR-⸢*ka*$_{4}$⸣ ⸢*ep*⸣-*ra* ⸢*ša*⸣
08) 2 ⸢GÌR⸣.⸢MEŠ⸣-*ka*$_{4}$ [LÚ *kàr*]-⸢*tap*⸣-⸢*pí*⸣
09) ⸢*ša*⸣ ANŠE.KUR.[RA].⸢MEŠ⸣-*ka*$_{4}$
10) *a-na* 2 GÌR.MEŠ ⸢LUGAL⸣ EN-*ia*
11) ^{d}UTU *ša iš-tu*
12) AN *ša*$_{10}$-*mì-i* 7-*šu*
13) *u* 7-*ta-a-an*
14) *lu-ú iš-ta-ḫa-ḫi-in*
Lo.ed. 15) LÚ.‹MÁ›ŠKIM \ *ra-bi-iṣ*
Rev. 16) *ša* LUGAL EN-*ia*
17) *ša iš-tap-ra-am*
18) LUGAL EN-*ia* ^{d}UTU
19) *iš-tu* AN *ša*$_{10}$-*mì*
20) *a-na ia-a-ši*
21) *iš-te*$_{9}$-*me*
22) [*a*]-⸢*wa*⸣-›*wa*‹-*te*$^{⸢MEŠ⸣}$-*šu*
23) [*ma*]-*gal ma-gal*

---

24) [*u*] ⸢*a*⸣-*nu-ma a-na-ṣa-ru*
25) [*aš*]-⸢*ri*⸣ LUGAL *ša*
26) [*it*]-*ti-ia*

EA 321

TRANSLATION

(1–14) [T]o the king, my lord, my deity, my sun god, the sun god from heaven, the message of Yidia, the ruler of the city of Ashkelon, your servant, the dirt that is under your two feet, [the gr]oom of your horses: At the two feet of the king, my lord, the sun god from heaven, seven times and seven times have I verily prostrated.

(15–23) As for the commissioner of the king, my lord, which the king, my lord, the sun god from heaven sent here to me, I have heeded his [wo]rds [ve]ry carefully.

(24–26) [And] now I am guarding the [pl]aces of the king which are in my charge.

EA 322

TRANSCRIPTION

Obv. 01) *a-na* ^{I}L[UGAL E]N-*ia* DIN[GIR.MEŠ-*i*]*a*
02) ^{d}UTU-[*i*]*a* ^{d}UTU *ša*
03) *iš-t*[*u* AN] *ša*$_{10}$*-mì*
04) *u*[*m-m*]*a* ^{I}*Y*[*i-i*]*d-ia* LÚ
05) *ša* U[R]U *A*[*š-q*]*a-lu-na*^{KI}
06) ÌR-*k*[*a ep-r*]*i ša*
07) UZU.G[ÌR.MEŠ-*k*]*a*
08) ⸢LÚ⸣ *k*[*àr-tap-p*]*í ša* ANSE.KUR.RA-*ka*
09) *a-na* G[ÌR.MEŠ L]UGAL EN-*ia*
10) ^{d}UTU *ša iš-tu* AN *ša*$_{10}$*-mì*
11) 7-*šu u* 7-*ta-a-an*
12) ⸢*lu*⸣-*ú iš-ta-ḫa-ḫi-in*
13) ^{UZU}*ka-bat-tum-ma*
14) *u* ^{UZU}*ṣe-ru-ma*
15) *a-nu-ma a-na-ṣa-ru-mì*
16) *aš-ri* LUGAL *ša it-ti-ia*
17) *u ma-an-nu* LÚ *kal-bu*

Rev. 18) *ša la-a yi-i*[*š-m*]*u*
19) *a-na* LÚ.MÁŠKIM LUGAL
20) *a-nu-ma iš-te*$_{9}$*-ma-aš-šu*
21) *ma-gal ma-gal*
22) *a-na* ^{I}LÚ.MÁŠKIM *ša* LUGAL
23) *be-li-ia* DUMU ^{d}UTU
24) *ša iš-tu* AN *ša*$_{10}$*-mì-i*

EA 322

TRANSLATION

(1–14) To the k[ing,] my [lo]rd, my dei[ty], [m]y sun god, the sun god who is fro[m] heaven; the me[ssag]e of Y[i]dia, the ruler of the c[it]y of A[shk]elon, yo[ur] servant, [the dir]t under your feet, the g[roo]m of your horse: At the feet of the king, my lord, the sun god who is from heaven, seven times and seven times, I have verily prostrated myself on the stomach and on the back.

(15–16) Now I am guarding the places of the king that are in my charge.

(17–19) But who is the dog that would not li[sten] to the commissioner of the king?

(21–24) Now I am heeding him very diligently, viz. to the commissioner of the king, my lord, the son of the sun god who is from heaven.

EA 323

TRANSCRIPTION

Obv. 01) ⸢*a*⸣-*na* ^{I}LUGAL EN-*ia* DINGIR.MEŠ-*ia*
02) ^{d}UTU-*ia* ^{d}UTU *ša iš-tu*
03) AN *ša*$_{10}$-*mì um-ma* ^{I}*Yi-id-ia*
04) ÌR-*ka ep-ri ša* 2 GÌR.MEŠ-*ka*
05) LÚ *kàr-tap-pí ša* ANŠE.KUR.RA-*ka*
06) *a-na* 2 GÌR.MEŠ LUGAL EN-*ia lu-ú*
07) *iš-ta-ḫa-ḫi-in* 7-⸢*it*⸣-*šu*
08) *u* 7-*ta-na ṣe-ru-ma*
09) *u ka-ba-tu-ma a-nu-ma*
10) *i-na-ṣa*-⸢*ru*⸣ ⸢*a*⸣-*šar* LUGAL ⸢EN⸣-*ia*
11) *u* URU.KI LUGAL *ki-ma qa-bi*
12) LUGAL EN-*ia* ⸢^{d}⸣UTU *ša iš-tu*
13) AN ⸢*ša*$_{10}$⸣-*mì* ⸢*i*⸣-*nu-ma qa-ba*
14) LUGAL EN-*ia a-na* NA$_{4}$.MEŠ ⸢*eḫ*⸣-⸢*lu*⸣-⸢*pa*⸣-⸢*ak*⸣-*ku*
15) ⸢*a*⸣-*lu-ú uš-ši-ir-ti a-na* L[UGAL EN]-*ia*
16) 30(?) NA$_{4}$.MEŠ *eḫ-lu-pa-ak-k*[*u*]
Rev. 17) ⸢*ša*⸣-*ni-tam mi-ia-mi*
18) LÚ UR.GU *u la-a*
19) *yi-iš*-⸢*te*⸣-⸢*mu*⸣ *a-wa*-⸢*ta*$_{5}$⸣
20) LUGAL ⸢EN⸣-⸢*ia*⸣ ^{d}UTU *ša*
21) *iš*-⸢*tu*⸣ ⸢AN⸣ *ša*$_{10}$-*mì*
22) ⸢DUMU⸣ ⸢^{d}⸣⸢UTU⸣ ⸢*ša*⸣ *ti-ra-am*
23) ^{d}⸢UTU⸣

EA 323

TRANSLATION

(1–9) To the king, my lord, my deity, my sun god, the sun god from heaven, message of Yidia, your servant, the dirt at your feet, the groom of your horses: At the two feet of the king, my lord, I have verily prostrated myself seven times and seven times, on the back and on the stomach.

(9–13) Now, I am guarding the [p]lace (temple?) of the king, my lord, and the city of the king, just as the king, my lord, the sun god from heaven, has said.

(13–16) Inasmuch as the king, my lord, spoke about raw glass, behold, I have sent to the k[ing], my [lord], thirty(?) (pieces) of raw glass.

(17–23) Furthermore, who is the dog that he would not heed the word of the king, my lord, the sun god from heaven, the son of the sun god whom the sun god loves?

EA 324

TRANSCRIPTION

Obv. 01) ⸢*a*⸣-*na šàr-ri* EN-*ia*
02) ⸢^{d}⸣UTU-*ia* DINGIR.MEŠ-*ia* ^{d}UTU
03) ⸢*ša*⸣ ⸢*iš*⸣-*tu* AN *ša*$_{10}$-*mi*
04) *um-ma* ^{I}*Yi-id-ia* ÌR-[*k*]*a*
05) *ep-ri ša* 2 GÌR.MEŠ-*ka*
06) ^{LÚ}*kàr-tap-pí ša* 2 ANŠE.KUR.RA-*ka*
07) *a-na* 2 GÌR.MEŠ LUGAL EN-*ia*
08) *lu-ú iš-ta-ḫa-ḫi-in* 7-*šu ù* 7-*ta-na*
09) *ṣe-ru-ma ù ka-ba-tu*-⸢*ma*⸣
10) *a-nu-ma i-na-ṣa-ru a-wa-t*[*a*$_{5}$]
11) LUGAL EN-*ia* DUMU ^{d}UTU *ù*
12) *a-nu-ma šu-ši-ir-ti* NINDA.MEŠ
13) KAŠ.MEŠ Ì.MEŠ ŠE.MEŠ GU$_{4}$.MEŠ
14) ÙZ.MEŠ *a-na pa-ni* ÉRIN.MEŠ LUGAL EN-*ia*
15) ⸢*be*⸣?-*it-ti gáb-ba a-na* ÉRIN.MEŠ LUGAL EN-*ia*
16) ⸢*mi*⸣-*ia-mi* LÚ ⸢UR⸣.GU
17) ⸢*ù*⸣ *la-a yi-iš-te-mu*

Rev. 18) *a-wa-te* LUGAL EN-*ia*
19) DUMU ^{d}UTU

EA 324

TRANSLATION

(1–9) To the king, my lord, my sun god, my deity, the sun god from heaven; message of Yidia, your servant, the dirt at your two feet, the groom of your two horses: At the two feet of the king, my lord, I have verily prostrated myself seven times and seven times, on the back and on the stomach.

(10–11) Now, I am guarding the word of the king, my lord.

(11–15) And now I have prepared bread, beer, oil, cattle, small cattle, towards the arrival of the troops of the king, my lord. I have *stored/sought out* everything for the troops of the king, my lord.

(16–19) Who is the dog that he would not obey the words of the king, my lord, the son of the sun god?

EA 325

TRANSCRIPTION

Obv. 01) [*a-na*] LUGAL EN-⸢*ia*⸣ DINGIR.MEŠ-*ia*
02) ⸢^{d}⸣⸢UTU⸣-*ia* ^{d}UTU ⸢*ša*⸣ *iš*-⸢*tu*⸣[AN *ša*$_{10}$-]*mi*
03) *um-ma* ^{I}*Yi-id-ia* ÌR-*ka*
04) *ep-ri ša* 2 GÌR.MEŠ-*ka*
05) LÚ *kàr-tap-pí ša* 2 ANŠE.⸢KUR⸣.⸢RA⸣-⸢*ka*⸣
06) *a-na* 2 GÌR.MEŠ LUGAL EN-*ia am-qú-ut*
07) 7-*šu ù* 7-*ta-na*
08) *lu-ú iš-tu-ḫu-ḫi-in*
09) *ṣe-ru-ma ù ka-ba-tu-ma*

* * *

10) ⸢*a*⸣-*nu-ma i-na-ṣa-ru a-šar*
11) LUGAL EN-*ia ù* URU.KI LUGAL EN-*ia*
12) ⸢*ša*⸣ *it-ti-ia mi-ia-mi*
13) [LÚ] UR.GU *ù la-a yi-iš-te-mu*
14) *a-wa-te* LUGAL ^{d}UTU *iš-tu* ⸢AN⸣ ⸢*ša*$_{10}$⸣-*mi*

* * *

15) ⸢*a*⸣-*nu-ma šu-ši-ir-ti gáb-bi m*[*i-i*]*m*-⸢*mi*⸣
16) [NÍG].MEŠ KAŠ.MEŠ GU$_{4}$.MEŠ ÙZ.MEŠ
17) [Š]E.MEŠ IN.MEŠ *gáb*-⸢*bi*⸣ *mi*-⸢*im*⸣[-*mi*]
18) ⸢*ša*⸣ *qa-ba* LUGAL EN-⸢*ia*⸣ [*ù*?]

Lo.ed. 19) [*a*]-⸢*nu*⸣-*ma šu-ši-ir-ti*

- - - - - - - - - -

Rev. 20) ⸢*ù*⸣ *a-nu-ma* ⸢*i*⸣?-[*šu-ši-ru*(?)]
21) GUN ^{d}UTU *ki-ma qa-b*[*i*]
22) LUGAL EN-*ia* ^{d}UTU ⸢*iš*⸣-⸢*tu*⸣ [AN *ša*$_{10}$-*mi*]

* * *

EA 325

TRANSLATION

(1–9) [To] the king, my lord, my deity, my sun god, the sun god from heaven, message of Yidia, your servant, the dirt at your two feet, the groom of your two horses: At the two feet of the king, my lord, I have fallen, seven times and seven times, I have verily prostrated myself, on the back and on the stomach.

(10–12) Now, I am guarding the place (temple?) of the king, my lord, and the city of the king, my lord, which are in my charge.

(12–14) Who is the dog that he would not obey the words of the king, the son of the sun god?

(15–19) Now I have prepared every commodity: [br]ead, beer, cattle, small cattle, [gr]ain, straw, all the commodities which the king, my lord, said, [and] now I have prepared.

(20–22) And now I am [preparing(?)] the tribute of the sun god according to the command of the king, my lord, the sun god from [heaven].

EA 326

TRANSCRIPTION

Obv. 01) *a-na* ^{I}LUGAL EN-*ia* DINGIR.MEŠ-*ia* ^{d}UTU-[*ia*]
02) ^{d}UTU *ša iš-tu* AN *ša*$_{10}$!(Ú)-‹*me*›
03) *um-ma* ^{I}*Yi-id-ia* ÌR-*ka ep-*⸢*ri*⸣
04) *ša* 2 GÌR.MEŠ-*ka* ⸢LÚ⸣ ⸢*kàr*⸣-*tap*!(DU)-*pí*
05) *ša* 2 ANŠE.KUR.RA-*k*[*a*] *a-na* 2 ⸢GÌR⸣.MEŠ LUGAL
06) EN-*ia* 7-*šu u* 7-*ta-na*
07) *lu-ú iš-ta-ḫa-ḫi-in ṣ*[*e-ru-m*]*a*
08) *u ka-ba-tu-ma*

---

09) *a-nu-ma i-na-ṣa-ru* U[RU.KI LUGAL EN-]*ia*
10) DINGIR.MEŠ-*nu ša* LUGAL EN-*i*[*a li-ṣú-ru*]
11) URU.DIDLI-*šu u* 2 ŠU *ša* [LUGAL EN-*ia dan*]-*nu-tu-ma*
12) *li-ṣú-ru gáb-*⸢*bi*⸣ KUR-⸢*te*⸣-⸢*šu*⸣

---

13) *iš-te-mé a-wa-te ša* LUGAL EN-*ia*
14) *a-na* LÚ⸣⸢MÁŠKIM⸣-*šu i-nu-ma la-a*
15) *yi-la-ú na-ṣa-ar* KUR-*te* LUGAL EN-*ia*
16) *u a-nu-ma ša-ka-an* LUGAL ⸢EN⸣-*ia*
17) ^{I}*Re-a-na-pa* LÚ⸣⸢MÁŠKIM⸣ *ša* LUGAL EN-*ia*
18) *ša dam-qá a-na pa-ni* LUGAL EN-*ia*
19) ⸢*i*⸣-*pá-lu a-na* SAG.⸢DU⸣-[*ia*]

Rev. 20) ⸢*mi*⸣-*im-ma ša it-ta-a*[*ṣ*]
21) *iš-tu pí-i* LUGAL EN-*ia*
22) *a-nu-ma i-*⸢*na*⸣-*ṣa-ru* KAM^{v}.UD
23) *u mu-ša*!(MA)

Faint hieratic sign in black ink on reverse.

EA 326

TRANSLATION

(1–8) To the king, my lord, my deity, [my] sun god, the sun god which is from heaven, the message of Yidia, the dirt under your two feet, the groom of your two horses: At the two feet of the king, my lord, seven times and seven times have I verily prostrated, on the b[ac]k and on the stomach.

(9–12) Now I am guarding the ci[ty of the king,] my [lord. May] the gods of the king, m[y] lord, [protect] his cities, and may the two [str]ong hands of [the king, my lord,] protect all of his lands.

(13–19) I have heard the words of the king, my lord, to his commissioner, that he is unable to protect the lands of the king, my lord. And now the king, my lord, has appointed Reʿ-anapa commissioner of the king, my lord. That which is good in the sight of the king, my lord, I reply, "On [my] responsibility!"

(20–23) Whatever has co[me] forth from the mouth of the king, my lord, now I am protecting day and night.

EA 327

TRANSCRIPTION

	11)	⸢*iš*⸣*-te-mé* [*a*]*-wa-ti* MÁŠ[KIM]
	12)	^{I}LUGAL *a-*⸢*na*⸣ *ia-ši*
	13)	*a-na na-*⸢*ṣár*⸣ URU.DIDLI.KI.ḪI[.A *a-n*]*a*
	14)	^{I}*šàr-ri* BAD-*ia* [*ù*]
	15)	*ú-na-ṣár ma-gal š*[*a-ni-ta*$_5$]
	16)	[^{I}]*šàr-ru* BAD-*ia* ⸢*ša*⸣[*-pár*]
Lo.ed.	17)	⸢*a*⸣*-na ia-ši a-na*
Rev.	18)	⸢NA$_4$⸣ ⸢*eḫ*⸣*-li*!(TU)*-pá-ak-ku*
	19)	⸢*a*⸣*-nu-um-ma ú-ba-a*[*l*]
	20)	50 MEŠ NI LAL \ *maš-qa-al*[*-šu-nu* (?)]
	21)	*a-na* ^{I}LUGAL EN-*ia*

Joins EA 235, q.v.

EA 327

TRANSLATION

(11–15) ⸢I⸣ have heeded the [wo]rds of the king's com[missioner] to me to guard the cities [fo]r the king, my lord, [and] I have guarded diligently.

(15–21) Fu[rthermore] the king, my lord has wr[itten] to me about raw glass. Now I have sent 50 (units), [their] weight, to the king, my lord.

EA 328

TRANSCRIPTION

Obv. 01) ⸢*a*⸣-⸢*na*⸣ ^{I}LUGAL EN-*ia* DINGIR.MEŠ-*ia*
02) ^{d}UTU-*ia* ^{d}UTU *ša*
03) *iš-tu* AN *ša*$_{10}$*-mì-i*
04) *um-ma* ^{I}*Ia-ab-ni*-DINGIR
05) LÚ *ša* URU *La-ki-ša*
06) ÌR-*ka ep-ri ša*
07) UZU 2 GÌR.MEŠ-*ka*
08) LÚ *kàr-tap-pí ša*
09) ANŠE.KUR.RA.MEŠ-*ka*
10) *a*-⸢*na*⸣ UZU.GÌR.MEŠ LU[G]AL EN-*ia*
11) DINGIR.MEŠ-*ia* ^{d}UT[U-*i*]*a*
12) ^{d}UTU *ša iš*-⸢*tu*⸣ ⸢AN⸣ ⸢*ša*$_{10}$⸣-[*m*]*ì*
13) 7-*šu u* 7-⸢*ta*⸣*-a-an*
14) *lu-ú iš*-⸢*ta*⸣*-ḫa-ḫi-*[*in*]
15) [^{U}]^{ZU}*ka-bat-tum-ma*
16) [*u* ^{U}]^{ZU}*ṣe-ru-ma*
17) [*ù*] LÚ [*ra*]*-bi-iṣ*
18) [*ša*] LUGAL ⸢EN⸣-*ia*

Rev. 19) [*š*]*a iš-p*[*u-*]*ra-am*
20) [L]UGAL EN-*i*[*a*] *a-na i*[*a-ši*]
21) *a-nu-ma iš-te*$_{9}$*-me*
22) *gáb-bi a-wa-te*^{MEŠ}
23) *ša yi-iq-bi*
24) ^{I}*Ma-ia* LÚ.‹MÁ›ŠKIM LUG[AL]
25) *a-na ia-ši a-nu-ma*
26) *i-pu-šu gáb-ba*

EA 328

TRANSLATION

(1–16) To the king, my lord, my deity, my sun god, the sun god who is from heaven; the message of Yabni-ilu, the ruler of the city of Lachish, your servant, the dirt under your two feet, the groom of your horses: At the feet of the king, my lord, my deity, [m]y sun [god,] the sun god who is from heaven, seven times and seven times verily I have prostrated myself of the stomach and on the back.

(17–26) [And] as for the ‹com›missioner [of] the king, my lord, [th]at the [k]ing, m[y] lord sent to m[e], now I have heard all the words that Maya, the ‹com›missioner of the ki[ng] said to me. Now I am carrying out everything.

EA 329

TRANSCRIPTION

Obv. 01) ⸢*a*⸣-⸢*na*⸣ LUGAL EN-*ia*
02) DINGIR.MEŠ-*ia* ^{d}UTU-*ia*
03) ^{d}UTU *ša iš-tu*
04) AN *ša*$_{10}$*-mì-i*
05) ⸢*um*⸣-⸢*ma*⸣ ^{I}*Zi-im-re-di*
06) LÚ *ša* URU *La-ki-ša*
07) ÌR-*ka ep-ri*
08) *ša* GÌR.MEŠ-*ka*
09) *a-na* GÌR.MEŠ ⸢LUGAL⸣ EN-⸢*ia*⸣
10) ^{d}UTU *i*[*š*-]*t*[*u* A]N ⸢*ša*$_{10}$⸣-*mì-i*
11) 7-*šu* [*ù* 7-]⸢*ta*⸣-⸢*a*⸣-⸢*an*⸣
12) [*i*]*š-ti*-⸢*ḫa*⸣-⸢*ḫi*⸣-*in*
13) LÚ.DUMU *ši-ip-ri*
Rev. 14) ⸢*ša*⸣ LUGAL EN-*ia*
15) *ša iš-tap*-⸢*ra*⸣-⸢*an*⸣-*n*[*i*]
16) ⸢*iš*⸣-*te*$_{9}$*-me a-wa-te*$^{⸢MEŠ⸣}$-*š*[*u*]
17) [*m*]*a*-⸢*gal*⸣ *ma-gal*
18) ⸢*ù*⸣ *a-nu-ma*
19) *ú*-⸢*še*⸣-*ši-ru-mì*
20) *ki-ma ša qa*-⸢*bi*⸣-⸢*šu*⸣

EA 329

TRANSLATION

(1–12) To the king, my lord, my deity, my sun god, the sun god from heaven, the message of Zimreddi, the ruler of the city of Lachish, your servant, the dirt under your feet: At the feet of the king, my lord, the sun god from heaven, seven times [and seven] times have I prostrated.

(13–20) As for the emissary of the king, my lord, which he sent to me, I have heeded his words very carefully and now I am preparing in accordance with his order.

EA 330

TRANSCRIPTION

Obv. 01) ⸢*a*⸣-⸢*na*⸣ ^{I}*šàr-ri* EN-*ia*
02) *qí-bí-ma um-ma*
03) ^{I}*Ši-ip-ṭì*-^{d}IŠKUR ÌR-*ka*
04) ⸢*ù*⸣ *ep-ri ša* GÌR *šàr-ri*
05) ⸢EN⸣-*i*⸢*a*⸣ *a-na* GÌR *šàr-ri* EN-*ia*
06) ⸢*ù*⸣ DINGIR.MEŠ-*nu-ia ù* ^{d}UTU-*ia*
07) ⸢7⸣ *ù* 7 *mi*-⸢*la*⸣-⸢*ma*⸣
08) ⸢*am*⸣-^{qú}*qut a-na* GÌR *šàr-ri* EN-*ia*
09) *ù yi-de-mi šàr-ru*
10) ⸢EN⸣-*ia i-nu-ma*
11) [*iš*]-⸢*te*⸣-*mé gáb-bi*

Lo.ed. 12) [*a*]-*wa-at šàr-ri*

Rev. 13) ⸢EN⸣-*ia ša-ni-tam a-mur*-⸢*mi*⸣
14) ^{I}*Ia-an-ḫa-ma* ÌR *ki*-⸢*ti*⸣
15) ⸢*šàr*⸣-⸢*ri*⸣ *ù ep-ri*
16) *ša* GÌR *šàr-ri*
17) *ša-ni-tam yi-de-mi*
18) *šàr-ru* EN-*ia*
19) *i-nu-ma šul-ma-at*
20) URU.KI *šàr-ri*
21) *ša it-ti-ia*

EA 330

TRANSLATION

(1–8) Speak t[o] the king, my lord, the message of Shipṭi-Baʿlu, your servant, and the dirt at the feet of the king, my lord: At the feet of the king, my lord and my deity and my sun god, seven and seven times have I fallen at the feet of the king, my lord.

(9–13) So may the king, my lord, be apprised that [I] have heeded every word of the king, my lord.

(13–16) Furthermore, look, Yanḫamu is the loyal servant of the king and the dirt at the feet of the king.

(17–21) Furthermore, may the king, my lord, be apprised that the city of the king that is in my charge is safe and sound.

EA 331

TRANSCRIPTION

Obv.	01)	[*a-n*]*a* ^{I}*š*[*à*]*r-ri* EN[-*ia*]
	02)	DINGIR.MEŠ-*ni-ia* ^{d}UTU[-*ia*]
	03)	^{d}UTU *ša iš-tu* A[N *ša*$_{10}$-*m*]*i*
	04)	*um-ma* ^{I}*Ši-ip-ṭi*$_{4}$-⸢^{d}⸣⸢IŠKUR⸣
	05)	⸢ÌR⸣-*ka ep-*[*r*]*i ša* 2 GÌR.MEŠ-*ka*
	06)	LÚ *kàr-tap‹-pí› ša* ANŠE.KUR.RA-*ka*
	07)	*a-na* 2 GÌR.MEŠ ^{I}*šàr-ri* EN-*ia*
	08)	DINGIR.MEŠ-⸢*ni*⸣-*ia* ^{d}UTU-*ia* ^{d}UTU
	09)	⸢*ša*⸣ *iš-tu* AN *ša*$_{10}$-*mi* 7-*š*[*u*]
	10)	*ù* 7-*ta-a-ni l*[*u*]-*ú i*[*š-t*]*u-*
	11)	⸢*ḫa*⸣(?)-[*ḫ*]*i*-⸢*in*⸣ ⸢*ka*⸣-*b*[*at-t*]*u*-⸢*ma*⸣
	12)	*ù* ⸢*ṣe*⸣-*r*[*u-*]*ma a-nu-ma*
	13)	*i-na*-⸢*ṣa*⸣-*ru a-šar* LUGAL EN-*ia*
	14)	*ù* URU.KI LUGAL *a-šar*
	15)	[*i*]-*ba-ša-ti u i-nu-ma*
	16)	[*qa-*]*ba šàr-ri* EN-*ia*
	17)	[*a-n*]*a* N[A$_{4}$] *eḫ*-⸢*li*⸣-*pá*-⸢*ak*⸣-⸢*ku*⸣
Lo.ed.	18)	*m*[*i*]-*i*[*m-ma*] *ša i-b*[*a-*]*ši*
Rev.	19)	[*a-na i*]*a-ši u al-lu-ú*
	20)	[*uš-š*]*i-ir-ti a-na*
	21)	[*šàr-*]*ri* EN-*ia* DINGIR.MEŠ-*ia*
	22)	^{d}[U]TU-*ia* ^{d}[UT]U *ša iš-tu*
	23)	AN *ša*$_{10}$-*mì*

EA 331

TRANSLATION

(1–12) [T]o the k[i]ng, [my] lord, my deity, [my] sun god, the sun god who is from H[eaven]; the message of Shipṭi-Baʿlu, your servant, the dirt under your two feet, the groom of your horse: At the two feet of the king, my lord, my deity, my sun god, the sun god who is from heaven, seven tim[es] and seven times I have v[e]rily p[ro]str[at]ed myself on the stom[a]ch and on the bac[k].

(12–15) Now I am guarding the place of the king, my lord and the city of the king where I [a]m.

(15–23) And inasmuch as the king, my lord, [spo]ke [o]f raw glass, as much as ⸢I⸣ ha[v]e, now behold, I have [sen]t to [the ki]ng, my lord, my deity, my [s]un god, the [sun] god who is from heaven.

EA 332

TRANSCRIPTION

Obv. 01) [*a-na* LUGAL] ⌜EN⌝‹-*ia*› ᵈU[TU-*ia* DINGIR.MEŠ]-*ia*
02) [ᵈUTU *š*]*a* ⌜*iš*⌝-⌜*tu*⌝ A[N *ša₁₀-me*]
03) [*um-ma*] ᴵ*Ši-ip-ṭi₄*-⌜ᵈ⌝[IŠKUR LÚ URU *L*]*a-ki*-⌜*ša*⌝⌜KI⌝
04) [ÌR-*k*]*a* ⌜*ep*⌝-⌜*ri*⌝ [*ša* GÌR.MEŠ-*k*]*a*
05) [LÚ *kàr-tap*-]⌜*pí*⌝ *š*[*a* ANŠE.KUR.RA-]*ka*
06) [...........]*ka*[..............]

EA 332

TRANSLATION

(1–6) [To the king,] ‹my› lord, [my] s[un god,] my [deity, the sun god] from h[eaven; the message of] Shipṭi-B[aʿal, the ruler of the city of L]achish, [yo]ur [servant,] the dirt [of] yo[ur feet, the groo]m of your [horse…] your […]

EA 333

TRANSCRIPTION

Obv. 01) [*a-na* L]Ú.GAL *qí-*⸢*bí*⸣*-m*[*a*]
02) [*um-ma* ^{I}*P*]*a-*⸢*a*⸣*-pí*
03) ⸢*a*⸣-⸢*na*⸣ ⸢GÌR⸣.MEŠ-*ka am-qú-ut*
04) *lu-ú ti-i-de i-nu-ma*
05) *tu-ša-ṭú-na* ^{I}DI.KUD.^{d}IŠKUR
06) *ù* ^{I}*Zi-im-re-da*
07) *pu-uḫ-ri-iš ù*
08) *iq-ta-bi-mi*
09) ^{I}DI.KUD.^{d}IŠKUR *a-na* ^{I}*Z*[*i-i*]*m-re-da*
10) ⸢*a*⸣*-bi* URU *Ia-ra-mi*
11) [*š*]*a-pár-mi a-na ia-a-ši*
12) [*i*]*d-na-ni-mi*
Rev. 13) [x+]10+1 GIŠ.PAN *ù* 3 GÍR.URUDU
14) *ù* 3 *nam-*⸢*ṣa*⸣*-ru-ta*
15) *šum-ma-mi a-na-ku*
16) *uṣ-ṣú-na* UGU KUR
17) *ša* LUGAL *ù a-na ia-ši*
18) *in*$_{4}$*-né-ep-ša-ta* ⸢*it*⸣*-t*[*i-i*]*a*
19) *ù a-di-mi ú-ti-ru-m*[*i*]
20) *šu-uṭ mu-ul-ka*
21) *ša ú-ša-aṭ mil-ka*
22) [^{I}]*Pa-a-pu ù uš-ši-ir-*[*š*]*u*
23) [*a-n*]*a pa-ni-ia ù*
24) [*i-na-an-n*]*a* ⸢^{I}⸣*Ra-pí*-DINGIR *ú-wa-ši-*[*i*]*r*
Up.ed. 25) [*lu*]-⸢*ú*⸣ *yi-pal-šu*
Lft.ed. 26) [*i-na*] *a-wa-ti an-ni-ti*

EA 333

TRANSLATION

(1–3) Speak [to the] senior official; [thus says P]a'api: At your feet I have fallen.

(4–7) May you be apprised that Shipṭi-Baʿlu and Zimredda are stirring up sedition together.

(7–18) And Shipṭi-Baʿlu has said (been saying) to Zimredda, "The father of the town of Yarami has written to me, (saying) 'Furnish me with [*x*] + eleven bows and three bronze daggers and three swords, since I am starting out against the land of the king and you will be my ally alongside me.'"

(19–22) And still he retorts, "Commit high treason! The one who is plotting treason is Pa'apu."

(22–26) So send him [t]o confront me! So [no]w I have sent Rapi-ilu. [Le]t](!) him answer him [with regard to] this matter.

EA 334

TRANSCRIPTION

Obv. 01) [*a*]-⸢*na*⸣ *š*[*àr*]-⸢*ri*⸣ EN-*ia*
02) [*qí*]-⸢*bí*⸣-⸢*ma*⸣ *um*-⸢*ma*⸣
03) ⸢I⸣[.......]⸢*ya*⸣ ⸢LÚ⸣ URU *Ṣú-uḫ-ra* [K][I]
04) [*a-nu-ma ša-pa-a*]*r*
05) [*šàr-ru* E]N-⸢*ia*⸣
06) [*ú-ṣú-ur-mì* URU.]KI.⸢ḪI⸣.⸢A⸣
07) [[I]*šàr-ri ša i*]*t-ti-ka*
08) [*ù a-na-ṣa-ru a-*]*di a-ṣé*
09) [[I]*šàr-ri*] EN-*ia*
10) [*ù* [I]]⸢*šàr*⸣-*ru*
11) [*yi-il*$_5$*-ma-*]*ad* ⸢KUR⸣.⸢MEŠ⸣-*šu*

EA 334

TRANSLATION

(1–3) [Sp]eak [t]o the king, my lord, the message of [...]ya, the ruler of Ṣuḫ̮ra.

(4–9) [Now, the king,] my [lo]rd, [has writt]en, "[Protect the cit]ies [of the king that are]in your charge." [And I am guarding un]til the coming forth of [the king,] my lord.

(10–11) [So], [may] the king [lear]n of his territories.

EA 335

TRANSCRIPTION

Obv. 00) [*a-na* ^{I}*šàr-ri* EN-*ia qí-bí-ma*]
01) [*um-ma* ^{I}ÌR-^{d}INNIN ÌR-*ka*]
02) [*a-na* GÌR.MEŠ EN-*ia* 7 *ù* 7 *mi-la*]
03) [*ma-aq-ti-ti ù ka-ba-tu-ma ù*] *ṣú-uḫ-ru-‹ma›*
04) [*a-na* GÌR.MEŠ ^{I}*šàr-ri* E]N-*ia*
05) [*li-il*$_{5}$*-ma-ad* ^{I}*šà*]*r-ri* EN-*ia*
06) [*ki-ma* 1-*en i-ba*]*-šu-ti*
07) *li-i*[*l*$_{5}$*-ma-ad* ^{I}*šàr-r*]*i* EN-*ia*
08) *ki-ma* G[AZ.M]EŠ \ *mi-ḫi-ṣa*
09) ^{I}*Tu-u*[*r-ba-ṣú ù*] ^{I}*Ia-ap-ti-ḫa-da*
10) *ù nu*-K[ÚR URU *L*]*a-ki-ši*
11) *li-i*[*l*$_{5}$*-ma-ad* ^{I}*šà*]*r-ri* EN-*ia*
Rev. 12) *ù i*[*l*$_{5}$*-qé* LÚ] *ar-ni*
13) *gáb-bi* ŠEŠ! SIG$_{5}$-*ia*
14) *li-il*$_{5}$-⸢*ma*⸣-*ad*
15) ^{I}*šàr-ri* ⸢EN⸣-*ia ki-ma*
16) ⸢*na*⸣-*ki-ra-at* URU *La-ki-ši*
17) ⸢*ù*⸣ ⸢*ṣa*⸣-⸢*ab*⸣-⸢*ta*⸣-⸢*at*⸣ URU *Mu-ú*ʾ*-ra-aš-ti*
18) ⸢*ù*⸣ [*na-ki-r*]*a-at*
19) [URU *Ú-ru-sa-l*]*im*⸢^{KI}⸣
20) [*ù yu-uš-ši-r*]*a* ^{I}*šàr-ri*
21) [EN-*ia* ÉRIN.MEŠ *pí-ṭá-ti*]

EA 335

TRANSLATION

(0–4) [Speak to the king, my lord; the message of ʿAbdi-Ashtarti, your servant. At the feet of the king, my lord, seven times and seven times have I fallen, both on the stomach and] on the back, [at the feet of the king], my lord.

(5–6) [May the kin]g, my lord be [apprised that] I a[m all alone].

(7–10) May [the kin]g, my lord, be ap[prised] that Tu[rbaṣu and] Yaptiḫ-Hadda have been ki[lle]d \ smitten and [the city of L]achish is hos[tile].

(11–13) May [the ki]ng, my lord, be a[pprised] that the tra[it]or ha[s taken] all my loyal colleagues (brothers).

(14–21) May the king, my lord, be apprised that the city of Lachish is hostile and the city of Mo'rašti is captured and [the city of Jerusal]em [is host]ile. So may the king, [my lord, sen]d [regular troops].

EA 336

TRANSCRIPTION

Obv. 01) [*a-na š*]*à*[*r*]-⌜*ri*⌝ ⌜EN⌝[-*ia*]
02) [*qí*-]⌜*bí*⌝-⌜*ma*⌝
03) [*um-ma* ᴵ]*Ḫi-zi*-⌜*ri*⌝ ÌR[-*ka*]
04) [*a-na* G]ÌR.MEŠ ⌜EN⌝-⌜*ia* ⌝[7]
05) [*ù*]⌜7⌝-⌜*ta*⌝-⌜*an*⌝ ⌜*ma*⌝-*aq-t*[*a-ti*]
06) [............]⌜*bi*⌝-⌜*ni*⌝
07) [...............]⌜*ia*⌝
08) [..............]*a*[....]

---

09) [...........]

EA 336

TRANSLATION

(1–5) Sp[eak to the ki]ng, [my] lord; [the message of]Ḫizziri, [your] servant. [At the f]eet of my lord [seven (times) and se]ven times have ⸢I⸣ fallen.

(6–8) [.............]

---

(9) [.............]

EA 337

TRANSCRIPTION

Obv.	01)	*a-na* ^{I}LUGAL EN-*ia*
	02)	^{d}UTU-⸢*ia*⸣ DINGIR.MEŠ-*ia*
	03)	⸢*qí*⸣-⸢*bí*⸣-*ma*
	04)	*u*[*m-m*]*a* ^{I}*Ḫi-zi-ri* ÌR-*ka*
	05)	⸢*a*⸣-[*n*]*a* ⸢GÌR⸣.MEŠ ^{I}⸢LUGAL⸣ ⸢EN⸣-*ia*
	06)	⸢7⸣-⸢*šu*⸣ [7]-*a-an* ⸢*am*⸣-⸢*qut*⸣
	07)	^{I}LUGAL EN-*ia* ⸢*ša*⸣-*pár*
	08)	*a-na* ⸢*ia*⸣-*ši šu*-⸢*ši*⸣-*ir-mì*
	09)	IGI.KÁR.MEŠ *ma*-[*aṭ*]-*ni-a*
	10)	⸢*a*⸣-[*na*] *pa-ni* ÉRIN.MEŠ
	11)	\ ⸢*pí*⸣-[*ṭ*]*á*-⸢*ti*⸣
	12)	⸢*ša*⸣ ^{I}⸢LUGAL⸣ ⸢EN⸣-⸢*ia*⸣
	13)	⸢*yi*⸣-*di*-⸢*in*$_{4}$⸣
Lo.ed.	14)	⸢DINGIR⸣ ⸢*ša*⸣ LUGAL ⸢EN⸣-*ia*
	15)	⸢*ú*⸣ *yi-ta-ṣa*
Rev.	16)	^{I}LUGAL EN-*ia qa-du*
	17)	ÉRIN.MEŠ.GAL-*šu ú yi-ìl-ma*-⸢*ad*⸣
	18)	KUR.ḪI.A-*šu ú an-nu-ú*
	19)	*ki-ia-am šu-ši*-⸢*ir*⸣-*ti*$_{7}$
	20)	IGI.KÁR.MEŠ GAL.MEŠ
	21)	\ *ma-aṭ-ni-a a-na*
	22)	*pa-ni* ÉRIN.MEŠ.GAL LUGAL
	23)	EN-*ia*

---

	24)	*ú* LUGAL EN-*ia ša-pár*
	25)	⸢*a*⸣-⸢*na*⸣ *ia-ši ú-ṣur-mì*
	26)	^{I}*Ma-a-ia*
	27)	LÚ.MÁŠKIM *ša* LUGAL EN-*ia*
	28)	*a-di ú-ṣur-ru*
Up.ed.	29)	^{I}*Ma-a-ia ma-gal*
	30)	*ma-gal*

EA 337

TRANSLATION

(1–6) Speak to the king, my lord, my sun god, my deity; the m[essa]ge of Ḫizzīri, your servant: at the feet of the king, my lord seven times and [seven] times have I fallen.

(7–18) The king, my lord, wrote to me: "Prepare supplies for the arrival of the regular army of the king, my lord." May the god of the king, my lord, grant that the king, my lord, come forth with his great army that he may learn about his lands.

(18–23) And, behold, thus I have prepared abundant supplies for the arrival of the great army of the king, my lord.

(24–30) And the king, my lord, wrote to me: "Protect Maya, the commissioner of the king, my lord." I am still protecting Maya most diligently.

EA 338

TRANSCRIPTION

Obv.	01)	⌜*a*⌝-⌜*na*⌝ LUGAL [*be-li-ia*]
	02)	⌜*um*⌝-*ma* [I]⌜*Zi*⌝[......ÌR-*ka*]
	03)	⌜*a*⌝-⌜*na*⌝ ⌜GÌR⌝⌜MEŠ⌝ ⌜*be*⌝[-*li-ia am-qut*]
	04)	⌜*ù*⌝ [...]⌜*ša*⌝ [...........]
	05)	‹*qa*›-⌜*bi*⌝(!)-⌜*mì*⌝ ⌜*a*⌝-⌜*ṣí*⌝ ⌜ÉRIN⌝.⌜MEŠ⌝
	06)	⌜*iš*⌝-⌜*tu*⌝(?) *qà-bi* ⌜LÚ⌝[......]
	07)	[*šum*]-⌜*ma*⌝ ⌜*a*⌝-*ṣí l*[*a*...]
	08)	[*iš*]-⌜*tu*⌝ ⌜*qà*⌝-⌜*bi*⌝ [.......]
	09)	[......]⌜*šum*⌝(?)-⌜*ma*⌝(?) [...]
	10)	⌜*ma*⌝-*a* ⌜*im*⌝(?)[...........]
Lo.ed.	11)	[.......................]
Rev.	12)	⌜*nu*⌝(?) [................]
	13)	[*a*]-⌜*mur*⌝ [..............]

EA 338

TRANSLATION

Obv.	01)	To the king, [my lord,]
	02)	the message of Zi[.....your servant]
	03)	At the feet of [my] lo[rd have I fallen.]
	04)	and[...]of [...........]
	05)	‹Comm›and the coming forth of the troops
	06)	by the command(?) of [the senior official(?)]
	07)	If they have not come forth [...]
	08)	at the command of [.......]
	09)	[......] If(?)[...]
	10)	???[..........]
Lo.ed.	11)	[....................]
Rev.	12)	?[..............]
	13)	[L]ook, [.............]

EA 339

TRANSCRIPTION

Obv.
01) [*a-na* LU]GA[L EN-*ia*]
02) ⌜DINGIR⌝.⌜MEŠ⌝-⌜*ia*⌝ [ᵈUTU-]*i*[*a*]
03) *qí*-[*bí-ma*]
04) *um*-⌜*ma*⌝ ᴵ[..............]
05) ⌜LÚ⌝ ⌜URU⌝[...........]
06) ⌜*ša*⌝-[*ni*]-⌜*tam*⌝ ⌜*lu*⌝ *ti*-[*i-de i-nu-ma*]
07) ⌜DINGIR⌝ [.............]
08) [......................]
09) [......................]
10) [......................]
11) [......................]
12) [......................]
13) [......................]
14) [......................]
15) [......................]

EA 339

TRANSLATION

Obv. (01) [To the ki]n[g, my lord,]
(02) my deity, [my sun god,
(03) sp[eak:]
(04) The message of [.............]
(05) the ruler of the city of [...........]
(06) Furthermore, may you [be apprised that]
(07) the god [...............]
(08) [......................]
(09) [......................]
(10) [......................]
(11) [......................]
(12) [......................]
(13) [......................]
(14) [......................]
(15) [......................]

EA 362

TRANSCRIPTION

Obv. 01) ⸢^{I}⸣*Ri-ib-ed-di qí-bi-mi*
02) *a-na* LUGAL *be-li-ia*
03) *a-na* KI.TA GÌR.MEŠ *be-li-ia*
04) 7-*ta u* 7 *am-qut*^{ut}
05) *a-nu-ma ša-mi-ti*$_{7}$ *a-wa-te*^{MEŠ}
06) LUGAL *be-li-ia ù ḫa-di lìb-bi*
07) *ma-gal yu-ḫa-mi-iṭ be-li*
08) *uš-šar* ÉRIN.MEŠ *pí-ṭá-te ki-ma*
09) *ar-ḫi-iš šum-ma* LUGAL *be-li*
10) *la-a yu-ša-ru* ÉRIN.MEŠ *pí-ṭá-ta*$_{5}$
11) *ù ni-nu-mi* BA.ÚŠ.MEŠ *ni-mu-ut*
12) *ù* URU.MEŠ *Gub*^{ub}*-li*
13) *tu-ul*$_{11}$*-qú ma-an!-ga-mi*
14) *tu-ma-al ša-al-ša-mi*
15) *ma-an-*⸢*ga*⸣*-am-mi i-na-an-na*
16) *tu-ma-al ša-al-ša-mi*
17) *ti*$_{7}$*-iq-bu-ni ia-a-nu-mi*
18) ÉRIN.MEŠ *pí-ṭá-ta*$_{5}$ *ù aš-pu-ur*
19) *ù tu-ṣa* ÉRIN.MEŠ *pí-ṭá-tu*
20) *ù ti*$_{7}$*-ìl-qé* ˡ*a-ba-šu-nu*
21) *a-nu-ma i-na-an-na ti*$_{7}$*-iq-bu-na*
22) *la yi-iš-pu-ra-am ù*
23) *nu-ul*$_{11}$*-qa-am-mi ù a-nu-ma*
24) *ti*$_{7}$*-ba-ú-na ṣa-bat* URU.MEŠ *Gub-li*
25) *ù ti*$_{7}$*-iq-bu-ni ṣa-bat-mi*
26) *ni-nu-u*$_{16}$ URU.MEŠ *Gub*^{ub}*-li*
27) *ù dan-na-nu-u*$_{16}$ *a-mur-mi*
28) ⸢*ṣa*⸣*-bat-mi šu-nu* URU.KI *Gub-li*
29) *ù da-an-nu ia-nu-am-mi*
Lo.ed. 30) LÚ-*la ti*$_{7}$*-i-ṣa a-na ša-*⸢*šu*⸣*-n*[*u*]

EA 362

TRANSLATION

(1–4) Rib-Eddi:—speak to the king, my lord: Beneath the feet of my lord seven times and seven (times) have I fallen.

(5–13) Now I have heard the words of the king my lord and my heart rejoiced greatly. May my lord hasten to send the regular army with all due haste. If the king, my lord does not send the regular army, then we must perish and the towns of Byblos will be taken.

(13–23) There was distress previously; there is distress now. Previously they said to me, "There is no regular army," so I wrote and the regular army came forth and took their father. Now they are saying, "Let him not write that we be taken."

(23–30) And now they are seeking to seize the towns of Byblos and they said to me, "If we seize the towns of Byblos then we will be strong." Look, they have taken a town of Byblos and they are strong. There was no man. It was too weak for them.

31) *a-nu-ma a-na-ku a-na-aṣ-ṣa-r*[*u*]
Rev. 32) ⸢URU⸣.⸢MEŠ⸣ ⸢*Gub*⸣^{ub}-⸢*li*⸣ ⸢URU⸣.⸢KI⸣ L[UGAL]
33) *mu-ša ur-ra-am i-nu-*⸢*ma*⸣
34) *i-ka-ša-da-am* KUR.MEŠ.KI
35) *ù ti*$_{7}$*-pa-ṭi*$_{4}$*-ru-na* LÚ.MEŠ-*tu*
36) *a-na la-qé* KUR.MEŠ-*i-mi*
37) *a-na ša-a-šu-nu ù ia-nu-am*
38) LÚ.MEŠ-*li a-na na-ṣa-ri* URU.KI *Gub-li*
39) URU.KI LUGAL *be-li-ia*
40) *ù yu-ḫa-mi-ṭá be-li*
41) ÉRIN.MEŠ *pí-ṭá-ta*$_{5}$ *ù ni-*ÚŠ.BA
42) *i-nu-ma ša-ṭe*$_{6}$*-er be-li*
43) *a-na maḫ-ri-ia ù a-nu-mi*
44) *ù i-du i-nu-ma ta-mu-tu-na*
45) *ù ti-ba-ú-na i-pé-eš*$_{15}$ *ar-ni*
46) *i-nu-ma yi-iq-bu a-na pa-ni* LUGAL
47) BA.ÚŠ \ *mu-tu-mi a-na* KUR.MEŠ
48) *la-a yi-iš-mé* LUGAL *be-li*
49) *a-wa-te*^{MEŠ} LÚ.MEŠ *ša-nu-te ia-nu-mi*
50) *mu-ta-na a-na* KUR.MEŠ *ša-lim iš-tu pa-na-‹nu›-um*
51) *ù be-li i-de i-nu-ma*
52) *la-a aš-pu-ru a-wa-at*
53) *ka-az-bu-te a-na be-li-ia*
54) *ù gáb-bi* LÚ.MEŠ *ḫa-za-nu-te*
55) *la-a ra-i-mu i-nu-ma*
56) *tu-ṣú* ÉRIN.MEŠ *pí-ṭá-tu*
57) *i-nu-ma pa-ši-iḫ a-na šu-nu*
58) *ù a-na-ku i-ba-ú a-ṣé-ši*
59) *i-nu-ma ma-ri-iṣ ia-ši*
60) ⸢*ù*⸣ *yu-ṣa-am* LUGAL *be-li-ia yi-*⸢*mur*⸣
61) ⸢KUR⸣.MEŠ-*šu ù yi-ìl-qé gáb-ba*
62) ⸢*a*⸣-⸢*mur*⸣-*mi a-na ú-mi tu-ṣú*
Up.ed 63) *ù i-né-pu-ša-at gáb-*⸢*bi*⸣
64) ⸢KUR⸣.KUR.MEŠ *a-na* LUGAL *be-li-ia*
65) *mi-ia* ⸢*yi*⸣-⸢*zi*⸣-*zu a-na pa-ni* ÉRIN.MEŠ LUGAL
Lft.ed. 66) *la-a yu-wa-šar* LUGAL *be-li* MU \ *ša-ni-ta an-ni-ta*$_{5}$
67) *a-na* DUMU.MEŠ ^{I}ÌR-*A-ši-ir-ti ù ti-dì-šu-*⸢*na*⸣ DUMU!‹MEŠ›
68) ⸢*gáb*⸣-*bi-šu-nu a-na* KUR.MEŠ LUGAL *be-li-ia mi-ia šu-nu*
69) *i-nu-ma i-pu-šu ar-na ù da-a-ku* LÚ.MÁŠKIM *sú-ki-na* ^{I}*Pí-wu-ri*

(31–39) Now, I am guarding the towns of Byblos, the ki[ng's] city, night and day. If I go forth to the territories, then the personnel will depart to take territory for themselves and there will be no men to guard the city of Byblos, the city of the king, my lord.

(40–45) So may my lord hasten the regular army lest we perish. Since the king wrote to me, then now they know that they will perish so they are seeking to commit treason.

(46–53) Inasmuch as he (Aziru) said before the king, "There is a plague in the land," may the king, my lord, not listen to other men. There is no plague in the lands. It has been healthy for a long time. And my lord knows that I do not write a word of falsehood to my lord.

(54–65) But all the city rulers don't like it that the regular army is coming forth since it is tranquil for them. But I am seeking its coming forth because it is bitter for me.

(60–65) So may the king, my lord, come forth that he may see to his lands and that he may (re)take it all. Look, on the day that you come forth, then all the territories will be joined to the king, my lord. Who can stand before the army of the king?

(66–69) Assuming that the king does not send (the army) this year against the sons of ʿAbdi-Ashirta, then the son‹s› will tread on all of them, against the lands of the king, my lord. Who are they that they have committed treason and slain the commissioner, Piwuru?

EA 363

TRANSCRIPTION

Obv. 01) *a-na* LUGAL EN-*ia* DINGIR-*ia* ^{d}UTU-*ia*
02) *qí-bí-ma*
03) *um-ma* ÌR-*re-ša* ÌR-›⸢UT⸣‹-*ka*
04) ⸢LÚ⸣ URU *E-‹ni›-ša-sí a-na šu-pa-li*
05) *up-ri* GÌR-*pí* LUGAL EN-*ia*
06) 7 *ù* 7 *am-qú-ut*
07) *a-mur-mi ni-i*$_{15}$*-nu i*$_{15}$*-ba-ša-‹nu›*
08) *a-na* KUR *Am-qí* URU.DIDLI.ḪI.A LUGAL EN-*ia*
09) *ù a-li-ik*!(UK) ^{I}*E-tá-ka*$_{4}$*-ma*
10) LÚ URU KUR *Qí-in-sà*
11) *a-na pa-ni* ÉRIN.MEŠ *Ḫa-at-ta*
12) *ù ša-ka*$_{4}$*-an* URU.DIDLI.ḪI.A
13) LUGAL EN-*ia*
Lo.ed. 14) *a-na i*$_{15}$*-ša-ti*$_{7}$
Rev. 15) *ù li-de-mi*
16) LUGAL EN-*ia*
17) *ù li-di-na* LUGAL EN-*ia*
18) ÉRIN.MEŠ *pí-ṭá-a-ta*
19) *ù ni-pu-uš*
20) URU.DIDLI.ḪI.A ⸢LUGAL⸣ EN-⸢*ia*⸣
21) *ù ni-*⸢*ša*⸣*-ab*
22) *a-na* URU.DIDLI.ḪI.A
23) LUGAL EN-*ia* DINGIR-*ia*
\\$^{d}$UTU-*ia*

EA 363

TRANSLATION

(1–7) Speak to the king, my lord, my god, my sun god; the message of ʿAbdi-rēša, your servant, the ruler of the city of ʿÊ‹ni›-šâsi: Beneath the dirt under the feet of the king, my lord, seven (times) and seven (times) have I fallen.

(7–14) Look, we are in the land of ʿAmqi, the cities of the king, my lord and Etakama, the ruler of the city of Qinsa (Qedesh) came at the head of the Hittite army and he set the cities of the king, my lord, on fire.

(15–23) So may the king, my lord be apprised and may the king, my lord, provide regular troops that we may (re)gain the cities of the king, my lord, and so that we may dwell in the cities of the king, my lord, my god, my sun god.

EA 364

TRANSCRIPTION

Obv. 01) *⸢a⸣-na* LUGAL EN-*ia*

02) *um-ma A-ia-ab*

03) ÌR-*ka a-na*

04) GÌR.MEŠ EN-*ia*

05) 7-*šu* 7-*ta-an*

06) *am-qut a-na-ku* ÌR

07) LUGAL EN-*ia ù*

08) SAḪAR \ *a-pa-ru ša*

09) 2 GÌR.MEŠ-*šu*

10) *iš-te-mé ša-pár*

11) LUGAL EN-*ia*

12) *a-na ia-ši i-na*

13) *qa-ti* ^{I}*A-taḫ-ma-ia*

14) *⸢a⸣-di aṣ-ṣur-r*[*u*]

Lo.ed. 15) [*m*]*a-gal ⸢ma⸣-g*[*al*]

Rev. 16) [URU].MEŠ ⸢LUGAL⸣ EN-[*i*]*⸢a⸣*

17) *ša-ni-tam a-mur*

18) LÚ URU *Ḫa-ṣú-⸢ra⸣*

19) *il-te-qé*

20) 3 URU.DIDLI.KI *iš-tu ⸢ia⸣-ši*

21) *i-na* UD *aš-mé ù ⸢a⸣-ma-ru*

22) *i-pé-eš*$_{15}$ *nu-kùr-ti*

23) *i-na ša-a-šu*

24) *a-di-mi li-de-mi*

25) LUGAL EN-*ia*

26) *ù* LUGAL EN-*ia*

27) *li-im-lu-uk-mi*

28) *a-na* ÌR-*šu*

EA 364

TRANSLATION

(1–9) To the king, my lord, the message of Ayyāb, your servant: At the feet of my lord seven times and seven times have I fallen. I am the servant of the king, my lord, and the dirt under his two feet.

(10–16) I have heard the message of the king, my lord, by the hand of Ataḫmaya. I am still guarding most diligently the [town]s of the king, [m]y lord.

(17–23) Furthermore, look, the ruler of Hazor has taken three towns from me. From the day that I heard, then I have been seeing hostile activity by him.

(24–28) Again, may the king, my lord, be apprised and may the king, my lord, take counsel concerning his servant.

EA 365

TRANSCRIPTION

Obv. 01) [*a-na šà*]*r-ri* EN-*ia*

02) *u* ⸢^{d}⸣⸢UT]U-*ia qí-bí-ma*

03) *um-ma* ^{I}*Bi-ri-di-ya*

04) ÌR *ki-it-ti ša šàr-ri*

05) *a-na* GÌR.MEŠ LUGAL EN-*ia*

06) *u* ^{d}UTU-*ia* 7-*šu*

07) *ù* 7-*ta-a-an am-qut*

---

08) *li-de-mi* LUGAL EN-*ia*

09) *a-na* ÌR-*šu u a-na* URU.KI-*šu*

10) *a-nu-um-ma a-na-ku-ma*

11) *er-ri-šu* \ *aḫ-ri-šu*

12) *i-na* URU *Šu-na-ma*⸢^{KI}⸣

Lo.ed. 13) *u a-na-ku-ma*

14) *ub-ba-lu* LÚ.MEŠ ⸢*ma*⸣-*as*-⸢*sà*⸣^{ME}[^{š}]

Rev. 15) *u a-mur-mì*

16) LÚ.MEŠ *ḫa-za-nu-ta*^{MEŠ}

17) *ša it-it-ia*

18) *la-a ti-pu-šu-na*

19) *ki-ma ia-ti-ia la-a*

20) *te-er-ri-šu-na*

21) *i-na* URU *Šu-na-ma*^{KI}

22) *u la-a tu-ub-ba-lu-na*

23) LÚ.MEŠ *ma-as-sà*^{MEŠ} *ù*

24) *a-na-ku-ma* \ *ya-ḫu-du-un-ni*

25) *ub-ba-lu* LÚ.MEŠ *ma-as*-⸢*sà*⸣^{MEŠ}

26) *iš-tu* URU *Ia-pu* ^{K}[^{I}]

27) ⸢*yi*⸣-*la-ku iš-tu* ŠU-[*ti-ia*]

28) *an-ni-ki-ma iš-t*[*u*]

Up.ed. 29) [UR]U *Nu-ri-ib-da*^{K}[^{I}]

30) [*u*] *li-de-mi*

Lft.ed. 31) [L]UGAL EN-*ia a-na* URU.KI

\-*šu*

EA 365

TRANSLATION

(1–7) Speak [to the ki]ng, my lord, and my [sun g]od; the message of Biridiya, the loyal servant of the king: At the feet of the king, my lord, seven times and seven times have I fallen.

(8–9) May the king, my lord, be apprised concerning his servant and concerning his city.

(10–14) Now, it is I who am cultivating in the town of Shunem and it is I who is bringing corvée men.

(15–29) Look, the city rulers that are with me are not doing as I am doing; they are not cultivating in the town of Shunem and they are not bringing corvée workers. But I, by myself, am bringing corvée workers. From Yapo (Joppa) they are coming, from [those under my] authority here, and fro[m the to]wn of Nuribda.

(30–31) [So] may [the k]ing, my lord, be apprised concerning his city.

EA 366

TRANSCRIPTION

Obv. 01) ⸢*a*⸣-*na* ^{I}*šàr-ri* EN-*ia* ^{d}UTU-*ia*

02) DINGIR.MEŠ-*ia qí-bí-ma*

03) ⸢*um*⸣-⸢*ma*⸣ ^{I}*Šu-wa-ar-da-ta*

04) ⸢ÌR⸣-*ka* ÌR *ša šàr-ri*

05) *ù* SAḪAR-*ru ša* 2 GÌR.MEŠ-*šu*

06) *qa-aq-qa-ru ša ka-ba-ši-ka*

07) *a-na* GÌR.MEŠ *šàr-ri* ⸢EN⸣-⸢*ia*⸣

08) ^{d}UTU *iš-tu* AN *ša*$_{10}$-*me*-⸢*e*⸣ ⸢7⸣-*šu*

09) 7-*ta-a-an uš-ḫé-ḫi*-⸢*in*⸣ ⸢*ù*⸣

10) ^{UZU}*ka-bat-tu-ma ù ṣe-ru-ma*

---

11) *li-il-ma-ad šàr-ru* EN-⸢*i*⸣*a*

12) *i-nu-ma* LÚ.SA.GAZ ⸢*ša*⸣

13) *yi-na-aš-ši* \ *na-aš-ša-a*

14) *i-na* KUR.KI.ḪI.A *na-da-an*

15) DINGIR-*lu*$_{4}$ *ša šàr-ri* EN-*ia a-na ia-ši*

Lo.ed. 16) *ù i-du-uk-šu ù*

17) [*l*]*u-ú yi-ìl-ma-ad šàr-ru*

Rev. 18) ⸢EN⸣-*ia* ⸢*i*⸣-⸢*nu*⸣-*ma iz-zi-bu-ni*

19) *gáb-bi* ŠEŠ.ḪI.A-*ia ù*

20) *a-na-ku-ma ù* ^{I}ÌR-*Ḫe-ba*

21) *nu-kúr-tu*$_{4}$ *i-na* LÚ.⸢SA⸣.GAZ

22) *ù* ^{I}*Sú-ra-ta* ⸢LÚ⸣ URU *Ak-ka*^{KI}

23) *ù* ^{I}*In*$_{4}$-*tár*!(AŠ+DA)-⸢*ú*⸣-⸢*ta*⸣ LÚ URU *Ak-ša-pa*

24) *šu-ni-ma in*$_{4}$-*né-ri-ru* \ *na-az-a-qú*

25) *i-na* 50 GIŠ.GIGIR.ḪI.A

26) *a-na mu-ḫi-ia ù a-nu-ma*

27) *i-ba-aš-šu it-ti-ia*

28) *i-na nu-kúr-ti ù li*-⸢*it*⸣-*ru-uṣ*

EA 366

TRANSLATION

(1–10) Speak to the king, my lord, my sun god, my deity: Thus Shuwardata, your servant, the servant of the king and the dirt under his two feet, the ground of your treading: At the feet of the king, my lord, the sun god from heaven, seven times (and) seven times have I prostrated both on the stomach and on the back.

(11–16) May the king, my lord, be apprised that as for the *ʿapîru* man who rose up in the territories, the god of the king, my lord, gave him over to me and I smote him.

(17–28) And may the king, my lord, be apprised that all my colleagues (brothers) have abandoned me and I and ʿAbdi-Ḫeba are at war with the *ʿapîru* man. But Surata, the ruler of Acco, and Intaruta, the ruler of Achshaph, the two of them, were called forth with fifty chariots against me (or: to me) and now they are at war with me (or: Now they are with me in the war).

29) *i-na pa-ni šàr-ri* EN-*ia ù*
30) *lu-ú yu-ši-ra* ^{I}*Ia-an-ḫa-ma*
31) *ù lu-ú ni-pa-aš gáb-bu-ma*
32) *nu-kúr-ti ù lu-ú tu-te-er*
33) KUR.KI.Ḫ̮I.A *ša šàr-ri* EN-*ia*
Up.ed. 34) ⸢*a*⸣-*na* ZAG!.Ḫ̮I.‹A›-*ši* \ *up-sí* Ḫ̮I.‹A›

(28–34) So may it seem right in the sight of the king, my lord and may he send Yanḥamu and so that we may all wage war and so that you may restore the territory of the king, my lord, to its full extent.

EA 367

TRANSCRIPTION

Obv. 01) *a-na* ^{I}*In-tar-ú-tá* LÚ URU *Ak-ša-pa*
02) *qí-bí-ma um-ma* LUGAL-*ma*
03) *a-nu-ma ṭup-pa an-na-a uš-te-bi-la-ku ‹a-na› qá-bé-e*
04) *a-na ka-a-ša ù uṣ-ṣur lu-ú na-ṣa-ra-ta*
05) *aš-ru* LUGAL *ša it-ti-ka*

---

06) *a-nu-um-ma* LUGAL *um-te-eš-še-ra-ku*
07) ^{I}*Ḫa-an-ni* DUMU ^{I}*Ma-i-re-ia*
08) LÚ.PA.TÙR *ša* LUGAL *i-na* KUR *Ki-na-aḫ-ḫi*
09) *ù ša i-qáb-bá-ku ši-ma-aš-šu*
10) SIG$_5$-*iš dan-níš la-a i-kaš-ša-dak-ku*
11) LUGAL *ar-na a-wa-ta gáb-bá*
12) *ša i-qáb-bá-ku ši-ma-aš-šu* SIG$_5$-*iš dan-níš*
13) *ù e-pu-uš* ⸢SIG$_5$⸣-*iš dan-níš*
14) *ù uṣ-ṣur* ⸢*uṣ*⸣-*ṣur la-a tá-mé-ek-ki*
15) *ù lu-ú šu-šu-ra-tá a-na pa-ni*
16) ÉRIN.MEŠ *pí-ṭa-ti* LUGAL NINDA *ma-a-ad*
Rev. 17) GEŠTIN *gáb-bu mi-im-ma ma-a-*⸢*ad*⸣
18) *a-nu-um-ma i-kaš-ša-dak-ku*
19) *ar-ḫi-iš ar-ḫi-iš*
20) *ù i-na-ak-ki-ís* SAG-⸢*ad*⸣
21) *a-ia-bé-e ša* LUGAL

---

22) *ù lu-ú ti-i-de*$_9$ *i-nu-ma*
23) *ša-lim* LUGAL *ki-*⸢*ma*⸣ ^{d}UTU-*aš*
24) *i-na* AN *ša*$_{10}$*-me-e* ÉRIN.MEŠ-*šu* GIS.GIGIR-*šu*
25) *ma-a-du ma-gal šul-mu*

EA 367

TRANSLATION

(1–5) Speak to Intaruta, the ruler of Achshaph; thus (spoke) the king: This tablet have I sent to you ‹to› say to you, "Guard! May you be on guard in the place of the king that is in your charge."

(6–21) Now, the king has sent to you Ḫanni, the stable master of the king in the land of Canaan and as for what he says to you, heed it most diligently, lest the king find in you a fault. Every word that he says to you, heed it most diligently and carry out most diligently. And guard! Guard! Do not be slack and may you verily be prepared before the arrival of the king's regular troops, the bread being abundant, the wine (and) every supply being abundant.

Now he is coming to you very quickly and he will cut off the head(s) of the enemies of the king.

(22–25) And may you be apprised that the king is well like the sun god in heaven; his vast troops and his chariotry are exceedingly well.

EA 369

TRANSCRIPTION

Obv. 01) *a-na* ^{I}*Mil-ki-li* ⸢LÚ⸣ URU *Gaz-r*[*i*]

02) *um-ma* LUGAL-*ma a-nu-um-ma ṭup-pa an-na-am*

03) *ul-te-bi-la-ak-ku a-na qa-bé-e*

04) *a-na ka-a-ša a-nu-um-ma*

05) *um-te-še-ra-ak-ku* ^{I}*Ḫa-an-ia*

06) LÚ ‹PA›.TÙR ÉRIN.MEŠ *pí-ṭá-ti*

07) *qa-du mi-im-ma a-na la-qé-e*

08) MUNUS.DÉ \ *ša-qí-*tu_4 SIG_5

09) KÙ.BABBAR.ḪI.A KÙ.GI.ḪI.A GADA.MEŠ \ *ma-al-ba-ši*

10) ^{NA_4}GUG ⸢*ka*⸣-*li* NA_4.MEŠ GIŠ.GU.ZA GIŠ.ESI.MEŠ

11) *qa-tam-ma ka-*⸢*li*⸣ *mi-im-ma* SIG_5

12) ŠU.NIGIN-*ma ša* 1 *me šu-ši ṭì-ba-an*

13) ŠU.NIGIN-*ma* MUNUS.DÉ 40

14) 40 ⸢KÙ⸣.BABBAR ŠÁM MUNUS.DÉ.MEŠ

15) *ù uš-ši-ra* MUNUS.DÉ.MEŠ

16) SIG_5 *da-an-ni-iš*

17) *ša ṣa-bu-ur-ti i-ia-nu*

18) *i-na lìb-bi-šu-nu*

19) *ù li-iq-ba-ak-ku*

20) ⸢LUGAL⸣ ⸢EN⸣-*ka*

Lo.ed. 21) *ši-ia-*tu_4 ⸢*ba*⸣-*an-*⸢tu_4⸣

22) KA *ši-*pir_6*-ti*

Rev. 23) *iš-pu-ru-ka*

24) *ù lu-ú ti-*⸢*i*⸣*-de i-nu-ma*

25) *ša-lim* LUGAL *k*[*i-m*]*a* ^{d}UTU

26) ÉRIN.MEŠ-*šu* ⸢GIŠ⸣.⸢GIGIR⸣.MEŠ-*šu*

27) ANŠE.KUR.RA.MEŠ-⸢*šu*⸣ *ma-gal šul-mu*

28) *a-nu-um-ma yi-*⸢*ta*⸣*-din*

29) ^{d}*A-ma-nu* KUR *i-li-ti*

30) KUR *šap-li-ti ṣi-it* ^{d}UTU

31) *e-re-eb* ^{d}UTU *i-na šu-pa-al*

32) 2 GÌR LUGAL

EA 369

TRANSLATION

(1–2) To Milkilu, ruler of Gezer; thus the king:

(2–14) Now, this tablet have I sent to you in order to say to you: Now I have dispatched to you Ḫanya, ‹commander of› the stable of the regular army, with everything for the acquisition of beautiful female cupbearers, viz. silver, gold, linen garments, carnelian stones, all (kinds of) precious stones, an ebony chair; likewise, all of excellent quality.

Total: one hundred and sixty *diban*.

Total: 40 female cupbearers.

Forty (shekels of) silver is the price of one female cupbearer.

(15–23) So send very beautiful female cupbearers in whom there is no malice among them, so that the king will say to you, "This is excellent," according to the requisition that he sent you.

(24–27) And may you be apprised that the king is hale, l[ik]e the sun god; his army, his chariotry, his horses are all very well.

(28–32) Now Amon has placed the upper land, the lower land, (from) the coming forth of the sun god (to) the entering in of the sun god beneath the two feet of the king.

EA 370

TRANSCRIPTION

Obv.

01) *a-na* ^{I}*-dì-ia* LÚ URU *Aš-qá-lu-*⸢*na*⸣⸢^{KI}⸣
02) *qí-bí-ma um-ma* LUGAL*-ma a-nu-*⸢*ma*⸣
03) *ṭup-pa an-na-a uš-te-bi-la-ku ‹a-na›*
04) *qá-bé-e a-na ka-a-ša ù* ⸢*uṣ*⸣*-*⸢*ṣur*⸣
05) *lu-ú na-ṣa-ra-ta aš-ru* LUGAL
06) *ša it-ti-ka*

---

07) *a-nu-ma* LUGAL *um-te-eš*$_{17}$(MEŠ)-⸢*ši*⸣[*-ra-ku*]
08) ^{I}*I-ri-ia-ma*[*-aš-ša*]
09) ⸢LÚ⸣?.⸢MÁŠKIM⸣? ⸢*ša*⸣? [LUGAL]

10–22) Lower part of obv. and upper part of rev. broken off

Rev.

23) ⸢*ù*⸣ *lu-ú* [*ti-i-de*$_{9}$ *i-nu-ma*]
24) *ša-lim* LUGAL *k*[*i-ma* ^{d}UTU]
25) *i-na* AN *ša*$_{10}$*-me-*⸢*e*⸣ [ÉRIN.MEŠ*-šu*]
26) GIŠ.GIGIR.MEŠ-⸢*šu*⸣ ⸢*ma*⸣*-a-d*[*u šul?-mu?*]
27) *i-na* KUR UGU*-tì* ⸢*a*⸣*-d*[*i* KUR GAM*-tì*]
28) *ṣi-it* ^{d}UTU*-aš a-di e-re-*⸢*eb*⸣ ⸢^{d}⸣⸢UTU⸣*-aš*
29) *ma-gal šul-mu*

EA 370

TRANSLATION

(1–6) To (Y)idia, ruler of the city of Ashkelon, speak: Thus (says) the king: Now this tablet have I sent to you ‹to› say, "Guard, may you be on guard in the place of the king that is in your charge."

(7–9) Now, the king has sen[t to you] Irima[šša], ⸢commissioner⸣(?) of [the king].....

(10–22) *Lower part of obv. and upper part of rev. broken off*

(23–29) And may [you be apprised that] the king is fine l[ike the sun god] in heaven. [His infantry and] his chariotry are great (or: very [well?]). From the upper land to [the lower land], from the sunrise to the sunset, it is very well.

EA 371

TRANSCRIPTION

Obv. 01–09 Missing

10) [......]⸢*ú*⸣? ⸢*ul*[.....]
11) [......]⸢*i*⸣?-*na* ŠU.MEŠ ⸢EN⸣-[*i*]⸢*a*⸣ ⸢*ù*⸣
12) [......]⸢*a*⸣? *a-na-ṣa-*⸢*ar*⸣*-šu-nu*
13) [LÚ.MEŠ]⸢GAL⸣-*tu a-di* LUGAL ^{d}UTU
14) [..*yi-ma-*]⸢*lik*⸣ *a-na* ÌR.MEŠ-*šu*
15) [......]x? EN-*ia a-di*
16) [*a-na-ṣa-a*]*r aš-ri-šu ù*
17) [......]x? EN-*ia ki-ma*!?
18) [......]*ia-nu lìb-bá ša-na-am*
19) [......]y? ÉRIN.MEŠ URU *Še*$_{20}$*-eḫ-la-li*
20) [.....*li-*]*de i-nu-ma la-a* DÙG.GA
21) [*šu-nu*..]*ù ti-iṣ-ba-tu-ni*$_{7}$
22) [URU *Ṣu-mur*]^{KI} *qa-du* LÚ.MEŠ *ša*

Lo.ed. 23) [.....*a-*]⸢*la*⸣*-ki a-na pa-ni-šu-*⸢*nu*⸣
24) [*a-na-ṣa-*]*ru* LÚ.MEŠ.MÁŠKIM EN-[*ia*](?)
25) [*šum-ma ul*] *en-né-ri-ir*

Rev. 26) [*a-na-ku*]*qa-du* GIŠ.GIGIR.ḪI.A-*i*⸢*a*⸣
27) [*qa-du* ÉRIN.MEŠ-]⸢*i*⸣*a ù ša-ar-pu*
28) [URU.KI *ù* É.GAL-]*ši ù ma-aḫ-ṣú-ni*$_{7}$
29) [*gáb-ba* LÚ.MEŠ] *ša i-na lìb-bi* É-*ti*
30) [......]URU.KI LUGAL EN-*ia iš-tu*
31) [......*m*]*a-ḫi-iṣ ma-ḫi-iṣ ù*
32) [......]⸢*li*⸣ *i-na* KÙ.BABBAR.ḪI.A
33) [....*iš-*]*tu pa-ni* LUGAL.MEŠ
34) [*ù i-na*]^{UZU}*pí-šu-nu yi-iṣ-bat*
35) [.....U]RU.KI *ù ap-lu-*$_{uḫ}$
36) [......*a-n*]*a* UGU-*ia ù*

EA 371

TRANSLATION

Obv. about 9 lines missing.

(10) [......]and not[......]
(11) [......]in the hands of m[y lord] ⸢and⸣?
(12) [......]I guard them
(13) senior [officials] until the king, the sun god
(14) [takes coun]cil concerning his servants
(15) [......]? my lord, until/still
(16) [I guar]d his places and
(17) [......]? my lord,
(18) [......]there is no other intention
(19) [......]? the troops of Šeḫlal
(20) [may he kn]ow that it is not good
(21) [......]and they captured
(22) [the city of Ṣumur] with the men who

Lower edge
(23) [....go]ing before them
(24) [I am guar]ding the commissioners of [my] lord
(25) [If I had not] come to (their) aid

Reverse
(26) [myself] together with my chariots (and)
(27) [together with] my [infantry] then they would have burnt
(28) [the city and]its [palace] and they would have smitten
(29) [all of the men] who were within the house (palace)
(30) [......] the city of the king, my lord, from
(31) [......k]illed, killed, and
(32) [......]? from the silver
(33) [......fr]om the kings
(34) [and by] their order he captured
(35) [..the c]ity. So I was afraid(?)
(36) [......]? against me and

37) [......ME]Š-⸢*šu*⸣-*nu i-na* KÙ.BABBAR
38) [......]x LÚ.MEŠ.MÁŠKIM-ka_4
39) [......]⸢*ša*⸣?[.....*m*]*a*

(37) [......]their [...]s for silver
(38) [......]? your commissioners
(39) [......]which[......]?

EA 372

TRANSCRIPTION

Obv. 01') [...] broken [...]
02') [...*t*]*im* ⸢*ki*⸣-⸢*a*⸣-⸢*am*⸣ [...]
03') [...]*ú-ša-al-l*[*i-im*...]
04') [...*t*]*im te-ru-ub*[...]
05') [..*i-n*]*a pa-ni-k*[*a*(?)...]
06') [..*š*]*a* ⸢*ki*⸣(*?*)[...]

EA 372

TRANSLATION

(1'–6') [...] thus [...]...he pai[d...] you entered [...] in ⸢your⸣(?) presence [...]

EA 378

TRANSCRIPTION

Obv. 01) [*a-na*] LU[GAL EN]-⸢*ia*⸣ DINGIR.MEŠ *i*[*a*]
02) [^{d}UTU-*ia*] ⸢^{d}⸣UTU *ša iš-t*[*u*]
03) [AN] ⸢*ša*$_{10}$⸣-*mì*-⸢*i*⸣ ⸢*um*⸣-⸢*ma* ⸣ ^{I}*I*⸢*a*⸣[*-pa-ḫi*]
04) [L]Ú *ša* URU ⸢*Gaz*⸣-*ri*^{K}[^{I} ÌR-*ka*] ⸢*ep*⸣-*ri* ⸢*ša*⸣ ⸢^{UZU}⸣GÌR.MEŠ[-*ka*]
05) ⸢*a*⸣-*na* ^{UZU}GÌR.MEŠ LUGAL EN-*ia*
06) DINGIR.MEŠ-*ia* ^{d}UTU-*ia* ^{d}UTU *i*[*š-tu*]
07) AN *ša*$_{10}$-*mì-i* 7-*šu u* 7-⸢*ta*⸣-⸢*a*⸣-⸢*an*⸣
08) *lu-ú iš-ta-*[*ḫ*]*a-ḫi-in*
09) ^{UZU}*ka-bat-tum-ma u*
10) ^{UZU}*ṣe-ru-ma a-nu-ma*
11) *a-na-ṣa-ru-mì a-šar* LUGAL EN-*ia*
12) ⸢^{d}⸣UTU *iš*-⸢*tu*⸣ AN *ša*$_{10}$-*mì-i*
13) ⸢*ša*⸣ *it-ti*-⸢*ia*⸣
14) *u gáb-bi mì-im-mì ša*
15) *ša-pár* LUGAL EN-*ia*
16) ⸢*a*⸣-*na ia-ši gáb-ba*
17) ⸢*lu*⸣-*ú ep-pu-šu-mì*
18) [*u m*]*a-an-nu-mì a*-⸢*na*⸣-*ku* UR.GI$_{7}$
Lo.ed. 19) [*u ma-*]*an-nu* ⸢É⸣-*ia*
Rev. 20) ⸢*u*⸣ [*m*]*a*-⸢*an*⸣-*nu* ⸢URU⸣.⸢KI⸣-*ia*
21) [*u m*]*a-an-nu* ⸢*gáb*⸣-⸢*bi*⸣
22) *mi-im-mì ša* ⸢*i*⸣-⸢*ba*⸣-*aš-ši*
23) *a-na ia-ši u a-wa-te*^{MEŠ}
24) LUGAL EN-*ia* ^{d}UTU ⸢*iš*⸣-*tu*
25) AN *ša*$_{10}$-*mì-i ú*-⸢*ul*⸣
26) ⸢*il*⸣-*te*$_{9}$-*né-em-me*

EA 378

TRANSLATION

(1–10) [To the ki[ng], my [lord], ⸢my⸣ deity, [my sun god], the sun god from heaven, message of Ya[paʿi] the ruler of the city of Gezer, [your servant], the dirt at [your] feet: At the feet of the king, my lord, my deity, my sun god, the sun god f[rom] heaven, seven times and seven times I have verily prostrated myself, on the stomach and on the back.

(10–17) Now I am guarding the place of the king, my lord, the sun god from heaven, which is in my charge, and as for every thing that the king, my lord, has written to me, I am verily doing it all.

(18–26) [And w]hat am I, a dog, [and wh]at is my house, [and w]hat is my city, [and w]hat is everything that belongs to me, that I should not continually heed the words of the king, my lord, the sun god from heaven?

EA 380

TRANSCRIPTION

Obv.	01')	[*um*]-*ma* ^{Id}[IŠKUR-?? *a-na*]
	02')	[ŠEŠ]-*ia qí-b*[*í-ma*]
	03')	[*a-n*]*u-ma a-qá*[*b-bi*]
	04')	[*u*]*m-ma-a u*[*ṣ-ṣur*]
	05')	[*l*]*u-ú ša-l*[*i-im*]
	06')	*am-mì-ni la*[*ta-aš-pur*]
	07')	*šul-ma*[*-ni-ka*]
Lo.ed.	08')	*lu-ú šul*[*-mu a-na ka-ša*]
	09')	*am-mì-ni l*[*a tu-še-bi-la*]
	10')	*i-na* ŠU [^{I}...ÌR]
Rev.	11')	*ša* LUGAL *a*[*-na-ku*]
	12')	*ù šu-t*[*e-ši-ir*]
	13')	*šum-ma pa-*[...]
	14')	*um-ma-a* [^{I}...]
	15')	LÚ.DUB.S[AR⌉

EA 380

TRANSLATION

(1'–2') [Mes]sage of [Baʿl-??] spe[ak to] my [brother].

(3'–5') [N]ow I sa[y a]s follows, "Gu[ard! M]ay it be we[ll!]

(6'–10') Why [have you] not [written concerning your] welf[are]? May it be we[ll with you]. Why [have you] n[ot sent] by the hand of [...].

(10'–13') [The servant] of the king [am] I, so ex[pedite...] if [...]."

(14'–15') Thus (says) [...] the scribe.

VAT number assigned by Klengel 1974:262. EA number assigned by Heintz 1996:72.

EA 381

TRANSCRIPTION

01’) [....................................]
02) [....................................]
03’) [.......]x ⌜*ru*⌝ ⌜*e*⌝(?) [..................]
04’) [..........................]⌜*ma*⌝[.....]
05’) [........................]⌜*še*⌝[........]
06’) [....................................]
07’) [....................................]
08’) [....................................]
09’) [.......]*aš-te* [*-mé*.....................]
10’) [.......*a*]*d š*[*i*[........................]
11’) [.......]*yi-ìš-m*[*é*......................]
12’) [.......*a*]*d* x[..........................]
13’) [.....................................]
14’) traces

EA 381

TRANSLATION

01') [.................................]
02) [.................................]
03') [.......]??????????/ [.................]
04') [.........................]???[......]
05') [.......................]???[........]
06') [.................................]
07') [.................................]
08') [.................................]
09') [.......]I have [heard.................]
10') [........]???[........................]
11') [.......]he heard[.....................]
12') [.......]???[.........................]
13') [.................................]
14') traces

VAT number assigned by Klengel 1974:262. EA number assigned by Heintz 1996:72.

EA 382

TRANSCRIPTION

Obv. 01’) [...]
02’) [...]
03’) [................]x ⸢*ru?*⸣ ⸢*e?*⸣[...............]
04’) [.................................] *ma?*[....]
05’) [.............................] *še?*[........]
06’) [...]
07’) [...]
08’) [...]
09’) [............] *aš-te*[*-mé?*.....................]
10’) [...........*a*]*d? š*[*i*.........................]
11’) [........]*yi-ìš-m*[*é*..........................]
12’) [...........*a*]*d?* x[..........................]
13’) [...]
14’) traces

EA 382

TRANSLATION

Obv. 01') [...]
02') [...]
03') [................] ? ? ? ? ? ? [...............]
04') [...............................] ? ? [....]
05') [............................] ? ? [........]
06') [...]
07') [...]
08') [...]
09') [............] I have[heard?................]
10') [...........] ? ? [.........................]
11') [.......]may he listen[.....................]
12') [...........] ? ? [..........................]
13') [...]
14') traces

VAT number assigned by Klengel 1974:262. EA number assigned by Heintz 1996:72.

GLOSSARY

Alice Mandell

Introduction to Glossary

The glossary requires a few words of introduction as it was prepared after the passing of Professor Rainey. Rainey suggested that a glossary should be included, but he was not able to oversee its preparation. Here we outline some of the aspects of its preparation.

The principle language of the Amarna Letters is Akkadian, yet there is great influence from the diverse substrate languages and scribal traditions represented in this corpus of letters. The lists in the glossary are limited to the Akkadian letters in the Amarna corpus and do not include the lexemes in the literary or lexical texts discovered at Tell el-ʿAmarna, nor in the Hurrian (EA 24) and Hittite letters (EA 31–32). The letter order of the Akkadian glossary is as follows: *a, b, d, e, g, ḫ, i, k, l, m, n, p, q, r, s, ṣ, š, t, ṭ, u, w, y, z*. We mark initial *yod* as *y-* following English convention as opposed to *j-*, which follows German convention, e.g., *yānu* "there is not" vs. *jānu* (CAD i/j 323). The Akkadian glossary includes terms that are written using logograms as well as syllabic cuneiform, whereas the list of logograms is restricted to those terms attested solely in the Amarna Letters in logographic form.

The lexemes in the Amarna Letters that reflect an Akkadian or Akkadianized root are listed in the Akkadian section of the glossary; likewise, lexemes that may not be of Akkadian origin but occur in peripheral Akkadian, and are included in major works such as the AHw and the CAD, are likewise included in the Akkadian section of the glossary. When appropriate, the presumed language of origin is specified in parenthesis, e.g., *tumunsallu* "¼ shekel weight" (Am. < Hurr.); *maḫan* "a wooden chest" (< Eg. *mhn*). Similarly, the designation WS indicates that the lexeme is a WS term, loan, or calque, e.g., *anuki* "I" (Am. < WS); *bâʾum* II; G "to come" (Am. < WS).

The glossary attempts to be faithful to Rainey's translation, yet in certain cases when his translation deviates, or provides a slightly more nuanced translation than that listed in other lexicons, the more standard translation is included, e.g., *dudittu* (*tudittu*) "toggle pin" (Rainey), "pectoral" (CAD).

When a variant, rare orthography (e.g., an alternative spelling resulting from dental or sibilant confusion, b/p alternation, and/or consonant doubling etc.), or by-form of a lexeme occurs in the Amarna corpus, the standard form and/or variant form listed in the major lexicons is provided in parenthesis. This is intended to guide readers to the appropriate entry in the dedicated Akkadian dictionaries, e.g., *duḫnu*, (*tuḫnu*) "millet;" *bikru* (*pikru*) "a bead, gemstone." Likewise, when two forms of a word are attested, both are included in the glossary. For example, both *angurinnu* (EA 13 rev. 23) and *angurbinnu* (EA 15:III:15) ("a metal household object") are attested Rainey's work, yet the form *angurbinnu* is not listed in the CAD or AHw. The glossary provided here lists both forms of this word in line with Rainey's transcription. Accordingly, on occasion the reader is directed to a separate entry in the glossary that may clarify the root or origin of the lexeme, e.g., *untu* see *undu* (from the root *emēdu*). Verbal roots that are formally identical but semantically distinct are listed separately, e.g., *abātu* I G "to destroy;" *abātu* II G "to flee, run away;" N "to escape; hide." When appropriate, the reader will be directed to the historically "fuller" verbal root, or in the case of derived forms, the G infinitive. This is particularly pertinent for I-*w* verbal roots, verbs with by-forms, and derived forms, e.g., *abālu* see *wabālu; arādu* see *warādu*; *babālu* see *wabālu; ibašši* see *bašû; gummuru* see *gamāru* etc. Again, this is intended to make the corpus more accessible to non-Akkadian specialists.

Rainey's new transliteration renders a number of words obsolete. There are a small number of lexemes, mainly unidentified or ill-understood objects, or *hapax legomena* (particularly in the lists of gifts), that are tentatively listed as being part of the phenomenon of peripheral Akkadian represented in the el-ʿAmarna corpus (EA) that Rainey did not include in this publication. Some of these terms were eliminated in Rainey's updated transliterations, as his segmentation of the signs altered certain words; in other cases, Rainey's analysis and translation of these terms differed from other publications. These lexemes are not included in this glossary, as it only reflects the readings attested in Rainey's manuscript. For example, the CAD lists the term *ta-aḫ-ba-ṣí* (EA 36:7) "meaning unknown" (CAD *t*:48); likewise, the AHw does not offer a definition of this term, other than identifying it as being derived from the root *ḫabāṣu*, and relating to some type of gift (AHw *t*: 1301). Rainey, on the other hand, interprets *ta-aḫ-ba-ṣí* as a 2nd person prefix conjugation verb derived from the root *ḫabāṣu*, rendering the translation "you will rejoice." This term is thus listed in the Akkadian list as a G stem of *ḫabāṣu*. Another example is the term *makkasu* (in EA 22:II:59), which Rainey interprets as a type of axe (from the verb *nakāsu*), following AHw (*m*:589), whereas the CAD (*m*-1:132) lists this object under *makkasu* B, as a type of metal bowl.

Since the discovery of the Amarna Letters, the field has traditionally viewed the language of the Amarna Letters as a reflection of the various "dialects" of Akkadian operating in the periphery. As such, the Akkadian list provided here includes terms that may have originally been of foreign origin but are listed by their Akkadianized forms in the designated Akkadian dictionaries. This will aid readers locate the appropriate entries in the dedicated Akkadian dictionaries. In particular, the CAD and AHw include attestations underneath the definition that they provide which may prove helpful to the reader. This is particularly relevant for the numerous lexemes in the letters from the southern Levant that reflect the influence of the WS spoken language substratum. For convenience, if a lexeme is listed in the designated Akkadian dictionaries, it is likewise listed in the glossary by its Akkadianized form, as opposed to the WS list. Such terms are designated WS in parenthesis in order to alert the reader to their potential WS origin, e.g., *zuruḫ* "arm" (Am. < WS). This is also done to reflect the ambiguity of the term, as there are numerous lexemes shared by both WS and Akkadian dialects. Moreover, in some cases it is unclear whether or not the lexeme was considered to be an Akkadian word or a WS calque or loanword by the scribe, or was perhaps a term unique to peripheral Akkadian.

The WS list, on the other hand, comprises of lexemes found in glosses, the lexemes that Rainey analyzed as WS or as showing WS influence in his publications, and terms that are not included in the designated Akkadian lexicons (as they are not Akkadian, or do not have Akkadian cognates, or are unattested elsewhere in Akkadian texts). Such lexemes are unambiguously derived from the local WS languages spoken by the Canaanite scribes, i.e., the WS lexemes in the Amarna glosses that are essentially marked as non-Akkadian terms, e.g., *ḥmh* "wall"; *kwn* "to establish, to make ready, prepare"; etc. Such lexemes are listed in the WS list by their tri-literal root following the conventions established in *Koehler-Baumgartner* (*KB*).

Likewise, there is a separate list for the Egyptian terms in the Amarna Letters that were written in Egyptian and/or are considered to be Egyptian loans or technical terms. Again, the Egyptian lexemes or Egyptian loans that are written in cuneiform in the Amarna letters and are included in the designated Akkadian lexicons are listed by their Akkadianized form in the Akkadian list, e.g., *we'u* (*weḫu*) troops (Am.‹Eg.). Whereas, the lexemes written in the Egyptian language and script in the Amarna Letters can be found in the Egyptian list according to their Egyptian root, e.g., *ꜣbd* "month."

As this work reflects Rainey's academic journey, and in a sense, the history of cuneiform scholarship since the discovery of the Amarna Letters in 1887, the contributors have decided to include some variant sign values in the logogram glossary to guide readers. Due to the dynamic changes in the field of Assyriology the current sign values of certain logograms are not reflected in the classic sign lists (such as Borger and Labat), nor in the previous publications of the Amarna Letters. As such, Rainey's "older" sign readings, e.g., GUŠKIN or KUG.GI for *ḫurāṣu* "gold," have been updated (e.g., to KÙ.GI) although an even more updated reading might be KÙ.SIG$_{17}$. Likewise, Rainey lists certain signs by both their longer and shorter sign values, e.g., both GUD as well as GU$_4$ (EA 248:16, 280:27) for *alpu* or "ox" in Akkadian. When combinations of signs for the same lexeme deviate slightly, they are grouped together under the principle sign that makes up the word for the sake of convenience, e.g., the entry for ŠE is as follows: ŠE, ŠE.ḪI.A, ŠE.IM.ḪI.A, IM.ŠE.ḪI.A *šeʾu, uṭṭatu* "grain, barley"; ŠE-*tu uṭṭatu* "grains"; immediately, i.e., "after 10 grains."

The logograms in the glossary reflect the system of transliteration in place in Rainey's manuscript, which does not usually distinguish determinatives from other logograms, e.g., NA$_4$.GUG [Rainey] vs. ^{NA4}GUG, whereby the determinative NA$_4$ "stone" is in superscript. The one exception is the DINGIR sign in deity names, which is raised in superscript in Rainey's transliteration, e.g., ^{d}A for Aten. Determinatives such as GIŠ "wood," LÚ "man," and NA$_4$ "stone" are usually not considered part of the lexemes that the precede, but rather identify the semantic group to which the lexemes belong. For example, in the logogram sequences NA$_4$.GUG (*sāmtu* "carnelian") the determinative NA$_4$ indicates that GUG is a type of stone. At times the line between the determinative and the actual word is ambiguous. For example, Rainey understood the signs KUR "land" and URU "city" in place names as actual words, rendering "land of/city of X," as opposed to mere determinatives designating the following names as a region/city. The logograms are arranged alphabetically in the glossary following the conventions of the English alphabet. Since the determinatives are not differentiated in Rainey's manuscript, the reader should look for the logogram alphabetically by the first logogram in the sign sequence, e.g., GIŠ.GIGIR (*narkabtu*) "chariot" is listed under the sign GIŠ.

Lexemes that rare or are unique to the Amarna corpus are designated as Am. for "Amarna." This designation signals to the reader that this term or usage is not standard in Middle Babylonian (MB). Such lexemes are either best attested in the Amarna corpus and/or in peripheral Akkadian at sites such as Nuzi or Ugarit. In some cases, they are unique to the Amarna corpus and most likely derived from local substrate languages or the product of local scribal conventions. For example, certain words are attested in texts produced by Akkadian scribal centers in the periphery but are not well attested in contemporary Middle Babylonian or Middle Assyrian dialects, e.g., *sakku* "a bronze object" is attested in the Amarna corpus, Nuzi and in Neo-Assyrian, yet, not in MB. Therefore, it is marked as Am. In many cases, lexemes that are mainly found in peripheral Akkadian are loans or calques from a foreign language. For example, the specific meaning of the D stem of *banû* as "to erect/establish a city" is unique to the Amarna corpus and is thought to be a calque from WS. Other examples include *baqāmu* G "to pluck; to harvest"; *agrūtu* "wages," which are also thought to be derived from WS. *išuḫḫu*, which appears to be a type of garment, is attested once in a list of gifts in a letter from Tušratta (EA 25:IV:41) and thus is most likely a Hurrian term. The designation Am. is also used to highlight orthographies that are either best attested, or only attested in the EA corpus, e.g., *tumālu* (*timālu*) "yesterday" (Am. < WS). The word *timālu* occurs in Akkadian from the OA on; however, the form *tumālu* is only attested in the Amarna Letters and is presumably derived from WS.

In creating this glossary, we debated where to place the verbs in the Canaanite Letters that do not neatly fall into the Akkadian or WS verbal paradigm. Current discussions of such forms are central in debates as to whether or not the language underlying the Amarna Letters from the southern Levant should be classified as Akkadian, as opposed to WS. Rainey viewed the language of the Canaanite Letters as a "code" between various groups, but argued that it is impossible to tell whether or not it was spoken: "Was it due to some dominant, creative personality in one of the scribal school? Did this result in, or was it the result of, a spoken 'interlanguage' that developed among the local administrators?" (A. Rainey and R. Steven Notley, *The Sacred Bridge* [Jerusalem: Carta, 2006]:88.) Though, in his own analysis of the Amarna Letters, he approached the differences in orthography as a reflection of a phonological, spoken reality, classifying the verbs of the Canaanite Letters as "mixed" Akkadian/Canaanite forms. In contrast to Rainey, who classified the Canaaanite Letters as part of the phenomenon of Peripheral Akkadian (albeit with heavy Canaanite influence), a trend in recent scholarship divorces writing from speech, calling into question the assumption that Peripheral Akkadian reflects the existence of various concurrent "dialects" of spoken Akkadian. However, as the main goal of the glossary is to provide information as to the verbal stems attested in the letters in a way that reflects Rainey's own interpretation of the verbal system, moreover, to honor him as a scholar and his exhaustive writings on the subject, the glossary follows Rainey's analysis of the language of the Canaanite letters. Rainey viewed "Canaanite Akkadian" as a hybrid language drawing from the prestige of Akkadian as well as the local WS languages spoken by Canaanite scribes during this period, as is reflected by the title of his grammar of the Canaanite corpus: *Canaanite in the Amarna Letters: A Linguistic Analysis of the Mixed Dialect Used by the Scribes from Canaan* (CAT). In order to resolve the issue of how to classify such forms, we turned to Rainey's writings, in particular CAT, which reflects Rainey's life work on the Canaanite verbal system. Rainey wrote extensively the verbal system in the Canaanite letters, which presents several interesting problems due to archaic and anomalous forms. Rainey argued that Canaanite Akkadian verbs were "hybrid" forms that used elements from both the Akkadian and WS verbal systems: the verbal roots were derived from Akkadian, whereas, the affixes that code tense, aspect, and modality were derived from WS. In CAT II, Rainey parses the "mixed" verbal forms as though Akkadian verbs, in accordance with the verbal stems in Akkadian (G, D, Š, N). Since he approached the verbs as "mixed" forms, he interpreted anomalous forms such as the internal passives Gp and Dp, and use of the H-stem (Causative), which are not attested in Akkadian, as reflections of the WS substratum language of the Canaanite scribes.

When the verbal stem employs an anomalous form that reflects a WS as opposed to an Akkadian verbal stem, such as an internal passive (Gp), we note this in the Akkadian glossary. The Canaanite Letters are also characterized by the use of WS affixes on Akkadian verbal bases to code tense and/or modality, e.g., EA 114:42 *ša [m]a-an-ni yu-pa-šu ki-a-ma* "why is he being treated thus?" The verb here is a 3ms G passive (Gp) present indicative derived from the Akkadian verbal root *epēšu* "to do." However, the Gp is a WS verbal stem (corresponding to the Akkadian N stem). Moreover, *yv-* is the WS 3ms pronominal prefix, as opposed to *i-* in Akkadian (*iprus* [3ms preterite], *iparras* [3ms durative], *iptaras* [3ms perfect] etc.), e.g., EA 138:38 *yi-iṣ-bat* "he seized" (WS prefix) vs. *iṣbat* (the 3ms Akkadian preterite). In the Canaanite letters WS pronominal suffixes are affixed to the suffix conjugation *qatala* (which corresponds to the Akkadian stative), e.g., WS 1cs *-ti* vs. 1cs Akkadian *-āku*. The suffix conjugation denotes actions in the past, e.g., EA 127:34 where the Akkadian 1cs stative *ma-ṣa-ku* is followed by the Canaanite gloss *ṣí-ir-ti* "I am hard pressed." Rainey classified such verbs as Canaanized or Canaanite Akkadian, a dialect or written form of Akkadian that was heavily influenced by WS, yet, not WS. We have accordingly included such "hybrid" verbs in the Akkadian list by their Akkadian infinitives as listed in the designated Akkadian dictionaries.

The hope is that this glossary will prove useful to scholars and readers, in particular, those new to the Amarna Letters. The glossary is not intended to be exhaustive, but to be an accessible reference and a guide to Rainey's updated transliterations and translations, particularly where his translations differ from previous publications of the Amarna Letters. More involved researchers should consult the excellent lexicons already in circulation, such as the *Akkadisches Handwörterbuch* (AHw) and the *Chicago Assyrian Dictionary* (CAD) etc., which contain the bulk of lexemes in the Amarna corpus. In particular, the CAD offers a useful list of attestations for each entry that will prove invaluable to further study of this corpus. In addition, *A Concise Dictionary of Akkadian* (edited by J. Black, A. George, and N. Postgate) is a useful and quick reference work that utilizes both CAD and AHw.

Glossary

â, ai, yâ	not; may not; do not (before a prohibitive)
abu	father [A; A.A; AD; AD.DA; AB.BA]
abālu	see *wabālu*
abašmû	a greenish colored precious stone
abātu I	**G** to destroy
abātu II	**G** to flee, run away; **N** to escape; to hide
abnu	stone, rock [NA4]
abūbu	flood, deluge
abullu	gate [KÁ.GAL]
adaḫa	a type of cloth
addu	a type of throw stick (Am.)
adi	until, up to, until the time that; along with; indeed, truly (Am.); still (Am. < WS)
agāmi	today
agannu	a bowl
agarḫu	a piece of jewelry
agru	hireling, hired man
agrūtu	wages (Am.)
aḫāmiš	each other, one another
aḫāru	**G** to be late, be delayed; **D** trans. to hold back, delay (Am.)
aḫātu	sister
aḫāzu	**G** to take, seize; to marry
aḫennâ	separately, by itself
aḫītu	side
aḫita	on one side; aside
aḫu I	brother [ŠEŠ]
aḫu II	side, arm [ZAG]
aḫḫūtu	brotherhood, brotherly relations

aḫû II	**Gt** to fraternize, have brotherly relations with
aḫuzzatu	marriage gift; marriage-like relationship
aigalluḫu	a type of horned animal
akalu	food, sustenance [NINDA; NÌG]
akālu	**G** to eat
akkannama	similarly
akanna	so, thus
akunu	(*akūnu*) jar, vessel (< Eg.)
alāku	**G** to go; **GT** to go forth; **GTN** to roam, wander
allû	presentation particle (Am. < WS); certainly, indeed, furthermore
ālu	city, town (in Am. can be treated as a f. noun); pl. *ālānu* [URU]
ālu II	(*ēlu*) ram, ram-shaped ornament
alpu	bull, ox [GU4]
alta(p)pipu	a chest, box (Am.)
-am	to me (1cs dative)
amāru	**G** to see
amartu	board, sideboard; partition (between homes)
amātu	(*awātu*) word; matter [INIM]
amê ṣabi	red colored(?) (< Eg. *ỉmꜣw*)
amēlu	(*awīlu*) male, man, human, person [LÚ]
amēltu	(*awīltu*) female, woman [MUNUS]
ami	see *amê*
amīlūtu	(*awīlūtu*) personnel, servants (coll. pl.)
ammal	as much as, in accordance with
ammīni	why?
ammiu	f. *ammītu*; that
ammu	people
amtu	female servant [GÉME]
amur	see *amāru*; behold (introduction particle) (Am.)
amūtu	a type of precious metal
ana	to, for; belonging to
anaḫu	a golden object (*ʿnḫ* shaped?)
anāḫu	**G** to become tired, weary
anāku	1cs; I, me
angurbinnu	see *angurinnu*
angurinnu	a metal household object
anmûtti	(pl. of *anmû*) these things
annāma	likewise
annânum	here, from here
annikâ	**anni(u)+ kīam*; here
anīna	now
anniš	(*annuš*) **annû+ ištu*; here, hither
annû	this, those; fs. *annītu* this one; mp. *annûtu* these, those; in this manner
annû	behold (Am. < WS)
annûš	look! (Am. < WS)
anṣabtu	(*inṣabtu*) earing

anuki	see *anāku*; 1cs I (Am. < WS)
anumma	now
apālu	**G** to pay; to answer; **N** to be paid off
ʿapîru	see *ḫāpiru*
apisāmūš	a type of bow (?)
appu	nose; spout (vessel)
appanannu	a type of metal object (Am.)
appūna	(*appunnāma, appunāna*) moreover
apsasu	a type of animal (bovine?)
aqra	(*waqāru*) rare, scarce
aqarḫu	a type of jewelry (Am.)
arādu	see *warādu*; **G-D** to serve (Am.)
arāku	**G** to be long; **D** to lengthen, make long
arānu II	**G** to be guilty (Am.)
arapšannu	an unidentified object (Am.)
arāru	**G** to curse
araššannu	a type of bird, a bird-shaped object (?) (Am.)
ardu	(*wardu*) m. slave, servant
ardūtu	service; to (be of) service to; vassalage; slavery [ÌR]
arḫiš	quickly, hastily
arḫu	month [ITI]
arku	long, tall [GÍD.DA]
arnu	see *arāru*; guilt, sin, crime
asīru	captive, prisoner
asu	myrtle [ŠIM.AZ]
assaštaranni	the cloth streamers on a fly-whisk (Am.)
assuri	if (for neg. probability); in case that; on no account
ašallu	a type of bowl
ašar	(*ašru*) place, site; here; from
ašāšu	**G** to be angry, enraged
ašbu	see *wašābu*
aširi	a person of rank (Am < WS)
aškirušḫu	a type of utensil used in pairs (Am. < Hurr.)
ašnugallu	alabaster [NA4.GIŠ.NU_{11}.GAL]
ašrānu	see *ašar*; there
ašša	a type of jar with sweet oil (related to Late Egyptian ʿš?)
aššatu	wife [DAM]
aššiyannu	a type of garment, textile (Hurr. *maššiyannu*?)
aššum	because of
aššûtu	marriage [DAM-*ut*]
ašû	physician [A.ZU]
atteru	companion, friend (Am. < Hurr.)
atterūtu	friendship
atḫû	see *aḫu I*; partners
atḫûtu	brotherly relations; partnership
atru	(*watru*) extra, surplus
attū-	belonging to, e.g., *attūka* (2ms) your (used in possessive constructs)

awatamulušhe	an unidentified ivory object (Am. < Hurr.)
awatu	see *amātu*; word, matter [INIM]
a(y)yabba	the sea
ayyābu	(*yābu*) enemy
ayyaka	(*yaka*) where?
ayyalu	deer, stag [DÀRA.MAŠ]
ayyāmi	where? (Am.)
ayyānu	see *yānu*
ayyâši	(*yâši*) to, for, with me
ayyigalluḫu	(*haigallathe*) a type of horned animal (Am. < Hurr)
ayyimme	(*ēm*) wherever, whatever
ayyu	which, that; *ayyītu* fs; *ayyūtu* m.pl.
ayyumma	(*ayyummê*) any, anyone
azida	a type of sweet oil
bābu	door, gate [KÁ]
babālu	see *wabālu*; **G** to carry, bring
bakû	**G** to cry, weep
bali	see *balu*; without (Am.)
balāṭu I	life; provisions (Am.) [TI; TI.LA; TIN.ZI]
balāṭu II	**G** to live, be alive; **D** to rejuvenate, revive; **Š** to give life to (Am.) [TI; TI.LA]
balṭānumma	alive (Am.) [TI.LA]
ballukku	styrax [ŠIM.BÚL]
balu	(*bali*) without
banû I	good
banû II	**G** to be good; to be beautiful
banû III	**G** to build, create; **D** to erect, establish (a city) (Am.)
baqāmu	**G** to pluck; to harvest (Am.)
bašālu	**G** to be cooked; **Š** to cook
baštu	(*baltu*) dignity, pride, honor [TÉŠ]
bašû	(*ibašši*) **G** to exist
bâ'um II	**G** to come (Am. < WS)
bazā'um	**D** to treat harshly, deal with unreasonably
bēlu	lord, master, owner of [EN; BAD]
bēltu	lady, mistress [NIN; BAD-*tu*]
betatu	(*betātu*) a decoration on cloth and leather (Am.)
bibrû	a rhyton
bikru	(*pikru*) bead, gemstone
biltu	load, the load that a donkey can carry; talent (unit of weight) [GUN; GÚ]
biri-	(*beri-*) among, between
bītu	house; container [É]
bubūtu	a wooden section of a chariot (a beam on the side?)
buginnu	trough; wooden container [BUGIN]
bultu	a type of blanket, cover (Am.)
bumer	a measuring vessel
buqūmu	see *baqāmu*; plucking, (sheep) shearing [ZÚ.SI.GA]

burḫu	*ša b.* an object set in gold (?) (Am.)
burḫiš	(*burḫu*) a type of buffalo (Am.)
burku	(*purku*) knees, loins; *ša b.* loincloth
burrumu	multicolored; speckled [GÙN.(A)]
bušlu	see *bašalu*; molten
būšu	see *bašû*; (*bušû*) goods, property
butinnu	(*putinnu*) button (Am.)
bu’’û II	**D** to seek, search for; to ask for; to seek out (a result); to intend
dabābu	**G** to speak, talk, tell; **GTN** to repeatedly ask, inquire about
daba’uḫ I	a type of eye paint receptacle
dagālu	**G** to see, look; to show reverence to (Am.)
daḫû	**G** to beat down; to be pushed down
dâku	**G** to kill, defeat [GAZ]
dalāḫu	**G-D** to disturb, to interfere with; **D** to hurry (Am.)
daltu	door [(GIŠ).GI.IG]
dāmu	blood; *ša dama šūlû* "reddish"
damāqu	**G** to be good, make agreeable, pleasant; **D** to behave favorably towards
damqu	good, beautiful; notable
dannu	strong [KAL; GA.KAL, KAL.GA]
danniš	very, greatly
dapāru	see *ṭapāru*
dāru	era; eternity; *ana d.* forever (Am.)
dārītu	*ištu d.* of old, from time immemorial (Am.); *adi dāriāta* forever (Am.)
darû	**G** to last, live forever
dardara	a type of ornament (Am.)
daši	a type of beer jar (< Eg. *dś*[*y*])
dayyanu	see *diānu* (*diyānu*), a judge
dekû II	**G** to call up; to lift, levy
diānu	**G** to judge, to give or pass judgment [DI.KUD]
diban	(*tiban, deben*) a weight measurement (Am. < Eg.)
dimtu II	tears; *d.+ alāku* "to flow"
dīnu	legal case, legal ruling, decision, trial
dinīta	a bowl or vase (< Eg.)
diqāru	pot, large vessel
dišpu	honey [LÀL]
dūdu	a metal vessel, kettle
dudittu	see *tudittu*
duḫnu	(*tuḫnu*) millet
dullu	(*tullû*) work, labor; *dullu qatnu* "delicate labor," "handiwork"
du(*l*)*luḫu*	urgency; *dulluḫiš* "rushed, hurried" (Am.)
dūltu	(*tūltu*) worm
dumqu	goodness, a good thing [SIG$_5$]
dunnu	see *dannu*; power, strength
duppuru I	(*ṭapāru*) **D** to move away, to drive away so.
dūru	wall [BÀD]

dušû	a type of stone (agate?) [NA$_4$.DU$_8$.ŠI.A; NA$_4$.DUḪ.ŠI.A]
ē	(*ai*) not; *ē lā* "certainly not"
ebbu	pure, clear [SIKIL]
ebēru	**G** to cross over; **Š** to bring across, to transport
ebūru	harvest; summer, harvest month [BURU14]
eddāttu	(*eddittu*) a type of thorn bush
edēlu	**G** to shut, bolt; **Gp** locked
ēdēnu	alone, sole
edēšu	**G** to become new; **D** to rebuild, repair [GIBIL]
edû	(*idû*) **G** to know; to recognize; *e. ana* "to care for" (Am.)
eḫlipakku	(*eḫlupakku, eḫlapakku*) raw glass
ēkallu	palace [É.GAL]
ēkallû	palace official
ekēmu	**G** to save, deliver, rescue
el	(*elu, eli*) on, over, above
elammakku	a type of precious wood
elēnu	see *el*; above, over, more than (Am.)
eleppu	ship, boat, vessel [GIŠ.MÁ]
eliš	above [AN.TA]
elû I	upon, above; high, tall, exalted
elû II	upper (body part; geographic feature) [UGU]
elû III	**G** to go up, arise; **D** to raise, make higher, lift up; **Š** (caus. of **G**) to bring up; *ša dama šūlû* "enhanced blood-red" i.e., "reddish (gold)" (Am.); **Št** +*ana* to make as high as (dowry) (Am.)
ēm	wherever; whatever part of; whatever time
emu	father-in-law
emqu	wise
emēqu	**G** to be wise
emūqu	strength, force; *ina e.* "by force, violently"
emqūtu	wisdom (Am.)
emūtu	betrothal; marriage alliance (Am.)
enēnu I	**G** to grant favor, be favorable to; to be merciful (Am.)
enēnu II	**G** to punish
enēšu	**G** to be weak [SIG]
enūma	(*inūma*) when; because
enzu	goat [ÙZ]
epru	(*eperu*) earth, soil, dust [SAḪAR]
epēšu	**G** to do, make; *āla e.* to take a city; to fortify a city (Am.); to make into (king, son) (Am.); **Gtn** to continuously do; **N** pass. of **G**
eqlu	field [A.ŠÀ]
eratti(*ya*)*nnu*	a part of a weapon (?) (Am.)
erēbu	**G** to enter; **D** to inscribe on a tablet; **Š** to deliver; to cause to enter; to post troops
erēnu	cedar [GIŠ.EREN]
erbe	(f. *erbēt*) four
erbēšerû	fourteenth (Am.)
erbu II	(*e. šamši*) sunset

erēšu I	**G** to sow, cultivate, plow
erēšu II	**G** to request, wish, desire; to seek; **N** to be demanded, requested
eršu	bed [GIŠ.NÁ]
erṣētu	earth, land [KI]
erû	eagle, vulture; augury [Á.MUŠEN]
erû	(*werû*) copper [URUDU]
esēpu	**G** to gather up, collect
eṣēdu I	harvest [ŠE.KIN.(GUR$_{10}$).KU$_5$]
eṣēdu II	**G** to harvest, reap
ešēru	**G** to be straight; to go directly towards, to attack; **Š** to get in order, to prepare (Am.); N to put in order
ešer, (f.) ešeret	the number 10 [U]
ešmekku	malachite
eššu	(*edēšu*) new
etēqu	**G** to pass, cross over; **Š** to cause to cross; to transgress, break (oath, treaty); **Štn** iterative of **Š**
eṭlu	youth, young man
ezēbu	**G** to leave, abandon; **Gtn** to abandon; **Š** to save, deliver
gabbu	all of
gabīdu	(*kabīdu*) liver
gallābu	barber [LÚ.ŠU.I]
gamāru	**G** to complete, finish
gamru	complete, full; *ana g.* "in its entirety"
gamrūtu	entirety; *ana g.* "completely"
garādu	(*qarādu*) **G** to pluck, tear out
galtu	(*galdu*) a type of vessel (< Eg.?)
giltû	(*gištû*) rung
gilāmu	(*kilāmu*) a type of ivory
gimru	totality, everything
gištappu	footrest, footstool [GIŠ.GÌR.GUB]
guduppiānu	(*kuduppānu*) pomegranate (?)
guggubu	(*gubgubu*) an ornament set with a precious stone
guḫaṣṣu	(*guḫaššu*) wire, cord; torque
gumiru	see *gamāru*; completely, totally
gumūru	dagger hilt (Am.)
gummuru	see *gamāru*; **D** to finish off
gungubu	(*gungupu*) a part of a chariot (Am.)
gunte memētu	unknown object (housed in storerooms)(Am.)
gursipu	helmet [GUR.SI.IB]
guštappu	(*kuštappu*) the part of a harness (?) (Am.)
guzi	stable boy
ḫabālu I	injury, act of wrongdoing
ḫabālu II	**G** to damage; to do wrong; to oppress; **D** to wrong
ḫabālu III	**G** to be in debt, owe; to borrow
ḫabalkinnu	(*ḫabalginnu*) a metal alloy used for weapons
ḫabannatu	a container for oil
ḫabāṣu	**G** to be elated, carefree; **Š** to cause to rejoice

ḫabātu	**G** to rob, plunder, raid
ḫabbātu	bandit, raider [LÚ.SA.GAZ]
ḫadû	**G** to be joyful, rejoice; **D** to make happy
ḫalāqu	**G** to disappear, be lost; to be destroyed; **D** fact. of G
ḫalṣu	fort, fortress, camp
ḫalzuḫlu	district governor; fortress commander
ḫamāṭu	**G** to hurry, hasten; **D** to hurry (troops) (Am.)
ḫamṭu	quick sudden
ḫamuttu	haste; *ana/ina h.* "hastily"
ḫamutta	(*ḫamittu*) at once, soon
ḫamuttiš	quickly
ḫanāpu	**G** to act basely; to be sacrilegious (Am. < WS)
ḫannipu	see *ḫanpu*; sacrilege, impiety (Am.)
ḫanpu	see *ḫanāpu*; baseness (Am.)
ḫanūnu	box; chest; *ḫanūnu šāḫû* "upright chest" (< Eg. *hnu* or *hnn śʿḥʿ*)
ḫāpiru	(*ʿāpîru*) bandit, raider [LÚ.SA.GAZ]
ḫaragabaš	a type of gold/silver goblet (Am.)
ḫarranu	road [KASKAL]
ḫarāšu	see *erēšu*; **G-D** to bring together, to collect; to plow (WS)
ḫarušḫu	a type of animal; an animal-shaped ornament (?) (Am.)
ḫaṣṣinu	axe
ḫaṣuru	a type of garment
ḫašāḫu	**G** to desire, want, wish for
ḫašḫuru	apple tree [GIŠ.ḪAŠḪUR]
ḫatanu	in-law, relation by marriage
ḫatānu	son in law
ḫatappi	meaning unknown (a golden object)
ḫaṭû	**G** to do wrong, to be faulty, negligent
ḫāwiru	(*ḫāʾiru*) husband, consort [NITLAM$_4$]
ḫazannu	(m.pl. *hazannūte*) mayor, chief official
ḫedûtu	see *ḫadû*; (*ḫidûtu*) joy, rejoicing
ḫerizzi	a type of precious stone (Am. < Hurr.)
ḫidumû	(*ḫudumû*) a type of garment (Am. < Nuzi)
ḫilibû	a type of precious stone
ḫin	(*ḫina*) a type of stone (?) (< Eg.?)
ḫindu	(*ḫiddu*) (pl. *ḫintuna, ḫintena*) bead
ḫīrtu	wife, spouse [NITLAM$_4$]
ḫīṭu	error, negligence, fault
ḫubullu	damaged (< WS *ḥbl*)
ḫubunnu	a type of container
ḫubūtu	thicket (Am. < WS)
ḫuḫāru	a bird snare
ḫulālu	a type of precious stone [NA$_4$.NÍR]
ḫuliam	helmet (Am.)
ḫullu	(*ullu*) neck ring; torque; yoke (< WS *ʿwl*)
ḫunima	a type of vessel (Am. < Eg)
ḫurādu	soldiers; elite troops

ḫurru	Hurrian
ḫurāṣu	gold [KÙ.GI]
ḫuppalû	(*ḫutpalû*) mace [GIŠ.TUKUL.SAG.NA_4]
ḫupšu	yeomen workers; a member of the lower classes; rabble (pejorative)
ḫuššû	red [ḪUŠ.A]
ḫuttu	a type of stone jar (Am.)
ḫuzzi	a type of linen garment, cloth
ḫuzunu	a golden object (animal shaped?) (Am.)
-ī, -a, -a, -ya	1cs. suffix "my"
iaruttu	a type of oil (Am.)
ibaššu	see *bašû*; to be, exist
iduzzarra	an unidentified object (Am.)
idru	(*itru*) a band, belt (?), quality of cloth (?) (Am.)
i'lu	wrap, blanket [TÚG.SIG_4.ZA= OB TÚG.GUZ.ZA?]
ilu	deity determinative; god [DINGIR]
imdu	see *emēdu*; (*indu*) support; imposition, obligation
imittu	a type of spear
imēru	donkey [ANŠE]
immati	see *mati*; interrogative "when?"
immēru	sheep, flock of sheep; a ram shaped rhyton [UDU; UDU.‹A›.LUM]
ingana	(*gana*) "come on!" (Am.)
inu	(*enu*) when, at the time of
īnu	eye [IGI]
indu	see *imdu*
inūma	(*enūma*); when; since, because; that; now (for *anumma*) (Am.)
ina	in, into; (away) from; *ina* + PN "at the time of PN"
inanna	now
ipru	ration
ipšu	see *epēšu*; deed, action; behavior (Am.)
ipṭiru	see *paṭāru*; ransom money
irpi	an Egyptian official, army commander (Am. < Eg. *ḥry-pḏ*[*t*])
irtu	breast, chest; breastplate
isinnu	festival; *isinni kimiri/gimiri* (Heb. *ḥag hā'āsiḇ*) "feast of completion"(?) [EZEN]
iṣṣūru	bird [MUŠEN]
iṣû	wood; timber; tree [GIŠ]
išdu	base, foundation
išḫunnatu	(*isḫunnatu*) a cluster of grapes
išuḫḫu	a type of garment (Am.)
išātu	fire [IZI]; *ša i.* brazier (Am.)
išmekku	(*ešmekku*) malachite
išpatu	quiver [KUŠ.É.MAR.URU_5 (Am.)]
išqillatu	an oil container (Am.)
ištēn	one (unit), person, object
ište(n)nūtu	for the first time (Am.); single entity, set
ištu	from; on; around; with (Am.)
iššuḫu	(*išuḫḫu*) a type of garment (Am.)

išû	to have, possess; to exist (Am. < WS)
itbāru	friend, colleague
itquru	spoon [GIŠ.DÍLIM]
itti	with; *itta-* (Am.)
ittiltu	see *ištēn*; one time, once
itussarra	(*ituzzarra*) a type of ornament (Am.)
izirtu	help (Am. < WS *ʿzr*)
izuzzu	(*uzuzzu*); **G** to stand; *z.* + UGU to attack; **Š** to cause to be present; to substitute
-ka	you (2 ms. acc suffix)
kaballu	a type of fabric
kabāšu	(*kabāsu*) **G** to tread, trample (**kabāšu* [Am.])
kabātu	**G** to be heavy; to be honored, respected; **D** to treat honorably, to respect; **Dtn** to repeatedly honor, be complementary of [DUGUD]
kabattu	liver; stomach [UZU.UR$_5$]
kabattuma	see *kabattu*; on the stomach, front of the body (used in prostration formula) (Am.)
kabtu	heavy, weighty, important; a dignitary [DUGUD]
kabbuttu	counterweight
kadrû	greeting gift; bribe
kaḫšu	throne (Am. < WS; Ug. *kḫṯ*)
kakkaru	an ingot, disk of metal
kakkusu	a type of precious stone
kakkû	(*kakkūtu*) lentil [GÚ.TUR]
kalbu	dog [UR; UR.GI$_5$; UR.GI$_7$; UR.GU]
kalû I	all, totality
kalû II	**G** to hold back; to detain; to withhold; **N** pass. of **G**
kallātu	daughter-in-law; bride [É.GI.A]
kallû	express messenger; *ina/ana kallê* "in haste"
kamiru	(*gamiru*) a noble, elite (Am.)
kamû	**G** to be bound; to be a prisoner; **D** to bind
kamû II	**G** to bind
kâmma	so, thus (by-form of *kīam*)
kammaru	a type of gold, an ornamental design (?) (Am.)
kammuššakku	a type of bed (Am.)
kannu	a vessel stand
kanna	(*akanna*) so thus, similarly, just so
kannama	(*akannama*) similarly, likewise
kanāšu	**G** to bow; to submit; **D** to subject, to submit
kanatku	an aromatic tree; the aromatic substance from this tree [ŠIM.GIG]
kapālu	**G** to curve, curl up; **D** to bend, twist
kapissuḫḫu	(*kapizzuḫḫu*) a type of ornament (Am. < Hurr.)
karašu	camp, expeditionary force [ÉRIN.MEŠ KAL.BAD.KASKAL]
karašku	funerary chapel, mausoleum (Am. < Hurr.?)
karatnannu	a golden ornament (Am.)
karpatu	pot, clay vessel [DUG]
karaṣu	**G** to break off; to pinch off

karṣu	slander; *ākil k.* "to slander"
kartappu	groom, animal driver
kāsu	cup [GÚ.ZI; GAL]
kaspu	silver [KÙ.BABBAR]
kašādu	**G** to arrive; **D** to drive off, send away (messenger); **Š** caus. of **G**
kašāšu I	**G** to control, acquire (property); to take control of an enemy (Am.); **N** to be held, to serve for a debt
kâša	(*kâšim*) to you, for you (2sg dat.)
katāmu	**G** to hide, cover; **D** to cover with, cover over, close; to conceal (Am.)
katappû	bridle [KUŠ.KA.TAB]
kâti	you (2 sg acc., gen.)
kayyānu	constant, regular; constantly, regularly
kazābu II	**G** to lie, tell lies (Am. < WS)
kazbūtu	see *kazābu; awât k.* lies (Am.)
kazīru	curl fringe; a type of figurine (Am.)
kezēru	**G** to style hair; to style a certain type of hairdo
kī	like, how, as, according to
-ki	you (2 fsg. acc.)
kiā'im	see *kiām*
kiām	thus, in this manner; *kiām ... kiām* here and there (Am.)
kibbu	a type of ornament
kika	(*kikā*) thus, like (Am. < WS)
kilallū	(*kilallān*) both
kilūbu	a cage, trap (Am. < WS)
kima	like, as; *k*+ adv. "as ... as possible" (Am.)
kimê	like; as that; as soon as
kimru	a type of festival (?) (Am.)
kīnanna	(*kī+inanna*) so, thus (Am.)
kīnātu	see *kīnu*
kinattūtu	personnel (Am.)
kīnu	true, reliable, loyal
kinṣu	(*kimṣu, kiṣṣu*) leggings
kinūnu	braizer
kipalallu	a type of furniture (Am.)
kirdib	(*kirdippu, kartappu*) groom (of an animal)
kirru	a pot, big jar [GIŠ.KIRI$_6$]
kirissu	pin
kišādu	neck, back of neck; back [UZU.GÙ]
kišādu	scarf [GÚ.GADA]
kiškanu	a type of wood (Am.)
kišūma	thus, so (< WS *kī*)
kitini	a type of eye paint receptacle
kittu	see *kīnu*; truth, reliability; *kīma kitti* "by consent"
kitû	linen [GADA]
kizzu	a type of jewelry (in phrase *kizzi wušru*) (Hurr.)
kuba	see *kūbu*
kubbutu	see *kabātu* heavy, weighty; honored

kubbuttu	see *kabātu*; pl. *kubbutāti*; an honorific gift (Am.)
kubbuttu	a counterweight (?); a part of a necklace (?)
kuba	see *kūbu*
kūbu	(*kûbu*) jar (< Eg. *qbw*)
kûbu	see *kūbu*
kuiḫku	a type of oil container (Am. < Eg.)
kukubu	(*kukkubu*); rhyton
kukutu	a reed implement (?) (Am.)
kulu	see *kalû* II; all, totality of
kuldu	a bronze object (part of a brazier?) (Am.)
kunāšu	(pl.) emmer [ŠE.ZÍZ.ḪI.A]
kuninnu	a type of bowl, basin
kunukku	cylinder seal [KIŠIB]
kurru	a measure of a dry-good [GUR]
kursinnu	ankle
kuru(m)mānu	an ivory object (fruit-shaped?)(Am.)
kurû	short [LÚGUD]
kussû	throne, chair, seat [GIŠ.GU.ZA]
kušītu	(*kusītu*) robe; linen garment (Am.) [TÚG.BAR.DUL]
kuššudu	to chase away; *ša zubbī k.* "fly whisk"
lā	not, no; un- (negation) [NU]
labīru	old, ancient; elder
labīrūtu	old age
labittu	(*libittu*) brick [SIG_4]
lalû	plenty, abundance; wealth
lama	(*lām*) before, in front of (location, person); before (temporal)
lamādu	**G** to learn
lam(a)ḫuššû	a type of ceremonial garment [TÚG.NÍG.LAM]
lamassu	a female deity; figurine of a female deity [^{d}LAMMA]
lapātu	**G** to touch; to fashion an object
laqāḫu	see *leqû*; **G** to take, seize; **Gp** taken (Am. < WS)
leḫēmu	**G** to eat, consume (Am. < WS)
lemēnu	**G** to become bad, evil; **Dt** to become angry (with one another); to become embroiled in a dispute
lemnu	bad, evil; hostile [ḪUL, ḪUL.GÁL]
leqû II	**G** to take, take away, deliver
leû	**G** to be able to
lē'u	a board, plaque
libbu	stomach, heart, mind; *ša libbi-* "according to the desire of;" *ana l.* "in, throughout" [ŠÀ]
līmu	family, tribe, nations
līm	thousand [LIM]
līmu	(*lawû* II) environs
limītu	neighboring, in the surrounding area
limûtu	encirclement
lišānu	tongue; blade of a tool; ingot(?)
lū	or; indeed (asseverative particle); if (Am.)

lubāšu	clothing; *lubulti šarri* "royal linen," i.e., "byssus" (< Eg. *sšr nswt*)
lulīmu	stag, deer, ram [LU.LIM]
lulūtu	a type of animal-shaped vessel (Am.)
lullû II	to enrich, make luxurious, beautiful
lūqu	see *luqāḫu*; "taken," i.e., a hostage (Am. < WS)
lurimtu	f. of *lurmûm* pomegranate
-ma	(*-me*) enclitic particle; the conjunction "and"
mādu	many, much
mâdu	a great deal, much
mādūtu	see *mādu; kī m.* very much (Am.)
magāgu	**G** to be tense, to be distressed; to have cramps, spasms
magal	very much, greatly
magāru	**G** to consent, agree; to be amenable to; **Gt** to be in agreement; **Š** to cause to agree, to reconcile
maḫan	a wooden chest (< Eg. *mhn*)
maḫāru	**G** to accept, receive
maḫāṣu	**G** to smite, strike, beat; to overlay; **D** to inlay, cover with gold (Am.); **Gtn** to continuously strike, beat
māḫāzu	town, settlement; center of city
maḫda	a type of hand bracelet
maḫru	front; presence; *ina/ana m.* "in the presence of, before"
maḫīru	emporium, market [GÁN.BA]
maḫzirāmu	(pl) requirements, needed things (Am. < WS)
makkasu	a type of axe, cutting implement
makû III	**G** to be absent, missing, to be lacking
mala	as much as, in accordance with
malāku II	**G** to discuss; to advise, to look after
malû	full, complete; *malē libbāti* "full of anger" [DIR]
mamma	(*mamman*) somebody, someone; *la mamman* "no one"
māmīnu	why?; what? (Am. < WS *mā+mīnu*)
māmitu	oath; curse [NAM.RU]
mangu	see *magāgu*; stiffness, paralysis
maninnu	a type of necklace
manû II	mina weight measurement [MA.NA]
manû IV	**G** to count; to recite
māni	how much? how many? (Am. < WS); *ana lā māni* "countless"
mannu I	who, whosoever; each, every
mannu II	what? (Am. < WS)
mannummê	who(so)ever; *m*+neg. no one
manṣartu	see *maṣṣartu*
maprû	a type of vessel (Am.)
maqû	see *makû*
maqqibu	(*maqqabu*) hammer (Am. < WS)
maqqītu	(pl. *maqqû*) libation vessel [BAL]
māru	son; man/resident of (city/region) [DUMU]
mārtu	daughter [DUMU.MUNUS]
marbadu	blanket (Am. < WS; [Ug. *mrbd*; Heb. *marbaddîm*])

marḫatu	wife, spouse [NITLAM$_4$]
marḫa(l)lu	carnelian
marāru III	**G** to go away, depart; **Š** to drive away, chase away (Am.)
marāṣu	**G** to be sick, in distress; **Š** to cause distress, to hurt, offend; **ŠD** *m+ libbum* to distress (Am.)
mari(y)annu	a caste of warriors
maršītu	see *rašû*; property, possessions
masdariš	(*masdara*) *ana m.* always, continuously (Am.)
massu	corvée, conscript laborer (<WS)
maṣṣartu	see *naṣāru*; guard, watchman; watch, watch post; [UN]
maṣṣaru	see *naṣāru*; guard, watchman; *m. šarri* the royal guard, king's guard (Am.)
maṣiqta	a type of container, pouring vessel (Am.)
mâṣu	**G** to be/come a small amount; **Š** caus. of **G** (Am.)
maṣû	**G** to correspond with; be equal to; to be sufficient; **Š** to cause to be sufficient
mašaddu	chariot-poles (?) [NÍG.GÍD.DA GIGIR]
mašḫu	a type of ring (Am.)
mašḫalu	sieve
mašku	animal skin, hide; sack [KUŠ]
maškanu	see *šakānu*; threshing floor, granary [KISLAḪ]; place, site; settlement, residence
maškittu	see *maškanu*; residence
mašālu	**G** to be equal, become equal
mašlu	half
mašqalu	weight (Am. < WS)
mašqaltu	balance, scales; weighing out
maša'u	**G** to rob, take away forcibly; **N** be taken by force, stolen
maššu	polished, shining
mašû I	(f. *mašītu*) forgotten, left behind
mašû II	**G** to forget, leave behind
mašuya	a golden ornament (Am.)
mati	when
matimê	whenever
mātu	country, land (KUR; KUR.KI)
mâtu	**G** to die, be dead; **Š** to put to death, kill; **H** to put to death [BA.ÚŠ; BA.UG$_7$]
maṭru	(*maṭrû*) a pole, stick, handle(?) (Am.)
maṭû	**G** to become little, less; **D** to reduce
maû	**G** to push away; to refuse; **D** to hurl, throw
mē	(*mētu*) one hundred
-mê II	particle used in indirect iterrog. (e.g., *matimê* "whenever")
meḫru	equal, colleague, peer (Am.)
meḫrūtu	of equal rank
mekku	glass
mekû V	**G** to neglect; **Dt** = **G**
Meluḫḫa	(*meluḫḫu*) adj. of *m.*

mēqītu	eye-paint (Am.)
mēreštu II	(*erēšu*) wish, request, demand
mesukku	a type of bird of prey; bird shaped obj. (Am.)
mešēnu	sandal, shoe
-mi	particle of direct speech
miḫṣu	weave, woven textile, fabric
miḫḫuṣ	see *maḫāṣu* (*muḫḫuṣ*) covered with, "studded"
mīya	(*mīati, ema'e*) who? (Am. < WS)
miammu	see *mimma*; (*mimmû*) all, anything, something, everything; possessions, property; supplies (Am.)
mila	times (in 7x7 prostration formula) (Am. < WS)
milku	advice, counsel; LÚ-*m.* advisor, counselor
mimma	anything, something, everything; with pron. suffix "all that belongs to" (Am.)
mimmû	see *miammu*
minde	(**mīn+īde*) perhaps
minu	interrogative pronoun "who?" (< WS)
mīnu(*m*)	what; *ana m.* "why?"
mīnummê	all of, each of
minûtu	counting number
mirûtu	for seeing, viewing (Am. < WS)
mīṣu	(*wīṣu*) a small amount
mīṣūtamma	a small escort (Am.)
mišu	troops, expeditionary force; (Am < Eg. *mšʿ*)
miši	see *mišu*
mišlu	half [BAR]
mītu	see *mâtu*; dead
mitḫār	corresponding to; equally
mitḫāriš	likewise
muballit(*t*)*u*	a type of bottle that holds aromatics (Am.)
mūdû	see *edû*; wise, knowing, expert
muḫḫu	skull, top; with regard to, referring to, concerning (often *muḫḫi* in Am.)[UGU]
mulūgu	a type of dowry gift
mulku	kingship; *šûṭ m.* treason (Am. < WS)
mulṭu	see *mušṭu*; comb
mumerrītu	a type of scraper, tool
mūraku	see *arku*; length
murru	myrrh
musalliḫtu	a libation vessel
muṣalil	fan bearer, parasol bearer (Am. < equivalent of Eg. *ḥbśw bn*[*.t*])
mūṣû	see *waṣû*; exit, going out; setting (sun); produce (Am. < WS)
mušālu	mirror
mūšu II	(*mīšu*) night [GI_6]; *mūša* "at night" (Am.)
muššaru	(*mušgarru*) a semi-precious stone; serpentine, onyx (?) [(NA_4.)MUŠ.GÍR; NA_4.NÍR.MUŠ.GÍR; NA_4.MUŠ.GÍR.TAB]
muššuru	([*w*]*uššuru*) released, freed

muššuru	see *wašāru* **D**
muššurūtu	"chased?" (of gold) (Am.)
muškēnu	a poor man, dependent
mušṭu	comb [GIŠ.RÍG; GA.ZUM]
mūtānu	epidemic, plague
mutu	man; husband
muttû	pole
muštu	(*mulṭu*); comb [GIŠ.GA.RÍG, GA.ZUM]
mû	water [A]
na'ādu	**G** to be attentive; **Gt** to notify, inform; **Dtn** to continually alert; to start wars repeatedly (Am.)
na'arruru	**N** to bring help, aid, reinforcements (Am.)
nabalkutu	**N** to cross over; to defect, revolt; **Š** to send across, bring across; to allow to defect; to overthrow
nabāsu	a red wool [SÍG.GAN.ME.TA]
nabû	**G** to name; to decree, to proclaim
nadānu II	**G** to give; to get ready to travel to (Am.); **Gp** to be given (Am. < WS); **Gtn** to give repeatedly
nadû I	placed, laid down
nadû II	**G** to throw down; to lay down; to be incorporated (of metal) (Am.); **D** to expel, cast out (Am. < WS)
nagāru	carpenter [NAGAR]
naglabu	razor
naḫbû	a type of vessel; pail
naḫlaptu	a Hurrian style shirt [TÚG.GÚ; TÚG.GÚ.Ì(.A)]
naḫra	a material used for mirror making
naḫāsu	**G** to recede, to withdraw; to halt, stop s.o. (Am.)
naḫāšu	**G** to return, recede; to halt, delay
nâḫu	meaning unknown (Am.)
nâḫu	**G** to rest, be at rest, be calm
nakāmu	**G** to heap, pile up, amass
nakāru	**G** to become different, strange; to grow hostile, be angry, deny; **D** to change (trans.); to remove, eliminate
nakkaru	hostile
namḫāru	a storage jar [NAM.ḪA.RA]
namlu	(*namālu*) ant
nakāsu	**G** to cut down, sever; to kill, slaughter; to block, cut off a path; **N** pass. of **G**
nakāšu	**G** to set aside; to turn away
naktamu	cover, lid
nakû	(*naqû*) stopper, plug
nalbašu	cloak (Am.)
nalpattu	a metal tool, spatula,
namandu	(*madaddu*) measuring bowl
nāmaru	(*amāru*) mirror
namsû	(*nemsû, nemsētu*); pl. *namsītu*; washbasin [NÍG.ŠU.LUḪ.ḪA]
namṣāru	sword [GÍR.GAL]

namāšu **G** to set out, start a journey, campaign; **D** to dispatch; **Dtn** to continually dispatch (iterative)
namša jar (Eg. *nmśt*)
namur see *nawāru*; to be/become bright (Am.)
nunnû command
narkabtu chariot [GIŠ.GIGIR]
narmaktu washbowl, basin; ewer
napādu clasp
napḫaru the sum of, total, entirety of [ŠU.NIGÍN]
napālu III **G** to fall (Am. < WS)
napāqu **G** to harden, solidify
napāšu **G** to breath; **D** to let breath freely; to make productive, make fertile
napīšu breath
napištu life, soul; throat [ZI]
naprušu II **N** to fly; to speed, rush (messenger) (Am.)
napultu (*napuštu*) life; throat; corpse(?)
naqû **G** to sacrifice, pour a libation, make a ritual celebration
nasāḫu **G** to tear out, uproot
nasāku **G** to throw, eject; to reject
naṣābu II **Gt** to place, set, put (Am. < WS)
naṣāru **G** to guard, protect (Am. **G** = **D**); **Š** to obey, observe
naṣriš (*naṣāru*) safely
naṣû **G** to despise, revile, look down on
nâšu **G** to despise, look down on
našāku **G** to bite, gnaw
našši a type of vessel (Am. < Eg. *nšw*)
našû I lifted, raised up
našû II **G** to raise, lift up, carry
nattullu part of a harness
nawāru **G** to be/become bright, shine; to be glad; **D** to make bright, illuminate; **N** to brighten (eyes) (Am.)
nazāmu **G** to moan, complain; **Dt** to raise complaints against, be angry with
nēbeḫu sashes [TÚG.ÍB.LÁ]
nēḫû calm, peace
nemsētu see *namsû*; wash basin
ne'rāru aid, help, reinforcement; *bēl n.* "helper" (Am.)
nešuru see *ešēru*
nēšu lion [UR.MAḪ]
nimru panther
nīnu we (1c.s)
nīqu see *naqû*; sacrifice, libation, ritual celebration
niqiptu (*nikiptu*) a medicinal shrub
nīru yoke
nišu (*nīšu, nešu*) people, population, humanity [UN]
nukarippu gardener [NU.GIŠ.KIRI$_6$]
nurmû (*nurimdu*) pomegranate [NU.ÚR.MA.A]

nukurtu	hostility; act of aggression; *bēl n.* "enemy" (Am.) [KÚR.NU]
nūru	lamp [IZI.GAR]
pabbu	(*pappu*) lock of hair(?)
pagūtu	(*pagû*)(f.sg) monkey
paḫāru	**G** to be gathered, assembled; **D** to assemble, gather (trans.)
palāḫu	**G** to fear, be afraid
palḫu	fearsome; frightened
palāsu	(*palāšu*); **G** to look at, to look towards; **N** to look at, gaze at
palāšu	**G** to perforate, break through, pierce through; **N** pass. of **G**
pānānu	previously, before; since
pānītu	earlier time, previously; *kī p.* "as before"
pānu	face, front; presence; in the presence of
pappardilû	stone, a type of chalcedony (agate?) [(NA$_4$.)BABBAR.DILI]
paqa	a fine linen (Am. < Eg. *p(ꜣ)qt*)
paqādu	**G** to entrust; to command; to allocate; to take care of [NU (Am.)]
paqāru	(*baqāru*) **G** to claim, make a claim
parakku	throne, dais
parakkatannu	(*parakkatānu*) a golden ornament (Am.)
parāsu	**G** to cut off; to decide; **N** passive of **G**
parṣu	cultic ordinance; custom, practice
paršīgu	headdress; [TÚG.BAR.SIG]
parattitinnu	part of a tool; whip handle? (Am.)
parūtu	a type of alabaster
parzillu	iron [AN.BAR]
pasitu	(*pazitu*) vizier (Am. < Eg. *p3-ṯ3ty*)
paskāru	head-binding, headdress (Am.)
pašāḫu	**G** to be cool, calm, tranquil; to be at rest; **Š** cause to be at rest, pacify
pašāqu	**G** to be narrow, difficult; **Š** to make difficult
pašāru	**G** to free; release captives (Am.); to ransom; to become calm
paššuru	tray
pašû	**G** to break up, smash
patru	sword, dagger [GÌR]
pāṭu	(*paṭṭu*) border, edge; hem (of a garment); 1-*en paṭi* "even to the slightest extent, "even one" [ZAG]
paṭāru	**G** to loosen, release, free; to leave, move off (Am.); to unpack; **D** trans. of **G**
pawuru	prince, noble (< Eg. *p3 wr*)
pendu	mole; birthmark; a red, specked stone (?) [NA$_4$.ŠI.TIR]
per'azu	(*peḫḫazu*) a type of precious metal, a metal alloy (?)
peršantu	(*piršantu*) a type of aromatic plant; oil from the *peršantu* plant
perazu	(see *mumerritu*) (*piazu, pur'asu*?) a type, or part of a tool(?)
pessû	cripple, lame; a type of figurine
peṣû	white [BABBAR]
petû	**G** to open; to develop, bring into cultivation
pīḫātu	province, area under jurisdiction
pīru	(*pīlu*) elephant
pišaiš	(*piša'iš*[*hu*]) a type of material (Am.)

piššatu ointment; ointment container; spoon (Am.)
pitinkak a pair of gloves (Am.)
piṭ(ṭ)ātu (pl) regular troops (Am. < Eg.)
puati (*buati*) a type of bracelet, ring
pû mouth [KA, KAxPU]
puḫīlu (*puḫālu*) m. animal, stud, (Am.)
puḫriš see *puḫru, paḫāru*; together, to be in assembly
puḫru see *paḫāru*; to be gathered, assembled
puḫtu reckoning, account
pulluštu a bronze vessel (Am.)
punnugu (*panāgu*) capped, mounted, overlaid
puqdatu (*puquttu*) thorn, spike
pušqu narrow place; trouble
puwanaḫ a type of vessel (for oil?) (Am. < Hurr.)
qablītu center, middle
qablu centerpiece [MURUB; $MURUB_4$]
qablû middle, center of [MÚR; MURUB; MÚRUB; $MURUB_4$]
qabû **G** to say, speak
qadu(m) with, together with, including
qadmu former time
qadamiš as before, formerly
qalālu G to be small, light, weak; to be despised; D to diminish, belittle [SIG]
qalû II G to roast, burn
qâlu G to pay attention; to be silent (Am.)
qanû reed; tube [GI]
qâpu (*qiapu*) G to trust, entrust, believe
qaqqadu head [SAG; SAG.DU]
qaqqaru ground, earth
qarādu **G** to be warlike; **D** to strengthen, encourage, urge
qardu hero, warrior [UR.SAG]
qarnu an animal horn; rhyton [SI]
qaštu bow [(GIŠ.)BAN]
qātu hand; handle; measure of; item; set; *ša q.* "for the hand" i.e., bracelet [ŠU]
qātamma in the same way as; just as
qebēru **G** to bury
qerēbu **G** to be/become close to, to approach; to take action against (Am.)
qerbu I near
qerbu II center, interior
qēṣu summer (Am. < WS)
qiāpu **G** to trust, entrust; to encumber, impose a task upon
qinnāzu (*qi*[*n*]*nanzu*) whip [GIŠ/KUŠ.ÙŠAN]
qīpu representative (e.g., of king)
qiššû cucumber; *aban q.* cucumber-shaped oil container (Am.)
qištu gift, present [NÌG.BA]

qu''û	**D** to await, to wait for
qubbatu	(*qubbû*) mourned
quppû	chest
qurdu	heroism
ra'ābu	**G** to be angry; to shake
ra'amuttu	friendship, loving relationship
rabāṣu	**G** to sit, camp; **Š** to cause to sit, to camp
rabiṣ	crouched, seated
rābiṣu	royal official, commissioner (Am.) [MÁŠKIM]
rabû I	(fs. *rabītu*) big, great; chief, senior [GAL]
rabû II	**G** to be big, to grow, to become adult
rabûti	senior officials [LÚ.MEŠ GAL.GAL.MEŠ]
rādû	guide
ragābu	**G** to be afraid (Am. < WS)
raḫda	(*raḫta*) a metal kettle (< Eg. *rhdt*)
raḫāṣu	**G** to devastate, overwhelm; to smite, to crush (Am. < WS *rǵṣ*)
raḫāšu	**G** to move, set in motion; **H** to move so., to mobilize (troops) (Am. < WS)
rakābu	**G** to ride (an animal, vessel, chariot); to mount a chariot
rakāsu	**G** to bind, tie, attach; **Š** caus. of **G**
raksu	bound, tied
rakāšu	see *rakāsu*
ramāku	**G** to bath
ramānu	self (reflexive particle)
rāmu	(fs. *raimtu*) beloved
râmu	love
râmuttu	(*ra'āmuttu*) friendship (Am.)
râmu II	**G** to love; **Gtn** to continually show love to, to love one another (Am.)
raqqu	thin, fine (band)
raṣāpu	**G** to build; to layer a structure
râṣu	**G** to go the aid of
rašû	**G** to acquire, get
rē'û	shepherd, herdsman [SIPA]
rēdû	soldier
redû	**G** to lead, to accompany; **D** to add to, to make additional payment to
reḫūtu	(pl.) the rest; the remainder
rēšu	head, beginning of [SAG]
rettu	an unidentified object (Am.)
riaḫu	**G** to remain, be left over; **D** to leave over, allow to remain
rīḫu	(*rēḫu*) remaining left over, the rest
riksu	see *rakāsu*; treaty
rīmu	auroch [AM]
rīmtu	wild cow [SÚN]
ripûtu	healing (Am. < WS)
rīqu I	(*riāqu*) empty; nonentity (pejorative)

rīqu II (*riqqu*) aromatic substance [ŠIM]
riqqu (*ruqqu*) metal vessel (Am.)
rittu (*rettu*) hand; handful of, scoop of; handle
rubû prince, ruler [NUN]
rukūbu a vehicle; boat
ruqqu pot [URUDU.ŠEN]
sabnakû (*zabnakû*) a type of vessel (Am. < Eg)
saddinu (*šaddi*[*n*]*nu*) a shirt, cloth (Am. < WS)
sâ (*sa; zâ*[*h*]) a container made of precious wood (< Eg. *ṯꜣy*)
saḫāmu **D** to oppress, give trouble
saḫāru **G** to search for; to turn, turn back; **Gtn** to constantly seek out; **D** to send; to make return, turn back
saḫḫa(*r*)*ru* a type of bowl
sakānu **G** to see, to care for (Am. < WS)
sakāpu I **G** to push off, away; to push off (ship from land)
sakāpu II **G** to rest, lie down
sākinu prefect, governor
sakku a bronze object (Am.)
samû (*šamû*) sky, heavens
sāmtu carnelian [NA_4.ZA.GUG]
sankallu (*sagkallu*) a type of precious stone [NA_4.SAG.KAL]
sankallu foremost
sanāqu I **G-D** to check, test
sarāru **G** to be false, lie, betray
sarru I criminal, dishonest, false [LÚ.LUL]
sarruttu (*sarrūtu*) criminal, dishonest
sarra (*šarra*) a type of vessel (alabaster)
sartu (*sarāru*) falsehood
sassu chariot platform [KI.KAL.GIGIR]
sebe seven
sekēru **G** to block; to shut
semeru bracelet [ḪAR]
sennu see *šennu*
siḫpu (*seḫpu*) covering; overlay (gold) (Am.)
simānu occasion, period
simiu statue (< Eg. *śmꜣw* ?)
sinuntu swallow
sinnništu (*sinniltu*) woman [MUNUS]
sipparru bronze, copper [ZABAR]
sisû horse [ANŠE.KUR.RA]
su'adi (*suādu*) an aromatic plant; oil from the *su'adi* plant
suḫsi in the expression *s.* ^{d}INANNA; a type of golden vessel (for the goddess)
sūkinu see *sākinu*; prefect, governor (Am. < WS)
sumbiru (*ṣumbiru*) an unidentified object (made of jasper?) (Am.)
summuḫu mixed, assorted; studded with, encrusted with (Am.)
sūnu I loin, lap [ÚR]

sūnu II	hem, trim (related to Ug. *si'n*)
surru	deceit, falsehood, treachery
sūqu	road [SILA]
Sutû	Suteans; nomads
ṣābu	military force, army, troops [ÉRIN]
ṣabāru I	**G** to blink, to twinkle; to mutter maliciously
ṣabru	a gossip, one who mutters maliciously,
ṣabātu	**G** to seize; **D** to bind, capture; **Dt** Pass. of **D** (Am.)
ṣabītu	gazelle
ṣaburtu	see ṣabāru; falsehood; malice
ṣâdu II	**G** to melt down; **D** to melt, refine
ṣaduq	true, right, righteous (Am. < WS)
ṣaḫu	(*ṣaḫātu*) pure, pressed oil
ṣaḫāru	(*ṣeḫēru*) **G** to become small, little; to be hard pressed (Am.); **D** to reduce, to decrease
ṣaḫātu	**G** to press, squeeze oil
ṣahtu	pressed, squeezed
ṣâlu	(*ṣêlu*) **G** to fight, quarrel; **Gt** to be quarrelsome, angry
ṣalālu	**G** to sleep, rest, lie down
ṣalmu	statue, figurine [ALAM]
ṣamādu	**G** to tie up, yoke, bind; to be equipped
ṣapānu	**G** to shelter; to recover, rescue (Am. < WS)
ṣarāḫu III	**G** to heat up; **D** to keep warm (horse)
ṣeḫru	small, young; few (number) [TUR]
ṣēru	back; steppe; to be up against, opposing (Am.) [EDIN]
ṣēnu	small cattle [UDU]
ṣētu	bright light; *ina* ṣ. in the broad daylight, open air (Am.)
ṣillaḫta	(*zillaḫta*) type of bowl (Am. < WS.)
ṣimittu	team of horses; yoke, pair of oxen [LÁ, LAL]
ṣippar(r)ātu	cosmetics (ointment?); *bīt* ṣ. an ointment container (Am. < Eg.)
ṣīru	high, elevated [MAḪ]
ṣītu	exit; in ṣ. *šamši* "sunrise"
ṣubātu	textile, cloth [TÚG]
ṣuḫaru	boy; male servant
ṣuḫartu	girl, young woman; female servant
ṣupru	claw; claw-shaped
ṣu'ru	(*ṣūru*) back (Am. < WS)
ṣurru	obsidian, flint [NA_4.ZÚ(KA); NA_4.GÍR.ZÚ; NA_4.GÍR.ZÚ.GAL]
ṣurû	a type of plant, balsam
ša	of, who, whom, which
šabattu	a type of garment
šadû	mountain, open country; desert [KUR; ḪUR.SAG]
šadādu	**G** to drag, to tow
šaḫāḫu	**G** to fall
šaḫānu	**G** to be/become hot; **D** to warm, heat up (trans.)
šaḫarru	jar, clay pot [SAR]
šaḫātu III	**G** to be afraid, in awe; **D** to scare, intimidate

šaḫātu IV	**G** to wash off; to be cleared of debts, obligations
šaḫāṭu	**G** to jump on; to attack, raid
šaḫpu	a substance used in decoration (Am.)
šaḫru	gate (Am. < WS)
šāḫû	see *ḫanūnu*; upright (Am. < Eg. *hnn sʿḥʿ*)
šā'iru	see *šāru* II; hostility (Am.)
šakānu	**G** to place, set down; to issue an order, command, statement, oath; *š+ išātu* to put fire to, to set on fire (Am.); **N** to come together with s.o.
šaknu	governor, appointee
šakru II	handle (bucket, vessel) [KIN]
šakattû	girdle [GADA.ŠAG$_4$.DÙ.A]
šâlu	**G** to ask, inquire about; **Gt** to ask about, to reflect about someone/thing
šā'ilu	see *šâlu*; diviner (Am.)
šalāḫu	**G** to pull out, uproot; to withdraw, to back out
šalālu	**G** to plunder, spoil, carry off
šalāmu I	wellbeing, health, welfare (in the greeting letter formula); peace
šalāmu II	**G** to be healthy, well
šalaš	(f. *šalāšat*) three
šālinnu	a type of vessel (bronze) (Am. < WS)
šalmiš	in peace; *alāku+ š* to go in peace
šalmu I	see *šalāmu*; completed, carried out
šalmu II	(*šalīmu*) peace (Am. < WS)
šalšāmu	(*šalšūmu*) the day before yesterday (Am. < WS)
šâmu	**D** to redden
šammu	plant(s)
šamnu	oil, fat [Ì]
šamû	heavens, sky [AN]
šanānu	**G** to be/become equal to; to fight, rival; **D** = **G** to fight, rival (Am.); **Dt** to struggle, dispute (Am.)
šanāṣu	**G** to sneer at, mock, insult; **Gtn** to continuously jeer, mock (Am.)
šanītu	a second time
šanû I	another, a second; pl. *šanûtu* "others"
šanû III	**G** to do twice, to repeat
šanû IV	**G** to be changed, become different; **D** to change so.
šanûti	see *šanû*; adv. a second time
šanûtu	see *šanû* I; (pl.) "others"
šanzātu	adj. from *šanzu* (in reference to a semi-precious stone) exact meaning unknown (Am.)
šapāku	**G** to heap up, pour out; **D** to cast bronze
šapālu	**G** to be low, lowly, humble
šapāru	**G** to send; to write to; **Gt** to send a message to, to write to; **Gtn** to repeatedly send to, write to; **Gp** to be sent (Am. < form WS); *mār š.* envoys, delegates [LÚ.MEŠ. DUMU. KIN; LÚ.KIN]
šapku	see *šapāku*; cast (metal) (Am.)
šaplānu	underneath, below; *š. šēpī* "sole of the foot"

šapliš	below, downwards
šaplītu	see *šaplû*; (adj.) lower part [GAM]
šaplu	bottom [KI.TA]
šaplû	lower part, side [KI.TA]
šapru	envoy, messenger
šāqītu	female cup-bearer [MUNUS.DÉ (Am.)]
šaqû I	**G** to be high, elevated
šaqû II	**G** to become high, elevated
šaru I	wind, breath [ĪM]
šāru II	(pl. *šārūtu*) hostile, enemy; lying (< WS)
šâru	**G-D** to slander (Am. < WS)
šarāḫu	**D** to make proud; to glorify
šarāpu	**G** to burn, burn down
šarāqu	**G** to steal, rob
šarmu	trimmed, cut (of ornaments) (Am.)
šarqu	stolen
šarru	king [LUGAL]
šarrumma	see *šurrumma*; indeed, certainly; promptly
šarrūtu	kingship
šašallu	heel; back
šâšu	to/of him
šâšuna	to/of them
šattu	year [MU; MU.KAM]
šatû II	**G** to drink
šâṭu II	**G** to despise, ignore; **Gp** to be disloyal (Am. < WS)
še'u	grain, barley [ŠE]
šēḫu	wind; breath (of the king.) (Am.)
šemû	**G** to hear, listen; to obey; **Gt** (iterative) to continually obey; N to be heard
šēnu	sandals, shoes
šennu	kettle [URUDU.ŠEN]
šēpu	foot [GÌR]; "foot soldier" [LÚ.GÌR]
šēru	morning star; dawn
šerdanu	(*širdanu*) Sherdanu (Am.)
šeršerretu	(*šuršurrātu*) chain, fetters [ŠÈR.ŠÈR]
šērtu	(*šārtu*) hair
šī	she, it
šiāti	(f) of her; it; that; this same
šib'ettān(a)	(*sebîšu*) seven times (Am.)
šību	(pl. *šībūtu*) old person, elder; witness
šībūtu	old age; testimony
šikaru	beer [KAŠ]
šikkatu	flask
šīmu	price, purchase; purchased (of goods, property) [ŠÀM]
šīmāti	payment due [ŠÀM.MEŠ]
šimtu	fate, destiny [NAM (TAR)]; *ana šimtu* "to die"; *sarratu* "a criminal fate" [NAM]

šina (3 fp) they, those
šina two
šinnu tooth; ivory [ZÚ; ZU9 (KAxUD) (Am.); ZÚ.SÚN]
šīpātu wool, fleece [SÍG]
šipku heaping up; casting (metal)
šipru work; envoy; message; shipment; mission; *mār š.* messenger, envoy [KIN; LÚ.MEŠ. DUMU. LÚ.KIN]
šiqlu shekel-weight [SU (variant of GÍN)]
šīru flesh [UZU]
širinnatu snaffle, horse's bit
šistu cry, outcry, shout
šīt she (3fs); that, this (f)
šītû see *šatû* II; drinking (Am. < WS)
šū he, it
-šu 3ms (gen. and acc.)
šu x-times (in multiplication)
šububu a type of weapon (Am.)
šūbultu (*šūbiltu*) consignment, shipment
šubtu a type of garment
šuḫenḫunu see *šukênu*; to prostrate (Am. < Hur.)
šuḫītu a type of chariot (Am.)
šuḫû II adj. describing a bed, couch (precise meaning unknown)
šuḫītu a type of chariot (Am.)
šuḫuppatu (*suḫuppatu; šuḫuptu*) boots
šu'ibta a type of libation vessel, dipper
šukênu Š to prostrate, to do obeisance
šukudu a type of arrow (Am.)
šukkuku strung, threaded (bead)
šulmu see *šalāmu*; wellbeing, health; good wishes, greeting gift
šulmānu greeting; greeting gift
šūlû I see *elû*; raised, heightened; *ša dama šūlû* "reddish;" *ša mê šūlî* "water dipper"
šuluhtu shipment (Am. < WS)
šumu name; repute, reputation
šumma if; behold; because, since; when
šumrușu (*marāșu*) pain, distress
šunī they (m. dual) (Am.)
-šunī them two; of them two (m. dual suffix)
šūnu they (3 mpl)
-šunu 3 mpl oblique pron. suffix
šupālītu undergarment (Am.)
šupālu below; *ana š. šēpī* "beneath the feet of"; "in submission to" (Am.); *š. šēpī* "footstool"
šuqultu weight (of object.)
šurkusu *rakāsu*; *ša š.* "for attaching"
šuruḫtu a type of ornament (Am.)
šurrumma see *šarrumma*; indeed, certainly; promptly (Am.)

šusuppu	a type of undergarment, cloth [ŠU.ZU.UB]
šūši	(f. *šūšti*) sixty
šušinnu	a type of garment (Am.)
šuššūgu	a type of wood
šūšuru	see *ešēru*; to prepare; to cause something to be in order
šūt	he; it; that (3ms); *šūtma* (emphatic form)
šūtû IV	see *šatû*; drinking (Am. < WS)
šūtuqu	see *etēqu*; to proceed, to pass on through
šuzuta	a golden hand ornament (Am.)
tabāku	**G** to pour out
tabarru	a hue of red; red wool [SÍG.GAN.ME.TA; HÉ.ME.TA (Am.)]
taḫta	under (Am. < WS); *tahtamu* * *taḫta*+3ms (< WS) "beneath them"
taḫtamu	see *taḫta*; beneath, under (them) (< *WS* * *taḫta+3mp*)
tāḫāzu	battle, combat [MÌ]
taḫbātu	a type of cloth overlay, leggings (?)
takālu	**G** to trust
takiltu	(blue-)purple colored
takmussû	(*muṣû*) a type of garment (Am.)
tallu	a container, jar [(DUG.)DAL]
tamû II	**G** to swear, to make an oath; **D** to cause to swear, to bind by oath
tāmartu	see *amāru* (*tāmurtu*) audience gift; contribution; *š. tāmarti* "mirror" [IGI.DU$_8$]
tamkāru	merchant, trader [DAM.GAR]
tamlû	inlay
tâmtu	sea [A.AB.BA]
tāpalu	pair of (object)
tappû	friend, companion; colleague, partner
tāpatu	oil container, stone vessel for oil
taptu	(*tapatu*) a type of stone container (Am.)
târu	**G** to turn, return; **D** to restore, return, send back; to change something into; **Š** = **D** (Am.) [GUR]
tarabbanu	(*tarambānu*; *tarabānu*) a material to make glass; a type of colored glass
tarāṣu I	**G** to stretch out; to point; *tariṣ pani* "to be determined, set out to"
tarāṣu II	**G** to be/ become in order, be correct; **D** to confirm, establish (Am.)
tārītu	lady in waiting [MUNUS.EME.DA]
taskarinnu	(*taškarinnu*) boxwood [GIŠ.TÚG = TASKARIN]
taṣraḫu	horse groom (Am.)
tašlu	metal object listed as part of horse equipment (exact meaning unknown) (Am.)
tatbīku	of plating, coating (gold) (Am.)
tebû	**G** to set out
telannu	a type of vessel (alabaster) (Am.)
terḫatu	bride price [NÍG.BA.MEŠ MUNUS.UŠ.MEŠ]
terinnu	cone
terṣu	see *tarāṣu*; stretching out; *ina tarṣu* "at the time of, era of"
tērsītu	equipment, necessities

tērubtu	entry, entrance
tibnu	straw [IN, IN_4.NU]
tikku	necklace
tillatu	help, reinforcement, support; military reinforcements (auxiliary force)
tilpānu	a type of bow (Am.)
tiṣbutu	see *ṣabātu*; attached, clasping (Am.)
tudittu	(*dudittu*) toggle pin, pectoral
tuḫnu	(*duḫnu*) millet
Tukriš	a style of garment?
tumālu	(*timālu*) yesterday (Am. < WS)
tumunsallu	¼ shekel weight (Am. < Hurr.)
tunzu	a type of cloth, cloak
tupninnu	box
turāḫu	wild goat; ibex
turru	(*târu*) turned
tutturru	leaf; gold leaf (decorative)
ṭābu	(*ṭâbu, ṭiābu*) good, sweet [DÙG.GA]
ṭābūtu	friendship, goodwill
ṭapālu	**G-D** to slander, insult, humiliate
ṭapāru	**G** to press towards; **D** to drive away
ṭarādu	**G** to send off, drive away, expel; **D** to drive away so.
ṭeḫû	**G** to be near approach; **D** to bring close, to bring before, to approach (trans.)
ṭēmu	judgment; plan; report; agreement; good relations (Am.)
ṭemû	(*ṭamû*) braided, twisted
ṭiābu	see *ṭābu*
ṭīdu	(*ṭīṭu*) clay, mud [IM]
ṭimbuʾu	(*ṭubbuttu, ṭubbūtu, ṭūbātu, ṭubbātu*) cricket
ṭūbu	goodness, happiness; *ana ṭ*. "as a favor"
ṭulemu	a part of a chariot (exact meaning unknown) (Am.)
ṭuppu	tablet [DUB]; GIŠ-*ṭuppu* plaque; *bīt ṭuppim* archive, tablet house; school [É.DUB.BA]
ṭupšarru	scribe [DUB.SAR]
u	conjugation and (used between clauses); *u* … *u* … "both … and …" (Am.)
ubānu	finger, toe; measurement corresponding to a finger's width; *ubān* abs. "all but, by a narrow margin"
ubāru	foreigner, foreign guests
ūbilu	porter; *u*. KASKAL.ḪI.A caravaneers (Am. < WS)
uddû	see *edû*; **D** to identify, make known
ugāru	meadow, cultivable lands [AGÀR]
uḫatati	(pl) a leather object (Am.)
uḫinnu	date; NA_4-*u*. a date-shaped stone
uḫḫuzu	see *aḫāzu*; plated, set in metal [GAR; GAR.RA]
uḫūlu	a plant used as a source of alkali
ūl	not

ula	not (used to negate main clauses)
ūla	or
ulluru	(*ullūru*) an object made of precious stone (exact meaning unknown) (Am.)
ullû I	that, those; distant (of time)
ullû III	a type of linen cloth (Am.)
ultu	see *ištu*; from, out of; since
umāmu	animals, beasts
umma	thus
ummānu	military force, army, troops [ÉRIN]
ummu	mother [AMA]
ūmu	day [UD]
ūmišam	daily, day by day
undu	when, then (Am.)
unqu	ring [ŠU.GUR]
untu	see *undu*
unūtu	tools, equipment; goods
uppuqu	massive, solid (of gold) (Am.)
upru II	dust (Am. < WS)
upṭa	a type of ivory box (< Eg.)
uqnû	lapis lazuli [NA_4.ZA.GÌN]
urḫu	way, path
ūru	beam; roof
urru	day, daytime
urdu	see *ardu*, *wardu*; servant, slave
urukmannu	the part of a shield (Am.)
urrāšena	(pl.) desiderata, requests (Am.)
uršānu II	wild dove
uršu	bedroom; *bīt u.* "bedchamber"
uruššu	headrest
uṣultu	a type of knife, dagger [GÍR.TUR]
uškār	(*ušqār*) the crescent moon [U_4.SAKAR]
ušû	ebony, a hard wood [GIŠ.ESI]
utuppu	a type of ornament (?) (Am.)
uṭṭatu	(*uṭṭetu*) grain, barley [ŠE; ŠE.BAR]; *uṭṭatu* "grains;" idiom "after 10 grains" i.e., "immediately" [ŠE-ti]
uznu	ear; handle (on a vessel)
uzzapnannu	a type of ornament (Am.)
wabālu	**G** to carry, bring; **Dtn** = **Gtn** (Am.); **Š** to send, deliver
wadû	**D** to identify, recognize
wadḫa	a type of oil container (< Eg.)
waqû	**G** to wait; **D** to wait for, await
warādu	**G** to descend, go down; **Š** to send, bring down
wardu	(*ardu*, *urdu*) (m.) slave, servant [ÌR]
wardūtu	service; vassalage; slavery
warkû	(*arkû*) behind, rear; (*w*)*arka* afterwards, later [EGIR]
warû	**G** to go up to; to confront, go up against

waṣû	**G** to go out; **Gt** to go out, go away from; **Gtn** to continuously go out
wašābu	**G** to settle, reside
wašāru	see *muššuru*; **G** to be obedient to a deity; **D** to send, send forth; release, set free, liberate; **Gp/Dp** to be freed, liberated; to be sent (Am. < WS)
watāru	**G** to increase; to be in surplus; **D** to increase property, to make something surplus; **Dtn** (= **Dtt** Am.) to repeatedly increase
watru	(*atru*) additional, surplus, excess, extra [DIRI]
we'u	(*weḫu*) troops (Am. < Eg.)
wiaṣu	see *mâṣu*
wizza	(*uizza*) an ornament set with precious stones (*wedjet*-eye?) (Am. < Eg.)
wušru	see *ḫerizzi*; an unknown object (Am.)
wutru	a bronze object (Am.)
yakītu	a javelin, spear (Am.)
yānu	(*ayyānu*) there is no, there is not
yānummâ	(variant of *yānu*) there is no, there is not
yapu	beautiful (Am. < WS)
yâšia	(*yâši*) to, for me (1cs. dat.) (Am.)
yâšinu	to/for us (1cp. dat.) (Am.)
yâtia	(*yâti*) to/for you (1cs acc.) (Am.)
yâtinu	us (1cp acc.)
zakāru	**G** to speak, say; to mention; to remember, acknowledge (Am. < WS)
zakû I	clear, pure; refined (of metal)
zakû II	**G** to become clear, pure; **D** to make clear, purify; to use a refined material (Am.)
zallewe	a type of knife (Am. < Hurr.?)
zallulu	an unidentified object (Am.)
zamiri	(*zamirītu*) a type of material used in bow-making (?), or a bow made according to the style of *zamiri* (a city, region?) (Am.)
zaqāpu	**G** to fix, plant, erect; to be upright; to rise up (i.e., attack)
zâru	**G** to twist, turn
zarku	(*sarku*) a type of soldier; a type of official(?) (possibly related to Hittite LÚ.MEŠ *šarikuwa-*, or to the Assyrian *zarīku*)
zēru II	seed, offspring
zēru	(*zerretu, zâru*) braided, plaited; braided leather (?) [KUŠ.SUG]
zêru	**G** to hate, dislike
zikaru	(*zikru*) male; virile; sexuality [NITA]
ziminzu	(*zimizzu*) bead, stone of a certain shape
zimiu	a metal object (Am. < Eg.?)
zubbu	(*zumbu, zunbu*) fly; *ša zubbī kuššudi, ša zubbī šūli* "fly whisk" [NIM]
zukkatu	physical disability, illness (?)
zuruḫ	arm (Am. < WS)

NWS

ʾēb	enemy
ʾbd	to perish; to be lost
ʾḫr	to be behind; to be late, delayed
ʾnk	I (1cs.)
ʾny	ship, vessel
ʾsr	captive, prisoner
bd	(*bâdi* < **ba-yadi*) in the possession of
bṭḥ	to be confident, secure
bṭn	stomach
bnh	to build
dbr	pestilence
gg	roof
-hî, -ši	3fs. suffix
hnh	(Akk. *annû*) behold, look! (presentation particle)
-hû	3ms. suffix
hr	mountain, mountainous region
ḥyh	life; alive; to be alive
hṭr	branch, rod; scepter
ḥmd	precious, desirable
ḥmh	wall
ḥnn	favor; to be merciful, to grant favor
ḥrš	to plow, cultivate
ḥṣl	to eat away, consume; to despoil
ḫbh	to hide
ḫsr	requirement; lack, need
ypq	to send out; be issued(?)
yn, yyn	wine
ypʾ	beautiful, fine; beauty
yṣʾ	to go out; to take out (causative)
kbd	honor; to honor; (see Akk. *kabattuma*) internal organ, liver, stomach
kzb	(*kazābu*) to lie, deceive
kikā	thus, like
kl	all, the totality of
klb	cage, trap
kwn	to establish; make ready, prepare
lbnt	brick
ll, llh	night
lqḥ	to take
mhr	*pamahâ* foot soldier (WS. *mhr*; originally from Eg. **pꜣ mhr*)
my	who?
mila	times (in 7x7 prostration formula)
mṭnʾ	provisions supplies
mlbš	garment, clothing
mrʾh	(*rʾh*) face, countenance; appearance

mrbd(*t*)	(*rbd*) blanket, bedding?
ms	corvée, conscript laborer
mw, my, mym	water
mwt	(*mâtu*) death; to die
-nu	us, our (1cs. pronominal suffix)
ngʿ	to strike, smite
nwḫ	rest; to rest, be at rest
nḥš	copper, bronze
npl	to fall
nsk	(*nasāku*) to cast, throw, pour out
ʿbd	(*ubudu*) service
ʿôḏ	again, still
ʿzr	help, aid; to help, aid
ʿnh	to answer
ʿpr	dust
ʾps	extremity, edge, end
ʿṣr	detained, stopped; to detain, to stop
ʿwl	yoke
qyṣ	summer
qll	to treat with contempt; be treated with contempt
qṣp	to be angry
qṣr	to harvest
qwh	(*quʾʾû*)to wait
rʾš	head
rwm	to raise, lift
rʿh	friend; associate
sws	horse
syr	pot
skn	(*sākinu, sūkinu*) commissioner, prefect, governor
ṣlḫt	(*saḫarru*) plate, bowl
ṣdq	righteous; to be good
ṣʾn	sheep, flock
ṣʿq	to call out, yell; to summon
ṣpn	north
ṣr	hard-pressed, surrounded; narrow; in idiom *ana ṣ*. "against"
šdh/y	open field, agricultural lands, countryside
šlḥ	to send
šlm	peace; to be completed
šʿr	gate
šmm, šmym	sky, heavens
šrr, šwr	to slander
šs, šsh	to plunder, rob
tḥt	under, underneath
tmwl šlšm	(*tumālu*) idiom "formerly, before"
zkr	remember, acknowledge
zrʿ	arm

Egyptian

ꜣbd	month
ꜣḫt	horizon
ỉꜣ-rꜣ- šꜣ	Alashia (Cyprus)
ỉw	proclitic particle
ỉn	by (prep. of agent)
ỉry-pꜥt	hereditary prince, nobleman
ỉrpỉ	an official
ỉkn	jar, amphora
y3	yea, verily; repeated in exclamation for emphasis
wꜥw	soldier
wpwt	envoy, mission
wr	prince
bḫn	country mansion; palace
pꜣ	definitive article (Late Egyptian)
pr	house
prt	growing (season)
pḏt	(*piṭ*(*ṭ*)*ātu*) archers; military troops
m	in
n	belonging to; to, for
nwt	town
mỉtt	(*mỉt; mỉtw*) copy
(*pꜣ*) *mhr*	(*pamahâ*) warrior, soldier
mšꜥ	(see *miši*) expedition; soldiers
rsy	southern (adj)
hrw(*w*)	content, happy
ḥꜥ	(*ḥꜥwt*) enjoyment, rejoicing
ḥsbt	(*ḥꜣt sp*) year (in date formulae)
ḫpš	strong arm
ḥry-pḏ(*t*)	(transcribed as ᴵ*iḫ-ri-pí*) army commander
sr	noble man
sš	scribe; to write
šꜥt	letter
šnwt	granary
kṯn	(see *guzi*) (Egyptian) chariot driver; stable boy, groom (Am.)
tw	he
dbn	weight measurement (aprox. 91 grams)

Logograms

A	*mû* water
A, A.A	*abu* father
A.AB.BA	*tâmtu* sea
Á.MUŠEN	*erû* vulture, eagle; augury

A.ŠÀ	*eqlu* field
AB.BA	*abu* father
AD; AD.DA	*abu* father
AGÀR	*ugāru* cultivable lands
ALAM	*ṣalmu* statue, figurine; winged disk
AM	*rīmu* wild bull, auroch
AMA	*ummu* mother
AN	*šamû* heavens, sky
AN.BAR	*parzillu* iron; *ḫabalkinnu* (*ḫabalginnu*) a metal alloy used for weapons
AN.TA	*eliš* above
ANŠE	*imēru* donkey
ANŠE.KUR.RA	*sisû* horse
AŠ	*ištēn* one (unit), person, object
BA.ÚŠ, BA.UG$_7$	*mâtu* dead; to die
BABBAR	*peṣû* white
BAD	*bēlu* lord; BAD-*tu bēltu* mistress
BÀD	*dūru* wall
BAL, BAL.MEŠ	*maqqītu*; pl. *maqqû* libation vessels
BAR	*mišlu* half
BUGIN	*buginnu* trough; wooden container
BURU$_{14}$	*ebūru* summer, summer months, harvest season
DAM	*aššatu* wife; DAM-*ut aššûtu* marriage
DAM.GÀR	*tamkāru* merchant, trader
DÀRA.MAŠ	*ayalu* deer, stag
DIDLI	plural marker
DINGIR	*ilu* god, deity; deity determinative
^{d}A	Aten
^{d}DA.MU	Adonis
^{d}EŠDAR	Ishtar?
^{d}INNIN	female goddess (Shaushka, Ishtar, etc.)
^{d}LAMMA	*lamassu* female deity; figurine of a female deity
^{d}LAMA$_2$	see ^{d}LAMMA
^{d}MAŠ.MAŠ	Nergal
^{d}NIN.IB	Ninurta
DIR	*malû* full, complete
DIRI	(*w*)*atru* additional, surplus, excess, extra
DUB	*ṭuppu* tablet
DUB.SAR	*ṭupšarru* scribe
DUG	*karpatu* pot, clay vessel; vessel determinative
DUG.DAL	*tallu* a container, jar
DÙG.GA	(syl. *tu-ka*) *ṭābu, ṭâbu* good, sweet; well-meaning, friendly; *ṭābūtu* friendship, brotherhood; goodwill
DUGUD	*kabātu* **G** to be heavy; to be honored, respected; **D** to treat honorably, to respect; **Dtn** to repeatedly honor, be complementary of; *kabtu* heavy, weighty; important; a dignitary
DUMU	*māru* son, man (resident) of

DUMU.MUNUS	*mārtu* daughter
É	*bītu* house; container, receptacle
É.DUB.BA	*bīt ṭuppim* archive, tablet house; school
É.GAL	*ekallu* palace
É.GI.A	*kallātu* daughter-in-law; bride
E.NE	Sumerian plural marker (animate)
É NIN.IB	*Bīt Ninurta* the temple of Ninurta
EDIN	*ṣēru* plain, steppe
EGIR	*(w)arkû* behind, rear; *warka* afterwards, later
EN	*bēlu* lord, master
EN.NUN	*maṣṣartu* garrison
ÉRIN	*ṣābu, ummānu* military force, army, troops
ÉRIN.MEŠ GÌR.MEŠ = LÚ.GÌR	*ṣābē šēpšū* infantry
ÉRIN.MEŠ KAL.BAD.KASKAL	*karāšu* expeditionary force?
EZEN	*isinnu* festival
GA.KAL, KAL.GA	*dannu, dunnu* strong
GA.ZUM	see GIŠ.GA.RÍG; *mušṭu, mulṭu* comb
GADA	*kitû* linen
GADA.ŠAG$_4$.DÙ.A	*šakattû* girdle
GAL	*rabû* big, great; chief, senior official; *kāsu* cup (see also GÚ.ZI)
GAM	*šaplītu* lower
GÁN.BA	*maḫīru* emporium, market
GAR, GAR.RA	*uḫḫuzu* plated, set in metal; *šakānu* **G** to set, place
GAZ	**G** *dâku* to kill, defeat
GÉME	*amtu* female servant
GI	*qanû* reed; arrow
GI$_6$	*mūšu* night; determinative for black objects
GIBIL	*edēšu* **G** to be/become new; **D** to rebuild, repair
GÍD.DA	*arku* long
GÍN	*šiqlu* weight
GÍR	*patru* sword, dagger
GÌR	*šēpu* foot; LÚ.GÌR foot soldier
GÍR.GAL	*namṣāru* sword
GÍR.TUR	*uṣultu* a type of knife, dagger
GIŠ	*iṣû* wood, tree, timber; determinative for trees, wooden objects
(GIŠ).BAN, PAN	*qaštu* bow
(GIŠ).BUGIN.TUR, BÚGIN.TUR	*buginnu ṣeḫru; sussullu*? a trough used for liquids(?)
GIŠ.DÍLIM	*itquru* spoon
GIŠ.EREN	*erēnu* cedar
GIŠ.ESI	*ušû* ebony, a hard wood
GIŠ.ÉŠ.SAG.KUL	*ebel sikkūri* a rope lock
GIŠ.GA.RÍG	see GA.ZUM; *mušṭu/ mulṭu* comb
GIŠ.GIGIR	*narkabtu* chariot
GIŠ.GÌR.GUB	*gištappu* footrest, footstool
GIŠ.GU.ZA	*kussû* throne, chair, seat
GIŠ.ḪAŠḪUR	*ḫašḫuru* apple; apple tree

GIŠ.GI.IG	*daltu* door
(GIŠ).KIRI$_6$	*kirû* orchard; *kirru* a large jar
GIŠ.MÁ	*eleppu* ship, boat, vessel
GIŠ.MURUB$_4$	a wooden object (meaning unknown)
GIŠ.NÁ	*eršu* bed
GIŠ.PAN	see GIŠ.BAN
GIŠ.TASKARIN/TAŠKARIN	*taskarinnu, taškarinnu* boxwood
GIŠ.TÚG	see GIŠ.TASKARIN
GIŠ.TUKUL.SAG.NA$_4$	*ḫuppalû, ḫutpalû* mace
GIŠ/KUŠ.ÙŠAN	*qinnā, qi(n)nanzu* whip
GÚ, GUN, GÚ.UN	*biltu* load, donkey load; talent (unit of weight); tribute
GU$_4$, GUD	*alpu* ox
GÚ.GADA	*kišādu* scarf
GÚ.TUR	*kakkû, kakkūtu* lentil, lentil shaped
GÚ.ZI	*kāsu* cup (see also GAL)
GÙN	(SU$_4$) *pelû* red
GÙN.(A)	*burrumu* multicolored, speckled
GUR	*kurru* measure, capacity of; *târu* **G** to return, become
GUR.SI.IB	*gursipu* helmet
KÙ.GI	see KÙ.GI; *ḫurāṣu* gold
ḪAR	*semeru* bracelet
ḪÉ.TUR	meaning unknown
ḪUL, ḪUL.GÁL	*lemnu* bad, evil, hostile
ḪUR.SAG	see KUR; *šadû* mountain; hill country; open country, desert
ḪUŠ.A	*ḫuššû* red
I	*ištēn* one (unit), person, object
Ì	*šamnu* oil, fat; Ì DÙG(.GA) *šamnu ṭābu* good oil
IGI	*īnu* eye
IGI.DU$_8$	*tāmartu* audience-gift; contribution
IGI.KÁR, IGI.KÁR(.MEŠ)	*barû* **G** to examine, inspect; aširtu inspection; provisions, supplies
IM	*ṭīdu, ṭīṭu* clay, mud
IM.ŠE.ḪI.A	see ŠE
IN, IN$_4$.NU	*tibnu* straw
INIM	*amātu, awātu* word
ÌR	(*w*)*ardu, urdu*; m. slave, servant; *wardūtu* service, vassalage; slavery
IŠ+BI (= ŠIM!.ZAR.MEŠ)	*murru* myrrh
ITI	(*w*)*arḫu* month
ITI.NE.NE.GAR	the month of Ab
ITI.ŠU.NUMUN.NA	the month of Tammuz
IZI	*išātu* fire
IZI.GAR	*nūru* lamp
KA	*pû* mouth; word, command; advice
KÁ	*bābu* door
KÁ.GAL	*abullu* gate
KAL, KAL.GA	*danānu, dannu, dunnu* strong, mighty, powerful

KASKAL *ḫarranu* road; *gerru* caravan; military campaign

KAŠ *šikaru* beer

KEŠDA *kiṣru* group; troop, band (soldiers, bandits)

KI *erṣētu* earth, land; determinative for land/region of; *itti* with

KI.KAL.GIGIR *sassu* chariot platform

KI.KAL.KASKAL, KAL.BAD.KASKAL *karašu* military camp, expeditionary force

KI.LÁ, KI.LAL.BI *šuqultu* weight (of obj.)

KI.TA *šapliš* below; downward; *šaplu* bottom, underside; *šaplû* lower part, side; *šaplītu* (adj.) lower part

KIN *šipru* work; message; envoy; shipment, mission; *šakru* handle

KIN (for KIN.‹NIM›) *šēru* morning star, dawn

KISLAḪ *maškanu* threshing floor, granary

KIŠIB *kunukku* cylinder seal

KÙ.BABBAR *kaspu* silver

KÙ.GI *ḫurāṣu* gold; KÙ.GI GAR.RA *ḫ. uḫḫuz* inlaid (gold)

KU.TI.TI (= GÙ.[UN].DI$_6$.DI$_6$?), (KU.TI.TI as a syllabic reading) *ābilāt bilti* tribute bearers

KUR *mātu* land; *šadû* mountains, open country; desert; genuine (of lapis lazuli, i.e., "of the mountains")

KUR.KI *mātu* land

NU.KÚR see KÚR.NU; *nukurtu* hostility, act of aggression

KUŠ *mašku* animal skin, hide; sack

KUŠ.É.MAR.URU$_5$ *išpatu* quiver

KUŠ.KA.TAB *katappû* bridle

KUŠ.SUG *zēru, zerrutu* braided leather (?)

KUŠ.ÙŠAN see GIŠ.ÙŠAN; *qinnāzu* (*qi*(*n*)*nanzu*) whip

LÁ *ṣimittu* team of horses; yoke, pair of oxen

LÁL *dišpu* honey

LIM *līm* thousand

LÚ *amēlu, awīlu* man

(LÚ.)A.ZU *ašû* physician

LÚ.(MEŠ).DUMU. KIN, DUMU LÚ.KIN, LÚ.KIN *mār šipri* envoy, delegate

LÚ.GIR$_5$+PA see MAŠKIM

LÚGUD *kurû* short

LÚ IGI.KÁR *āširu* inspector

LÚ.ÌR.MEŠ *ardūtu* service; to (be of) service

LU.LIM *lulīmu, lulimmu* stag, deer, ram

LÚ.LUL *sarru* criminal, dishonest, false

LÚ.MEŠ GAL.GAL.MEŠ *rabûti* senior officials

LÚ.NU.GIŠ.KIRI$_6$ *nukarippu* gardener

LÚ.PA.TÙR (*w*)*akil tarbaṣi* stable master (calque for Eg. *ḥry iḥw*)

LÚ.SA.GAZ *ḫabbātu, ḫāpiru, ʿapîru* bandit, raider

LÚ.SIPA.ANŠE.HI.A donkey herders

LÚ.ŠU.I *gallābu* barber

LUGAL *šarru* king

MA.NA *manû, mina* a weight measure

MAḪ *ṣīru* high, elevated

MAR.TU Amurru

(LÚ.) MÁŠKIM; LÚ.GIR$_5$+PA *rābiṣu* royal official, commissioner

MÈ *tāḫāzu* battle, combat

MEŠ plural marker

MU, MU.KAM *šattu* year

MUNUS *sinništu, sinniltu* woman; *amēltu* woman; female determinative

MUNUS.DÉ *šāqītu* a female cup-bearer

MUNUS.EME.DA *tārītu* lady in waiting

MÚR, MÚRUB, MURUB, MURUB$_4$ *qablû* midst, middle of; *qablu* centerpiece

MUŠEN *iṣṣūru* bird

NA$_4$ *abnu* stone; determinative for stone objects, precious stones

NA$_4$.AN.GUG.ME a type of stone

NA$_4$.BABBAR.DILI, NA$_4$.BAR$_6$.BAR$_6$.DILI *pappar(dil)dali, pappar(dil)dalû* a type of stone (chalcedony, agate?)

NA$_4$.DU$_8$.ŠI.A, NA$_4$.DUḪ.ŠI.A *dušû* a type of stone (agate?)

NA$_4$.GÍR.ZÚ, NA4.GÍR.ZÚ.GAL *ṣurru* flint, obsidian

NA$_4$.GIŠ.NU$_{11}$.GAL *ašnugallu* alabaster

NA$_4$.GUG *sāmtu* carnelian

NA$_4$.MAR type of stone (*mar*-stone?)

NA$_4$.NÍR *ḫulālu* a type of precious stone

NA$_4$.NÍR.MUŠ.GÍR, NA$_4$.MUŠ.GÍR.TAB, NA$_4$.MUŠ.GÍR *muššaru* (*mušgarru*) (a semi-precious stone; serpentine, onyx?)

NA$_4$.SAG.KAL *sankallu* a type of precious stone; foremost

NA$_4$.ŠI.TIR, NA$_4$.ŠE.TIR *pendu* a red, specked stone(?)

NA$_4$.ZA.GÌN *uqnû* lapis lazuli

NA$_4$.ZA.GÌN KUR *uqnī šadi* genuine, natural lapis lazuli

NA$_4$.ZA.GUG, GUG (ZA+GUL) *sāmtu* carnelian

NA$_4$ZÚ(KA) see NA$_4$.GÍR.ZÚ; *ṣurru* obsidian, flint

NAGAR *nagāru* carpenter

NAM.(TAR) *šimtu* fate

NAM.ḪA.RA *namḫāru* a storage jar

NAM.TIL.LA *balāṭu* life

NAM.RU, NAM.‹NE›.RU *māmītu* oath

NÍG determinative for object, thing

NÍG.BA *qīštu* present, gift

NÍG.BA.MEŠ MUNUS.UŠ.MEŠ *terḫatu* dowry, bride price

NÍG.GÍD.DA GIGIR see GIGIR; *mašaddu* chariot-poles(?)

NÍG.ŠU.LUḪ.ḪA *namsû, nemsû*, pl. *namsītu* washbasin

NIM *zibbu* fly

NIN *bēltu* lady, mistress

NINDA *akalu* food, sustenance

NITA *zikaru, zikru* male

NITLAM$_4$ *ḫīrtu, marḫatu* wife, spouse

NU *paqādu* **G** to entrust; command; allocate, take care of (Am.); *lā* negation, not, no, (un-)

NU.KÚR, KÚR.NU *nukurtu* hostility, act of aggression

NU.ÚR.MA.(A) *nurmû* pomegranate

NUN *rubû* prince, ruler
NUNUZ *erimmatu* egg-shaped, ovoid (of ankle?)
PA (*w*)*aklu* overseer
PA.TÙR *akil tarbaṣi* stable master
SAG, SAG.DU *rēšu, qaqqadu* head; self, person
SAḪAR *eperu, epru* earth, soil, dust
SAR *šaḫarru* jar, clay pot
SI *qarnu* animal horn; rhyton
SIG *qalālu* G to be small, light, weak; to be despised; D to diminish, belittle
SÍG *šīpātu* wool, fleece
SIG$_4$ *libittu, labittu* brick
SIG$_5$ *dumqu* goodness, good thing
SIG$_7$ numeric value 10,000
SÍG.GAN.ME.TA *nabāsu, tabarru* red wool
SILA *sūqu* road; determinative for road
SIPA *rē'û* shepherd, herdsman
SU (for GÍN) see GÍN; *šiqlu* shekel-weight
SÚN *rīmtu* wild cow
ŠÀ *libbu* stomach, heart, mind
ŠÁM *šīmu* price, purchase
ŠÀM.MEŠ *šīmāti* payment
ŠE, ŠE.ḪI.A, ŠE.IM.ḪI.A, IM.ŠE.ḪI.A *še'u, uṭṭatu* grain, barley; ŠE-*tu uṭṭatu* grains; immediately, i.e., "after 10 grains"
ŠE.BAR *uṭṭatu, uṭṭetu* grain, barley
ŠE.KIN (GUR$_{10}$).KU$_5$ *eṣēdu* to harvest
ŠE.ZÍZ.ḪI.A *kunāšu* emmer (pl)
ŠÈR.ŠÈR *šeršerretu* chains, fetters
ŠEŠ *aḫu* brother
ŠIM *rīqu, riqqu* aromatic plant, substance
ŠIM.AZ *asu* myrtle
ŠIM.BÚL *ballukku* styrax
ŠIM.GIG *kanatku* tree; the aromatic substance from this tree
ŠU *qātu* hand; measure of; item; set
ŠU.GUR *unqu* ring
ŠU.NIGÍN *napḫaru* the sum of, total, entirety
ŠU.ZU.UB *šusuppu* a type of undergarment
TA.ÀM determinative following distributive numbers; each
TÉŠ *baštu, baltu* dignity, pride, honor
TI, TI.LA, TE.LA *balāṭu* life; to live, be alive
TIN.ZI *balāṭu* provisions (Am.)
TÚG *ṣubātu* textile, garment
TÚG.BAR.DUL *kusītu, kušītu* robe, linen garment
TÚG.BAR.SIG *paršīgu* headdress
TÚG.GÚ, TÚG.GÚ.È(.A) *naḫlaptu* a Hurrian style shirt
TÚG.ÍB.LÁ *nēbeḫu* sashes
TÚG.NÍG.LAM *lam*(*a*)*huššû* a type of ceremonial garment

TÚG.SIG$_4$.ZA, (TÚG.GUZ.ZA?) wrap, blanket
TUR *ṣeḫru* small, young; servitor
TÙR *tarbaṣu* animal stall, stable
U *ešer, ešeret* the number 10
U$_4$.SAKAR *uškār, ušqār* crescent moon
UD *umu* day
UDU *immeru, ṣēnu* sheep, flock
UDU.‹A›.LUM *immeru* ram; rhyton
UDU.SIR$_4$ *puḫīlu, puḫālu* a breed ram; rhyton
UGU *elû* upon, upper; *muḫḫu* skull, top; with regard to, referring to
UN *nišu, nešu* people; population; humanity; *maṣṣartu* garrison
UR, UR.GI$_5$ (= KI), UR.GI$_7$, UR.GU, UR!(UŠ).GI$_7$!(GU) *kalbu* dog
ÚR *sūnu* loin, lap
UR.MAḪ *nēšu* lion
UR.SAG *qardu* hero, warrior; *qarādu* **G** to be warlike
URU *ālu*; pl. *ālānu* city, town
URU.PÚ.ḪI.A, URU.KI A.PÚ.ME, A.PÚ.MEŠ Beirut
URUDU *erû* copper
URUDU.GAG.Ú.TAG.GA *šiltāḫ(ḫ)u* arrow
URUDU.ŠEN *ruqqu, šennu* kettle
ÙZ *enzu* goat
UZU *šīru* flesh; determinative for body part
UZU. GÙ *kišādu* neck, back of neck; back
UZU.UR$_5$ *kabattu* stomach (Am.)
ZABAR *sipparru* bronze, copper
ZAG *ahu* side, arm; *pāṭu, paṭṭu* border, district
ZI *napištu*
ZI.KÍL (= SIKIL) *ellu* pure (oil)
ZU see SU
ZÚ, ZU$_9$ (KAxUD); ZÚ.SÚN *šinnu* tooth; ivory
ZÚ.SI.GA *buqūmu* plucking, (sheep) shearing
ZU.ZU (for GÍN.GÍN) (pl.) *šiqlū* shekel weight